What's New in This Edition

The first edition of *PowerBuilder Unleashed* deals with the then-current version of PowerBuilder, Version 4.0. This edition has been dramatically reworked to cover *all* the new features and products that are available in PowerBuilder 5.0.

Some of these new features include

- Direct DataWindow data and object access
- The new object-oriented features of PowerScript
- The new window controls (Tab, TreeView, ListView, and so on)
- The new and improved Script painter
- Distributed PowerBuilder
- PowerBuilder and OLE 2.0: Client/server technology
- OCX controls
- How to create truly compiled executables

In addition, in this edition some of the simpler examples and descriptions from the first edition have been reworked. This means even more in-depth and advanced concepts for you to use.

We have also added some additional chapters that address such issues as

- Client/server case studies
- Cross-platform PowerBuilder
- The ORCA interface
- Making 32-bit API calls

Above all, we hope that this edition of *PowerBuilder Unleashed* will be your definitive reference guide for your PowerBuilder development efforts.

PowerBuilder® 5

UNLEASHED

Simon Gallagher & Simon Herbert

SAMS PUBLISHING

201 West 103rd Street
Indianapolis, IN 46290

SECOND EDITION

International Standard Book Number: 0-672-30907-6

Library of Congress Catalog Card Number: 95-72340

99 98 97 96 4 3 2 1

Interpretation of the printing code: the rightmost double-digit number is the year of the book's printing; the rightmost single-digit, the number of the book's printing. For example, a printing code of 96-1 shows that the first printing of the book occurred in 1996.

Composed in AGaramond and MCPdigital by Macmillan Computer Publishing

Printed in the United States of America

Trademarks

Publisher and President *Richard K. Swadley*

Acquisitions Manager *Greg Wiegand*

Development Manager *Dean Miller*

Managing Editor *Cindy Morrow*

Marketing Manager *John Pierce*

Assistant Marketing Manager *Kristina Perry*

Acquisitions Editors
Brad Jones
Rosemarie Graham

Development Editor
Todd Bumbalough

Software Development Specialist
Steve Flatt

Production Editor
Kitty Wilson

Technical Reviewers
Marion Sternstein
P.J. Stewart-Martin
Jay Stevens

Editorial Coordinator
Bill Whitmer

Technical Edit Coordinator
Lynette Quinn

Formatter
Frank Sinclair

Editorial Assistants
Carol Ackerman
Andi Richter
Rhonda Tinch-Mize

Cover Designer
Tim Anrhein

Book Designer
Gary Adair

Copy Writer
Peter Fuller

Production Team Supervisor
Brad Chinn

Production
Stephen Adams, Ginny Bess, Mona Brown, Charlotte Clapp, Judy Everly, Jason Hand, Clint Lahnen, Paula Lowell, Donna Martin, Cheryl Moore, Beth Rago, Laura Robbins, Bobbi Satterfield, Laura A. Smith, Andrew Stone, Susan Van Ness, Colleen Williams

Overview

Contents

Part II Programming with PowerBuilder

Part III Creating PowerBuilder Applications

Dedications

To my parents, Paul and Hilary, for their intelligence, gentleness, sense of humor, patience, and understanding that have been so inspirational in my life. And to my grandparents, Cyril and Joy Lowther and George and Audrey Gallagher, who have been so supportive and loving over the years. Last but never least, to Andrea, my wife and constant companion in life's little journey. This book is for all of you who have been a guiding light and influence in my life.

—Simon Gallagher

To my son, Malcolm, and wife, Rebecca, for being my inspiration. Also, to my parents, Ann and Alan Herbert, for their guidance and love.

—Simon Herbert

Acknowledgments

This book is the combined effort of a number of people, and we would like to take this opportunity to thank Rosemarie Graham and Brad Jones, our Acquisitions Editors, and Todd Bumbalough, the Development Editor, for their help and guidance through the process of writing this book.

Thanks to Brad Jones, Kellsey Le, Jim LeValley, and Bill Hatfield, who coerced us into writing the first edition of this book. To all those who have sent encouraging e-mails for that edition, many thanks for keeping our spirits up whilst writing this new edition. It made it all the more enjoyable!

Many thanks go to my mother, Hilary, for her impromptu transatlantic French lesson. Thanks to Chris Fotiadis for his ideas for the book. Special thanks to Kevin Penner for help with cc:Mail and VIM. Thanks to Charlie Hensler for his bug spot on the print dialog, and his other useful suggestions on the previous edition.

Special thanks to Ulric (my 1½ year old collie) for being a late-night (early-morning) writing companion.

To Mike Mangin and Lance Gordon for their always-down-to-earth views on PowerBuilder development, thanks for keeping my feet on the right path when it was required. Many thanks to Dennis Prothero, for allowing me to be part of his development team, and for his contributions to Chapter 2.

Thanks to all the people involved at Sams Publishing, especially Kitty Wilson. Thanks to our technical editors Jay Stevens and Scott Virtue for catching our stupid mistakes. A special thanks to a very insightful technical editor P.J. Stewart-Martin—good work, P.J.! Many special thanks to Cathy Col at Powersoft for holding up a torch to the darkness of our ignorance, and the many technical resources she pulled together, not the least of which was Ruth Ann Donaldson. Also, thanks to Jane Cantz of Powersoft for eleventh-hour help in getting InstallBuilder for the authors to review.

Thanks to the staff at NewMedia, Inc., for their ideas, thoughts, and suggestions, especially for helping Simon and me keep going through all the pressure and deadlines. Many thanks to Joe Quick for keeping the client happy while I was off writing, and to Bob Hunchberger for his views on the current computing environment and his knowledge in all things object oriented. Also, thanks to Scott Cunningham for a lot of useful ideas for the book and sharing relevant and interesting information.

The most special thanks go from all the authors to all our families, near and far, who have been supportive of our efforts.

—Simon Gallagher

In addition to the individuals noted above, I would like to thank some additional people. First off, I would not have had the motivation or patience to attempt either book without the love and support of my family. Rebecca, thanks for giving me the time to work, letting me stay at home, and making sure that I was working and not goofing off. A huge thanks also goes to my son, Malcolm, for providing much-needed distractions and making the pressure bearable. To the rest of my family, the Herberts and the Josons, thank you for all your encouragement.

Thanks to Joe Quick, Jim O'Connor, Leasa Bridges, Kellsey Le, Terry McConahay, and the rest of the staff at NewMedia for all your support, help, and putting up with my whining and bad moods.

—Simon Herbert

We would both like to recognize the time and effort of Kurt Sundling and Chris Urbanek for their parts in the writing of the first edition of this book.

About the Authors

Simon Gallagher

Simon Gallagher graduated in 1991 from the University of Kent at Canterbury, England, with a first-class bachelor of science with honors degree in computer science. He is currently a senior consultant and technical lead for the Indianapolis office of NewMedia, Inc. Simon is also a Certified PowerBuilder Associate and still hopes to find time to become a Certified PowerBuilder Professional. He is also a Microsoft Certified Professional.

Simon has been programming in PowerBuilder since Version 2.0 and has successfully fielded a number of different applications, ranging from a property tax reporting system to an order entry system. He has been involved with a number of different hardware platforms and operating systems, and has a broad knowledge of databases and development languages. As part of the PowerBuilder 2.0 project team, he was working to help debug the first Informix 5.0 DBMS interface for PowerBuilder.

You can reach Simon on the Internet at `raven@iquest.net`. You can also explore his web pages at `http://www.iquest.net/~raven/raven.html`.

Simon J.A. Herbert

Simon Herbert graduated in 1991 from the University of Notre Dame with a bachelor of arts degree in economics and computer applications. He is a technical instructor and senior analyst in the Indianapolis branch of NewMedia, Inc. Simon is a Certified PowerBuilder Developer Associate and Certified PowerBuilder Instructor. He is also a Microsoft Certified Professional and Certified Trainer in Visual Basic.

Simon has been developing client/server applications over the past five years. These applications encompass several different business systems, including sales reporting, order entry, financial reporting, and diabetes patient tracking. These systems were developed using Visual Basic, Access, and PowerBuilder running against a variety of different DBMSs (Sybase, MS SQL Server, and Oracle).

You can reach Simon on the Internet at `herbs@iquest.net`. You can also explore his web pages at `http://www.iquest.net/~herbs/sjah.html`.

Kurt Sundling

Kurt Sundling graduated from Ball State University with a B.S. in computer science and history. During the last four years, Kurt has been involved in the development of CASE tool technology for a consulting firm and has implemented a variety of client/server applications, ranging from maintenance systems to an order entry system.

Introduction

Since 1994 there has been a steady succession of PowerBuilder books, ranging from beginner-oriented books to more advanced. However, the majority of them fail to provide very much in-depth knowledge. In 1995 the first edition of *PowerBuilder Unleashed* was released with the aim of providing an all-encompassing book, one that would really allow you to unleash the power in PowerBuilder.

PowerBuilder Unleashed was written not as a tutorial or replacement for the PowerBuilder manuals, but as a complement to them. It provides a depth of knowledge based on real-world experience not found in other books, and we hope you will turn to this book as your central repository of information on PowerBuilder.

While this book does not spend time creating a fanciful application that is of little real use to people, it *does* show many of the advanced concepts, and includes a number of reusable objects that can be incorporated into your existing framework. If you don't have a framework yet, then these can be used to start building the foundations for one. Sample code from relevant chapters has been made available on the disc included with this book, and you should find some of it sufficiently useful to drop it into your existing framework or class library.

We recognize that there are some beginner and intermediate developers out there who learn very quickly, and some of the early chapters were written with you in mind. These chapters help bridge the gap for all PowerBuilder developers and include information for those of you who consider yourselves of an advanced level. While we were writing this book we all managed to surprise each other with little pieces of information that you might have expected seasoned developers to know.

Throughout this book you will encounter a small variety of naming and coding standards. We did not want to constrain ourselves to any one particular style, as there are so many different standards in use. The code you will see uses the standards that we use in our everyday application development, and you might want to adopt some or all of the standards used.

A great deal of thought, time, and effort has been poured into making this the best book we could produce. *PowerBuilder Unleashed* addresses the advanced concepts the PowerBuilder community is crying out for. We hope that this will be *the* reference and guide you turn to first while you are developing your PowerBuilder applications.

PowerBuilder 5.0 has incorporated some significant changes, which means we were discovering new features after this book was submitted for editing. We have managed to include all the new features that we had learned during the review stage. We would like to thank those members of the CompuServe Powersoft Beta forum for sharing their findings and knowledge.

One last thing before you delve into this book: If you do find any discrepancies, bugs, or outright lies, we *want* to know, and you can send your findings to us either in care of Sams Publishing or to the Internet accounts listed in the author biographies. The feedback from the first edition has been great and we hope to hear of *your* PowerBuilding experiences.

Happy reading, and may you expand your knowledge.

—Simon Gallagher & Simon Herbert

PART I

Understanding PowerBuilder

IN THIS PART

New Features in PowerBuilder 5.0

1

IN THIS CHAPTER

Powersoft has put a lot of thought into what the development community has been saying they needed to put in the next release of PowerBuilder, and together with directions in the tool market and computing environment as a whole, they have rolled out PowerBuilder Version 5.0.

This chapter provides a brief overview of the new features as they relate to particular areas.

Overall Enhancements

Powersoft has incorporated a number of enhancements throughout the different objects and painters available. PowerBuilder has adopted many of the standards of Windows 95 to make the product easier to use (assuming you find Windows 95 easier to use!). The migration process from previous releases to 5.0 has been improved and now provides batch migration. Batch migration allows for the unattended migration of your application, and all errors are reported at the end of the attempt. And of course, as Powersoft has promised, the execution of your application will be faster with the introduction of true machine code executables. Explore Chapter 18, "Application Implementation, Creation, and Distribution," for some speed comparisons.

Ease of Use

Powersoft has added a number of features that make it easier to use PowerBuilder: drop-down toolbars, docking toolbars, customizable PainterBars, property sheets, and unlimited undo levels. Powersoft has also made a conscious effort to reduce the number of modal painters (such as the Structure painter) in PowerBuilder.

The drop-down toolbars consist of a number of toolbar buttons accessible via one button on the toolbar. They are used to conserve real estate on the various toolbars. In prior versions of PowerBuilder, you were able to move the toolbars to different locations (top, left, floating, and so on). In 5.0, toolbars can still be moved to a new location, but you can click on a toolbar and drag and drop it onto another toolbar that combines the two toolbars (referred to as docking). PowerBuilder has given you ultimate control in the customization of your toolbars by allowing you to define up to eight new PainterBars and four new PowerBars.

In compliance with the Windows 95 standard, attributes are now referred to as *properties* and are accessed almost exclusively as tab pages, which are known as property sheets. Property sheets are tab pages that provide access to the different object values. The property sheets replace the complex pop-up menus of prior releases.

Another feature expands on the much-needed undo capabilities of Version 4.0. PowerBuilder supports an unlimited number of undos in the majority of the painters, but still only for specific operations.

Migration

Powersoft has added some new features to the migration process along with some much-needed detailed error reporting.

Batch mode allows unattended migration, with all errors and informational messages appearing at the end of the process. Unfortunately it has not been written to allow multiple applications to be migrated in one go.

The PowerBuilder 5.0 compiler generates warning messages regarding syntax that is now obsolete and syntax that will potentially be removed in later versions. It detects function name changes and conflicts between existing variable names and the new parameters available for some events.

Performance

Machine code executables and DLLs can now be created, but only from within a 32-bit operating system (currently Windows 95 and Windows NT). You can create 16-bit executables, but again only from within the 32-bit environment.

The creation of a machine code executable requires additional time and resources, and it runs best on a powerful machine with plenty of memory. The compilation process actually generates ANSI C code and uses the Watcom C++ compiler technology, which is recognized as one of the industry's leaders.

PowerBuilder Painters

PowerBuilder has revamped the majority of the painters, which are described in the following sections.

The Script Painter

The PowerScript painter has been greatly enhanced to provide some of the basic functionality of a programmer's editor. Most notably, your script will be color-coded to indicate the types of syntax (for example, comments are red, keywords are blue, and so on). PowerBuilder also supports auto-indentation, which maintains indentation from line to line and also indents automatically for flow-of-control statements. The syntax colors and the indentation behavior are fully customizable, as is the specification of different Paste drop-down list boxes at the top of the painter.

In addition to the environmental settings you can specify for the Script painter, the painter includes a context menu (pop-up) that allows you to cut, copy, paste, clear, select all, undo, and execute context-sensitive help. You can also select text and drag it to cut and paste the text (holding the Ctrl key copies the text).

The Object Browser has undergone a complete revision for Version 5.0. Instead of two different dialogs to view PowerBuilder objects and your own objects, there is only one browser that uses the tabbed metaphor to provide a much easier-to-use interface.

The new tab pages allow you to view the different application objects and system classes, their properties, events, functions, variables, and the object hierarchy. The properties and functions that are inherited from higher up in the hierarchy are shown, as are the access levels. In addition to allowing you to view different objects' definitions, the Object Browser allows you to create a rich text format (RTF) document that details the selected information about a particular object.

For more information on the PowerScript painter, see Chapter 7, "The PowerScript Environment."

The Application Painter

The Application painter has been modified to include the new property sheets for access to the different attribute settings. The application tree has been converted to use the new TreeView control. The application object has also gained a new attribute for internationalization and two new events for use in a distributed application environment.

The most significant change to the Application painter is that it no longer gives you the ability to create an executable. This is now exclusively done through the Project painter. For more information on the Application painter, see Chapter 8, "Application Objects and the Application Painter."

The Window Painter

To become compliant with the Windows 95 interface, Powersoft has added a number of controls to those already available in the Window and User Object painters:

- The Tab control—The Tab control consists of a number of *pages* that can be accessed using the tab areas of the control. This control eliminates the need to rely on the wide variety of third-party implementations of the tab metaphor.
- The Rich Text Edit (RTE) control—The RTE control allows you to effectively place a simple word processor in your PowerBuilder applications. It includes such features as font choice and point size, text color, font style (bold, italic, strikethrough), and justification.

- The TreeView control—The TreeView control is used to implement the hierarchical lists that you see throughout Windows 95. With this control you can do the following: expand and collapse nodes; make representations of bitmaps and textual nodes; use drag and drop; copy, paste, delete, and insert nodes; and edit node text.
- The ListView control—The ListView control closely mirrors the file system directory windows in the Windows 95 operating system. This control allows you to present the user with graphical as well as textual information. Four different views are provided: Large Icon, Small Icon, List View (tabular), and Report (name and defaults).
- The PictureListBox control—With the PictureListBox control you can add a graphical representation next to the text value that you find in a standard list box control.
- The DropDownListBox control—The DropDownListBox control is similar to the new PictureListBox control in that it enhances a standard drop-down list box by allowing the display of a graphic representation next to the list's text value.

As you would expect, each of these new controls has a number of new functions, events, and attributes. These are detailed in Chapter 11, "Windows and the Window Painter."

The Menu Painter

The creation of menus in PowerBuilder is significantly faster than in prior releases. The toolbar icon specifications in the Menu painter that were modal dialog boxes in earlier versions are now easier-to-use tab pages. You have the ability to create your own drop-down toolbars for implementation in your applications. The Menu painter also has an attribute specific to cross-platform development with the Macintosh. Since the Mac uses different text for standard menu items (for example, instead of Exit, the Mac uses Quit), you can specify that the text be automatically changed on the Mac for specific menu items. See Chapter 12, "Menus and the Menu Painter," for more information.

The DataWindow Painter

The DataWindow objects are now fully OLE 2.0 compliant. You can now add OLE objects, including OCX controls, to your DataWindow presentation. The OLE objects can then be activated in place instead of just off-site. The painter still allows you to access a binary large object (blob) column, but blob columns are now implemented using OLE 2.0 instead of 1.0. PowerBuilder has also added an OLE 2.0 presentation style that allows you to place database-retrieved information in an OLE-compatible server application such as Word or Excel.

In addition to the OLE 2.0 presentation style, the DataWindow object has gained a second new presentation style: Rich Text Edit. The RTE presentation acts much in the same manner as the RTE control in the Window painter, but it allows you to more easily merge retrieved data with a document inside a word processor. The RTE presentation reduces the necessity to interact with an outside application to implement business functionality such as a mail merge.

Powersoft has added several other features to the DataWindow painter such as Retrieve Rows to Disk, AutoScrolling, drop-down toolbars, and SQL syntax formatting. The Retrieve Rows to Disk option is available in the 32-bit environment and writes rows to a temporary disk file for faster access. AutoScrolling gives you the ability to automatically scroll with the cursor when dragging, resizing, and using the lasso select. Many of the common menu items and the multitude of PainterBar icons have been implemented using the new drop-down toolbars, which eliminate the need for menu access and rid the PainterBar of a multitude of icons. A useful enhancement is if you convert your SQL to syntax from the graphical environment, PowerBuilder now formats the SQL instead of placing the whole statement on one line.

For more information on these and other DataWindow painter enhancements, see Chapter 9, "The DataWindow Painter."

The Database Painter

The Database painter remains almost the same as in previous versions except for two modifications: the Table painter and access to the Pipeline painter.

The Table painter is used to make any modifications to a table's definition and extended attributes. The interface is essentially the same as the Create/Alter Table dialog box in prior releases, but you can now access this non-modal painter directly.

The Database painter now gives direct access to the Pipeline painter. The Data Pipeline painter gives you multiple data source options (Quick Select, SQL Select, Query, and Stored Procedures) and the ability to perform blob transfers.

The supported database connectivity has also changed for PowerBuilder 5.0. Windows 3.*x* supports DB/2, Informix 5 and 7, MDI Database Gateway for DB/2, Oracle 6 and 7, Microsoft SQL Server 4.2 and 6.0, Sybase System 10 (`ctlib` and `dblib`) and System 11 (using System 10 `ctlib`), Sybase Net Gateway for DB/2, and ODBC (dBASE, Watcom 5.0, Netware SQL, Btrieve, and Paradox 5).

NOTE

The following native database drivers have been discontinued: SQLBase, HP Allbase, Informix 4, and XDB. They can still be accessed via ODBC if you so require.

Windows NT supports Informix 5 and 7, MDI Database Gateway for DB/2, Oracle 7, SQL Server 4.2 and 6.0, Sybase System 10 (`ctlib` and `dblib`) and System 11 (using System 10 `ctlib`), Sybase Net Gateway for DB/2, and ODBC (dBASE and Watcom 4 and 5).

Windows 95 supports SQL Server 4.2 and 6.0, Sybase System 10 (`ctlib` and `dblib`) and System 11 (using System 10 `ctlib`), and ODBC (Watcom 5).

The Debugger

The Debugger has been modified to provide support for overloaded functions (see the section "Object Orientation" later in the chapter) as well as access to the `This` and `Parent` pronouns. The inclusion of these pronouns simplifies the debugging of instance variables, parent relationships, and current object variables.

PowerScript

Parameterized events allow you to send parameters to an event and to use parameters for the PowerBuilder defined events within your script. This means that some functions are now considered obsolete and may result in some considerable code review before an application truly uses the 5.0 features. These functions include `GetClickedColumn()`, `GetClickedRow()`, `dbErrorCode()`, `dbErrorMessage()`, and `GetSQLPreview()`. You can also create your own events to use the new parameters' functionalities. This effectively blurs the delineation between object functions and events so that they truly become object methods. For a detailed review of this feature and what it means for your code and performance, see Chapter 6, "The PowerScript Language."

Most of the system events now return a Long value, and if you use the `Return` statement, PowerBuilder will assume `Return Message.ReturnValue` if you do not specify a value.

PowerBuilder now assumes `Message.Processed = TRUE` for all non-zero return values, and you must specifically state `Message.Processed = TRUE` for a zero value to prevent the default processing from occurring.

Some of the DataWindow custom events that Powersoft provided previously were never actually fired, and these have been removed in 5.0. You should use the following instead:

Old Event	*New Event*
pm_dwnlbuttondown	Clicked
pbm_dwnmbuttonclk	N/A
pbm_dwnmbuttondblclk	N/A
pbm_dwnrbuttonclk	N/A
pbm_rdwnbuttondown	N/A

There are several new keywords for use when you're declaring variables: `CONSTANT`, `READONLY`, `PROTECTEDREAD`, `PROTECTEDWRITE`, `PRIVATEREAD`, `PRIVATEWRITE`, `SYSTEMREAD`, and `SYSTEMWRITE`. These allow you to further restrict and refine the access you allow external scripts to your objects' variables.

For additional information on the new capabilities of PowerScript, see Chapter 6.

A number of functions have been implemented to support PowerBuilder's cross-platform capabilities. Many of these functions were available in the later releases of PowerBuilder 4.0 for the Macintosh and UNIX Motif. Most noticeably added to Version 5.0 is the support of the Windows Registry. PowerBuilder enables you to read and write information to the Registry, which is heavily used by Windows 95 and NT. For more information, see Chapter 21, "Cross-Platform PowerBuilder."

DataWindow Scripting

You can now directly manipulate DataWindow objects from within PowerScript. This includes direct reference and modification of single data items. Nested reports and OLE objects are also directly accessible.

The DataWindow has now gone nonvisual with the introduction of the `DataStore` object. This object acts just like a regular DataWindow, and you can access the same properties and methods (except those that are visual in nature).

`Case` statement support in DataWindow expressions as well as SQL-based expression operators (`LIKE`, `NOT LIKE`, `IN`, `NOT IN`, `BETWEEN`, `NOT BETWEEN`, `EQUAL`, and `NOT EQUAL`) have been added to expand the power and flexibility of DataWindow scripting.

You can now write a generic `Retrieve()` call because PowerBuilder 5.0 allows you to supply more parameters than are required by the DataWindow object.

`SetActionCode()` is now an obsolete function because scripts written for DataWindows conform with those of your other scripts by making use of the `Return` statement.

For more information on DataWindow scripting, see Chapters 10, "DataWindow Scripting," 25, "Advanced DataWindow Techniques I," and 26, "Advanced DataWindow Techniques II."

Internationalization

Recognizing the demand for multilingual applications, PowerBuilder has implemented several new functions and attributes to ease the development of international applications.

The `Reverse()` function is used to reverse the order from left to right of a specified string argument (for example, `simon` would become `nomis`). The `IsArabic()` and `IsHebrew()` functions are used to determine whether a specified character is Arabic or Hebrew. PowerBuilder also supports international and double-byte characters and allows you to specify right-to-left orientation for alignment and cursor movement via the `RightToLeft` attribute of most objects.

Object Orientation

PowerBuilder has continued to develop its object-oriented capabilities in Version 5.0. As you saw in the "PowerScript" section, there are numerous keywords that can be specified for a variable declaration that are used to control objects' access to that variable.

If a global variable is being hidden because a local, a shared, or an instance variable has been declared with the same name, you can reference the global variable by prefacing it with double colons (for example, `::count`).

With the introduction of parameterized events, a new syntax has been introduced that allows you to pass parameters to events. These events and now functions can be posted for later execution.

In previous versions of PowerBuilder, to achieve function overloading (the ability to call the same function for an object with different parameters) you had to resort to inheritance and declaring one version of the function at each level. New to PowerBuilder 5.0 is the ability to write functions with the same name, but either a different number of parameters or parameters with different data types in the same object. You also have the ability to call dynamically bound functions and events. For more information on PowerBuilder and its object-oriented capabilities, please see Chapter 15, "Programming PowerBuilder."

PowerBuilder is now fully OLE 2.0 compatible in both the DataWindow and Window painters. OLE 2.0 objects allow access to any OLE automation server as well as to the OCX technology for component-based development. PowerBuilder 5.0 also allows you to create OLE servers via nonvisual user objects. This means that you can create a business object in PowerBuilder that is accessible from other OLE-enabled applications. For more information on OLE, see Chapter 36, "OLE 2.0 and DDE."

Additional Products

Sybase SQL Anywhere is the new name for the Watcom relational database since the merger of Powersoft and Sybase, Inc. SQL Anywhere was modified to fill the desktop gap in Sybase's product line. SQL Anywhere provides language compatibility with Sybase Transact-SQL and replication as well as the additions to Version 4.0.

The PowerBuilder Foundation Class (PFC) library was developed as a starting point for developers. You can use the PFC library for your base objects or to create your own framework.

ObjectCycle is a new Powersoft utility for version control and source management of your PowerBuilder applications. ObjectCycle incorporates labeling and version control for use in a multideveloper environment. ObjectCycle differs from many of the existing file-based version control packages in that it uses SQL Anywhere to store all its information.

PowerBuilder is packaging three galleries that can be used to enhance and simplify application development. The Component Gallery is a collection of basic OCX controls. Additional OCX controls can be purchased as part of the Component Pack, which is the result of a 1995 merger with the company Visual Components, which develops OCX component ware. The Art Gallery is a collection of bitmap images that can be used for toolbars, picture buttons, and picture controls. The Samples Gallery contains numerous code examples and sample applications that can be pulled from to learn the different PowerBuilder features.

Additional Features

The Open Server Executable option has been added to the Project painter to enable the creation of distributed PowerBuilder applications that use the Sybase Open Server product. Distributed PowerBuilder supports the following network drivers: Named Pipes, Winsock, and Open Server. Two additional objects have been introduced for constructing distributed PowerBuilder applications: Connect object and Transport object. The initial release of Distributed PowerBuilder supports only a driver-based implementation between a PowerBuilder client and a PowerBuilder server.

To become truly Windows 95 logo compliant, PowerBuilder will also ship with such features as Uninstall and Silent Install.

Summary

In creating Version 5.0 of PowerBuilder, Powersoft has listened to the needs of the development community and the direction of current technology. PowerBuilder has increased its object-oriented capabilities and at the same time decreased execution time by creating machine code executables. With this new release, PowerBuilder ensures its place as a leader in the application-development tools market.

The Client/Server Arena and PowerBuilder

2

IN THIS CHAPTER

PowerBuilder from its first inception has been positioned as a client/server application development tool. In this chapter you will learn what is special about the client/server arena and how PowerBuilder provides some of the functionality required to field a truly client/server-based application.

Client/Server Overview

Client/server is currently the predominant architecture used for downsizing or rightsizing projects. The term actually covers a wide range of different methods, not all of which adhere strictly to the client/server paradigm. This architecture is one of many that is being used by the software engineering community.

The simplest architecture, two-tier, involves a single client machine, a single server machine, and a network connection between the two. The client machine is used to carry out independent processing from the server and uses the server as a source of information as the end user requires it. Obviously, as you extend this definition to include multiple clients and servers, you increase the number of places from which information can be gathered. The next two sections define the responsibilities of client and server machines.

Servers

A server involves a piece of hardware that serves data to a client PC. This is not unlike a waiter (server) in a restaurant serving you what you request. In fact, within a client/server environment a client may request files and data from multiple servers.

Many organizations caught up in the downsizing hype of the late '80s and early '90s allowed business units to dictate their hardware and software requirements to M.I.S. (also now known as Information Technology, or I.T., departments). Some departments even maintained servers and client machines outside the control, or at least direct control, of the M.I.S. departments. This permitted the department to benefit from making use of computing resources appropriate to its problem domain. But it also introduced problems of its own, not the least of which is the difficulty of maintaining controllable standards for software purchasing and development.

In the late '80s this caused information management problems. Recently, however, numerous software solutions allowing access to heterogeneous data sources and file systems have become available. Now a knowledgeable worker using a PC or Apple Macintosh has access to mainframe data, from the other side of the world if necessary, at the touch of a button.

Choosing hardware for a server requires careful planning to provide a secure, reliable server. The specific task that the server is being acquired for will influence the vendor choices somewhat. For example, if you want a very high-performance database server that is readily upgradable, you might consider a UNIX box from Hewlett-Packard or Sun Microsystems. Communication, file, database, and even the more recent entries into this fold such as online analytical processing (OLAP) require different considerations in their hardware requirements.

Clients

The real workhorses of client/server systems are the client machines (or PCs). It is this piece of hardware that has enabled the explosion of graphics tools and utilities that enhance end user productivity. The intense computing power required to drive a GUI would choke most mainframes if they had to provide this service for a typical organization. Not only does the client machine carry out the processing of data within the original problem domain, but it can also be exploited for additional uses, such as word processing, spreadsheets, and e-mail. All this and a friendly graphical user interface—surely this is heaven?

The exact requirements for a desktop client machine have changed considerably in only a few years. It used to be acceptable to place a 386 processor PC on an end user's desk and expect him or her to be content with the performance. But not today. The end user community has demanded increased performance from machines and software, to the point where in some organizations the end user is working with machines that are superior to those of the developers. This is actually the intention in some organizations, where some of the machines used by developers are lower-powered than the intended end-user machines. If the developers can make the application work at an acceptable level on these lower-powered machines, then the deployment to the end users can be achieved more easily. Carrying out upgrades to a department full of PCs can be an expensive and time-consuming prospect. Was it worth the migration from the mainframe? The answer is usually yes. But not from a cost perspective. The increased productivity and improved tools for accessing data justify the cost, and this has enabled improved customer responsiveness. Communication between employees and departments is usually higher, due to sharing of applications and data. This can lead to some interesting partnerships that might never have been thought of within the confines of the old mainframe system.

The most common complaints from end users seem to be about the responsiveness of the display and the speed of obtaining data from the server. You can increase application graphics speed by purchasing a relatively inexpensive Windows accelerator card or by altering your application code so the end user perceives that the window is opening faster than it actually is.

The Network

Network throughput has a great influence on the performance of the client/server environment. Some of the factors affecting throughput include the physical distance over which the network extends (network segments and nodes per segment), the type of cabling used, the client and server network protocols, network topology, bridging versus routing, and overall network loading.

The physical cable distance that separates a client machine from a server might be greater than the actual distance from box to box. The distances the two machines may communicate over can vary between local area networks (LANs), metropolitan area networks (MANs), and wide area networks (WANs). As the network grows, additional pieces of specialized hardware are needed to grow and expand the network (repeaters, routers, bridges, and so on). These can introduce their own performance problems, which may require the whole network to be re-architected.

If applications will be developed that utilize a MAN or WAN, you might want to consider special versions of the software to provide additional caching or simpler functionality, because there is a great difference in communication rates between these and LANs.

One factor not often given serious consideration is the physical cabling. There are a number of different grades of cable that give better performance at greater cost. You may even consider fiber-optic cabling as a solution. Always try to purchase the grade of cable that you can envision using more than a few years into the future, and keep network expansion foremost in mind.

The network protocol used by the client and server can affect the rate at which data can be transferred. Some protocols carry greater overhead than others but are less error prone and can be used to carry larger packet sizes. The protocol you decide on will be influenced by the types of applications that will be using the network.

The type of network technology used can also affect communication rates, and is again a trade-off between cost and performance. For example, Ethernet technology exhibits a performance drop off as the utilization of the bandwidth approaches 50% but is very fast under light to medium loading. Token Ring, on the other hand, has a fixed response time to client requests and does not experience the same performance degradation at higher utilization. However, there is an associated implementation cost, as well as problems such as a failure at a point in the ring that will cause the whole network to fail.

Why Client/Server Systems?

Client/server is well suited to the implementation of decision support systems (DSSs) that are used to access legacy data. *Legacy data* is usually business-critical data that is being used by older back-office types of applications on the mainframe. The use of those costly mainframe cycles can be greatly reduced using a PC-based DSS. Mainframe data is downloaded to a server on a one-time basis and then updated periodically; this is the only cost incurred on the mainframe. This data can then be loaded into a PC-based database server for access by any number of clients at a significant cost savings.

Sounds simple, doesn't it? It usually isn't. What was not taken into consideration in the previous paragraph is that there is a cost involved in writing the mainframe export program, having it run periodically, buying and administering the server, buying the client machines, possibly training the users on their new machines, writing the DSS program, and writing the data import program. Did I miss anything? Probably. There is certainly more to it than the simple statements suggest, and you should be prepared to tackle each issue before you start.

Each client/server application must be carefully analyzed before development starts. Will there be a cost savings? Wouldn't it be simpler to give the end user a PC and a terminal emulator so he or she can still access the mainframe data directly? This would provide the end user with a powerful workstation to use word processing, perform spreadsheet calculations, use e-mail, and so on, but still have access to the central data store on the mainframe.

As you start looking at client/server systems in detail, there are going to be more questions. Carefully consider each step you make into this brave new world.

Implementing Client/Server Systems

Most companies start with small pilot projects to examine aspects of client/server systems before fully committing time and resources to larger projects. The structured approach that is common in the mainframe world is sometimes abandoned as developers embrace new development tools that allow rapid changes to be made. This often leads to several false starts and different teams heading off in new directions.

You cannot use the same procedures you would when developing mainframe applications, but some of them can be reworked for client/server systems. Maintaining a structured approach to application design is still paramount within this new technology, and ensuring that you have the right components will help your projects get off to the right start.

The choice of different components can be a predominant factor in the success of any project. Hardware for the three main components has been previously discussed for two-tier client/server, but this is only one part of the puzzle. The other part, the software, can be much harder to decide.

The decisions that need to be made regarding what to include in a project toolset are often considered after the system requirements stage. The findings in this stage are a driving factor in which tools are chosen. In some organizations there might not be an option, and you must use the corporate standard tools. In this case you might have to be ingenious with the application of these tools rather than use the tools you would have chosen. A good place to start exploring the available tools is with the people you have access to from other projects. They will be able to explain to you their hands-on experience with a range of products and give you their relative strengths and weaknesses. Of course, nothing beats trying it for yourself. So once you have isolated a couple contenders for the tool of choice, start to experiment with them yourself. Vendors are usually more than happy to provide evaluation versions of their products. Important questions sometimes left unanswered are What is the market direction and trend? What is the latest and greatest? In what direction is a particular tool market heading? Be very careful buying into technology on the trailing or bleeding edge; keeping up with the rest of the industry is usually a strong position to be in.

Hopefully you have already decided what development tool you will be using, and hopefully it is PowerBuilder. While we might be biased toward using PowerBuilder as the tool of choice, we always consider what other tools or development languages might be a better fit for the task. Indeed a combination of tools and languages will often be used to provide an optimal solution.

Once you have decided on the components you will use for each of the facets of implementing a client/server system, your next step is to build a team of designers, developers, and engineers.

When building your team, look for people who have an underlying understanding of what is going on, and not just the fact that they can produce PowerBuilder code. The team members should consider concepts before syntax. This will allow the team to tackle a variety of projects, whether they are PC, Macintosh, or UNIX based. Enlist original systems staff and incorporate them into teams, because these people often have an in-depth knowledge of not just the systems you are replacing, but of the underlying business concepts. Some may resist change and you should try to ease their way into a team by placing them in advisory positions, usually with some sort of stake in the success of the system. Others may try to take on development, even though they are ill-equipped at this time to take on the new challenges new tools bring. Encourage them to experiment with the tools. Provide training and allow them to work on less critical components as they learn.

Often companies do not have the special skills required for their first client/server projects, and they'll look for outside help. Consulting firms can provide you with several benefits. One of these benefits is knowledge transfer from them to your project members. You will have gained nothing but a client/server system that you are unable to support if you do not get your company's employees involved in all stages of a project.

The techniques you will use to develop client/server applications are covered in Chapter 14, "Analysis and Design."

Client/Server Case Studies

The next two sections describe actual accounts from two large corporations that made a move to a client/server architecture, the methods chosen to tackle each individual business problem, and their reasons behind the move to client/server.

Case Study 1: Health Care Company Moves to Client/Server

In an attempt to curtail expensive, resource-intensive mainframe processing, a Fortune 500 health care corporation made the decision to migrate several key application systems to a client/server environment. The hope for the projects was to cut costs, provide the user community with a more flexible interface, and integrate new technology into all facets of the workforce.

In the process of determining which systems would be migrated, the company decided that it would avoid the mission-critical applications and opt for several smaller subsystems. The reasoning behind this decision was that since the company did not have any client/server applications yet, it made sense to test the process on one or more small systems that would not affect crucial day-to-day business activities. This would allow for any difficulties encountered in a technology switch and extra time needed to establish standards. Therefore, the first systems chosen were used for reporting purposes. In addition, it was agreed that once the client/server applications were in place, the mainframe equivalent would continue to operate for at least one month.

A high-level timetable was implemented using recommended schedules determined by benchmarking other companies attempting to move to client/server systems. Since the data that was to be used by the new applications was generated from other applications on the mainframe, the development team needed to create a method to extract the data from the necessary mainframe files and databases. The data was then downloaded to a network server from which the users could run an application for ad hoc queries and the generation of reports. The mainframe extract program was easily implemented, as was the automated download process from the mainframe, since this functionality had been used in other projects. But once it was sent down to the communications server, how was the data going to be queried and from what application?

The choice was to purchase a server-based relational database management system (RDBMS) and access the data in the tables from a Windows-based application. Several prewritten application software packages were evaluated for the front end. It was decided that the best direction to take was to purchase a Windows development tool and create a custom application that could access the RDBMS and its corresponding tables. By developing an in-house application, M.I.S determined that they were laying the groundwork for future applications and giving employees exposure to new technology.

After the tools had been decided on and the development team had been trained in using the products, two issues remained: how to populate the relational database with the downloaded mainframe files and how to create an interface that would not frighten users unfamiliar with Windows. In addition to populating the database, a process needed to be developed for daily and weekly updates of static data, such as code tables. Time and budget dictated that the solution the development team adapted was based on batch files executed using the network operating system's scheduler. These batch files started a copy routine from the communication server to the SQL server and then populated the appropriate tables.

While the table population proved trying, the creation of a Windows interface was even more frustrating. The initial pass-through had an uncanny resemblance to the existing mainframe system that the team wanted to move away from. This was because the project team focused on the functionality of the system (retrieving the data and providing queries) before they designed the interface. To assist in this process, the project team decided to incorporate techniques from other Windows applications and bring in a consultant to review the system and make suggestions on the interface and coding techniques. This combination of recommendations and examination of other applications resulted in an interface (non-MDI) that gave the users a Windows application, but still guided them through the system so as not to intimidate them in a new environment.

The application was tested by other M.I.S. employees not on the immediate project team to determine the ease of use and find unexpected problems. The application was then demonstrated to several of the key users, who gave recommendations on functionality and the interface. The changes were reworked and shown to the users again for a final sign-off. The distribution of the application was provided via sneaker-net (that is, the developers installed the application from disk one machine at a time). The response from the users was positive, and overall the project was viewed as a success.

The company's plan succeeded for several reasons. The initial decision to start with a small part of the business removed considerable stress and extra work from the development team. It gave the team the ability to focus on learning the technology necessary for the client/server environment. The company was willing to provide training for the development team and the cost of a consultant, if needed. Finally, the project team made sure that other M.I.S. members as well as the users were involved and had input in the application's development. The procedures determined by these first applications became the standard that was used for other applications and proved a good foundation for later, more complex applications.

While overall this was a success story, there were some problems that the company encountered. The project ran over budget due to the cost of new equipment, software, training, double processing on the server and mainframe, consulting fees, and downtime due to unexpected errors. The process was not particularly efficient on the client, server, or network, and resulted in an application that did not meet the speed expectations of the users. The system was not well documented, and there were not many standards in place between developers. There was also no process established to handle problem resolution. Also, bad feelings were created between the new client/server team and the old mainframe support teams because the client/server team was able to learn and use new technology.

This situation is not uncommon in many companies and often results in an unsuccessful client/server migration. Companies must be committed to the process and have realistic expectations of the new system and their development teams. Also, because the technology and standards are continually evolving, a company must keep an eye on the future and what it may bring.

Case Study 2: Use of Client/Server by a Fortune 500 Manufacturing Company

In 1991 the Bemis Company, a major supplier of flexible packaging and pressure-sensitive materials with annual sales of $1.4 billion, realized that their information systems were becoming antiquated. Their mainframe-based business systems, some of which were more than 20 years old, were becoming increasingly difficult to enhance and maintain. These systems, used at 4 divisional headquarters and more than 40 plant locations throughout the United States, were a major source of dissatisfaction among the users throughout the company.

The corporate officers decided to change how information systems were delivered. A strategy was set to replace the central information systems staff with development groups at each of the divisions and to make a major investment to replace the aging business systems. Committees of financial and technical personnel from the corporate offices and each division were established to set hardware and software standards and to coordinate the effort.

These committees agreed on a number of principles:

- The company will implement PC-based client/server systems rather than mini-mainframe applications.
- The company will prefer purchasing packaged applications over developing custom applications.
- The company will use PCs on the desktop and prefer PCs as back-end servers.
- The company will use Microsoft's SQL Server database.
- Custom applications will be developed using Powersoft's PowerBuilder.

Selecting PowerBuilder over C or other procedural languages was a strategic decision. PowerBuilder, with its painter-based, event-driven model allowed Bemis to employ developers with primarily analyst skills who could also operate as programmers, rather than employing dedicated programmers. This was done with the knowledge that the resulting programs would require additional PC hardware resources. Powersoft's PowerBuilder was specifically chosen as the development suite because PowerBuilder has a strong development toolset and Powersoft has a dominant position in the marketplace.

With these principles established, each division began to staff its information systems group and set a strategy for the implementation. Some divisions purchased an integrated package, and then internally modified it to their specifications; others contracted with a software company to incorporate their unique requirements into their existing packages.

One division had a large divisional plant with 700 to 800 employees and two smaller 100-employee plants. In the beginning of 1993, the division purchased a fifth medium-sized plant (400 employees) in Pennsylvania. This plant was using custom-developed mainframe-based systems outsourced to a large systems house.

In May the division hired an information systems manager from another division in the company. After much discussion, the division set a strategy to develop its own applications for its order and production control systems (that is, order entry, inventory management, production control). This decision was made due to the uniquenesses of their business and because there were virtually no applications being marketed in 1993 in the chosen environment. The division also hired two developers, both skilled in procedural languages but without knowledge of PowerBuilder or SQL-based databases.

The first project was to eliminate the outsourcing contract for the Pennsylvania plant. This required that the division train its staff while developing four major applications over a six-month period, as well as transferring the financial systems and other supporting systems to the corporate mainframe. These tasks began in August 1993 with two four-person development teams, one located at the corporate headquarters and one made up of the two newly hired developers and two contractors. Both teams used training contractors to train the company's developers and to help develop the applications. The division constructed its own framework, set a number of development standards, and began developing. The headquarters-based team developed an order-entry system and a pricing system. The team at the divisional headquarters developed a production reporting system and a raw materials inventory system for the Pennsylvania plant. A version of the production reporting system was also installed at the large divisional plant.

By February and March 1994, the newly developed systems were implemented and the financial and other systems were migrated from the outsourced mainframe to the corporate mainframe. During this project, a number of smaller applications were also developed to transfer information between the corporate mainframe and the new PowerBuilder systems. This amount of development could never have been accomplished in such a short time with a procedural language. Even though the toolset and hardware platform was somewhat immature, it proved to be sufficiently stable to accomplish the team's objectives.

By mid-1995 the division had implemented an order-costing system at the Pennsylvania plant and the divisional headquarters, an order-entry system at the divisional headquarters, and a number of smaller applications. In the division's migration from the mainframe, the next goal is to develop a finished goods application, an invoicing application, and a sales reporting application. These applications will be bolted onto both of the existing order entry systems.

A third project was completed mid-1995 that established a divisional server containing customer and order information used for reporting. The division purchased an information transfer program to assist in transferring the data between the plant servers onto the divisional server.

There are still a number of projects to accomplish before Bemis completely frees itself of the mainframe. When the finished goods application and invoicing application are running at the divisional headquarters, these will then be implemented at the Pennsylvania plant. The final step will be to install the entire order-control system at the two smaller plants.

With some help from corporate headquarters with the financial systems, the division should be finished with the migration in the second half of 1996, just over three years from the beginning of the first project.

Case Study Conclusions

Both of these case studies show that as a company starts to investigate client/server systems as an alternative, it is implemented in carefully phased stages. The remaining sections of this chapter introduce PowerBuilder as a client/server tool and explain why you will want to use its powerful features in your development efforts.

PowerBuilder as a Client/Server Tool

PowerBuilder provides a graphical user interface (GUI) development tool. In fact, it offers much more than just the ability to paint GUIs. Developers make use of a visual integrated development environment (IDE) to produce GUI applications. PowerBuilder uses a painter paradigm to tackle each object and development requirement. Painters provide a point-and-click environment where objects can be built, modified, and managed.

The "glue" used to do the actual work within objects is written in PowerScript, an enhanced version of BASIC. PowerScript is very similar to Visual Basic and SQL Windows Application Language (SAL).

However, PowerBuilder only provides one piece of the puzzle. You can only develop client applications. There is no direct access or support for network components, and only limited access to database server structures. There is a good reason for this: There is such a wide variety of networks and databases that can be used that PowerBuilder would have to be huge in order to cope with only a fraction of them. Instead, developers make use of database-specific tools (for example, SQL Object Manager for Microsoft SQL Server).

Powersoft has designed PowerBuilder to be an open system and has built some strategic partnerships through its client/server open development environment (CODE) partners. This is an agreement between Powersoft and its partners to establish and maintain a transfer of technical information and work toward tighter integration of products.

In the past year, Powersoft has rapidly expanded its product line to include a number of new tools; S-Designor is one of these. Powersoft is positioning itself to provide solutions to all phases of the software development life cycle with what it calls *best-of-breed products.*

PowerBuilder lends itself to cooperative teamwork within a corporate environment, provided that there is someone able to direct and control the effort. PowerBuilder also lends itself to the development of both component and solution products. This makes it a very powerful tool that can produce low-cost, efficient applications in short periods of time.

Why Use PowerBuilder?

Developers can become productive in a very short period of time with PowerBuilder. It requires less training to produce a finished product than would be required with some of the other development tools. This does not mean that the best solution will be found or that the developer's knowledge is complete because there are numerous advanced topics in PowerBuilder that only come with experience (and reading this book!).

PowerBuilder provides developers with the means to write event-driven applications in an object-oriented manner or to produce procedural applications. PowerBuilder can be used for "good" or for "evil"; it is the developer's choice. If you delve a little under the surface of PowerBuilder, you will find a world of classes, inheritance, ancestors, descendants, encapsulation, polymorphism, overloading, and overriding. Purists will argue that PowerBuilder is not a true object-oriented tool. They have a valid case in places. However, PowerBuilder does make use of object-oriented techniques and technology and allows developers to be as object oriented as they want to be.

Applications can be developed very rapidly by experienced developers. By taking advantage of PowerBuilder's intuitive environment, developers can participate in rapid application development (RAD) sessions to quickly produce functioning prototypes that end users can touch and feel. This is further aided by use of numerous reusable objects that can be built with PowerBuilder.

Probably one of the biggest selling points of PowerBuilder is the DataWindow. This object is the focal point of data interaction in PowerBuilder and is used for reporting as well as data entry tasks. DataWindows have numerous built-in functions, such as handling communication with the database server, data validation, and complex report presentations. Integral with the database communication is submission of `SELECT` statements (which are graphically painted by the developer) to retrieve data and the appropriate generation of database `UPDATE`, `INSERT`, and `DELETE` statements to reflect the data changes made by an end user. This might be reason enough to make use of a DataWindow, but it also offers a number of other advantages. Using other development tools, a number of controls must be used to construct a data entry screen, whereas the DataWindow is actually one control with simply a graphical representation of the desired controls. This places fewer demands on the graphic resources of the operating system and is faster to render on the screen.

Another attractive feature of PowerBuilder is Powersoft's commitment to provide a multi-platform tool that requires little or no additional code to run. PowerBuilder is currently available for 16-bit Windows, Windows 95, Windows NT, Macintosh, and UNIX. Objects in library files can be accessed directly by PowerBuilder running on each platform without any migration.

PowerBuilder supports object linking and embedding (OLE) Version 2.0 as well as Version 1.0, dynamic data exchange (DDE), access to external functions and objects, VBX support, and standard file I/O operations.

All these features make PowerBuilder a very scalable product, moreso than the majority of the other client/server tools available.

PowerBuilder Basics

Now that we have discussed what PowerBuilder is and what it can do for you, let's run through a quick guide to the various parts of the PowerBuilder environment and some useful shortcuts.

Figure 2.1 shows a typical painter window.

FIGURE 2.1.
A typical painter window.

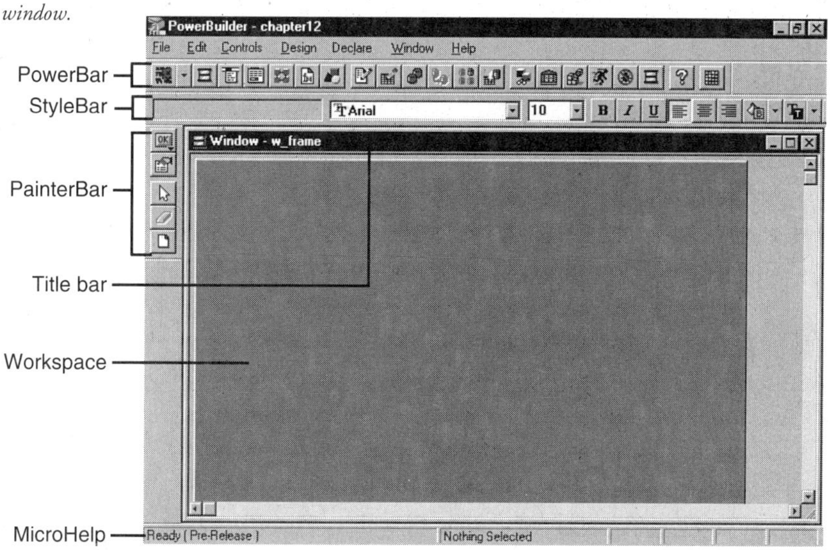

Actions in a painter are usually controlled by using one of the available painter toolbars:

- The PowerBar provides access to other painters and tools.
- The PainterBar allows you to manipulate controls and objects in the current painter.
- The StyleBar allows you to change text attributes (for example, font, size).
- The ColorBar allows you to change the color of controls and define custom colors.

These options are also available through the painter menus, and the toolbars can be modified to carry out any action available in a painter menu. Obviously, not all the same options are available in different painters. Indeed, some toolbars may be irrelevant and therefore unavailable in some painters (for example, the ColorBar cannot be accessed in the Menu painter).

In some of the painters, most notably in the Window painter, you can get a context-sensitive menu by right-clicking. The menu displays a list of actions that are appropriate to the object you have right-clicked. This provides a shortcut to some of the most frequently accessed actions. On a Macintosh this menu can be opened by holding down the Ctrl key and clicking the mouse button. The menus and commands available in a painter depend on which painter is currently open.

The title bar for a painter identifies the currently open object, whereas the title bar for PowerBuilder identifies the current application.

The basis of each PowerBuilder painter is the workspace where you actually interact with the object.

The MicroHelp line running along the bottom edge of PowerBuilder displays a variety of information, from what action is currently occurring to the position and size of an object.

Shortcuts to Open Painters

You can open painters by either clicking on the corresponding button on the PowerBar or by using one of the hotkeys shown in Table 2.1.

Table 2.1. Painter hotkeys.

Painter	*Hotkey*
Application painter	Shift+F1
Window painter	Shift+F2
Menu painter	Shift+F3
DataWindow painter	Shift+F4
Structure editor	Shift+F5
File editor	Shift+F6
Database painter	Shift+F7
Query painter	Shift+F8
Function painter	Shift+F9
Library painter	Shift+F10
User Object painter	Shift+F11

Getting Help

PowerBuilder provides a complete reference manual in its online help. Help is easily accessed via the familiar F1 key. The help contains a number of topics, from connecting to your database to PowerScript function descriptions, definitions, and examples. You can get context-sensitive help from within the Script painter of an object by highlighting a word and pressing Shift+F1.

Summary

This chapter describes client/server technology and its components. The necessary resource considerations in terms of people, money, and tools are introduced, and you have also been warned that client/server is not the solution to every problem.

You have learned a little about PowerBuilder and the components that make up the painters. This chapter describes the major features in PowerBuilder and why you would want to consider PowerBuilder as the development tool of choice for all your client/server applications.

PART II

IN THIS PART

Programming with PowerBuilder

Database Management Systems

3

IN THIS CHAPTER

In response to the pressure of end users who want accessible data, the client/server platform has become the dominant computing architecture of the 1990s. Corporate departments have felt the need to develop applications for their own specialized purposes, whereas organizations need information systems to support the overall business system. The client/server platform allows the distribution of components across a network to create a flexible architecture that meets the needs of departments as well as those of the organization. This architecture enables companies to use differing database management systems, network protocols, and end-user tools together effectively.

The database management system (DBMS) enables shared access to data within a database. The DBMS maintains the security, integrity, and reliability of the database. Deciding on a development tool is important, but just as important is the choice of DBMS. When you make that choice, you need to consider a number of points, including scalability, platforms support, and technical support.

PowerBuilder provides native connections to a number of DBMSs. To connect to a specific DBMS, three components need to be installed (see Figure 3.1). First is the Powersoft-supplied database interface, which usually consists of a single dynamic link library (DLL). The name of this DLL should be PB*xxx*050.DLL, where *xxx* is a three-character description of the DBMS. For example, PBMSS050.DLL is the Microsoft SQL Server database interface. The next layer is the DBMS vendor-supplied interface files. These files provide the API with which the Powersoft DLL interacts; for example, W3DBLIB.DLL is the SQL Server–specific DLL. The third and final layer is the database network support. These files vary depending on what type of network the DBMS server is located in; for example, for SQL Server listening on Named Pipes, the database network file is DBNMP3.DLL.

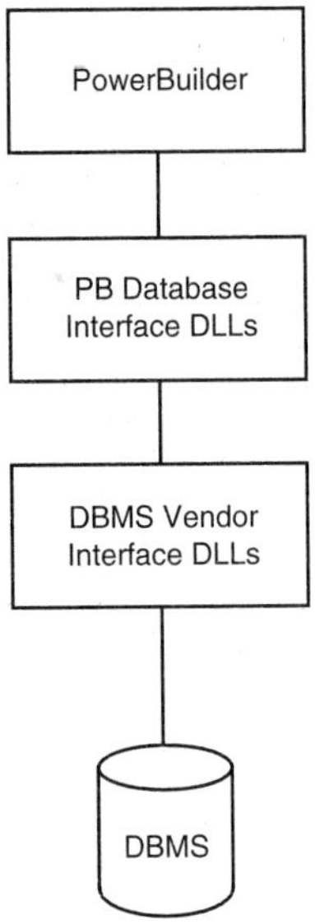

FIGURE 3.1.
Components required to connect to a DBMS.

The installation of each of the layers is too varied to be described here, but adequate instructions are available with each piece of software.

TIP

Each layer might support only a certain version of one or another of the additional layers. Your best bet is to get the most up-to-date version of all the drivers. You should, however, always make backup copies of older drivers when you upgrade.

What follows is an overview of a number of DBMSs that are directly supported by the PowerBuilder native drivers.

The supported database connectivity has changed for PowerBuilder 5.0.

Windows 3.*x* supports Informix 5.*x*, 6.*x*, and 7.*x*, Oracle 6.*x*, 7.0, 7.1, and 7.2, Microsoft and Sybase SQL Server 4.*x* (using `dblib`), Microsoft SQL Server 6.0, Sybase System 10 (`ctlib` and `dblib`), Sybase System 11 (`ctlib`), IBM, Sybase InformationCONNECT Gateway for DB2, Sybase Net-Gateway for DB2, and ODBC (dBASE, Sybase SQL Anywhere, Excel, text, NetWare SQL, Btrieve, and Paradox 5).

NOTE

In Version 5.0, PowerBuilder has dropped the native driver access of several DBMSs: Gupta SQLBase, HP AllBase, Informix 4, and XDB. These databases are now accessible via ODBC. These DBMSs are still covered in this chapter, but the "Connecting to PowerBuilder" section has been removed from each.

Windows NT supports Informix via INET 5.*x*, 6.*x* and 7.*x*, MDI Database Gateway for DB2, Oracle 7.*x*, Microsoft and Sybase SQL Server 4.*x*, Microsoft SQL Server 6.0, Sybase System 10 (`ctlib` and `dblib`), Sybase System 11 (`ctlib`), Sybase InformationCONNECT Gateway for DB2, ODBC (Intersolv 2.11 drivers and Sybase SQL Anywhere).

Windows 95 supports Microsoft and Sybase SQL Server 4.*x*, Microsoft SQL Server 6.0, Sybase System 10 (`ctlib` and `dblib`), Sybase System 11 (`ctlib`), Sybase InformationCONNECT DB2 Gateway, Oracle 7.*x*, Informix 5.*x*, 6.*x*, and 7.*x*, and ODBC.

One definition that is useful to learn before looking at the features of your particular DBMS is that of isolation levels. Isolation levels vary greatly among DBMSs in their names as well as their precise meaning. An *isolation level* specifies the degree to which one transaction operation is visible to another concurrent transaction, and determines how the DBMS isolates and/or locks data from other processes.

This overview covers everything from available features and platforms to the requirements of connecting PowerBuilder.

ALLBASE/SQL

The HP ALLBASE/SQL Version G.0 database server from Hewlett-Packard is an open, mission-critical relational database management system (RDBMS).

Hewlett-Packard sells ALLBASE/SQL as providing a functionally rich, high-performance, relational database management system for HP 3000 MPE/iX and HP 9000 HP-UX business servers and workstations. The company also boasts of giving HP users single-vendor support and worldwide-response availability 7 days a week, 24 hours a day.

ALLBASE/SQL is tightly integrated with HP's MPE/iX and HP-UX operating systems and Precision Architecture Reduced Instruction-Set Computing (PA-RISC) architecture. It is engineered to support very large databases, with well over 100GB and thousands of online users, without compromising application performance. Microsoft's open database connectivity (ODBC) and Gupta's API are supported in HP's PC API, which is bundled with ALLBASE/SQL. ALLBASE/SQL meets the ANSI SQL-92 entry-level requirements.

Features

Data consistency is maintained by way of the HP/ALLBASE/Replicate database shadowing capability that ensures 24-hour uptime, disaster recovery, and remote unattended backup. Forward, backward, and online transaction recovery are also available. Several locking levels are offered: row-level, page-level, and table-level. ALLBASE/SQL uses the isolation feature to support assorted database-lock options. In PowerBuilder you can use the `Lock` attribute of the transaction object to set the isolation level when you connect to the database. The isolation level (lock) values supported by ALLBASE/SQL are CS (cursor stability), RL (release locks), and RR (repeatable read).

DB2

DB2 (Database 2) from IBM is one of the more well known and established relational databases in the computer industry, largely due to its presence in the mainframe environment. The DB2 product family provides high levels of data availability, integrity, security, recovery, reliability, and performance capabilities for small- to large-scale application management. Each product provides the same basic functionality and SQL commands, regardless of the platform.

One of the goals and strong points of DB2 is its scalability. IBM has expanded the available platforms beyond IBM's own PCs, AS/400s, RISC System/6000 hardware, and IBM mainframe computers to non-IBM machines from Hewlett-Packard and Sun Microsystems. This gives you the ability to grow from a single-user environment to an environment that provides shared access to hundreds or thousands of users.

DB2 employs data staging, which enables host data to be easily downloaded to a LAN database server. This enables client/server users and LAN-based application programs to access host data for informational purposes, making the database appear local and the remote connection appear transparent. DB2 provides the database server and database client with functions for LAN environments using OS/2, DOS, and Windows applications.

Features

The latest version of DB2 (MVS/ESA) has increased its network support in a variety of ways. The maximum number of distributed users that can be connected has been increased from 10,000 to 25,000 per DB2 subsystem. In relation to the number of connections being increased, up to 2,000 threads can be active simultaneously, which gives you the ability to have 200,000 concurrent connections with 16,000 active threads in an 8-way data-sharing configuration. The ability to manage the threads has been enhanced by allowing you to assign different dispatching priorities to each distributed application. Remote environments can access DB2 data via stored procedures, which can be called from local DB2 applications or remote distributed relational database architecture (DRDA) applications.

DB2 includes implicit row-level locking, explicit table-level locking, deadlock detection, and data-isolation functions. Type 2 indexes are now supported; they are used to avoid index locking, which removes problems of deadlocks and timeouts on an index. Creation of unique and clustered indexes can be accomplished on any field with an almost unlimited range.

Information is stored as linear ESDS VSAM data sets for DB2. Integrity is assured by providing forward recovery permit restoration of all changes made in a database since the last backup was performed. These backups can include either the entire database or the database changes, using the transaction log. DB2 now gives you the ability to recover indexes, display databases, and obtain diagnostic information. Rules for referential integrity can be defined during or after table definition. The database security is handled by an internal table manager.

DB2 is well known for having a very thorough query optimizer. Queries have been improved with added functions such as outer joins to allow result sets to include unmatching rows as well as matching rows from all tables or for specific tables. For CPU-intensive queries that generate several tasks, DB2 allows parallel processing to occur. This, combined with the ability to reclaim unused or wasted DASD space by reorganizing the catalog and indexes, is part of IBM's enhancements to make DB2 a higher-performing product.

PowerBuilder Support

Powersoft provides three database interfaces to access a DB2 server: IBM, Sybase InformationCONNECT DB2 Gateway Interface, and Sybase Net-Gateway Interface (16-bit PowerBuilder only). These gateways enable an interface to distribute relational database information to open client/server platforms, which includes protocols for communications between applications and remote databases, as well as between databases.

Connecting to PowerBuilder

The IBM interface (previously IBM DRDA) is the connection protocol for IBM relational database products. The following databases are accessible: Database Manager, Database 2 for OS/2, Database 2 for MVS, and Database 2 for RS/6000. DB2 scalar and aggregate functions can be used in SQL syntax, although aggregate functions are used only in summary-only SQL statements. The basic software components to access IBM databases differ from database to database, but all require PBDBL050.DLL, PBIBM050.DLL, PCDRDLL.DLL, DB2W.DLL, and NetBios, IPX/SPX, or TCP/IP. Database Manager, or DB2/2, requires the `NetHeapSize` parameter in the `[386Enh]` section of the SYSTEM.INI file to be set to `76`. Part of the requirements and setup for connecting to the IBM DRDA database is the process of binding PowerBuilder to the desired database. This binding procedure is accomplished by the Client Application Enabler, which you can obtain from IBM.

The InformationCONNECT DB2 Gateway and Sybase Net-Gateway are the two Powersoft connection gateway software packages for DB2. The basic software components to access DB2 using InformationCONNECT DB2 are PBMDI050.DLL or for Net-Gateway, PBNET050.DLL (Net-Gateway is only available for 16-bit). In addition, you need W3DBLIB.DLL and the appropriate gateway software.

Table 3.1 lists the unique values for each database interface profile setup definition.

Table 3.1. DB2 interface profile setup definitions.

Field	*IBM DRDA*	*InformationCONNECT Database Gateway*	*Sybase Net-Gateway*
DBMS	IBM DB2	MDI Gateway	NETGATEWAY
User ID	The ID depends on the CAE version in use. CAE 1.0 or 1.1: The value is the authorization ID used in the `SQLLOGN2` command to log on to IBM Communication Manager. CAE 1.2: The value is the DB2USERID environment variable in the \SQLLIB\SETUP.BAT script.	Not applicable	Not applicable

Field	*IBM DRDA*	*InformationCONNECT Database Gateway*	*Sybase Net-Gateway*
Database Name	The alias name of the accessed IBM database, which must match the cataloged entry for the database.	Only specify the name of the DB2 database if you want to create a table in a database that is not the default database.	Only specify the name of the DB2 database if you want to create a table in a database that is not the default database.

Informix

The Informix database server from Informix Software, Inc., comes in two different packages: Informix-SE and Informix-OnLine.

Informix-SE is available for the UNIX and Windows NT platforms and is designed for small to midrange applications. It is sold as the low-maintenance, high-reliability solution for small businesses or self-contained departments that do not have vast database-administration expertise.

Features

Informix-SE uses a cost-based optimizer to produce the best performance for queries and enables the creation of unique and clustered indexes. Indexes can include up to eight fields of varying data types, up to a maximum of 120 bytes. Data consistency is maintained (as it is by most other DBMSs) by the use of transaction logging, but it is further enhanced by audit trails that provide additional information to restore a table and all completed transactions. Databases are restored by use of the transaction log and a backup of the database. Several locking levels are available, from row-level to table-level, and even database-level locking (although the latter has to be specifically requested by a user application). Informix-SE also provides read-only isolation control so that a `SELECT` can request the data `FOR UPDATE` and still make the data available for viewing while reserving the right to make modifications to it. Business rules can be specified on columns, which specify acceptable values, defaults, and column-to-column relationships enforced by integrity constraints and triggers. The Informix implementation of integrity constraints is ANSI-SQL compliant and is specified in the `CREATE TABLE` syntax. Triggers can be written for the standard three cases: `INSERT`, `DELETE`, and `UPDATE`.

Security is provided in two levels of access privileges: database privileges that control object creation and table privileges that specify allowable user actions. Informix-SE security controls alter, insert, and delete at the table level and enable `SELECT` and `UPDATE` privileges to be specified on a column-by-column basis. No separate database login is required; Informix-SE relies on login security at the operating-system level. Stored procedures are supported and provide an additional security mechanism by enabling users to execute procedures that work on tables they would not normally have access to. This enables a DBA to assign procedure-level security. In a UNIX environment, Informix-SE uses the native tools for backing up databases so that system maintenance requires no additional skills.

Informix-SE meets most of the ANSI SQL-92 Entry Level requirements and even claims some SQL3 features and functions. Two notable omissions from the package, however, are delimited identifier support and serialization of transactions. Informix-SE has passed a subset of the NIST SQL 127-2 test suite, currently the only test for ANSI-SQL compliance.

Migration of your data is made easy because Informix uses the X/Open XPG3 specification of Native Language Support and enables the collation of character strings and date and currency transformations required by the country of use.

Within a UNIX environment, Informix-SE requires 1.2MB of memory and 6MB of disk space—very modest usage compared to that of other systems. Each user process requires (on average) 180KB, but this varies by application. Pricing is charged by the seat, with a development seat being twice as expensive as a user seat. Minimum purchases for both of these are required.

The Informix-OnLine Dynamic Server provides a multithreaded server that can exploit symmetric multiprocessor and uniprocessor architectures and is aimed at a different market than Informix-SE.

Using a multithreaded architecture enables Informix-OnLine to utilize each hardware resource to its fullest. Informix-OnLine can be dynamically reconfigured to tune the system for different types of work loads, maintaining high availability of the server. For example, shared memory is parceled out on demand and can be changed without needing the server to be brought down first; memory can also be released back to the operating system. OnLine tries to minimize memory fragmentation by allocating large chunks as they are required.

The server uses a configurable pool of processes, which Informix calls *virtual processors*, and multiple concurrent threads (MCTs), which simply means that a process can carry out multiple tasks at the same time. OnLine's multithreaded algorithms schedule processor usage by threads—a method called *context switching*—to make the best use of resources. By using these methods, Informix-OnLine can undertake many of the major database tasks, such as input/output (I/O), queries, index building, and backups in parallel. Informix-OnLine enables the partitioning of tables across multiple disks, which increases I/O performance and also enables parallel I/O operations to be carried out. The data for the table can be partitioned using two methods: round robin or by expression. Round-robin data partitioning allows you to evenly spread the database across multiple devices (for example, a database is evenly distributed across five different devices). Using expression data partitioning lets you specify which devices the database is distributed across based on the expression (for example, the database spans only even-numbered devices: 2, 4, and 6). These methods allow for distributed database I/O, so that you can tailor performance to the available hardware and access requirements.

The multithreading and parallel processing of OnLine were built into the core architecture and give it great scalability. The virtual processors have built-in intelligence to control and redirect MCTs. With the use of threads, so-called lightweight processes, only a small number of UNIX processes are required to manage a large number of user requests. Therefore, with less operating-system context switching, the whole server, not just OnLine, runs more efficiently. OnLine then goes a step further and assigns the virtual processors into classes, such as I/O and CPU, in order to further prioritize the operations.

Every DBMS runs into the I/O limitation in its performance. In an attempt to alleviate this, OnLine uses its own asynchronous I/O (AIO) package or, where available, the operating system's own AIO. This enables a virtual processor to continue working on a new request while the I/O is undertaken. To keep data throughput high, OnLine can be configured to read several pages ahead of what is currently being processed. OnLine also supports disk mirroring, which gives added security and performance gains. Because queries are the statements most frequently issued in a DBMS, OnLine provides Parallel Data Query, which enables the breakdown of a query into subtasks that can be executed in parallel, thus giving much faster processing and execution times. This includes sorting, scanning, aggregation, and even joining of the data.

To help the DBA get the most out of OnLine, Informix bundles several administration tools. The memory grant manager gives dynamic control over the priority settings for the system. Two system-performance monitors are provided: OnPerf and SMI. The System Monitoring Interface (SMI) tracks systemwide information from disk, CPU, and lock usage to user process status. OnPerf effectively replaces `tbstat` and provides a graphical view of system-performance metrics. A graphical DBA tool named DB/Cockpit provides the capability to set alarms on system resources, as well as a very useful history recorder and analyzer. This enables the DBA to be forewarned against impending system problems or overloads and can also be used against remote servers.

Deletes that need to be cascaded from a parent to all its children can now be done automatically, which eliminates the need to code the operation within an application or referential rule. OnLine handles the entire operation and rolls back the entire operation if a failure occurs.

OnLine provides server replication in its High Availability Data Replication, which enables a primary server to replicate itself by means of transaction log transmittal to a secondary server.

Informix-OnLine has gained full C2-level security as set forth by the U.S. National Computer Security Center and can trace any database objects manipulated by a user. This can be configured for certain tasks and individual users.

Within a UNIX environment, Informix-OnLine requires around 4MB of memory and 22MB of disk space. Each user connection requires 35KB, and an average session requires 250KB. Pricing is charged by the seat, with a minimum user license purchase required.

PowerBuilder Support

PowerBuilder does not support the Byte, Text, and Varchar data types of Informix-SE, but it does support all the others.

Connecting to PowerBuilder

Connecting PowerBuilder to Informix requires a number of components. The first is provided by Powersoft and is PBIN5050.DLL (Informix-SE 5.*x*, 6.*x*, or 7.*x* or Informix-OnLine 5.*x*, 6.*x*, or 7.*x* with Informix-NET 5.*x*). Informix-NET supports the IPX/SPX and TCP/IP network protocols and consists of the following three files: LDLLSQLW.DLL, SETNET.EXE, and REMSQL.EXE. The Windows interface for Informix is LDLLSQLW.DLL, and 5.*x* is dated 1994 or after. You inform PowerBuilder of the database interface by specifying IN5-I-Net v5.*x*.

Oracle

The Oracle 7.*x* database from Oracle Corporation is a cooperative server and an open RDBMS used to support mission-critical applications. It is fully portable to more than 80 distinct hardware and operating-system platforms, from desktop systems to mainframes and supercomputers. These platforms include UNIX, VMS, MVS, VM, HP MPE/XL, Siemens, ICL, OS/2, Macintosh, Windows 3.1, Windows 95, NT, and Novell NetWare. This portability enables the freedom to select database server platforms that meet current and future needs without affecting already existing applications. Oracle provides extensive 8-bit and 16-bit national language support for European and Asian languages.

Oracle delivers scalable high performance for a large number of users on all hardware architectures, including Symmetric Multiprocessors, Clustered Multiprocessors, Massively Parallel Processors, and Loosely Coupled Multiprocessors. Performance is achieved by eliminating CPU, I/O, memory, and operating-system bottlenecks and by optimizing the Oracle RDBMS server code to eliminate all internal bottlenecks.

Oracle now comes packaged as a desktop database (Personal Oracle) that gives you the power of Oracle on your local machine.

Features

With Oracle 7.1's release, Oracle introduced the *paralleled query option.* This option is designed to improve the performance of lengthy, data-intensive operations associated with data warehousing, decision support applications, and other large database environments. The paralleled query option enables Oracle to split up query execution, data loading, and index-creation tasks, and execute them concurrently on multiple CPUs. Release 7.3 extends the functionality by allowing parallel-aware optimization, bitmapped index queries, unlimited star queries, partition-level optimization, adaptive parallel queries, and parallel hash joins.

Oracle employs a self-tuning, multithreaded server architecture in which the number of database server processes dynamically adjusts to the current work load. A shared SQL cache enables all users executing the same SQL statement to share a single in-memory copy, which minimizes memory usage. Dynamic SQL, static SQL, and stored procedures are shared across all users. The PL/SQL (Oracle's procedural language) procedures are stored in a shared, compiled format within the Oracle7 database. These procedures can be called explicitly from other tools or other procedures, or they can be triggered when rows are inserted, updated, or deleted. This shared SQL cache feature means that stored procedures do not generate result sets. These features minimize operating system overhead and memory usage.

Other performance highlights in Oracle include a resource limiter with which DBAs can control the system resources a user can consume. DBAs can set maximum levels for such resources as CPU time, logical disk I/O, and connect time. This solves problems such as runaway queries. Oracle also has an intelligent, cost-based query optimizer that determines the most efficient access path.

Oracle employs full, unrestricted row-level locking and contention-free queries to minimize contention wait times. Oracle provides row-level locking for both data and indexes with no lock escalation and no limit on the number of locks per transaction, table, or database. These contention-free queries maintain complete data integrity and consistency without read locks, so updates and queries don't block each other. Multithreaded sequence number generation is also included.

Oracle's support for loosely coupled and fault-tolerant hardware platforms enables you to isolate applications from hardware failures. In addition, you are able to replicate commonly used data to multiple nodes and automatically have changed data refreshed to read-only copies at user-defined intervals.

Oracle is 100% ANSI/ISO compliant, and it fully supports declarative integrity constraints. With PL/SQL stored procedures and triggered PL/SQL procedures, complex business rules can be enforced at the server level. Triggers can execute either before or after the triggering statement and can execute either once per row or once per statement. Release 7.2 permits multiple triggers of the same type on a single table.

Oracle has transparent distributed database architecture. This means that a physically distributed database can be treated as a single logical database. To ensure database integrity, a transparent two-phase commit mechanism is employed. Multisite transactions are committed with one standard SQL `COMMIT` statement, whereas Oracle automatically detects and resolves all failures to ensure that all sites either commit or roll back together.

Database security is role based. Roles are a named collection of privileges. This enables you to group together privileges on tables and other objects and grant them to individual users or groups of users. Oracle roles enable organizations to have multiple DBAs and precisely control the special privileges given to each DBA.

PowerBuilder Support

Supported PowerBuilder data types are Char, Date, Float (Oracle 7.*x* only), Long, Longraw, Number, Raw, Varchar (Oracle 6 only), and Varchar2 (Oracle 7.*x* only).

To ensure concurrency control in DataWindow objects, PowerBuilder supports the following SQL clauses:

- `FOR UPDATE OF` (Oracle 6 interface only)
- `FOR UPDATE` (Oracle 7.*x* interface only)

If the data source for a DataWindow object is a SQL `SELECT` statement, you can change the `SELECT` statement to include the `FOR UPDATE OF` clause. Including the `FOR UPDATE OF` clause locks the rows selected from the table until a `COMMIT` or `ROLLBACK` is executed.

You can define DataWindow objects and reports that use an Oracle PBDBMS stored procedure as their data source. To do this, you must first change the `TerminatorCharacter` value in the PowerBuilder Database preferences to ` (a back quote). You also must install special software on the database server. Special PBDBMS `Put_Line` function calls must be used in the SQL `SELECT` statements of the stored procedures. Oracle stored procedures as a data source cannot have any output parameters, and the `SELECT` statement is limited to 25,500 characters.

Connecting to PowerBuilder

PowerBuilder supports two versions of Oracle: Version 6 (OR6) and Version 7 (OR7). Connecting PowerBuilder to Oracle requires a number of components. Powersoft provides the PBOR6050.DLL module for Version 6, PBOR7050.DLL for Version 7.0, PBO71050.DLL for Version 7.1, and PBO72050.DLL for Version 7.2 (for both 16- and 32-bit environments). Oracle provides ORA6WIN.DLL for Version 6, and ORA7WIN.DLL and COREWIN.DLL for Version 7. You must install the SQL*Net client software from Oracle also. The configuration file is named CONFIG.ORA if you are using SQL*Net for DOS, and ORACLE.INI if you have SQL*Net for Windows. If you are using the 32-bit version of PowerBuilder, you must also install the 32-bit version of SQL*Net.

Along with the DLLs, AUTOEXEC.BAT must be modified to include the `SET CONFIG` environment variable:

```
"SET CONFIG = ORACLE_configuration_file_pathname".
```

This information is required for the appropriate SQL*Net driver. This information also needs to be specified in the Oracle server connect string of the database profile. Table 3.2 lists frequently used network protocols and their corresponding SQL*Net for DOS and SQL*Net for Windows drivers.

Table 3.2. Network protocols and their required SQL*Net drivers.

Network Protocol	*SQL*Net for DOS Driver*	*SQL*Net for Windows Driver*
DECnet	SQLDNT.EXE	SQLDNT.DLL
Local	SQLPME.EXE	SQLPME.DLL
Named Pipes	SQLNMP.EXE	SQLNMP.DLL
NetBios	SQLNTB.EXE	SQLNTB.DLL
Novell	SQLSPX.EXE	SQLSPX.DLL
TCP/IP	SQLTCP.EXE	SQLTCP.DLL
Vines	SQLVIN.EXE	SQLVIN.DLL

You inform PowerBuilder 5.0 of the database interface by specifying OR6 for Version 6 or OR7 for Version 7 as the DBMS attribute.

The `Server Name` attribute is required only when you're using a networked version of the Oracle database server. If you are using a local version, the Server Name field is blank. When the `Server Name` attribute is required, it must contain the proper connect string or connect descriptor. The connect string or connect descriptor specifies the connection parameters the Oracle Windows API uses to access the database. The SQL*Net client software you are using determines whether you should specify an Oracle connect string or connect descriptor in the `Server Name` attribute.

If you are using SQL*Net for DOS or SQL*Net for Windows Version 1.0 (SQL*Net V1), use the connect string. If you are using SQL*Net for Windows Version 2.0 (SQL*Net V2), use the connect descriptor. The syntax for SQL*Net for DOS is `"@identifier : LogicalServerName"`. The syntax for SQL*Net for Windows Version 1.0 is `"@identifier : LogicalServerName : ORACLEInstanceName"`. The syntax for SQL*Net for Windows Version 2.0 is `"@TNS : ORACLEServiceName"`.

SQLBase

SQLBase from Gupta Corporation began life as a single-user PC database. It has grown into a full-fledged database server that is now available for the DOS, Windows, OS/2, Novell NetWare, and Sun UNIX operating systems. The most common flavor is the NetWare NLM, where it is a solid performer. SQLBase provides enterprisewide connectivity out of the box, with support for IPX/SPX, TCP/IP, NetBeui, and others. Previous versions of SQLBase proved to be somewhat difficult to configure, but this was addressed by Version 6.0, and installation, configuration, and management are made simpler by the use of a detailed install menu with easy-to-understand options.

The SQLBase product family consists of the SQLBase Server, which is a robust LAN-based server designed for workgroup solutions; the SQLBase Desktop, a configurable standalone server; and SQLBase Ranger, a programmable data mover.

Features

SQLBase stored procedures are coded using the SQLWindows Application Language (SAL), which is Gupta's rival development tool to PowerBuilder. The idea is to provide a more consistent interface for client/server developers; unfortunately, this means PowerBuilder developers will need to learn the Gupta folding editor and SAL language. You can write transactions to run against multiple servers with SQLBase, and it handles transaction integrity transparently with a two-phase commit protocol.

Gupta has designed SQLBase with client/server development very much in mind. One of the special enhancements is optimistic locking, which gives applications the highest possible level of concurrency. SQLBase also tries to minimize network traffic by improving the synchronization of client and server result set cursors. The implementation of cursors enables the fetching of data in any order and maintains the cursor's position even after committing a transaction.

A number of tools are included with SQLBase. One of these is Gupta's renowned Quest product, an advanced data-query and manipulation tool that is easy for novices to use but still powerful enough to be considered by the more advanced user. It enables the import and export of data, the management of database definitions, and the creation of data capture and query forms. SQLConsole is a graphical database administration tool that enables the installation, configuration, and management of SQLBase. SQLConsole can be set up to react to server events, and, by the use of alarms, to escalate a series of actions. The Scheduling Manager, which enables the automation of routine maintenance and backups, is built into SQLConsole. Remote management tools are also part of the SQLConsole tool suite. The Database Object Manager provides graphical management of each of the database components, including stored procedures and triggers. Tools called SQLTrace and Replay are provided to help in the tuning and debugging of the server, and SQLActivity with online monitoring windows provides access to current server status.

SQLBase Server is available only for NetWare 3.11, 4.0, or higher and requires 12MB of memory and 10MB of disk space. SQLBase Desktop Server is available for OS/2 2.1 or higher, Windows, Windows NT, and Windows 95 and requires 12/4/12/12MB of memory respectively, and 10/4/10/10MB of disk space, respectively.

Microsoft SQL Server 6.0

SQL Server 6.0 from Microsoft is a high-performance relational database management system that operates entirely within Microsoft's Windows NT operating system. Previous versions of MS SQL Server could also run under IBM's OS/2; this support has now been dropped. SQL

Server for NT provides a database engine that can be used for small to large systems development, and combines high availability, security, transaction processing and fault tolerance, server-side data integrity, remote stored procedures and logins, connectivity services, and an integrated enterprisewide server administration tool. SQL Server 6.0 also provides tight integration with OLE object technology and Visual Basic.

Microsoft continues to extend its product and it now has improved ANSI SQL support including declarative referential integrity and server cursor support that exceeds the ANSI standard. Since splitting with Sybase on the joint development of the SQL Server product, Microsoft has also introduced its own set of enhancements to Transact-SQL.

Features

Because SQL Server 6.0 is so tightly integrated with the NT operating system, there are a number of inherent benefits. SQL Server uses the threading and scheduling services of NT. The same performance monitor and event viewer can be used, and NT logons can be set up to provide an automatic login for the SQL Server. This simplifies the management of users and allows you to centralize access assignment for both the network and SQL Server.

SQL Server provides stored procedures for repetitive SQL, extended stored procedures using custom dynamic link libraries, triggers enforcing referential integrity, and validation rules for fields or data types. Rules and user-defined data types are bound to individual columns or data types. Security includes system procedures, system tables, and extended stored procedures to maintain user information. Login security for NT consists of three different types: standard, integrated, and mixed. Standard security requires specification of a login ID and password. Integrated security uses Windows NT security to authenticate users. Mixed is a combination of the other two types, enabling access with a valid SQL Server login ID and password.

New to Version 6.0 is built-in replication between Microsoft SQL Servers through an easy-to-understand publish-and-subscribe metaphor. A publishing server broadcasts the data to the servers that subscribe to certain pieces of data. SQL Server 6.0 replication makes use of a transaction log reader and automatically distributes logged transactions that are associated with marked tables, for asynchronous updates on the subscribing servers. The broadcast of the data can occur either continuously as data is entered into the transaction log or at specified intervals from a captured log. The captured log is maintained in a special database called `distribution`. Because the replication process is transaction based, the SQL Server remains available for normal user access. The data that is replicated can be an entire database, a table, or a vertical or horizontal partition of a table; this is called an *article* and is the base unit of replication. A *publication* is a collection of one or more articles that can then be subscribed to; this is used in cases where you need to maintain referential integrity. To make use of the replication features of SQL Server, you must install the MS ODBC 32-bit drivers. There is a minimum memory requirement of around 32MB for the servers involved in replication.

Microsoft has integrated all its previous tools into one: the Enterprise Manager. This provides the ability to set alerts for SQL Server events and to have them automatically responded to (for example, executing a set task or sending e-mail or pager notifications to specified operators). You can also create server tasks and then schedule them for execution at specified times (either a single specified time, recurring, or when initiated by an alert). This information is held in the `msdb` database.

SQL Server 6.0 is now constructed around a parallel architecture that allows internal database functions to be executed in parallel and provides improved performance and scalability.

SQL Server writes all database modifications to a transaction log that is associated with an individual database. Transaction logging is write ahead, which ensures that the commands are logged before any database changes occur. This logging process is used during automatic recovery, and transactions are rolled forward and backward to leave the database in a consistent state. Nonautomatic recovery requires the use of database backups (dumps) and logs, which can be scheduled using SQL Enterprise.

The data dump and load processes have been greatly enhanced and now include the ability to perform parallel dumps or loads to multiple devices (allowing data striping), to undefined dump devices, named pipe dump devices, and network dump devices that use universal naming conventions (UNCs). Data can also be appended to existing dump devices, and you can even create dumps to removable media such as floppy disks (but more usually to CD-ROMs).

Like the other large database vendors, Microsoft has finally recognized the requirements from the development community for a standalone version of its product. Microsoft's answer is the SQL Workstation. This has the same features and functionality as the Server version, except it is a single-user product that supports up to 15 simultaneous connections. SQL Workstation is intended for use as a development platform and also includes the DB Library and ODBC SDK files.

The latest version of SQL Server is Version 6.5 and promises new data warehousing enhancements and a new technology TransAccess.

Microsoft SQL Server 6.0 can be installed on computers that are based on the following microprocessor architectures:

- Alpha AXP microprocessors
- Intel 32-bit *x*86–based microprocessors (such as the 80486 or the Pentium)
- MIPS microprocessors

Installation of SQL Server requires a minimum of 16MB and about 60MB of disk space. For replication you need a minimum of 32MB of memory.

PowerBuilder Support

The Char, Bit, Binary, Time, Timestamp, Money, and Arithmetic data types are supported in DataWindows, reports, and embedded SQL. The `AutoCommit` attribute of a transaction object must be set to `FALSE` to update image or text columns within a transaction.

Connecting to PowerBuilder

SQL Server 6.0 now provides the Multi-Protocol Net-Library to take advantage of the remote procedure call (RPC) facility of Windows NT. The Multi-Protocol Net-Library communicates over most interprocess communication (IPC) mechanisms supported by Windows NT. However, you should note that for SQL Server 6.0, currently only TCP/IP Windows Sockets, NWLink IPX/SPX, and named pipes are considered tested and supported.

The basic software components to access SQL Server are PBSYB050.DLL (for 4.*x*) or PBMSS050.DLL (for 6.*x*) and W3DBLIB.DLL. Further files are required depending on the network protocol and client used. For example, a Windows 3.*x* client, DBNMP3.DLL, is required for a named pipes connection, and DBMSSPX3.DLL, NWNETAPI.DLL, and NWIPXSPX.DLL are required for IPX/SPX. The DBMS field in the profile setup should be set to either MSS or SYB-SQL Server v4.*x*.

Sybase System 11

Sybase System 11 is composed of a family of components used to provide security and support for large database system development within a client/server environment on a UNIX or NT platform. All Sybase System 11 products are built on the Open Client and Open Server Architecture foundation and share the same interfaces. This architecture enables the development of departmental client/server applications and integration of the mainframe into a client/server environment. Modularizing the software into clients, servers, and interfaces enables the integration of the framework with different data sources, applications, and services. System 11 addresses many of the issues of Sybase System 10, particularly the fact that it could not scale up to support hardware that used more than four processors.

Features

Open Client and Open Server provide a set of application programming interfaces (APIs) and libraries, enabling integration with Sybase and non-Sybase data sources and services. Open Client manages all communications between any client application or tool and the SQL Server or any application using Open Server. These APIs include DB-Library, Client-Library, Embedded SQL, XA Library, ODBC interface, and Net-Library. Open Client supports MS DOS, MS Windows, Macintosh, Windows NT, NetWare, OS/2, a variety of UNIX implementations,

VMS, and mainframe CICS operating systems. This interface enables system-independent development without knowledge of specific network operating systems, transport protocols, or data access methods. Open Server enables the transformation of data sources into multithread servers supporting UNIX, VMS, Windows NT, NetWare, OS/2, MVS, CICS, and MVS IMS/TM. This technology lends itself to creating multitiered solutions such as gateways.

Sybase Enterprise CONNECT products resolve any differences between client applications and target data sources, including SQL dialects, data representations, and error codes. This is accomplished by data conversions and SQL translations. The Powersoft database interface uses the Client Library (`CT-Lib`) API or the DB-Library (`DBLIB`) API to connect to the database. Part of the CONNECT product family is Sybase's replication server, which allows for the automatic replication of data between multiple databases.

Sybase System 11 manages data integrity enforcement through triggers, stored procedures, rules, defaults, and domains. Passing the National Institute for Standards and Technology test, SQL Server 11 is in compliance with 1989 and 1992 ANSI standards. Part of this compliance involves additional features such as declarative integrity constraints and cursors. A nonprocedural way of defining integrity as part of the table definition, declarative integrity constraints require much less code than procedural integrity demands. In addition, column default values and column constraints enforce declarative integrity with the Sybase 11 system. All standard cursor operations (declare, open, fetch, position update and delete, and close) function with System 11. Using some extensions, System 11 can also return multiple rows within a fetch statement, which improves performance over record-at-a-time processing. A cursor can now be kept open across multiple transactions and be specified as read-only or updateable.

The query optimizer for Release 11 makes use of index-only access for queries that request all columns that are part of an existing index, and has also increased the probability of using a nonclustered index to avoid record-sorting overhead.

System 11 maintains a transaction log for backup and recovery purposes. The log is used for forward and backward rolling of transactions to keep the database in a consistent state. A standard component of System 11, the backup server provides high-speed data-backup and data-loading facilities. The backup server offers multiple backups on a single volume, backups across multiple volumes, and parallel backups, with minimal impact on running applications. Backups occur through scheduled or user-defined thresholds. These thresholds are set by an administration tool or by triggers or stored procedures. System 11 safeguards against database failure by giving you the ability to perform disk mirroring for your transaction logs and databases.

System 11 enables accounting of system resources for chargeback purposes. The costs monitored can be allocated based on the per-session usage of the CPU or I/O resources.

Security complies with C2 standards from the U.S. Government Trusted Computer System Evaluation Criteria and is upgradable to a B1 trusted DBMS for the highest level of security, as mandated by government agencies. System procedures, system tables, and extended stored procedures enable System 11 to maintain positive login and user identification and information.

All server events, including system events, user events, and data-defined events, are logged into a complete auditing facility with a secondary audit trail. The audited events are stored in a special database for later analysis. Security also provides named system administrators and encrypted minimum-length passwords and password expirations.

System 11 has improved its scalability to handle symmetric multiprocessing machines. Improvements have also been made to the dynamic logical memory manager; the memory resources have been optimized. The performance of the database access can also be improved using Sybase SQL Server Monitor. For environments using symmetrical multiprocessing (SMP), Sybase's Virtual Server Architecture (VSA) allows you to control how much of the CPU's resources are allocated to the RDBMS.

Sybase has also introduced web.sql to provide relational database access from Internet web pages. web.sql is used to generate HTML pages with SQL statements and Perl scripts. When a user requests the web page, the queries are executed and return the data to the Web browser as HTML text. SQL Server works with any web server via the Common Gateway Interface (CGI), but also supplies a link to web servers using Netscape's API, which provides faster access.

PowerBuilder Support

The Char, Bit, Binary, Time, Timestamp, Image, Money, and Arithmetic data types are supported in DataWindows, reports, and embedded SQL.

Connecting to PowerBuilder

The software components to access Sybase System 11 are PBSYC050.DLL for the `CTLib` interface, WCTLIB.DLL, WCSLIB.DLL, and WNLWNSCK.DLL. If you are using Sybase SQL Server 4.*x* (`dblib`), you need to install PBSYB050.DLL (16-bit) or PBSYT050.DLL (32-bit). Sybase Open Client Client-Library for Windows and the Sybase Net-Library for Windows must be Release 10.0.1 or higher. The network layer must be Windows Sockets–compliant TCP/IP software. The SQL.INI configuration file must be correctly configured for the individual environment. The basic format is as follows:

```
[server_name]
Win3_Query = driver, address, port_number
```

The DBMS field for connecting PowerBuilder needs to be set to SYC-Sybase System 11, and the `ServerName` field must exactly match the server name specified in the SQL.INI.

Sybase SQL Anywhere

Sybase SQL Anywhere is a complete client/server DBMS that ships with PowerBuilder. SQL Anywhere is the replacement for Watcom-SQL and has become the desktop DBMS for Sybase, Inc. Many PowerBuilder developers are familiar with this standalone database but do not realize that SQL Anywhere also has a multiuser SQL network server. The standalone SQL Anywhere is available for Windows 3.*x*, Windows 95, Windows NT, OS/2, NetWare, and DOS. In addition to all the features that SQL Anywhere delivers, the best part is the relatively low cost of the product. The standalone is packaged with PowerBuilder, and the multiuser server version can be purchased for a relatively low cost, depending on the number of user connections required.

Features

The SQL Anywhere database includes stored procedures; before and after action triggers; cascading updates and deletes; bidirectional, scrollable, updateable cursors; row-level locking; and updateable multitable views. It is ANSI SQL89 Level 2 and IBM SAA compatible. SQL Anywhere also supports multimedia data types such as blobs.

The SQL Anywhere engine was compiled to use the 32-bit instruction set and designed to take advantage of instruction pipelining and superscalar architecture of 486 and Pentium processors. Optimization is performed each time a query is run against a database. The optimizer learns about the data structure and access to provide for faster performance and less disk access and processing.

SQL Anywhere includes extensive data type conversion. Data types can be compared with or used in any expression with all other data types. SQL Anywhere enables the use of date fields in simple arithmetic calculations with integers and other date and time fields. In addition, numerous functions are included for date and time manipulation. The Date, Time, and Timestamp data types maintain a high degree of precision—up to a fraction of a second.

SQL Anywhere supports entity and referential integrity, which is specified in the `CREATE TABLE` and `ALTER TABLE` commands. To reduce the complexity of the `WHERE` clause, automatic joins can be used based on foreign-key relationships. In SQL statements, subqueries can be specified wherever expressions are allowed, as opposed to being restricted to just the right side of a comparative operator. Watcom SQL supports four different ANSI-standard isolation levels to ensure that each transaction executes completely or not at all: RU (read uncommitted), RC (read committed), RR (repeatable read), and ST (serializable transactions). The isolation levels differ with respect to dirty reads, nonrepeatable reads, and phantom rows.

SQL Anywhere also includes savepoints or subtransactions. A savepoint acts as a checkpoint within a transaction. Changes can be made after a savepoint and can be undone by rolling back to that savepoint (multiple savepoints can be defined for one transaction). Savepoints make use of the rollback log, one of the three database logs that SQL Anywhere utilizes, and cannot be used in bulk operations mode. SQL Anywhere provides full transaction processing through the use of these logs. The other two database logs are the checkpoint log and the forward transaction log. The forward transaction log records standard database activity and can be converted into a SQL command file to be used as an audit trail of changes made to the database.

A SQL Anywhere database can be up to 12TB (terabytes) in size. Each table can be up to 1024GB in size, with a potential 999 columns. The index entry size is limited to 32.767, and data can be imported from ASCII, dBASEII, dBASEIII, DIF, FoxPro, Lotus, and WATFILE file formats.

PowerBuilder Support

SQL Anywhere provides transparent portability from the standalone to multiuser platform, and vice versa. SQL Anywhere has ODBC Level 2 support and built-in user- and group-level security. All versions of SQL Anywhere come equipped with an interactive SQL facility and database-administration tools. You can create a SQL Anywhere database from within the PowerBuilder environment and run it as PowerBuilder's native database.

The system requirements for the standalone version of SQL Anywhere are an IBM i386 or higher and Windows 3.*x*. The client uses a minimum of 1MB of memory and additional memory for caching (set up when the database specifications are defined). For the SQL Anywhere Network Server, the client must be an IBM-compatible PC running DOS Version 5.0 or later, Windows 3.1 or higher, Windows NT 3.5, or OS/2 2.*x*. The database server must be at least an IBM-compatible PC 80386 processor with 4MB of RAM and running either Windows 3.1 or DOS 5.0 or later. For OS/2 and Windows 95, the server requires 8MB. Windows NT and Novell NetWare 3.11 and up require at least 16MB of memory. The network requirements are NetBios, TCP/IP, or Novell IPX for Windows 3.*x*, NT, Windows 95, and OS/2 database servers, NetBios and IPX for DOS servers, or Novell NetWare IPX or TCP/IP for Novell database servers.

In addition, SQL Anywhere is fully compatible with Sybase SQL Server. This gives users the flexibility to access the Sybase Replication Server to maintain multiple synchronized copies of a database. SQL Anywhere is also compatible with Sybase's Transact-SQL via the Transact-SQL API.

Connecting to PowerBuilder

The following files need to be distributed when you're using a SQL Anywhere database: PBODB050.DLL (ODBC interface), ODBC.DLL (ODBC driver manager), and WOD50w.DLL (16-bit) or WOD50t.DLL (32-bit) (SQL Anywhere driver). You will usually use the deployment disks that come with PowerBuilder to set up the required SQL Anywhere files.

XDB

The XDB product line from XDB Systems, Inc., provides a standalone database (XDB-SQL RDBMS) as well as a full-blown, multiuser, networked database system (XDB-Server). The greatest appeal of the XDB systems is to companies requiring a database system that has full compatibility with DB2 and a variety of platforms.

Features

The XDB-SQL RDBMS runs under DOS, Windows, and OS/2, and is 100% compatible with IBM's mainframe DB2 SQL. The XDB-SQL Engine was designed with speed in mind and minimizes the amount of workstation memory needed. The database engine also optimizes queries based on data statistics and indexes. The multithreaded SQL Engine was created as a DLL that enables multiple tasks to share the same engine. In addition to supplying full support for DB2, SAA, and ANSI SQL standards, the XDB-SQL Engine also provides cascading referential integrity, bidirectional cursors, distributed database access, backup and recovery, concurrency control, transaction processing, and updateable views. Any application written to run against XDB-SQL RDBMSs can easily be migrated from a standalone to the full-scale XDB-Server multiuser environment with no code modifications. This scalability of XDB applications is an attractive feature for companies needing to downsize or run on multiple platforms.

XDB-Server runs under multiple platforms: DOS, Windows, OS/2, NT, and with Version 5.0 under NetWare and UNIX. XDB-Server maintains the same functionality as the XDB-SQL RDBMS and enables three-part name and ALIAS support, global security, and server-to-server connectivity. The global security can be maintained on one database for all servers in a distributed environment. XDB-Server also maintains full compatibility with DB2 SQL.

XDB databases have a limit of 750 columns in a table with no limit on the number of tables per database. An individual column can be up to 32,767 bytes in length, and an indexed column can be up to 4,056 bytes. There can be up to 750 fields in a `SELECT` clause, and there is no limit to the number of tables in a SQL command or the number of nested query levels.

With the use of XDB-Link, any of the XDB products can be used as a gateway to enable applications to access data in multiple locations, including mainframe DB2 tables via APPC LU6.2 protocols. XDB-Link uses distributed relational database architecture to access IBM's relational databases. In addition to the PC/server component of XDB, a CICS/host component provides remote procedure call access to nonrelational databases on the mainframe. Because XDB is portable and DB2 compliant, development can be done on a local version of XDB and then migrated to access mainframe DB2 tables with no code modifications.

In the multiuser version, XDB uses different isolation levels to support various database lock options. These levels are RR (repeatable read), EU (exclusive use), LC (lock current), DR (dirty read), and CS (cursor stability). The isolation level to be used is specified in the `Lock` attribute of the transaction object during initialization. To run XDB, the machine must be at least an IBM AT, PS/2, or 100% compatible microcomputer. A minimum of 4MB of RAM is required for OS/2 1.3 or higher, 2MB of RAM for Windows 3.0 or higher (including Windows 95), and 1MB of RAM for DOS 3.1 or higher.

Summary

This chapter covers all the leading database-management systems for PowerBuilder. You have learned about each of their features and drawbacks, along with the individual quirks that PowerBuilder has with them. Table 3.3 is a list of the connection attributes for each of the DBMSs, which are required when connecting through the PowerBuilder development environment and also when deploying an application.

Table 3.3. DBMS login requirements.

Database	*DBMS*	*User ID*	*DB Pass*	*Server Name*	*Log ID*	*Log Pass*	*Database*
Database Manager and DB2/2	IBM DB2	CAE-specific	Y	•	N	•	CAE-specific
DB2/MVS	IBM DB2	CAE-specific	Y	•	N	•	CAE-specific
DB2/6000	IBM DB2	CAE-specific	Y	•	N	•	CAE-specific
Informix v5.*x*/6.*x* with I-NET v5.*x*	IN5-I-Net v5.*x*	opt.	opt.	opt.	•	N	Y
Micro Decisionware Database Gateway for DB2	MDI Gateway	•	N	Y	Y	Y	optional
Oracle v6.*x*	OR6-Oracle v6.*x*	•	N	Y	Y	Y N with local	N
Oracle v7.*x*	OR7-Oracle v7.0, O71 for 7.1, or O72 for 7.2	•	N	Y	Y	Y N with local	N

continues

Table 3.3. continued

Database	*DBMS*	*User ID*	*DB Pass*	*Server Name*	*Log ID*	*Log Pass*	*Database*
SQL Server	SYB-SQL Server v6.*x*	•	N	Y	Y	Y	Y
Sybase NetGateway Interface for DB2	NETGATEWAY (16-bit)	•	N	Y	Y	Y	optional
Sybase SQL Server System 11	SYC-Sybase System 11	•	N	Y	Y	Y	Y

Databases and the Database Painter

4

by Kurt Sundling

IN THIS CHAPTER

PowerBuilder provides developers a means to manage databases against which they have database administration rights: the Database painter. It enables the management of

- Tables
- Columns and their extended attributes
- Indexes
- Primary and foreign keys
- Views

With the Database painter you can create, alter, and drop tables along with their primary and foreign keys. Each column in a table has *extended attributes*, which define additional information that is used within DataWindows. These attributes can be defined and altered in this painter. You can create and drop indexes and views.

Five related painters can be accessed from the Database painter: the Create and Alter Table painter, the Data Manipulation painter, the Database Administration painter, the View painter, and the Data Pipeline painter (which is elaborated on further in Chapter 29, "Data Pipelining").

This chapter discusses the creation of tables and their associated characteristics, such as primary and foreign keys. It also shows you how to create and maintain table column extended attributes, of which three are very important: edit styles, display formats, and validation rules.

Using the Database Painter

You can manipulate database tables from within the Database painter. To open the Database painter, click the Database painter button in the PowerBar or PowerPanel or use the hotkey Shift+F7. PowerBuilder will attempt to connect to the database listed in the current profile and, upon a successful connection, the Select Tables dialog box appears (see Figure 4.1).

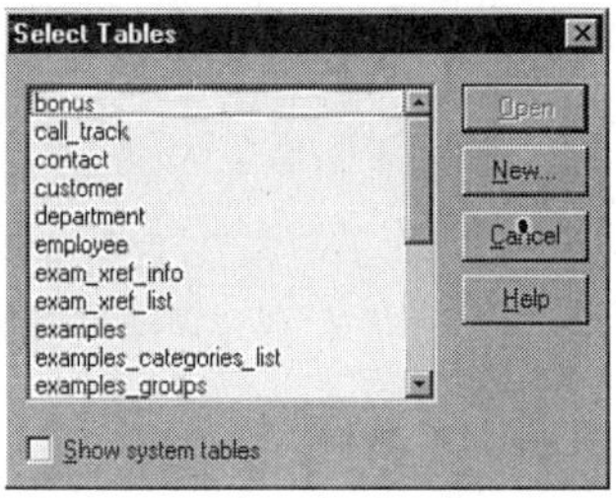

FIGURE 4.1.
The Select Tables dialog box.

After you select the desired tables, they are displayed in the Database painter's workspace (see Figure 4.2). The table columns and the table's primary and foreign keys and indexes are displayed. The keys and indexes are signified by identifiable icons marking the columns and lines drawn to show connections to other tables.

FIGURE 4.2.
The Database painter workspace.

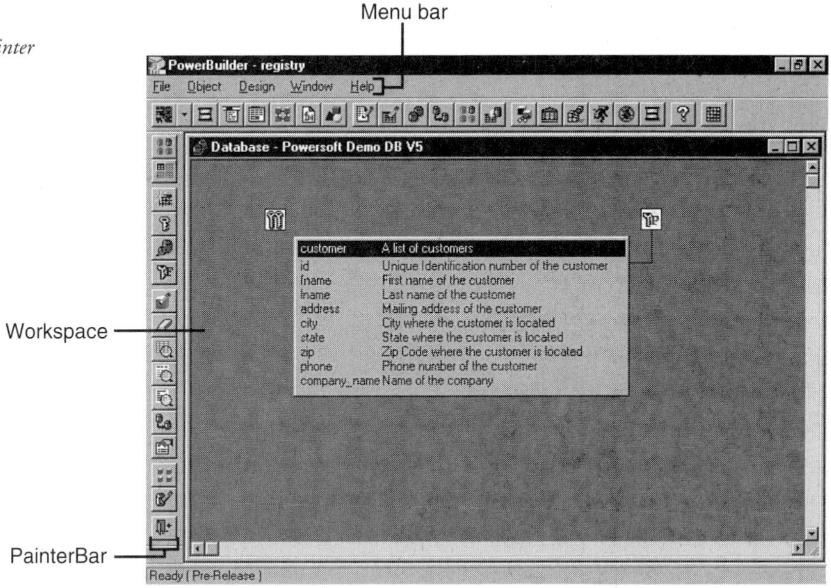

If a table has more than eight columns, a vertical scrollbar appears to enable you to scroll through all the columns. Or you can simply resize the table window to show as much or as little as you want. The default number of columns to display in the Database painter workspace is saved in the database section of the PB.INI file.

You can dictate how the tables are displayed in the workspace by right-clicking on the painter workspace to access a pop-up menu. This pop-up menu has three display options: Show Comments, Show Index Keys, and Show Referential Integrity. The table columns are shown at all times.

You can also open the Select Tables dialog box and arrange the tables from this pop-up menu.

You can move and resize tables while you're in the Database painter workspace. To move a table, move the cursor to the title bar and drag the table to the desired location. You can resize a table by dragging a side of the table to the desired size.

Table maintenance consists of the creation and alteration of table definitions. The table definitions give details about the table and column characteristics. To alter a table you must first have access to the table.

Opening a Table

From the Select Tables dialog box you can either select one or more tables in the painter workspace or indicate that you would like to create a new table. To select a table you can click each table and then click Open, or you can double-click each table and then click Cancel. The double-click automatically opens the table you clicked. You can also open multiple tables at once by selecting each of the tables and clicking the Open button.

A repository list of tables and views is built from the database and is refreshed every 1800 seconds. This refresh rate, `TableListCache`, is stored in the database section of the PB.INI file.

If a table is dropped without using the Database painter, the information pertaining to the table will still exist in the repository list until the next automatic synchronization. To manually refresh the list, select Synchronize PB Attributes from the Design menu. Click OK to confirm the synchronization of the attributes.

Initially only the non-system tables are displayed, but the Select Tables dialog box also enables you to display the database system tables. You do this by checking the Show system tables check box (see Figure 4.3). There are two kinds of system tables: DBMS system tables and PowerBuilder repository tables.

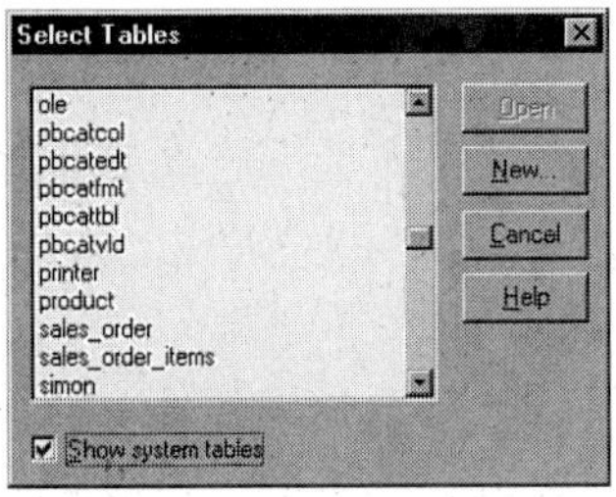

FIGURE 4.3.
The Select Tables dialog box with the Show system tables check box checked.

These are the five PowerBuilder system tables, referred to as *the Powersoft repository*:

System Table	*Application Information for the Database*
`PBCatCol`	Information on each of the table columns
`PBCatEdt`	Edit styles
`PBCatFmt`	Display formats
`PBCatTbl`	Tables in the current database
`PBCatVld`	Validation rules

These five system tables contain all the extended attribute information for the tables and their columns for a database. PowerBuilder will update these tables accordingly whenever the tables, columns, or extended attributes are altered only within PowerBuilder. The repository is not updated if tables are altered outside of PowerBuilder and might contain orphaned information. You have to use the Synchronize PowerBuilder Attributes menu option to perform housekeeping on the repository.

While in PowerBuilder you can view the contents of these tables in the same manner that you view the other tables, but it is highly recommended that you do not alter these tables from the workspace and leave them to PowerBuilder to maintain. There are third-party products, such as ERWin/ERX for PowerBuilder and S-Designor, that can be used to synchronize and maintain the repository with information such as column labels, headings, edit styles, formats, and validation rules.

The `PBCatTbl` table contains the table information used in PowerBuilder. The index for this table is based on `pbt_tnam`, which is the column with the table name, and `pbt_ownr`, the owner of the table.

The `PBCatCol` table contains information on table columns and their extended attributes. The table name and owner columns are `pbc_tnam` and `pbc_ownr`, respectively. The index, like for the `PBCatTbl` table, is based on these two columns, with the addition of `pbc_cnam`, which is the name of the column. Each column in the table can be associated with the three remaining repository tables (`PBCatFmt`, `PBCatVld`, and `PBCatEdt`) through three individual columns. The following list shows the three columns that are the keys to the three extended attribute tables:

- `pbc_mask`—The display format name from the `PBCatFmt` table
- `pbc_ptrn`—The validation rule name from the `PBCatVld` table
- `pbc_edit`—The edit style name and sequence number from the `PBCatEdt` table

The `PBCatFmt` table contains all the display formats available in the current database. `pbf_name` is the name of the display format. The `PBCatVld` table contains all the validation rules for the database table columns. The validation rule names are in the `pbv_name` column. The `PBCatEdt` table has the edit styles for the database; `pbe_name` and `pbe_seqn` designate the key for this table. `pbe_name` is the edit style name and `pbe_seqn` is the sequence number if edit types require more than one row.

These last three repository tables contain the most powerful of the extended attributes. The creation and utilization of display formats, validation rules, and edit styles is discussed in detail later in the chapter.

Closing a Table

To close a database table and remove it from the workspace, click the right mouse button in the title of the table. This is not the same as dropping the table; it just removes it from the workspace area. A pop-up menu appears (see Figure 4.4).

FIGURE 4.4.
The table pop-up menu.

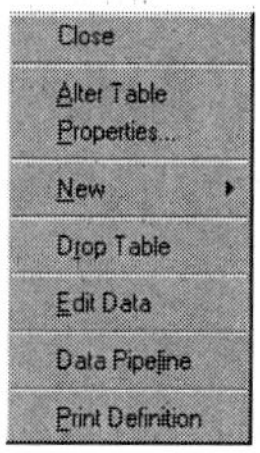

Select Close from this menu and the table is removed from the workspace.

Creating a Table

To create a database table, click the New button in the PainterBar, click the Table button in the PowerBar, click the New command button in the Select Tables dialog box, or select New Table from the Object menu. Powersoft has given you a number of ways to enter the Create Table painter (see Figure 4.5) depending on where you currently are within PowerBuilder.

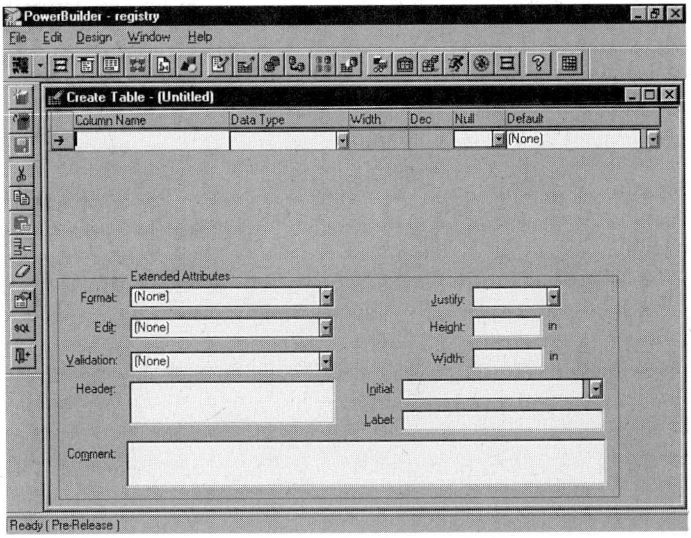

FIGURE 4.5.
The Create Table painter.

From here you are required to specify the following information: a table name, column names, and column data types and sizes. You can also define the fonts for the table, comments about the table, primary and foreign keys, and the extended attributes for the columns at creation or modification time.

When you have completed the required information, you have two options: to create the table or to save the `CREATE TABLE` SQL statement to a file. To create the table, select Save or Save As from the File menu while in form view of the Table painter (refer to Figure 4.5). If you switch to the SQL Syntax view, PowerBuilder will prompt you for the table name. You can then select Save from the File menu to tell PowerBuilder to build the `CREATE TABLE` SQL code and submit it to the DBMS. To save the `CREATE TABLE` SQL statement to a file, select Save As from the File menu while in the SQL Syntax view of the Table painter; the SQL statement is written, once the table has been named, to a file, which you can use at a later time to submit to the DBMS. You can use both options during the `ALTER TABLE` procedures. The Table painter is explained in greater detail later in the chapter.

Either way, you are returned to the Database painter workspace from this painter.

Altering a Table

To alter a database table, double-click on an open table's title bar or right-click the table name and select Alter Table from the pop-up menu.

The Alter Table painter appears (see Figure 4.6).

FIGURE 4.6.
The Alter Table painter.

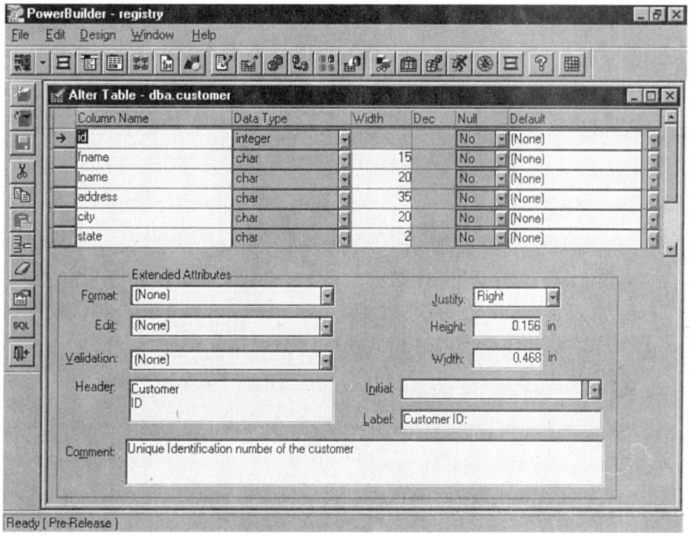

A table can have columns appended only at the end of the column list, but they can be deleted from anywhere (depending on your DBMS). You can alter the table fonts, comments, and primary and foreign keys. You can also alter the extended attributes of the columns. In some DBMSs you are permitted to increase the number of characters and allow `NULL` values for a column. You can only increase, not decrease, the number of characters. Also, you cannot prevent `NULL` values in these columns because the `NULL` option is disabled for the columns. The `NULL` option is disabled because any new columns will not have any data in them when the table is altered. If you were permitted to alter a column to be `NOT NULL`, the alter would probably fail, and certainly will if the column has just been added. Most of the alter options are dependent on the DBMS being used.

When these changes are completed you can have PowerBuilder submit the `ALTER TABLE` SQL statement or save the statement to a file in the same fashion as with the `CREATE TABLE` SQL statement.

Dropping a Table

To drop a database table, open and select the table in the workspace. Then click the Drop button from the PainterBar or select Drop from the Object menu. The Drop option acts on the object that currently has focus; this can be a table, view, or key. You can also right mouse click on the table title bar and choose Drop Table from the pop-up menu. PowerBuilder will then display a message for you to confirm the action. Clicking Yes submits the `DROP TABLE` statement to the DBMS.

Table Definition Properties

The *table definition* consists of table and column characteristics. The Create/Alter Table painter displays the column characteristics. To access and alter the table properties (see Figure 4.7) you must either select Properties from the table pop-up menu (see Figure 4.4), select Properties from the Object menu in the Database painter, or select Table Properties from the Edit menu in the Create/Alter Table painter.

NOTE

The dialog opened within the Create/Alter Table painter contains two additional tabs, Indexes and Foreign Keys, that are not available in the dialog opened by the Database painter.

Table Characteristics

These are the *table properties* that can be entered or changed in the Create/Alter Table painter (refer to Figure 4.5):

- Fonts for the data, headings, and labels
- Comments about the table
- Table name
- Table owner (only in the Create Table painter)
- Primary key
- Foreign key
- Indexes

These characteristics are displayed and maintained in the Table Properties dialog box (see Figure 4.7). The Table Properties property sheet utilizes the tab format to access the different table characteristics.

The Data Font tab enables you to change the font, point size, and style for data in the tables, column heading identifiers for certain DataWindow objects, and column label identifiers for freeform DataWindow objects. Click OK to save the font changes. As with all font selections, make sure the fonts you choose are available on the user's machine. If the font is *not* available, the operating system will determine a font closest to the selected font; this will be the font PowerBuilder will use.

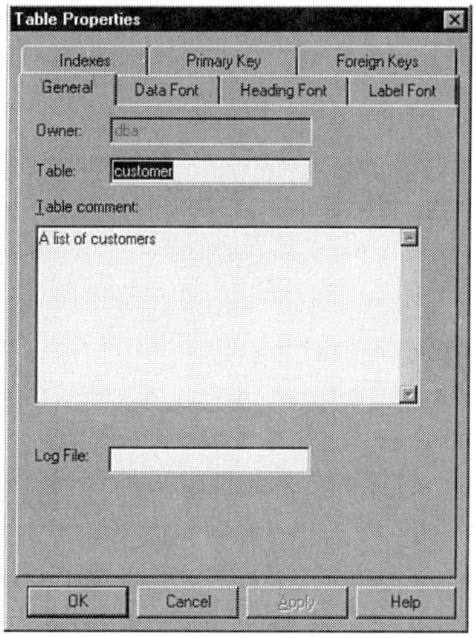

FIGURE 4.7.
The Table Properties property sheet.

Clicking the General tab makes the Owner, Table, and Table Comments appear. You can enter or alter the comments and table name at any time, but only the owner can be entered at the creation of the table. To save the changes click OK in the Table Characteristics dialog box. There is also a new edit field that allows you to specify a log file to capture SQL statements to.

Primary and foreign keys are used to enforce referential integrity of the tables within a database. These keys can ensure that valid values are being entered into the tables. A *primary key* uniquely identifies a single row within a table, and a *foreign key* signifies a relationship between a row in one table and a row in the related table.

For example, if a `product` table and `sales_order_items` table are related by a product identifier, the relationship might be the `prod_id` field (a product) in the `sales_order_items` table that is directly related to the `id` in the `product` table. To relate these two tables, the `prod_id` field would be designated as a foreign key that points to the product table `id` field (see Figure 4.8).

The primary key `order_no` identifies a row in `order_header` and the `sold_to` field identifies a customer from the `customer` table as a foreign key.

Clicking the Primary Key tab displays the table and the existing primary key (if there is one). You can then click the columns in the order in which you want to make the primary key. Clicking OK creates the key within the database and places a primary key icon within the Database painter workspace, connecting to the columns of the table selected as being part of the primary key.

The primary key icon of a table can be used to open all the tables referencing it as a foreign key. You accomplish this by clicking the right mouse button on the primary key icon. A pop-up menu appears (see Figure 4.9).

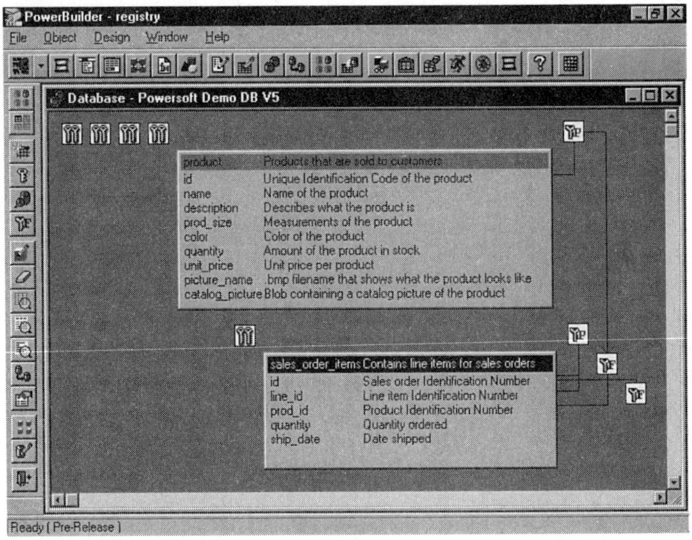

FIGURE 4.8.
The `product` *and* `sales_order_items` *tables in the Database painter workspace displaying the referential integrity with the* `product_id` *and* `id` *columns.*

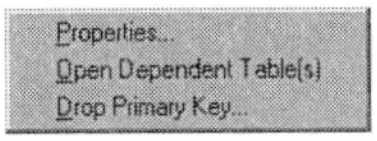

FIGURE 4.9.
The primary key pop-up menu.

Select Open Dependent Table(s), and the tables are opened in the workspace.

Clicking the Foreign tab displays the table and the existing foreign keys (if there are any). You can then click the New command button or select Foreign Key from the New menu in the table's pop-up menu to display the Foreign Key Definition dialog box (see Figure 4.10).

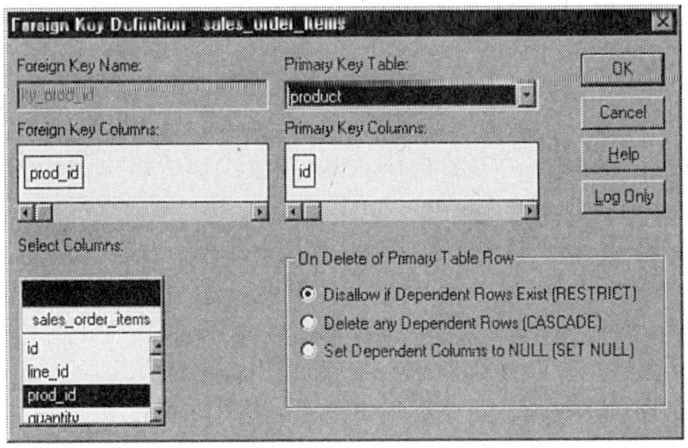

FIGURE 4.10.
The Foreign Key Definition dialog box.

Name the new key and select from the current table the columns that will make up the foreign key. You then need to select a primary key table that contains the appropriate primary key referenced by the foreign key. Select the appropriate DBMS-related information and click OK. This brings you back to the Foreign Key Selection dialog box, where you click the Done button to save the key and place a foreign key icon within the Database painter workspace connecting to the columns of the table selected as part of the foreign key.

You can also use foreign keys to open related tables. You do this by clicking the right mouse button on the foreign key icon. A pop-up menu appears (see Figure 4.11).

FIGURE 4.11.
The foreign key pop-up menu.

Select the Open Referenced Table, and the table is opened in the workspace.

To drop a primary or foreign key, select the appropriate primary or foreign key icon from a table in the workspace. Then click the Drop button in the PainterBar or select Drop Table/View/Key from the Object menu. PowerBuilder then displays a message for you to confirm the action. Clicking Yes submits the appropriate SQL statements to the DBMS.

Clicking the Indexes tab displays the table and the existing indexes (if there are any). You can then click the New command button or select Index from the New menu in the table's pop-up menu to display the Index Definition dialog box. The Create Index dialog box appears (see Figure 4.12) with some DBMS-related information.

FIGURE 4.12.
The Create Index dialog box.

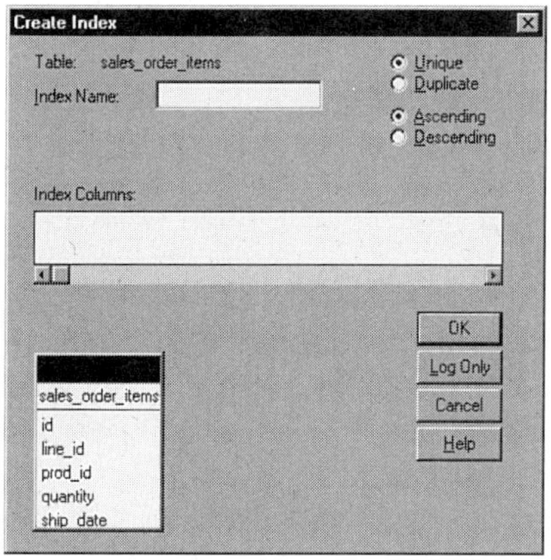

You specify the required information, such as the name, unique or duplicate index, and specific DBMS-related information. You then select the columns that are displayed in the Index On box.

When you are finished you can have PowerBuilder submit the `CREATE INDEX` SQL statement or log the statement.

Indexes cannot be changed, but you can view them by either double-clicking on the index icon or selecting Browse from the index icon's pop-up menu (see Figure 4.13).

FIGURE 4.13.

The index pop-up menu.

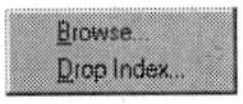

The Browse Index dialog box appears (see Figure 4.14).

FIGURE 4.14.

The Browse Index dialog box.

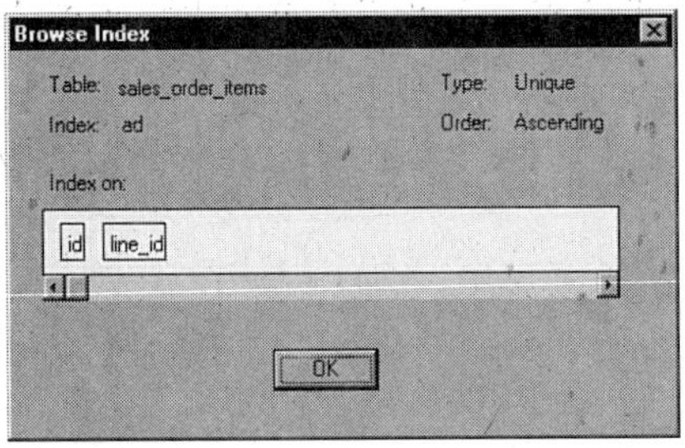

Because an index cannot be directly altered, you must delete the index and then re-create it to modify it.

To drop an index, select the icon of the index to be dropped and either click the Drop button from the PainterBar or select Drop Index from the index icon's pop-up menu (refer to Figure 4.13). PowerBuilder will then display a message for you to confirm the action. Clicking Yes submits the appropriate SQL statements to the DBMS.

Column Characteristics

The column characteristics can be entered in the Create Table painter or changed in the Alter Table painter. Collectively known as the *extended attributes*, they are stored in the Powersoft repository (PowerBuilder system tables) and are the following:

Extended Attribute	*Description*
Comment	Describes the column and can be displayed in the workspace when a table is opened
Header	Default header of the column
Label	Default label of the column
Display Format	Format of the data when displayed
Height, width	Default height and width of the column
Initial value	Default initial value of the column
Justify	Default alignment justification of the column
Validation rule	Default criteria to validate against entered values
Edit style	Format of the column during user interaction

These attributes can also be accessed through the pop-up menu (see Figure 4.15). This menu displays when you click the right mouse button while over a column.

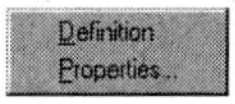

FIGURE 4.15.
The table column pop-up menu.

Select Properties from the pop-up menu, and the Column Characteristics dialog box appears (see Figure 4.16).

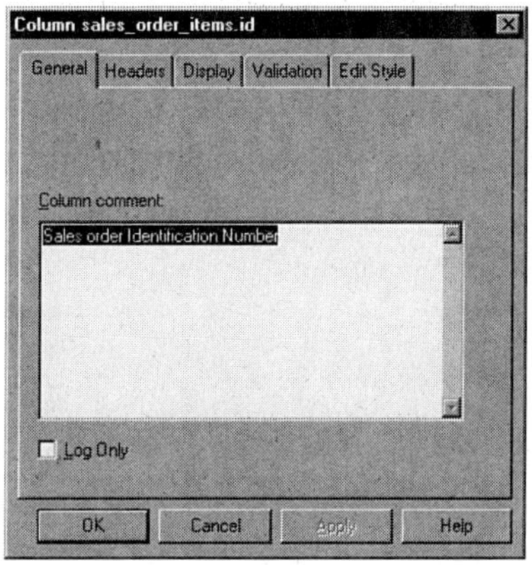

FIGURE 4.16.
The Column Characteristics dialog box.

You can enter or change comments for a column by selecting the General tab from the Column Characteristics dialog box. Comments are stored as the `Tag` attribute of the column in a DataWindow object. Also in the General tab page is the Log Only check box; if it is checked and the OK button of the Column Characteristics dialog box is clicked, all changes made while the Column Characteristics dialog box was open are logged. Checking the Log Only check box will also start the log if it is stopped.

You can specify the header and label and their position by selecting the Headers tab (refer to Figure 4.16) from the Column Characteristics dialog box. You specify the text and position of the header and label for a column when it is displayed in a DataWindow object.

Clicking the Display tab (refer to Figure 4.16) enables you to specify the display format, justification, case, height and width, and whether the column is to be a picture.

The case can be set to Any, UPPER, or lower. In the case of a picture, PowerBuilder expects the column to contain either a BMP or WMF filename. When a picture is specified, the height and width are set to `0`; you are required to specify these values accordingly.

You can also create or edit a display format from this dialog box by selecting the Display tab. The display format is used in the DataWindow object to display data. Selecting either the Edit or New button makes the Display Format Definition dialog box appear (see Figure 4.17).

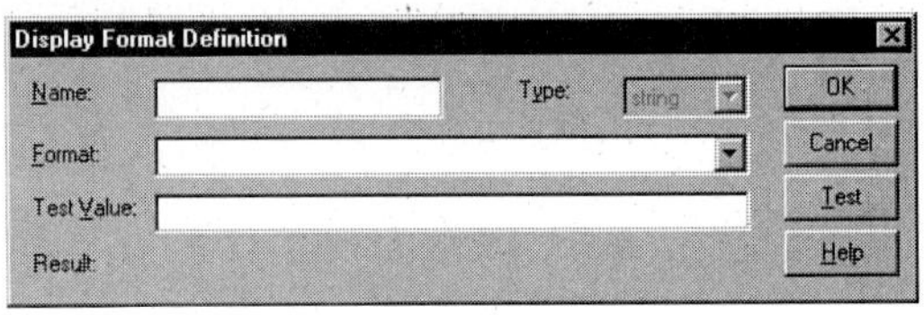

FIGURE 4.17.
The Display Format Definition dialog box.

From here you can create or alter a display format to fit your needs.

To specify the validation of the column, select the Validation tab, which enables you to specify the validation rule and initial value for a column. (The initial value is the default value for the column for each new row.)

You can also create or edit a validation rule from here. The validation rule is used in the DataWindow object to validate that the data being entered by the user meets certain criteria. Selecting either the Edit or New button makes the Input Validation dialog box appear (see Figure 4.18).

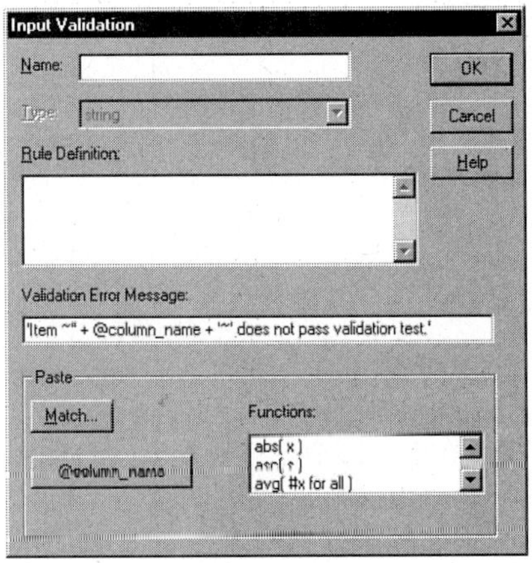

FIGURE 4.18.
The Input Validation dialog box.

From here you can create or alter a validation rule to fit your needs.

To specify the edit style of the column, select the Edit Style tab, which enables you to specify a new or alter an existing edit style.

You can also create or edit an edit style from here. These styles are used by the DataWindow object to have an edit presentation style affixed to a column that will dictate how the user enters data. Selecting either the Edit or New button makes the Edit Style dialog box appear (see Figure 4.19).

See the section "Displaying, Editing, and Validating Data" later in this chapter for a more complete description of the extended attributes.

FIGURE 4.19.
The Edit Style dialog box.

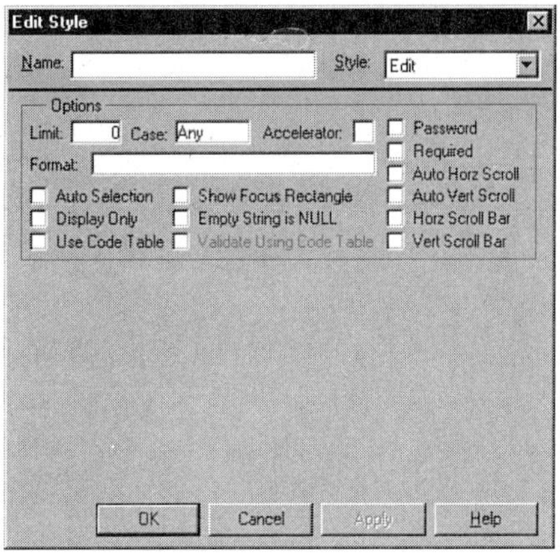

Logging the SQL Statements

During your database manipulation you might want to log your SQL work. You can accomplish this by various means in the Database painter. By having an ongoing log, you can record all SQL generated in the Database painter, which you can reuse at a later date or modify to complete other tasks.

To start the logging, select Start/Stop Log from the Design menu when in the Database painter. A log file is opened and the Activity Log icon appears in the bottom-left corner of the Database painter workspace. You can view this log by double-clicking the Activity Log icon.

To stop the logging, select Start/Stop Log from the Design menu or close the activity log. If the Database painter was not closed and the log is reopened, logging will continue from its last logged position in the log.

To save the log to a file, select Save Log As from the Design menu. This enables you to submit the SQL statements to the DBMS later. You can also clear the log by selecting Clear Log from the Options menu.

You can also export table information to a log file. First select a table or view from the workspace and select Export Syntax To Log from the Object menu. After you select a table, a DBMS dialog box for the destination DBMS appears. From here you select the desired destination DBMS. Exporting to a different DBMS requires PowerBuilder to have the proper interface for that DBMS. If you select the ODBC DBMS, PowerBuilder will prompt you for a data source.

The syntax is exported to the log with the table-related Powersoft repository information.

The Table Painter

The Table painter (refer to Figures 4.5 and 4.6) gives you the capability (as described in the "Creating a Table" and "Altering a Table" sections) to specify the following information: a table name, column names, column datatypes and sizes, fonts for the table, comments about the table, primary and foreign keys, and the extended attributes for the columns.

The following buttons are used in the painter:

Button	*Description*
	Create New Table
	Open Another Table
	Save Changes to Database
	Cut Column
	Copy Column
	Paste Column
	Insert Column
	Delete Column
	Table Properties
	SQL Syntax View
	Close Painter

The painter is used to create or alter tables in the current DBMS. The syntax view of the Table painter provides the SQL scripts for the visual representation of the table in the form view. The Table painter is used in as described earlier in the "Creating a Table" and "Altering a Table" sections of this chapter.

To create or alter a table from the Form view in the painter, you select Save or Save As from the File menu. If you are creating a table and the table is not named yet, PowerBuilder prompts you for the name of the table. Using the Save As from the File menu also requires you to enter the table name.

The Data Manipulation Painter

The Data Manipulation painter gives you the capability to retrieve and manipulate data from the database. You can create, delete, or alter rows and save the changes back to the database. Being a DataWindow, the Data Manipulation painter presentation style is either grid, tabular, or freeform (see Chapter 9, "The DataWindow Painter"). Any time you are in the painter you can print or preview the displayed data.

To open the Data Manipulation painter, click one of the three Preview buttons or select Edit Data from the Object menu. Both of these options allow you to decide in which of the three formats (grid, tabular, or freeform) you want to have the data displayed. When the painter opens, all rows are retrieved (see Figure 4.20).

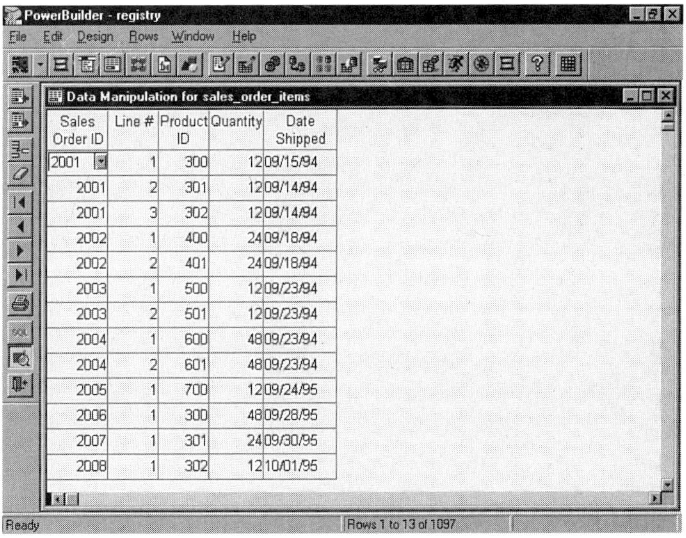

FIGURE 4.20.
The Data Manipulation painter.

During the retrieval, the Retrieve button changes to a hand to signify a cancel. You can click this Cancel button to stop the retrieval process at any time. When the retrieval is finished, the hand reverts to the Retrieve button.

The columns in the rows utilize all of the appropriate display formats, validation rules, and edit styles defined for them.

The following buttons are used for modifying the data in the painter:

Button	*Description*
	Retrieving data
	Saving changes to the database
	Inserting a row
	Deleting a row
	Go to first row
	Next row
	Previous Row
	Go to last row
	Print
	SQL Syntax
	Preview
	Close Painter

From the Data Manipulation painter you can also filter and sort the data. You select either Filter or Sort from the Rows menu item, and the appropriate dialog box—Specify Filter (see Figure 4.21) or Specify Sort Columns (see Figure 4.22)—appears.

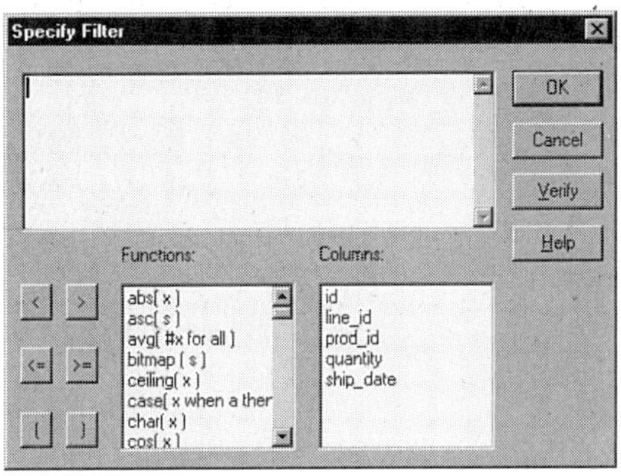

FIGURE 4.21.
The Specify Filter dialog box used to filter data in the Data Manipulation painter.

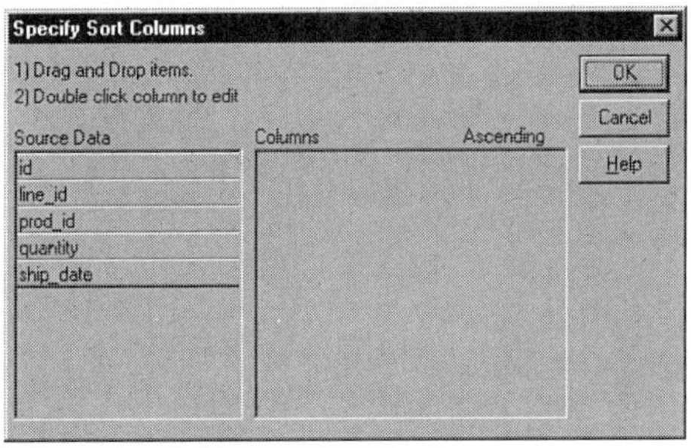

FIGURE 4.22.
The Specify Sort Columns dialog box used to sort data in the Data Manipulation painter.

The filter process requires a Boolean expression used against the rows to determine which rows will be displayed.

Here's an example of this Boolean expression:

```
customer_id  <= "2000000"
```

The sort process involves selecting columns, and sometimes expressions, to sort the displayed rows. You declare expressions by double-clicking on an item in the Sort Columns box, and the Modify Expression dialog box appears (see Figure 4.23).

The Data Manipulation painter enables the importation of data from external sources. These sources are listed in the List Files of Type drop-down list box in the Select Import File dialog box. To open this dialog box, select Import from the Rows menu.

When you have selected the file, PowerBuilder loads the data and displays it in the painter.

As well as importing data, you can save data to an external file. To do this, select Save Rows As from the File menu. The Save As dialog box appears (see Figure 4.24).

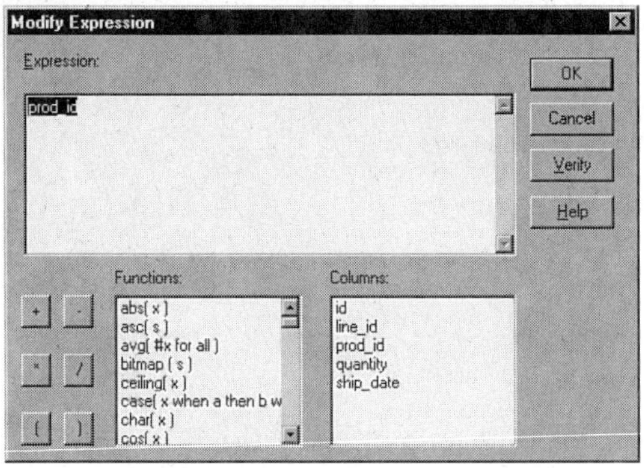

FIGURE 4.23.
The Modify Expression dialog box.

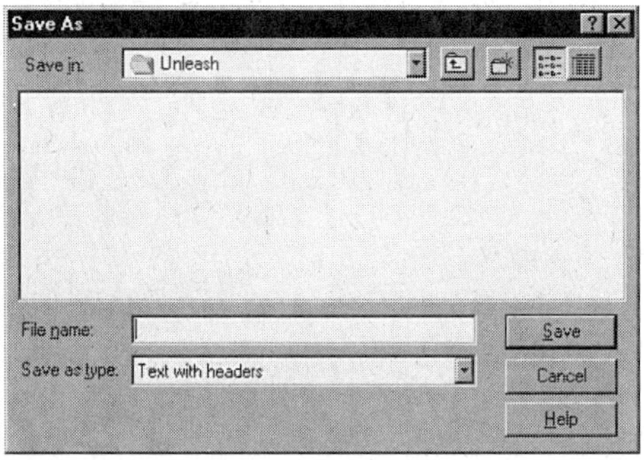

FIGURE 4.24.
The Save As dialog box.

You can now choose the appropriate format and save the file. Some of the more commonly used formats are Excel, Text, CSV, and SQL Syntax.

You can return to the Database painter workspace by closing the Data Manipulation painter (by selecting Close from the File menu). Alternatively, you can minimize the window or select Database Painter from the Window menu. If any changes have occurred that have not yet been saved, you will be asked if you require the database to be updated. After this, the painter is closed and you return to the Database painter. Another additional option is to uncheck Preview from the Design menu or toggle the Preview button on the toolbar.

The Database Administration Painter

The Database Administration painter enables you to control database and table access, create and execute SQL statements, and manage users.

To open the Data Administration painter (see Figure 4.25), click the Admin button or select Data Administration from the Design menu.

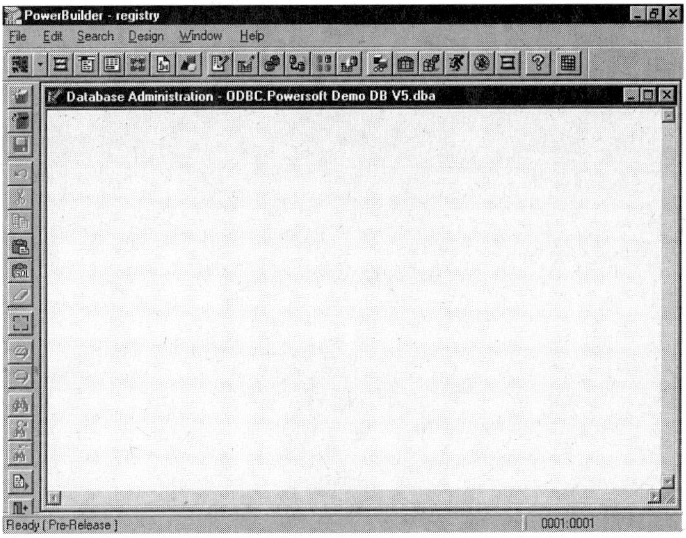

FIGURE 4.25.
The Data Administration painter.

This painter acts similarly to the PowerScript painter in its editing capabilities, except that you write SQL statements, not scripts. The SQL statements are written in the workspace. The editing toolbar buttons and menu items match the ones in the PowerScript painter.

You enter and execute SQL statements from the workspace. You must use the termination character (;) in the workspace the same way you would in PowerScript. However, for this painter only you can redefine the termination character. This termination character, `TerminatorCharacter`, is stored in the database section of the PB.INI file.

SQL statements are entered in one of three ways:

- Entering the statement into the workspace via the keyboard
- Pasting the statement using the Paste SQL button
- Opening a SQL script file

Typing the SQL statement is the most direct way. It enables you to enter statements that cannot be pasted.

Pasting statements limits you to the `SELECT`, `INSERT`, `UPDATE`, and `DELETE` SQL statements.

Clicking the Paste SQL button or selecting Paste SQL from the Edit menu displays the SQL Statement Type dialog box (see Figure 4.26). The SQL painter is detailed in Chapter 5, "SQL and PowerBuilder."

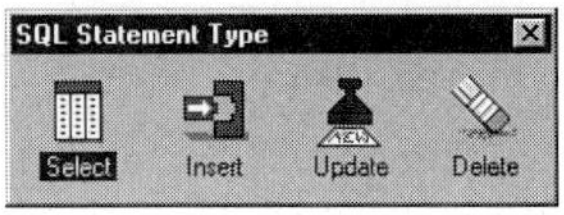

FIGURE 4.26.
The SQL Statement Type dialog box.

If you double-click on the desired SQL statement, the Select Tables dialog box appears. Select the tables you want, and PowerBuilder guides you through the process, with dialog boxes to help input the required information to build the syntax. When you return to the Data Administration painter, the created syntax is displayed in the workspace.

You can import script files into the Data Administration painter by selecting Import from the File menu. If you have created any log files, this is usually where they are loaded.

To execute these SQL statements, click the Execute button or select Execute SQL from the Design menu (Ctrl+L). The statements will then be submitted to the DBMS.

You can create and alter views within the Database painter. Views are used to retrieve data from a database in a restricted manner that enables easy access to complex queries and an additional level of security. Every time a view is accessed, its `SELECT` statement is submitted to the DBMS.

Existing views are accessed from the Database painter and displayed in the View Definition dialog box with the complete `SELECT` statement. Views cannot be altered within this dialog box. This can only be done by dropping and re-creating the view. Within the View painter you can create views using the same SQL toolbox that is used in DataWindow `SELECT` statement creation (see Chapter 5).

Database Profiles

PowerBuilder provides you with a way to set up numerous database profiles that make changing from one data source to another easy. The active database profile defines the current data source.

A Database Profile button in the toolbar gives you a shortcut to opening the Database Profiles dialog box.

To define a profile within the Database painter, select Connect from the File menu. A menu appears with the currently defined profiles, a Prompt option, and a Setup option (see Figure 4.27). Select Setup from the menu, and the Database Profiles dialog box appears (see Figure 4.28).

You can click New to define a new profile or click Edit to edit the profile of the highlighted profile. Clicking either button produces the Database Profile Setup dialog box (see Figure 4.29).

From here you enter the profile name, the DBMS, and DBMS-related information. Click OK to save the profile, and PowerBuilder attempts to connect with the DBMS. If the connection is successful, this profile becomes the active profile. If it's unsuccessful, PowerBuilder displays a message indicating that it could not connect to the database.

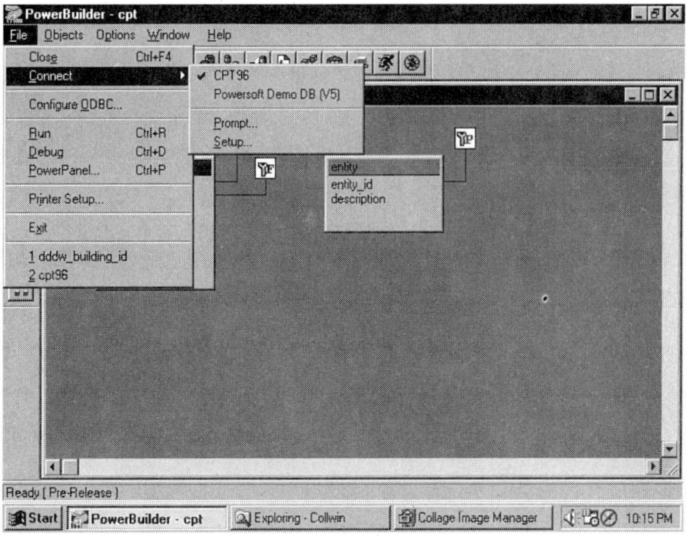

FIGURE 4.27.
The Database connect menu.

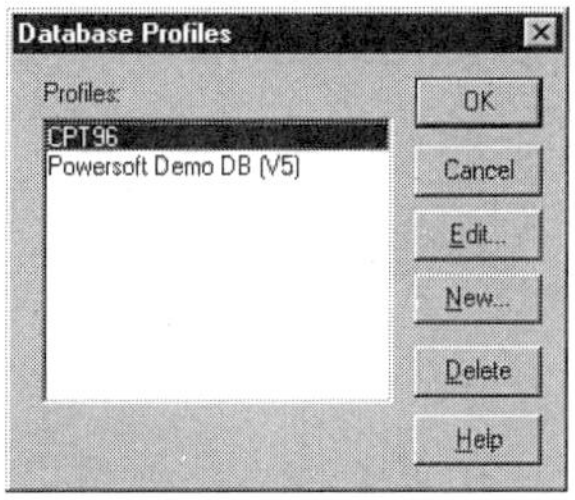

FIGURE 4.28.
The Database Profiles dialog box.

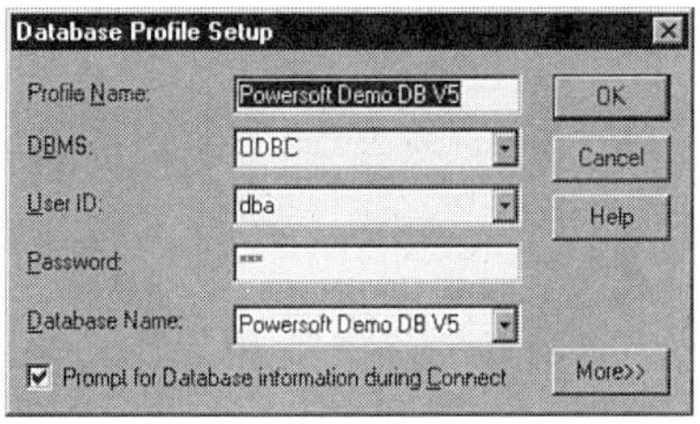

FIGURE 4.29.
The Database Profile Setup dialog box.

From the Database Profiles dialog box you can also delete profiles, regardless of whether they are the active profile. To do this, select the profile and click the Delete button. Even though the profile no longer exists, the connection is still active.

The Database Trace Log

A *database trace* can be set up within the Database Profiles dialog box. This trace enables you to troubleshoot the database connection while developing your application. You can only trace one DBMS and one connection at a time. When you're running the Database Trace tool, it logs the information that it gathers to a file, PBTRACE.LOG, in the \Windows directory. The information gathered by the Database Trace tool and written to the log file is described in Chapter 5.

To start the Database Trace tool from the database profile, enter the word `trace` and a space before the DBMS name in the DBMS box in the Database Profile Setup dialog box. When you click the OK button, a message appears informing you that the Database Trace has been enabled and the output will be written to the PBTRACE.LOG file in the \Windows directory. Click OK, and you are connected to the database with PowerBuilder, beginning the trace of the database connection. To stop tracing the database connection remove the word `trace` from the DBMS field in the Database Profile Setup dialog box. This will break the connection to the DBMS and create a new connection. Click OK and you are connected to the database with the Database Trace turned off.

Displaying, Editing, and Validating Data

Being able to control the displaying, editing, and validating of data in the DataWindow provides a powerful and easy-to-use interface for the user. You can control the way data will be entered and displayed. You do this with the extended attributes defined for columns in the Database painter and stored in the Powersoft repository, or directly within the DataWindow painter.

As stated earlier, the repository consists of five PowerBuilder system tables, and each column can have only one edit style, one display format, and one validation rule.

The DataWindow is the primary user of the Powersoft repository and uses it to define the way the data is edited, displayed, and validated. For a further explanation of how these attributes are used in the DataWindow, refer to Chapter 10, "DataWindow Scripting."

This section concentrates on how to create, modify, and delete edit styles, display formats, and validation rules.

Because these attributes are stored in the Powersoft repository for a database, they can be used throughout the columns in the database. Although assignment of these attributes to the database columns was discussed when describing the Create and Alter Table dialog boxes, later in this section you will also see how the definition and assignment can occur simultaneously in the Database painter.

You maintain these three extended attributes by selecting the appropriate Edit Style Maintenance, Display Format Maintenance, and Validation Maintenance menu items from the Objects menu (see Figure 4.30).

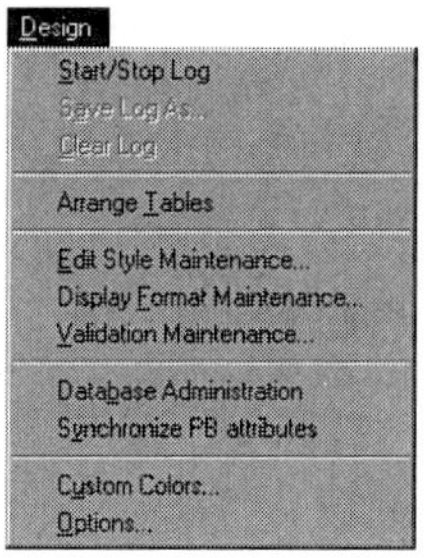

FIGURE 4.30.
The Design menu with Edit Style Maintenance, Display Format Maintenance, and Validation Maintenance options.

From this menu you can access these three extended attributes, and you can make changes without affecting any current column assignments or existing DataWindows.

TIP

Part of the Advanced PowerBuilder Utilities provided by Powersoft is a program called the DataWindow Extended Attribute Synchronizer, or DWEAS for short. This program syncs existing DataWindows with the attributes in the PowerBuilder repository tables.

When these three attributes are defined and associated with a column while you're in the Database painter, they become the column's default for that particular attribute each time it is painted on a DataWindow object. These can be overridden in the DataWindow painter.

Edit Styles

Edit styles dictate the way column data is entered by the user and presented by the DataWindow.

These are the six edit styles:

Edit Style	*Description*
`DropDownListBox`	Enables users to select or enter a value
`DropDownDataWindow`	Enables users to select a value from another DataWindow object
`CheckBox`	Specifies values for on, off, or sometimes a third state
`RadioButton`	Enables users to make a selection from a series of exclusive options
`EditMask`	Specifies allowable characters that the user can enter
`Edit`	Enables users to enter a value

Figure 4.31 is a DataWindow example showing all six edit styles.

FIGURE 4.31.
The DataWindow example of the six edit styles.

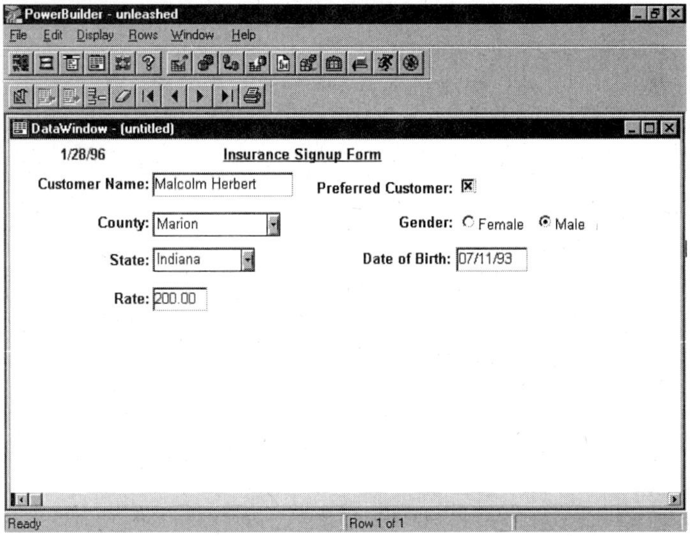

Defining and Modifying Edit Styles

To define an edit style, open a table having the column to be assigned an edit style and click the right mouse button over that column to display the column pop-up menu (refer to Figure 4.15).

Select Properties, and the Column Characteristics dialog box appears (refer to Figure 4.16). Selecting the Edit Style tab allows you access to either select an edit style and click Edit to modify an existing style or click one of the six edit style buttons in the New group box to create a new style. Either way, Edit Style dialog box appears (refer to Figure 4.19).

From here you name the style, enter the attributes, and click OK to return to the Column Characteristics dialog box. To apply either the new or modified edit styles, click OK and the style is assigned to the column.

You can always select an existing edit style for a column in a similar manner. Position the cursor over the column to be assigned and click the right mouse button. As before, the Column Characteristics dialog box appears. In the Edit Style tab page select an edit style and click Done. The edit style has now been applied to the column.

To remove an edit style from a column, position the cursor over the column to be assigned and click the right mouse button. As before, the Column Characteristics dialog box appears. From the Edit Style tab page deselect the highlighted edit style and click OK. The column no longer has an associated edit style.

The `DropDownListBox` Edit Style

The `DropDownListBox` edit style provides the user with a column that displays as a drop-down list box (refer to Figure 4.31).

When an edit style is defined and the style is `DropDownListBox`, the DropDownListBox Edit Style dialog box appears (see Figure 4.32).

FIGURE 4.32.
The DropDownListBox Edit Style dialog box.

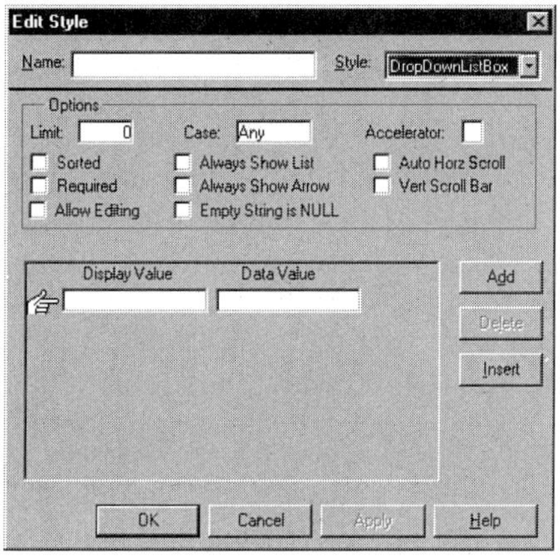

A drop-down list box has a set of values that you predefine for the user to select. These values are known as a *code table*. These are internal tables used by edit styles. Besides the drop-down list box, code tables can be assigned to the `DropDownDataWindow`, `RadioButton`, `EditMask`, and `Edit` edit styles.

Code tables have a display value, which the user will see and can select, and a data value, which the user will not see. This data value is what is stored in the database table. The data value in the code table must match the data type of the column for the data value to be stored. You can use an internal PowerBuilder code `NULL!` as a data value to signify a `NULL` value. When you do this you should give it an associated display value.

Because code tables are case-sensitive, the data values in the code table must exactly match the DataWindow's data. This means that if the data values match, the display value is displayed, or else the DataWindow's actual value is displayed.

Because only one display value will display at a given time, you can have multiple display values in the code table for different data values. Processing of the code table is done from the top down, so only the first of multiple display values that are equal will display. This gives you the flexibility to check for multiple data values when using a DataWindow, yet still use the same code table for a list box.

The following is an example:

Display Value	*Data Value*
`Sundling`	`SUN`
`Sundling`	`sun`
`Sundling`	`Sun`
`Gallagher`	`GAL`
`Gallagher`	`gal`
`Gallagher`	`Gal`

For this example, uppercase is the preferred way of storing the data. PowerBuilder will use the first data values listed for the same display values (which in this example will be uppercase). This enables the list boxes to use the first display values, `Sundling` and `Gallagher`, and the associated uppercase data values, `SUN` and `GAL`. But data can be stored in any form in the database table, so an allowance is made to give a DataWindow the flexibility to choosing one of the data value forms, uppercase, lowercase, or both (`SUN`, `sun`, `Sun`).

You can further dictate the `DropDownListBox` edit style by defining its attributes:

- The Limit box imposes the number of characters the user can enter. The default is 0, which indicates an unlimited amount. The maximum is 32,767 characters.
- The Accelerator box enables you to define an accelerator key.
- To enable the user to enter a value, select the Allow Editing check box, or you can restrict values from being entered by deselecting the check box. The user will always have the capability to select from the list.
- To make the column a required field, select the Required Field check box and you are required to enter a valid value into the column before you leave it.
- To make the column value a `NULL` if an empty string is entered, select the Empty String is `NULL` check box; otherwise, the column value will be left as an empty string. Your database table requirements will dictate whether you can use this option for the column.
- You can have automatic scrolling and scrollbars if the appropriate check boxes are selected.
- You can always have the list and/or arrow appear via the Always Show List check box and the Always Show Arrow check box.
- You can control the case of the entered text using the Case drop-down list box. The case can be Any, UPPER, or lower.

The `DropDownDataWindow` Edit Style

The `DropDownDataWindow` edit style provides the user with a column that displays the same as a `DropDownListBox`, except the values originate from a DataWindow (refer to Figure 4.31) and are therefore dynamic, as opposed to list box values, which are static.

This style is often used in association with validation tables. For example, it can consist of an order-type table column for an order number to a customer identification number for a shipping label. Providing the order-type column and the customer identification number to a DataWindow via the `DropDownDataWindow` allows the most recent information in the database tables to be available to the user.

Of course, you must define the DataWindow that will be used in the DropDownDataWindow before you can define the DropDownDataWindow edit style. You define a DataWindow object with the columns that will be used in the edit style. You usually select two columns: the display column and the data column. The *display column* is the value the user views; the data column is the value stored in the table.

When an edit style is defined and the style is a `DropDownDataWindow`, the DropDownDataWindow Edit Style dialog box appears (see Figure 4.33).

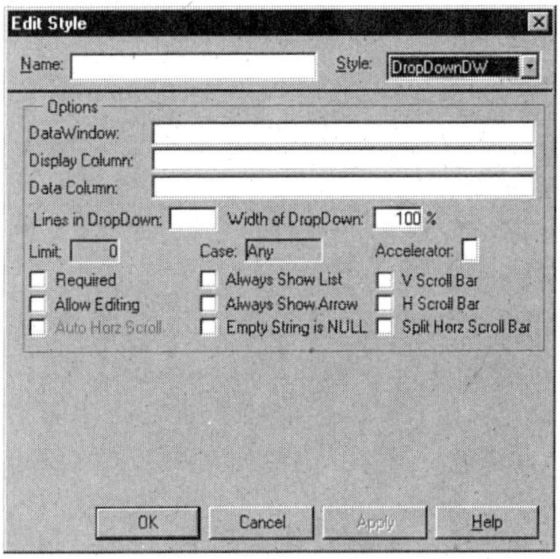

FIGURE 4.33.
The DropDownDataWindow Edit Style dialog box.

From this dialog box you enter the DataWindow, display column, and data stored column. You also define the attributes of the `DropDownDataWindow` edit style much as you do for the `DropDownListBox` style. (A *drop-down list box* is a combination of a single-line edit box and a list box that drops down.) An additional attribute is the Width of Drop Down box. You can enter a value that dictates the width percentage of the drop-down list box. This enables you to display the drop-down list box area either wider or narrower than the single-line edit box, which is the default width.

The `CheckBox` Edit Style

The `CheckBox` edit style provides the user with a column that can accept one, two, or three values. Users can check or uncheck a box representing the column (refer to Figure 4.31).

When an edit style is defined and the style is `CheckBox`, the `CheckBox` Edit Style dialog box appears (see Figure 4.34).

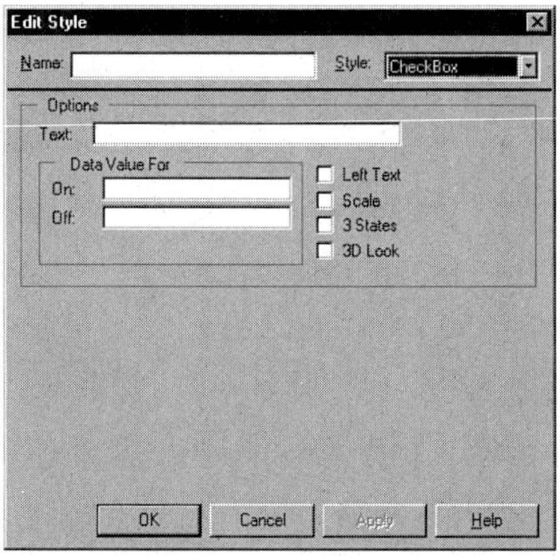

FIGURE 4.34.
The `CheckBox` *Edit Style dialog box.*

From this dialog box you enter the text that will appear next to the check box. Then you enter the values for on (checked), off (unchecked), and other if 3 States is checked. These entered values are the values that are stored in the database. You can also define presentation-style attributes specific to a check box, such as 3D presentation, Left Text, and Scale Box. The Left Text attribute enables you to make the check box label appear to the left of the box. The Scale attribute causes the actual check box to change in size as you stretch the column within the DataWindow painter. The Scale Box check box and 3D check box cannot be checked at the same time.

The `RadioButton` Edit Style

The `RadioButton` edit style provides the user with a column that has a small number of different values (refer to Figure 4.31).

When an edit style is defined and the style is `RadioButton`, the `RadioButton` Edit Style dialog box appears (see Figure 4.35). From this dialog box you enter the display and data values for the individual buttons. (The data value is the value stored in the column.) You will also enter the number of buttons across a single line. This determines how many buttons will be displayed per single line. And as with the CheckBox edit style, you can define the attributes of the radio buttons, such as 3D, Left Text, and Scale Box.

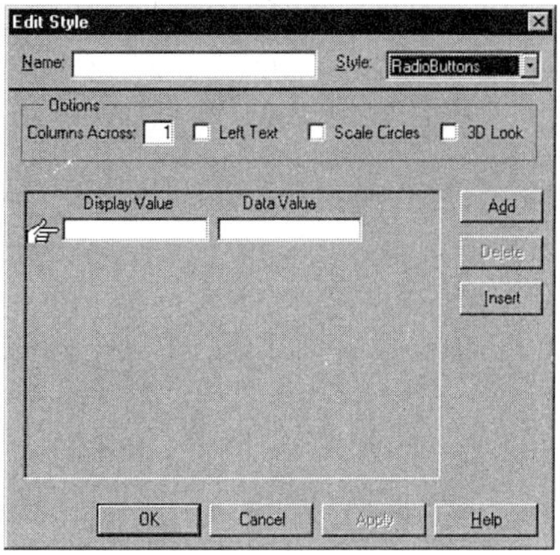

FIGURE 4.35.
The `RadioButton` *Edit Style dialog box.*

The `EditMask` Edit Style

The `EditMask` edit style provides the user with a column that has a fixed format. These edit masks contain special characters that determine what information can be entered and what information cannot. A column with the `EditMask` edit style is drawn the same as the SingleLineEdit Window control (refer to Figure 4.31).

When an edit style is defined and the style is `EditMask`, the `EditMask` Edit Style dialog box appears (see Figure 4.36).

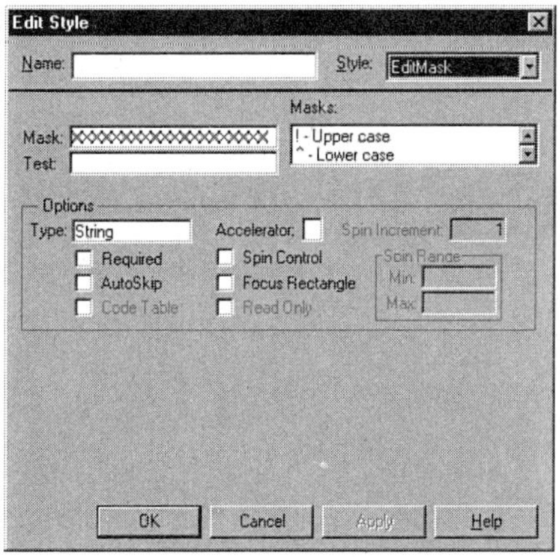

FIGURE 4.36.
The `EditMask` *Edit Style dialog box.*

From this dialog box you enter the desired special characters and the character's type for the mask. You can also specify options to be associated with the edit mask.

When you select the Focus Rectangle check box, PowerBuilder places a rectangle around the column when the column gains focus.

The Autoskip check box is used to specify whether to skip to the next column when the last character is entered.

The Spin Control check box enables you to utilize a code table for the user to cycle through values using up and down arrows. For a numeric column you can enter a Spin Range with a Spin Increment. This control acts similarly to a drop-down list box except that only one value appears at a time and the user can cycle through them using both the up- and down-arrow keys. You define the values and other attributes of the spin control in an extension to the `EditMask` Edit Style dialog box (see Figure 4.37).

FIGURE 4.37.
The `EditMask` Edit Style dialog box with the Spin Control extension.

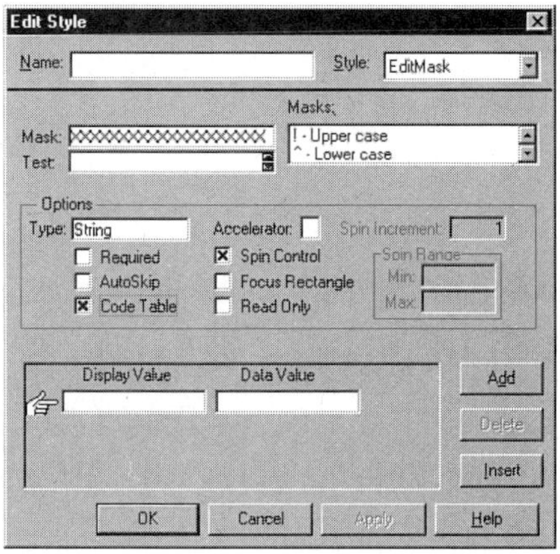

The special characters for the Mask box are described in the section "Display Formats" later in this chapter.

While you are defining the mask you can use the Test box and button to enter a value and make sure it produces the desired result.

There are certain behaviors you should be aware of in this edit style's actions and values.

The `Date`, `DateTime`, and `Time` edit masks are interpreted as `NULL` if the value entered into the mask contains only zeros. If the first entered number is greater than the maximum day, hour, or month, it is placed in the second position, preceded by a zero. If the values entered are a number followed by a delimiter, the value is altered so that a zero is placed before the number (for example, 4/22/88 would be changed to 04/22/88).

The Backspace key deletes only the preceding character, regardless of whether the Shift key is used. The Delete key deletes only what is selected.

The `Edit` Edit Style

The `Edit` edit style is the default edit style in a DataWindow. A column with this edit style in a DataWindow has the same appearance as the `Edit Mask` (refer to Figure 4.31).

When an edit style is defined and the style is `Edit`, the `Edit` Edit Style dialog box appears (see Figure 4.38).

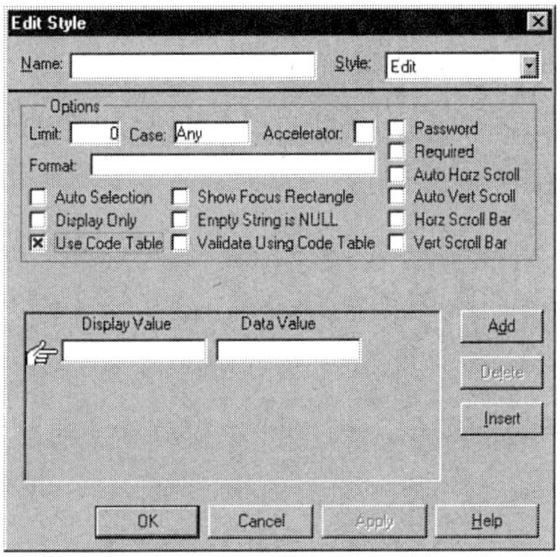

FIGURE 4.38.
The `Edit` *Edit Style dialog box.*

In addition to having previously described attributes, the `Edit` edit style enables you to enter data, such as sensitive information or passwords, that will display as asterisks by selecting the Password check box. You can use the Display Only check box to set the column as display only and stop the user from making changes to the data within the field. A display format mask can be entered in the Format box; this determines how the data is displayed once the user leaves the field.

Display Formats

Display formats are used to affect how the data is displayed to the user. Unlike edit styles, display formats are for display only. When the user is editing the column, the display format is not applied to the column. It is applied when the focus has left the column.

A display format can be used to display entire month names, different colors for negative numbers, dollar signs for money values, and phone numbers with parentheses around the area code and a dash after the exchange. Figure 4.39 shows an example of some of these display formats.

When the data does not have a display format, the information appears in the format in which the value is stored in the database.

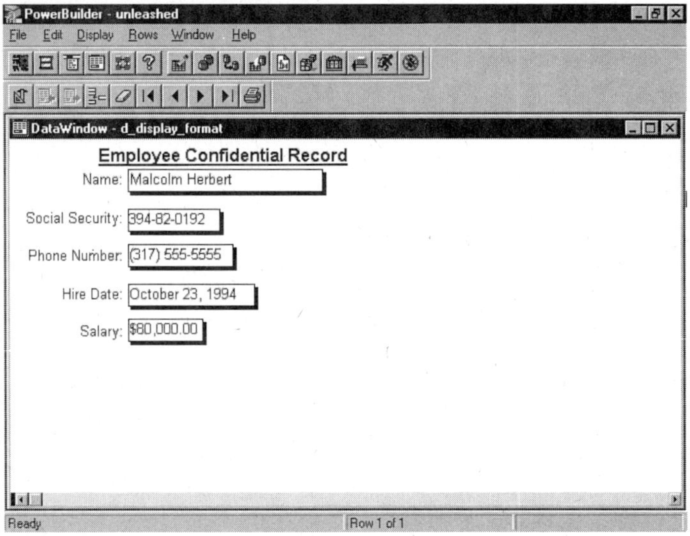

FIGURE 4.39.
Examples of display formats.

Defining and Modifying Display Formats

To define a display format, open a table having the column to be assigned a display format and click the right mouse button over that column to display the column pop-up menu (refer to Figure 4.15).

Select Properties, and the Column Characteristics dialog box appears (refer to Figure 4.16). Selecting the Display tab allows you access to either select a display format and click Edit to modify an existing format or click New to create a new format. Either way, the Display Format Definition dialog box appears (refer to Figure 4.17).

From here you can define and test the display format. If this is a new format, name it and click OK. If you are just modifying an existing one, click OK to save the modification. Clicking the OK button brings you back to the Column Characteristics dialog box with the defined format highlighted. To apply either the new or modified display format, click OK and the format is assigned to the column.

You can select an existing display format for a column in a similar fashion to that described previously. Position the cursor over the column to be assigned and click the right mouse button. As before, the Column Characteristics dialog box appears. Select the desired display format and click OK. The display format has now been applied to the column.

To remove a display format from a column, position the cursor over the column to be assigned and click the right mouse button. As before, the Column Characteristics dialog box appears. Deselect the highlighted display format to remove the highlight; then click OK. The column no longer has an associated display format.

Describing the Formats

There are four different kinds of display formats:

- Numbers
- Strings
- Dates
- Times

These four formats can be combined to create a combined format. Here's an example:

```
MM/DD/YY HH:MM:SS
```

This format is an example of combining the `MM/DD/YY` month format with the `HH:MM:SS` time format. A space is used to differentiate the two masks.

You can also have more than one section to a format. The sections are divided by a semicolon (;) and are used for different cases of the data. Here's an example:

```
$#,##0.00;[RED]($#,##0.00);ZERO;NULL
```

This currency format displays a positive number with the first format (`$#,##0.00`), a negative number with the second format (`[RED]($#,##0.00)`), a zero value with the third format (`ZERO`), and a `NULL` value with the fourth format (`NULL`).

Square brackets are used to enclose keywords. Keywords range from the term `[GENERAL]` to color names. Each display format has its own individual set of keywords. The following color keywords can be used in any of the four formats:

- `[BLACK]`
- `[BLUE]`
- `[CYAN]`
- `[GREEN]`
- `[MAGENTA]`
- `[RED]`
- `[WHITE]`
- `[YELLOW]`

You also can use the numeric representation of these colors or alter the numbers to create a different color. The numeric representation can be entered in the display formats in a similar fashion to that of the color names. The advantage of using the numeric representation is that you control the actual color via the formula for the color. Therefore, you can create more than the standard colors by altering these values. This is the formula for creating the various colors:

```
[256*256*blue + 256*green + red]
```

Each primary color has a range from 0 to 255.

Number Display Formats

As shown in an earlier example, the number display has four potential formats:

- Positive format
- Negative format
- Zero format
- Null format

Number display formats have four sections: positive, negative, zero, and `NULL` value sections. The *positive section* is the format that is displayed when a positive value is in the column. The *negative section* is the format that is displayed when a negative value is in the column. The *zero section* is the format that is displayed when the value equals zero. The *null section* is the format that is displayed when the column is a `NULL` value.

TIP

To prevent a zero value from displaying anything, you can use the format `#,###0;;;`. You should also place a space after the last semicolon.

The number display has many special characters than can be used in the format. Decimal points, dollar signs, parentheses, percent signs, and spaces are position based and display in the value where they appear in the format. These are the two most important display format special characters:

Character	*Description*
`#`	A number value
`0`	A required number value for each 0 in the format, if no value is given a 0 is displayed

The keyword `[GENERAL]` enables PowerBuilder to determine the correct format for the number display.

The following are examples of different numeric display formats:

Number Display Format	*68*	*-68*	*.68*	*0*
`[GENERAL]`	68	-68	.68	0
`0`	68	-68	1	0
`0.0`	68.0	-68.0	0.7	0.0
`0.00`	68.00	-68.00	0.68	0.00

Number Display Format	*68*	*-68*	*.68*	*0*
`#,##0`	68	-68	1	0
`#,##0.00`	68.00	-68.00	0.68	0.00
#,##0;(#,##0)	68	(68)	1	0
`$#,##0.00;($#,##0.00)`	$68.00	($68.00)	$0.68	$0.00
`0%`	6800%	-6800%	68%	0%
`0.00%`	6800.00%	-6800.00%	68.00%	0.00%
`0.00E+00`	6.80E+01	-6.80E+01	6.80E-01	0.00E+00
`0;(0);ZERO`	68	(68)	1	ZERO

String Display Formats

The string display has two formats:

- String format
- Null format

The string format is required, but the null format is optional. All characters within the format represent themselves except the following character:

Character	*Description*
`@`	A string format representing each character

Here are examples:

String Display Format	*462369800*	*This is a test*
`(@@@@@-@@@@)`	(46236-9800)	(This -is a)
`@@@@@@@ NOT@@@@@@@`	4623698 NOT00	This is NOT a test

Date Display Formats

The date display has two formats:

- Date format
- Null format

The date format is required and the null format is optional.

The date display has many special characters used in the format:

Character	*Description*
`d`	A day number
`dd`	A day number with leading zeros if applicable
`ddd`	A day name abbreviation
`dddd`	A day name
`m`	A month number
`mm`	A month number with leading zeros if applicable
`mmm`	A month name abbreviation
`mmmm`	A month name
`yy`	A two-digit year number
`yyyy`	A four-digit year number

The keywords `[GENERAL]` and `[ShortDate]` instruct PowerBuilder to use the short date format description defined in the Microsoft Control Panel for the date display. The keyword `[LongDate]` designates the long date display description defined in the Microsoft Control Panel for the date display and is the default.

Here are examples:

Date Display Format	*Saturday April 22, 1995*
`mm/dd/yy`	04/22/95
`mmmm dd yyyy`	April 22 1995
`mmm-dd-yyyy`	Apr-22-1995
`mmmm d,yyyy`	April 22,1995
`ddd, mmmm d`	Sat, April 22
`dddd, mmmm dd, yyyy`	Saturday, April 22, 1995

Time Display Formats

The time display has two formats:

- Time format
- Null format

The time format is required and the null format is optional.

The time display also has many special characters that can be used in the format. These are the special characters:

Character	*Description*
`A/P`	A or P as applicable
`a/p`	a or p as applicable
`AM/PM`	AM or PM as applicable
`am/pm`	am or pm as applicable
`ffffff`	A microsecond
`h`	An hour
`hh`	An hour with leading zeros if applicable
`m`	A minute
`mm`	A minute with leading zeros if applicable
`s`	A second
`ss`	A second with leading zeros if applicable

The keyword `[Time]` instructs PowerBuilder to use the time format description defined in the Microsoft Control Panel for the time display.

Here are examples:

Time Display Format	*10:23:59:123456 AM*
`h:mm AM/PM`	10:23 AM
`h:mm:ss`	10:23:59
`h:mm:ss AM/PM`	10:23:59 AM
`h:mm:ss:fff AM/PM`	10:23:59:123 AM
`h:mm:ss:ffffff am/pm`	10:23:59:123456 am

Validation Rules

Validation rules are used to validate the data being entered by the user. Each column can have a single validation rule assigned to it. These rules contain a set of criteria that evaluates to `TRUE` or `FALSE`. The DataWindow uses this evaluation to determine which event (`ItemChanged` or `ItemError`) to fire (see Chapter 10 for further explanation).

Figure 4.40 is an example of entered data that did not pass validation.

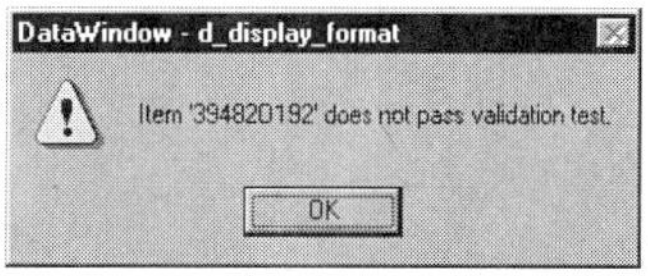

FIGURE 4.40.
The failed validation message.

Defining and Modifying Validation Rules

You can define and modify validation rules in the Database painter.

To define a validation rule, open a table having the column to be assigned a validation rule. Click the right mouse button over that column to display the column pop-up menu (see Figure 4.15).

Select Properties, and the Column Characteristics dialog box appears (refer to Figure 4.16). Selecting the Validation tab allows you access to either select a validation rule and click Edit to modify an existing rule or click New to create a new rule. Either way, the Input Validation dialog box appears (refer to Figure 4.18). From here you define the validation rule, which can use any valid PowerScript expression.

You can enter an initial value for the column in the Initial Value drop-down list box; this value appears when a new row is inserted in a DataWindow. If this is a new rule, name it and click OK. If you are just modifying an existing one, click OK to save the modification. Clicking the OK button brings you back to the Column Characteristics dialog box with the defined rule highlighted. To apply either the new or modified validation rule, click OK and the rule is assigned to the column.

You can select an existing validation rule for a column in a similar manner. Position the cursor over the column to be assigned and click the right mouse button. As before, the Column Characteristics dialog box appears. Select the desired validation rule and click OK. The validation rule has now been applied to the column.

To remove a validation rule from a column, position the cursor over the column to be assigned and click the right mouse button. As before, the Column Characteristics dialog box appears. Deselect the highlighted validation rule to remove the highlight and then click OK. The column no longer has an associated validation rule.

Describing the Rules

The validation rule is an expression that returns either `TRUE` or `FALSE`. The expression can be composed of any valid PowerScript expressions, PowerBuilder functions, and user-defined global functions.

The Input Validation dialog box (refer to Figure 4.18) contains a list box with the most commonly used PowerScript functions that can be pasted into the validation expression. The Match button is used only with string values. If you click Match, the Match Pattern dialog box appears (see Figure 4.41).

You can enter a match pattern or select one of the available match patterns. To test the pattern, enter a value in the test box and click the Test button. PowerBuilder evaluates it and determines whether the test value is valid or invalid. Clicking OK will paste the pattern into the `Rule Definition` section.

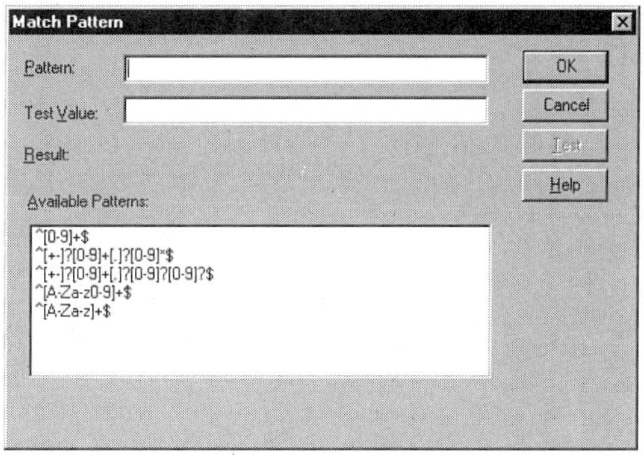

FIGURE 4.41.
The Match Pattern dialog box.

The @placeholder button pastes the current column name or @col into the `Rule Definition` section. Even though the current column appears in the rule, it really is only a placeholder, and the column the expression is attached to is substituted at runtime. This button enables the generic definitions of rules to accommodate their reuse with other columns.

Within the Input Validation dialog box you can define the error message that will appear when the validation rule fails. PowerBuilder enters a default one:

```
'Item ~'' + @col + '~' does not pass validation test.'
```

You can modify this message or create one of your own and enter it into the validation error message box.

Here are examples of validation rules:

```
Not IsNull( GetText())
```

```
IsNull( @col) OR @col = 'O' OR @col = 'N' OR @col = 'H'
```

The first example determines whether the value in the column to which the rule is attached is not a `NULL` value. The second example requires the value entered into the column with the validation rule to be either `NULL`, `O`, `N`, or `H`.

Summary

This chapter shows how you can use the Database painter to maintain table and column characteristics. Manipulation of the column extended attributes is covered, and the three most important extended attributes (edit styles, display formats, and validation rules) are detailed.

SQL and PowerBuilder

5

IN THIS CHAPTER

After you have created the database with tables and views based on the conceptual schema, the next step is to communicate with the database system in order to manipulate or modify the data. Each database management system (DBMS) has its own *Data Manipulation Language* (DML), but all DMLs are based on a single language—*Structured Query Language* (SQL), pronounced either "sequel" or "S-Q-L." The precursor to today's SQL was originated by Dr. E.F. Codd in the 1970s as a means of accessing his new concept, relational databases. The first implemented version of the query language theorized by Codd was developed by D.D. Chamberlin in 1976 and was known as Sequel. SQL was first adopted for IBM's System R project, a research prototype that was to yield SQL/DS and DB2 and has since been approved as the official relational query language standard by the American National Standards Institute (ANSI). SQL can be found in many different forms throughout PowerBuilder, from the most obvious (embedded SQL) to the least obvious (DataWindows).

There are three main types of SQL statements. The most common is the *query*, which is a request for information. Next are the statements for *data modification*—the adding, deleting, or updating of data. The last type covers the administration of the system and transactions (for example, creating tables, granting security permissions, committing, and rolling back transactions).

Before diving into the mysteries of SQL, you need to understand a number of terms. Database tables can be called entities, tables, or relations. Tables contain *rows*, or records of data, and describe one occurrence of that entity. Within each row are a number of attributes, fields, or columns. The usage of each term is related to the area of description. When discussing a conceptual data model, you use the terms entities, attributes, and relationships. When using DMLs, however, the correct terms are tables and columns.

SQL is based on *tuples* (record occurrences) and tuple-oriented relational calculus. What this means to you, the programmer, is that when two tables are joined, a multiplication occurs. For example, table A has 10 records and table B has 20 records. If the two tables are simply joined (that is, without a `WHERE` clause), the result will consist of 200 records; each record from table A joins with each of the records from table B. This is important because the multiplication factor can cause the novice SQL programmer some problems when join conditions are not quite correct. This also means that you need to adjust your mind-set. Instead of dealing with a procedural language or method to solve problems, you need to think in a relational way, and you need to remember that you can now operate collectively on sets of data.

This chapter details aspects of SQL from the basics of the `SELECT` statement through advanced SQL constructs. The Powersoft demonstration database (PSDEMODB.DB), which comes with PowerBuilder, is used to illustrate examples of SQL. Some additional examples are written to use the `pubs` database that comes with Microsoft and Sybase SQL Server.

SQL

Before we show you how to incorporate SQL into PowerBuilder applications, we will first examine the different kinds of SQL statements that are available. The following sections describe the `SELECT`, `INSERT`, `UPDATE`, and `DELETE` statements and how they are constructed and used.

Understanding Queries

The basis of a query is the SELECT statement. You will find a number of variations and limitations among the various DBMSs you will encounter, but in its simplest form, it is structured as follows:

```
SELECT target list
FROM list of relations
```

target list is a projection (the columns that will be used as opposed to the columns that will not be used) of a subset of the columns from one or more tables, or, put simply, the names of the values to retrieve. A *join* links the rows of two or more tables (this provides the relations of a query).

This is the most common form of a query:

```
SELECT target list
FROM list of relations
WHERE conditions
```

The values of certain columns (usually primary or foreign keys) are compared in the conditions clause. This provides a link between two tables and a method to restrict the resulting rows from a table. Sometimes this linkage is automatically carried out by the DBMS if the columns are key values. Watcom-SQL is an example of this automatic linkage, and it helps reduce the complexity of the WHERE clause. The syntax used in Watcom-SQL requires you to specify a NATURAL or KEY JOIN in the FROM clause of a query. You can find more information on this feature of Watcom-SQL by exploring the Sybase SQL Anywhere documentation that comes with PowerBuilder.

To retrieve attributes emp_lname and city from a single relation employee with no selection criteria, thus returning all rows in the table, the WHERE clause is omitted and the statement appears as follows:

```
SELECT emp_lname, city
FROM employee
```

These might be the results from running this query (in the Database Administration painter):

```
Last Name          City
Whitney            Needham
Cobb               Waltham
Chin               Atlanta
Jordan             Winchester
Breault            Milton
```

You can place selections (or restrictions) on this query within the WHERE clause. For example, to list just the employees from California, the query becomes

```
SELECT emp_fname, city
FROM employee
WHERE state = "CA";
```

NOTE

Users of Sybase SQL Anywhere must use a single quote (') instead of the double quote (") in the previous and following examples.

However, to create a link between multiple relations, another WHERE clause is added:

```
SELECT employee.city, customer.city
FROM   employee, customer, sales_order
WHERE  employee.emp_id = sales_order.sales_rep AND
       sales_order.cust_id = customer.id;
```

The results of this query are shown below, but you should note that if you run this query against the demo database, you will get a succession of the same first city for just one employee (because there are multiple entries of an employee in the sales_order table):

```
City            City
Atlanta         Raleigh
Atlanta         South Laguna
Atlanta         Bohemia
Atlanta         Winnipeg
Atlanta         Lakewood
```

Note in this example that two columns of the same name (City) are retrieved. Also note that the table name prefixes the column name; this is to inform the DBMS from which tables to pull the values and in what order. Also note that there are three tables involved in the join, and the WHERE clause has now become a compound statement. Multiple conditions are related using AND or OR and enable the construction of complex truth conditions.

Understanding NULLs

SQL is based on three state logic: TRUE, FALSE, and Unknown. The unknown value is represented by RDBMSs as NULL, and you have to be as aware of NULLs in your SQL as you are in your PowerScript. NULLs are used to represent a missing or unknown value, or to indicate that a value for that column in a record is not applicable. The NULL value is not the empty string or a zero; it is the absence of a value. Like PowerBuilder, the DBMS provides you with a means to check the equality of a value to NULL, because a NULL is never equal to anything, including itself. So, for example, the following query will produce some unexpected results:

```
SELECT emp_lname
FROM   employee
WHERE  city = "Indianapolis" OR
       NOT city = "Indianapolis";
```

This query does not return all employees. If some employees' cities have NULL values, their records will not appear in the result set. To check whether a column equals NULL you use the special phrase IS NULL. Using any other operator will give a FALSE value if used against a NULL value, and the join will fail. A negation of the WHERE clause does not solve the problem (as can be demonstrated by running the previous query), because three-valued logic (TRUE, FALSE, and Unknown), not two-valued logic (just TRUE and FALSE), is in operation. Therefore, NOT Unknown values are also Unknown (at least in SQL!). The correct syntax for the sample query is this:

```
SELECT emp_lname
FROM   employee
WHERE  city = "Indianapolis" OR
       NOT city = "Indianapolis" OR
       city IS NULL;
```

NOTE

Obviously, you would not code a query to return all the employees in this way; this is shown only to illustrate the correct way to handle NULL values. You will also notice that you get the same number of results in the demo database since there are no NULL city values.

If you want to default NULL to a usable value, say for the purpose of grouping your result set, use the ISNULL() function. ISNULL() takes two parameters: the column or expression you suspect might be NULL and the value to which you want it to default. For example, this:

```
SELECT emp_lname
FROM   employees
WHERE  ISNULL( salary, 0) = 0;
```

will return all employees who have a zero salary, together with all employees who have yet to be assigned a salary (new hires) and therefore have a NULL salary amount.

NOTE

As noted earlier, not all DBMSs support the same syntax. For example, Oracle uses an NVL() function instead of ISNULL() (for example, NVL(salary, 0)).

The SELECT Statement

Because each DBMS has its own variations, what follows is a generalization of the complete SQL SELECT statement:

```
SELECT { DISTINCT } select_list
FROM [ table_list | view_list ]
WHERE search_conditions
GROUP BY non_aggregate_expressions
HAVING search_conditions
ORDER BY column_list { [ ASC | DESC ] }
```

The DISTINCT keyword removes duplicate rows from the result set. A row is considered *duplicate* if all values in the select list completely match those of another row. NULL values are considered to be equal for the DISTINCT keyword. Most systems include the opposite keyword ALL in their syntax, which explicitly asks for all rows. This is the default behavior of a query and the keyword is only included for backward compatibility with earlier versions of the SQL language.

The Retrieval List

select_list contains a comma-separated list of columns, constants, expressions, or an asterisk (representing all columns). *Expressions* are functions, subqueries, arithmetic operators, or any combination of columns, constants, and expressions. The asterisk selects all columns in all tables, but can also be qualified with a table name to select all the columns in only that table.

The WHERE Clause

The WHERE clause can include the standard comparison operators (such as =, >, <, and !=), ranges (BETWEEN), lists (IN), pattern matches (LIKE), and the unknown value operator (IS NULL). Each condition can be combined using the standard logical operators (AND, OR) and also nested within parentheses. The DBMS will most often make the appropriate data conversion when comparing values of differing data types. Here's an example:

```
WHERE date_entered = "12/06/69"
```

NOTE

This example will work against a SQL Server environment, but against Sybase SQL Anywhere you are required to phrase it as '1969-12-06'. Other databases may require other specific formats to work, and you should refer to the appropriate DBMS SQL book.

The NOT keyword can be applied before any of these operators to negate the expression. For example, this:

```
SELECT emp_lname
FROM   employee
WHERE  start_date NOT BETWEEN '86/1/1' AND '86/12/31';
```

returns all employees that did not start in 1986.

Joins

There are three main types of join conditions used in the WHERE clause: the natural join, the outer join, and the self-join.

A *natural join* is the linking of two tables on matching column names using the equality operator, such as

```
SELECT employee.emp_fname
FROM   employee, department
WHERE  employee.dept_id = department.dept_id;
```

An *outer join* is used in queries to return all rows from an outer table, with any values taken from the inner table being `NULL` if no join condition exists. The construction of an outer join varies from one DBMS to another; with SQL Server the syntax is `*=` and `=*` specified in the `WHERE` clause, whereas Watcom-SQL uses `LEFT ¦ RIGHT OUTER JOIN` in the `FROM` clause. For example, to list all the department names with everyone in that department, and to allow for cases in which no one belongs to a department (a new department, say), the query against SQL Server might be

```
SELECT dept_name, emp_lname, emp_fname
FROM   department d, employee e
WHERE  d.dept_id *= e.dept_id;
```

or in Watcom-SQL

```
SELECT dept_name, emp_lname, emp_fname
FROM   department KEY LEFT OUTER JOIN employee;
```

NOTE

This SQL statement will give you an error with the demo database using Sybase SQL Anywhere because there is more than one way the database engine can join the two tables. This SQL `SELECT` is purely to illustrate the differences in approach between DBMSs.

Some DBMSs place restrictions on outer joins that prevent other joins on either (or both) inner and outer tables; SQL Server restricts regular joins on the inner table.

Another type of join is the *self-join*. This is when values are compared within a column of a table. To construct this type of join requires *table aliasing*—renaming a table within the `SELECT`. Here's an example:

```
SELECT DISTINCT e1.emp_fname, e1.emp_lname, e1.zip_code
FROM   employee e1, employee e2
WHERE  e1.state = 'MA' AND
       e1.zip_code = e2.zip_code AND
       e1.emp_id <> e2.emp_id
ORDER BY e1.zip_code;
```

This returns all the employees from Massachusetts who live in the same ZIP code. `DISTINCT` eliminates the duplicate records found due to the self-join, and the not-equality operation on the `employee_id` removes any self-matches (to give only a list of multiple employees who live in the same area, thus eliminating any employees who are the only ones in a specific ZIP code).

Subqueries

A *subquery* is a SELECT that exists within another statement (for example, SELECT, INSERT, UPDATE, or DELETE) and is used to provide one or more rows to be used in the outer statement's evaluation. You use a subquery for three main purposes:

- To generate a list for use with the IN operator
- To generate a single value
- With the EXISTS, ANY, and ALL operators

A subquery can be used anywhere an expression can be used.

Subqueries with IN

A subquery is used with the IN keyword to produce a set of values against which a value or column can be compared to check whether it is a member. Membership inclusion is stated using the IN keyword and membership exclusion by use of NOT IN. Here's an example:

```
SELECT id, line_id
FROM   sales_order_items
WHERE  prod_id IN ( 300, 301, 302, 303);
```

The following query is a check for what sales order items have been entered for products that are currently out of stock:

```
SELECT id, line_id
FROM   sales_order_items
WHERE  prod_id IN
       ( SELECT id
         FROM product
         WHERE quantity = 24);
```

Single-Value Subqueries

A single-value subquery, as its name suggests, has sufficient restrictions placed on it such that only one row with only one value (column, expression, or constant) is returned:

```
SELECT id, line_id, quantity, ship_date
FROM   sales_order_items
WHERE  prod_id =
       ( SELECT id
         FROM product
         WHERE name = "shorts" );
```

Correlated Subqueries

A subquery that depends on the outer query for values is known as a *correlated* subquery. The subquery is executed repeatedly, once for each row being selected by the outer query, and cannot be resolved independently:

```
SELECT emp_fname, emp_lname
FROM   employee e1
WHERE  city =
       ( SELECT city
         FROM employee e2
         WHERE e2.emp_id = e1.manager_id );
```

This query returns all employees who live in the same city as their managers. The subquery is dependent on the `manager_id` being supplied for each row by the outer query. The equality operator can be used because there is only one manager per employee.

Subqueries with EXISTS

A subquery with `EXISTS` is used to test the existence of rows returned by the subquery by a parent query, and is usually constructed using a correlated subquery.

This example returns all products that have sold more than 100 items in a single sale:

```
SELECT name
FROM   product
WHERE  EXISTS
       ( SELECT id
         FROM sales_order_items
         WHERE sales_order_items.prod_id = product.id AND
               quantity > 40);
```

Subqueries can appear outside of the `WHERE` clause. They can be expressions in the select list, or even in the `HAVING` clause, and they provide a clean way of carrying out additional checks and/or restrictions on the data to be included in the results. You can construct a wide variety of subqueries and, depending on the database, there might be other operators (such as `ANY`, `ALL`, and `SOME` in Watcom-SQL) that you can use.

Aggregate Functions

Each DBMS provides its own set of functions, but a number of them are common. The common aggregate functions are `COUNT()`, `SUM()`, `AVG()`, `MAX()`, and `MIN()`. There might be additional functions within your specific DBMS (for example, Watcom-SQL also provides a `LIST()` function). They are detailed in Table 5.1.

Table 5.1. Aggregate functions and their results.

Aggregate Function	*Result*
`AVG( [DISTINCT] expression)`	Produces an average of the numeric values in the expression.
`COUNT( [DISTINCT] expression ¦ *)`	Returns the number of records that fall within the expression.

continues

Table 5.1. continued

Aggregate Function	*Result*
`MAX( expression)`	Gives the highest value of the expression.
`MIN( expression)`	Gives the lowest value of the expression.
`SUM( [DISTINCT] expression)`	Totals the numeric value in the expression.

Note that `SUM()` and `AVG()` only work on numeric values, and all except `COUNT()` ignore `NULL`s.

The GROUP BY and HAVING Clauses

Aggregate functions return summary results and are usually used with the `GROUP BY` and `HAVING` clauses. The `GROUP BY` clause collects the data into related groups. For example, this:

```
SELECT id, SUM( quantity)
FROM   sales_order_items
GROUP BY id;
```

returns one record for each product with the total number of sales. If you leave off the `GROUP BY`, you will get a database error informing you that the nonaggregate columns must be included in a `GROUP BY` clause.

The `HAVING` clause sets conditions on which groups will appear in the result set and is comparable to the `WHERE` clause, except that it only works on aggregate expressions. For example, this:

```
SELECT DISTINCT name, COUNT( product.id), SUM( sales_order_items.quantity)
FROM   sales_order_items, product
WHERE sales_order_items.prod_id = product.id
GROUP BY name
HAVING SUM( sales_order_items.quantity) > 4000;
```

returns a list of all the products, the number of orders for each, and total quantity ordered for each product that has sold more than 4,000 items. Another example is useful in determining the presence of duplicate data within a table:

```
SELECT emp_fname, emp_lname
FROM   employee
GROUP BY emp_fname, emp_lname
HAVING COUNT(*) > 1;
```

The ORDER BY Clause

The last clause of a `SELECT` is the `ORDER BY`, which is used for sorting values in either ascending (`ASC`) or descending (`DESC`) order. If multiple columns are listed, the results are sorted in the column order, left to right. The results of an `ORDER BY` are affected by the sort order that your DBMS imposes. This might mean uppercase values appear before lowercase, or numbers appear after alphabetic characters. If the `ORDER BY` is left off a query, the DBMS usually returns rows in the physical order in which they exist in the table (for example, a table with a clustered index will return rows in the index key sequence).

The INSERT Statement

The INSERT statement is used to enter new rows into a table. In most DBMSs you can also use INSERT, along with UPDATE and DELETE against database views, usually with certain restrictions. One common restriction to using these commands against a view is that they can only affect one table of the view at any one time. So to insert values into a two-table view you are required to issue two INSERT statements. Each DBMS will impose a different set of restrictions on what operations can be carried out against a view. The syntax for an INSERT is as follows:

```
INSERT [INTO] { table_name ¦ view_name }
[( column_list )]
{ VALUES ( constant_expressions ) ¦ select_statement }
```

column_list can be any number of columns from the table, but must include those columns that are specified as NOT NULL and do not have a default bound to them. Neglect to do this and you will get an error telling you that the offending column cannot be NULL. The VALUES clause requires a list of constants that are of the same data type as those listed in *column_list*. This clause can be replaced by a SELECT statement that returns any number of rows with a column list that matches that of the INSERT. The *column_list* of the INSERT is not required if all of the columns are to receive values, but it is advisable to list the columns anyway. If the table structure were to change—for example, if a column were added—and you had not coded the SELECT statement to return the additional information, the INSERT could fail depending on that column's specification (for example, NOT NULL). You are also taking a leap in the dark by not explicitly specifying the order of the columns, because you are relying on the physical ordering of the receiving columns. Following are examples of both kinds of INSERT:

```
INSERT INTO authors
( name, book)
VALUES
( "Gallagher", "PowerBuilder Unleashed");

INSERT INTO authors
( name, book)
SELECT name, book
FROM   new_authors
WHERE  name LIKE "G%";
```

Using the SELECT clause of the INSERT, you can even populate a table based on itself. An INSERT of data must conform to any rules or triggers that might be defined on the table and columns.

The UPDATE Statement

The UPDATE statement is used to modify existing rows of data. This is its syntax:

```
UPDATE { table_name ¦ view_name }
SET column = { expression ¦ NULL ¦ ( select_statement ) }
```

```
  [,column = { expression ¦ NULL ¦ ( select_statement ) } ]
[ FROM { table_list ¦ view_list } ]
[ WHERE search_conditions ]
```

The `SET` clause specifies the column to be modified and the *value*, or expression, to be used as the new data. The expression cannot be an aggregate function, but it might be an aggregate result returned by a `SELECT`, on the condition that only one value is returned. If the sub-`SELECT` returns more than one row, an error is produced stating that more than one row was returned by a subquery. This type of update is known as a *correlated update*. The `FROM` clause permits the expression to use columns from other tables, and the `WHERE` clause controls which rows are affected by the `UPDATE`. If you omit the `WHERE` clause from an `UPDATE` statement, all the rows in the table will be affected. Some examples are the following:

```
// Set all author royalty values to zero
UPDATE authors
SET    current_month_royalties = 0;
//
// Set the sales of authors with Gallagher as their name to 100,000
//
UPDATE authors
SET    sales = 100000
WHERE  name = "Gallagher";
//
// Update the quantity sold and date modified with data from the sales table
//
UPDATE authors
SET    sales = authors.sales + sales.quantity,
       change_date = GetDate()
FROM   authors, sales
WHERE  authors.author_id = sales.author_id;
//
// Carry out same modification except for authors that had a last shipment
// before the last day in the sales table
//
UPDATE authors
SET    sales = authors.sales + sales.quantity,
       change_date = GetDate()
FROM   authors, sales
WHERE  authors.author_id = sales.author_id AND
       authors.last_shipped < ( SELECT MAX( ship_date )
                                FROM   sales );
```

As with the `INSERT` statement, new values must conform to the table's triggers and the column's rules.

The `DELETE` Statement

The last data-manipulation statement is the most destructive—the `DELETE`. This is the syntax:

```
DELETE
FROM [ table_name ¦ view_name ]
{ WHERE search_conditions }
```

The WHERE clause restricts the rows affected by the DELETE, just as it does with the other statements. The DELETE must pass any triggers that are attached to the affected table. After a DELETE is issued there is no way to recover the records affected other than to cause an explicit ROLLBACK or if a trigger fails (which does its own ROLLBACK).

Good SQL Practices

This section covers a few practice exercises to help with the readability of SQL you write and to provide a better interface to canned queries, stored procedures, and views.

You should capitalize the SQL statements to make them stand out from the column names, table names, and other expressions. See the many code examples in this chapter.

Wherever a computed value or expression is returned, it is considered good manners to give it a name related to the value. For example, the following SELECT returns a salesperson and the number of items sold:

```
SELECT employee.emp_lname, COUNT(*)
FROM   employee, sales_order
WHERE  employee.emp_id = sales_order.sales_rep
GROUP BY employee.emp_lname
ORDER BY COUNT(*);
```

These are the results for this query:

```
emp_lname      Count(*)
Kelly          47
Dill           50
Poitras        52
.
.
Clark          57
Overbey        114
```

As you will see next, if the SELECT is modified to alias the columns, the meaning of the query is much clearer, and if you alias the tables, the join conditions don't look as awkward. It is advantageous to use table aliases with very large statements that join and select columns from many tables. The overall size of the statement is much smaller, which reduces network traffic somewhat, but the main benefit is that it aids in the readability and therefore maintainability.

For example, the following query is the same as the previous query except that it names the two returned values and aliases the tables used:

```
SELECT e.emp_lname LastName, COUNT(*) TotalSales
FROM   employee e, sales_order s
WHERE  e.emp_id = s.sales_rep
GROUP BY LastName
ORDER BY TotalSales1
```

This query produces the same results, but the computed column is now named as follows:

```
LastName       TotalSales
Kelly          47
```

```
Dill            50
Poitras         52
.
.
Clark           57
Overbey         114
```

Always list the columns that you will use repeatedly in a `SELECT` or an `INSERT` statement instead of relying on `*` or implicit column order. The column names, order, and even existence might vary without the `SELECT` or `INSERT` being appropriately modified, and you can get unexpected results by relying on the column order and existence.

SQL Within PowerBuilder

The SQL statements just described can be embedded directly into your PowerScript, and will perform in the same manner as they would from the Database Administrator. However, embedded SQL enables you to include PowerScript variables in various areas of the commands, whereas you cannot include them if you work from the Database Administrator.

The `SELECT` statement gains an `INTO` clause that enables the specification of bind or host variables for the placement of the results. *Bind variables* are PowerScript variables that are prefixed by a colon (`:`) and are treated the same as any other column or value by the SQL. All embedded SQL is terminated by a semicolon (`;`), the same as within the Database Administrator. This means that you do not need to, in fact PowerBuilder will not allow you to, use the line continuation character (`&`) if your SQL extends over many lines.

Therefore, the following query:

```
SELECT COUNT( books), SUM( sales)
INTO   :nTotalBooks, :nSales
FROM   authors
HAVING SUM( sales) > 15000 AND
       name = :szName;
```

uses the PowerScript variable `szName` to find the appropriate author and then the variables `nTotalBooks` and `nSales` to hold the values returned. The `szName` is used to restrict the query to returning just one row; otherwise a database error will occur on subsequent SQL commands because there are still additional rows in the result set waiting to be fetched. If no rows are found, you will get either a zero or `NULL` value in the PowerBuilder variables (this is DBMS specific).

> **NOTE**
>
> In the `[DataBase]` section of your PB.INI you will find the entry `TerminatorCharacter=;`. This enables you to change the terminator character, but only for the Database Administrator. The ; must still be used for all embedded SQL.

Transaction Objects

PowerBuilder controls both embedded SQL and DataWindows through *transaction objects*, of which the `SQLCA` is the default and globally available transaction object. The `SQLCA` (SQL Communications Area) is a nonvisual object that contains relevant information on a connection to the database. The first 10 attributes contain information necessary to connect, and the last 5 are used to receive information from the DBMS on the last operation executed. The default transaction object contains the attributes listed in Table 5.2.

Table 5.2. Attributes of the default transaction object.

Attribute Name	*Data Type*	*Description*
`DBMS`	String	The name of the database vendor
`DataBase`	String	The name of the database
`UserId`	String	The user name to connect by
`DBParm`	String	Specific to the DBMS
`DBPass`	String	The password to be used with the user ID
`Lock`	String	The isolation level
`LogId`	String	The user name to connect by
`LogPass`	String	The password to be used with the log ID
`ServerName`	String	The database server name
`AutoCommit`	Boolean	The automatic commit indicator:
		`TRUE`—Commit automatically after every action
		`FALSE`—Do not commit automatically (the default)
`SQLCode`	Long	The success or failure code of the last operation:
		`0`—Success
		`100`—No results
		`-1`—Error
`SQLNRows`	Long	The number of rows affected
`SQLDBCode`	Long	The database vendor's error code
`SQLErrText`	String	The database vendor's error message
`SQLReturnData`	String	Specific to the database vendor

Not every one of the first 10 attributes needs to be given a value. For example, Sybase SQL Anywhere only requires the `DBMS` and `DBParm` attributes to be filled. `DBParm` is used to hold the relevant data source name and login information, instead of `LogPass`, `LogId`, and the similarly related attributes (for example, database and server names). For native database interfaces `DBParm` is used to specify DBMS-specific options. (See the online help under DBParm for further information.)

The AutoCommit attribute must be set to TRUE in order to create temporary tables or for any other database statements that require execution outside of a PowerBuilder-controlled transaction. The reasons for this are to ensure database consistency during execution and to improve database performance. The AutoCommit attribute affects only Micro Decisionware Database Gateway Interface for DB2, some ODBC, SQL Server, and Sybase SQL Server database management systems. If the Micro Decisionware Database Gateway Interface for DB2 is being used and is configured for long transactions, changing AutoCommit has no effect. If the gateway is configured for short transactions, setting AutoCommit to FALSE changes the gateway configuration to support long transactions.

SQLNRows is filled by the DBMS and varies in meaning from vendor to vendor, but is usually checked after DELETE, UPDATE, or INSERT to ensure that the correct number of records were affected. The SQLCode is usually sufficient to check after executing a SELECT command.

Situations will arise that require an additional connection to the database, such as a need to issue UPDATE, SELECT, or DELETE inside an open cursor that is already making use of the SQLCA. You create it by declaring a variable of type Transaction and assigning it the SQLCA attributes. A straight assignment cannot be made, as this then becomes a pointer to the SQLCA and that already has an open connection! Once you have populated the new transaction object, it needs to be connected to the database.

For example, you might expect the following to work, but it doesn't:

```
Transaction trCursor

trCursor = CREATE transaction
trCursor = SQLCA
```

You will instead have to use the following:

```
Transaction trCursor

trCursor = CREATE transaction
trCursor.DBMS = SQLCA.DBMS
trCursor.Database = SQLCA.Database
// Etc. for the remaining transaction object attributes
```

As you will learn in Chapter 6, "The PowerScript Language," it is important to destroy anything you create. With this in mind, you should issue a DESTROY trCursor just before the previous cursor leaves scope.

Connecting and Disconnecting

After the transaction object has been populated, the next step is to connect it to the database. You most often do this in the startup of an application, either in the application Open event or a login window. This is the syntax:

```
CONNECT [USING transaction_object];
```

where the transaction object is either the default (SQLCA) or one that you have previously defined and initialized. It is good practice to explicitly state that the transaction object to be used is the SQLCA when doing a CONNECT, even though the USING clause is optional. This improves the readability of your code and gives novice programmers a clearer understanding of what is happening. It is also a good habit to get into because if you ever omit a transaction object that you have created, it can be quite difficult to track down the problem.

To drop the connection to the database, a similar statement is used:

```
DISCONNECT [USING transaction_object];
```

Again, in this case the transaction object is either the SQLCA or one you have declared. Remember that the USING clause is optional for the SQLCA, but it is best to specify it explicitly.

Logical Units of Work

Interaction with a DBMS is broken down into *logical units of work* (LUWs), or transactions. Transaction processing by the DBMS ensures that when a transaction is completed all the changes are reflected in the database, or that if the transaction fails, the changes are rolled back or undone to the point where the transaction started.

The classic example used to describe units of work is a bank account fund transfer: If a clerk makes a debit to an account and for some reason the debit process fails (say the database connection is lost) the actual debit of funds that took place is undone. Without a logical unit of work the account could be left with a debited balance, but the clerk could not be sure the transaction had been completed and that other tables that were possibly affected were appropriately updated.

PowerBuilder provides two commands to carry out transaction processing: COMMIT and ROLLBACK. The syntax for these is as follows:

```
COMMIT [USING transaction_object];

ROLLBACK [USING transaction_object];
```

The transaction object is again optional, but it is advised even if it is the SQLCA and required if using a programmer-defined transaction. COMMIT tells the DBMS to accept all changes and to go ahead and make them permanent, whereas a ROLLBACK indicates that any changes since the last COMMIT should be undone. PowerBuilder uses the COMMIT and ROLLBACK statements as the basis of database transactions, which you will see later is not always a good thing. When a DISCONNECT is issued, an automatic COMMIT is executed. You might want to code the COMMIT yourself or even issue a ROLLBACK in case Powersoft decides that this is a bug rather than a feature.

Using the PowerBuilder transaction-management statements means that transactions cannot be nested as they can be natively with some DBMSs.

Checking for SQL Failures

To check for the failure of an embedded SQL statement, consult `SQLCA.SQLCode`. If the `SQLCode` is `0`, the previous command succeeded and a `COMMIT` should be issued. (A `COMMIT` should be issued even after a `SELECT` because it frees DBMS resources, such as locks and buffers.) If the code is –1, the SQL failed and a `ROLLBACK` should be issued, which again frees DBMS resources and leaves the application in a state to continue processing the next transaction. Here's an example:

```
UPDATE employee
SET    emp_fname = "Simon"
WHERE  emp_id = 95
USING  SQLCA;

If SQLCA.SQLCode = 0 Then
   COMMIT USING SQLCA;
Else
   szError = SQLCA.DBErrText
   ROLLBACK USING SQLCA;
   MessageBox( "Update Failure", szError)
End If
```

Occasionally, the developer checks the `SQLCode` for the value `100`. This value signifies that no data was returned as a result of the previous statement, and is checked after a singleton `SELECT` or a `FETCH`. `FETCH` statements usually occur in loops; the indicator for the end of the result set is a `SQLCode` value of `100`.

NOTE

A *singleton* `SELECT` is a query that returns only one record of information.

The specific DBMS error code and error message are taken from the transaction object attributes `DBCode` and `DBErrText`, respectively. These two values are the ones usually reported in any error-message dialog box. In most systems the DBMS error code is checked against a hard-coded list or another database table to replace `DBErrText` with a more user-friendly message. Of course, if the error message is an indication of a lost or not-connected transaction, the error script that generates the new message must be able to handle this case. This is usually done by hard coding the connection error messages into the script while leaving the rest of the messages in a database table.

DECLARE and FETCH

In the case of embedded SQL, which produces multiple-row result sets, or in the case of a stored procedure that requires execution, you use a different set of statements. The object used for traversing a multirow result set is called a *cursor* and provides a movable, single-row view of the results (the result set).

The DECLARE Statement

The DECLARE statement is comparable to a variable declaration, and as such it is not executed—it is only used to prepare the transaction object.

> **NOTE**
>
> You can declare the same cursor only once in the same script. If you have a declared cursor that is outside the local scope, the same scope rules that apply to standard variables (for example, String, Integer) also apply to cursor declarations.

This is the syntax for a SELECT:

```
DECLARE cursor_name CURSOR FOR select_statement
{ USING transaction_object };
```

In this example, note the use of a bind variable in the WHERE clause:

```
DECLARE employee_data CURSOR FOR
SELECT  emp_fname, emp_lname
FROM    employee
WHERE   birth_date < :dtCutOff
USING   SQLCA;
```

For a stored procedure, the syntax is similar:

```
DECLARE procedure_name PROCEDURE FOR database_procedure_name
        @parmameter1 = value1, @parameter2 = value2,...
{ USING transaction_object };
```

Here's an example:

```
DECLARE employee_data CURSOR FOR
sp_employee_by_birth_date @cut_off = :dtCutOff
USING SQLCA;
```

The actual stored procedure would be written as

```
CREATE PROCEDURE sp_employee_by_birth_date @cut_off DATETIME
AS
SELECT *
FROM employee
WHERE birth_date <= @cut_off;
```

Not all DBMSs support stored procedures. The Sybase SQL Anywhere DBMS does not accept the use of @ to signify parameters and instead uses the IN, OUT, and INOUT keywords.

SQL Server and Sybase stored procedures support the use of OUT to denote a parameter used as an output from the procedure. Some DBMSs require you to specify the result set if one is generated by the stored procedure (for example, Watcom-SQL's RESULT clause in the stored procedure declaration). This is the syntax:

```
DECLARE procedure_name PROCEDURE FOR database_procedure_name
@parmameter1 = value1, @parameter2 = value2 OUT,...
{ USING transaction_object };
```

Even though the `DECLARE` statement is only a declaration, it is part of a specific order of SQL statements and must be terminated with a ;. There is no need to check—indeed no point in checking—the `SQLCode`, because a `DECLARE` is simply that, a declaration, and not an action.

Using OPEN, EXECUTE, and FETCH

When the SQL statement has been declared, the next step is to execute it. For declared cursors the `OPEN` statement is used:

```
OPEN cursor_name;
```

For declared procedures the `EXECUTE` command is used:

```
EXECUTE procedure_name;
```

The `SQLCode` of the transaction object, defined in the `DECLARE`, should be checked for SQL failure after either an `OPEN` or an `EXECUTE`. If the `OPEN` or `EXECUTE` is successful and a result is generated, the data cursor is placed before the first row of the result set. The `FETCH` statement is used to step to the first row and then subsequent rows, and it does the actual retrieve of the data into host variables. If either the `OPEN` or `EXECUTE` fails, you should close the cursor and process the error. This is the syntax for the `FETCH`:

```
FETCH cursor_name ¦ procedure_name INTO host_variable_list;
```

Some DBMSs permit the use of `FETCH FIRST`, `FETCH PRIOR`, implicit `FETCH NEXT`, and `FETCH LAST`, which (as their names imply) fetch the first row, the previous to current row, the next row, and the last row, respectively. If no direction is indicated, PowerBuilder assumes `FETCH NEXT`. The `FETCH` statement is usually used inside a loop to collect the data into other PowerBuilder structures, such as arrays or even DataWindows. When a `FETCH` is issued against the result set and the last record has already been retrieved, `SQLCode` takes the value `100`, indicating that there are no more result rows. Here's an example:

```
nCount = 0
Do
   nCount ++
   FETCH employee_data INTO :szFirstName[ nCount], :szLastName[ nCount];
While SQLCA.SQLCode = 0
```

To finish the processing of the cursor or procedure and to release both client and server resources, a `CLOSE` statement is executed. This is the syntax:

```
CLOSE cursor_name ¦ procedure_name;
```

`SQLCode` should be checked after this statement, although a failure at this stage probably indicates wider server problems.

WARNING

You should be careful not to place a `COMMIT` or `ROLLBACK` within an open cursor or stored procedure that is returning multiple rows because it will close the cursor or procedure.

Dynamic SQL

Now that you've mastered the basic syntax of embedded SQL, the next step is to explore dynamic SQL. *Dynamic SQL* enables the execution of database commands that are not supported directly as embedded SQL, such as *Database Description Language* (DDL), `CREATE TABLE` and `DROP TABLE`, or SQL where parameters or results are unknown at the time of development.

Dynamic SQL can be categorized into four types:

- No result set or input parameters
- No result set but requires parameters
- Known result set and input parameters
- Unknown results and parameters at development time

PowerBuilder only supports the main SQL statements (`SELECT`, `INSERT`, `UPDATE`, and `DELETE`), together with its transaction statements (`CONNECT`, `DISCONNECT`, `COMMIT`, and `ROLLBACK`), because these are common in all databases. To execute SQL syntax that is specific to a database you will have to resort to one of the forms of dynamic SQL.

Type 1

This type of dynamic SQL is often used for the execution of DDL and other database-specific code. This is the syntax:

```
EXECUTE IMMEDIATE sql_statement { USING transaction_object };
```

For example, to drop a table, type this:

```
EXECUTE IMMEDIATE "DROP TABLE employee" USING SQLCA;
```

Type 2

The second type is used for SQL statements that require one or more parameters that are unknown at development time and do not return result sets. It is also used for DDL statements that require runtime-defined parameters. Here are the syntax and sequence:

```
PREPARE dynamic_staging_area FROM sql_statement { USING transaction_object };
EXECUTE dynamic_staging_area USING parameters;
```

The Type 2 syntax makes use of one of the other SQL objects defined in PowerBuilder, the SQL *dynamic staging area* (SQLSA). The SQLSA is used to store SQL in preparation for later execution. The SQL is stored together with the number of parameters and the transaction object to be used. The attributes of the SQLSA are protected and cannot be accessed at runtime. As with the SQLCA, the SQLSA is a default object instantiated from the DynamicStagingArea class, and user-defined classes or variables can be used in its place.

The PREPARE statement is used to prepare the SQLSA for the execution of the SQL statement. Within the PREPARE statement's SQL, the ? character is used to indicate the placement of all PowerBuilder variables that will be supplied during execution. These characters are called *placeholders*. When the SQL statement is executed, the ? characters are replaced by the values signified by the EXECUTE's USING clause. These values can be PowerBuilder variables or object attributes. The order of the placeholders and the order of the EXECUTE parameter list must be the same. Here's an example:

```
PREPARE SQLSA FROM
"UPDATE employee SET termination_date = GETDATE() WHERE emp_id = ?"
USING SQLCA;

EXECUTE SQLSA USING :nEmployeeId;
```

Another example looks like this:

```
PREPARE SQLSA FROM
"INSERT INTO employee ( emp_id, manager_id ) VALUES ( ?, ?)"
USING SQLCA;

EXECUTE SQLSA USING :nNewEmployeeId, :sle_assigned_manager_id.text;
```

Type 2 syntax can be reduced to Type 1 syntax by using string concatenation to put the parameters into the SQL statement. However, most uses of Type 2 have the statement declared outside of a script's local scope. This allows the SQL statement to be prepared once and used multiple times. The execution of the code is faster, but you can obviously have only one statement prepared to run at any one time (unless you are making use of variables declared as type SQLSA and preparing the statements for these instead of the SQLSA).

Type 3

The third type of dynamic SQL is probably the most frequently used after Type 1. The SQL statement produces a known result set for a known number of parameters. These are the syntax and statement order:

```
DECLARE cursor_name DYNAMIC CURSOR FOR dynamic_staging_area;

PREPARE dynamic_staging_area FROM sql_statement { USING transaction_object };

OPEN DYNAMIC cursor_name { USING parameter_list };
```

```
FETCH cursor_name INTO host_variable_list;

CLOSE cursor_name;
```

For a stored procedure, the syntax uses different `DECLARE` syntax and an `EXECUTE` statement instead of an `OPEN`:

```
DECLARE procedure_name DYNAMIC PROCEDURE FOR dynamic_staging_area;

PREPARE dynamic_staging_area FROM sql_statement { USING transaction_object };

EXECUTE DYNAMIC procedure_name { USING parameter_list };

FETCH procedure_name INTO host_variable_list;

CLOSE procedure_name;
```

A popular use for the Type 3 syntax is populating an internal table or drop-down list boxes (DDLBs) with data from a database table. You can perform the same functionality using a DataWindow, but you might not want the overhead of this object. The dynamic SQL is written as a function, either global or attached to a specific object (as a user object). The following example is of a function attached to a DDLB user object that takes a SQL `SELECT` string as a parameter that it uses in the `PREPARE`. During the `FETCH` cycle it issues `AddItem()` calls to fill the list box. The code is shown in Listing 5.1.

Listing 5.1. Sample code for Type 3 dynamic SQL.

```
String szValue

DECLARE listbox_values DYNAMIC CURSOR FOR SQLSA;

PREPARE SQLSA FROM :a_szSelect USING SQLCA;

OPEN DYNAMIC listbox_values;

If SQLCA.SQLCode < 0 Then
   MessageBox( "DataBase Error", &
               "Unable to open dynamic cursor in PopulateList function " + &
               SQLCA.SQLErrText)
   Return SQLCA.SQLCode
End If

this.SetRedraw( FALSE)
this.Reset()

Do While SQLCA.SQLCode = 0
   FETCH listbox_values INTO :szValue;

   If SQLCA.SQLCode = 0 Then
      this.Additem( Trim( szValue))
   ElseIf SQLCA.SQLCode < 0 Then
      MessageBox( "DataBase Error", &
                  "Unable to fetch row from table specified" + &
```

continues

Listing 5.1. continued

```
                SQLCA.SQLErrText)
   End If
Loop

this.SetRedraw( TRUE)
CLOSE listbox_values;
```

When the `FETCH` reaches the end of the result set, the `SQLCA.SQLCode` becomes `100` and the loop is left. The redraw for the list box or drop-down list box object is turned off, so that the object does not flicker on the screen each time the `AddItem()` method is called.

Type 4

The fourth type of dynamic SQL is the most complicated, because it is coded with no knowledge of the input parameters or the return result set. The SQL *dynamic description area* (`SQLDA`) is used to hold information about the parameters and result set columns, and like the `SQLCA` and `SQLSA` it is the default object instantiated from a system class—in this case, the `DynamicDescriptionArea` class. Table 5.3 describes the attributes that are available for investigation after a statement is described in the `SQLDA`.

Table 5.3. Attributes of the default `SQLDA`.

Attribute Name	*Description*
`NumInputs`	The number of input parameters
`InParmType`	An array of the input parameter data types
`NumOutputs`	The number of output parameters
`OutParmType`	An array of the output parameter data types

The input parameters are specified in the `DECLARE` statement in the same manner as before, using the `?` character. The actual values are set using the `SetDynamicParm()` function. The function takes the index position of the parameter and the value. The value can be of Integer, Long, Real, Double, Decimal, String, Boolean, Unsigned Integer, Unsigned Long, Date, Time, or DateTime data type. The appropriate data type is stored in the `InParmType` array, and the value is stored in a data type–specific array. After execution, the result set is gathered value by value using one of the five functions listed in Table 5.4.

Table 5.4. Type 4 dynamic SQL functions.

Function Name	Used For
GetDynamicNumber()	TypeInteger!, TypeDecimal!, TypeDouble!, TypeLong!, TypeReal!, TypeBoolean!
GetDynamicString()	TypeString!
GetDynamicDate()	TypeDate!
GetDynamicTime()	TypeTime!
GetDynamicDateTime()	TypeDateTime!

These are the syntax and statement order for Type 4 dynamic SQL:

```
DECLARE cursor_name ¦ procedure_name DYNAMIC CURSOR ¦ PROCEDURE
FOR dynamic_staging_area;

PREPARE dynamic_staging_area FROM sql_statement { USING transaction_object };

DESCRIBE dynamic_staging_area INTO dynamic_description_area;

OPEN DYNAMIC cursor_name USING DESCRIPTOR dynamic_description_area;

EXECUTE DYNAMIC procedure_name USING DESCRIPTOR dynamic_description_area;

FETCH cursor_name ¦ procedure_name USING DESCRIPTOR dynamic_description_area;

CLOSE cursor_name ¦ procedure_name;
```

NOTE

The help pages in PowerBuilder 4.0 incorrectly state that the `OPEN DYNAMIC` statement is also used with a procedure, and that the `EXECUTE DYNAMIC` statement is also used with a cursor. A cursor is opened and a procedure is executed.

The order of the statements is critical. Successive statements are dependent on the completion of the previous ones.

After the `FETCH` has occurred, a `Choose...Case` statement is usually entered to determine the data type and then to extract the value. Listing 5.2 shows an example.

Listing 5.2. An example of Type 4 dynamic SQL.

```
Long lValueCount = 0

DECLARE customer_data DYNAMIC CURSOR FOR SQLSA;
```

continues

Listing 5.2. continued

```
PREPARE SQLSA FROM "SELECT company_name FROM customer WHERE state = ?"
USING SQLCA;

DESCRIBE SQLSA INTO SQLDA;

SetDynamicParm( SQLDA, 1, "IN")

OPEN DYNAMIC customer_data USING DESCRIPTOR SQLDA;
If SQLCA.SQLCode <> 0 Then
   MessageBox( "Database Error", "Unable to open dynamic cursor.")
   Return
End If

FETCH customer_data USING DESCRIPTOR SQLDA;
If SQLCA.SQLCode = 100 Then
   MessageBox( "Select Error", "Unable to retreive data.")
   CLOSE customer_data;
   Return
End If

Do
   lValueCount ++
   Choose Case SQLDA.OutParmType[ lValueCount]
      Case TypeLong!
         nValue = SQLDA.GetDynamicNumber( lValueCount)
         //Process value
      Case TypeString!
         szValue = SQLDA.GetDynamicString( lValueCount)
         //Process value
   End Choose
Loop While lValueCount <> SQLDA.NumOutPuts

CLOSE customer_data;
```

Error checking should be carried out after the `OPEN` or `EXECUTE`, `FETCH`, and `CLOSE` statements. It was not included in the example so that the dynamic SQL syntax and statement flow would be more obvious. The `SELECT` statement that is prepared is usually constructed by the application or user at runtime.

As an alternative to using dynamic SQL Type 4, you can make use of a dynamically created DataWindow to achieve the same effect. You should be aware, however, that accessing the retrieved columns using the dynamic DataWindow will require some additional processing because you will be required to check the data type of the column (because you have to use the Type 4 syntax) before you can extract a piece of data.

Paste SQL Statements

So that the syntax of the embedded SQL statements does not need to be fully memorized, PowerBuilder provides a SQL Statement painter (see Figure 5.1). This is accessed from the PowerScript painter toolbar or the Edit menu. As you use embedded SQL in PowerBuilder you will find yourself typing the syntax straight in rather than using these painters, but is useful to know they are there to fall back on when your memory fails.

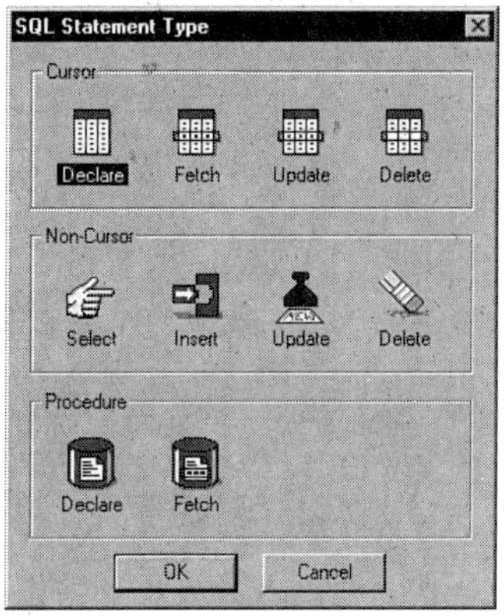

FIGURE 5.1.
The SQL Statement Type dialog box.

Cursor and procedure declarations can also be painted from the variable declaration dialog boxes.

There are three types of SQL statements that can be created: cursors, non-cursors, and procedures. The non-cursor statements are composed of the singleton `SELECT` (returns only one row), `INSERT`, `UPDATE`, and `DELETE`. The following sections use the `SELECT` as an introduction to the SQL painter, and then introduce just the differences for the subsequent statement types.

Pasting a SELECT

If you double-click the `SELECT` icon in the statement painter, a dialog box appears listing the available tables in the current database (see Figure 5.2). Make your selection by clicking on the table name (multiple tables can be selected if a join is required) and then clicking on the Open button.

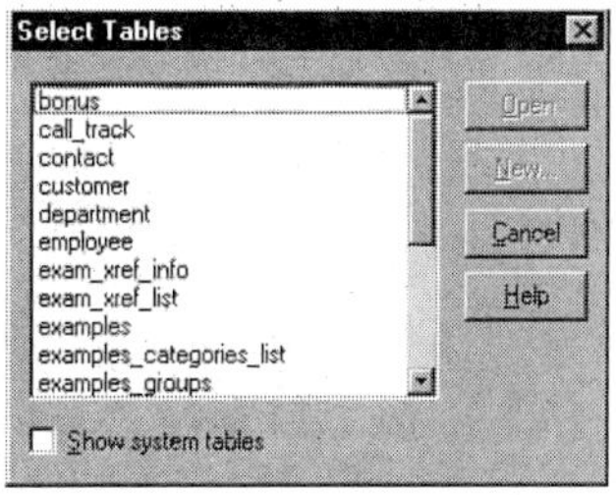

FIGURE 5.2.
The Select Tables dialog box.

PowerBuilder queries its own system tables for extended information on the tables selected and displays each table in a child window (see Figure 5.3) showing the column names, labels, data types, and extended comments. The attributes displayed in the child windows are controlled from the Design menu or by right-clicking on the background of the SQL Select painter.

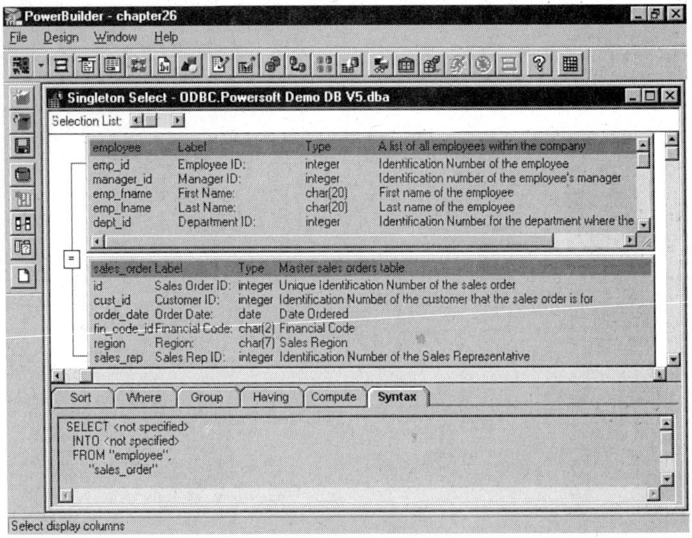

FIGURE 5.3.
Table child windows.

In addition to the child windows that have opened, access is now granted to the painter toolbar and the tab control at the bottom of the SQL painter main window. You can see in Figure 5.3 that the two tables selected are connected by key values and that PowerBuilder automatically draws the relationship and defaults the operator to equality. Clicking on the box that contains the equal sign opens the Join painter (see Figure 5.4), which enables you to alter the joining condition. With PowerBuilder 4.0, the specification of outer joins was simplified considerably. Instead of having to figure out which side of a relationship is outer or on which side of an operator another character appears (SQL Server uses `*=` and `=*` to signify outer joins), PowerBuilder displays the join condition in plain English that is context sensitive to the tables involved in the join.

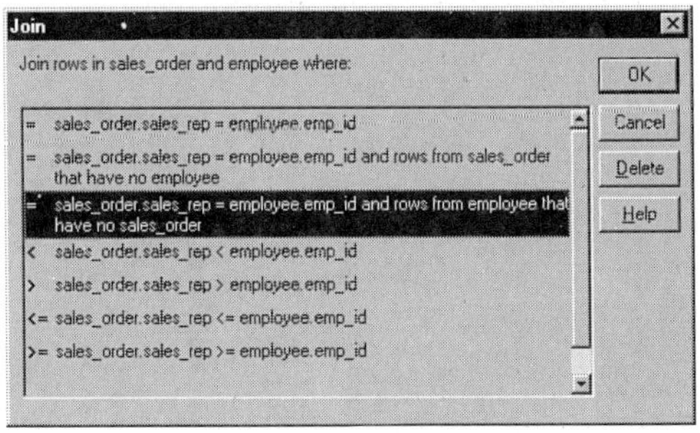

FIGURE 5.4.
The Join painter.

Additional `WHERE` conditions are specified from the Where tab page (see Figure 5.5). Clicking on the first column displays a drop-down list of all the columns. The next column is a drop-down list of standard operators, and the third column is the value to use in the comparison. If another column, function, or other value is to be used, you can either type it in or make use of a pop-up menu. The last column is a list of the logical operators to join multiple conditions.

FIGURE 5.5.
The Where tab page.

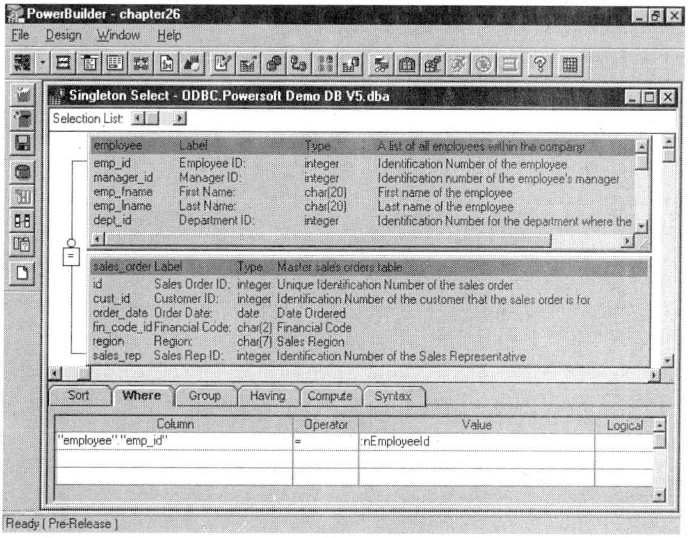

The pop-up menu available on the Value column provides six options and can also be used in the Having and Compute tab pages:

- Columns provides a list of all the columns available from the tables currently selected.
- Functions provides a list of the functions supported by the current DBMS.
- Arguments provides a list of all the objects and their attributes that are accessible from the script that the SQL will be pasted into.
- Value becomes active once a column is specified, and can be used to provide a list of distinct values from the actual database table.
- Select opens another instance of the query painter so that you can define a subquery.
- Clear clears the current text from the field.

The next step is to select which columns are to be returned. Do this by clicking on the appropriate column names from the table child windows. As you select the columns, they appear at the top of the window to the right of the Selection List horizontal scrollbar (see Figure 5.6). You can alter the columns' order after selection by clicking on the boxed column names that have appeared and dragging left or right. If the column does not appear in the list, the Selection List scrollbar can be used to move through the columns until it appears.

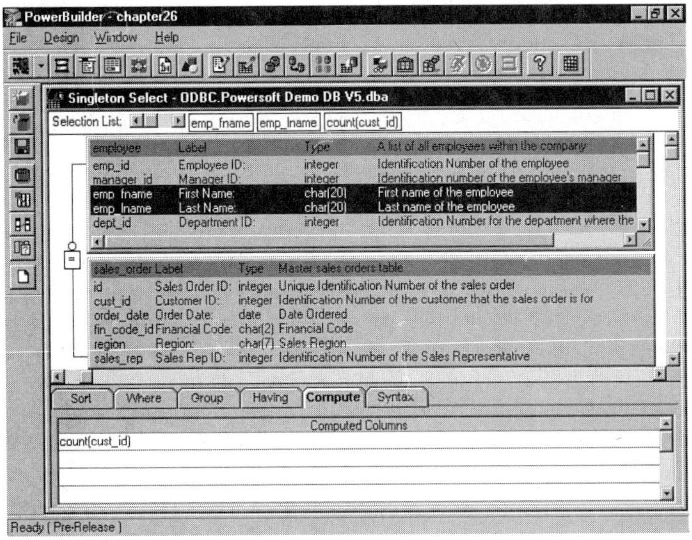

FIGURE 5.6.
The selection list.

To add aggregate or other database functions, select the Compute tab page. This opens a notes area below the tab where you can enter the function. If a different tab page is selected or the Enter key is pressed, the Compute column appears at the end of the selection list.

With the addition of the `COUNT(cust_id)` column to the `SELECT`, you must specify a `GROUP BY` to return the data correctly. The Group tab page shows a list of all columns from all selected tables. To generate a grouping, drag the columns from the left side to the right side (see Figure 5.7).

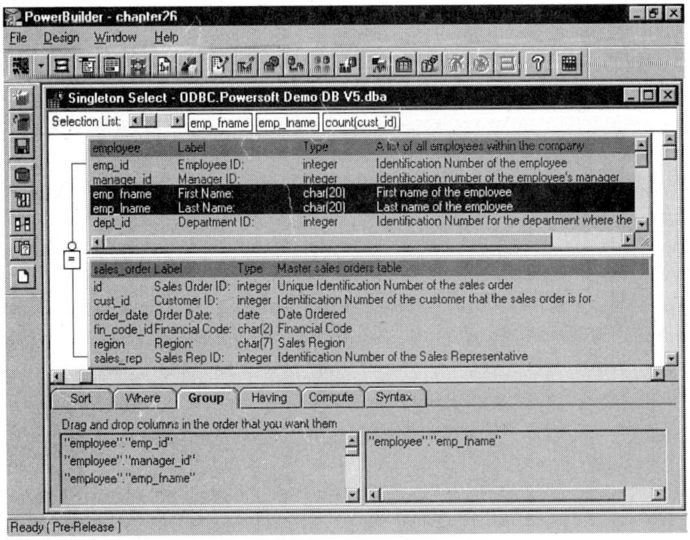

FIGURE 5.7.
The Group tab page.

As mentioned at the beginning of this chapter, conditions are sometimes placed on the grouping of data using a HAVING clause. You enter the HAVING clause using the Having tab page, which displays the same grid as the Where tab page (see Figure 5.8). The HAVING clause is constructed in the same way as a WHERE.

FIGURE 5.8.

The Having tab page.

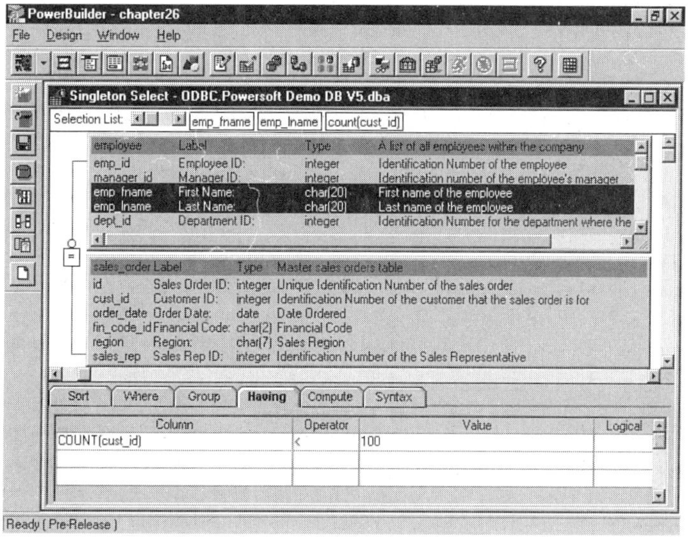

Use the Sort tab page to specify an ordering of the values. As with specifying the grouping requirements, sorting also involves dragging the columns from left to right (see Figure 5.9), with the first column on the right being the first column sorted on, and so on down the list. Choose an ascending or descending sort by using the check box to the side of the column name.

The last operation before returning to the Script painter is to specify the PowerBuilder variables into which the SELECT will return data. Open the Into Variables dialog box (see Figure 5.10) from the toolbar (a red arrow pointing away from a grid) or from the Design menu.

Displayed in the lower area of the dialog box is a list of the currently defined application variables that are accessible from the script into which the SQL statement will be pasted. (Local variables do *not* appear.) You can make your selections from this list or enter them manually into the program variable field next to each column name. If you have not yet declared the variables, you can still type them in at this point because no error checking or compilation is carried out.

When you have constructed the SELECT and have clicked on the Return button or selected the menu option, the complete SQL syntax is pasted into the script at the current cursor position (see Figure 5.11).

FIGURE 5.9.
The Sort tab page.

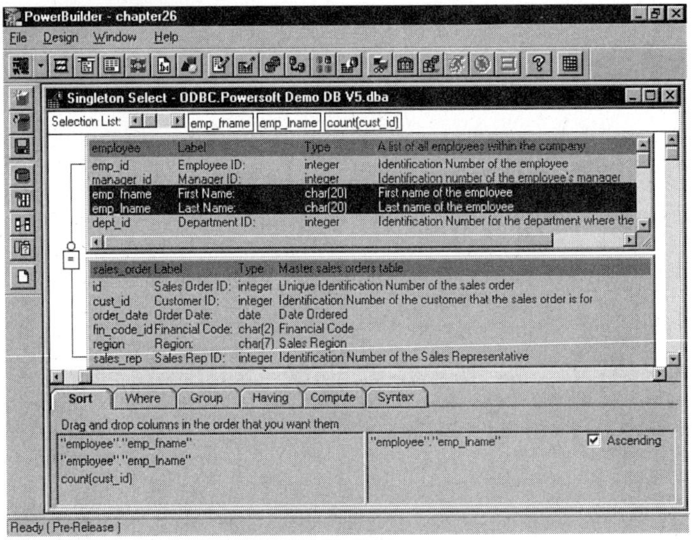

FIGURE 5.10.
The Into Variables dialog box.

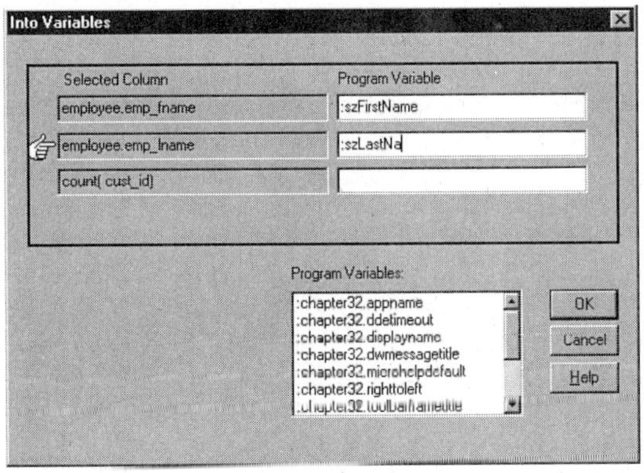

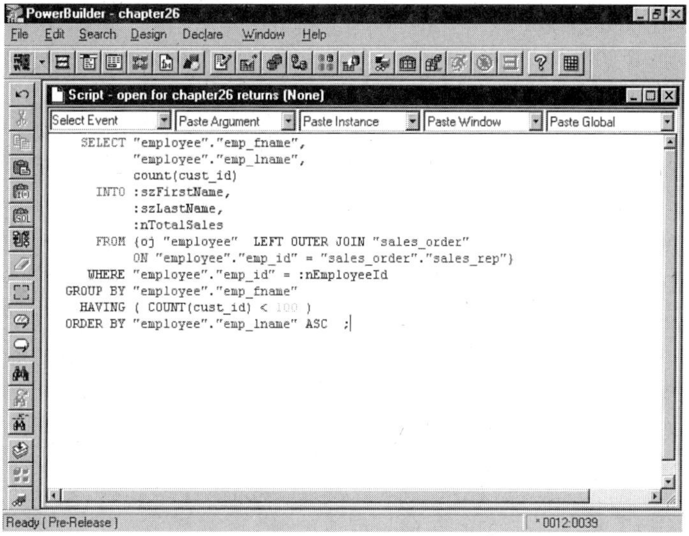

FIGURE 5.11.
The pasted SELECT *statement.*

Pasting an INSERT

Choosing INSERT from the SQL Statement Type dialog box displays the Table Selection dialog box as you saw with the SELECT, except that only one table can be selected. If you select more than one, the first one in the chosen list is used. The Insert Column Values dialog box appears automatically after you choose a table (see Figure 5.12). This dialog box is split into five main areas. The top area is editable and shows the columns to be used in the statement together with the constants or PowerBuilder variables that will be used to specify the values. The next area is a representation of the table for which the statement is being generated; this is where you select the columns to be included in the INSERT. PowerBuilder selects all the columns by default. To the right of this is the list of accessible program variables, and as you did with the Into Variables dialog box for the SELECT, you can enter variables that have yet to be declared.

Along the left set of the dialog box are three buttons: Null, Select, and Clear. The Null button inserts the appropriate NULL specification into the current cursor position in the column value field. The Clear button resets all the column values. The Select button enables the construction of a SELECT as the source of the values and opens the same painter used for the SELECT specified at the start of this section. After you have specified the SELECT and have filled in and disabled the column values for the INSERT, you can make changes only through the Select painter (see Figure 5.13). The SELECT result set must exactly match the one specified for the INSERT.

FIGURE 5.12.
The Insert Column Values dialog box.

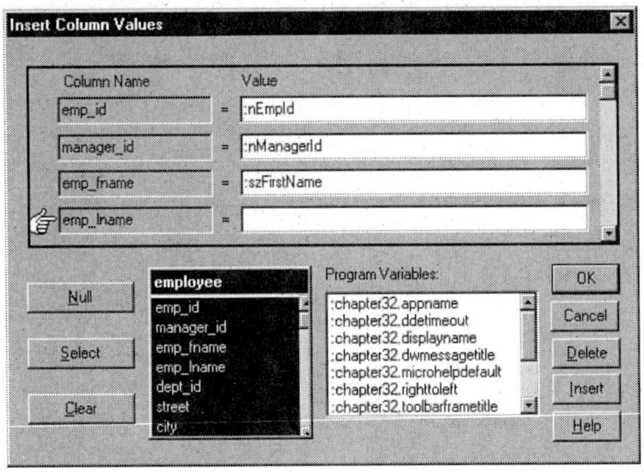

FIGURE 5.13.
A completed Insert Column Values dialog box.

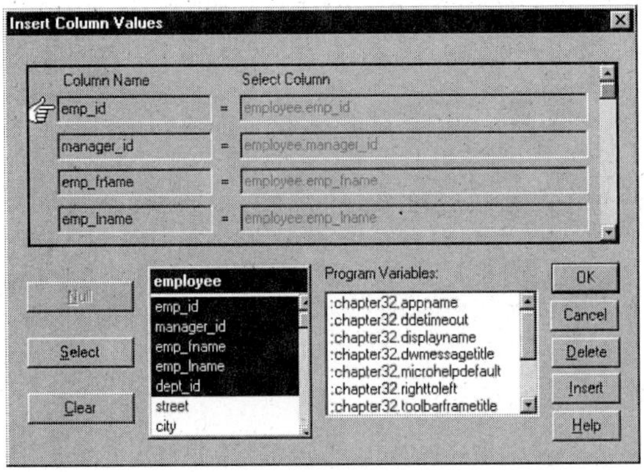

When the `INSERT` has been defined, it is pasted back into the script using any of the methods described for the `SELECT` (see Figure 5.14).

Pasting an UPDATE

Declaring an `UPDATE` statement follows very much the same process as declaring an `INSERT`, and after you understand and master the basic painter layout you will be able to generate the statements quickly. As with the `INSERT`, only one table can be selected, after which the Update Column Values dialog box appears (see Figure 5.15). As a default, PowerBuilder does not select any of the columns for the table. When you select a column, it appears in the list at the top of the dialog box, together with a field that specifies the value to be assigned. This value can be a PowerBuilder variable (either from the list or directly entered) or a constant.

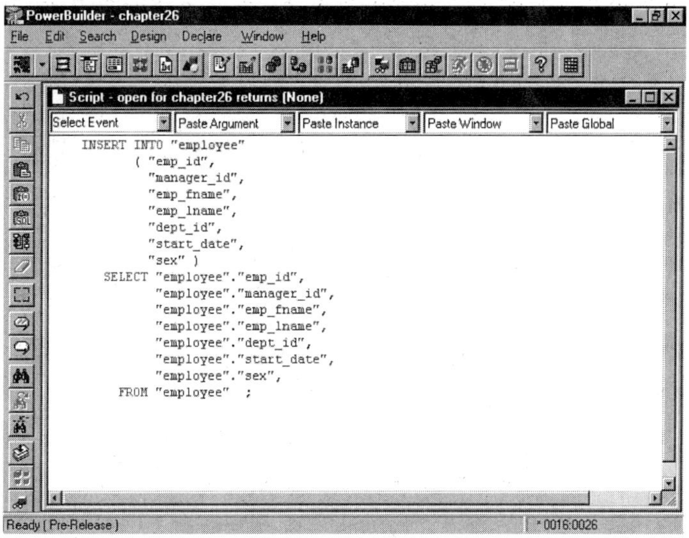

FIGURE 5.14.
The pasted `INSERT` *statement.*

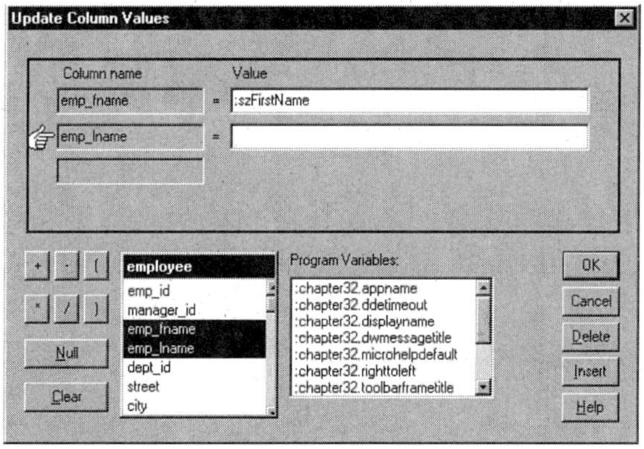

FIGURE 5.15.
The Update Column Values dialog box.

You can specify a `WHERE` clause by selecting the Where tab page. The finished `UPDATE` is then pasted back into the Script painter (see Figure 5.16).

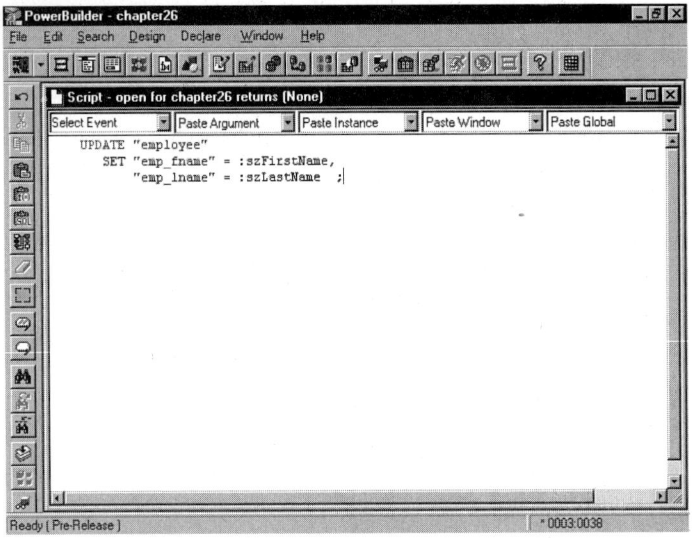

FIGURE 5.16.
The pasted UPDATE *statement.*

Pasting a DELETE

The DELETE statement is the easiest of all the statements to create because it only requires the selection of a single table and (optionally) specifying a WHERE clause.

Cursor Painting

You define the four types of cursor statements using steps similar to those in the previous sections. You use the same dialog boxes to declare a cursor as you used for the singleton SELECT, except that when the declaration is finished, a dialog box prompts for the name of the cursor (see Figure 5.17). The completed statement is then pasted back into the Script painter (see Figure 5.18).

When you declare a FETCH on a cursor, a dialog box appears, which enables you to select from a set of predefined cursors (see Figure 5.19). These cursors must be declared in one of the global, shared, or instance variable sections. Cursors that are declared locally are not listed. The source for the currently highlighted cursor is shown in the lower section of the dialog box.

After the cursor is selected, the Into Variables dialog box automatically appears (see Figure 5.20) so that you can define the INTO variables. The INTO variables section is not intelligent and enables you to define a maximum of only 25 variables; for that reason the cursor source appears in the lower-left corner of the dialog box to provide a preview of the expected results.

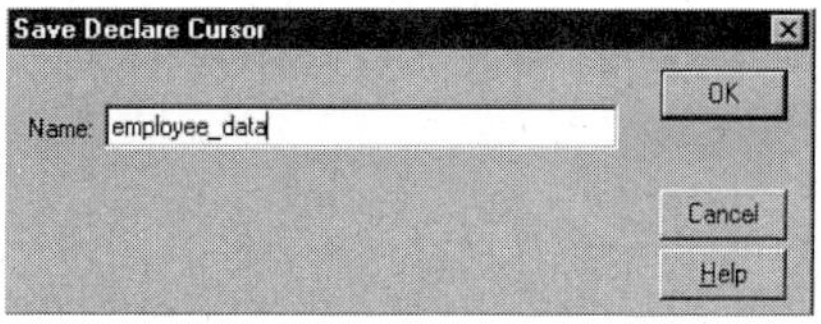

FIGURE 5.17.
The Save Declare Cursor dialog box.

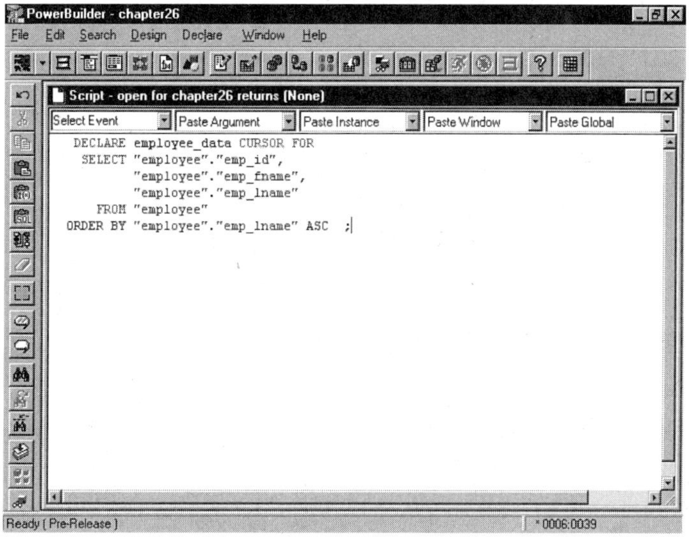

FIGURE 5.18.
The pasted DECLARE *statement.*

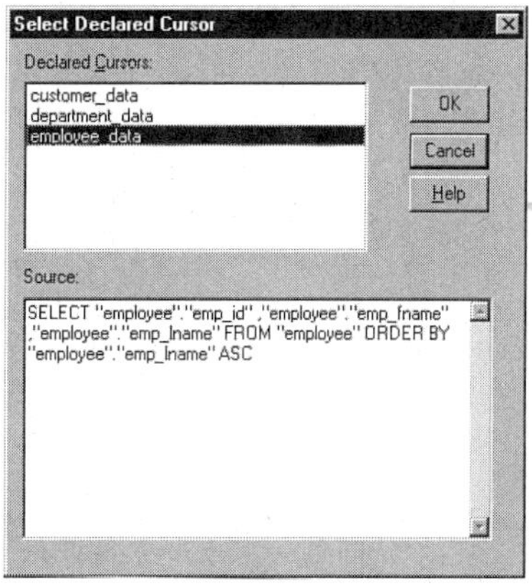

FIGURE 5.19.
The Select Declared Cursor dialog box.

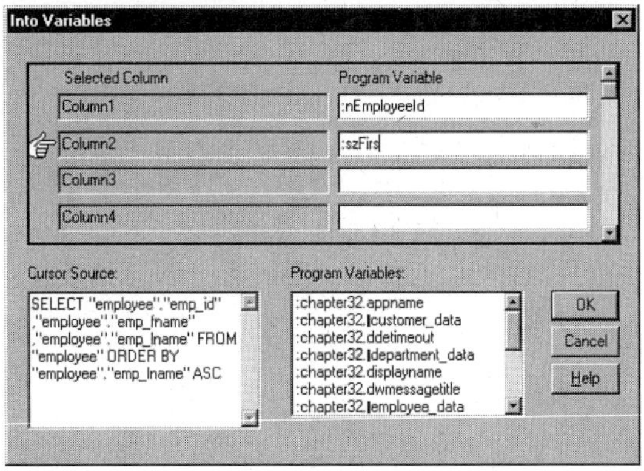

FIGURE 5.20.
The Into Variables dialog box.

> **NOTE**
>
> For `FETCH` statements that are manually coded into PowerScript there is no limit on the number of `INTO` variables.

The resulting code is then pasted back into the Script painter (see Figure 5.21), but unless the cursor result set is not known or is not immediately accessible, it takes considerably more time to paint the statement than it takes to code it directly.

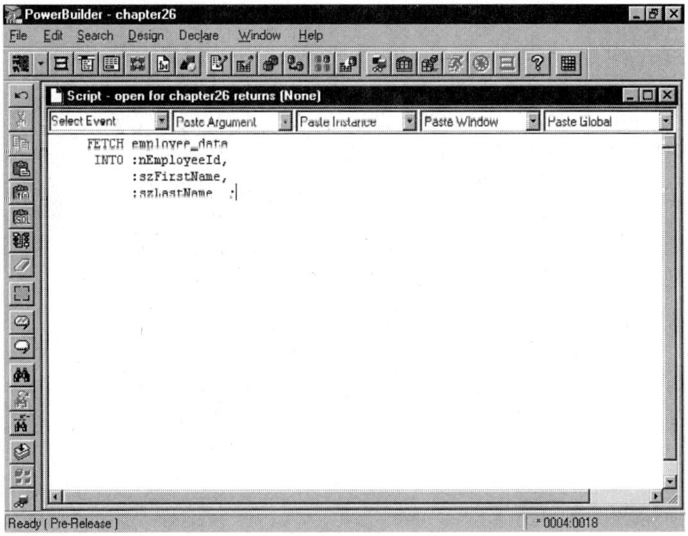

FIGURE 5.21.
The pasted `FETCH` *statement.*

UPDATE WHERE CURRENT OF

To make a modification to the data that you are accessing through a cursor, you can use the UPDATE WHERE CURRENT OF statement.

To paint an UPDATE that acts on a cursor, select Cursor Update from the SQL Statement Type dialog box. As with the FETCH, a list of the available cursors is displayed together with the selected cursor source. When a cursor is selected, a second dialog box automatically appears (see Figure 5.22) where you can define the update column values.

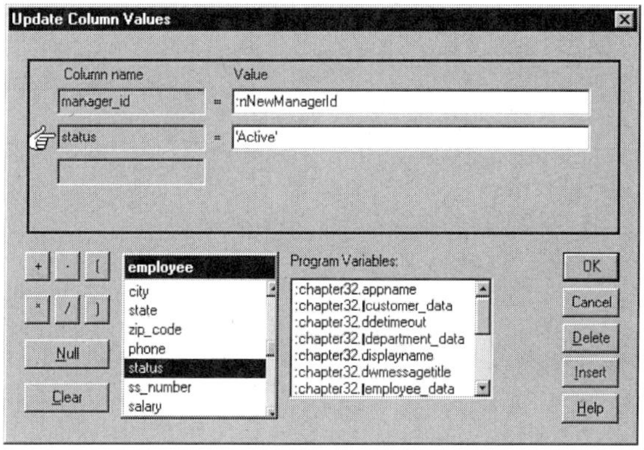

FIGURE 5.22.
The Update Column Values dialog box.

The Column Value definition dialog box works exactly the same way in this situation as it does for the FETCH. Leaving this dialog box pastes the statement into the Script painter (see Figure 5.23).

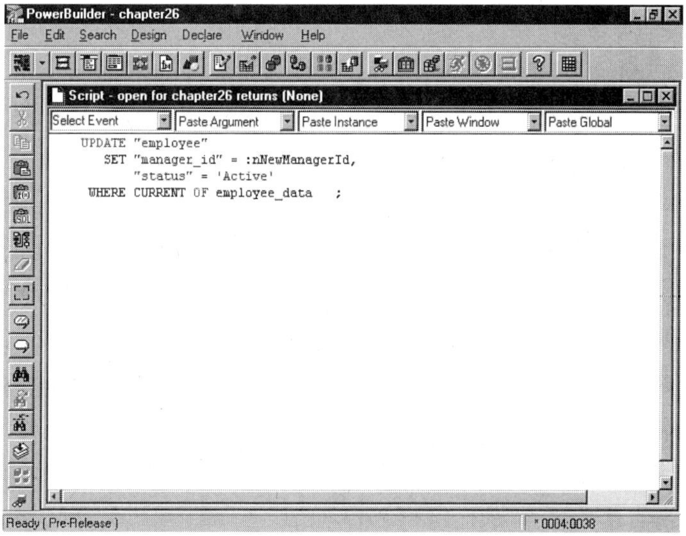

FIGURE 5.23.
The pasted UPDATE *statement.*

DELETE WHERE CURRENT OF

As with the UPDATE statement that acts on the current record of a cursor, there is also a statement that allows you to delete the record.

To paint a DELETE that acts on a cursor, select Cursor Delete from the SQL Statement Type dialog box. As with the FETCH and the UPDATE statements, a list of the available cursors is displayed together with the selected cursor source. When a cursor is selected, the dialog box closes and leaves a screen empty of everything but the Syntax tab. The only options are to select a different cursor or return to the Script painter (see Figure 5.24).

DECLARE PROCEDUREs

Painting stored procedure DECLAREs and FETCHs is very similar to painting the previous cursor statements. Selecting DECLARE PROCEDURE displays a dialog box of stored procedures in the current database, together with the source (see Figure 5.25).

FIGURE 5.24.

The pasted DELETE *statement.*

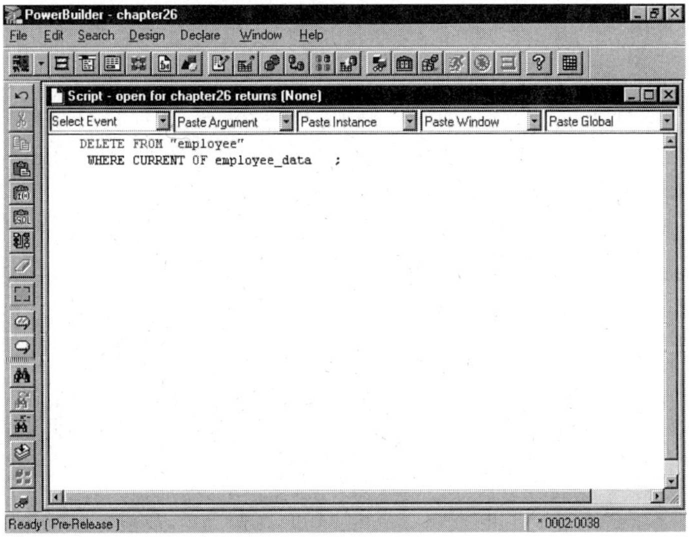

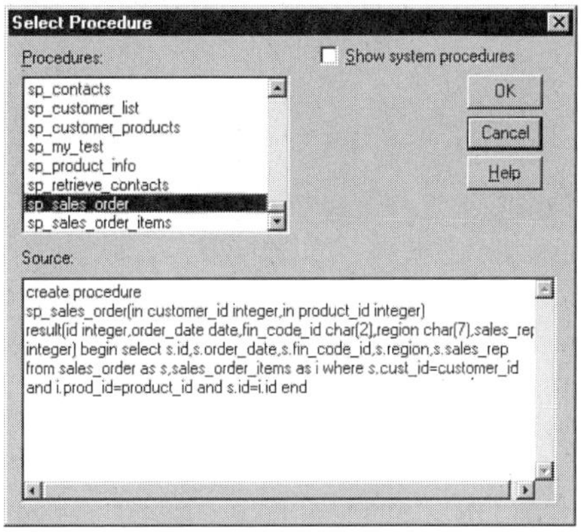

FIGURE 5.25.
The Select Procedure dialog box.

The Parameters dialog box is displayed next, with PowerBuilder automatically prompting you to fill in the parameters that require values (see Figure 5.26).

When you attempt to leave the dialog box, you are prompted for a name (see Figure 5.27) before PowerBuilder will paste the statement into the Script painter (see Figure 5.28).

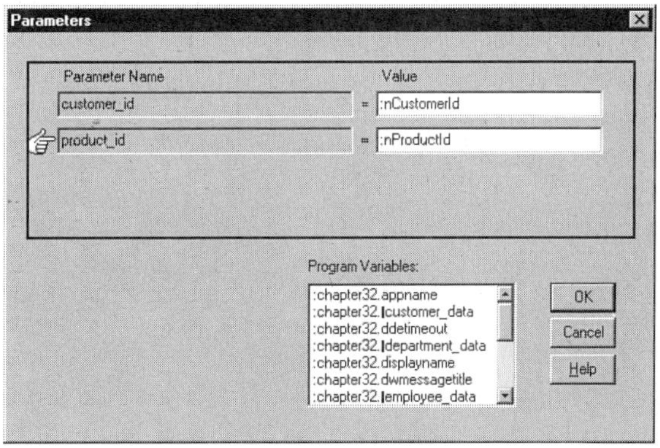

FIGURE 5.26.
The Parameters dialog box.

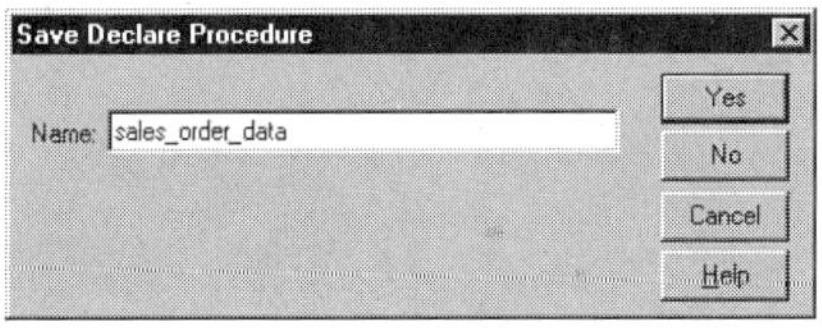

FIGURE 5.27.
The Save Declare Procedure dialog box.

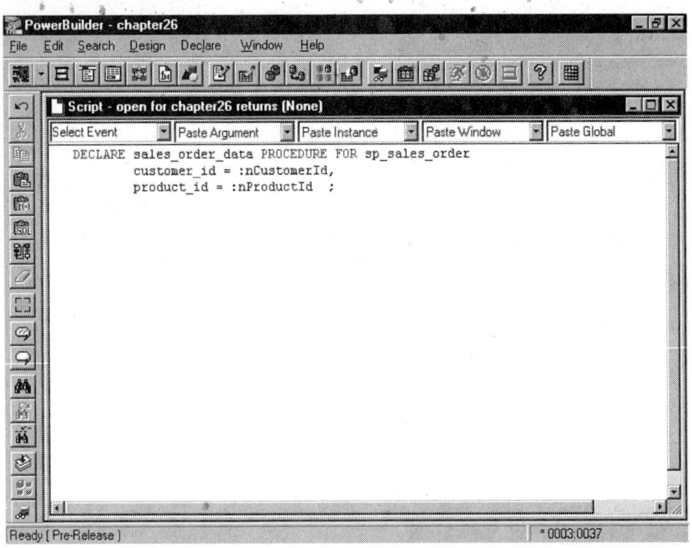

FIGURE 5.28.
The pasted DECLARE *statement.*

FETCH FROM PROCEDURE

This is identical to using FETCH from a cursor (see Figure 5.29), except that in the parameter specification window it maintains the parameter awareness demonstrated during the DECLARE (see Figure 5.30).

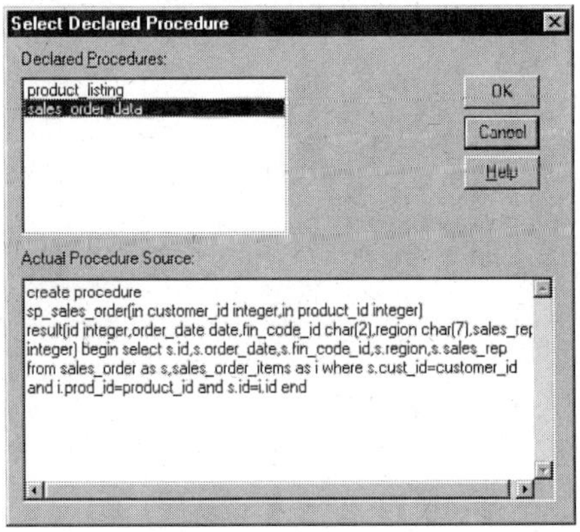

FIGURE 5.29.
The Select Declared Procedure dialog box.

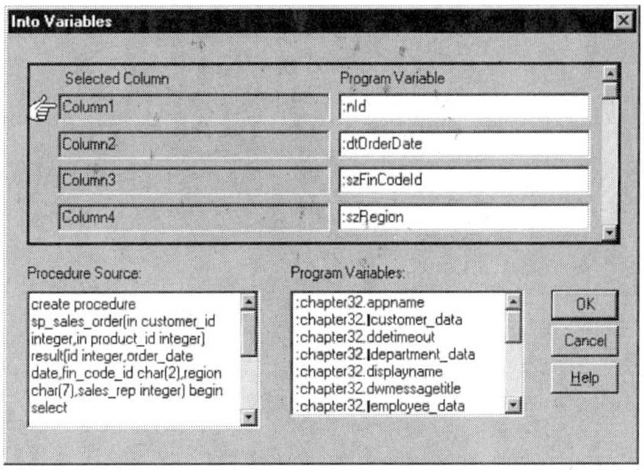

FIGURE 5.30.
The Into Variables dialog box.

As with the `FETCH`, it is more time-consuming to generate the syntax than it would be to enter it directly (see Figure 5.31).

As you can see from the majority of these statements, it is more time-consuming to paint the statements than to directly type them. The various painter windows are only of any use during the initial stages of a project before developers become familiar with the syntax of stored procedures and the other SQL statements.

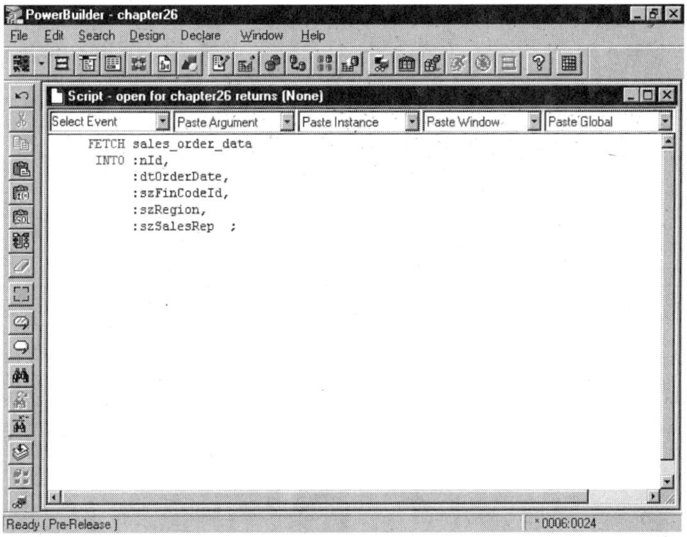

FIGURE 5.31.
The pasted `FETCH` *statement.*

Advanced Concepts

This section explores some of the tricks of using SQL to carry out complex tasks and some tips on how to write good client/server applications.

Logical Units of Work, Revisited

An important consideration in application development is effective transaction management, which is essential to maximizing concurrency and ensuring consistency.

When a PowerBuilder `CONNECT` is issued, a transaction is started—work is carried out and `COMMIT`s and `ROLLBACK`s are executed. After each `COMMIT` and `ROLLBACK` the old transaction is closed and a new transaction is begun. This might sound like an acceptable situation, but the DBMS has a problem with long-running transactions. In the following discussion, the SQL Server DBMS is used as an example, but the concepts and problems apply to any of the other DBMSs as well, unless very special transaction logging is available for a DBMS.

A running PowerBuilder application will always have an open transaction. For example, a user logs into the application and retrieves some data into a DataWindow. If the DBMS has read locks on the data, they will not be released until a `COMMIT`, `ROLLBACK`, or `DISCONNECT` is issued. Because most novice PowerBuilder developers only issue `COMMIT`s and `ROLLBACK`s after data-modification statements, these locks will be held for an excessive amount of time. That is why Powersoft states that a `COMMIT` or `ROLLBACK` should be issued after every piece of SQL or every instance of DataWindow access, to free any server resources that might have been consumed.

NOTE

This is not the case for DataWindows that are set up to use the `SetTrans()` function instead of `SetTransObject()`. For a discussion of the differences, see Chapter 10, "DataWindow Scripting."

With a typical production system, the transaction log (a constant record of all actions carried out in the database that is used in database recovery procedures) is either automatically or manually dumped a couple times per day. When a transaction log is *dumped*, the DBMS removes all records up to the last one that is still active. If the application detailed previously is left on all day and is used only for read-only queries, the transaction started when the PowerBuilder `CONNECT` was issued will be open all day. Any attempts to dump or truncate the log will have no effect and the log will eventually fill up, causing databasewide problems.

The solution is to take the task of transaction management away from PowerBuilder and manage it more effectively. To do this, set the `AutoCommit` attribute of the transaction object to `TRUE` and then when a unit of work begins, the developer needs to explicitly tell the SQL server. This is achieved by making use of Type 1 dynamic SQL and issuing an `EXECUTE IMMEDIATE` for `BEGIN TRANSACTION` and then an `EXECUTE IMMEDIATE` for either `ROLLBACK TRANSACTION` or `COMMIT TRANSACTION` at the end of the unit of work. For example, to update a DataWindow the code becomes the following (note that error checking for the embedded SQL has been ignored only for clarity):

```
EXECUTE IMMEDIATE "BEGIN TRANSACTION" USING SQLCA;

If dw_1.Update() = -1 Then
   EXECUTE IMMEDIATE "ROLLBACK TRANSACTION" USING SQLCA;
Else
   EXECUTE IMMEDIATE "COMMIT TRANSACTION" USING SQLCA;
End If
```

By controlling when a transaction is active, better performance can be expected from the server *and* the database administrator. Therefore, try to code for concise transactions and make sure you finish a transaction before giving control back to a user. For example, do not begin a transaction, save some data, and then prompt the user that an error occurred during the save without first rolling back the transaction. Be aware, though, that issuing a `ROLLBACK` will destroy the contents of the `SQLCA` that pertain to the error that occurred, so make a copy of the information before issuing that command. This makes transaction processing the short-lived process that it is supposed to be.

You can easily build this functionality into a user-defined transaction object (see Chapter 24, "Building User Objects").

It might be tempting to try to flip the value of the `AutoCommit` attribute or just place `COMMIT`s after every `SELECT`, but both of these options have hidden side effects. Changing the value of `AutoCommit` to `TRUE` automatically issues a `COMMIT`, and when set to `FALSE` it automatically issues a `BEGIN TRANSACTION`. A `COMMIT` after a `SELECT` does finish the current transaction, but unfortunately it also starts a new one.

NOTE

Remember that only Micro Decisionware Database Gateway Interface for DB2, some ODBC, SQL Server, and Sybase SQL Server database management systems are affected by the `AutoCommit` attribute.

Using Stored Procedures

If your DBMS supports stored procedures you can usually extract information using one of three mechanisms. In fact, you may be able to use all three at one time. The remainder of this section focuses on the SQL Server DBMS, although the concepts are similar for other DBMSs.

Stored procedures can return data in any or all of the following ways:

- As a result set of the stored procedure. A statement in the stored procedure is a `SELECT` statement that returns data; this is usually the last statement. With some DBMSs you can return multiple result sets, where the last statement is not the only `SELECT` statement within the stored procedure. Note that you can only use one result of a stored procedure as the source for a DataWindow.
- As an output parameter. Using the `OUTPUT` keyword after a stored procedure's argument, when defining it in the database, allows data to be returned via the argument.
- As a return value. Using the `RETURN` statement in the stored procedure, you can pass back a single numeric value; this is exactly the same as the PowerScript `Return` statement.

The `DECLARE`, `EXECUTE`, `FETCH`, and `CLOSE` statements that were introduced earlier in the chapter are used to access the different returned information.

Accessing a Return Value

To make use of a return value passed back by a stored procedure, you must first alter the declaration for the stored procedure. The `DECLARE` statement now becomes this:

```
DECLARE ProcedureName PROCEDURE
FOR @ReturnValue = DBProcedureName USING SQLCA;
```

The name you give to *ReturnValue* is irrelevant; PowerBuilder is using it purely as a placeholder for its own internal use.

You will then use the `FETCH` command to retrieve the returned value. A combined example is shown in the section "Accessing Returned Data from a Stored Procedure."

Accessing an OUTPUT Variable

To specify a parameter or multiple parameters that will be used to return values by the stored procedure, you need to modify the `DECLARE` statement so that it looks like this:

```
DECLARE ProcedureName PROCEDURE
FOR DBProcedureName @InParameter = :PBVariable1, @OutParameter = :PBVariable2
OUTPUT
USING SQLCA;
```

Again, the names you give *InParameter* and *OutParameter* are irrelevant, but it is a good practice to give them the same, or similar, names as the actual stored procedure. The bindings to PowerBuilder variables are only used to pass values to the stored procedure during the EXECUTE, and you must still use the FETCH command to access the values.

Accessing Returned Data from a Stored Procedure

The first task is to retrieve all the rows for the result set or result sets returned by the stored procedure. If there are none, you just code for the return value and/or output parameters.

The result set of a stored procedure is retrieved by executing a loop and carrying out a FETCH until there are no rows left. At the end of each result set, the SQLCA.SQLCode will become 100.

The values for a RETURN or an OUTPUT parameter are retrieved after the last row of the last result set of the stored procedure using a FETCH statement. The RETURN value is first and then any OUTPUT parameters:

```
FETCH ProcedureName INTO
:ReturnValue, :OutParameter1, :OutParameter2, .. :OutParameterN;
```

To demonstrate how this works, consider the following stored procedure that has a return value and two parameters (one of which is defined as an OUTPUT), and that produces two result sets of differing sizes and columns:

```
CREATE PROCEDURE sp_results_demo @InParmInt Int, @OutParmInt Int OUTPUT
AS
BEGIN
   SELECT 1, 2, 3, 4

   SELECT uid, id
   FROM sysobjects
   WHERE type = 'U'

   SELECT @OutParmInt = 69

   RETURN 16
END
```

This is a very simple stored procedure, but one that demonstrates each of the features. The PowerScript you would use to access each of the returned values is as simple:

```
Long lReturnValue, lParm1, lParm2, lResult1, lResult2, lResult3, lResult4
Long lResult5, lResult6

DECLARE results_demo PROCEDURE FOR
@return = sp_results_demo @InParmInt = :lParm1, @OutParmInt = :lParm2 OUTPUT
USING SQLCA;
```

```
EXECUTE results_demo;

//
// Retrieve the values for the first result set
//
Do While SQLCA.SQLCode = 0
  FETCH results_demo INTO :lResult1, :lResult2, :lResult3, :lResult4;
Loop
//
// Setup to retrieve the values for the second result set.
// NOTE: The SQLCA.SQLCode will be 100 before this next line executes.
//       Therefore preload the first row, if there is one.
//
FETCH INTO :lResult5, :lResult6;

Do While SQLCA.SQLCode = 0
   FETCH results_demo INTO :lResult5, :lResult6;
Loop
//
// Capture the return value, and output parameter value
//
FETCH results_demo INTO :lReturn, :lParm2;

CLOSE results_demo;
```

When you try to compile this PowerScript the PowerBuilder compiler may give you some compilation warnings concerning the return value. You can safely ignore any such warning, and you will not be prompted again.

NOTE

If you are trying to use output parameters with a SQL Server DBMS and keep getting the SQLDBCode 179 and the error message `Can't use the OUTPUT option when passing a constant to a stored procedure.`, set your transaction objects `UserId` property to an empty string. You must do this before connecting the transaction.

Caching SQL

As you saw in the previous section, Oracle provides caching of SQL statements for faster execution. Some ODBC databases also provide the ability to cache SQL, and both of these are controlled by the `SQLCache` parameter in the `DBParm` attribute of the transaction object. SQL statements generated by a DataWindow or report or embedded SQL are all cached.

Optimizing Queries

Each DBMS claims to have the best query optimizer—the one that outperforms all competitors in terms of speed. The performance of SQL, however, is very much dependent on the developer. Of course, the optimizer can make a poorly written query run at an acceptable speed, but is that really the point? SQL should be written with the best possible performance and optimization built in. A developer would not intentionally write inefficient program code, and should not do it with SQL either.

Before introducing some of the techniques, let's first explore the steps involved in processing a SQL statement:

- *Parsing* verifies the SQL to make sure it is syntactically correct and creates a query tree; this step is also known as *query detachment*. A *query tree* is an internal representation of the original query, decomposed into a sequence of subqueries involving either a single relation or two relations. The target lists of the queries are either used in subsequent queries or are part of the target list of the original query. With the latest versions of DBMSs, parallel query processing is a major enhancement and these smaller queries can sometimes be carried out at the same time.
- In the *normalization* phase the query tree is manipulated using a set of database-independent rules to remove redundancy.
- *Optimization* is where the vendor's optimizer will vary from the rest of the pack. Using a number of rules, the optimizer will look at each clause in the query tree to optimize joins to limit the amount of data scanned. As you will see next, not all SQL operators (notably, the <> operator) allow a query to be optimized.
- The optimizer will generate an *execution plan*. This plan determines which indexes, if any, will be used to retrieve the data. Associated with each index and processing clause is a cost. If the cost is too high, the optimizer will generally perform a full-table scan instead of using the index to go directly to the desired records. This means that the DBMS will read each data page of a table from start to end. Careful consideration of the indexes on a table is an important stage of your database design and implementation duties.
- By the *physical access* stage the optimizer has looked at a number of query trees and has come up with a *query plan,* which is used by the DBMS to access the necessary data pages, collect the intermediate results, and package them for transport to the client.

The developer can improve the performance of the query optimizer using the following techniques:

- A query optimizer depends on indexed columns to make the best choice. When an index is created, statistics on the data distribution are stored by the DBMS. To try to force the use of an index, name one of the indexed columns in the `WHERE` clause.

- Generally, the lefthand rule is applied for composite indexes, so use the leftmost column from the index to improve the chances of index usage. For example, if a table has an index of `id, lname, fname`, you need to make use of any of the following combinations: `id, lname, fname; id, lname;` or `id`.
- When examining a `WHERE` clause, the optimizer places penalties against conditions making use of `NOT`, `NOT IN`, `!=`, or `OR`. The use of these conditions will likely result in a full-table scan rather than the use of an index. Where possible, try to reverse the logic to use `IN`, `=`, and `AND` to get an index to be used.
- The optimizer does not, generally, undertake algebraic logic on `WHERE` conditions. For example, `age > 100 / 5` will run faster than `age * 5 > 100` because it can use an index to pull values greater than 20, instead of having to pull each age and multiply it by 5.
- When possible, place as many restrictions as you can on each table so that joins are made using a smaller subset of the data than if no restrictions were imposed.
- If the tables involved in the join are different sizes, try to select a column from the smaller of the tables. This will aid the optimizer by reducing the potential result set.
- Do not perform unnecessary sorting or grouping. These operations require time and resources on top of that required by the query to just locate and collect the data.
- If appropriate, use a temporary table for intermediate results. Because you can create indexes on temporary tables, you can make a performance gain when dealing with a large result set. Just remember to create the index after inserting all the data. Selective use of a temporary table with very large queries allows the query as a whole to be broken down into smaller and better-optimized steps.
- Watcom-SQL allows the explicit specification of a row return percentage with each condition. For example, if a > condition is used, the optimizer deduces that about 25 percent of the rows will match; if the result is closer to 1 percent, the query will perform poorly. If it is known that the results are more likely to be 1 percent, they can be specified in the condition. For example, `sales > 10000, 1`.
- Sybase SQL Anywhere's optimizer is self-tuning on equality constraints, and a query that is run a second time will be optimized differently and might perform better. The optimizer learns from any mistakes it makes in the execution estimate and stores the results in the database.

Occasionally, PowerBuilder makes use of a series of SQL statements to carry out a task—for example, initializing a window. When possible these should be collected together and, as the DBMS permits, made into a stored procedure. Because execution of the statements is now made with only one call and the results are returned in one go, network, client, and server utilization are greatly reduced.

One last place to look for a performance gain, especially when retrieving large result sets, is the network. By adjusting the packet size used by the network protocol, you can get more data transferred per packet. You will need to change this on both the server and client machine protocol setups.

These tips are not meant to encompass every DBMS but are tricks that might be useful in the DBMS you are using. The best place to look for tips is in a DBMS-specific book or in one of the reference books supplied with the DBMS.

Useful Queries

As part of any data migration or SQL debugging you will inevitably run into the need to carry out some kind of analysis or check on data and tables. The following sections describe some of the more useful queries that you can use and manipulate to track down even the most elusive data or SQL problem.

Table Comparison

To compare the data values in one table with those in a second, you can use either of two methods. The simplest to write and understand uses the `NOT EXISTS` operator. For example, suppose that you just loaded an updated employee list into `employee_load`. This table looks identical to the original `employee` table. This approach does not require any indexes on the temporary load table. The query would look something like this:

```
SELECT emp_id, emp_fname, emp_lname
FROM employee_load
WHERE emp_id NOT EXISTS
      (SELECT emp_id
       FROM employee);
```

You could then capture the returned ID into another table, which you can then use in a join to add the new employees to the original `employee` table.

The second approach is conceptually a little more complex and makes use of the outer join. By joining the `employee` and `employee_load` tables in an outer join, you can collect a list of all the employee IDs in the two tables. However, due to the way you will join the two tables, new employees will show up with a `NULL` for the `employee` employee ID value. This would be the code:

```
INSERT INTO new_ids (el_emp_id, e_emp_id)
SELECT el.emp_id, e.emp_id
FROM employee_load el LEFT OUTER JOIN employee e;
```

You can then run a second query on the values in `new_ids` to determine the new employee IDs:

```
SELECT el_emp_id
FROM new_ids
WHERE e_emp_id IS NULL;
```

This second method may seem like additional work, but it will actually perform the same function with fewer I/O requests (logical or physical) because the DBMS does not have to run comparisons over the whole range of the subquery.

FALSE WHERE Conditions

As part of a table-to-table copy you will often need to query the table for its column list. Every DBMS enables you to query tables for their structure in different ways, but most often the resulting information requires extensive editing to provide the comma-separated column list you are after. The following `SELECT` generates a heading list; you can quickly use Ctrl+right arrow to go through the list, placing commas where needed:

```
SELECT *
FROM table_name
WHERE 0 = 1;
```

Finding Duplicate Values

Occasionally things will take a turn for the worse and you will load the same or similar data into a table while you have the indexes removed. In fact, it is highly recommended when importing large amounts of data that you first remove triggers and indexes from a table, and then reapply the same functionality after the load. Once you have determined that there are duplicate records, usually on the failure of your primary key rebuild, you need to track down the culprits and transfer the affected records to a temporary table. Once you have the affected records saved, you can delete them from the primary table. The query to find the duplicate data would be similar to the following:

```
SELECT emp_id
FROM employee
HAVING COUNT( emp_id) > 1
GROUP BY emp_id;
```

There are obviously a number of other techniques and queries that make up your repertoire of data massage tools, and this chapter has covered only the most commonly used ones. You will learn about the others with practice and need. Just remember to record them for your future use, as well as for those who follow in your steps to support a system with such requirements.

Data Type Choices

One of the major stumbling blocks during application development is the correct matching of database and PowerBuilder data types. Table 5.5 shows the PowerBuilder data types and the supported data types of Sybase SQL Anywhere and Microsoft SQL Server.

Table 5.5. PowerBuilder-to-DBMS data type matching.

Data Type	*PowerBuilder*	*SQL Anywhere*	*SQL Server 4.21*
Double	2.2e–308 to 1.7e308	same	1.7e–308 to 1.7e308
Integer	–32768 to 32767	2e31–1 to –2e31	2e31–1 to –2e31
Long	2e31–1 to –2e31		
Real	1.17e–38 to 3.4e38	same	3.4e–38 to 3.4e38
String	65536	32767	255

As you can see in Table 5.5, PowerBuilder and the DBMSs support a wide variety of accuracies and sizes—even two of the major PowerBuilder-supported DBMSs have this variety! You need to be careful to match up the expected maximum sizes of fields, and you need to be aware that if a PowerBuilder Long data type is used, it is actually referencing a DBMS Integer data type.

PowerBuilder will not report any problems it encounters with placing values into data types that have a lesser accuracy. For example, placing a SQL Server integer value of 40,000 into a PowerBuilder variable that is also an integer will actually result in the variable holding the value `-25,535`. This is because the value *overflows* the variable size, loops off the positive end, and starts back at the largest negative number. With strings, a size difference is not as noticeable because the value is truncated to fit into the available space.

If an application is to be run against multiple DBMSs, the lowest common size should be used when determining the data types of tables and of PowerBuilder variables.

Primary Key Generation

Not all tables have a single column or multiple columns (a compound key) that will make a unique key into the table, so a system-defined key needs to be generated and assigned to a record. Codes that are system generated and have no real meaning are commonly known as *surrogate keys*. There is some controversy over the use of surrogate keys—E.F. Codd being one of the many antagonists—but these are more a conceptual problem than a practical one. There are a number of different ways to generate such keys, and indeed some database management systems include facilities such as a special data type to save the developer from any extra work:

- Use a key lookup table, which is a single table that consists of two columns, a table name, and the last key used. When a new key is required, the table is locked to prevent another user from generating a key at the same time. The value is incremented and saved to a variable. This requires that all tables have the same data type as a key—usually an Integer. Sometimes an upper and lower boundary are specified to roll over a sequence. This is often used when the sequence number is combined with other values. This is the correct sequence of commands to lock and update the table:

1. Begin a transaction that can be rolled back if any part fails.
2. Issue an update that increments the key value by 1. This read locks the table against any other user.
3. Select the new key value back into a variable.

- On a success, commit the transaction; on a failure of the `UPDATE` or `SELECT`, roll it back.
- Use the `MAX()` aggregate function and increment the value by one within a `SELECT` that holds a lock on the table using `HOLDLOCK` (this is not supported by some DBMSs). This requires an index on the column to produce acceptable speed. The `SELECT` should be part of the data `INSERT`.
- Use either a DBMS or client random-number generator. If the data fails to save, simply generate a new number, and as long as the collisions are few and far between it will produce good performance (but also nonsequential keys).

There are a number of additional ways to generate sequence numbers, but they tend to be very DBMS specific. The most commonly used, and widely accepted, method is the key lookup (or sequence table).

Troubleshooting SQL in PowerBuilder

Powersoft has very thoughtfully added to PowerBuilder a feature that enables the capture of database commands. For native database drivers, the Database Trace tool records all the internal commands that are performed during a connection. The trace can be done during development or at runtime, and is written out to a log file called PBTRACE.LOG (which is in the Windows directory).

The trace file documents the following information:

- Connection parameters
- Execution time (measured only in a granularity of 55ms)
- Internal commands issued by PowerBuilder, such as SQL preparation and execution, getting table and column descriptions, binding variables, and disconnecting from the database

This is the format of the trace file:

```
COMMAND: (time)
{additional_information}
```

`COMMAND` is the command executed (for example, `PREPARE`, `FETCH NEXT`, `DISCONNECT`); `(time)` is the execution time in milliseconds; and `additional_information` is optional text describing the command. If the execution time appears as `0`, the execution actually took between 0ms and 54ms to complete. Here's an example of a trace:

```
LOGIN: (1154 MilliSeconds)
```

```
CONNECT TO trace Sybase:
USERID=gallagher_simon
DATA=oe_010
LOGID=gallagher_simon
LOCK=RL
DBPARM=appname='PB App',host='RAVEN-PB',dbgettime='20',async='1'
SERVER=falcon (0 MilliSeconds)
PREPARE: (0 MilliSeconds)
PREPARE:
SELECT DISTINCT  maintenance_tables.table_name
FROM maintenance_tables
ORDER BY maintenance_tables.table_name          ASC   (55 MilliSeconds)
DESCRIBE: (0 MilliSeconds)
name=table_name,len=31,type=CHAR,pbt1,dbt1,ct0,dec0
BIND SELECT OUTPUT BUFFER (DataWindow): (0 MilliSeconds)
name=table_name,len=31,type=CHAR,pbt1,dbt1,ct0,dec0
EXECUTE: (0 MilliSeconds)
FETCH NEXT: (0 MilliSeconds)
table_name=payment_terms
FETCH NEXT: (0 MilliSeconds)
table_name=product_classes
FETCH NEXT: (0 MilliSeconds)
table_name=resin_codes
FETCH NEXT: (0 MilliSeconds)
table_name=unit_of_measures
FETCH NEXT: (0 MilliSeconds)
Error 1 (rc 100)
COMMIT: (55 MilliSeconds)
DISCONNECT: (0 MilliSeconds)
SHUTDOWN DATABASE INTERFACE: (0 MilliSeconds)
```

This trace shows a successful connect, the selection of four pieces of data from a table, and then a disconnect.

To begin a trace on a connection, the keyword `trace` is placed at the start of the transaction object's DBMS attribute (that is, `SQLCA.DBMS = "trace Sybase"`).

The trace is halted by disconnecting from the current database or connecting to another database.

To trace an ODBC data source, you can use the ODBC Driver Manager Trace to record information on ODBC API calls. The default log is named PBSQL.LOG, but can be user specified with a change to the entry in the `[PBCONNECTOPTIONS]` section of the PBODB040.INI:

```
[PBCONNECTOPTIONS]
PBTrace='ON'
PBTraceFile=C:\PB4\PBSQL.LOG
```

Changing the PBTrace entry is the only way to start (`'ON'`) and stop (`'OFF'`) the trace file from being generated. The trace file produced is more complex than the trace generated for native drivers:

```
SQLDriverConnect(hdbc53CF0000, hwnd369C,
"DSN=Powersoft Demo DB;UID=dba;PWD=***",-3,szConnStrOut,513,pcbConnStrOut,1);
SQLGetInfo(hdbc53CF0000, 6, rgbInfoValue, 512, pcbInfoValue);
SQLGetInfo(hdbc53CF0000, 2, rgbInfoValue, 512, pcbInfoValue);
```

```
.
SQLGetInfo(hdbc53CF0000, 46, rgbInfoValue, 2, pcbInfoValue);
SQLGetConnectOption(hdbc53CF0000, 102, pvParam);
SQLGetInfo(hdbc53CF0000, 8, rgbInfoValue, 4, pcbInfoValue);
.
SQLAllocStmt(hdbc53CF0000, phstmt56F70000);
SQLGetTypeInfo(hstmt56F70000, 0);
SQLBindCol(hstmt56F70000, 1, 1, rgbValue, 129, pcbValue);
.
SQLFetch(hstmt56F70000);
.
SQLFreeStmt(hstmt56F70000, 1);
SQLAllocStmt(hdbc53CF0000, phstmt56F70000);
SQLTables(hstmt56F70000, "(null)", 0, "dba", 3, "pbcattbl", -3, "(null)", 0);
SQLFetch(hstmt56F70000);
.
SQLDescribeCol(hstmt56EF0000, 20, szColName, 129, pcbColName, pfSqlType,
pcbColDef, pibScale, pfNullable);
SQLBindCol(hstmt56EF0000, 1, 8, rgbValue, 40, pcbValue);
.
SQLBindCol(hstmt56EF0000, 6, 1, rgbValue, 41, pcbValue);
.
SQLBindCol(hstmt56EF0000, 20, 1, rgbValue, 2, pcbValue);
SQLFetch(hstmt56EF0000);
SQLFetch(hstmt56EF0000);
.
SQLFetch(hstmt56EF0000);
SQLFreeStmt(hstmt56EF0000, 1);
SQLDisconnect(hdbc53CF0000);
SQLFreeConnect(hdbc53CF0000);
SQLFreeEnv(henv552F0000);
```

This (partial) log shows how much more verbose ODBC is during its interaction with a data source. The listing was considerably edited from a file size of 26KB to the lines you see here, and all this code does is bring up the table list in the Database painter, select the employee table, and pull up data manipulation. The data source ODBC documentation is required to interpret the ODBC API calls.

To aid in the debugging of embedded SQL at runtime as well as during development, embedded SQL should always be followed by a `SQLCode` check. The only pieces of SQL that do not require a check are the `PREPARE` and `DECLARE` statements.

Advanced SQL

This section covers SQL code, solving some of the trickier query problems: rotating data, hierarchy navigation, wildcards as data, and pseudo `IF` statements.

Rotating Data

Sometimes a series of data needs to be represented as a single line. One approach is borrowed from matrix mathematics (and was described by Steve Roti in the August 1990 issue of *DBMS* magazine). A *pivot*, or rotating matrix, is used to multiply (or in the case of SQL, to join) the set of data that is to be compressed. For example, if there is data that needs to be combined to give a weekly total for each week for a number of weeks, the pivot table would be built as follows:

```
Day  Mon  Tue  Wed  Thu  Fri  Sat  Sun
Mon   1    0    0    0    0    0    0
Tue   0    1    0    0    0    0    0
Wed   0    0    1    0    0    0    0
Thu   0    0    0    1    0    0    0
Fri   0    0    0    0    1    0    0
Sat   0    0    0    0    0    1    0
Sun   0    0    0    0    0    0    1
```

The data table is structured like this:

```
Week          Day           Amount
1             Mon           230
1             Mon           320
2             Mon           10
1             Tue           20
2             Tue           50
```

The following `SELECT` statement then multiplies (joins) this matrix with the data table:

```
SELECT week, Mon = SUM( data * Mon), Tue = SUM ( data * Tue) ....
FROM   weekly_data, pivot
WHERE  weekly_data.day = pivot.day
GROUP BY week;
```

to give the following results:

```
Week       Mon         Tue         Wed ....
1                      550         20
2                      10          50
```

Hierarchy Expansion

A common problem encountered in manufacturing applications is *parts explosion*, or the expansion of a hierarchy. The following information and code are based on an example found in the *Transact-SQL* reference manual that comes with Microsoft's SQL Server, but it is widely applicable because it contains the most elementary Transact-SQL statements that should be found in other DBMS scripting languages.

To demonstrate this technique, assume that an employee table contains a circular relationship: A manager is an employee and has employees underneath him; that group also includes managers with employees under them, and so on:

```
ManagerLastName               EmployeeLastName
Gallagher                     Herbert
Gallagher                     Sundling
Herbert                       Quick
Sundling                      O'Connor
Quick                         Urbanek
```

This gives the following hierarchy:

```
Gallagher
   Herbert
      Quick
         Urbanek
   Sundling
      O'Connor
```

The following code expands the hierarchy down to any depth and uses a temporary table as a stack to hold intermediate results. The variable `@current` defines the value at which to start expansion (that is, `Gallagher`):

```
INSERT INTO #stack values (@current, 1)

SELECT @level = 1

WHILE @level > 0
BEGIN
   IF EXISTS ( SELECT * FROM #stack WHERE level = @level )
   BEGIN
      SELECT @current = item
      FROM   #stack
      WHERE  level = @level

      SELECT @line = SPACE( @level - 1) + @current

      PRINT @line

      DELETE FROM #stack
      WHERE level = @level AND item = @current

      INSERT #stack
      SELECT EmployeeLastName, @level + 1
      FROM employee
      WHERE ManagerLastName = @current

      IF @@rowcount > 0
         SELECT @level = @level + 1
   END
ELSE
   SELECT @level = @level - 1
END
```

This example uses the `PRINT` function to display the information to the screen but can easily be modified to store the information and level to another temporary table. This can then be used to return the data via a `SELECT` at the end of the code. This information could then be used to populate a DataWindow that has been set up to display hierarchical information.

Wildcard Tables

An interesting feature of SQL is the capability to store data that contains wildcards and then, during a join, make use of a wildcard to match multiple values. For example, if a certain type of report needs to be generated per account group, this might be the code table:

```
Account_Type                Report_Type
425%                        1
5432.%                      1
65%                         2
```

This table is then joined to the main data table using a `LIKE` to determine which account numbers are required for a given report type. For example, if the data table `opars_data` looked like this:

```
Account_Number          Beg_Balance      End_Balance
4256.1                         1000                0
5432.2                        10000             3455
5431.2                        60000            63455
6534.6                       324253           232111
6634.6                        89754           459873
```

you could issue the following statement to generate a list of data from the `opars_data` table for a report type of 1:

```
SELECT od.*
FROM   opars_data od, code_table ct
WHERE  od.account_number like ct.account_type AND
       ct.report_type = 1;
```

The resulting rows from the `opars_data` table would be account numbers 4256.1 and 5432.2.

Pseudo IF

A very useful trick is to emulate a simple `IF` statement within a query. This is often used in SQL import procedures to convert from one data value and data type to another while preserving the meaning. For example, the column "completed" in the raw data is either a C or a blank. The actual table structure makes use of a bitfield; it stores a C as a `1` and a blank as a `0`. The following code was written to use SQL Server functions, but should be easily convertible to any DBMS that provides comparable functions:

```
SUBSTRING( "01", 1 + ISNULL( DATALENGTH( RTRIM( completed) ), 0), 1)
```

This statement first trims off all spaces, leaving an empty string for the case of an empty completed column value. The `DATALENGTH` function returns the length of the string; if the string is `NULL`, a `NULL` is returned. In case of a `NULL` value, the `ISNULL` function is used to turn the `NULL` into a `0`. The length of the string is added to 1 to give the starting position in the code string to extract. The `SUBSTRING` function then removes the single character at the specified starting position. The return value from the `SUBSTRING` would then be put through a `CONVERT` function to arrive at the desired numeric value. This statement can be combined into the `SELECT` column list as just another expression. The SQL code is identical to the following PowerScript:

```
If szCompleted = "C" Then
   nCompleted = 1
Else
   nCompleted = 0
End If
```

Longer codes can be placed into the code string. For example, if the completed column were converted to YES and NO, the code string would become "NO YES" and the SUBSTRING would be set to select three characters out of the string. The starting position for the SUBSTRING would be calculated as three times the DATALENGTH plus 1:

```
SUBSTRING( "NO YES", 1 + 3 * ISNULL( DATALENGTH( RTRIM( completed) ), 0), 3)
```

You can use a number of additional methods to implement decision-making processes in your SQL. An additional method you might be able to employ uses the CHARINDEX() SQL function.

The CHARINDEX() function takes two parameters: the string you want to search for and the string you want to search. It then returns the position within the second string at which the first occurs. You can use this to turn the return value into a Boolean 1 or 0.

For example, consider trying to conditionally summate a single column based on another value. In the following SQL code, department_group is a single-character column, so you can easily pattern match and multiply the counter column by the return value. This gives a conditional value for each record you are operating on, which is then correctly summed:

```
SELECT SUM( counter2_elapsed * CHARINDEX( 'C', department_group)) converted,
       SUM( counter2_elapsed * CHARINDEX( 'P', department_group)) printed
FROM summary_production
```

You might be lucky enough to get away with this, but you might have to perform some additional manipulation of the CHARINDEX() return value to get a 1 or 0 value.

TIP

Remember that you can use similar techniques in the expressions you can code for DataWindows.

Summary

This chapter covers each of the basic SQL statements (SELECT, INSERT, UPDATE, and DELETE) and shows you how they can be combined to undertake complex tasks. You have learned about how PowerBuilder uses SQL, the process of using simple SQL statements in PowerScript, and how to dynamically construct and execute such SQL at runtime. Tracing problems for both native and ODBC interfaces is covered, and you've gotten some suggestions for where and when to generate error messages.

The PowerScript Language

6

IN THIS CHAPTER

This chapter introduces you to both basic and advanced PowerScript concepts and syntax, object-oriented concepts and the syntax and methods available to implement them, and some additional features such as error handling and file processing.

PowerScript is the language used by PowerBuilder and is written using a collection of statements, commands, and functions, together with user-defined functions and embedded SQL statements. You write PowerScript for the object events whose actions you want to direct when a user triggers them. For example, if you want to close a window when the user presses a certain command button, you code the appropriate PowerScript statements in the command button's `Clicked` event.

Objects

A PowerBuilder *object* is an application component that has a number of characteristics called *attributes* and behaviors called *methods* (which is the collective name for *events* and *functions*).

In PowerBuilder there are a number of types of objects: applications, windows, menus, global functions, structures, user objects, queries, pipelines, and even projects. Within windows and visual user objects you can place an additional type of object: a control. Each of these objects has a different number of attributes, events, and functions.

Attributes

An object's *attributes* describe how the object will look (for example, whether it is visible, the color of the text) and the position in which it will appear. Some of the attributes enable or disable certain behaviors of the object, such as allowing it to be dynamically resized by the user. Most of an object's attributes can be set when the object is created and can also be dynamically changed at runtime using PowerScript.

To access an object's attributes in PowerScript, you use a *dot notation*. The syntax for dot notation is *object.attribute*, and you can extend off the left side as many objects as you need to point to the correct object/attribute. For example, to access a command button (`cb_close`) within a window (`w_connect`) from a different window, the syntax would be

```
w_connect.cb_close.Enabled = TRUE
```

PowerScript Basic Concepts

This might seem like an odd section to include in an advanced book; it is really intended for accomplished beginners to intermediate-level developers, and even those among you who are studying for CPD tests. This short section speeds through a number of basic ground rules and topics for PowerScript.

Identifiers

An identifier, which can be anything from an object to a variable, must start with a letter and can include the following characters:

- Dash (-)
- Underscore(_)
- Dollar sign ($)
- Pound sign (#)
- Percent sign (%)

The identifier can be up to 99 characters in length. The PowerBuilder documentation states a limit of 40, but if you are really desperate for a descriptive name, you can go all the way to 99!

The fact that PowerBuilder allows a dash in an identifier is strange, and to prevent yourself from making errors in your expressions you will want to exercise your right to turn this feature off. In the `[pb]` section of the PB.INI file is an entry called `DashesInIdentifiers`, and to turn the feature off set it equal to `0`.

WARNING

Remember that by default PowerBuilder uses dashes in the identifiers for separator lines in the Menu painter. If you turn the dashes in identifiers off, you will be unable to save a menu until you rename each of the separators.

Labels

A label enables you to branch to a certain point within a script and is used with the `GOTO` statement. A label is an identifier followed by a colon (:), and you can place any number of labels within a script, although each must be unique. You cannot jump to a label in a different script—only to one in the current local scope. For example, to jump to a central point of error handling, you could code the following statements after a SQL statement:

```
If SQLCA.SQLCode <> 0 Then
   Error.Line = 12
   Goto DBError
End If

//
// More of the script here ....
//

Return

DBError:
   error.Object = this.ClassName()
```

```
error.Number = SQLCA.SQLDBCode
error.Text = SQLCA.SQLErrText
SQLCA.RollbackTran()
Open( w_error)
```

Some developers consider GOTO statements to be "evil" and avoided at all costs, but consider that the low-level machine code commands continually branch to implement the desired logic. If you don't use an excessive number of labels—say no more than three or four—and they are well named and documented in the code, you should not hesitate to use a label and GOTO to make your code more concise. If you consider the situation presented in the code example, you would have to code similar statements after each embedded SQL statement rather than the two lines that set the line number and jump. Not only does your code become more concise, but you have fewer places where you need to make code changes if they are required.

The one important statement to remember is RETURN. It was used in the code example just before the label to prevent the code from "dropping through" into the conditional code. A RETURN statement immediately terminates the execution of the script and returns to whatever script called the current code. Occasionally you might have to use a GOTO and associated label to leap around areas of code that will be reached using other GOTO statements; this might be grounds for reconsidering your logic structure.

Operators

An *operator* symbolizes the operation that is performed on either one or two operands. In PowerScript there are four types of operators: arithmetic, relational, logical, and concatenation.

Arithmetic Operators

Arithmetic operators are used for mathematical calculations. Table 6.1 lists the base arithmetic operators and gives an example of each.

Table 6.1. Base arithmetic operators.

Operator	*Meaning*	*Example*	*Description*
+	Addition	n1 = n1 + n2	Adds n2 to n1
-	Subtraction	n1 = n1 - n2	Subtracts n2 from n1
-	Negative	n1 = -n1	Changes the sign of n1—either from negative to positive or vice versa
*	Multiplication	n1 = n1 * n2	Multiplies n1 by n2
/	Division	n1 = n1 / n2	Divides n1 by n2
^	Exponentiation	n1 = n1 ^ n2	Raises n1 to the n2th power

Table 6.2 shows the extended arithmetic operators. These operators act on only one operand, and you cannot combine them with other operators.

Table 6.2. Extended arithmetic operators.

Operator	*Meaning*	*Example*	*Description*
`++`	Increment	`n1 ++`	Increments `n1` by 1
`--`	Decrement	`n1 --`	Decrements `n1` by 1
`+=`	Plus Equals	`n1 += n2`	Adds `n2` to `n1`
`-=`	Minus Equals	`n1 -= n2`	Subtracts `n2` from `n1`
`*=`	Times Equals	`n1 *= n2`	Multiplies `n1` by `n2`
`/=`	Divide Equals	`n1 /= n2`	Divides `n1` by `n2`
`^=`	Power Equals	`n1 ^= n2`	Raises `n1` to the `n2`th power

NOTE

If you have the `DashesInIdentifiers` option turned on you must place spaces around the subtraction (`-`), negative (`-`), and decrement (`--`) operators. Otherwise, PowerBuilder will produce an error when compiling the script because it interprets the expression as an undeclared variable.

As with all arithmetic operations there are certain types of operations that will cause runtime errors to occur: attempting to divide by a zero value, causing a Double or Real to overflow, or raising a negative value to a non-integer power. Overflowed integer values cause the resulting value to wrap around to the other end of the range (for example, `32767 + 1` results in the value `-32768`).

WARNING

Overflowing decimals have a much stranger affect: the resulting value becomes `-(Null)`. This cannot be detected using `IsNull()`, and any expressions that use this value may also result in `-(Null)` or some other unexpected value.

Relational Operators

Relational operators make a comparison between two operands, which do not have to be numeric. The result of this evaluation can be TRUE, FALSE, or NULL. Table 6.3 lists the relational operators.

Table 6.3. The relational operators.

Operator	*Meaning*
=	Equals
>	Greater than
<	Less than
<>	Not equal
>=	Greater than or equal to
<=	Less than or equal to

If you are comparing strings, the comparison is case and length sensitive. So in order to ensure string matches, you might want to employ either the `Upper()` or `Lower()` functions together with either `RightTrim()`, `LeftTrim()`, or `Trim()`.

NOTE

C programmers should be aware that the evaluation of an `If` expression using relational or logical operators in PowerBuilder is not the same as in C. Each expression is evaluated, and not just up to the point in the expression where it fails (known as short-circuiting). Therefore, you might want to consider using a `Choose...Case` construct to evaluate complex, interdependent conditions.

Logical Operators

Logical operators are used to form Boolean expressions, which are expressions that evaluate to either TRUE or FALSE. Table 6.4 lists the logical operators and gives an example of each.

Table 6.4. The logical operators.

Operator	Meaning	Example
NOT	Logical negation	`this.Checked = NOT this.Checked`
		`If NOT nActive Then wf_Activate()`
AND	Logical and	`If nValue > 1 AND nValue < 9 Then`
OR	Logical or	`If nValue = 1 OR nValue = 9 Then`

NOTE

Unless you are building a simple expression, it always makes good sense to enclose related parts within parentheses. This helps other developers understand the expression more easily without having to figure out the order of operator precedence.

Concatenation Operators

The *concatenation operator* (+) is used to join the contents of two variables that must be either both String or both Blob data types. Here's an example:

```
String szString1, szString2, szString3

szString1 = "First "
szString2 = "Second"

// szString3 now contains: "First Second"
szString3 = szString1 + szString2
```

Operator Precedence in Expressions

In mathematics the operators used in expressions are evaluated in a particular order of precedence. You will commonly use parentheses to group expressions to aid readability and expected results. Nested groups are evaluated from the inside outward. When operators have the same precedence, they are evaluated from left to right. Table 6.5 lists the operators in descending order of precedence.

Table 6.5. The descending order of operator precedence.

Operator	Meaning
+, -	Unary plus and unary minus
^	Exponentiation

continues

Table 6.5. continued

Operator	*Meaning*
`*, /`	Multiplication and division
`+, -`	Addition, subtraction, and concatenation
`=, >, <, >=, =<, <>`	Relational operators
`NOT`	Negation
`AND`	Logical and
`OR`	Logical or

ASCII Characters

PowerBuilder enables you to use special ASCII characters in your strings. The most commonly used ones allow you to force new lines, include tabs, and include quotation marks in a string that is already using the same quotation mark type. The tilde character (~) is used in PowerBuilder to introduce special characters. Table 6.6 lists how to specify ASCII characters in PowerBuilder.

Table 6.6. ASCII characters available in PowerBuilder.

String	*Resulting ASCII Character*
`~n`	New line
`~t`	Tab
`~v`	Vertical tab
`~r`	Carriage return
`~f`	Form feed
`~b`	Backspace
`~"`	Double quote
`~'`	Single quote
`~~`	Tilde
`~000` to `~255`	The ASCII character with the stated decimal value
`~h01` to `~hFF`	The ASCII character with the stated hexadecimal value
`~o000` to `~o377`	The ASCII character with the stated octal value

You usually use these characters when you are creating the display strings for message boxes or writing out values to a file.

NOTE

Another way to assign a double (") or single (') quotation mark to a variable is to embed it within the opposite kind of quotation marks (for example, `szSingle = "'"` and `cDouble = '"'`).

Continuing Strings

The continuation character (`&`) can be used to extend not only statements, but strings, over multiple lines. You can place the `&` character at the end of a string without closing quotation marks, and then continue the string onto the next line. However, you must be aware that any spaces and tabs that appear before the `&` and also at the start of the additional lines are also included. Unless you do not care about the extra space, for example in a `Modify()` function call, you should close the string and use the concatenation operator (+).

Standard Data Types

The standard data types that are available in PowerBuilder are common across many different programming languages and databases servers. However, you should carefully match PowerBuilder's data type definition with that of the intended target or source. A good example of this difference in definitions can be seen by comparing integer data types between Microsoft SQL Server and PowerBuilder.

In SQL Server an integer is defined as a 32-bit signed value that ranges from -2,147,483,648 to +2,147,483,647. In PowerBuilder, an integer is defined as a 16-bit signed value that ranges from -32,768 to +32,767. SQL Server's integer definition actually matches that of the PowerBuilder Long data type. You must take great care when you are matching PowerBuilder variables to those of a database. Table 6.7 lists all the standard data types and their definitions and gives an example of each.

Table 6.7. PowerBuilder standard data types.

Data Type	*Definition*	*Example*
Blob	Binary large object. Used to store large amounts of data.	A bitmap
Boolean	A truth value, either `TRUE` or `FALSE`.	`FALSE`
Character or Char	A single ASCII character.	`A`

continues

Table 6.7. continued

Data Type	*Definition*	*Example*
Date	The date, consisting of the full year, the number of the month, and the day.	`1969-06-13`
DateTime	The date and time combined into a single data type.	`1969-12-0612:10`
Decimal or Dec	Signed decimal numbers with up to 18 digits of precision.	`3463346.5247`
Double	A signed floating-point number with 15 digits of precision and a range from 2.2E-308 to 1.7E+308.	`6.342E+3`
Integer or Int	A 16-bit signed number with a range of -32,768 to +32,767.	`7,533`
Long	A 32-bit signed number with a range of -2,147,483,648 to +2,147,483,647.	`4,699,247`
Real	A signed floating-point number with six digits of precision and a range from 1.17E-38 to 3.4E+38.	`3.6E+7`
String	Any ASCII characters with a variable length of 0 to either 59,999 or as large as your system can provide.	`"Ulric"`
Time	A time value in 24-hour format: hour, minute, second, and fractions of a second (up to six digits).	`19:18:29.435214`
UnsignedInteger or UnsignedInt or Uint	A 16-bit unsigned number with a range of 0 to 65,535.	`6,324`
UnsignedLong or Ulong	32-bit unsigned number with a range of 0 to 4,294,967,295.	`43,234,54`

Data Type Conversions

PowerBuilder provides a number of data type conversion functions (see Table 6.8) that allow you to easily change from one data type to another.

Table 6.8. PowerBuilder conversion functions.

Data Type	*Definition*
Char	Convert Blob, Integer, or String to a Char.
Dec	Convert a String to a Decimal.
Double	Convert a String to a Double.
Integer	Convert a String to an Integer.
Long	Convert a String to a Long.
Real	Convert a String to a Real.
Date	Obtain the Date portion of a DateTime value.
DateTime	Convert a Date and a Time to a DateTime value.
String	Convert Blob, Date, DateTime, numeric, and Time to String.
Time	Obtain the Time portion of a DateTime value.

Strings and Characters

Characters are single ASCII elements and strings are collections of 0 or more characters. In the 32-bit implementation of Version 5.0 you can build strings as large as you want. In previous versions of PowerBuilder, and also in the 16-bit implementation of PowerBuilder 5.0, the maximum size of a string is 59,999 characters. If you assign a string value to a character variable, only the first ASCII value is stored. The special characters listed in the section "ASCII Characters" can be assigned to character variables using an implicit string-to-character conversion. For example, to assign the representation of a tab the statement is

```
cTabCharacter = "~t"
```

Arrays of characters can also be assigned to string variables, and they obey the following rules:

- You can directly copy a string to an unbounded character array.
- A string that you copy to a bounded array will be truncated to the array's upper boundary.
- If the string is shorter than the upper boundary, the unused elements are initialized to empty strings.

Character arrays can be converted back into strings by assignment to a variable of data type String. Characters are copied until an empty character (equal to '') is found.

All PowerBuilder functions will accept strings and characters or character arrays.

Dynamic Variable Assignment

Variables can be initialized with a value when they are declared. The value set can either be a constant value or the result of an expression. If you make an assignment during a variable's declaration, the value set is determined at compile time and not during runtime execution. For example, the following code sets the variable to the time the application was compiled, and the variable will not be updated each time this code is called:

```
String szTime = String( Now())
```

The only obvious use for this kind of initialization is if you want to capture the time that an application is compiled for auditing or other purposes.

> **WARNING**
>
> If you try to dynamically assign to a variable from the attribute of an object, you will get an error.

Arrays

You use an *oi* to collect related pieces of information of the same data type under one name. Each element in the array has a unique index to distinguish it from the others. There are two types of arrays: single-dimensional and multidimensional. Multidimensional arrays must have a fixed size, whereas single-dimensional arrays can be either a fixed or an unbounded size.

You declare an array by first stating the data type of the elements, the name of the variable, and then the size of the array, enclosed in square brackets.

Single-Dimensional Arrays

A single-dimensional array is similar to a list of related items and is declared using a single size or using the `To` statement to specify a range. Here are two examples:

```
String aszThis_Is_An_Array[ 30]
Integer anAnother_Array[ 10 To 20]
```

The first example declares an array of 30 Strings, with indexes from 1 to 30. The second example declares an array of 11 Integers, with indexes starting at 10 and going up to and including 20. Both of these examples are of fixed size, and any index reference outside the valid range will produce a runtime error.

The To notation is used to override the default start index of 1 and requires that the first number specified be less than the second number of the range. Negative index ranges are also valid, as are indexes that begin negative and end positive. Following are some examples, all of which define arrays of 21 elements:

```
String aszArray1[ -10 To 10]
Integer anArray2[ -21 To -1]
Real arArray3[ 0 To 20]
```

Unbounded Arrays

Unbounded or *variable-size* arrays are single-dimensional arrays for which no index boundaries are defined. The memory requirements and usage are controlled by PowerBuilder at runtime. An unbounded array starts at index 1, which cannot be changed. The upper boundary is controlled by the largest index assignment that has been made at the point where you check the boundary. When an unbounded array is first created, the upper index is 0 and the lower is 1. For example, a declaration for an array containing any number of integers is as follows:

```
Integer anArray4[]
```

Following the declaration of such an array, any index reference over 1 is fully valid. However, the manner in which PowerBuilder assigns memory to the unbounded array is worth noting:

```
anArray4[ 200] = 100
anArray4[ 250] = 50
anArray4[ 350] = 25
anArray4[ 299] = 12
```

The first use of the array causes PowerBuilder to create a 200-element array, of which it initializes the first 199 elements to the default integer value of 0 and then assigns the value 100 to the 200th element. The second assignment to the array causes an additional 50 elements to be created and added to the array; these are initialized to 0 except for element 250, which takes the value 50. The third assignment causes an additional 100 elements to be added; they are initialized to 0 except for element 350, which takes the value 25. The last does not cause any additional memory allocations because it is referencing an already created element.

Keep in mind the manner in which PowerBuilder creates memory for the unbounded arrays. Any usage of an unbounded array is optimally written if it starts at the largest value and works backward. Each time PowerBuilder is required to allocate more memory, it must deal with the Windows operating system, which is a time-expensive operation. Therefore, causing the maximum size of the array to be created once will produce faster execution. This is not always possible, but it is worth considering if the array can be populated in reverse.

NOTE

Accessing an element of an unbounded array that is outside the current range will cause a runtime error. Of course, the upper boundary might change as execution commences, such that the following code will give an error:

```
Integer anArray4[]
anArray4[100] = 10
If anArray4[ 101] = 10 Then
End If
```

Determining Array Boundaries

Two PowerBuilder functions are available for determining the upper and lower boundaries of arrays: `UpperBound()` and `LowerBound()`, respectively. `LowerBound()` always returns 1 for unbounded arrays. `UpperBound()` is usually used before iterating through the array, but a common misuse of this function is to place it in the loop condition:

```
For nCount = 1 To UpperBound( anArray4)
   // Do some processing
Next
```

Powersoft states that the `UpperBound()` function is very expensive to execute, and because any function calls in a loop condition are executed each time, this code calls `UpperBound()` for every element! The correct way to use this function is to assign the value to a variable first, like this:

```
nNumberOfElements = UpperBound( anArray4)
For nCount = 1 To nNumberOfElements
   // Do some processing
Next
```

Array Initialization

Arrays can be assigned values during their declaration, similarly to other data types, and the same syntax can be used after the declaration line if required. The initialization values must be of the same data type as the array, and for a fixed-size array must be of the correct value. The syntax is a comma-separated list enclosed by braces. Here's an example:

```
Real arArray5[ 5] = { 1.2, 2.1, 3.2, 2.3, 4.3 }
```

The following is also valid:

```
Real arArray5[ 5]
arArray5 = { 1.2, 2.1, 3.2, 2.3, 4.3 }
```

Unbounded arrays can also be initialized in the same manner, and this sets the initial number of elements.

TIP

A quick and elegant way to reinitialize an array back to default values is to declare another array of the same data type and index boundaries, and then assign the new array to the old array. Here's an example:

```
Real arCleanArray[6]

// An array a_arValuesIn is passed as an argument to this function
a_arValuesIn = arCleanArray
```

The only disadvantage to this method is the extra memory of the second array, but this will usually outweigh the time taken to iterate through the original array to reset each element.

Multidimensional Arrays

Multidimensional arrays can only be of fixed size and contain more than one dimension in the declaration. For example, to model points in 3D space, an array could be created to hold the X, Y, and Z coordinates. Here's an example:

```
Real arPoints[ 100, 100, 100]
```

The `arPoints` array consists of 100×100×100, or 1 million, elements. The rules for declaring the range for single-dimensional arrays also apply to multidimensional arrays. The following are all valid declarations:

```
Real arAxis[ -10 To 10, 20]
Integer anCoOrds[ 2, 0 To 200, -1 To 3]
String aszDrawer[ 0 To 100, 0 To 100]
```

Multidimensional arrays cannot be initialized. The number and size of a dimension is only limited by available memory. You access elements by specifying the dimensional indexes in a comma-separated list. Here's an example:

```
arAxis[ 4, 5] = 43.5
anCoOrds[ 1, 43, 2] = 69
aszDrawer[ 34, 54] = "Ulric"
```

Arrays in Function Parameters

An array can also be declared for a function argument, but not for the return value. The argument declaration is modified to include the square brackets and the upper boundary for a fixed-size array. Unbounded arrays can be defined for function arguments. Although arrays cannot be defined for the return value, an argument can be declared as a pass by reference argument for the purposes of returning an array. In fact, you should always pass arrays by reference so PowerBuilder doesn't copy the entire array.

NEW 5 in PowerBuilder

You can now pass arrays into the new parameterized events of PowerBuilder 5.0. They are treated and declared in the same manner as for functions.

NULL Values

A NULL value, as you saw in Chapter 5, "SQL and PowerBuilder," can be tricky to deal with. The same is also true in PowerScript.

A NULL is an undefined value—it is an unknown value. PowerScript variables can become NULL if they are retrieved from a database, by using the PowerScript function SetNull() or by calling a PowerScript function or external function that returns handle information to an object.

Like SQL, PowerScript also provides a method for testing for a NULL value, in this case the IsNull() function. This function returns a Boolean value, which is TRUE if the value being tested is NULL and FALSE otherwise.

To check that a returned object handle is not a NULL-object reference you need to use the IsValid() function. For example, to see if an object is currently selected, use this:

```
GraphicObject hControl

hControl = GetFocus()

If IsValid( hControl) Then
   MessageBox( "Focus", "Something has focus")
Else
   MessageBox( "Focus", "Nothing has focus!")
End If
```

You must also be careful when you are adding two variables, whether they are Integer or String data types. If one of them is a NULL, the result will be a NULL.

The SetNull() function allows you to set PowerScript variables to a NULL value. Care must be taken to cast the NULL into a variable of the correct data type if you are going to place it in a DataWindow or use it elsewhere. A NULL integer is not interchangeable with a NULL string, and even though the DataWindow SetItem() function allows you to specify a string variable set to NULL to be placed into an integer column, the actual modification will fail with no error.

Classes and Objects

Classes and objects are related but separate concepts. Objects are instances of a class, and classes can have zero or more instances. An *object* is a package of related functions and data. A class is simply a template from which particular instances can be created. All windows that you create in PowerBuilder are in the class Window. Objects are the actual physical representation of a class and are what you create and destroy.

PowerBuilder defines each class—the system classes as well as the classes that you create—as a data type and maintains these as a class hierarchy.

Using the Object Browser, shown in Figure 6.1, you can set the specific class type that you want to zoom in on.

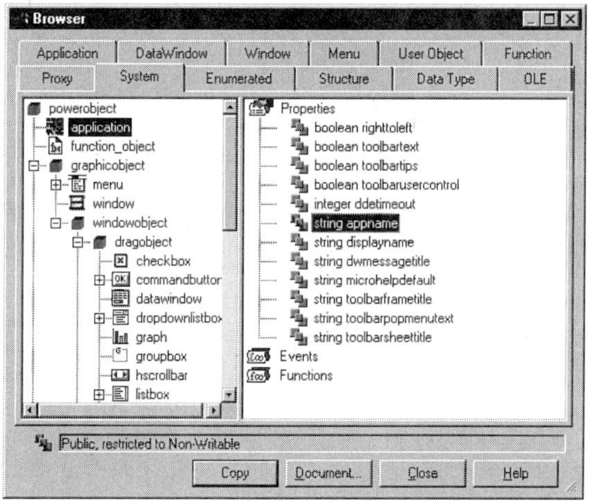

FIGURE 6.1.
The Object Browser.

Using Object Pointers

To further illustrate the point that objects can be declared as variables (which are in fact pointers to an object), this section examines how to implement a doubly linked list in PowerBuilder.

For those of you who have not heard of a linked list, let alone a doubly link list, a brief word of description. A linked list is a list representation of data values that are not necessarily sequentially stored. Access to data is made through links, which are pointers stored with each data value that point to the next data value in the list. For a doubly linked list, the data value is also associated with a pointer to the previous data value. The collection of data and pointer(s) is called an *atom*. Linked lists are frequently used in such languages as C, C++, and Pascal to store related data values.

The atom is implemented as a custom class user object that contains three instance variables:

- `Any aData`
- `u_n_atom ptrNext`
- `u_n_atom ptrPrevious`

The `aData` variable is used to store the actual data value. The two pointers, `ptrNext` and `ptrPrevious`, are defined of the same type as the user object they are in.

NOTE

You will need to save the user object before you can declare the two pointer variables!

To implement a doubly linked list you will provide a custom class user object: `u_n_doubly_linked_list`. This object will maintain a pointer to the head (first item) and tail (last item) of the list using two instance variables:

- `Public ProtectedWrite u_n_atom ptrHead`
- `Public ProtectedWrite u_n_atom ptrTail`

These variables are protected from outside modification but are made available for other objects to traverse the list.

Two functions are provided to add and remove atoms from the list. The function for adding an atom (see Listing 6.1) creates the atom and then makes the appropriate pointer assignments to link it into the list. This function simply appends to the end of the list, which is defined by the `ptrTail` variable. You can easily enhance this function to allow a new atom to be inserted after a specified atom. This function has only one special case, which is when the first atom is added. This is checked by looking at the value of `ptrHead` and to see whether it is valid.

Listing 6.1. `AddAtom( ReadOnly Any a_aData)` for `u_n_doubly_linked_list`.

```
u_n_atom Atom

Atom = Create u_n_atom

Atom.aData = a_aData

If Not IsValid( ptrHead) Then
   ptrHead = Atom
Else
   ptrTail.ptrNext = Atom
   Atom.ptrPrevious = ptrTail
End If

ptrTail = Atom

Return Atom
```

As mentioned previously, the `AddAtom()` function only appends to the list. To illustrate more complex operations on the list, you can use the `DeleteAtom()` function (see Listing 6.2). This function destroys a specified atom and reassigns the pointers for related atoms. If there is another atom after the one to be deleted, this is assigned as the next atom of the previous atom, and vice versa. There are then two special cases to catch. If you have just deleted the head item or tail item from the list, then you need to update the appropriate pointers.

Listing 6.2. `DeleteAtom( Ref u_n_atom a_unAtom)` for `u_n_doubly_linked_list`.

```
u_n_atom ptrPrevious, ptrNext

If Not IsValid( ptrHead) Then
   // Empty List
   Return
End If

ptrPrevious = a_unAtom.ptrPrevious
ptrNext = a_unAtom.ptrNext

If IsValid( ptrNext) Then
   // Point from the atom after the one to be deleted to the atom previous
   ptrNext.ptrPrevious = ptrPrevious
End If

If IsValid( ptrPrevious) Then
   // Point from the atom previous to the one being deleted to the atom after
   ptrPrevious.ptrNext = ptrNext
End If

If a_unAtom = ptrTail And IsValid( ptrPrevious) Then
   // Move the tail pointer to the previous atom if there is one
   ptrTail = ptrPrevious
End If

If a_unAtom = ptrHead And IsValid( ptrNext) Then
   // Move the head pointer to the next atom if there is one
   ptrHead = ptrNext
End If

Destroy a_unAtom
```

The case of an empty list is automatically handled by PowerBuilder as both the `ptrHead` and `ptrTail` variables become invalid, and you can check against just one of these using `IsValid()`.

The `u_n_doubly_linked_list` user object can be set up to be auto-instantiating, and for the following examples we will assume a variable `unDll` of this user object type that is already instantiated. We will also use a pointer to a position within the list, `ptrCurrentAtom`, which is declared of type `u_n_atom`.

The code to add a value to the list is simply

```
ptrCurrentAtom = unDll.AddAtom( "SimonG")
```

This code can be issued multiple times to add multiple atoms to the list. Since the data type of the linked list is Any, you can store anything you want in the list. This is much more versatile than linked lists in C or Pascal, which can store only one data type (for single-value atoms).

To remove the current atom from the list, you'd use this code:

```
If IsValid( ptrCurrentAtom) Then
   unDll.DeleteAtom( ptrCurrentAtom)
End If
```

To navigate through the list you can start at either the head or tail end, using the appropriate variable. For example, to go to the previous atom from the current, this would be the code:

```
If IsValid( unDll.ptrHead) Then
   If Not IsValid( ptrCurrentAtom) Then
      ptrCurrentAtom = unDll.ptrHead
ElseIf IsValid( ptrCurrentAtom.ptrPrevious) Then
      ptrCurrentAtom = ptrCurrentAtom.ptrPrevious
End If
Else
   MessageBox( "Linked List", "You are already on the first atom in the list!")
End If

//Extract the data value - in this case assume numeric
lValue = Long( ptrCurrentAtom.aData)
```

You can traverse in the other direction simply by changing the `ptrPrevious` references to `ptrNext`.

Class and Instance Pools

PowerBuilder maintains three separate memory pools that are used to track class, instance, and Windows manifestation information.

The first time you instantiate a particular class, the class definition is loaded into the class pool, and then an instance is created in the instance pool. Subsequent instantiations of that object take their definition straight from the class pool. Depending on how you instantiate the object, a pointer to the instance will be either in global memory or at the scope level of the variable used. PowerBuilder then uses one additional pool, the Windows pool, to hold information about the actual Windows manifestation of an object. This last pool is only used for visible classes, such as windows, menus, and user objects.

NOTE

The way the class pool works is somewhat of a mystery, and Powersoft has said that the current operation might well change in future releases. Currently, when you close a visual object or destroy a nonvisual object, the memory for the instance is freed immediately. The class information (mostly the methods) go away at some random (for all practical purposes) time in the future if there are no other instances. It is, however, possible that the class definition will remain in memory until the application terminates. Only auto-instantiate classes (structures in 4.0 and now `NVO`s marked `autoinstantiate` in 5.0) are freed immediately when there are no references. The implementation details have changed in 5.0, but the behavior is essentially the same as in 4.0. The part of the behavior that might change is with respect to classes that have shared variables declared. Currently, the class definition is "pinned" into the class pool until the application's termination.

For example, consider opening a window `w_sheet` using two local variables and another window `w_about` that you open directly:

```
w_sheet wInstance, wInstance2

Open( w_about)
//
Open( wInstance, "w_sheet")
Open( wInstance2, "w_sheet")
```

As you know, this script will open three windows. Now let's explore what happens in the class and instance pools, and in global and local memory:

1. If this is the first time the class `w_about` has been opened, the class definition is loaded into the class pool.
2. An instance of the class is created in the instance pool.
3. An entry is made into the global memory area of the application that points to the instance. This is what is checked when you directly open a window to see if it is already instantiated.
4. The `w_sheet` class definition is loaded into the class pool.
5. An instance of `w_sheet` is created in the instance pool.
6. The local variable `wInstance` now points to the instance just created.
7. Another instance of `w_sheet` is created in the instance pool.
8. The local variable `wInstance2` points to this instance.

This can be seen more easily in Figure 6.2, which shows the two pools and two memory areas.

During the second run of the same script, a slightly different set of operations takes place:

1. The `w_about` class is already loaded and there is a global memory pointer to an instance of the class, so nothing further is done for the `Open( w_about)` statement.
2. An instance of `w_sheet` is created in the instance pool.
3. The local variable `wInstance` now points to the instance just created.
4. Another instance of `w_sheet` is created in the instance pool.
5. The local variable `wInstance2` points to this instance.

This can be seen more easily in Figure 6.3, which shows the final state of the two pools and two memory areas.

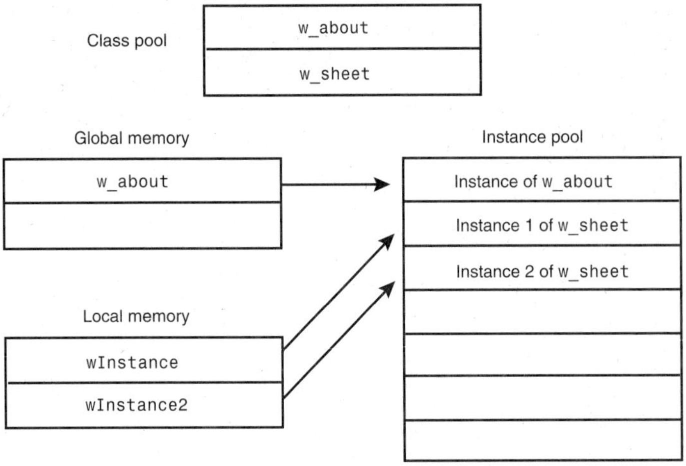

FIGURE 6.2.
The first run of a script.

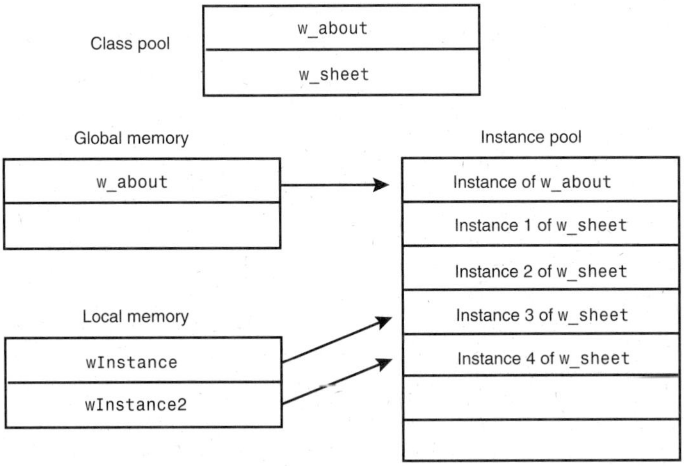

FIGURE 6.3.
The second run of the script.

This mechanism for creating class instances is an important concept to grasp and will allow you to anticipate heavy-use class hierarchies that you might want to preload at the start of the application.

NOTE

PowerBuilder handles DataWindows in a completely different manner. This is because DataWindow objects do not have associated scripts, object references, and so on. During runtime execution, DataWindows are managed by a DataWindow engine that handles all service requests. The engine creates a template of what the DataWindow will look like, an instance of the DataWindow, and a Windows manifestation. If another instance of a DataWindow is requested, the engine creates another template, instance, and Windows manifestation. Storage for these templates and instances is managed on an as-needed basis and not by using the pools previously discussed.

Variables

You define variables for use within your scripts, and they are made up of a type, a scope, a data type, and an initial value. Variables can be declared using a simple data type (for example, string, integer), as an object (for example, window, `w_about`, `cb_connect`), or as a structure (for example, `Message`, `s_my_vals`). In the next sections you will see the different scopes at which you can declare variables, and you'll learn what access restrictions can be placed on them.

Object Access Levels

Object-level variables and functions can have their accessibility restricted to allow you to build more encapsulated objects. There are three settings: `Public`, `Protected`, and `Private`, in descending order of accessibility. Instance variables for an object can use these keywords in their declaration. If no access is specified, `Public` is the default, but you will usually include a `Public` section to make your intentions clear for other developers. Here's an example:

```
Public:
   Integer i_nCount
Protected:
   String i_szTitle
Private:
   Time i_tNow
```

The object-level function declaration window provides a drop-down list with the three access levels; `Public` is the default value.

The `Public` access level allows the function or variable to be used and changed from anywhere in an application. All global functions and variables are at the `Public` access level, and this cannot be changed; in fact, it does not make much sense to even try.

`Protected` variables and functions can only be used within the class that declared them and any of its descendants. No access is allowed from outside the class.

The highest level of restriction is `Private`. Only scripts in the class that declares the function or variable can access them. Access from outside the class, including all of its descendants, is *not* allowed.

When you are creating highly encapsulated objects, you will make the most use of the `Private` and `Protected` levels and provide access to certain of the variables through `Public` access–level functions. These allow you to completely control any modifications to a variable (for example, to disallow certain values or trigger particular processing if the variable is set to a certain value).

NEW in 5 PowerBuilder

PowerBuilder 5.0 has introduced an additional four access levels that can be used only with instance variables: `ProtectedRead`, `PrivateRead`, `ProtectedWrite`, and `PrivateWrite`. These are used to optionally control the read and write access for variables.

To further restrict which scripts can read a variable's value, you use the `ProtectedRead` and `PrivateRead` keywords. With `ProtectedRead`, only scripts for the object that the variable is declared in and any descendant objects can read the variable. For `PrivateRead`, only the object that declared the variable can read from it. These access levels mesh with the overall access levels in the following manner:

- If the variable's scope is `Public`, either `ProtectedRead` or `PrivateRead` can be used.
- If the variable's scope is `Protected`, only `PrivateRead` can be used. The variable is already implicitly `ProtectedRead`.
- If the variable's scope is `Private`, neither can be used. The variable is already implicitly `PrivateRead`.

If the read access of a variable is not defined, any script in the variable's scope can read its value.

The write access of a variable can also be further restricted using the `ProtectedWrite` and `PrivateWrite` keywords. With `ProtectedWrite`, only scripts for the object that the variable is declared in and any descendant objects can change the value of the variable. For `PrivateWrite`, only the object that declared the variable can change its value. As with the read restrictions, these access levels also mesh with the overall access levels in the following manner:

- If the variable's scope is `Public`, either `ProtectedWrite` or `PrivateWrite` can be used.
- If the variable's scope is `Protected`, only `PrivateWrite` can be used. The variable is already implicitly `ProtectedWrite`.
- If the variable's scope is `Private`, neither can be used. The variable is already implicitly `PrivateRead`.

If the write access of a variable is not defined, any script in the variable's scope can change its value.

Variable Scope

A variable can de defined to have one of four different scopes. The scope dictates how the variable must be accessed, when it can be accessed, and which variable takes precedence if it is declared within different scopes. The scopes are global, shared, instance, and local.

Global Variables

Global variables are defined to be accessible applicationwide and are stored in the actual application object. As you would with any other programming language, you should keep the number of global variables to a minimum because anywhere in any script a variable could be modified, which would make debugging a trickier proposition. The variables also use a piece of memory for the duration of the application's execution. Global variables are initialized when the application is first opened.

NOTE

New in PowerBuilder 5

For those developers that have not decided on naming conventions for the scope of their variables and run into a situation where they have a local variable declared with the same name as a global variable, PowerBuilder 5.0 provides an easy way to use both. To refer to a global variable that is "hidden" by a local or shared variable, prefix the variable name with the global scope operator (::).

Instance Variables

Instance variables are defined in an object (application, window, user object, or menu) and are therefore directly accessible anywhere within that object. They are also available, depending on the access level, to outside objects by using the dot notation. Instance variables effectively become attributes of the object on which they are defined, and are initialized when the object is created by the application. When the object is destroyed, the instance variables are destroyed along with it.

The value of an instance variable is not shared between two instances of the same class.

NOTE

Remember that multiple occurrences of the same window are called *instances* of the window and this should not be confused with instance variables.

Shared Variables

Shared variables are also defined in the same type of objects as instance variables. However, shared variables are associated with the actual class definition and not with the object instances. This means that all instances of the same class share the same variable.

Shared variables always have a `Private` access level that cannot be changed because they can only be accessed in the class in which they are defined.

The variable is initialized the first time an object of that class is created. When you then destroy the object, the shared variable retains the last value it was set to, so that when you create another instance of the object, the shared variable will again hold the last value it was set to. If you have multiple instances of the same object created at the same time, they all access the same variable.

TIP

You can use the persistence property of shared variables to hold on to information between different creations of the same window. For example, you have a pop-up window that displays some status information for another window. In the `Open` event of the pop-up set the window's `X` and `Y` attributes to the values of two shared variables. Then in the `Close` event of the pop-up save the current `X` and `Y` attributes of the window to these variables. Once you have initialized the shared variables to some starting position, the window will remember where it was last positioned for the duration of the application's run. You should remember that the memory used by shared variables remains until the application closes, so you should carefully consider how you use them.

Local Variables

Local variables are those that are defined at the script level. They can be used only within that script and are destroyed at the end of the script. Local variables are used as a scratch pad for holding intermediate data values.

Order of Precedence

If during the execution of a script PowerBuilder finds an unqualified reference to a variable, it searches for the location of the variable using the following search order:

- Local variables
- Shared variables
- Global variables
- Instance variables

If PowerBuilder cannot find the variable at any of these levels, it searches up the object's inheritance chain, looking at the instance variables.

Controlling Variable Access

An as-yet unsupported feature that is available in both PowerBuilder 4.0 and 5.0 is the ability to provide get and set functions for an instance-level variable. This allows you to control any direct access that is made to the variable through `get` and `set` functions, without forcing the developer to explicitly use these functions.

For example, the class object `uo_order_nos` provides a variable `nCounter` that will be publicly accessible. In PowerBuilder you have two ways to achieve this:

- You can declare a public variable that can be read from and written to without any control.
- You can declare the variable as private and then provide a `get` function and a `set` function that the developer must use in order to access the variables value.

The second mechanism is the one that all object-oriented purists insist be used because it provides a means to control access and modifications to the variable.

Using the `Indirect` syntax, you now have a third mechanism to use. This is the current syntax for this:

```
Indirect DataType PropertyName{ SetFunction( *value), GetFunction()}
```

`DataType` is the actual data type of the property you want to create. *`PropertyName`* is the name that external scripts will reference. *`SetFunction`* and *`GetFunction`* are the names of the methods you will supply that PowerBuilder will use whenever an external script attempts to read from or write to the property.

As the syntax suggests, all we are doing is a bit of trickery and redirecting references to one thing through some access functions to the real object. The previous syntax is declared as `Public` and the actual variable is declared as `Private`. To illustrate this better, let's explore the actual syntax required to make this work.

Consider the string property *`szOrderNo`*, which holds specific information for a particular class user object that you want to control access to. The following code would be placed in the `Declare Instance Variables` section of the class user object:

```
Public:

   Indirect String szOrderNo{ set_orderno( *value), get_orderno()}

Private:

   String i_szOrderNo
```

This declares the actual variable, `i_szOrderNo`, and the publicly accessible property, `szOrderNo`. The final step is to provide the two object-level functions specified.

This would be the code for the set function `set_orderno()`:

```
i_szOrderNo = a_szValue
```

`szValue` is a string argument defined for the function.

This would be the code for the get function `get_orderno()`:

```
Return i_szOrderNo
```

You can add as many additional checks and restrictions as you want to in these two functions. Just remember that these will be called *every* time that particular property is accessed.

You can use this syntax anywhere that you can define an instance scope variable. It makes less sense in anything other than a class user object because the controls in other objects (for example, a window) can still access a private scope variable.

NOTE

Support for this syntax varies from one version of PowerBuilder to another. For example, the use of such a variable in a `Choose...Case` statement will cause a GPF in PowerBuilder 4.0. PowerBuilder 4.0 will also prevent you from compiling a script if you try to use the variable in, for example, a call to the `MessageBox()` function. Both of these cases work without a problem in PowerBuilder 5.0.

It is a good bet that the syntax will remain close in future releases of PowerBuilder that do support this functionality. This is because the proxy objects used in distributed PowerBuilder make use of this syntax. Powersoft would have to migrate any existing proxy objects if they were to change the syntax.

WARNING

Remember that this is unsupported syntax and Powersoft will provide any technical support on problems you might encounter due to it. Powersoft also reserves the right to change the syntax and availability of this syntax at any time. You have been warned.

Constants

The ability to declare constants has finally been introduced into PowerBuilder Version 5.0. Any variable declaration that can be given an initial value in its declaration can be turned into a constant with the addition of the keyword `Constant`. You *cannot* modify the value of a constant after its declaration. Here's an example:

```
Constant Integer ORDER_HEADER = 1
```

Then within all your scripts you can use these constants without having to remember which value meant what. As you can see in the following example, your code becomes a great deal more readable, and because you declare the constant in one place, maintaining the value of the constant is simple:

```
If i_nArea = ORDER_HEADER Then
   i_nArea = PRINTING
End If
```

The new PowerBuilder 5.0 constants eliminate the overhead associated with the pseudo constants that developers have used in previous versions, either using global variables or class user objects. The value of the constant is substituted at compile time wherever the constant is referenced.

Constants will also correctly state their access properties within the Object Browser—that the object is readable but not writeable.

WARNING

You cannot make multiple declarations on one line. For example, the following one-line declaration only declares one constant, `ORDER_HEADER`. Both `CUSTOMER_DIMENSIONS` and `PRINTING` are declared as normal integers and can be modified:

```
Constant Integer ORDER_HEADER = 1, CUSTOMER_DIMENSIONS = 2, PRINTING = 3
```

You have to split them into single-line declarations:

```
Constant Integer ORDER_HEADER = 1
Constant Integer CUSTOMER_DIMENSIONS = 2
Constant Integer PRINTING = 3
```

Functions

You use PowerScript to write global and object-level functions, and these will make use of a number of the statements and system functions provided by PowerBuilder. See Chapter 7, "The PowerScript Environment," for the how-to of constructing functions.

As you would expect with a major release of PowerBuilder, there are some new functions available. The majority of the functions, for example registry access functions, are covered in the chapters to which they are relevant. Some of the functions are general purpose and are introduced here.

Handle()

The `Handle()` system function has now been removed; more accurately, it's been moved to be a method for the `GraphicObject` super class. This makes the function available for all visual objects, such as windows and single-line edits, and makes more architectural sense with the class hierarchy.

IsArabic() and IsHebrew()

The `IsArabic()` and `IsHebrew()` system functions are part of the International Support that is being introduced with PowerBuilder 5.0 and indicate which language is being used by the operating system.

GetParent()

The `GetParent()` is used to acquire the parent of a specified object and can be used against any visual object (`PowerObject` class descendant). The syntax is

```
ObjectName.GetParent()
```

where `ObjectName` indicates the window, user object, or menu item of which you want the parent object to be. The function returns a value of type `PowerObject`. Often you will simply use `Parent` and `ParentWindow` to access the immediate parent object. However, sometimes you will need to traverse the parent chain to access the overall parent and its attributes.

NOTE

You might think the return type of `PowerObject` is a little strange when dealing with only visual objects, and that a return type of `GraphicObject` would make more sense. The function was implemented this way because of inheritance constraints encountered by Powersoft.

For example, a control in a tab page that is itself a child of a tab control would need to execute a call to `GetParent()` to obtain the tab control:

```
// Event script within the control sitting in the tab page
Tab tTab

tTab = Parent.GetParent()
tTab.SelectTab( 1)
```

TIP

You do not need to check the return value of the `GetParent()` function because every object has a parent of one kind or another (even if it's the Windows desktop).

Reverse()

NEW in PowerBuilder 5

The `Reverse()` function is an addition to the string manipulation functions and provides the ability to reverse a string. Here's an example:

```
String szTest = "George"

szTest = Reverse( szTest)
// Now szTest contains "egroeG"
```

This function and `IsHebrew()` and `IsArabic()` constitute the new functions for use with internationally sensitive applications.

Function Search Chain

When you call your PowerScript a function that is not qualified with an object name, PowerBuilder searches for the function in the following order:

1. Global external function
2. Global function object
3. Local external function
4. Object level function
5. System function

As you can see from this search chain, you can override PowerBuilder's system functions with your own. Obviously, to speed up the execution of your function calls you should qualify, where possible, with the object name. It is interesting to note that global functions will be executed faster (for unqualified function calls) than object-level functions, although you might expect the reverse.

The `Message` Object

The basis of Microsoft's Windows system, and other GUI environments, is the capture and reaction to events, either system or user.

A majority of the Windows messages are mapped to PowerBuilder events, but there is occasionally a message that needs to be trapped that isn't mapped. The `Message` object is used to determine the message ID and optional parameters. This code is usually placed in a special event found in objects called the `Other` event. You should use the `Other` event carefully, though, because it adversely affects performance by sending *every* unmapped message to that event!

The `Message` object can also be used to pass additional parameters on the open or close of a window, using the `OpenWithParm()`, `OpenSheetWithParm()`, `OpenUserObjectWithParm()`, or `CloseWithReturn()` functions.

The `TriggerEvent()` and `PostEvent()` functions both take optional parameters that are stored in the `Message` object (these are introduced in the "Events" section).

The `Message` object has nine attributes: The first four directly map to the Microsoft message structure, the next three are used to pass PowerBuilder data type parameters during an open or close of a window, and the last two communicate to PowerBuilder that the event was handled. Table 6.9. lists the attributes.

Table 6.9. The `Message` object attributes.

Attribute	*Data Type*	*Description*
`Handle`	Integer	The control/window handle
`Number`	Integer	The (MS Windows) event ID
`WordParm`	UnsignedInt	The word parameter
`LongParm`	Long	The long parameter
`DoubleParm`	Double	A number or numeric variable
`StringParm`	String	A string or string variable
`PowerObjectParm`	PowerObject	Any PowerBuilder object
`ProxyName`	String	Part of a distributed application
`Processed`	Boolean	Part of the script to indicate that the event was processed
`ReturnValue`	Long	The value to return to Windows if it is processed

If the `Processed` attribute is not set to `TRUE`, default Windows event processes will be executed.

To find the appropriate Windows message ID, you either need to consult a Windows API book or have a copy of a Windows C/C++ compiler that provides a copy of windows.h. The code required to trap a Windows message in the `Other` event is straightforward as long as you have the correct message ID (and have converted it from hexadecimal to decimal if the value is taken from windows.h).

For example, to detect when the application goes into an idle state, you would place the following script in the `Other` event:

```
If Message.Number = 289 Then
   // WM_ENTERIDLE 0x0121
   // Do some processing
   Message.Processed = TRUE
End If
```

You could use the new PowerBuilder 5.0 constant feature in the comparison to make it more readable and eliminate the need for the comment.

Events

Events are triggered when actions are performed against an object. The script that you write for an event determines what processing will take place in response. PowerBuilder provides a number of default event handlers for the more commonly called events. For example, when you open a window, PowerBuilder handles the creation and screen painting of all the window's controls. An event originates either from the user performing an action or because of the execution of a

PowerScript statement. Events caused by PowerScript statements can occur at one of two times: either immediately or when a request is placed in the Windows event queue that will be executed after the current processing is complete.

You can also use events to allow objects to be loosely coupled with other objects. This means that you can attempt to execute events that an object might have without causing an error if they don't exist; this allows you to generalize code, thus making it more reusable.

As you already know, some PowerScript statements, such as `MessageBox()` and `this.X = 1200`, will cause events to be triggered. These are always processed before anything further in the processing queue will take place. To directly control the origination of events, you use the two PowerBuilder functions `TriggerEvent()` and `PostEvent()`. Both of these functions can be used to originate events in an application object, providing that it has at least one open window; otherwise, there is no event queue to post to.

The event types in PowerBuilder 4.0 are

- Predefined object events that are already mapped to `pbm_ event` IDs
- User-definable object events that you map to `pbm_ event` IDs
- Custom object events that you map with the `pbm_custom` IDs

PowerBuilder 5.0 has these event types as well as an additional type:

New in PowerBuilder 5

- Custom object events that have multiple parameters and a definable return type

The first two types of events have also changed slightly in PowerBuilder 5.0, because the relevant parameters for the event are now made available instead of just `WordParm` and `LongParm`. The custom object events (`pbm_custom`) still provide only the `WordParm` and `LongParm` parameters.

In the next sections you'll see how to call each of the types. Remember that the first three are still triggered the same way they were in PowerBuilder 4.0, only the new type requires a different syntax.

TriggerEvent()

When you require an event to be executed before continuing with the remainder of a script, you need to use the `TriggerEvent()` function. This function bypasses the object's current event queue and processes the event immediately. The syntax for this function is

```
ObjectName.TriggerEvent( Event {, WordParm, LongParm })
```

`Event` can be either a string that identifies a user event or a value of the `TrigEvent` enumerated data type. The optional *`WordParm`* and *`LongParm`* are both of the Long data type and used to pass values to events. The data type has changed from PowerBuilder 3.0 for cross-platform compatibility. These two values are stored in the `Message` object's `WordParm` and `LongParm` attributes, and can be retrieved in the event triggered.

The `LongParm` parameter can also be used to pass a single string value to the event. Within the triggered event this string can be retrieved by using the `String()` function. For example, in the calling event the code might be

```
cb_ok.TriggerEvent( Clicked!, 0, "DO IT")
```

> **NOTE**
>
> For some reason, in PowerBuilder 4.0 the `Event` parameter cannot be specified of enumerated type `TrigEvent` and must be a string if you specify the additional parameters. This has now been fixed in PowerBuilder 5.0 with additional overloaded `TriggerEvent()` and `PostEvent()` functions, and the previous example will work.

The `Clicked` event for the object `cb_ok` command button would then include the following code:

```
string szStringPassed

szStringPassed = String( Message.LongParm, "address")
// Other event code
```

> **WARNING**
>
> If you are going to use these two parameters, you should retrieve them from the `Message` object at the earliest opportunity in the triggered event. This is because the `Message` object is used continuously by PowerBuilder in the processing of events, and the contents may have changed if you take your time getting to them.

If you want to use the `LongParm` parameter you need to remember that both parameters are required, and therefore you must set `WordParm` to a value, usually `0`.

The `TriggerEvent()` function returns `1` if it is successful and the event script is run and `-1` if the event is not a valid event for `ObjectName`, or if no script exists for that event. This obviously keeps you from returning any information directly using `TriggerEvent()`. The attributes of `Message` cannot be used to return information from the called event, because they are cleared out at the end of that event's script processing.

> **NOTE**
>
> You can extend the standard `Message` object using your own user object to include some additional fields that do allow you to return information. See Chapter 24, "Building User Objects," for more information.

PostEvent()

To cause the origination of an event after all the currently queued events have completed, you use the `PostEvent()` function. The `TriggerEvent()` function causes the desired event to be executed synchronously with the calling script, but `PostEvent()` is used to cause the event to be processed asynchronously. This causes posted events to be processed in the order in which they are posted. The syntax for this function is

```
ObjectName.PostEvent( Event {, WordParm, LongParm } )
```

The parameters are the same as for the `TriggerEvent()` function.

The fact that the events happen in the order in which they are issued can lead to some strange happenings when you have posted some events and also caused others to be triggered. The triggered events will occur before the posted ones. You are not guaranteed of the order in which the event will be processed when you post it. For example, a posted event earlier in the queue may cause additional events to be triggered, and this may cause some unexpected side effects.

New Method Calling Syntax

NEW in 5 PowerBuilder

For PowerBuilder 5.0 a new syntax has been introduced to combine the PowerScript statements required to access both functions and events (in other words the *methods* of an object). This has also allowed Powersoft the means to more elegantly support parameters for events, rather than trying to extend the existing `TriggerEvent()` and `PostEvent()` functions. Powersoft did not stop at just adding the parameterized event mechanism, but also allows dynamic binding and the ability to post functions. This is the new method syntax:

```
[Trigger ¦ Post] [Static ¦ Dynamic] [Function ¦ Event] MethodName( [Arguments])
```

NOTE

The keywords `Trigger`, `Static`, and `Function` are the defaults for this syntax, but you are advised to explicitly state `Trigger` and `Function` in order to make your code more readable.

The only keywords you will be unfamiliar with are `Static` and `Dynamic`. The `Dynamic` keyword allows you to write a call for a method that might not currently exist, but will be available at runtime. PowerBuilder does a runtime search for the function, and will produce an error if it is unable to locate it. For example, if you have a base class user object but only define certain methods in descendant class objects, you would use the `Dynamic` keyword:

```
// uo_1 is an ancestor class object that does not have a uf_calculate() function
// This script can be called with either uo_2 or uo_3, both are descendants
// and do have a uf_calculate() function.
uo_1 unObject
```

```
Integer nValue

unObject = Create Using a_szObjectClass

nValue = unObject.Dynamic uf_calculate()
```

You would receive a compilation error in the PowerScript editor if you did not use the `Dynamic` keyword. This is because the data type of `unObject` is `uo_1`, which does not have a `uf_calculate()` function. However, the class that `unObject` will be at runtime does have this function.

The keywords can appear in any order, and this is the calling syntax for dot notation calls:

```
ObjectName.[ Keywords] MethodName( [Arguments])
```

In this case `Keywords` is a combination of `Trigger`, `Static`, and so on.

The `Trigger` Event and `Trigger` Function

To call parameterized methods in a synchronous manner you are required to use the following syntax:

```
ObjectName.Trigger Event EventName( {Parameter1, Parameter2, ..})
```

`EventName` is the name that was specified in the Events dialog box of the object *`ObjectName`*. Notice the spacing between `Trigger`, `Event`, and *`EventName`*. These commands must be separated from each other or PowerBuilder will misinterpret the line as an invalid attribute of the object.

As an example of the new syntax, consider triggering an event on a single-line edit field, `ValidateItem`, that expects two strings. The event script takes these two values, compares them with the value in its `Text` attribute, and returns a Boolean response. The code in the `ValidateItem` event would be

```
// Where a_szValue1 and a_szValue2 are the parameters defined for the event.
If this.text = a_szValue1 Or this.text = a_szValue2 Then
   Return TRUE
End If

Return FALSE
```

The calling script would look like this:

```
Boolean bReturn

bReturn = sle_order_no.Trigger Event ValidateItem( "1059", "1050")

If bReturn Then
   // Acceptance processing
Else
   // Some other processing
End If
```

As you can see from the two scripts, it looks as though you have suddenly gained a whole lot of programming power. That's not completely so in this case. The event call is tightly coupled;

this means that the event `ValidateItem` must exist in the object `sle_order_no` and must take two parameters. In this case, the event is actually little more than a normal function. You will actually get a compilation error `C0051: Unknown function name:` if you try to call the `ValidateItem` event for an object that does not have it defined.

NOTE

With the introduction of event parameters, you may get informational messages indicating that parameters are now hiding a global, a shared, or an instance variable. That is why it is a good idea to use variable-scope prefixes. In the previous example, event arguments are prefixed with `a_`.

As you can see, the area between object-level functions and the object's events is blurred in PowerBuilder 5.0. Which method, function, or event you use to implement a given piece of functionality is left to your own preference. These are the key differences between events and functions:

- Calling a nonexistent function at runtime produces an error; calling a nonexistent event simply yields a return value of `-1`.
- Events can extend ancestor processing. Functions override their ancestors processing (although you can call the ancestor using the `Super` keyword).
- Events have public accessibility that cannot be changed. Object-level functions have a definable access level.

NOTE

It is up to 30 percent faster to run a simple 5,000- and 10,000-iteration loop to call the same functionality in an event than in a function. This is true even with a fully qualified function call.

NEW in PowerBuilder 5

The same syntax for triggering a parameterized event can also be used to trigger functions; the only benefit to this that we have found is a slight performance gain (the 10,000-iteration loop takes 9 seconds rather than 10 seconds). The syntax is

```
ObjectName.Trigger Function FunctionName( {Parameter1, Parameter2, ..})
```

You might be asking yourself What use is a parameterized event to me? The speed gain is worth it, even if it's not always measurable, but the real benefit comes with the ability to post this event into the message queue for later processing. You'll learn more about this in the next section. Probably the best feature of parameterized events is the encapsulation they allow you to achieve with objects. Instead of having to declare a window function to carry out some processing, you can now collect this with the object that it affects or uses.

> **NOTE**
>
> If you are using a parameterized event that is inherited, each level of the event uses the initial value of the arguments. Modifications to a parameter you make in a level are *not* reflected at the other levels of the inheritance chain for the event.

The `Post` Event and `Post` Function

PowerBuilder 5.0 provides a new syntax that mirrors the `PostEvent()` function and allows posting parameterized events (and even functions) to the event queue for asynchronous execution:

```
ObjectName.Post Event EventName( {Parameter1, Parameter2, ..})
```

The parameters are the same as for `Trigger Event`, and the syntax is identical except for the keyword change from `Trigger` to `Post`. Again, the event call is tightly coupled to the object that you are posting to.

The blurring between object-level functions and the object's events continues with the ability to now post functions into the processing queue. This is done using the syntax

```
ObjectName.Post Function FunctionName( {Parameter1, Parameter2, ..})
```

The only restrictions on posting both events and functions is that they *cannot* return a value; in fact, PowerBuilder will not allow you to compile the script containing such a call.

Chaining Calls

This syntax can be extended even further by chaining together multiple calls using the dot notation. The return value of the function or event becomes the object for the next call, and so on. Each call must return an object, except the last, which can return anything. This is the syntax:

```
Function1ReturnsObject().Function2ReturnsObject().Function3ReturnsAnything()
```

The following conditions and restrictions apply to the keywords:

- A posted method must be the last method in a chain of calls.
- You cannot assign the returned value of a posted method call or pass it as an argument.
- If you post an object function that is not available at runtime you will get a runtime error.
- The `DYNAMIC` keyword can only be used with functions.

- You must use the REF keyword before any argument that is passed by reference in a call using DYNAMIC.
- The DYNAMIC keyword can only be specified once in a statement, and carries over additional calls.

As you might imagine, you can concoct some pretty hairy calling sequences, and you should fully comment what a chained call is meant to be doing. You should also note that since you have chained calls together, you cannot test for the failure of a single call before attempting the next. If you need to (and it is usually a good idea to), check the return value of a call. Before making further calls, you should break the statement into its constituent pieces.

To illustrate the new syntax, here are some examples together with comments of what each call is achieving:

```
// Posting a call to a global function
Post f_calculate_weight( rTarePercent, nQuantity)
//
// Making a call to a dynamic function of a user object
uo_bag_calcs.Dynamic uf_bag_width( Ref rWidth, nLength, szProductCode)
//
// Assigning a variable to the return of a chained call
nLength = uo_bag_calcs.uf_return_bag( szProductCode).uf_bag_length()
```

Send()

There are two additional ways to send event messages to objects. These make use of the `Send()` and `Post()` functions. You will want to use these two functions if you wish to originate an event for an object that PowerBuilder does not have direct control over (for example, another Windows application or an external user object).

The syntax for the `Send()` function, which is comparable to the `TriggerEvent()` function in its execution, is

```
Send( Handle, Message#, WordParm, LongParm)
```

The *Handle* parameter is the Windows handle to the object that you want to send a message to. The message ID is passed in the *Message#* parameter as an unsigned integer. The *WordParm* and *LongParm* parameters are used in the same manner as for the `TriggerEvent()` and `PostEvent()` functions.

For example, if you wanted to change the text of a window, in this case controlled by PowerBuilder, the code would be

```
Send( Handle( w_frame), 12, 0, "This is the new window title")
```

To change the title of a window that is outside PowerBuilder, you first need to acquire its Windows handle using the Windows `FindWindow()` API function. For this example, we can alter an open Windows calculator window title using the following code:

```
uInt hWnd
hWnd = FindWindow( "scicalc", "calculator")
Send( hWnd, 12, 0, "This is the new window title")
```

Post()

The corresponding function to `PostEvent()` is the `Post()` function. The syntax is

`Post( `*`Handle`*`, `*`Message#`*`, `*`WordParm`*`, `*`LongParm`*`)`

The parameters are the same as for the previous functions.

Pronouns

In PowerBuilder there are four *pronouns*. These four reserved words (`This`, `Parent`, `ParentWindow`, and `Super`) have a special meaning that depends on where they are used. Pronouns are used extensively when building objects for inheritance or that are encapsulated (which is the aim of every object). Just like in English, pronouns are used to provide a generic reference to an object, and in PowerBuilder they make your code more reusable.

This

The pronoun `This` is used in PowerScript to generically reference the object for which the script is written. This enables you to write code without tying the script to a specific object name. For example, `this.width = this.width * 2` has the same functionality as `cb_delete_row.width = cb_delete_row.width * 2`, except that if the button is renamed, the first piece of code would still work, but the second would require updating to the new button name.

`This` should be used in place of all object self-references, usually attribute access, within the object's scripts. The pronoun can also be used in function call arguments in place of the object's name, as long as the argument is not being passed by reference (although you can pass it as a `ReadOnly` argument). For example, the following code sample calls a window function for the object `w_frame` and passes itself as an argument:

```
w_frame.RegisterMe( this)
```

> **NOTE**
>
> Most objects have a reference passed by value when the argument type is by value. The exceptions to this are structures and auto-instantiating objects, which have their contents passed by value. If an object is passed by reference, this is a reference to the passing variable.

Parent

Nearly every object in PowerBuilder, and for that matter in Windows itself, has a parent. To reference an object's owner, the `Parent` reserved word is used. The meaning of `Parent` changes depending on where it is used: in an object on a window, in an object in a custom user object, or in a menu item.

When used in a window control, `Parent` refers to the window. The most common use is in a Close button, where it is used to make the code generic. The following two examples are functionally the same, but the first is generic and makes the object a good candidate for reuse:

```
Close( Parent)
Close( w_script_window )
```

Inside a custom user object, any control that uses `Parent` is in fact referencing the user object itself, not the window on which the user object is placed. This permits controls in the user object to make changes to the parent. The user object's name will most likely be different on each window on which it's placed. In order to access the user object's parent object, you can use the new `GetParent()` function. You may have to make successive calls until you reach either the window or user object you want. Of course, this will only allow you access to the attributes and methods that are defined for the `PowerObject` class. Sometimes you might want to restrict the kind of object your user object can be placed on and set this instance variable to the appropriate class data type.

When used within a menu item, `Parent` references the menu item on the next level up. The parent depends on the level of cascading. (See Chapter 12, "Menus and the Menu Painter," for a discussion on menu item cascading.)

ParentWindow

The reserved word `ParentWindow` is used only in menus. `ParentWindow` is used to refer to the window to which the menu is attached and can be used anywhere in the menu. For example, under the menu item `m_close` the code might be

```
Close( ParentWindow)
```

`ParentWindow` refers to the window the menu is assigned to at runtime, and although this does not preclude the hard coding of a specific window name, a single menu might be associated with multiple windows. This is especially true when you're coding an MDI application, because most sheets usually share a single menu.

Super

The `Super` pronoun is used only when dealing with inheritance, and is used to refer to the ancestor from a descendant object. The name of the ancestor object can be explicitly stated, but is more commonly (and more clearly) referred to in generic terms as `Super`.

`Super` can be used with the `CALL` statement to cause execution of ancestor events from a descendant object. The syntax for `CALL` is

```
CALL AncestorObject {'ControlName}::Event
```

`AncestorObject` is the ancestor object of the descendant, and you can replace it with the `Super` keyword. The optional *`ControlName`* specifies the name of the control in an ancestor window or custom user object of which you want to trigger the event specified by *`Event`*. In this case, *`AncestorObject`* needs to specify a window or user object. Here's an example:

```
CALL super::Show
```

It also can be used directly to access an ancestor function that has been overridden by the descendant:

```
Super::wf_function()
```

PowerBuilder Version 4.0 restricts the accessibility of ancestor scripts from previous versions, so only the ancestor of the current object can be referenced. The following code has been made illegal in PowerBuilder 5.0, and the Script painter will produce a compilation error. For example, the following code inside the `cb_open` command button to trigger another button's `Clicked` event is now illegal:

```
CALL cb_close'::Clicked
```

To produce the same functionality, a user event needs to be added to the object `cb_close`, which then calls its own ancestor script. This user event can then be triggered by other controls or objects.

By using the `CALL` statement you can cause the execution of the ancestor script anywhere in your descendant script. Execution of the descendant will then continue after the ancestor script has finished. This allows you to carry out descendant processing before allowing the ancestor script to execute. Unfortunately, you do not have access to the local variables in the ancestor script and you will have to make use of larger scope variables to pass information backward and forward.

Statements

PowerScript provides a number of statements that range from control-of-flow through halting the application. The following sections detail the more complex of these; it is assumed that you are familiar with basic coding concepts and syntax.

Choose...Case

We wanted to include this flow-of-control statement so that we could describe a particular style of use that not many people seem to be aware of and that has some practical application.

The following is an example of a Choose...Case control structure that uses a Boolean test to check whether a certain key was pressed:

```
Choose Case TRUE
   Case KeyDown( KeyPageUp!)
      wf_SynchPageUp()
   Case KeyDown( KeyPageDown!)
      wf_SynchPageDown()
   Case KeyDown( KeyUpArrow!)
      wf_SynchUpArrow()
   Case KeyDown( KeyDownArrow!)
      wf_SynchDownArrow()
End Choose
```

Create and Destroy

You use the Create statement to generate an instance of an object class. The only classes you need to use this statement for are nonvisual user objects, such as the standard classes (for example, Transaction and Error) or for pop-up menus. Visual user objects and windows should be created using the appropriate Open() functions. You must instantiate an object variable using the Create statement before you can make any access to the object's attributes or methods. For example, to create a local version of the Error object, the code is

```
Error eMyError

eMyError = Create Error
eMyError.Line = 1
```

The object variable is eMyError and the object class is Error.

When you use the Create statement, PowerBuilder allocates memory for the object; this memory remains in use until it is freed using the Destroy statement. For example, at the end of the script started in the previous example, the code required is

```
Destroy eMyError
```

Creating Objects Dynamically

In previous versions of PowerBuilder you could use the Create statement to dynamically create user objects. You were, however, limited to creating objects of a stated type. Here's an example:

```
u_n_application g_App

g_App = Create u_n_application
```

This has been extended in PowerBuilder 5.0 to allow the object type to be defined using an expression. This is the syntax:

NEW in 5 PowerBuilder

```
ObjectVariable = Create Using Expression
```

This allows you to make the decision of what object to create at runtime, and the value of *Expression* can be one of the following:

- A String variable
- An Any variable containing a String
- A function that returns a String
- A function that returns an Any (which must be a String at runtime)

You will want to declare the data type of *ObjectVariable* to be some base class that you can make generic calls on based on the expected values of *Expression*.

For example, to dynamically create a database connection, perform an operation, and then close the connection without regard for which DBMS is being used you could code it this way:

```
u_n_transaction unTran

unTran = Create Using a_szTransactionClass

unTran.MakeConnection()

unTran.BeginTran()

If unTran.ProcessValues() Then
   unTran.CommitTran()
Else
   unTran.RollbackTran()
End If

unTran.CloseConnection()

Destroy unTran
```

All the methods used will be declared in the base class `u_n_transaction` as virtual functions and then overridden and defined within each descendant class (for example, in `u_n_sqlserver_transaction`). The descendant class is what would be passed in the argument `a_szTransactionClass`. For example, if the preceding code were written as a function, you would call it using this:

```
f_special_database_process( "u_n_sqlserver_transaction")
```

WARNING

If you use either of the CREATE statements you must remember to pair that call with a DESTROY. This will release the resources used by the object. PowerBuilder will not do this for you, and you have to be responsible for any objects that you create. This does not apply to user objects that are set up to be auto-instantiating (see Chapter 23, "The User Object Painter").

HALT and Return

The HALT statement is used to immediately terminate an application. You can optionally use the keyword CLOSE with HALT to cause the Close event of the application object to be executed before finishing. The normal use for this statement is to stop an application after a serious error that cannot be recovered from or after a security violation occurs (for example, on a login screen).

The Return statement halts the current execution of a script as if the script had completed, so that the application either waits for further user interaction or returns to the calling script. This statement is used in functions to send a value back to a calling script.

Placement of Script

To get full use of object-oriented programming, you should code your objects with complete encapsulation as your goal. Is this always feasible or desired? Sometimes it's not, so what you must decide on, along with your naming conventions and other standards, is the placement of script.

Some developers will code everything into a window's events or functions and call these from within the other controls on the window.

What we have tended to do is code object-specific functionality in the object itself and then place the actual business and calculation processes in window functions since the window is usually considered a business function in its own right. With parameterized events this can, in some places, be moved back to the object level rather than being defined at the window level.

The remaining sections explore some specific areas of the PowerBuilder scripting environment.

PowerBuilder Units

All sizes in PowerBuilder are measured in PowerBuilder units, or PBUs. The only exceptions to this are the Window and DataWindow painter grid sizes, which are measured in pixels.

Why does Powersoft do this? Simply so your application looks similar running on a VGA, an EGA, or an SVGA monitor. Powersoft uses the same technique that Windows itself uses. This is based on the system font, where sizes are defined in terms of $^1/_4$ the character width and $^1/_8$ the character height. PowerBuilder, however, uses $^1/_{32}$ the width and $^1/_{64}$ the height, to provide eight times greater resolution than you get with Windows.

Do you need to worry about this fact? Not unless you are making external function calls that require position or size information of a PowerBuilder object, in which case you will need to convert to the expected measurement units. There are two PowerScript functions provided to carry out conversions between PBUs and pels (or pixels or picture elements).

UnitsToPixels()

The `UnitsToPixels()` function is used to convert PBUs to pels in either the horizontal or vertical direction:

```
UnitsToPixels( Units, ValueDirection)
```

The *`Units`* parameter is an integer PBU value that will be converted to pels. The *`ValueDirection`* parameter is of the `ConvertType` enumerated data type and indicates what axis the value belongs on. The valid values for *`ValueDirection`* are `XUnitsToPixels!` and `YUnitsToPixels!`. The function's return value is the converted value in pels.

PixelsToUnits()

The `PixelsToUnits()` function is used to convert pels to PBUs in either the horizontal or vertical direction:

```
PixelsToUnits( Pixels, ValueDirection)
```

The *`Pixels`* parameter is an integer pel value that will be converted to PBUs. The *`ValueDirection`* parameter is of the `ConvertType` enumerated data type and indicates what axis the value belongs on. The valid values for *`ValueDirection`* are `XPixelsToUnits!` and `YPixelsToUnits!`. The function's return value is the converted value in PBUs.

The `PixelsToUnits()` function is useful when you're accessing the screen size attributes from the `Environment` object, and allows you to correctly center a window within the display (see Chapter 24).

File Functions

PowerBuilder provides a number of functions to read and write text and blobs to files. Additional functions provide other ways to manipulate files and also provide a user interface for specifying filenames.

File Access Modes

Files can be read or written to through one of two methods: line mode or stream mode. When reading in line mode, characters are transferred until a carriage return (CR), a line feed (LF), or an end of file (EOF) is encountered. Writing in line mode causes a carriage return *and* a line feed to be appended to each line of text written. Stream-mode reading will transfer up to 32,765 bytes from a file or until an EOF is found. Writing in stream mode enables up to 32,765 bytes (characters) to be written at a time and does *not* append CR or LF characters.

Opening a File

When PowerBuilder opens a file, it assigns a unique number to each request, and your PowerScript uses this value in all file operations to indicate the required open file. This value is an integer and is returned from the `FileOpen()` function on a successful open. `-1` is returned on a failure to open.

> **NOTE**
>
> A return of `-1` does not indicate that the file does not exist when you're opening it to write. PowerBuilder will create a new file if the one specified cannot be found. This may not always be the case, depending on the type of network you are developing with, and you may want to make use of the `FileExists()` function to check for existing files just in case.

The syntax of the `FileOpen()` function is

```
FileOpen( FileName{, FileMode{, FileAccess{, FileLock{, WriteMode }}}})
```

The following is a description of the `FileOpen()` arguments:

- *`FileName`*—This is either the complete path to the file or a filename that exists in the machine's search path.
- *`FileMode`*—This is the mode discussed in the section "File Access Modes" and can be either of the two enumerated types `LineMode!` or `StreamMode!`. PowerBuilder uses `LineMode!` as the default if no file mode is specified.
- *`FileAccess`*—This is the reason the file is being opened, either to read or write. The enumerated types `Read!` and `Write!` are used, with `Read!` being the default.
- *`FileLock`*—This determines if any other users can access the file being operated on, and if so, what kind of access they have. This is an enumerated type, either `LockReadWrite!`, `LockRead!`, `LockWrite!`, or `Shared!`. `LockReadWrite!` is the default and permits access only to the user who opened the file. `LockRead!` gives other users write access, but not read. `LockWrite!` gives other users read-only access. `Shared!` permits everyone to read and write. The behavior of this parameter depends on the network you are using.
- *`WriteMode`*—If the file being opened for writing already exists, the write mode determines whether the file is appended to or overwritten. The enumerated types `Append!` and `Replace!` are used, with `Append!` being the default. *`WriteMode`* is ignored when you're opening for read.

Closing an Open File

As with database connections, an open file also needs to be closed. The `FileClose()` function closes the specified file and restores full access to other users. The syntax is

```
FileClose( FileNumber)
```

FileNumber is the same integer value returned from `FileOpen()` and is used in all file operations to distinguish between multiple open files.

Reading from a File

After you have opened a file, you can read information from it for use in an application by using the `FileRead()` function. Its syntax is

```
FileRead( FileNumber, StringOrBlobVariable)
```

FileNumber is the integer value returned from the `FileOpen()` function call. *StringOrBlobVariable* is used to hold the characters or bytes read from the file.

`FileRead()` returns one of four values:

- `-100`—If an EOF is encountered
- `-1`—If an error occurs
- `0`—If CR or LF is the first information read (`LineMode!` access only)
- *x*—Where *x* is the number of characters or bytes read into the variable

If the file mode is `LineMode!`, `FileRead()` reads characters until a CR, an LF, or an EOF is found. The end-of-line characters are skipped and PowerBuilder positions the file pointer at the start of the next line.

If the file mode is `StreamMode!`, `FileRead()` reads to the end of the file or the next 32,765 characters or bytes, whichever occurs first. If the file is longer than 32,765 bytes, `FileRead()` positions the pointer after each read operation so that it is ready to read the next section of information.

Here's an example:

```
Integer nFile, nCount = 0
String szFileLines[]

nFile = FileOpen( "G:\test.out", LineMode!, Read!, LockReadWrite!)
Do
   nCount ++
Loop While FileRead( nFile, szFileLines[ nCount]) > 0
FileClose( nFile)
```

This example opens a file on the G: drive called test.out for reading, and locks out all other access to it. The `FileRead()` is used in a loop condition to read lines into a string array.

NOTE

All the parameters are specified in this example, even if they are the default. This makes your code more obvious. Write mode is not specified because this is a read.

Writing to a File

To write information to a file, use the `FileWrite()` function. Its syntax is

```
FileWrite( FileNumber, StringOrBlobVariable)
```

If the write mode is `Append!`, the file pointer is initially set to the end of the file and is repositioned to the new end of file after each `FileWrite()`. If the file mode is `LineMode!`, `FileWrite()` writes a CR and an LF after the last character of the line. The file pointer is set after these.

If the write mode is `Replace!`, the file pointer is set to the start of the file. After each `FileWrite()` call, the pointer is positioned after the last write.

The `FileWrite()` function returns the number of characters or bytes written to the file, or `-1` if an error occurs.

NOTE

Because `FileWrite()` can only write a maximum of 32,766 bytes at a time, if the length of the variable exceeds 32,765, which includes the string terminator character, `FileWrite()` only writes the first 32,765 characters and returns 32,765.

Here's an example:

```
Integer nFile, nCount = 0, nLoop
String szFileLines[]

// Fill the string array with test data
For nLoop = 1 To 10
   szFileLines[ nLoop] = "Cyril,Joy,George,Audrey"
Next

nFile = FileOpen( "G:\test.out", LineMode!, Write!, LockReadWrite!, Append!)
For nCount = 1 To 10
   FileWrite( nFile, szFileLines[ nCount])
Next
FileClose( nFile)
```

There are a couple other ways to read and write information from a PowerBuilder application, but they are specific to DataWindows and are discussed in both Chapter 25, "Advanced DataWindow Techniques I," and Chapter 26, "Advanced DataWindow Techniques II."

Using Windows Dialog Boxes

Windows provides two dialog boxes that give the user access to a number of controls to specify the exact directory and filename for the desired file.

Use `GetFileOpenName()` to obtain a valid filename and path for an existing file (see Figure 6.4).

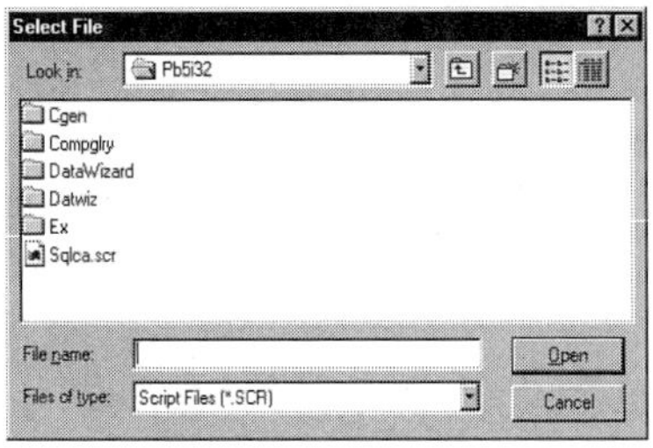

FIGURE 6.4.
The Select File dialog box.

The syntax for this function is

```
GetFileOpenName( Title, PathName, FileName {, Extension {, Filter}})
```

The following is a description of the `GetFileOpenName()` arguments:

- `Title`—A string that you would like to appear as the title for the dialog box.
- `PathName`—A variable that will hold the full path and filename returned from the dialog box.
- `FileName`—A variable that will hold just the filename (and extension) returned from the dialog box.
- `Extension`—A string of up to three characters that will be used as the default file extension. The default is no extension.
- `Filter`—A string containing a description of the files to include in the file type list box and the file mask to associate with it.

The function returns one of three integer values:

- `1`—On a success
- `0`—If the user clicks Cancel (or for some reason Windows cancels the dialog box)
- `-1`—If an error occurs

The filter argument is used to limit the type of files displayed in the list box. For example, to list only Script Files (*.SCR), the filter would be

```
"Script Files (*.SCR),*.SCR"
```

Multiple filters can be specified by using a comma after each set. Here's an example:

```
"Script Files (*.SCR),*.SCR,Data Files (*.DAT),*.DAT"
```

The `GetFileOpenName()` does *not* open the file the user selects; you must still code a `FileOpen()` call.

An example of a complete call to `GetFileOpenName()` is as follows:

```
nFile = GetFileOpenName("Select File", szFullPath, szFile, "SCR",  &
                        "Script Files (*.SCR),*.SCR,Data Files (*.DAT),*.DAT")

If nFile = 1 Then FileOpen( szFullPath)
```

If the user tries to enter a file that does not currently exist, a message window is displayed (see Figure 6.5).

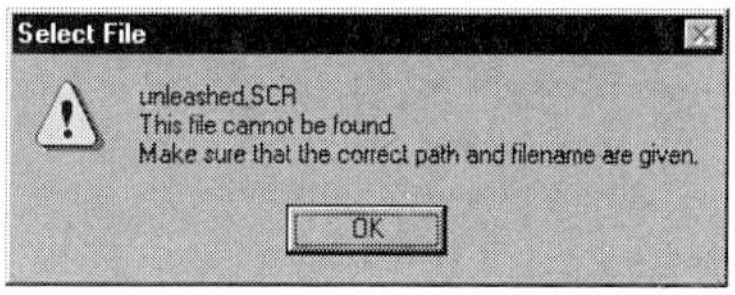

FIGURE 6.5.
An invalid file selected message box.

`GetFileSaveName()` is used to obtain a filename and path that will be used as the save destination, and uses the same dialog box shown in Figure 6.4. The syntax for this function is

```
GetFileSaveName( Title, PathName, FileName {, Extension {, Filter}})
```

The parameters and action of the dialog box are the same as for the `GetFileOpenName()` function, with one difference: Even a nonexistent file can be specified because the file and path being built are to be saved to and not read from.

Checking for File Existence

There are occasions when the existence of a file needs to be verified, and for this task you use the `FileExists()` function. The syntax is

```
FileExists( FileName)
```

`FileName` is a fully qualified path and filename, or just a filename if the check is being made against the machine's search path and the function returns either `TRUE` or `FALSE`. Here are two examples:

```
FileExists( "PB.INI")
FileEXists( "WIN.INI")
```

Both of these examples will return `TRUE` if the directories \PB4 and \WINDOWS exist on the machine running the application, and these are both included in the machine's PATH.

NOTE

The search path might vary from one machine to another, so using fully qualified filenames is advisable. The path is searched in order, so you might find a file in a different directory than the one you were expecting.

A nice trick to remember is that you can place PowerBuilder in a loop to wait for the appearance of a certain file. When you execute a `Run()` command in PowerBuilder, processing continues immediately without waiting for the executable or batch file to finish. However, if you modify the batch file or executable to create a temporary file at the end of the batch, PowerBuilder can check for this file before continuing. A DOS executable can be run from a BAT file to get the same functionality if required.

Deleting a File

To delete a file, use the `FileDelete()` function. Its syntax is

```
FileDelete( FileName)
```

`FileName` can be either fully qualified or just the name. It is *highly* advisable that you specify the full path when deleting a file, for obvious reasons. The function returns either `TRUE` or `FALSE` upon successful deletion of the file.

Finding the Length of a File

To find the length of a file, use the `FileLength()` function. Its syntax is

```
FileLength( FileName)
```

This function returns a Long that is the length (in bytes) of the file. If the file does not exist, `-1` is returned.

`FileLength()` is usually called around the `FileOpen()` call to check the number of characters that can be expected from a `FileRead()`.

NOTE

If the file is being shared on a network, you must call `FileLength()` before `FileOpen()`; otherwise, a sharing violation will occur.

The following example returns the length of the file SIMON.TXT in the current directory:

```
FileLength( "SIMON.TXT")
```

Positioning Within a File

The file pointer can be moved backward and forward within a file and specifies the point at which the next read or write begins. The syntax is

```
FileSeek( FileNumber, Position, Origin)
```

The following is a description of the `FileSeek()` arguments:

- *`FileNumber`*—The integer file number returned from `FileOpen()`.
- *`Position`*—A Long that specifies the new position relative to the *`Origin`*.
- *`Origin`*—A `SeekType` enumerated data type that specifies a position in the file. The values are `FromBeginning!`, `FromCurrent!`, and `FromEnd!`. `FromBeginning!` is the default.

The function returns a Long that is the file pointer position after the seek has completed or a `-1` if the file does not exist.

The following example moves the file pointer 95 bytes in from the start of the file:

```
Integer nFile

nFile = FileOpen( "simon.txt")
FileSeek( nFile, 95. FromBeginning!)
```

NOTE

Immediately after a `FileOpen()`, the positions of `FromBeginning!` and `FromCurrent!` are the same.

The `Error` Object

The `Error` object contains all the relevant information about an error situation needed for reporting to the user. Powersoft only ever shows the use of the `Error` object in conjunction with the `SystemError` event, but there is no reason not to make use of this structure for error information passing in the rest of the applications events.

The attributes of the `Error` object are listed in Table 6.10.

Table 6.10. The `Error` object attributes.

Attribute	*Data Type*	*Description*
`Number`	Integer	The error number
`Text`	String	The error message text
`WindowMenu`	String	The window or menu where the error occurred

continues

Table 6.10. continued

Attribute	*Data Type*	*Description*
`Object`	String	The object where the error occurred
`ObjectEvent`	String	The event where the error occurred
`Line`	Integer	The line where the error occurred

A number of errors can occur at the time of an application's execution. The errors listed in Table 6.11 will cause the `SystemError` event to be called.

Table 6.11. System errors that can be trapped in the `SystemError` event.

`Error.Number`	`Error.Text`
1	`Divide by zero`
2	`Null object reference`
3	`Array boundary exceeded`
4	`Enumerated value is out of range for function`
5	`Negative value encountered in function`
6	`Invalid DataWindow row/column specified`
7	`Unresolvable external when linking reference`
8	`Reference of array with NULL subscript`
9	`DLL function not found in current application`
10	`Unsupported argument type in DLL function`
12	`DataWindow column type does not match GetItem type`
13	`Unresolved attribute reference`
14	`Error opening DLL library for external function`
15	`Error calling external function`
16	`Maximum string size exceeded`
17	`DataWindow referenced in DataWindow object does not exist`
18	`Function doesn't return value`
19	`Cannot convert` *`name`* `in Any variable to` *`name`*
20	`Database command has not been successfully prepared`
21	`Bad runtime function reference`
22	`Unknown object type`
23	`Cannot assign object of type` *`name`* `to variable of type` *`name`*
24	`Function call doesn't match its definition`
25	`Double or real expression has overflowed`

Error.Number	Error.Text
26	Field *name* assignment not supported
27	Cannot take a negative to a non-integer power
28	VBX Error: *name*
30	Does not support external object data type *name*
31	External object data type *name* not supported
32	Name not found calling external function *name*
33	Invalid parameter type calling external object function *name*
34	Incorrect number of parameters calling external object function *name*
35	Error calling external object attribute *name*
36	Name not found accessing external object attribute *name*
37	Type mismatch accessing external object attribute *name*
38	Incorrect number of subscripts accessing external object attribute *name*
39	Error accessing external object attribute *name*
40	Mismatched Any data types in expression
41	Illegal Any data types in expression
42	Specified argument type differs from required argument type at runtime in DLL function *name*

If the `SystemError` event has not been overridden, PowerBuilder will display a standard message box with an OK button that details the specifics of the error. (See Figure 6.6.)

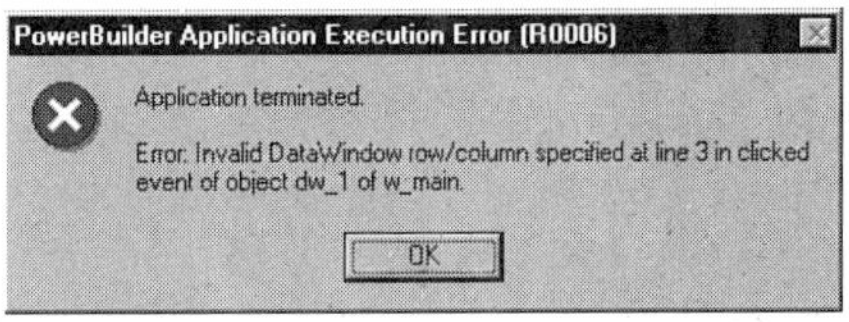

FIGURE 6.6.
The PowerBuilder Application Execution Error message box.

Ten errors do not cause the `SystemError` event to be triggered; they cause the application to be immediately terminated (see Table 6.12).

Table 6.12. Errors that do not trigger the `SystemError` event.

`Error.Number`	`Error.Text`
50	`Application reference could not be resolved`
51	`Failure loading dynamic library`
52	`Missing ancestor object` *`name`*
53	`Missing ancestor object` *`name`* `in` *`name`*
54	`Conflicting ancestor object` *`name`* `in` *`name`* `and` *`name`*
55	`Window close occurred processing yield function`
56	`Database interface does not support remote procedure calls`
57	`Database Interface does not support array variables (function` *`name`*`)`
58	`Blob variable for` *`name`* `cannot be empty`
59	`Maximum size exceeded`

The `SignalError()` function is used to trigger the `SystemError` event programmatically. This is used in the case of errors that are severe enough to halt the application (for example, the database connection was lost and the server went down). If `SystemError` has not been coded to respond to the error value passed in via the `SignalError()` call, the message will be ignored.

To provide a consistent interface to an error situation, many applications make use of a single window to display and handle the problem. The `Error` object is often used to pass to the window information from the script in which the error occurred. Here's an example:

```
If SQLCA.SQLCode = -1 Then
   error.Number = SQLCA.DBErrCode
   error.Text = SQLCA.DBErrText
   error.WindowMenu = "w_sql_tasks"
   error.Object = this.ClassName()
   error.ObjectEvent = "clicked"
   error.Line = 10
   Open( w_error)
End If
```

The window, in this case `w_error` (see Figure 6.7), then takes the values from the `Error` object in the `Open` event and places them into the appropriate single- and multiline edit controls. `w_error` gives the user the capability to halt the application or to try to recover from the error and return to the calling code. The Halt command button can be disabled by passing in a negative line number; this forces the user to return to the calling code. This can be used if the calling script determines that there is a recoverable option to the situation, a need to disconnect other database connections, or a need to free up some memory usage before halting the application.

FIGURE 6.7.
An example of an error window.

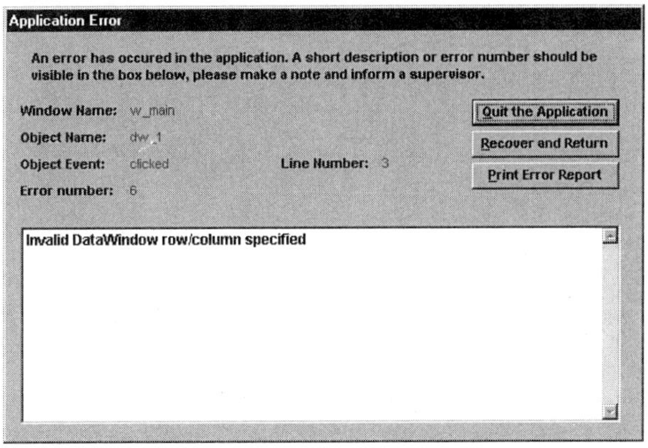

After error processing has been captured in a single area, other processing can also be carried out. The sample window has been MAPI enabled and will create and send an e-mail message to a specified user. This functionality is invaluable during user acceptance testing and final deployment to catch any small problems that only end users ever encounter. Another enhancement is that you can code in understandable English so the user can understand many of the cryptic database errors. You would do this with a `Choose...Case` on the DBMS to provide a more generic (and therefore reusable) error window.

Only two other events specifically trap error events. They are `DBError` and `ItemError` and are only found in the DataWindow control. These events are discussed fully in Chapter 10, "DataWindow Scripting."

Summary

In this chapter the basic concepts used in PowerBuilder and its programming language PowerScript are defined. This chapter also covers more advanced topics such as events and messages, file functions, and error handling.

The PowerScript Environment

7

IN THIS CHAPTER

When you have mastered the basics of the PowerScript language (see Chapter 6, "The PowerScript Language"), you need a place to write your code. Since PowerBuilder is event driven, your code will be dispersed across events for the different objects that make up your PowerBuilder application. Scripts can be written for many of the PowerBuilder objects: the application object, windows, window controls, menus, user objects, and functions. It doesn't matter if the script you are writing is for a menu's `Clicked` event or a DataWindow control constructor event—the interface will be the same. The PowerScript painter is the editor you use throughout PowerBuilder to enter PowerScript statements.

In conjunction with writing scripts for objects, it is often necessary to write user-defined functions to incorporate all the business rules and commonly used procedures. The PowerScript painter is the underlying foundation for the Function painter. Functions can be written on the global, application, menu, window, and user-object levels.

This chapter takes a look at the Structure painter. Structures are commonly used in both event scripts and user-defined functions. Structures, like functions, can be created globally or at an object level. Regardless of the structure's scope, the interface to create a new structure class is the same.

This chapter explores the PowerScript painter, the Function painter, and the Structure painter.

The PowerScript Painter

The PowerScript painter enables you to write scripts for object events and for functions. You can enter the PowerScript painter in several different ways. Because scripts are written for events, which are part of objects, you access the Script painter via another PowerBuilder painter (Application, Window, Menu, User Object, or Function). Although this might appear to be an unnecessary extra step, it enforces encapsulation for each of your objects.

The most common method for accessing the Script painter is the Edit Script icon in the PainterBar (see Figure 7.1). You first select the object for which the script is to be written (for visual objects only) and then click on the icon. After a script has been written for an event, the icon's appearance changes to indicate that the object now contains one or more events with script written for them (see Figure 7.1).

FIGURE 7.1.
The Edit Script PainterBar icon with no script written on it (left) and with script written on it (right).

For those of you who prefer to use the keyboard, Ctrl+K produces the same desired effect as clicking on the PainterBar. The PainterBar and keyboard methods can be used in any of the aforementioned PowerBuilder objects to open the Script painter.

The Window and User Object painters offer an additional method of opening the Script painter. This method is to use the right mouse button pop-up menu to select the script option at the top of the menu.

When you have used your favorite access method, you are presented with the PowerScript painter (see Figure 7.2).

FIGURE 7.2.

The PowerScript painter.

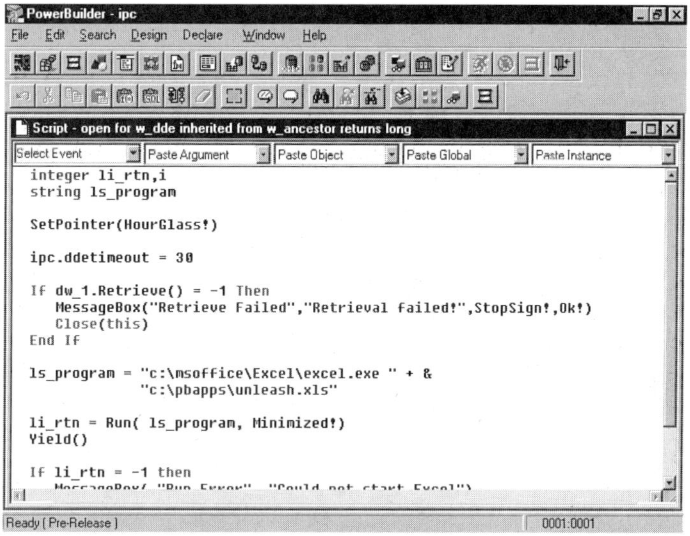

Where Am I?

If you are coding the first script for your object, PowerBuilder will place you in the most commonly used or default event for that object (for example, the `Clicked` event for a command button). The PowerScript painter title bar identifies the object and the event that will cause the script to execute (see Figure 7.3).

FIGURE 7.3.

The PowerScript painter title bar.

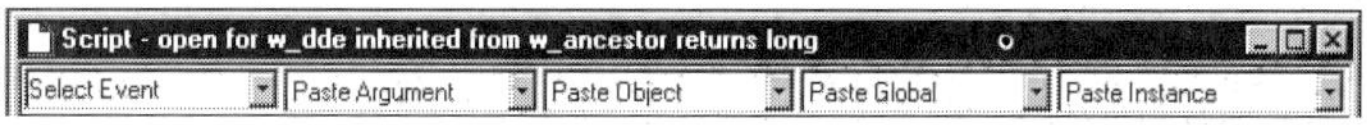

It is likely that you will want to code a script for a different event for the same object. To do so, click on the Select Event drop-down list box located at the top of the painter and select an event (see Figure 7.4).

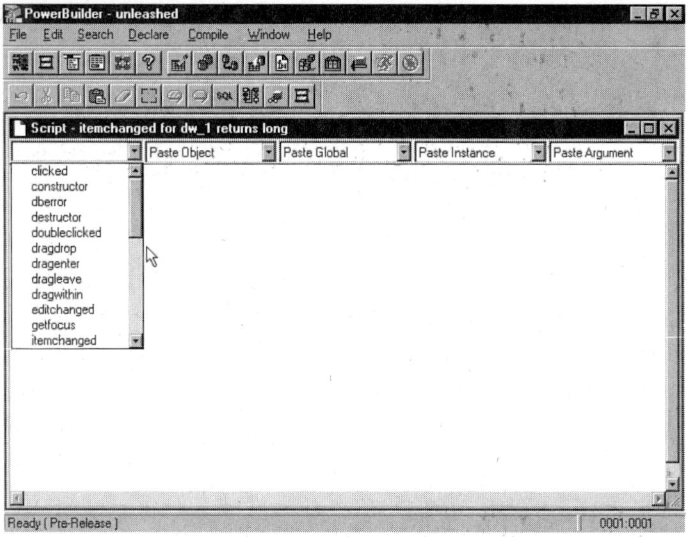

FIGURE 7.4.
The Select Event drop-down list box.

You can also activate the list by pressing Ctrl+1. The arrow keys enable movement up and down through the list. Pressing Enter when your choice is highlighted takes you to the script for the event and pressing Esc closes the drop-down list. The PowerScript painter indicates whether code has been written for an event by placing a picture of a sheet of paper with lines on it next to the event name. The icon will appear three different ways:

- All white. This indicates that there is script written for an event for the current object only.
- All purple. The icon appears purple only when the current object is inherited and indicates that script has been written in an event for the ancestor.
- Half white/half purple. The combination, as you might expect, means that there is script written in the current descendant and in the ancestor.

For more information on accessing the script, see the section "The Design Menu" later in this chapter.

The PowerScript Property Sheet

New in PowerBuilder 5.0 is the ability to customize the Script painter. You do this selecting Options from the Design menu. This opens the Properties for Editor property sheet (see Figure 7.5).

The property sheet for the Script painter allows you to specify general settings, the font used, syntax color specifications, and the Paste drop-downs that are available.

FIGURE 7.5.
The Properties for Editor property sheet.

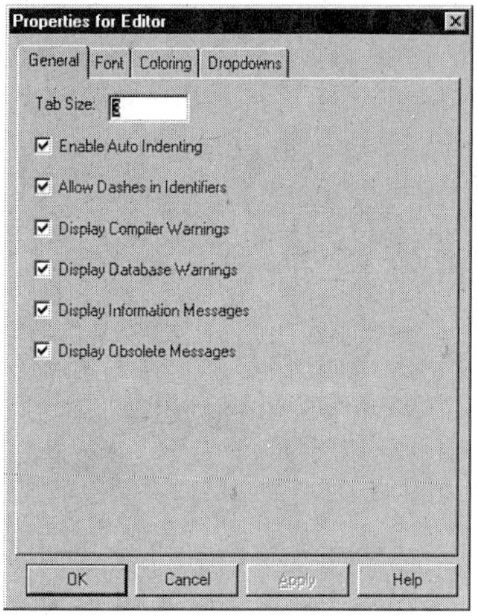

The General Tab Page

The General tab page (see Figure 7.5) is used to specify general settings for the Script painter's behavior. You can define for the auto-indentation how many spaces you want to equal one tab (the default is three). It also contains the Enable Auto Indenting check box, which is used to enable/disable the ability for PowerBuilder to automatically perform indentation on flow-of-control statements. For example, previously on a `Choose...Case` statement, you would specify the test expression to be evaluated by the `Choose...Case` statement, press Enter, press Tab, and then place the first `Case` statement. With Auto Indent you do not need to press the Tab key because PowerBuilder recognizes the flow-of-control statement and indents for you.

NOTE

Auto Indent does not backward indent, meaning that it does not line up automatically the `Choose...Case` and the `End...Choose` statements.

In addition to providing the auto-indentation settings, the General tab page has several options that you can turn on or off. The Allow Dashes in Identifiers check box when checked allows you to create variable names containing dashes. The other four check boxes are used to indicate what type of warnings and messages the script compiler displays: compiler and database warnings and obsolete and informational messages.

The Font Tab Page

The Font tab page (see Figure 7.6) allows you to specify the font that is used in the Script painter. You can specify not only the font, but also the font style, size, strikeout, underlined, and the text and background colors. When you have made your selections, you can click OK to close the property sheet or click the Apply button, which automatically applies your changes but does not close the property sheet.

FIGURE 7.6.
The Font tab page.

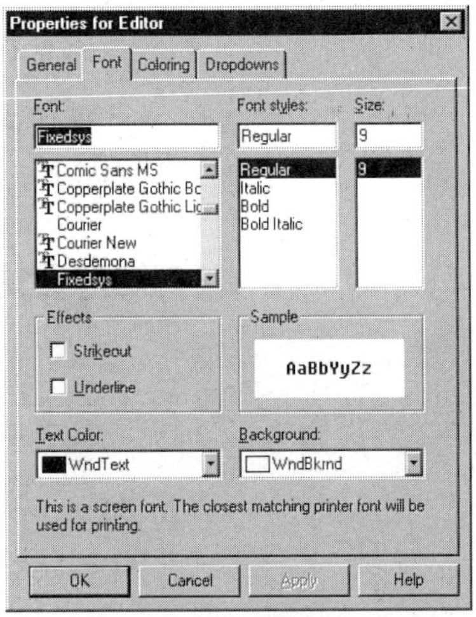

NOTE

The property settings for the Script painter are global settings. The settings are applied to all scripts for all applications.

The Coloring Tab Page

One of the other features that PowerBuilder developers have been asking for is a color-coded script editor. You probably noticed this as one of the first new features in the Script painter. Depending on the settings you specify on the Coloring tab page (see Figure 7.7), PowerBuilder uses different colors to indicate keywords, comments, data types, and so on.

As you can see in Figure 7.7, you have the ability to turn off the color coding by deselecting the Enable Syntax Coloring check box. If it is checked, though, you have 15 different types of PowerScript statements, such as enumerated data types and keywords, that you can specify be colored differently. For each of the specified PowerScript statements, you can set the text color and the background color. This is extremely useful since you now can differentiate comments, keywords, errors, and data types just based on their colors.

FIGURE 7.7.
The Coloring tab page.

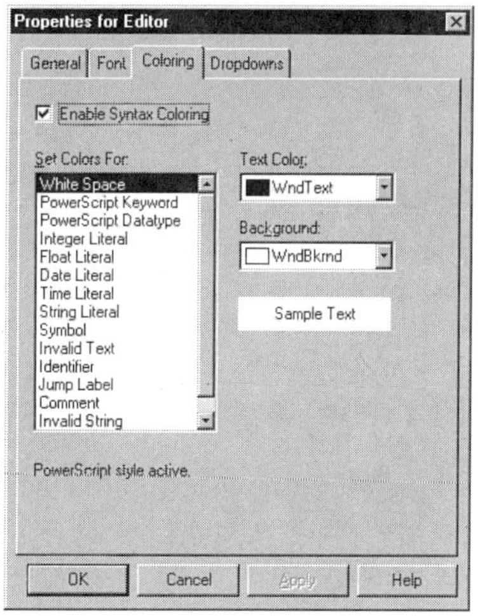

TIP

One use of a color-enabled editor is to make comments appear as very light gray so that they blend into the background and allow you to see the actual code statements.

The Dropdowns Tab Page

The last tab in the property sheet is the Dropdowns tab page (see Figure 7.8).

FIGURE 7.8.
The Dropdowns tab page.

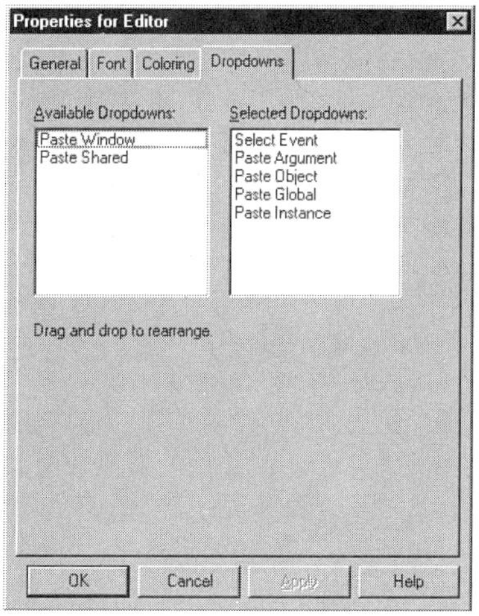

The purpose of this tab page is to specify which drop-down list boxes appear at the top of the Script painter (for example, the Select Event drop-down discussed earlier). The other options are Paste Argument, Paste Global, Paste Instance, Paste Object, Paste Shared, and Paste Window. Each of these Paste drop-down list boxes gives you the ability to paste the specified application component name (function argument, global variable, instance variable, PowerBuilder object name, shared variable, or window name) into your script. These are useful when you need to refer to a particular object in your script (for example, calling an object function or referencing an attribute). By clicking on an item that appears in the drop-down list, you paste the item name into your script where the cursor is positioned. This saves you from having to type in the name or remember a multitude of object names.

NOTE

The use of these drop-downs points out one of the many reasons it is important to give your objects and controls meaningful names instead of accepting the defaults. It is difficult to remember the difference between `cbx_1` and `cbx_22` from one of the drop-down lists, but you can easily remember `cb_insert` and `cb_delete`. For information on naming conventions, see Chapter 22, "Standards and Naming Conventions."

These list boxes can be accessed via the mouse or by using the keyboard combinations Ctrl+the position of drop-down across the top, from left to right. For example, if the Event, Object, Global, and Instance drop-downs are displaying, Ctrl+1 activates Select Event, Ctrl+2 activates Paste Object, and so on.

WARNING

When you use the drop-down list boxes to paste information into your script, PowerBuilder copies the selected object or variable to the Windows Clipboard. Therefore, anything that has been previously copied to the Windows Clipboard is destroyed.

You can specify which of the list boxes appears at the top of the Script painter by dragging the list box name from the Available Dropdowns list box to the Selected Dropdowns list box. You can specify the order in which the list boxes appear based on the order in the Selected Dropdowns list box.

While all the other property tab pages have a global effect on the Script painter, the Dropdowns tab page applies to the current object type. Therefore, you can have a different set of drop-downs for your menu objects than for your window objects. You will need to use different drop-downs with the different objects you are writing scripts for.

After you have specified all the preferences for the Script painter, click OK or Apply to have the changes made to your scripting environment.

The Script PainterBar

To assist you in writing scripts for your application, the PainterBar contains several options to provide standard text editor functionality (for example, Cut, Copy, and Paste) as well as some shortcuts useful in writing code.

Text Manipulation

Because the Script painter is essentially a text editor, it provides the standard Windows capability to undo changes, cut, copy, paste, erase/clear, and select all text (see Figure 7.9). These text-manipulation options are also available in the Edit menu.

FIGURE 7.9.
The PowerScript PainterBar.

In addition to the PainterBar and Edit menu, all of the previously mentioned utilities are available by right-clicking and choosing the appropriate option from the pop-up menu.

NOTE

PowerBuilder 5.0 now has two very useful features: draggable text and multilayer undo. You can select text, click on it, and drag it to a new location. By holding down the Ctrl key using the same process, you can copy the selected text. The Undo option in the Script painter now remembers more than one level of changes for some options.

Comments

Also located on the PainterBar are two icons that provide the capability to comment out and uncomment selected text. The comment icon uses the single-line comment (`//`) for all lines selected as opposed to the multiline comment (`/*`). This provides a quick method of commenting out large blocks of code.

All the PainterBar icons, thus far, assist in manipulating the text that you have typed into the Script painter. Wouldn't it be useful to have a development tool that assists in writing the code? The PowerScript painter provides this capability with four more PainterBar icons. The Paste Function, Paste SQL, Paste Statement, and Object Browser icons increase productivity and reduce the need for memorization of exact syntax by using a graphical interface to assist in code generation.

Paste Function

The Paste Function menu item opens a dialog box that lists all the PowerBuilder functions, user-defined global functions, and global external functions and enables you to select one and paste it into your script (see Figure 7.10). The only detractions to using this method are that only the function name is pasted into your script and not the full function syntax and the length of time elapsed before the dialog box opens. You must access online help to find the syntax for the pasted function.

FIGURE 7.10.

The Paste Function dialog box.

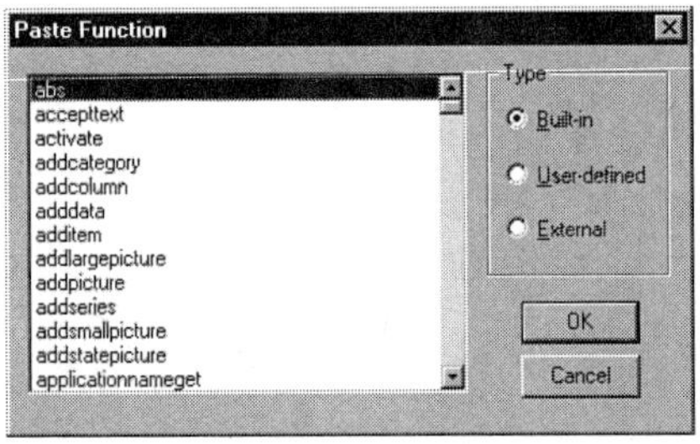

Paste SQL

The Paste SQL icon provides a method for graphically creating cursor, noncursor, and stored procedure SQL statements. When the SQL statement has been coded to the developer's satisfaction, it is pasted into the Script painter. For detailed information on Paste SQL's capabilities, see Chapter 5, "SQL and PowerBuilder."

Paste Statement

To insert the syntax for PowerScript statements such as `IF...THEN`, `FOR...NEXT`, and `CHOOSE CASE`, select the Paste Statement PainterBar icon or the Paste Statement option in the Edit menu.

Select the type of statement that you want to paste into your script. The statement's framework is then inserted after the cursor in your script. You must then modify the statement to suit your particular business logic. For example, if you cannot remember the exact syntax for the `Choose Case Else` statement, select it from the Paste Statement dialog box (see Figure 7.11), and you will see the following appear in your script:

```
CHOOSE CASE <expression>
CASE <item>
<statementblock>
CASE ELSE
<statementblock>
END CHOOSE
```

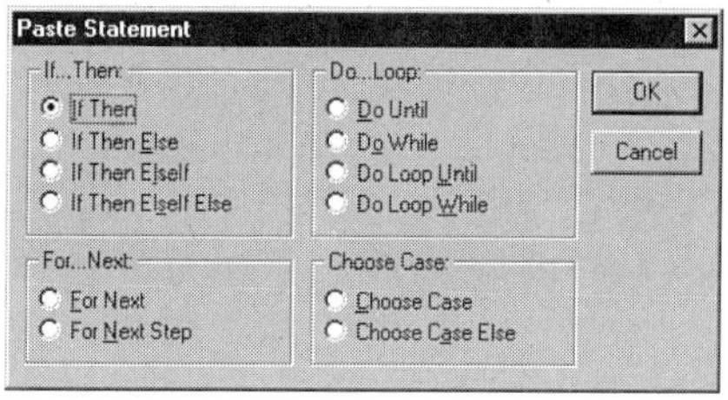

FIGURE 7.11.
The Paste Statement dialog box.

The Object Browser

The Browser dialog box gives extra assistance in development by giving you the ability to paste any attribute, object, variable, or function into your application. This can be an extremely useful tool when you consider that the PowerScript language contains more than 400 different functions. In addition to each of these functions, there are multiple objects and controls that have attributes you must learn. It becomes increasingly difficult to remember object names, attributes, and functions as your application continues to grow. The object browser provides you with a means to reduce the amount of information you must memorize (and that you have to type into your event script).

The Browser dialog box enables you to view all objects and the properties, functions, global variables, instance variables, names, shared variables, and structures associated with them (see Figure 7.12).

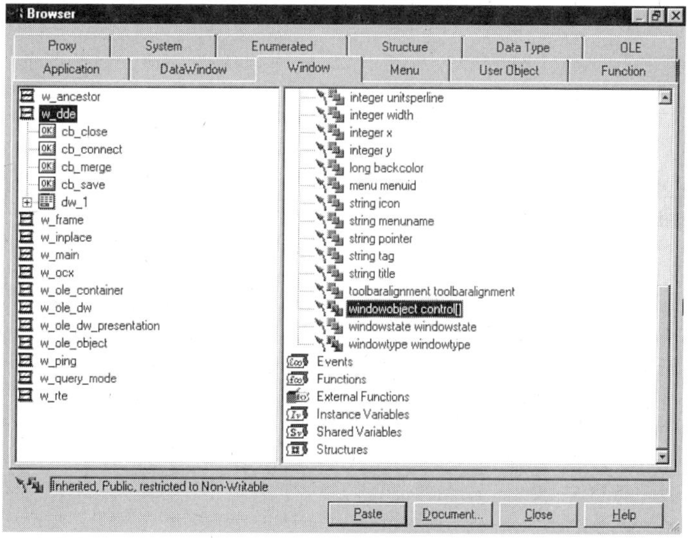

FIGURE 7.12.
The Object Browser.

The Object Browser uses several tab pages to access each of the different types of objects you can have in your application. In the majority of the tab pages, the Object Browser is divided into two list boxes. The list box on the left indicates all objects in your application that are of the object type selected (you get this information by clicking on a tab). The default object is the object you are currently editing (in this case, `w_dde`). The list box on the right displays detailed information or categories about the selected object, such as properties, events, functions, variables, and structures. For each category, the browser indicates the inheritance and access designation. In Figure 7.12 the blue arrow next to a property indicates that it is inherited. The squares next to a property indicate scope, access designation, and read and write access by using different numbers of squares and coloration. While you can memorize what each graphical representation means, it is considerably easier to view the legend at the bottom of the Object Browser (in this case, the selected property is Inherited, Public, and restricted to Non-Writable). You can also view the object inheritance tree in your application by right-clicking and selecting Show Hierarchy.

After selecting the desired attribute or function, click on the Paste button to have the information inserted into your script. Notice that if you choose the name of the object you are currently editing, the object name is not pasted into the script, but the pronoun `This` is used, followed by the attribute or function. For further information on pronouns, refer to Chapter 6.

To reference controls in a window, select Window as the object type, which provides a list of all window objects in the current application. Locate the desired window and double-click on the object's name. This expands the list with the window name followed by the name of the controls that appear on the window. You can use the same method for user objects and to reference the menu-item hierarchy (see Figure 7.13).

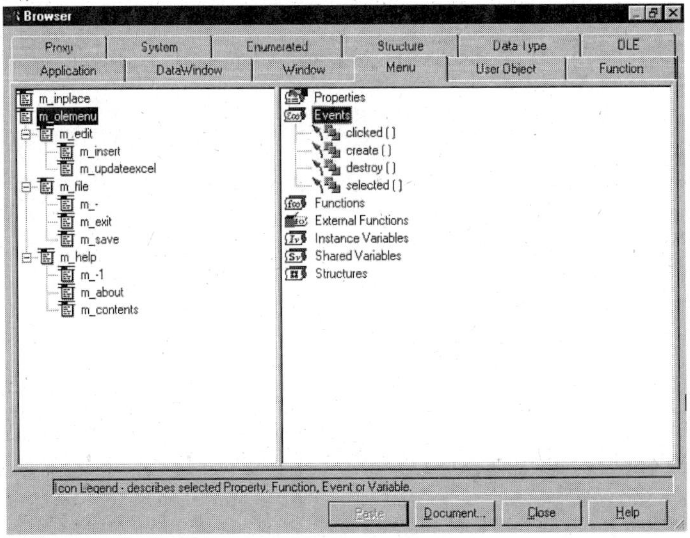

FIGURE 7.13.

An expanded menu hierarchy using the Object Browser.

The Object Browser is also the best place to find all the valid enumerated data types. If you select an object type as Enumerated, the Object Browser shows all of PowerBuilder's enumerated data types and the possible values for each.

Also new to Version 5.0 is the ability to create a rich text format (RTF) document that displays the selected object and the corresponding category details (see Figure 7.14).

FIGURE 7.14.
The Document dialog box.

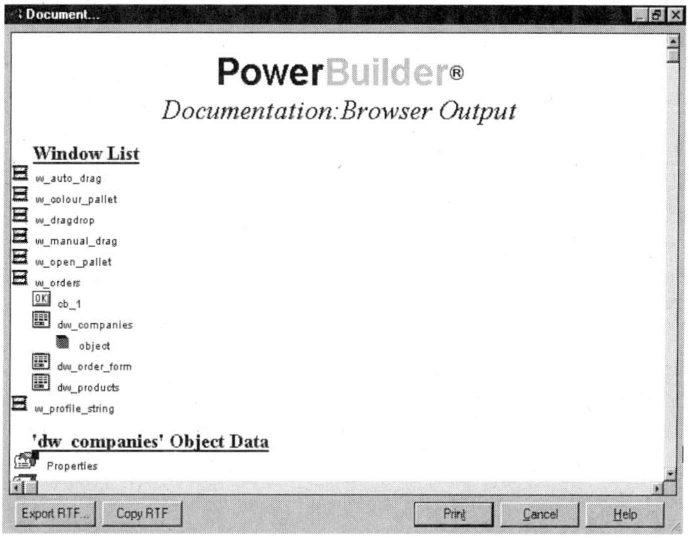

From this dialog box you can export the RTF document to a file, copy it to the Clipboard, or print it.

After closing the Document dialog and the Object Browser, you are back in the Script painter. The final PainterBar icon for the Script painter is the Return icon. Use it to exit the painter and return to the object painter for which you were writing the script. When you exit the Script painter, PowerBuilder automatically compiles the script you just wrote. If an error is encountered, an error message will be displayed and you will be unable to leave the Script painter.

Search and Replace

The Search menu as well as three new PainterBar icons give you the capability to search for specified text and ask whether to match upper- and lowercase letters. The Find Text dialog box has been greatly enhanced in 5.0 to incorporate case matching, expressions, searching forward and back, and wrapping the search when the beginning or end is met. In addition to a search facility, the Replace Text dialog has been changed; this is useful for making variable name changes throughout a script. Changes can be made all at once or can be verified before each replacement is made. Under the Search menu only, the Go To Line menu item (also accessible by pressing Ctrl+Shift+G) opens a dialog box requesting a line number for where you want to move the cursor.

> **NOTE**
>
> At the bottom-right corner of the Script painter is a counter that indicates the line where the cursor is positioned and the number of positions from the far-left side of the painter. The line counter enables easy movement to a particular line number. An asterisk also appears if PowerBuilder has detected any change to the script.

Compiling the Script

The script editor automatically compiles any code when the Return icon is clicked, when the control menu is double-clicked, or when a different script or object is selected. If you prefer to have the code compile as it is coded, pressing Ctrl+L, selecting the PainterBar icon, or selecting Script from the Design menu will immediately compile the code. If the script compiles cleanly, PowerBuilder will permit you to move on and work on something else. If the code is not flawless, the Script painter will display in a separate window an error code and a message stating what the problem is (see Figure 7.15).

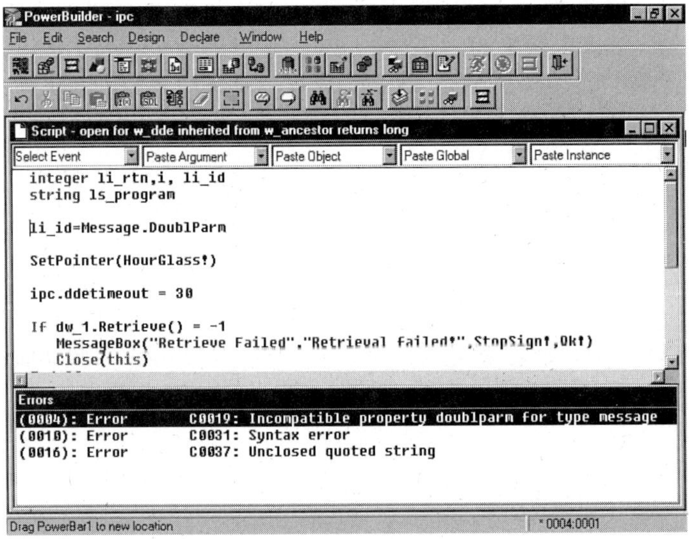

FIGURE 7.15.
The compile error message window.

The error message at the bottom of the Script painter provides you with the line number on which the error occurred, the PowerScript error code, and the PowerScript error message. To correct the problem, you must first go to the line in error. You could start at the beginning and count lines, but that might get tedious if the script is more than 10 lines long. The row number and column number are also displayed in the MicroHelp area of the Script painter in the bottom-right corner. The best method to jump to the line in error is to click on the error message for the error you want to fix, and the cursor will move to that line number.

After jumping to the line in error, you need to determine the error and what fix is required. If the problem is with the syntax of a PowerScript statement or function, position the cursor within the keyword and press Shift+F1. Context-sensitive help will be displayed for the PowerScript statement. A very common (and unhelpful) error message is `Error C0031: Syntax error`. This only indicates that PowerBuilder has found an error, but it will not often give a clear indication of where the problem might be. Typically, the culprit causing the error is a missing keyword or punctuation mark. Occasionally, the syntax error message points to the number of a line with no code. This situation often occurs when you're using a flow-of-control statement such as an `If...Then` statement with the `End...If` not coded.

If a compile error occurs, your first reaction probably is to move on and deal with the compile error later. No problem, right? Wrong! Remember, PowerBuilder will not let you leave the Script painter until the problem has been resolved. If you are going to leave the problem until later, select the lines of code causing the error (or even easier, use the Select All PainterBar icon) and click on the Comment PainterBar icon. You can now exit the Script painter and return later to uncomment the erroneous code and fix the problem.

You can also capture compiler warnings, database warnings, informational messages, and obsolete syntax messages by selecting the corresponding menu items under the General tab page for the script editor (accessed from the Design|Options menu item). All messages display in the same window as the compile errors, but unlike with compile errors, you are not forced to address a warning message in order to leave the Script painter or save the object. With the database warnings, PowerBuilder actually validates embedded SQL against the current database (see Chapter 4, "Databases and the Database Painter"), which may or may not be the intended database and might not have had the referenced database objects created in it yet. The obsolete syntax message is useful if you are migrating an existing application or are used to coding in earlier versions of PowerBuilder. You should aim to fix this last type of errors because Powersoft might stop supporting some of the function names and syntax that have been carried through from previous versions.

WARNING

The compile message window does not have scrolling capabilities, so portions of error text get cut off.

Menu Structure in the PowerScript Painter

Although many options in the Script painter can be evoked from the PainterBar and keyboard, there are additional options that can only be accessed from the menu bar. The following discussion is not exhaustive, but covers the important items.

The File Menu

There are many times when an event script needs to be saved to a text file: documentation, code walk-throughs, book writing, or code stealing. PowerBuilder includes the capability to save scripts to a text file with an .SCR extension; you use the Export menu item. To insert an SCR file, use the Import menu item. Scripts can also be printed via the Print menu item, which prints the object name and the event name with the code. If you want to print multiple objects at the same time, you can do it using the Library painter.

The Design Menu

The Select Object menu item (also available on the PainterBar) enables you to jump between scripts for different objects in all object Script painters except the Application painter. When you select this menu item, a dialog box opens that lists the valid objects you can select (see Figure 7.16).

FIGURE 7.16.
The Select Object dialog box.

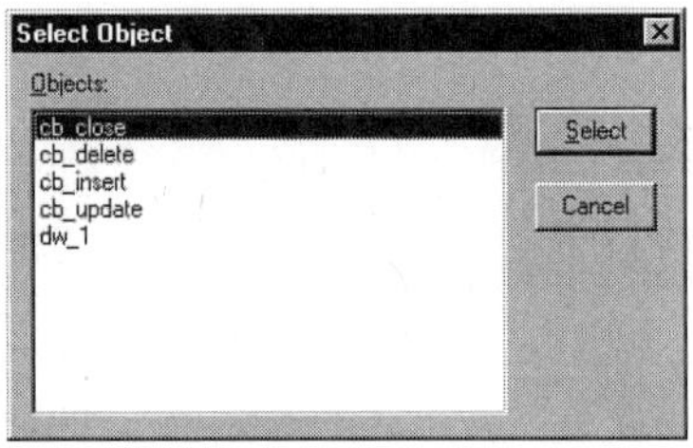

The Compile Script menu item (also accessible by pressing Ctrl+L and on the PainterBar), as you saw previously, is how PowerBuilder syntax checks any statements written (see the section "Compiling the Script"). From this menu you can also turn on and off the compiler messages.

The Design menu deserves additional attention with respect to the Window, Menu, and User Object painters. If inheritance is being used, the Compile menu has an additional three new menu items: Extend Ancestor Script, Override Ancestor Script, and Display Ancestor Script. These options are used to determine how PowerBuilder will handle any scripts written for each of these events in the ancestor object. If an event contains code in the event for the ancestor, the Page icon in the Select Event drop-down list box will be purple. If the same icon is half purple and half white, the event contains code in both the ancestor and the descendant objects' scripts for that event.

To view an ancestor script, click on the menu option Display Ancestor Script (see Figure 7.17).

FIGURE 7.17.
The Display Ancestor Script dialog box.

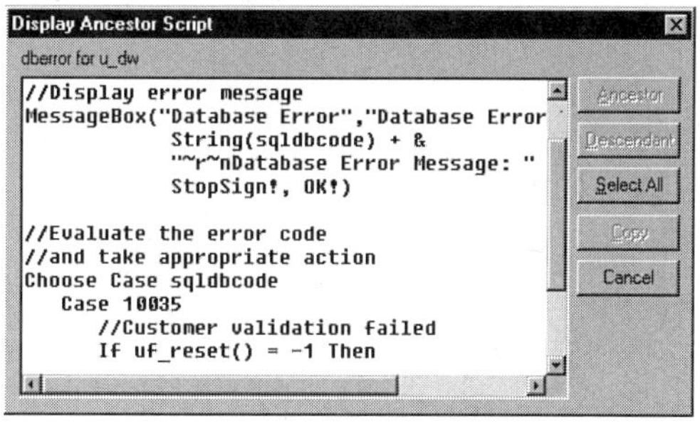

The Display Ancestor Script dialog box enables you to view ancestor or descendant scripts. The Ancestor and Descendant buttons give you the ability to move forward and backward through multiple levels of inherited scripts. The Select All button highlights the entire ancestor script, and the Copy button gives you the ability to copy it. You also can select specific lines just as you would in any text editor.

NOTE

The order of execution of inherited scripts is as follows: The initial ancestor script is executed first and then the rest are executed in order down through the tree, ending with the bottom-most descendant. If you do not want the scripts to execute in this order, you must select the Override Ancestor script menu item and code the statements to explicitly execute each ancestor script (see Chapter 6).

For more discussion on inheritance, see Chapter 11, "Windows and the Window Painter."

The Declare Menu

The Declare menu enables the declaration of global, instance, and shared variables; object functions and structures; global and local external functions; and user-defined object events.

Declaring Variables

Regardless of whether the scope of a variable is global, shared, or instance, the same interface is used to declare it (see Figure 7.18).

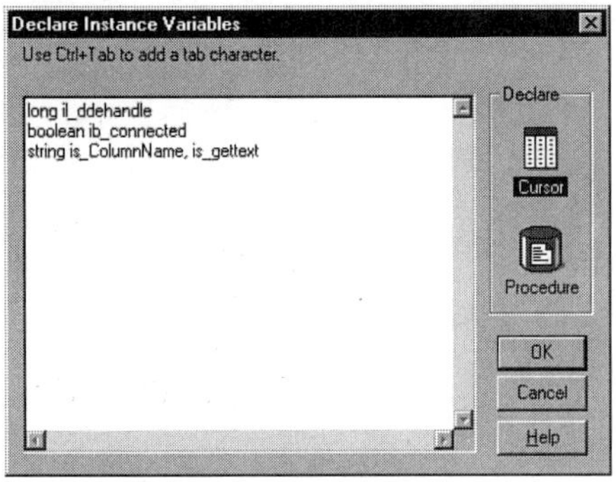

FIGURE 7.18.
The variable declaration dialog box.

In the multiline edit control on the dialog box, type in the data type(s) and variable name(s). To enter multiple variables, press Enter to move to a new line (in previous versions, pressing just Enter closed the dialog box and Ctrl+Enter had to be used to move to a new line!). You can also use Ctrl+Tab to space your declarations by inserting a tab character. The variable declaration dialog box also has a graphical interface to generate the `DECLARE` statement for cursors and stored procedures. The cursor declaration takes you into the SQL painter; the stored procedure declaration takes you into the Select Procedure dialog box (see Chapter 5).

Declaring Functions and Structures: An Introduction

Just as you can declare variables, you can also define object-level functions and structures. Depending on the object you have selected, the menu will reflect the object type in the menu text (for example, in the Window painter, the menu will read Window Functions and Window Structures). Use these options to create user-defined procedures and user-defined data types. For more information on each of these options, see the sections "The Function Painter" and "The Structure Painter" later in the chapter.

Declaring Global and Local External Functions

Both menu items open an identical dialog box with a multiline edit in which you write your dynamic link library (DLL) function call syntax. You make API calls to the Windows SDK and third-party vendor DLLs via this method (see Figure 7.19). For more information on the calling syntax, see Chapter 33, "API Calls."

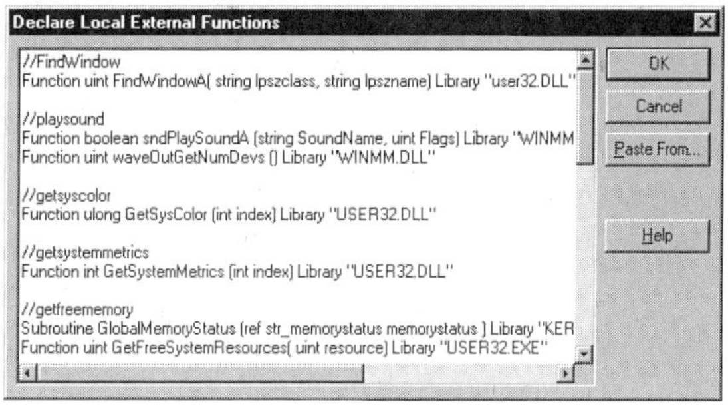

FIGURE 7.19.
The Declare Local External Functions dialog box.

User Events

When you initially write scripts for various PowerBuilder objects, you have a set list of events for each given object. You can, however, specify additional events for a window, window controls, or a user object by capturing the underlying Windows messages. You can also create custom events that Windows does not trigger automatically, but that you can manually trigger via your code.

The first thing to do when defining a new user event is select the object for which you want the event defined. Click on the User Event menu item (in the Window and User Object painters) to make the Events dialog box appear (see Figure 7.20).

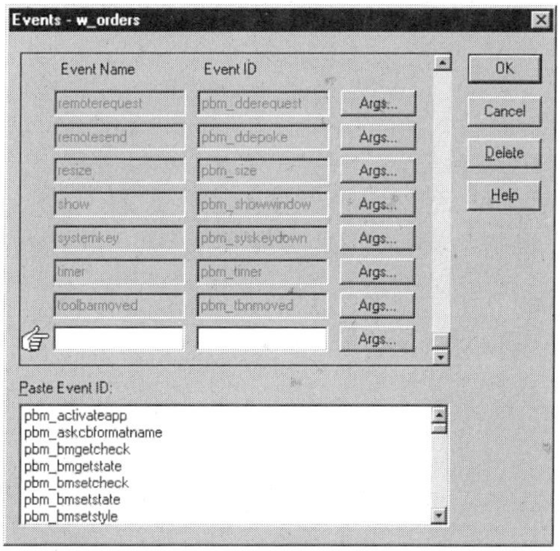

FIGURE 7.20.
The define user events dialog box.

The dialog box title bar shows objects for which the list of events are defined. The events shown are those currently defined for the object and the corresponding Windows messages that are captured. The predefined PowerBuilder events are disabled because you cannot alter them. The blank single-line edits at the bottom of the list are where your custom events can be defined.

The first column specifies what the name of the event will be. This name will appear in the Select Event drop-down list box with all of the currently defined events and will be used to refer to the event. The naming standard for user-defined events is to begin the event name with `ue_` followed by a descriptive name (for example, `ue_keypressed`). The second column has the event ID that is assigned to the event name. You can enter the event ID by either typing it in, or if you do not know the correct spelling of the event, using the Paste Event ID list box. To use the Paste Event ID list box, scroll to the event ID you want and double-click on it to paste it into the Event ID single-line edit. After you have defined an event, you cannot change its name or its event ID; you must delete it first and re-create it. (Note that doing so deletes all script written for that event.)

TIP

In previous versions of PowerBuilder, all user events were appended to the Select Event drop-down list box. With Version 5.0, the event name is placed alphabetically in the Select Event drop-down. If you name your user events beginning with `ue_`, all your defined events will be placed together in the list. This makes your application easier for maintenance and documentation.

The list of event IDs corresponds to specific Windows messages. None of the PowerBuilder manuals offer definitions of these IDs, but the names are similar to the Windows message names (for example, `pbm_mousemove` maps to the Windows message `wm_mousemove`). These are referred to as *object events.*

In addition to the PowerBuilder object events you can define, you can create a user event that you can trigger manually and Windows does not trigger. PowerBuilder provides 75 custom user event IDs you can use. These event IDs all begin with `pbm_custom` and can be used to perform application-specific processing such as updating a DataWindow control.

New to Version 5.0 is the definition of arguments for events. The Args button by each event displays the arguments that are being passed to the event. Clicking on the button opens the Event Declaration dialog box, which is shown in Figure 7.21.

FIGURE 7.21.
The Event Declaration dialog box.

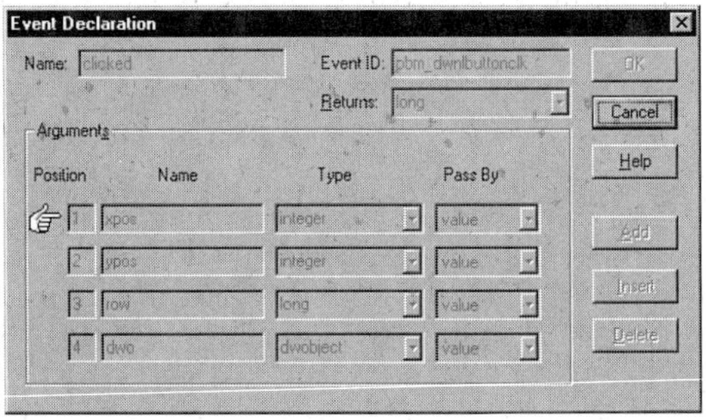

You can use this to view the arguments passed for any of the existing events or any of the user events you add. For all the predefined PowerBuilder event IDs the arguments are already defined and cannot be modified. These arguments can be directly referenced in your script, thus reducing having to check the `WordParm` and `LongParm` attributes of the `Message` object.

Previous versions of PowerBuilder allowed you to create the aforementioned object and user events, but Version 5.0 gives you the ability to create custom events. Custom events are effectively functions and treated as such by PowerBuilder. These events are not associated with one of the PowerBuilder event IDs. They allow you to define the arguments and return a value from the new event.

To create your own custom event and specify the argument's passed and return value, type in an event name and leave the event ID single-line edit blank. Clicking on the Args button then opens an editable Event Declaration dialog box (see Figure 7.22).

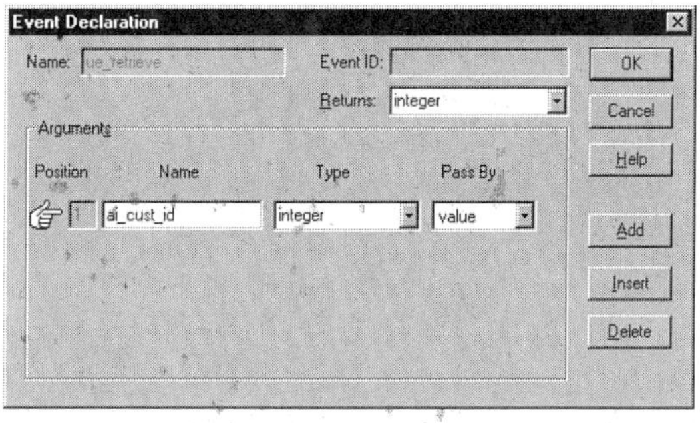

FIGURE 7.22.
The Event Declaration dialog box using user-defined parameters.

Within the Event Declaration dialog box, you can specify as many arguments as you like. The arguments can be of any valid PowerBuilder data type and passed by reference or value. You can also specify a return value data type for the event. For information on how to call the new event and pass arguments, see Chapter 6.

After a user event has been defined, click OK in the Event dialog box to return to the PowerScript painter. Select the new event name from the Select Event drop-down list box (see Figure 7.23) and begin coding your script.

Once you have defined all of your events, you may need to code the script to execute them (for user and custom events). The user events are executed using `TriggerEvent()` or `PostEvent()`. The custom events have their own syntax for passing arguments. See Chapter 6 for descriptions of each of these functions.

If a desired Windows message is not located in the list of PowerBuilder event IDs, PowerBuilder defines an event for you that's known as the `Other` event. These unmapped Windows messages trigger the `Other` event for the particular object. Through PowerScript code and use of the `Message` object, the Windows message can be trapped and appropriate actions can be coded.

FIGURE 7.23.
The Select Event drop-down list box with user events.

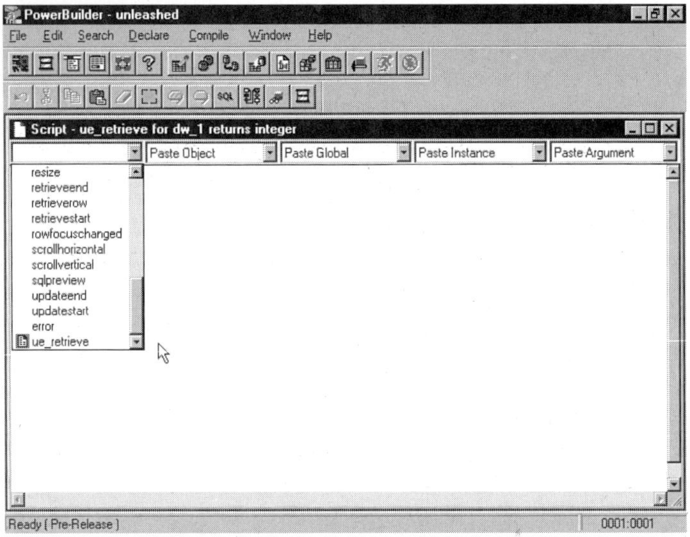

> **WARNING**
>
> Because the `Other` event is triggered for all unmapped Windows messages, writing substantial script for this event can slow the application's performance.

Context-Sensitive Help

To ease in your learning and understanding of the PowerScript language, PowerBuilder has incorporated context-sensitive help into the Script painter. To invoke help, place the cursor within a PowerScript function name or keyword and press Shift+F1. The help is then activated for that particular PowerScript statement. An alternative method for getting context-sensitive help is to right-click on the desired PowerScript statement and select Help from the pop-up menu.

Keyboard Command Reference

For you keyboard enthusiasts, Table 7.1 is a list of valid keystrokes that can be used while in the PowerScript painter.

Table 7.1. Keyboard commands that can be used in the PowerScript painter.

Keyboard Shortcut	*Action*
Ctrl+n (n = 1 through 7)	Paste drop-down list boxes
Ctrl+F4	Close painter
Ctrl+A	Select all
Ctrl+C	Copy
Ctrl+F	Find text
Ctrl+G	Find next text
Ctrl+Shift+G	Go to line
Ctrl+L	Compile script
Ctrl+Q	Exit PowerBuilder
Ctrl+V	Paste
Ctrl+X	Cut
Ctrl+Z	Undo
Shift+F6	Text editor
Shift+F1	Context-sensitive help for selected function

The Function Painter

Although the PowerScript language provides many functions to accomplish a variety of tasks, most applications need to perform additional processing that PowerBuilder does not supply. Functions and subroutines enable the creation of modularized and reusable code. Both functions and subroutines are created using the Function painter and can be defined on an object or a global level.

Functions Versus Subroutines

The only difference between a function and a subroutine is that a function always returns a value of a specific data type (for example, an integer). Subroutines, on the other hand, do not return values and therefore have no return type. An important but occasionally confusing point is that subroutines and functions are both created using the Function painter. For each subroutine or function, there are some common components that must be specified in its definition: the function/subroutine name, any arguments to be passed, whether the arguments are passed by reference or by value, access designation (only for object-level functions), and the data type of the return value (for functions only).

Access Privileges

There are three access privileges you can specify for an object-level function or subroutine: public, private, and protected. The access privileges determine from where a function can be called.

A designation of *public*, valid for global and object-level functions, means that the function can be called from any script in the application. *Private* means that the function can only be called from scripts in the object in which it was declared. *Protected* is an extension of private in that in addition to being called from the object in which it was declared, the function can be called from the object's descendants as well.

Arguments

Arguments can be any valid data type or class within PowerBuilder—they include all standard and enumerated data types, variables, controls (such as a DataWindow control), objects (such as windows), specific objects (`w_order_detail`, for example), and arrays of all of the above. You can specify as many arguments as you need.

Arguments can be passed by reference or by value. In passing an argument by reference, PowerBuilder is actually passing the memory location of the argument. This enables the function or subroutine to modify the value of the argument. If an argument is passed by value, PowerBuilder passes a copy of the current value of the argument. The argument can be changed by the function or subroutine, but the change will not be reflected in the script that executed the function.

An example of passing by reference versus by value is demonstrated in the following code:

```
Int A, B, C
A=2
B=3
C=f_calculate( A, B)
```

The function `f_calculate()` takes two arguments, `X` and `Y`. The return type is an Integer. The body of the text increments `X` and `Y` each by 1 and returns the value of `X` multiplied by `Y`:

```
//Args: X - Integer
//      Y - Integer
//Returns an Integer

X++
Y++
Return X * Y
```

To understand how passing by reference and by value affects the values of `A`, `B`, and `C`, see Table 7.2.

Table 7.2. Passing values by reference versus by value.

Variable	`X` *by Val/*`Y` *by Val*	`X` *by Ref/*`Y` *by Ref*	`X` *by Val/*`Y` *by Ref*
A	2	3	2
B	3	4	4
C	12	12	12

Return Values

The last component of the function declaration is to specify the return type. Because a subroutine does not return a value, select (None) from the drop-down list box for return type. If you are planning to specify a return type, you must include the keyword `Return` followed by an expression of the correct data type in the body of the function script. If `Return` is omitted, PowerBuilder will display a compile error requesting that a `Return` statement be coded.

NOTE

When using conditional logic and returning values based on those conditions, be sure to include a `Return` statement for each condition. Omission of a `Return` statement will not be flagged as a compile error as long as one `Return` statement exists within the function script. Therefore, at runtime you will get an application error when the function tries to exit without a `Return`. To ensure that this does not happen, assign a value to a variable and place a `Return` statement at the end of the function. You are then always passing back a default value if you forget to code the `Return` in your script.

Global Functions

You can access the Function painter from the PowerBar by clicking on the icon showing a sheet of paper with `f(x)` written on it. Clicking on this icon brings up a dialog box where you can view an existing function or create a new one.

The New Function dialog box is the main tool you use to create or declare a function or subroutine (see Figure 7.24).

FIGURE 7.24.
The New Function dialog box.

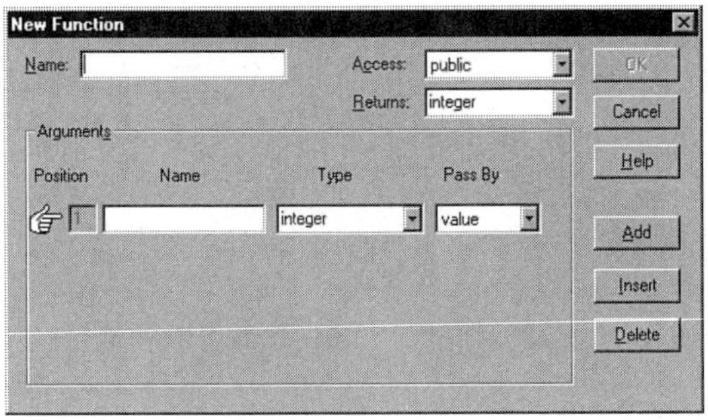

The first step is to name the function or subroutine. Global function names begin with `f_` followed by a descriptive name of the processing. Access designation for global functions is always public. The Returns drop-down list box shows all of the valid return types and the (None) specification for a subroutine. After you decide what arguments are needed for the function, use the Add, Insert, and Delete buttons to provide the appropriate number of arguments. Naming standards for arguments are the same as for other variables with the addition of adding `a_` or `arg_` to the front. After declaring the argument name, choose from the list of argument types and whether the arguments should be passed by reference or by value. When you have completed this step, click the OK button to open the Script painter.

The Script painter within the Function painter acts the same in almost every way as it does with object events. Two major differences are the Paste Argument drop-down list box and the Function Declaration PainterBar icon and menu item. The Paste Argument drop-down list box is in place of the Select Event list box and pastes the selected argument name into the script when chosen. The Function Declaration icon and menu item open the initial dialog box shown in Figure 7.24.

Global functions are best suited to processing that spans multiple objects. For that reason, global functions cannot be encapsulated into one object and therefore are saved as separate objects in your PowerBuilder library.

Object-Level Functions

In contrast to global functions, object-level functions and subroutines are encapsulated and stored within the object for which they are declared (for example, stored with a window's definition). Local functions can be written for the application object, windows, menus, and user objects. To declare an object-level function, click on the Declare menu and select the object function (where *object* means application, window, menu, or user object).

NOTE

In the Application painter the Declare menu is only available within the Script painter.

When you select the function menu item, a Select Function in Window dialog box appears (see Figure 7.25). The Select Function in Window dialog box provides a list of all valid functions defined for the current object. From this dialog box you can create, edit, or delete functions and subroutines.

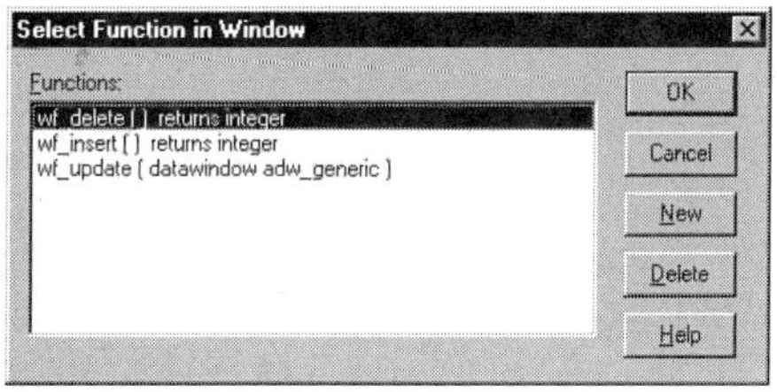

FIGURE 7.25.
The Select Function in Window dialog box.

The Structure Painter

You use a structure to create a collection of one or more related variables. You might be familiar with structures from other languages, where they are known as structs, user types, or records. Creating a structure gives you a high-level reference to these related variables instead of using the separate entities. A common use for structures is to pass multiple values between objects (see Chapter 6). Structures, like functions, can be created globally or on an object level. The Structure painter enables the creation of a new data type or structure class. You then use the structure class to create structure instances for use in PowerBuilder scripts.

Global Structures

You can access the Structure painter via the PowerBar using the icon with four squares joined in a square pattern with a black line (between the Menu and Function painter icons). Clicking on the icon opens the Select Structure dialog box, which gives you the choice of editing an existing structure or creating a new one. The interface for creating and changing a structure in 5.0 now consists of a non-modal window (see Figure 7.26).

The first column is where you enter the names of each variable or field within the structure. Use the second column to specify the data type of each field. The data type can be any standard or enumerated data type, another structure, or a class. Variables can be inserted and deleted using the new PainterBar icons. When you have declared all of the variables, click on the Save PainterBar icon, which will prompt you to specify a name. Global structure names begin with s_ followed by a descriptive name. A global structure is saved as a separate object in your PowerBuilder library.

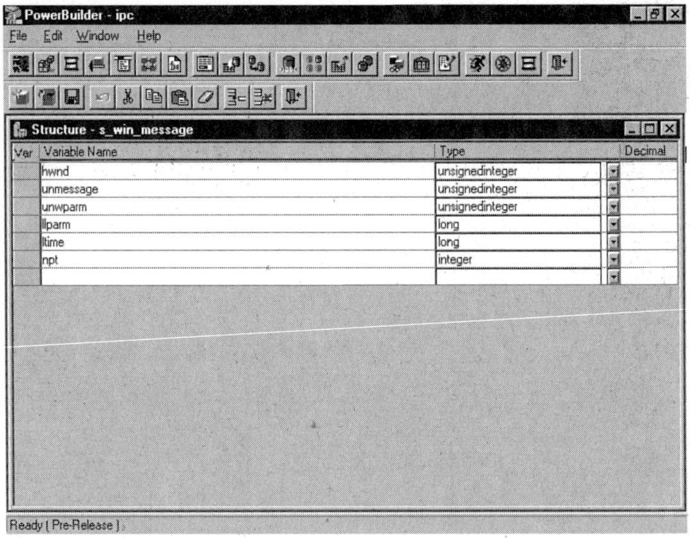

FIGURE 7.26.
The Structure painter.

Object-Level Structures

Structures can be declared for the application object, windows, menus, and user objects. As with object-level functions, object-level structures are defined from the Declare menu (which is only accessible from the Script painter for the application object). The interface is the same for both object-level and global structures. Object-level structures are saved with the object for which they were defined and therefore are not a separate object in your PowerBuilder library.

Summary

The PowerScript environment consists of three main components: the PowerScript painter, the Function painter, and the Structure painter. The PowerScript painter is PowerBuilder's built-in text editor that enables the developer to write scripts for object events. The Script painter also lays the foundation for the Function painter, where user-defined procedures can be declared and written. Using functions increases productivity by enabling you to modularize and reuse code. Finally, in order to define new multivariable data types for use in scripts and passing data between objects, PowerBuilder supplies the Structure painter. The PowerScript environment aids developers by providing an easy-to-use interface equipped with tools that decrease the amount of time spent coding.

Application Objects and the Application Painter

8

IN THIS CHAPTER

When working with any development tool, you need a context to work within and, more importantly, an entry point for the application. For you, the PowerBuilder developer, the application object defines the framework in which you begin to create your application.

This chapter defines what an application object is and how to change each of its components through the Application painter. It examines the attributes, events, methods, and uses of the application object. In addition, this chapter examines some processing that can be incorporated into a nonvisual user object for use with the application object.

What Is an Application Object?

An application object is a nonvisual object that maintains high-level information about your application and is the entry point into your application. What does *high-level information* mean? The main components that are stored with the application object are as follows:

- Default font specifications
- The application icon
- The library search path
- Default global class variables
- Application structures
- Application functions
- Application instance variables
- Global variables
- Global external functions

Whenever an application is executed (at runtime or design time), the `Open` event of the application object is the first script executed. If the script is empty, your application does absolutely nothing and PowerBuilder prompts you to write a script for the `Open` event. Therefore, this script must tell PowerBuilder what to do—for example, open the first window (which is explored later, in the section "The Open Event").

Application Painter Basics

The Application painter enables you to open existing PowerBuilder applications or create new ones. To access the Application painter, click the PowerBar icon that looks like a series of gears or press Shift+F1.

This brings up the Application painter, as shown in Figure 8.1.

FIGURE 8.1.
The Application painter.

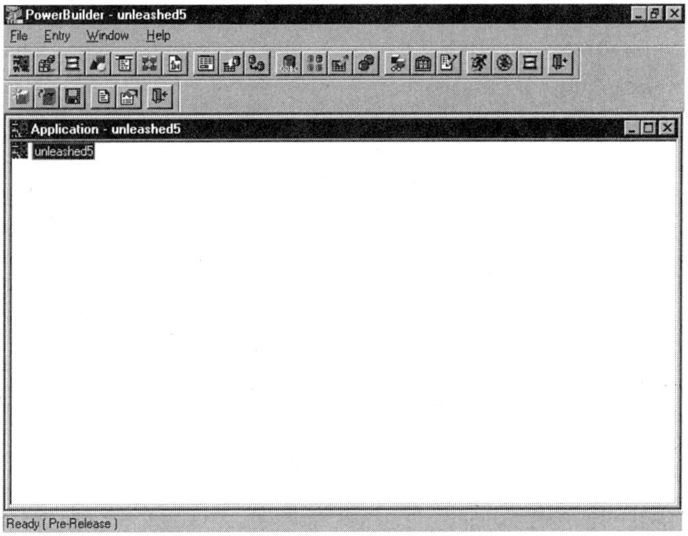

The title bar of the Application painter contains the name of the current application. The same holds true for PowerBuilder's title bar. For example, the title in the figure is PowerBuilder - unleashed5; unleashed5 is the name of the currently open application. Each application maintains a list of PowerBuilder library files (PBLs) from which objects can be read and modified. This is important because it defines the scope of objects accessible from other painters. It is possible to view objects from PBLs outside of your application via the Library painter, but they are read-only. You can only edit objects that are within the list of PBLs defined by your application object, and you can have only one application open at a time in PowerBuilder. There are two methods for changing the current application: opening an existing application object and creating a new one.

NOTE

You can only change the application object when no other painters are open in PowerBuilder.

To open an existing application object, select Open from the File menu or click the Open icon (the open box) on the PainterBar. The Select Application Library dialog box appears (see Figure 8.2) and requests the name of the application object.

After selecting the appropriate directory and library, click OK. This opens the Select Application dialog box (see Figure 8.3). If any application objects exist in the library you selected in the Select Application Library dialog box, the names are shown in the list box. As you will see later, it is a good idea to have only one application object per PBL file. Select the application object you want to open and click OK. The application object now appears in both PowerBuilder's and the Application painter's title bars. If no application object names appear in the list, click the Cancel button and choose Open from the File menu or the PainterBar and start the process over.

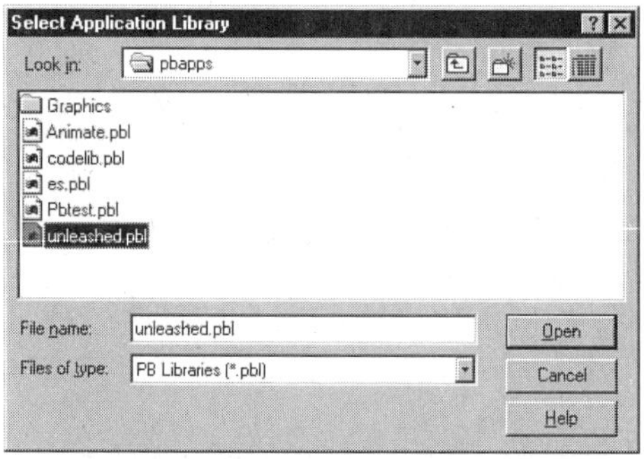

FIGURE 8.2.
The Select Application Library dialog box.

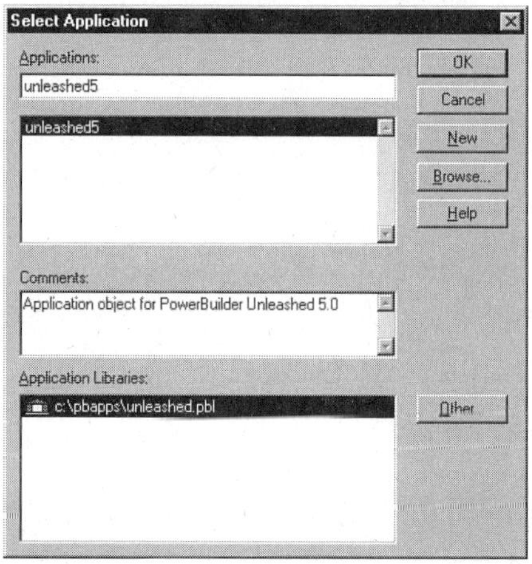

FIGURE 8.3.
The Select Application dialog box.

To create a new application object, choose New from the File menu or click the new application PainterBar icon. This opens the Select New Application Library dialog box (see Figure 8.4). This dialog box prompts you to specify the name of a new PBL and the directory in which you want the file created.

After typing in a name, click the OK button to open the Save Application dialog box (see Figure 8.5). Specify the name of the new application object (it can be different from the PBL name). The application object name has the same restrictions as any other object or variable name (up to 40 characters, no embedded spaces, and so on). Descriptive text can be added in the Comments list box to provide additional information about the application (this is typically a high-level business description).

FIGURE 8.4.
The Select New Application Library dialog box.

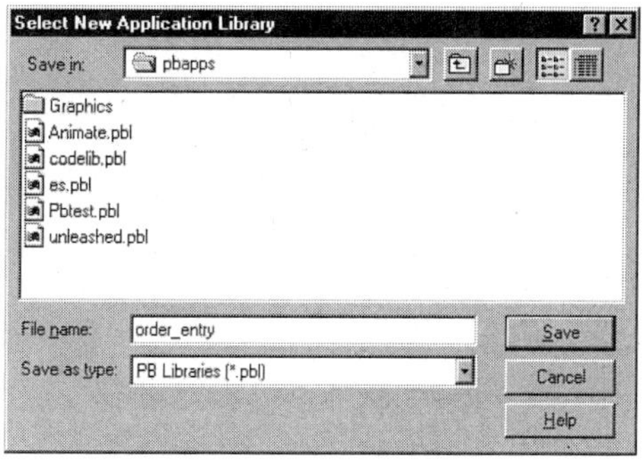

FIGURE 8.5.
The Save Application dialog box.

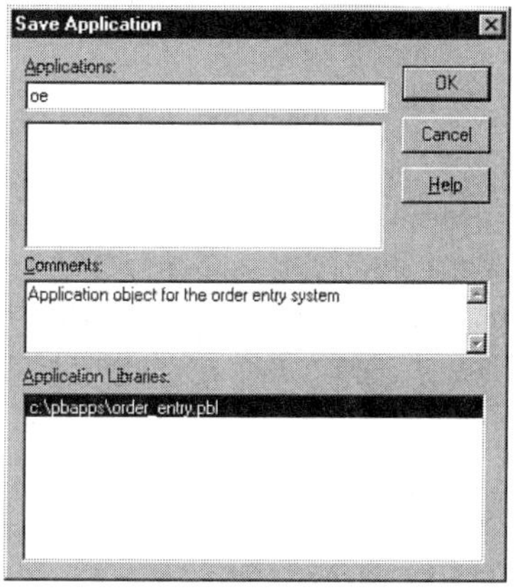

After you specify the library name and the application object name, PowerBuilder asks whether you would like to create an application template (see Figure 8.6).

FIGURE 8.6.
The create application template message box.

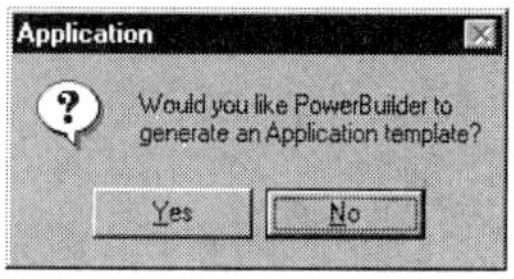

If you select Yes, PowerBuilder generates six objects (four windows and two menus), complete with code (see Figure 8.7). The application template is a quick way to generate a prototype and learn how to create an MDI (multiple-document interface) application in PowerBuilder. The template creates an MDI frame with MicroHelp, a generic sheet, a window for manipulating the toolbars, an About window, a menu for the frame, and an inherited menu for the sheet. This provides a useful framework for the beginning developer. For those with more experience, the application template has some useful functionality that can be incorporated into your objects. (Notice that the window, `w_genapp_toolbars`, does include a nice interface to include in an MDI application.)

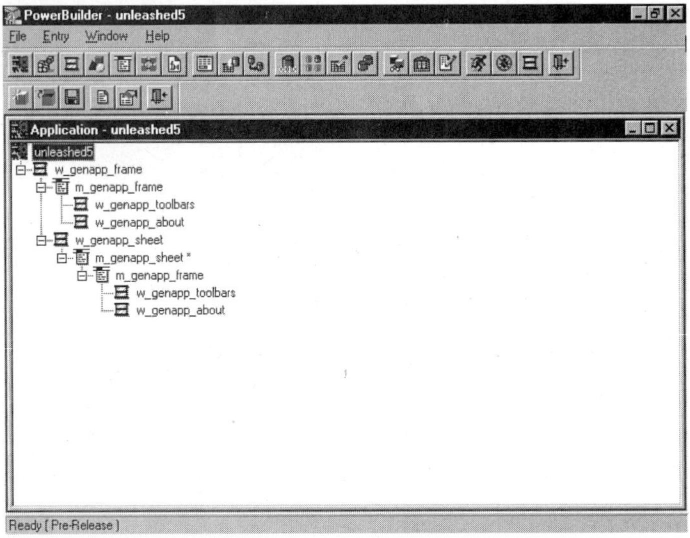

FIGURE 8.7.
A list of PowerBuilder template objects in the Application painter.

If you want to modify the template that PowerBuilder generates, you can change the definition of the default objects. The way Powersoft implemented the template generation is very clever. In the PowerBuilder directory, locate a file named PBGEN050.DLL. Make a copy of the file to PBGEN050.PBL and look at the PBL in the Library painter. Surprise! There are the objects PowerBuilder uses to create its default Application template (see Figure 8.8).

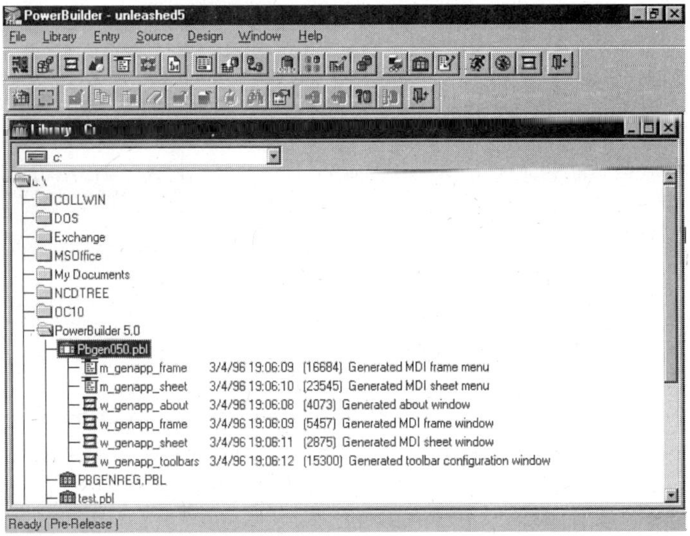

FIGURE 8.8.
The PBGEN050.PBL object listing in the Library painter.

You can modify the default PowerBuilder template quite simply. Make a backup of PBGEN050.DLL (you might want it later), modify the default objects, and rename your template PBL to PBGEN050.DLL. You now have your own specific application template.

WARNING

If you try to generate a template from PBGEN050.DLL that does not include the default PowerBuilder template objects, you will get an error when creating the new application object. PowerBuilder copies a script for the `Open` event of the application object that references `w_genapp_frame` and copies only the six specified objects from PBGEN050.DLL (even if more are included in the PBL).

After you have specified whether you wish to create a template, the Application painter opens. It has the name of the application object in the title of the painter.

Components of the Application Object

After you have created or selected the application object you want to use, you are ready to set the default information about your application: application icon, default fonts, library search path, and default global variables. You can access these attributes by selecting the Properties PainterBar icon, selecting Properties from the Edit menu, or right-clicking on your application object name next to the Application Object icon. This displays the Application property sheet (see Figure 8.9).

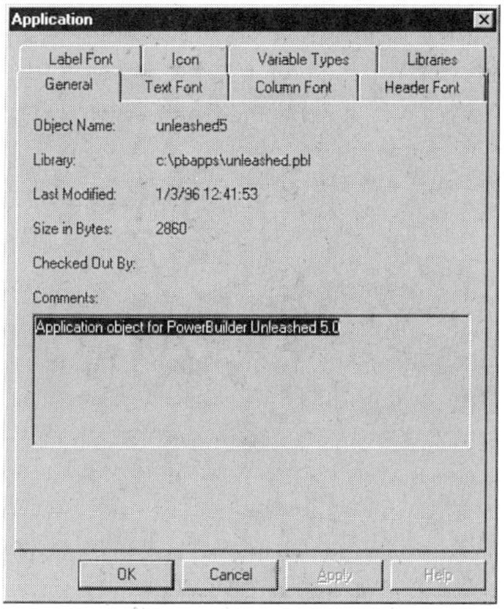

FIGURE 8.9.
The Application property sheet.

The General tab page (see Figure 8.9) displays specific information about the current application: the object name, the PowerBuilder library file in which the application object resides, any comments about the application, the date and time stamp of the last modification, the size of the object in bytes, and who checked out the object from the Library painter.

Setting the Default Fonts

Within the Application painter you can specify the default fonts, text colors, sizes, and styles for the application. Different settings can be applied to all text, columns, headings, and labels that appear in your application. By enabling you to choose this information at a high level, PowerBuilder reduces the need for you to set the font properties every time you create a new object (such as a window). What you set at this time will be the standard font used throughout the application.

> **NOTE**
>
> An important thing to remember, however, is that after an object is created it no longer has any knowledge of the default fonts. In other words, there is no link maintained for the fonts after an object is created, so changing the default font on the application object after objects have already been created does not affect the created objects.

To change the default fonts, select the appropriate tab page for the object for which you wish to set a default (see Figure 8.10).

FIGURE 8.10.
The Text Font tab page

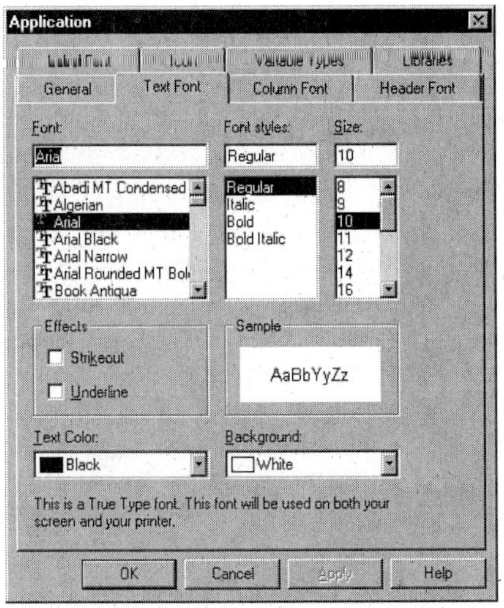

The tab page interface is the same for text, columns, headings, and labels, with the only difference being that you can only change the text and background colors on the Text Font tab page.

The Application Icon

The application icon is the icon that represents the application when you set up a new item in the Windows Start menu. To select an icon for your application, click the Icon tab page (see Figure 8.11).

FIGURE 8.11.
The Icon tab page.

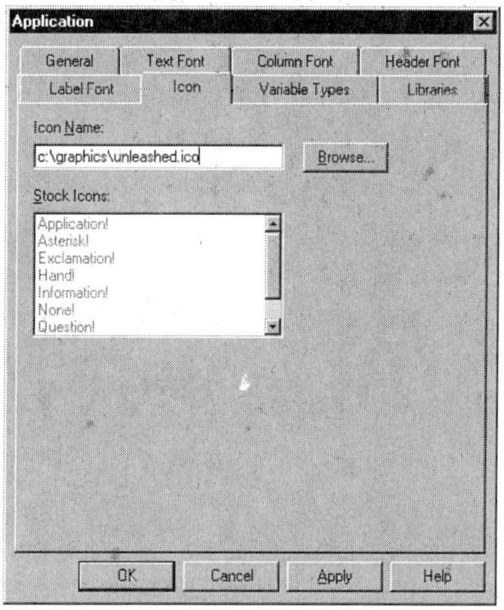

You can choose one of the stock icons that PowerBuilder supplies or specify your own ICO file. PowerBuilder ships with a handful of icons to choose from and also gives you the capability to create your own icons using the Watcom Image Editor.

NOTE

The Watcom Image Editor can only be used to create 16-color bitmaps and icons.

The icon file you choose is also used as the default icon for all the windows in that application. Whenever a window is minimized in the application, the application object icon is the default. You can override this in the Window painter (see Chapter 11, “Windows and the Window Painter”).

Default Global Variables

PowerBuilder enables you to use your own customized versions of the default global objects (`SQLCA`, `SQLDA`, `SQLSA`, `Error`, and `Message`). First, you must create a standard class user object inherited from one of the aforementioned global objects. (For more information on how to create user objects, see Chapter 23, "The User Object Painter.") After you have created the user objects for the global variable you want to change, select the Variable Types tab page (see Figure 8.12).

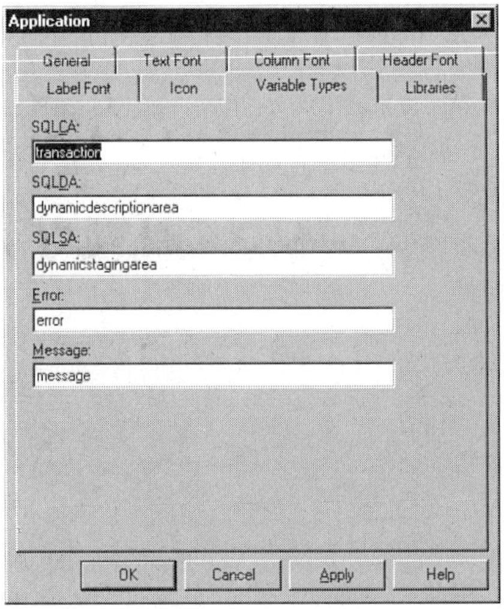

FIGURE 8.12.
The Variable Types tab page.

The names of the default objects (for example, `Transaction` or `Error`) can be changed to the names of the user objects you have created. If you specify a new object associated with the default global variable, PowerBuilder automatically creates an instance of your standard class user object for use within your application. Thus, you can have a customized error object with built-in error routines or SQLCA that contain methods to log you into your database and trap any errors.

The Library Search Path

The library search path is one of the most important aspects of the application object because it defines which objects can be accessed for the current application object. An application comprises multiple objects (windows, menus, and so on) that can be stored in one or several PowerBuilder libraries. The library search path defines a list of libraries from which PowerBuilder can pull objects to be used in the application.

The library search path works in the same way as the DOS search path. If PowerBuilder cannot find an object referenced in the first library, it searches through the library list until the specified object is found. Because PowerBuilder starts at the top and works down, it is recommended that you list the libraries with the more frequently used objects near the top to increase performance.

There are three common uses of the library search path. The first is to have quick and easy access to a library that contains objects that are used across all applications in a company (for example, a logon window or user objects). The second use is for each developer to maintain a private test library containing checked-out copies of objects that are being modified. By placing the test library at the top of the list, all objects the developer is modifying in the test library will be used instead of any other versions. Finally, multiple library files are used to logically arrange the objects that comprise your application. For an in-depth look at how to arrange your objects in your libraries, see Chapter 13, "The Library Painter."

To define the library search path, click the Libraries tab page. This tab page (see Figure 8.13) enables you to specify which libraries—local or networked—you want to include.

FIGURE 8.13.
The Libraries tab page.

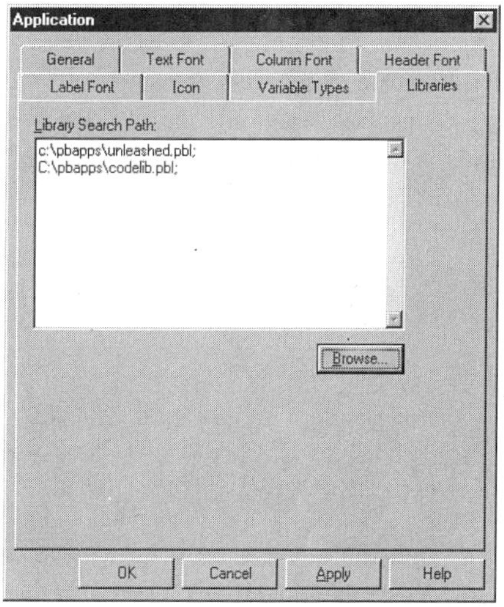

To add a library to the search path, click the Browse button, locate the library's directory, and select the library's name, which pastes it in the search path list box. If you prefer to manually type in the library names, use Enter to move to a new line. To remove a library name from the search path, select the PBL name in the edit box and press the Del key.

NOTE

The library search path is maintained for each developer using the application, so it must be set up for each developer individually for the application to function correctly. This also allows for the use of the private test library mentioned previously. The library search path is stored in the [Application] section of your PB.INI file. The search path can be modified here as well as in the Preferences painter.

Global Variables and Global External Functions

Global variables are variables that can be accessed from any script for any object within an application. Global external functions are calls to function libraries that are stored in dynamic link libraries (DLLs).

All global variables and global external function declarations are stored within the application object. This is not overly exciting or surprising by itself, but it brings up an important point. You should not have more than one application object per application or per library. This is important when migrating applications from previous releases of PowerBuilder. If you have one object (such as a window) referencing a global variable in application A and another object referencing another global variable in application B, a problem can occur. In migration, you must choose which application object you want to migrate, because only one application object is migrated at a time. If you have objects in your library that are accessing global variables in the unmigrated application object, you will receive multiple errors, and migration of those objects will fail.

The Application Object Tree

When you open the Application painter, the current application object name appears next to the application icon at the top of the painter. By using the mouse or a series of keyboard commands, you can see how the various objects in your application are related. Double-click the application icon or name to display the names of all objects referenced in the application's Open event. Each of these objects can then be expanded to show what additional objects it references. The application tree enables you to view how the objects in your application are interrelated (refer to Figure 8.8).

The application tree can be expanded and collapsed by double-clicking on any of the object icons or names in the tree. Compliant with the Windows 95 standard, the application object tree is now a tree view. You can single-click on the + and – signs to expand and collapse each branch. Each object can be opened in the appropriate painter by selecting Edit from the pop-up or the Entry menu, or by pressing Enter. In addition, if any of the objects are ancestor objects in an inheritance chain, the Inheritance Hierarchy menu option on the pop-up and Entry menus is enabled. This dialog box displays the inheritance chain for the selected ancestor object.

Application Object Attributes

Now let's explore each of the application object's attributes. To reference any of the attributes, use the standard dot notation, which is introduced in Chapter 6, "The PowerScript Language."

AppName and DisplayName

The `AppName` attribute contains the name of the application object. `DisplayName` is an alternate name for your application that is easier for an end user to read. For example, when using OLE, any dialog boxes displaying the application's name would use `DisplayName`. If nothing is specified, `DisplayName` defaults to `AppName`. It is important to note that `AppName` is read-only at runtime. If you try to assign a value to this attribute in your script, you will get a compile error.

DDETimeOut

`DDETimeOut` indicates the number of seconds PowerBuilder (as the client) will wait to get a response from a DDE (dynamic data exchange) server before giving up on communicating. The default response time is 10 seconds.

DWMessageTitle

This attribute is used to change the default title of DataWindow message boxes that display at runtime. For example, rather than using the system default title for a column validation rule error, you would place the application name in the title to provide a cleaner interface.

MicroHelpDefault

`MicroHelpDefault` sets the default text of the status bar (or, as it is known in PowerBuilder, MicroHelp). The PowerBuilder (and MDI standard) default is `Ready`.

RightToLeft

`RightToLeft` is used to display text characters from right to left. This is important in multilingual applications that read from the right of the screen to the left.

ToolbarFrameTitle

`ToolbarFrameTitle` specifies the title bar of your application's MDI frame toolbar when it is floating. The default is `FrameBar`.

ToolbarPopMenuText

If you have ever wanted to change the text that displays in the toolbar pop-up menu for an MDI application, this is the attribute for you. If you prefer to change the standard menu text from `Left`, `Top`, `Right`, and so on, set `ToolbarPopMenuText` equal to `Move toolbar to the Left`, `Move toolbar to the Top`, and so on. This changes the text attributes of the toolbar, but not the functionality. This is particularly useful for applications that are to be released in a foreign language. For more information, see Chapter 12, "Menus and the Menu Painter."

ToolbarSheetTitle

The `ToolbarSheetTitle` attribute works the same way that the `ToolbarFrameTitle` attribute does. The only difference is that the title of the floating toolbar is different from the frame toolbar for the sheet.

ToolbarText and ToolbarTips

`ToolbarText` specifies whether the toolbar icons are increased in size to display descriptive text on the buttons. It must be either `TRUE` or `FALSE`. `ToolbarTips` specifies whether PowerTips display when the mouse is over a toolbar icon. (Note that `ToolbarText` must be equal to `FALSE` for PowerTips to display.)

ToolbarUserControl

If any of you don't like giving your users any more flexibility than is necessary, set `ToolbarUserControl` to `FALSE`. Doing so disables the pop-up menu on the toolbar in an MDI application and disables the capability to drag the toolbars to different locations.

Application Object Events

The application object has six possible events in which you can code scripts: `Open`, `Close`, `Idle`, `SystemError`, `ConnectionBegin`, and `ConnectionEnd`. The Script painter can be accessed by clicking the icon showing a sheet of paper in the PainterBar, selecting Script from the Edit menu, or by pressing Ctrl+S.

The Open Event

The `Open` event has a script for each and every application. When an application is run (either at design time or runtime), the first thing to be executed is the `Open` event. If nothing is coded, PowerBuilder pops up a message box stating that you must place code in the `Open` event. In Version 5.0, the `Open` event has an argument called `commandline`. This is used in place of `CommandParm()`, which retrieves any information typed on a command line when executing the application EXE. Standard uses for the `Open` event are to populate transaction objects, connect to a database, and open the first window. Because Powersoft knew developers would want to access a database, it provided a script in the PowerBuilder directory called SQLCA.SCR. This script initializes SQLCA by using the function `ProfileString()` against the PB.INI file, as shown in the following code lines:

```
// This script will read all the database values from PB.INI
//   and store them in SQLCA.
SQLCA.DBMS        =ProfileString("PB.INI","Database","DBMS",             " ")
SQLCA.Database    =ProfileString("PB.INI","Database","DataBase",         " ")
SQLCA.LogID       =ProfileString("PB.INI","Database","LogID",            " ")
SQLCA.LogPass     =ProfileString("PB.INI","Database","LogPassword",      " ")
SQLCA.ServerName  =ProfileString("PB.INI","Database","ServerName",       " ")
SQLCA.UserID      =ProfileString("PB.INI","Database","UserID",           " ")
SQLCA.DBPass      =ProfileString("PB.INI","Database","DatabasePassword", " ")
SQLCA.Lock        =ProfileString("PB.INI","Database","Lock",             " ")
SQLCA.DbParm      =ProfileString("PB.INI","Database","DbParm",           " ")
```

You can paste the SQLCA.SCR file into the `Open` event. If the application is using a logon window, the `Open` event might populate some of the transaction object attributes and then open the logon window. After successfully logging into the database, it might set an application instance Boolean variable to indicate a successful connection.

The `Close` Event

The `Close` event is triggered when the user shuts down the application (that is, closes the last window or MDI frame). The standard use is to disconnect from the database and provide any necessary cleanup of any objects created via PowerScript. It is a good idea to check a flag variable in your script to see if the application is successfully logged on. If so, disconnect from the database and destroy any globally defined objects you might have created (for example, user-defined transaction objects). If the disconnect is unsuccessful, consider writing the database error code and message to a log file or, even better, send an e-mail message that states the problem to the database administrator. If the database is down, it is quite possible that the network is down, too, so you can't send an e-mail. Therefore, it might be a good idea to implement both solutions!

The `Idle` Event

The `Idle` event is triggered when the `Idle()` function has been explicitly called with an idle time in an object script. The `Idle()` function specifies the number of seconds of inactivity that must pass before the `Idle` event is triggered. After the number of seconds specified by the function has elapsed with no mouse or keyboard activity, the `Idle` event is triggered. For example, in the `Open` event, coding `Idle(300)` causes the `Idle` event to trigger after 5 minutes (300 seconds) of inactivity. You use the `Idle` event for several reasons. If you want to prevent long-running transactions from occurring due to inactivity, use the `Idle` event to perform a rollback. For an application containing secure data, the `Idle` event can trigger a password-protected screen saver. Another use is for a kiosk that provides a demonstration—if no one touches the keyboard or mouse for more than a few minutes, the `Idle` event kicks in to stop the demonstration. The `Restart()` function can be coded in the `Idle` event, which then restarts the application from the beginning.

The `SystemError` Event

The `SystemError` event is used to trap severe runtime errors. Two common reasons for this event being triggered are if you refer to an object that does not exist or if an error occurs while you are trying to communicate with a DLL. Typically, the `SystemError` event consists of a `Choose...Case` statement that evaluates the `Number` attribute of the `Error` object. For more in-depth information about this event and the `Error` object, see Chapter 6.

The `ConnectionBegin` Event

The `ConnectionBegin` event is triggered when a client application tries to make a connection to a server application using the new PowerBuilder 5.0 distributed processing environment. `ConnectionBegin` only occurs in the server application. For more information on distributed PowerBuilder, see Chapter 19, "Distributed Processing and Application Partitioning."

The `ConnectionEnd` Event

`ConnectionEnd` is triggered in a distributed processing environment when a client application attempts to terminate a connection to a server application. `ConnectionEnd` occurs only in the server application. For more information on distributed PowerBuilder, see Chapter 19.

Application Object Methods

The application object has only five methods or functions associated with it. They are `ClassName()`, `PostEvent()`, `TriggerEvent()`, `TypeOf()`, and `SetLibraryList()`. `PostEvent()` and `TriggerEvent()` are used to execute events and are covered in depth in Chapter 6. The `ClassName()` function returns the name of the application object, and `TypeOf()` returns the enumerated data type of the application object, `Application!`. These two functions are available to most PowerBuilder objects and are not used frequently with the application object.

Dynamic Library Lists

The last function, `SetLibraryList()`, is unique to the application object. It is used to change the list of dynamic library files in the library search path. The function works only when the application is being run outside the PowerBuilder development environment. The `SetLibraryList()` function accepts a comma-separated list of filenames and uses this list to search for specified objects. One reason you would use this is to increase performance for different users. If user A used your application for editing purposes and user B used the same application for reporting, it would make sense to place the library containing the objects for editing before the library containing the reporting object for user A. The opposite would be true for user B. By switching the library order in the search path, the performance will be better for both users because the library that is needed the most is found first in the search path. This is also intended for use with cross-platform support. You might have a PBL that contains objects for use with Windows and another PBL for use with the Mac. At runtime, you can point to the appropriate PBL, depending on the operating system.

If you needed to implement this functionality, you could hard code the dynamic library list into your application. A better approach would be to create a function in a custom class user object that is instantiated in your application object. This would provide the same logic that could be reused for all applications. For more information on an application user object, see Chapter 24, "Building User Objects."

One way to implement the dynamic modification of the library search path would be to read in values from an application INI file with the structure in Listing 8.1.

Listing 8.1. INI file layout for a dynamic library list.

```
[LibraryList]
NumberOfLibraries = Number of PBD's to be in the search path
Library1 = The first PBD to be in the search path
.
.
LibraryN = The last PBD to be in the search path where N = LibNum
```

The idea is that only the INI file needs to be changed and that the code can remain generic. There would be as many library entries (`LibraryN`) specified as the number indicated by `NumberOfLibraries`. Each group of end users would maintain a different INI file with a different PBD list order.

> **NOTE**
>
> The dynamic library modification has been implemented so far by reading an INI file, which does not work on all platforms. An alternative method of maintaining this list would be to place it in a table in your database. Then, based on the user's security, read the table and assign the appropriate PBD order to the application.

However the PBD list is maintained, the user object function in Listing 8.2 can be used to dynamically build the library search path. This function cycles through the INI file and creates the library list. The application user object has an instance variable, `i_application`, of type Application that is initialized to the current application object.

Listing 8.2. Public subroutine `uf_LibraryList()` in `u_n_application`.

```
int li_libbnum, li_rtn, I
string ls_liblist, ls_appname

ls_appname = i_application.AppName
li_libnum = ProfileInt(ls_appname + ".ini", "LibraryList", &
                     "NumberOfLibraries", 0)

For I = 1 to li_libnum
   Choose Case I
      Case 1            //For the first entry in the list
         ls_liblist = ProfileString(ls_appname + ".ini", &
                      "LibraryList", "Library", String(i) + " ", "")
      Case li_libnum    //For the last entry in the list
         ls_liblist = ls_liblist + ", " + ProfileString(ls_appname + ".ini", &
                      "LibraryList", "Library", String(i), "")
      Case Else         //For all other entries
         ls_liblist = ls_liblist + ", " + ProfileString(ls_appname + ".ini", &
                      "LibraryList", "Library", String(i) + " ", "")
   End Choose
Next
```

`uf_LibraryList()` can be called from the `Open` event of your application object so that the more commonly used PBDs are placed at the top of the library search path.

Another function is often used with the application object: `GetApplication()`. This function returns a handle of data type Application to your script so that you can reference the application object without having to hard code the application name into your script. Here's an example:

```
application   app
app = GetApplication()
app.DDETimeOut = 30
```

Summary

One of the first things you do when developing a PowerBuilder application is create an application object. Every PowerBuilder application must have one, because it is the entry point into the application. Without this object, PowerBuilder will do absolutely nothing. In addition, the application object stores high-level information about the application and provides a point of reference for all other objects. The application object is often an underutilized object in PowerBuilder and can give you the ability to prevent long-running transactions and dynamically change your library search path.

The DataWindow Painter

9

IN THIS CHAPTER

One of the main reasons PowerBuilder is among the strongest application-development software packages on the market is the DataWindow. A *DataWindow* enables you to present data in several different styles for data entry or reporting. It is a unique object that retains knowledge of the data that is being viewed, and it is therefore a powerful means of providing an application with a high degree of database transaction processing.

This chapter explores what a DataWindow object is, potential data sources, the different presentation styles, enhancing and changing your DataWindow objects, and associating a DataWindow object with a DataWindow control.

The DataWindow Object

With the plethora of application-development software packages available these days, there are a number of different ways to retrieve and display data. Unfortunately, these packages are concerned only with developing an easy method to access data and neglect the presentation of the data, or vice versa. PowerBuilder includes a unique object that combines the best of both worlds. A *DataWindow object* incorporates two major components: data intelligence and a number of different user presentations.

A DataWindow object stores considerable information about the data it is displaying. Obviously, the most important data information is the source of the data. A DataWindow object can display data from a number of sources: a relational database, text or dBASE files (with .TXT or .DBF extensions), user input, or dynamic data exchange (DDE) with another Windows application. In addition to knowing the data source, a DataWindow object tracks when data has been changed, whether the data is of the correct data type, whether the data is required, and whether the data passes any specified validation rules. A DataWindow object automatically performs each test and makes sure all data passes the tests.

Developers of many applications would be happy to stop with the data-intelligence component, but the people who created PowerBuilder also provided an environment to create a wide range of user interfaces. The DataWindow painter presents a number of predefined presentation styles that generate default formats for your data. These styles include composite, freeform, graphs, grids, labels, group reports, tabular, N-Up, rich text, OLE 2.0, and crosstabs. Within each of these styles, PowerBuilder provides standard report bands (header, detail, footer, summary, and group headers and footers), display formats, sorting, grouping, and combination presentation styles (such as a spreadsheet user interface with an associated graph). (See Figure 9.1.)

FIGURE 9.1.
An example of a DataWindow's presentation.

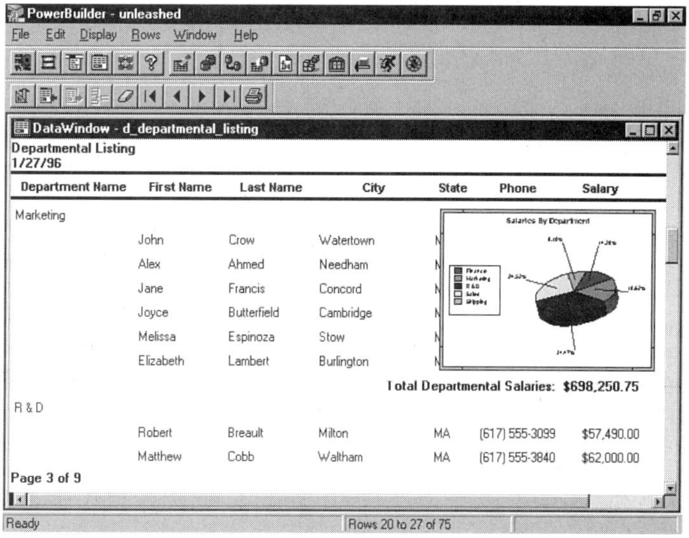

Creating a DataWindow Object

To open the DataWindow painter, simply click the PowerBar icon. This brings up the Select DataWindow dialog box (see Figure 9.2).

FIGURE 9.2.
The Select DataWindow dialog box.

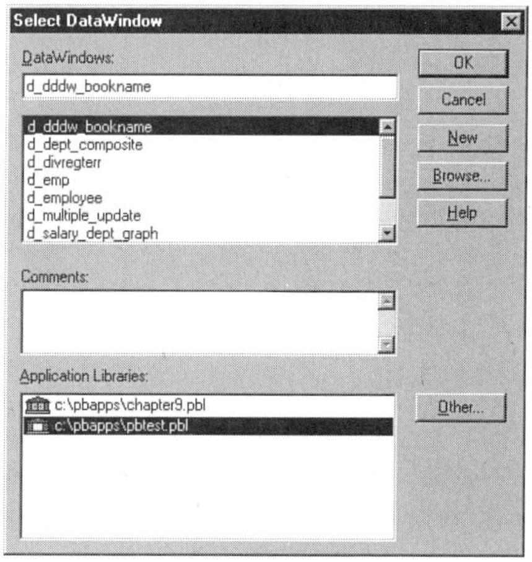

From the Select DataWindow dialog box, you can edit any existing DataWindow object or create a new one. Selecting the New button opens the New DataWindow dialog box (see Figure 9.3).

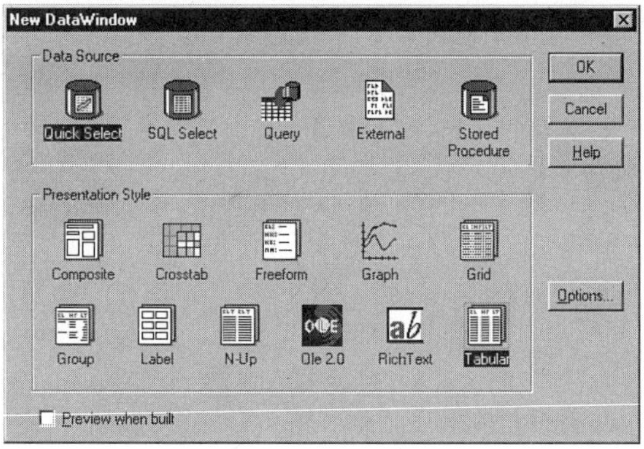

FIGURE 9.3.
The New DataWindow dialog box.

The New DataWindow dialog box consists of four main sections: the data source, the presentation style, Generation Options, and the Preview when built check box. Let's take a look at each of these pieces.

DataWindow Data Sources

Five data sources can be selected for a DataWindow object. These are methods for specifying how PowerBuilder obtains the data you want to display to your user. The different data source choices are Quick Select, SQL Select, Query, External, and Stored Procedure.

Quick Select

The Quick Select data source is used to generate a SQL statement against one or more tables sharing a key relationship. You would typically use Quick Select if you wanted to retrieve data from a single table and potentially retrieve additional information from related tables. After the tables have been selected, you can also specify sorting and `WHERE` clause criteria to limit the amount of data retrieved.

When you choose Quick Select, PowerBuilder displays the Quick Select dialog box (see Figure 9.4).

All the tables that exist in the database you are currently connected to are listed in the Tables list box in the dialog box. Search the list to locate the table from which you want to obtain data. When you select one of the tables (for example, `Employee`), all the columns for that table are displayed (see Figure 9.5).

Also notice that if there are any foreign-key relationships to or from the table that was selected, those related tables are listed in the Tables list box (in Figure 9.5, it is the `Sales_Order` and `Department` tables). The type of relationship is specified by the blue arrow located next to the table name. For example, the arrow pointing down next to the `Sales_Order` table means that a column in the `Employee` table is a primary key in `Sales_Order`. When the arrow points down, it indicates that the selected table's primary key is a foreign key in another table. Any of these related tables can be selected, which in turn show their columns and any relationships (see Figure 9.6).

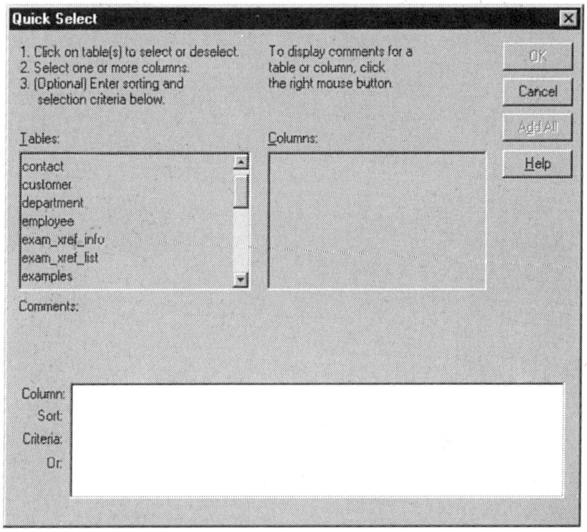

FIGURE 9.4.
The Quick Select dialog box.

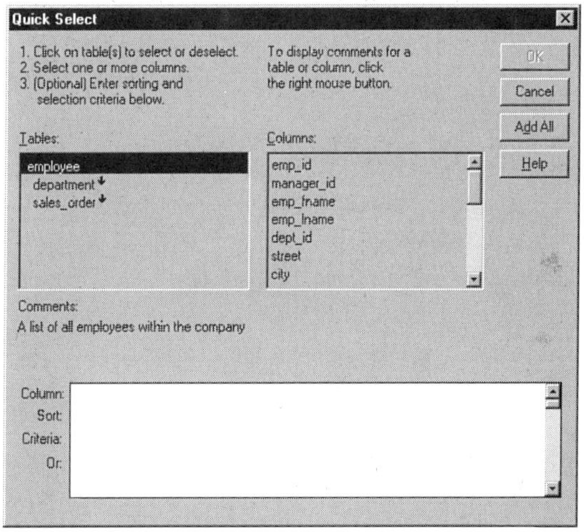

FIGURE 9.5.
The list of columns for the `Employee` *table.*

When all tables have been selected, you can select column names from the Columns list box. If you decide that you made a mistake in selecting columns or tables, just deselect the column or table name. To return to the initial list of tables in your database, deselect the table listed at the top of the Tables list box. Selecting columns from the Columns list box causes the columns to appear in the selected columns box at the bottom of the dialog box (see Figure 9.7). If you want to retrieve all the columns, click the Add All button.

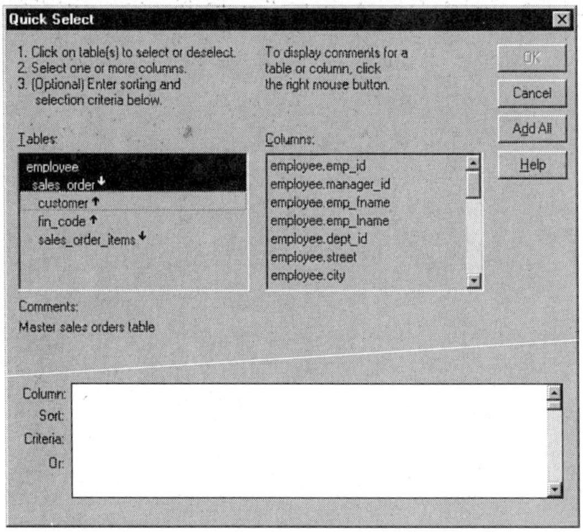

FIGURE 9.6.

Selecting multiple tables using the Quick Select dialog box.

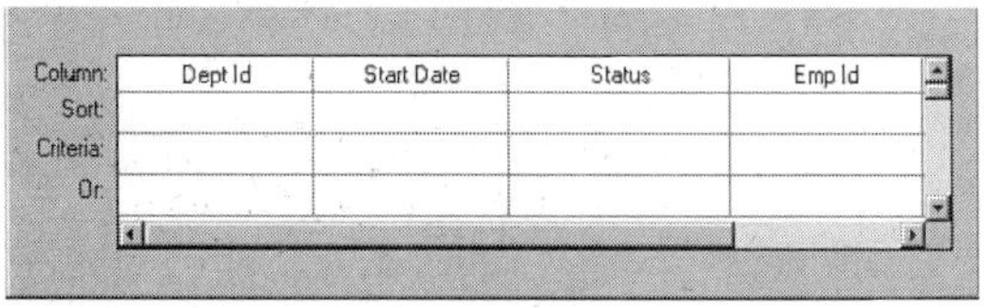

FIGURE 9.7.

The selected columns list in the Quick Select dialog box.

Beneath each of the selected columns you can specify sort criteria and selection criteria. To specify sorting, click the Sort row under the column on which you want the sort performed. A drop-down list box appears, enabling you to choose Ascending, Descending, or not sorted (the default). To specify selection criteria, type an expression under the column you want to have limited. If a column has a drop-down list box or drop-down DataWindow edit style defined on the database (see Chapter 4, "Databases and the Database Painter"), the drop-down list can be used to select a value in the Criteria rows. Criteria specified on the same row generate a logical `AND` in the SQL `WHERE` clause. Criteria specified on different rows generate a logical `OR` in the `WHERE` clause (see Figure 9.8).

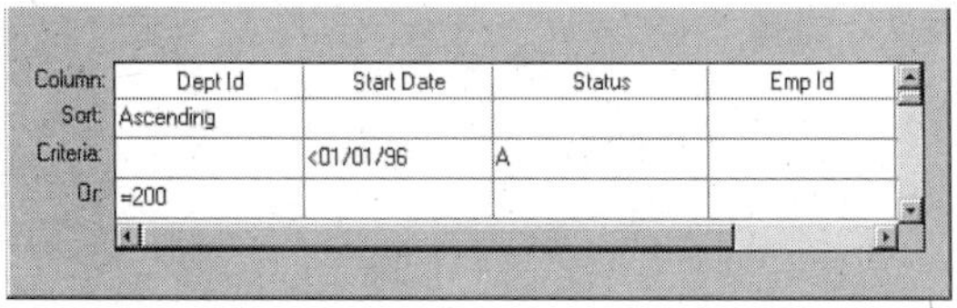

FIGURE 9.8.

The selected columns list with `WHERE` *criteria specified.*

The criteria generated in Figure 9.8 would be as follows:

```
WHERE (start_date < 01/01/96   AND status = 'A')
OR (dept_id= 200)
```

The order in which the columns are selected is the way PowerBuilder arranges the columns on the DataWindow. If you don't like the current order, you can click on a column and drag it to the desired position. After you have specified all the information you want, click OK and PowerBuilder generates the SELECT statement and default user interface for your DataWindow object (see Figure 9.9).

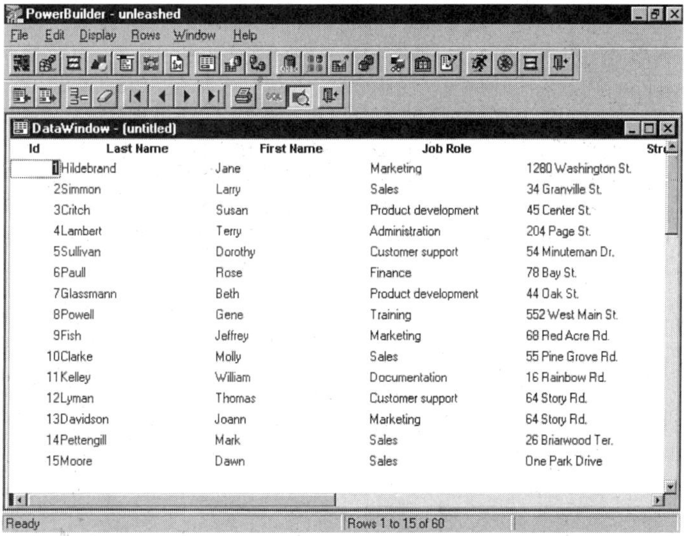

FIGURE 9.9.
The default DataWindow presentation (tabular).

If you decide later that you want to update the SQL statement (that is, add or delete a column or change a logical AND to an OR), click the SQL Select button on the DataWindow PainterBar or select Data Source from the Design menu.

Instead of the Quick Select dialog box appearing again, PowerBuilder takes you into a new interface called the SQL Select painter, which is also the second data source in the New DataWindow dialog box.

The SQL Select Painter

The SQL Select painter is another method you can use to graphically generate a SQL statement in order to retrieve data from an RDBMS. The SQL Select painter is used in several different places in PowerBuilder and is the most frequently used data source for a DataWindow object. The SQL Select painter is shown in Figure 9.10.

The SQL Select painter displays the available tables from which you can retrieve data. The tables that display are those that exist in the database to which you were most recently connected in the Database painter. Select the table(s) from which you want to retrieve data and click the Open button. To select a column, click the column name in the table list, and it is placed in the Selection List at the top of the painter.

FIGURE 9.10.

The SQL Select painter.

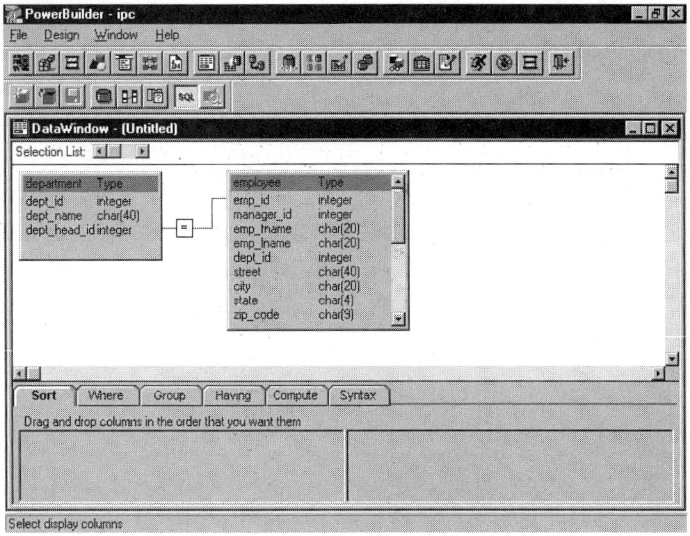

At the bottom of the SQL Select painter is the SQL toolbox. The SQL toolbox consists of a series of tabbed pages that enable you to specify the different clauses of a `SELECT` statement (for example, `HAVING` and `WHERE`). Using the SQL Select painter is covered in detail in Chapter 5, "SQL and PowerBuilder."

In addition to the procedures outlined in Chapter 5, other features of the SQL Select painter are active in the DataWindow painter.

If you feel more comfortable typing the SQL statement as opposed to graphically creating it, select Convert to Syntax from the Design menu. You can toggle back and forth between syntax and graphic modes so you can work in the mode where you are the most comfortable.

NOTE

If you make significant changes while in syntax mode, PowerBuilder might not be able to convert back to the graphic mode.

The other important component of the SQL Select painter that is heavily used by DataWindows is retrieval arguments. From the Design menu select Retrieval Arguments to open the Specify Retrieval Arguments dialog box (see Figure 9.11).

A *retrieval argument* is a variable that you can reference in the `WHERE` clause of your `SELECT` statement, and will be given a value at runtime. In the Specify Retrieval Arguments dialog box, specify the name of the variable and the data type. If the field is a numeric data type, the data type of the retrieval argument is Number. You can specify as many retrieval arguments as you need. When all retrieval arguments have been defined, click OK. If you try to leave the SQL Select painter at this point, you will get a message stating that the retrieval arguments have not been referenced.

FIGURE 9.11.
The Specify Retrieval Arguments dialog box.

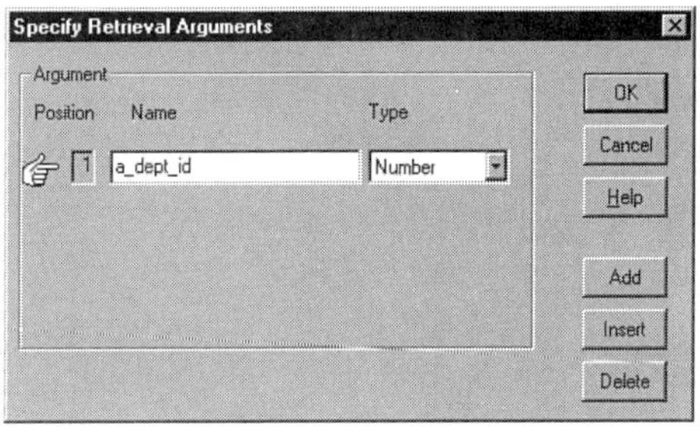

A retrieval argument can be referenced in the `WHERE` and `HAVING` clauses and in computed columns. The most common place is in the `WHERE` clause. For example, instead of specifying the `WHERE` clause `order_no = 12345`, you could use a retrieval argument (defined as `a_order_no number`) and then construct the clause as `WHERE order_no = :a_order_no`. When the DataWindow is previewed, you are prompted to specify a value for the retrieval argument. To place the retrieval argument in the `WHERE` clause, click the Where tab. Next, select the column name from the list box in the Column column, specify an operator, and then right-click on the Value column. From the pop-up menu select Arguments, which opens a dialog box listing all the defined retrieval arguments. Select the retrieval argument you want and click the Paste button.

After you have specified all the information you want to be in the SQL `SELECT` statement, click the SQL icon on the PainterBar to go to the DataWindow object design mode or select Data Source from the Design menu.

Query Object

The Query data source uses a predefined PowerBuilder query object. A query object consists of a SQL `SELECT` statement generated in the Query painter. The Query painter interface is, in essence, the SQL Select painter. The difference is that the query object is saved as a separate object into a library. Query objects are useful if you have a `SELECT` statement that needs to be used as a source for multiple DataWindow objects. This way, you don't have to keep reconstructing the SQL for every DataWindow (which is particularly useful for complex `SELECT` statements).

> **TIP**
>
> If you are going to share data across your DataWindows, query objects ensure that you start with the same query for each DataWindow.

When you select the Query data source, PowerBuilder prompts you with the Select Query dialog box (see Figure 9.12).

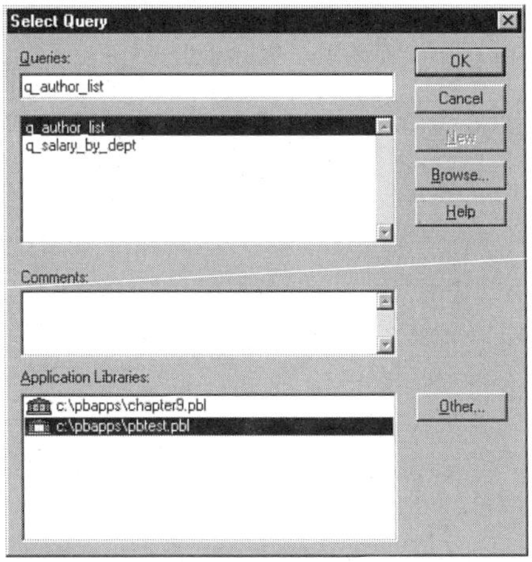

FIGURE 9.12.
The Select Query dialog box.

After initially choosing a query object, you can modify the SQL statement just like the Quick Select and SQL Select data sources. Any changes you make to the SQL statement are not reflected in the query object.

> **NOTE**
>
> Once a DataWindow has specified a query object as a data source, any changes made to the query object are *not* reflected in the DataWindow.

External Data Source

The *External data source* is the catchall for those data sources that are not accessible via the other four data sources (that is, external to a database). This includes such things as embedded SQL, user input, DDE with another Windows application, and remote procedure call (RPC). Instead of the standard relational/SQL-driven data sources you have seen so far, the External data source, when chosen, prompts you for a result set description (see Figure 9.13).

Click the Add button for each distinct field that you want to be a part of the DataWindow. Specify a field name, the data type, and the length of the field (if applicable). The order in which the fields are typed is important because this is the way PowerBuilder creates the user interface (the top field is the farthest to the left, and so on). With the External data source, additional code must be written to populate the DataWindow (for example, direct syntax, `SetItem()`, or any of the File or Import functions).

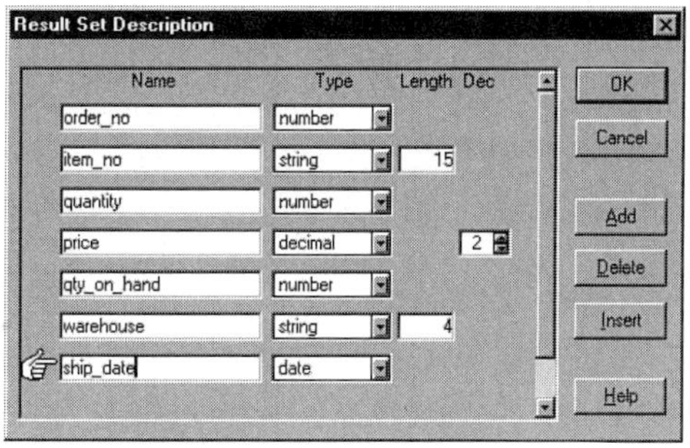

FIGURE 9.13.
The Result Set Description dialog box.

Stored Procedures

The Stored Procedure data source might or might not be available to you when you create a new DataWindow object. The Stored Procedure data source appears only when the DBMS you are using supports stored procedures (for example, SQL Server). A *stored procedure* is precompiled SQL that resides in the DBMS. Stored procedures are very useful if you have a long-running or complex SQL statement or series of statements. When you select this data source, the Select Stored Procedure dialog box appears (see Figure 9.14). In the title bar of the dialog box is the name of the database to which you are currently connected.

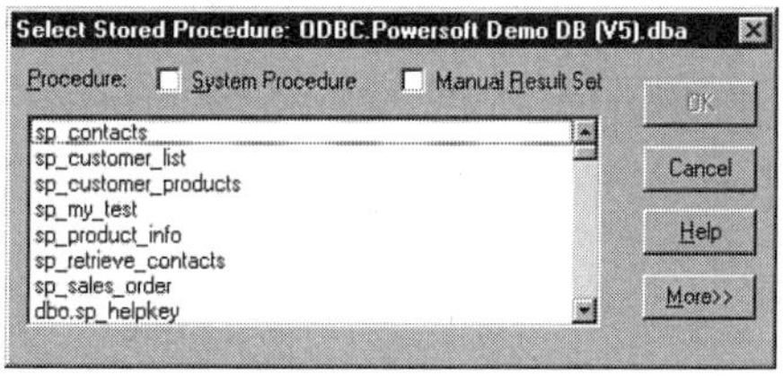

FIGURE 9.14.
The Select Stored Procedure dialog box.

By default, the dialog box shows only the stored procedures that have been created for the specified database. If you want to display system-stored procedures, click the System Procedure check box. The second check box, Manual Result Set, specifies whether you want PowerBuilder to generate the result set description based on the last `SELECT` statement found in the stored procedure or whether you want to do it yourself.

If you are unsure about what each stored procedure is doing, select a procedure name from the list and click the More button. This expands the dialog box to display the SQL statements used to generate the stored procedure (see Figure 9.15).

If you decide to define the result set manually, the Result Set Description dialog box opens (refer to Figure 9.13). As with the External data source option, you specify the fields, data types, and lengths of those fields that the stored procedure will be returning. Because stored procedures can become quite complex, you might need to specify additional information.

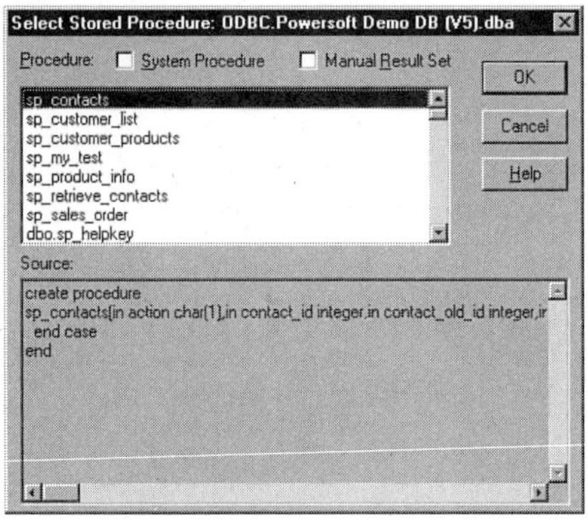

FIGURE 9.15.
The expanded Select Stored Procedure dialog box.

DataWindow Presentation Styles

You have seen that the DataWindow object can retrieve data from a number of different sources (the most common is a relational database). When you have determined where the data will be coming from (you should know this location long before you get to this point), the next step is to choose how the information is displayed to the user. Will it be a graph or a spreadsheet? Is it to be used to display summary or detail information? PowerBuilder supplies 11 different presentation styles to assist in developing an attractive and intuitive user interface.

The Tabular Style

The *tabular* presentation style is a common data layout that displays headings across the top of the page and the data in columns under the headings (see Figure 9.16).

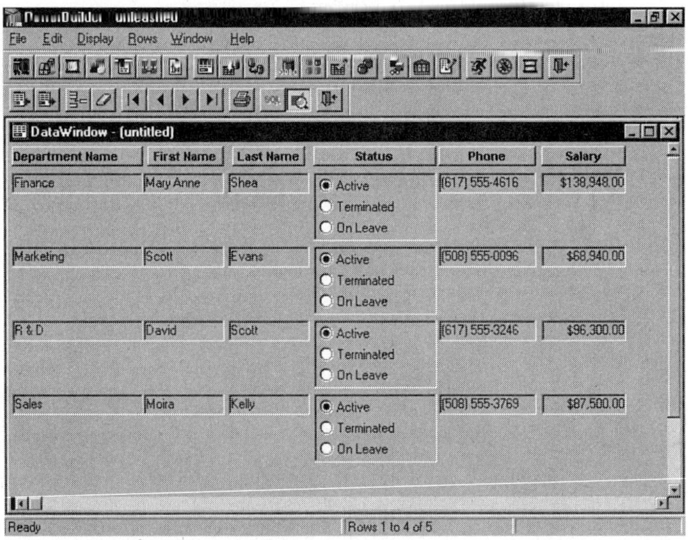

FIGURE 9.16.
The tabular presentation style.

The tabular presentation style is useful for displaying high-level or summary information. From this summary data, the application code enables the user to access the detailed records for the summary row.

The Grid Style

Similar to the tabular presentation style is the *grid* style. The grid style displays headings along the top and columns under the headings, but it also includes lines separating the columns. The grid style looks and acts much like the standard spreadsheet software packages (for example, Microsoft Excel and Lotus 1-2-3), as shown in Figure 9.17.

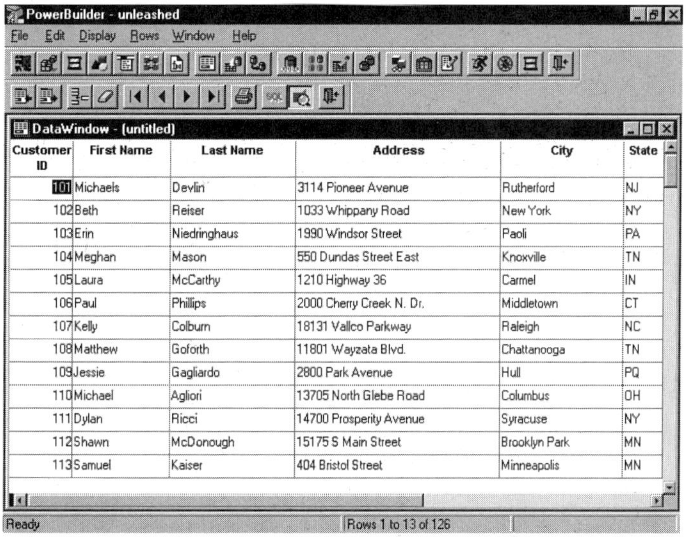

FIGURE 9.17.
The grid presentation style.

The grid style also provides the capability to resize the column widths and row heights, reposition the order of the columns, and split scroll. All this is available at runtime and can be done without any coding.

> **NOTE**
>
> With a grid presentation, you are locked into the grid format and cannot drag the DataWindow objects to a new location to create a different presentation (for example, converting a tabular to a freeform style).

The Group Style

The *group* presentation style also extends the definition of the tabular presentation style. The group style does what the name suggests—it logically groups the data according to a specified column (for example, a list of customers in a particular region, with the region specified as the group field). Every time the value for the region changes, the DataWindow enables you to specify some type of calculation (for example, a count of customers or a summary of sales) before it displays the next value (see Figure 9.18).

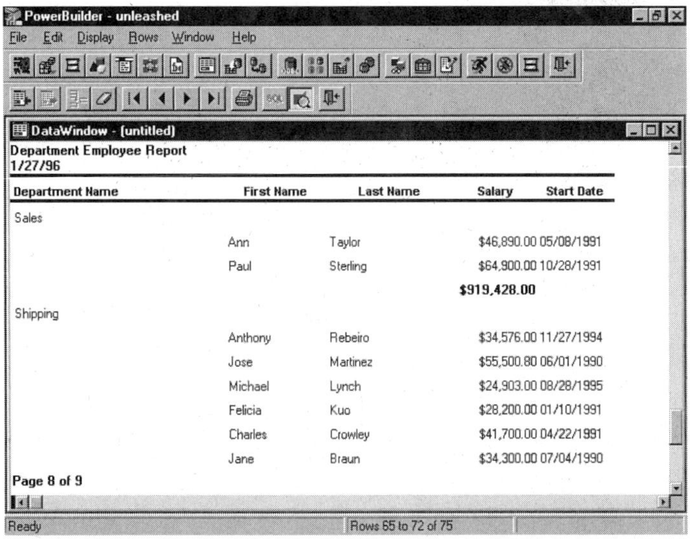

FIGURE 9.18.
The group presentation style.

With the group presentation style, only one level of grouping can be specified initially (however, the group can be a compound group). A compound group consists of two or more columns specified for a single group. After the result set is defined, PowerBuilder opens the Group Report property sheet (see Figure 9.19).

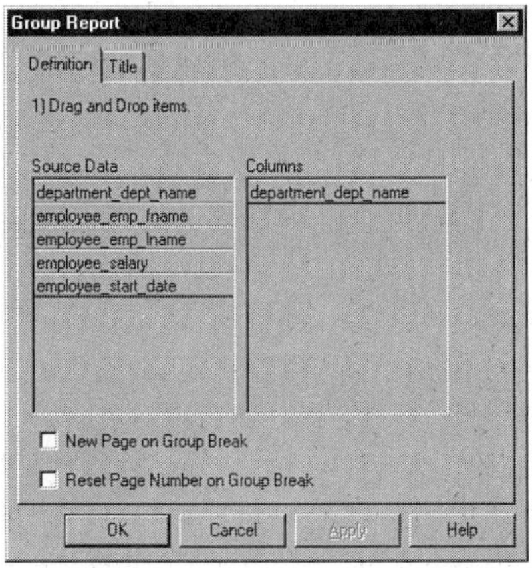

FIGURE 9.19.
The Group Report property sheet.

The Definition tab page asks you to specify on which columns to base the group. To select a column, just drag the column from the Source Data list box and drop it into the Columns list box. You can also specify whether a new page is generated every time the group column's value changes and whether the page number is reset on a group break.

The Title tab page (see Figure 9.20) allows you to specify a page header, which it places in the header band of the DataWindow object.

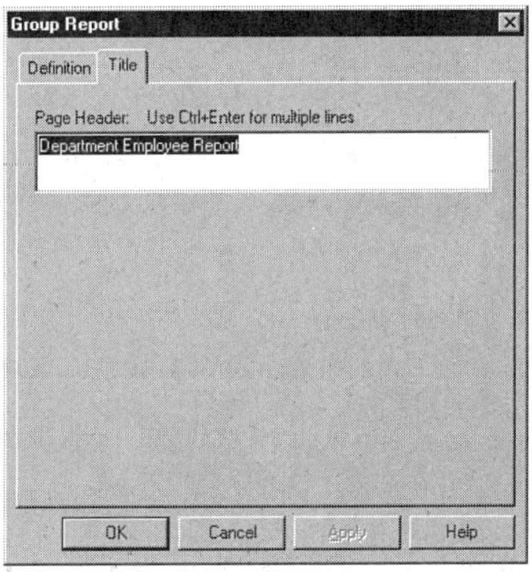

FIGURE 9.20.
The Title tab page.

The default page header is the names of all selected tables specified in the data source and placed before the word Report. Many times this is a perfectly acceptable title, but if not, you can edit the title in the Page Header multiline edit.

Note that this presentation creates only one group. Because more are often desired, see the section titled "Groups" later in the chapter to learn how to create multiple grouping layers.

The Freeform Style

The styles discussed so far are typically used for displaying multiple rows at one time. In the case of detail-level data, you might want to edit one row at a time. To achieve that functionality, the *freeform* presentation style provides a format for single-row editing. Instead of the headings-over-columns layout, the freeform style places labels to the left of the associated column (see Figure 9.21).

The Label Style

If you need to generate mailing labels, the *label* presentation style is an easy way to create them (see Figure 9.22). PowerBuilder supports many different label types and forms so that the DataWindow objects can be specified to match your label sheets.

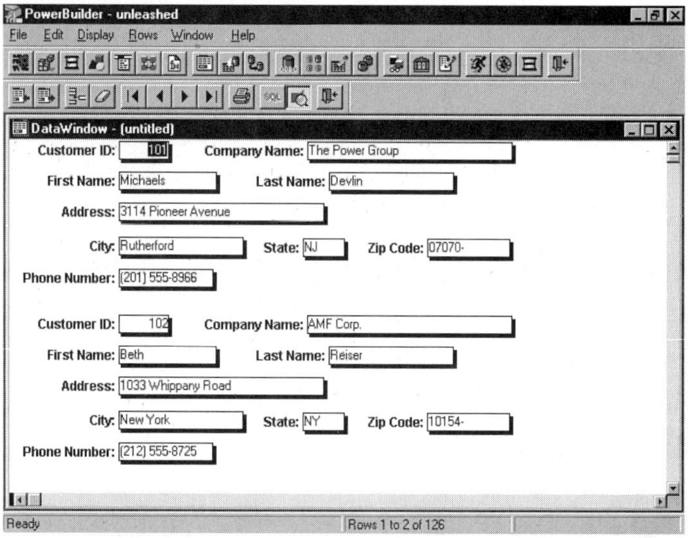

FIGURE 9.21.
The freeform presentation style.

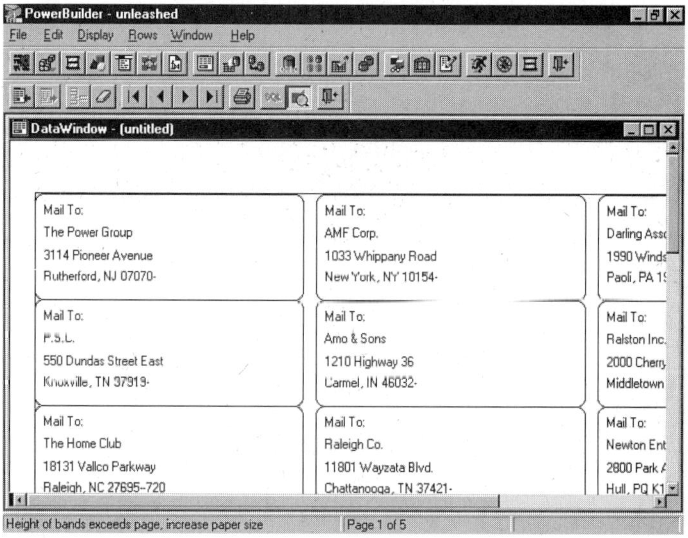

FIGURE 9.22.
The label presentation style.

After you select the label presentation style, the Specify Label Specifications dialog box opens (see Figure 9.23).

In this dialog box you specify the label form on which you want to print your labels. You can also change the height and width of each label, the number of labels across and down a page, whether the label paper is in continuous or single sheets, the page margins, the margins between label columns and rows, and whether you want the labels to print from left to right or from top to bottom.

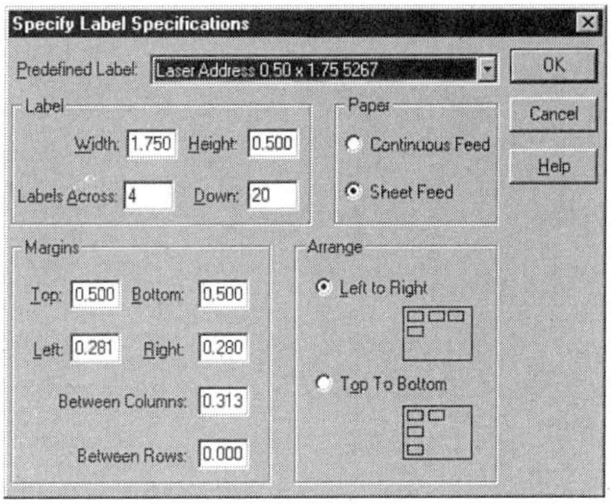

FIGURE 9.23.
The Specify Label Specifications dialog box.

If you need to change the definition after the labels have been created, open the property sheet for the DataWindow and select the Definition tab page.

The N-Up Style

At first glance, the *N-Up* presentation style appears to be an excellent style for displaying two or more columns on a page. Although you can display the data in a multicolumn layout, the data reads from left to right across the columns instead of down the columns (see Figure 9.24).

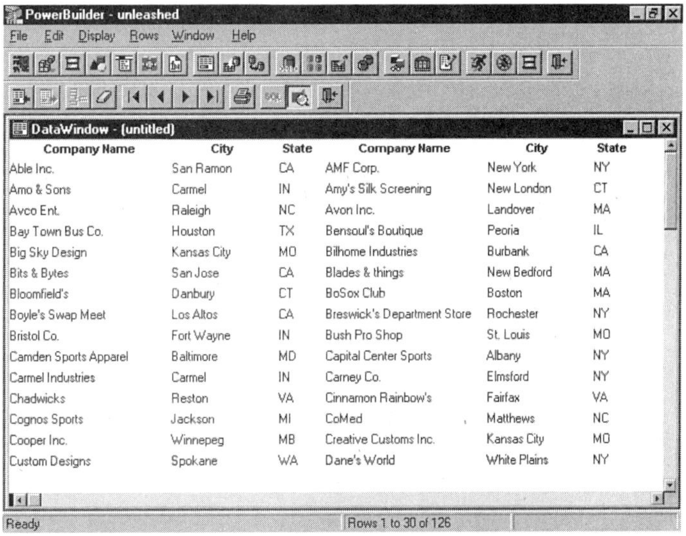

FIGURE 9.24.
The N-Up presentation style.

After you specify the data source, the DataWindow painter opens the Specify Rows in Detail dialog box (see Figure 9.25), which asks how many columns you want created in the detail band (two is the default).

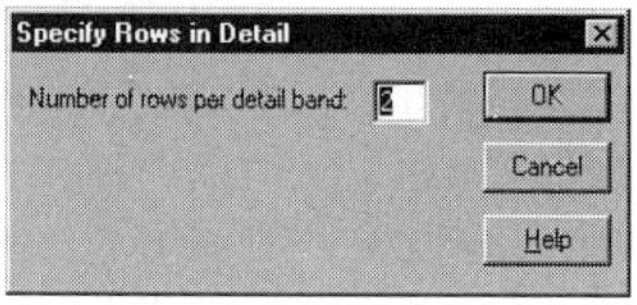

FIGURE 9.25.
The Specify Rows in Detail dialog box.

Most people expect the data to read down each column before moving to the next column of information (as in a newspaper or telephone directory). Because of this, the N-Up presentation style is usually not used except to build a calendar report. If you need to create a newspaper-style report, the DataWindow painter enables you to do so, as you will see later.

The Crosstab Style

The *crosstab* presentation style is very popular with users who need to analyze data. A crosstab enables the user to view summary data as opposed to multiple rows and columns. An easy way to define a crosstab is to specify an example. In a sales application, you can summarize the year's sales for each particular product (see Figure 9.26).

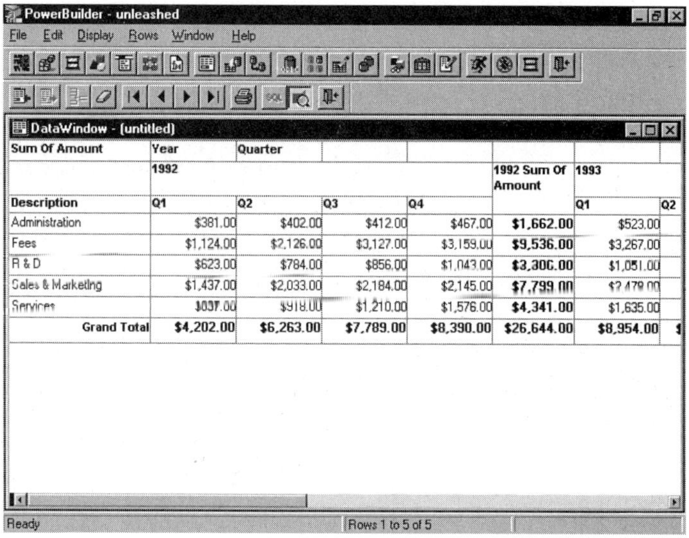

FIGURE 9.26.
The crosstab presentation style.

After you have selected the crosstab presentation style and the data source information, the Crosstab Definition dialog box opens (see Figure 9.27).

Click and drag the source data to the appropriate location. The column (or columns) you want displayed along the top of the crosstab table should be dragged to the column's list box (in this case, year). The same holds true for the data to be displayed on each row (that is, product). Finally, the data you want to perform the calculation on (usually a summary or count) should be dragged to the Values list box (see Figure 9.28). The Rebuild columns at runtime check box tells PowerBuilder whether to re-create the crosstab headings at runtime or use the headings that you specify at design time (in case the runtime headings are nondescriptive).

FIGURE 9.27.
The Crosstab Definition dialog box.

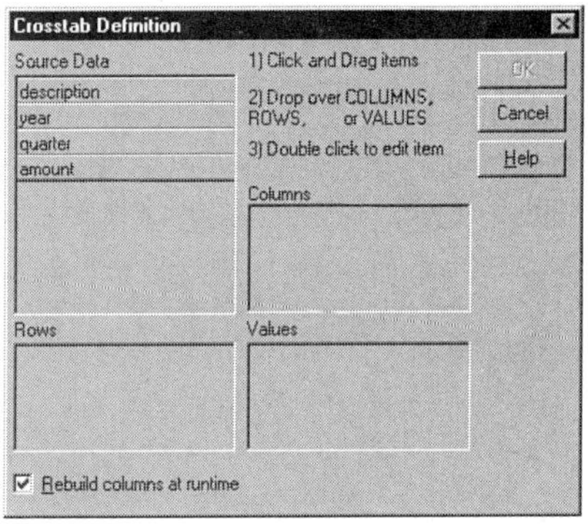

FIGURE 9.28.
The Values list box in the Crosstab Definition dialog box.

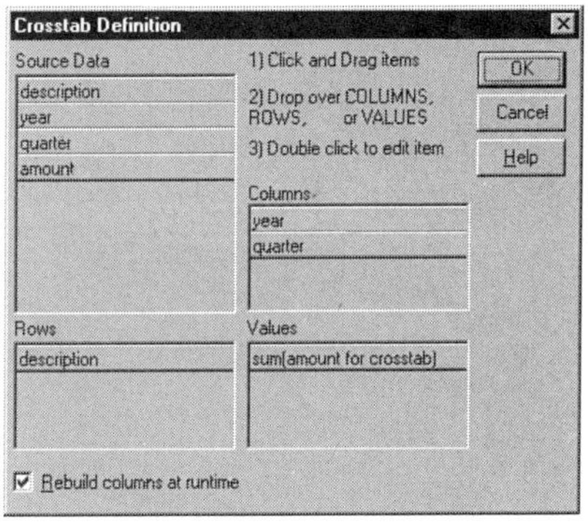

If you do not like the default calculation for the value, double-click the calculation to open the Modify Expression dialog box (see Figure 9.29).

FIGURE 9.29.
The Modify Expression dialog box.

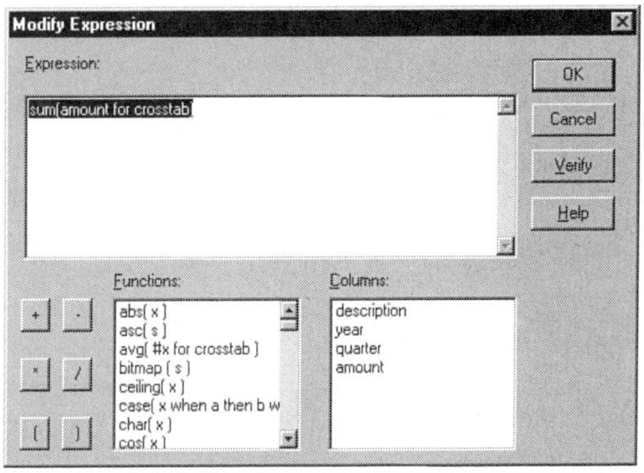

In this dialog box you can change the computed expression that appears at the junction of the specified row and column. To change the definition from the DataWindow design, right-click on the design and select Crosstab from the pop-up menu.

The Graph Style

The *graph* presentation style enables you to display the data using a wide range of different graph types (3D pie, bar, scatter, area, and so on). Figure 9.30 shows an example of a 3D pie graph.

FIGURE 9.30.
The graph presentation style.

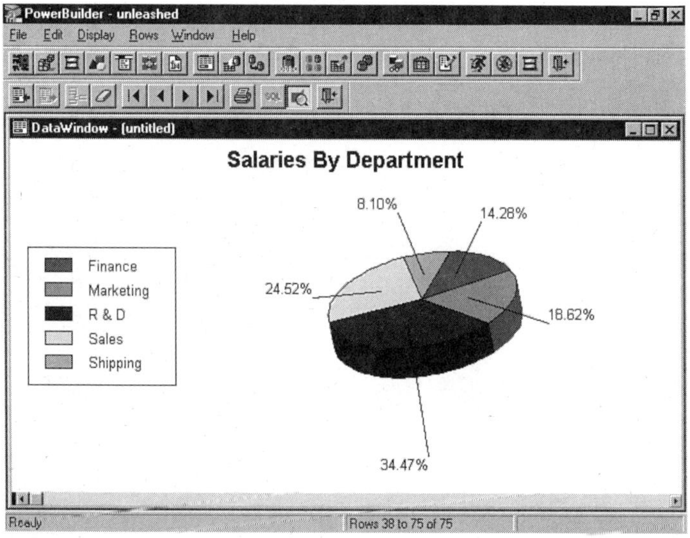

When a data source has been defined, the Graph Object Data property sheet opens, requesting additional information (see Figure 9.31).

With the graph presentation style, all rows are included. (Graphs can be defined in another DataWindow and thus include a subset of the rows, as you will see later in the chapter.) The Category refers to the X axis or the major independent divisions of the data. These divisions are also known as *datapoints*. The Value refers to the Y axis or the dependent data. An optional Series adds another layer of depth to a graph and refers to a set of datapoints. When this information has been specified, PowerBuilder generates the default column graph (which can be changed later). For an in-depth look at graphing, see Chapter 27, “Graphing.”

The Composite Style

The *composite* style differs from the rest of the presentation styles in its source of data. Notice that when you select the composite style, the DataWindow data sources become disabled. This is because the composite presentation consists of multiple, predefined DataWindow objects. After you click OK, you are presented with the Select Reports dialog box (see Figure 9.32), which contains a list of all of the DataWindow objects found in your current application library list.

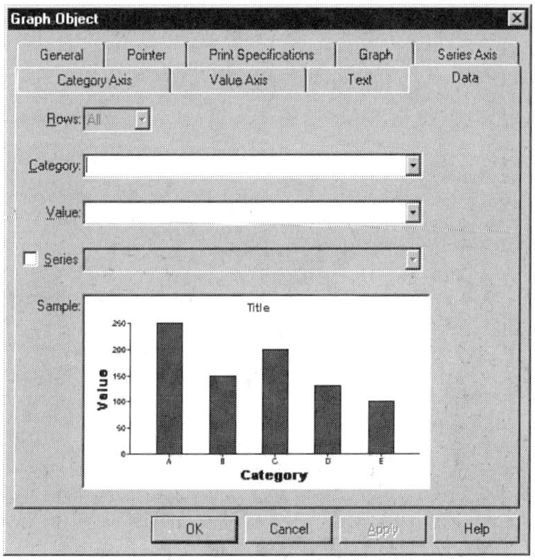

FIGURE 9.31.
The Data tab page of the Graph Object property sheet.

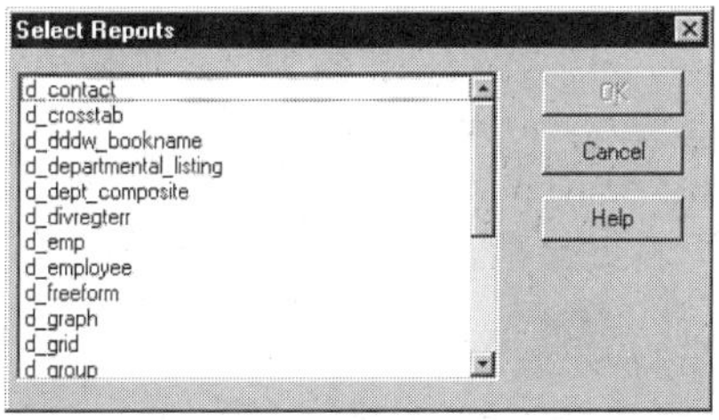

FIGURE 9.32.
The Select Reports dialog box.

NOTE

The dialog box in Figure 9.32 is called Select Reports, which indicates that the DataWindows are just reports and are not editable. The DataWindows that are specified *cannot* be edited using the composite presentation style.

When all the DataWindows have been selected, PowerBuilder places each one in the painter as a bar and labels each with the name of the DataWindow object. These selected DataWindow objects cannot be modified from within the composite style (you must bring up each individual DataWindow to make modifications). Why is this a useful presentation style? In previous releases of PowerBuilder, it was difficult to print multiple DataWindows on the same page without writing some tricky code. Also, it provides an easy method of grouping reports for users, even if the reports are not directly related.

The Rich Text Edit Style

The rich text edit (RTE) presentation style is new in PowerBuilder 5.0. It allows you to place data columns in a rich text document (see Figure 9.33), thus removing much of the need to interact with a word processor outside PowerBuilder.

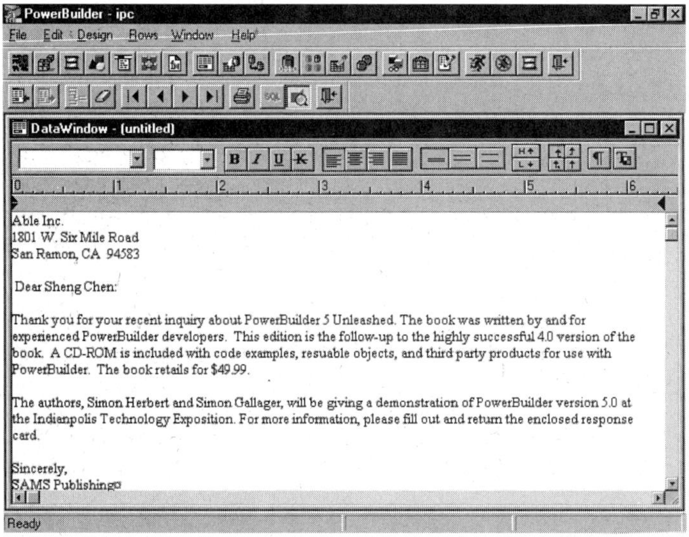

FIGURE 9.33.
The rich text edit presentation style.

After you have specified your data source, the RichText Definition dialog box opens (see Figure 9.34).

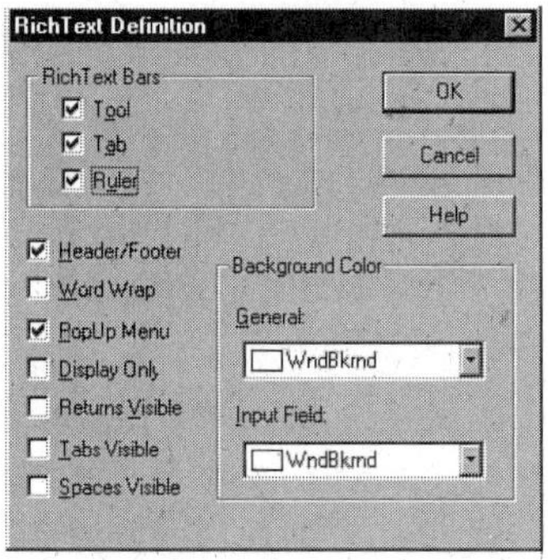

FIGURE 9.34.
The RichText Definition dialog box.

In this dialog box you define how the rich text dialog box will appear. The initial text for the document can be from one of two sources: an existing RTF document or the default (which is empty). After you decide what the text will be, there are a number of additional options that affect the appearance and how the user will interact with the document. The rich text presentation gives you the ability to include headers and footers, have automatic word wrapping, include a pop-up menu (which includes Properties, Insert File, Cut, Copy, Paste, and Clear), and specify whether the whole DataWindow is read only.

The document can include paragraph formatting such as displaying markers for carriage returns, tabs, and spaces. You can also specify which rich text bars are shown: the toolbar, tab bar, and ruler. As with most DataWindows, you can also specify the general background color and the color of each input field.

When the rich text edit DataWindow presentation is opened, the columns appear with their corresponding labels defined in the data repository in the database. The columns appear within braces. You can then treat the DataWindow as you would any document in a word processor and type in the desired text information. To place a column in the text, click on the Column toolbar icon, which opens the Select Column dialog box, allowing you to specify a particular column. Once the layout has been defined, the Rich Text DataWindow is treated like any other, with data retrieved and allowing you to step through the data a row at a time. The user can interact with the text (provided that it is not display only) to make modifications to the text, alignment, font, and so on, as they would in other mail merge applications.

There are a number of new functions specifically for use with RTE. The functions are the same as those for the Rich Text Edit control in the Window painter. For more details, see Chapter 11, "Windows and the Window Painter."

The OLE Presentation Style

PowerBuilder 5.0 now supports OLE 2.0 in the DataWindow painter as an OLE column and as a presentation style. For a detailed look at OLE, see Chapter 36, "OLE 2.0 and DDE." The OLE 2.0 presentation style allows you to incorporate data with an OLE Version 2.0–compliant application. With this presentation, you can embed or link applications such as an Excel spreadsheet, a Word document, or a graph that utilize the data retrieved via the DataWindow (see Figure 9.35).

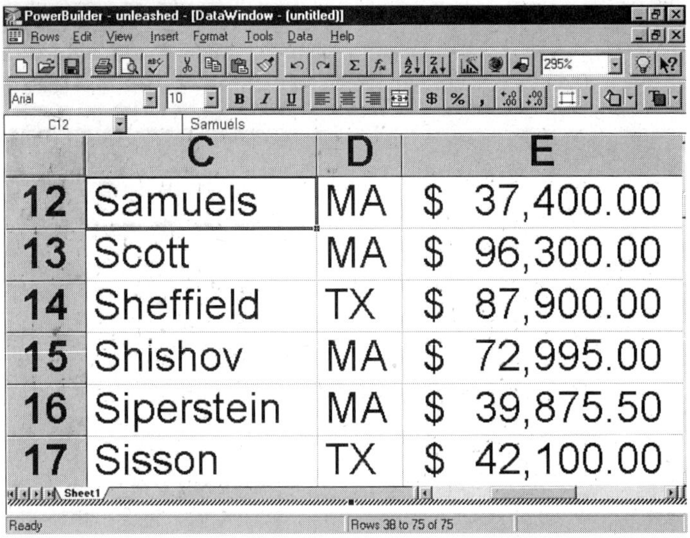

FIGURE 9.35.
The OLE 2.0 presentation style.

After you have specified the required data, the Insert Object property sheet is opened (see Figure 9.36).

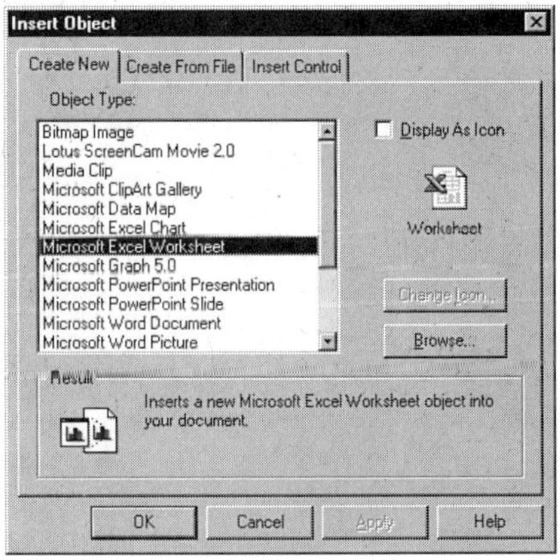

FIGURE 9.36.
The Insert Object property sheet.

Using the different tab pages, you can specify how your OLE object is to be created: as a new object or from an existing object, or with a control (an OCX) inserted. You can also specify whether the object is embedded or linked, and if the object is displayed as an icon or not.

After you specify the OLE object source, the DataWindow design is displayed with the OLE object server environment activated in-place. Click outside the OLE server on the DataWindow to open the OLE object property sheet (see Figure 9.37).

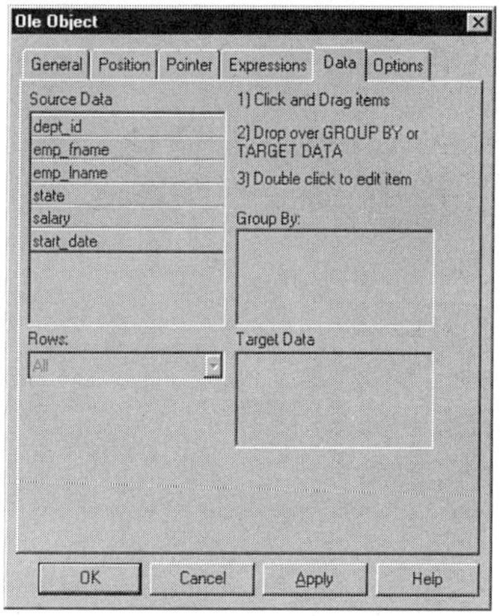

FIGURE 9.37.
The OLE Object property sheet.

The two tabs that are important for defining the OLE interaction are the Data and Options tab pages. The Data tab page (Figure 9.37) defines how the retrieved data is to interact with the OLE server. If you want data to be grouped, click the desired columns and drag them to the Group By list box. With one or more columns specified in the Group By list box, any columns dragged to the Target data are incorporated into a computed column (string columns are counted and numerics are summed). If there is no grouping to be performed, drag the desired columns to the Target Data, which then appear as the column values (no computations).

The Options tab page allows you to specify how the server is activated, the display type, the client name, the object contents, and how the link is updated. Once the OLE definition is complete, the DataWindow retrieves the data and supplies it to the OLE server to manipulate as specified. For more details on OLE, see Chapter 36.

A Sample DataWindow

Let's continue with the creation of a tabular DataWindow and see some of the additional functionality the DataWindow painter provides.

After you specify the tabular presentation and the data source, the default DataWindow design is created (see Figure 9.38).

Notice that the order of the columns (from left to right) corresponds to the order of the fields specified in the data source result set.

Report-Level Formatting

If you are not familiar with standard report-writing software, the design of a DataWindow might be a bit frightening. The design of a DataWindow is broken up into a number of areas referred to as *bands* (similar to a standard report). Figure 9.39 shows the bands of the DataWindow object.

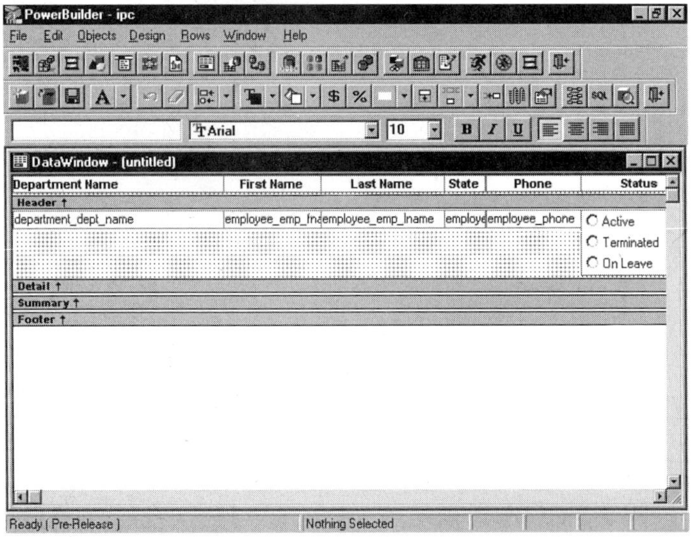

FIGURE 9.38.
The default tabular DataWindow design.

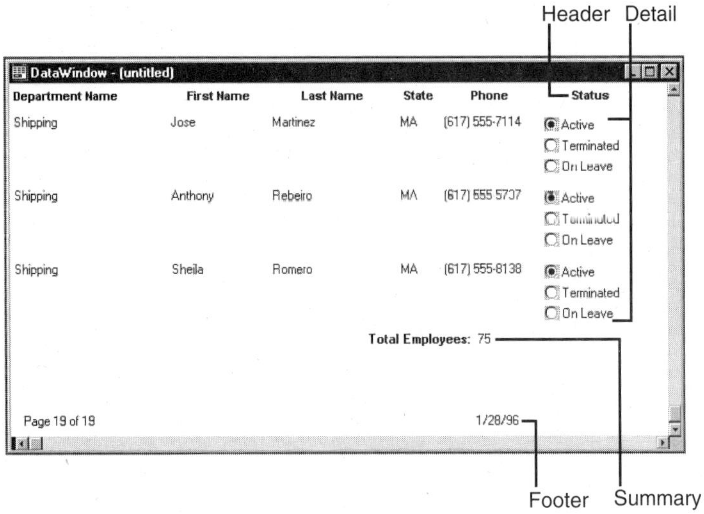

FIGURE 9.39.
DataWindow bands.

In design mode (shown in Figure 9.38), each band is marked with a gray bar below it that holds the name of the band and an arrow pointing to it (for example, Header). The header, detail, footer, and summary bands appear for each of your DataWindows (except the graph and label presentation styles, for which the bands do not apply). The typical uses for each are as follows:

Report Band	*Description*
Header	Appears at the top of every page and is used to display titles and column headings.
Detail	Contains the body of the DataWindow object. Displays rows of data and associated labels. The detail band repeats as many times as necessary within the constraints of the DataWindow object's height.
Footer	Appears at the bottom of each page and is used to display text and page numbers.
Summary	Appears on the last page of the DataWindow object and is used to display totals and summaries for the entire DataWindow object.

In addition to the standard four report bands, a DataWindow object can contain bands such as group headers and group trailers. These bands appear only if you create one or more groups for your DataWindow object (either using the group presentation style or by specifying your own group).

Each of the bands can be resized to accommodate any layout you desire. To resize, just click the gray bar associated with the band you want to resize, and drag.

Remember, though, that any additional white space you leave at the top and bottom areas of the band appears in the DataWindow during execution.

Changing Colors and Borders

Because the default color scheme might not be exactly as you had hoped it would look, you might find that you often have to change the look and feel of your DataWindow object.

To change the background color of the whole DataWindow object, right-click the DataWindow (make sure you are not on a column, heading, or similar location) and select Properties from the pop-up menu. The DataWindow Object property sheet opens (see Figure 9.40).

Select the color you want from the color drop-down on the General tab page; this color is applied to the rest of the report. Notice that on the same tab page you can also specify the units of measurement used in the DataWindow and the timer interval if you are using the DataWindow's internal timer. The Pointer tab page is used to specify the pointer that appears in the DataWindow (the default is an arrow). In addition to being able to set the color and the pointer for the whole report, you can specify the same information for each individual report band (right-click the gray band marker and select Properties).

When you have specified the color of the report and the report bands, it might be necessary to change the appearance of the columns and headings. To accomplish this, right-click on the desired column and select Properties. On the Font tab page (see Figure 9.41), you can select the background or text color and the font and font's style.

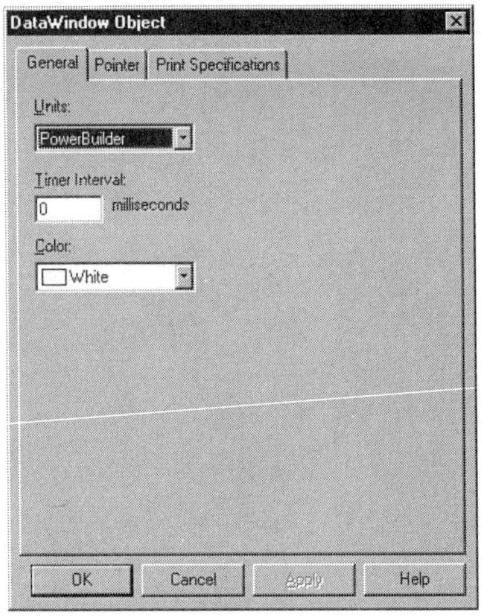

FIGURE 9.40.
The DataWindow Object property sheet.

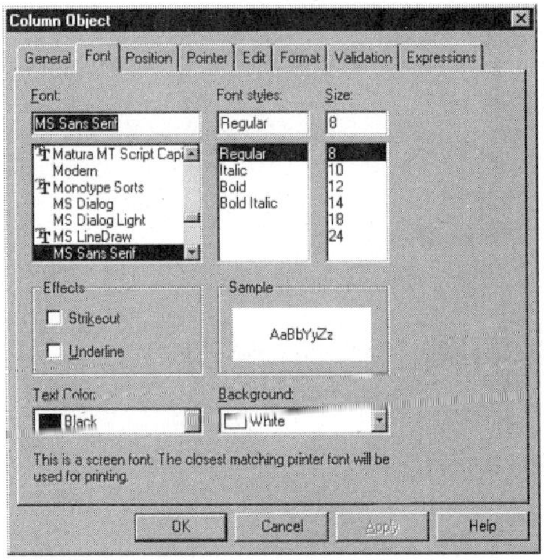

FIGURE 9.41.
The Column Object property sheet Font tab page.

In addition to changing the text and column colors, you can change the border of the column by selecting the General tab page and accessing the Border drop-down list box. The valid options are None, Underline, Box, Resize, Shadow box, 3D Raised, and 3D Lowered. For columns on a tabular presentation, 3D Lowered is a very popular choice. You can do the same thing for the headings; 3D Raised is quite common for headings.

You can use a couple methods to simplify this process. Instead of opening the property sheet for every column and every heading, you can select all the headings or all the columns and format them all at the same time. To select multiple objects on the DataWindow, click one object, hold down the Ctrl key, and click all the other objects to select them. You can also click the left mouse button on a blank space on the report and drag the pointer. Doing this creates a lasso that selects all objects that are touched by or are within the rectangle created by the lasso. A third method is through the Edit menu: Click the Select cascading menu. This enables you to select everything on the DataWindow; everything to the right, left, above, or below a selected object; all columns; or all text (that is, headings and labels). This is a very powerful method of selecting objects and can save you a lot of time during development.

NOTE

A new feature in PowerBuilder 5.0 that assists in the resizing of objects is AutoScrolling. This means that you are no longer required to size an object, stop, move the scrollbars, and continue sizing an object. Movement of objects and their edges is not restricted to the visible screen.

Once all the objects you want to modify are selected, you are ready to apply the format changes. You do this by using the new drop-down toolbars for the border or colors (see Figure 9.42).

FIGURE 9.42.
The border and color drop-down toolbars.

NOTE

In 5.0 the only way to change the colors or borders of multiple objects simultaneously is by using the drop-down toolbar options.

The second method to simplify the color and border designation is from the Generation tab page on the DataWindow Options property sheet (see Figure 9.43).

This tab page is accessed when you create a new DataWindow object. The Options button in the New DataWindow dialog box opens the DataWindow Options property sheet. In the Options tab page you can specify the default colors and background styles for the whole report, text, and columns. If you constantly use the same formatting for a particular presentation style, specify it in this tab page so that it will always be the default. This DataWindow Options property sheet can also be opened by choosing Options from the Design menu in the DataWindow painter.

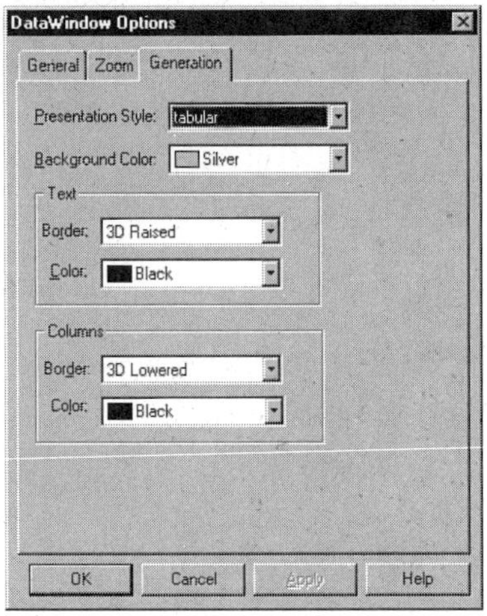

FIGURE 9.43.
The Generation tab page.

> **NOTE**
>
> The Options button is only available for some of the presentation styles (tabular, form, grid, label, N-Up, crosstab, and group), and for those available, a different set of defaults can be specified for each of the other presentation styles. These are stored in the PB.INI file.

Previewing the DataWindow

If you selected the Preview when built check box in the New DataWindow dialog box, the DataWindow automatically executes the SQL statement and displays the tabular DataWindow, complete with data. If not, you are placed in design mode. Either way, you can view the DataWindow as it would appear at runtime with data.

To see the runtime version of your DataWindow, click the PainterBar Preview icon.

Clicking this button retrieves data into the DataWindow layout you created. If you specified one or more retrieval arguments in your SQL statement, PowerBuilder prompts you for them now. At this point, you are in preview mode. If no data is found to satisfy your request, or if you are using an external data source, there is no data displayed. You can always tell you are in preview mode by the different appearance of the PainterBar (see Figure 9.44).

The same icon that took you into the DataWindow preview takes you back into design mode so that you can modify the appearance of the DataWindow (pressing Ctrl+Shift+P also takes you back to design mode). The first time you enter preview mode, the data is retrieved from the database, but each additional time you enter preview mode, the retrieval is not reexecuted. This is because the default option for PowerBuilder is to cache the data in preview mode. Since preview mode is typically used to view how the finished DataWindow object will appear, this removes the overhead of constant database retrieval. These values can be change by modifying your PB.INI file (see Appendix A which is on the book's CD-ROM) or by using the General tab page on the DataWindow Options property sheet. If you want to reretrieve data from the database, click the icon on the PainterBar that shows an arrow pointing toward a DataWindow. The SQL statement is executed and the Retrieve toolbar icon changes to a red hand. Clicking the icon when the hand displays cancels the retrieval of data.

FIGURE 9.44.

The PainterBar in preview mode.

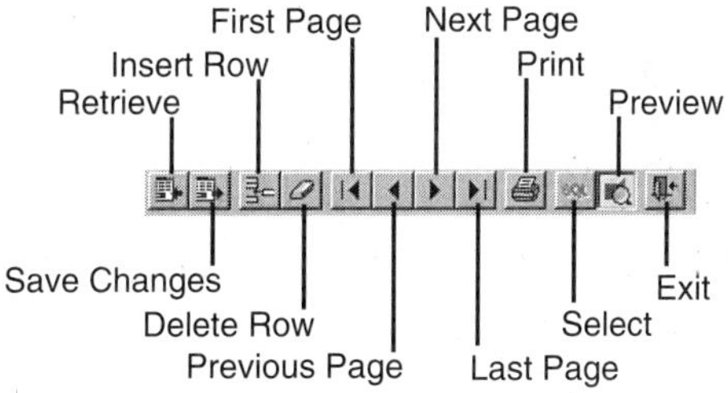

If you are creating an editable DataWindow, you can now modify the data. To do so, click a column and change it. To insert a new row, click the Insert Row icon (the one displaying a series of rows with a new row being inserted). This inserts a blank row above the current row (where your cursor is). To delete an existing row, click the icon with the picture of an eraser. If you try to exit the DataWindow or return to design mode, PowerBuilder prompts you to save the changes back to the database. You can also update the database by selecting the Save Changes icon on the PainterBar (a red arrow pointing away from the DataWindow). The DataWindow generates the appropriate SQL to insert, update, and delete rows in the database. For more information on how PowerBuilder does this, see the section "Update Characteristics."

The next four PainterBar icons are used for movement through the result set displayed in the DataWindow. They enable you to move to the first record, the preceding page (a *page* is defined as what can be viewed on the screen), the next page, and the last record.

You have the ability to print your DataWindow using the Print PainterBar icon. The last two enabled icons on the PainterBar (Select is disabled) are Preview and Exit icons. The Preview icon acts as a toggle that will take you back to the DataWindow design. The Exit icon closes the DataWindow painter.

Sizing, Aligning, and Spacing

After previewing the DataWindow, you might decide that the columns do not look exactly as you had hoped they would. Some of the columns might be truncated, there might be large gaps between columns, or maybe columns and their corresponding headings are not lined up correctly.

Just as in the Window painter, the DataWindow painter gives you the capability to change the size, alignment, and spacing of all objects in the current DataWindow.

To make any changes to an object, you must first select it. As you have already seen, there are many different ways to select several objects. For alignment, sizing, and spacing, the order in which the objects are selected is extremely important. Therefore, do not use the lasso select to select all your fields, because you cannot be sure of the order in which PowerBuilder will decide to select them. You must first select a single object; then you can use the lasso.

To align objects in the same band or across different bands, select the object with which you want all other objects to be aligned. When you have done this, hold down the Ctrl key and manually select each additional object by clicking it (or, because you have already selected one object, you can now use the lasso select for all other objects). You can also choose the Select option in the Edit menu if you need to select a large number of fields. When all desired fields have been selected, click Align Objects in the Edit menu. A cascading menu appears, with pictures specifying how the selected objects will be lined up: on the left, in the center vertically, on the right, on the top, in the center horizontally, or on the bottom. The selected objects jump to their new position in alignment with the first selected object. If you accidentally choose the wrong option, select Undo from the Edit menu, which returns the selected objects to their original positions.

NOTE

In Version 5.0, the undo facility is now multilevel, whereas in previous versions the undo facility was only one change deep.

To size an individual object, select the desired object and move the mouse pointer to the edge of the object so that the pointer changes to the double-arrowed line. Click and drag the object's edge to the desired size. If you cannot see the edge of an object because a border specification is None, turn on the Show Edges option by selecting Options from the Design menu and clicking on the General tab page (see Figure 9.46). To make two or more objects the same size, select one object that has the size (height and width) that you want the other objects to have. Then, using the selection method you prefer, select the other DataWindow objects. From the Edit menu, click the Size Objects option to open the cascading menu. The two options in the Size Objects menu are sized according to the first selected object's width or to its height.

To ensure that the spacing between objects is consistent, position two objects with the desired spacing between them. Select these two objects and then select any objects to which you want to copy the spacing. From the Edit menu, click Space Objects to open the cascading menu, which enables you to specify that the spacing be copied horizontally or vertically. Remember, the spacing is based on the space between the first two objects selected.

Aligning, sizing, and spacing columns can also be accomplished using the new drop-down toolbar in Version 5.0 (see Figure 9.45).

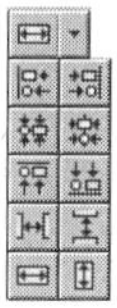

FIGURE 9.45.
The alignment, spacing, and sizing drop-down toolbar.

Keyboard Shortcuts

Table 9.1 shows the keyboard shortcuts that are available in the DataWindow painter.

Table 9.1. Keyboard shortcuts available in the DataWindow painter.

Keyboard Commands	*Description*
	Selecting Objects
Ctrl+up arrow	Select above
Ctrl+down arrow	Select below
Ctrl+left arrow	Select left
Ctrl+right arrow	Select right
Ctrl+A	Select all
	Text Functions
Ctrl+B	Bold
Ctrl+I	Italicize
Ctrl+U	Underline
	View Mode
Ctrl+Shift+P	Toggle Preview/Design mode

Grid, Ruler, and Zoom

To assist you in arranging columns, headings, and any other objects on the DataWindow, the DataWindow painter provides some additional features: the grid, the ruler, and zoom.

The grid displays in the DataWindow workspace and enables you to position objects more easily. The ruler appears on the left and top of the painter and helps to position objects in relation to inches. To turn the grid or ruler on, select Options from the Design menu, which brings up the DataWindow Options property sheet shown in the section "Changing Colors and Borders."

NOTE

The property sheet shown in Figure 9.43 is accessible via the Options button on the New DataWindow dialog box.

To set the grid and ruler, select the General tab page (see Figure 9.46).

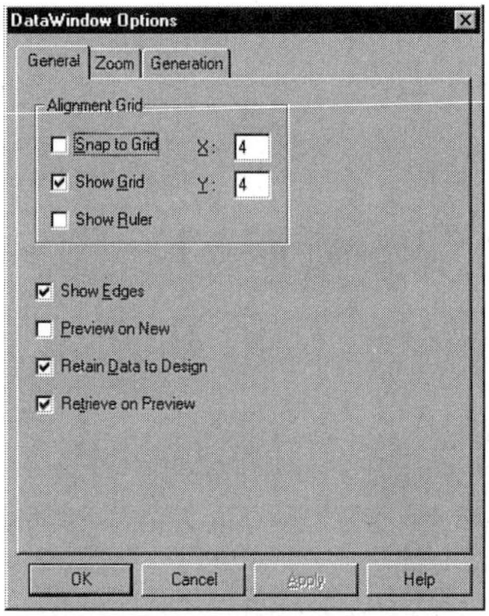

FIGURE 9.46.
The General tab page.

The default size of the grid is 8×8 pixels. For most practical purposes, this is too large; make it 4×4 instead. Another option in the General tab page is Snap to Grid. When this option is activated, objects in the DataWindow automatically align themselves with the grid when they are moved or placed on the DataWindow. The Show Ruler option displays a ruler vertically and horizontally, which is useful for determining margins.

The Zoom tab page enables you to change the scale of the DataWindow workspace so that you can see more of the object or view more detail. The Zoom tab page (see Figure 9.47) is useful for a couple reasons.

If you have a large DataWindow object, you can reduce the workspace scale to view more of the object. Conversely, you can enlarge the workspace to see the DataWindow in more detail. Zoom is view-only (you cannot make changes to the DataWindow) and does not affect the actual size of the DataWindow object. Zoom is also available in preview mode under the Display menu.

FIGURE 9.47.
The Zoom tab page.

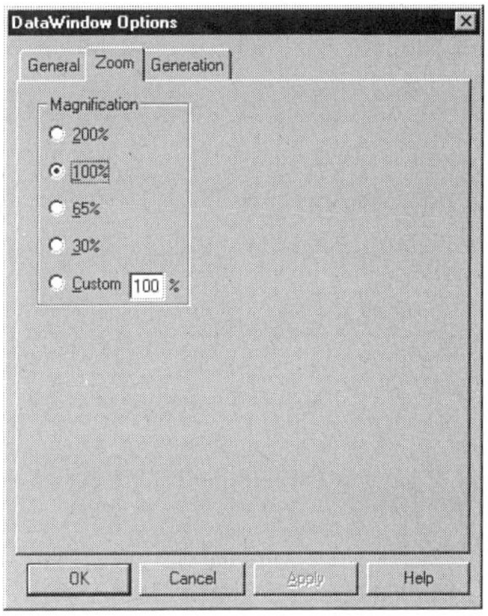

Display Formats, Edit Styles, and Validation Rules

When you previewed the DataWindow object, several of the columns had different formatting (for example, drop-down list boxes, radio buttons, and edit masks). In addition to the data appearing differently, some of the columns displayed an error message when incorrect data was entered. Where did the formatting and validation rules come from? Why is this consistent across all the DataWindow objects that reference these columns? If you recall, in the Database painter you specified extended attributes for some of the columns in the database. All this information is stored in the data repository and is used in all subsequent DataWindow objects that reference the columns.

NOTE

In addition to display formats, edit styles, and validation rules being specified in the data repository, some additional extended attributes are used: justification, height, width, header, and label. These can be modified to be the defaults so that manual manipulation does not have to be performed each time a column is placed on a DataWindow object.

Let's take a look at using existing display formats, edit styles, and validation rules, modifying them, and creating new ones.

Display Formats

A *display format* controls how a DataWindow is presented to the user. When a user clicks a field with a display format, the display format disappears. Display formats are used to keep unnecessary formatting from being stored in the database and taking up valuable space. A display format is useful for those columns that the user is not able to modify.

To use a display format, open the Column Object property sheet and choose the Format tab page (see Figure 9.48).

FIGURE 9.48.
The Format tab page.

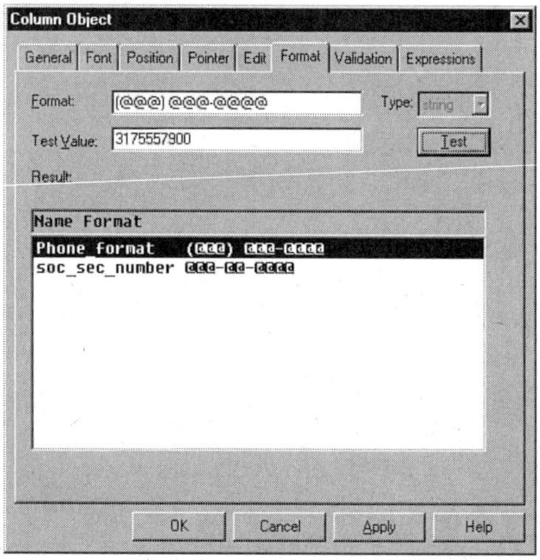

If display formats exist for the data type of the column (for example, String), they display in the list box at the bottom of the dialog box. To apply an existing format, click the format name and click OK. If you want to see what a value will look like with the display format applied to it, enter a value of the correct data type in the Test Value single-line edit and click the Test button. For more information on creating a display format, see Chapter 4.

Edit Styles

Like a display format, an *edit style* changes the way the data is presented to the user. Unlike a display format, though, an edit style does not disappear when the column has focus. An edit style affects the way the user interacts with the data. There are six different types of edit styles: Edit, Edit Mask, RadioButton, CheckBox, DropDownListBox, and DropDownDataWindow. To select an edit style, open the Column Object property sheet and click the Edit tab page.

If an edit style was assigned to the column in the Database painter, the style name is the selected name in the Name drop-down list box. To select another existing edit format from the data repository, select a name from the drop-down list box. If none of the existing edit styles fit your application's requirements, you can modify an existing edit style or create a new one.

To modify an existing edit style, select a style name and choose the options you require.

NOTE

As soon as you modify an existing style, the edit style name disappears from the Name drop-down list box. This is because you have defined a new style (the edit style defined on the database is not changed).

The other option is to create a new edit style from scratch. To learn how to create the different edit styles, see Chapter 4. There is one edit style available only in the DataWindow painter, Display as Bitmap, which is covered next.

The Display as Bitmap Style

One additional edit style that is not available in the Database painter is the Display as Bitmap style. This style enables you to display pictures instead of text in the DataWindow column. The database column stores the name of the bitmap file (BMP) that is to be displayed. When data is retrieved into the DataWindow, PowerBuilder searches for the corresponding bitmap file and displays the picture in the column instead of the name of the file. The BMP file does not need to be accessible at design time. At runtime, PowerBuilder searches the user's DOS search path to locate the appropriate file. To use the Display as Bitmap style, click the check box on the General tab in the Column Object property sheet.

Validation Rules

A column on the DataWindow object can have a validation rule associated with it that ensures that the information the user is typing in is valid. As with the display formats and edit styles, validation can be defined in the Database painter and extended to apply to the column on the DataWindow. To access a column's validation rules, click the Validation tab page on the Column Object property sheet (see Figure 9.49).

In this tab page you can specify a number of different expressions that contain column names, arithmetic operators, function names, and the like. The validation rule must evaluate to a Boolean value—either `TRUE` or `FALSE`. You can test the validation rule for correct syntax by clicking on the Verify button. If the data being entered does not pass the validation rule specified, the error message defined in the Error Message Expression multiline edit is displayed. (See Chapter 8, "Application Objects and the Application Painter," to find out how to set the title bar of the error message window.)

In addition to typing in an expression for the validation rule, you can specify a global user-defined function to perform validation as long as it returns `TRUE` or `FALSE`. A global function for a validation rule is extremely useful for performing functions not supported on the Validation tab page, such as embedded SQL. For more information on creating validation rules, see Chapter 4.

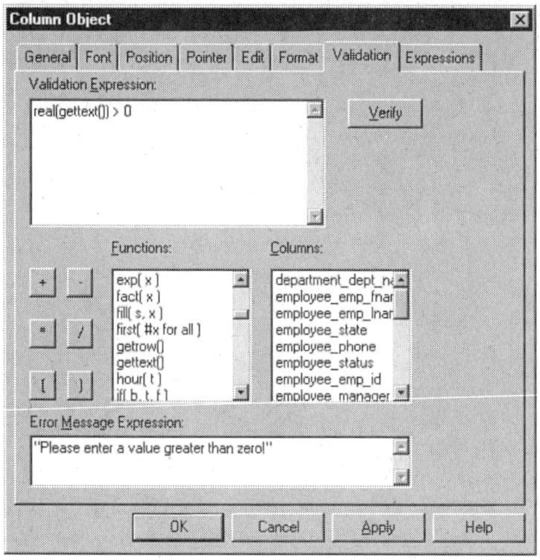

FIGURE 9.49.
The Validation tab page.

Adding and Deleting Columns

After a DataWindow object has been created, you might find that you want to add a column to the DataWindow or delete a column from it.

If a column is not currently specified as part of the data source, the first step in adding a column is to add it to the data source specification. To do so, click the PainterBar icon with SQL on it or select Data Source from the Design menu. This takes you into the appropriate data source definition painter (either the SQL Select painter, the Stored Procedure dialog box, or the Modify Result Set Description dialog box). When the new column has been added to the result set, return to the design mode of the DataWindow object. The new column is placed after the last column on the right in the detail band. Notice that no header or label is placed on the DataWindow with the column.

If a column is being retrieved and is no longer needed, it should be removed from the result set specification in the same way that a column is added. Ensuring that unnecessary data is not retrieved helps to increase your application's performance.

So far, you have examined adding and removing a column from the data source. There are times when you might want to add or keep a column from being displayed on the DataWindow but still retrieve the value into memory. An example of when you would retrieve a field and not display it is in the case of a key field. If a table contains a key field that is not deemed useful information to the user (for example, a customer ID), that column does not need to be shown. If the column is important because it uniquely identifies a row in the DataWindow, however, it should continue to be retrieved. To remove a column, select the column and press the Delete key or select Clear from the column's pop-up menu.

Another common situation is to accidentally delete or remove a column and then actually find out you need it in the DataWindow. You can add the column back by clicking the Add Column icon in the object drop-down toolbar (see Figure 9.58) on the PainterBar.

After clicking this icon, click the DataWindow in the location where you want to place the column. Clicking one of the report bands opens the Select Column dialog box (see Figure 9.50).

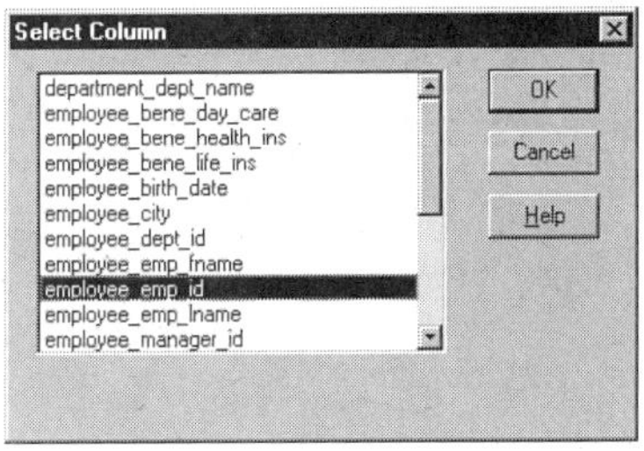

FIGURE 9.50.
The Select Column dialog box.

The list box displays all columns that are specified in the result set definition for your DataWindow. Select the column that you want to place on the DataWindow object and click the OK button to place it in the report band.

TIP

Although you can add additional columns to a DataWindow object by using computed columns, if you want the user to be able to enter values that you might not be saving, you can add dummy values to the result set of the DataWindow `SELECT` (for example, `0` for a Numeric and `""` for a String). Pad the string with spaces to the required size. Some databases, such as SQL Server, might require you to use a conversion function to get the right size (for example, `CONVERT( CHAR(5), "")`).

Tab Order

Just as in the Window painter, a DataWindow object has a tab order that controls how you move about the screen when you press the Tab key. There is a difference between the Window painter tab order and that of the DataWindow painter. In the Window painter, a tab order of `0` means that a control was skipped when the user pressed the Tab key. The control can still be clicked on and used. In the DataWindow painter, a tab order of `0` not only disables that control in the tab sequence, but it also does not allow the user to access the column at all. Use this feature when you want to prevent your users from being able to update or edit a column (this is particularly useful for key columns).

To set the tab order, select Tab Order from the Design menu. As in the Window painter, you are now in tab mode (see Figure 9.51).

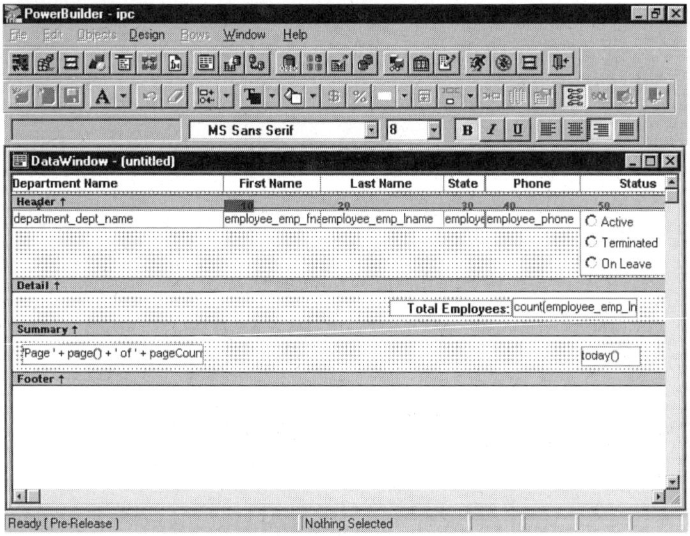

FIGURE 9.51.
Tab mode in the DataWindow painter.

The tab order is specified by the red numbers over each of the columns in the result set. Only data columns can be included in the tab sequence (notice that computed columns, text objects, and so on have no red number labels). To modify the tab order, click the red numbers and type the new order sequence (from 0 to 999). PowerBuilder renumbers the tab order in increments of 10. To turn off the tab mode, click the Tab Order menu item again.

NOTE

If the DataWindow is a join between two or more tables, the default tab order on all columns is `0`. This is because a DataWindow object can update only one table. To learn how to specify how the DataWindow updates, see the "Update Characteristics" section later in this chapter.

NOTE

If a column's ability to be edited changes based on a user's security, the preferred method to render a column uneditable is by using the `Protect` attribute, which preserves the tab order.

Groups

You have seen how to easily create a DataWindow with one group on it using the Group presentation style. At times you might want to create more than one group. Select Create Group from the Rows menu, which opens the Band Object property sheet (see Figure 9.52).

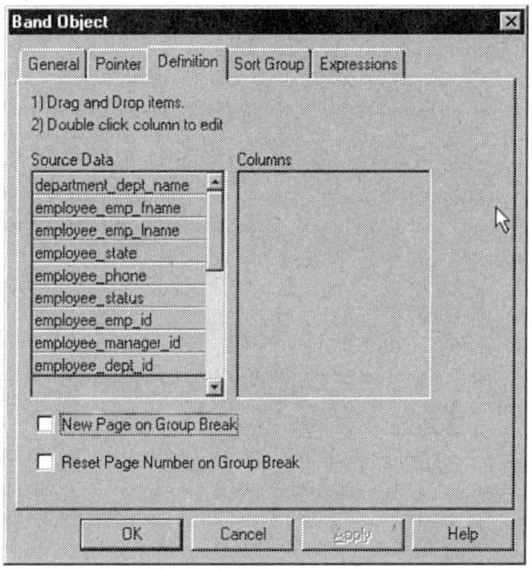

FIGURE 9.52.
The Band Object property sheet.

On the Definition tab page you can specify one or more columns as a group by clicking the column name from the Source Data list box and dragging it to the Columns list box just as for the Group presentation style. Two options on the bottom of the tab page are New Page on Group Break and Reset Page Number on Group Break. If you want each group to appear alone on one or more pages, click the New Page on Group Break check box. If you want the page numbers to be reset when this break occurs, select the second check box (this should be used only in conjunction with the New Page on Group Break check box).

> **NOTE**
>
> To have grouping work effectively, you must include an `ORDER BY` clause for the grouped column on your SQL statement. This ensures that the data is sorted before the grouping takes place. If this is not done, the resulting report may contain multiple breaks for the same value.

The Sort Group tab page is used to specify how the groups will be sorted based on any computed columns in the group trailer. For example, if a group break was specified for the `department_name` column and a computed column counting the number of employees was placed in the `group` trailer band, the Sort Group tab page could be used to indicate that the order of the groups should be based on the computed column. Therefore, you could have the department listed first with the greatest number of employees followed by the second highest number of employees, and so on. The other three tab pages (General, Pointer, and Expressions) are used to further define the appearance and behavior of the group header band such as the height, color, pointer, and attribute expression value (which is discussed in more detail in the section "Object Attributes").

After a new group has been created, you can create a second group by selecting the Create Group menu item again. The DataWindow painter sequentially numbers the groups as they are created. When you create an additional group, do not be alarmed to see that in the Specify Group Columns dialog box your previous groups are not listed in the Columns list box. If at any point you want to modify the definition of one of the groups you have created, select Edit Group from the Rows menu and select the number of the group in question. If you are not sure of a group's number, look on the associated bands, which are numbered (see Figure 9.53).

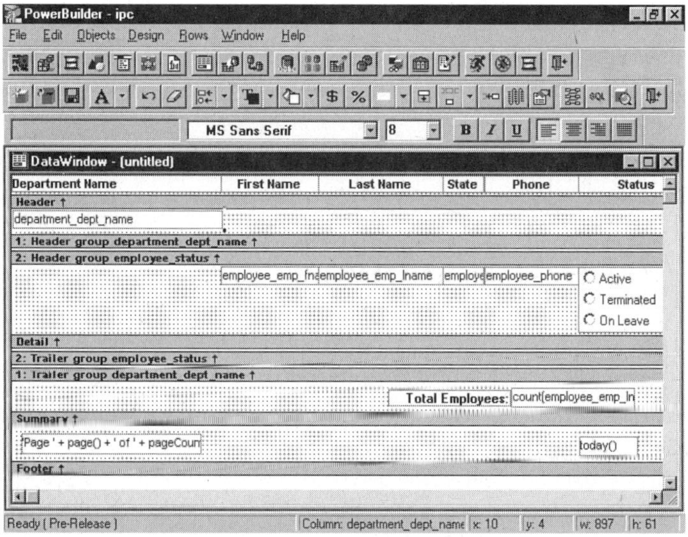

FIGURE 9.53.
Numbered bands indicating the different groupings.

These bands, in their initial state, have no information in them. Unlike in the Group presentation style, creating a group from within the DataWindow painter does not create any computed columns in the group footer bands (see the section "Computed Columns" later in the chapter). You must do this, as well as move the columns into the respective bands, manually.

If at some point you decide that a group is no longer needed, you can select Delete Group from the Rows menu.

WARNING

If you have any objects in the group header or footer when you specify Delete Group, they are deleted also. Therefore, if you want to continue to display any of this information, you must move it to another report band before the deletion. If you forget, you must re-create the objects.

Suppressing Repeating Values

An option that can be used instead of creating a group report, but that still gives the appearance of grouping, is Suppress Repeating Values. For example, you might have a report that doesn't need to perform any calculation when a new group is processed, but a certain column value is repeated over and over (see Figure 9.54).

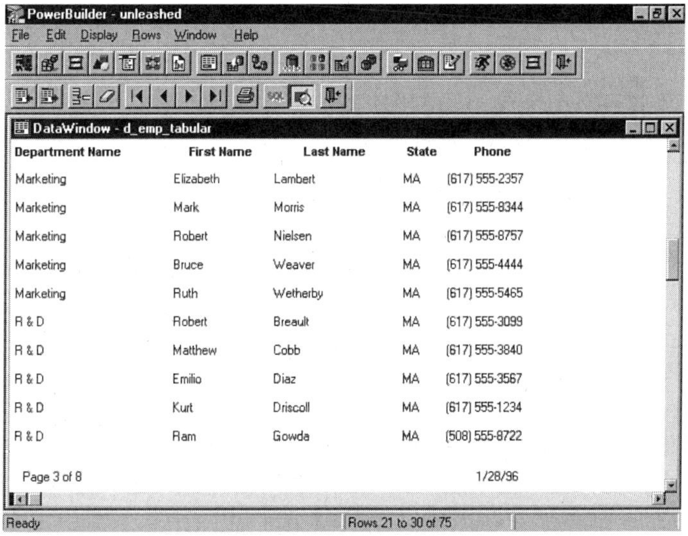

FIGURE 9.54.
A DataWindow object displaying a repeating value (department name).

The department name in Figure 9.53 is repeated for each row. To prevent this from happening, click Suppress Repeating Values on the Rows menu, which opens the Specify Repeating Value Suppression List dialog box (see Figure 9.55).

Again, a drag-and-drop interface enables you to specify those columns for which you don't want the values to be repeated for every row. In this example, you would want to click dept_name from the Source Data list box and drag it over to the Suppression List area. You can do this for as many columns as you want. This example would result in the DataWindow shown in Figure 9.56. As for a group break, the data should be sorted on those columns for which the value is to be suppressed.

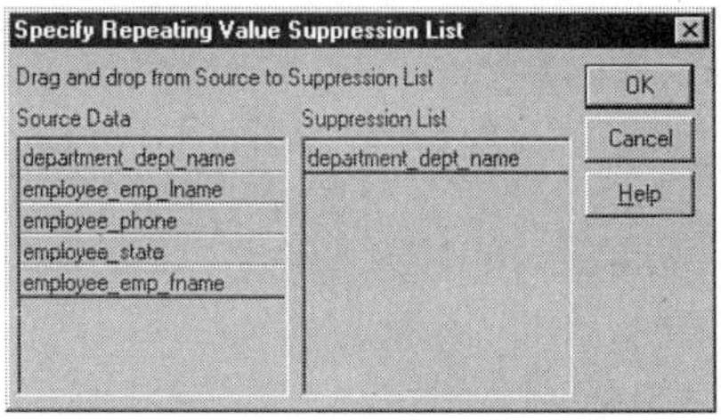

FIGURE 9.55.
The Specify Repeating Value Suppression List dialog box.

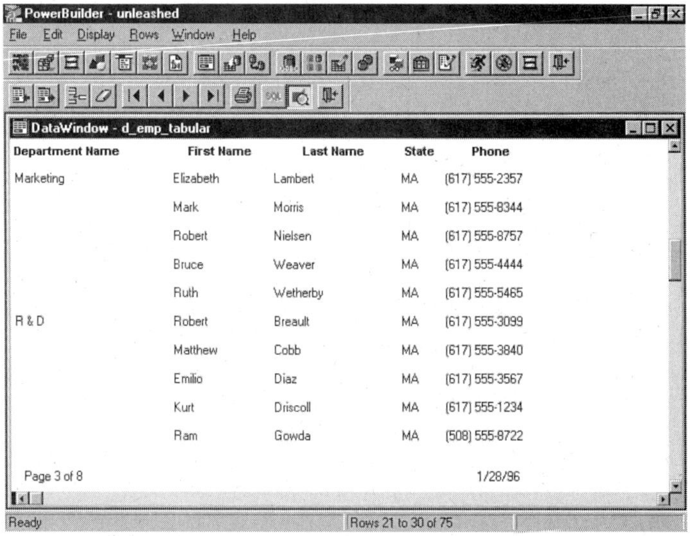

FIGURE 9.56.
The DataWindow object suppressing the repeating value (department name).

Sliding Columns

To remove spaces between columns, open the Column Object property sheet and select the Position tab page. On this tab page, specify one of the available Slide options: Left, All Above, or Directly Above. For example, suppose you are creating mailing labels with first name, last name, address1, address2, city, state, and zip. The size of the name and city fields varies, and there might be no value specified for address2. If sliding columns were not used, there would be gaps between the fields, creating an unattractive label. Figure 9.57 shows two labels, the first with no sliding and the second with sliding.

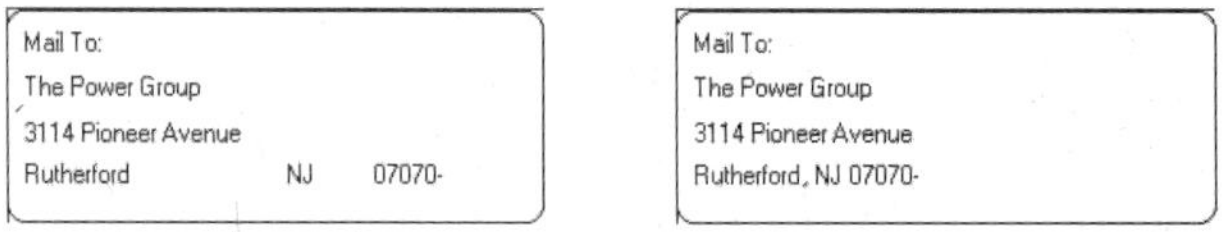

FIGURE 9.57.
The mailing label on the left shows no column sliding. The mailing label on the right shows the same columns with Slide Left turned on.

If you specify sliding columns, you can clean up the unnecessary spaces between the columns. For the last name, state, and zip, you would choose Left from the Position tab page. This forces the specified columns to slide to the left and removes the gaps between the columns. To correct the address problem, on the city, state, and zip columns, select Slide/Directly Above to make all three slide up when there is nothing specified in the address2 column. On the address2 column, you must turn on the option Autosize Height from the Position tab page. This causes the address2 column to collapse if there is no data in it. If you do not specify Autosize Height, the DataWindow object maintains the size of the address2 column even if it is empty.

DataWindow Enhancements

In addition to all the formatting you have seen so far (for example, edit styles and colors), several additional objects can be placed on a DataWindow to enhance its functionality and interface. These objects include static text, computed columns, bitmap images, graphs, graphic objects, nested reports, and OLE objects. In Version 5.0, these objects are accessed from a drop-down toolbar (see Figure 9.58).

FIGURE 9.58.

The new object drop-down toolbar.

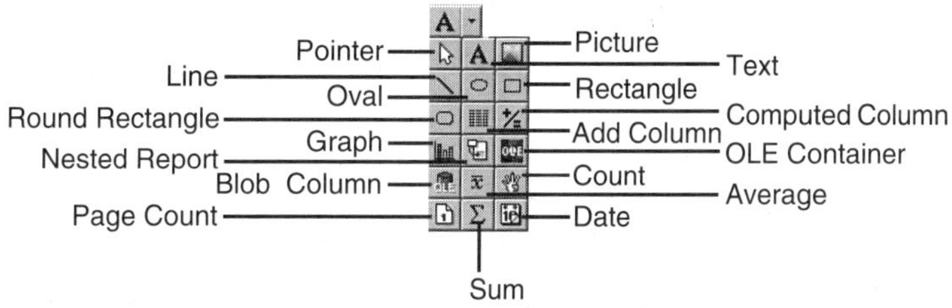

Let's take a look at each of these objects and how to create them.

Static Text Objects

By default, PowerBuilder places some static text fields on DataWindow objects such as headings and labels. Additional static text fields can be placed on the DataWindow object to enhance the user presentation.

If a new column is added to one of the report bands, a label or heading is not created for the column. Therefore, you must create one. Another use for static text objects is report headings. To add a text object to a DataWindow, click the drop-down toolbar Text icon and click somewhere on the DataWindow object to place the text. After the text has been placed on the DataWindow, you can manipulate it to match the formatting of the other fields.

NOTE

To copy the format of an existing text object or column, select the object before placing the new text or column in the DataWindow. Any text object or column placed into the DataWindow object automatically assumes the formatting of the object that was previously selected (this does not include the border style, however).

To modify the information in the text (that is, change the font, the justification, or the verbiage in the text object), you can use the StyleBar located at the top of the DataWindow painter (see Figure 9.59).

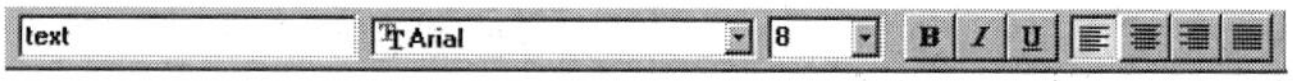

FIGURE 9.59.
The StyleBar.

On the StyleBar you can change the default text value of `text` to something a little more meaningful. Click the single-line edit on the left side of the StyleBar to change the text. If you want the text to span more than one line, all you need to do is resize the object so that the desired text is forced to the next line. If you need to force text to the next line (if you can't position the values as desired), you need to use the ASCII characters for a carriage return (~r) and new line (~n).

In addition to changing the text value on the StyleBar, you can also change the font type, the font size, whether the font is bold, italicized, or underlined, and the alignment of the text (left, centered, right, or the new option, justified).

Computed Columns

Earlier in this chapter you saw a reference to creating computed columns in the DataWindow object result set. This computed column is calculated on the server and is static until the data is retrieved again. In addition to the columns that are specified in the result set for your DataWindow, you can add client-side computed columns. Similar to the server-side computed columns, these columns are used to perform calculations. These computed columns are different from the calculated columns that were defined in the SQL Select painter because they are not static fields. The values in a computed column change as the data displayed in the DataWindow object is changed.

The decision to use a client-side column versus a server-side column depends on the functionality of the DataWindow and the type of calculation. If you anticipate that the user will be able to change data and will expect to see the changes reflected in the computed column, use a client-side computed column.

To create a computed column on your DataWindow, click the Computed Column icon on the drop-down toolbar. Next, determine where on the DataWindow you want to place the computed column, and click that report band. Clicking the DataWindow opens the Computed Object property sheet (see Figure 9.60).

FIGURE 9.60.
The Computed Object property sheet.

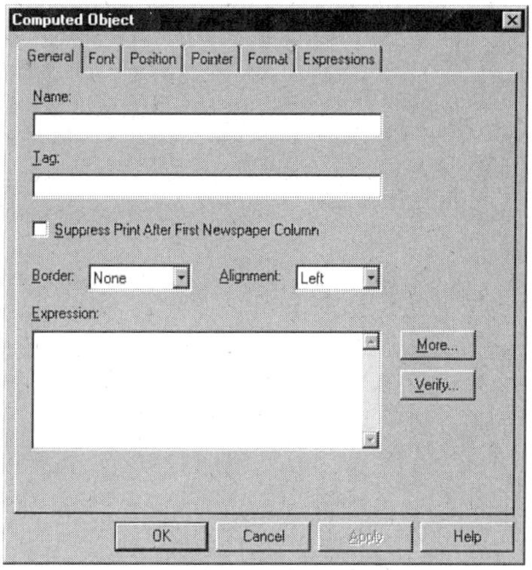

Where you place the computed column depends on what you want that particular field to accomplish. If you want the computed column to appear for every row in the result set, place the column in the detail band. To show summary statistics for a group, place the column in the group header or footer. Any summarization that you want for the whole report should be placed in the summary band, and if it is to be repeated on each page, use the header and footer bands.

In the Computed Object property sheet, specify a name for the computed column on the General tab page. This enables you to reference the column in your scripts and in other computed columns and sort on the column. At the bottom of the tab page is a multiline edit box where you write the column expression. The expression can consist of the other columns being retrieved, other computed columns, PowerScript operators, and PowerScript DataWindow functions.

To place a column or function in the expression box, click the More button, which opens the Modify Expression dialog box (see Figure 9.61).

FIGURE 9.61.
The Modify Expression dialog box.

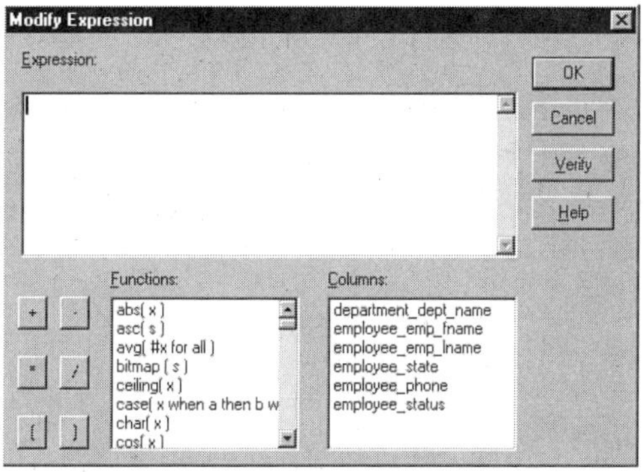

Specify the desired function name in the Function list box or click the desired column in the Column list box. The function and column are pasted into the expression box. When a function is pasted into the expression box, the arguments that the function is expecting (if any) are highlighted (see Figure 9.62).

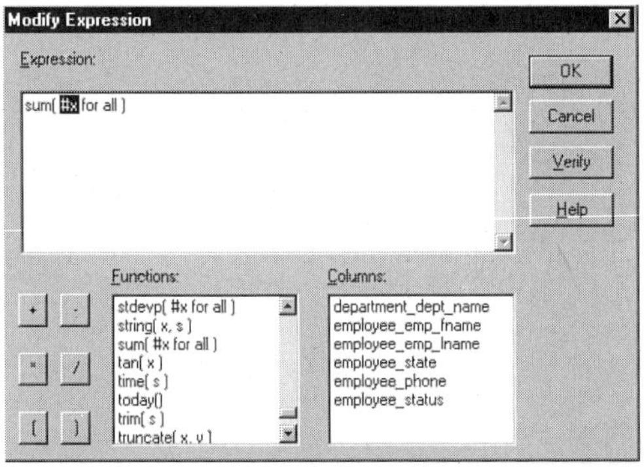

FIGURE 9.62.
The Modify Expression dialog box using the `Sum()` *function.*

The required data type is designated by the character specified in the argument list (for example, `s` = String, `#` = Number, and `b` = Boolean). When all arguments and functions have been specified for the column, click the Verify button to determine whether the expression is valid. PowerBuilder kindly tells you that the expression is invalid and might give some hint as to what is wrong (for example, `Function is expecting a string value`). If you do not know a function or the syntax, you can look in the online help to find all the functions listed in the Function list box. After the expression has been verified successfully, click OK to return to the General tab page. The rest of the Computed Object property sheet allows you to define the font, position, pointer, format, and attribute expressions for the new column just as you would for any other DataWindow column. To modify a computed column definition, select the column and double-click it to open the Computed Object property sheet.

TIP

A common need for a computed column that is not an obvious calculation is creating a total for a column based on specific criteria. For example, an application needs to compute the total number of active customers (indicated by the value `A` for the column *status*). The computed column would be `sum(if(status = 'A', 1, 0) for all)`. A value `1` is generated for each row with an active status and then each row with a value of `1` is included in the sum to give a total count.

In addition to giving you the capability to create your own computed columns, PowerBuilder provides a number of commonly used computed columns to save you the time and effort of having to redefine the field every time you want it. These columns are available as icons on the PainterBar and from the Objects menu (as you will soon see).

To add the page number to the bottom of each page, use the Page Computed Field icon from the drop-down toolbar or select Page n of n from the Objects menu and click in the footer band.

The page number computed column generates the expression

```
'Page ' + page() + ' of ' + pageCount().
```

Another predefined computed field is the current date. This field is usually placed in either the header or the footer band. To place it on the DataWindow, click the Today's Date drop-down toolbar icon or select Today() from the Objects menu and then click the appropriate band. The computed column definition consists of the PowerScript function `Today()`.

The Sum computed field enables you to summarize a detail band column containing a number or amount (for example, salary). To create a summary column, you must first select the field in the detail band that you want to summarize. Click the Sum drop-down toolbar icon or select Sum from the Objects menu.

If your DataWindow object contains group bands, the computed column sums by group and is placed in the group footer band. If not, the column calculates the sum for the whole report in the summary band.

Working under the same principle as the summary computed column, you also have the capability to create computed columns that determine the average value of a column or count the number of occurrences of an item. To create either column, you must access the Objects menu or click the drop-down toolbar icons Average or Count.

Pictures

Another object that can be added for display purposes only is a *picture object*. The picture object is often used to show a company logo in the background of the report. To place a picture on your DataWindow object, click the Picture drop-down toolbar icon and click the band in which you want the picture to appear. This brings up the Picture Object property sheet (see Figure 9.63).

The picture you want included in your DataWindow is specified in the File Name single-line edit. You can specify three different types of graphics files: BMPs, RLEs, and WMFs. If you do not know the directory and filename of the graphics file you want to display, click the Browse button to locate the desired file.

On the General tab page, you can give the picture object a name (so you can reference the object in your code) and you can select whether you want the original size of the graphics file shown and if you want the image inverted. If you select Original Size for the graphics file, you still have the capability to increase and decrease the size of the picture (this turns off the Original Size check box). The Invert Image check box reverses the colors of the graphics file (that is, it creates a negative image).

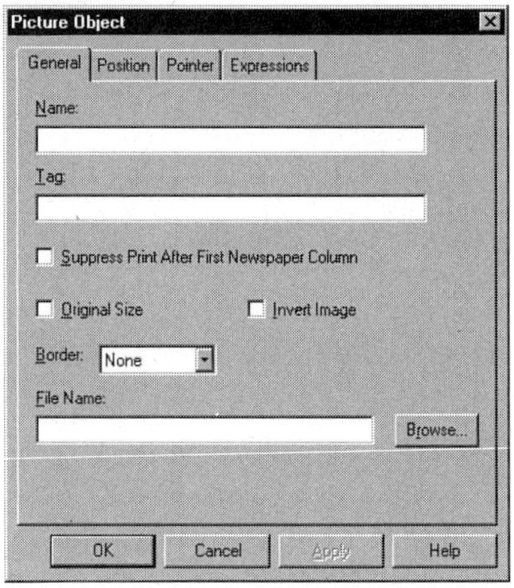

FIGURE 9.63.
The Picture Object property sheet.

The problem that now exists is how to get the picture object to not overlay your columns and headings. To do this, you must place the picture object in the background layer of the DataWindow. PowerBuilder provides you with a series of layers that control what objects can be placed on top of other objects.

Layers

The DataWindow object has three levels of depth, or *layers*, to it: the background, the band, and the foreground (see Figure 9.64).

The *background layer* is usually used for placing picture objects (for example, a company logo). The *band layer* contains the report itself (this is the default location for almost all objects, except graphs). The *foreground layer* is most often used for objects that are for display purposes rather than for printing. The most common example of an object that resides in the foreground is a graph (see the next section for more information on graphs).

If an object is created in the band layer and you want it to appear in either the foreground or background, open the object's property sheet and select the Position tab page. Within the Layer drop-down list box are the options to specify a DataWindow object in the Foreground, Band, or Background layer. Select the appropriate layer and rearrange the DataWindow to appear as desired (for example, if a picture is sent to the background layer, all other objects can be placed on top of it).

WARNING

A common use of the background layer is to place drawing objects behind columns so that the columns appear to be grouped together. This is a problem when you're using a nested report. Since the nested report resizes depending on the data retrieved, it will dynamically change in size and the drawing objects do not automatically move with it.

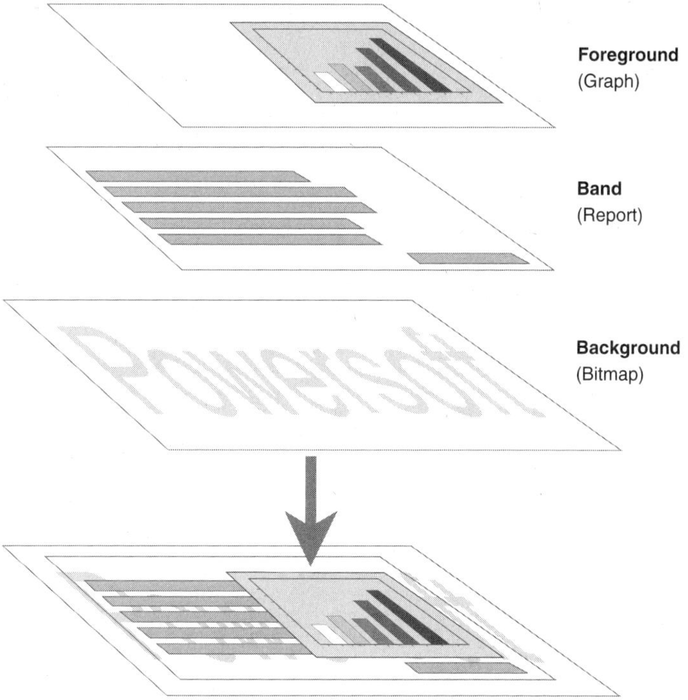

FIGURE 9.64.
DataWindow layers.

Graphs

In addition to the Graph presentation style, you also can add a graph to any existing DataWindow object (see Figure 9.65).

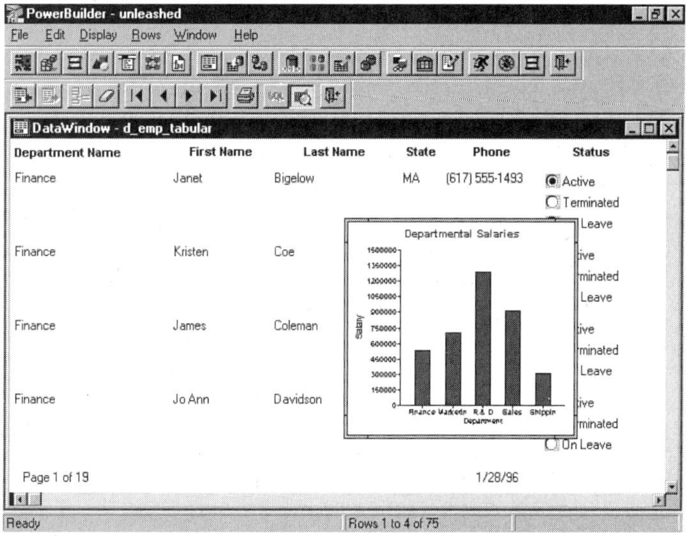

FIGURE 9.65.
A tabular DataWindow object with a graph object in the foreground layer.

To add a graph, create your base DataWindow object and then click the Graph drop-down toolbar icon or select Graph from the Objects menu. Click where you would like the graph to appear, which opens the Graph Object property sheet (see Figure 9.66).

FIGURE 9.66.
The Graph Object property sheet.

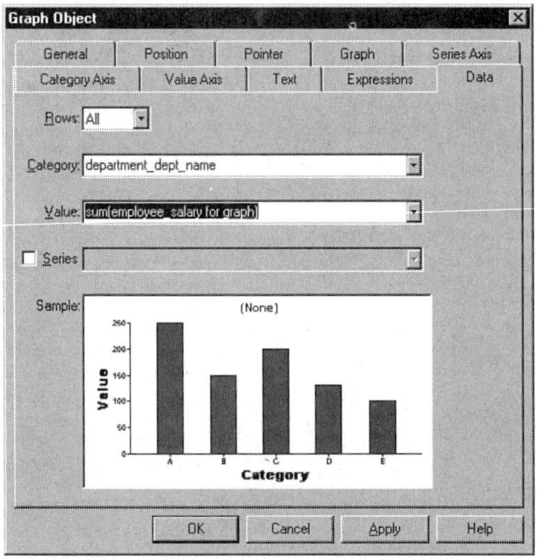

This is the same property sheet that is used in the Graph presentation style. From the Rows drop-down list box on the Data tab page, specify which rows the graph corresponds to: All (all rows in the DataWindow object) or Page (all rows on the current page). Specify the Category, Value, and optional Series, and click OK. PowerBuilder then creates the default column chart. The graph can be modified just like the Graph presentation style (for more information on graphing, see Chapter 27).

To provide a more friendly interface, you can allow the user to move the graph and still view the underlying report. To incorporate this functionality, open the property sheet and select the Position tab page. Make sure the graph is in the Foreground layer and select Moveable and Resizable. The user is now able to click the report and drag it to a new location and resize the graph to make it larger or smaller.

Drawing Objects

Several objects exist in the DataWindow painter that simply add artistic value to the DataWindow object. These are rectangles, lines, ovals, and round rectangles. None of these objects have any major significance to the DataWindow, but they are useful for grouping different parts of the report logically. You can also use static text objects for drawing purposes. For example, a 3D raised or lowered text object with no text is useful for grouping objects because it gives you border effects without having to use the line objects.

Nested Reports

In addition to placing nested graphs, you can also place (or nest) an entire report on a DataWindow object (see Figure 9.67).

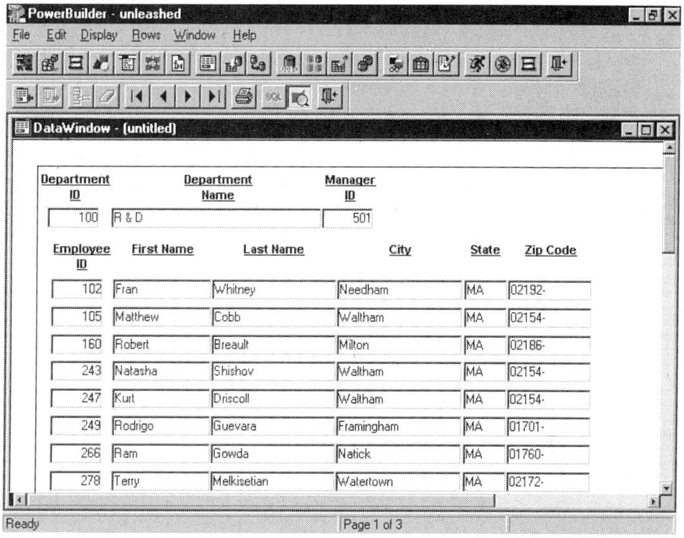

FIGURE 9.67.
A nested report.

To place a nested report on your existing DataWindow object, click the Nested Report drop-down toolbar icon or click Report on the Objects menu.

A nested report simply consists of another DataWindow object. The report can be dropped in any band of the DataWindow object. When you have clicked the location for the nested report, the Report Object property sheet opens (see Figure 9.68). Select the DataWindow object you want from the Select Report tab page, and click OK.

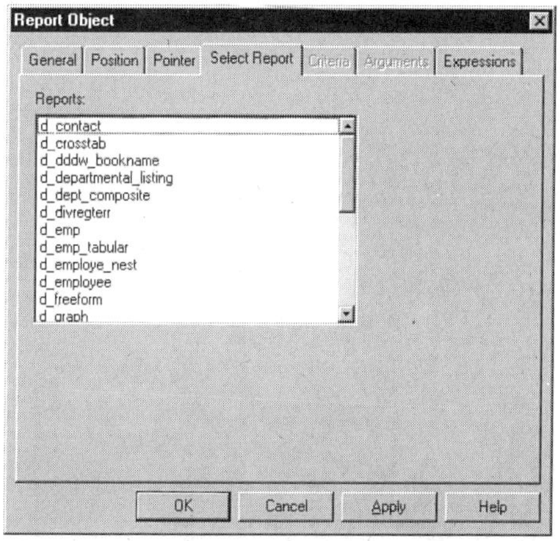

FIGURE 9.68.
The Report Object property sheet.

In design mode the nested DataWindow appears as a blank box with the DataWindow object name on it. This box can be moved and resized to appear exactly as you want it.

As the name implies, you are creating a nested *report*. This means that neither the newly created DataWindow object nor the one just dropped on your DataWindow is editable. Therefore, a nested report is for view-only purposes.

Initially, each report retrieves and displays its data independently of the other DataWindow. Although this might be acceptable in some cases, more often than not you will want to establish a relationship between the two reports. You create the association between the two reports by using retrieval arguments or specific criteria.

To associate the reports using retrieval arguments, the nested report must have one or more retrieval arguments defined. The data from the base report is then used to feed data to the retrieval arguments. After defining the retrieval arguments in the nested report (see the section "The SQL Select Painter"), open the property sheet for the nested report and choose the Arguments tab page (see Figure 9.69). (Note that if no retrieval arguments are specified for the nested report, this tab page is disabled.)

FIGURE 9.69.
The Arguments tab page.

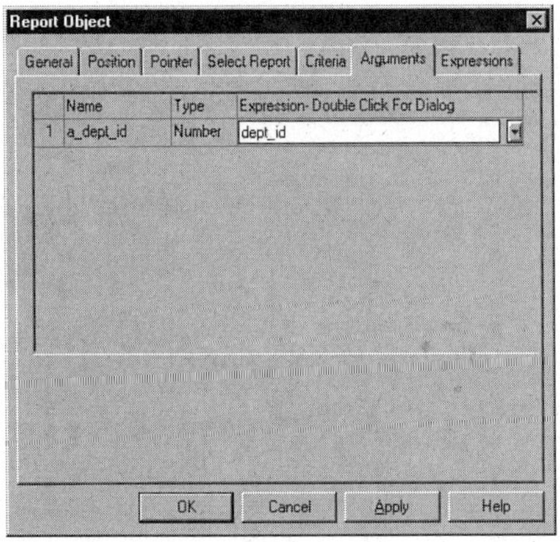

The tab page lists all the retrieval arguments in the nested report and their corresponding data types. The last column asks for an expression that you want the retrieval argument to equal. You can type something in, select a column name from the drop-down list box (current columns in the base report), or double-click the column to open the (by now familiar) Modify Expression dialog box.

You can create any expression in this dialog box using column names, functions, and arithmetic operators. Most likely, you will choose one of the column names from the base report. When this is done, the two reports will be in sync.

The other way to associate the two reports is using criteria. To accomplish this, select the Criteria tab page (see Figure 9.70).

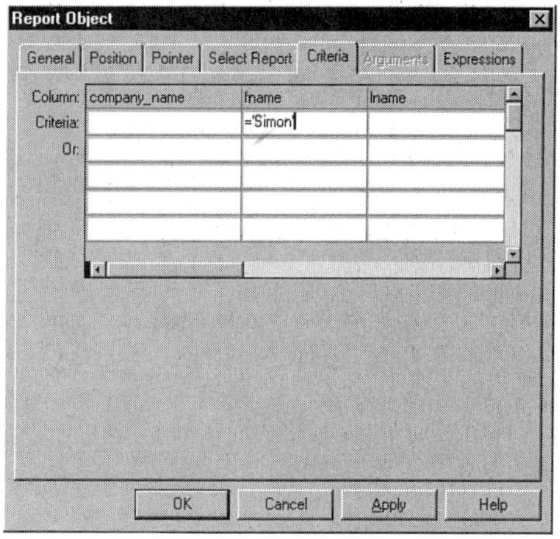

FIGURE 9.70.
The Criteria tab page.

This tab page behaves in the same way as the Quick Select data source. Criteria specified on the same line are joined by an AND operator, and criteria on different lines are joined by an OR. This is useful if the DataWindows being used do not have retrieval arguments defined. PowerBuilder then retrieves the data according to the specifications in the tab page.

OLE Objects

The last object that you can place on a DataWindow object is the *OLE object.* Object linking and embedding (OLE) is a Windows technology for interprocess communication (IPC) between Windows applications. OLE enables two Windows applications to talk to each other and integrate with one another (for example, using Excel to perform calculations and pass data to your PowerBuilder application). In Version 5.0 of PowerBuilder, the DataWindow painter supports OLE Version 2.0; in previous versions of PowerBuilder only OLE 1.0 is supported.

To create an OLE database column on your DataWindow, select OLE Database Blob from the Objects menu or the Blob Column drop-down toolbar and click the DataWindow to place the OLE column. The Database Blob Object dialog box opens (see Figure 9.71), requesting that you specify information about the database column to which the OLE object is saved and the OLE class description.

You can also add an OLE container object to your DataWindow presentation by clicking on the OLE Container icon on the object drop-down toolbar or selecting OLE Object from the Objects menu. This opens the Insert Object property sheet (see Figure 9.36), which allows you to specify an OLE server object that is embedded or linked into your DataWindow object. (For a more in-depth look at OLE, see Chapter 36.)

FIGURE 9.71.
The Database Blob Object dialog box.

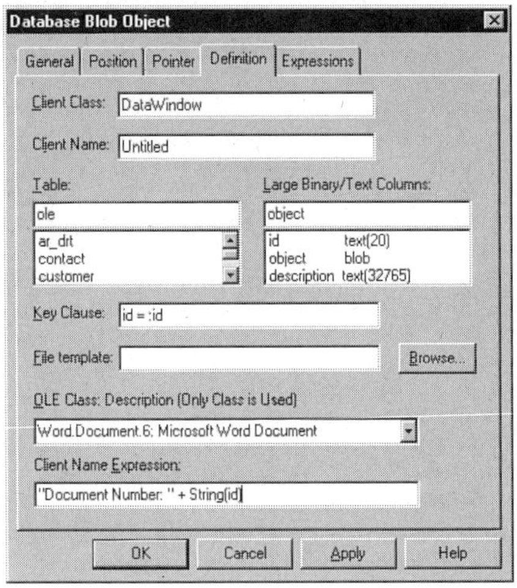

Object Attributes

You have seen that several different objects can be placed on a DataWindow object (for example, headings, columns, and pictures). Each of these objects has attributes you can modify at design time or runtime. To access these attributes, open the object's property sheet and select the Expressions tab page (see Figure 9.72).

FIGURE 9.72.
The Expressions tab page.

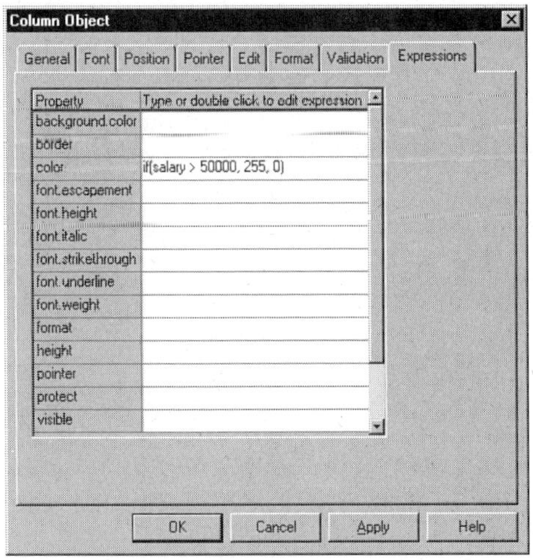

In this tab page all the attributes are listed for the selected object. You can create an expression for each attribute to manipulate the values assigned to that attribute. For example, a salary column might have the following expression associated with it for the `Color` attribute:

```
if(salary > 50000, 255, 0)
```

This expression evaluates the value of the column salary to see if it is greater than 50,000. If the expression is `TRUE`, the color of the text for the column is red (RGB value of `255`); otherwise the color is black (RGB value of `0`).

All other attributes can also have their values modified as the result of an expression. In some cases, specifying an expression at design time achieves the desired result. Unfortunately, this is not always the case. You might need to dynamically set the expression to modify an attribute of an object on the DataWindow. This is accomplished by using the new direct access syntax or the PowerScript function `Modify()` (see Chapter 25, "Advanced DataWindow Techniques I," on how to use both of these methods).

Column Specifications

In the Rows menu click the Column Specifications option to open the dialog box of the same name (see Figure 9.73).

FIGURE 9.73.
The Column Specifications dialog box.

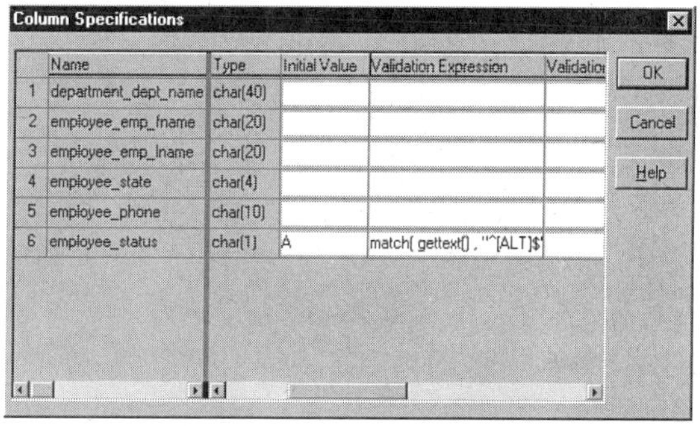

This dialog box displays information about the columns specified in the DataWindow result set. It lists the names of the objects in the DataWindow, their data types, initial values, validation rules, and validation messages, and the corresponding database column name. Not all fields are specified or need to be. This provides a quick and easy way to add or change validation information and initial values. Both the validation rules and the initial values will default from PowerBuilder repository tables situated on the database, if specified, and can then be changed.

Row Manipulation

When you have added all the objects you need to your DataWindow object and have customized their appearance, you can use some additional functions that enable you to manipulate the rows retrieved from the data source. From within the DataWindow painter, you can perform sorting and filtering, import and export data, prompt the user to specify retrieval criteria, retrieve data only as you need it, and update specifications.

Sorting

Sorting can be performed on either the client side or the server side. On the server, the sorting is specified by the `ORDER BY` clause in a SQL `SELECT` statement. The sorting is handled by the DBMS, and the result set is returned in the sort order to the DataWindow.

An alternative to using the `ORDER BY` clause on your SQL `SELECT` is to carry out the sorting within the DataWindow object. Sorting on the client is often desirable because it simply re-sorts the data in memory as opposed to issuing another `SELECT` statement against the database, which could be expensive and an unnecessary waste of resources. Determining where the processing should occur is often a difficult task and is often dictated by the requirements of the system, the hardware available for both server and client, and the server load. You should perform testing to determine whether one location provides better performance than the other.

Specifying sort criteria on the client can be done in design mode and preview mode in the DataWindow painter. In both cases, select Sort from the Rows menu. This opens the Specify Sort Columns dialog box (see Figure 9.74).

FIGURE 9.74.
The Specify Sort Columns dialog box.

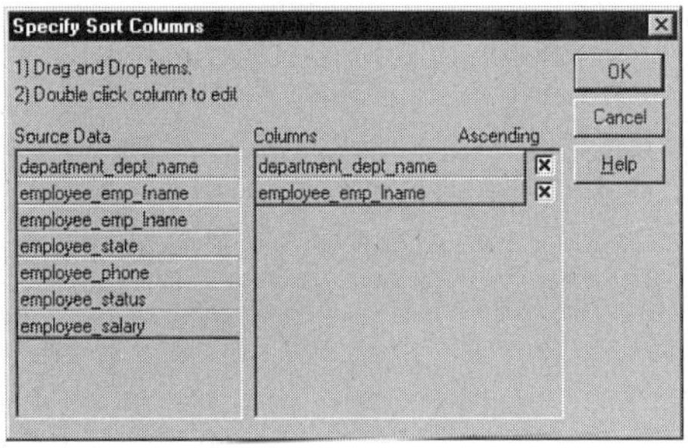

To specify sorting on one or more columns, click the column name in the Source Data list box and drag and drop it into the Columns list box. To specify an ascending sort, make sure the Ascending check box is checked. When the columns have been placed in the Columns list box, you can change the order by clicking and dragging the columns within the list box. To remove a column from the sort order, just click and drag it outside the Columns list box.

In addition to sorting based on a column, the sort criteria can also be based on an expression. To sort on an expression, double-click a column that has been placed in the Columns list box. This opens the Modify Expression dialog box.

Although it's nice that you can specify sorting in the DataWindow painter, it is more likely to be the user who wants to change the sorting of the data. The same process can be performed at runtime if you use the `SetSort()` and `Sort()` functions. See Chapter 26, "Advanced DataWindow Techniques II," for more information on these functions.

Filtering

Similar in concept to performing a client-side sort, the DataWindow object also enables you to do client-side filtering. A *filter* is an expression that evaluates to a Boolean value (`TRUE` or `FALSE`) and is used to limit the data that the user sees. You can limit the data from the server using the `WHERE` or `HAVING` clauses in your `SELECT` statement. However, if your user wants to continually change the data displayed, continually sending new queries to the database would not be an effective or efficient method. Instead, it would make more sense to retrieve all the required data into memory and enable the user to filter out the data he doesn't want to see. Doing this reduces network traffic in the long run with a one-time performance hit and gives your users more flexibility.

To create a filter in the DataWindow painter, select Filter from the Rows menu in either design or preview mode. This opens the Specify Filter dialog box (see Figure 9.75).

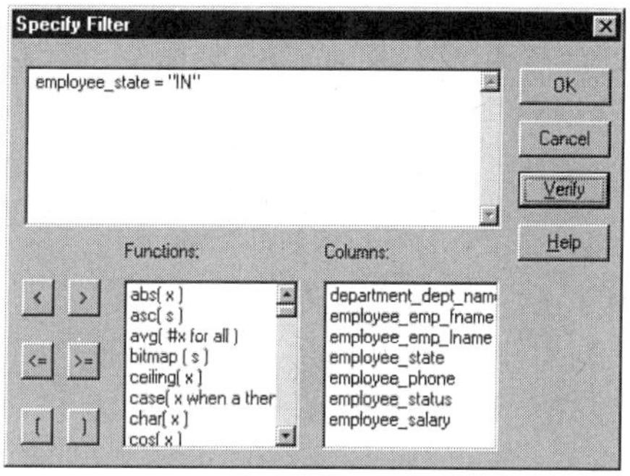

FIGURE 9.75.
The Specify Filter dialog box.

The Specify Filter dialog box is similar to many of the other dialog boxes you have already seen that are used to create expressions. The expression, as previously mentioned, must evaluate to either `TRUE` or `FALSE`. The expression can consist of columns, relational operators, functions, and values. The expressions can be connected using the `AND` and `OR` operators and can also contain `NOT` for negating expressions. You should make judicious use of parentheses to specify which expression is evaluated first. In addition to using the functions specified in the Specify Filter dialog box, you can also use an application global function. After the expression has been written, click the Verify button to check whether the expression is valid.

The data that is filtered out is still in memory (see Chapter 10, "DataWindow Scripting," for more information on DataWindow buffers) and can be redisplayed to the user if you redefine or remove the filter expression. Just as sorting can be done at runtime, so can filtering, if you use the `SetFilter()` and `Filter()` functions. See Chapter 26 for more information on these functions.

Importing and Exporting Data

You can both import data to and export data from a DataWindow object. To import data, select Import from the Rows menu in preview mode in the DataWindow painter. The Select Import File dialog box (see Figure 9.76) asks you for the name of either a tab-separated text file or a dBASE II or III (DBF) file. If the file layout matches the columns specified for the DataWindow, the data is imported into the DataWindow layout. If the columns do not match, PowerBuilder displays a message box indicating the mismatch and asks if you wish to continue inserting rows from the file. After this is done, you must click the Save Changes to Database icon on the PainterBar to save the data back into the current database.

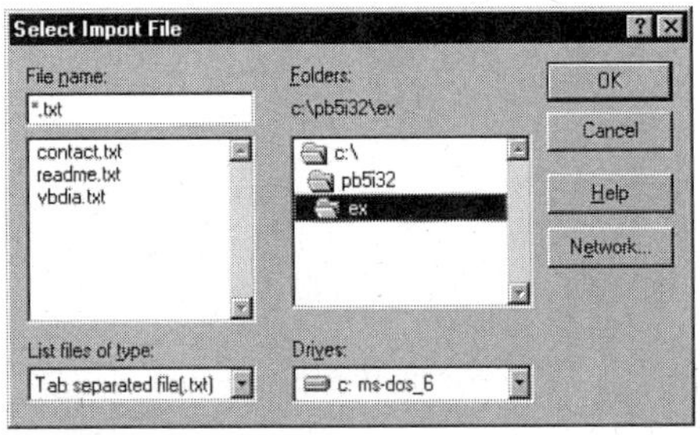

FIGURE 9.76.
The Select Import File dialog box.

To export data, select Save Rows As from the File menu, while in preview mode. This opens the Save As dialog box (see Figure 9.77), which lists a number of different file formats in which the data can be saved (for example, as an Excel spreadsheet, a SQL statement, or a tab-separated text file). The default file is UNTITLED plus the extension of the file type chosen using the File Format radio buttons.

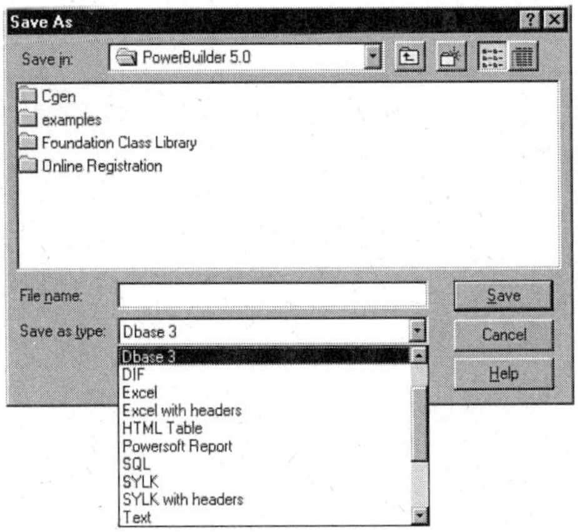

FIGURE 9.77.
The Save As dialog box.

NOTE

Powersoft has added a number of new file formats available for the data to be saved as. One of them is as an HTML table. This is useful when you're creating a web page using some data because PowerBuilder generates the Table tag (`<TABLE></TABLE>`) and the corresponding detail tags utilizing the DataWindow data.

See Chapter 10 for a full description of the file formats and the `SaveAs()` function, which gives you the capability to display the Save As dialog box at runtime.

Prompting for Criteria

Similar to specifying a retrieval argument, prompting for criteria enables the selection of data to be more dynamic because the user can specify selection criteria. To implement selection criteria, select Prompt For Criteria from the Rows menu in the DataWindow object design mode. The Prompt For Criteria dialog box (see Figure 9.78) opens, showing a list of the columns in your DataWindow object.

FIGURE 9.78.
The Prompt For Criteria dialog box.

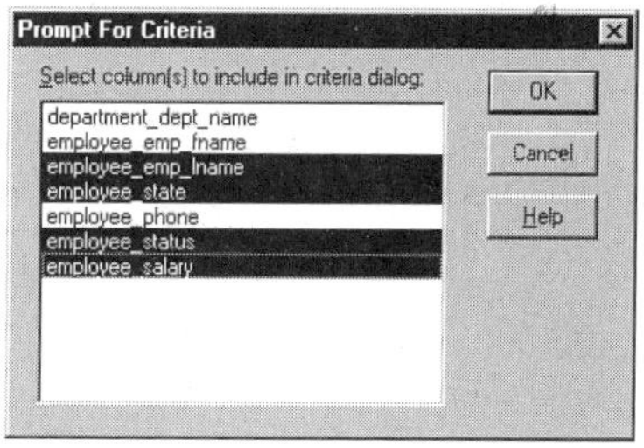

Select those columns for which you want the user to be able to specify additional selection criteria and click OK. When you preview the DataWindow or specify the `Retrieve()` function, the Specify Retrieval Criteria dialog box opens (see Figure 9.79).

FIGURE 9.79.
The Specify Retrieval Criteria dialog box.

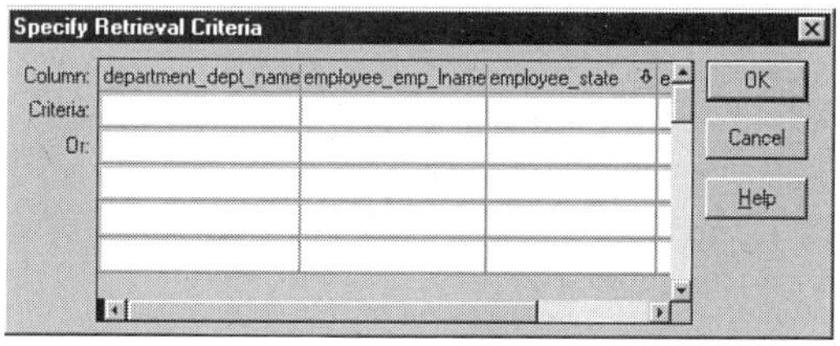

The Specify Retrieval Criteria dialog box works similarly to the Quick Select data source. The column names that you selected in the Prompt For Criteria dialog box appear along the top of the dialog box. Under any of the columns, the user can specify criteria to limit the data that is retrieved from the database. Any criteria that is typed in is used in the WHERE clause of the SQL statement.

> **WARNING**
>
> When using Prompt For Criteria, you should not specify a WHERE clause on the data source. This is because anything specified in the Specify Retrieval Criteria dialog box is added with a logical AND onto your WHERE clause; thus you could end up with conflicting retrieval criteria and have peculiar results.

To specify criteria, type your criteria on the rows beneath the column names. If criteria are typed on the same line, they are joined by a logical AND. If the criteria are on different lines, they are joined by a logical OR. When criteria have been specified, click OK to execute the SQL SELECT statement with the new WHERE clause. Note that if no criteria are specified, the SELECT statement runs like a standard DataWindow retrieval.

Retrieving Rows as Needed

You have just seen that by using filters and prompting the user for additional criteria you can limit the amount of data being retrieved from the database. It is generally a good idea to limit what is retrieved in order to reduce long-running queries that consume resources and, worse yet, frustrate the user because he has to wait to see the data.

You have several options to prevent a SELECT statement from running too long and retrieving excessive amounts of data. A very simple option is to select the Retrieve | Rows As Needed menu item in the Rows menu. This option retrieves only as many rows as necessary to display data in the DataWindow. Therefore, PowerBuilder needs to retrieve only a small number of rows, and control is returned to the user much more quickly. As the user scrolls through the data using a result set cursor, PowerBuilder continues to retrieve the data necessary for display purposes until the end of the result is reached.

Although this is a good option because it provides the appearance of increased performance, it does have its drawbacks. Because PowerBuilder is getting data as it needs it, it is maintaining a connection and, therefore, holding resources on the server. Also, if you are using aggregate functions in your SQL SELECT statement, such as Avg() and Sum(), Retrieve Rows As Needed is overridden.

NEW 5 in PowerBuilder

New to Version 5.0 is the ability to retrieve rows to disk. This means that you can write rows out as they are retrieved to a temporary file on the hard drive to free up your client's memory. The benefit of this option is it increases the number of rows that can be retrieved from the database. While this might be useful, you suffer a performance hit because PowerBuilder has to read and write to the hard drive to access the data during the retrieve and any client-side aggregate functions such as filtering and sorting.

Update Characteristics

One reason the DataWindow object is so powerful is the ease of modifying the database. After you have modified data, inserted new rows, and deleted rows, all you need to do is call the `Update()` function. This generates the necessary SQL statements (`INSERT`, `UPDATE`, and `DELETE`) and sends them to the database.

For DataWindow objects that have one table as a data source, PowerBuilder uses defaults for how the SQL statements are to be created. Many times this is satisfactory, but there are times when you might want to change the defaults. When more than one table is specified in the data source, you must specify how the DataWindow object is going to perform updates to the database. How you change the update options depends on your application's needs for concurrency and data integrity.

To change how updates are performed for the DataWindow object, select Update Properties from the Rows menu, which opens the Specify Update Characteristics dialog box (see Figure 9.80).

FIGURE 9.80.
The Specify Update Characteristics dialog box.

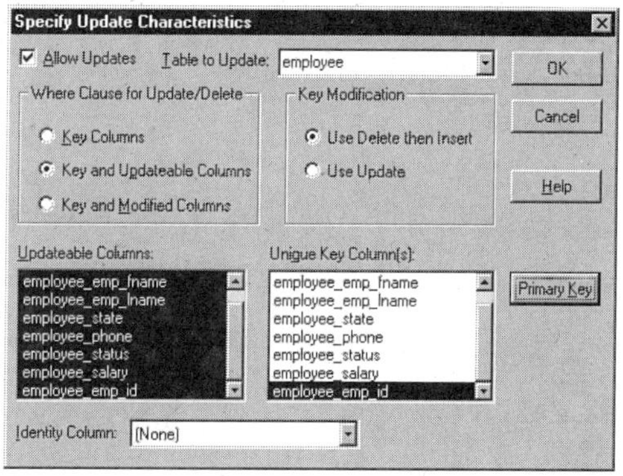

When you first create the DataWindow, PowerBuilder decides whether the DataWindow object is updateable. It bases its decision on whether the data is coming from one or more tables and if the primary keys are being retrieved. The Allow Updates check box in this dialog box indicates whether you can update the DataWindow object.

Notice that the list box next to the Allow Updates check box says Table to Update. This means that only one table can be updated in a DataWindow via this method (to see how to update multiple tables on a DataWindow object, see Chapter 10). If your result set pulls data from multiple tables, PowerBuilder automatically specifies the DataWindow as not updateable and sets the tab order of all columns to `0`.

After checking the Allow Updates check box, select the table that you want the DataWindow to update from the Table to Update drop-down list box.

The next step is to identify which columns on the DataWindow can be updated. Click on the columns you want to be able to update in the Updateable Columns list box. Remember, if you have more than one table in your data source, you can update columns on only one of those tables even though all column names appear in the list.

After you have selected what columns you want to update, use the Unique Key Column(s) list box to select the columns that make a row unique. If the primary keys have been specified in your SQL Selection List, you can click the Primary Key button, which checks the specified update table and selects those primary key columns.

The Where Clause for Update/Delete group box contains three radio buttons that tell PowerBuilder how to build the `WHERE` clause in the `UPDATE` and `DELETE` SQL statements. The three buttons provide different options for maintaining data integrity and provide a different option from database locking. Instead of locking a row or page (depending on the database-locking granularity) when a row is selected and preventing other users from retrieving the row, you can provide integrity protection via the DataWindow object. The three options are Key Columns, Key and Updateable Columns, and Key and Modified Columns.

Key Columns

If you specify Key Columns, the DataWindow uses only the key columns specified in the Unique Key Column(s) list box. This option is often used with single-user applications. When PowerBuilder generates an `UPDATE` or a `DELETE` statement, it compares the value of the originally retrieved key column for a row against the value of the key column of that row in the database. If the two values are equal, the update or delete is successful.

For example, suppose that Malcolm and Jonathan retrieved the following row from the customer table, where `Customer_ID` is the primary key, and the name, status, and region are updateable:

```
Customer ID: 110
Customer Name: Simon Herbert
Status: Preferred
Region: Midwest
```

If Jonathan changed the region from Midwest to Southeast, the following `UPDATE` statement would be generated using key columns:

```
UPDATE customer
SET region = "Southeast"
WHERE customer_id = 110
```

This `UPDATE` statement will be successful. There will be a problem if Malcolm also makes changes to the row (for example, changes the region to Northwest). Jonathan's changes would be overwritten because the key column has not been changed. Therefore, in this example you have high concurrency (both users could access and change the data), but your data integrity is poor.

Key and Updateable Columns

When the Key and Updateable Columns option is specified, PowerBuilder creates UPDATE and DELETE statements that compare the originally retrieved value for the key columns and the originally retrieved value of any column specified as updateable against the same values in the database. If the values are equal, the update or delete takes place. This is the preferred method because it provides high data integrity.

Using the same example, Jonathan's change to the region generates the following SQL statement:

```
UPDATE customer
SET region = "Southeast"
WHERE customer_id = 110
AND name = "Simon Herbert"
AND status = "Preferred"
AND region = "Midwest"
```

Jonathan's update would be successful. If Malcolm again made his change to the region and tried to update, the update would fail because the WHERE clause would not have changed, but the value of the region would now be Southeast instead of Midwest. Data integrity is much higher using key and updateable columns even though concurrency is lower.

Key and Modified Columns

When the Key and Modified Columns option is specified, PowerBuilder creates UPDATE and DELETE statements that compare the originally retrieved value for the key columns and the originally retrieved value of any updateable column that was modified against the same values in the database. If the values are equal, the update or delete takes place. This method is a trade-off between key columns and key and updateable columns.

Using the same example, if both Malcolm and Jonathan make changes to the same column (for example, region), the end result is the same: The first update will be successful and the second will fail. The SQL statement would be as follows:

```
UPDATE customer
SET region = "Southeast"
WHERE customer_id = 110
AND region = "Midwest"
```

You would have a problem if the preceding UPDATE were run and then later the status were changed from Preferred to Exceptional. This would be the SQL statement:

```
UPDATE customer
SET status = "Exceptional"
WHERE customer_id = 110
AND status = "Preferred"
```

This update would be successful even though the data had changed (region is different). Therefore, the data integrity is lower but the concurrency is higher. This option is used when it is okay for two users to modify the same row simultaneously as long as they are changing different data.

Timestamps

If your DBMS supports timestamps, you can maximize data integrity by including the timestamp in your result set for the DataWindow object. PowerBuilder automatically includes the timestamp in the `WHERE` clause for your updates and deletes and does not display it in the updateable column list. Oracle handles timestamps entirely on the server and no extra work is required in the DataWindow.

Key Modification

The last component to specify in the Specify Update Characteristics dialog box is how modification will take place if the user changes the value of a key column (the key column or columns must be specified as updateable). The two options are Use Delete then Insert and Use Update.

The first option deletes the row and then inserts a new one using the new key value. This option reduces the number of reorganizations needed on the database, but it has some potential problems. If a primary key is a foreign key in another table and is specified to use a cascading delete, you probably don't want to use Use Delete then Insert.

WARNING

In addition to the possibility of triggering cascading deletes, the Update option is useful if you only retrieve some of a table's columns. If you have only retrieved 5 of 20 columns from a table and change a primary key value, using the Delete then Insert options causes the whole row to be deleted and any data in the 15 columns that were not retrieved to be lost.

The second option, Use Update, updates the key value in the row (only some DBMSs allow key column updates). The new key value is included in the update along with the rest of the data. This prevents the problem with the foreign keys and cascading deletes.

A new option on the Specify Update Charateristics dialog box is the Identity Column drop-down list box. This list box is used to specify sequence number generation for the column specified in the drop-down list (usually the key column). This option is only applicable to DBMSs that support sequence number generation.

Printing

You can set a number of options to print a DataWindow object. In design mode, select the Print Specifications tab page on the DataWindow object property sheet (see Figure 9.81).

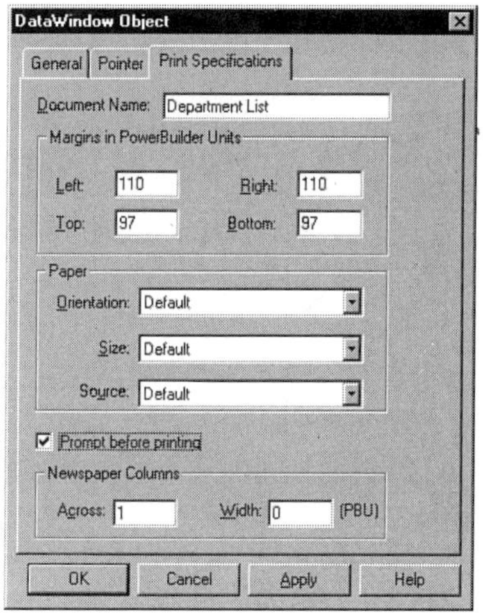

FIGURE 9.81.
The Print Specifications tab page.

Document Name is the name that appears in the print queue when the DataWindow is printed. The margins (in PowerBuilder units) can be changed for left, right, top, and bottom. The paper orientation, size, and source can also be specified. When checked, the Prompt before printing check box displays the Printer Setup dialog box before printing begins.

The bottom section of the Print Specifications dialog box is where you can specify a Newspaper column effect. If you want a report with two columns that read top to bottom rather than left to right (opposite of the N-Up presentation style), you would specify 2 in the Across single-line edit box and the column width in the Width single-line edit box. In addition to specifying this information to get the newspaper columns, you will probably want to use the Suppress After First check box on the General tab page for the Column Object property sheet. (Suppress After First should be used on objects such as column headings and page numbers so that they are printed only once per page and not on every newspaper column on the same page.)

In design mode, if you choose Print from the File menu, the design of the DataWindow object is printed. Several additional printing options appear under the File menu in preview mode. In this mode, Print sends the DataWindow object, complete with data, to the printer. If you would rather view the DataWindow object first, select Print Preview. When in Print Preview mode, you can select Print Preview Rulers, which places horizontal and vertical rulers on the edges of the DataWindow to help with alignment and spacing. Print Preview Zoom enables you to zoom in or out to view the DataWindow up close or from a distance. For more details on DataWindow printing techniques, see Chapter 26.

DataWindow Objects Versus DataWindow Controls

Now that you have created your DataWindow object, you need to place a DataWindow control on a window in the Window painter and associate the DataWindow object with the control. This can be done at design time in the Window painter (see Chapter 11) or at runtime by setting the `DataObject` attribute of the DataWindow control. The purpose of the DataWindow control is to act as a frame or viewport into the data that the DataWindow object retrieves. To learn more details about how the two link together, see Chapter 10.

Summary

In this chapter you have seen how to create PowerBuilder's most powerful object, the DataWindow object. A DataWindow object has a wide range of presentation styles to choose from to provide an attractive and appropriate user interface. In addition to providing different ways to display data, the DataWindow object can pull information from several different sources. New to PowerBuilder 5.0 is support for the rich text edit and OLE 2.0 presentation styles. The DataWindow painter is now fully OLE 2.0 compliant and has been updated with features such as AutoScrolling and additional PainterBar icons, resulting in an easier-to-use interface.

The DataWindow painter provides a means to create an interface that enables easy access to data (particularly data in a relational database). The DataWindow manages the data and generates all the necessary SQL statements to apply a user's changes to the database. In addition to supplying a method to update a database, the DataWindow painter can be used to create complex reports and graphs.

DataWindow Scripting

10

IN THIS CHAPTER

After you have placed a DataWindow control onto a window or a user object, you need to interact with it. PowerBuilder provides many PowerScript functions that act only on DataWindow controls.

A common misunderstanding of people new to PowerBuilder is the difference between a DataWindow object and a DataWindow control. The DataWindow *object* is what you create using the DataWindow painter and what is stored in your libraries. The DataWindow *control* is a control, just as a command button is a control, that is placed in a window or a user object. The DataWindow control acts as a viewport onto a DataWindow object, which is an attribute of the control. This is the `DataObject` attribute.

The DataWindow Control

Throughout this chapter you will encounter code that can be placed in a DataWindow control user object, or even in a base DataWindow control user object, which is then inherited from to give special-purpose DataWindows—for example, those that enable multiple selections with drag and drop. For more information about DataWindow control user objects, see Chapter 24, "Building User Objects."

Buffers

NEW 5 in PowerBuilder

There are four buffers in a DataWindow control, and now in PowerBuilder 5.0 you can directly access all of them. The most important of the buffers is the *Primary* buffer. This buffer holds all the currently available (displayed in the DataWindow control) rows, as well as the status of these rows and individual columns. These statuses are used in the generation of the appropriate SQL during a DataWindow save. The second of the buffers is the *Delete* buffer, which holds all the rows that have been deleted from the Primary buffer using either the `DeleteRow()` or the `RowsMove()` function. The `RowsMove()` function can be used to move rows between DataWindows and/or between the various buffers. The rows from the Delete buffer are used in the generation of `DELETE` statements when the DataWindow data is saved. The third buffer is the *Filter* buffer, which is used to hold all the rows that the current DataWindow filter has removed. These rows are included in a save of the data, generating the appropriate `INSERT` or `UPDATE` statements, along with the rows in the Primary buffer. The fourth buffer (which used to be hidden prior to Version 5.0) is called the *Original* buffer, and is used by PowerBuilder to store the values of the rows as they were retrieved from the database. These values are then used to build the `WHERE` clause on the SQL modification statements. You can also access the original value of a column through the `GetItem` functions by specifying a `TRUE` value as a fourth parameter.

Many DataWindow control functions can access specific buffers. The enumerated data type for specifying which DataWindow buffer to act on is `dwBuffer`, which has the values `Delete!`, `Filter!`, and `Primary!`.

Within the Primary and Filter buffers each row and each column within a row maintains an *edit status flag*. This flag indicates whether the row or column is new or has been modified. The value of this flag is used by the DataWindow to determine what type of SQL statement to generate for a row. This flag is of the `dwItemStatus` enumerated data type and can have the following values:

- `NotModified!`—The row or column is unchanged from the values that were originally retrieved. If a row has this status, it does not need to be saved. If a column has this status, it is not included in a `DELETE`, an `UPDATE`, or an `INSERT` statement.
- `DataModified!`—The specified column or another of the columns for that row has changed. The row is saved and the columns that have changed are made part of the `UPDATE` statement. If the row has this status in the Delete buffer, a `DELETE` statement is generated.
- `New!`—The row has been inserted into the DataWindow after a retrieve, but no values have been specified for any of the columns. This status applies only to rows. The row does not generate an `INSERT` statement, nor does it generate a `DELETE` statement if the row is in the Delete buffer.
- `NewModified!`—This status applies only to rows. It indicates that the row has been inserted into the DataWindow after a retrieve, and values have been assigned to some of its columns. A new row also gets this status if one of its columns has a default value. The row generates an `INSERT` statement that includes all the columns that have `DataModified!` status. The row does not generate a `DELETE` statement if the row is in the Delete buffer.

The `GetItemStatus()` function is used to determine the current status of either a row or a column. The syntax is

```
DataWindowControl.GetItemStatus( Row, Column, DWBuffer)
```

The *`Row`* parameter identifies the row from which the status will be obtained. *`Column`* specifies the column (either by number or name) for which you want the status; if this is a zero it returns the status of the row. The *`DWBuffer`* parameter identifies the DataWindow buffer you want to check. The function returns a value of type `dwItemStatus`.

The `SetItemStatus()` function is used to change the modification status of a row or column to a different value. You use this function to influence the type of SQL statements that will be generated for a row. The syntax is

```
DataWindowControl.SetItemStatus( Row, Column, DWBuffer, Status)
```

The *`Row`* parameter identifies the row for which the status will be changed. *`Column`* specifies the column (either by number or name) whose status you want to change; if this is a zero, the status of the row is changed. The *`DWBuffer`* parameter identifies the DataWindow buffer you want to change. The status is of type `dwItemStatus`.

If you change the status of a row's modification flag, it also affects the flags of all the row's columns, and vice versa. That is, setting a row to `NotModified!` or `New!` will cause all the columns to become `NotModified!`. You must be aware that not all status changes are legal, and you might have to go through an additional step to set a row or column to a particular status. The status might actually change to a third value that is different from both the original and the intended values.

Table 10.1 shows the effect of changing from one status to another. An entry of Yes means that the translation is allowed. An entry of No means that there is no change made. If a specific `dwItemStatus` value is shown, it is the new status of the row or column rather than the desired one.

Table 10.1. Valid item status modifications.

Original Status	*Desired Status*			
	`New!`	`NewModified!`	`DataModified!`	`NotModified!`
`New!`		Yes	Yes	No
`NewModified!`	No		Yes	`New!`
`DataModified!`	`NewModified!`	Yes		Yes
`NotModified!`	Yes	Yes	Yes	

You can reach a desired status that is not allowed directly by changing the status to an allowable intermediary one. For example, to change a status of `New!` to `NotModified!`, you first must make it `DataModified!`.

This table can be encapsulated into a function (see Listing 10.1) to be used throughout an application, either as a global or DataWindow user object function. This function is very useful for controlling DataWindow updates; it can cause some rows not to save or direct others to become updates rather than inserts.

Listing 10.1. `uf_ChangeRowStatus()` for the `u_dw` object.

```
// Parameters:
//    dwItemStatus a_state    (The new state)
//    Long a_lStartRow        (The start row)
//    Long a_lEndRow          (The end row)

Long lRow
dwItemStatus dwStatus

If a_lStartRow > a_lEndRow Then
  Return
End If
```

```
For lRow = a_lStartRow To a_lEndRow
  dwStatus = this.GetItemStatus( lRow, 0, Primary!)

  Choose Case a_State
     Case New!
        Choose Case dwStatus
           Case NewModified!, DataModified!
              this.SetItemStatus( lRow, 0, Primary!, NotModified!)
              this.SetItemStatus( lRow, 0, Primary!, New!)
           Case NotModified!
              this.SetItemStatus( lRow, 0, Primary!, New!)
        End Choose
     Case NewModified!
        Choose Case dwStatus
           Case New!, DataModified!, NotModified!
              this.SetItemStatus( lRow, 0, Primary!, NewModified!)
        End Choose
     Case DataModified!
        Choose Case dwStatus
           Case New!, NewModified!, NotModified!
              this.SetItemStatus( lRow, 0, Primary!, DataModified!)
        End Choose
     Case NotModified!
        Choose Case dwStatus
           Case New!, NewModified!
              this.SetItemStatus( lRow, 0, Primary!, DataModified!)
              this.SetItemStatus( lRow, 0, Primary!, NotModified!)
           Case DataModified!
              this.SetItemStatus( lRow, 0, Primary!, NotModified!)
        End Choose
     End Choose
Next
```

You could use this function, for example, if you were saving the data outside the DataWindow and then wanted to carry out a normal DataWindow update. In this case, you would want to alter any `INSERT` statements to `UPDATE`s instead. This is sometimes a business requirement and cannot always been achieved using separate DataWindows.

The `GetNextModified()` function enables you to find the rows that have been modified in a specific buffer. The syntax is

`DataWindowControl.GetNextModified( Row, DWBuffer)`

`Row` is the row number after which to start searching and *`DWBuffer`* indicates which of the DataWindow buffers is to be examined. To search from the beginning and include the first row, *`Row`* should be set to `0`. The function returns a Long value for the first modified row found and `0` if no modified rows are found after the start row. A row is considered modified if it has a status of `NewModified!` or `DataModified!`.

NOTE

Remember that `GetNextModified()` begins searching after the row you specify, whereas most other DataWindow functions begin at the specified row.

Accessing the Data

NEW in PowerBuilder 5

In previous versions of PowerBuilder, interaction with the data could be achieved only through the `SetItem()` and various `GetItem` functions. PowerBuilder 5.0 allows direct access to all DataWindow data via PowerScript. You can access all the buffers and operate on the entire DataWindow, single rows, or arrays of rows.

This is the syntax for this new type of access:

```
dw_control.Object.Data[.Buffer[.WhichValue]][Range]
dw_control.Object.Data[Range]
dw_control.Object.Column[RowRange]
```

In this code

- *Buffer* is either `Primary` (the default), `Filter`, or `Delete`.
- *WhichValue* is either `Current` (the default) or `Original`. This allows you to access the original value of a column as it came in from the database.
- *Range* can be any of the following: `0` for all rows, `>0` for a specific row, `[Row, Column]` for a specific column, `[Row1, Column1, Row2, Column2]` for a range of rows and columns, or `.Selected` for all selected rows.
- *RowRange* can be any of the following: `0` for all rows, `>0` for a specific row, `[Row1, Row2]` for a range of rows, or `.Selected` for all selected rows.

You should note that some forms of syntax that you might expect to work are in fact invalid. For example, you cannot use the syntax `dw_1.Data.Buffer.ColumnName[ Row]`.

These are some examples that demonstrate this new syntax:

```
// Extract the original value of the 3rd column of the first row
dw_1.Object.Data.Primary.Original[ 1, 3]
//
// Extract all of the rows that have been filtered out
dw_1.Object.Data.Filter[ 0]
//
// Extract all the currently selected rows
dw_1.Object.Data.Selected
//
// Extract the values for the column emp_fname for rows 1 through 5
dw_1.Object.emp_fname.Primary[ 1, 5]
```

You can use the dot notation that was just introduced to both read and write data in a DataWindow control. Here's an example:

```
Real rRaise = 1.05
Long lCount, lRows

lRows = dw_1.RowCount()

For lCount = 1 To lRows
   // pre 5.0 method: lSalary = dw_1.GetItemNumber( lCount, "emp_salary")
   lSalary = dw_1.Object.Data.emp_salary[ lCount]
   lSalary = lSalary * rRaise
   // pre 5.0 method: dw_1.SetItem ( lCount, "emp_salary", lSalary)
   dw_1.Object.Data.emp_salary[ lCount] = lSalary
Next
```

The `SetItem()` function and the `GetItem` functions are still available with PowerBuilder 5.0, but as you will see later in this section, there is little purpose in continuing to use them. The only time you will want to fall back on these two functions is when you do not know the column name at the time the code is written (for example, a generic function that acts on data in a particular way). You cannot use the new syntax for accessing the data because it requires the column to be specified in dot notation (or accessed through the array index using the column number). Unlike with the `SetItem()` function, PowerBuilder steps away from a true object-oriented implementation when you have to access data using the `GetItem` functions, because it forces you to explicitly state the data type of the value. Rather than issuing a simple `GetItem()` function call, you have to use one of the functions shown in Table 10.2.

Table 10.2. The `GetItem` functions.

Function	*Description*
`GetItemDate`	Get a value from a Date column
`GetItemTime`	Get a value from a Time column
`GetItemDateTime`	Get a value from a DateTime column
`GetItemNumber`	Get a value from a Number column (Decimal, Double, Integer, Long, Real, or ULong)
`GetItemDecimal`	Get a value from a Decimal column
`GetItemString`	Get a value from a String column

Although PowerBuilder provides numerous functions for taking data out of a DataWindow, it provides only one for putting data back in: `SetItem()`. The `SetItem()` function takes a row, a column, and a data value as parameters:

```
DataWindowControl.SetItem( Row, Column, DataValue)
```

`Column` can either be a column number (integer) or a column name (string), and `DataValue` must match that of the receiving DataWindow column. The function returns `1` if it is successful and `-1` if an error occurs.

> **NOTE**
>
> A call to `SetItem()` validates only that the data type of the value matches the column. Any validation rules on the column or coded within or called from the `ItemChanged` event are not executed.

Here's a useful trick to remember if your DataWindow makes use of the radio button edit style for a column: After a value is selected for the radio button group, there is no way to deselect the checked value. You need to provide a way for the user to deselect the radio button. Use the `SetItem()` function with a `NULL` variable as the data value. You need to take this into consideration for the non-editable DropDownListBox edit style as well.

> **NOTE**
>
> The variable you use in the `SetNull()` call must match the data type of the column you will be affecting in the `SetItem()` call; otherwise, it will not work.

To test the speed benefits of the various methods, a test window was created consisting of three DataWindows and related command buttons and single-line edits to control the timing and operations. All the DataWindow controls make use of an external-source DataWindow object containing a numeric column and two 10-character string columns. Two of the DataWindows are prefilled with 1000 rows (`ImportString()` inserts its own rows). The write operation consists of looping through all 1000 rows and setting the three columns with dummy values. The read operation again loops through all 1000 rows and stores the values into dummy variables. The results of the test are shown in Table 10.3.

Table 10.3. Speed comparisons of different access methods.

Operation	`GetItem/SetItem`	`Direct`	`ImportString`	`Redraw`
Writing	1885ms (1.9s)	89538ms (89.5s)	30347 (30.3s)	On
Writing	1007ms (1s)	1382ms (1.4s)	1244 (1.2s)	Off
Reading	999ms (1s)	1331ms (1.3s)	N/A	N/A

As you can see from Table 10.3, the state of the redraw option for the DataWindow control has a dramatic effect on the time taken for the direct access and `ImportString()` methods. The timings were taken on a 120MHz Pentium running Windows 95.

This direct access syntax can also be used to manipulate objects in the DataWindow object. This includes column attributes, nested reports, and OLE objects. With nested reports there is no limit placed on the number of levels (a nest within a nest) that you can refer to, as long as the previous level exists.

Also new to PowerBuilder 5.0 is the capability to load DataWindows by assignment to and from structures. The only restriction is that you must have the structure built to the same specifications as the DataWindow (column data types and order).

Here's an example of this type of assignment:

```
ws_assign sAssign
//
// You can assign to existing rows
//
dw_1.InsertRow( 0)
dw_1.InsertRow( 0)
//
// Setup the data values
//
sAssign.value1 = "Simon"
sAssign.value2 = "Gallagher"
//
// Load row 1 of the DataWindow
//
dw_1.Object.Data[1] = sAssign
//
// Setup some more data
//
sAssign.value1 = "Nomis"
sAssign.value2 = "Rehgallag"
//
// Load these into row 2 of the DataWindow
//
dw_1.Object.Data[2] = sAssign
//
//
//
sAssign = dw_1.Object.Data[ 1]
```

From a few simple tests, it looks as though using this method of loading data outperforms any of the other methods by almost a factor of two. It is well worth experimenting with the various methods to find the optimal performer for any heavy DataWindow access code you develop.

The Edit Control

One of the most important concepts to understand when dealing with DataWindows is the edit control (see Figure 10.1). The main reason that DataWindows use fewer resources than a window with a similar number of controls is that the DataWindow is only a graphical representation of data on a single control. The user actually interacts with the DataWindow through the edit control, which floats over the DataWindow and validates the user's input before accepting it and moving to the next field.

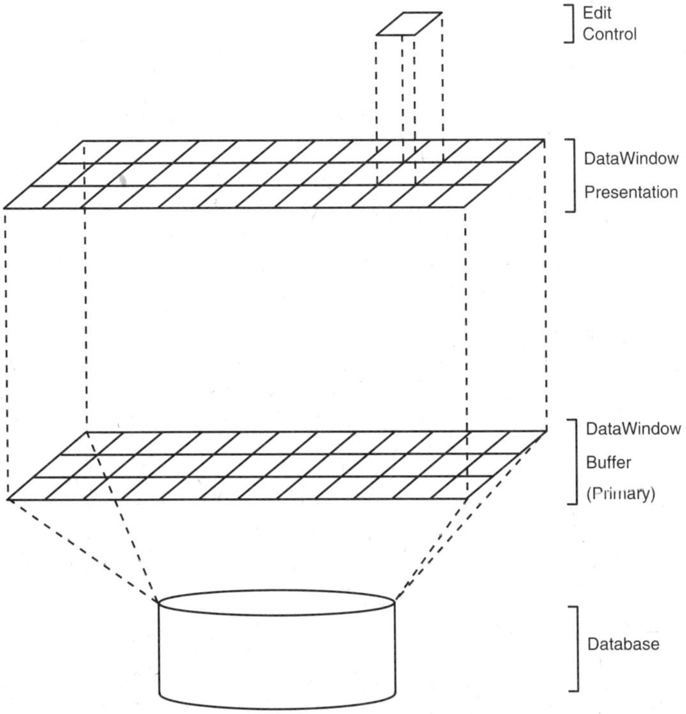

FIGURE 10.1.
How a DataWindow handles data entry and presentation.

For those who are familiar with Microsoft Excel, the edit control can be likened to each cell in the grid. When you type a formula into the cell, it is not accepted and calculated until you move to a new field or select the checkmark button next to the formula. If the formula is wrong, you cannot move to a new location. The DataWindow control uses the same concept.

There are occasions when you need to obtain the value that the user has just entered before it becomes accepted and is placed into the column and buffer. Use the PowerScript function `GetText()` for this purpose:

```
DataWindowControl.GetText()
```

The edit control is text based, and the value returned is the string the user entered. If the value is of a different data type, you must convert the returned value yourself. If there are no editable columns in the DataWindow, the function returns an empty string. This function is usually called in the `ItemChanged` and `ItemError` DataWindow control events and within any validation rules these events might call. A different set of functions (the `SetItem()` function and the `GetItem` functions described earlier) are used after the value leaves the edit control and is placed in the column for the Primary buffer. This transfer occurs when the user moves from one column to another or when a script calls `AcceptText()`. If the user clicks a control other than the DataWindow, the last value entered remains in the edit control (and is not validated).

If you ask a PowerBuilder developer (or Powersoft, for that matter) how to ensure that the last column in a DataWindow is accepted when focus has left the DataWindow control, you will receive a myriad of solutions. The majority of them do not work or are so unwieldy as to be laughable. This section addresses one of the correct solutions, which does not require a lot of coding, is encapsulated, and does not cause the double message box problem, which occurs when the value fails a validation check and causes an error message box to appear. When the user clicks the OK button in the message box, focus flashes back to the DataWindow, and another message box appears. This usually causes another application to be brought in front of the PowerBuilder application. This is because the usual solution is to code an `AcceptText()` in the `LoseFocus` event, which causes the following problem: When the user leaves the DataWindow the `LoseFocus` event causes the `AcceptText()`, which fails and opens the message box. This causes the DataWindow to receive a second `LoseFocus` because it has now lost the focus to the message box. When the user closes the message box the DataWindow processes the new `LoseFocus` event, which causes the same thing to happen. You might expect this to loop indefinitely, but it doesn't for some unexplainable reason; it possibly has something to do with the way Windows queues events.

The `AcceptText()` function applies the contents of the DataWindow's edit control to the current column in the Primary buffer, as long as the value passes the validation rules for that column:

```
DataWindowControl.AcceptText()
```

The function returns `1` if it succeeds and `-1` if the validation fails. `AcceptText()` can trigger the `ItemChanged` and `ItemError` events and so should never be coded in those locations.

The following code is something you should build into your framework's DataWindow base object. First, declare two Boolean variables:

```
Public:
Boolean  bFailedAccept = FALSE

Private:
Boolean  bInAcceptText = FALSE
```

The `bFailedAccept` Boolean is accessible from outside the DataWindow and is used by other scripts to query the DataWindow regarding the success or failure of the last triggered `AcceptText`. The `bInAcceptText` Boolean is used as a semaphore to indicate whether PowerBuilder is still executing an `AcceptText`.

A user event, AcceptText, is added to the DataWindow, and the following is placed in the event:

```
If Not bInAcceptText Then
   bInAcceptText = TRUE
   If this.AcceptText() = -1 Then
      bFailedAccept = TRUE
      this.SetFocus()
      this.PostEvent( "PostAccept")
      Return
   Else
      bFailedAccept = FALSE
   End If
End If

bInAcceptText = FALSE
```

This code relies on the factor that causes the double message box problem: the triggering of an additional LoseFocus event. The first time into this event, the Boolean bInAcceptText is FALSE and the IF statement is executed. This immediately sets this Boolean to TRUE to indicate that PowerBuilder is now executing the accept. The AcceptText() function is then called, and the return value is checked. This call might invoke an error window if one of the validation checks fails. If this happens, this event is again entered. Because the Boolean bInAcceptText is now TRUE, PowerBuilder drops to the end and resets the Boolean to FALSE. Execution then continues in the first called AcceptText event, which sets the Boolean bFailedAccept to TRUE and then sets the focus back to the DataWindow control. A custom event, PostAccept, is called, which will reset the bInAcceptText flag once you are safely finished accepting the text. The additional code is required only when the user tabs from a column but stays within the DataWindow and the edit value fails a validation check. This particular series of events would cause the double message box problem. If the user moved to another control, the simple (and commonly accepted) way of ensuring that the text is accepted is to post to an event from the LoseFocus event, which then carries out the AcceptText() call.

The AcceptText user event is triggered by posting the message from the LoseFocus event:

```
this.PostEvent( "AcceptText")
```

If a validation error occurs, an ItemError event is triggered:

```
bInAcceptText = TRUE
```

The last event is a user-defined custom event that is called from the AcceptText event. The code simply resets one of the Boolean flags:

```
bInAcceptText = FALSE
```

In order to complete the family of functions that act on the edit control of a DataWindow, one more function should be mentioned. There will be times, usually outside the DataWindow, when you will want to replace the value of the edit control with a new one. For example, the user enters a partial string on which you carry out a lookup, which you then use to replace the value in the DataWindow. The `SetText()` function is used for this purpose:

```
DataWindowControl.SetText( StringValue)
```

The *`StringValue`* must be in a format that is compatible with the data type of the column on which the edit control is currently located. The function returns `1` if it succeeds and `-1` if an error occurs.

Most of the time, you modify data using the `SetItem()` function.

The Validation Process

When the user changes a value in a DataWindow column, there are four stages of validation. The first two are the responsibility of PowerBuilder; the last two are coded by the developer.

The first check is whether the value has actually changed from the value that existed before the edit. If the value has not changed, no processing occurs.

The second check is to see if the value is of the correct data type for the column. If the data types do not match, an `ItemError` event is triggered and the value is rejected. This is needed because the value of the edit control is a string and PowerBuilder has to perform an internal conversion to check the original data type of the column.

The third check tests the value against any validation rules (see Chapter 4, "Databases and the Database Painter," and Chapter 9, "The DataWindow Painter") that might be attached to that DataWindow column. If the rule fails, the value is rejected and an `ItemError` event is triggered.

The fourth, and final, check is the script the developer has written in the `ItemChanged` event. What occurs depends on the value that is assigned to something known as an action code. The *action code* is used to direct what PowerBuilder should do at the end of the DataWindow event. This used to be achieved using `SetActionCode()`, but in Version 5.0 the preferred method is to use `Return`. If the value is `0`, the value is accepted and the focus is allowed to change. If the value assigned is `1`, the value is rejected and the `ItemError` event is triggered. If the value is set to `2`, the value is rejected, the original value is placed back where it was, and the focus is allowed to change.

The flowchart in Figure 10.2 summarizes the validation process.

FIGURE 10.2.
Validation process flow.

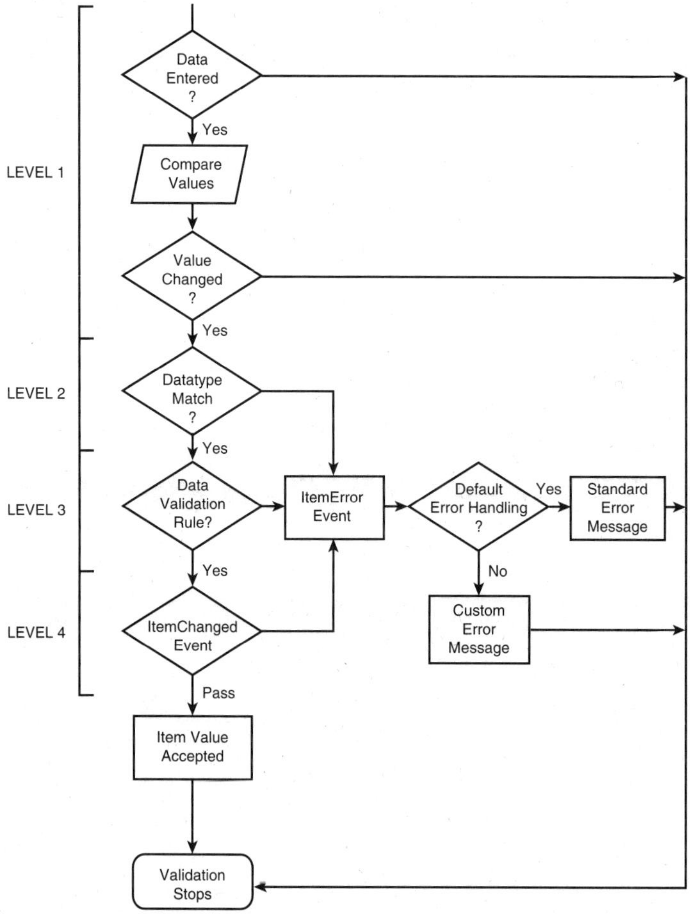

There are numerous methods of placing and removing data from a DataWindow, and these are covered in the next section. Accessing data from the database is covered in the section "Database-Related Functions."

Adding and Removing Rows

The two functions that add and remove rows from the Primary buffer are `InsertRow()` and `DeleteRow()`.

Three other functions also add and remove rows. These are `RowsMove()`, `RowsCopy()`, and `RowsDiscard()`. Each of these is fully described in Chapter 26, "Advanced DataWindow Techniques II."

Inserting a Row

The `InsertRow()` function inserts a row into a DataWindow or child DataWindow. As detailed in Chapter 4, the PowerBuilder data repository can be set up to specify defaults for individual columns. If any columns have such defaults, they are set before the row displays. The syntax for this function is

```
DataWindowControl.InsertRow( lRow)
```

The only parameter is the row before which you want the new row to be inserted. To insert a new row at the end of the DataWindow, *lRow* needs to be `0`. The function returns a Long data type that is the row number that was added. If an error occurs, `-1` is returned.

NOTE

When a new row is added, the current range of rows displayed in the DataWindow control is not altered. (Unless, of course, you add the row after a row that is currently visible on the DataWindow, barring the last row.) The current row remains unaltered, and the new row is not made current.

To scroll to the new row and make it the current row, call the `ScrollToRow()` function. This enables you to show the newly added row to the user, especially if it was added out of sight. To make the new row the current row without moving to it, use the `SetRow()` function.

Deleting a Row

The `DeleteRow()` function deletes a row from a DataWindow or child DataWindow. The syntax for this function is

```
DataWindowControl.DeleteRow( lRow)
```

The only parameter is the row you want to delete. To delete the current row, *lRow* needs to be `0`. The function returns `1` if the row was removed and `-1` if an error occurred.

When a row is deleted, it is moved from the Primary buffer into the Delete buffer. The DataWindow row is not deleted from the database table until the `Update()` function is called and the database transaction is committed.

NOTE

If the DataWindow object is set up as not updatable, all storage (the memory used by the buffers) that is associated with the row is cleared when a `DeleteRow()` is issued.

The Delete buffer is emptied and any associated storage resources are released only after a successful update and reset of the update flags.

Saving Data

The `Update()` function makes the actual changes in the database to reflect the changes made in the DataWindow object. The syntax is

```
DataWindowControl.Update( { AcceptText {, ResetFlag}})
```

`Update()` takes two optional parameters. The first enables you to force an `AcceptText()` to occur and the validation to be passed successfully before the DataWindow can save. `AcceptText` needs to be `TRUE` to force this. The second parameter is a Boolean that enables you to control the updating of the modification flags. If `ResetFlag` is `TRUE`, the modification flags (covered in the "Buffers" section) for each row are reset. `TRUE` is the default for both parameters.

There will be times when you need to control the status of the modification flags. For instance, during multiple DataWindow updates you need to leave everything in the state it was in before the update in case an error occurs. By default, `Update()` resets the flag after a successful save.

NOTE

Remember that if `SetTrans()`, rather than `SetTransObject()`, has been used, you cannot carry out synchronized DataWindow updates, and `ResetFlag` is not used in this case.

The `Update()` function returns `1` if it succeeds and `-1` if an error occurs. Calling `Update()` might trigger the events `DBError`, `SQLPreview`, `UpdateEnd`, and `UpdateStart`. In addition, if `AcceptText` is `TRUE`, `ItemChanged` and `ItemError` might also be triggered.

NOTE

If for some reason you need to call the `Update()` function in an `ItemChanged` event, you must set the `Accept Text` parameter to `FALSE` to avoid stack faulting the application. Stack faulting occurs when code goes into an infinite loop and fills the system-maintained function call stack. Also, because the current edit has not yet been validated, you must use `SetItem()` to place the value in the DataWindow before calling `Update()`.

There are cases in which you will want to synchronize the update of DataWindows with the database.

The first case occurs when you want to update multiple tables from one DataWindow. This is achieved by using the `Describe()` and `Modify()` functions, which are discussed in Chapter 25, "Advanced DataWindow Techniques I," to change the `Update` attribute of the columns for each table.

NOTE

In the Listing 10.2 you should notice the use of both of the new syntax for direct access and the appropriate uses of `Describe()` and `Modify()`.

You need to preserve the status of the modification flags between each `Update()` call by using the optional flags for the function. The code in Listing 10.2 shows a DataWindow object-level function that performs an update to a multitable DataWindow. The function takes two parameters: a table to update and the key fields for the table.

Listing 10.2. `uf_UpdateTable()` for object `u_dw`.

```
// Function takes:
//    String a_szTableName - the table to be updated
//    String a_szKeyFields - a concatenated list of key fields for the table
Integer nColumns, nCount
String szDBName, szTableName, szColumnName, szModify

nColumns = Integer( this.Object.DataWindow.Column.Count)
a_szTableName = Lower( a_szTableName)
a_szKeyFields = Lower( a_szKeyFields)

For nCount = 1 To nColumns
   szDBName = this.Describe( "#" + String( nCount) + ".DBName")
   szColumnName = this.Describe( "#" + String( nCount) + ".Name")
   szTableName = Lower( Left( szDBName, Pos( szDBName, ".") - 1))

   If szTableName = a_szTableName Then
      szModify = szColumnName + ".Update = Yes"
      If Pos(a_szKeyFields, szColumnName) > 0 Then
         szModify = szModify + " " + szColumnName + ".Key = Yes"
      Else
         szModify = szModify + " " + szColumnName + ".Key = No"
      End If
   Else
      szModify = szColumnName + ".Update = No " + szColumnName + ".Key = No"
   End If

   If this.Modify( szModify) <> "" Then
      Return FALSE
   End If
Next
```

continues

Listing 10.2. continued

```
this.Object.DataWindow.Table.UpdateTable = a_szTableName

If this.Update( TRUE, FALSE) > 0 Then
   Return TRUE
Else
   Return FALSE
End If
```

There is only one caveat: The database column names must be prefixed with the table name they relate to. For example, a DataWindow object created with the following syntax:

```
SELECT "product"."id", "product"."name", "sales_order_items"."id",
       "sales_order_items"."line_id", "sales_order_items"."prod_id",
       "sales_order_items"."quantity"
FROM "product", "sales_order_items"
WHERE ( "sales_order_items"."prod_id" = "product"."id" )
```

can update itself using the following lines of code:

```
If this.uf_UpdateTable( "product", "product_id") Then
   If this.uf_UpdateTable( "sales_order_items", "id, line_id") Then
      this.ResetUpdate()
   End If
End If
```

The column names you pass in as the key fields are the names as they appear in the DataWindow and not the database version. The only statement you must remember to add is to the `ResetUpdate()` function (see next case) to place the DataWindow back into an unmodified state, since the `Update()` did not do this for you. In the second case you are updating multiple DataWindow controls that need to be completed as one transaction. For this reason the modification flags for each DataWindow control need to be left until all DataWindows have successfully completed. If any one of the updates fails, the DataWindows are left in such a state that the user can fix the problem and try again.

In both cases, when the updates have been successfully completed, you need to reset the modification flags. For this task you use the `ResetUpdate()` function. Its syntax is

DataWindowControl`.ResetUpdate()`

This function resets the modification flags in the Primary and Filter buffers and clears all the rows in the Delete buffer of a DataWindow control. After calling this function, the flags are all reset to the status `NotModified!` or `New!`. Rows that already have the status `New!` retain the same status, but the status of all other rows is changed to `NotModified!`. The reason for this is that all modifications that have been made to `DataModified!` and `NewModified!` will be successfully handled. However, a `New!` has not been saved because there is nothing to save. For the possibility of future updates where PowerBuilder needs to generate an `INSERT`, the row maintains the `New!` status.

If you call `Update()` with the `ResetFlag` parameter set to `FALSE` and have not called the `ResetUpdate()` function, the DataWindow will issue the same SQL statements the next time you call `Update()`, which will most likely produce numerous errors.

An example of coordinated DataWindow updates is shown in the following code, which ensures the success of the updates to both `dw_customer_dimensions` and `dw_customer_dimensions_wall`. Note that it uses a custom transaction object that was introduced in Chapter 5, "SQL and PowerBuilder," and is further discussed in Chapter 24:

```
Integer nUpdateStatus
Boolean bSuccess = FALSE

SQLCA.BeginTran()

nUpdateStatus = dw_customer_dimensions.Update( TRUE, FALSE)

If nUpdateStatus = 1 Then
   //
   // If this update fails the flags will automatically be left alone
   //
   nUpdateStatus = dw_customer_dimensions_wall.Update()
   If nUpdateStatus = 1 Then
      SQLCA.CommitTran()

      dw_customer_dimensions.ResetUpdate()
      dw_customer_dimensions_wall.ResetUpdate()

      bSuccess = TRUE
   End If
End If

If Not bSuccess Then
   SQLCA.RollbackTran()
End If

Return bSuccess
```

The final piece of the data-saving mechanism is seldom of interest and is therefore often overlooked, but it involves the order in which the DataWindow control buffers are saved. There may be occasions when you need to sequence the order in which rows are being saved, and a useful technique is to filter out the subset of the rows you are interested in so that their data modifications occur last. The sequence of the buffers is Delete, Primary, and then Filter.

An example of this requirement is if you undertake sequencing or resequencing of row keys that reuse values from rows that have been deleted. In this particular case you will want to let the deleted and existing rows be updated first and then any new rows saved from the Filter buffer.

Update Events

The `UpdateStart` event is triggered before any changes are sent to the database but after you have issued an `Update()` function call for a DataWindow object. You can control whether the update proceeds or stops without doing any processing by setting the return value. The return values for this event are as follows:

- `0`—Continue with the update (the default).
- `1`—Do not perform the update.

The `UpdateEnd` event occurs after all the updates for a DataWindow object have been completed in the database.

You can use both of these events to place additional control on an update. For example, if the DataWindow can be updated only if certain fields or options are set, you can encapsulate these checks into a place that will always get executed rather than coding them at every point where you do an update.

Scrolling in the Primary Buffer

Six PowerScript functions enable you to scroll around a DataWindow control. Each of the scroll functions can trigger any of the following events: `ItemChanged`, `ItemError`, `ItemFocusChanged`, or `RowFocusChanged`. There are also two scroll-specific events—`ScrollVertical` and `ScrollHorizontal`—that are triggered whenever the DataWindow scrolls in the appropriate direction.

The `Scroll()` and `ScrollToRow()` functions enable relative and direct movement, respectively. The syntax for these functions is

```
DataWindowControl.Scroll( lNumberRows)
```

The only parameter is the number of lines to scroll. The direction of the scroll is specified by using a positive integer to scroll down and a negative integer to scroll up. This function returns the line number of the top line displayed, or returns `-1` on an error. If you specify a value that would put the scroll past the beginning or end of the control, the function will stop at that boundary. The current row is not affected by this function.

To scroll to a specific row rather than to a relative row, you need to use the `ScrollToRow()` function:

```
DataWindowControl.ScrollToRow( lRow)
```

The parameter specifies the row where you want to scroll. As with `Scroll()`, if the row value is outside the boundaries, the function will stop on the boundary. The function returns `1` on a successful scroll and `-1` on an error.

NOTE

`ScrollToRow()` affects only the current row, not the current column. This function also does not highlight the row. To indicate the current row, use the `SelectRow()` or `SetRowFocusIndicator()` functions.

If the row scrolled to is already visible, the display does not change. If the row was not visible, the displayed rows change to display the row at the top unless the row is the next one after the bottom row displayed, in which case PowerBuilder simply scrolls down one row to display the required line.

The functions `ScrollNextPage()` and `ScrollPriorPage()` work in a similar manner, except that they display the next or previous page of rows. A page is the number of rows that can display in the control at one time.

NOTE

Both of these functions change the current row, but not the current column:

```
DataWindowControl.ScrollNextPage()
DataWindowControl.ScrollPriorPage()
```

Both of these functions return the number of the topmost row displayed after scrolling; `-1` is returned on an error.

The functions `ScrollNextRow()` and `ScrollPriorRow()` work similarly. These functions scroll only one row, either forward or backward. The current row is changed each time. These are the functions:

```
DataWindowControl.ScrollNextRow()
DataWindowControl.ScrollPriorRow()
```

Both of these functions return a Long data type that is the number of the topmost row displayed. If the new current row is not visible, the display is moved up to show the current row. If an error occurs, `-1` is returned.

Changing the Current Edit Focus

Because a DataWindow is essentially a spreadsheet, an individual field is referenced by a row and column pairing known as an *item*. The DataWindow control maintains knowledge of the current column and the current row. These are changed every time a user presses the Tab or Enter keys, clicks the mouse on another field, or uses the up- and down-arrow keys or the Page Up and Page Down keys. The current row and column can also be changed by some of the DataWindow functions, and explicitly by using the `SetRow()` and `SetColumn()` functions. If there is at least one editable column, a DataWindow will always have a current column, even when the DataWindow control is not active.

The `SetColumn()` function sets the current column of a DataWindow control:

```
DataWindowControl.SetColumn( Column)
```

The *Column* parameter can be either the number of the column or a string containing the column name. The function returns `1` if it succeeds and `-1` if an error occurs. If the column number is outside the valid range of columns, or if the column name does not exist, the call fails.

`SetColumn()` moves the cursor to the specified column but does not scroll the DataWindow control to that column if it is not currently visible. You can set only an editable column to be current.

If you try to set a column to be current and none of the columns in the DataWindow object are editable (have a tab value), `SetColumn()` returns a value of `1`. Any subsequent calls to `GetColumn()` return `0`, and `GetColumnName()` returns the empty string (`""`). If you try to set a uneditable column and there are other editable columns in the DataWindow object, `SetColumn()` returns `-1` and `GetColumn()` and `GetColumnName()` return the previously current column.

A call to `SetColumn()` can trigger these events: `ItemChanged`, `ItemError`, and `ItemFocusChanged`. You should avoid coding a call to `SetColumn()` in these events because it will cause a stack fault due to the iterative calls.

The `SetRow()` function sets the current row for a DataWindow control:

```
DataWindowControl.SetRow( Row)
```

The *Row* parameter is a Long data type that is the row number to set as current. The function returns `1` if it succeeds and `-1` if an error occurs. If the row is outside the valid range of row numbers, the call fails.

`SetRow()` moves the cursor to the current row but does not scroll the DataWindow control if the row is not currently visible. You must use the scroll functions described earlier.

A call to `SetRow()` might trigger the same three events as `SetColumn()`, as well as a fourth: `RowFocusChanged`. As with `SetColumn()`, you should avoid calling `SetRow()` from within these events.

The two preceding functions have the following reciprocals that return the current row and column: `GetRow()`, `GetColumn()`, and `GetColumnName()`.

The `GetRow()` function returns the row number of the current row in a DataWindow control:

```
DataWindowControl.GetRow()
```

The function returns the number of the current row in the DataWindow, `0` if no row is current, and `-1` if an error occurs. The current row is not always visible in the DataWindow.

The `GetColumn()` function returns the number of the column that currently has focus. The syntax is

```
DataWindowControl.GetColumn()
```

If no column is current, the function returns `0`, or `-1` if an error occurs. A `0` return value can happen only if all the columns have a tab value of `0`.

The `GetColumnName()` function returns the name of the column that currently has focus. The syntax is

```
DataWindowControl.GetColumnName()
```

If no column is current or an error occurs, an empty string is returned.

To indicate which row is current, rather than relying on the user to spot the focus rectangle in a field (this is also optional for DataWindow columns), you can specify a pointer or indicator to appear in the DataWindow pointing at the current row. This is achieved using the `SetRowFocusIndicator()` function. The syntax is

```
DataWindowControl.SetRowFocusIndicator( Indicator {, Xlocation {, Ylocation }})
```

The *`Indicator`* parameter can be of either the `RowFocusInd` enumerated type or the name of a picture control. `RowFocusInd` can be of the following types: `Off!` (no indicator), `FocusRect!` (a dotted-line rectangle around the row—no effect on a Macintosh), or `Hand!` (the PowerBuilder pointing hand).

Frequently the indicator is customized and a picture control is used instead. This control is made invisible after being placed on the same object (Window or user object) as the DataWindow control.

The *`Xlocation`* and *`Ylocation`* parameters enable you to set the position (in PowerBuilder units) of the pointer relative to the upper-left corner of the current row. The indicator position defaults to `(0,0)`.

NOTE

If the `DataObject` attribute is modified for a DataWindow control, the row focus indicator will be turned off. You have to reissue a `SetRowFocusIndicator()` call after changing this attribute. If the connection between the DataWindow control and a transaction is broken, the row indicator will remain; it gets turned off only when the DataWindow object is swapped out.

Selecting by Mouse

A DataWindow is a kind of mini window, having some but not all of the same behaviors as a window. One of the similar behaviors is the capability to react to a user clicking an area of the object—in this case, the DataWindow. PowerBuilder provides a number of functions you can use to react to a user's mouse movements and actions.

The `GetClickedColumn()` function returns the column number that the user clicked or double-clicked in a DataWindow control and is used in the `Clicked` and `DoubleClicked` events:

```
DataWindowControl.GetClickedColumn()
```

The function returns `0` if the user did not click or double-click on a column. The column clicked on becomes the current column after the `Clicked` or `DoubleClicked` event has finished. Therefore, the return values of `GetClickedColumn()` and `GetColumn()` are different within these events.

NEW 5 in PowerBuilder

`GetClickedRow()` is a function similar to `GetClickedColumn()` that determines the row on which the user has just clicked. This function is obsolete in PowerBuilder 5.0 because the row is passed as an argument to both `Clicked` and `DoubleClicked` events. The syntax is

```
DataWindowControl.GetClickedRow()
```

As with the `GetClickedColumn()` function, this also returns `0` if the user clicked outside the data area—that is, outside the detail band. The row selected becomes the current row after the `Clicked` or `DoubleClicked` event. As before, the `GetRow()` and `GetClickedRow()` functions return different values during these scripts.

The `SelectRow()` function is used to highlight and unhighlight a row or multiple rows of a DataWindow control. It has no further action except to make the rows stand out in the control, and it does not affect the current row:

```
DataWindowControl.SelectRow( Row, Boolean)
```

The *`Row`* parameter is a Long data type signifying the number of the row on which you wish to change the highlighting. To select or deselect all rows, set *`Row`* to `0`. The *`Boolean`* parameter determines whether the row is to be highlighted (`TRUE`) or unhighlighted (`FALSE`). Any rows that are already highlighted and are highlighted again do not change; similarly, an unselected row remains unselected.

The `IsSelected()` function is used to check whether a particular row is currently selected. The syntax is

```
DataWindowControl.IsSelected( Row)
```

The function returns a Boolean value that is `TRUE` if the row is selected and `FALSE` if it is not. If the specified row is outside the valid range of rows, the function returns `FALSE`.

Whereas the `IsSelected()` function is used to check a particular row, the `GetSelectedRow()` function is usually used in a loop and returns the number of the first row selected after a given row. Rows are selected only with the `SelectRow()` function:

```
DataWindowControl.GetSelectedRow( StartRow)
```

The function returns `0` if no row is selected after *`StartRow`*.

The following code uses most of the functions that have just been described. This example enables the user to click individual rows in one DataWindow, click a copy button, and have those rows appear in another DataWindow. This code is placed in the `Clicked` event of the primary DataWindow:

```
// Make use of the event paremeter: Row
//
this.SelectRow( Row, TRUE)
```

The code behind the button to copy the rows is as follows:

```
Long lRow = 0

dw_1.SetRedraw( FALSE)
dw_2.SetRedraw( FALSE)

Do
   lRow = dw_2.GetSelectedRow( lRow)

   If lRow <> 0 Then
      dw_2.RowsCopy( lRow, lRow, Primary!, dw_1, 1, Primary!)
   End If
Loop While lRow <> 0

dw_1.SetRedraw( TRUE)
dw_2.SetRedraw( TRUE)
```

As you can see, this code is not very sophisticated and can be greatly enhanced. The copy code could, in fact, be placed in a `DragDrop` event to remove the need for a button completely.

The following is a more sophisticated version of the `Clicked` event script that enables the user to use the Ctrl key to select individual rows and the Shift key to select ranges:

```
Long lRow, lStartRow, lEndRow

If KeyDown( KeyControl!) Then
   If Row > 0 Then
      this.SelectRow( Row, TRUE)
   Else
      Return
   End If
ElseIf KeyDown( KeyShift!) Then
   this.SetRedraw( FALSE)
   lStartRow = this.GetRow()
   lEndRow = Row
   //Be able to range select backward as well as forward
```

```
    If lStartRow > lEndRow Then
        For lRow = lStartRow To lEndRow Step -1
            this.SelectRow( lRow, TRUE)
        Next
    Else
        For lRow = lStartRow To lEndRow
            this.SelectRow( lRow, TRUE)
        Next
    End If
    this.SetRedraw( TRUE)
Else
    //If the user simply clicks on a row - deselect any selected row(s)
    this.SelectRow( 0, FALSE)
    // and highlight the clicked row
    this.SelectRow( Row, TRUE)
End If
```

The `GetBandAtPointer()` function is used to find out which band the mouse pointer is currently within, and is usually placed in the `Clicked` event of a DataWindow (Chapter 9 discusses the bands of a DataWindow):

```
DataWindowControl.GetBandAtPointer()
```

The function returns a string that consists of the band, a tab character, and the number of the row associated with the band. The empty string (`""`) is returned if an error occurs. The string can consist of the information shown in Table 10.4.

Table 10.4. `GetBandAtPointer` return values.

Band	*Location of Pointer*	*Associated Row*
detail	Body of the DataWindow	Row at pointer
header	Header of the DataWindow	The first row visible in the body
header.n	Header of group level n	The first row of the group
trailer.n	Trailer of group level n	The last row of the group
footer	Footer of the DataWindow	The last row visible in the body
summary	Summary of the DataWindow	The last row before the summary

The row value within the string when the pointer is in the detail band is dependent on the number of rows filling the body. If there are not enough rows to fill the body because of a group with a page break, the first row of the next group is the value returned. If the body is not completely filled because there are no more rows, the last row is returned.

In a DataWindow are a number of objects that mostly consist of columns and labels but also include graphic objects such as lines and pictures. The `GetObjectAtPointer()` function returns the name and row number of the object currently under the mouse pointer in a DataWindow:

```
DataWindowControl.GetObjectAtPointer()
```

The returned string contains the name of the object, a tab character, and the row number. The empty string is returned if an error occurs or the object does not have a name.

DataWindow Events

A DataWindow control has a number of events in common with other controls. In addition to these are a few unique events, which are defined in the following sections.

The `ItemChanged` Event

The `ItemChanged` event is the last level of edit validation. It is triggered whenever the user modifies a field and tries to enter another field and the value entered has passed the previous three levels of validation.

> **NOTE**
>
> The only variation on this is when the field is of the DropDownListBox, DropDownDataWindow, CheckBox, and RadioButton edit styles. `ItemChanged` is triggered when an item is selected.

New in PowerBuilder 5

Both the row and the data value are available as parameters of the `ItemChanged` event, which saves you from having to call the appropriate PowerScript functions to obtain these commonly used values.

As with many DataWindow events, you can set the return value to control what happens when the execution of the event has finished. The valid return codes for `ItemChanged` are as follows:

- `0`—Accept the data value (the default).
- `1`—Reject the data value and trigger the `ItemError` event.
- `2`—Reject the data value but allow the focus to change. The value in the column is replaced with the original value.

The `ItemError` Event

The `ItemError` event is triggered whenever a field has been modified and any of the validation steps fail. The return codes for this event are as follows:

- `0`—Reject the data value and show an error message (the default).
- `1`—Reject the data value, display no error message.
- `2`—Accept the data value.
- `3`—Reject the data value but allow the focus to change. The original value of the column is replaced.

NEW 5 in PowerBuilder

As with the `ItemChanged` event, both the row and the data value are available as parameters of the `ItemError` event.

Some sample code (that is actually from a production application) for `ItemChanged` (see Listing 10.3) and `ItemError` (see Listing 10.4) show how you use both of these events and how they interrelate. The `print_loc_code` case is the one you want to examine closely, because it will trigger the `ItemError` event.

Listing 10.3. The ItemChanged event.

```
Boolean bProcess = FALSE
String szColumnName, szValue

szColumnName = this.GetColumnName()
szValue = this.GetText()

Choose Case szColumnName
   Case "use_increments"
      i_u_n_BagWizard.sBagParms.bUseIncrements = ( szValue = "1" )
      bProcess = TRUE
   Case "print_loc_code"
      If dw_extruding_spec_header.GetItemString( 1, "film_type") = "JS" And &
         szValue = "2" And Not m_mfg_order.m_activities.m_keyedentry.Checked Then
         Return 1
      End If
      i_u_n_BagWizard.sBagParms.nSidesPrinted = Integer( szValue)
      bProcess = TRUE
   Case "figure_unwind_pattern_num"
      If IsNumber( szValue) Then
         dw_customer_dimensions.SetItem( 1, "figure_unwind_pattern", Integer(
szValue))
      End If
   Case "press_cylinder_circumference"
      i_u_n_BagWizard.sBagParms.decCylinderSize = Real( szValue)
      bProcess = TRUE
   Case "color_1", "color_2", "color_3", "color_4", "color_5", "color_6"
      i_u_n_BagWizard.sBagParms.nNoOfColors = wf_CountPrintColours()
      bProcess = TRUE
End Choose

If bProcess Then
   this.PostEvent( "bagcalculate")
End If
```

Listing 10.4. The ItemError event.

```
String szColumnName

szColumnName = this.GetColumnName()
//
// Check the current column - the one that caused the error
//
```

```
If szColumnName = "print_loc_code" Then
   MessageBox( "Print Location Error", "You cannot specify a 2 side print for J-
Sheeting.")
   // We have handled the error message
   Return 1
Else
   // Open the default message box
   Return 0
End If
```

One of the features of PowerBuilder DataWindows is the capability to set an empty string to `NULL`. This prevents wasting space when you save the data back into the database, because most databases have a special representation for a `NULL` that takes up a minimal amount of space.

NOTE

You might think that a `NULL` is a `NULL` is a `NULL`, but in fact PowerBuilder makes a point of distinguishing between data types, so you must declare a variable for each data type you will be setting to `NULL`. This is one of the little idiosyncrasies of PowerBuilder that make it so beloved.

The `SQLPreview` Event

The `SQLPreview` event is triggered after a call to `Retrieve()`, `Update()`, or `ReselectRow()`, but immediately before that function carries out any processing. This event is triggered every time a SQL statement is sent to the database, which means that it is triggered for each row that is updated via the `Update()` function.

Using the return value from this event you can control what action takes place following the `SQLPreview` event for an `Update()` function call. The return codes are as follows:

- `0`—Continue (the default).
- `1`—Stop processing.
- `2`—Skip this request and execute the next request.

Inside this event you can capture the SQL that is about to be submitted. Before Version 5.0 you had to use the `GetSQLPreview()` function, but the event now supplies the following parameters:

- *`request`* (`SqlPreviewFunction`)—This is the type of function that is requesting database access; for example, `PreviewFunctionReselectRow!`, `PreviewFunctionRetrieve!`, or `PreviewFunctionUpdate!`.
- *`sqltype`* (`SqlPreviewType`)—This is the type of SQL statement that is about to be submitted; for example, `PreviewDelete!`, `PreviewInsert!`, `PreviewSelect!`, or `PreviewUpdate!`.

- `sqlsyntax` (String)—the actual SQL statement that is being submitted.
- `buffer` (dwBuffer)—The DataWindow control buffer that is to be used in the request; for example, `Delete!`, `Filter!`, or `Primary!`.
- `row` (Long)—The row in the DataWindow that will be used in the SQL statement.

The `GetSQLPreview()` function can be called only in the `DBError` and `SQLPreview` events. The syntax is

```
DataWindowControl.GetSQLPreview()
```

This function returns either a string that is the current SQL statement or an empty string if an error occurs.

When a DataWindow generates SQL and binding is enabled for the database being used, the syntax might not be complete. The bind variables have not yet been replaced with the actual values and will appear as question marks. If you need to see the complete SQL statement, you should disable binding for the DBMS being used. This is achieved by setting the `DBParm` variable `DisableBind` to `1`.

In the `SQLPreview` event you can also modify the SQL statement returned by `GetSQLPreview()` and then call `SetSQLPreview()` to place the updated SQL statement into the DataWindow control.

The `SetSQLPreview()` function specifies new SQL syntax for the DataWindow control that is about to execute a SQL statement. The syntax is

```
DataWindowControl.SetSQLPreview( SQLSyntax)
```

The string specifying the `SQLSyntax` must contain a valid statement. This function can be called only in the `SQLPreview` event.

NOTE

If the data source is a stored procedure, you will see the `EXECUTE` command in the previewed SQL.

The `DBError` Event

The `DBError` event is triggered whenever a database error occurs because of a DataWindow action. By default, this event displays an error message window, but by setting the return code to `1` you can disable this feature and carry out some other processing.

Inside the `DBError` event you can obtain the database-specific error code and error text from the event parameters:

- *`sqldbcode`* (Long)—The DBMS vendor's specific error code.
- *`sqlerrtext`* (String)—The DBMS vendor's error message.
- *`sqlsyntax`* (String)—The SQL statement that caused the error.
- *`buffer`* (dwBuffer)—The DataWindow control buffer that was being used at the time of the error.
- *`row`* (Long)—The row within the DataWindow that caused the error.

In previous versions of PowerBuilder you had to use the functions `DBErrorCode()` and `DBErrorMessage()`. The syntax for the `DBErrorCode()` function is

```
DataWindowControl.DBErrorCode()
```

The syntax for the `DBErrorMessage()` function is

```
DataWindowControl.DBErrorMessage()
```

Both of these functions should be called only from the `DBError` event because this is the only place they will return anything meaningful.

In both the `SQLPreview` and `DBError` events, you have access to the current row and buffer (in previous versions of PowerBuilder you can make use of the `GetUpdateStatus()` function to find the row number and buffer of the row that is currently being updated to the database). This is obviously very useful in the `DBError` event because you can now point out to the end user the line causing the problem and allow him or her to fix it before trying to save again. Of course, if the problem row is in the Filter buffer you must first give the user access to it.

The previous method using `GetUpdateStatus()` has the syntax

```
DataWindowControl.GetUpdateStatus( Row, DWBuffer)
```

`Row` and *`DWBuffer`* must be variables of type Long and dwBuffer respectively, so that the function can assign the value of the current row's number and buffer.

The following code is placed in the `DBError` event. It scrolls to the offending row and sets the focus to the DataWindow:

```
If Buffer = Primary! Then
   this.ScrollToRow( Row)
   this.SetFocus()
   // Additionally you could make use of the ReselectRow() function to re-
   //retrieve the row from the database if the error so requires. You would trap
   //on a per DBMS error code for this case.
End If

Return 1
```

The `Error` Event

The `Error` event is used to trap runtime errors that occur as a result of using the direct-access syntax, and allows you to handle them gracefully. The event provides access to the following information as parameters:

- *`ErrorNumber`* (uInt)—The PowerBuilder error number.
- *`ErrorText`* (String)—The PowerBuilder message describing the error.
- *`ErrorWindowMenu`* (String)—The window or menu that caused the error.
- *`ErrorObject`* (String)—The object that caused the error.
- *`ErrorScript`* (String)—The event within the object causing the error.
- *`ErrorLine`* (uInt)—The line within the event causing the error.
- *`Action`* (ExceptionAction)—What the application will attempt to do after your `Error` script has finished. This can be one of the following: `ExceptionFail!`, `ExceptionIgnore!`, `ExceptionRetry!`, and `ExceptionSubstituteReturnValue!`.
- *`ReturnValue`* (Any)—A return value that is used with the `ExceptionSubsituteReturnValue!` action.

For DataWindows, when an error occurs while evaluating a data or property expression, error processing occurs in the following order:

1. The `Error` event is triggered.
2. If the `Error` event has no script or the *`Action`* argument is set to `ExceptionFail!`, the `SystemError` event is triggered.
3. If the `SystemEvent` has no script, an application error occurs and the application is terminated.

DataWindow Functions

As with other controls, the functions available for the DataWindow control can be broken down into three major groups: database, information acquisition, and modification.

Database-Related Functions

These are functions that direct the DataWindow control to carry out a specific task: connect the control to the database.

Connecting to the Database

The majority of DataWindows are attached to some form of database, and therefore require a connection to be made between them. This is done through either the `SetTrans()` or

`SetTransObject()` function. If you are unfamiliar with the concept of database transactions, you should read Chapter 5 before continuing with this section.

There is one distinct difference between these two functions. With `SetTrans()` you do not have to carry out any database initialization or transaction management. You just fill in a transaction object, which does not need to be currently connected, and then inform the DataWindow about it. `SetTrans()` copies the information in the transaction object into a transaction object internal to the DataWindow. The syntax is

```
DataWindowControl.SetTrans( TransactionObject)
```

This syntax means that the DataWindow will now issue a `CONNECT` each time a database request is carried out, an automatic `ROLLBACK` on any error, and a `DISCONNECT` at the end of the transaction. Remember that Powersoft currently does a `COMMIT` after a disconnection. Because database connections are generally very expensive (in terms of time and resources) operations to execute, you can see that if you will be making numerous calls, this function will give the worst performance. However, there might be times when you will need to use this function rather than `SetTransObject()`—usually when you have a limited number of available connections to the database or when the application is being used from a remote location.

NOTE

If you use the `SetTrans()` function, you must remember that you cannot coordinate multiple DataWindow updates because the data has already been committed at the end of the update for each DataWindow.

The most commonly used version of the two database connection methods is `SetTransObject()` because it maintains an open connection to the database and therefore is far more efficient. There is a one-time connection and disconnection, and the developer has control of the transaction and can commit or roll back the DataWindow's save. This gives you optimal performance when carrying out any database operations on the DataWindow. The syntax is

```
DataWindowControl.SetTransObject( TransactionObject)
```

As with `SetTrans()`, you must supply a transaction object. `SetTransObject()`, however, must have the transaction object connected to the database either before the function call or before any DataWindow database operations are executed.

Also unique to `SetTransObject()` is that if the DataWindow control's data object is changed or if you disconnect and reconnect to a database, the connection between the DataWindow control and the transaction object is broken. You must call `SetTransObject()` again to rebuild the association.

Both of these functions return `1` if they succeed and `-1` if an error occurs.

NOTE

You will receive an error if the DataWindow control has not had a DataWindow object assigned to it before calling either of the `SetTrans` functions.

Two little-used functions are mentioned here for completeness. The first, `GetTrans()`, enables you to access the DataWindow's internal transaction object and copy it into another transaction object. The syntax is

```
DataWindowControl.GetTrans( TransactionObject)
```

If the `SetTrans()` function has not been called for the DataWindow, `GetTrans()` will fail. If the DataWindow has been connected using `SetTransObject()`, `GetTrans()` will not report any information.

The second little-used function is `ResetTransObject()`, which terminates a DataWindow connection to a programmer-defined transaction object that was set up via `SetTransObject()`. After a call to `ResetTransObject()`, the DataWindow reverts to using its internal transaction object. The syntax is

```
DataWindowControl.ResetTransObject()
```

`SetTrans()` must then be called before any database activities can begin. This function is rarely used because you are very unlikely to mix the connection types in a single execution of the application.

Retrieving Data

The `Retrieve()` function is used to request rows from the database and place them in a DataWindow control. If the DataWindow object has been set up to use retrieval arguments, you must either specify them as parameters of the call or if the arguments are not specified, PowerBuilder will open a window for the user to enter them at runtime. The syntax is

```
DataWindowControl.Retrieve( { Argument, . . . })
```

The arguments must appear in the same order in which they were defined for the DataWindow object. New to PowerBuilder 5.0 is the capability to specify more parameters in your call to `Retrieve()` than the DataWindow object expects. This is no longer considered an error condition, and will allow you to write a generic retrieval script. You cannot specify fewer parameters than are expected because this is still an error. The function returns a Long data type that is the total number of rows retrieved into the Primary buffer and returns `-1` if it fails. If the DataWindow has a filter specified, this is applied after the rows are retrieved, and these rows are not included in the return count.

A call to `Retrieve()` might trigger the following events: `DBError`, `RetrieveEnd`, `RetrieveRow`, `RetrieveStart`, and `RowFocusChanged`.

Retrieve Events

The `RetrieveStart` event is triggered after a call to `Retrieve()` but before any database actions have been taken. You can control whether the retrieve can proceed, whether it stops without doing any processing, or whether it appends the new rows to the existing ones by setting the return value of the event. The return codes for this event are as follows:

- `0`—Continue with the retrieve (the default).
- `1`—Do not perform the retrieve.
- `2`—Do not reset the rows and buffers before retrieving data.

The `RetrieveRow` event is triggered every time a row is retrieved and after the row has been added into the DataWindow. Coding anything in this event can adversely affect the performance of a data retrieval. The retrieval can be stopped by setting the return code as follows:

- `0`—Continue with the retrieve (the default).
- `1`—Do not perform the retrieve.

The `RetrieveEnd` event is triggered when the retrieval has completed.

Canceling a Retrieve

One of the most common end-user solutions to an application that does not seem to be progressing anymore and is thought to be hung is to use Ctrl+Alt+Delete to kill the process. This might, however, still tie up a number of server and network resources while the query continues to run. To prevent this from happening, you should provide the end users with a way to cancel long-running queries or, even better, provide them with an estimate of the time or records remaining.

NOTE

If the `Async` `DBParm` parameter is set to allow asynchronous database operations (`1`) the query can be halted before the first row is returned. Only some databases support this capability, and you should refer to the database-specific documentation in PowerBuilder. If the DBMS does not support `Async`, you will be unable to cancel a retrieval before the database has finished building the result set.

PowerBuilder provides a PowerScript function, `DBCancel()`, to halt the row retrieval currently being processed by a DataWindow. This function must be called from the `RetrieveRow` event in order to interrupt the retrieval. The syntax is

```
DataWindowControl.DBCancel()
```

`DBCancel()` returns `1` if it succeeds and `-1` if an error occurs.

The most common method of providing a way to cancel a retrieval operation is to give the user a dialog box or pop-up window that displays a row indicator and a Cancel pushbutton.

This window is a pop-up–style window that has two static text controls (`st_percent` and `st_rows_retrieved`), one pushbutton (`cb_cancel`), and two rectangular drawing controls (`r_total_percent` and `r_percent_done`). The window also has three private instance variables:

```
Private:
Long i_lTotalRows, i_lCurrentRow
Boolean i_bCancel = FALSE
```

The `Open` event for this window extracts information from the message object that influences the type of cancel window to display (see Listing 10.5).

Listing 10.5. The `Open` event for `w_retrieve_cancel`.

```
i_lTotalRows = Message.DoubleParm

If IsNull( i_lTotalRows) Then
   r_total_percent.visible = FALSE
   r_percent_done.visible = FALSE
   st_percent.visible = FALSE
Else
   st_rows_retrieved.visible = FALSE
   r_percent_done.width = 0
End If

Timer( 1)
```

If the script that opens the retrieve's cancel window specifies the total number of rows that will be retrieved (which is sometimes possible by running a `SELECT COUNT(*)` statement), the window sets itself up to display a percentage bar using the rectangle controls. Usually this value will be `NULL` to indicate that the window should just display the number of rows retrieved so far in the operation. A 1-second timer is started to make the cancel window update its display (see Listing 10.6).

Listing 10.6. The `Timer` event of `w_retrieve_cancel`.

```
Double dPercent

If Not IsNull( i_lTotalRows) Then
   dPercent = i_lCurrentRow / i_lTotalRows
   st_percent.text = String( Truncate( dPercent * 100,0)) + "%"
   If (dPercent * 100) <= 100 Then
      r_percent_done.width = 700 * dPercent
   End If
Else
   st_rows_retrieved.text = "Rows: " + String( i_lCurrentRow)
End If
```

The `Timer` event inspects its instance variable, `i_lCurrentRow`, which is updated from the calling window's DataWindow. Depending on the type of display, this value is used either to calculate the new width of the percentage rectangle or to display with the `"Rows: "` text string.

The Cancel button simply closes the retrieval window:

```
Close( Parent)
```

The only thing remaining for the retrieve window to do is shut down the timer resource in the `Close` event using `Timer(0)`.

The retrieve cancel window also has a number of simple window functions defined; they act on the instance variables.

The `wf_UpdateRowCount()` function takes a single numeric argument, which is the current total number of rows:

```
If a_lCurrentRows > i_lCurrentRow Then
   i_lCurrentRow = a_lCurrentRows
End If
```

The DataWindow using this retrieve cancel window requires code in two of the three retrieve events: `RetrieveRow` and `RetrieveEnd` (see Listings 10.7 and 10.8).

Listing 10.7. The `RetrieveRow` event of the retrieve cancel DataWindow.

```
If IsValid( w_retrieve_cancel) Then
   // Stop - user wants to cancel
   this.DBCancel()
Else
   // Continue - increment row counter in retrieve cancel window
   w_retrieve_cancel.wf_UpdateRowCount( row)
End If
```

Listing 10.8. The `RetrieveEnd` event of the retrieve cancel DataWindow.

```
If IsValid( w_retrieve_cancel) Then
   Close( w_retrieve_cancel)
End If
```

The `RetrieveRow` event is used to check whether the user has clicked the Cancel button on the pop-up window by seeing whether the retrieve cancel window is still open. If the retrieve has not been canceled, the pop-up window variable `i_lCurrentRow` is incremented by the current row count by calling the `wf_UpdateRowCount()` and passing the event parameter `row`. If the user wants to cancel, the `DBCancel()` function is called to tell PowerBuilder to stop the retrieve.

The `RetrieveEnd` event closes the pop-up window. The `IsValid()` function is used to make sure the window is still open before closing to prevent a runtime error.

The following code should be placed wherever the retrieve is to be started. As mentioned earlier, to display a percentage bar, the total number of rows to be returned should first be determined. It would then be passed as the parameter instead of `lNull`:

```
Long lNull

SetNull( lNull)
OpenWithParm( w_retrieve_cancel, lNull)
dw_1.Retrieve()
```

Refreshing Data Rows

If your DBMS and DataWindow object make use of timestamp data types, the timestamp value occasionally needs to be refreshed from the database. This might be required if the data were retrieved a long time before any changes are made. If the data fails to save and you want to give the user the opportunity to view the new information and possibly update it instead, you can use the `ReselectRow()` function.

This function retrieves values from the database for all updatable and timestamp columns for a specified row in a DataWindow control. The old values are then replaced with the newly retrieved ones:

```
DataWindowControl.ReselectRow( lRow)
```

The function returns `1` if it is successful and `-1` if the row cannot be reselected. The row cannot be reselected if it has been deleted from the database or if the DataWindow is not updatable.

This function is most often used when a DataWindow update fails because of a changed timestamp, which occurs when the row has been changed between the times of its retrieval and its attempted update.

Informational Functions

Informational functions are used specifically to obtain information about the DataWindow and DataWindow objects. A very important and useful function that is covered in the detail it deserves is `Describe()`; you can find out more about this in Chapter 25.

Data Extraction

If you need to access all the data in the DataWindow, you can use the `SaveAs()` function to avoid having to go through repeated calls to the appropriate `GetItem` functions or directly accessing the data.

The `SaveAs()` function enables you to save the contents of not only a DataWindow, but also graphs, OLE 2.0 controls, and OLE storage. For DataWindows and graphs, the data can be saved in a number of formats, from tab- and comma-delimited to Excel files and even SQL statements. To save the data from a DataWindow or child DataWindow, the syntax is

```
DataWindowControl.SaveAs( { FileName, SaveAsType, ColumnHeadings})
```

If the *FileName* parameter of the output file is omitted, PowerBuilder will prompt the user at runtime for it. The *SaveAsType* parameter is of the `SaveAsType` enumerated data type and can take one of the following values (if none is specified, `Text!` is taken as the default):

SaveAsType	*Description*
`Clipboard!`	Save to the Clipboard
`CSV!`	Comma-separated values, terminated with a carriage return
`dBASE2!`	dBASE II format
`dBASE3!`	dBASE III format
`DIF!`	Data Interchange Format
`Excel!`	Microsoft Excel format
`PSReport!`	PowerBuilder report format
`SQLInsert!`	SQL `INSERT` statements
`SYLK!`	Microsoft Multiplan format
`Text!`	Tab-separated values, terminated with a carriage return
`WK1!`	Lotus 1-2-3 format
`WKS!`	Lotus 1-2-3 format
`WMF!`	Windows MetaFile format

The *ColumnHeadings* parameter is a Boolean that specifies whether the DataWindow column names should be included at the beginning of the file.

NOTE

With the `SQLInsert!` format, the table name used for the `INSERT` is not the original table name but the name of the file. This is not an issue when you're using an operating system that supports long filenames, because you can use the whole name of the table as the filename.

To save the data from graph controls in windows, user objects, or DataWindow controls, the syntax is

```
ControlName.SaveAs( {GraphControl,} { FileName, SaveAsType, ColumnHeadings})
```

`ControlName` is the name of the actual graph control, or the name of the DataWindow that contains the graph. The `GraphControl` optional parameter is used only for DataWindow controls and specifies the name of the graph.

If no parameters are specified for the `SaveAs()` function, at least for these two syntaxes, PowerBuilder displays the Save Rows As dialog box (see Figure 10.3), which enables the user to specify values for each of the parameters.

FIGURE 10.3.
The Save As dialog box.

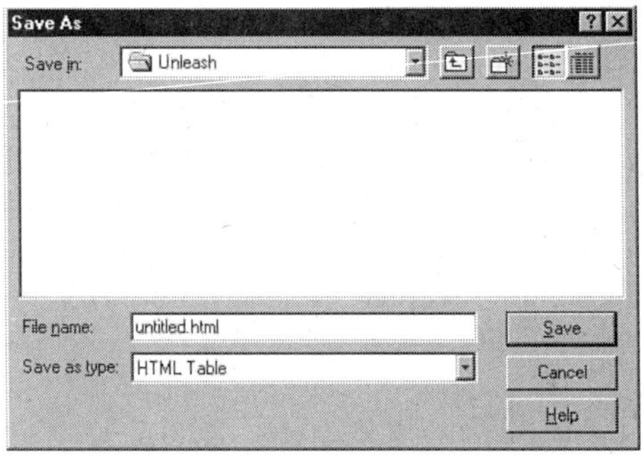

For example, to save the data from the DataWindow `dw_employees` to the file C:\DATA\EMP.SQL in a SQL syntax format that can be loaded into another database, the call would be

```
dw_employees.SaveAs( "C:\DATAEMP.SQL", SQLInsert!, FALSE)
```

To save the contents of a graph object sitting within this same DataWindow, the syntax might be

```
dw_employees.SaveAs( "dept_graph", "C:\DATAEMP.CSV", CSV!, TRUE)
```

The `SaveAs()` function has a number of other formats that all relate to OLE controls; see Chapter 36, "OLE 2.0 and DDE," for more information.

Counting Rows

Four functions return the number of rows in each of the buffers, or a count of rows with a modified status. The first two functions usually appear in a `CloseQuery` event of a window to inform the user that there are modified records in the DataWindow that have not yet been saved.

The `DeletedCount()` function returns the number of rows that have been deleted from the DataWindow but have not been deleted from the database. This is the number of rows in the Delete buffer. The syntax is

```
DataWindowControl.DeletedCount()
```

This function returns a Long data type of the number of rows, `0` if none are waiting for deletion from the database, or `-1` if the function fails.

The `ModifiedCount()` function returns the number of rows that have been changed in the DataWindow but have not been updated in the database. The syntax is

```
DataWindowControl.ModifiedCount()
```

This function returns a Long data type of the number of rows, `0` if none are waiting for updating in the database, or `-1` if the function fails. The function counts the rows in both the Primary and Filter buffers.

NOTE

Prior to PowerBuilder 4.0 this was not the case: `ModifiedCount()` counted rows only in the Primary buffer.

The `FilteredCount()` function returns the number of rows that have been placed into the Filter buffer of the DataWindow. The syntax is

```
DataWindowControl.FilteredCount()
```

This function returns an Integer data type of the number of rows in the Filter buffer, `0` if all rows are currently displayed, or `-1` if the function fails.

NOTE

This function returns an Integer, not a Long like the other count functions. If, in the unlikely event that you do have more than 32,767 rows in a DataWindow and filter them out, you will receive a negative count from this function.

The most common row-counting function is `RowCount()`, which can be found in a majority of DataWindow scripts and object scripts that are operating on the DataWindow. The syntax is

```
DataWindowControl.RowCount()
```

This function returns a Long data type of the number of rows currently in the Primary buffer, `0` if no rows are currently available, and `-1` if an error occurs.

Crosstab Messages

Unique to crosstab-style DataWindow objects is the generation of messages that detail what the DataWindow is doing. The `GetMessageText()` function can be used to capture these processing messages as a string, which can then be redisplayed to the user to inform him or her of what actions the DataWindow is currently making. The syntax is

```
DataWindowControl.GetMessageText()
```

If there is no text or if an error occurs, the function returns an empty string. This function can be used only in a user-defined event for the PowerBuilder event ID of `pbm_dwnmessagetext` for the DataWindow. The most common messages are `Retrieving data` and `Building crosstab`, and these are usually redisplayed in the MicroHelp area of an MDI frame. Here's an example:

```
w_frame.SetMicroHelp( this.GetMessageText())
```

Modification Functions

An often-used function is `Modify()`, which is covered in detail in Chapter 25. The next few sections describe some of the other DataWindow modification functions.

Code Table Functions

DataWindow columns that have edit styles of CheckBox, RadioButton, DropDownListBox, EditMask, and Edit can have associated value lists or code tables. A value list is simply a list of constants. A code table provides a translation between a visible display value and an invisible data value. The user sees and enters display values, and the DataWindow acts on and saves data values. This kind of validation can be called *proactive validation* because it undertakes validation at the time of entry instead of when the data is saved, which is reactive. PowerBuilder provides extraction and modification functions that act on the column's code values.

The `GetValue()` function extracts the value from a column's code table at a specified index:

```
DataWindowControl.GetValue( Column, ValueIndex)
```

`Column` is either the name or number of the column that has the code table.

This function returns a string that contains the item at the specified index of the code table. If the value has an associated display value, it is prepended to the return string with a tab character separator and then the code value. If the index is invalid or the column has no code table, an empty string is returned. This function cannot be used to obtain values from a DropDownDataWindow code table.

NOTE

The new direct access syntax to access the code table of a column is

```
dwControl.Object.ColumnName.Values
```

This returns you to the complete code table, not to specific indexes.

The `SetValue()` function enables you to programmatically affect the values of a code table or ListBox edit style. The syntax is

```
DataWindowControl.SetValue( Column, ValueIndex, Value)
```

The *`Value`* parameter is a string that contains the new value for the item specified by *`ValueIndex`*. To specify a display value, you must separate the display value and data value with a tab, in the same manner as detailed in the `GetValue()` function. The data value must be converted from a data type that matches the column's data type to a string; this ensures that when PowerBuilder has to convert back within the DataWindow it will not fail.

The `SetValue()` function can be used inside a cursor loop to fill a code table from the values returned by a `SELECT`. You can use drop-down DataWindows to achieve the same effect. The following is a combined example of calls to the `GetValue()` and `SetValue()` functions that retrieve a value from a code table, modify it, and place it back:

```
String szStatus

// Extract the code value
szStatus = dw_employee.GetValue( "status", 2)
// Find the status data value
szStatus = Mid( szStatus, Pos( szStatus, "~t") + 1)
// Set the 'Newly Employed' display value to the status data value
szStatus = "Newly Employed~t" + szStatus
// Place it back into the DataWindow
dw_employee.SetValue( "status", 2, szStatus)
```

The `ClearValues()` function is used to remove all the items from a value list:

```
DataWindowControl.ClearValues( Column)
```

A call to this function does not affect the data of the associated column in any way other than removing the value list.

Column Format Functions

You can use the `GetFormat()` function to extract the display format for a DataWindow column:

```
DataWindowControl.GetFormat( Column)
```

This function returns a string containing the display format and an empty string if an error occurs. This value is usually stored during a temporary modification of the format using the `SetFormat()` function:

```
DataWindowControl.SetFormat( Column, NewFormat)
```

NOTE

When the new format for a column is for a number, the format must be constructed using the U.S. number notation (that is, using a comma as a thousands separator and a period for decimals). When the application is running, the U.S. delimiters and symbols are replaced by the local symbols as required. This is true of both the `SetFormat()` function and the `GetFormat()` functions.

For example, to save the format of a unit price column and change it to display cents, the code would be as follows:

```
String szOldFormat, szNewFormat = "$#,###.00"
szOldFormat = dw_product_item.GetFormat( "unit_price")
dw_product_item.SetFormat( "unit_price", szNewFormat)
```

The old format would have to be stored in an instance variable or some other variable to allow it to exist outside this script. It is shown as a local variable here simply to avoid confusion.

Column Validation Rule Functions

Validation rules can be defined in the Database painter or the DataWindow painter; they are discussed in Chapters 4 and 9. PowerBuilder provides two functions to enable the modification of existing validation rules or the specification of a validation rule where one did not previously exist.

`GetValidate()` is another of the functions made obsolete for PowerBuilder 5.0. It is used to extract the validation rule for a column, and its behavior is similar to that of the `GetFormat()` function:

```
DataWindowControl.GetValidate( Column)
```

It can be now be rewritten as follows:

```
DataWindowControl.Object.ColumnName.Validation
```

This function returns a string containing the validation rule and an empty string if there is no validation rule. This value is usually stored during a temporary modification of the input rule using the `SetValidate()` function:

```
DataWindowControl.SetValidate( Column, NewRule)
```

This is very useful when you have to deal with exception validation (where only one business unit requires special processing).

For example, to save the current validation rule of the unit price column and modify it to accept only values between 0 and 100, the code would be

```
String szOldRule, szNewRule= "Long(GetText()) >= 0 And Long(GetText()) <= 100"
szOldRule = dw_product_item.GetValidate( "unit_price")
dw_product_item.SetValidate( "unit_price", NewRule)
```

Setting Tab Orders Programmatically

Most applications are used by multiple user groups, and users usually have different security access to different parts of a DataWindow. You sometimes have to turn off a column's editability at runtime, depending on the current user.

Protecting a column can be done in one of two ways: modifying the `Protect` attribute of the column or setting the column's tab order to `0`.

The `SetTabOrder()` function is used to change the tab sequence value of a specified column in a DataWindow control:

```
DataWindowControl.SetTabOrder( Column, NewTabValue)
```

or with the new syntax:

```
DataWindowControl.Object.ColumnName.TabSequence = NewValue
```

The *`NewTabValue`* parameter is the new tab sequence number for the column and can range from 0 to 9999. Remember, if you want to disable a column so that the user cannot enter data into it, set the tab value to `0`. The function returns the column's original tab value if it succeeds, and `-1` if an error occurs. This original tab value can be used to reset the column so that it can be made editable or appear in the original tab order again.

You can set the `Protect` attribute of a DataWindow column to override any tab order settings. While a column is protected, the user cannot edit it even when the tab order of the column is greater than 0. Here's an example:

```
DataWindowControl.Object.ColumnName.Protect = 1
```

This is the preferred method for disabling a DataWindow column because the tab value is not destroyed.

Column Border Style Functions

To provide a more proactive user interface, use the `SetBorderStyle()` function to indicate certain conditions for columns, such as being required or having a bad value. The conditions might not be known at design time but can be programmed into the application using the functions described in this section. For example, if a particular department is allowed read-only access to a column, you could turn off the border for that column.

Use the `GetBorderStyle()` function to extract the current style of a column's border:

```
DataWindowControl.GetBorderStyle( Column)
```

The return value is of the `Border` enumerated data type and can have the following values: `Box!`, `NoBorder!`, `ShadowBox!`, or `Underline!`. Be aware that the function returns a `NULL` if it fails.

You can use the `SetBorderStyle()` function to change the border style of a column:

```
DataWindowControl.SetBorderStyle( Column, NewBorderStyle)
```

You can replace both functions with the direct access syntax:

```
DataWindowControl.Object.ColumnName.Border
```

The border style is an integer value representation: None (`0`), Shadow (`1`), Rectangle (`2`), Resize (`3`), Line (`4`), 3D Lowered (`5`), and 3D Raised (`6`).

Changing the Height of Detail Rows

To change the height of an individual detail row or a range of detail rows, you can use the `SetDetailHeight()` function:

```
DataWindowControl.SetDetailHeight( StartRow, EndRow, NewHeight)
```

The *`StartRow`* and *`EndRow`* parameters define an inclusive range of row numbers for which you want to change the height to the *`NewHeight`* value. The *`NewHeight`* value is specified in the units of the DataWindow object.

The most common use of this function is to hide certain rows from view by setting their height to `0`.

Resetting a DataWindow

To throw away all the data from a DataWindow or child DataWindow, use the `Reset()` function. The `Reset()` function has three forms. The form for a DataWindow has the following syntax:

```
DataWindowControl.Reset()
```

`Reset()` does not merely transfer rows to a different buffer; it completely and irrecoverably clears out all the DataWindow's buffers. It will not make any changes to the database, regardless of row and column update status flags.

DataWindow Performance

You can realize a number of performance gains from using a DataWindow, and most of these are covered in Chapter 35, "Configuring and Tuning." However, you must still consider the script that you write for DataWindow events.

There are three groups of DataWindow events for which you need to carefully consider not only what is coded, but how much.

If anything is coded in the `RetrieveRow` event, it is executed every time a row is retrieved. Depending on the amount of code, this could dramatically increase the time to retrieve data. You should avoid coding anything in this event, even a comment, if at all possible. If you need to code anything in this event, try to keep it as succinct and optimal as possible. If you put any code in this event, PowerBuilder does an asynchronous retrieval, which you can cancel and keep working through.

Similarly, if you place any code in the `Clicked` event, you should try to make it as short as possible because a second click might be missed and the `DoubleClicked` event might never get fired.

The `RowFocusChanged` and `ItemChanged` events will also degrade in performance as the length of their scripts increases. This is important because they are triggered far more frequently by a user entering data.

If you will not be using all the columns retrieved into a DataWindow, eliminate them from the DataWindow `SELECT` to increase the retrieval performance.

Do not code redundant error checking. If a check is carried out at one level of the validation sequence, do not repeat it at a lower level.

With each release of PowerBuilder the developers at Powersoft continue to enhance the performance and behind-the-scenes functionality of DataWindows. In PowerBuilder 5.0 two new features have been added:

- DataWindow now uses *describeless* retrieves by constructing column lists from the DataWindow structure rather than going to the database interface. This feature is available when you're using Oracle, ODBC, and Sybase interfaces.
- There is now a *Rows to disk* option in the 32-bit implementations of PowerBuilder. This allows the retrieved rows to be written to a temporary file for faster subsequent access.

Summary

This chapter introduces a number of functions and events that are specific to the DataWindow control and the DataWindow object. You should now understand the difference between the control and the object and how they interact. This chapter also covers the different components of the control: the buffers, events, and functions. This chapter gives a grounding in functionality of DataWindows, which is expanded on in Chapters 25 and 26.

Windows and the Window Painter

11

IN THIS CHAPTER

The window object is the primary graphical user interface for an application, and consists of attributes, events, and controls. Depending on the operating system you are developing for, there are a number of different styles and associated characteristics for windows. This chapter concentrates on the Windows environment; for GUI design information you should see Chapter 21, "Cross-Platform PowerBuilder."

Application Styles

There are two standard ways to construct PowerBuilder applications: as a single-document interface (SDI) or as a multiple-document interface (MDI). You can also build contortions of both by incorporating styles from one to the other. As already stated, you should try to conform with the operating system standards that you are developing for.

SDI applications can be likened to text-based programs where there is a completely controlled flow of windows. The name comes from the fact that the user can interact with only one window at a time. The choices given to the user on a particular window limit the user to a fixed number of choices.

MDI applications require a lot more thought to program because the user can interact with multiple windows (referred to as *sheets*) at any one time. This kind of interface is a lot more intuitive to the way that a user works, allowing him to open a window to carry out a quick modification or lookup while keeping his main piece of work visible and accessible. Sheets are usually related in functionality and depend on no set sequence of actions for their processing.

The main advantage of MDI over SDI application styles is that they are more consistent in their presentation of a user interface. SDI applications tend to have distinct personalities and are therefore a lot harder for an end user to get familiar with quickly. An excellent example of the contrasts between MDI and SDI can be seen by looking at Word and Excel, and then at the Notepad and Control Panel applications. Both of the MDI applications, Word and Excel, use the same user interface paradigms, whereas Notepad and the Control Panel are completely different types of SDI applications.

Modal, Modeless, and Non-Modal Windows

A window is modal if it requires the user to interact with it before allowing him access to the other windows of the application. Modal windows are used to force the user to make an important decision before the application can continue. This is called *application modal*. Another version of modal windows, called *system modal*, requires user interaction before anything further in Windows can occur. An example is the Windows System Error window.

A modeless window is a dialog box that enables access to the application while asking for user interaction. The best example of this type of window is the floating toolbar window.

Most windows, or sheets, are non-modal and do not force the user to interact with them.

When a window is opened by another, it becomes a child of that window (not of the child style), which then becomes the parent.

Window Instances

Each object in PowerBuilder belongs to, or defines, a particular class (or for those of you who are a little unsure on the subject of classes, a data type). You can declare variables using the name of any of these classes, and this is how you can create multiple instances of a window. As with the more normal data types (such as String), the window is declared in a script as follows:

```
w_parent wParent
```

The variable `wParent` is an instance of the class `w_parent`. Once you have instantiated the variable by using one of the `Open()` window functions, you can use this variable to access properties and functions for the window.

The only problem with instances of a class is in accessing a particular instance. Since there is no global handle to reference a window instance, you must decide whether you need to manage the instances yourself. Methods for this are discussed in the "MDI-Specific Functions" section.

Window Types

When you create each window object, you set a style that determines how it will appear to the user (for example, whether it has a thick border or if it can float outside of its parent window).

In PowerBuilder there are six distinct types that you can set a window object to:

- Main
- Pop-up
- Child
- Response
- MDI frame
- MDI frame with MicroHelp

The next six sections describe the features and characteristics of each of these window types as well as provide specific examples of each.

Main Windows

Main windows are independent of all other windows, which allows them to overlap and be overlapped with other windows. Main windows optionally have a menu and a control menu, and can be minimized, maximized, or resized. They always have borders.

The main type of window is used in one of two roles, which depends on the type of application you are developing. In an SDI application main windows are used for the first window that you open; from this point you will usually use the other window types. All the windows you will be opening as sheets (most of the windows used within an MDI application) will be of the main type. Some inexperienced developers use the child type for sheets, which means that you cannot attach a menu to the window.

The main type is a generic window (also the default type), which is what the majority of an application's windows are.

Pop-up Windows

A pop-up window is used to provide supporting information to another window. A pop-up window overlaps its parent and can be displayed outside the parent window. A pop-up window maintains a close relationship with its parent, and will minimize and close with the parent. A pop-up window optionally has a menu, a control menu, and a border, and can be minimized, maximized, or resized.

You can specify a parent for the pop-up that is different from the window that is opening it by using a different format for the `Open()` function, which is introduced later in the chapter.

Pop-up windows are used for a variety of uses, from find windows to help cue cards. The next section describes a common use for this type of window.

Progress Windows

There are usually numerous points in an application where a great deal of processing occurs, during a save or load, printing complex reports, or undertaking calculations. Some of these are good candidates for showing a progress status to the user because the progress status gives users something to watch and can help reduce user-perceived response time.

The basis of this encapsulated, reusable window is the pop-up style, as this will allow the placement of the window over the parent while allowing the parent to keep executing.

The window has two static text controls (`st_percent` and `st_text`) and two rectangular drawing controls (`r_total_percent` and `r_percent_done`). The window also has two private instance variables:

```
Private:

Long i_lTotal, i_lCurrent = 0
```

The `Open` event for this window centers the window on the display.

Access to the window is then restricted to three window functions: `wf_SetTotal()`, `wf_SetText()`, and `wf_UpdateDisplay()`.

NOTE

Remember to change the return value of the following functions to `[None]` from the default `Integer` setting. Otherwise, you will be prompted for a return value when you save the function script.

The function `wf_SetTotal()` is the first that the parent should call because this is used to set the total number of points that you are going to be sending progress reports from, and it takes a Long variable as its parameter and simply sets the variable `i_lTotal` to this value.

The next function, `wf_SetText()` (see Listing 11.1), is used to set the text value on the window at points where you are not updating the percentage done. The function takes a single string, which it uses to set the text attribute of the static text object, `st_text` . The total number of characters for this window is 25, but feel free to make it larger if you want. Just remember to measure it with the *W* character because you are using a nonproportional font to get the maximum number of wide characters in the area.

Listing 11.1. The `wf_SetText()` function for `w_status`.

```
If Len( a_szText) > 25 Then
   a_szText = Left( a_szText, 25)
End If

st_text.text = a_szText
```

The last function on the window, `wf_UpdateDisplay()`, is the heart of the process and is used to update the percentage bar. The function takes two parameters—a Long to indicate the amount to increment the bar by and a String, which is the new text for the next stage:

```
Double dPercent

i_lCurrent += a_lIncrement

dPercent = i_lCurrent / i_lTotal
st_percent.text = String( Truncate( dPercent * 100,0)) + "%"
If (dPercent * 100) <= 100 Then
   r_percent_done.width = 700 * dPercent
   r_percent_done.Visible = TRUE
End If

wf_SetText( a_szText)
```

The following script shows an example of using these functions:

```
w_status wStatus
Open( wStatus)

wStatus.wf_SetTotal( 4)
wStatus.wf_SetText( "Beginning Processing")
// Carry out some processing
wStatus.wf_UpdateDisplay( 1, "Step 2")
// Carry out some processing
wStatus.wf_UpdateDisplay( 1, "Step 3")
// Carry out some processing
wStatus.wf_UpdateDisplay( 1, "Step 4")
// Carry out some processing
wStatus.wf_UpdateDisplay( 1, "Finished")

Close( wStatus)
```

As you can see in this code, the `wf_SetText()` function is usually going to occur only once, after the `wf_SetTotal()` call. The reason that they have been left separate is to try to adhere to object-oriented coding principles and provide access methods to individual object components, rather than combine them into one method.

Child Windows

Child windows, as their name implies, are always opened from another window, either a main or a pop-up. A child window only exists within the area of its parent and is clipped to the parent (you can't move it outside this area). If you maximize the window, it takes up the entire parent area, and when you minimize it, it becomes an icon on the bottom edge of the parent. Child windows maintain a strict relationship with their parent, and will move, minimize, and close with the parent. Child windows optionally have a control menu and a border and can be minimized, maximized, or resized.

A child window is never considered to be an active window.

> **NOTE**
>
> A child window's position is always relative to its parent and not to the screen.

Child windows are rarely used because if you want this kind of functionality, you will usually make use of an MDI frame and sheets, in which window management is automatic.

Response

Response windows are used to force the user to answer a question before the application will continue. In other words, they are application-modal windows. The window overlaps all of the application's open windows, cannot be minimized or maximized, and optionally have a control menu.

About Windows

The infamous About box, or credit window, is an integral part of every application and allows the development team a moment of fame and glory (or maybe that should be infamy and ignominy!).

This is where you can make use of the fact that functions called as an initialization for a variable are executed one time during compilation (see Chapter 6, "The PowerScript Language," for more information). You assign a string variable in the `Constructor` event of a static text object to the value of `Today()` concatenated with `Now()`, and then set the object's text value to the data and time the executable (or PBD) was compiled. You can do it just to show those end users that developers usually work long hours and compile at something close to midnight!

NOTE

If you are using PBDs, you will probably want to do the assignment inside the application object and then make it globally accessible.

Message Boxes

Using the PowerScript function `MessageBox()` you can open predefined application-modal windows. They allow you to set the window's title and text and select from a list of command buttons and pictures to customize the window.

WARNING

If either of the string arguments in the function call is `NULL`, the window will not open.

This is the syntax for the function:

```
MessageBox( Title, Text {, Icon {, Button {, Default}}})
```

The *`Title`* parameter is the text that appears in the window's title. The *`Text`* parameter is what will be displayed in the window, and this can be a Number, a String, or a Boolean value. The

Icon parameter determines what picture shows on the left side of the window and is a value of the `Icon` enumerated data type, the valid values of which are `Information!` (the default), `StopSign!`, `Exclamation!`, `Question!`, and `None!`. The *Button* parameter is of enumerated data type `Button` and is used to control which type of buttons display in the window. The valid values for `Button` are `Ok!` (the default), `OkCancel!`, `YesNo!`, `YesNoCancel!`, `RetryCancel!`, and `AbortRetryIgnore!`. The *Default* parameter is used to set the button that will be the default (responds to the Enter key), and this defaults to the first button.

NOTE

Instead of passing a String value for the *Text* argument you can pass a Boolean or a Number. PowerBuilder will automatically convert this for you and display it in the window. This is a very useful trick during debugging, when you want to display the value of a variable.

`MessageBox()` returns the number of the button that was selected, or `-1` if an error occurs. The buttons are numbered sequentially from left to right in the order listed in the enumerated data type.

Since the message box generated is an application-modal window, you must be careful where you use it. Using `MessageBox()` in the `Modified`, `GetFocus`, `LoseFocus`, `ItemFocusChanged`, `ItemChanged`, `Activate`, and `Deactivate` events will cause problems in your application because of the focus changes that are occurring.

In Windows 3.*x* controls capture the mouse when performing certain event processing, and if a message box is invoked during this time, Windows will become unstable. To prevent some of these problems, PowerBuilder will not open a message box as requested and you must instead use window titles, MicroHelp, StaticText objects, and any of the other controls to display information.

The `MessageBox()` function can also cause strange behavior if it is used after a `PrintOpen()` call. For more information, see Chapter 10, "DataWindow Scripting."

MessageBox Manager

An ideal way to manage messages, warnings, and errors for applications, especially when you start to field more than one, is to place them into a central database table. You can then write a reusable function or nonvisual user object that interprets a request and retrieves and displays the correct message in the desired style. This makes your application messages more consistent between applications.

MDI Frames

The MDI frame window is the basis of an MDI application in that it defines the working area for the whole application and is the overall manager for open sheets. The frame must have a menu associated with it, can optionally have a control menu, and can be minimized, maximized, or resized.

> **NOTE**
>
> In PowerBuilder 4.0 specifying an MDI frame window type forces you to associate a menu with the window. This constraint has been dropped in PowerBuilder 5.0, but you will still want to make an association with a menu. This is because MDI frames work with many sheet windows and you need to provide a means to open, close, and arrange them. These operations are normally all carried out from menu options.

NEW 5 in PowerBuilder

MDI frames can also be set to include a MicroHelp area, which appears at the bottom edge of the window and is used to display application information. This is actually a different window type, rather than a property for the window.

An MDI application has six key components, which are shown in Figure 11.1.

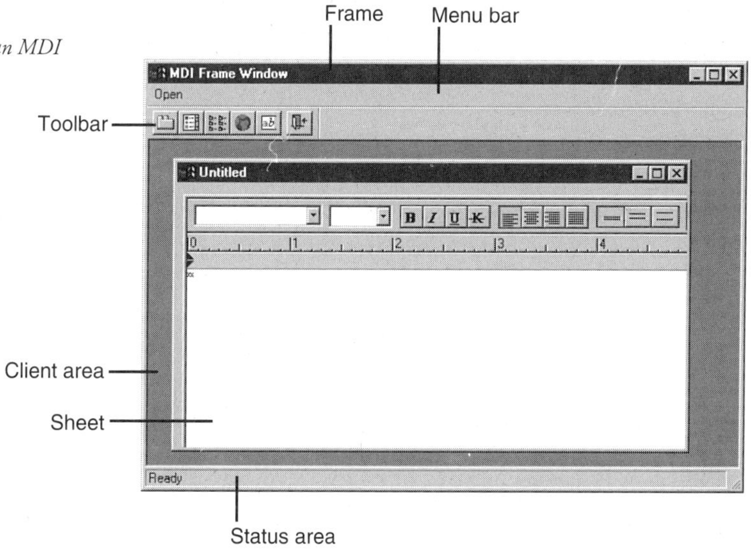

FIGURE 11.1.
Key components in an MDI application.

Sheets in an MDI frame can exist only in the client area and a sheet is active only when the frame is. Sheet windows are only considered active in the context of the frame. In nearly all respects, sheets act like the child window type.

The Client Area

The client area is specified by a special control, called `mdi_1`, in the frame window. The client area rarely has any other controls placed on it, but when it does the MDI frame is said to be *customized.* When you customize, you must programmatically alter the size of the `mdi_1` control to fit inside the area on the frame that has been left free (not in use by other controls). You must place code in the `Resize` event of the frame to handle this.

> **NOTE**
>
> If you do not resize the `mdi_1` control and then try to open any sheets, you will be unable to see them.

For example, if you customized the frame by adding a row of command buttons along the top edge, the `Resize` script would look something like this:

```
Uint uiX, uiY, uiW, uiH

uiX = WorkspaceX()
uiY = cb_1.Y + cb_1.Height
uiW = WorkspaceWidth()
uiH = WorkspaceHeight() - uiY - mdi_1.MicroHelpHeight
mdi_1.Move( uiX, uiY)
mdi_1.Resize( uiW, uiH)
```

In a standard frame PowerBuilder automatically manages sizing the `mdi_1` control.

MicroHelp

MicroHelp is used to display information for the application. This information can be set either using a function or automatically by PowerBuilder.

Menu items can have text set that will be shown in the MicroHelp as the user passes the mouse pointer over them. This is used to provide a longer description of the menu item's purpose.

To set the MicroHelp text from within your code you need to use the `SetMicroHelp()` function, which takes one parameter, the text you want displayed.

Most developers use the `Tag` attribute of window controls to hold similar information and then place a call to the function with `w_frame.SetMicroHelp( this.Tag)`. This call is usually made in the `GetFocus` event for the object. See the "Tag Values" section later in this chapter for a discussion on tag values.

Menus

There are two common styles of providing menus for MDI sheets: sharing a single menu between the frame and each sheet or providing a menu for the frame and each individual sheet. You can of course mix the two styles together.

NOTE

If a sheet is opened that does not have an associated menu, the frame menu becomes the active menu.

Menus are an integral part of an MDI application and are used to carry out actions and navigate through the application screens. There are some issues that you should be aware of in the interaction between menu objects and sheets. Chapter 12, "Menus and the Menu Painter," provides a detailed discussion on menus in MDI applications.

In most Windows applications you will have noticed a Window menu title on the menu bar. The menu items listed in this drop-down menu allow the user to perform a variety of actions on opened MDI sheets—from arranging open sheets to lining up iconized sheets along the bottom edge of the frame.

These actions are all carried out using one function, `ArrangeSheets()`. This function can only be used on MDI sheets and has the following syntax:

```
MDIFrameWindow.ArrangeSheets( ArrangeType)
```

The single parameter, *`ArrangeType`*, is of the `ArrangeTypes` enumerated data type, and can take the following values:

Value	*Description*
`Cascade!`	Overlap the open sheets so that the title bars are all visible.
`Layer!`	Completely overlap the open sheets one on top of the other.
`Tile!`	Arrange the open sheets in a tile pattern, from left to right.
`TileHorizontal!`	Arrange the open sheets so that they are side by side.
`Icons!`	Arrange just the minimized sheets along the bottom of the frame.

All but the last value also arrange the minimized sheets along the bottom of the frame in addition to completing their other actions.

NOTE

On the Macintosh, sheets cannot be iconized, so `Icons!` has no effect.

Toolbars

A number of attributes on MDI frame windows relate to the display of toolbars:

- `ToolbarVisible`—Whether the toolbar is visible on the frame
- `ToolbarTitle`—The title that displays on the floating toolbar window
- `ToolbarHeight`—The height of the floating toolbar
- `ToolbarWidth`—The width of the floating toolbar
- `ToolbarX`—The X location of the floating toolbar from the frame
- `ToolbarY`—The Y location of the floating toolbar from the frame
- `ToolbarAlignment`—Where the toolbar is attached, or if it is floating

Each attribute except `ToolbarAlignment` is either a Number, a String, or a Boolean value. `ToolbarAlignment` accepts values from the enumerated data type of the same name. The acceptable values are `AlignAtBottom!`, `AlignAtLeft!`, `AlignAtRight!`, `AlignAtTop!`, and `Floating!`.

Another of the menu items that you will find under the Window menu title that was previously mentioned is one that opens a dialog box that gives access to some of these toolbar attributes. The application template that PowerBuilder will generate for you comes with such a window, or you can create your own. Toolbars are covered in more detail in Chapter 12.

MDI Sheets

When you open a window as a sheet, using the `OpenSheet()` function, regardless of the window's style, it will open as a sheet with its control menu, minimize, maximize, resize, title bar, and even the visibility attributes overridden. Depending on the parameters you pass `OpenSheet()`, the size and location of the window may also be overridden.

Any alterations you want to make to a sheet's appearance have to be done once it is opened. You may end up deciding to create a sheet manager that can handle these kinds of modifications. Later in this chapter you will see how to achieve this with some simple API calls.

MDI-Specific Functions

One of the most important functions of an MDI application is the control of the open sheets. Most of the sheet management that you want in an MDI is automatic; to carry out additional work you often need to maintain information on the sheets that are open.

There are two approaches you can take to manage your MDI sheets. In the first approach, you can track each sheet as you open it and close it, usually through an MDI sheet manager object.

TIP

You would build the MDI sheet manager as a custom class user object (otherwise referred to as a *nonvisual user object*, or *NVO*) and make it an instance variable of the frame window.

There are two methods of opening instances that such a manager can use. The first uses an array for holding instances of the same window class. For example, an array declared of type `w_sheet` (declared at the appropriate scope) would be used in the following code to open three sheets:

```
Open( awSheet[1])
Open( awSheet[2])
Open( awSheet[3])
```

Access to these open sheets can now be made using the pointer value in the array at the appropriate index.

The second method of the MDI manager allows you to open instances of the same window class or of different windows that are descendants of a base class. You can do this if you will not be using individual window class attributes and functions or if you have defined the functionality (via virtual functions or public and protected variable declarations) in the base class. The following code opens three instances of different window classes that have all been inherited from the base class `w_sheet`:

```
Integer nIndex
String aszWindowClass[3] = { "w_sheet1", "w_sheet2", "w_sheet3" }
w_sheet awSheet[3]

For nIndex = 1 To 3
   Open( awSheet[ nIndex], aszWindowClass[ nIndex])
Next
```

Both of these methods used to handle sheet instances require you to manage the arrays. For example, what happens when a window is closed? Do you blank out the index and reuse it or do you just keep expanding at the end of the array for each sheet?

In the second approach, you can open and close sheets without tracking them and resort to using the MDI sheet functions that PowerBuilder provides. This is referred to as a *reusable reference variable.*

One of the most frequently used functions in an MDI application is the `GetActiveSheet()` function, which returns a handle to the currently active sheet, if there is one. The syntax for the function is

```
mdiFrameWindow.GetActiveSheet()
```

You should always check the returned handle from this function using the `IsValid()` function to ensure that a handle to a sheet was actually returned.

The method you choose very much depends on the type of application you are developing and what operations you want to carry out on sheets.

Maintaining Frame Settings

You can provide a feature for when the user reopens an application that causes the frame to appear in the same location and size as when the user left the application. This would also happen with an MDI toolbar that would then remember all the settings of when it was last active. There is very little code involved in doing this, and it's extremely straightforward. In fact, what we have done in our own framework is to place this in a nonvisual user object that we use for all the general application functionality, and so it is available to each new project with two lines of code (which are themselves inherited, but that is another story!).

Within the nonvisual application user object there are four functions that carry out all the work of saving and setting the options for the frame window and associated toolbar.

The first function is called `uf_SetApplication()` and takes the application object as its only parameter. This is saved into an instance variable for use in other functions. Four toolbar-related attributes are associated with application objects: `ToolbarFrameTitle`, `ToolbarSheetTitle`, `ToolbarText`, and `ToolbarTips`. This is the code for this function:

```
i_application = a_application

i_application.ToolbarFrameTitle = ProfileString( i_szINIFile, "Application", &
                                        "ToolbarTitle", "Frame Menu")
i_application.ToolbarSheetTitle = ProfileString( i_szINIFile, "Application", &
                                        "ToolbarSheetTitle", "Sheet Menu")
i_application.ToolbarText = ( Upper( ProfileString( i_szINIFile, "Application", &
                                        "ToolbarText", "FALSE")) = "TRUE")
i_application.ToolbarTips = ( Upper( ProfileString( i_szINIFile, "Application", &
                                        "ToolbarTips", "TRUE")) = "TRUE")
```

The `uf_SetApplication()` function is called in the `Open` event of the application. For example, using the global variable `g_App`, which is defined of type `u_n_application`, the code in the `Open` event might be the following:

```
// This is only required if the user object is not setup to be
// auto-instantiating.
g_App = Create u_n_application
//
// Set some default values
g_App.i_szINIFile = "PCS.INI"
g_App.i_szApplication = "Order Entry"
g_App.i_szApplicationName = "Order Entry - Version 1.1 (Terre Haute)"
//
g_App.uf_SetApplication( this)
```

The next step in setting the environment back to the way the user left it is to modify the frame. This is done using the `uf_SetMDIFrame()` function, which takes one parameter: a pointer to a window. Again the object is stored into an instance variable for later use in the object and throughout the application to reference the MDI frame. The frame also holds a number of properties that are specific to a toolbar—not just its own toolbar—that can be used in the application for setting global toolbar information. The code for this function is the following:

```
String szAlignment

i_hWndFrame = a_hWnd

szAlignment = ProfileString(i_szINIFile,"Application","ToolbarAlignment","Top!")

Choose Case Upper( szAlignment)
   Case "ALIGNATBOTTOM!"
      i_hWndFrame.ToolbarAlignment = AlignAtBottom!
   Case "ALIGNATLEFT!"
      i_hWndFrame.ToolbarAlignment = AlignAtLeft!
   Case "ALIGNATRIGHT!"
      i_hWndFrame.ToolbarAlignment = AlignAtRight!
   Case "ALIGNATTOP!"
      i_hWndFrame.ToolbarAlignment = AlignAtTop!
   Case "FLOATING!"
      i_hWndFrame.ToolbarAlignment = Floating!
End Choose

i_hWndFrame.ToolbarVisible = (Upper( ProfileString( i_szINIFile, "Application", &
                                     "ToolbarVisible", "TRUE")) = "TRUE")
i_hWndFrame.ToolbarX = ProfileInt( i_szINIFile, "Application", "ToolbarX", 60)
i_hWndFrame.ToolbarY = ProfileInt( i_szINIFile, "Application", "ToolbarY", 60)

Choose Case Upper(ProfileString(i_szINIFile,"Application","FrameState","Top!"))
  Case "MAXIMIZED!"
    i_hWndFrame.WindowState = Maximized!
  Case "MINIMIZED!"
    i_hWndFrame.WindowState = Minimized!
    i_hWndFrame.X = ProfileInt( i_szINIFile, "Application", "FrameX", 0)
    i_hWndFrame.Y = ProfileInt( i_szINIFile, "Application", "FrameY", 0)
    i_hWndFrame.Height = ProfileInt(i_szINIFile,"Application","FrameHeight",600)
    i_hWndFrame.Width = ProfileInt(i_szINIFile,"Application","FrameWidth",400)
  Case "NORMAL!"
    i_hWndFrame.WindowState = Normal!
    i_hWndFrame.X = ProfileInt( i_szINIFile, "Application", "FrameX", 0)
    i_hWndFrame.Y = ProfileInt( i_szINIFile, "Application", "FrameY", 0)
    i_hWndFrame.Height = ProfileInt(i_szINIFile,"Application","FrameHeight",600)
    i_hWndFrame.Width = ProfileInt(i_szINIFile,"Application","FrameWidth",400)
End Choose
```

This function is called in the `Open` event of the frame window itself.

In order to capture the relevant information from the MDI frame as it closes, the `uf_ClosingMDIFrame()` function is called in the `Close` event of the frame. All you do is capture the same information that you load in using the previous function, making the appropriate data type changes. This is the code:

```
Choose Case i_hWndFrame.ToolbarAlignment
   Case AlignAtBottom!
      SetProfileString( i_szINIFile, "Application", "ToolbarAlignment", &
                                                    "AlignAtBottom!")
```

```
   Case AlignAtLeft!
      SetProfileString( i_szINIFile, "Application", "ToolbarAlignment", &
                                                          "AlignAtLeft!")
   Case AlignAtRight!
      SetProfileString( i_szINIFile, "Application", "ToolbarAlignment", &
                                                         "AlignAtRight!")
   Case AlignAtTop!
      SetProfileString( i_szINIFile, "Application", "ToolbarAlignment", &
                                                           "AlignAtTop!")
   Case Floating!
      SetProfileString( i_szINIFile, "Application", "ToolbarAlignment", &
                                                             "Floating!")
End Choose

If i_hWndFrame.ToolbarVisible Then
   SetProfileString( i_szINIFile, "Application", "ToolbarVisible", "TRUE")
Else
   SetProfileString( i_szINIFile, "Application", "ToolbarVisible", "FALSE")
End If

SetProfileString( i_szINIFile, "Application", "ToolbarX", &
                                              String( i_hWndFrame.ToolbarX))
SetProfileString( i_szINIFile, "Application", "ToolbarY", &
                                              String( i_hWndFrame.ToolbarY))

Choose Case i_hWndFrame.WindowState
   Case Maximized!
      SetProfileString( i_szINIFile, "Application", "FrameState", "Maximized!")
   Case Minimized!
      SetProfileString( i_szINIFile, "Application", "FrameState", "Minimized!")
      SetProfileString( i_szINIFile, "Application", "FrameX", &
                                                    String( i_hWndFrame.X))
      SetProfileString( i_szINIFile, "Application", "FrameY", &
                                                    String( i_hWndFrame.Y))
      SetProfileString( i_szINIFile, "Application", "FrameHeight", &
                                                    String(i_hWndFrame.Height))
      SetProfileString( i_szINIFile, "Application", "FrameWidth", &
                                                    String( i_hWndFrame.Width))
   Case Normal!
      SetProfileString( i_szINIFile, "Application", "FrameState", "Normal!")
      SetProfileString( i_szINIFile, "Application", "FrameX", &
                                                    String( i_hWndFrame.X))
      SetProfileString( i_szINIFile, "Application", "FrameY", &
                                                    String( i_hWndFrame.Y))
      SetProfileString( i_szINIFile, "Application", "FrameHeight", &
                                                    String(i_hWndFrame.Height))
      SetProfileString( i_szINIFile, "Application", "FrameWidth", &
                                                    String( i_hWndFrame.Width))
End Choose
```

The last function called in the application's `Close` event is `uf_CloseApplication()`, which captures the current state of the relevant application object attributes and stores it in the INI file. This is the code for this function:

```
If i_application.ToolbarText Then
   SetProfileString( i_szINIFile, "Application", "ToolbarText", "TRUE")
Else
   SetProfileString( i_szINIFile, "Application", "ToolbarText", "FALSE")
```

```
End If

If i_application.ToolbarTips Then
   SetProfileString( i_szINIFile, "Application", "ToolbarTips", "TRUE")
Else
   SetProfileString( i_szINIFile, "Application", "ToolbarTips", "FALSE")
End If
```

You might want to consider using the Windows Registry instead of an INI file to store this information (you could use `HKEY_CURRENT_USER` so that each user has different settings).

TIP

If you are looking at developing applications across platforms, you might want to consider constructing a custom class user object that handles making the appropriate access to either an INI file or to the registry. This object can sense which operating system it is running in (by using the `GetEnvironment()` function) and makes the appropriate choice.

Window Attributes

Some of the more useful window attributes that have not been covered yet are `Control[]`, `MenuID`, and `WindowState`.

The `Control[]` attribute is an array of the controls that are defined for a window, and you use it in a purely read-only manner. This attribute is very useful when you are trying to make widespread changes to the controls on a window. A common function is to reset the controls on a window, when, for example, the user needs to enter a fresh set of data. Using the `Control[]` array you can use the code in Listing 11.2 to reset the controls.

Listing 11.2. Using the `Control[]` attribute to reset window controls.

```
Integer nCount, nTotalControls
DataWindow ptrDw
DropDownListBox ptrDdlb
RadioButton ptrRb

nTotalControls = UpperBound( wParent.Control[])

For nCount = 1 To nTotalControls
   Choose Case wParent.Control[ nCount].TypeOf()
      Case DataWindow!
         ptrDw = wParent.Control[ nCount]
         ptrDw.Reset()
      Case DropDownListBox!
         ptrDdlb = wParent.Control[ nCount]
         ptrDdlb.SelectItem( 0)
```

continues

Listing 11.2. continued

```
      Case RadioButton!
         ptrRb = wParent.Control[ nCount]
         ptrRb.Checked = FALSE
         .
         // Any other controls you wish to affect
         .
      Case Else
        // An object we can't or don't need to affect
   End Choose
Next
```

You can make this more object oriented by sending a message or calling a method in the object to be executed instead of doing it directly from this function. This would also allow the object to carry out more specific processing.

The `MenuID` attribute is the window's pointer to its associated menu. In an MDI application, multiple sheets can cause this pointer to reference other instances of the menu and even to become a `NULL` object pointer. This attribute, together with solutions to this problem, are discussed in Chapter 12.

The `WindowState` attribute is an enumerated data type that can take the following values: `Maximized!`, `Minimized!`, and `Normal!`. This attribute tells you what the current state of the window is, and you can also use it to set a new window state.

Window Events

Window events are where you will trap and process user and system actions that affect the whole window. A number of window events are discussed in other chapters or other areas of this chapter; the more important ones that are not covered elsewhere are discussed in this section.

The `Activate` event is triggered just before a window becomes active and receives focus. This event is often used to update a sheet manager as to which sheet is the current one being used. There is also a corresponding `Deactivate` event that is triggered when the window loses focus and becomes inactive.

The `Clicked` event is triggered whenever a visible area of the window that is not covered by a control is clicked on. There is also a `DoubleClicked` event for when the user double-clicks the primary mouse button. If you want to trap when the mouse button is clicked and held down, you need to use `MouseDown` and the corresponding `MouseUp` events.

In a window the three events that (nearly) always have code in them, unless you are inheriting, are `Open`, `Close`, and `CloseQuery`.

The `Open` event is triggered when the window is first opened and after the `Constructor` events of all the controls have finished. The script you write in the `Open` event is usually for the initialization of window attributes, variables, and controls.

The CloseQuery event is triggered just before the Close event and is often used as a safety net to check that the user is absolutely certain that he wants to close the window. In this event you can check the status of DataWindows to make sure their data is saved, and to prompt the users using a message box to check that they want to close the window, possibly with unsaved data. PowerBuilder checks the value of Message.ReturnValue to determine if the close has been aborted (a value of 1) or if it should continue and trigger the Close event (a value of 0).

Just before a window is closed, the Close event is the very last event to occur before the Destructor events for each control execute. The Close event is used for destroying any objects the window has created. You can *still* access all the window's controls, properties, and variables within the Close event.

NOTE

When you close a window that is a parent for another window, that window will also be closed with the parent. Any of these child windows may halt the entire process by setting Message.ReturnValue to 1 in its CloseQuery event.

The final event to be introduced in this section is SystemKey. This event is triggered when the Alt key is pressed and the current focus is not in an edit field.

There may be times when you want to precisely control the method with which a user closes down the windows of an application. To enforce this, you must first disable the appropriate menu item from the system menu. This requires two Windows API calls (see Chapter 33, "API Calls," for a discussion on using API functions): GetSystemMenu() and ModifyMenuA().

These functions are declared in PowerBuilder as

```
Function uInt GetSystemMenu( uInt hWindoq, boolean bResetFlag) &
                             Library "user32.dll"
Subroutine ModifyMenuA( uInt hMenu, uInt unItem, uInt Flags, uInt unId, &
                        string szText) Library "user32.dll"
```

Then in the Open event of the window you would use the following code, either directly or as a function:

```
// Declare the handle for the system menu
Uint hMenu
// Define the constant values
Integer MF_BYCOMMAND = 0, MF_GRAYED = 1
Long SC_CLOSE = 61536
// Declare the text for the menu item we are affecting
String szMenuItem = "Close~tAlt+F4"

// Get the handle to the windows system menu
hMenu = GetSystemMenu( Handle(this), FALSE)

// Carry out the modification using the handle
ModifyMenu( hMenu, SC_CLOSE, MF_BYCOMMAND + MF_GRAYED, 0, szMenuItem)
```

You should note that in the Windows operating system the main windows use Alt+F4 as the shortcut to close, and sheet windows use Ctrl+F4. However, some of Microsoft's Windows 95 applications seem to be setting a new standard with Ctrl+W for sheets (for example, Word and Excel).

The code required for the `SystemKey` event in the frame window is actually quite short:

```
If KeyDown( KeyF4!) Then
   Message.Processed = TRUE
End If
```

The event checks whether the F4 key is also pressed with the Alt key, and if so, tells the window that the keys have been processed already. This prevents Windows from even realizing that the key combination has occurred. This code has to be placed in the frame and all sheet windows; otherwise, the Alt+F4 keys can be used in a sheet to close the frame.

To prevent a sheet window from closing (for example, the Windows 3.*x* File Manager prevented you from closing the last sheet), you need to place the following code in the `CloseQuery` event of the sheets:

```
Long lReturn

If KeyDown( keyf4!) Then
   lReturn = 1
End If

Return lReturn
```

You will also need to use the same code as in the frame window's `Open` event to disable the menu option. Just remember to change the menu text to reflect Ctrl+F4 and not the frame's Alt+F4.

You can also place additional control or behavior around the window's minimize and maximize events by mapping a user event to the `pbm_syscommand` event identifier. In this script you can then trap various events:

```
If message.WordParm = 61472 Then
   // Trap the minimize event
   Message.Processed = True
   // Carry out some alternative processing
Else If message.WordParm = 61488 Then
   // Trap the maximize event
   Message.Processed = True
   // Carry out some alternative processing
End If
```

A situation in which you require this functionality is introduced in the section "Window Manipulation Techniques."

PowerScript Window Functions

A number of PowerScript functions can be used to manipulate windows, and the more important and commonly used ones are introduced in the following sections.

Opening and Closing Windows

PowerBuilder provides you with a number of functions to create and destroy window objects.

The parent of a window can be either explicitly or implicitly defined when the window is opened, and is dependent on the type of window. If the parent window is not named when a dependent window (pop-up, child, or response) is opened, the last active window becomes the parent.

NOTE

Remember that MDI sheet windows are never considered to be active windows, and the parent in these cases will be the MDI frame window.

In the following sections on the functions for opening windows, you will see how to specify the parent window.

The `Open()` Function

The `Open()` function is used to load a window and display the window and its associated controls. The controls on the window, along with its own attributes, functions, and variables are not accessible until it has been opened. There are four versions for the `Open()` function.

The first two versions of `Open()` are defined using this syntax:

```
Open( WindowVariable {, Parent})
```

The *`WindowVariable`* parameter can be either a window object or a variable of the desired window class. In the latter PowerBuilder places a reference to the opened window in *`WindowVariable`*. The optional *`Parent`* parameter allows you to specify the parent of the opened window if you do not want it to be the currently active window. The *`Parent`* parameter can only be used for pop-up and child windows.

The `Open()` function returns `-1` if the call fails, and `1` if it succeeds.

An example of each type of call is shown here:

```
w_edit wInstance

// Open the window object class w_edit
Open( w_edit)
```

```
// Open an instance of the window object class w_edit
Open( wInstance)

// Open an instance of the window object class w_edit and make w_frame the parent
Open( wInstance, w_frame)
```

> **NOTE**
>
> To understand how PowerBuilder manages the class and instance pools, see Chapter 28, "Frameworks and Class Libraries."

The last two versions of `Open()` are defined using this syntax:

```
Open( WindowVariable, WindowType {, Parent})
```

The *`WindowVariable`* and *`Parent`* parameters are the same as in the first versions of the `Open()` function. *`WindowType`* is a string value that is the window object class that you want to open. The data type of *`WindowType`* must be an equal or descendant member of the inheritance tree of the *`WindowVariable`* class.

An example of each type of call is shown here:

```
String szWindowType = "w_single_edit"
w_edit wChild

// Opening the window instance wChild with a string, szWindowType, indicating
// the window data type
Open( wChild, szWindowType)

// Opening the window instance wChild with a string, szWindowType, indicating
// the window data type and a parent window, wParent
Open( wChild, szWindowType, w_frame)
```

Using these last two versions requires you to ensure that the window object class specified in the *`WindowType`* parameter is included in the compiled version of the application, either in a PowerBuilder dynamic library (PBD) or listed in a PowerBuilder resource file (PBR).

If you use the *`Parent`* parameter with the `Open()` function and specify a child or sheet window as the parent, PowerBuilder will search up the open window hierarchy from the current window until it finds a window that can be a parent.

The `OpenSheet()` Function

Like the `Open()` function, the `OpenSheet()` function is used to load and display a window; in this case it is specifically an MDI sheet. Also like the `Open()` function, there is an optional parameter that allows you to specify the window class of which you want to open an instance by string. This is the syntax for this function:

```
OpenSheet(SheetReference {,WindowType},MDIFrame {,MenuPosition {,ArrangeOpen}})
```

The *SheetReference* and *WindowType* parameters carry out the same function as the *WindowVariable* and *WindowType* parameters in the `Open()` function. The *MDIFrame* parameter is the name of the application's MDI frame window and is required in the same way *Parent* is used for `Open()`. *MenuPosition* is used to add the sheets name onto an open sheet list, usually under the Window menu title. The default behavior is to list the sheet names under the next-to-last menu title. This will also occur if you pass a value greater than the number of menu titles or a zero. The *ArrangeOpen* parameter is used to force the sheet to display in a certain way. The value is of the `ArrangeOrder` enumerated data type and can take these values:

- `Cascaded!`—Open the sheet so that the other open sheet title bars are still visible (this is the default). All sheets are sized the same.
- `Layered!`—Open the sheet so that it overlays previous sheets and fills the client area of the frame.
- `Original!`—Allow the sheet to open to its original size and cascade it.

Some examples of calls to `OpenSheet()` are shown here:

```
String szWindowType = "w_special_sheet"
w_sheet wInstance

// Open a cascaded instance of the class w_sheet as a sheet in the MDI w_frame
OpenSheet( wInstance, w_frame)

// Open an instance of the class w_sheet in MDI w_frame with its original size
OpenSheet( wInstance, w_frame, 0, Original!)

// Open an instance of class w_special_sheet in MDI w_frame with original size
OpenSheet( wInstance, szWindowType, w_frame, 0, Original!)
```

The `Close()` Function

To shut down a window and free all the resources that it is using, you use the `Close()` function. As already discussed in the "Window Events" section, this function triggers the `CloseQuery` and `Close` events. This is the syntax:

```
Close( WindowObject)
```

Passing Parameters to Windows

The three functions that have just been introduced (`Open()`, `OpenSheet()`, and `Close()`) all have modified versions that allow parameters to be passed between windows. These functions use the `Message` object to hold the passed information. Three of the `Message` object's attributes are used to hold the data being passed from an object to the opening window:

- `Message.DoubleParm`—Used to pass Numeric values
- `Message.StringParm`—Used for String values
- `Message.PowerObjectParm`—Used for passing PowerBuilder objects

You can send additional data types by converting them to a String or Numeric value first, and you can send structures via the PowerObjectParm attribute.

NOTE

There are a number of other methods for passing information to a window; they are covered in the section "Other Parameter Mechanisms."

The window that is being opened and that will receive the parameter needs to retrieve the value from the Message object in its Open event before it carries out any additional processing. This is because Message is a globally used object and is used every time an event is triggered or posted, and therefore it runs the risk of being overwritten.

NOTE

The only way to pass multiple parameters is to use a structure and pass that via the PowerObjectParm attribute.

You should always validate the parameter attribute of the Message object you are using to make sure a value was passed.

The OpenWithParm() Function

The OpenWithParm() function is identical to the Open() function, with the exception of an additional parameter:

```
OpenWithParm( WindowVariable {, WindowType}, ValueToPass {, Parent})
```

The *ValueToPass* parameter is used to pass the data value as a parameter to the window being opened. The appropriate attribute in the Message object is set.

An example of the two scripts that you would use to pass a structure to a window follows.

Within the calling script, you'd use this:

```
s_character sCharacter

sCharacter.Name = "Ulric Von Raven"
sCharacter.Age = 32
sCharacter.Profession ="Templar"

OpenWithParm( w_character_detail, sCharacter)
```

Then within the Open event of the opened window, w_character_detail, the script to retrieve the structure would be this:

```
s_character sACharacter

If IsValid(Message.PowerObjectParm) Then
   sACharacter = Message.PowerObjectParm
End If
```

The OpenSheetWithParm() Function

The `OpenSheetWithParm()` function, like the two `Open()` functions, is similar to the `OpenSheet()` function, again with only an additional parameter:

```
OpenSheet( SheetReference, ValueToPass {, WindowType}, MDIFrame {, &
                                         MenuPosition {, ArrangeOpen}})
```

The same statements that are valid for the `OpenWithParm()` function are valid for this function.

The CloseWithReturn() Function

The twin to the `Close()` function is the `CloseWithReturn()` function, which can only be used in conjunction with response windows. The `CloseWithReturn()` function can pass a value, or using the `PowerObjectParm` attribute of the `Message` object, multiple values, and pass the values back to the script that opened the response window. This is the syntax for this function:

```
CloseWithReturn( WindowObject, ValueToReturn)
```

This function closes the response window and places the return value in the `Message` object, from where the calling script should immediately remove it.

NOTE

Remember that response windows are modal. This is what allows you to return a value to a calling script.

You should also be careful not to return an object that exists in the response window, because these are always passed by reference and the object that they referenced has been destroyed. Attributes or variables can be returned because these are passed by value.

The execution sequence using the `CloseWithReturn()` function is shown in the following example:

```
String szName

// Open a response window that will return a customer name
Open( w_select_customer)
//
// Once the response window closes execution returns to this
// point and we can retrieve the value from the Message object.
szName = Message.StringParm
```

The script in the method used for closing `w_select_customer` would be this:

```
CloseWithReturn( Parent, i_szCustomerName)
```

In this case the script is in an object other than the window, and the value being returned is a window instance variable `i_szCustomerName`. Since the variable will be passed back by value, you don't care that the actual variable is destroyed with the window.

Other Parameter Mechanisms

There are several other options you can use if you are passing more complex pieces of data (ones that cannot be adequately described in a structure). In general, though, you will use structures or class objects to pass your data to a window.

The obvious solution is to use global variables or publicly accessible window instance variables and to set these immediately after you open the window. You must of course make the opened window carry out a post event retrieval of the data, since the controlling window will not have assigned the values yet.

Another parameter-passing mechanism is to call a function on the window, passing the parameters you need, and in PowerBuilder 5.0 you can also use parameterized events for the same purpose.

NOTE

For more information on this new feature of PowerBuilder 5.0, see Chapter 6.

These mechanisms should rarely, if ever, be used. They are unreliable and depend completely on certain events occurring in a certain order. Using a structure to pass information is well defined and the data is immediately accessible in the `Open` event of the window.

Printing Windows

You can print the contents of a window using the second format of the `Print()` function. This is the syntax for this format:

```
ObjectName.Print( PrintJobNumber, X, Y {, Width, Height})
```

`ObjectName` can be an object that is descended from the `DragObject` class type, which includes windows and window controls. The *`X`*, *`Y`*, *`Width`*, and *`Height`* parameters are all used to specify a starting location and scaling factor to apply to the printed image. The call to `Print()` must be encompassed by a valid `PrintOpen()` and `PrintClose()` function pairing.

Here's an example of printing the `w_about` window:

```
Long lJobNo

lJobNo = PrintOpen()
If lJobNo <> -1 Then
   w_about.Print( lJobNo, 1, 1)
   PrintClose( lJobNo)
End If
```

To print an entire screen you would use the `PrintScreen()` function, which takes identical parameters as does the `Print()` function defined previously. The only difference between them is that you do not specify an object name to print. Here's an example of using this function:

```
Long lJobNo

lJobNo = PrintOpen()
If lJobNo <> -1 Then
   PrintScreen( lJobNo, 1, 1)
   PrintClose( lJobNo)
End If
```

The Window Painter

When you open the Window painter, you are first greeted with the Select Window dialog box (see Figure 11.2), which allows you to either create a new window, open an existing one, or inherit from an existing window to create a new one.

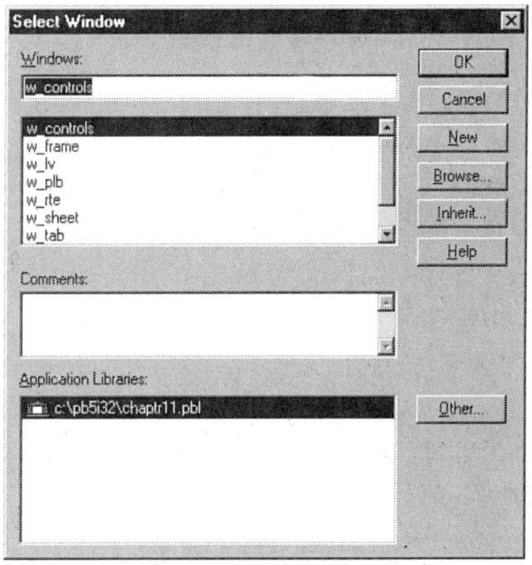

FIGURE 11.2.
The Select Window dialog box.

Once you have made your selection, the Window painter workspace is opened (see Figure 11.3), which shows the window area and associated toolbars.

FIGURE 11.3.
The Window painter.

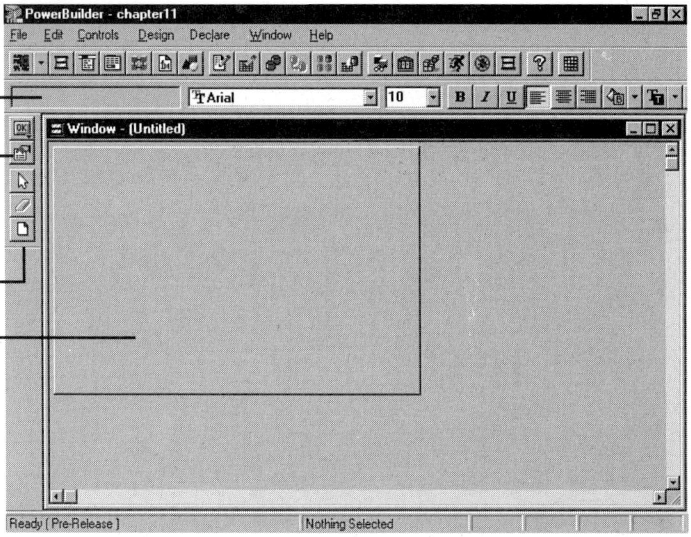

The painter will look familiar to those of you who have used PowerBuilder before, with the exception that the controls are now "hidden" under a drop-down toolbar item and there is a new button for accessing the window's properties.

TIP

Developers familiar with PowerBuilder 4.0 might want to go ahead and customize the PainterBar and place the controls back on the toolbar.

Accessing Properties

You access the properties for the window and any of its controls either from the Properties button, the Properties option on the pop-up menu (opened by right-clicking on the object), or more easily by double-clicking on the object. These are the only ways to affect the properties of a control or window now. In this respect PowerBuilder 5.0 is less flexible than the previous versions of PowerBuilder. For example, you are now unable to make multiple controls invisible or have a similar style setting.

To affect the properties of multiple controls, you use the mouse to drag a rectangle (known as a *rubberband* or *lasso*) over the controls you want to affect. Each selected control then displays the modification handles in the corners. You can individually add or remove controls from the selected group by using the Ctrl key and the mouse. In PowerBuilder 5.0 you can only affect the font settings (size, bold, alignment, and so on) and the text and background colors for a group of controls. These options are accessed from the StyleBar of the Window painter.

The property sheet for a window or control uses the tab metaphor to allow access to different related settings. The window's property sheet (see Figure 11.4) provides all the settings that were previously scattered across a couple different dialog boxes and pop-up menu settings.

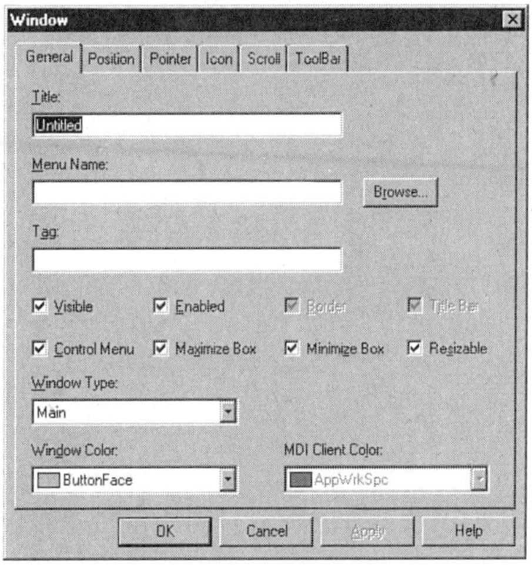

FIGURE 11.4.
A window's property sheet.

The General tab page allows you to change the type of window, colors, window style, and the associated menu. The Position tab page (see Figure 11.5) allows you to set the initial position and state of the window.

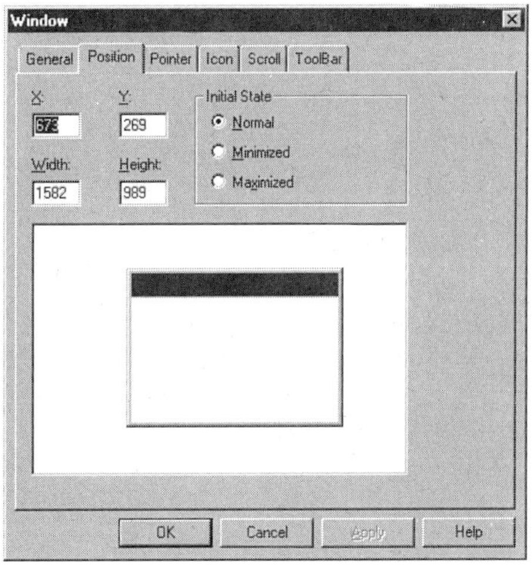

FIGURE 11.5.
The Position tab page.

TIP

At first glance you might think you have lost the functionality of the center horizontally and vertically (PowerBuilder used two check boxes in previous versions). To bring up these two options, right-click in the preview area of the tab page. However, you should not rely on this because a user might be using a different resolution than the one you set the centering with. Instead, you should use a function to center the window when it opens (see the description of the `uf_CentreWindow()` function in Chapter 33).

The Pointer and Icon tab pages provide you with a way to specify the mouse pointer graphic when the mouse is over the window and the icon of the window when minimized, respectively. The Scroll tab page (see Figure 11.6) allows you to customize the way the window is scrolled and whether it has scrollbars.

FIGURE 11.6.
The Scroll tab page.

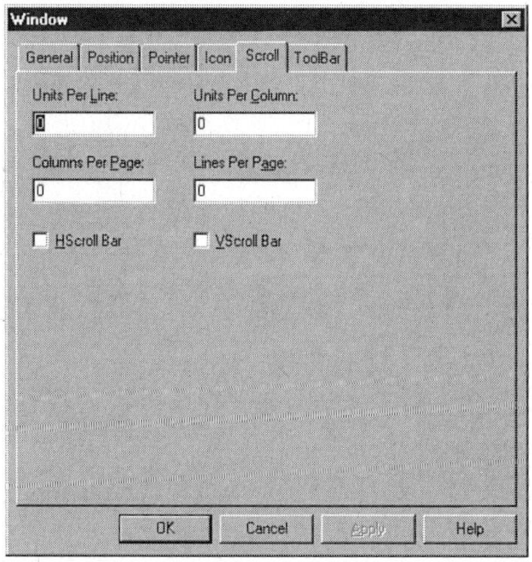

The ToolBar tab page (see Figure 11.7) allows you easy access to the toolbar-related properties of the window. In previous versions of PowerBuilder these could only be set from within PowerScript.

The property sheets for controls are very similar to each other, with only the General tab page being different for each, and some of the more complex controls (for example, rich text edit) also insert an additional tab page after General. The General tab page for a command button is shown in Figure 11.8.

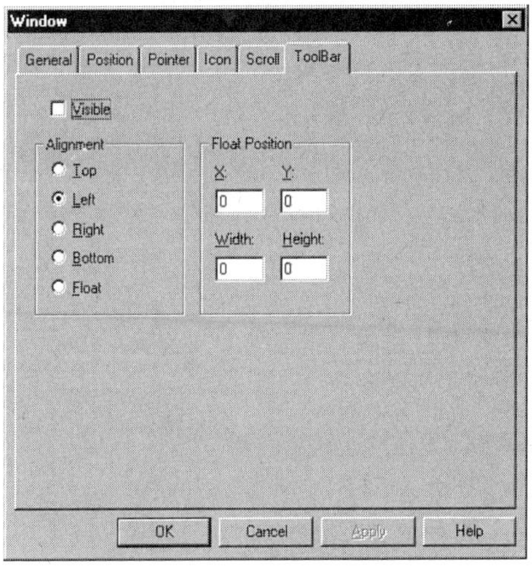

FIGURE 11.7.
The ToolBar tab page.

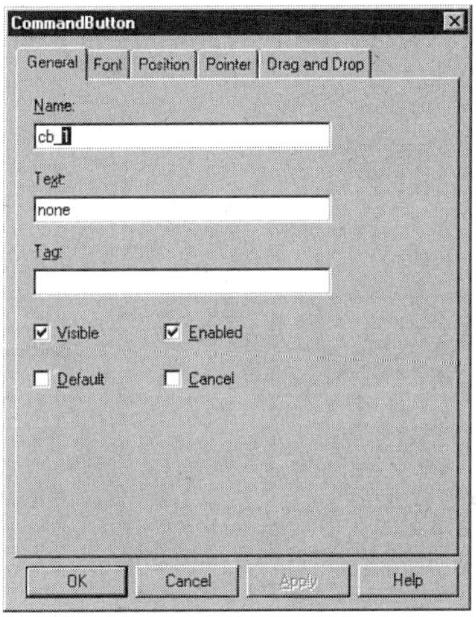

FIGURE 11.8.
The General tab page for a command button.

The Font tab page (see Figure 11.9) allows you to change the font, font style and size, effects, and colors for the text used in the control.

The Position tab page provides four edit fields for you to manually change the `X`, `Y`, `Width`, and `Height` properties of the control. You will usually do this from within the painter using the mouse. The Pointer tab page allows you to set the pointer graphic as it passes over the control. The Drag and Drop tab page (see Figure 11.10) lets you set the drag icon for the control and whether it should be set to automatic drag (see Chapter 31, "Drag and Drop").

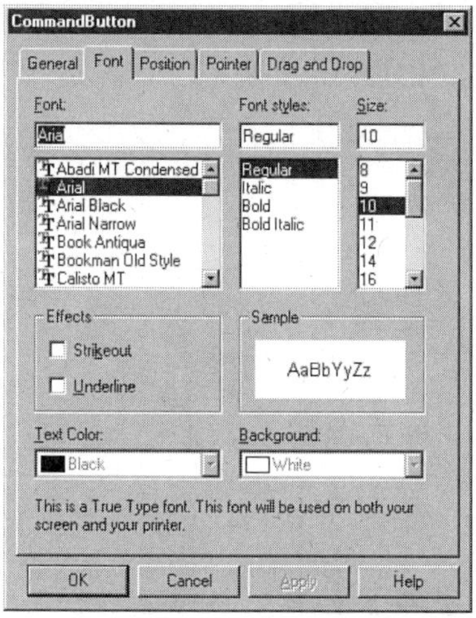

FIGURE 11.9.

The Font tab page.

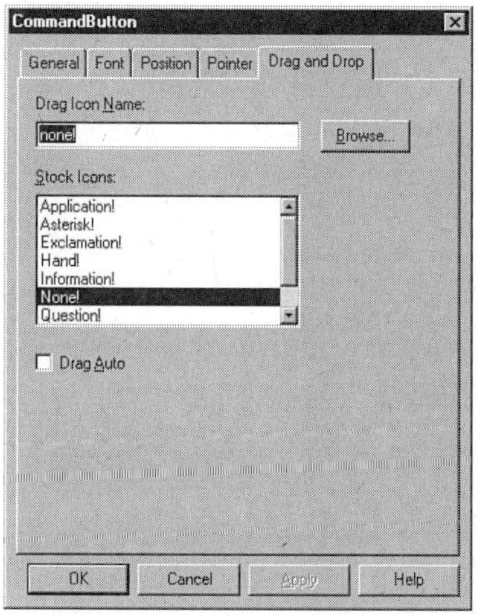

FIGURE 11.10.

The Drag and Drop tab page.

Manipulating Controls

You can use three options from the Edit menu to control the size and placement of controls with respect to other controls in the window.

Align Controls

To align a number of controls with a base position, first select the control you want to align with, and then select the others (either using a rubberband or Ctrl+Click). Once you have all the controls you want to affect selected, access the Edit menu and choose the Align Controls cascading menu (see Figure 11.11).

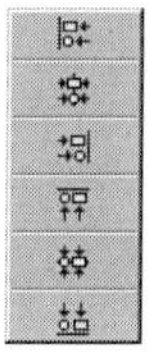

FIGURE 11.11.
The Align Controls menu.

These pictures look different from the ones that developers are used to in previous versions of PowerBuilder, but the exact same functionality is available.

WARNING

There is an important consideration when spacing, aligning, or sizing controls: The appropriate value is taken from the first (or first two in the case of spacing) control selected and then applied to the second, third, and so on controls. You will get very unpredictable results if you use the rubberband/lasso method of selecting controls and then carry out one of these operations.

Space Controls

To produce uniform spacing between controls in either the horizontal or vertical direction, you will use the Space Controls cascading menu (see Figure 11.12) from the Edit menu.

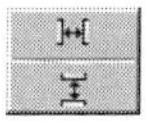

FIGURE 11.12.
The Space Controls cascading menu.

Size Controls

To resize a control or group of controls to a uniform width and/or height you use the Size Controls cascading menu (see Figure 11.13) from the Edit menu.

FIGURE 11.13.
The Size Controls menu.

This works in the same manner as the align option.

Duplicating Controls

You can easily duplicate a control within the Window painter by selecting a control and using the Ctrl+T key combination. This will place a new control under the selected one. You can use this key sequence as many times as you want, and this will continue to stack the controls underneath each other.

NOTE

New 5 in PowerBuilder

This operation in PowerBuilder 5.0 retains the correct width and height of the control being copied, rather than using some default value.

Setting the Tab Order

You set the tab order for controls by selecting the Tab Order option under the Design menu or the appropriate toolbar button. This disables all other options and control access while you are in tab sequence mode (see Figure 11.14). The current tab sequence order of the controls is shown as a red number by the upper-right corner of each control.

FIGURE 11.14.
A window in Tab Sequence mode.

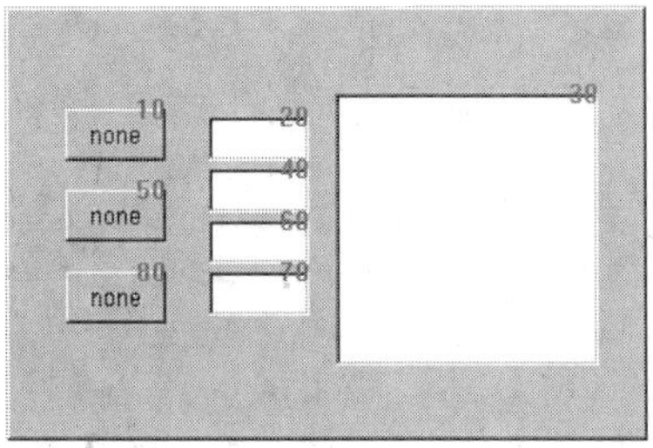

You can change the value by clicking on it and entering a new number. When you leave the tab sequence mode (by selecting the menu option again), PowerBuilder resequences the values in increments of 10.

Showing Invisible Controls

New 5 in PowerBuilder

By selecting Options under the Design menu, you will open an options dialog box that allows you to display controls that have been made invisible. This used to be easily accessible from the Design menu, but is now removed into this dialog box.

TIP

You can customize your toolbar to include the Design Options button to take you straight to this dialog.

Testing the Window

You can preview the window either by selecting Preview from the Design menu or using the Run Window button on the PowerBar. This shows the window as it will appear at runtime, and you can check the tab orders and initial styles of the controls.

To test the window without running the whole application, you can use Ctrl+Shift+W (PowerBuilder 4.0) or place the Run Window toolbar button on the PowerBar (PowerBuilder 5.0) to cause execution of scripts and controls on the window.

NOTE

Only use preview mode for checking simple changes you make. During a normal run the window may act differently.

Controls

Controls are *the* components of an application that an end user interacts with to perform the desired activities. PowerBuilder provides you with a range of controls that exist in the operating system, plus a few additional ones like DataWindows.

There are five types of controls:

- Controls that initiate actions (for example, command buttons)
- Controls that indicate states (for example, radio buttons)
- Controls that display and allow manipulation of data (for example, DataWindows)
- Controls that enhance a window's appearance (for example, lines)
- User object controls that can combine all of the above

You should make appropriate use of each, and only use a control for the task for which it is intuitively meant. For example, do not use a command button to toggle the state of something—use a check box or radio button instead.

To create a control on the window, simply select it from the control list and click on the window area. PowerBuilder will draw the control and give it a default name.

Control Names

It is important to maintain standards not only within your code, but also with control names and even labels. Most developers stick with the Powersoft control type prefixes, but usually little attention is given to the rest of the identifier. By setting a standard (for example, placing underscores between each logical word of the identifier), you can help a team of developers considerably.

> **NOTE**
>
> In PowerBuilder 5.0 the prefixes for controls can be set in the Options dialog, which is opened from the Design menu in the Window painter. In previous versions of PowerBuilder these could be set through the Preferences painter. The current settings are held in the PB.INI file.

The labels you use should be end-user–accepted names and descriptions. This makes end users' tasks easier since they know what the field should be used for, and makes your task easier when describing the system to the end user and other developers. This may force you to "write the manual" on the names used, but it is a worthy exercise.

Where possible, you should avoid using abbreviations. In fact, in one case, a client had a big book of abbreviations that were used on the mainframe. This was enforced on the client/server pilot project much to the dismay of the PC development team, as we had to use three- and four-letter words where we would normally have used the full word. There are extremes, and where possible you should make a system intuitive for not only the existing end users, but for future end users who will be using the system with possibly no background knowledge of how the system really works.

With Version 5.0 of PowerBuilder, Powersoft has introduced a number of new controls into the Window painter's palette. They all owe their inclusion to the Windows 95 interface standards introduced by Microsoft, and their use and properties are described in the following sections.

> **NOTE**
>
> Due to the complexity of these new controls, you should explore the accompanying examples that come with PowerBuilder for code examples. Powersoft has provided some excellent and well-thought-out examples that demonstrate the use of the events, functions, and properties that are introduced next. We felt that we could make better use of the space allocated for this chapter by providing tips and tricks rather than trying to duplicate or create additional examples for these controls.

The Tab Control

The tab control uses a new metaphor, the tab page, which is the basis of all interactions with the tab control itself (see Figure 11.15). Each tab page is effectively a container for other types of controls; user objects can also be included using a different process.

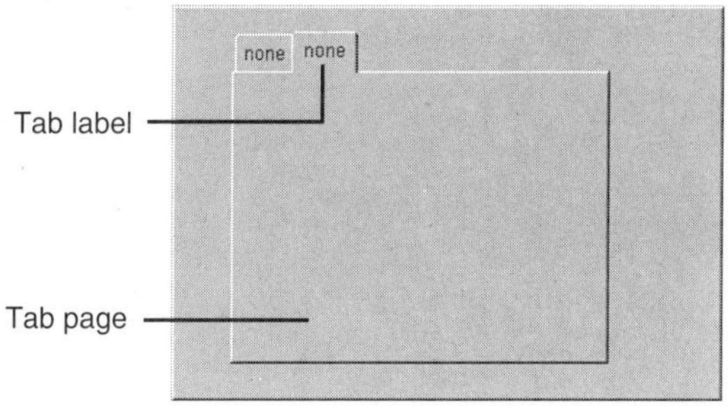

FIGURE 11.15.
The tab control.

Tab pages share the same font settings and all of the properties that can be set in the property sheet for the tab control. These include the following:

- `Alignment` (Alignment)—An enumerated value that specifies the text label alignment on the tab pages: `Left!`, `Center!`, and `Right!`.
- `BoldSelectedText` (Boolean)—Whether to bold the text for the currently selected tab page: `TRUE` (bold the text), `FALSE` (text is the same as other tab pages).
- `Control[]` (UserObject)—This is an array of the controls in the object. If the object is a tab control, it contains the tab pages, and if it is a tab page, it contains the visual controls on that page.
- `CreateOnDemand` (Boolean)—This determines whether the objects that exist in the tab pages are instantiated when the tab control is created (`FALSE`), or when the tab page is first selected (`TRUE`). The trade-off in performance is that you cannot access the controls or their properties before the tab page is selected. This is useful if the controls in a tab page are self-contained; otherwise, you will have to make sure the object has been instantiated using the `IsValid()` function.
- `FixedWidth` (Boolean)—Whether the tab label has a fixed width or shrinks to the length of the text label. When `TRUE` all tab label widths are determined by the longest text label, and when `FALSE` the tab label width adjusts to fit the length of its own text.
- `FocusButtonDown` (Boolean)—Determines whether the current tab page has a dotted focus rectangle.
- `MultiLine` (Boolean)—Whether the tab control can show the tab labels in more than one row. If there is not enough room to display all the tab labels in one row and this property is `TRUE`, the tabs will be arranged in multiple rows. If there is not enough room for all the tab labels and this property is `FALSE`, a double-arrow control will be displayed to allow the user to scroll the tab labels.
- `PerpendicularText` (Boolean)—If this property is `TRUE` you will get narrow perpendicular tab labels on the tab page, otherwise the tab labels run along the edge of the tab pages.
- `PictureOnRight` (Boolean)—Specifies the position of the picture for the tab pages. When `TRUE` the picture is on the right; otherwise, it appears to the left (`FALSE`).

- `PowerTips` (Boolean)—Indicates whether a PowerTip will display when the mouse pointer pauses over a tab label. You can specify `PowerTipText` values for each individual tab page. These are useful if you are using only pictures for labels.
- `RaggedRight` (Boolean)—Determines whether the tab labels are stretched to fill the whole space along the edge of the control (`FALSE`) or if they remain the size determined by the label text and `FixedWidth` property (`FALSE`).
- `SelectedTab` (Integer)—Sets the index number of the selected tab page that is shown when the tab control is created.
- `ShowPicture` (Boolean)—Whether the tab label pictures are displayed.
- `ShowText` (Boolean)—Whether the text for each tab label is displayed.
- `TabPosition` (TabPosition)—Determines which edges of the tabs are displayed on the control. The values for this property are shown in Table 11.1.

Each of these attributes is available in the Window painter and also at runtime for modification.

Table 11.1. Values for the `TabPosition` enumerated data type.

Enumerated Value	*Resulting Effect*
`TabsOnBottom!`	Tabs are at the bottom.
`TabsOnBottomAndTop!`	The selected tab and those after it are displayed along the bottom. Tabs before are arranged along the top.
`TabsOnLeft!`	Tabs are on the left.
`TabsOnLeftAndRight!`	The selected tab and those before it are displayed on the left. Tabs after are on the right.
`TabsOnRight!`	Tabs are on the right.
`TabsOnRightAndLeft!`	The selected tab and those before it are displayed on the right. Tabs after are on the left.
`TabsOnTop!`	Tabs are on top.
`TabsOnTopAndBottom!`	The selected tab and those after it are displayed along the top. Tabs before are arranged along the bottom.

Each tab page also has its own properties that are used to individually customize their appearance. These properties can be accessed in the Window painter and at runtime:

- `Name`—The PowerBuilder object name for the tab page.
- `Text` (String)—The text to be displayed as the tab page's label.
- `Tag` (String)—A tag value to be used for whatever purposes you want.

- `BackColor` (Long)—The background color of the tab page.
- `TabBackColor` (Long)—The color of the tab label background.
- `TabTextColor` (Long)—The color of the tab label text.
- `PictureName` (String)—The picture to use in the tab label.

Each tab page also has a couple properties that you can access at runtime:

- `ObjectType` (`UserObjects`)—This is a read-only reference to the user object that is used for the tab page.
- `Control[]` (`WindowObject`)—This is a read-only array of the controls within the tab page. The `Control[]` and `ObjectType` properties are mutually exclusive.

You can place any of the normal window controls, including user objects, on a tab page. You can even use a standard visual user object of type tab, which you use instead of inserting a normal page into the tab control (see the "Painting Tab Controls" section for more information). This allows you to define standard colors and tab label behavior for all of your tab controls.

The tab control has a number of specific functions:

- `CloseTab(` *`UserObjectReference`*`)`—Removes a tab page from the control. The tab page must have been added using either the `OpenTab()` or `OpenTabWithParm()` functions. This function will trigger the `Destructor` event for the user object. Once a tab page has been closed, all resources associated with it are released. If you attempt to reference the object or any of its attributes, you will get an error.
- `MoveTab(` *`nSourceIndex`*`,` *`nDestinationIndex`*`)`—Moves a tab page with the specified index, *`nSourceIndex`*, to a new position and changes its index value. The *`nDestinatioIndex`* argument specifies the index before which the tab page will be moved. If this value is `0` or greater than the total number of pages, the tab page is moved to the end.
- `OpenTab(` *`UserObjectReference`*`,` *`nIndex`*`)`—Creates a new page using a user object of a known class type, *`UserObjectReference`*. You can use either a user object name or variable of the required data type. This function places a reference to the opened user object into *`UserObjectReference`*, similarly to other PowerScript `Open()` functions. However, using the `OpenTab()` function, you can specify that the same user object be opened again and again, and each is opened as a new page. The new tab pages do not become selected, and the `Constructor` events for the controls in the user object are not triggered until the tab page is selected.
- `OpenTab(` *`UserObjectReference`*`,` *`szUserObjectType`*`,` *`nIndex`*`)`—This is the second format for the `OpenTab()` function, which you will use when you need to dynamically determine the type of user object to open.
- `OpenTabWithParm()`—This function comes in a number of flavors that allow either of the two previously described open methods along with a Numeric, a String, or a `PowerObject` parameter.

- `SelectTab(` *`DragObject`* `¦` *`nIndex`* `¦` *`szUserObject`*`)`—Selects the specified tab page and displays it in the tab control.
- `TabPostEvent(` *`szEvent`* `{,` *`lwParm`*`,` *`llParm`* `¦` *`szValue`*`})`—Posts the *`szEvent`* message to each tab page in a tab control. You can also specify an enumerated value as the only argument; you cannot specify additional arguments. This is similar to the `PostEvent()` function, which is covered in Chapter 6.
- `TabTriggerEvent(` *`szEvent`* `{,` *`lwParm`*`,` *`llParm`* `¦` *`szValue`*`})`—Triggers the *`szEvent`* message for each tab page (in index order) in a tab control. You can also specify an enumerated value as the only argument; you cannot specify the additional arguments in this case.

Tab Control Guidelines

Since a tab control only displays a single row of tabs by default (you must set the `MultiLine` property if you want more), you should try to avoid multiple row and scrolling tab styles, because these add complexity to the interface and can be confusing to work with. As an alternative to using multiple lines or scrolling, you might want to consider breaking the tab pages into groups and provide a means to toggle between these.

Accessing Tab Controls from Scripts

Accessing a tab control, the associated tab pages, and each of their respective controls is not as complex a task as you might first think. Using dot notation, you refer to the tab control, and then the tab page, and then the control on the page. Here's an example:

```
TabControl.TabPageName.ControlName
```

For example, to access the text of a pushbutton `cb_choice` that sits on the `tp_configuration` tab page of the tab control, `t_selection` would be coded as

```
t_selection.tp_configuration.cb_choice.text = "Push Me!"
```

Using the same notation, you can access tab control– or tab page–specific attributes. For example, to change the enabled state of a tab page, you would use the following:

```
t_selection.tp_configuration.Enabled = FALSE
```

Painting Tab Controls

To paint a tab control, choose the tab control tool from the toolbar and click on the window; this will create a tab control with one tab page. If you now right-click on the control, you will see a list of the available actions, as well as the Properties option. One of the action options is Insert TabPage, which you use to add additional tabs to the control. The next option down is Insert User Object, which allows you to add a custom visual user object as a new tab page to the control.

Tab pages that were *not* created from a user object can then have additional controls placed on them. You will get a warning if you attempt to drop a control on a tab page created from a user object.

The tab pages that you create in the User Object painter can have the following attributes set in the TabPage tab page of the object's properties dialog box:

Attribute	*Description*
`Tab Text`	The text to be displayed on the tab
`Tab Picture`	The picture for the tab with or instead of the text
`PowerTipText`	Text for the PowerTip message window
`Tab Background`	Color of tab background
`Tab Text Color`	Color of the tab's text
`Picture Mask`	Color of the picture's mask

You cannot alter the attributes of any of the controls from within the Window painter, and you must use the User Object painter for these tasks. The property sheet for user object tabs (on the right) are different from normal tabs (on the left), as shown in Figure 11.16.

FIGURE 11.16.
The different property sheeets.

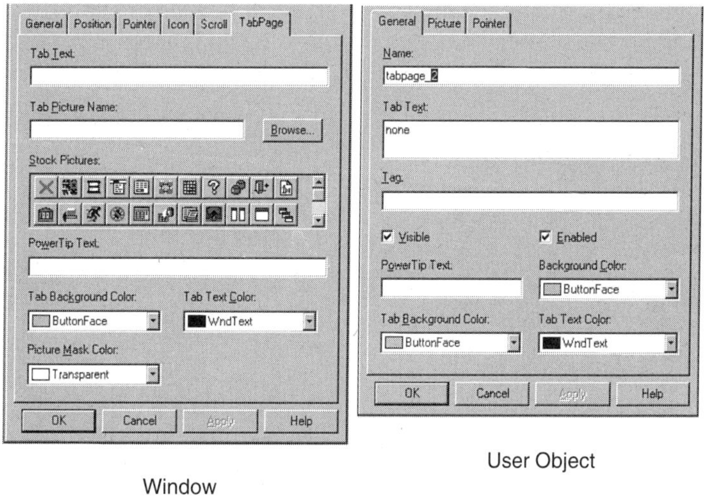

You can move between the different tab pages by clicking on the tab label. This will cause the tab page to be brought to the front. You should note that the tab labels will be rearranged according to the settings you have made for the tab control. This behavior is exactly what the user will see during runtime execution.

You can alter the properties for the tab control by double-clicking on the tab page area, and you can reach the tab page's properties by double-clicking on the corresponding tab label.

To remove a tab page from the control, right-click to bring up the context-sensitive menu and select either Clear or Cut.

You can place and move controls in tab pages as you would in a window, and you can use the pop-up menu to cut, copy, and paste the controls between tab controls and tab pages.

WARNING

You must remember that this will change the control's parent, and any script you have written for that control may be made invalid. This is one of the reasons you should try to write generic code by using the `This` and `Parent` pronouns. It is also worth noting that placing a new control onto a tab control's active page and dropping a control onto the window and then moving it to the tab control are subtly different. The first operation assigns the control's parent to be the tab control, and in the second the window remains the parent.

The Picture List Box and Drop-Down Picture List Box Controls

NEW 5 in PowerBuilder

Both the list box and drop-down list box visual controls (see Figure 11.17) have been made into ancestor objects in the PowerBuilder object hierarchy, because each now has a corresponding picture-enabled descendant. The new properties and functions for each of these controls are all related to pictures.

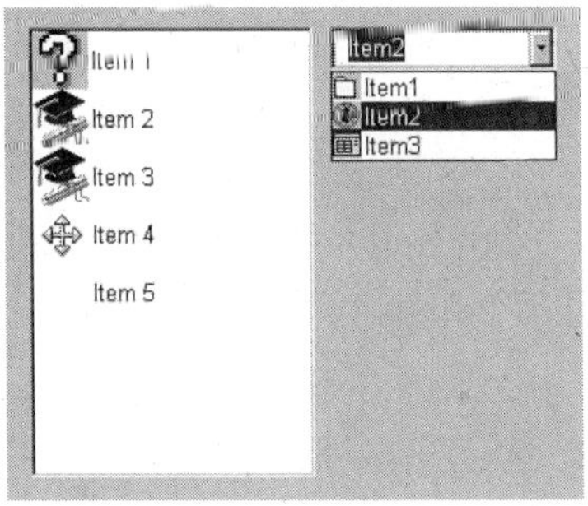

FIGURE 11.17.
The picture list box and drop-down picture list box controls.

These are the new properties for these controls:

- `ItemPictureIndex[]` (Integer)—This is a read-only array that holds the picture index for each item in the item list. It is modified by use of the `AddItem()` and `DeleteItem()` functions.
- `PictureHeight` (Integer)—The height at which the pictures appear in the control. This can only be set when there are no items currently in the controls list.

- `PictureWidth` (Integer)—The width at which the pictures appear in the control. If this property is `0` (Default), the size of the first image added with the `AddPicture()` function is used; otherwise, the image is scaled to the specified size. This property will only have an effect if it's set before the first picture is added using `AddPicture()` or after a call to `DeletePictures()`.
- `PictureMaskColor` (Long)—This allows you to specify the mask color (this makes the specified color transparent on the bitmap) for a picture. This attribute is used when a bitmap is added and can be changed between `AddPicture()` calls.
- `PictureName[]` (String)—This is a read-only array that corresponds to the values in the `ItemPictureIndex` array. You can modify this array only through the use of the `AddPicture()`, `DeletePicture()`, and `DeletePictures()` functions.

These functions have been added to handle these new properties:

- `AddItem(` *`szValue`*`,` *`nPictureIndex`*`)`—This is similar to the `AddItem()` function for normal list boxes, except that you specify the index of the picture in the `PictureName[]` array, using the `nPictureIndex` argument.
- `AddPicture(` *`szPictureName`*`)`—Adds a bitmap to the main image list and returns the index at which it was added.
- `DeletePicture(` *`nPictureIndex`*`)`—Removes the bitmap at the specified index from the image list.

WARNING

You will have strange repaint problems if you delete a picture already in use by the list box.

- `DeletePictures()`—Deletes all the pictures in the image list.
- `InsertItem(` *`szValue`*`,` *`nPictureIndex`*`,` *`nIndex`*`)`—Allows you to specify the index at which you want to add a new item and associated picture to the list.

The ListView Control

The ListView control is another of the new controls that can be used in your PowerBuilder 5.0 applications. It is used when you need to show a collection of items consisting of a label and an icon. This control allows you to present a set of information in one of four ways:

- Icon—Item appear as icons, each with a label below. The user can drag icons within the view.
- Small icon—Items appears as small icons, each with the label to the right. The user can also drag these icons within the view.

- List—Items appear as small icons, each with the label to the right in a columnar and sorted presentation.
- Report—Items appear in a multicolumn list, with the leftmost column displaying the icon and label.

These presentations look the same as they do when you select them from the View menu for a Windows 95 drive window. An example of each is shown in Figure 11.18.

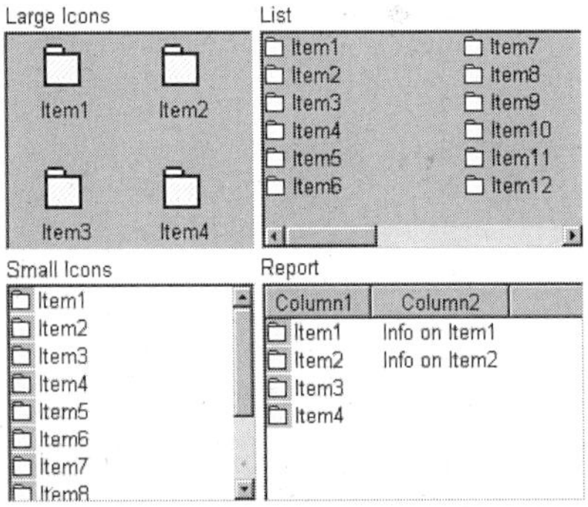

FIGURE 11.18.
The four styles of a ListView control.

> **NOTE**
>
> In order to use the Report view of this control, you *must* specify at least one column. This can only be done through a PowerScript function, `AddColumn()`. Otherwise, nothing will display.

As you might imagine, there are a number of new properties, events, and functions that apply exclusively to ListView controls. These are the properties:

- `AutoArrange` (Boolean)—Automatically arranges icons in large/small icon view.
- `ButtonHeader` (Boolean)—The header in report view appears as buttons instead of just labels.
- `DeleteItems` (Boolean)—Allows items to be deleted from the list using the Del key.
- `EditLabels` (Boolean)—Allows the item labels to be modified by the user.
- `ExtendedSelect` (Boolean)—Allows the user to select multiple list items.
- `FixedLocations` (Boolean)—Stops the user from dragging large/small icons to new positions.
- `Item[]` (String)—The label for each list item.
- `ItemPictureIndex[]` (Integer)—The picture index for each list item.
- `LabelWrap` (Boolean)—Whether the item text is word wrapped or displayed as a single line.

- `Scrolling` (Boolean)—Whether the control can be scrolled.
- `ShowHeader` (Boolean)—Whether the header should appear in the report view.
- `SortType` (grSortType)—The sort order for the list items. If `SortType` is `UserDefinedSort!`, the `Sort` event will be triggered.
- `View` (ListViewView)—Changes the display type between the four styles.
- `LargePictureHeight` (Integer)—The height of the large icons. This property, together with the width, can only be set if there are no images currently in `LargePictureName[]`. If this value is `0` when the first image is added, the size of that image is used to set the height and width properties.
- `LargePictureWidth` (Integer)—The width of the large icons.
- `LargePictureMaskColor` (Long)—The masking color to use with non-system bitmaps.
- `LargePictureName[]` (String)—The images to be used for the large icon view.
- `SmallPictureHeight` (Integer)—The height of the small icons.
- `SmallPictureWidth` (Integer)—The width of the small icons.
- `SmallPictureMaskColor` (Long)—The masking color to use with non-system bitmaps.
- `SmallPictureName[]` (String)—The images to be used for the small icon view.
- `StatePictureHeight` (Integer)—The height of the state pictures.
- `StatePictureWidth` (Integer)—The width of the state pictures.
- `StatePictureMaskColor` (Long)—The masking color to use with non-system bitmaps.
- `StatePictureName[]` (String)—The images to be used for the state pictures.

The *state pictures* are used in the control to indicate that an action has been or is about to be performed on the item. For example, the currently selected item can have a state picture associated with it, which will appear to the left of the item's picture, that indicates that it will be part of a group deletion.

These are the ListView control–specific events:

- `BeginDrag`—The user uses the left mouse button to start dragging. The index the user is attempting to drag is available as an event argument.
- `BeginLabelEdit`—Triggered when the user begins to edit an item label. The edit can be prevented by returning a value of `1` from this event. The index of the item is available as an argument.
- `BeginRightDrag`—The user uses the right mouse button to start dragging. The index the user is attempting to drag is available as an event argument.
- `ColumnClick`—Triggered when the user clicks on a column. The column is passed as a parameter.
- `DeleteAllItems`—Triggered when all the items in the list are deleted.

- `DeleteItem`—Triggered when an item is deleted by the user using a PowerScript function.
- `EndLabelEdit`—The user has finished editing a label. You can return `1` to discard the change. The item index and the new label are available as parameters.
- `InsertItem`—Triggered when an item is added. The new index is available as a parameter.
- `ItemChanged`—Something in the item has changed. These are the available parameters to determine the change:
  - `Index`—The item that is changing
  - `FocusChange`—The focus state that is changing
  - `HasFocus`—The new focus state
  - `SelectionChange`—The item selection that is changing
  - `Selected`—The new selection state
  - `OtherChange`—Some other change that is affecting the item
- `ItemChanging`—Something in the item is in the process of changing. You can return `1` to prevent the change. The same parameters as the `ItemChanged` event are available.
- `RightClicked`—The control was right-clicked.
- `RightDoubleClicked`—The control was double-right-clicked.
- `Sort`—To define your own sort order for the items, you need to set the `SortType` property to `UserDefinedSort!` and then return the following return value for the two parameters:
  - `-1`—Index1 is less than Index2
  - `0`—Index1 is equal to Index2
  - `1`—Index1 is greater than Index2

Now that we have examined the properties and events that are available to use when developing a ListView control, let's explore the associated functions and how they interact with the events and properties.

Before we do that, the `ListViewItem` data type needs to be introduced. This structure is used to hold information on each item in the ListView control, and it has the following properties:

- `Data` (Any)—The data value you want to associate with the item.
- `CutHighLighted` (Boolean)—The item is highlighted and is the target of a cut operation.
- `DropHighLighted` (Boolean)—The item is highlighted and is the target of a drag and drop.
- `HasFocus` (Boolean)—The item currently has the focus.
- `Selected` (Boolean)—The item has been selected.

- `ItemX` (Integer)—The item's X coordinate in the ListView control.
- `ItemY` (Integer)—The item's Y coordinate in the ListView control.
- `OverlayPictureIndex` (Integer)—The index number of the picture in the overlaying image list.
- `PictureIndex` (Integer)—The index within the control's image list to use as the item's icon.
- `StatePictureIndex` (Integer)—The index in the control's state image list.
- `Label` (String)—The text label of the item.

Overlay pictures are pictures that appear over the top of the item's picture and are used to relay additional information about the status of the item.

These are the ListView-specific functions:

- `AddItem(` *`lviItem`*`)`—Adds an item of type `ListViewItem` to the ListView control. Returns the index at which the item was added.
- `AddItem(` *`szLabel`*`,` *`nPictureIndex`*`)`—This form of the function is used only to set the label and picture for the item. To specify more information, use the previous format. This function also returns the index at which the item was added.
- `Arrange()`—Arranges the icons in rows and is only effective in large icon and small icon views.
- `DeleteItem(` *`nIndex`*`)`—Deletes the item at the specified index. This function does *not* cause the other items to change index.
- `DeleteItems()`—Deletes all the items from a ListView control.
- `EditLabel(` *`nIndex`*`)`—Places the specified item to be placed in label edit mode. The ListView control also has a Boolean property, which enables all items to be editable. By setting this property to `FALSE` you can use the `EditLabel()` function to isolate certain labels for editing or editing at controlled points.
- `GetItem(` *`nIndex`*`,` *`nColumn`*`,` *`szValue`*`)`—This function is used when the ListView control is set to the Report view style. *`nColumn`* represents the report column index, and together with *`nIndex`* provide a cross-reference in the control to extract the value into *`szValue`*.
- `GetItem(` *`nIndex`*`,` *`lviItem`*`)`—This function retrieves a complete `ListViewItem` object into *`lviItem`* from the specified index in the control.
- `InsertItem(` *`nIndex`*`,` *`lviItem`*`)`—Allows you to specify a complete `ListViewItem` structure to be inserted at the index specified.
- `InsertItem(` *`nIndex`*`,` *`szLabel`*`,` *`nPictureIndex`*`)`—This allows you to just specify a label and picture for the item that you want to insert at the index specified.
- `SetItem(` *`nIndex`*`,` *`nColumn`*`,` *`szValue`*`)`—This function is used when the ListView control is set to the Report view style. *`nColumn`* represents the report column index,

and together with `nIndex` provides a cross-reference in the control to set the value to `szValue`.

- `SetItem( nIndex, lviItem)`—Sets the item at the index with the values from a `ListViewItem` structure.
- `FindItem( nIndex, Direction, bFocused, bSelected, bCutHighlighted, bDrophighlighted)`—This function searches for the next item that matches the criteria you specify using the four Boolean parameters. You can specify the direction of the search relative to the index by setting Direction to one of the following: `DirectionAll!`, `DirectionUp!`, `DirectionDown!`, `DirectionLeft!`, or `DirectionRight!`. The search criteria are the following: Does the item have focus (`bFocused`), is the item selected (`bSelected`), is the item the target of a cut operation (`bCutHighLighted`), and is the item the target of a drag-and-drop operation (`bDropHighlighted`). Like other PowerScript search functions, this one starts at the specified index plus 1, so to start from the beginning the index needs to be `0`.
- `FindItem( nIndex, szSearchLabel, bPartial, bWrap)`—Used to search for the next item that has the same label as `szSearchLabel`. `bPartial` allows the search to perform a partial match, and `bWrap` makes the index return to the first item after the function call. `nIndex` is the index to start searching after (remember to state `0` to include the first item in the search). The function returns the index of the item if one is found, and `-1` if an error occurs.
- `Sort( SortType)`—Sorts the items in the ListView control using an enumerated value of type `grSortType`: `Ascending!`, `Descending!`, `Unsorted!`, and `UserDefinedSort!`.
- `Sort( SortType, nColumn)`—When the ListView control is in report mode this function allows you to sort on a specific column.
- `AddLargePicture( szPicture)`, `AddSmallPicture( szPicture)`, `AddStatePicture( szPicture)`—These functions add the specified picture into the appropriate image list.
- `DeleteLargePicture( nIndex)`, `DeleteSmallPicture( nIndex)`, `DeleteStatePicture( nIndex)`—These functions delete the specified picture from the appropriate image list.
- `DeleteLargePictures()`, `DeleteSmallPictures()`, `DeleteStatePictures()`—These functions delete all the pictures from the appropriate image list.
- `SetOverLayPicture( nOverlayIndex, nImageIndex)`—This function is used to map an overlay picture to a large or small image list index. Instead of maintaining an additional image list, the overlays are mapped into the main image list of the control.
- `AddColumn( szLabel, Alignment, nWidth)`—Adds a new column with the specified label, alignment, and width.
- `DeleteColumn( nIndex)`—Deletes the column at the specified index.
- `DeleteColumns()`—Deletes all the columns.

- `GetColumn( nIndex, szLabel, Alignment, nWidth)`—Extracts information about the column at the specified index.
- `InsertColumn( nIndex, szLabel, Alignment, nWidth)`—Inserts a new column at the requested index, with the label, alignment, and width specified.
- `SetColumn( nIndex, szLabel, Alignment, nWidth)`—Sets the label, alignment, and width values for the specified column. This only displays during the Report view style for the control.
- `TotalColumns()`—Returns the number of columns in the control.
- `GetOrigin( nX, nY)`—Used to find the X and Y coordinates of the upper-left corner of the ListView item. The parameters *nX* and *nY* are used to receive the coordinates.
- `SelectedIndex()`—Returns the index of the selected item in the ListView control. If more than one item is currently selected, the function returns the index of the first item. Otherwise, it returns `-1` on an error or when there are no items selected.

NOTE

The `SelectedIndex()` function is only intended for controls allowing single selections, and you should write your own loop to individually check the `State` property of each item.

- `TotalItems()`—Returns the total number of items in the control.
- `TotalSelected()`—Returns the total number of selected items in the control.

The TreeView Control

The TreeView control (see Figure 11.19), also known as an outline control, along with the tab control, has been the focus of a number of third-party controls. Powersoft made use of it in Version 4.0 of PowerBuilder and now supplies it as part of the controls available in the development environment.

FIGURE 11.19.
The TreeView control.

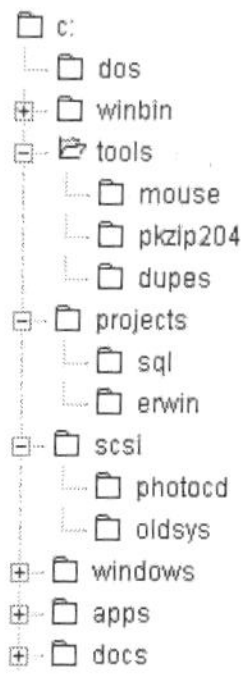

TreeView controls have some of the following functionality:

- Traversing data via tree nodes that can be expanded or collapsed.
- Graphical and textual node representation.
- Drag-and-drop manipulation.
- Node manipulation that includes cut, copy, and paste.

The TreeView control has a number of unique properties:

- `DeleteItems` (Boolean)—Allows items to be deleted from the list using the Del key.
- `DisableDragDrop` (Boolean)—Prevents items from being dragged.
- `EditLabels` (Boolean)—Allows the user to edit an item's text.
- `HasButtons` (Boolean)—Shows the +/- buttons next to parents.
- `HasLines` (Boolean)—Shows connecting lines between related items.
- `Indent` (Integer)—The number to indent child items (in PBUs).
- `LinesAtRoot` (Boolean)—Shows lines connecting all root items.
- `SortType` (grSortType)—The sort order for the list items. If `SortType` is `UserDefinedSort!`, the `Sort` event will be triggered.
- `PictureHeight` (Integer)—The height of the images. This property, together with the width, can only be set if there are no images currently in `PictureName[]`. If this value is `0` when the first image is added, the size of that image is used to set the height and width properties.
- `PictureWidth` (Integer)—The width of the images.
- `PictureMaskColor` (Long)—The masking color to use with non-system bitmaps.
- `PictureName[]` (String)—The images to be used at the nodes.
- `StatePictureHeight` (Integer)—The height of the state icons.
- `StatePictureWidth` (Integer)—The width of the state icons.
- `StatePictureMaskColor` (Long)—The masking color to use with non-system bitmaps.
- `StatePictureName[]` (String)—The images to be used for the state icons.

These are the events for a TreeView control:

- `BeginDrag`—The user uses the left mouse button to start dragging. The index the user is attempting to drag is available as an event argument.
- `BeginLabelEdit`—Triggered when the user begins to edit an item label. The edit can be prevented by returning `1`. The index of the item is available as an argument.
- `BeginRightDrag`—The user uses the right mouse button to start dragging. The index the user is attempting to drag is available as an event argument.
- `DeleteItem`—Triggered when an item is deleted either by a PowerScript function or a user action.

- `EndLabelEdit`—The user has finished editing a label. You can return `1` to discard the change. The item index and the new label are available as parameters.
- `ItemCollapsed`—A user has collapsed an item.
- `ItemCollapsing`—The user is attempting to collapse an item. You can return `1` to prevent the collapse from occurring or `0` to allow it to continue.
- `ItemExpanded`—The user expands an item.
- `ItemExpanding`—An item is expanding. If you need to populate the child items each time the item is expanded, this is the event to do it in. If no child items are created during either the `ItemPopulate` or this event, the item will not expand. You can prevent the item from expanding by returning `1`.
- `ItemPopulate`—Triggered the first time an item is expanded. This event or `ItemExpanding` should be used to populate the child items.
- `SelectionChanged`—The user has changed the currently selected item.
- `SelectionChanging`—The selection is changing between items. You can return `1` for this event to prevent the selection from changing.
- `Sort`—To define your own sort order for the items, you need to set the `SortType` property to `UserDefinedSort!`, and then return the following return value for the two parameters:
  - `-1`—Index1 < Index2
  - `0`—Index1 = Index2
  - `1`—Index1 > Index2

Now that we have examined the properties and events that are available to use when developing a TreeView control, let's explore the associated functions and how they interact with the events and properties.

Before we do that, the `TreeViewItem` data type needs to be introduced. This structure is used to hold information on each item in the TreeView control and has the following properties:

- `Data` (Any)—The data value you want to associate with the item.
- `Bold` (Boolean)—Whether the label text should be bold.
- `Children` (Boolean)—Whether the item has any child items.
- `CutHighLighted` (Boolean)—Whether the item is highlighted when it is part of a cut operation.
- `DropHighLighted` (Boolean)—Whether the item is highlighted when it is part of a drag-and-drop operation.
- `Expanded` (Boolean)—Whether the item is currently expanded. If the node has items below it that are visible this property is `TRUE`; otherwise, it is `FALSE`.
- `ExpandedOnce` (Boolean)—Whether the item has been expanded at least once during the current execution.

- `HasFocus` (Boolean)—Whether the item currently has the focus.
- `Selected` (Boolean)—Whether the item is currently selected.
- `Level` (Integer)—The level of the item within the hierarchy.
- `OverlayPictureIndex` (Integer)—The picture index from the overlay image list.
- `PictureIndex` (Integer)—The index within the controls image list to use as the items icon.
- `SelectedPictureIndex` (Integer)—The picture index to use to indicate that the item is selected.
- `StatePictureIndex` (Integer)—The picture index from the state image list.
- `ItemHandle` (Long)—A unique reference to the item.
- `Label` (String)—The text label of the item.

The following are functions for a TreeView control:

- `AddPicture( `*`szPictureName`*`)`—Adds the picture (icon, cursor, or bitmap) to the main image list.
- `AddStatePicture( `*`szPictureName`*`)`—Adds the picture to the state image list.
- `CollapseItem( `*`lHandle`*`)`—Collapses the item specified by the handle *`lHandle`*.
- `DeleteItem( `*`lHandle`*`)`—Deletes the item specified by the handle *`lHandle`*.
- `DeletePicture( `*`nIndex`*`)`—Deletes the picture from the main image list at the specified index.
- `DeletePictures()`—Deletes all the pictures from the main image list.
- `DeleteStatePicture( `*`nIndex`*`)`—Deletes the picture from the state image list at the specified index.
- `DeleteStatePictures()`—Deletes all the pictures from the state image list.
- `EditLabel( `*`lHandle`*`)`—Places the item specified by *`lHandle`* in edit mode.
- `ExpandAll( `*`lHandle`*`)`—Expands all the specified item's child items recursively.
- `ExpandItem( `*`lHandle`*`)`—Expands just the specified item to show its child items.
- `FindItem( treenavigation, `*`lHandle`*`)`—Finds a matching item using a navigation code that is of the enumerated type `TreeNavigation`: `ChildTreeItem!`, `CurrentTreeItem!`, `DropHighLightTreeItem!`, `FirstVisibleTreeItem!`, `NextTreeItem!`, `NextVisibleTreeItem!`, `ParentTreeItem!`, `PreviousTreeItem!`, or `PreviousVisibleTreeItem!`.
- `GetItem( `*`lHandle`*`, `*`tviItem`*`)`—Retrieves the data for the specified item into a `TreeViewItem` structure.
- `InsertItem( `*`lParentHandle`*`, `*`lAfterHandle`*`, [ `*`szLabel`*`, `*`nPictureIndex`*`] ¦ [`*`tviItem`*`])`—Inserts the specified item into the TreeView control after the item specified by *`lAfterHandle`*, and makes the item with *`lParentHAndle`* the parent. You can either specify the label and picture or a whole `TreeViewItem` structure for the item.

- `InsertItemFirst( lParentHandle, [ szLabel, nPictureIndex] ¦ [tviItem])`—Makes the specified item the first child of its parent. You can specify either a label and picture, or a complete item using the `TreeViewItem` structure. The function returns the handle of the item if it succeeds. If *`lParentHandle`* is `0`, the item is added at the root level.
- `InsertItemLast( lParentHandle, [ szLabel, nPictureIndex] ¦ [tviItem])`—Similar to `InsertItemFirst()` except that the item is added as the last child item to the parent.
- `InsertItemSort( lParentHandle, [ szLabel, nPictureIndex] ¦ [tviItem])`—Inserts an item as a child of a parent item in sorted order.
- `SelectItem( lHandle)`—Selects the specified item and makes it the current item.
- `SetDropHighLight( lHandle)`—Highlights the specified item as the drop target.
- `SetFirstVisible( lHandle)`—Sets the specified item to be the first visible item in the control.
- `SetItem( lHandle, tviItem)`—Sets the information for an item using the values from a `TreeViewItem` structure.
- `SetLevelPictures( nLevel, nPictureIndex, nSelectedPictureIndex, nStatePictureIndex, nOverlayPictureIndex)`—Sets the picture indexes used by all items at a specified level.
- `SetOverlayPicture( nOverlayIndex, nImageIndex)`—Maps an overlaying picture to a large or small image list index.
- `Sort( lHandle, grSortType)`—Sorts the children of the item specified by *`lHandle`*. *`grSortType`* specifies the sort method you want to use: `Ascending!` or `Descending!`. This function only sorts the immediate level beneath the specified item. If you want to sort multiple levels, you need to make use of the `SortAll()` function.
- `SortAll( lHandle, grSortType)`—Recursively sorts all the child items under the specified item using the *`grSortType`* method.

The Rich Text Edit Control

New in PowerBuilder 5

A rich text edit (RTE) control (see Figure 11.20) is an extension of the single- and multiline edit controls and supports font properties (type face, size, bold, italic, and so on), character and paragraph formatting (alignment, indents, and so on), and printing of its contents. In effect, it is a simple word processor.

You can control initial settings for the control using the Document tab page (see Figure 11.21) of the RichTextEdit property sheet.

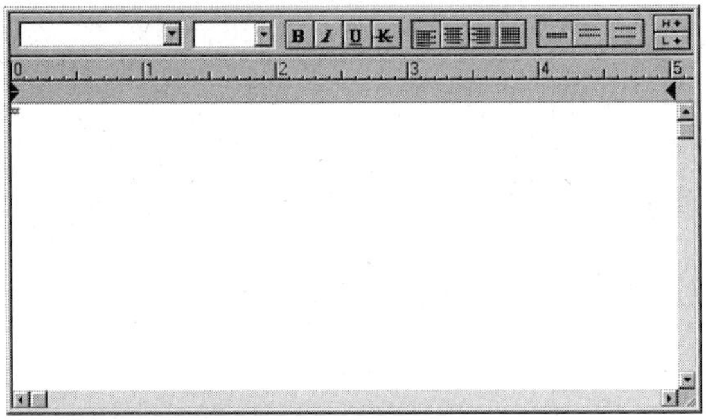

FIGURE 11.20.
A rich text edit control.

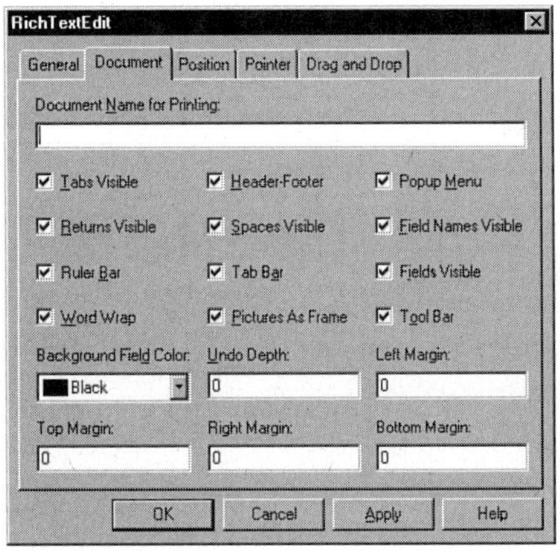

FIGURE 11.21.
The Document tab page.

The properties on the Document tab page can also be modified at runtime either by direct interaction by the user or programmatically by using PowerScript functions or direct property alterations. These are the properties specific to the rich text edit control:

- `HeaderFooter` (Boolean)—Whether the header and footer areas are displayed.
- `InputFieldNamesVisible` and `InputFieldsVisible` (Boolean)—For use when data is being supplied from a DataWindow. Control whether the user can see the data fields and names.
- `InputFieldBackColor` (Long)—Background color for input fields.
- `RulerBar`, `TabBar`, `ToolBar`, and `PopMenu` (Boolean)—Control whether certain features are visible to the user.
- `ReturnsVisible`, `SpacesVisible`, and `TabsVisible` (Boolean)—Determine whether the three types of nonvisible control characters are shown.
- `PicturesAsFrame` (Boolean)—Controls whether graphics are displayed as frames.
- `Modified` (Boolean)—Specifies whether the control has been edited since it was last saved. As soon as the first change is made, this property is set to `TRUE` and the `Modified` event is triggered.

- `Resizable` (Boolean)—Whether the RTE control itself can be resized.
- `WordWrap` (Boolean)—Whether text wraps automatically when the end of a line is reached.
- `BottomMargin`, `LeftMargin`, `RightMargin`, and `TopMargin` (Long)—Specify and control the positions of the margins for the document when printed.
- `UndoDepth` (Integer)—The maximum number of undoable operations.
- `DocumentName` (String)—The name that will display in the print queue when the control's contents are printed.

The rich text edit control also uses a number of specialized functions:

- `CopyRTF( {bSelected})`—Returns the text, pictures, and input fields from an RTE control. The *`bSelected`* argument determines whether only selected text is copied. The default is `TRUE` (only selected text); otherwise, the function copies all of the control's text. If there is no text currently selected, the function will return an empty string. See the `PasteRTF()` function for an example of `CopyRTF()`.
- `GetAlignment()`—Returns the alignment of the paragraph at the insertion cursor position.
- `GetSpacing()`—Returns the line spacing of the paragraph at the insertion cursor position.
- `GetTextColor()`—Returns the numeric value of the selected text's color.
- `GetTextStyle( tsStyle)`—Used to find out what styles are set within the selected text. You query the text by passing in different text styles. The function returns a Boolean value depending on whether the text has that style. For example, to determine if the currently selected text is bold and italic, the code would be this:

  ```
  Boolean bBoldItalic

  bBoldItalic = rte_1.GetTextStyle( Italic!)
  bBoldItalic = rte_1.GetTextStyle( Bold!) And bBoldItalic
  ```
- `InsertDocument( szFileName, bClear, {ftFileType})`—Used to either insert or replace text in the control with text from a file (either RTF or TXT). The *`bClear`* argument controls whether the text is inserted (`FALSE`) at the current insertion point or replaces the existing contents (`TRUE`). The optional argument *`ftFileType`* indicates what type of file is being opened: `FileTypeRichText!` or `FileTypeText!`. If you do not specify the type, PowerBuilder tries to determine the type from the file's extension, and defaults to trying to read it as rich text.
- `InsertPicture( szFileName)`—Places the picture specified into the RTF document at the current insertion point.
- `PageCount()`—Returns the total number of pages in the document for the control. If the control contains no text, it returns `1`. The number of pages in the control is determined by the amount of text and the layout specifications (margins, page size, and so on).

- `PasteRTF( szString {, Band})`—This function is used to paste rich text data into the control. The `Band` argument is used when the `RTF` string is being pasted into a rich text edit DataWindow and can be `Detail!`, `Header!`, or `Footer!` (Note that this style of DataWindow does not contain summary, trailer, group header, or group footer bands.) The return value of this function indicates the number of characters pasted upon success or `-1` if an error occurs.
- `Preview( bSetting)`—Toggles the display of the RTE control contents between print preview (`TRUE`) and edit view (`FALSE`). In preview mode the page is sized to fit within the control and also provides edit fields for the user to enter paper dimensions and margins. The user cannot directly modify the text, but you can affect the text using any of the control's functions. You should make sure that the RTE control is large enough to handle the preview mode's additional controls. You can use the `IsPreview()` function to see if the RTE control is in preview mode.
- `Print( nCopies, szPageRange, bCollate, bCancelDialog)`—Used to print the contents of an RTE control. You can specify the number of pages, the page range, whether to collate the copies, and if the print cancel dialog box should be displayed.

NOTE

If the RTE control is sharing data with a DataWindow, the total number of pages is the page count per row times the number of DataWindow rows.

You can control the page numbers printed by adding an input field to the footer or header, and then using the `InputFieldChangeData()` function in either the `PrintHeader` or `PrintFooter` events, you can set whatever value you want.

- `SaveDocument( szFileName {, FileType})`—Saves the contents of the control to a specified file in either RTF or ASCII text format. The format is either `FileTypeRichText!` (default) or `FileTypeText!` (or the filename extension is .TXT). If the file already exists, the RTE control's `FileExists` event is triggered.
- `SelectedColumn()` and `SelectedPage()`—The currently selected column and page number, respectively.
- `SelectText( lFromLine, lFromChar, lToLine, lToChar)`—Selects the text between two specified lines and two specified character positions. `lToChar` specifies the character before which the selection ends. The return of this function is the number of characters selected.
- `SelectTextAll()`—Selects all of the RTE control's contents. Returns the number of characters selected.
- `SelectTextLine()`—Selects the line containing the insertion point and returns the number of characters selected. If the control has a multiline text selection, the line

selected is the bottom line of the selection. This function does not select line-ending characters.

- `SelectTextWord()`—Selects the word containing the insertion point. If there is white space after the selection point, nothing is selected and the function returns `-1`.
- `SetAlignment( Alignment)`—For the selected paragraphs this function will set the alignment (`Left!`, `Right!`, `Center!`, or `Justify!`).
- `SetSpacing( Spacing)`—For the selected paragraphs or the paragraph at the current insertion point the line spacing can be changed to one of the values: `Spacing1!` (single spacing), `Spacing15!` (one and a half), or `Spacing2!` (double spacing).
- `SetTextColor( lColorNo)`—Sets the color of the selected text in the control.
- `SetTextStyle( bBold, bUnderLine, bSubScript, bSuperScript, bItalic, bStrikeThrough)`—Each of the Boolean arguments specifies the new text formatting for the selected text in the control. If you specify both subscript and superscript, the text will be subscripted.
- `ShowHeadFoot( bEditHeadFoot)`—Displays (`TRUE`) or hides (`FALSE`) the header and footer panels for editing. If the control is in preview mode and you call this function, the control will return to edit mode. You can use the `PrintHeader` and `PrintFooter` events to provide values for header and footer input fields (for page numbers and dates).
- DataSource`( DataStore ¦ DataWindow ¦ DataWindowChild)`—The document displayed in the rich text edit control can include input fields that are linked to either a data store, a DataWindow, or a DataWindow child. In this case, there is an instance of the document in the control for each row in the DataWindow. If the name of an input field matches that of a column in the DataWindow, it is filled with data from the current row.

PowerBuilder provides five additional functions for the RTE control that allow you to manipulate input fields:

- `InputFieldChangeData( szInputFieldName, szInputFieldValue)`—This function allows you to modify the data value of a specified input field.
- `InputFieldCurrentName()`—Returns the name of the input field that the insertion point is currently in. If the insertion point is not in an input field, an empty string is returned.
- `InputFieldDeleteCurrent()`—Deletes the input field that is currently selected. Even though input fields can share the same name (and therefore the same data), you can delete them independently of each other. If you delete all the fields for a given name, the control still retains the data value for future use. If other text is selected along with the input field, the deletion will fail.
- `InputFieldGetData( szInputFieldName)`—Gets the data from the requested input field and returns it as a string.

- `InputFieldInsert( szInputFieldName)`—Inserts a new input field with the name specified by *`szInputFieldName`* at the insertion point. If there is currently text selected, the function places the new field at the beginning of the selection.

You will use these functions to modify the information retrieved from the data source, either by adding new input fields that you populate from other controls or dynamically altering the input fields visible in the control.

The following rich text edit functions operate on or report information about an instance of the document: `LineCount()`, `PageCount()`, `InsertDocument()`, `SaveDocument()`, `SelectedPage()`, `SelectedStart()`, `SelectedLine()`, `SelectText()`, and `SelectTextAll()`. `Print()`is the only function that affects the collection of documents.

The following events are unique to rich text edit controls:

- `FileExists`—If you attempt to save the contents of the controls to file and that file already exists, this event is triggered. The filename of the file is available as an event parameter.
- `InputFieldSelected`—Triggered when the user selects an input field (using a double-click or pressing Enter in the field). The field name is available as an event parameter.
- `Modified`—Triggered when the first change is made to the contents of the control.
- `PictureSelected`—Triggered when the user double-clicks or presses Enter on a bitmap.
- `PrintFooter`—Triggered when each page's footer is about to be printed. The current page and row as well as the total number of pages are available as event parameters.
- `PrintHeader`—Triggered when each page's header is about to be printed. The same parameters as for `PrintFooter` are available.
- `RButtonDown`—Triggered when the right mouse button is pressed over the control and the pop-up menu option is disabled.

Tag Values

Each control on a window contains an attribute known as the tag value, `ObjectName.Tag`. The tag value is frequently used by developers to store an object description that is displayed in the MicroHelp area of an MDI frame by the `GetFocus` event. The tag value is set in the properties dialog box for an object. A number of developers have extended the use of the tag value from just containing a description to holding additional style information. This is usually the case when general-purpose objects have been built that can be told to act in different ways depending on certain settings.

Take, for example, a DataWindow user object called `u_dw`. There is a requirement to allow for either a single row to be selected, or in some cases multiple rows. Along with this behavior, you also wish to sometimes allow the DataWindow to be drag/drop enabled.

There are two solutions to this problem, and the choice between them is dependent on your programming philosophy, knowledge background, and ultimately how the object(s) will be used. The first involves setting up an inheritance chain, as shown in Figure 11.22.

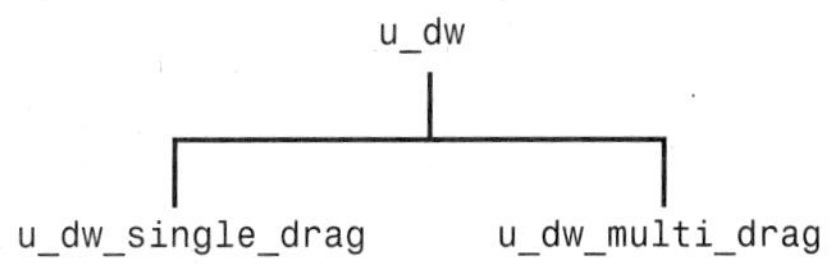

FIGURE 11.22.
A DataWindow inheritance solution.

As you can see from this diagram, we have had to duplicate code between the objects `u_dw_single_drag` and `u_dw_multi_drag` to incorporate the ability for drag and drop.

The second solution, often called the "Big Object" approach, is to place the functionality for single selects, multiselects, and drag/drop functionality in one object (in this case `u_dw`), and to then use switches to turn the appropriate behavior on and off. Obviously, this second approach allows complete encapsulation of the code.

For both of the approaches that use the object's tag value, you can use the following scripts to turn behavior on and off.

First, you need to define a tag value delimiter standard that you can use to separate the individual pieces of the tag. A good one is the back quote character (`). For example, here is a tag value that has a MicroHelp description, allows multirow selections, and can participate in drag/drop:

```
Enter customer information here'MULTISELECTABLE'DRAGGABLE'
```

In the object's `Constructor` event you would then code the following script to disassemble the tag string into the component parts:

```
Integer nCount, nTotalValues
String szValues[]

nTotalValues = f_tokenize_to_sz_array( this.Tag, '`', szValues)

For nCount = 1 To nTotalValues
   Choose Case szValues[ nCount]
      Case "SINGLESELECTABLE"
         i_bSingleSelectable = TRUE
      Case "MULTISELECTABLE"
         i_bMultiSelectable = TRUE
      Case "DRAGGABLE"
         i_bDraggable = TRUE
      Case Else
         // It is the MicroHelp description
         this.Tag = szValues[ nCount]
   End Choose
Next
```

You also have two choices with the MicroHelp value: You can either assign it to an object-level instance variable or assign it back to the `Tag` attribute, where most developers would expect to find it.

The function `f_tokenize_to_sz_array()` breaks the tag value into the respective tokens, and is shown in Listing 11.3.

Listing 11.3. The `f_tokenize_to_sz_array()` function.

```
Integer nCount = 0
String szMisc

Do
    szMisc = f_get_token( a_szToSearch, a_szDelimiters)
    If szMisc <> "" Then
       nCount = nCount + 1
       a_aszReturn[ nCount] = szMisc
    End If
Loop Until szMisc = ""

Return nCount
```

This function takes three parameters: `a_szToSearch`, `a_szDelimiters`, and `a_szReturn`. All three are strings, with the last being declared as a string array passed by reference. The function returns the number of values that were stored in the string array `a_szReturn`.

The `f_get_token()` function called by `f_tokenize_to_sz_array()` is as straightforward, and is shown in Listing 11.4.

Listing 11.4. The `f_get_token()` function.

```
Integer nPosition
String  szReturn

nPosition = Pos( a_szSource, a_szSeparator)

If nPosition = 0 Then                                 // if no separator,
   szReturn = a_szSource                              // return whole source string
   szSource = ""                                      // and original as 0 length
Else
   szReturn = Mid( a_szSource, 1, nPosition - 1) // o/w, return just the token
   szSource = Right( a_szSource, Len( a_szSource) - nPosition)  // strip it and
                                                                // separator
End If

Return szReturn
```

This function takes two string parameters—`a_szSource` and `a_szSeparator`—and returns a string that is the value found within `a_szSource`. The `a_szSource` parameter is passed by reference and is updated to contain only the remaining part of the string after the value and separator have been removed.

Using these methods you can make extensive use of the tag value for many purposes.

Window Manipulation Techniques

You can use a number of tricks and techniques to manipulate or control your windows. Some have been introduced in other areas of this chapter, and in the following sections you will see how to control windows with no title bar and automatic scrollbars, and how to repaint windows correctly.

Moving a Window Without a Title Bar

You may require a window in your application to not have a title bar (for example, some form of menu or pop-up window). This of course means that you will be unable to move it around the screen by the normal method of picking it up and dragging it. To allow the user to move this kind of window around, you need to use the following script.

In the event code for `MouseDown` you need to send the window a message, `WM_SYSCOMMAND (274)`, with `WordParm` set to `SC_MOVE + 1 (61457)`. This is done with the following one line of code:

```
Send( Handle(this), 274, 61458, 0)
```

This informs the window that the mouse is being moved on to move itself along with it.

Scrolling Within Sheets

You may have already noticed that when a DataWindow is dynamically resized within a window at runtime, it automatically turns vertical and horizontal scrollbars on as they are required, provided of course that you have set those particular style attributes. You might further have observed that MDI sheets do not exhibit the same behavior, but it would be great if they would. Well, using two API calls and a little creativity, you can get your sheets to act as they should.

These are two API function declarations:

```
Subroutine GetScrollRange( uint hWnd, int nScrollBarFlag, ref int nMin, &
                                      ref int nMax) Library "user32.dll"
Function int GetScrollPos( uint hWnd, int nScrollBarFlag) Library "user32.dll"
```

These will be used to find the range that a scrollbar is operating over and find the exact position in that range where the scroll box (thumb) is located. This little bit of API "magic" is required in case the user has scrolled the region of a window before resizing it back to an area that can fully display the window's controls.

We will also be using two window instance variables and a few constants for the API calls. These are defined as the following:

```
Integer i_nMinWidth, i_nMinHeight

// CONSTANTS:
Constant Integer SB_HORZ = 0
Constant Integer SB_VERT = 1
Constant Integer SB_TOP = 6
Constant Integer WM_HSCROLL = 276
Constant Integer WM_VSCROLL = 277
Constant Long SC_MINIMIZE = 61472
```

These two instance variables are set in the `Open` event of the window, and set the minimum allowable width and height of the window before scrollbars are required. The code for this is

```
i_nMinWidth = this.Width
i_nMinHeight = this.Height
```

The actual code is split between two functions, with the majority of it in the `Resize` event. This event is triggered once the user has resized the window, whether it is using the window edges or control options (such as minimize). At this point, we need to check the new window width and height against the minimum values we have previously set.

If the width is below the minimum allowed value and the relevant scrollbar is not already showing, we turn the scrollbar attribute on. Note the first `If` statement, which traps when the user minimizes the window (in this case we do not want to carry out any processing). In fact, the scrollbars have already been turned off in the `SysCommand` event, which you will see a little later.

The code for the `Resize` event is

```
UInt hWnd
Integer nScrollPos, nMinPos, nMaxPos

If this.WindowState = Minimized! Then
   Return
End If

this.SetRedraw( FALSE)

// Store the window handle so we don't have to keep calling Handle()
hWnd = Handle( this)

// Is the current window width less than the allowable width?
If this.Width < i_nMinWidth Then
   // Turn on the horizontal scrollbar
   this.HScrollBar = TRUE
// Is the horizontal scroll bar currently on?
ElseIf this.HScrollBar Then
   // Get the current position of the thumb within the scrollbar
   nScrollPos = GetScrollPos(hWnd, SB_HORZ)

   // Get the range of the scroll bar
   GetScrollRange(hWnd, SB_HORZ, nMinPos, nMaxPos)
```

```
    // Has the user scrolled the window horizontally?
    If nScrollPos > nMinPos Then
       // Tell the window to scroll back to the far left edge
       Post( hWnd, WM_HSCROLL, SB_TOP, 0)
    End If
    // Turn the scroll bar off
    this.HScrollBar = FALSE
 End If

 // Is the current window height less than the allowable height?
 If this.Height < i_nMinHeight Then
    // Turn on the vertical scroll bar
    this.VScrollBar = TRUE
 // Is the vertical scrollbar currently on?
 ElseIf this.VScrollBar Then
    // Get the current position of the thumb within the scrollbar
    nScrollPos = GetScrollPos(hWnd, SB_VERT)

    // Get the range of the scroll bar
    GetScrollRange(hWnd, SB_VERT, nMinPos, nMaxPos)

    // Has the user scrolled the window vertically?
    If nScrollPos > nMinPos Then
       // Tell the window to scroll back to the top edge
       Post( hWnd, WM_VSCROLL, SB_TOP, 0)
    End If
    // Turn the scroll bar off
    this.VScrollBar = FALSE
 End If

 this.Post Function SetRedraw( TRUE)
```

As mentioned earlier, you need to trap the point at which the user minimizes the window and turn off the scrollbars. This is done in a user event `SysCommand`, which is mapped to `pbm_syscommand`. The code is

```
If Message.WordParm = SC_MINIMIZE Then
   this.VScrollBar = FALSE
   this.HScrollBar = FALSE
   Return
End If
```

With these two simple scripts you can provide some missing functionality to your MDI sheet windows.

Painting Problems

Whenever you resize a control or a window, you should turn off the screen redraw for the appropriate object. This is done using the `SetRedraw()` function. Passing a `FALSE` value as an argument turns the screen paint off for the object, and `TRUE` causes the object to be immediately painted and repainted every time a change is made.

The `Control[]` array property of a window holds references to the controls defined in the window, and it is also used to process the order of the screen paints. If you leave the redraw on for a window, you can sometimes see the controls as they paint on the window. The order of the painting can be altered by sending controls to the background. This change in the Z-order (front-to-back ordering) of the control also corresponds to a movement within the `Control[]` array.

If you have problems with controls flickering or leaving odd pieces of graphics on the window, check how you have the screen painting set up during the operation. It will also make an operation, especially successive visual changes, much faster because the operating system only has to draw the screen one time (when you have finished) instead of with each change.

For example, if you need to change the size or position of a window's controls when the window is resized, you'd use this script in the `Resize` event:

```
this.SetRedraw( FALSE)
//
// Call an application level function that broadcasts the message
// to each control on the window.
g_App.BroadCast( "ParentResize")
//
this.SetRedraw( TRUE)
```

Object Orientation in Windows

This section shows how windows conform to the big three object-oriented terms: encapsulation, inheritance, and polymorphism.

Encapsulation

Windows are naturally encapsulated. They contain the controls and objects to achieve their processing purposes. Windows and its controls encapsulate their functionality within the scripts that you write for events and window-level functions. Window instance variables and functions can be made as accessible or inaccessible as you want using the protection statements introduced in Chapter 6.

Inheritance

Inheritance of a window makes the ancestor controls, events, and public or protected instance variables and functions available to a descendant. You can inherit from a previously constructed window by selecting the Inherit button in the Select Window dialog box.

An ancestor window can have an unlimited number of descendants, but a descendant window can have only one ancestor; this is called *single inheritance*. PowerBuilder provides the Object Browser to view the ancestor and descendant windows in your application in a hierarchical display (you need to have Show Hierarchy turned on; otherwise, you will get an alphabetical list of the objects).

Descendant windows can be modified to fit specific functional requirements, and the attributes of the inherited controls can be overridden. Additional controls can be added to descendants, but you cannot remove ancestor controls from the descendant. You can only hide unwanted controls from view (set the `Visible` attribute to `FALSE`). The control is still created and takes up resources, which is an important reason you should set up an efficient inheritance structure.

Changes you make to inherited controls do not have to be permanent. You can always reset the inherited properties by selecting Reset Attributes from the Edit menu. This resets the attributes of the selected object to be those defined in the ancestor.

After making any modifications to an ancestor, it is a good idea to regenerate the descendants in case the modifications adversely affect a descendent.

Polymorphism

Polymorphism is the ability of different objects to react to the same request, usually in different ways. Requests are made on windows using functions or events. Which mechanism you use depends on whether you want loose or tight coupling. Loose coupling uses non-parameterized events and allows the window to respond to the request if it has an event that is declared for it. If no event is defined, no error is generated. For tight coupling you use window-level functions or parameterized events, and these must exist for the call to be made.

Summary

This chapter shows you the available window types and styles, as well as some techniques for using each type. The properties and events covered should help you determine which type of window best matches the functionality you wish to provide in your user interface. The new controls for PowerBuilder 5.0 and their uses are introduced, along with their functions and events. The techniques learned for controlling and manipulating windows combined with the new controls will allow you to provide strong user interfaces for the end user.

Menus and the Menu Painter

IN THIS CHAPTER

A *menu* provides a list of choices or actions that the user can choose from to initiate an action. In this chapter you'll learn about the Menu painter and the benefits and problems of using menus in an application. A menu can be used in both multiple-document interface (MDI) and single-document interface (SDI) applications.

Menu Basics

Several concepts, warnings, and terms need to be introduced before you can fully understand the description of the actual Menu painter.

Menu Types

There are three types of menus. The first type is a *drop-down menu* (see Figure 12.1); this is a menu on a menu bar.

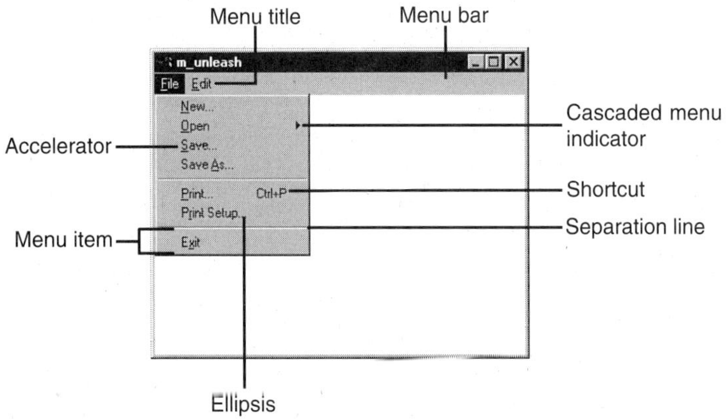

FIGURE 12.1.
A drop-down menu.

Drop-down menus are represented by a menu title in the menu bar of a window, which can be accessed either by clicking the title with the mouse or by pressing Alt and the underlined character in the title.

The second type is a *pop-up menu* (see Figure 12.2), which appears in relation to an object and is also known as a *contextual menu.*

The pop-up menu usually appears at the mouse pointer position and is invoked when the user performs an action, which is usually clicking the right mouse button. The menu contains context-sensitive options relating to the object that it was invoked on and provides an efficient means to access methods associated with an object. The menu should be kept short, and there should not be multiple cascading levels.

The third type, the *cascading menu* (see Figure 12.3), can appear on either of the two preceding types of menus.

FIGURE 12.2.
A pop-up menu.

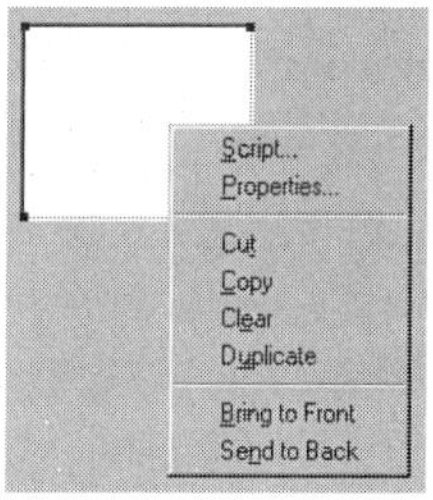

FIGURE 12.3.
A cascading menu.

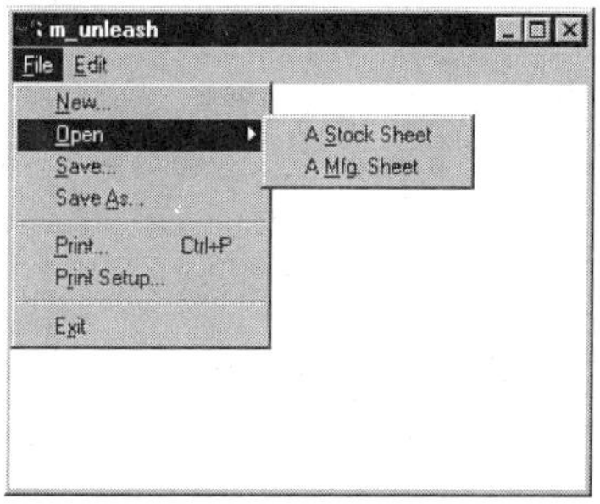

Cascading menus are indicated by a right-pointing arrow on the parent menu item and are accessed by the user selecting this menu item. A cascading menu is used when you group similar actions together under a heading (for example, the Align Objects menu in the Window painter). Cascading menus enable you to simplify your top-level menus and hide a multitude of options in the submenus. You should try to keep the level of cascades to no more than two so that the user can see all the options simply by selecting a top-level menu item; otherwise, menus become difficult to navigate.

Menu Items

The menu items of a menu usually describe an action or command that is executed when selected, but they can also include open window names or changeable options.

You might have heard the terms *accelerator* and *shortcut key*, and many novice developers confuse the two.

An *accelerator key* is signified by the underline that appears beneath a letter in a menu item, or even some controls. You select the item by pressing the Alt key (which activates the menu bar) and the character that is underlined. These can be accessed only if the item is visible.

A *shortcut key* is always accessible when the window is in focus, no matter where the associated menu item resides in the menu structure. The shortcut key for a menu item appears to the right of the menu item. For example, Ctrl+P is usually used for printing. Shortcut keys directly access the menu item and are used for common actions.

NOTE

The particular keystrokes for an action are determined by the operating system that the application is being written for, and you should examine the design guide for that system. You can also examine existing commercial applications to see what hotkeys they use.

If the menu item causes a dialog box to be opened, the convention is to use an ellipsis (...) following the item text. This provides a visual cue that the action described will not immediately happen, and the user has the chance to either modify the behavior or cancel the operation.

As mentioned previously, some menu items indicate settable options for the application, such as the visibility of a ruler in a word processor. There is no standard for indicating that a menu item is an option as opposed to an action, unless it is currently selected, in which case a checkmark appears to the left of the menu item text.

Most options are logically grouped under a particular menu title. You can provide further subdivisions by using separation lines. These are lines that appear horizontally in the menu.

Menu Conventions and Guidelines

When you add a menu to a window, you must remember that you have just lost some of your screen real estate, and when you add a toolbar (or two), you have lost even more. You must bear this in mind when you are creating your application windows and allow sufficient space for menus and toolbars to be accommodated. If you do not, controls will start to disappear off the bottom of the window.

Try to limit the number of items you place in a cascading menu so you don't overwhelm a user with a multitude of options.

As mentioned earlier, you should try to keep the number of cascading menus to only one level, or at most two.

You should disable (gray out) a menu item or even a menu title if the user should not have access to it. For example, you could disable the Save menu item until a change has actually been made.

The descriptions of menu titles and items should be kept short and descriptive. Try for just a couple words—four being a maximum—while still fully describing the item. Remember to include the ellipsis (...) if the option opens a dialog box.

Developers of Windows-based systems should purchase *The Windows Interface—An Application Design Guide*, a book published by Microsoft Press, which you can use to reference the standard names, positions, and construction of menus. Try to follow these guidelines as much as possible. If you cannot get this book, you should explore other commercial Windows applications, such as Microsoft Word or Excel, and examine their menu structures. This also applies to other development environments: You should work with an accepted design guide or adopt another widely used application as your template.

If you are going to use a menu item that toggles between one state and another, you should use a checkmark next to the item and also set the associated toolbar button to the appropriate up or down state. A checkmark and a button in the down state signify that the option is in effect.

NOTE

You should avoid changing the text of menu items at runtime because it can be very confusing to an end user.

You should make sure each menu item can be reached by the keyboard by using either accelerator or shortcut keys. Some people, especially in data entry applications, hate to move their hands away from the keyboard to grab a mouse just to access a menu. You should make any keypresses unique and consistent within the application, and you should use the accepted standards of the operating system being used.

Use the MDI frame toolbar to display the most common menu items for quick user access.

The Menu Painter

You open the Menu painter by clicking the menu button in the PowerBar or PowerPanel. This opens the Select Menu dialog box (see Figure 12.4), which enables you to open an existing menu, create a new one, or inherit from an existing menu object.

FIGURE 12.4.
The Select Menu dialog box.

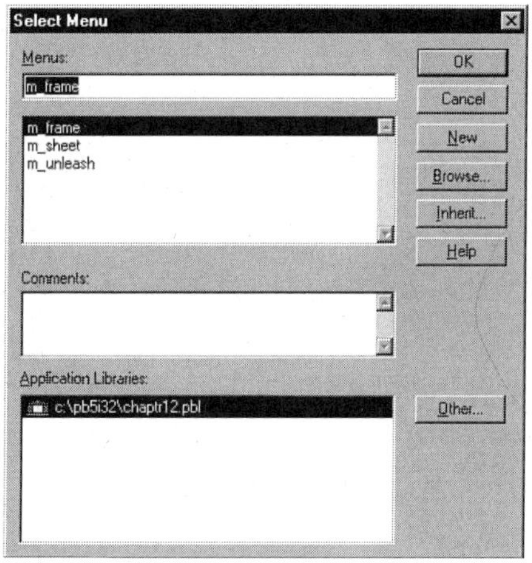

After you close the Select Menu dialog box, the actual Menu painter workspace is accessible (see Figure 12.5).

FIGURE 12.5.
The Menu painter workspace.

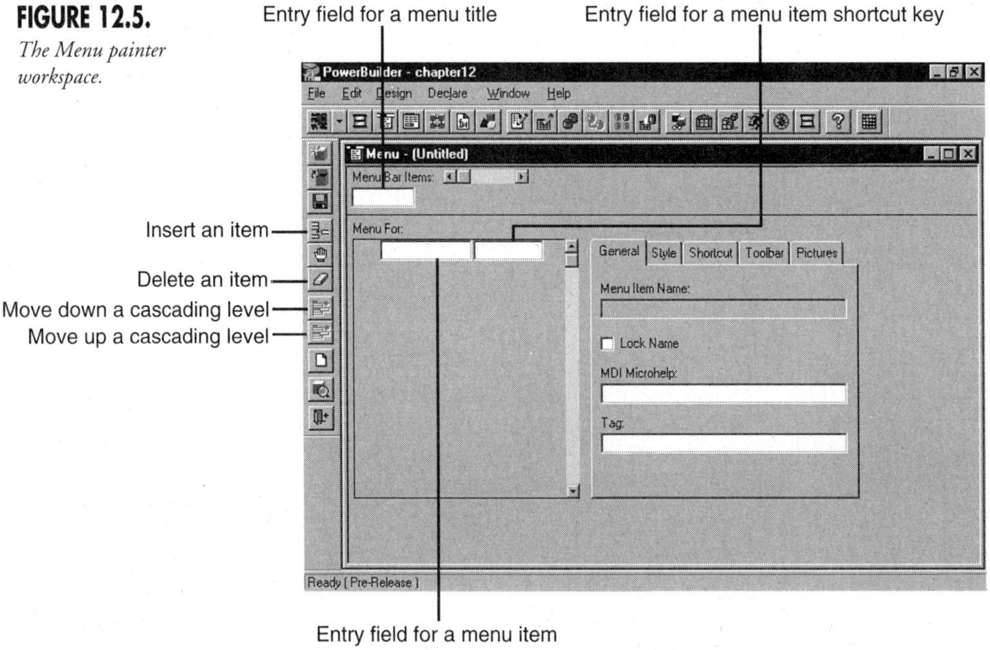

The topmost edit field is where you enter menu titles, and after you have typed the text into the field you can create a new title to the immediate right. If you enter a significant number of menu titles, or if you are running at a low resolution, you will have to use the horizontal scrollbar above the menu title line to scroll backward and forward.

As you enter the text for each menu title, it is named by PowerBuilder; you can see the assigned name in the Menu Item Name box on the right side of the window. If you come back to the menu item and alter the text, the object's name also changes. This is obviously undesirable when the menu is in use by an application; you need to turn on the Lock Name option (the check box below the Menu Item Name field) to retain the original name.

NOTE

PowerBuilder turns on the Lock Name option any time you return to an already entered menu item. All new menu items are entered with the Lock Name option off. If you turn the option off, this state exists only for the duration of your edit on the menu item and is reset as soon as you change focus to another menu item.

The menu items for the drop-down part of the menu are entered in the scrolling area on the left of the window. Each line is split into two fields; the first is for the menu item text and the second is for the assigned shortcut key. As with the menu titles, after you have entered a menu item line, a new line is made available below it for you to continue the menu (see Figure 12.6).

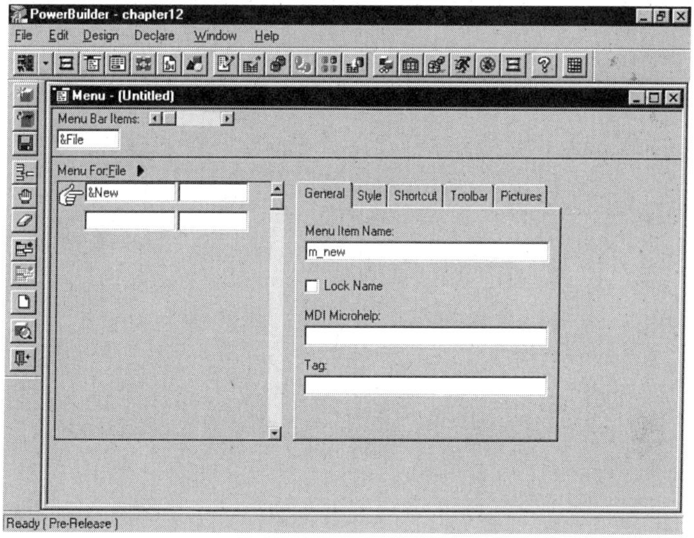

FIGURE 12.6.
A menu title and menu item.

You can change the order of menu titles and menu items by using the yellow hand button in the PainterBar. Then when you click a field, the mouse pointer turns into a big white hand and you can drag the item to the location in the menu layout where you want it to appear.

> **NOTE**
>
> You cannot drag a menu item into the menu title area or vice versa. You also cannot directly move a menu item in a descendant menu; you'll read more on that in the "Menu Inheritance" section later in this chapter. Attempting to drag a menu item past the top of the menu results in different behavior in Version 5.0; the menu item is moved to the bottom of the menu rather than to the top, as it was in previous versions.

You can insert menu titles and menu items before the current area by using the Insert Item button on the PainterBar. You also can remove items by using the Delete Item button.

As you might have noticed in Figure 12.6, you assign the accelerator for a menu item the same way you do for window controls: by using the ampersand character (`&`). The shortcut key for a menu item is assigned by using the controls in the bottom-left group box. You can assign the key and whether it is associated with the Ctrl, Alt, and/or Shift keys. These options are not available for menu titles.

To create separator lines in PowerBuilder menus, you enter a single minus sign (-) as the item's text (see Figure 12.7).

FIGURE 12.7.
The separator item has the hand pointer pointing to it.

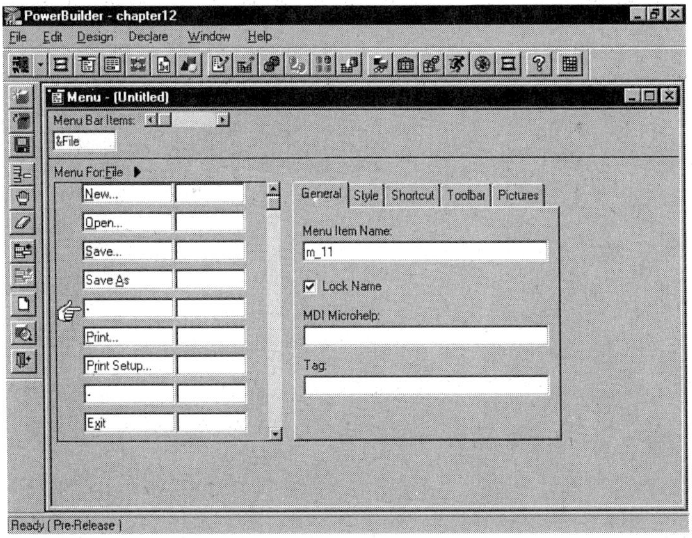

As you can see in Figure 12.7, the name PowerBuilder constructs is `m_-`. Because this name clashes every time you create a new separator line, you should number separator lines in increments of 10 so that you can insert new separator lines as required.

WARNING

One of the options that many developers turn off when they have been using PowerBuilder for a while is Dashes in Identifiers. This enables you to use the dash (-) in variable and object names and is quite a confusing option if you actually do name objects with it. Inside the Menu painter, PowerBuilder quite happily generates names with dashes in them, and even enables you to do the same. However, when you try to save the object, you get an error detailing some `Forward Declarations`. This is because the dash option has been turned off and the menu contains dashes. The same error appears when you're migrating menus between versions of PowerBuilder. A useful naming scheme is to number each separator with numbers, the first being the menu title index, and the second some unique number within that index. For example, in the example above the separator would be named `m_11`.

NEW in PowerBuilder 5

The `Enabled` and `Visible` attributes for each menu title and menu item, in addition to the `Checked` attribute for menu items, are accessible on the Style tab (see Figure 12.8). The other options in this area are dealt with in the "Menu Inheritance" section in this chapter. The Type option is used when developing cross-platform applications, and informs PowerBuilder to make the necessary changes for Exit and About menu items for the operating system in which the menu is running.

FIGURE 12.8.
The Style tab.

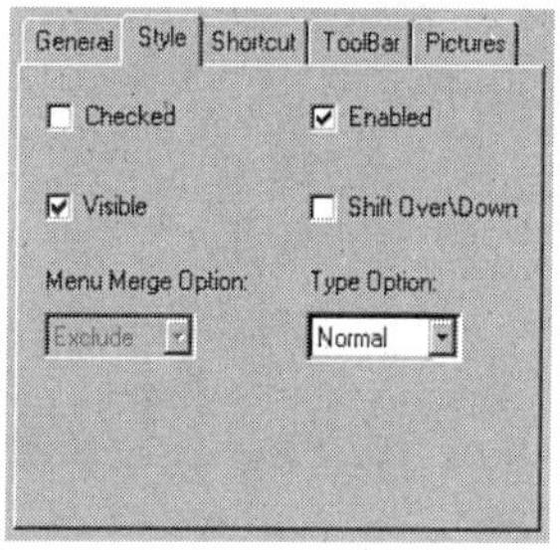

If you want to turn a menu item into a submenu title with its own cascading menu, you use the Down a Cascading Level button in the PainterBar. This places you either in a new area for defining menu items or in the menu items you have already defined.

WARNING

If you delete a submenu title, you are not warned that there are menu items existing in the cascading menu, and everything is removed.

It is not very obvious that a cascading menu exists under a menu item because the only indicator is a small black triangle on the far right of the menu item area, which can be easily overlooked by novices. When you go down a level, the text area directly above the menu items changes to show the path taken to get to the current level (see Figure 12.9).

You can traverse between levels of a cascading menu by using the Down and Up Cascading Level buttons in the PainterBar or by double-clicking the little black triangle (which only takes you down a level).

You can assign a MicroHelp value for each piece of the menu. PowerBuilder uses this value to automatically display in an MDI frame's MicroHelp area (if available) as the user traverses the menu. You enter the value in the MDI MicroHelp edit field, and you are permitted to enter quite long descriptions. This saves you from having to write scripts to carry out the same functionality.

Each menu item can have a corresponding toolbar icon that is displayed when you create an MDI application. To access these properties select the Toolbar tab (see Figure 12.10).

FIGURE 12.9.
A cascaded menu.

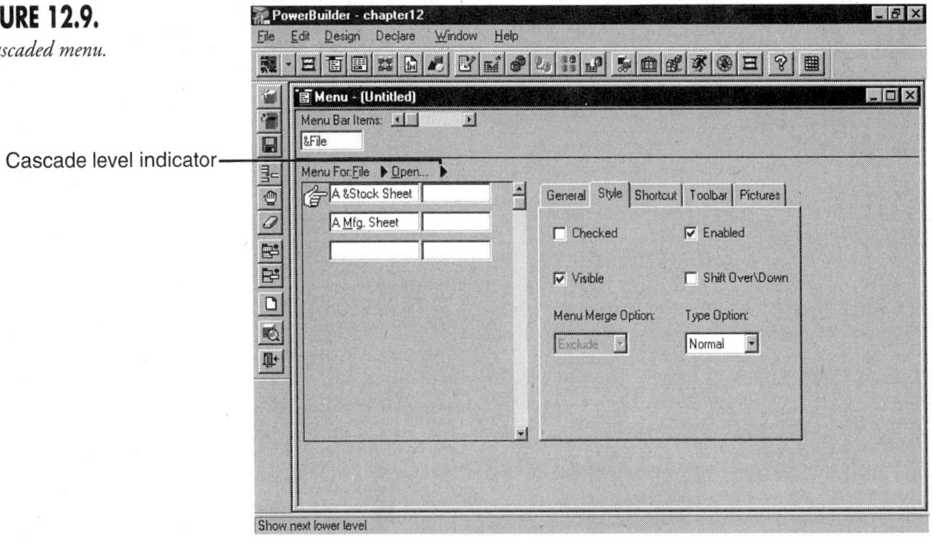

FIGURE 12.10.
The Toolbar tab.

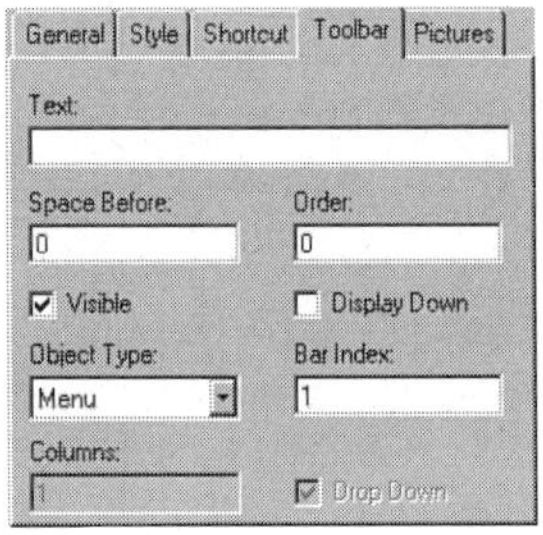

In the Toolbar tab you can specify the text displayed when the Show Text option is on or with PowerTips, the positioning of the button on the toolbar, and drop-down toolbar properties.

The Text box enables you to specify the text that displays on the toolbar button and also the text that appears in the PowerTip. Button text is displayed when the `ToolbarText` attribute of the application object is `TRUE`, and PowerTips are displayed only when this attribute is `FALSE`. You specify the two pieces of text with a comma-separated string, such as `Button Text, PowerTip Text`. If you specify only one piece of text, it is used for both the button and the PowerTip.

> **NOTE**
>
> You should limit the actual button text to no more than eight or nine characters. The PowerTip text, however, can be quite extensive.

To separate a toolbar button from the preceding button, you need to enter an integer value into the Space Before box. This is done to logically group related buttons together. The usual value is `1`, and the default (no spacing) is `0`. This attribute is ignored when the toolbar is set to display button text.

If, for some reason, you need to change the order of the buttons on the toolbar, you can use the Order box to set an ordering value. This defaults to `0`, and the buttons are displayed in menu order.

NOTE

Remember that PowerBuilder defaults menu item orders to `0`, so you might have to set all the Order values for menu items to get the desired result. Otherwise, all of the `0` Order value menu items appear first, and then the menu items with Order values greater than `0`. Number each item in increments (`5`, `10`) to give you more flexibility in changing the order or adding new options.

NEW 5 in PowerBuilder

New to this version of PowerBuilder is the ability to provide drop-down toolbar items (see Figure 12.11). This allows you to make your toolbars shorter so that they can be more easily used and are easier to dock (see the "Toolbars and PowerTips" section). You can provide drop-down toolbar items for menu titles such that all of their subordinate menu item toolbar entries appear underneath the parent's drop-down. You can specify the number of columns that the drop-down should use when displaying the toolbar pictures by entering a value in the Column field.

NOTE

The Bar Index option allows you to open multiple toolbars for the one menu. Each toolbar is independent of the other. You can control which toolbar a menu item appears in by setting this value.

NOTE

You must specify the drop-down toolbar items within a level of menu inheritance. You cannot extend a drop-down toolbar from within an inherited menu. Any that you specify within the child menu become their own drop-down toolbars.

In the Pictures tab you can specify the pictures displayed on the toolbar and when the button is pressed down.

FIGURE 12.11.
Drop-down toolbar items.

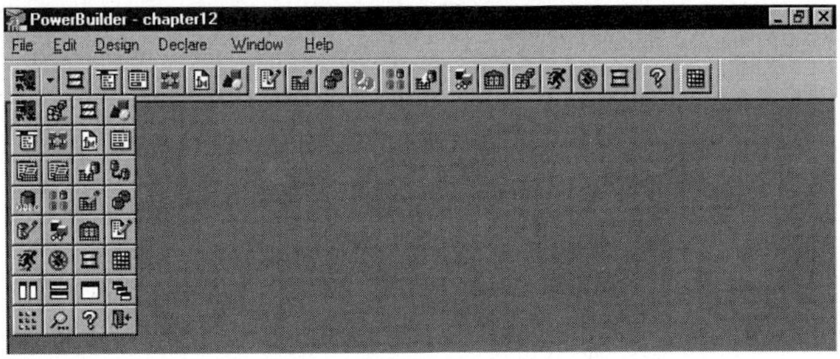

You can either enter the filename and path of the graphics file (in BMP, RLE, or WMF file formats) to be used for the button and down pictures or use the appropriate button to bring up a file dialog box. The stock pictures that come with PowerBuilder are also accessible in this tab. The Picture attribute is used in the button's normal state, and the Down Picture is used when the button is clicked. If you want the Down Picture to remain when the user releases the mouse button, click the Display Down check box. When the button is in the down state, you must use code to alter the `ToolbarItemDown` attribute of the menu item to set it back to the normal picture. The value `FALSE` resets the button. You use this functionality with menu items that can be checked and unchecked.

NOTE

The picture file should be 16 pixels wide by 15 pixels high. Otherwise, PowerBuilder compresses or expands the picture, and you get some ugly results.

When you have finished constructing your menu, or even during construction, you can see what the finished menu will look like by selecting Preview from the Design menu or by pressing Ctrl+Shift+P. This opens the design preview window and enables you to traverse the menu structure. No PowerScript that you have written will be executed.

NOTE

Any drop-down toolbars that you have specified will not be displayed, and all pictures appear contiguously across the toolbar.

The only step left when you have finished the menu and saved it is to attach it to a window—unless you are dynamically using the menu for creating pop-up menus.

Menu-Specific PowerScript

Several functions, attributes, and events specific to menus are covered in this section.

Opening a Pop-up Menu

Now that you can create a menu, two things can be done with the object. The menu can be attached to a window, in which case it becomes a drop-down menu and is created and destroyed by PowerBuilder. The menu can also be used as a pop-up menu for which you have control and responsibility. Pop-up menus can also be opened for menu items that exist in the window's current menu.

To create a menu at a certain location, you use the `PopMenu()` function. The syntax is

```
MenuItem.PopMenu( XLocation, Ylocation)
```

The *MenuItem* argument is a fully qualified name of the desired menu title for the menu and is created at the coordinates (in PowerBuilder units) indicated by the *Xlocation* and *Ylocation* arguments (from the left and top of the window, respectively). Be careful, because these coordinates are relative to the currently active window. Remember that MDI sheets are not active—only the frame is.

If the menu is not already open and attached to a window, you must declare and instantiate a variable of the correct menu type before calling the `PopMenu()` function.

> **NOTE**
>
> If for some reason the menu title you are going to use for a pop-up is not visible, you must make it visible before it can be displayed as a pop-up.

To illustrate the points made earlier, let's explore some examples.

The first example opens a pop-up menu of a menu title that already exists as part of a window. The two functions that return the current coordinates of the mouse pointer are used to open the pop-up menu at the mouse's position:

```
m_sheet.m_file.PopMenu( PointerX(), PointerY())
```

The second example opens the same menu that is not currently attached to any of the open windows:

```
m_sheet mPopUp

mPopUp = Create m_sheet
mPopUp.m_file.PopMenu( PointerX(), PointerY())
```

However, if you are opening the pop-up menu in an MDI sheet, you need to prefix both `PointerX()` and `PointerY()` with the name of the MDI frame window:

```
mPopUp.m_file.PopMenu( w_frame.PointerX(), w_frame.PointerY())
```

When the user has made a selection, the menu action is carried out and the pop-up menu is destroyed by PowerBuilder.

NOTE

Remember that both `PointerX()` and `PointerY()` return the coordinates from the upper left of the object that you prefix the functions with, and *not* from the window corner.

Menu Attributes

As mentioned in the description of menu items, you can provide items that can be checked and unchecked. This is an attribute of a menu item; it can be accessed either directly by using the dot notation (`.Checked`) or by using the `Check()` and `UnCheck()` functions. You cannot check a menu title.

PowerBuilder does not automatically handle turning the checkmark on and off. You must place the following line of code in the `Clicked` event:

```
this.Checked = Not this.Checked
```

Like other controls, a menu item (and even a menu title) can be disabled and enabled at runtime. As before, PowerBuilder provides two ways to alter the state: using the dot notation (`.Enabled`) and using the `Enable()` and `Disable()` functions.

The `ParentWindow` Pronoun

Often you need to refer to the window that owns the menu in which you are coding. This special relationship can be written using the `ParentWindow` pronoun. For example, to code the exit menu item, the code would be

```
Close( ParentWindow)
```

The `ParentWindow` pronoun, however, points only to an object of type window, and you cannot make specific references to controls or other developer-defined attributes of the menu's parent window.

Menu Events

Menu items have only two events: `Clicked` and `Selected`.

The `Clicked` event occurs when the user clicks a menu item and releases the mouse button.

The `Selected` event occurs when the user is browsing through the menu and is on the current menu item but has yet to trigger the `Clicked` event. This event is very rarely used but is provided if you want to code some specific functionality into your application.

By placing code in the `Clicked` event of a menu title, you can dynamically enable and disable the menu items in the cascading menu every time a user selects it. You can provide dynamic security based on application parameters or transaction object settings, or more usually a cascading menu that is sensitive to the current state of the window it is associated with. For example, you want to enable an MDI frame menu Save option only if the current sheet has been modified. The sheet maintains an instance variable `i_bModified` for this purpose. The code in the `Clicked` event of the File menu title would then be

```
w_sheet wInstance

wInstance = ParentWindow.GetActiveSheet()

// Disable it for the cases 1) no sheet and 2) no modifications
this.m_file.m_save.Enabled = FALSE

If IsValid( wInstance) Then
   // Note that these are split into two tests, because PowerBuilder will
   // evaluate both regardless of the success or failure of the first
   // expression. This means if there was no active sheet
   If wInstance.i_bModified Then
      this.m_file.m_save.Enabled = TRUE
   End If
End If
```

Accessing Menu Items

Accessing a particular menu item can require coding an extensive dot notation chain, depending on from where you are calling. The format is

```
Window.MenuName.MenuTitle.MenuItem{.MenuItem etc.}
```

The chain can be shortened depending on from where you are accessing the menu. For example, a menu function needs to specify only *`MenuTitle`* and *`MenuItem`*. You can also make use of the Object Browser to paste the calling chain for menus.

Menu Functions and Structures

Menus are one of the four objects (along with applications, windows, and user objects) that can have local functions and structures declared for them. These are created and maintained using the same painters as the other objects, and are covered in Chapter 7, "The PowerScript Environment."

Menu Inheritance

As with other PowerBuilder objects, menus can also be inherited. You specify this in the Select Menu dialog box before you enter the Menu painter workspace.

With a descendant menu you can append items to the end of a cascading menu or modify existing menu items. You cannot insert new items between ancestor items or remove ancestor items. As with inherited windows, you can make only the unnecessary menu items invisible.

There is, however, a method for inserting new menu items between ancestor menu items in a limited fashion. Within the ancestor menu, you must set the Shift Over/Down attribute for the menu titles you want to move right and for menu items you want to move down. In the descendant menu, any appended menu titles or menu items are placed before the moved ancestor titles and items at runtime. You also can check this in the Preview window. So the order of the menu items is Ancestor, Descendant, Moved Ancestors.

If you have made changes to an ancestor menu item within the descendant and then decide you actually want to retain the original settings, you can use the Reset Attributes menu option in the File menu. You cannot reset the attributes for the whole menu but only on an item-by-item basis.

Changing the visibility of menu items in inherited and normal menus has performance problems in all the current releases of PowerBuilder (this may be fixed in the next release). This is because every time a menu item is hidden, it is actually destroyed, and the whole menu is re-created and drawn on the screen. Creating a menu at runtime is a very expensive operation because each menu item is an individual object within the Windows system. If you start hiding items, you are going to cause a significant amount of rebuilding, and depending on the machine's speed you might or might not notice the impact.

NEW 5 in PowerBuilder

NOTE

Microsoft appears to have spent some significant effort increasing the speed of opening and modifying menus within the Windows 95 operating system. We carried out a simple test using a two-level inherited menu with 7 menu titles, 3 cascaded menus, 51 menu items, and a total menu object size of over 70KB. Each of the menu items contained code, which was taken from a production system. The menu appeared almost twice as fast as it did in PowerBuilder 4.0, and modifications to the menu did not cause any visible performance slowdown.

Menus and MDIs

Powersoft has again changed the restriction on creating an MDI window and having to associate a menu with it. In PowerBuilder 4.0, when you create an MDI frame you have to associate a menu with it. This is supposed to lead you into creating a menu that will open sheets and be capable of closing the frame. With PowerBuilder 5.0 this restriction has been removed and you can again create an MDI frame without a menu. The sheets in an MDI application do not have to have menus associated with them. If a sheet has its own menu, it displays in the menu bar of the frame window when the sheet is active. The frame's menu, if there is one, is used when a sheet does not have its own menu.

PowerBuilder uses two internal attributes of a window to track which menu is associated with it. These attributes are `MenuID` and `MenuName` and can be only indirectly affected by using the `ChangeMenu()` function.

The `ChangeMenu()` function enables you to programmatically change the menu associated with a window:

```
Window.ChangeMenu( Menu {, SheetPosition})
```

The *`SheetPosition`* argument is used when the window is an MDI frame. It indicates the menu title position to which you append the currently open window list. The default is `1`, and all opened sheets appear at the bottom of the first menu title's drop-down menu.

NOTE

If a sheet is currently open in the MDI frame with its own menu, the new menu is not visible until the sheet is closed or the user activates a sheet without a menu.

Whenever you create or open an object at runtime, PowerBuilder creates a global variable of that type and points it at the instance you just created. However, when you open multiple instances of a window with a menu, PowerBuilder creates a global variable of that menu type and an instance of the menu for each window instance. You might not immediately see a problem with this, but the global variable points to the last instance that was created. This means that anywhere you specifically code that menu's object name you are potentially accessing the wrong menu. For example, imagine that you have an MDI frame that has three open sheets—A, B, and C—and each sheet is an instance of the same window and all have menus (`w_menu`). If you have the following piece of code in the `Clicked` event of a menu item, it affects the menu pointed to by window C until you close sheet C:

```
w_menu.w_save.Enabled = FALSE
```

You receive a `Null Object Reference` error message the next time you try to access the menu. There are two solutions to this problem.

The first solution forces you to use good coding practices and use only pronoun references within your menu scripts. This means using the `Parent` keyword throughout your code, which makes the script work on the current instance rather than the last one created.

The second solution requires you to maintain an instance variable on each window instance that holds its menu. You do this by placing the following code in the `Open` event of the window:

```
// Instance declaration: m_mfg_order mMyMenu

mMyMenu = this.MenuID
```

This example assumes you know that the window's menu is of a certain class, in this case `m_mfg_order`.

If the window makes any access to its menu, it can now carry out the calls using the local instance variable. However, if there is any need to fully qualify a menu item, such as from another window, you will have to code a method for the window to provide its menu—or better still, code a method that carries out this external request within the window itself.

The following list includes some general information and guidelines on using menus within an MDI application:

- If the current sheet does not have a menu, one of two things occurs: In 3.0 applications, the menu that was available on the previous sheet remains in place; in 4.0 and 5.0 applications the sheet takes the frame's menu.
- To prevent user (and developer) confusion, if you are going to give one sheet a menu, you should provide all sheets with a menu (because the active menu can change depending on the previous sheet).
- If the current sheet's menu does not have a toolbar, but the previously active sheet did, the menu is the active sheet's. However, the space where the previous sheet's toolbar appeared is still there, even though the toolbar itself is not visible.
- Once again, to prevent confusion, if you code one sheet with a toolbar, code all the sheets with a toolbar.
- The open sheet list menu title must have at least one menu item; otherwise, the list will not appear. If you do not intend to place any menu items under this title, you can code a menu item with a single dash, but this will cause two lines to appear in the menu when a sheet is opened. Usually you have options to tile or arrange the open sheets in some fashion (for example, layered, tiled).

Toolbars and PowerTips

Unique to MDI frames and their sheets is the capability to provide a toolbar based on selected menu items. You read about the rules for specifying a toolbar earlier in the section "The Menu Painter." In this section you'll discover how to use toolbars and you'll learn about some of the restrictions and problems associated with toolbars.

First, let it be quite clear that toolbars can be used only in MDI frames and MDI sheets. If you open a sheet with a menu and toolbar outside the MDI frame, the toolbar does not show. Each button on a toolbar is directly associated with a menu item, and clicking the button simply triggers the `Clicked` event for that menu item.

You have control over these toolbars only through attributes (see Table 12.1) on the application and on the frame window.

Table 12.1. Toolbar attributes of an application object.

Attribute	*Data Type*	*Description*
`ToolbarFrameTitle`	String	The title text for a floating FrameBar
`ToolbarPopMenuText`	String	The text on the pop-up menu for toolbars
`ToolbarSheetTitle`	String	The title text for a floating SheetBar
`ToolbarText`	Boolean	Whether the menu item text shows on the button
`ToolbarTips`	Boolean	Whether PowerTips show when the `ToolbarText` is not active
`ToolbarUserControl`	Boolean	Whether the toolbar pop-up menu can be used

When a user right-clicks the toolbar, PowerBuilder provides a default pop-up menu that provides options to manipulate the toolbar. In fact, it is the same menu you use inside PowerBuilder on the PowerBar and PainterBar. The `ToolbarPopMenuText` attribute enables you to alter the text on the menu, but not the functionality. This attribute is really used only in the construction of multilingual applications. The first two items on the pop-up menu display the titles set for the `ToolbarFrameTitle` and `ToolbarSheetTitle` attributes.

You set the `ToolbarPopMenuText` attribute by using a comma-separated list constructed as follows:

```
&Left, &Top, &Right, &Bottom, &Floating, &Show Text
```

These are the default values for the pop-up menu. For example, the French equivalent, with appropriate accelerators (`&`), would be as follows:

```
"A'&Gauche, En &Haut, A'&Droite, Au &Fond, F&lottant, Montrer Le &Texte"
```

The toolbar properties for window objects are shown in Table 12.2.

Table 12.2. Toolbar properties of MDI frame and sheet window objects.

Attribute	*Data Type*	*Description*
`ToolbarAlignment`	`ToolbarAlignment`	Where the toolbar displays
`ToolbarHeight`	Integer	Height of a floating toolbar

Table 12.2. continued

Attribute	*Data Type*	*Description*
`ToolbarVisible`	Boolean	Whether the toolbar displays
`ToolbarWidth`	Integer	Width of a floating toolbar
`ToolbarX`	Integer	X coordinate of a floating toolbar
`ToolbarY`	Integer	Y coordinate of a floating toolbar

NOTE

The following two properties for window objects are available in Version 4.0 of PowerBuilder and are not available in Verison 5.0:

`ToolbarItemsPerRow`	Integer	Maximum items per row of a floating toolbar
`ToolbarTitle`	String	Title of a floating toolbar

An MDI frame window also has one event that is associated with toolbars: `ToolbarMoved`. This event is triggered in an MDI frame window when the user moves the FrameBar or SheetBar. The `Message.WordParm` and `Message.LongParm` attributes contain information on what was moved and to where it was moved:

`Message.WordParm` *Value*	*What It Means*
`0`	The FrameBar has been moved
`1`	The SheetBar has been moved

`Message.LongParm` *Value*	*What It Means*
`0`	Moved to the left
`1`	Moved to the top
`2`	Moved to the right
`3`	Moved to the bottom
`4`	Set to be a floating toolbar

NOTE

A toolbar control window that demonstrates the use of the preceding attributes is constructed in Chapter 11, "Windows and the Window Painter."

One of the nonstandard effects displayed by the menu toolbars that PowerBuilder 4.0 provides occurs when you disable a menu item. This action also causes the associated toolbar button to be disabled, but the appearance of the button remains unchanged. PowerBuilder does not provide you with a means to specify a disabled bitmap for the button, and you must code such functionality into your application. This means replacing the `ToolBarItemName` attribute value with a bitmap that shows the option grayed out.

NOTE

In PowerBuilder 5.0 the toolbar picture is grayed out for you when the menu item is disabled. This conforms with the Microsoft Windows 95 interface standards and is available in the Windows 3.*x*-based PowerBuilder 5.0, as well.

Hiding a menu item does not cause the toolbar button to become disabled or to disappear. Again, you must code specifically for this occurrence. However, if you disable a menu title, it disables, but does not remove, the toolbar buttons for all of the menu items under it.

Both of these kinds of processing are best encapsulated into either the menu itself or a nonvisual user object built for managing menus.

One of the sometimes annoying toolbar effects in PowerBuilder applications is the double toolbar. When the frame and the sheet both have toolbars, the frame toolbar displays above the sheet's. Both toolbars are active, and options can be selected from either.

A simple way around this is to not construct a toolbar for the sheet menus and have the options you want to make available at the sheet level part of the frame's menu, but disabled. Obviously, this is not always practical. With each type of sheet there is usually a different menu, and therefore you can use this method only if the number of types of sheets is small.

Another more complex method requires you to turn off screen redraws while you hide the frame toolbar when a sheet opens. You then have to track when the last sheet is closed to re-enable the frame toolbar. This is best achieved by using a controlling function on the MDI frame window. Within this function it can update a window instance variable as you open and close sheets. When this counter is decremented back to `0`, the function makes the frame toolbar visible again.

With Version 5.0 of PowerBuilder your user has the ability to dock these menus together onto one line, thus reclaiming some of the screen space that had been lost (see Figure 12.12).

FIGURE 12.12.
Two menu toolbars docked.

In the Window painter you have access to some of the attributes for the initial position of the window's toolbar. This is accessed via the Window property sheet, under the ToolBar tab (see Figure 12.13).

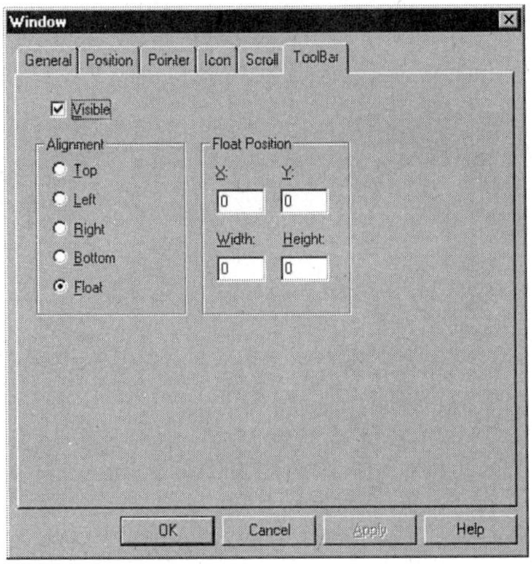

FIGURE 12.13.
The window toolbar properties.

The X, Y, Width, and Height options only have an effect when the toolbar alignment is set to floating.

Controlling Toolbars

PowerBuilder 5.0 hasintroduced some new functions that allow developers to control and query the state of a toolbar for a window. Using these functions you can also make a toolbar dock onto the frame window's toolbar.

The `GetToolbar()` function allows you to query a window for basic toolbar information. If the window does not have a toolbar, the function returns `-1`. The function syntax is

```
wWindow.GetToolbar( nIndex, bVisible {, aAlignment {, szTitle}})
```

There are two versions of the `GetToolbarPos()` function that allow you to extract further information about the toolbar:

```
wWindow.GetToolbarPos( nIndex, nRow, nOffset)
wWindow.GetToolbarPos( nIndex, nX, nY, nWidth, nHeight)
```

The first version returns information about the row the toolbar appears on and the offset from the row's left origin. The second returns the size and position information for a floating toolbar.

The `SetToolbar()` function allows you to set basic toolbar values and has the following syntax:

```
wWindow.SetToolbar( nIndex, bVisible {, aAlignment {, szTitle}})
```

There are two versions of the `SetToolbarPos()` function that allow you to set further information for the toolbar:

```
wWindow.SetToolbarPos( nIndex, nRow, nOffset, b)
wWindow.SetToolbarPos( nIndex, nX, nY, nWidth, nHeight)
```

The first version allows you to set the row the toolbar will appear on and the offset from the row's left origin. The second sets the size and position information for floating toolbars.

Saving and Restoring Toolbar Settings

Using the toolbar functions just described, you can construct generic save and restore functions for preserving the state of a window's toolbars. This information can be written to a number of different places: an INI file, a database table, or the system registry.

The code shown in Listing 12.1 uses an INI file, but it should require minor changes to store the data elsewhere. The reason you might still want to use an INI file over the registry is the same as the reason that PowerBuilder still uses a PB.INI: cross-platform compatibility. Macintosh and UNIX platforms do not have a corresponding registry structure, but the PowerBuilder INI access functions work in either case.

So that you can store (Listing 12.1) and restore (Listing 12.2) multiple windows' toolbars, make a new section for each toolbar using each window's class name. If the section does not already exist, the `SetProfileString()` function will create it for you; the only requirement is that the INI file must already exist.

Listing 12.1. `SaveToolbar( ReadOnly Window a_wWindow).`

```
Integer nRow, nOffset, nX, nY, nWidth, nHeight
Boolean bVisible
ToolbarAlignment aAlignment
String szTitle, szAlignment, szSection

// If the toolbar does not exist, this will return -1
If a_wWindow.GetToolbar( 1, bVisible, aAlignment, szTitle) = 1 Then
   // The window's class is the section we will save the toolbar's state under
   szSection = a_wWindow.ClassName()
   // Convert the boolean to a string representation
   If bVisible Then
      SetProfileString( g_App.i_szINIFile, szSection, "Visible", "TRUE")
   Else
      SetProfileString( g_App.i_szINIFile, szSection, "Visible", "FALSE")
   End If

   // Convert the toolbars alignment to a string representation
   Choose Case aAlignment
      Case AlignAtLeft!
         szAlignment = "Left"
      Case AlignAtTop!
         szAlignment = "Top"
```

continues

Listing 12.1. continued

```
      Case AlignAtRight!
         szAlignment = "Right"
      Case AlignAtBottom!
         szAlignment = "Bottom"
      Case Floating!
         szAlignment = "Floating"
   End Choose
   SetProfileString( g_App.i_szINIFile, szSection, "Alignment", szAlignment)

   // Extract the row and offset values and save them
   a_wWindow.GetToolbarPos( 1, nRow, nOffset)
   SetProfileString( g_App.i_szINIFile, szSection, "Row", String( nRow))
   SetProfileString( g_App.i_szINIFile, szSection, "Offset", String( nOffset))

   // Extract the size and position values and save them
   a_wWindow.GetToolbarPos( 1, nX, nY, nWidth, nHeight)
   SetProfileString( g_App.i_szINIFile, szSection, "X", String( nX))
   SetProfileString( g_App.i_szINIFile, szSection, "Y", String( nY))
   SetProfileString( g_App.i_szINIFile, szSection, "Width", String( nWidth))
   SetProfileString( g_App.i_szINIFile, szSection, "Height", String( nHeight))
End If
```

Notice that the function argument was declared using the new `ReadOnly` parameter passing mechanism. This allows the function to be called using the `this` PowerBuilder pronoun. For example, to save the state of a windows toolbar within the `CloseQuery` event the code would be

```
g_App.SaveToolbar( this)
```

NOTE

In this case we have implemented the toolbar save and restore functions in a base class user object. The calls to both this and the following function can be placed in a base class window object. The information for each window's toolbar is stored under a class name and so will not clash with another.

Listing 12.2. `RestoreToolbar( ReadOnly Window a_wWindow).`

```
Integer nRow, nOffset, nX, nY, nWidth, nHeight
Boolean bVisible = FALSE
ToolbarAlignment aAlignment
String szTitle, szAlignment, szVisible, szSection

// If the bar does not exist, this will return -1
If a_wWindow.GetToolbar( 1, bVisible, aAlignment, szTitle) = 1 Then
   // The window's class is the section that we saved the toolbar's state under
   szSection = a_wWindow.ClassName()

   // Try and retrieve the toolbars visiblity
   szVisible = ProfileString( g_App.i_szINIFile, szSection, "Visible", "")
```

```
   // If we failed to find the toolbars visible state then do NOT overwrite
   // the current settings of the toolbar.
   If szVisible <> "" Then
      szAlignment = ProfileString( g_App.i_szINIFile, szSection, "Alignment",
"Top")
      szTitle = ProfileString( g_App.i_szINIFile, szSection, "Title", "")

      If Upper( szVisible) = "TRUE" Then
         bVisible = TRUE
      End If

      // Convert the string back into an alignment value
      Choose Case Lower( szAlignment)
         Case "left"
            aAlignment = AlignAtLeft!
         Case "top"
            aAlignment = AlignAtTop!
         Case "right"
            aAlignment = AlignAtRight!
         Case "bottom"
            aAlignment = AlignAtBottom!
         Case "floating"
            aAlignment = Floating!
      End Choose
      // Set the base settings for the toolbar
      a_wWindow.SetToolbar( 1, bVisible, aAlignment, szTitle)

      // Obtain the other settings for the toolbar ...
      nRow = ProfileInt( g_App.i_szINIFile, szSection, "Row", 1)
      nOffset = ProfileInt( g_App.i_szINIFile, szSection, "Offset", 0)
      nX = ProfileInt( g_App.i_szINIFile, szSection, "X", 0)
      nY = ProfileInt( g_App.i_szINIFile, szSection, "Y", 0)
      nWidth = ProfileInt( g_App.i_szINIFile, szSection, "Width", 0)
      nHeight = ProfileInt( g_App.i_szINIFile, szSection, "Height", 0)

      // ... and then set them for the toolbar
      a_wWindow.SetToolbarPos( 1, nRow, nOffset, FALSE)
      a_wWindow.SetToolbarPos( 1, nX, nY, nWidth, nHeight)
   End If
End If
```

Tricks with Menus

Using Powersoft functions and attributes, there are a number of little tricks to using menus. Following are some examples to illustrate these functions and attributes.

Implementing an Edit Menu

In Windows 95 applications the operating system already provides a full pop-up edit menu for editable controls. For developers using other operating systems, these features might not be available and a brief description of the code required is given next.

The code listed for each of the edit actions could be incorporated into a base-level menu ancestor or implemented as global or nonvisual object functions.

The standard Edit menu consists of Undo, Copy, Cut, Paste, and Clear. Only the code for the Undo option is shown in detail because the other options only require a function name change. This edit functionality can be applied only to DataWindows, drop-down list boxes, edit masks, multiline edits, single-line edits, and OLE 2.0 controls.

Undo

An Undo menu option should cancel the last edit that was made to an editable control. You use the PowerBuilder `Undo()` and `CanUndo()` functions.

The `Undo()` function cannot be used with drop-down list boxes or OLE 2.0 controls. To see if the last action can be undone, use the `CanUndo()` function:

```
GraphicObject goObject
DataWindow dwUndo
EditMask emUndo
MultiLineEdit mleUndo
SingleLineEdit sleUndo

goObject = GetFocus()        // Saves us calling the f() multiple times

If Not IsNull( goObject) Then
   Choose Case TypeOf( goObject)
      Case DataWindow!
         dwUndo = goObject
         If dwUndo.CanUndo() Then
            dwUndo.Undo()
         End If
      Case EditMask!
         emUndo = goObject
         If emUndo.CanUndo() Then
            emUndo.Undo()
         End If
      Case MultiLineEdit!
         mleUndo = goObject
         If mleUndo.CanUndo() Then
            mleUndo.Undo()
         End If
      Case SingleLineEdit!
         sleUndo = goObject
         If sleUndo.CanUndo() Then
            sleUndo.Undo()
         End If
   End Choose
End If
```

You have to set a variable of the correct object type to the current object because the `GraphicObject` object does not have either `Undo()` or `CanUndo()` as object functions.

Copy

The Copy menu option nondestructively (that is, leaves the highlighted text alone) duplicates the value in the current control into the Windows Clipboard. Only the part that is highlighted is copied. For this you use the PowerBuilder `Copy()` function.

If the control is a drop-down list box, the `AllowEdit` attribute must be set to `TRUE`; otherwise, the control is effectively a list box. Here's an example:

```
Case DropDownListBox!
   ddlbCopy = goObject
   If ddlbCopy.AllowEdit = TRUE
      ddlbCopy.Copy()
   End If
```

For a DataWindow control, the text value is copied from the edit box, not from the column.

If for some reason you need to trap when nothing was copied or trap what happened with an OLE 2.0 control, you can examine the return value of `Copy()`. For the edit controls, the number of characters copied is returned: If the control was empty, the value is `0`, and on an error it is `-1`. If it was an OLE 2.0 control, the return value is `0` for a success, `-1` if the control is empty, `-2` if the copy fails, and `-9` for all other errors.

Cut

The Cut menu option destructively (that is, removes the highlighted text) moves the value in the current control into the Windows Clipboard. Only the part that is highlighted is moved. For this you use the PowerBuilder `Cut()` function.

The same restrictions for the `Copy()` function apply to `Cut()`.

The return value for `Cut()` is identical to that of `Copy()`. The return values if it was an OLE 2.0 control are the same except that `-2` means the cut failed. Cutting an OLE object breaks any connection between it and the source file or storage.

Paste

The Paste menu option inserts into the current text or overwrites the highlighted section, or with OLE controls, completely replaces the object. For this you use the PowerBuilder `Paste()` function.

For DataWindow controls the text is pasted into the edit field, not the column. If the value does not match the data type of the column, the whole value is truncated so that an empty string is inserted. For all controls, `Paste()` copies only as many characters as will fit in the control; the rest are truncated. When an OLE object is pasted into an OLE 2.0 control, the data is only embedded, not linked.

The return value for `Paste()` is the number of characters that were pasted. If the Clipboard does not contain a textual value, the function does nothing and returns `0`. With OLE 2.0 controls, the function returns `0` on success, `-1` if the Clipboard contents are not embeddable, and `-9` on all other errors.

Clear

The Clear menu option deletes the selected text or OLE 2.0 control and does not place it in the Clipboard. For this you use the PowerBuilder `Clear()` function.

Clearing an OLE 2.0 control's object deletes all references to it, does not save any changes that were made, and breaks any connections.

The return value for `Clear()` is `0` on success and `-1` on an error. For OLE 2.0 controls, `0` also indicates success, but `-9` indicates that an error occurred.

You can place a controlling script in the `Clicked` event for the Edit menu title that enables and disables the appropriate menu items, depending on the object that has current focus or whether there is anything to paste. You might expand this menu to include the capability to use the `PasteSpecial()` and `PasteLink()` functions.

Accessing the Open Sheet Menu

Maybe you are going to track the open sheets using the dynamic window list menu, or perhaps you need access to other window titles. Whichever it is, the following piece of code can be used to traverse a cascaded menu.

These API functions will be used and should be declared either globally or locally:

```
FUNCTION uInt GetMenu( uInt hWnd) LIBRARY "user32.dll"
FUNCTION uInt GetMenuItemID( uInt hWnd, int nPosition) LIBRARY "user32.dll"
FUNCTION uInt GetMenuItemCount( uInt hWnd) LIBRARY "user32.dll"
FUNCTION uInt GetSubMenu( uInt hWnd, int nPosition) LIBRARY "user32.dll"
FUNCTION uInt GetMenuStringA( uInt hWnd, uInt nItem, REF string szItem, &
                              int nMax, uint nByCommand) LIBRARY "user32.dll"
```

NOTE

Developers using Windows 3.*x* need to replace the user32.dll filename with user.exe and change the name of the `GetMenuStringA()` function to `GetMenuString()`.

The code that makes use of these functions would probably be placed in a menu function. Listing 12.3 is an example of a menu function used to traverse an open sheet menu.

Listing 12.3. Code for traversing the open sheet menu.

```
uInt hMainMenu, hMenuTitle, hMenuItem
Integer nLength, nMaxSize = 32, nNoOfMenuItems, nItem, nItemPosition
String  szBuffer

szBuffer = Space( nMaxSize)

// Get main menu handle of a window passed as an argument
hMainMenu = GetMenu( Handle( ParentWindow))

// GetSubMenu()'s second argument is the position of the menu
// title that you want the handle. Within this menu we maintain
// a menu instance variable that is used in all OpenSheet() calls.
// However, PowerBuilder is based from 1 onwards, Windows is 0 based.
hMenuTitle = GetSubMenu( hMainMenu, i_nWindowList - 1)

// Get a count of the menu item for the menu title
nNoOfMenuItems = GetMenuItemCount( hMenuTitle)

// We can now loop through the menu and explore each item
Do While nItem < nNoOfMenuItems
   // Get the handle of a menu item
   hMenuItem = GetMenuItemID( hMenuTitle, nItem)

   // The menu item text is returned into the string szBuffer
   // The last argument is MF_BYCOMMAND (0) so that we can use hMenuItem
   nLength = GetMenuStringA( hMainMenu, hMenuItem, szBuffer, nMaxSize, 0)

   nItem ++
Loop
```

The value of `nLength` is the length of the text that was copied into `szBuffer`. For menu items that are line separators, `nLength` is `0`, and `szBuffer` contains an empty string.

NOTE

Remember that the text value contains an ellipsis (...) and the accelerator indicator (`&`). It also contains the number of the sheet (that is, if the menu item is 1 Stock Sheet, the value returned is `&1 Stock Sheet`).

Similar in concept to the previous example is the capability to scan through a menu to find a particular menu item. You can do this easily and without having to resort to API functions by using the `MenuID` attribute of a window and its associated array of menu items.

For example, the code shown in Listing 12.4 is built into a window-level function that takes a menu title and item, locates that item, and disables it.

Listing 12.4. Traversing the MenuID attribute.

```
Integer nMenuTitle, nTotalTitles, nMenuItem, nTotalItems

// Get a count of the top level menu titles
nTotalTitles = UpperBound( this.MenuID.Item)

For nMenuTitle = 1 To nTotalTitles
   // Locate the required menu title
   If this.MenuID.Item[ nMenuTitle].Text = a_szTitle THEN
      nTotalItems = UpperBound( this.MenuID.Item[ nMenuTitle].Item)
      For nMenuItem = 1 To nTotalItems
         // Locate menu item
         If this.MenuID.Item[ nMenuTitle].Item[ nMenuItem].Text = & a_szItem Then
            Disable( this.MenuID.Item[ nMenuTitle].Item[ & nMenuItem])
            nMenuItem = nTotalItems
            Exit
         End If
      Next
      Exit
   End If
Next
```

You can use this technique when you do not know the name of the menu with which the window is associated. It also prevents the need to hard code menu names.

Menus and OLE

With OLE 2.0 in-place activation, the OLE server's menu becomes the active menu to enable you to work on the object within its own context. The server menu can be merged into the current PowerBuilder application's menu by making use of the `MergeOption` attribute for each menu title. This attribute can be found in the Menu Merge Option drop-down list in the Style tab page of the Menu painter:

Enumerated Data Type	*Description*
`Exclude`	Do not include it in the OLE server menu.
`Merge`	Add this menu title and cascading menu into the OLE server menu, appearing after the first menu title of the server.
`File`	This menu title is leftmost on the menu bar. The server's File menu is not used.
`Edit`	The server's Edit menu displays in place of this Edit menu title.
`Window`	The menu that lists the open window. The server's Window menu is not used.
`Help`	The server's Help menu displays instead of this Help menu title.

The default value for the `MergeOption` attribute is `Exclude`.

The In Place settings cause the menu bar to display the PowerBuilder application's File and Window menus and the server's Edit and Help menus. Any menus that you label as Merge are added into the other server menu titles. For more information on OLE see Chapter 36, "OLE 2.0 and DDE."

Summary

In this chapter you have explored how to physically create menus and logically create better menus. You have examined a number of guidelines that will lead to the construction of better menus. You have also taken a detailed look at the use of menus in an MDI application and some of the tricks and traps of using toolbars.

The Library Painter

IN THIS CHAPTER

As you already know, when you create a new application object, you can also create a PowerBuilder library file with the extension .PBL (pronounced "pibble"). Any other objects you create for your application are also stored in a PBL. A common scenario for an application is that your objects are stored across multiple PBLs. Since library files are a repository for all of your objects, you will need some method of managing these libraries and the objects that are contained in them. You do this using the Library painter.

Because libraries are an integral part of any PowerBuilder application, there are some structure guidelines you should follow to get the optimum performance out of your libraries. This chapter looks at some of the library file guidelines and then explores how to manipulate your library files and PowerBuilder objects using the Library painter.

When creating your application, you should decide where the PowerBuilder library files should reside, both for performance reasons and source management. There are also some guidelines that help increase the performance and ease of use of your library files. These guidelines are covered in the following sections.

Library Placement

Before any development begins, it is important to decide where you are going to store the actual PBLs (that is, in what drive and directory). There are some special considerations when creating a project that involves multiple developers.

Speed is an important part of any application. Placing your PBLs locally (on your machine) will increase the speed with which your application runs. With a single-developer application, this is not a problem because the lone developer is the only one who requires access to the objects.

With a project involving multiple developers, the location of the files becomes more of an issue. If everyone were to keep a copy of the libraries locally, no one would have the most recent changes and developers could be overlaying each other's work. Even if the developers were careful and communicated with one another, they still would have to copy their objects manually to each of the other machines to keep themselves in sync. This does not seem like a productive solution. To work effectively with multideveloper projects, you should place the PowerBuilder libraries on a common network drive.

Table 13.1 shows a standard configuration of a directory structure on a network drive (in this case n:\). (This could also be used on a local drive for a single-developer application.)

Table 13.1. The project directory structure.

Directory	*Description of the Use of the Directory*
N:\PROJECTS	Common objects for multiple applications (for example, ancestors, user objects, functions).

Directory	*Description of the Use of the Directory*
\PROJECT_NAME	High-level reference directory for the following subdirectories: \VERSION—Current version number of *PROJECT_NAME.* \DEV—PBLs containing objects being developed. \TEST—PBLs containing completed objects that are ready for integration testing. Changes are not made to this directory. \PROD—Production files for current version of the application. Contains PBLs, PBDs, PBR, EXE, and any other miscellaneous file needed. Developers do not have access to this directory.

If each developer uses the PBLs located in the DEV directory to make changes, all the code will be maintained in one place. Unfortunately, this can cause a severe impact on the speed of execution and testing due to additional network traffic. To avoid this problem, each developer should maintain a PBL on his own workstation that is used to hold objects on which he is currently working.

NOTE

You may get the message `Save Failed - Probable file I/O Error` when you try to save an object. This typically is because someone else is using the library you are writing to. One way to fix this is to make sure the network recognizes the library files as shared files.

The library search path can be used to list the developer's personal development PBL first and then include all the networked PBLs. This is possible because the library search path is stored in each developer's PB.INI file. By placing the test PBL at the top of the library search path, you are ensuring that PowerBuilder uses your copy of the object and not one found in the network PBLs.

NOTE

The library search path is very important in the performance tuning of your PowerBuilder application. Frequently used objects should be placed near the top so that PowerBuilder does not have to search through multiple PBLs to find the requested object. For more information, see Chapter 8, "Application Objects and the Application Painter," and Chapter 18, "Application Implementation, Creation, and Distribution."

Source Management

The directory structure in Table 13.1 is useful when multiple PowerBuilder library files need to be maintained, but it is also quite useful for managing your source code. As you have seen, the directory structure breaks down each project by version number, and within that version are copies of development, test, and eventual production versions of the PBLs. This structure, or one similar to it, is commonly used across all client/server application-development projects.

Although the placement of libraries in the different directories is useful for determining the different phases of a project and maintaining source code, it does not prevent developers from overlaying one another's code in the DEV directory. To prevent accidental modifications to a particular object, you should have three things in place: communication between team members, version control management, and a mechanism to track work in progress.

Communication between members of the development team is crucial for the success of any application. Information on who is working on each portion of an application should be readily accessible. Unassigned and undefined tasks are the areas in which potential problems can arise. Many of these problems can be avoided with a good plan for application version control. Version control can range from using a directory structure like the one previously described or purchasing a specific software package such as PVCS or LBMS. Powersoft has also created its own source management package, called ObjectCycle, for use with PowerBuilder. For more information on ObjectCycle, see Chapter 20, "Application Maintenance and Upgrades."

In addition to communication, there should be a mechanism to track whether work is being done on a particular object. PowerBuilder provides a simple interface to check objects in and out to prevent a developer from modifying the same object another developer is working on. For example, using the standard project directory structure, a developer would check out an object from a public library (DEV) and copy it to a local work library. The test library would be placed at the top of the library search path and changes would be made to the checked-out object. After all changes have been made, the developer would then check the object back in. If another developer tried to access the object while it was checked out, PowerBuilder would display a message indicating the name of the developer who had checked out the object. You'll learn more about the check-in/check-out facility later in this chapter.

Library Guidelines

There are several recommended guidelines for use with PowerBuilder library files, both for tuning and ease of use. These guidelines include library organization, library size, and library optimization.

After you have a structure in place for storing your libraries, you will also want to decide how to divide the objects logically in your application. In a small application, it is common to have one PBL that contains all the objects for the application. In a large application, however, it can be confusing and very inefficient to have a single, large PBL containing all objects. The two common organization schemes for libraries are by object type and by application functionality.

Organizing your application by object type means that you maintain separate PBLs for the different object types. For example, suppose one PBL contains all window objects; a second PBL contains menus; a third contains structures and functions; a fourth has all DataWindow objects; and the last contains the application and project objects. Using this method, you know which objects are located in each library.

The downside to this method is that some of the PBLs could get very large (for example, the window library) and subsequently become difficult to manage. You should keep PBL files at less than 800KB in size. As the number of objects stored in the PBL increases, so do the sizes of your library files. As this happens, PowerBuilder must access the disk drive for longer periods of time as it moves through the PBL file to satisfy a request for an object. In addition, if the number of objects increases to more than 40 or 50 in one library file, the Library painter and the list boxes that display objects in a library (for example, the Select Window dialog box) become difficult to work with because you are always scrolling up and down.

What is an alternative, then, to organizing libraries by object type? Organize by business functionality! One PBL might contain all objects common to the whole application (for example, user objects and the logon window). Another PBL might contain objects for daily sales calculations, and another the quarterly forecast objects. Although this method can decrease the number of entries in a library file, it can also affect the number of library files. Having too many library files can make them difficult to keep track of and can appear cluttered, and PowerBuilder would have to search through many different libraries to find an object, which can have a negative effect on performance.

Because both methods of organization have their faults, using a combination of both can be implemented. Separate your objects by higher-level business functionality, and within that functionality, divide the PBLs into groups of different objects. One setback is that unless you have support for long filenames, the library names become cryptic and confusing.

The last recommendation for getting the highest performance out of your libraries is to frequently optimize them. Just like your hard drive, a library file can become fragmented over time, which increases the amount of time needed to access the objects in the library. By using the Optimize option under the Library menu in the Library painter, you can reorganize your PBL so that PowerBuilder will run more efficiently.

Once you have determined what is the best structure for your library files, you need a tool to manage the library files. This is done in the Library painter.

Using the Library Painter

You can access the Library painter by clicking on the PowerBar icon or by pressing Shift+F10.

The Library painter opens, revealing an interface that looks and feels very much like the Windows 3.*x* File Manager. The painter displays a directory listing of the current drive, the libraries located in the directories, and the objects in the libraries. The current drive, directory, and even library are dictated by the current application object. When you open an application in PowerBuilder from the Application painter, you have to specify the library that the desired application object resides in. Whatever drive the selected library file is located on is the current drive in the Library painter. Each of the directories is displayed as a file folder (see Figure 13.1).

FIGURE 13.1.
The Library painter.

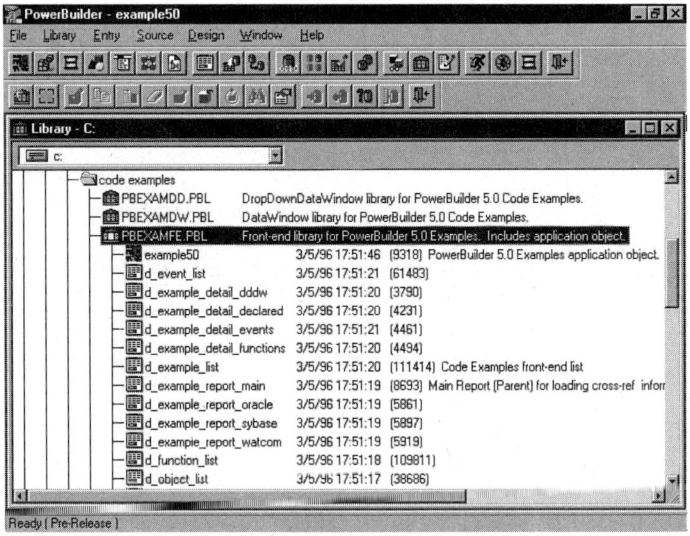

For the directories that contain PBLs, the painter displays the library icon followed by the library filename. The PBL containing the current application is expanded so that it displays all the objects contained within the library file. Each object is identified by the object name and an icon to the right indicating the object type. Table 13.2 displays the icons and the corresponding object types.

Table 13.2. Library painter object icons.

Icon	*Object Type*
	Application
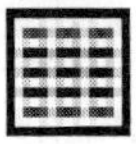	DataWindow

Icon	*Object Type*
	Function
	Project
	Menu
	Pipeline
	Query
	Structure
	User Object
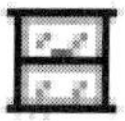	Window

By default PowerBuilder displays all objects that are contained in a particular PBL and all the object information. You can easily modify what is displayed by clicking Options under the Design menu, which opens the Options property sheet. You can specify whether the check-out status, comments, last modification date, and compiled object size information display on the General tab page (see Figure 13.2). The General tab page also allows you to choose whether informational and obsolete compiler messages are displayed, if backups of library files are created when you optimize the library, and whether you are prompted on any delete action.

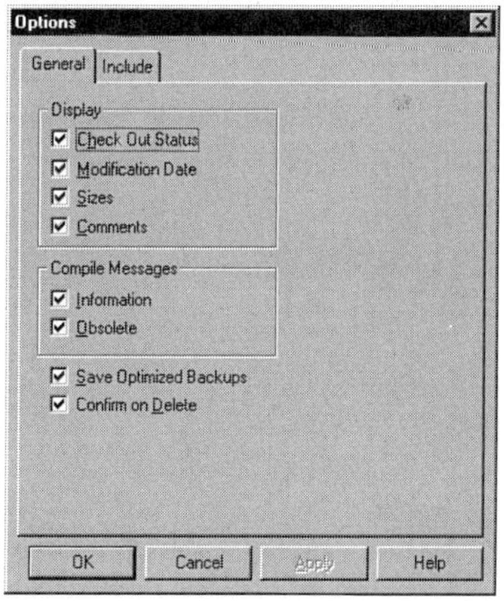

FIGURE 13.2.
The General tab page.

The Include tab page (see Figure 13.3) allows you to specify what PowerBuilder objects you would like to see.

FIGURE 13.3.
The Include tab page.

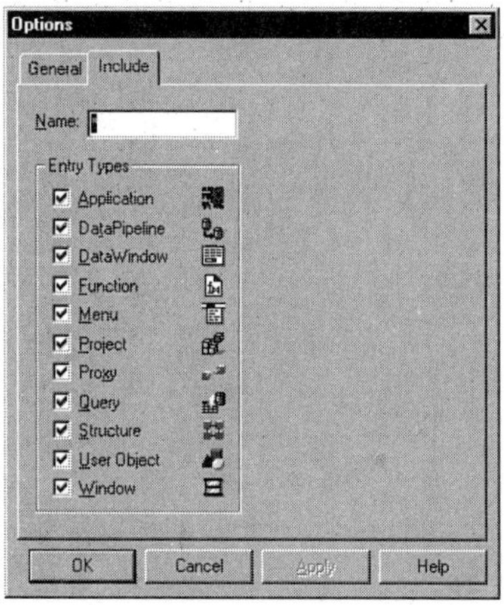

With the Include tab page you can specify what object types you wish to view as well as place a mask on what object names you view. For example, if you typed `*ex*` in the Name edit box, the only objects that would display would be those with `ex` somewhere in the object name. The criteria you specify for the painter will be saved for the next time you use the painter.

Once you have decided what information you want to view, you need to be able to move about the painter. To change to a new drive, you can click on the Drive list box or click the Select Device menu under the Design menu. Directories and libraries can be expanded and collapsed by double-clicking the library or directory name, by using the arrow keys to move to the desired location and pressing the Enter key, or by selecting Expand/Collapse Branch from the Design menu. If a directory is expanded, the file folder opens and if a library is expanded, the library doors are opened. If you are on an object in a PBL and press the Enter key or double-click the object, PowerBuilder will try to open the object in its respective painter.

These are the basic components and methods of movement in the Library painter. Let's now take a look at some of the different functionalities provided by the Library painter.

Maintaining Libraries

As you saw earlier, a number of guidelines should be followed for performance reasons as well as for ease of use. To successfully implement these guidelines, you need to know how to create, delete, and optimize your libraries.

Creating a Library

The method of creating a library that most people are familiar with is in the Application painter. The only problem with that method is that you are required to create an application object at the same time. Under the Library menu in the Library painter, you can create a new PBL by selecting Create or you can click on the Create icon on the PainterBar (see Figure 13.4).

FIGURE 13.4.
The Library painter PainterBar.

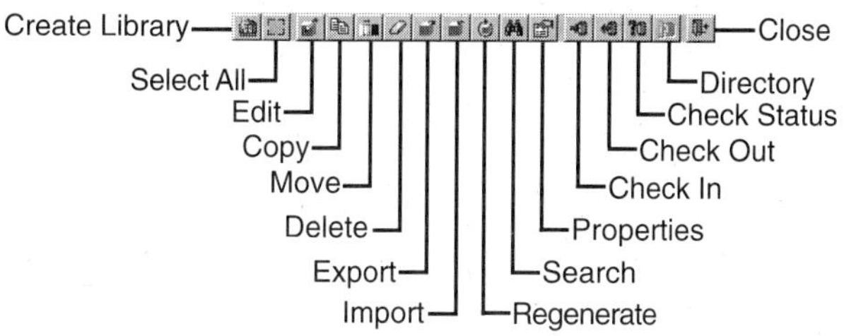

Selecting the Create icon and menu options causes the Create Library dialog box to open (see Figure 13.5).

FIGURE 13.5.
The Create Library dialog box.

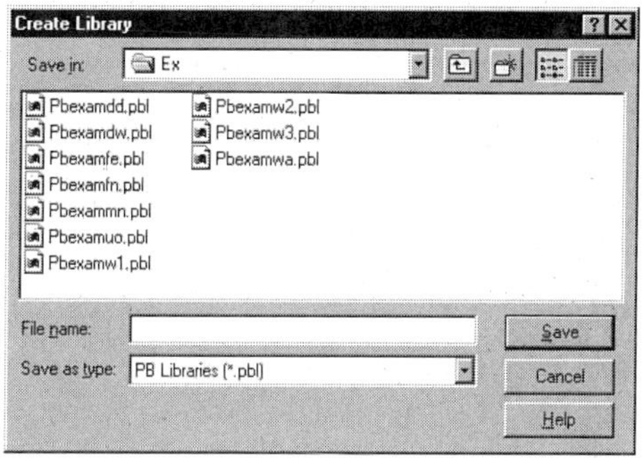

After you specify the new name for your library, clicking the Save button opens the property sheet for the library (see Figure 13.6).

FIGURE 13.6.
The Library property sheet.

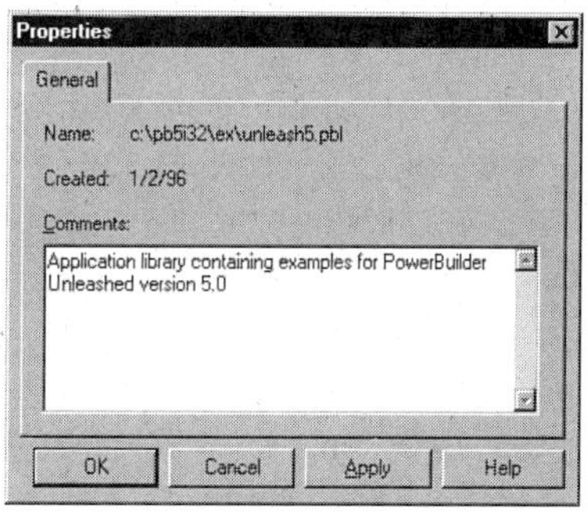

With the property sheet you can add comments about the purpose of the library file. This property sheet can also be accessed by selecting Properties from the Library menu or by right-clicking on the library file and choosing Properties from the pop-up menu.

Deleting a Library

You may, during the course of your application's development, need to delete one or more library files. This is easily done by selecting Delete from the Library menu or from the library's pop-up menu. Clicking on Delete brings up a message box that asks for a delete confirmation. If you prefer not to be prompted for deletion of your libraries or any objects, you can specify this by clicking the check box on the General tab page shown in Figure 13.2.

WARNING

Deleting a library deletes the physical file and all objects contained in the file. The library file cannot be retrieved via PowerBuilder.

Library Optimization

Because objects are constantly being inserted, deleted, and updated in your library files, the library file is constantly being fragmented. In a fragmented library there are areas of unused space and objects that are not stored contiguously to your hard drive. This can have an adverse effect on performance. In addition to the areas of unused space, PowerBuilder sometimes creates something known as a *dead object*, which is an object that has been specified for deletion within PowerBuilder, but for some reason it still physically exists in the library. By optimizing your libraries regularly, you can remove the fragmentation and dead objects.

To optimize a library, select Optimize from the Library menu or from the pop-up menu. Previous versions of PowerBuilder asked for confirmation before performing optimization, which is no longer the case in 5.0. To have PowerBuilder create a backup of your library before performing optimization, select Save Optimize Backups from the General tab page on the Options property sheet. PowerBuilder then creates a copy of your library file with the extension .BAK in the same directory as the selected library to be optimized.

Maintaining Entries

Once you have created a new library file, you will often need to copy or move objects from one library to the new one. You may also need to delete an object from a PBL, which has to be done through the Library painter.

To copy an entry from one library to another, you need to select the desired object or objects to be copied. The Library painter gives you the ability to perform extended selects using the Ctrl and Shift keys. The extended select can also be used to span libraries so that by holding the Ctrl key down you can click on objects in two or more different libraries and have the objects copied to the new library. If you need to select all objects in a library, click on the library name and choose the Select All icon from the PainterBar, click Select All from the Library menu or pop-up menu, or press Ctrl+A.

Once the desired objects are selected, choose Copy from the Entry menu, click the Copy icon on the PainterBar, press Ctrl+C, or if you have only one object selected, you can choose Copy from the pop-up menu. This opens the Select Library dialog box (see Figure 13.7), which asks for the name of the destination library.

FIGURE 13.7.
The Select Library dialog box.

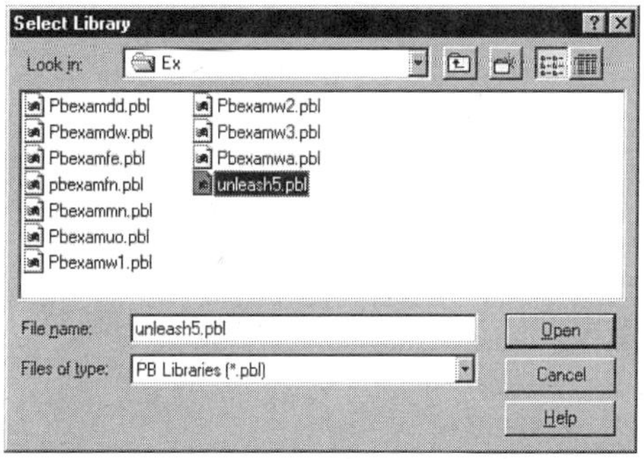

Similar to copying objects is the process of moving entries from one library to another. When you specify that you want to move an object, PowerBuilder copies the object to the destination library and then deletes it from the source library. To move one or more entries, select the desired objects and select Move from the Entry menu, press Ctrl+M, or click the Move icon on the PainterBar. If you are moving just one object, you can select Move from the object's pop-up menu. Choosing Move will open a dialog box identical to the one used for copying objects (refer to Figure 13.7).

If you have erroneously copied or moved an object or just have an extra object hanging around, the only way to delete that object is through the Library painter. Select the object(s) and click Delete from the Entry menu, press the Del key, or click the Delete icon on the PainterBar. Delete is also available in the object's pop-up menu. After you specify one or more objects for deletion, PowerBuilder will ask you to confirm the deletion if you have the Confirm on Delete option checked on the Options property sheet General tab page.

NOTE

If you have multiple objects selected for deletion, you will be prompted for delete confirmation for each entry.

In addition to copying, moving, and deleting objects, you can also view the general property information about the object. You do this by selecting the desired object and clicking Properties from the Entry menu or pop-up menu. This opens the entry property sheet (see Figure 13.8).

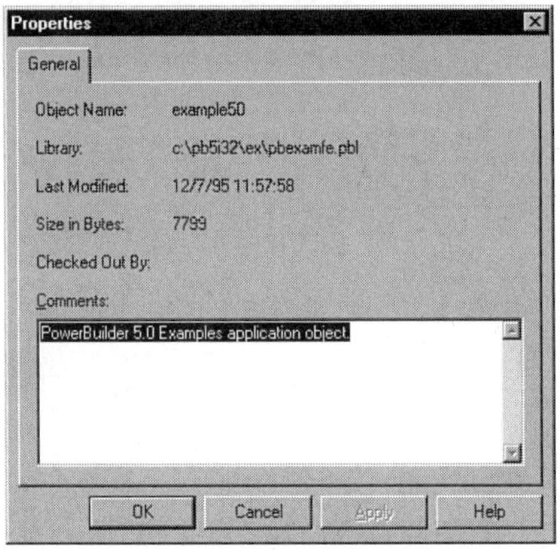

FIGURE 13.8.
The entry property sheet.

Although most of the information on the sheet is read-only, you can modify the comments for the object.

Searching Objects

It is often necessary to search through an object or multiple objects for a specific function name, variable, or whatever. You usually need this functionality when you are in the Script painter. Unfortunately, PowerBuilder only allows you to search in the current script from that painter. The Library painter gives you the ability to look for a search string across multiple objects.

To browse for a specified string, select one or more objects and then click the Search icon on the PainterBar, select Search from the Entry menu or pop-up menu, or press Ctrl+B. This brings up the Search Library Entries dialog box (see Figure 13.9).

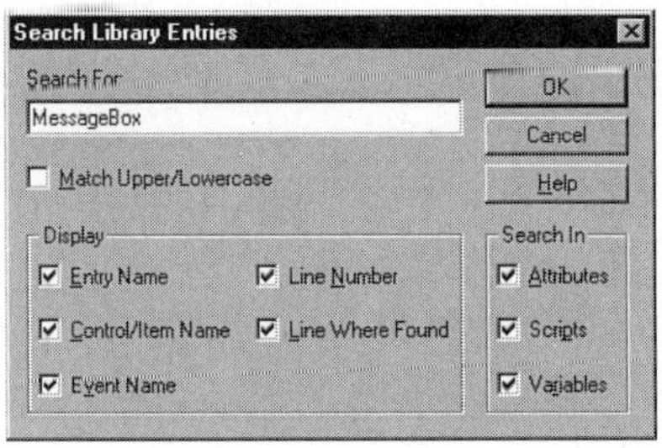

FIGURE 13.9.
The Search Library Entries dialog box.

Specify the desired string to search for in the Search For edit box (the string cannot contain any wildcards or placeholders). If you want to match upper- and lowercase, select the Match Upper/Lowercase check box. Once the desired string is specified, you can select what parts of objects are to be searched (attributes, scripts, and variables) and what information you want displayed if there is a match found. After you have specified everything, click the OK button to process your search.

If any matches are found for the search criteria, the Matching Library Entries dialog box is opened (see Figure 13.10).

FIGURE 13.10.
The Matching Library Entries dialog box.

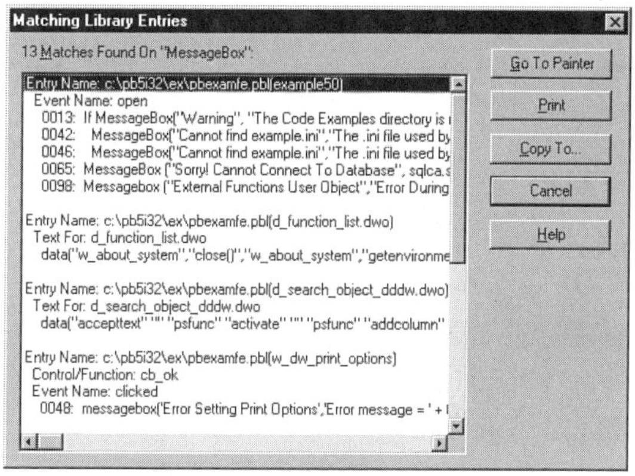

What was specified on the Search dialog box will affect what is displayed in the search results. If you left the defaults (everything chosen), you will see the entry name, the event/attribute/variable, and the usage of the search string. PowerBuilder allows you to perform several functions from the Matching Library Entries dialog box:

- If you double-click on an entry or click on the Go To Painter button, PowerBuilder launches the entry's painter and opens the object.
- Clicking on the Print button sends the search results list from the Matching Library Entries dialog box to the printer.
- The Copy To button allows you to specify the name of a text file to save the search results to.

Once you are done, click Cancel to return to the Search Library Entries dialog box.

Exporting and Importing Entries

Exporting and importing library entries gives you the ability to convert your PowerBuilder objects to an ASCII file format and vice versa. This can be useful for viewing the object syntax as well as modifying the object's definition. To learn how to read the exported code syntax, see Appendix F, "Investigating Exported Code," which is on the book's CD.

Exporting

Exporting an object to a file takes the source code definition of your PowerBuilder object (event scripts and object attributes) and creates an ASCII file.

To export an object, select the object and click the Export icon on the PainterBar or select Export from the Entry menu or pop-up menu. This opens the Export Library Entry dialog box (see Figure 13.11).

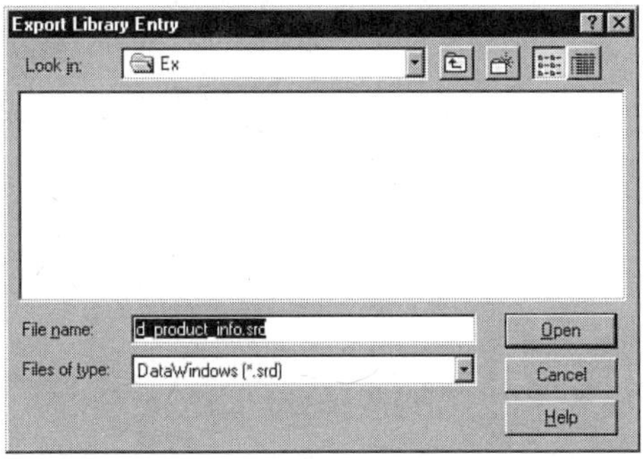

FIGURE 13.11.
The Export Library Entry dialog box.

PowerBuilder provides a default name for the exported object based on the object's name. The extension for the objects is .SR*x*, where *x* represents the object type (in this case a d for a DataWindow object).

NOTE

If you're running on a platform that does not support universal naming conventions (UNCs), the object name is truncated to comply with the local naming conventions.

The exported file can then be pulled up in any text editor and viewed or modified. While modifying an exported file is typically not recommended, there are times when you may need to do so.

Importing

If you have an exported file in ASCII format, you can import the file, which converts the source code back into a compiled PowerBuilder object.

To import an ASCII file, click the Import PainterBar icon or select Import from the Entry menu. This opens the Select Import Files dialog box (see Figure 13.12).

This dialog box looks for files with the extension .SR*. After selecting the desired text file, you are prompted with the Import File Into Library Entry dialog box (see Figure 13.13).

Select the destination library for the imported object and click OK.

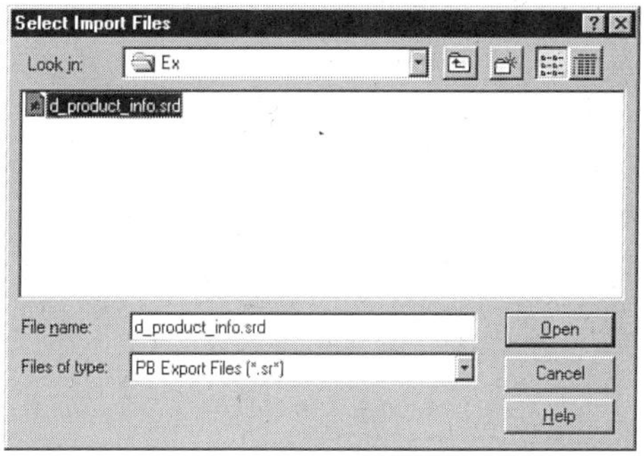

FIGURE 13.12.
The Select Import Files dialog box.

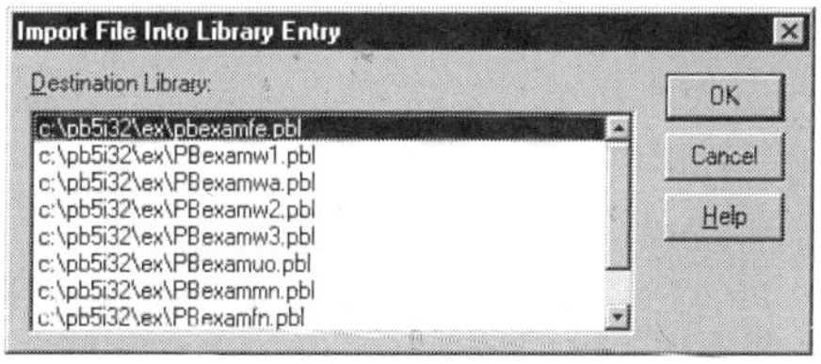

FIGURE 13.13.
The Import File Into Library Entry dialog box.

WARNING

If an object with the same name already exists in the destination library, the import will overwrite the existing object with the new object. Be aware that PowerBuilder does not notify you of this fact. Also, if the import fails, the original object is deleted.

Regeneration

A PowerBuilder library file contains both the compiled version and the source code for an object. Regeneration is the process of deleting the existing complied object and recompiling the source code. There are many times when you will need to regenerate your library objects (for example, when you migrate your application from one version of PowerBuilder to another). Another, more common, case is when you're using inheritance; if a modification has been made to an ancestor object you will want to regenerate the ancestor and all descendants to ensure that all changes are propagated through the inheritance tree. The Object Browser enables you to easily regenerate descendants of an altered ancestor object.

NOTE

In prior versions of PowerBuilder, if you deleted a control from an ancestor window, you were forced to open the Window painter and resave the object. Regeneration did not propagate these changes through to the descendants. In 5.0, regeneration makes sure the descendant objects are updated. The same holds true for inherited menus.

To regenerate your objects, select the objects desired and click the Regenerate PainterBar icon or select Regenerate from the Entry menu or the pop-up menu.

One of the difficulties of regenerating with inheritance is remembering all the objects that are involved. An easy way around this is to use the Object Browser.

The Object Browser can be used not only to view your application's objects (see Chapter 7, "The PowerScript Environment," for more details), but you can also view the class hierarchies of PowerBuilder's system classes, menus, user objects, and windows.

To open the Object Browser, click Browse Objects from the Utilities menu. The Object Browser appears, displaying the Application tab page as the default. Click on the System tab and check the Hierarchy check box to view the system class hierarchy (see Figure 13.14).

FIGURE 13.14.
The Object Browser.

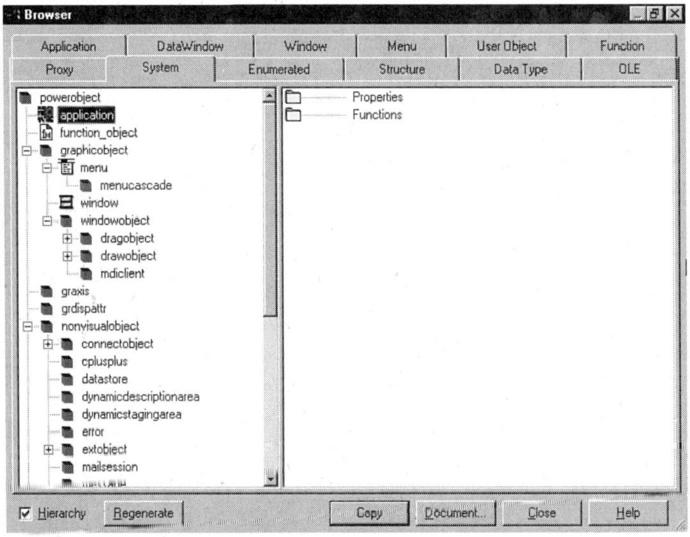

Four of the tab pages allow you to view a hierarchy, either class or object: Menu, System, User Object, and Window.

From the three object tab pages, you can regenerate the objects and their descendants. This is easier than regenerating each object individually because you can regenerate all objects in an inheritance tree in one go. Select the ancestor object and click on the Regenerate button. This regenerates the ancestor object and all its descendants.

Printing

From within the Library painter you can create several different printouts. You can print a library directory of the objects that it contains and you can print out object details. To print a library directory, select a library and choose Print Directory from the Library menu or the pop-up menu. The printout shows all the objects in the library, the size, the modification date, and comments.

To print out the object details, select the object(s) and click the Print menu item under the Entry menu or on the pop-up menu. The Print Options dialog box opens (see Figure 13.15).

FIGURE 13.15.
The Print Options dialog box.

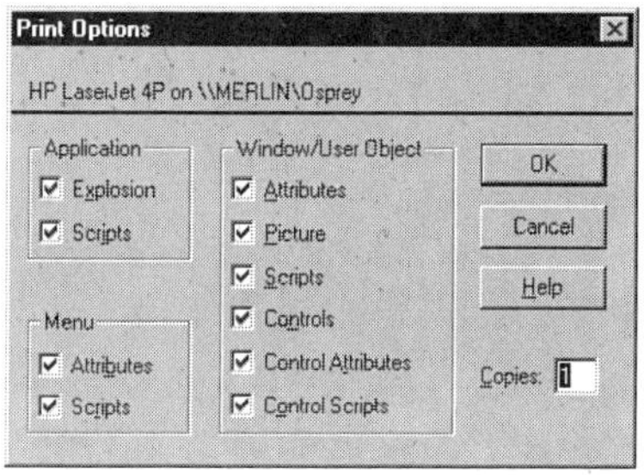

Clicking OK generates a report with the specified options. The objects that are selected when you chose Print from the menu should dictate what information is printed. As you can see, you can print attributes, scripts, control details, and so on.

Source Management

Any application development should include a plan for source management. PowerBuilder gives you a method to control the access of your library entries. This ensures that only one developer is working on a library entry at any given time. To best implement this, a centralized test library should exist that contains the completed objects. Each developer should maintain individual libraries that are used to make changes to copies of the original objects.

Objects can be extracted and inserted from the test library via the check-out and check-in facilities in the Library painter. When an object is checked out, only the developer who checked it out can modify or change the object. It cannot be modified in the public test library or be checked out by another developer. Only after the object is checked back in can modifications be made to the object.

Checking Out an Object

When an object is checked out of a library, only the developer who checked it out can make modifications to it. After the object has been modified and tested, it is checked back into the public test library.

During the check-out process, PowerBuilder copies the selected object to a specified destination library (typically the developer's private library). PowerBuilder stores with the checked-out object information on where the object was taken from and who checked it out. It then sets the status of the object to checked out. This status prevents the original object from being altered and allows only the working copy to be modified.

To check out an object, select the desired object and click the Check Out PainterBar icon or select Check Out from the Source menu or pop-up menu.

If this is the first time you have checked out an object, PowerBuilder will prompt you to enter a user ID (see Figure 13.16).

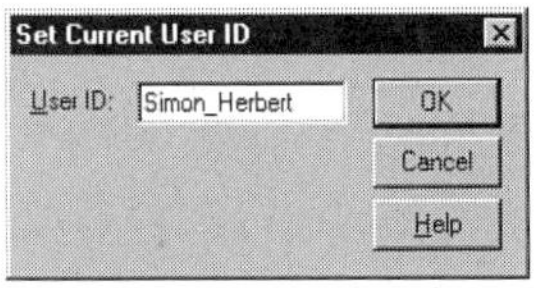

FIGURE 13.16.
The Set Current User ID dialog box.

The user ID is stored in the `[Library]` section of your PB.INI file. This ID is used for check-in and check-out identification purposes. You are only asked once to specify a user ID and have to manually change the PB.INI file to make any alterations to the ID.

After you enter the User ID, the Check Out Library Entries dialog box opens (see Figure 13.17).

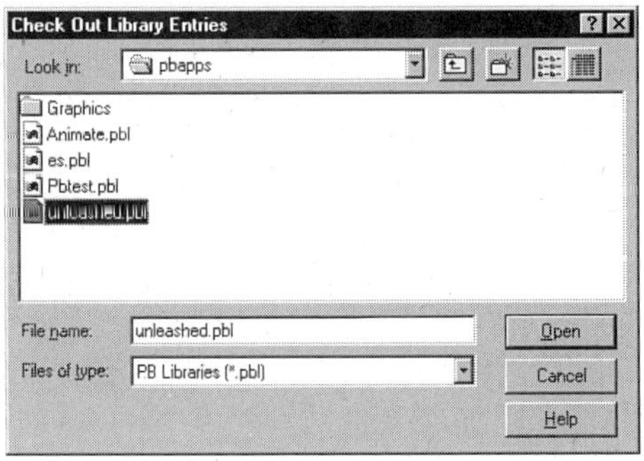

FIGURE 13.17.
The Check Out Library Entries dialog box.

Specify the destination library and click Open. If the entry is not already checked out, PowerBuilder creates a working copy in the destination library. If the entry is checked out, PowerBuilder displays a message indicating that the object is checked out and by whom and asks whether you want to continue (in which case PowerBuilder will open a read-only copy of the object for you).

To find out the check-out status of an entry, click the Check Status icon on the PainterBar or select View Check Out Status from the Source menu. The View Entries Check Out Status dialog box appears (see Figure 13.18).

FIGURE 13.18.
The View Entries Check Out Status dialog box.

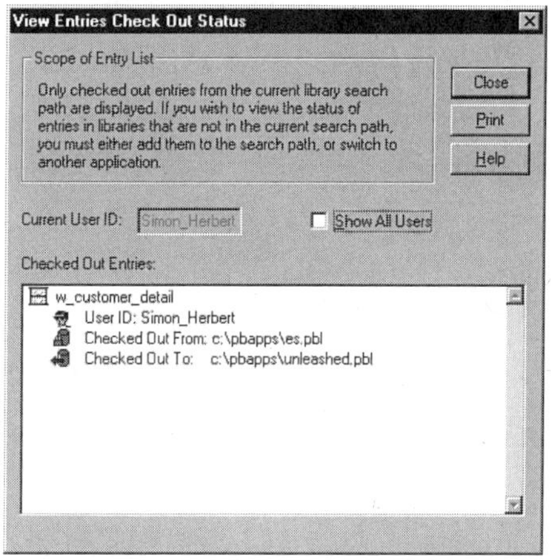

This dialog box can be used to display all the checked-out objects as well as print a list of the checked-out objects.

There are some implications of checking out objects that you need to keep in mind. Checked-out objects are locked and therefore they cannot be moved to a different library. This is because a move deletes the entry from the originating library. These objects can be copied, but the copy will not retain the check-out status.

Figure 13.19 shows the icon in the Library painter's workspace that symbolizes the locked check-out status of the original object. This figure also shows the icon in the Library painter's workspace that symbolizes the working copy of a checked-out object.

FIGURE 13.19.
The icons indicating checked-out objects in the Library painter workspace.

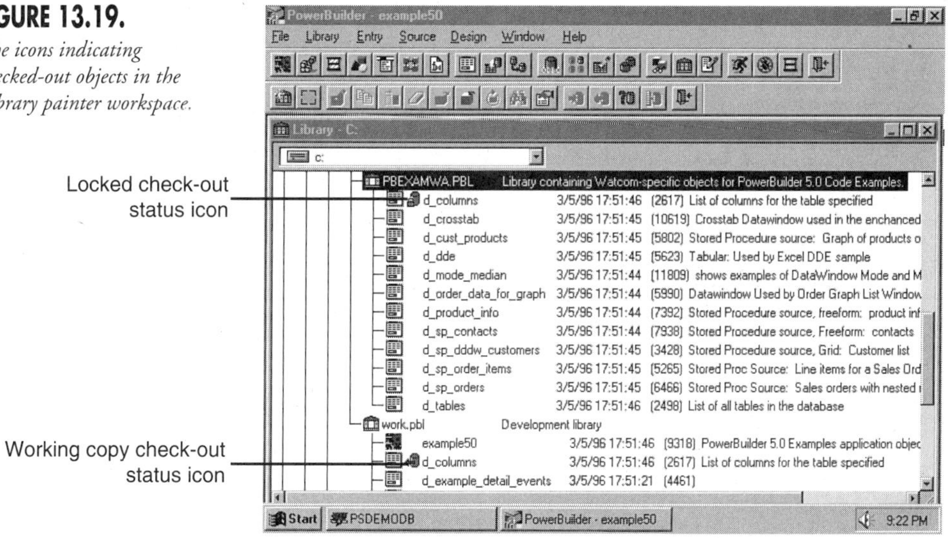

After checking out an object and making modifications to it, you are ready to check the object back into the public test library.

Checking In an Object

When you check in an object, the original copy is replaced with the working copy. The checked-out object is copied over the original object and then deletes the working copy in the development library.

To check in the working copy, click the Check In icon on the PainterBar, select Check In from the Source menu, or press Ctrl+I.

Multiple objects can be checked out and checked in at the same time.

NOTE

You can create a new PBL and copy objects to it to remove check-out status if something goes wrong during a check in. Of course, this can be frustrating in a multideveloper system because everyone has to check their objects back in first!

Clearing the Check-Out Status

If for some reason you no longer want to use the checked-out copy, you can clear the check-out status and delete the object from your private development library.

To clear the check-out status, select Clear Check Out Status from the Source menu. PowerBuilder prompts you to see if you want to clear the check out status of the library entry.

Click OK to clear the check-out status. PowerBuilder then asks whether you want to delete the library entry's working copy. Click Yes to delete it or No to leave the copy.

The Library painter should not be relied on as a version-control system because it is only as effective as the techniques and standards followed by the development team. PowerBuilder does provide an interface for an external version-control system such as PVCS or LBMS; the options for interacting with such a system are provided in the Source menu.

Creating Dynamic Libraries

The Library painter gives you the ability to create PowerBuilder dynamic libraries (PBDs or DLLs). To create a dynamic library, select Build Dynamic Library from the Library menu or the pop-up that appears when you right-click on a library name. The Build Runtime Library dialog box opens (see Figure 13.20).

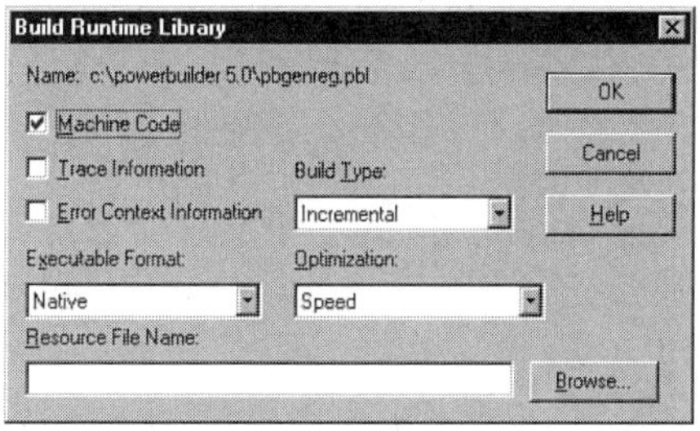

FIGURE 13.20.
The Build Runtime Library dialog box.

This dialog box has been modified in Version 5.0 to incorporate the ability to generate machine code. You can specify if the PBD will be machine coded and contain debug information with the Trace and Error Context Information check boxes. You can specify the runtime library's format as 16-bit or native (32-bit) and the optimization type: No Optimization, Space, or Speed. You can also specify a resource file in the Resource File Name box if needed. Click OK and PowerBuilder will create the dynamic library. It will have the same name as the source library, but with a .PBD extension for a 16-bit dynamic library and .DLL for a machine code library.

A further discussion of the advantages of using dynamic libraries is found in Chapter 18.

Application Migration

When you move from a prior release of PowerBuilder to Version 5.0, you must migrate all your applications. The migration process takes place in the Library painter. If you try to open an application object created in an earlier release in the Application painter, PowerBuilder will open the Library painter and the migrate current application dialog box (see Figure 13.21).

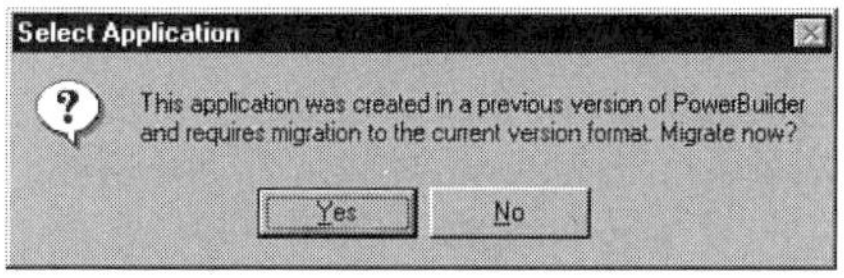

FIGURE 13.21.
The migrate current application dialog box.

This migrate application dialog box can also be opened from the Design menu by selecting the Migrate menu item. From this dialog box you can specify what type of error messages are processed. PowerBuilder will capture syntax errors, but can also display informational messages and obsolete syntax messages. PowerBuilder allows you to specify a library search path for the selected application object. Click on the Browse button to open the Select Library dialog box. In this dialog, you can select any PBLs you want to include in the search path.

PowerBuilder 5.0 runs the migration process in what Powersoft refers to as *batch mode.* This means that PowerBuilder tries to migrate all objects and displays any messages after all objects have been processed. This is useful in that you do not have to review each message as it is processed. Before migration occurs, PowerBuilder indicates that you should perform a backup of any libraries before proceeding with migration.

If you get any errors, they will be displayed in a compiler errors window (see Figure 13.22).

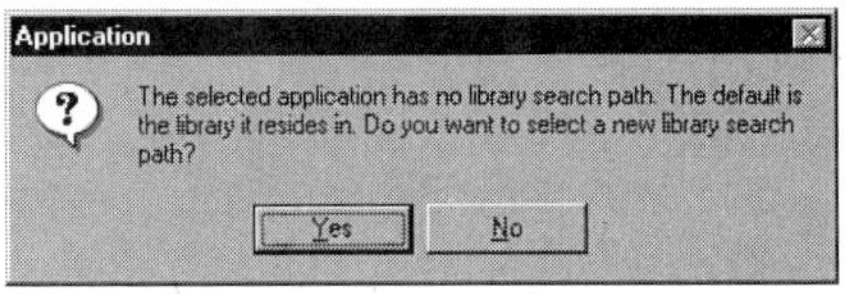

FIGURE 13.22.
The compiler errors window.

This window displays the object, event, and line number(s) that were in error. The type of message is indicated next to the actual error message. These messages can be sent to the printer or the Clipboard, or can be written to a text file. If the migration process encounters an error (noninformational and obsolete), migration of that object does not occur and the problem must be corrected in the older version of PowerBuilder before the object can be used in 5.0. Those objects can also be exported from within 5.0, modified, and reimported if you know what needs to be changed.

PowerScript

There are a number of PowerScript functions that you can incorporate into your application to access library files: `LibraryCreate()`, `LibraryDelete()`, `LibraryDirectory()`, `LibraryExport()`, and `LibraryImport()`.

The `LibraryCreate()` function is used to create an empty PowerBuilder library. The syntax for this function is

```
LibraryCreate( LibraryName {, Comments})
```

`LibraryName` is the name of the library that you want to create. The library is created in the current directory if a path is not included. If no extension is specified, the .PBL extension is added for you. The *`Comments`* argument is used to create a description entry for the library. The function returns `1` if it succeeds and `-1` if an error occurs.

`LibraryDelete()` is used to delete either an entire library file or a DataWindow object from a library. The syntax is

```
LibraryDelete( LibraryName {, ObjectName, ObjectType})
```

`LibraryName` is the name of the library file. To delete a DataWindow object instead of the library, you must include the *`ObjectName`* parameter (a string containing the DataWindow

object name), as well as *ObjectType*. *ObjectType* is of enumerated data type LibImportType (currently this only supports the value ImportDataWindow!). The function returns 1 if it succeeds and -1 if an error occurs.

The LibraryDirectory() function is used to return a list of the objects contained in a PowerBuilder library. The list contains the name, the date and time of the last modification, and any comments for each object. The list can be restricted to a particular object type if required. The syntax is

```
LibraryDirectory( LibraryName, ObjectType)
```

The *ObjectType* argument is of the enumerated data type LibDirType and identifies the type of objects to be included in the list. Table 13.3 lists the possible values and their descriptions.

Table 13.3. LibDirType values and descriptions.

Value	*Description*
DirAll!	All objects
DirApplication!	Application objects
DirDataWindow!	DataWindow objects
DirFunction!	Function objects
DirMenu!	Menu objects
DirPipeline!	Pipeline objects
DirProject!	Project objects
DirQuery!	Query objects
DirStructure!	Structure objects
DirUserObject!	User objects
DirWindow!	Window objects

The function returns a string containing a tab-delimited list with each object, with multiple objects separated by the ASCII value for a new line (~n). Here's an example:

```
w_customer_detail~t1/2/96 17:58:04~tCustomer detail list
```

The general format is

```
object_name ~t date/time modified ~t comments ~n
```

The LibraryExport() function is used to export an object from a library to a text file. The syntax is

```
LibraryExport( LibraryName, ObjectName, ObjectType)
```

`ObjectType` is of the enumerated data type `LibExportType` that identifies the type of object to be exported. Table 13.4 lists the possible values and their descriptions.

Table 13.4. `LibExportType` values and descriptions.

Value	*Exported Object*
`ExportApplication!`	Application object
`ExportDataWindow!`	DataWindow object
`ExportFunction!`	Function object
`ExportMenu!`	Menu object
`ExportStructure!`	Structure object
`ExportUserObject!`	User object
`ExportWindow!`	Window object

The function returns a string containing the syntax of the object if the operation succeeds. This syntax is the same as the syntax generated when the object is exported from within the Library painter. The only difference is that this function does not include an export header. An empty string (`""`) is returned if an error occurs.

The `LibraryImport()` function is used to import objects into a library. Currently, only DataWindow objects are supported. The syntax for this function is

```
LibraryImport( LibraryName, ObjectName, ObjectType, Syntax, Errors {,Comments})
```

The `ObjectType` parameter is of the `LibImportType` enumerated data type, and currently only supports `ImportDataWindow!`. The `Syntax` parameter is a string containing the syntax of the DataWindow object to import. The `Errors` parameter is a string variable that is filled with a description of any errors that occur. `Comments` is an optional string that is used as the comment for the library entry. The function returns `1` for success and `-1` if an error occurs. This function is particularly useful for DataWindows that are created dynamically.

Summary

As you have seen, the Library painter allows you to manage libraries and their entities to improve performance and accessibility. With the Library painter you can create, delete, and optimize your PowerBuilder libraries. The entities of the libraries can be manipulated as well.

The check-out and check-in facilities provide a useful interface that is designed to protect the development environment. Finally, there are several PowerScript functions that can be implemented into your application to interface with your application library files.

PART III

Creating PowerBuilder Applications

IN THIS PART

Analysis and Design

14

by Kurt Sundling

IN THIS CHAPTER

When approaching the development of a successful client/server application you must consider the entire development process from start to finish. Applications developed in the client/server arena use a continuous development life cycle to create, maintain, or improve solutions they provide.

Client/Server Application Development Methodology

This circular life cycle is but an inner piece of a much larger methodology that includes total quality management and continuous improvement techniques, as well as client/server technology concepts. This methodology is displayed in Figure 14.1 and handles the different aspects of the solutions needed to create a successful client/server application.

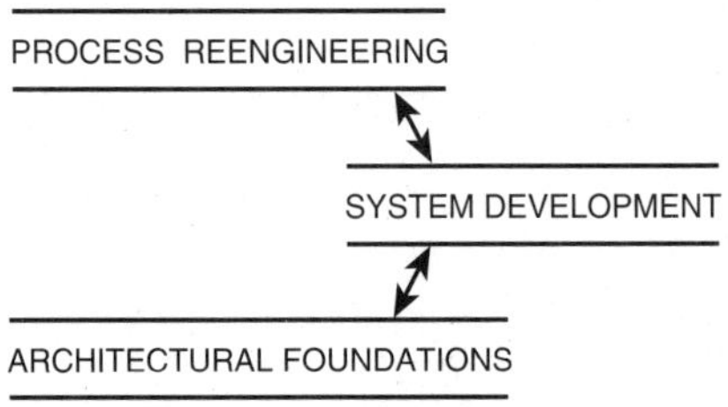

FIGURE 14.1.
The client/server application development methodology.

The three pieces of the client/server application development methodology are as follows:

- Process re-engineering
- Architectural foundations
- Systems development

Even though each piece reflects a different approach to the solution, the pieces interact and utilize the products of the other pieces to form a completely rounded approach.

Process re-engineering is the existing problem definition and solution piece of the methodology. It gathers information about the current situational application problems and determines optimal solutions for those problems. It incorporates those solutions into the system and continually monitors and improves the system through the problem identification, definition, and solution process.

Architectural foundations are the tools used to build the application piece of the methodology. This involves defining the packaging of the application, including the interaction between the application and data sources and external interfaces. It is also responsible for monitoring and optimizing database performance and application resource usage.

The final piece of the methodology is *systems development*, the phase when you discover needs or problems and model this information to determine an optimal solution. The solution is then developed and implemented into the application. This includes defining a plan and requirements that will be utilized in the design, creation, and implementation of a system. The system is continually monitored and enhanced through maintenance and development.

Even though the pieces interact as shown in Figure 14.1, they have their own individual life cycles. Within each of these pieces is the development life cycle, which allows for discovery, creation, and enhancement. This is illustrated in Figure 14.2.

FIGURE 14.2.
The client/server application development methodology with the individual life cycles.

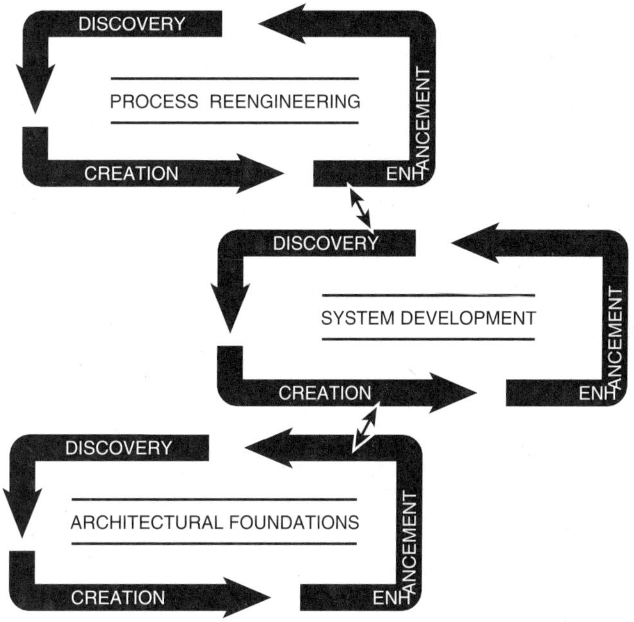

After this brief introduction to the basic methodology behind client/server application development, this chapter concentrates on analysis and design phases of these three pieces.

There are many types of analysis and design approaches, some of which are waterfall, object orientation, joint application development (JAD), rapid application development (RAD), rapid iterative prototyping (RIP), and business process engineering. Another method is the Capability Maturity Model (CMM), which is an ever-growing method. Tools such as computer-assisted software engineering (CASE) assist development teams with these processes. This chapter gives a brief synopsis of some of these different approaches and their place in the client/server application development methodology. It then discusses the procedure of matching the analysis and design phases with PowerBuilder functionality and characteristics. Finally, it concentrates on the cornerstone of all successful client/server applications: the database design.

Object-Oriented Analysis and Design

Object-oriented analysis and design (OOA and OOD) is an approach to application development that emphasizes object development and de-emphasizes procedure development. This approach is based on the concept of modularity. *Modularity* provides a means of decomposing a system into smaller, more manageable units with well-defined interfaces between them. Both OOA and OOD evolved from this concept.

Using *modularity* as the base, the object-oriented approach encapsulates information into separate modules for easier definition and manageability. These modules are related pieces of information grouped together. Encapsulating the information led to the idea of *information hiding*, which is the process of eliminating the use of globally accessible data. So these modules are self-contained, manageable, modifiable, understandable, and most importantly reusable.

The object-oriented approach contains three ideal pieces:

- Objects
- Classes
- Inheritance

These pieces can be viewed as

```
OBJECTS + CLASSES + INHERITANCE
```

Because they are the information hiding modules, objects are designed to be as generic as possible while still encapsulating the information. They conceptually communicate by means of messages that correspond to an operation in the object. Classes are an object type and are considered templates for objects. An object is an instance of a class, which makes the class a module type. Classes may be specialized using inheritance. Inheritance is a mechanism for sharing and reusing attributes and code between classes. A child class adapts the structure (encapsulated data and attributes) and behavior (operations and events) of its parent class for its own use by adding new or redefining existing attributes, operations, events, and instance variables as the developer sees appropriate.

This method is becoming more and more popular in the client/server realm. It allows for the gathering of information for problem definition and solution. With the emergence of more object-oriented programming and development environments and tools, this appears to be the most viable approach to analysis and design for most organizations.

The Waterfall Development Methodology

The waterfall methodology is generally considered the conventional or "classic" software life cycle. It follows the structured analysis and structured design approach in development. A model of the waterfall methodology is displayed in Figure 14.3.

FIGURE 14.3.
The waterfall development methodology model.

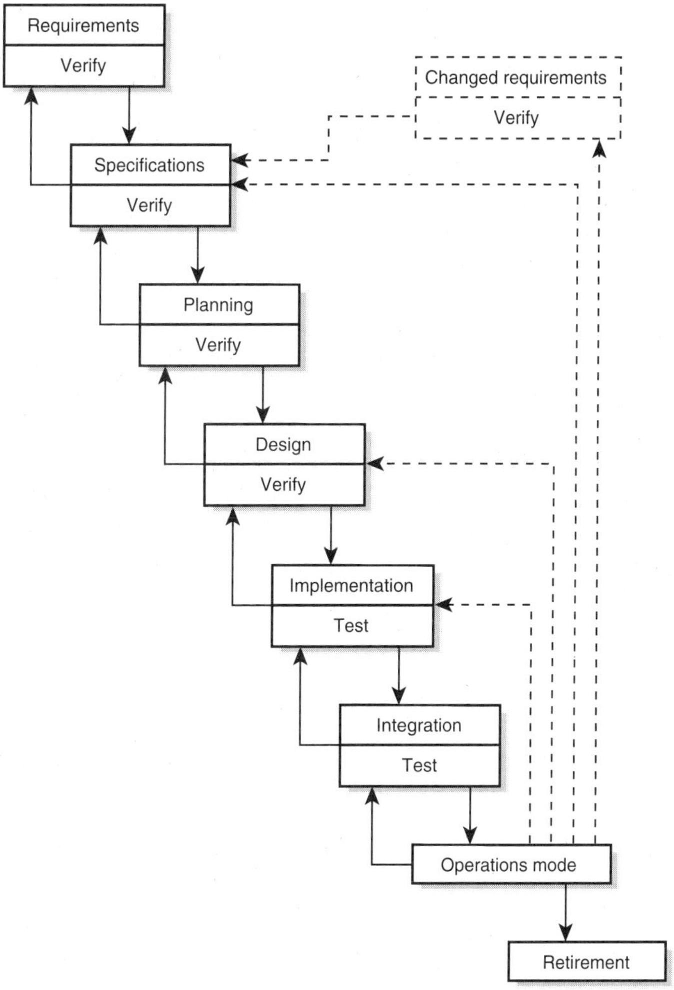

The first step in this model is the analysis and identification of the user requirements. The software requirements are then specified in a requirement specifications document, which is a complete description of system external behavior that does not describe how the system works internally. The architectural design is the structuring of the system into concurrent tasks, with an emphasis on decomposition into tasks, modules, or both. An important factor at this point in the design is the behavioral aspect of the system. You need to define the sequence of events and what the system is experiencing. The detailed design is done in a Program Design Language (PDL) notation, also referred to as Structured English or pseudocode.

Two things occur when you're operating in this model: testing and documentation. Testing is performed continuously throughout the software process, either in the form of verification or actual testing. Documentation is constantly produced, maintained, and updated throughout each phase. The model produces a specifications document, a design document, a code document, and many other documents, including the database, user, and operations manuals that are essential for maintenance of the system.

There are a number of potential problems with this approach. One is that requirements are not properly tested until a working system is operational, at which time the system demonstrates to the users what the specifications have produced. Errors in the requirement specifications document are the last to be detected and are the most costly to correct. Since the working model comes late in the development life cycle, major design or performance issues and concerns are not encountered until the system is almost operational.

Client/server architecture is supplying, in essence, a standalone system on a user's desk. Users are looking for systems that can be produced quickly and effectively. Because the waterfall method produces a working model of the system late in the development cycle, it has a difficult time finding space in the client/server development methodology. One of the solutions to the problems of using the waterfall model is the prototyping approach.

The Prototyping Methodology

The prototyping methodology is an analysis and design approach in which the system designer and the end users work together very closely. They participate in interactive meetings where design versions of the system are modeled, modified, and updated until the system designers get a complete understanding of the needs and requirements of the system and the users see what the final product will look like. The final prototype reflects the needs and requirements of the application and can generally be developed and expounded on to produce the final product.

The development of a prototype after preliminary requirement specifications gives the users the capability of exercising the prototype to develop valuable feedback to the systems development team. Based on this feedback, a revised requirement specifications document can be prepared along with a new or revised prototype. Prototypes can be thrown away and rebuilt with each revised set of specifications or the process can be evolutionary or incremental in nature, in which case the prototype evolves through several intermediate systems into the final delivered system. The latter prototype version provides a working subset to build on. All through these prototype iterations a new or revised prototype and requirement specifications document are produced and used until the final product is complete.

Figure 14.4 is a visual model of the working evolutionary or rapid iterative prototype (RIP) methodology.

This rapid iterative prototyping process encompasses all development phases from planning to delivery and fully utilizes the waterfall methodology model, with the addition of the prototype iteration. The analysis phase is not complete until after the prototype iteration cycle, during which the prototype is continually modified until an end requirement specifications list and a final prototype are agreed on by the development and user teams.

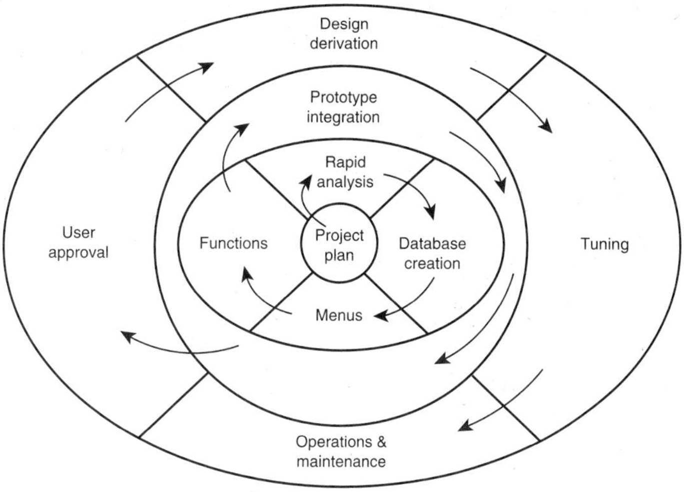

FIGURE 14.4.
The rapid iterative prototype development methodology model.

This model works very well in organizations where the end users can allocate a sufficient amount of time to working with the development team. The users also gain the benefit of seeing and working with multiple versions of the system as it flows through the prototype iterations. This allows for problem identification, and feedback is immediately provided so that solutions in the software or hardware can be made. This also minimizes the amount of training for the users, as they will already be familiar with the application and its components.

Joint Application Development

Joint application development (JAD) is an extended form of rapid iterative prototyping, in which the client (end user) team plays an active, rather than reactive, role. The joint team represents both the development and client teams.

The teams work together to form a group with an impartial leader. The team leader should not have a vested interest in the outcome of the project. That person's job is to be a mediator and obtain consensus among the various proposed alternatives without having a specific interest in the final choice.

The joint team discusses the needs of the client, designs screens and reports, builds rapid prototypes, and draws up the requirement specification document. In this manner the client team plays an active, rather than a reactive, role in the analysis and design. This technique places members of both the development and client teams together to function and work to produce the requirements and specifications with joint responsibility.

As you can see, this requires a great deal of dedication by both the development and user groups. The rewards from such a partnership are similar to the benefits of the prototype development methodology, but the user group will be much more involved and more knowledgeable about the developed system, and therefore will have a vested interest in it and its success.

Rapid Application Development

Rapid application development (RAD) is not so much a new methodology as it is an integration of several currently used techniques. The main objective is quicker development of higher-quality systems. The goal is to quickly develop a working system that meets all requirements but with, hopefully, fewer bugs per 1000 lines of code (a measurement in some areas of the system development world of quality assurance in coding).

The five components of RAD are

- Project scheduling
- Joint resource planning and development
- Prototyping
- CASE tools
- Reusable code

Project scheduling involves the client team. The idea is to utilize the fewest people for the project. You staff the project in a manner that maximizes the overlapping of functions with developers and determines the duration of the project based on the function complexities.

Joint resource planning and development consists of joint requirement planning and joint application design. This is the combined effort of the client and development teams. Requirement planning is the structured analysis and application design phase as described earlier in the chapter in the section "The Waterfall Development Methodology."

Prototyping is an integral part of the design in RAD. As stated earlier in the chapter, some prototyping processes evolve into parts of the production system. In RAD, prototyping is essential to building the final system because the prototype will be used as the main building block of the application.

CASE tools are heavily used in RAD because they are capable of integrating existing reusable code. Reusable code integrates with the CASE tools to reshape existing code, thus minimizing errors in and centralizing the code.

CASE Tools

CASE is not a software development process, but rather a set of tools used in the process. The tools enable you to capture business rules and functional requirements in an electronic format that can be related, associated, and presented much more quickly and in an orderly fashion to a variety of audiences such as client teams and senior management. These tools are used for storing and accessing system objectives, requirements, process specifications, and so on online. You must eventually determine your analysis and design technique and how these tools will play a part in that technique.

Capability Maturity Model

The Capability Maturity Model, known as CMM, is not a software process model, but a strategy for improving the software process, regardless of the process model being used. When organizations introduce new processes to solve existing software development problems, it does not always work. The introduction of a new process will not always result in an increase in productivity and profitability, because the cause of many problems is the way software processes are managed.

The idea of CMM is to achieve disciplined and mature levels of the software processes. These processes comprise the activities, techniques, and tools utilized to build and create software applications incorporating both technical and managerial elements. In CMM, if you improve the management of the process, the improvement in techniques will follow as a natural consequence.

An organization advances through these maturity levels in a series of small, evolutionary steps. Changes only occur incrementally. CMM has five levels of maturity, which are displayed in Table 14.1.

Table 14.1. The capability maturity model's five levels of maturity.

Level	*Name*	*Description*
1	Initial	Ad hoc process
2	Repeatable	Basic project management
3	Defined	Process definition
4	Managed	Process management
5	Optimizing	Process control

At the *initial* level no sound software project management practices exist. All systems are created on an ad hoc basis. The software process is completely unpredictable.

The *repeatable* level demonstrates that basic software engineering management practices are in place. Planning and management techniques are based on the experience with similar products, hence the term *repeatable*.

The *defined* level illustrates that the process for software production is completely documented. Both managerial and technical aspects of the software process are clearly defined and continually updated with improvements.

At the *managed* level, quality and productivity goals for each individual project are set. They are continually monitored and measured, and corrective action is taken where deviations occur. This level begins the statistical quality control of the software process itself.

In the *optimizing* level, there are continuous process improvement statistical quality and process control techniques guiding the organization. Knowledge transfer between projects and teams occurs. The software process incorporates positive feedback to continually improve the process.

Of course, all these methods and techniques have pluses and minuses and must be evaluated according to organization requirements. By no means are these the only software development methodologies. The rest of the chapter illustrates a type of development process that is very viable with PowerBuilder development.

Analysis

This section covers the analysis processes in the client/server application development life cycle. You will determine system requirements, analyze data, design system requirements, and match the designed system requirements with PowerBuilder functionality.

The systems analysis phase consists of determining system requirements and analyzing data. This process consists of gathering all pertinent information about the desired application and determining what the application does when used. It includes looking at the existing system and talking with users. This entails doing a walk-through with the users of the desired or existing system to determine the components of the application. These walk-throughs provide information from different perspectives on the flows, processes, data, and usage of the application.

During these walk-throughs and gathering of information, you create the system requirements. You review the existing system, determine the user needs, and define the functional requirements of the system application. The entire process produces information that needs to be collected and organized in a manageable fashion.

One suggestion for a manageable organization of data encompasses three categories:

- Input
- Output
- Processing

The *input* category consists of all inputs the application receives. This includes user and data source input. User input is the data being created, manipulated, or deleted by the user through a user interface. Data source input embodies disparate data sources accessed by the application to supply the data that the user and the application will process, manage, and manipulate.

The *output* category covers the output the application produces. This includes the creation of multiple detailed reports, the updating of the data source, and the generation of different types of files.

Both the input and output categories determine what data is needed. The data is then modeled from this gathered information. This information modeling identifies, organizes, and quantifies the data used by the application. This is further discussed in the section "Data Analysis."

The *processing* category reflects the application control flow and the required additional services from other programs. The operations performed by the application include displaying and updating data. This category also includes the process of connecting to other programs to access their data or functions.

The information gathered in these three categories needs to be stored in a way that allows it to be easily updated and maintained throughout the entire client/server application life cycle. This consolidated information provides analysts, developers, and managers with a central repository of information they can use to construct applications. There are several different approaches to the collection and organization of this information.

One approach to creating the application requirements is putting the information into a specification document. This document usually states the requirements in the terms used by the analyst. The terms are agreed to by the client or the owner of the system application. The developer uses this document information to design and match the requirements to the application's creation and modification.

Another approach to storing the collected information is the use of workflow models. Such models as data flow diagrams, entity relationship diagrams, and structure charts store the information in visual as well as textual ways.

A type of collection utilizing a combination of these approaches is the CASE tool. This type of tool encompasses the use of workflow models and structured documents, as described earlier in the chapter.

Once the system requirements are defined and you have a working information model, you can determine the optimal solution. This entails a complete, documented set of requirements describing the functionality of the system. At this point you can begin to determine the system data needs.

Throughout this process you can develop windows and menus giving the users a visual representation of your understanding of the system. These will provide you with multiple prototypes that you may or may not utilize in the development of the final application.

Data Analysis

The data analysis process is concerned with the logical and physical database construction. This stage identifies, inventories, organizes, and quantifies the information the application uses. It captures all the user information in a way that enables you to analyze and classify it. This results in a model that can be transposed directly to a database schema.

We use an information modeling technique, where the information is defined through three basic objects:

- The entity
- The attribute
- The relationship

An *entity* is a collection of related characteristics that you need to maintain and use. An *attribute* is a quality, feature, or characteristic of an entity. A *relationship* is an associative link between two entities. The relationship models an association between records (instances) of the entities and how they interact with each other.

An example of this type of modeling is the entity relationship diagram shown in Figure 14.5.

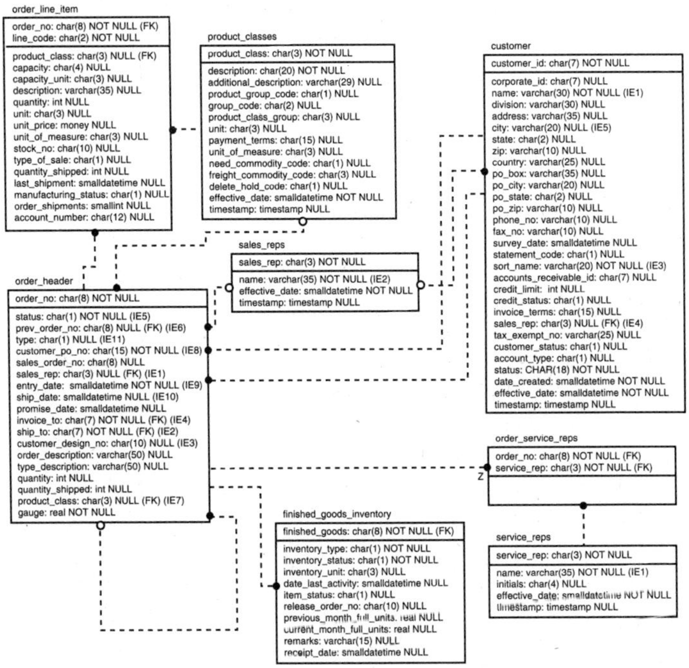

FIGURE 14.5.
An entity relationship diagram.

An excellent development tool used to create Figure 14.5 is the entity relationship window, which is a part of ERWin/ERX for PowerBuilder by LogicWorks. Several other tools, such as System Architect, S-Designor, and LBMS, can also be used to create similar diagrams. LBMS is more of a full-scale CASE tool, whereas ERWin/ERX, System Architect, and S-Designor are purely data modeling, design, and implementation tools. The new versions of these tools claim that they can be used to prototype simple windows and DataWindows.

The relationship diagram, like the one in Figure 14.5, helps you complete a full picture of the desired database schema. You identify objects, classify the objects, quantify the entities and relationships, quantify classification schemes, and validate the completed model. The information gathered during this identification and classification process is incorporated into the information model as the entities, attributes, and relationships. This will assist you in your analysis and design of the data.

The first step in creating a relationship diagram is to identify the objects. You must identify the primary or major information objects. These are usually directly related to the potential system data. You can review and study the previous system data, the user interviews, and the general information to determine what the system data is. All this data is eventually classified as entities, attributes, or relationships in the model.

Next, you need to classify the individual objects. You must determine whether an object is an entity, an attribute, or a relationship. This includes associating attributes with an entity and specifying relationships between associated entities. There are many ways to determine these three objects, but the following are some rules of thumb for each:

- If the object appears to have many characteristics or values, it is probably an entity. For example, the entity `Order` entails many values or attributes, such as the status of the order, the order number, where the order goes, and the ordered date. This makes `Order` an entity.
- If the object appears to have only one characteristic or value, it is probably an attribute. For example, the attribute `Order Number` is the identifying number of an order, and that is all. The attribute `Order Entry Date` is the date the order was entered. Both of these examples are attributes.
- If the object description contains a verb phrase, it is probably a relationship. For example, the phrase `Customer Requests Order` exemplifies a relationship between a `Customer` entity and an `Order` entity.

You then quantify the entities and relationships. You must determine the individual entities and their associated attributes. You ascribe a full business-related description and an individual usage requirement for each object. This also includes whether the entity is a necessary permanent requirement for the application. Identification of the cardinality of every relationship makes use of the business definition and requirements associated with the relationship.

During your determination of the attributes associated with an entity, you also want to determine keys, and therefore indexes, of the entities and how you will be organizing the attributes in each of the entities. In addition, you need to determine the datatype of the attribute and whether it can be a null value. At an advanced level of the attribute-describing process you may also want to identify all the extended attribute information, including length, format, edit style, validation rules, and initial values, that can be stored in the PowerBuilder repository tables.

Once the attributes are organized for the individual entities, you can begin classifying the entities in an organized fashion.

You must quantify the classification scheme by grouping the entities via associations. This is the initial phase of *abstraction*, or hiding obscure information to heighten understanding of the analysis. By classifying the data in groups, you produce types of classes for the associated groups (see Figure 14.6), which are more easily viewed and analyzed.

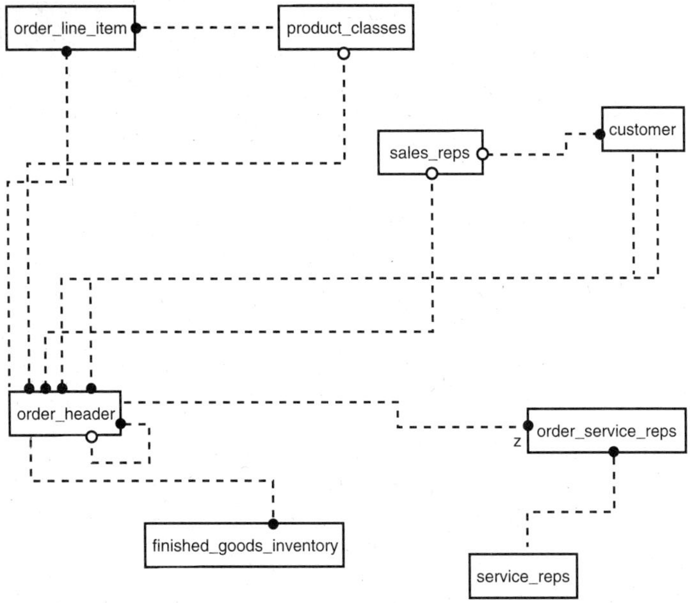

FIGURE 14.6.
Groups of related entities.

Now you can group these entities into a single class, which is much easier to view and manipulate (see Figure 14.7).

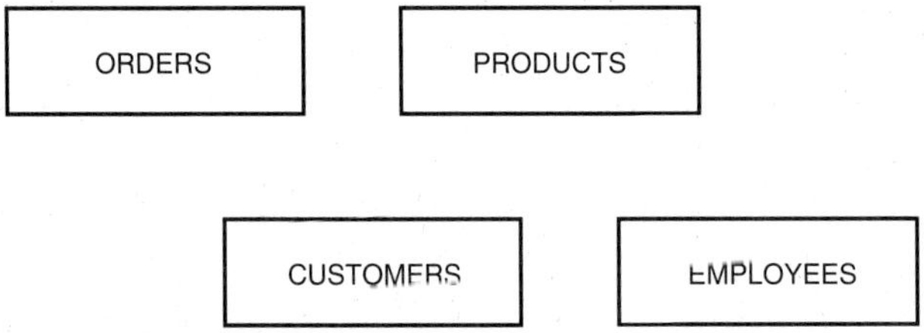

FIGURE 14.7.
Classes of the grouped entities.

Next you determine the correct classifications for the entities. You can generalize multiple entities into single classifications. See if there are any similarities in their functionality and attribution. If there are similarities, you can classify them into a single common entity without losing either of the entities' meanings. Make sure the scope and purpose of combined entities are not diminished or sacrificed during this classification and combination of entities.

Because the classification process is the most important process, you spend most of your data analysis time in this phase. This phase of classification and generalization of the entities prepares the data for the design phase. In the design phase you use other methods, such as normalization, which is described later in the chapter in the "Normalization" section, to complete the entire data analysis scenario with a fully functional database information model.

After the classification step, you need to validate the information to make sure it still coincides with the information the users manage. In the validation phase you ensure that all entities have been captured and identified correctly with their associated relationships and attributes.

This concludes the analysis phase of the system development life cycle. With the plethora of functionality information and the modeled data, you are prepared to begin designing your application.

System Design

The system design phase consists of designing the system requirements and matching the designed system requirements with PowerBuilder functionality. In this phase you complete the information model to produce a fully functional database schema, and a designed physical form of the system emerges from the three categories of the system requirements. This is accomplished through normalizing the data to produce a database schema. The application design can be attacked from different angles. One of these approaches is rapid prototyping; this is discussed briefly earlier in the chapter. The chapter mainly concentrates on matching the system requirements with PowerBuilder characteristics, thus creating a physical form that can be used as a blueprint for developing and implementing an application. As part of this process, attention should be given to the appropriate use of stored procedures and triggers for certain processing and enforcing referential integrity.

Matching System Requirements to PowerBuilder Characteristics

From the system analysis you have the input, output, and processing requirements deciphered and described. Each of these categories can now be matched to a PowerBuilder characteristic. This entails breaking down the categories into individual parts and mapping those parts to PowerBuilder features that best support their functionality.

Designing the Input Category

The input category consists of the user interface and the data sources. The database design is described later in the section "Normalization," but there are other considerations involved with the data source's access by the application. This part of the design process is concerned only with the PowerBuilder features associated with the user interface and data source access.

The user interface requires the specification of the creation, manipulation, and deletion of data by the user. You need to provide the user with the means to accomplish these actions. During design of the user interface, your primary concerns are with data organization and presentation and the user's interaction with the application and the presented data.

The user interface controls the entering and manipulation of data while navigating through a series of organized screens and menus used to present the data. PowerBuilder provides windows and DataWindows to display and manipulate the data.

There are different types of windows (refer to Chapter 11, "Windows and the Window Painter," for a further description on the types of windows), but two useful window types are the *MDI frame* and *main* windows. The multiple-document interface (MDI) enables the user to interact with multiple sheets (windows) within the frame. A user can perform different tasks on multiple windows at the same time. The other type of interface is a single-document interface (SDI). This provides the user with one main window to perform a specific task. If the user requires a different task, a different main window must be accessed. The method of designing and developing the application is solely dependent on the type of application required and is driven by the system requirements previously defined.

When designing the user interface, you should decide whether you plan to create a multiple-document interface or a single-document interface. To do this you must decide how the data will be organized and presented and how the user will move around in the application. This will dictate how the application user interface should be designed.

Within these different types of windows you can map desired functionality to controls. Event-driven processing puts the user in control of how an application operates and uses controls to display and interact with the data. You can also refer to Chapter 11 for further description of the types of controls for windows.

Menus provide another way of manipulating data or interacting with the application. The user selects menu items to initiate an action. Menus can be accessed from a menu bar, an MDI Frame toolbar, or a pop-up menu. For a more complete description of menus refer to Chapter 12, "Menus and the Menu Painter."

For example, you might want to create an order entry application that allows users to have more than one order open at the same time. Users may want to compare multiple orders or create a repeat order. The MDI style provides this functionality very easily, but additional code would be required in an SDI application.

Data source requirements include the accessing of tables from one or more databases on one or more DBMSs. PowerBuilder provides two ways of accessing this data:

- SQL statements
- DataWindows

SQL statements are embedded in the application, whereas DataWindows are special objects used to interface with the database. An easy method of data row manipulation and presentation is accomplished through DataWindows. You can also refer to Chapter 9, "The DataWindow Painter," and Chapter 10, "DataWindow Scripting," for a further description on the workings of DataWindows. By designing the DataWindow objects, you create a user interface that can be utilized by windows.

You can design these SQL statements and DataWindows without prior knowledge of the DBMS because PowerBuilder places the DBMS-specific access information in a different software layer. This layer of database interfaces comes with the installation of PowerBuilder. It provides the database interfaces for many different DBMSs, including Watcom and SQL Server. Thus, the application's database presentation and manipulation can be developed independently of the DBMS.

NOTE

You can bypass this isolation level and place in the DataWindow query DBMS-specific keywords and actions that will make it less portable to another DBMS.

Designing the Output Category

The output category consists of all output produced by the application, such as detailed reports, data written to the database, and data written to external files. This is the base function of the application, because a system is usually designed to produce some form of output.

Detailed reports can be online, printed, or written to a file for future access. The full definition of the report and how the report is to be delivered should already be captured by the analysis phase. In the design phase you need to match the data with the report and design how the report will look. Using DataWindows is an excellent way of designing reports. You can also refer to Chapter 9 for further description of using DataWindows as a reporting tool.

You can also use SQL statements and DataWindows to update the database. When designing a DataWindow user interface, you also set up how to handle updating the database after the data has been modified.

PowerBuilder gives you the ability to generate different types of files, such as Excel spreadsheets, text files, and dBASE files.

Designing the Processing Category

The processing category consists of all processing flow and logic internally and externally. Because PowerBuilder is event driven, the processing must be designed to control the flow and follow the logic of the processing requirements, while allowing the user to dictate the actions of the system.

You write scripts for events to react to the actions the user wishes to make. During the design phase of the application, you need to decide which of the events will be used. Then you can provide the logic in these events to control the processing flow. This is the most important part of the processing design. If you didn't identify all the events and place the appropriate logic in them, some of the requirements for processing could be lost.

The external process control requirements contain any requirements to share data with other programs or to access additional services.

PowerBuilder supports two approaches to data sharing:

- Dynamic data exchange (DDE)
- Object linking and embedding (OLE)

DDE enables the sharing of data and commands between programs. OLE provides more powerful functionality than DDE. Refer to Chapter 36, "OLE 2.0 and DDE," for further description of these two approaches.

Database Design

Even though database design is part of both the analysis and design phases of an application, this chapter discusses database design in these phases separately because the database creation and maintenance are extremely important to the overall development of an application.

The database is the central hub of your application. The quality of the database design and maintenance will greatly determine the quality and success of your application. Since PowerBuilder will design the application around the database, spending quality time in analysis and design on the database will assist in the development of the application.

Database design can be broken down into four parts:

- Creating the data's physical schema
- Normalization and finalizing table relationships
- Creation of triggers, stored procedures, and indexes
- Documentation of the database design

Creating the data's physical schema consists of using the products of the data analysis to form the tables, columns, and relationships between tables. Columns are assigned a datatype. Also during this phase you can define the extended attributes of the columns, such as the edit style, initial value, validation, display format, and so on. For a more complete description of the extended attributes, refer to Chapter 4, "Databases and the Database Painter."

Table relationships as well as the primary and foreign keys can be defined here. The keys will be expounded on later in the "Triggers, Stored Procedures, and Indexes" section. The data analysis determines most of the table relationships and is represented accordingly, but to optimize these relationships you will use the *normalization* process.

Normalization

During the data design phase, which is an extension of data analysis, an important goal is that data be stored in exactly one place. This eliminates redundancy, simplifies database updates, improves database integrity, and reduces storage requirements.

Normalization is the process of eliminating duplicate entries by moving data into its own entity. Database tables are described as having a certain *normal form* if they satisfy particular criteria. Each level of the normal forms builds on the previous level.

To best describe normalization, each step is followed by an example.

The five levels of data normalization are as follows:

- Eliminate repeating groups (1NF, or first normal form)
- Eliminate redundant data (2NF, or second normal form)
- Eliminate columns not dependent on key (3NF, or third normal form)
- Isolate independent multiple relationships (4NF, or fourth normal form)
- Isolate semantically related multiple relationships (5NF, or fifth normal form)

The example this chapter uses to illustrate the normalization method consists of the following information:

Unnormalized attributes for an order entry system
Order number
Order date
Order description
Customer number
Customer name
Customer address
Product number 1_n
Product name 1_n
Product unit price 1_n
Product order quantity 1_n
Order discount 1_n

First Normal Form

To eliminate repeating groups, create a separate entity for each group of related attributes and give the entity a primary key.

In the sample unnormalized attributes, each order can have multiple products but only one customer. So an order could have five different products going to one customer. If you move the `Product` attributes into a separate entity, the other information needs to be repeated for each product (see Table 14.2). At this point, these entities are in the first normal form. You can now use `Order Number` to easily access both entities: the `Order` entity and the `Product` entity. `Order Number` acts as a primary key in the `Order` entity and a foreign key in the `Product` entity.

Table 14.2. The `Order` entity and `Product` entity, with `Order Number` being the primary key and relationship between the two entities.

`Order` *Entity*	`Product` *Entity*
`Order Number`	`Order Number`
`Order Date`	`Product Number`
`Order Description`	`Product Name`
`Customer Number`	`Product Unit Price`
`Customer Name`	`Product Order Quantity`
`Customer Address`	`Order Discount`

Second Normal Form

To eliminate redundant data, you need to create separate entities for attributes that do not fully depend on an entity's multivalued key.

In the example of the order entry system, the `Product` entity attributes `Product Name` and `Product Unit Price` are dependent only on the `Product Number`, whereas `Product Order Quantity` and `Order Discount` are dependent on both the `Order Number` and the `Product Number`. Therefore, you can remove the `Product Name` and `Product Unit Price` and create their own entity, like the one in Table 14.3. These entities are in second normal form.

Table 14.3. The addition of the `Product` entity.

`Product Order` *Entity*	`Product` *Entity*
`Order Number`	`Order Number`
`Product Number`	`Product Name`
`Product Order Quantity`	`Product Unit Price`
`Order Discount`	

Third Normal Form

To eliminate columns not dependent on keys, create a separate entity for the attribute.

`Customer Name` and `Customer Address` are not dependent on the `Order Number` key but are dependent on the `Customer Number`. You need to create a new entity, `Customer` (see Table 14.4), to house these two attributes and remove them from the `Order` entity. The entities are now in third normal form.

Table 14.4. The addition of the `Customer` entity.

`Order` *Entity*	`Customer` *Entity*
`Order Number`	`Customer Number`
`Order Date`	`Customer Name`
`Order Description`	`Customer Address`
`Customer Number`	

Third normal form is adequate for most database situations, but there are two additional normal forms. Some data models may require use of these additional normal forms to produce a better-designed database model.

Fourth Normal Form

The fourth normal form is concerned about isolating independent multiple relationships. Basically, an entity cannot have more than one one-to-many (1:n) or many-to-many (n:m) relationship that is not directly related to another relationship.

If each product order can have many sales representatives associated with it, you should place the attribute `Sales Representative` in the `Product Order` entity (see Table 14.5).

Table 14.5. The `Product Order` entity with the addition of the `Sales Representative` attribute.

`Product Order` *Entity*
`Order Number`
`Product Number`
`Product Order Quantity`
`Order Discount`
`Sales Representative`

The `Sales Representative` entity has a many-to-many relationship with `Product Order` and is not related to `Product Order Quantity` or `Order Discount`. Because this is a many-to-many relationship, you can place the attribute in its own entity with the `Order Number` and `Product Number`, with all three attributes acting as the primary key (see Table 14.6).

Table 14.6. The `Product Order Sales Representative` entity.

`Sales Representative` *Entity*	`Product Order` *Entity*
	`Order Number`
`Order Number`	`Product Number`
`Product Number`	`Product Order Quantity`
`Sales Representative`	`Order Discount`

The unrelated attributes are separated into the `Product Order` entity and the `Product Order Sales Representative` entity. The `Product Order Sales Representative` entity can have multiple values without affecting the `Product Order` entity, with the `Product Order Quantity` and `Order Discount` values being repeated, as in Table 14.5. The entities are now in fourth normal form.

Fifth Normal Form

Fifth normal form concentrates on isolating semantically related multiple relationships. You may want to separate many-to-many relationships that are logically related.

Each customer has many sales representatives and service representatives, as shown in Table 14.7 and Table 14.8. If a service representative is assigned to a sales representative in a many-to-many relationship, many of the sales representatives and service representatives are being duplicated in the `Customer` entity.

Table 14.7. The `Customer` entity with `Sales Representative` and `Service Representative` attributes.

`Customer` *Entity*
`Customer Number`
`Customer Name`
`Customer Address`
`Sales Representative`
`Service Representative`

Table 14.8. The `Customer` entity with sample data.

Customer Number	Sales Representative	Service Representative
1	Joe	Kurt
1	Joe	Simon
2	Jim	Kurt
2	Lloyd	Kurt
3	Joe	Simon
3	Jim	Kurt
3	Jim	Simon
4	Joe	Kurt
4	Joe	Simon
4	Jim	Simon

To alleviate this duplication, the two attributes—`Sales Representative` and `Service Representative`—can be split into two entities (see Table 14.9 and Table 14.10).

Table 14.9. The `Customer Sales Representative` entity.

Customer Number	Sales Representative
1	Joe
2	Jim
2	Lloyd
3	Joe
3	Jim
4	Joe
4	Jim

Table 14.10. The `Customer Service Representative` entity.

Customer Number	Service Representative
1	Kurt
1	Simon
2	Kurt

continues

Table 14.10. continued

Customer Number	Service Representative
3	Kurt
3	Simon
4	Kurt
4	Simon

This allows for fewer inserts with less duplication of data. The entities are now in fifth normal form.

As stated previously, third normal form is adequate for most databases, but some require further normalization. At this point you have a functioning database schema. All you need is a system to access it. You must now use the requirements gathered in the analysis phase to create a design that can be developed for implementation. This additional step creates a database design that is actually one step back from the final level of normalization. This process is called *denormalization* and takes the actual use of the tables and data into consideration by breaking some of the rules to provide for sample duplicate or unrelated attributes in some entities.

Creating Triggers, Stored Procedures, and Indexes

Triggers, stored procedures, and indexes enable the database to maintain referential integrity, easy accessibility, and adaptability. Triggers can be used to maintain data integrity, child–parent table relationships, and sometimes column validations, among other things. Stored procedures are used as a repetitive mechanism for working behind the scenes of an application, and provide precompiled forms of often-used SQL. Indexes are used to promote fast access to data via an ordering scheme.

Triggers are designed for individual tables for three types of operations:

- Deleting
- Inserting
- Updating

These operations can be represented in one trigger, two triggers, or more (the implementation of triggers is DBMS specific). The appropriate trigger is fired when one of these operations is performed on a table. Listing 14.1 is a delete trigger for a customer table written in Transact-SQL for Microsoft SQL Server.

Listing 14.1. The delete trigger for a customer table.

```
CREATE TRIGGER tD_customer ON customer FOR DELETE
AS
BEGIN
   DECLARE  @numrows int,
            @nullcnt int,
            @validcnt int,
            @mplscount int,
            @inscustomer_id char(7),
            @errno   int,
            @errmsg  varchar(255),
            @username varchar(30),
            @name varchar(30)

   SELECT @numrows = @@rowcount
   /* customer and customer_contacts ON PARENT DELETE CASCADE */
   DELETE customer_contacts
   FROM customer_contacts,deleted
   WHERE customer_contacts.customer_id = deleted.customer_id
   /* customer and plant_sales ON PARENT DELETE RESTRICT */
   IF EXISTS( SELECT * FROM deleted,plant_sales
              WHERE plant_sales.customer_id = deleted.customer_id)
   BEGIN
      SELECT @errno  = 30001,
             @errmsg = 'Cannot DELETE "customer" because "plant_sales" exists.'
      GOTO error
   END
   /* Who is the user initiating the trigger */
   SELECT DISTINCT @username = msl.name, @name = su.name
   FROM master..sysprocesses msp, sysusers su,
        sysalternates sa, master..syslogins msl
   WHERE @@spid = msp.spid AND msl.suid = msp.suid AND
         (( sa.suid = msl.suid AND su.suid = sa.altsuid) OR
          ( msl.suid = su.suid AND su.name = 'dbo') OR
          ( msl.suid = su.suid))

   IF @@rowcount < 1
      SELECT @username = 'SA', @name = 'DBO'

   IF @numrows > 1 and @name <> 'DBO'
   BEGIN
      SELECT @errno = 30020,
             @errmsg = 'Cannot DELETE more than one row at a time.'
      GOTO error
   END

   IF NOT EXISTS( SELECT * from change_log cl, deleted d
                  WHERE (cl.order_no = d.customer_id) AND
                        (cl.change_date = getdate()) AND
                        (cl.change_table = "customer"))
   BEGIN
      DECLARE @key CHAR(8), @row INT, @total INT

      SELECT @row = 0, @key = "", @total = count(*)
      FROM deleted
```

continues

Listing 14.1. continued

```
      WHILE @row < @total
      BEGIN
         SELECT @row = @row + 1, @key = MIN( customer_id)
         FROM deleted
         WHERE customer_id > @key
         /* customer record has changed, update change log */
         EXEC sp_new_change_log @key, @username, "customer", "D"
      END
   END
   return
error:
    raiserror @errno @errmsg
    rollback transaction
END
go
```

Stored procedures are used for repetitive tasks such as pulling down data from a different database to update another database. Listing 14.2 shows an example of this, with a stored procedure written in Transact-SQL for Microsoft SQL Server.

Listing 14.2. The stored procedure for updating monthly data from one table to another table.

```
/* Remove the following three lines if you do not want the object dropped. */
IF EXISTS (SELECT * FROM sysobjects WHERE id = object_id( "sp_create_so_out"))
   DROP procedure sp_create_so_out
GO
CREATE PROCEDURE sp_create_so_out
AS
BEGIN
   TRUNCATE TABLE sales_out
   INSERT INTO sales_out ( budget, type, name, amount, date_accrued,
                           sales_month, sales_year, operation, account_name,
                           product, user_name, debit_source
   SELECT b.budget, b.type, b.name, s.so_dollars, GETDATE(), inner_month,
          inner_year % 100, s.operation, s.Acct_name, s.inner_product,
          b.user_name, b.debit_source
   FROM sales_out_accruals s, budgets b, inner_calender i
   WHERE DATEADD( dd, -28, GETDATE()) BETWEEN start_ww AND end_ww AND
         s.so_dollars <> 0 AND
         b.user_name = s.user_name AND
         s.inner_product IN ( SELECT Product
                              FROM STAR_PMF
                              WHERE UPPER( operation) = "RETAIL" OR
                                    UPPER( operation) = "CONFERENCE" OR
                                    UPPER( operation) = "WHOLESALE" OR
                                    UPPER( operation) = "NETWORK")
END
```

Indexes are used to access data more quickly and easily. When you create a table you will want to set up a primary key. There may be one or more columns that provide a unique value or set of values that identify a single record of information. Creating an index on that primary key orders the data so that using the index in conjuncture with the table will allow you to search through the table's information much more quickly than if the key does not exist.

Indexes can also be created on columns other than the primary key. For example, if you wanted to access the alphabetical order of all customer names in a customer table where a customer ID is the primary key, you would index on a column that is not the primary key. Placing an index on the customer name column, which is not the customer ID column, would decrease the access time of displaying those names in order, or of accessing an individual record. Foreign keys, the primary keys from other tables, are also good candidates for indexes.

Of course you need to be selective about what columns should be indexed and what columns should not. Like everything, too much indexing will have a reverse effect on performance, especially when it comes to data updates because the DBMS has to make changes to each of the affected indexes.

Documenting the Database Design

You should always use some form of documentation for the database design. There are many tools and methods, as described earlier in the chapter, such as ERWin/ERX, S-Designor, Data Description Languages (DDLs), and so on that capture all this information for you. These types of tools usually provide a number of report formats that you can use to view the database design in various ways. Doing this will allow you to easily maintain the design with all its attributes.

Summary

This chapter briefly discusses system analysis and system design. These processes are only part of the system development life cycle, which is the inner piece of the client/server application development methodology. Both the analysis and design phases concentrate on creating a database schema, designing and determining system requirements, and matching those requirements to PowerBuilder functionality. The result is a design of the database and system requirements that can be used to develop and implement a client/server application.

Programming PowerBuilder

1

IN THIS CHAPTER

In Chapter 14, "Analysis and Design," you learned about the analysis-and-design phase of a successful client/server application. This chapter focuses on the system development phase of the system development life cycle.

You will be using the end product of the system design phase of the life cycle as a building block for the development process. The database design and the designed system requirements will be the basis for the development of the application.

The system development phase consists of molding the designed system requirements categories (input, output, and processing) into a working PowerBuilder application. The design will provide you with the indicators to the necessary PowerBuilder functionality for each of these categories. Now you must develop these application-required features using objects and scripts. Two different methods of developing are described: rapid application development and object-oriented programming. The latter usually follows a successful cycle of the former.

Rapid Application Development

Rapid application development (RAD) is a technique for creating as quickly as possible a working application that requires minor testing and can then be shown to the user. Updates and revisions, as well as testing, are commonly done in front of end users to get immediate feedback on the changes and application functionality. PowerBuilder lends itself to this approach of development because its painters enable you to rapidly create and modify objects that are used in the application.

A typical rapid application development work flow follows a pattern similar to that shown in Figure 15.1.

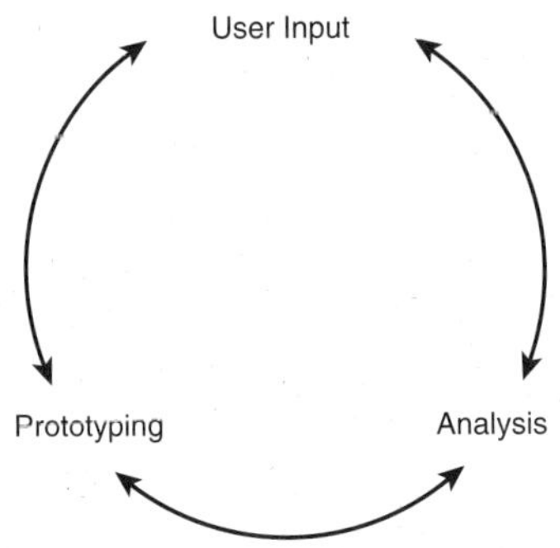

FIGURE 15.1.
A rapid application development work flow diagram.

In PowerBuilder the major concentration of work is in the development of the user interface portion of the input category of the designed system requirements. The RAD approach enables you to construct the user interface in a way that enables the users to interact with it and quickly provide feedback on the updates or revisions they require.

At this point, you basically have a working prototype that the user can manipulate. Not only does this expedite the development of the user interface, but it also enables the user to visualize and interact with the interface. This visualization and interaction contribute to the understanding of the application functionality and acceptance of the application itself. In RAD the users directly affect the development and appearance of the user interface by being a part of the initial design and testing phases.

RAD is an excellent way to continue the prototype design method. Because the skeleton of the system already exists in the prototype, you can just add the necessary objects and scripts to move the prototype to a first version of the final application. Often, though, the mistakes and pitfalls of the prototype require that you start from a solid base and that the prototype be used only as a model with only core functionality moving into the new generation of the application.

Because PowerBuilder provides the means to quickly create and modify objects and scripts in a working application, RAD is the preferred method of development for modules and small systems. The analysts involved during this stage must be aware of end user–influenced "scope creep." As the end user experiences and experiments with the prototype, he or she will consider What if? and How about? scenarios. This might lead to a more useful final application, but the time and monetary costs should be reconsidered and relayed to the end user. This will allow you to prioritize modules and features within the scope of the project budget.

Object-Oriented Programming

Object orientation is an extensive subject that cannot be totally covered in this book. You can find a number of books, in any good technical bookstore, that are completely dedicated to the topic. Probably one of the best-known and most well-respected books is *Object-Oriented Analysis and Design with Applications* by Grady Booch.

Object orientation is an extension of the information-modeling techniques discussed in Chapter 14. It further defines the entities that have been identified to include outside processes that act on these entities. These entities, along with services and data, become objects that are the basis for the program's functionality. The application is created and defined from the interaction of these objects. These interactions can be message- or function call–based and are requests to the object to carry out a particular task.

This type of programming makes use of three basic principles:

- Abstraction
- Encapsulation
- Inheritance

Abstraction is the hiding of detail. It allows you to view the problem or process as a black box so that the solution can be arrived at in a non-implementation-specific manner. *Encapsulation* is the grouping together of related ideas, characteristics, and operations into a single conceptual unit. It allows the hiding of object attributes and characteristics from other objects. *Inheritance* is the development of a hierarchy in related objects so that a child utilizes the characteristics of its parents.

In PowerBuilder you encapsulate an object's functionality mainly through the object's events, but also through the use of functions and the keywords `Private` and `Protected`. As you construct objects for your application, you should build each with an eye on where it will exist within the overall hierarchy of objects. This enables the creation of child objects that can utilize the scripts and functionality of their parents.

The system requirements dictate what you must develop. An important development practice is to decide what should not be developed. In other words, some of these matched functionalities are repetitive or unnecessary. You must decide which objects can be grouped together and developed into a hierarchy. In this manner, the objects can share functionality and scripts, utilizing a parent or ancestor as the base for their functionality.

Matching Categories to PowerBuilder Functionality

From the design system requirements, you match the three categories with PowerBuilder functionality. From here, you can develop the actual functionality of the application.

Both the input and output categories were determined in the database schema. This schema was constructed in the system design phase and must be synchronized into the chosen data sources before development of any of these three categories can occur. After the data source definitions and descriptions are implemented, the development of the application can proceed. Of course, some modification of the database schema will occur during development, but it should always be documented and approved before any changes occur. This will give you the opportunity to verify the impact of such changes throughout the application.

To build the components of the application for the input, output, and processing categories, you use different PowerBuilder painters. These painters provide the tools for creating and modifying objects.

Developing the Input Category

The *input category* consists of the user interface and data source access and is directly associated with windows, window controls, and DataWindows.

When you create a window in the Window painter, you define the attributes and properties of that window and add window controls for user interaction. Window controls such as command buttons, radio buttons, edit boxes, and list boxes enable the user to perform actions on the window.

The basic techniques employed in developing a user interface require you to know how to display a dialog box or message box, hide and show a window, open multiple instances of a window, enable and disable window controls, and perform drag and drop in a window.

For accessing data, you should develop retrieval techniques that can prompt the user to enter the selection criteria, retrieve multiple rows of information, and perform retrievals from multiple databases. This information should then be presented to the users in a consistent manner that enables them to perform either data entry–type actions or suitable formatting and printing functions for reports.

You can develop both windows and user objects that can be used to pass on functionality through inheritance to other windows and controls. This condenses future programming time and enables you to reuse code by inheriting the scripts and attributes from these objects.

One important fact that you will pull from the design is whether the PowerBuilder application will be constructed using a multiple- or single-document interface. This decision will be based on the perceived flow of information through the system, as you defined it in the system design phase.

As part of your initial foray into prototyping windows, you should carefully consider mapping business transactions or processes to individual windows. This is a worthwhile step and can save considerable time in the prototyping stage. There are other benefits of considering these relationships: you will refine task-time estimates, improve task assignment and ordering, and ensure that the design document encompasses all the perceived requirements.

Developing the Output Category

The *output category* consists of the information produced by the application. The system requirements have already defined the appropriate reports, data written to data sinks, and external files that will be created. You need to consider by what method you will implement these requirements in the application.

PowerBuilder provides *DataWindows* as an excellent way of reporting and saving information. A DataWindow can be specifically designed to accommodate either an online, a printed, or a file-written report. For a further explanation of the development of the DataWindow as a reporting device, refer to Chapter 9, "The DataWindow Painter."

Using a similar concept of mapping business transactions/processes to windows, you should also consider mapping database tables to DataWindows. As with windows, this may not be a one-to-one relationship, with more than one DataWindow retrieving and saving data from the same table. If there is considerable overlap of columns between DataWindows, the columns might become candidates for data sharing, or you might need to re-examine the underlying database structure to determine if the most optimal design has been achieved.

When dealing with data from a data source, you must determine whether you want to utilize a DataWindow or an embedded SQL statement to create, update, delete, and retrieve the data. For further information on developing the DataWindow for updating database information, refer to Chapter 10, "DataWindow Scripting." For further information on developing the SQL statements for updating database information, refer to Chapter 5, "SQL and PowerBuilder."

For updating data and managing DataWindows, you should develop objects that can update multiple rows, update multiple databases, manage master and detail DataWindow controls, accept the data from a user's last entry, work with the current and/or displayed row, share data with other DataWindows, dynamically change a DataWindow, and perform validation in the DataWindow.

For example, if a DataWindow will be used to display one or more rows of information, you need to consider from what source the data will be retrieved or entered, what validation will need to occur, what additional processing needs to be carried out, and where the data will be saved when the user has finished.

PowerBuilder also enables you to generate external files such as Excel spreadsheets and text files. You dictate which columns of data will be included and the order in which they will appear as the PowerBuilder application writes them out.

Using a DataWindow control to satisfy the input and output design system requirements can sometimes be overkill, and edit fields and other controls should be used instead.

For example, a connect window is designed to gather user information for the purpose of connecting to a database. The only required window controls are four single-line edits, two command buttons, and a check box. The window is gathering the user ID, password, database name, and server name through the four single-line edits. This input and output information could use a DataWindow, but you are performing no validation, formatting, data retrieval, or updates. Therefore, a DataWindow provides little more than a slight reduction in the use of Windows resources during the lifetime of the window, which in this case is very short-lived.

NOTE

You need to carefully consider the uses of each control and which one of the many provided will give you the desired functionality with the minimum of implementation and maintenance.

Developing the Processing Category

The *processing category* handles all internal and external system processing. For the most part PowerBuilder applications are event driven, and the flow and logic of processing must be controlled and manipulated inside object events. Obviously, you can also write procedural applications with PowerBuilder as you may have done in a more traditional language, but you will soon find the end user returning with additional requirements and needed flexibility. You write scripts using PowerScript to specify the processing that occurs when an event is triggered. For further explanation of object events, refer to Chapter 6, "The PowerScript Language," and Chapter 7, "The PowerScript Environment."

For example, windows have `Open` and `Close` events, window control buttons have `Clicked` events, edit boxes have `Modified` events, and DataWindow controls have `ItemChanged` events. All these events are commonly used to house the application-processing logic for these objects.

The `Open` and `Close` events are used to perform initialization and cleanup for a window object and its related controls and instance variables. `Clicked` events are scripted to perform a specific action such as a retrieve, an update, or a delete of data. When a user changes a value, the `Modified` event in an edit box and `ItemChanged` in a DataWindow are fired. This can be used to verify the new user value, trigger another event, or just enable other controls in the window or DataWindow object.

In any of these events, you determine how you are going to program the processing logic that was determined in the system design requirements. You can also define user events for specific processing of an object. For further explanation of the development of user events, refer to Chapter 7.

You can also move or perform certain parts of the processing by interacting with DLL functions, communicating via dynamic data exchange or object linking and embedding, or sending electronic mail (to name just a few ways). From the system requirements, you should be able to identify specific requirements that you know PowerBuilder will be unable to solve directly. This might require the use or access of external controls or software packages, some of which might directly integrate with PowerBuilder—for example, to perform imaging or special graphic tasks.

The scripts you write will reflect the application control flow and the additional services that are requested from other programs. This includes the process of connecting to other programs to access their data and functions.

The processing category exists as encapsulated code in appropriate objects. Business objects should be constructed for the encapsulation of specific functionality and implemented using class user objects.

Code and Validation Tables

Depending on the requirements of the supporting code and validation tables in your database schema, you should decide whether you can construct a generic table maintenance window and runtime-constructed DataWindow or a specific window and individual DataWindows that carry out additional checks or processing on the data entered.

Often the access to these types of code maintenance windows is restricted to a particular subset of the end user community, and the relevant security also needs to be considered.

Application Security

The security of certain application functions and the validity and security of the data is an often-forgotten or a postdevelopment consideration. As part of the design of input, output, and processing, the necessary security and access privileges also need to be gathered and implemented into the basic framework of the application.

A number of third-party add-on packages are available that will enable you to control a user's access to particular functions, objects, and even DataWindow columns. These products might be overkill in some applications, especially those with only a small number of user groups. In those cases, simple restrictions based on SQL group IDs can be used to disable menu options and controls in menu title `Clicked` events or window `Open` events, respectively.

Starting the Project

You should construct your project team to give yourself a good cross-section of the program-development knowledge that exists in your department or company. Early definition of each project member's role will help develop a cohesive team and application. Technical leader, technical writer, and tester are some of the roles to which you should allocate people. Project members can cover more than one of these positions, if required.

One of the most important roles that can be filled is that of a change controller. A smoothly running development process can be quickly derailed without some kind of change control. Especially during RAD sessions, users will try to make considerable changes to the system specifications that might have already been signed off on by an end user representative.

If other PowerBuilder or GUI projects have been completed successfully, you should examine their structure and approach. Even unsuccessful projects can provide valuable insight into the approaches you should take, what to avoid, and what should be done that wasn't done before. One thing you should not be afraid of when starting your first client/server application is making mistakes. Learn from the problems you encounter and grow stronger in your processes and knowledge. It is a mistake only if it occurs a second time!

While you are investigating other projects, you should look for naming conventions and GUI standards that have been used. You don't have to follow these blindly, but you should gauge the effects that any changes you make will have on future development efforts or on prospective end user groups. End users hate having to learn vastly different application interfaces, and developers hate having to alter the way they code.

Before any coding is even started on a production version of the application, you should have identified any frameworks or class libraries that will be used. This will have some effect on the method by which you identify ancestor objects—especially candidates for abstract and concrete class objects. For a full discussion on frameworks and class libraries, refer to Chapter 28, "Frameworks and Class Libraries."

If you are uncertain about any stage of the project—from starting it to carrying it through development or implementing and distributing the solution—you should look for outside help. This help can come from other areas of your company or from a recognized consulting firm that can show you a solid history of implemented client/server applications.

Summary

This chapter briefly covers system development. This process is only a part of the system development life cycle, which is the inner piece of the client/server application development methodology. The system development phase is concerned with creating a working application from the system design requirements. Using PowerBuilder objects and the PowerScript language, you can transform the input, output, and processing design system requirements into the desired client/server application. The ease with which you can design and implement applications using PowerBuilder will improve with experience.

Testing and Debugging

16

IN THIS CHAPTER

An integral part of every application-development process is testing. Without it, there can be no certainty that a quality application will be produced and provide the end user the necessary functionality to perform his or her job. In this chapter you will learn about a standard approach to testing, as well as techniques that will assist you in that process.

PowerBuilder comes equipped with several tools, such as the debugger and the /PBDEBUG option, that can be used to test and identify problem areas. Many developers utilize additional methods of testing logic and functionality within their applications; you will learn about these as well. Although PowerBuilder does contain several different means to test and debug, there is a suite of third-party products that complements the PowerBuilder application-development process.

The Testing Process

Before exploring the steps to successful application testing, let's review the goal of testing and how to get started.

The Goal of Testing

The most common misconception about testing is that its intention is to prove that the developer has created an application with no errors. Because creating an application with no errors is an improbability, you must approach testing with a slightly different mindset. Testing should mean running an application with the intent of finding errors. You have probably not had a successful test until you have found at least one error.

The process of finding errors in an application is referred to as *quality assurance*. This means that your application and its documentation are correct, complete, reliable, and easy to maintain in addition to meeting all the specifications and requirements as laid out by the users

Getting Started

One of the most difficult aspects of the testing process is creating a test plan. Many people do not have the slightest clue about where to begin and, therefore, panic at the thought of testing and ensuring that a quality product is delivered. The easiest way to approach the testing process is to formulate a test plan based on the functional design specifications of your application. You can then break down the testing process into small, manageable groups. Standard approaches to testing are as follows:

- Unit test—Tests each low-level (primitive) business process.
- System test—Tests each unit together as a whole entity/object.
- Integration test—Tests whether the whole application runs with all components of the application (network, server, and so on) and with other applications.

- Volume test—Tests whether the application can maintain production volume of data and keep to acceptable time limits.
- Acceptance test—Tests continuously throughout all stages of the testing process to determine whether the end user approves of the design and functionality of the system.

In a perfect world, each of these components would be completed before the next phase of testing began. More often than not, however, there are gray areas and overlap between each of the different test modes. Let's take a look at each test phase and see some common practices.

Unit Testing

In the unit test, you test the basic functionality of each low-level process of your system. Consider the following example: A basic requirement of a system is to calculate the net accounts receivable amount for specific customers based on the days of sales outstanding (DSO). This was implemented using a DataWindow that retrieves totals for all unpaid invoices and displays information based on each of the DSO totals (for example, 30 to 60 days). The test scenario asks whether the DataWindow correctly calculates the net accounts receivable. This information can be validated in several ways. If the developer has the appropriate business knowledge, he can manually determine what the correct amount will be for Customer ABC for 30 to 60 DSO. A better approach would be to obtain a copy of an existing report that calculates the figures for a given period of time (preferably a minimum of three months). The DataWindow could then be run against the data for the same time frame, and results from the application could be validated against the existing report.

Keeping this scenario in mind, the goal of the unit test is to tell the developer which scripts need to be corrected or better understood. This is done using two approaches: testing the code logic and examining the functional specifications. By testing the code logic, the tester should develop test cases that execute every line of code in the application component being tested. Code testing can be very time-consuming and, in a large system, difficult to formulate all test cases for. Even if all lines of code are executed, a bug-free application is not guaranteed because the overall functionality is not tested. Testing whether an application component meets the desired functional specifications must also be a part of unit testing. This is done by treating the component as a black box. This approach means that you do not care about what line of code is being executed when, but rather, if all aspects of the application perform as requested under different conditions.

As soon as a section of the application is completed, begin testing it to make sure that it provides all the necessary behavior. The initial test should be completed by the developer and subsequently by other individual team members. It is particularly useful if one of the other team members is an end user or has business experience similar to that of an end user. One of the most important reasons to get others involved as early as possible is that, as the developer, you have a tendency to try the same, tired routine each time. If you always use the same test scenario, you'll make sure that scenario works in those circumstances but potentially will miss testing other key areas. Each unit should also be constructed to include the appropriate error-handling tests to make sure the system will not crash.

For several reasons it is also important to get the end users involved in this early stage. They know what they need to do and can immediately tell you if something looks strange or acts incorrectly. If the interface is not what they want or the functionality is not completely there, wouldn't you rather know now than a week before implementation? By involving users from the beginning, you ensure that they will be happy with the application (they only have themselves to blame), and they are happy because they are contributing to the development process. Also, the users now have a stake in the application because their names and reputations are associated with it.

After all low-level units have been identified, tested, and approved by several members of the project team, it is time to assemble all pieces of the application and begin the next phase of testing—the system test.

System Testing

The system test combines all units of the application. This ensures that the application flows smoothly and that there is compatibility between the individual application components. Hopefully, by this time, each unit correctly provides the necessary business requirements. The system test ensures that navigation through the system is consistent, a common look and feel is maintained (good GUI), and the application provides the flexibility and components that the user has requested. It is essential that at least one or two of the end users be involved in the system test to ensure that no requirement has been left out of the application.

Also included in the system test is a process some people refer to as idiot testing. This is often one of the more fun parts of the testing process. Ask a developer from another project to take a few minutes to test your application. The developer's goal should be to try to break your application. In essence, the other developer should approach the application as if he is an idiot and try to do things that don't make sense, click everywhere, and question everything. You will be surprised at the number of unexpected results, potential pitfalls, and GPFs (general protection faults) or page faults that this testing approach uncovers.

When everyone has signed off on the application as it currently exists, you are ready to begin the later phases of the testing process: integration and volume testing.

Integration Test

The integration test takes the completed business application and places it in a mock production environment. The goal of the integration test is to make sure that the application functions properly with the network, database, hardware, and any other platforms or environmental factors specific to the company.

An important part of the integration test is running the application on your user's workstation. This can uncover multiple problems. For example, if all testing has been done on a 486/66 with 16MB of RAM, and the client workstation is a 386/25 with 4MB, you might notice a slight performance degradation. The resolution of the end user's monitor is also important because many developers run 800×600 or higher and most end users run standard 640×480. Application windows might be too large or have too-fancy color schemes, or graphical effects might be lost or look poor. This decision should be made before coding even begins, but it is a good idea to test anyway. In addition, you should check to see how the application looks with your user's Windows color scheme. You may be surprised at the results (for example, black text on a black background).

Another portion of the integration test is to make sure that the application executes and integrates with other company systems. Many times, new releases of software or patches to existing software are required. It is tempting to install the latest and greatest versions of the software. This can lead to problems if existing applications are on an earlier release that is not compatible with the new version (such as updates to DLLs). It is a good idea to find this out before the application is deployed into the production environment. A problem such as this also leads to another important aspect of the integration test: recovery. You should implement and test a procedure to back out your application and recover the previously existing application with a minimal amount of effort.

Integration testing identifies many unforeseen and previously untestable conditions: network traffic delays, long-running processing times (resulting in timeouts or missed availability time), data integrity and user concurrency issues, and the need for additional error handling. Pinpointing problems during integration testing can be challenging due to the fact that there are many components operating simultaneously. If a problem is encountered, determine what the problem is first and then try to nail down the component that is causing the problem. The integration test works hand-in-hand with the last phase: volume testing.

Volume Testing

The volume test (also called *load testing*) ensures that all components of the application can handle the production volume of data being processed. Most of the time, during application construction, developers use a scaled-down model of the production database. For applications dealing with small amounts of data, the volume test might not even be an issue, but for larger amounts of data it is crucial.

The goal of the volume test is to determine whether the application can handle the data without crashing or timing out and whether the current hardware configuration is robust enough to support the company's needs. Although testing the volume of data is important to the application's front-end developers, this test will greatly assist the individuals in charge of the servers, databases, and networks.

In conjunction with the test of high volumes of data, you should be aware of the issue of user concurrency. Do the users have sufficient access to the data? You must ensure that while using your application the users can retrieve and modify data without holding large numbers of locks on data or erroring out because of a timing or deadlock issue. You may find that your application can handle the large amounts of data but cannot handle the number of users concurrently accessing the data.

User Testing

As mentioned in each of the previous sections, the users' participation in the testing process is essential for a successful client/server application deployment. The users find problems not only with the functionality of the system, but also with the interface. Users typically respond to the system in ways you never dreamed of. They can tell you if the application process is natural to their way of thinking and approaching problems. By involving your users, you can maintain credibility, keep the users' expectations on track, and ensure that they have an application that suits their needs.

Identifying Problem Areas

One of the most difficult aspects about testing client/server applications is the involvement of multiple layers and components. It is important to determine which component is breaking down in order to identify and correct the problem. The components of a client/server application can be broken down into three main groups: the client, the network, and the server.

The client includes the following:

- The Windows operating system
- Your application executable
- Optional initialization (INI)
- Optional help (HLP) files
- A database library for database communication
- The PowerBuilder DLLs found in the Database Distribution and Deployment Kit
- The PowerBuilder database interface DLLs

Each of these components is crucial to your application functioning correctly. Misplacement of or mismatching versions of any of these files can result in unpredictable or incorrect behavior from your application. All of these components, including distribution and setup, are usually left as the responsibility of the application developer.

The network and server are typically out of the control of the developer in the production environment. Some common components that make up the network are access and permissions (security), resource dedication, and general processing and data-transfer times. The server contains the RDBMS software that manages table structures, triggers, rules, stored procedures, and backup and recovery procedures, just to name a few of its operations. It is important to familiarize yourself with both the network and the server to assist you in identifying where certain problems can occur.

Now that you have a general framework to use in an approach to the testing phase of your application development, it's time to examine some methods, tools, and techniques that you can utilize to maximize your test cases and minimize your testing time.

Testing Tools and Techniques

PowerBuilder comes equipped with several features to assist in the testing process. In addition to these features, there are some extra tips and techniques to use when testing a PowerBuilder application.

The Debugger

PowerBuilder comes with a built-in debugging tool that assists you in finding errors in any of your application's scripts. The debugger enables you to set stops (or breakpoints) within the different scripts you want to debug. When you execute your application in debug mode, PowerBuilder suspends processing right before it executes the PowerScript statement containing the breakpoint. At that point, you can step through each line of code and observe what code is executed, as well as examine variables currently in scope. Debugging enables you to watch what the values of variables are during breakpoints, and also gives you the capability to change the value of the variables.

To enter the debugger, click on the PowerBar icon that displays a bug with a slash through it. When you click on the debugger icon, one of two dialog boxes appears. If you have not used the debugger for your current application, the dialog box in Figure 16.1 appears, asking you to select a script.

FIGURE 16.1.
The Select Script dialog box.

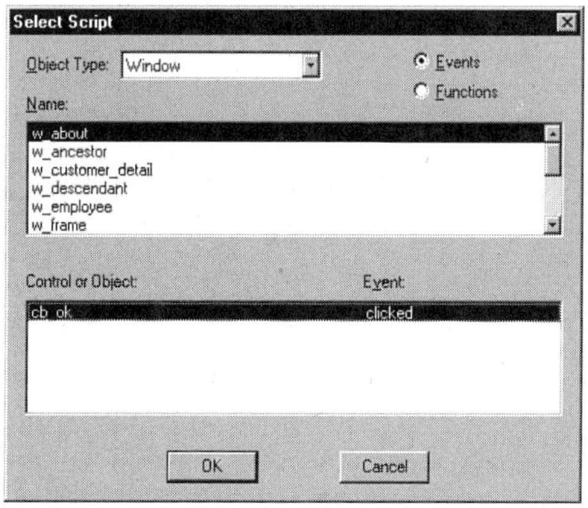

The Object Type drop-down list box at the top of the Select Script dialog box lists all five PowerBuilder objects that can contain scripts: Application, Window, Menu, User Object, and Function. Select the type of object for which you want to set a breakpoint. A list of all objects of that type that exist in your application appears in the Name list box. When you select a particular object name (such as `w_about`), all controls or objects that have a script written for them appear in the Control or Object list box. For all objects except a function object, you can specify whether you would like to view a list of events for the objects or functions by using the radio buttons at the top of the window. Choose a control or object and its associated event or function from the Control or Object list box and click OK.

When a script has been selected, it appears in debug mode. Double-click each PowerScript statement on which you want to set a breakpoint. A stop sign icon is displayed next to the lines that have breakpoints specified (see Figure 16.2). Remember that processing stops before executing the line with the breakpoint. It is also important to note that comments, variable declarations, and empty lines cannot contain breakpoints.

FIGURE 16.2.

Script with debugger breakpoints specified.

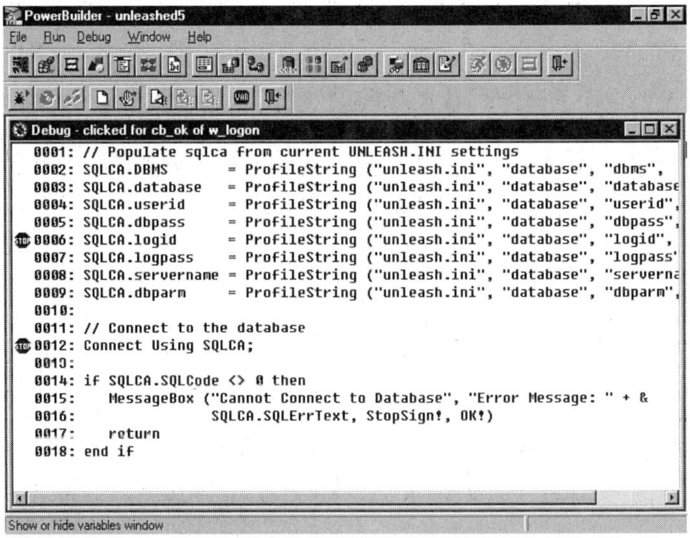

In PowerBuilder's debug environment it is not always intuitive as to how to view different variables and how to step through the code to find when each script happens. Let's examine a couple common scenarios to explore all the features of the debugger.

Connecting to a Database

One of the most important scripts in any PowerBuilder application that uses a relational database as its source of information is the script that connects that application to the database. Not only is it important, but if an error occurs, it can often be one of the trickier problems to solve. The problem could be caused by the script, communication on the network, or communication with the database.

Consider this scenario: For some reason an application will not connect to the database. The application object `Open` event opens the first window, `w_logon`. The logon window contains two single-line edits that prompt the user for his user ID and password. When that is done, the user clicks the OK button, which contains the script to populate the default transaction object, SQLCA, and connect to the database.

With this question in mind, let's see how to figure out what the problem is.

In the debugger, select the Window object type and choose `w_logon` from the list of windows and `cb_ok` (the OK command button) from the list of controls (see Figure 16.3).

FIGURE 16.3.
A selection of `cb_ok`*'s* `Clicked` *event in the Select Script dialog box.*

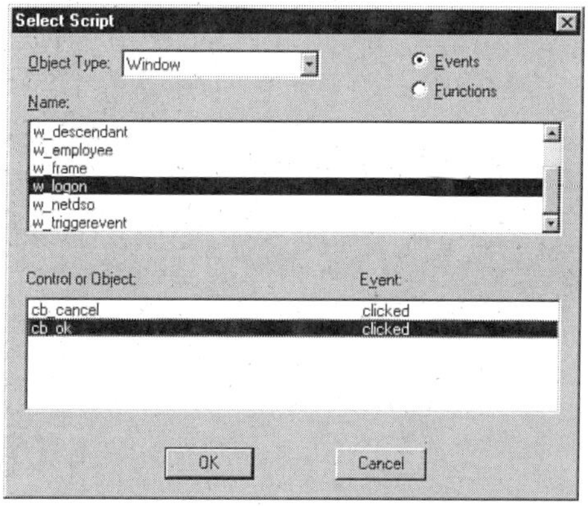

Because you are unsure of where the problem is occurring, place a breakpoint on the first line of code in the `Clicked` event script, as shown in Figure 16.4.

To start the application in debug mode, click the icon with a bug next to the green arrow on the top of the PainterBar, choose Start from the Run menu, or press Ctrl+T. The application runs as it normally would until the OK command button on `w_logon` is clicked. When you have triggered the script for the `Clicked` event for `cb_ok` and have hit the specified breakpoint, PowerBuilder goes into debug mode.

To find out what is wrong with the application, you need to step through each line of code and ensure that the attributes of the SQLCA object are being populated correctly. To execute one line at a time, click the second PainterBar icon, which displays a picture of footprints, select Step from the Run menu, or press Ctrl+S. The first time you click on the step icon, PowerBuilder executes the code marked with the breakpoint. To validate that SQLCA is being populated correctly, you need to view each attribute as it is being assigned a value. To do this, click the bottom icon with the VAR picture on it, select Show Variables from the Debug menu, or press Ctrl+V. The Variables window displays, as shown in Figure 16.5.

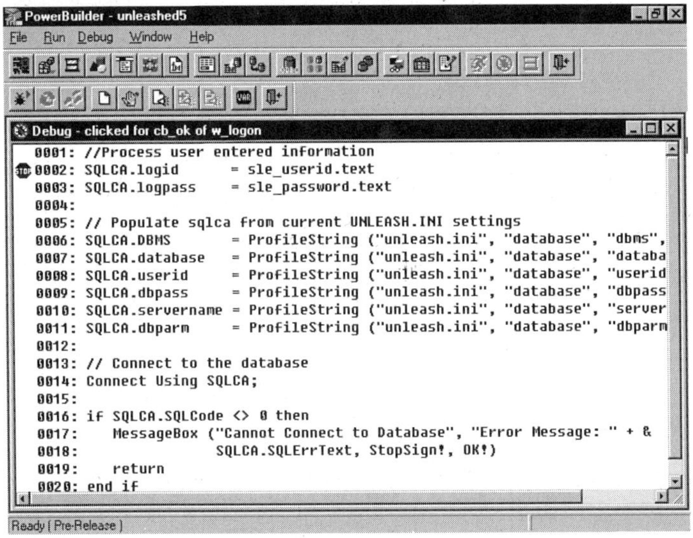

FIGURE 16.4.
A breakpoint set for the first line of the `cb_ok Clicked` *event.*

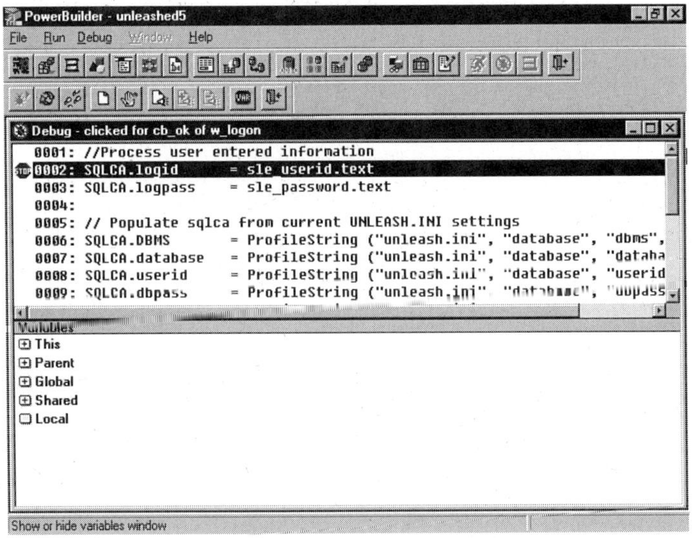

FIGURE 16.5.
The show variables window.

SQLCA is a global variable, so you need to look for it in the global variables section. Double-clicking on the global variables line in the Show Variables list opens the global variable tree to display the list of all application globals (see Figure 16.6).

FIGURE 16.6.
The global variable tree expanded.

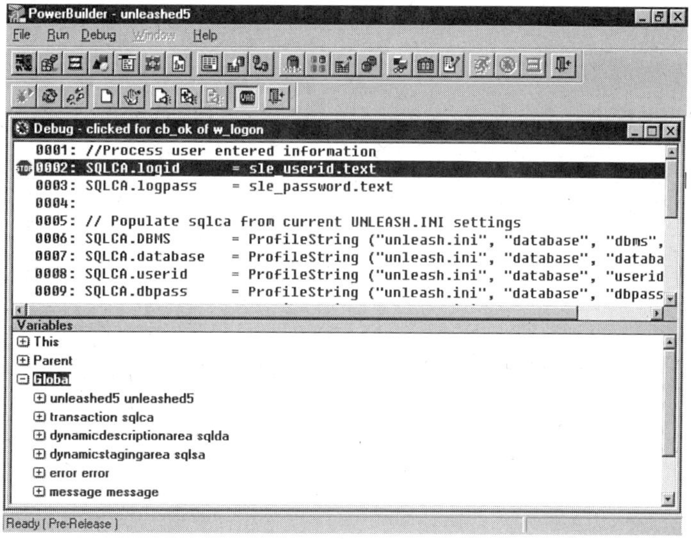

In the list, look at the transaction object SQLCA. Double-click on SQLCA to display a list of all of its attributes and their current values (see Figure 16.7).

FIGURE 16.7.
A list of attributes for SQLCA.

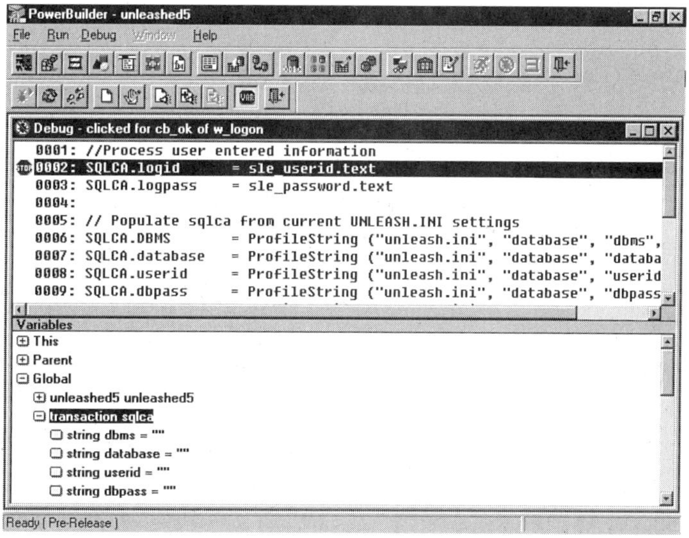

Because you are at the beginning of the script, only the default values are in SQLCA. To see what values the script is assigning to SQLCA, click the step PainterBar icon. The first two steps populate the `LogId` and `LogPass` attributes from the single-line edits on `w_logon`. Both values were assigned properly, although viewing the code might make you think that there should be some validation when the user enters a user ID and password before doing any more processing. If you need to stop debugging to code this script, the logical action would be to double-click the system menu and bring up `w_logon`. Unfortunately, clicking on the system menu and closing the debugger can make PowerBuilder very unstable, most of the time resulting in page faults. PowerBuilder will warn you of this with the message shown in Figure 16.8.

FIGURE 16.8.

The Debug termination warning dialog box.

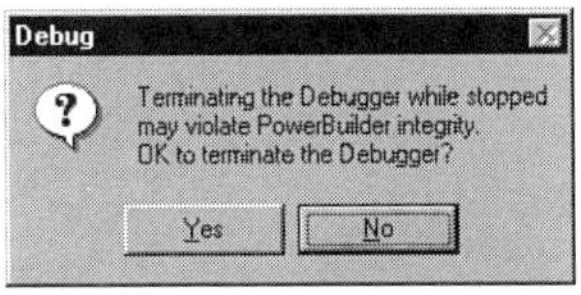

The best way to stop debug mode is to click the top PainterBar icon with the arrows pointing in a circle, click Continue from the Run menu, or press Ctrl+C. This takes you out of stepping through code and forces PowerBuilder to continue processing. Note that processing will stop, however, if PowerBuilder encounters another breakpoint. Once the application continues, exit the application normally (which returns you to PowerBuilder's debugger). Close the debugger and add the password and user ID validation checks.

After making the changes, start debugging again and see whether you can find the problem. The rest of the SQLCA's attributes are assigned from the values stored in an INI file. When the debugger reaches the `ServerName` attribute, you will immediately notice the problem (see Figure 16.9). The UNLEASH.INI file still contains the name of the test server.

FIGURE 16.9.

SQLCA's attribute values in debug mode.

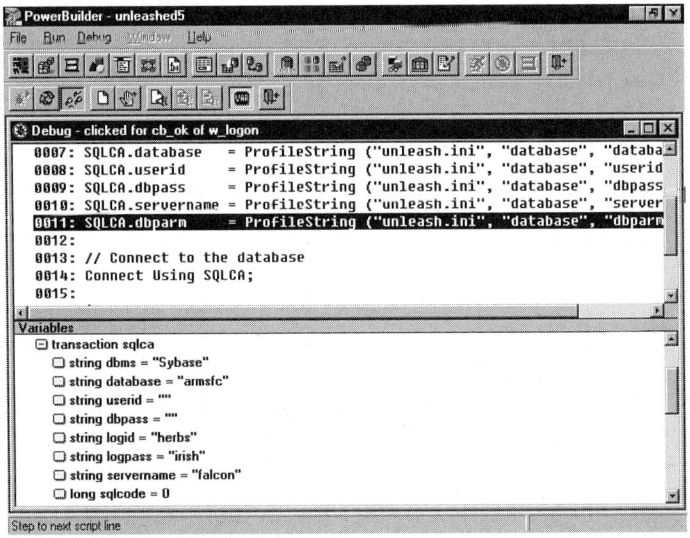

You could click the Continue icon, make the changes to the INI file, and restart the debugger to test this fix, but there is a better way to make sure no additional problems exist. Double-clicking on the `ServerName` attribute brings up the Modify Variable dialog box (see Figure 16.10).

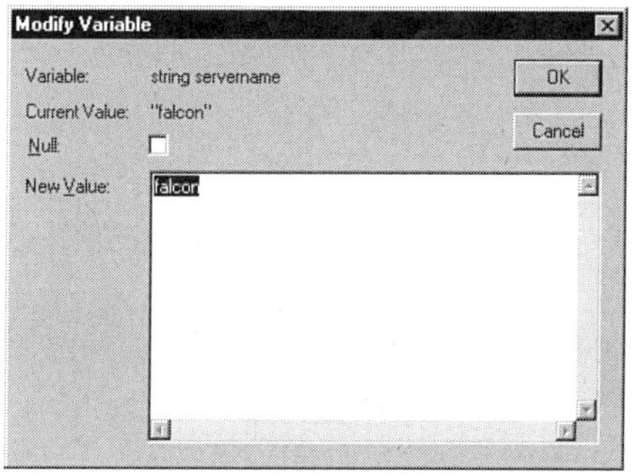

FIGURE 16.10.
The Modify Variable dialog box.

With this dialog box, you can modify the value of any variable. This gives you the capability to force PowerBuilder to test certain lines of code by mimicking test conditions. In this case, changing the `ServerName` attribute works and the application successfully connects to the SQL Server.

Watching Instance Variables

When debugging, it is easy to find the values of global, shared, and local variables because there is a section specified for each. There is no section specified for instance variables, so how do you check their values? Instance variables are displayed with the object in which they are declared. For example, the accounts receivable application has a window that displays net dollars for a specified division, region, and territory that are passed via a structure to the window. This information is stored in an instance variable, `istr_code`, in the window `w_netdso`. During testing, it was discovered that the net dollars were not being calculated correctly. You need to verify that the information passed to the window is correct and then determine whether any other scripts in the window modify `istr_code`.

Activating the debugger brings up the Edit Stops dialog box (see Figure 16.11), which lists all the current breakpoints that you have set for your application. From this dialog box, you can start the application in debug mode, add new breakpoints, remove existing breakpoints, enable and disable a breakpoint, clear all breakpoints, or go to an existing breakpoint. For this situation, you will remove the existing breakpoint and create a new one.

FIGURE 16.11.
The Edit Stops dialog box.

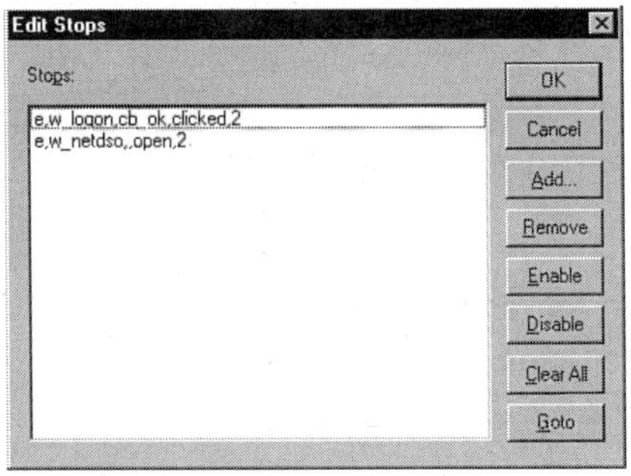

Select the existing breakpoint, which displays `e,w_netdso,,open,2`. To read this piece of information, break it down in this way: `e` stands for enabled (`d` stands for disabled), followed by the object name, the control name (in this case, there is no control), the event, and the line of code on which the breakpoint exists. Click the Remove button and then the Add button to set a new breakpoint. From the Select Script dialog box (refer to Figure 16.1), select `w_netdso` and the `Open` event for `w_netdso` from the object list. The second line of code contains the first assignment to your instance variable, `istr_code`, so place a breakpoint there (see Figure 16.12).

FIGURE 16.12.
A Breakpoint in the `Open` *event of window* `w_netdso`.

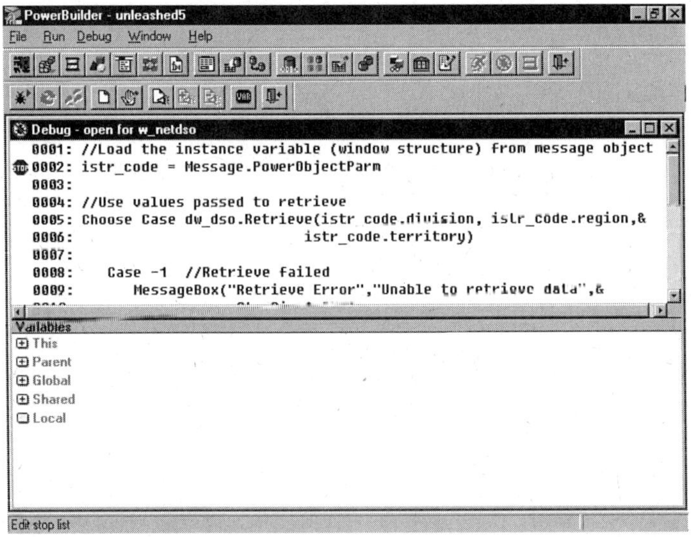

Click the Start icon to run the application. From a list of existing divisions, regions, and territories, double-clicking a row will open an instance of the window `w_netdso`. In each instance, `istr_code` is populated from the `Message` object in the window `Open` event and then used for retrieval arguments for the DataWindow retrieve. To find the values of an instance variable, you can look in one of two places. The first place to look is in the global variables section. When an instance of `w_netdso` is opened, PowerBuilder goes into debug mode and stops on the first breakpoint. Double-clicking on global variables displays a list of all global objects. At the bottom of the global list are some entries for the menus (`m_dso`) associated with your windows (see Figure 16.13). There are currently two entries for `m_dso`, which indicates that there are two instances of your window open. You must look in each of these instances to find the instance variables.

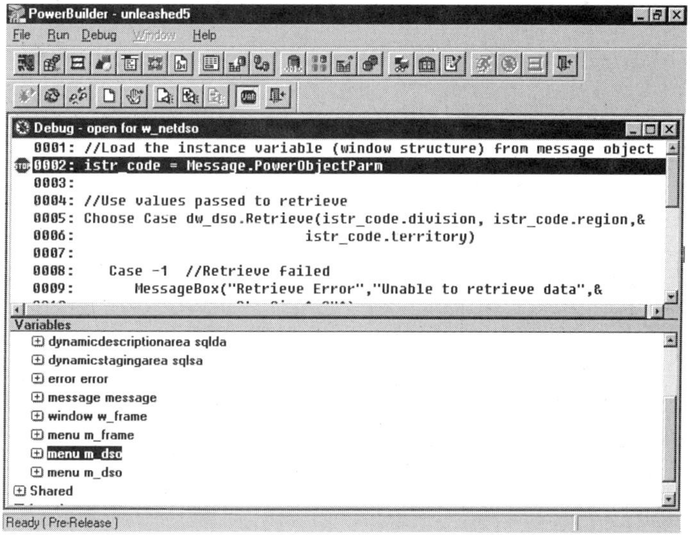

FIGURE 16.13.
A list of `m_dso` *(menu) entries for each instance of window* `w_dso`.

Double-clicking again on the variable menu `m_dso` expands the hierarchy tree by another level. Halfway down the list of components associated with the menu is the reference window, `ParentWindow` (see Figure 16.14). The pronoun `ParentWindow` refers to the window with which a menu is associated; it references an instance of `w_netdso` that is open.

Double-clicking on `window.ParentWindow` displays all the attributes and variables for that window instance. At the very bottom of the list for `ParentWindow` is your instance variable, `istr_code`. Because the instance variable is a structure, double-clicking on it enables you to view each of the fields that define the structure. When you have located the instance variable, you can step through the code to see what values are being passed (see Figure 16.15).

FIGURE 16.14.
The `ParentWindow` *pronoun under the instance of menu* `m_dso`.

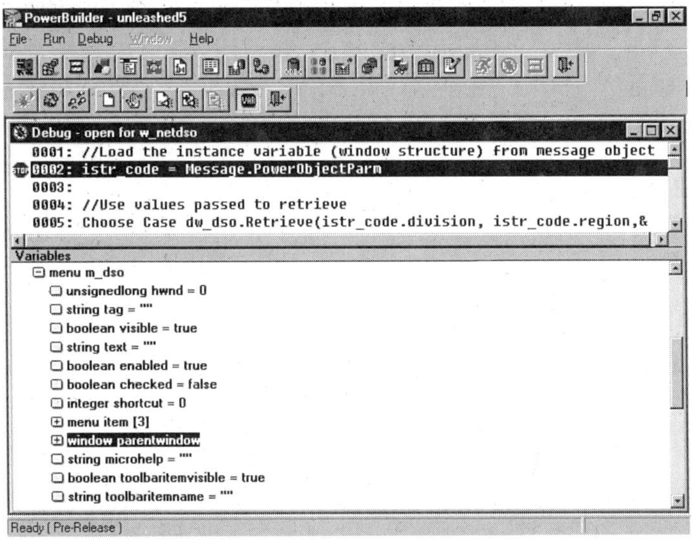

FIGURE. 16.15.
Values displayed in structure instance `istr_code`.

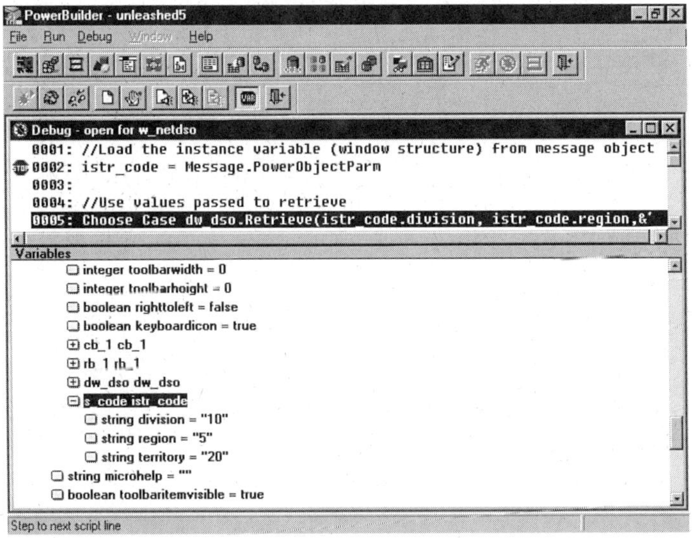

NEW in 5 PowerBuilder

The second place to find an instance variable is new to Version 5.0 of PowerBuilder. This is done using the two new entries in the variable list: the pronouns `This` and `Parent`. The pronouns hold the same meaning in the debugger as they would in any of your scripts. `This` refers to the object whose script you are debugging (for example, if you were debugging the `Clicked` event for `cb_ok`, this would refer to `cb_ok`). `Parent` can have several meanings depending on the object you are debugging. For controls on windows, `Parent` refers to the window on which they are placed. For controls placed in a custom visual user object, `Parent` refers to the user object. For menu items, `Parent` refers to the menu title the item is a child of.

In this case, because we are in the `Open` event of `w_dso`, we want to look under the pronoun `This`. Located at the bottom of the list is the instance variable `istr_code` (see Figure 16.16).

FIGURE 16.16.
Using `This` *to find the* `istr_code` *instance variable.*

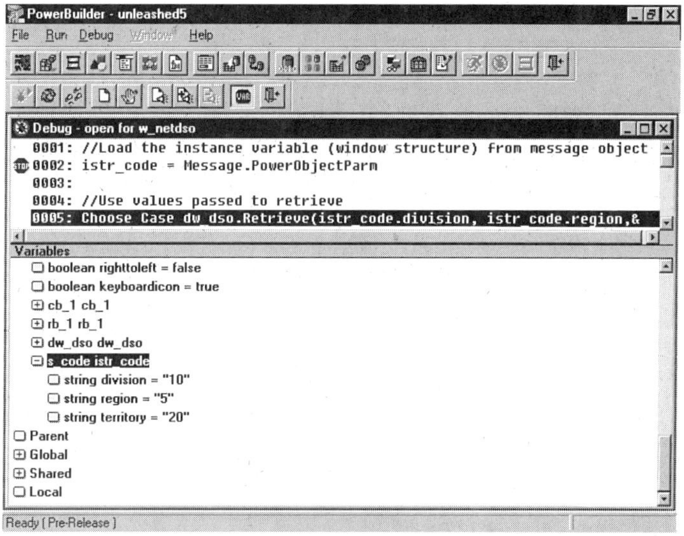

As you can see, the use of the pronouns considerably simplifies locating variables in the debugger.

The other thing you need to do is watch the structure to make sure that no other scripts are updating the values. Due to the limited space available within the debugger window, it can become confusing and annoying to constantly scroll back and forth and dig through the previous hierarchy each time you want to view `istr_code`. Powersoft provides the capability to watch a variable to see whether its value changes. To define a watch on a variable, you must first open the Watch list (see Figure 16.17). To open this list, you can click the icon with a piece of paper with an eye in the right-hand corner in the PainterBar, select Show Watch from the Debug menu, or press Ctrl+W.

If you have any watch variables defined from previous debug sessions, they will be listed in the Watch list. To add a variable to the Watch list, select the variable (in this case, `istr_code`) and click the watch icon with a plus sign on it, select Add Watch from the Debug menu, or hold the Shift key and click on the desired variable in the Variables window. This copies the variable to the Watch list (see Figure 16.18). You can now keep a constant eye on `istr_code` to see whether any other script in `w_netdso` makes modifications to it.

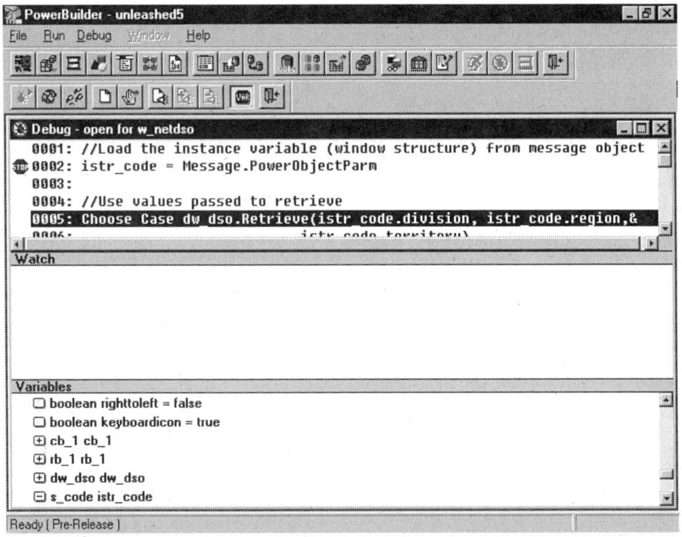

FIGURE 16.17.
The Watch list.

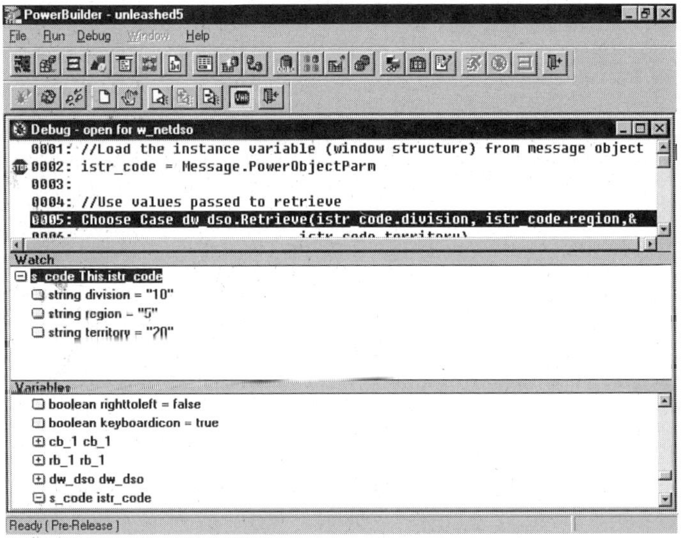

FIGURE 16.18.
A structure instance defined as a watch variable.

Any specified variables will remain in the Watch list until you specifically remove them by clicking on the wristwatch icon surrounded by four minus signs or selecting Remove Watch from the Debug menu. In addition to setting watch variables, the debugger enables you to print your variables. If you decide that you want to modify the Edit Stops list, click on the blue Edit sign on the PainterBar to open the Edit Stops dialog box.

Although the debugger is a very powerful utility, it does have limitations. You often need to make slight modifications to your code to display the information that you need. For example, when you are assigning a return value from a function in an expression with other values, you need to assign the return value to a new variable in order to view or modify it. The following:

```
Choose Case dw_1.Retrieve()
```

would become this:

```
long ll_rtn

ll_rtn = dw_1.Retrieve()
CHOOSE CASE ll_rtn
```

It is difficult use the debugger and breakpoints to track down focus change and timer problems. The debugger can trap you in an infinite loop and you will have to close PowerBuilder (Ctrl+Alt+Delete) or remove your breakpoints. Some different testing techniques that can be used to test this type of problems are covered later in the chapter.

PBDEBUG

In addition to the debugger, PowerBuilder comes equipped with another utility to assist in the testing and debugging process, the PBDEBUG option. PBDEBUG traces the creation and destruction of objects and the execution of scripts, system functions, global functions, object-level functions, and external functions. Your application must be made into an executable before you can make use of PBDEBUG. When you create your executable, you must select the Trace Information check box and Error Context check box (for machine code executables) in the Code Generation Options section of the Project painter (see Figure 16.19).

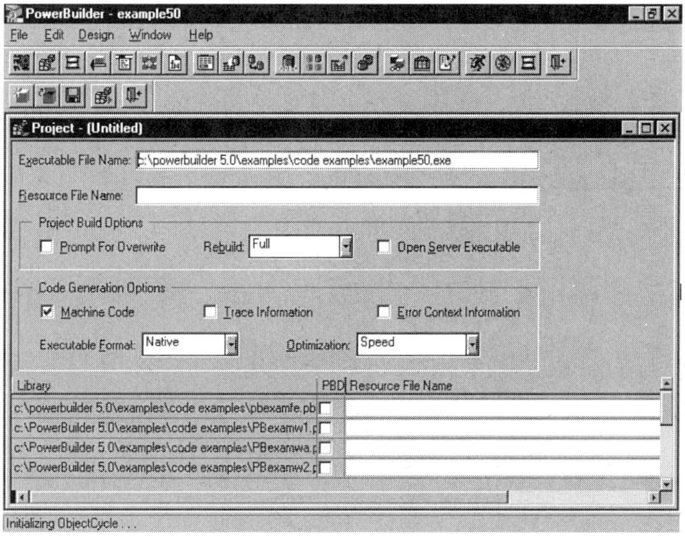

FIGURE 16.19.
The Code Generation Options section in the Project painter.

NOTE

In Version 4.0, executables were automatically created with the debug information built into them. In 5.0, if you leave the Trace Information and Error Context check boxes off, the DBG file will not be created. If you create an executable that is not machine code (in other words, p-code), the trace information is still automatically placed in the executable.

Once you have an executable, choose Run from the Start Menu and type the following:

```
C:\application_path\appname.exe /PBDEBUG
```

In this line, `application_path` is the location of the executable and `appname.exe` is the name of your application executable. The application will run as it normally does, but when you are finished there will be a new file created in the executable's directory. The new file will be named *appname*.dbg, where *appname* is the name of your executable file. Listing 16.1 shows a sample of what PBDEBUG generates.

Listing 16.1. A sample of a PBDEBUG file.

```
Executing event script CREATE for class UNLEASHED5, lib entry UNLEASHED5
  Executing instruction at line 2
  Executing instruction at line 3
  Executing instruction at line 4
  Executing instruction at line 5
  Executing instruction at line 6
  Executing instruction at line 7
End event script CREATE for class UNLEASHED5, lib entry UNLEASHED5
Executing event script OPEN for class UNLEASHED5, lib entry UNLEASHED5
  Executing instruction at line 6
  Executing event script CREATE for class W_LOGON, lib entry W_LOGON
    Executing instruction at line 2
    Executing instruction at line 3
    Executing instruction at line 4
    Executing instruction at line 5
    Executing instruction at line 6
    Executing instruction at line 7
    Executing instruction at line 8
  End event script CREATE for class W_LOGON, lib entry W_LOGON
End event script OPEN for class UNLEASHED5, lib entry UNLEASHED5
Executing event script CLICKED for class CB_OK, lib entry W_LOGON
  Executing instruction at line 1
  Executing instruction at line 2
  Executing instruction at line 3
  Executing instruction at line 4
  Executing instruction at line 5
  Executing instruction at line 7
```

```
Executing instruction at line 9
Executing instruction at line 14
Executing event script CREATE for class W_FRAME, lib entry W_FRAME
Executing instruction at line 2
```

The text file generated by running with the PBDEBUG option shows the order of each object as it is created (`W_LOGON`), the events that are executed (`CLICKED for class CB_OK`), the numbers of the lines of code that were executed for a particular event script (`Executing instruction at line 2`), and the destruction of each object. The PBDEBUG file can tell you much about what events and code are being run at what time. It also assists you in seeing how many times script/functions are executed. This can help identify areas for improving performance.

The PBDEBUG option enables you to track down focus and, to some degree, timer problems. The output file generated can quickly become very large, and it is advisable to get to the area of interest in the application as quickly as possible. Remember, when you create your executable to go into production, do not use trace execution since it increases the size of the executable and performance.

NOTE

Removing the debug options applies only when you are creating a machine code executable. A non-machine code executable will include the debug information anyway.

Database Tracing

Another technique that is useful in determining PowerBuilder and database connectivity is the trace facility. In the code in which you assign attributes to your transaction object, place the word `TRACE` before the DBMS attribute value (for example, Trace ODBC for Watcom or Trace SYB for Sybase). When you do this, PowerBuilder will generate a trace log text file that displays what SQL processing occurred during the execution of the code.

NOTE

If you are using an ODBC data source, you can also specify that a log file is generated to track the ODBC processing. This option is set up via the Windows Control Panel under the ODBC option.

For more information on this topic see Chapter 5, "SQL and PowerBuilder."

Additional PowerBuilder Testing Techniques

In addition to using the debugger and PBDEBUG to find errors, you can use a number of other common techniques to pinpoint problems in a PowerBuilder application.

Embedded SQL

If your application makes use of complex, embedded SQL statements, it is a good idea to test the SQL statements outside the Script painter before including them in the application. The first thing you need to do after you write the SQL statements is to test the SQL in the database administrator (see Chapter 4, "Databases and the Database Painter," for more about this painter). Run the SQL to make sure you have no syntax errors and also to validate any result sets to remove logic errors.

After the SQL has been tested, copy it into the appropriate script and compile the script.

WARNING

Just because the database administrator properly executed your SQL does not automatically mean that the SQL will require no changes when placed into a script. PowerBuilder will accept many of the standard data-manipulation language statements as is, but for more complex dynamic SQL and data-definition statements, you must incorporate additional code. (See Chapter 5 for more information on how to code embedded SQL in PowerBuilder.)

The `SQLPreview` Event

The previous section discusses how to ensure that your embedded SQL statements perform as desired, but it does not address the SQL statements that are generated when you're retrieving and updating data using a DataWindow. If you are unsure that the SQL being generated is correct, you can use the `SQLPreview` event of a DataWindow control to view the SQL before it is sent to the database.

The `SQLPreview` event is triggered after a `Retrieve()`, an `Update()`, or a `ReselectRow()` function is called, but before the SQL is sent to the database. For the `Retrieve()` and `ReselectRow()` functions, the `SQLPreview` event is obviously executed only once. For the `Update()` function, it is triggered for each row being updated.

The new Version 5.0 method used to capture the SQL statements is the `SQLPreview` event argument `SqlSyntax`. The `SqlSyntax` argument is a string that contains the SQL statement generated by the DataWindow. Instead of using the debugger to watch the value, place a multiline edit on the window with the DataWindow control in question and assign `SqlSyntax` to the text attribute.

NOTE

If your database engine uses bind variables (as do Watcom, Oracle, and Gupta), you might see lots of question marks in your SQL statement. If you would like to get rid of those for testing purposes, use the `DisableBind` option in `DBParm` when you connect: `SQLCA.DBParm = 'DisableBind=1'`.

The `SqlSyntax` argument replaces the need for using the `GetSQLPreview()` function.

The `DBError` Event

The `DBError` event can be used to determine the row in error when the `Update()` function is called for a DataWindow control and a SQL error triggers this event. The `GetUpdateStatus()` function was used in earlier versions of PowerBuilder. This can now be accomplished by using the `DBError` event arguments: `Row` and `Buffer`. These arguments indicate the row number in error and the DataWindow buffer (Primary, Delete, or Filter) in which the row exists. You can then look at the values being sent to the database and the SQL statement generated by the `Update()` function.

The `GetItemStatus()` Function

`GetItemStatus()` is often useful in conjunction with the `DBError` and `SQLPreview` events. `GetItemStatus()` returns the modification status of a row or column (`New!`, `NewModified!`, `NotModified!`, or `DataModified!`). This status identifies what type of SQL statement the `Update()` function will generate. When you know the status, you can determine whether PowerBuilder is generating the desired SQL statement for your application.

Displaying Messages to the Screen

Instead of using the debugger, you can display a message in a window to indicate PowerBuilder's position within a script or the value of certain key variables. Two common places to display these messages are to a single- or multiline edit control and to the MicroHelp (for MDI applications). The messages can consist of just about anything—for example, variable values or the function name currently being called.

The `MessageBox()` Function

In a way similar to displaying information on a window, the `MessageBox()` function can be called to tell the developer when a certain point in the script has been reached. Although displaying messages on a single-line edit might be quicker and easier to code, the `MessageBox()` function stops the script it is in (because a message box is modal) and does not continue until you click one of the buttons.

The `Beep()` Function

The `Beep()` function is used to indicate to the developer that a predetermined point in a script has been reached. `Beep()` brings additional attention to the developer because of the sound aspect. This technique is particularly useful in testing for focus events (`GetFocus`, `Activate`, `Deactivate`), where a message box will only cause additional focus changes.

SQA TeamTest

One of the more popular third-party products is SQA TeamTest from SQA, Inc. SQA TeamTest gives you the capability to test and track your application-development process. One main reason that this product is doing well is that it is tightly integrated with PowerBuilder objects (particularly DataWindows). SQA TeamTest can be used to plan test strategies and development, track test execution and results, track defects, and generate a multitude of reports. The engine for SQA TeamTest can use Visual Basic or SQA's own script language to create the test scenarios.

Many testing tools just track keystrokes and mouse movements. SQA TeamTest is a little different in that it tracks your application on an object level and therefore does not depend on extraneous information such as the appearance or location of a window. For this reason, SQA TeamTest works well across different versions of the same application.

Although setting up the test procedures might not seem worthwhile to smaller companies, there are many components that can be particularly useful. The SQA Robot enables you to record and play back various test scenarios. In playback mode, SQA TeamTest indicates whether an object's state has changed from the recorded scenario (perhaps a command button is now disabled when it was previously enabled). For DataWindows, SQA captures not only the format of the DataWindow, but also the columns and the data retrieved for a particular test case. SQA TeamTest will flag changes in the data as well, so that you can notify your DBA that there could be a potential problem on the database (see Figure 16.20).

FIGURE 16.20.
SQA TeamTest's test scenario.

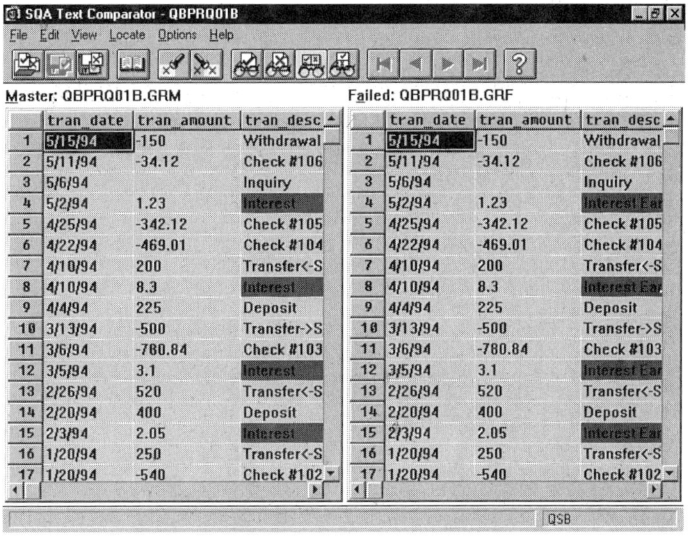

In conjunction with the SQA Robot for supplying test scripts, TeamTest comes equipped with an excellent defect tracker and reporting facility. To manually keep tabs on defects and their status can be an exhausting and complex ordeal (see Figure 16.21). TeamTest does a good job of simplifying this process.

FIGURE 16.21.
SQA TeamTest's defect report.

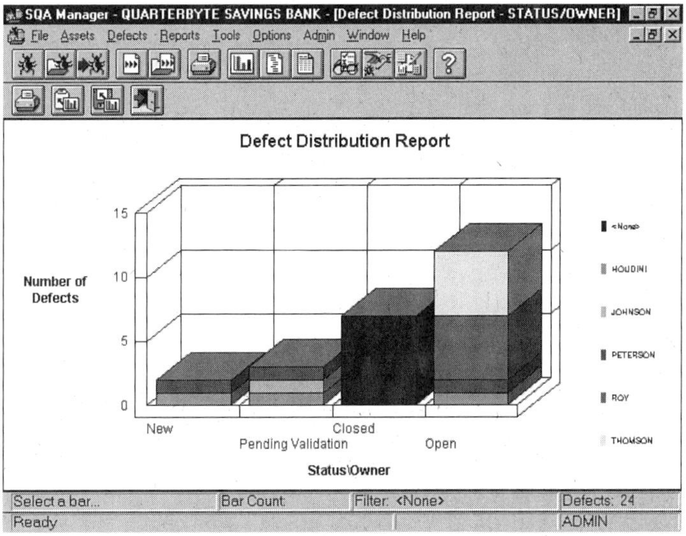

Relatively new to the SQA family is the product SQA LoadTest. LoadTest gives you assistance in volume testing and user concurrency testing. Traditionally, if you want to simulate 50 users running your application at the same time, you have to have 50 people involved in your testing or do an inadequate test. LoadTest gives you the ability to automate this process. All you need do is run the 50 machines with predefined scripts for your application without involving a large number of testers.

Additional Third-Party Tools

The list of tools that can be used to assist in the debugging and testing process is quite lengthy. Many applications are available as freeware products or can be purchased for a nominal amount. Some very common examples of these are WPS, DDE Spy, WinSnoop, and Rbrand. The following are some of the tools that we have used and are familiar with. There are number of other utilities available that perform the same or similar tasks:

- WPS can be found on the Microsoft tech net CD-ROM. It provides a memory dump of EXE, DLL, and DRV files that are currently loaded.
- DDE Spy allows you to watch DDE conversations taking place between two applications and is available on the Microsoft tech net CD-ROM.
- WinSnoop provides a variety of information on a window, from its handle to its parent. This program is freeware and is available almost anywhere.
- Rbrand is provided by Powersoft for checking the timestamps on the PowerBuilder DLLs.

Summary

In this chapter you have seen some standard approaches to the testing process. The methodologies for testing an application vary from project to project, but one key component—user involvement—should be maintained in all test procedures. After a test strategy has been agreed on, numerous tools and tricks can be used within PowerBuilder to ensure that the application fulfills all business requirements. The debugger and PBDEBUG option are two of the utilities with which PowerBuilder comes equipped to assist in identifying problem areas. In addition to these tools, several third-party tools are available for purchase or as freeware.

The testing and debugging process can be long and complicated. It is important to always identify where the process is breaking down (client, network, or server) and what component is causing the problem. Never jump to conclusions. In developing a detailed test strategy, you are ensuring the delivery of a quality application you can be proud of.

Documentation and Online Help

17

IN THIS CHAPTER

Just as there are a number of ways to code functionality into your application, there are a myriad of ways to document a client/server application. This problem is not a concern just for PowerBuilder development teams, but for all developers involved with client/server technology. In this chapter you will explore some possibilities for documenting your system. You will also look at providing online help for the end user, through either MicroHelp cues or full-blown Windows Help pages.

Probably the worst moment in the development cycle for a developer is when someone says "Okay, now we need to document the system!" If you have document templates and a procedure for creating the documentation, you can make life easier for all those involved and end up with a better-written and more organized piece of work. You should also try to make it as interesting and as varied as possible so that the developer can maintain at least some interest in the task.

System Documentation

System documentation should exist not only on paper but within the application itself. You should make use of the comment entries that are available in the Library painter to label each object—and even each library—with a short description. PowerScript functions and events should ideally have a comment block (or code header) at the start, and then short one- or two-line descriptions with logical blocks of code. See Chapter 6, "The PowerScript Language," for details on comment syntax.

The following is an example of a code header:

```
/*****************************************************************
* Function/Event Name: wf_SaveHeader()
* Date Created: 04/21/95 by Simon Gallagher
* Functional Description:
*    This function saves all the relevant header information
*    for an order.
* Modifications made:
*    04/30/95 by Simon Herbert
*           Missing validation check added for product_code
*****************************************************************/
```

NOTE

You can use the PBToolbox utility provided on the CD that accompanies this book to paste in a script comment block like the one just shown.

There are obviously many variations on this theme, and you will want to track several different pieces of information (for example, name, creation date, description, parameters, and modifications made). Make sure all members of the team create this kind of comment block; it will be a valuable source of information when someone is developing new versions of the software. Any in-line comments should be meaningful and not simply restatements of the obvious, because that just creates unnecessary clutter in your script. Comments should be short and concise, but should provide high-level information about the code.

NOTE

With the new PowerScript painter you can set the color of comments to a light gray, which causes the comments to fade into the background. This allows you to focus on the code and not be confused with what is code and what is a comment.

Some development teams provide on the network file server a file that can be imported into the Script painter that defines a standard comment block.

The actual system document should be structured to include an object's events, functions, variables, and even inheritance. If you are using a framework, the details of which ancestor objects are used can be especially helpful. In fact, documenting inheritance chains is an all-around beneficial task. If you are constructing your own framework or expanding on a framework, this kind of information can prove invaluable to a development team.

As with most of the other parts of a system's documentation, there are different styles of detailing PowerBuilder components. You might end up using different styles for different areas of your documentation. The most common style of system documentation is breakdown, otherwise known as drill down.

With this style, you take all the high-level objects—for example, global functions, top-level windows, and user objects —and detail all their attributes, events, and object functions. You should collect these top-level objects into groups based on the object type, and then arrange them alphabetically. When the topmost layer has been defined, go down to the next level, and so on, until you reach the actual windows that are used in the system. At this level, you should detail each of the controls on the window with a brief description.

Examples of both object-level and window-level system documentation using this style are shown in the following sections.

u_ddlb

`u_ddlb` is a standard drop-down list box user object that has been modified to provide some additional trappable events. The following are the variables and events used in `u_ddlb`:

Instance Variables	*Description*
`Boolean i_bModified`	Tracks whether the edit field has been modified. This variable is initialized in the `Constructor` event.
`Boolean i_bValidated`	Tracks whether the value in the edit field has passed the validation checks. This variable is initialized in the `Constructor` event.

Object Events	*Description*
`Constructor`	Initializes the instance variables.
`Destructor`	Clears out the edit field contents; this is due to the `Validate` event being triggered after the objects are destroyed. The `Validate` event should check for an empty field and return immediately.
`GetFocus`	Highlights the field contents upon getting focus.
`LoseFocus`	Trims the field contents upon leaving the field.
`Modified`	Sets the modified flag and triggers a `Validate` event.

User Events	*Description*
`Other`	Checks the message IDs coming from Windows and triggers a `Dropdown` event if one occurs.
`Dropdown`	Blank, for the child to override with specific code.
`Validate`	Blank, for the child to override with specific code.
`Invalid_entry`	Blank, for the child to override with specific code.
`Reset`	Resets the instance variables and clears the edit field.
`Refresh`	Blank, for the child to override with specific code.

u_ddlb_from_database

The `u_ddlb_from_database` object is inherited from the `u_ddlb` user object and has been modified to provide some additional trappable events:

User Object Function	*Description*
`uf_Populate( String szSQLSelect)`	Uses the supplied SQL `SELECT` string to populate the drop-down list box.

w_import

This window is used to import data from different sources:

Instance Variables	*Description*
`DataWindow i_dwImport`	The DataWindow to import to.
`String i_szPath`	The file path to read the data from.
`Long i_lStartRow`	The first row to start reading from.
`Long i_lEndRow`	The last row to read.
`Long i_lStartColumn`	The first column to use.

`Long i_lEndColumn`	The last column to use.
`Long i_lDWStartColumn`	The DataWindow column where you want to start inserting.

Window Functions	*Description*
`wf_GetParameters()`	Translates the edit field values into the instance variables.
`wf_ImportError()`	Takes an integer and opens an error window detailing the error code.

Window Events	*Description*
`Open`	Copies the passed DataWindow into the instance variable.

Controls	*Description*
`cbx_header`	Header information toggle.
`sle_file`	Holds the path and filename from which to read data.
`cb_file`	Opens the MS Open File dialog box; stores the returned value in `sle_file`.
`cb_from_file`	Reads the data from the specified file.
`cb_from_string`	Reads the data from `sle_string`.
`cb_from_clipboard`	Reads the data from the Clipboard.
`cb_cancel`	Closes the window.

This information can be arranged in a number of ways; the method selected here uses the table feature of Microsoft Word for Windows to provide a succinct but informative guide to the system. For documentation that goes into a little more depth, you might consider using a bulleted list and real paragraph structures. In addition, you can place any documentation with the object you are documenting. Create a custom user event for the object (for example, a user object) and call it `ue_Documentation`. Place all your documentation in this event and save your object. The beauty of this method is that the documentation will not get lost because it is stored with the object, and PowerBuilder will not include the information in the executable because it considers comments to be white space.

In PowerBuilder 5.0 you are able to generate simple documentation on any number of your application objects. You do this with the Object Browser (see Figure 17.1), which can be accessed from the PowerScript painter or the Library painter.

New in PowerBuilder 5

Select the object type you are interested in, expand the category details (Properties, Events, and so on) that you want to document, and click the Document button. By doing this, PowerBuilder creates an RTF (rich text format) document that displays the selected object(s) and the corresponding category details (see Figure 17.2). From this dialog box you can export the RTF document to a file, copy it to the Clipboard, or print it.

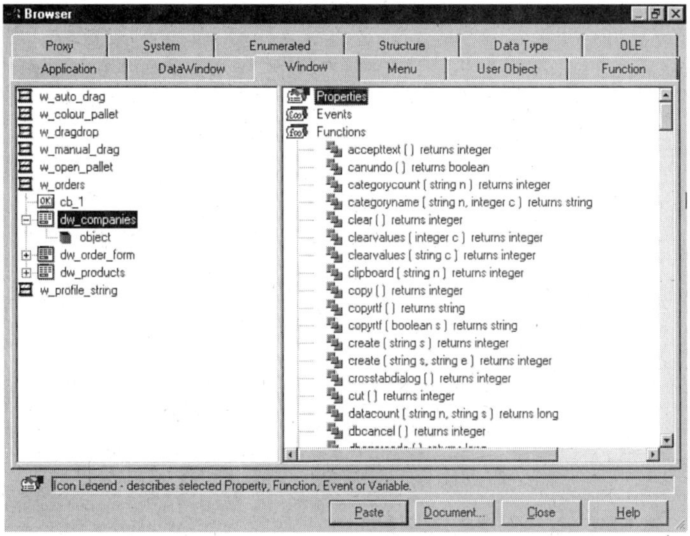

FIGURE 17.1.
The Object Browser.

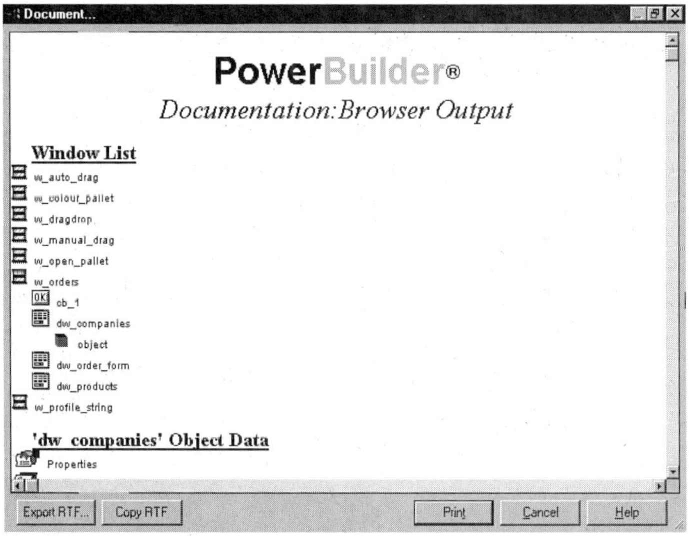

FIGURE 17.2.
The Document dialog box.

There are also some tools available for PowerBuilder that will produce object documentation for you quickly and easily and in a very readable format. One of these tools is PowerDoc from Catapult Systems (see Appendix B, "PowerBuilder Resources," on the accompanying CD for details), which creates a Microsoft Word document that includes a table of contents, an index, object pictures, and breakdown of all the PowerBuilder objects. The inheritance hierarchy is also included in the finished document. The only condition on using this product is that you must be running Microsoft Windows 3.1, PowerBuilder 4.0, and Microsoft Word 6.0.

WARNING

Because PowerDoc uses ORCA (see Chapter 34, "The Powersoft Open Library API: ORCA" for more details), you must have either the PowerBuilder Enterprise or PowerBuilder Team/ODBC products. Powersoft does not ship the required ORCA DLL with PowerBuilder Desktop.

The PowerDoc program is a one-window interface that uses a tabbed control to provide configuration options. Once you have PowerDoc configured to your liking, you simply click on the Document button and come back later to a fully documented system. The time it takes to document the system varies according to the number of objects, their size, and the levels of inheritance. For example, a seven-library project of about 2MB size and 40 objects took just over 20 minutes. (On average it seems to take about 1 1/2 to 2 times the time it takes to compile the project into an executable.) The resulting document was 150+ pages long and over 7MB in size!

For each DataWindow and window, PowerDoc produces a rendering of how the object looks and includes it in the documentation. The resulting picture is not overwhelming, but it gives an idea of what the object contains and how it is laid out. Functions, global or object level, are well documented with the inclusion of access levels, the return data type, and the parameter's name, data type, and passing type (by reference or by value). Menus are equally well presented, and they include an overview of the entire menu that shows an indented menu item hierarchy, accelerators, shortcut keys, and the object names. The documentation of a window includes instance variables, window functions, and structures, window events with code, and each control with the associated event scripts.

Another tool that can be used for documentation is PBToolbox (included on the CD), which includes a method of creating and extracting comments from your PowerBuilder objects. Not only can you create a comment block template that is pasted into your script, but you can also run PBToolbox to extract all comments and create a text file for documentation purposes.

User Documentation

The documentation for an end user should include a brief overview of what the system does and does not do, a detailed installation guide, and a detailed guide through the system—possibly with a tutorial.

Overview

The overview should use simple terms or terms the end user can understand and with which he or she will feel comfortable. You will not provide a very good first impression to the users if you use a lot of technical jargon. Keep it simple. The most complex ideas can be expressed much more clearly by using examples and graphics. If you can make appropriate use of graphics or even a simple flowchart to convey the reason the system has been built, you are much more likely to succeed. The concepts expressed should be based on the business functionality that is being proposed.

You should include brief descriptions of all the major functions that can be carried out in the application. It is not necessary to include pictures since the descriptions are short.

System Installation

Depending on how you are going to deploy your application, you might want to include a system installation guide in the user documentation. This is a useful source of reference for users and other developers.

This should include step-by-step instructions, making full use of screen shots and window captions to help the user through the installation. For example, use bold fonts when describing a button, window title, or menu option, as in the following example:

1. Click on the **OK** button.
2. Then, within the **Choose Printer** window, choose the **Database Connection** menu option.

As you can see in this example, this technique can really make the important information stand out. It can be a great help to more competent users who can just scan through the highlighted text and figure out what to do without having to read all the accompanying text.

Within the guide you may want to include the files and their locations that will be deployed during installation. This type of information is of more use to other developers, network personnel, and computer-knowledgeable end users than to your average end user.

Detailed Guide

The detailed guide can be broken into two distinct styles: by window or by business function.

With the first style, by window, you take a screen shot of each window and then describe it. If you decide to use this style, you should list all the functions available in each window. Include with the functions each of the controls on the window and any menu items that have particular relevance. Each window function should detail what it does, what effect it has on the current window, and any effects it has on the whole application. Navigation between the various windows should be stated, as should the relationship between the current window and other windows. That is, you should make it clear which windows you can open from the current window and how you open them.

A more logical style of presenting a system guide is by business function. With this style, you need to describe the business function and the flow through the major windows; that is, you enter an order in window X and then go into screen Y to assign a sales representative to it. Then, as mentioned before, you can use a screen shot with descriptions to detail the steps the user must take to use the function. Unlike before, however, you should ignore controls, fields, and menu items that have no bearing on the business function.

Problem Resolution

Whichever style you adopt for your application, you should provide a section in the guide that deals with problem resolution. This section should include how to recover from a particular error condition or message, or how to carry out a certain action that the system was not initially designed for, but that can be carried out with some careful interaction. Again, try to keep any error-message descriptions oriented toward the end users as much as possible, because users probably do not care very much about timestamps or other database-specific jargon.

When an error occurs, you will probably want to detail how to report the situation and possibly to whom it should be reported. See Chapter 30, "Mail Enabling PowerBuilder Applications," for a way to automate error reporting and make sure it gets reported to the right person.

Online Help

Online help that is accessible from within an application or development environment can save time spent chasing down the appropriate manual (and then making sure the information in it is up-to-date). The help provides the latest information on the application to the requester in a format that can be browsed easily. The next couple sections look at the different ways developers can provide information to users of an application.

MicroHelp

The MicroHelp area resides along the bottom edge of an MDI frame window. It is also known as a status bar within Microsoft circles (or should that be *outside Powersoft circles*!). This area is used to display useful information on the current state of the application and system. Most Windows applications make extensive use of this area to tell the user anything from the current mode of the application to the time and even what system resources are free. The most frequent use is to display short messages about what an object is (see Chapter 12, "Menus and the Menu Painter," for an example) or what processing is currently occurring.

PowerBuilder provides you with the function `SetMicroHelp()` to specify text to be displayed in the MicroHelp area on the MDI frame window (the text will be left justified). The syntax is

```
MDIWindow.SetMicroHelp( TextToDisplay)
```

As mentioned earlier, menus can be built to provide a short description of each menu item in the MicroHelp as you change focus between the items. You can provide the same functionality for the controls on a window, either by using the much-used and overworked `Tag` attribute or by declaring an instance variable for the ancestor object for each control (assuming that you have constructed a foundation class of all objects). Whichever method you choose, place a `SetMicroHelp()` call in the `GetFocus` and `LoseFocus` events for each control—or, if you are using inherited controls, just place the code once at the ancestor level.

For example, in the `GetFocus` event of the command button `cb_connect`, the script might be

```
g_App.i_wFrame.SetMicroHelp( "Use this to open the database connect window.")
```

Then within the `LoseFocus` event, it would be

```
g_App.i_wFrame.SetMicroHelp( "Ready")
```

Note the use of the `g_App` variable. This is a nonvisual user object that has been instantiated at the global level and contains all the important information for the application.

NOTE

In addition to this technique, you can also modify the default MicroHelp message (`Ready`) with your own message. This is done using the application object attribute `MicroHelpDefault`.

Windows Help Pages

A standard method of providing information to users is via online help, which is provided by almost all Windows applications. Help is commonly accessible under the rightmost menu item or by pressing the F1 key, either of which causes the WINHELP.EXE program to load and display a help file supplied by the application.

Windows help is based on the hypertext language, which enables the linkage of text, graphics, and sound into a multimedia document. A hypertext document is set up with a vast number of links that enable a user to jump from topic to topic with ease while following a particular train of thought or examining side issues. Before tackling the creation of a help file, there are some terms you need to learn because they are integral to a help file's creation.

A help file is a collection of *topics* (individual informational screens) that are interconnected via *hypertext jumps*. A *jump* is a word or phrase that when clicked takes the user to another topic.

Also defined within each topic are *keywords,* which are a series of words that point to one or more help topics. Keywords are used when the user clicks on the Search button and a keyword is entered, displaying all related topics. In addition to keywords, help files should provide definitions for commonly used terms. This is done using *pop-ups,* which appear as temporary windows when the user clicks on a particular word. A pop-up is different from a jump in that the pop-up does not change the current topic. The pop-ups should be accessible as a *glossary* via the online help engine.

The information used for building online help can be drawn from parts of previous documents (for example, design specs) or even from documents converted in their entirety. The opposite is also true; some help file generators can use a help file to produce polished documents with indexes and a table of contents.

The WINHELP.EXE program is used to display files with the .HLP extension, which are specially compiled document files. There are a number of commercial and shareware help compilers available to assist in the generation of help files.

The types of help file–generation applications can be divided into two main categories: word processor–based and standalone tools. The word processor–based tools are typically written as templates that add to the functionality of an existing word processing application such as Word for Windows. The prominent names in the word processor–based applications are RoboHelp, Help Breeze, and Doc-To-Help. The beauty of these programs is that they extend an environment that the developer of the help file is already familiar with. The downside of these tools is that they depend on additional software. The obvious benefit of the standalone help generators is that they run independently of any other software. Standalone help generators such as Help Ease, Fore Help, Windows Help Magician, and Visual Help provide more flexibility, but in the intricacy of their help files is limited.

Another tool you can use in help file creation is the Hot Spot Editor (SHED.EXE). The Hot Spot Editor is used to create hypergraphics, which are simply bitmaps with hotspots defined for them. A hotspot is an area of a graphic that executes a jump, pop-up, or help macro. The hypergraphic can then be placed in a help file.

Once you have decided on the tool you are going to use to create your help file, you need to design the layout of the help file. This process is often taken lightly and results in a very poorly written and laid out help file. After deciding what the individual topics will be, you need to know how they will be linked (which jumps are available), what words are keywords, and what words or phrases need to have pop-ups created. After deciding on the help file structure, use the help tool of choice to develop an RTF document.

The RTF is combined with a help project file (HPJ) and compiled to create the HLP you distribute with your application. You should break up your help into topics, and for each topic you might want to create a separate RTF file, depending on the size of each topic and the help tool chosen.

The following is a sample project (HPJ) file:

```
;**********************************************
;    Contents: sample Windows help project file
;    Use semi-colon to comment lines.
;**********************************************
 [OPTIONS]
;Enter the name of the context string for the first topic you want to
;display in your Help file.
CONTENTS=index_user_help

 [FILES]
;You list the topic (.RTF) files used in here

 [BITMAPS]
;You list the bitmap files used in here

 [CONFIG]
;Use BrowseButtons() to create WinHelp browse buttons in the button bar.
BrowseButtons()
```

When you have learned the intricacies of the help compiler that you have chosen to use and have an HLP file, how do you use it in PowerBuilder?

Help is usually accessed via several different methods in a Windows application. It is standard for an application to have either a Help button on each window or a Help menu option. Within the Help menu, there should at least be a Contents menu item that takes you to the main topic of the help file and a Search menu item that opens the Search tab (or dialog box) of the help file. Help can also be activated with a press of the F1 key. Depending on the sophistication of the application, this may open context-sensitive help or it may just open the Contents topic.

PowerBuilder provides a `ShowHelp()` function that you use to launch the Windows Help system and display the specified help file. The syntax is

```
ShowHelp( HelpFile, HelpCommand {, TypeID})
```

The *`HelpFile`* argument is the filename (optionally with a full path) that is the HLP file to be displayed. The *`HelpCommand`* argument is of the `HelpCommand` enumerated data type. The values are as follows:

Value	*Description*
`Index!`	Displays the top-level Contents topic in the help file.
`KeyWord!`	Goes to the topic identified by the keyword in *`TypeID`*.
`Topic!`	Displays the topic identified by the number in *`TypeID`*.

`TypeID` is an optional argument that identifies either a numeric topic if the *`HelpCommand`* argument is `Topic!` or a string keyword if the *`HelpCommand`* argument is `KeyWord!`.

To provide access to the help file in the Help menu item, you would code something like this:

```
ShowHelp( "OE_010.HLP", Index!)
```

which opens the help program and displays the index for the help file OE_010.HLP that is in the current directory or on the system path.

Context-Sensitive Help

You can provide context-sensitive help by using the other two *HelpCommand* values, `Topic!` and `KeyWord!`.

When you build the help project file, you will want to define unique topic identifiers. This enables you to open the help to a particular topic by passing in the numeric identifier:

```
ShowHelp( "OE_010.HLP", Topic!, 94)
```

The `KeyWord!` value can be used either to go straight to a topic that is associated with the string value or, if the string is not unique, to open the Search window (or in Windows 95, it opens the Index tab) (see Figure 17.3).

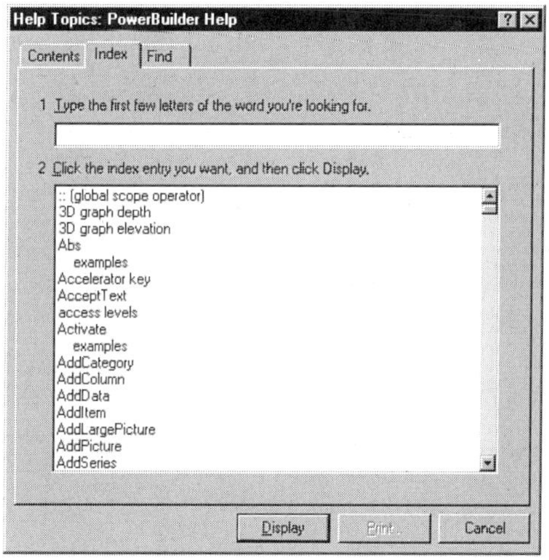

FIGURE 17.3.
The Help Index tab.

The big question is How do you open this dialog box in a window with a number of different controls and get the help for the object on which the user is currently focused? Actually, it is not too difficult. You use the `Key` event trapped inside a window.

The `Key` event is fired in a window whenever a key (except the Alt key) is pressed and the control with focus is not a line edit control.

WARNING

The PowerBuilder help page for the Key event really means that this event will not fire when the focus is in a DataWindow. The Key event *will* be triggered when you are in a single- or multiline edit control or drop-down list box.

Inside this event you can place a call to ShowHelp() with a topic identifier. The only problem now is to determine which topic to display. This information is set when the control first gains focus and can be placed globally, locally at the window level, within a global user object, or even in the window's Tag attribute. The following example makes use of a global application object that has a variable called i_nHelpTopic. An example of the code that might be placed in a command button, check box, or other online edit control's GetFocus event is

```
g_App.i_nHelpTopic = 20    // Display the help topic for the cb_connect button
```

Then within the Key event, the code would be

```
If KeyDown( KeyF1!) Then
   ShowHelp( g_App.i_szHelpFile, Topic!, g_App.i_nHelpTopic)
End If
```

For DataWindow controls, you need to capture the Key event yourself and then carry out the processing. This is only a matter of declaring a user event for the PowerBuilder message pbm_dwnkey. You can then use the same code that you used for the window Key event.

So that a help topic does not appear for objects on which you have not defined a specific help, you can code a statement in the LoseFocus that sets g_App.i_nHelpTopic = 0. Then in the Key event, you can use the KeyDown() function to check whether F1 was pressed and open the help index instead. Here's an example:

```
If KeyDown( KeyF1!) Then
   If g_App.i_nHelpTopic > 0 Then
      ShowHelp( g_App.i_szHelpFile, Topic!, g_App.i_nHelpTopic)
   Else
      ShowHelp( g_App.i_szHelpFile, Index!)
   End If
End If
```

You can implement the DataWindow's context sensitivity using the column's name as a KeyWord! search, as in this example:

```
String szColumnName

If KeyDown( KeyF1!) Then
   szColumnName = this.GetColumnName()
   If szColumnName = "" Then
      ShowHelp( g_App.i_szHelpFile, Index!)
   Else
      ShowHelp( g_App.i_szHelpFile, KeyWord!, szColumnName)
   End If
End If
```

An alternative to this is to enter a `Choose...Case` statement to generate a specific topic identifier on a column-by-column basis, and then perform a topic lookup.

The `WinHelpA()` API Function

As with some of the other API functions provided in PowerBuilder, Powersoft has managed to hide the complexities of the call, but in the process has lost some of the functionality. This is certainly the case with the `ShowHelp()` function, which is the wrapper around the API function `WinHelpA()`:

```
Integer WinHelpA( hWnd, lpszHelpFile, unCommand, lData)
```

The *`hWnd`* parameter specifies the window that is requesting that the help program be started, and is used to keep track of which applications have requested help. *`lpszHelpFile`* is a string that contains the path and filename of the help file, with the *`unCommand`* parameter indicating the type of help required. The *`lData`* parameter is used by some of the help types specified by *`unCommand`* to supply additional information.

NOTE

The filename specified in the *`lpszHelpFile`* parameter can be followed by an angle bracket (>) together with the name of a secondary window (rather than the primary window) that is to be used to display the topic. Secondary windows are used to present information without the full menus and all the buttons of the regular Windows help window. The secondary windows name must have been defined in the `[WINDOWS]` section of the HPJ file.

It is also important to note that even though the API help files state that `WinHelpA()` returns a Boolean, it in fact returns an Integer value that is a nonzero value if it is successful; otherwise it returns zero. This is the same as the PowerBuilder `ShowHelp()` function return value.

The possible values for the *`unCommand`* and *`lData`* parameters are shown in Table 17.1. The value in parentheses for each *`unCommand`* parameter is the numeric value for the constant. For all N/A entries in the *`lData`* parameter you should pass a zero value.

Table 17.1. Values for `unCommand` and `lData`.

unCommand	*lData*	*Description*
HELP_CONTEXT (1)	Context number for a topic	Displays help for the specified topic with a context number defined in the HPJ `[MAP]` section.

continues

Table 17.1. continued

`unCommand`	`lData`	*Description*
`HELP_CONTENTS (3)`	N/A	Displays the contents topic as defined in the HPJ `[OPTIONS]` section.
`HELP_SETCONTENTS (5)`	Context number for the topic to be designated on the contents page	Determines which contents topic is displayed when the user presses F1.
`HELP_CONTEXTPOPUP (8)`	Context number for a topic	Displays the topic in a pop-up window.
`HELP_KEY (257)`	A string containing a keyword for a topic	Displays the topic found on an exact match of the keyword. If there is more than one match per search, a dialog box is opened, with the topics in the Go To area.
`HELP_PARTIALKEY (261)`	A string containing a keyword for a topic	Displays the topic found on an exact match of the keyword. If there is more than one match, or if there are no matches, a search dialog box is opened with the topics in the Go To area.
`HELP_MULTIKEY (513)`	A pointer to a `MULTIKEYHELP` structure	Displays the topic identified by the keyword from the alternate keyword table.
`HELP_COMMAND (258)`	A string defining the help macro to execute	Executes a help macro.
`HELP_SETWINPOS (515)`	A pointer to a `HELPWININFO` structure	Positions the already open help window to the coordinates passed.
`HELP_FORCEFILE (9)`	N/A	If the current help file is not the default, this causes the correct one to be opened.

unCommand	*lData*	*Description*
`HELP_HELPONHELP (4)`	N/A	Shows the contents topic of a Using Help file.
`HELP_QUIT (2)`	N/A	Tells help to close down if no applications are currently using it.

NOTE

From Table 17.1 you can see that `lData` can be used to pass either a Numeric, a String, or a Structure data type. In PowerBuilder this means that you must declare four external function declarations, one with each of the different data types, for `lData`.

Only the `HELP_CONTEXT`, `HELP_INDEX`, `HELP_CONTENTS`, `HELP_KEY`, and `HELP_PARTIALKEY` functionality is accessible using the PowerBuilder `ShowHelp()` function.

NOTE

If you want to bring up the Search dialog box without starting the search with the keyword passed, send an empty string.

To conform with accepted Windows programming practices, before you close the requesting window you should send the `HELP_QUIT` message to `WinHelpA()` to allow help to close down when all applications have finished with it.

The structure's `MULTIKEYHELP` is defined in PowerBuilder as a regular structure with the following attributes:

Attribute Name	*Data Type*	*Description*
`unSize`	UnsignedInteger	The size of the structure.
`cKeylist`	Char	A Char that identifies the keyword table to search.
`szKeyphrase`	String	The keyword to find in the keyword table.

The `MULTIKEYHELP` structure is used to define a keyword table and an associated keyword that will be used by `WinHelpA()`.

The HELPWININFO structure is defined as follows:

Attribute Name	*Data Type*	*Description*
nStructSize	Integer	The size of the structure.
nX	Integer	The X coordinate of window's upper-left corner.
nY	Integer	The Y coordinate of window's upper-left corner.
nDX	Integer	The width of the window.
nDY	Integer	The height of the window.
nMax	Integer	Set to 1, it maximizes the window, and set to 0, it uses the previous attributes.
szWindowName	String	The window name.

The HELPWININFO structure is used to specify the size and position of a secondary help window for use with the HELP_SETWINPOS value for the *unCommand* parameter.

NOTE

The display is divided into 1024 units in both X and Y directions. Therefore, to fill the top half of the display, nX and nY should be 0 and nDX should be 1024 and nDY should be 512.

To declare the function within PowerBuilder you need to use the following:

```
Function Integer WinHelpA( uInt hWnd, String szHelpFile, uInt unCmd, &
    Long lData)  Library "user32.dll"
Function Integer WinHelpA( uInt hWnd, String szHelpFile, uInt unCmd, &
    String szData) Library "user32.dll"
Function Integer WinHelpA( uInt hWnd, String szHelpFile, uInt unCmd, &
    s_multikeyhelp sData)  Library "user32.dll"
Function Integer WinHelpA( uInt hWnd, String szHelpFile, uInt unCmd, &
    s_helpwininfo sData)  Library "user32.dll"
```

With the function defined, you can now call the WinHelpA() function anywhere you would have called the ShowHelp() function, and you'll get the same results.

For example, to open the help window and directly open the Search dialog box, you would use the following call:

```
WinHelpA( Handle( Parent), "pbhlp050.hlp", 261, "")
```

DataWindow Help Special Handling

At runtime you can customize the help topics related to any of the DataWindow dialog boxes that you have made accessible to your end users. The help can be altered using the `Help` attribute of a DataWindow object in a `Modify()` call.

The syntax required in the `Modify()` call (or a `Describe()` call) is

```
"DataWindow.Help.Attribute { = Value }"
```

The attributes of the `Help` attribute are the following:

Attribute	*Description*
`Command`	Type of help command specified in `TypeID` attributes. Values are `0` (Index), `1` (TopicID), and `2` (Search KeyWord).
`File`	The fully qualified name of the compiled help file. When a value is specified, the help buttons display on DataWindow dialog boxes.
`TypeID`	The default help command to be used when a help topic is not specified for the dialog box.
`TypeID.SetCrosstab`	The help topic for the Crosstab Definition dialog box (opened using `CrossTabDialog()`).
`TypeID.ImportFile`	The help topic for the Import File dialog box (opened using `ImportFile()`).
`TypeID.Retrieve.Argument`	The help topic for the Retrieval Arguments dialog box (opened when a `SELECT` statement is expecting arguments and none are given).
`TypeID.Retrieve.Criteria`	The help topic for the Prompt for Criteria dialog box (opened when the Criteria attribute has been specified for a column and a retrieve is executed).
`TypeID.SaveAs`	The help topic for the Save As dialog box (opened using `SaveAs()`).
`TypeID.SetFilter`	The help topic for the Set Filter dialog box (opened using `SetFilter()` and `Filter()`).
`TypeID.SetSort`	The help topic for the Set Sort dialog box (opened using `SetSort()` and `Sort()`).
`TypeID.SetSortExpr`	The help topic for the Modify Expression dialog box (opened when the user double-clicks on a column in the Set Sort dialog box).

Some examples of these attributes used in `Modify()` expressions are

```
dw_1.Modify( "DataWindow.Help.File='oe_010.hlp'")
dw_1.Modify( "DataWindow.Help.Command=1")
dw_1.Modify( "DataWindow.Help.TypeID.SetFilter='sort_topic'")
dw_1.Modify( "DataWindow.Help.TypeID.Retrieve.Argument='criteria_topic'")
```

NOTE

These DataWindow attributes can also be modified via the direct object syntax by just dropping `Modify()` and rearranging the quotation marks. For more information on the new DataWindow syntax, see Chapter 10, "DataWindow Scripting."

Documentation for Developers

One area of PowerBuilder online help that is often missed is the capability to expand the available help to include application- (or more often, framework-) specific functions, events, and objects. This enables the original writers to provide professional-quality help on their application/framework for those developers who will be either following in their footsteps or using the existing code.

If you look in the online help in PowerBuilder, you will see a button with the label User. This is where you can extend the PowerBuilder help to include your own. When you create your new help file, you must name a topic with the identifier `index_user_help`. This indicates the topic to access when the User button is clicked. This gives the same functionality as pressing F1 and then searching.

To provide context-sensitive help for your application/framework functions, you need to create a help topic that uses a single prefix (for example, `uf_`) and assign a search keyword that matches the function name. For example, the function `uf_SaveHeader()` would have the keyword `uf_SaveHeader`.

You can specify a single prefix for the functions that can have help topics using the `UserHelpPrefix` entry in the PB.INI file. The only requirement is that the prefix must end with an underscore character (for example, `wf_`).

When the user (developer) presses Shift+F1 on a user-defined function, PowerBuilder checks the prefix against the entry in the PB.INI and, if they match, opens the Help file specified by the `UserHelpFile` entry in the PB.INI file. PowerBuilder then does a keyword search using the function's name.

The `UserHelpFile` entry in the PB.INI file enables you to specify the Help file to be used in a user-function context-sensitive search, and it is set to only the filename and not the full path. If there is no value for this entry, the PBUSR050.HLP file will be loaded and searched instead.

Summary

In this chapter you have learned not only about the types of documents that should be produced during or at the end of an application's development cycle, but also how to incorporate the documents you create into online help that can be accessed at runtime and during development. By fully documenting your applications, you are providing an environment that will make maintenance easier and assist the user in learning the application.

18

Application Implementation, Creation, and Distribution

IN THIS CHAPTER

Up to this point in this book we have concerned ourselves only with the development environment. Obviously, the end user is not going to be running the development environment—well, not quite anyway; but the end user will use a number of the same DLLs. This chapter discusses the various component parts that you need to create and distribute for the successful deployment of a production copy of an application.

Creating the Components

Powersoft enables you to build an executable file in one of three ways. The first method is the production of one all-inclusive executable file that the user can run. The second method uses files called *PowerBuilder dynamic libraries* (PBDs) and a smaller executable file. PBDs are similar to DLLs; they enable demand loading of objects within the file to provide you with more control of memory consumption by the application. The third method is new to PowerBuilder 5.0 and allows you to compile to 16- or 32-bit machine code, for both the executable and PBDs; a PBL file can now directly be compiled into a DLL rather than a PBD. The remainder of this chapter refers to situations in which you can use either a PBD or DLL version of a PBL as a dynamic library.

> **NOTE**
>
> Even though the compiled machine code EXE is a true executable, the compiled DLL cannot be used by other applications. You are also still required to distribute a runtime environment (the PowerBuilder Deployment Kit) with the EXE and DLL files. This is because, as with the previous versions of PowerBuilder, large portions of PowerBuilder's functionality are contained in the DLLs and not directly in your application.

The PowerBuilder native executable file (not the machine code version) that is created actually contains a small bootstrap at the front of it that causes the PowerBuilder DLLs to be loaded. The code PowerBuilder has placed in the native EXE file, and optionally in the PBDs, is PowerBuilder-compiled code, not Windows-compiled code. The bootstrap causes the runtime PowerBuilder interpretation of the compiled code in the remainder of the EXE file and PBDs.

The Executable File

When the native executable file is created, PowerBuilder copies the compiled code (called *p-code*) into the EXE file in the order of the library search path specified for the application. P-code is the intermediate code that PowerBuilder compiles and stores with the objects in a library. This is the code that is interpreted by the runtime PowerBuilder DLLs.

For a machine code executable, PowerBuilder actually generates a true binary file that causes the runtime DLLs (PowerBuilder or your own) to be loaded as they are used; this is exactly like any other machine-native application.

The key difference is that the p-code has to be interpreted before it can perform an operation, whereas the machine code just does it.

As PowerBuilder is traversing the library search path, it copies only the objects that are explicitly referenced and are not in libraries that will be made into dynamic libraries (PBDs or DLLs). This means that graphic objects (bitmaps, icons, and pointers), windows, data pipelines, and DataWindows that are dynamically referenced are not copied. Many of these can be used by explicitly listing them in a resource file (detailed later).

The finished executable file contains the Windows bootstrap code, followed by the p-code versions of the objects, and then any dynamically assigned resources. In the case of a machine code version, you have just the executable and dynamically assigned resources.

Prior to PowerBuilder 5.0 you could create an EXE file in one of two places: the Application painter or the Project painter. Now you can create an executable only through the Project painter.

Creating a Resource File

The *resource file*, or *PBR file* as it is more commonly known, is created in any ASCII text editor. As mentioned earlier, objects (graphic or otherwise) that are not explicitly referenced in an application (except the application icon) are not included in the EXE file. All objects other than graphic objects are compiled into dynamic library files if you specify that compile option. This includes dynamically assigned DataWindows, windows, and so on. You still have to specify the graphic objects (bitmaps, icons, and so on) in a resource file.

The PBR file contains the name of each bitmap, icon, pointer, and DataWindow to be included. Depending on the project strictures placed on you, you have two options: either fully qualify the path of the resources or specify no path and place the objects in the same directory as that from which the executable file is constructed. If you fully qualify the path to the graphic objects, you must also fully qualify the path and library for DataWindows. If you choose not to specify the path, you might have to go through some extra steps when assigning bitmaps, drag/drop icons, and mouse pointers. An example of two resource files follows:

```
q:\projects\prs\prs_rept.pbl(d_stk199)
q:\projects\prs\prs_rept.pbl(d_stk430)
q:\projects\prs\prs_rept.pbl(d_stk754a)
q:\projects\prs\prs_rept.pbl(d_stk763)

q:\projects\shared\ptr.bmp
q:\projects\shared\logo.bmp
q:\projects\shared\next.bmp
q:\projects\shared\prev.bmp
q:\projects\shared\maint.ico
q:\projects\shared\entry.ico
q:\projects\shared\reports.ico
```

The first file contains dynamically assigned DataWindows; this resource file would be associated with the executable file. The second file contains bitmaps and icons that will be stored in a dynamic library file. This file is associated with the dynamic library at the time of the file's creation. The complete path and name are stored in the EXE or dynamic library file. The reason for this is discussed next.

NOTE

You *can* associate a resource file with each PBD that you create, but this can become a management nightmare. The solution is to collect all application-specific dynamic resources into one PBR and associate this with the executable. All shared/common dynamic resources that are used across applications should be collected into another PBR, which is then associated with the dynamic library that contains the shared/common objects.

If you place the resource file into either the EXE file or a dynamic library, PowerBuilder searches for the exact name of the resource. For example, if you have a picture button with the path C:\PBSTUFF\ULRIC.BMP, PowerBuilder attempts to match on the fully qualified path and name within the EXE or dynamic library files. That is why it is recommended that you fully qualify all references. It also means you will not inadvertently pick up resources from other than the intended location.

At runtime, PowerBuilder attempts to find the resource files using the Windows search path: the current directory, \WINDOWS, \WINDOWS\SYSTEM, and then the system search path. If the resource cannot be found, one of two things happens, depending on the type of resource. For graphic objects, PowerBuilder either uses a default or shows nothing. For DataWindow objects, the DataWindow control appears but has no assigned DataWindow object.

Creating Dynamic Libraries

A PBD, or a generated DLL, is similar in concept to Windows DLLs and contains all the compiled code for one *PowerBuilder library* (PBL) file. The PBD file can be used only in conjunction with a PowerBuilder-compiled executable file and must be part of the application's library search path to be accessed. Placing code in dynamic libraries enables you to partition your application into smaller related segments. By skillful consideration of which objects are placed in a PBL, you can speed up object load times and better economize resources when that PBL is made into a dynamic library. Like a DLL, only the code from a PBD that is required is loaded, which is different from an EXE file, where everything is loaded at once. See the section "Performance of EXEs Versus Dynamic Library Files" later in this chapter for a discussion of the trade-offs between EXE files and dynamic libraries.

By using a dynamic library you can share code between multiple applications, and it saves you from distributing redundant copies of the code if it was compiled into the EXE file each time. This also enables you to update the functionality of your application without having to distribute either a new EXE file or other files.

NOTE

Remember, the whole PBD is not loaded into memory—only the required object. In the PBDOC.NFO file that comes with the Enterprise edition of PowerBuilder, Powersoft states, "PowerBuilder doesn't load an entire PBD file into memory at once. Instead, it loads individual objects from the PBD file only when needed." As previously stated, this is the mechanism that is also used by DLL files.

PowerBuilder includes a copy of the library search path in the executable file and uses this to search for objects in the same manner that it does during development. If at runtime PowerBuilder cannot find an object in the EXE file, it searches through any available dynamic library files in the order of the library search path. For this reason you should store commonly used objects either in the executable file or in a PBL (and therefore PBD/DLL) that is positioned early in the search path.

Dynamic libraries have a number of advantages:

- Reusability—The dynamic library file is accessible by multiple applications.
- Maintainability—You can individually upgrade application component pieces, rather than redistributing the complete application.
- Completeness—Because a dynamic library contains all objects that were in the PBL file, you can use dynamic referencing more easily. In fact, the only dynamically created PowerBuilder objects that can be placed in the executable file are DataWindows, so you are required to place dynamically created windows, user objects, and so forth, in PBDs/DLLs.
- Efficiency—Better use can be made of the operating system memory. Only the object is loaded into memory, rather than the entire PBD. The executable stub will therefore be smaller, making it less intrusive on the OS resources and much faster loading.
- Modularity—Because each dynamic library corresponds to a PBL file, they enable easy partitioning of the application, which leads to better management of the application as well as all the preceding benefits.

You can create dynamic library files in the Library painter or in the Project painter.

The Build Dynamic Library option is available under the pop-up context menu for a library (see Figure 18.1), or from the Library painter menu.

FIGURE 18.1.

The library context menu.

When you select this menu item, the Build Runtime Library dialog box is opened (see Figure 18.2). The library name is the currently selected name in the Library painter or the first library in your library search path. Make sure you select the right one before continuing.

FIGURE 18.2.

The Build Runtime Library dialog box.

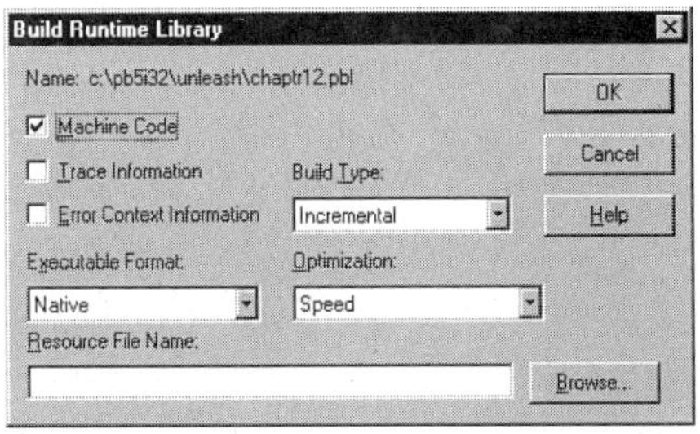

You can select a resource file to be compiled into the PBD or DLL by either typing directly into the field provided or by clicking the Browse button. You then have the option of choosing between a PowerBuilder native PBD or machine code DLL. See the next section, "The Project Painter," for more information on the various options. After specifying the dynamic library options, click the OK button; this creates a PBD or DLL file in the same directory as the PBL file.

The Project Painter

The Project painter creates a project object that stores all the information required to create an application. The Project painter is accessed from the PowerBar by clicking the Project Painter button.

This opens the Select Project dialog box (see Figure 18.3), which requires you to name the project object to be created.

From here you can create a new project or select an existing one. The Browse button provides you with a search feature to track down an existing project object within your libraries. To select an application object from a library outside your library search path, use the Other button. This enables you to temporarily add the library into the application libraries so that you can select the project object.

After you have clicked either OK or New, the actual Project painter opens, which first prompts you with the Select Executable File dialog box (refer to Figure 18.4).

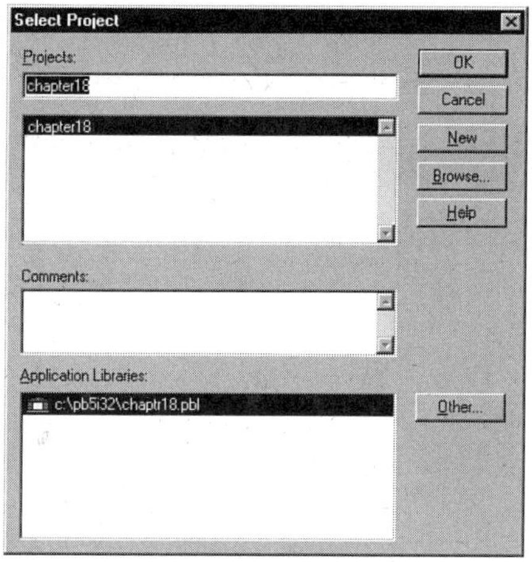

FIGURE 18.3.
The Select Project dialog box.

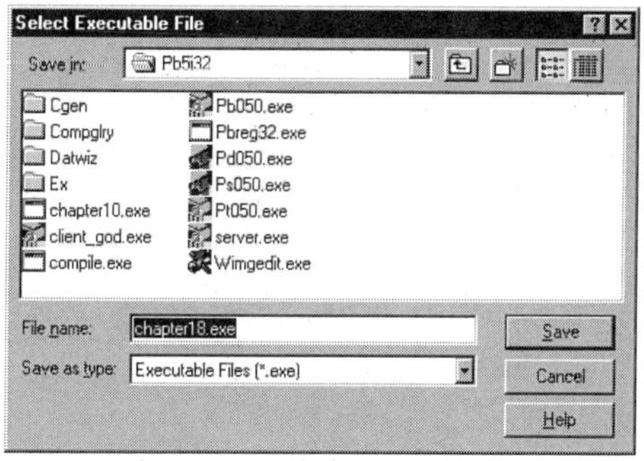

FIGURE 18.4.
The Select Executable File dialog box.

This dialog box enables you to specify the filename and location of the executable file to be created. When you click the Save button, you are placed in the Project painter proper (see Figure 18.5).

The painter provides an Edit menu (see Figure 18.6) that enables you to paste in values instead of typing them into the three edit fields: executable filename, resource filename, and library resource filename.

From the Design menu you can build the project or open a list of the objects used in the library (see Figure 18.7). This list details the library name, the object name, and the object type. The list can be sorted on any of these fields.

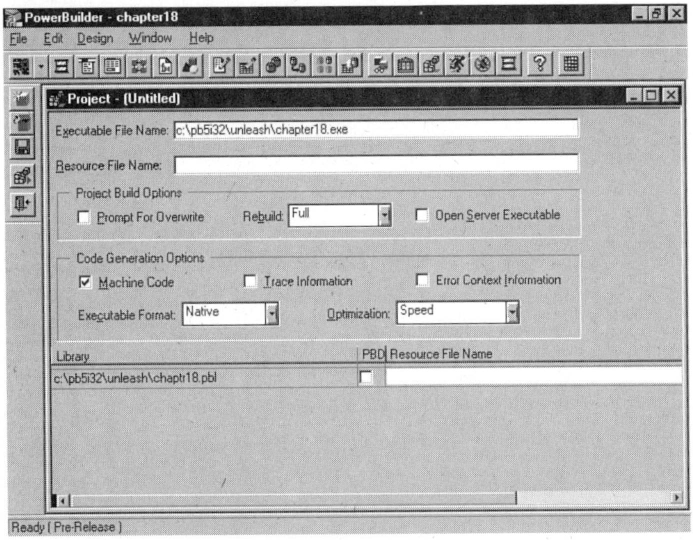

FIGURE 18.5.
The Project painter.

FIGURE 18.6.
The Project painter Edit menu.

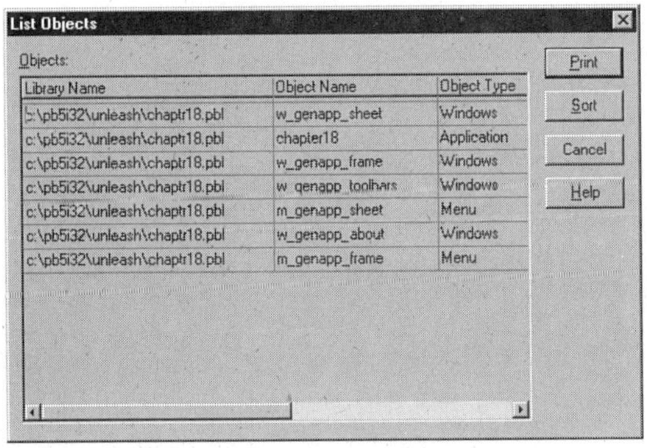

FIGURE 18.7.
The object list.

Within the Project painter you can tell the painter to prompt you before it overwrites the EXE file and whether to regenerate all of the objects in the listed libraries before compilation begins or to carry out an incremental rebuild of only the libraries that have changed. The incremental option is useful when you are creating an executable with dynamic libraries, because it allows you to check off the PBD box in the project painter and PowerBuilder will not rebuild the dynamic library unless the date of the PBL file is greater than the PBD/DLL date.

A new option for PowerBuilder 5.0 is the Open Server Executable, which allows you to create a PowerBuilder executable that can participate in a distributed computing environment (see Chapter 19, "Distributed Processing and Application Partitioning").

NOTE

You can only create an open server executable using the machine code generation option.

New to PowerBuilder 5.0 is the ability to generate machine code, and this is specified in the Code Generation Options area of the Project painter (or the dialog called in the Library painter for creating dynamic libraries). To turn machine code generation on make sure the Machine Code check box is checked; this allows you to toggle between native PowerBuilder code for the executable and dynamic libraries and the machine code versions.

NOTE

You can create machine code executables in only the Win95 and Win NT (32-bit) versions of PowerBuilder. However, you can create a 16-bit version for use in the Windows 3.*x* environment.

The other options in this area relate only to machine code generation:

- Trace Information—This option allows you to use the /PBDEBUG feature that you can use on PowerBuilder native executables, and works in the same manner. It slows performance of the code and should only be used for debugging purposes.
- Error Context Information—In p-code the line number and script information are easily obtainable; in machine code this is not the case. When this option is used, information about each line that is executed is captured. This slows the performance of the application and should only be used for debugging purposes.
- Executable Format—This option allows you to create either a 16-bit machine code version of your application and dynamic libraries or a native (32-bit) version.
- Optimization—You can tune the generation of your final machine code by having the compiler undertake optimization for size and speed. You can turn off optimization if you wish using the third option.

NOTE

When Powersoft bought Watcom, it also acquired one of the most highly regarded compilers on the market. This is the workhorse used by this compilation process, to provide you with the most optimized code possible.

If you are going to be creating machine code executables of any sizable application you should be aware that it can take a while and will run best on a high-powered machine. The C compiler optimizer has been stated by Powersoft to be "very aggressive about using memory," but you can reduce your compile times by significantly increasing the available physical memory available on the machine doing the compilation. P-code executables are much faster to create because they are simple copy routines that takes the compiled versions of the objects from the PBL files and places them into the EXE or PBD files. Powersoft recognizes that PowerBuilder developers are going to demand faster compilation and they are working to provide this in future releases. Such a speedup maybe affected by generating a C code version along with the p-code version that is stored each time you save an object into a PBL.

NOTE

The compilation of the machine code creates and deletes files in the directory specified in your `TEMP` environment variable. You can alter this directory by adding the following entry into the `[PB]` section of the PB.INI:

```
CodeGenTemp=c:\pb5i32\cgentemp
```

In the Project painter you can build an executable file that incorporates all the libraries, or you can make an executable stub by selecting all the libraries (except the library containing the application object) to be dynamic libraries.

WARNING

If you are going to use dynamic libraries, you should place the application object in a library by itself. This is because of the inheritance chains in your application. If ancestor and descendant objects are spread across the executable file and a dynamic library, you will get unexpected compiler errors or even GPFs. Therefore, the ideal situation is to create a small executable file from the library containing just the application object and create dynamic libraries out of the remainder (see the "Library Partitioning" section later in this chapter for more information).

You specify which libraries will be made into PBD/DLL files and any associated resource files. When you are ready to build, you can select Build Project from the Design menu or click the green Build button in the painter (see Figure 18.8).

FIGURE 18.8.

Ready to build with the Build button.

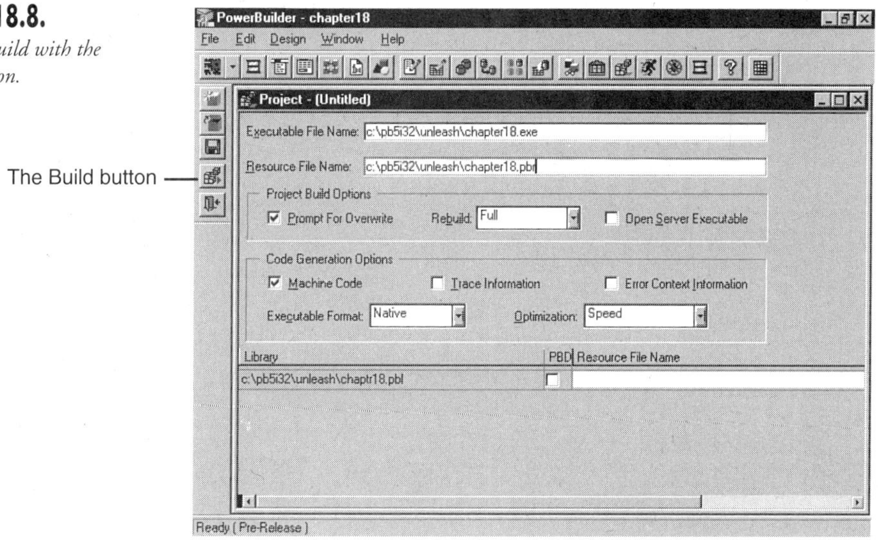

The Project painter regenerates the objects you requested and then builds the executable file and any dynamic libraries. If any problems occur during the compilation or regeneration process, you are shown an error window (see Figure 18.9). This window shows the error, the line number, the event, and the object where the error occurred.

FIGURE 18.9.

Compiler errors.

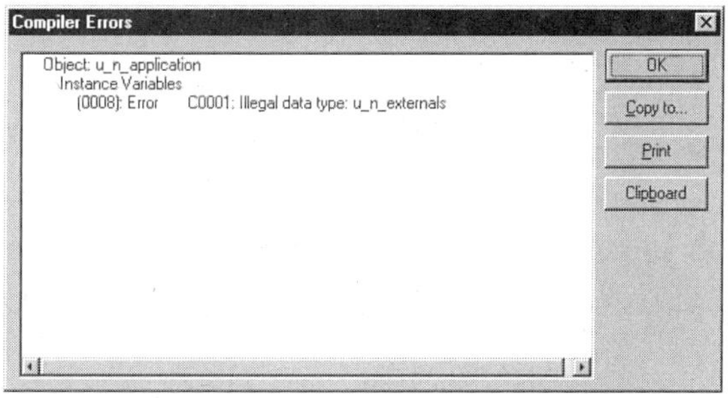

When you have made a successful compilation, or if you are just giving up for the moment, you are prompted to save the project when you leave the painter. The project object is then stored into the appropriate library.

Other Components

Now that you have compiled your PowerBuilder code into executable files and dynamic libraries, you need to distribute it. Because the code uses much of the functionality available in the development environment, you also need to distribute the runtime version of PowerBuilder with the EXE and PBD files. This is the PowerBuilder Deployment Kit (PBDK); it is provided with all product versions of PowerBuilder. If your application accesses a database, and most of them do, you need to distribute the necessary files from the database deployment kit as well.

Library Partitioning

You can use one of two philosophies when partitioning your objects into libraries: by object or by function. The collection of objects into libraries by object type might provide an easy means to navigate and find objects during development. However, when building an application, unless you are going for one big executable file, this provides a very inefficient split of objects. When the application is run using PBDs, you will probably force most of the PBDs into memory. Although this does not take up a great deal of actual memory (remember, only the objects are loaded), Windows resources are still consumed. The biggest hit to performance is that PowerBuilder now has to search through a number of PBDs to find the required object. When you partition by function, the majority of the objects to be used in any one business function are located together. More common objects should be placed at a higher level in the library search path.

Performance of EXEs Versus Dynamic Library Files

Placing every object into one big executable file gives you a small performance gain during execution, provided that the whole application can sit in memory at once and is not swapped out because of other Windows applications. There is a big initial speed penalty while the executable file is loaded into memory. During execution, the location of objects occurs entirely in memory (again not considering Windows swapping issues), unlike with dynamic libraries. With dynamic libraries, when PowerBuilder has determined where the object is located, it will more than likely have to load this from disk. As mentioned earlier, it is rarely practical to make a single EXE file, unless the application is quite small or the end users have high-performance machines.

As previously mentioned, several other issues need to be considered . The main one is that any modifications to the system require you to redistribute your entire executable file, whereas an application that uses dynamic libraries gives you the capability to replace just the necessary files. The main benefit of using dynamic libraries is that they enable the modularization of the application and all the benefits that entails, such as added security, cacheable small files, and responsibility assignment. Placing all the most frequently accessed objects (ancestors, functions, and so on) at the top of the library list can offset some of the speed loss of using dynamic libraries.

TIP

See Chapter 13, "The Library Painter," for a useful trick concerning the runtime alteration of the library search path.

The Powersoft recommended size for an executable file is between 1.2MB and 1.5MB, after which you should consider breaking it down to use dynamic libraries. You might want to set the upper limit to 1.44MB so that you can get it onto a disk without having to compress it.

Performance of Machine Versus Native Code

The questions on everyone's lips are What is the performance gain in speed for my application? Does my application now run lightning fast? The answers are a little faster to quite a bit faster. The speed difference you will see depends entirely on what operations your application carries out.

If your application is computationally intensive, you will see marked improvements in the execution of this type of code. For example, the following code took four times longer running as native PowerBuilder than 32-bit machine code compiled for speed:

```
Decimal {3} decValue1, decValue2, decValue3

For nCount = 1 To 1000
    decValue1 = decValue1 * 2
    decValue2 = decValue2 * decValue2
    decValue3 = Sqrt( decValue1)
Next
```

To get the best performance out of your application, you should still rely on the developers' experience to write the best code they can. You should attempt to optimize your own code as much as possible and use the best syntax or function for the job. Throughout this book are many hints and tips that point out which syntax or method of coding will provide you with the best results.

To examine the differences in build time and final binary size, an application was constructed using the PowerBuilder Application Template that PowerBuilder offers to construct for you when you create a new application. No additional code was added. The timings and sizes shown in Table 18.1 give an indication of the differences you might expect on larger applications.

Table 18.1. Comparison of build types.

Build Type	*Time to Build*	*Size*
PowerBuilder native (p-code)	6s	91KB
Machine code (No optimization)	42s	185KB
Machine code (Speed)	47s	155KB
Machine code (Space)	48s	148KB
Machine code (No optimization, full debug)	52s	231KB
Machine code (Speed, full debug)	59s	196KB
Machine code (Space, full debug)	57s	190KB
Machine code (No optimization, 16-bit)	51s	216KB

The times in Table 18.1 were taken using a Pentium 120 with 16MB RAM, running Windows 95. The amount of time to compile will vary from machine to machine. The final size of the application will also vary greatly and you may wish to consider different compilation options for each application you distribute. This is a very good reason for maintaining project objects for each application.

Accessing Executable File Command-Line Parameters

A useful feature available with most Windows programs is the capability to specify a parameter when you run the executable file and have it carry out some operation automatically, such as opening a particular file. PowerBuilder provides you with the `CommandParm()` function for this purpose. An example of a command-line parameter is `NOTEPAD C:\TODO.LST`, where `C:\TODO.LST` is the filename to open when the `NOTEPAD.EXE` file executes.

> **NOTE**
>
> If you are extracting the command-line parameters from the `Open` event of the application, you can instead use the `CommandLine` event parameter.

The `CommandParm()` function extracts the parameter string that occurs after the program name when the executable file is executed. The function always returns an empty string when you're using PowerBuilder on the Macintosh platform and is therefore only useful on the PC platform. The syntax is quite simply

```
CommandParm()
```

An empty string is also returned if the call fails for some reason or there was no parameter. In the previous example the function would return the string `C:\TODO.LST`. The function returns a single string even if there were multiple parameters, and you need to parse out the separate parts. The most common method of specifying multiple parameters (across multiple platforms) is to separate them with a space. This enables you to build a loop that breaks down the returned string using the `Pos()` function to search for a space:

```
String szCommandParm, szArguments[]
Integer nPos, nArguments = 1,

// Get a white space trimmed command line parameters
szCommand = Trim( CommandParm())

Do While Len( szCommand) > 0
   nNextPos = Pos( szCommand, " -", nPos + 1)
   // Unable to find a token, set position to end of string
   If nNextPos = 0 Then nNextPos = Len( szCommand) + 1

   i_nArgc ++

   // Extract the component parts of the argument
   szArgument = Trim( Left( szCommand, nNextPos—1))
   i_aszSwitches[ i_nArgc] = Left( szArgument, 2)
   i_aszParameters[ i_nArgc] = Mid( szArgument, 3)

   szCommand = Replace( szCommand, 1, nNextPos—1, "")
   nPos = Pos( szCommand, " -")
Loop
```

Deployment of the Application

Just as there are numerous ways to partition and build the runtime files for your application, so are there many methods of deploying those same files and their supporting files.

Probably one of the biggest decisions is which parts of the system should reside locally on a user's machine or be globally accessible from a network file server. The decision on how this partitioning occurs (either local or network, or sometimes even both) is highly dependent on the size and intended audience of the application; the hardware available for the client, network, and servers; the total number of users; and the number of concurrent users. Another big influence is how frequently you anticipate having to distribute not only application enhancements and fixes but also PowerBuilder DLL fixes, or even version migrations.

Methods for the distribution of maintenance and upgrade files are discussed in Chapter 20, "Application Maintenance and Upgrades."

For the best performance, you should place both the executable and the deployment kit files locally for every user. Obviously, this is feasible only if you have a small, easily accessible user group or have some method of distributing files. There might even be a corporate security policy that prevents you from doing this.

Application Execution Management

When an executable file is first run, PowerBuilder starts the Object Manager, which finds and loads the application object, stores the class definition, makes an instance (and global pointer), and then triggers that object's `Open` event. The Object Manager is used to locate and load all objects but more importantly to track what objects are already loaded and what objects have been instantiated.

When you make a request of the Object Manager, either by using an `Open()` function or by declaring a variable of an object type, it retrieves the class definition for the object from the EXE or dynamic library file and then creates an instance of that object in memory. Only one copy of the class definition is made in the class definition pool held in memory. Therefore, when you open or create a variable of a definition already in memory, the Object Manager uses that rather than accessing the EXE or dynamic library file again.

When you instantiate a class definition and create an actual instance of that definition, the Object Manager makes a copy of the class definition attributes that are dependent on that instance (instance variables). It keeps object functions and shared variables with the class definition. The class definition is not released until the application is terminated.

DataWindows are handled separately from all other objects. Because they have associated events or other PowerScripts, they are serviced by a DataWindow engine. This engine loads a template of the DataWindow into memory when a DataWindow is instantiated. If another instance of the same DataWindow is issued, a new template and instance are created. There are no class definitions, and the engine does not use a pool for the templates; storage is allocated on an as-needed basis.

Distribution

As we mentioned earlier, several other files have to be deployed along with your EXE and dynamic library files.

Installing the PowerBuilder Runtime Kit

PowerBuilder comes with a set of disks that contain the runtime DLLs (the PowerBuilder Deployment Kit). These often do not include any of the maintenance fixes you are running in your development environment. You must ensure that you also deploy any maintenance releases. Otherwise, your users might run into bugs that you didn't find during testing that Powersoft has fixed in a maintenance release. Occasionally your executable file can act unpredictably and causes a GPF if you provide different DLLs than the ones used during compilation.

The list of the runtime DLLs appears in the section titled "The PowerBuilder Runtime Files."

Installing the Database Interface

If your application uses a database, and most of them do, you also must set up the appropriate database interface files. This includes not only the PowerBuilder native or ODBC drivers, but also the drivers supplied by the individual DBMS vendors.

The native files required are listed in the section titled "PowerBuilder Database Interface Files."

Configuring ODBC Data Sources

If you use an ODBC data source, you must also install and configure the appropriate ODBC drivers and set up the data source.

The base ODBC files are listed in the section titled "Microsoft ODBC Driver Files."

Special Network Drivers

If the DBMS is located on a server that is running a different network protocol than the end user's machine, you have to install the appropriate network transport protocols. An example of this would be if a department used a Novell NetWare file server running IPX/SPX, and the division located the DBMS on a UNIX box that used TCP/IP.

Modifying the Operating System

Depending on the application, you might also need to distribute specific DLLs, such as for mapping or enhanced graphing capabilities. Depending on what other applications are running on the end user's machine, you might also make other adjustments to the system, such as adjusting disk caches, swap files, or video drivers. Most importantly, ensure that the machine's search path is properly configured.

Installing the Application

Remember to include all the necessary files for your application: EXE files, PBD/DLLs, initialization (INI) files, help (HLP) files, icons (ICO), graphics (BMP, RLE, WMF), cursors (CUR), and sound (WAV) files. You will not have to distribute any of the resources you stated in a PBR file when creating the executable file or dynamic libraries.

If you made use of a local database solution for your application, remember to distribute copies of the databases.

As a final step, make an entry into the Start menu, the Program Manager group, or another desktop area that enables these files to start up your application.

The Actual PowerBuilder Deployment Files

As you might have gathered from the previous section, a number of files must be deployed. These have been broken down into component parts and are listed in the following sections.

The PowerBuilder Runtime Files

The PowerBuilder runtime DLLs should be placed either in the same directory as the application or in a directory that is mentioned in the search path. These are the files:

PowerBuilder 4.0	*PowerBuilder 5.0*
PBBGR040.DLL	PBBGR050.DLL
PBCMP040.DLL	
PBDBI040.DLL	
PBDEC040.DLL	
	PBDPB050.DLL
	PBDSE050.DLL
PBDWE040.DLL	PBDWE050.DLL
PBDWO040.DLL	
PBECT040.DLL	
PBIDBF40.DLL	PBIDBF50.DLL
PBITXT40.DLL	PBITXT50.DLL
PBLMI040.DLL	
	PBNPC050.DLL
	PBNPS050.DLL
	PBOSC050.DLL
	PBOSS050.DLL (32 bit only)
PBOUI040.DLL	PBOUI050.DLL
PBPRT040.DLL	
	PBROI050.DLL
	PBRTC050.DLL
PBRTE040.DLL	PBRTE050.DLL
PBRTF040.DLL	PBRTF050.DLL
PBSHR040.DLL	PBSHR050.DLL
	PBSMI050.DLL
PBTRA040.DLL	
PBTYP040.DLL	PBTYP050.DLL (16-bit only)
	PBWSC050.DLL
	PBWSS050.DLL (32-bit only)

For 16-bit Windows-based applications, the PBVBX050.DLL (PBVBX040.DLL for Version 4.0) file might also be required. This file is not used with the Win32 version of PowerBuilder.

PowerBuilder Database Interface Files

The files for the Powersoft database interfaces that your application uses belong in the application directory or a directory that appears on the system path.

The following interface files are the ones required under Windows:

DBMS	*4.0 Files*	*5.0 Files*
Gupta SQLBase	PBGUP040.DLL	N/A
HP ALLBASE/SQL	PBHPA040.DLL	N/A
IBM DRDA	PBIBM040.DLL	PBMIBM050.DLL (16-bit only)
INFORMIX 4.*x*	PBIN4040.DLL	N/A
INFORMIX 5.*x*	PBIN5040.DLL	PBIN5050.DLL
MDI Database Gateway (DB2) Interface	PBMDI040.DLL and PBDBL040.DLL	PBMDI050.DLL PBDBL050.DLL
Oracle Version 6	PBOR6040.DLL	PBOR6050.DLL (16-bit only)
Oracle Version 7	PBOR7040.DLL	PBO7050.DLL (7.0) PBOR71050.DLL (7.1) PBOR72050.DLL (7.2)
Powersoft ODBC Interface	PBODB040.DLL and PBODB040.INI	PBODB050.DLL and PBODB050.INI
SQL Server 4.*x*	PBSYB040.DLL and PBDBL040.DLL	PBSYB050.DLL and PBDBL050.DLL and PBSYT050.DLL (32-bit only)
SQL Server 6.*x*	4.*x* files	PBMSS050.DLL
Sybase SQL Server System 10	PBSYC040.DLL	PBDBL050.DLL (32-bit only) and PBDBT050.DLL (32-bit only) with PBSYT050.DLL (`db-lib`) or (`ct-lib`)
Sybase Net-Gateway	PBNET040.DLL and either PBDBL040.DLL (DB2) or PBXDB040.DLL (XDB)	PBNET050.DLL (16-bit only) PBDBL050.DLL (16-bit only)

Microsoft ODBC Driver Files

If your application makes use of ODBC, you need PowerBuilder's database driver and INI file for ODBC (PBODB040.DLL and PBODB040.INI—these are usually in the Windows System directory, but you might want to keep them in the deployment directory to make upgrades easier. The only constraint is that these files must be in the client machine's path). You also need two ODBC INI files (ODBCINST.INI and ODBC.INI), which are found in the Windows directory and if they already exist must be updated during deployment.

For Windows, the following files need to be in the Windows System directory:

CPN16UT.DLL
ODBC32.DLL
CTL3DV2.DLL
ODBCCP32.DLL
ODBC.DLL
ODBCCURS.DLL
ODBC16UT.DLL
ODBCINST.DLL

For Win32, the following files need to be in the Windows System directory:

CTL3D32.DLL
ODBC32.DLL
DS16GT.DLL
ODBC32GT.DLL
DS32GT.DLL
ODBCAD32.EXE
MSVCRT10.DLL
ODBCCP32.DLL
MSVCRT20.DLL
ODBCCR32.DLL
ODBC16GT.DLL

In Windows 95 the ODBC INI settings are stored in the registry as well.

OLE System Files

The OLE system files are usually already installed on a Windows machine. If for some reason they do not exist, you need to copy the following files to the Windows System directory, \WINDOWS\SYSTEM:

COMPOBJ.DLL
OLE2NLS.DLL
CTL3DV2.DLL
OLE2PROX.DLL

OLE2.DLL
STORAGE.DLL
OLE2CONV.DLL
TYPELIB.DLL
OLE2DISP.DLL
STDOLE.TLB

To provide users with access to their OLE 1.0 applications, you need to merge the OLE2.REG file provided by Powersoft into the Windows system registry using Microsoft's REGEDIT program. Note that Windows NT and Windows 95 have OLE built into the operating system, so this step is unnecessary.

Powersoft's Installation Builder

Powersoft provided an application deployment utility that used to ship with the Enterprise Edition of PowerBuilder called PBSETUP. Powersoft has decided, due to its popularity, to make PBSETUP into a commercial application that they will sell separately; it will be called InstallBuilder.

This utility enables you to break your application into manageable components, such as program files, database files, and other system-related files, and then place them on disks in a compressed format.

When InstallBuilder is launched, it opens to the main window (see Figure 18.10). This window can be broken into two areas: components and install options.

FIGURE 18.10.
InstallBuilder's main window.

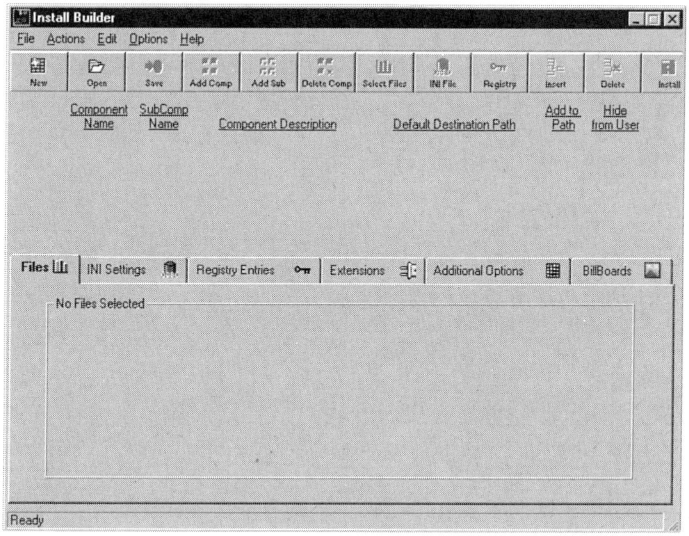

Configuration Files

Before you start, you need to create a *configuration file*, which is a textual representation of what is to be included in the deployment of the application. This is achieved by selecting New from the File menu, which opens the New File Name dialog box, where you can specify the location and name of the configuration file.

This file is altered as you make selections within the application. It contains information on the following: headings for the setup program, installation components, files for each component, paths for each component, system modification options, and INI file modifications.

Setup Program Defaults

Once you have saved the configuration file, you are prompted to enter installation caption information (see Figure 18.11).

FIGURE 18.11.

The Installation Captions dialog box.

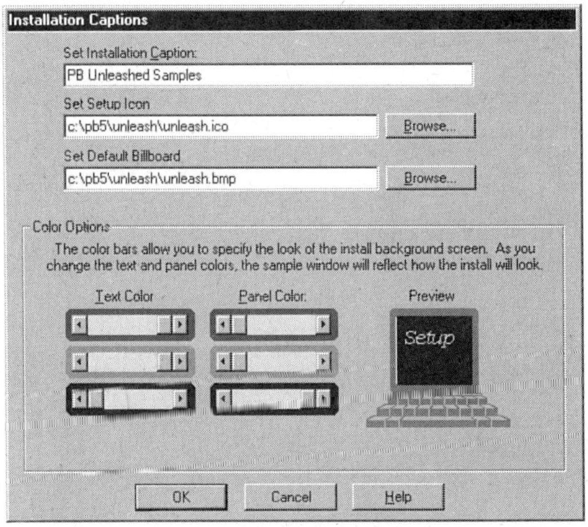

The icon you specify is the one that will be used for the actual installation executable file you will give the end user. The default billboard and installation caption are what appear when the setup program is run by the user. You can also customize the colors used by the setup program.

You are then prompted for the destination platform that the setup program will be compiled for (see Figure 18.12).

This tells InstallBuilder which setup executable file to include on your installation disks.

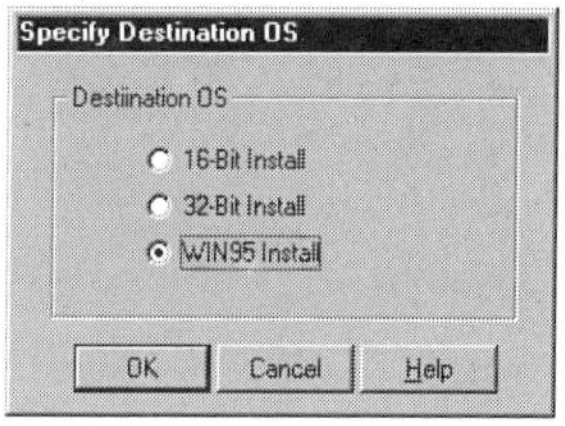

FIGURE 18.12.
The Specify Destination OS dialog box.

NOTE

Notice that there are separate options for Windows 95 and other 32-bit operating systems (NT). This is because Windows 95 handles paths in a slightly different manner. When you check AddToPath for a Windows 95 build, registry entries for AppPath are made to describe the application's search path rather than to add to the system search path. This is the way that PowerBuilder itself is now handling path issues. Also, internally the setup program has a few "quirks" that interact with Windows 95 differently than NT.

Defining Components and Component Files

The top part of the main window is used for defining all the components of the application, such as the application files, PowerBuilder deployment files, database files, and other miscellaneous files.

You must enter a description of the component, such as Order Entry Application, and the directory where the component's files will be installed. The directory field is a drop-down list box that lists Base, Component, System, and Windows. The directory you specify is considered the base directory for all the components with the Default Destination Path set to Base.

The first component you define is the base part of the application—that is, the application itself.

The actual files that make up the component are specified by clicking the Select Files button to open the Select Files for base Component dialog box (see Figure 18.13).

You have the freedom to select different files, file types, directories, and even drives to collate the required pieces for the current component. The files can be selected by double-clicking their filenames or by dragging them down to the Selected Files area. You can remove selected files by dragging them out of the bottom area or by highlighting the entry and clicking the Remove button. After you have all the files selected, click the OK button to return to the main window.

The following sections allow you to specify options for each component that you add to the install.

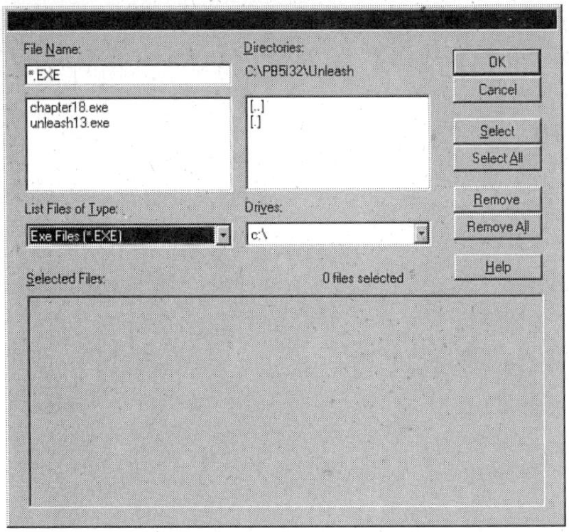

FIGURE 18.13.
The Select Files for Component dialog box.

INI File Settings

To set up an application's INI file as well as possibly the ODBC.INI or WIN.INI files, you need to specify any additional settings or entries that must be made. This is through the INI Settings tab page (see Figure 18.14).

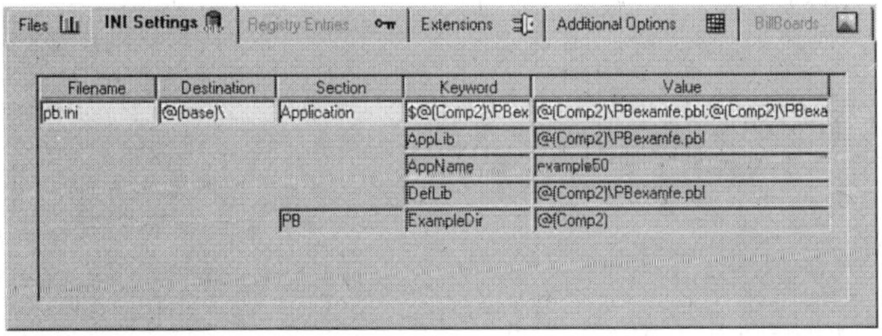

FIGURE 18.14.
The INI Settings tab page.

You can add and delete lines from this tab area using the corresponding toolbar buttons or Edit menu options. The new lines you add in the tab are where you set the filename of the INI file, the destination directory, INI section, keyword, and value. The value you declare can be of any data type and can even include files and pathnames.

NOTE

You can use a special syntax to allow more flexibility in the installation process. The string `@(base)` can be used as a placeholder for the base directory, which you initially set earlier, but which the user can change on the installation screen. The same syntax can be used to specify `@(windows)`, `@(system)`, and `@(component)`.

If you are using an ODBC data source in your application, you can use the Copy ODBC INI File button or select ODBC from INI file in the Edit menu to copy all the necessary settings into the configuration file. Clicking this button opens a list of all the current data sources listed in the ODBC.INI file as well as the corresponding entries. You can also specify that the database file is added to the base list of files by checking the Copy DB box. When you select OK the necessary entries are made into the INI tab page.

Registry Settings

To use the registry on those platforms that support it, you can specify any entries through the Registry Entries tab page (see Figure 18.15).

FIGURE 18.15.
The Registry Entries tab page.

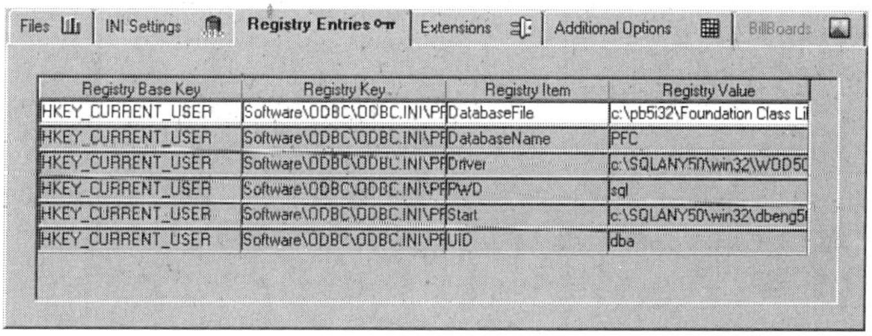

Files
INI Settings
Registry Entries
Extensions
Additional Options
BillBoards
Registry Base Key
Registry Key
Registry Item
Registry Value
HKEY_CURRENT_USER
Software\ODBC\ODBC.INI\PF
DatabaseFile
c:\pb5i32\Foundation Class Li
HKEY_CURRENT_USER
Software\ODBC\ODBC.INI\PF
DatabaseName
PFC
HKEY_CURRENT_USER
Software\ODBC\ODBC.INI\PF
Driver
HKEY_CURRENT_USER
Software\ODBC\ODBC.INI\PF
PWD
sql
HKEY_CURRENT_USER
Software\ODBC\ODBC.INI\PF
Start
c:\SQLANY50\win32\dbeng5
HKEY_CURRENT_USER
Software\ODBC\ODBC.INI\PF
UID
dba

You can add and delete lines from this tab page using the corresponding toolbar buttons or Edit menu options. The new lines you add in the tab page are where you set the base key, key, item, and value. The value you declare can be of any data type and can even include files and pathnames.

If you are using an ODBC data source in your application, you can use the Copy Registry button or select ODBC from Registry in the Edit menu to copy all the necessary settings into the configuration file. Clicking this button opens a list of all the current data sources listed in the ODBC section of the registry. You can also specify that the database file is added to the base list of files by checking the Copy DB box. When you select OK the necessary entries are made into the Registry Entries tab page.

Extensions

The Extensions tab page (see Figure 18.16) allows you to define the options used for each of the types of file extensions in your selected file list. You can control what occurs when a file is found to already exist in the destination directory. The available options are Make Backup, Overwrite, Prompt, Backup and Prompt, and Skip. You can also specify whether the installation procedure checks the file's date and time to determine which of the two files to use.

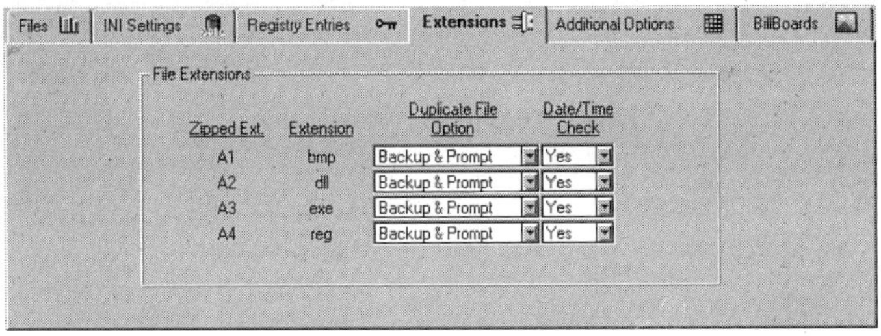

FIGURE 18.16.
The Extensions tab page.

Additional Options

The Additional Options tab page (see Figure 18.17) is used to control some of the settings displayed in the installation options dialogs.

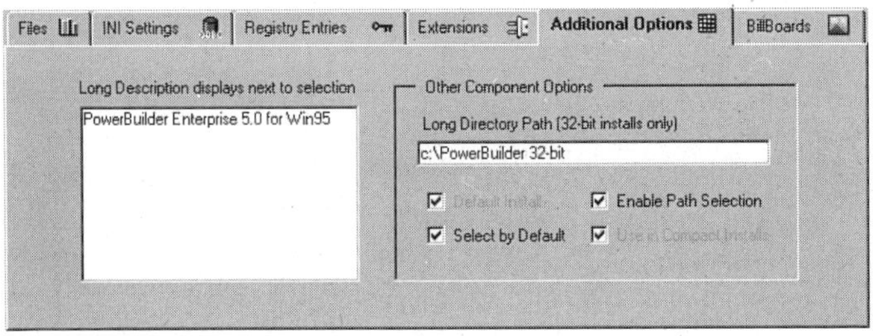

FIGURE 18.17.
The Additional Options tab page.

From this dialog you can specify additional comments, a long filename to be used instead of the Default Destination Directory fields, whether it is selected by default, and whether the component or subcomponent is included by default in typical and compact installs.

Billboards

As you probably noticed when you first installed PowerBuilder 5.0, Powersoft has added a very graphical interface while it installs the required files. You can achieve the same professional touch by constructing a list of bitmaps using the Billboards tab page (see Figure 18.18) that the installation program will display at regular timed intervals during the install.

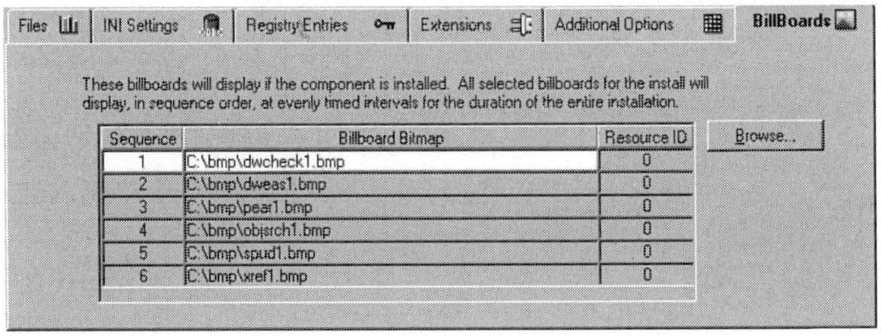

FIGURE 18.18.
The Billboards tab page.

The ID column in the Billboards tab page is used by PowerBuilder depending on the resource type. The resource can either be a bitmap file or a bitmap stored in a DLL.

Adding Components

When you have finished the previous steps, you can define additional components. These might include database files or runtime files and are added using the Add button in the component section of the main window.

Reusable Components

Rather than having to redefine a component each time you deploy a different application, you can set these up into reusable objects.

You do this by selecting Define Reusable Components from the Actions menu. This opens the Reusable Components window (see Figure 18.19), which looks very similar to the main window.

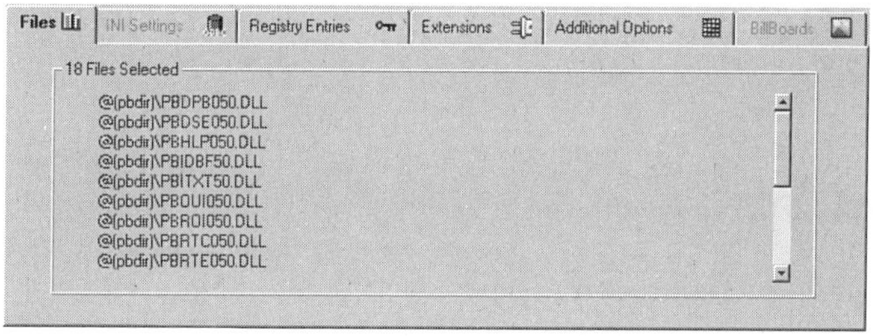

FIGURE 18.19.
The Reusable Components window.

The only difference is at the top of the window, where you specify the directory that is used to hold the compressed versions of the component files.

When you have finished defining the components, you must click the Save button, which saves the configuration information into the INSTBLDR.INI file. This must be done before the files can be compressed. After you have saved the files, the Compress button is enabled, and you can click this to create compressed versions of these component files.

NOTE

New to InstallBuilder is window-based compression. With it you do not have to worry about disturbing the minimized DOS window that used to appear.

Defining a Program Group and an Item

At the end of the installation you can direct the setup program to create a program group in Program Manager or the Start menu and add item entries to it. Select Define Program Group from the Actions menu to open the Define Program Group dialog box (see Figure 18.20).

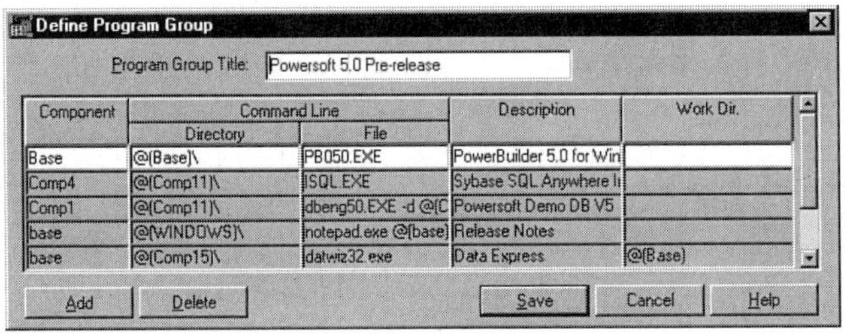

FIGURE 18.20.
The Define Program Group dialog box.

In this window you can set the program group's title and then use the Add button to create entries for each group item. For each item, you need to specify the component, installation directory, filename, item description, and working directory.

Component Shortcut—Project Object

You can use any project objects you have defined to provide the list of files for a component by selecting Read Project Object from the Actions menu. You are then taken to a selection dialog (see Figure 18.21) that enables you to choose the application and project object. When you have done this, InstallBuilder adds the files into the configuration.

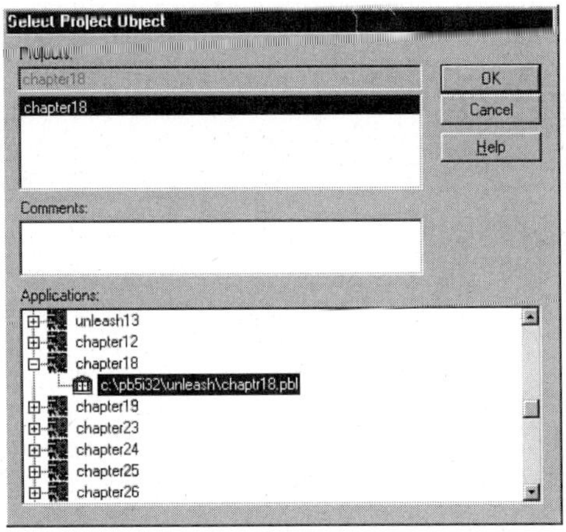

FIGURE 18.21.
The Select Project Object dialog box.

Creating Diskette Images

The option Create Diskette Images in the Actions menu is disabled until you have saved the configuration. When you select this option, the Create Diskette Images dialog box appears (see Figure 18.22), and you can select which components to include and the size of the installation disks being used.

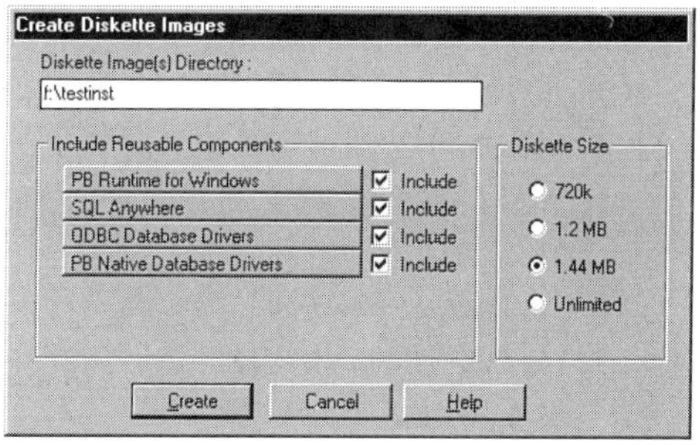

FIGURE 18.22.
The Create Diskette Images dialog box.

You must specify a drive and directory to hold the disk images. If the directory already exists, InstallBuilder warns you. When you click OK, InstallBuilder creates subdirectories DISK1, DISK2, and so on, and stores the relevant files in them.

NOTE

In PowerBuilder 5.0 you can create an unlimited size installation suitable for a network drive or CD installation, rather than the standard floppy disk configurations.

When you have the disk images, you can install them over the network, copy them onto disk yourself, or make use of the InstallBuilder program to make multiple copies at one time. You can do this by selecting Create Diskettes from the Actions menu, which opens the Create Diskettes dialog box (see Figure 18.23).

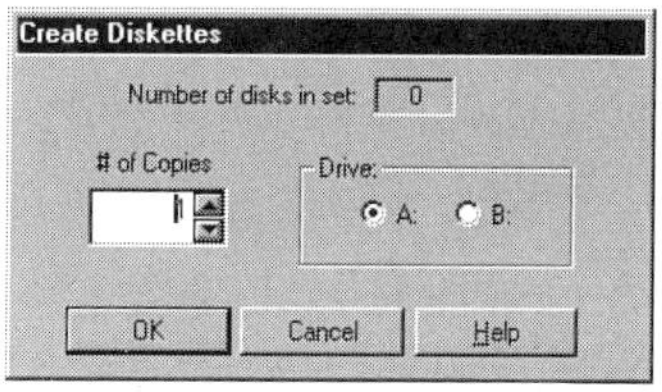

FIGURE 18.23.
The Create Diskettes dialog box.

NOTE

The size of the disks you copy to needs to match the size of the disk images.

Installing

You now have everything you need compressed onto a couple of installation disks that you can take to an end user's machine and install.

Guidelines for Application Installation

There are a number of guidelines you should try to follow when installing your application on another person's machine, most of which are commonsense. They allow you to maintain your applications more easily, and will result in fewer duplicate files (some of which may cause problems due to their versions). While the majority of these are directly related to Windows 95 and their interrelation with the registry, the naming and hierarchy structure can be adapted for other operating systems. These are the guidelines:

- You should avoid copying any files into system directories unless you are upgrading a common file that is used by applications outside of PowerBuilder (for example, the ODBC or native database drivers). This will help prevent operating system degradation by reducing the number of files within these areas. Any files that you place in a Windows 95 system directory should be registered in the SharedDLL subkey of HKEY_LOCAL_MACHINE.
- If the file is a common file that is only shared between your own applications you should create a subdirectory in the Common Files subdirectory of the Program Files directory. An alternative is to make an entry under Program Files itself for the shared files. Which ever method you use, the path should be registered with the Path subkey of the App Paths subkey of HKEY_LOCAL_MACHINE.
- You should always check that you are not replacing a newer version of the file with one of your own. This is true of your files as well as shared system ones.
- In Windows 95 and NT, you should place your application in its own directory under the Program Files directory. You can locate the appropriate directory by checking the ProgramFilesDir value in the CurrentVersion subkey of HKEY_LOCAL_MACHINE\Software\Microsoft\Windows.
- It is recommended for Windows 95 (and you may want to adopt this for other operating systems) that you partition supporting files (HLP, DLL, WAV, and so on) in a subdirectory of your application directory called System. You would then register its location in the registry in the App Paths subkey of HKEY_LOCAL_MACHINE\Software entry for your application.

- You should use the registry to store all the necessary information about your application, and you should not alter the autoexec.bat, config.sys, win.ini, or your own application INI file.
- Provide access to your application by making an entry in the appropriate launch engine of the operating system. For Windows 95 you should place a shortcut icon for the application in the Programs folder (found by checking the Shell Folders subkey of HKEY_CURRENT_USER\Software\Microsoft\Windows\CurrentVersion\Explorer.
- A number of commercial installation programs are available for your use. If you want to design your own, you should provide sufficient setup options for the user, as well as constant feedback on such things as percentage complete, disk space available, disk space used, and the ability to cancel the install. Remember that one of the logo compliance requirements for Windows 95 is the ability to uninstall an application; this maybe a useful feature to add, because it will allow you to back out changes you make to a users existing system.

These are just a few of the many points that deserve consideration during the deployment of your application.

Summary

In this chapter you have seen how to create the individual components of an application, the executable file and dynamic libraries, what occurs during runtime, and how you can use a project object to collect information on building the application together. The files that are required for the deployment of PowerBuilder and its database interfaces have been listed, and you have had a quick tour through the Install Diskette Builder application.

19

Distributed Processing and Application Partitioning

IN THIS CHAPTER

Distributed processing provides a means to decentralize the processing and location of business functions and the data that they act on in such a way that it appears transparent to the client. Applications will automatically make use of the best resources available from the network to complete their processing. The application can also make use of parallel processing to achieve greater performance by issuing multiple service requests to distributed servers.

The mostly commonly implemented computing architecture at present is client/server, and this is actually a form of distributed processing in which the client and server are cooperating in their processing.

This chapter explores what distributed processing provides for a computing environment and how PowerBuilder fits into this architecture.

TIP

If you would like to find out more about distributed computing, read *Client/Server Architecture* by Alex Berson from the McGraw-Hill series on computer communications.

Buzzword Definitions

The following are common buzzwords in the world of distributed computing and computer communications:

- *Advanced program-to-program communications* (APPC) provides peer-to-peer communication support and a generic API.
- The *distributed computing environment* (DCE) was developed by the Open Software Foundation (OSF) to provide a standards-based environment for heterogeneous platform portability and interoperability.
- *Distributed data management* (DDM) is an architecture that provides access to data stored on remote systems.
- The *distributed management environment* (DME) was developed by the OSF to provide a distributed management solution for DCE.
- The *distributed relational database architecture* (DRDA) was developed by IBM as a connection architecture that provides access to distributed relational databases.
- *Distributed transaction processing* (DTP) is transaction processing accomplished using LU6.2 protocols with synchronous communication. LU6.2 protocols include peer-to-peer communications, end-to-end error processing, and a generic API.
- A *distributed request* is a single SQL statement that requests data that is distributed over several DBMSs.

- A *distributed unit of work* (DUW) is a period of time from the start of a piece of work to the end, which spans several distributed DBMSs.
- *Remote data access* (RDA) is an ANSI standard (proposal) for accessing remote DBMSs.
- A *remote procedure call* (RPC) is a method of communication between a client (requester) and a server (remote service provider) that causes the execution of a procedure on the server.
- A *remote request* is a SQL statement that requests data from a single remote system.
- A *remote unit of work* (RUW) is similar to a DUW except that the data is requested from a single remote server.
- *Systems application architecture* (SAA) is a framework used for the design and development of consistent and portable applications in different environments.
- *Systems network architecture* (SNA) provides standards for the configuration and operation of networks that incorporates structures, formats, and protocols.

Open Systems

The preeminent goal of a computing architecture is to provide an open computing environment. This allows for the selection of the correct tools (hardware or software) for a given task, which can be made by end user groups or I.S. departments without having to be too concerned about the impact on existing systems and implementations.

Open systems allow the realization of distributed computing's potential by making possible the following:

- True application scalability
- Transparent data access and processing over networks
- Seamless resource sharing

They also offer the benefit of lower costs for both hardware and software vendors who will be able to develop from a firm base design rather than starting from scratch and building a proprietary product. This will also open the global marketplace for these and other products built on them because of the numerous countries that participate in an open system standard.

The true winners are of course the end users, who can pick the best hardware and software solution for their problem domain, budget, and overall requirements without being forced to buy expensive hardware and software that may not be fully utilized.

This vision is still just that—a vision. There are, however, two standards organizations that are working toward true open systems and are gaining interest from the various hardware and software vendors to their cause. The first organization is the Open Software Foundation, which has designed and encouraged the use of the distributed computing environment. The other organization is UNIX International (UI), which provides the open network computing (ONC) solution to open systems. Even though they are two different systems, they are fundamentally the same with only one major difference—the use and protocol of RPCs.

Due to the similarities between the architecture of the two standards, this chapter examines just one of them—DCE.

The Distributed Computing Environment

In 1990 the Open Software Foundation announced a suite of technologies that comprise the distributed computing environment. These technologies provided a foundation on which distributed applications could be built without regard to the underlying complexity of the computing network.

The distributed computing environment (see Figure 19.1) provides an integrated environment that is based on the Distributed File Services (DFS) component. Further components include a directory service, thread service, time service, and remote procedure calls.

FIGURE 19.1.
The architecture of DCE.

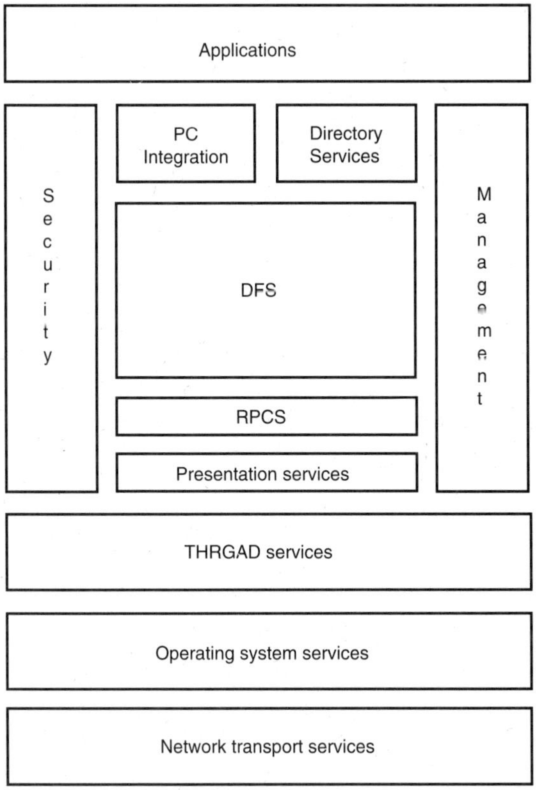

Figure 19.1 is simplified to show just the main components, which are explained in greater detail in the following sections.

The Distributed File System

A DFS allows a user to access and modify files or data from systems attached to a network. The system providing the file is the server and controls access to concurrent users by means of a token system. Clients can request the same file, which is cached at the client, for their own use. When one of the clients requires modification rights, the server grants a write token and informs other clients of the file that the status has changed and that their data is now out of date; the server possibly even revokes the users' existing tokens.

As you can see, this requires some extra features not usually inherent in a normal file system. File security access is provided in the form of user authentication (using security tickets) and an access list mechanism, and is assigned for both clients and servers. So that files/data have high availability and integrity, a replication service is used. This allows for the failure or maintenance of an area of the network without affecting the overall operation. Some slowdown will occur, but processing can continue uninterrupted. To track and manage all of the DFS's operations, DCE uses distributed databases that hold file locations and security information.

Directory Services

The directory service provides information on objects in the network that are accessed by a name and address, and is central to the DCE. The service provides information on an object so that the object can be moved or reconfigured without affecting how a client accesses it. The DCE directory service has been designed to interoperate with the X.500 worldwide directory service using global directory agents (naming gateways) that allow clients to look up names on the worldwide service. Access to this service is based on the X/Open Directory Services (XDS) API.

Remote Procedure Calls

The RPC mechanism is *the* means of access for all the DCE components and allows the execution of code on physically remote processors that are transparent to an application. The DCE RPCs are designed to allow transparent access to various network architectures and to support threads. Remote procedure calls are covered in greater detail later in this chapter in the section "What Are Remote Procedure Calls?"

Thread Services

Threads are used in parallel processing architectures to describe subprocesses of a single program that are making concurrent use of a processor. The thread service for the DCE is based on Digital Equipment's Concert Multithread Architecture (CMA), which is highly portable and is also POSIX 1003 compliant.

The other main components of the DCE architecture undertake services that you will find in most other computing architectures and provide the wraparound functionality to the core services. These components of the DCE model are placed between applications and the network layer at both the client and server. This molds very easily into the existing client/server paradigm, in which the service provider is considered a DCE server and the service requester the DCE client.

Distributed Systems

As you have just seen with the DCE, distributed systems consist of a number of components. These all interact to provide an environment for applications to be executed. Applications can be themselves broken down into components, which can then also be distributed across a network. These are the main components of an application:

- Presentation logic—This is the graphical user interface (GUI) component of the application that manages keyboard and mouse input, screen drawing, and window management. These are the services offered by Microsoft Windows, OS/2 Presentation Manager, and X Window, to name but a few. Presentation logic also includes the character-based world of CICS and other mainframe presentation facilities.
- Business logic—This is the embodiment of the business processes and functionality into a computerized form. The code is written using either third- or fourth-generation languages such as COBOL and PowerBuilder.
- Database logic—This encompasses two parts of the application: the code that is used to manipulate data within the application and the actual processing of the data by a DBMS.

Where these components reside dictates the type of computing environment. For example, the traditional host-based system runs all the components on the mainframe. The architecture of client/server, as has already been stated, is a form of distributed computing and provides a launching point for further distribution of services.

Distributed systems require additional planning and design to implement because you now need to decide where to divide the processing and then where to place each component object. This is also true to some degree with areas of client/server, in particular the business logic.

Client/Server Architecture

With client/server architecture, also now known as two-tier architecture, applications are split into two components: data and presentation (see Figure 19.2). These two areas can become indistinct when you consider the logic component that is split across them. The data component, the RDBMS, contains parts of the business logic in the form of defaults, rules, triggers, and stored procedures. The presentation also contains business logic in the form of functions and events, and additional presentation logic in windows and other visual objects.

FIGURE 19.2.
Two-tier architecture.

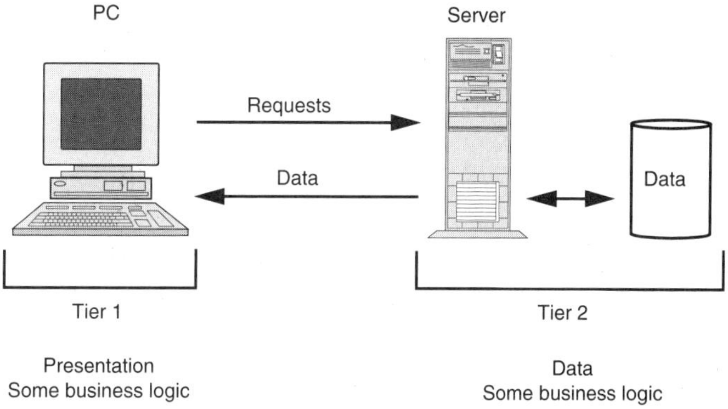

Obviously this blurring of the two components leads to the duplication of effort with some inherent problems such as Who is maintaining the server-based version and who the client-based? Which "object" should a developer use in a new application or when upgrading an existing one? What happens when a piece of the business logic changes—how many places now need to be updated with that information? This obviously results in an architecture that can be more difficult to maintain and in which to troubleshoot problems.

Advantages of Client/Server Computing

There are a number of inherent advantages to the client/server model over its predecessors and even over the current n-tier architectures that may eventually completely replace it:

- The utilization of desktop computing power and technology, which was previously centralized on mainframes.
- The implementation of GUI applications that make use of the PC hardware and software to provide easier navigation, multitasking, and enhanced visualization of data and reports.
- Client/server computing provides an introduction to the concepts behind open systems to both end users and I.S. departments. End users can be using a mix of PC hardware and software to access a variety of file and database servers that also exist on a variety of hardware types.
- Many people work in this area, and you can hire them to help with projects or bring them in for consulting help.
- Considerable knowledge within the computing industry now exists to provide the right help and proven tools as they are required.

Problems with Client/Server Computing

Of course, there are downsides to everything, and client/server architecture has the following:

- The architecture is only as good as it is designed. A client/server system can be configured similarly to a mainframe master/slave relationship, with a lot of the business logic embodied in the server. This can cause the server to become processor bound while it handles multiple client requests.
- You must invest resources into the acquisition of hardware and software for PC-based implementations—and you must incur the associated costs of training for end users, support staff, and development teams.
- You must invest in the construction or upgrade of a network that will support a wide bandwidth. Client/server applications generally send a lot of information back and forth over networks to accomplish their tasks, whether they're transaction processing or reporting.

N-Tier Architecture

The current cutting-edge architecture to be investing in is n-tier architecture (see Figure 19.3), which defines an application architecture that is separated into three logical components: presentation, logic, and data. It is called n-tier because there is no limit to the number of application servers you can use.

FIGURE 19.3.
N-tier architecture.

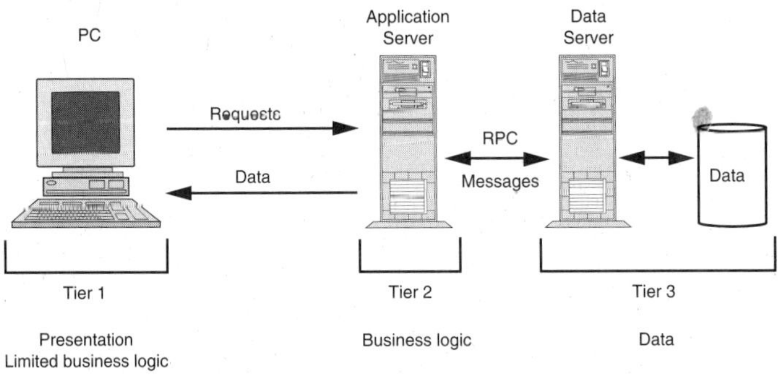

Advantages of Tier Architectures

Using a tiered approach to an application's architecture has many inherent benefits, which are discussed in the following sections.

Defined Division of Logic

The addition of a third tier to the architecture allows you to move all logic functions out of the other two components into a defined component. This allows the standardization of logic functions, with a defined set of standards and implementers. Modularization and encapsulation is the ultimate goal of any object-oriented system design, and logic division allows this to be attained with greater ease.

Resource Optimization

With the functionality of an application broken down into three areas, sometimes with different project teams addressing each component, the reduced view when carrying out implementation allows for the production of more optimized code. High-performance processors can be utilized for the processing of logic and different processors used for the retrieval of data. With these servers spread through an organization, access as well as installation and maintenance costs can be shared across departments.

As just mentioned, separate teams commonly attack the problems of each of the components. This allows the construction of teams that utilize the specific aptitudes of your developers with GUI design, data modeling, or business process acumen. Team members with good understanding of all the areas should be used to direct the component interfaces between the tiers.

Not only is there an optimization of team resources, but there is also a reduction in the hardware requirements for client machines. Client/server applications are no longer overly large, requiring fast CPUs and large amounts of memory. You can now optimize the application and slim it down to a more acceptable size using distributed objects that are used as they are required. A smaller client application places less demand on the client-side operating system.

Minimal Change Impact

Having distinctly isolated tiers allows modifications to be made within one that do not affect the others. Each tier is effectively a black box to the others, providing a set of interface functionality that can be used without an understanding of how the task is accomplished. For example, if a distributed object is used by multiple client applications, you only have to update the object at one location: on the application server on which the object is located.

Heterogeneous Data Sources

The presentation tier makes requests to the logic tier, which then decides which data source to use to satisfy the request. By using a similar calling interface to that used by the presentation layer, the logic tier can make requests against any of the available data sources.

Increased and Improved Security

Access privileges can be assigned or built in at each of the three tiers to provide three levels of security. Security can now be centralized to specific business logic objects.

Problems with Tier Architectures

As with the client/server architecture, multiple-tier architectures have inherent problems, which are discussed in the following sections.

Increased Network Traffic

Now that you have distributed business and data processing logic around the network, clients need to make numerous calls to achieve the required processing. This does not necessarily mean that the network will be brought down, but there should be an awareness of the potential increase in traffic. Any problems can usually be solved by revisiting the network's design and examining the various bridges and routers that exist.

Immature Technology

Compared to the history of host-based and now client/server systems, n-tier architectures and the tools required to implement them are newcomers. The tools currently available have some incompatibilities and do not yet provide the true openness of the ideal distributed system.

Increased Price

Additional software and hardware costs will be incurred as part of a tiered architecture. This will include the distributed system software for servers and clients, and the necessary upgrades in hardware (disk, memory, processor, and so on) to support it. The cost of hiring or training personnel that have expertise in the distributed system arena also needs to be considered.

Implementation Complexity

Obviously, as you increase the number of components and the number of access paths, the implementation and management complexities also increase. OSF is currently working on a proposed distributed management environment to offset some of these issues.

Transaction Monitors

The two-tier approach lacks the features that are needed to provide large-scale, industrial-strength, business-critical applications. These type of applications can be characterized by the following:

- A large number of users
- Business-critical data and processing
- High availability (24 hours a day, 356 days a year)
- Heterogeneous computing environments (UNIX, IBM, Macintosh, and so on)
- Heterogeneous database environments (Oracle, Sybase, DB2, and so on)
- Use of LANs, MANs, and WANs

This class of application (often known as online transaction processing, or OLTP) is ideally suited to the n-tier architecture and is often implemented with a transaction monitor "middleware" component as the second tier. Transaction monitors provide control and management of transaction execution, synchronization, and integrity. They also provide the following benefits:

- High transaction throughput
- Load balancing
- Support for a large number of users
- Transaction management and routing

What Are Remote Procedure Calls?

Remote procedure calls are one method currently used to implement three-tier architecture and allow applications to access *services* from remote systems. The services offered by a remote system can provide access to different communication protocols such as MAPI and TAPI, perform a business function, or access data. An RPC can be compared with the call and execution of a database stored procedure. Both are called from the client, which then optionally waits for results, and both are executed on a remote system without further interaction by the client machine (see Figure 19.4).

By using RPCs developers do not have to concern themselves with the underlying network protocols, data translation, and host languages because these are hidden by the RPC tool used. Specific RPC tools may support different network protocols. The only requirement for their use is the ability to locate a server that the procedure exists on, and this is achieved by use of the directory services of a distributed system.

RPCs are especially suited to client/server applications, and developers usually have access to tools for use in the construction of RPC-enabled applications.

The DCE implementation of RPC is one of the more commonly accepted and used. To create a DCE-compliant application, you use an Interface Definition Language (IDL) file. The syntax for IDL looks like a form of C that has been enhanced with networking functionality. IDL files are passed through a compilation stage that turns them into *stubs* that are bound to both server and client. The stub is used as a simulation of the missing piece—for example, on a client it would be the server-based functionality—and is similar to function/procedure stubs used in structured programming within a team environment.

FIGURE 19.4.
Remote procedure calls.

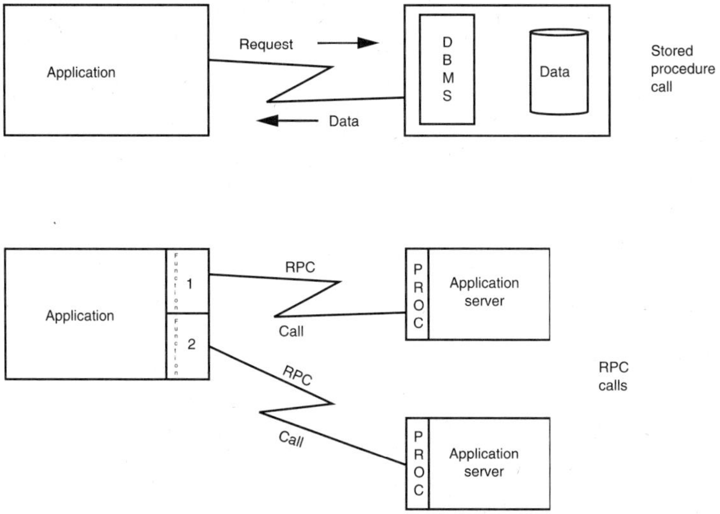

Application Partitioning

Application partitioning is, as its name suggests, the process of segmenting an application into components that can then be distributed across a network. The concept has been introduced in various ways in the preceding sections. However, in this section, we will examine some of the methods that can be used to decide where an application can, or should, be partitioned. The process of determining the application's architecture is separate from the design of the deployment architecture already discussed.

You have to tackle the problem of partitioning in the same manner that you would any other problem: with analysis, design, and implementation.

The first step is to look at the system to be implemented and begin collecting related data and functions. These different elements will form the basis of modules, which you continue to refine throughout the analysis and design stages. To help organize and identify the elements, you make use of domain analysis.

Domain analysis is used to collect elements into one of three domains—user interface (or presentation), problem (or business), and system (or management):

- User interface domain—This collects all the elements and specifications that detail what the interface looks like to the end user and other systems. This covers both graphical elements as well as the methods available to other systems to interact with it. Prototyping is the preferred method for capturing graphical elements.

- Problem domain—This contains the processes, concepts, and characteristics of the business functions that the application is being designed to implement.
- System domain—The elements in this domain define the system components that interact and manage the other two domains. This domain covers transaction management, error handling, security, and other similar management functions.

This is best illustrated in Figure 19.5, which also indicates that elements may lie along the boundary of multiple domains.

FIGURE 19.5.
The three domains of analysis.

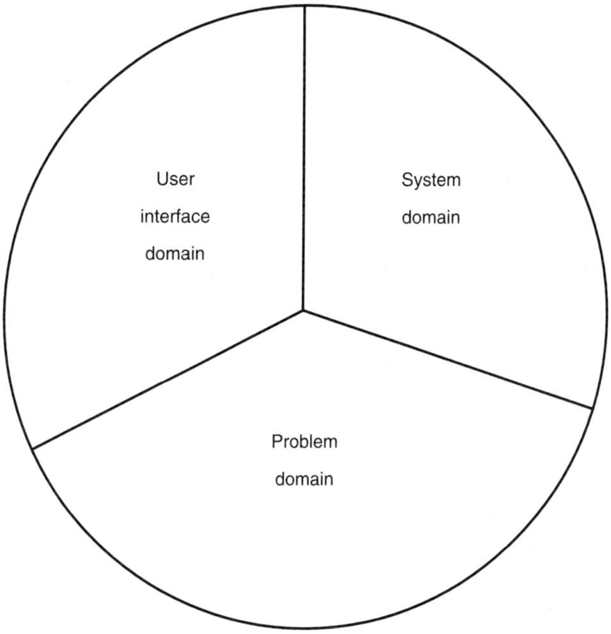

Once you have defined all the elements for each domain, you can start to construct modules from them. From these you will be able to determine the partitions of the application and their possible location within the distributed system.

Partitioned applications have more reusable classes that are truly encapsulated and can be easily used in cross-platform deployment.

Market Tools

A number of tools in the market provide access to remote procedure calls for PowerBuilder. The following sections give a brief overview and introduction to some of these.

Dazel from DAZEL Corporation

Dazel comes in two distinct packages: Dazel Express for the client side and Dazel Delivery for the server. The Dazel Delivery product is used to manage tasks in a distributed environment and is composed of several servers that can be accessed through an API, a command line, or Dazel Express.

Dazel is written to completely manage system output and deals in three types of objects:

- Documents—Files generated by Microsoft Word, WordPerfect, and so on
- Destinations—Printers, e-mail systems, and other output services
- Packages—A single structure containing at least one document and destination

The Dazel architecture allows the redirection of jobs, output format translation, notification of events, security management, load balancing, and tracking of jobs. Using the Dazel SDK product, you can integrate these features into PowerBuilder, Visual Basic, and C++ applications. The SDK product is available for both Windows and UNIX platforms and requires a network that supports TCP/IP (which it supports through the standard Windows Sockets, or WinSock, interface).

The Dazel Express product runs under Microsoft Windows or Motif. Dazel Delivery is provided by the output server, which runs on Sun SPARCs, IBM RS/6000, and HP9000 platforms. PostScript, PCL, and ASCII printers are supported, as are Group III Class 2 fax modems. Dazel supports e-mail systems that use the Simple Mail Transfer Protocol (SMTP) and either ONC or DCE architectures.

EncinaBuilder from Transarc

EncinaBuilder integrates Encina for Windows with the PowerBuilder Enterprise application development environment to streamline the development of Encina client applications. This tool provides a number of benefits for PowerBuilder developers. The main one is that PowerBuilder applications can now be truly scaled to the enterprise level using Encina's three-tier client/server architecture to support larger numbers of users and integrate a wide variety of data and resources.

Encina application servers make business functions available to client programmers through well-defined interfaces that are described in a Transactional Interface Definition Language (TIDL) file. This file is similar to the Interface Definition Language file used to define DCE remote procedure calls.

EncinaBuilder is used to select and convert Encina application server interfaces defined in the application server's TIDL file into PowerBuilder callable objects. These objects are placed in a PowerBuilder library and are then available for use within the development environment. Also included is a PowerBuilder library containing user objects that represent Encina transactional services (including `Begin`, `Commit`, and `Rollback`) and Encina Monitor functions (such as setting authorization and authentication defaults and application management functions such as initializing and terminating applications).

EncinaBuilder can also be used to create a fully functional PowerBuilder application that can be used to invoke the functions offered by the Encina application server. These generated applications are customized using standard PowerBuilder features to create graphical Encina client applications.

The Encina product family provides the full range of services for developing and deploying large-scale client/server and distributed online transaction processing systems. The most notable of these is the Encina Monitor, and includes the structured file system, the recoverable queuing service, and the peer-to-peer communications executive and gateway for mainframe connectivity.

The Encina Monitor provides the infrastructure for the development, execution, and management of large-scale client/server systems with such features as application server replication, load balancing, application monitoring, and restart.

Encina for Windows allows clients to participate in enterprisewide client/server and distributed online transaction processing systems by extending the power of the Encina Monitor to the desktop. Encina for Windows applications can be developed using visual development tools such as PowerBuilder or written to directly use the Encina Monitor API.

For more information you can contact Transarc by e-mail at `info@transarc.com` or by phone at 412-338-4400.

Encompass from OEC

Encompass is developed by Open Environment Corporation (OEC) and is otherwise known as the OEC Toolkit. It allows for the development of RPCs that communicate via TCP/IP or DCE protocols across heterogeneous platforms.

Encompass enables the creation of native language stubs that are then compiled with the source or imported into an interpreted environment (such as PowerBuilder executables). The process involves the creation of an IDL file that defines the information to be passed and the information expected back, together with the procedure's name and return type. This IDL file is then compiled using RPCMake into the native language code stubs for both the client and server.

The OEC Toolkit also provides a number of additional utilities that cover testing and monitoring of RPCs.

EZ-RPC from NobleNet, Inc.

NobleNet provides a number of middleware tools for client/server development, with their main product being EZ-RPC. This is an RPC compiler toolkit that features an enhanced XDR (packaged as an IDL), an IDL compiler, and various libraries. These tools allow the distribution of APIs to a variety of platforms without the need to use communication experts to provide network code.

EZ-RPC is used to generate the network communication code that clients and servers use to communicate with each other, and has three components:

- NobleNet's ANSI C–like IDL.
- An IDL compiler that generates C stub code and integrates the stub code with an application's source code.
- An RPC communication library that provides access to low-level communications functions and is linked into the client or server code.

EZ-RPCs have a number of notable features that make advanced communications programming easier:

- Extended data types
- Support for all six types of RPCs
- Rapid prototyping with "convenience routines"
- Advanced client-side memory-management tools
- Programmer participation features

EZ-RPC supports a broad range of data types: simple variables and arrays, binary, pointers, and strings.

The IDL supported also enhances the standard XDR data descriptors and does not require developers to rewrite complex structures to fit a network's limitations.

In addition to the basic asynchronous RPC, EZ-RPC supports all five advanced types of RPCs:

- No-wait RPCs—Allows the client to continue local processing without waiting for a response from the no-wait RPC. If a response is required, it is dispatched using a call-back RPC.
- Call-back RPCs—Reverses the client and server roles so that a server calls a function on the client.
- Broadcast RPCs—Sent to all nodes on the network instead of being directed to a specific server.
- Forking RPCs—Often used in UNIX environments to ensure that a unique server process is available to handle each client. Other operating systems usually use threads to achieve the same functionality.
- Batch RPCs—Used to optimize data transfers when several RPCs are being executed in sequence.

Key to the EZ-RPC Toolkit is the feeling of programmer participation. The EZ-RPC IDL compiler generates open, commented, readable C code. This allows developers to easily migrate existing applications and to tune EZ-RPC to handle specific data structures and semantics without caring about the underlying network details.

There are three ways a developer can customize or enhance EZ-RPC–generated code:

- Name redirection—Allows a programmer to place functions between an existing application and the generated functions.
- Programmer exits—These allow the access of routines outside of the client and server functions generated by EZ-RPC.
- Custom directives—These are used to insert a custom routine into the EZ-RPC–generated code.

The EZ-RPC product is available on more than 40 platforms, including most UNIX environments, most Windows environments (WinSock compliant), Mac, NetWare, OS/2, and VMS.

MitemView from Mitem Corporation

MitemView is a graphical toolset that is used for creating Mitem objects and managing host messages received by the client application. The terminal data stream API is used by MitemView to provide a distinctly different, and patented, communications framework that supports an unlimited number of multiple simultaneous sessions to heterogeneous systems. This allows the rapid construction of applications that run against UNIX, IBM 3270 and 5250, DEC, and Tandem computers. MitemView interfaces with client-based languages such as Powersoft's PowerBuilder and Microsoft's Visual Basic or Visual C++.

MitemView's architecture provides a generalized message monitor that is used to encapsulate and convert terminal- and transaction-based data streams into a standard transaction format. This format can then be used by client applications.

The MitemView technology is constructed to be loosely coupled and noninvasive to host and network environments. This is different from the normal relational client/server model and a number of other middleware implementations. The fact that MitemView is loosely coupled allows the introduction of new functionality into the client or the server without affecting existing functionality. It also allows for the migration of back-end systems or modules to different platforms and architectures without losing the time and resource investments already made in client applications.

Using asynchronous processes when communicating with remote systems, MitemView can communicate with multiple systems concurrently and respond to messages in the order in which they arrive. This decouples a client application from time-dependent message processing, which frees the developer from maintaining state information of remote systems. MitemView manages these parallel processes for client applications, which provides high levels of performance and simplified application development and maintenance.

MitemView supports the following:

- The MS/Windows 3.1 or 3.11 for Workgroups, NT, and Windows 95 (16-bit mode) operating systems
- Most networks, including TCP/IP WinSock, Novell SAA, TN3270, Serial, LAT, DECNet, and Twinax
- IBM, AS/400, DEC Vax, UNIX, HP, Unisys, Tandem, and Custom Transactions remote systems

You can find out more information from the Mitem Corporation web page at `www.mitem.com`.

RPC*painter* from Greenbrier & Russel, Inc.

RPC*painter* produced by Greenbrier & Russel, Inc., provides PowerBuilder support for the OEC Toolkit. This product tightly integrates PowerBuilder with RPCs by allowing the importation of RPC stubs into two objects:

- DataWindows using an RPC as the data source
- A nonvisual user object

RPC*painter* is accessed from PowerBuilder's PowerBar and is used to create both the DataWindow control and optionally the DataWindow object (see Figure 19.6). This is achieved by selecting an IDL file, which RPC*painter* reads and from which it generates the objects. Using the DataWindow Generation Profile, the developer can modify the finished DataWindow.

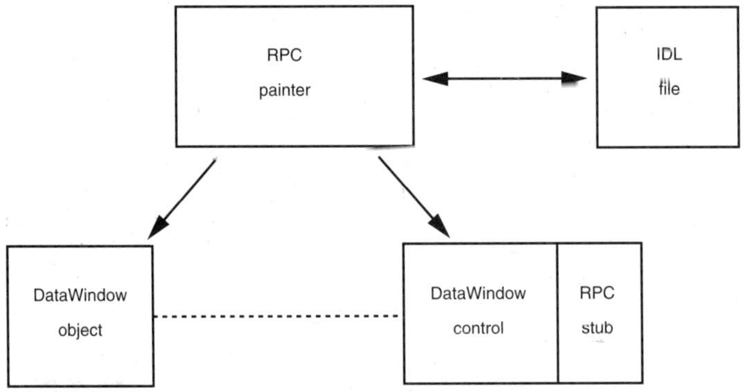

FIGURE 19.6.
Construction of an RPC-enabled DataWindow.

The DataWindow control is created with a function called RPCRetrieve, which is used in your PowerScript to invoke the RPC. This is used instead of the standard `Retrieve()` PowerScript function and can be used with function arguments in the same way. The DataWindow control is like any other DataWindow control, and all the standard PowerScript functions and PowerBuilder attributes are accessible to it.

The RPC-enabled nonvisual user objects are constructed in the same manner, allowing the developer to specify the appropriate IDL file and the required functions to be incorporated into the object.

Visual-DCE from Gradient Technologies

Gradient offers a number of OSF DCE-compatible ports and associated development and deployment tools, including Visual-DCE, PC-DCE, PC-DCE/32, and SysV-DCE.

Visual-DCE is a Microsoft Windows–based development environment that simplifies and accelerates the construction of DCE applications for the Microsoft Windows environment. Visual-DCE effectively eliminates the need to write C program code in typical applications, which allows development time and expenses to be reduced by hiding the details of Windows/DCE programming. Instead of allowing access to DCE functions through an API, it provides an object-based view.

Visual-DCE is primarily written for Visual Basic, but the custom controls used can also be used in PowerBuilder, Visual C++, and Borland C++. The additional controls simplify the creation of RPC interfaces, RPC bindings, and DCE login contexts. Visual-DCE has the following features:

- The RPC interface control simplifies the task of defining an RPC interface by displaying IDL interface attributes, allowing you to copy RPC argument and call definitions, and provides a list of all the operations (calls) for the interface.
- The RPC binding control allows you to define and modify RPC binding handle properties. These include its name, security attributes, communications timeout, CDS namespace entry name, and string binding attributes. This control eliminates the need for you to make explicit calls to the DCE RPC binding routines and to make allowances for threads or exceptions. The RPC bindings are linked with an RPC using the Visual-DCE RPC interface control.
- The DCE login context control is used to define DCE security-related properties for the client program, such as the principal name and password.

Visual-DCE uses a DLL to encapsulate the DCE layer so that your application is isolated from the RPC implementation. Gradient also provides a tool to create an RPC interface DLL from a standard IDL file. A comprehensive, well-indexed online help system is provided for complete reference information, step-by-step procedures, and advanced programming advice that can be used to guide you through the Visual-DCE application development process.

PC-DCE (DCE for Windows 3.1) is a peer client implementation of OSF's DCE. The implementation includes the core functions of RPC, distributed time service (DTS), threads, security, and the cell directory service (CDS).

PC-DCE/32 (DCE for Windows NT) is a peer client and server implementation of OSF's Distributed Computing Environment. The implementation includes the core functions RPC, DTS, threads, security, and the CDS. This includes both CDS and security servers.

SysV-DCE for UnixWare (DCE for Novell's UnixWare) is a full client/server implementation of DCE for Novell's UnixWare operating system.

For more information, you can contact Gradient by e-mail at `info@gradient.com` or by phone at 800-525-4343.

Distributed PowerBuilder

A new feature of PowerBuilder 5.0 is called *distributed PowerBuilder*, and gives you the ability to implement n-tier computing using a tool that you are already familiar with: PowerBuilder itself.

The key to distributed PowerBuilder is the class user object. The class user object allows you to implement functionality without a visual component. This object is then often reused throughout an application and across applications. Using distributed PowerBuilder, this object can be distributed onto an application server so that only one copy exists in a computing environment and which can be used by multiple users and applications. Once a developer has a basic knowledge of the construction and use of class user objects, it is a simple extension to make this into a distributable component: a remote object.

Distributed PowerBuilder can also be implemented in the local machine's environment. This allows developers to test their code on their local machine before the application is deployed, and the remote objects are placed on the application server.

Components of Distributed PowerBuilder

Distributed PowerBuilder makes use of four new class user object types, which follow this hierarchy:

```
NonVisualObject
   ConnectObject
      Connection
      Transport
   RemoteObject
Structure
   ConnectionInfo
```

Each of these new classes and the new structure are introduced in the following sections, and then all the concepts are drawn together into examples of both the client and server code required for distributed PowerBuilder.

`ConnectObject` is the base class for the `Connection` and `Transport` classes, which are used by the client and server applications respectively, and has the following properties:

- `ErrCode` (Long)—The error code value for the last error.
- `Handle` (ObjHandle)—Handle for the object.
- `Application` (String)—The name of the application.
- `Driver` (String)—The network driver to use when setting up to connect or listen.
- `ErrText` (String)—The error code description for the last error.
- `Location` (String)—An optional description of the location of the user.
- `Options` (String)—This is used to specify one or more comma-separated options that determine how data will be passed over the network. Note that this property is ignored when either the NamePipes or the Local driver is used.
- `ProxyName` (String)—This is the name you assigned when the custom class user object was saved in the User Object painter.
- `Trace` (String)—Allows the specification of trace options.

The `ConnectionInfo` structure is used by `GetServerInfo()` for the `ConnectObject` to retrieve information on the current connections into the server, and has the following structure:

- `Busy` (Boolean)—Whether the connection is currently busy making a request.
- `ConnectTime` (DateTime)—The date and time that the client connected.
- `LastCallTime` (DateTime)—The date and time that the client last made a request to the server.
- `CallCount` (Long)—The total number of calls made on the server by the client.
- `ClientId` (String)—The ID of the client on the server.
- `Location` (String)—The client location.
- `UserId` (String)—The user's ID.

If a client connects with a connect privilege of `ConnectWithAdmin!` (see the next section for details on setting this), the client can retrieve information on all clients connected to the server. The first instance of this structure is always the requesting client's connection information. Users with administrative privileges can also use the `RemoteStopConnection()` method to remotely disconnect clients. For example, you can use the following code to obtain all the current users and then single out the user "Andrea" for disconnection:

```
ConnectionInfo ciInfo[]
Integer nCount = 1, nTotalUsers

g_DPBConnection.GetServerInfo( ciInfo)

nTotalUsers = UpperBound( ciInfo)

Loop While nCount <= nTotalUsers
```

```
   If ciInfo[ nCount].UserId  = "Andrea" Then
      g_DPBConnection.RemoteStopConnection( ciInfo[ nCount].UserId)
      Break
   End If
   nCount ++
Do
```

In the following sections you will see the components of distributed PowerBuilder and how they all integrate together.

Server Applications

PowerBuilder applications can now participate in the computing environment as both clients and servers. The PowerBuilder *server application* is an application that contains a number of class user objects that are developed with the intention of allowing them to be invoked by one or more client applications. These types of class user objects are known as *remote objects*, and are covered in the section "Remote Objects." They may be called from any application in the distributed computing environment, on the same machine or across a network connection to another physically separate machine. The server piece is implemented using a transport object, which is covered in the section "Transport Objects."

One thing to remember when designing an application is that it can be made into a server and still be used as a normal PowerBuilder application, while serving requests for the class user objects that are defined for it. It can even be a client of another remote server.

The server application maintains separate variable spaces for each of the client threads that it is servicing, and it cannot be shared with other client threads. The variable space and object data are persistent in the client/thread context and obey the same scope rules as normal PowerBuilder. For example, a global variable will retain its value between successive remote calls. If you need to be able to share resources between client contexts, you will have to resort to one of the IPC mechanisms, such as DDE or OLE, database tables, or flat files.

NEW 5 in PowerBuilder

Two new events have been added to the application object for PowerBuilder 5.0 for use with applications acting as servers for distributed requests: `ConnectionBegin` and `ConnectionEnd`.

The `ConnectionBegin` event is triggered when a client makes a connection for services. Information on the client user is made available in this event so that you can carry out authentication if you so wish. The return value of this event determines the user's level of access as well as if he should be rejected. The return data type is of the enumerated value `ConnectPrivilege`, which can be either `ConnectPrivilege!`, `ConnectWithAdminPrivilege!`, or `NoConnectPrivilege!`.

The `ConnectionEnd` event is triggered when the client application requests that the connection be closed and can be used to carry out maintenance tasks for the server application.

Client Applications

A *client application* is a PowerBuilder application that requests services from a PowerBuilder server application by invoking remote objects. This is carried out through another of the new objects, the `Connection` object. You instantiate a client-side proxy of the object and then the object on the server. This will allow you to then use the object as if it were local to the application.

Remote Objects

A *remote object* is a special type of class user object that has been saved with a proxy name (proxies are covered in the section "Proxies"). Remote objects can only reference and accept as arguments nonvisual data types and PowerScript functions. They can also issue database commands and make use of the nonvisual DataWindow `DataStore`.

Transport Objects

The transport object is used by PowerBuilder server applications to receive incoming client requests for a particular communications connection type. This object, like the client's connection, is inherited from the `ConnectionObject` class. `Transport` only has one additional property to those that are inherited from its parent class: `TimeOut`. This property is used to control how long the server will wait before it considers a client connection to have been lost. If the value of the `TimeOut` property is greater than 0 before a `Listen()` call is executed, the application will start a timeout thread on the server. The timeout thread examines currently connected clients and will terminate their connections (and release server resources) if they have not made a call during the time period specified by `TimeOut`. This value is specified in milliseconds.

TIP

The `TimeOut` property will require tuning and careful consideration when your users are operating over WANs or other slow network connections.

There are also two additional functions declared for this object:

- `Listen()`—Once this method is executed by an application, it is able to accept client requests for the communication protocol for which the transport object was set up.
- `StopListening()`—This method prevents the application from accepting more client requests for the transport object.

Connection Objects

The connection object is used by PowerBuilder applications that wish to access remote objects on a server, and is set up using a particular communications connection type. This object is also inherited from the `ConnectionObject` class. `Connection` defines three additional properties to those inherited from its parent class:

- `ConnectString` (String)—This is additional information that can be passed to the server application at connection time. The value of this property could include application-specific information such as database connection parameters.
- `Password` (String)—The password used to connect to the server.
- `UserId` (String)—The name or ID of the user connecting to the server.

There are also a number of additional functions declared for this object:

- `ConnectToServer()`—This method is used to connect to a remote object server using the communications protocol specified for the `Connection` object.
- `DisconnectServer()`—This method is used to disconnect from a server when you have finished using the services and class user objects that were requested.
- `GetServerInfo( ciInfo[])`—This method is used to collect the current state of the server.
- `RemoteStopConnection( szClientId)`—This method is used by a supervisor login to kill the connection of another remote user.
- `RemoteStopListening()`—This method allows a client application to inform the server to stop listening for further client requests. You must be connected with administrative rights to issue this function call.

The `Connection` object usage varies by communication driver in the following ways:

- `NamedPipes`—Uses the `Application` and `Location` properties to specify the name of the pipe:

  `\\Location\PIPE\Application`

  or for a local pipe it is constructed this way:

  `\\.\PIPE\Application`

- WinSock—Uses the `Application`, `Location`, and `Options` properties to set up a TCP/IP connection:

  The `Application` property can be set using one of two formats. The first allows you to specify the service name as it appears in the service's file, and the second is used to specify the actual port number to connect to.

  The `Location` property can also be set using two formats. The first is the name of the server as it appears in the host's file, and the second is the actual IP address of the host.

  The `Options` property allows you to tune the TCP/IP protocol, and has the following settings available:

  `RawData`—Setting this option to `1` makes the WinSock driver pass raw data over the network. The value has to be set the same on both the client and

server, or they will be unable to communicate. By setting this to `1` you will get a slight performance increase, but the data will be in human readable form. The default is `0`, and the driver encrypts the data as it passes over the network.

`BufSize`—Sets the buffer sizes used by WinSock.

`NoDelay`—Causes each data packet to be sent without a delay. This setting can have severe performance implications, and should be used with care.

`MaxRetry`—The number of times the client will attempt to connect to a server if the listening port is busy before reporting a connection error.

These options should be set before calling either the `ConnectToServer()` or `Listen()` functions. Here's a sample option string:

```
"RawData=1, BufSize=4096, NoDelay=0, MaxRetry=10"
```

- Open Client/Server—Uses the `Application` and `Options` properties to set up the Sybase Open Client/Server protocol:

  The `Application` is set to the query service entry in the SQL.INI file.

  The `Options` property can be used for one setting, *`PacketSize`*. This will set the packet size option for the CTLIB.

The `Transport` object uses the same properties and option settings as the `Connection` object. The only exception is that both the `NamedPipes` and WinSock `Application` and `Location` settings specify where the application is to listen. The Open Client/Server protocol is different in the following ways:

- Open Client/Server—Uses the `Application` and `Options` properties to set up the Sybase Open Client/Server protocol:
- The `Application` is set to the server service entry in the SQL.INI file to use to listen for requests.
- The `Options` property allows you to tune the protocol with the following settings:

  `NetBufSize`—Sets the maximum size of the network I/O buffer used by client connections.

  `MaxServerThreads`—Sets the maximum number of threads that the Open Server has available to service requests.

Proxies

Proxy objects are created as stubs (see the section "What Are Remote Procedure Calls?") for the client application, and they define the available methods of the server-based remote object. These are created within the User Object painter by selecting Set Proxy Name in the context menu (see Figure 19.7).

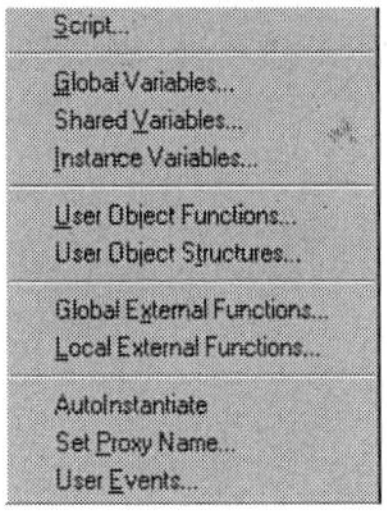

FIGURE 19.7.
The class user object context menu.

This will open the Save Proxy dialog box, where you name the proxy object and supply optional comments. Once the proxy name has been set, every time the user object is saved, a proxy object with the name you specified is also created in the same library.

> **NOTE**
>
> For more information on the `AutoInstantiation` property, see Chapter 23, "The User Object Painter."

You will use the proxy object in each client application as the class type for the remote object you connect to the server. The compiled proxy supports the *`ClientObject->Connection->ServerObject`* indirection when used with the `Connection` object. This is comparable to the IDL DCE definition and Microsoft's remote procedure calls.

Application Servers

As mentioned earlier, a PowerBuilder application that is used as a client in a typical client/server situation can also act as a server for distributed client requests. More often, you will create your application server, with either no visible component or more likely a simple interface that you can use to control the behavior of various settings of the application.

Development of such applications is undertaken using the skills developers have already acquired in PowerBuilder. Remote object construction and distribution to development teams is contained in the familiar PBL library file. The remote objects can be inherited from existing class user objects or created anew, stored in a PBL for compilation into a server application, and for distribution to development teams for use in their application construction.

The PowerScript required to set up an application to be a server for remote request is this:

```
// Declare at a global or instance level would be the following:
//    Transport g_DPBTransport

//Create the server transport object
g_DPBTransport = Create Transport

// Set the communications driver.
```

```
// This can be NamedPipes, Sockets, OpenClientServer, or Local.
g_DPBTransport.Driver = "NamedPipes"

// Set the application server name.
g_DPBTransport.Application = "Test1"

// Listen out for clients on the selected communication protocol.
g_DPBTransport.Listen()

If g_DPBTransport.ErrCode <> 0 Then
   Messagebox( "DPB Server Test1", "Failed to start!")
End If
```

As you can see from this example, the server application only makes use of the `Transport` object to become able to accept requests for its services. You would place this code in the `Open` event of the application or one of the application's windows.

NOTE

The only requirement for building a server application is that it is compiled as a 32-bit application.

Client Applications

Just as PowerBuilder applications can be easily turned into server applications, they can be made into clients that use remote objects in other applications. The actual PowerScript required is as straightforward and easy to set up as it was for the server, and will look like the following:

```
// Declared at a global or instance level would be the following:
// The connection object to connect to the app server for accessing
// the remote object
//    Connection g_DPBConnection
// The proxy user object p_service1 is used to declare the client side pointer
//    p_service1 g_roService1

g_DPBConnection = Create Connection
g_roService1 = Create p_service1

g_DPBConnection.Application = "Test1"

// A server IP address
//    g_DPBConnection.Location = "196.96.166.000"
// or a local test connection
//    g_DPBConnection.Location = "localhost"
// or some other named location.
g_DPBConnection.Location = "AppServer1"

// Change to the network driver you are using.
g_DPBConnection.driver = "NamedPipes"

If g_DPBConnection.ConnectToServer() <> 0 Then
```

```
   Messagebox( "Client", "Error Code = " + String( g_DPBConnection.ErrCode) + &
               "~r~nError Text = " + g_DPBConnection.ErrText)
   HALT CLOSE
End If

g_roService1.SetConnect( g_DPBConnection)
```

From this point on, within the scope of the remote object variable `g_roService1`, you can make use of any of the properties and methods that you have defined for this custom class user object.

Passing Data in Distributed PowerBuilder

One of the first remote objects you might try to build is a remote `DataStore` user object. This would give you easy access to remote data sources. You would join a majority of other developers in finding that PowerBuilder will not allow you to declare a remote user object of the standard object types. You can *only* create remote objects from custom class user objects. This might lead you to create a `DataStore` user object and declare it as an instance variable for a custom class user object. Unfortunately, PowerBuilder detects this subversive action when you try to save the proxy object, complains at you, and creates the proxy image without the instance variable. This prevents you from directly accessing the object as a property or returning the object from a method. This is also true of all other complex data types such as controls.

Do not despair; there is a way to transfer data between remote objects. This is achieved using arrays and the new DataWindow syntax that allows you to directly assign DataWindow rows into structures.

Let's use the customer table (see Table 19.1) from the demo database as an example.

Table 19.1. The Customer table structure.

Column Name	*Data Type*
`id`	Integer
`fname`	String
`lname`	String
`address`	String
`city`	String
`state`	String
`zip`	String
`phone`	String
`company_name`	String

The first object you will need to create is a structure, called `s_customer_data`, which has the same number of elements and data types as the customer table. The next two objects you will need to create are a DataWindow object and a DataStore user object. The DataWindow object, called `d_customer_data`, selects each column in the customer table. The DataStore object, called `u_ds_customer_data`, is associated with the new DataWindow object.

The final object is the actual remote object, a custom class user object called `ro_customer_data`. For this object, define a private instance variable called `ds_customer_data`, which is declared of type `u_ds_customer_data`. You also need to provide a method to extract and return the data from the `DataStore` object to a requesting client application. The method is implemented as a function that returns a value of type `s_customer_data`. The code for this function is

```
// s_customer_data GetCustomerData( a_lRow Long)
//
s_customer_data sCustomerData

sCustomerData = ds_customer_data.Object.Data[ a_lRow]

Return sCustomerData
```

As you can see, the function for returning a record of information is actually quite straightforward—or is it? Well not quite. You are returning a record's worth of data, but it is from the primary DataWindow buffer and you have lost the column and row modification status. For most cases this may not be a problem, but for those that do require this additional information, you will need to make use of additional reference variable arguments to the method to return structures for each buffer and structures for column and row status values.

All that is now left is to set the custom class user object to `AutoInstantiate` (using the pop-up menu) and save the proxy object, `p_customer_data`, with the user object. You should keep the proxy object and structure object in a common library that is used by both the server and client applications.

You can now make use of the remote object within your client applications using the code shown in the "Client Applications" section and instantiating a variable using the proxy object `p_customer_data`. You can then extract the data using the following code:

```
//
// Assume that there is a global variable of type p_customer_data
// called ro_customer_data
//
Long lRow, lRowCount
s_customer_data sCustomerData[]

//
// Also, assume that we coded an additional method that returns the current
// number of rows in the datastore object.
//
lRowCount = ro_customer_data.CustomerDataRowCount()
//
// Loop through the remote DataStore pulling into the array.
// NOTE: we back fill the array to get the best performance.
```

```
//
For lRow = lRowCount To 1 Step -1
   sCustomerData[ lRow] = ro_customer_data.GetCustomerData( lRow)
Next
```

Instead of populating a structure on the client, you can use a DataStore or DataWindow object or even make direct use of the data.

TIP

You can add a method to the custom class user object to control and restrict the retrieval carried out on the `DataStore` object held in the instance variable `ds_customer_data`.

Platform and Driver Requirements

Distributed PowerBuilder is currently only available in the Windows environment with the configurations shown in Table 19.2.

Table 19.2. Distributed PowerBuilder configurations.

Platform	*Communications Protocol*	*As a Server*	*As a Client*
Windows 3.*x*	NamedPipes	No	No
	Sockets	No	Yes
	OpenClientServer	No	Yes
Windows 95	NamedPipes	No	Yes
	Sockets	Yes	Yes
	OpenClientServer	No	Yes
Windows NT 3.51	NamedPipes	Yes	Yes
	Sockets	Yes	Yes
	OpenClientServer	Yes	Yes
PowerBuilder UNIX	N/A (support is planned for PB UNIX Version 5.0)		
PowerBuilder Mac	N/A		

NOTE

A Windows NT `OpenClientServer` server application cannot also function as a client to itself. The other limitation of this configuration is that only one `OpenClientServer` transport object can "listen" at any one time. The server transport object can, however, be listening on multiple protocols simultaneously.

Each of the different platforms and protocols supported by distributed PowerBuilder requires a variety of different drivers (see Table 19.3).

Table 19.3. Distributed PowerBuilder driver requirements.

Platform	*Communication Protocol*	*Drivers Required*
Windows NT	Named Pipes (Server)	PBNPS050.DLL
Windows NT, Windows 95	Named Pipes (Client)	PBNPC050.DLL
Windows NT, Windows 95	WinSock (Server)	PBWSS050.DLL as well as TCP/IP to be installed and configured
Windows NT, Windows 95	WinSock (Client)	PBWSC050.DLL as well as TCP/IP to be installed and configured
Windows 3.*x*	WinSock (Client)	PBWSC050.DLL as well as TCP/IP 32 for WFW
Windows NT	OpenClientServer (Server)	PBOSS050.DLL and PBOSRV050.EXE as well as Sybase Open Server to be installed
Windows NT, Windows 95	OpenClientServer (Client)	PBOSC050.DLL as well as Sybase Open Client
Windows 3.*x*	OpenClientServer (Client)	PBOSC050.DLL as well as Sybase Open Client for Windows
Windows NT, Windows 95, Windows 3.*x*	Local	PBDPB050.DLL

The following are some additional notes related to distributed PowerBuilder and the communication drivers:

- Security for distributed PowerBuilder is handled completely at the network protocol level and does not impose any additional checks.
- The server application cannot call client applications unless it is requesting a remote service that is being served by that application.
- Processing of remote requests is carried out synchronously. The client application will pause while it waits for a response from the server's remote object to return a result.

There was some discussion during the beta cycle for PowerBuilder 5.0 on whether asynchronous processing was going to be available, and the unofficial answer was "in a later release."

WinSock Driver Considerations

You will need to make entries into the hosts file for each machine that will be making use of distributed PowerBuilder objects. You will have an entry for each server that will be used.

You can also specify a loopback address to the local machine for testing purposes. This entry is by convention called localhost and has the IP address `127.0.0.1`.

NOTE

Microsoft supplies a hosts.sam file to show how to format the entries for the hosts file. It also supplies the localhost entry.

Asynchronous Distributed PowerBuilder

You developers who cannot wait until Powersoft provides an inherent mechanism for making asynchronous calls from a distributed PowerBuilder application might want to consider the following idea.

You could make use of a service application running on the client machine which communicates via DDE with the user's application. By making the appropriate requests of the service application, you can continue processing within the client application and then respond to DDE messages from the service application as they occur.

You could very easily build a single service application with this functionality for use by any number of client applications.

Debugging Distributed PowerBuilder

As you might expect, debugging a PowerBuilder application that is either a client or server in a distributed environment presents some unique difficulties. The main focus of any development work for either a server or a client application is to create it independently of the final platform that it will be deployed on. This allows the developer to develop and test the code on his own machine without having to worry about loading objects onto other machines. Distributed PowerBuilder provides some debugging and diagnostic tools to help you track down problems with remote calls. The most well known of these is the PowerBuilder debugger. You can use the familiar PowerBuilder debugger to watch the application code and variables, in the same manner that you would use any other PowerBuilder application.

The "Local" Driver

Since the PowerBuilder debugger can currently handle only single-process local debugging, a local loopback driver is available to enable single-process symbolic processing. This has the following effects on the client and server sides of an application: The server does not create a transport object, and the client uses the connection driver `"Local"`.

The `"Local"` driver then emulates a remote server locally and within the same process as the client application. The object reference indirections that normally occur during distributed processing are converted into references that are serviced locally, so that the variables and object data can be seen within the debugger.

WARNING

This also means that there is a single variable and data space used by both client and server applications, and this may lead to usage conflicts.

This method will not help you debug actual connection and communication problems, and you will have to use the methods outlined in the following sections with these.

Error Processing

Rather than force you to check each call you make to a remote object for possible errors, Powersoft has implemented error processing for distributed PowerBuilder using the `SystemError` event.

If an error occurs in the client-request context on the server, it is trapped and the `Error` structure is populated for that client thread. This is then sent back to the client side, where an application error is triggered. The developer has two locations that can be used to handle the error condition: the `Error` event for the `Connection` object and the `SystemError` event for the application.

NOTE

The `Error` event is modeled on the OLE error event mechanism.

The `Connection` object `Error` event can be set up to respond to different error conditions by setting the `Action` parameter to one of the following values:

- `ExceptionFail!`—Triggers the `SystemError` event.
- `ExceptionIgnore!`—Ignores the error and attempt to continue processing. You should use this value with caution, because the error you are processing may cause another error, ad infinitum.
- `ExceptionRetry!`—Attempts to re-execute the function or re-evaluate the expression.
- `ExceptionSubstituteReturnValue!`–Substitutes the return code with that in the `ReturnValue` event parameter and cancels the error condition.

The `ReturnValue` parameter is a value of the same data type as the value that would have been expected to be returned.

Using these options provides you with more flexibility than the `SystemError` events continue or halt options. For example, if an object or method is not available on the server you connected to, you can disconnect and reconnect to another server that does, and then retry the operation that failed.

For more serious errors, such as page faults or other fatal system conditions, distributed PowerBuilder attempts to save server applications by terminating the offending client thread. If the exception handler determines that the executing client thread caused the exception, it attempts to gracefully kill the thread, release acquired resources, and inform the client side of the problem. The client side can then respond in whatever manner you wish; it will probably attempt to reconnect to the server, and continue processing. If there is a more serious problem with the server application, the server may be terminated and client applications will receive "server no longer responding" messages on their next use of a remote object.

Trace Options

The `ConnectionObject` class (which encompasses the transport and connect objects) contains a `Trace` property, which you can use to obtain debug information during an applications execution. This property has the following options that can be specified for it:

- `Level`—Sets the level of information to capture. Setting this option to `1` will capture basic information (`Console`, `ObjectLife`, `ObjectCalls`, `ConnectInfo`).
- `ObjectLife`—By setting this to `1` you can capture the creation and destruction of objects. It will be written in this format:

```
DSE Create 'object class name' (object id), SUCCEEDED/FAILED
DSE Destroy (object id), SUCCEDDED/FAILED
```

- `ObjectCalls`—By setting this to `1` you can capture method calls for both the server and client. This is written in the following formats:

  Server method invocation:

  ```
  DSE (context id, object id) Called: Function name, SUCCEEDED/FAILED
  DSE Return(return type)
  Parm# (parm type) by Value/Reference
  ```

  Server attribute access:

  ```
  DSE Get/Set (context id, object id) attribute name, (attribute type)
  ```

  Client method invocation:

  ```
  DSE (object id) Call: object class name.function name
  DSE Return (return type), SUCCEEDED/FAILED
  Parm# (parm type) by Value/Reference
  ```

  Client attribute access:

  ```
  DSE (object id) Get/Set object class name.attribute name (attribute type),
  SUCCEEDED/FAILED
  ```

- `ThreadLife`—By setting this to `1` you can capture the creation and destruction of service threads.
- `Log`—Sets the filename and path of the log file. The file is opened in append mode.
- `Console`—Setting this to `1` enables the Win32 console log.

You can use these trace options to customize the log file generated. The following are some sample trace settings:

```
DPBConnection.Trace = "Log=c:\pb5i32\debug\app1.log, ObjectCalls=1, ObjectLife=1"
//
DPBConnection.Trace = "Console=1, ObjectCalls=1, ObjectLife=1"
//
DPBConnection.Trace = "Console=1, Level=1"
```

The task of debugging distributed PowerBuilder can be complex, but you can use the methods described in this section to make it easier on yourself.

Summary

As always, you have to decide between different methods of achieving the same result, and you not only need to choose the best tools for the job, but also the best architecture. Both client/server and n-tier architectures have benefits over each other, as well as accompanying disadvantages or issues. This chapter shows some of the n-tier tools available for use with PowerBuilder.

Distributed processing is going to force development teams to re-examine their conceptions of how their applications work and interact. This may, in fact, require some additional analysis work and design rework to make use of the advantages of the n-tier architecture.

Application Maintenance and Upgrades

20

IN THIS CHAPTER

An important part of the life cycle of a project is the maintenance and upgrade of the application code and runtime environment. As components of the application are enhanced or have bugs fixed, a properly controlled rollout of the new code is essential. This should include a plan for recovery back to the previously known working version if problems arise with the new code. This is true not only of upgraded application code, but of PowerBuilder runtime files and other supporting files (including network and database drivers). The iterative model used for software development allows the rapid release of application versions and it is more important than ever to manage these releases.

The one word that has not been mentioned yet is *quality*. One of the biggest reasons that release management and version control are used is to enforce *quality assurance*. This ensures the completeness, correctness, reliability, and maintainability of the product and ensures that it meets the design specifications and requirements with acceptable performance. For a detailed discussion on producing quality products, see Chapter 16, "Testing and Debugging."

Another reason for release management is to provide an audit trail of the changes made to an application, and by whom.

Team Management

An integral part of release management and version control is the procedures set in place for team members. These procedures should include the formalization of a directory structure to hold the various project files, from ER-diagrams, SQL scripts, bitmaps, sound files, and documents to the actual PowerBuilder libraries.

Members of the team or possibly from a variety of teams need to be assigned certain management responsibilities pertinent to the control and upkeep of object libraries, source code, and standards. Such titles as source librarian and object custodian are frequently used to describe the job functions.

With such procedures in place, the introduction and use of release management and version control can be introduced and utilized with minimal fuss and problems.

Release Management

Before a version of a software product is sent out for use by the end users it usually passes through a set of release steps (if it doesn't, maybe the following sections can convince you that it should). In fact, before even reaching a release status, the code is passed through a number of other tests such as unit testing and black and white box testing. For information on these methods see Chapter 16.

The release steps use two distinct types of testing: *verification* and *validation.*

The process of verification is to find errors within the code by executing it within a simulated/controlled environment. This step is more commonly known as *alpha testing*.

The process of validation is to find errors using real data in a live environment. This step is more commonly known as *beta testing*. The code is used to enter real transactions, but the users know that the system could fail at any point, and that they are to report any problems to the developers in as detailed description as they can.

As you can see in Figure 20.1, there are a number of steps and areas of potential management restrictions. The time that the whole process takes is completely up to each individual project. As you can see from some of the larger software houses such as Microsoft, the arrival of an actual version can take many months and many beta releases. One of the important aspects is compatibility with existing applications. For example, everyone has his or her own version of the OLE DLLs that aren't always compatible with the ones you need to install.

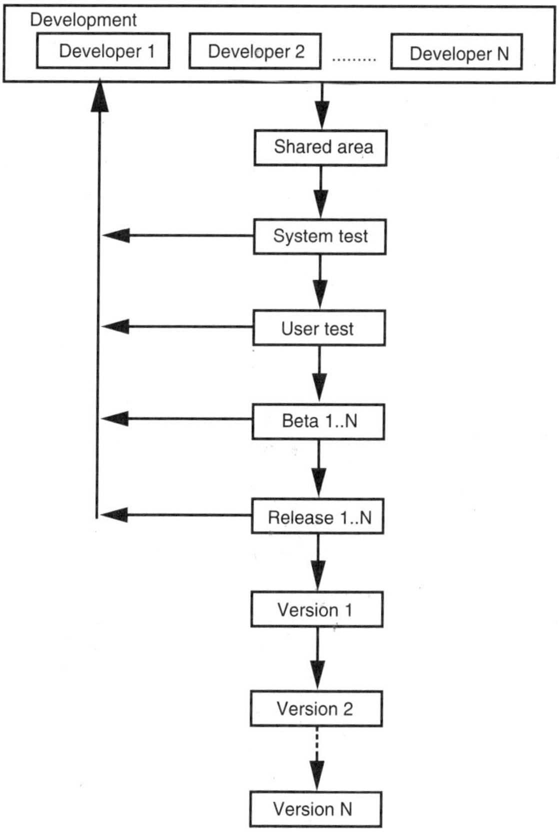

FIGURE 20.1.
The software release process.

Version Control

Once you have a release of your application that is a candidate for a version number and deployment, you need to consider at least the following questions:

- Does the application require upgrades of other software?
- Are additional files required to support the new version?
- Have the end users signed off on this version?

Version control software can be used to control the use and migration of all of an application's objects. However, the application is only the tip of the problem, and as in performance and design phases, you need to consider all the other contributing factors. To this end, you should make full use of your version control software to maintain versions of the following:

- Database objects (stored procedures, triggers, views, and so on)
- Database drivers (server and client)
- Network drivers (server and client)
- Printer drivers
- Project documentation

You might think that printer drivers are an odd addition to the list, but this one comes from experience. A client suddenly ran into some problems when printing a complex report. A structured troubleshooting session (these really pay off) led to the conclusion that an updated printer driver was the problem, and after a *lot* of searching, the original drivers were found and installed. The problem was fixed by the simple regression of the printer drivers. How much simpler it would have been to pull up a report of changes to the complete client/server system and pinpoint the problems, as well as have immediate access to the appropriate files.

When PowerBuilder or any other development tool moves to a new version, you must carefully consider the impact on your existing applications and development efforts. You may not have the resources or time to migrate every application to the latest version of PowerBuilder. In fact, some corporate departments were still using PowerBuilder 2.0 applications after Version 4.0 was released, which is purely a team resource problem. This can lead to a variety of application and runtime environment files that need to be tracked and maintained.

Each version of a piece of software that is released for use is denoted using a numbering scheme based on major and minor changes to the software. Software vendors all seem to have their own ideas about what the numbers mean and how the numbers are incremented. For example, Microsoft recently went from Version 4.21 of the SQL Server product to 6.0, while Powersoft numbers its maintenance releases at the third position (for example, 4.0.0.3).

These numbering schemes are based on whether a significant change has been made and are indicated by incrementation of the first number by one. Minor changes to the software, generally bug fixes and some additional functionality, are indicated by incrementing the second number. Occasionally the third is used internally by the developers for bug fixes, which are then rolled up until a released version and indicated by the second number.

A detailed log, an *audit trail*, of the changes made between releases is usually kept and maintained. This can be done either manually or preferably by a software package; the version control software is the usual location of this functionality.

The most common terms in version control are check-in and check-out; these are the basic procedures that make version control work. Before you start any work on an existing object, it must first be checked out to a work area. This process makes a copy of the object and locks the original so that no one else can work on it at the same time. When the developer has finished making modifications to the object, has tested it, and is ready to resubmit it for use in the application he checks it back in. Depending on what software you are using, a copy of the original object (a *delta*) is usually kept.

Version Control in PowerBuilder

PowerBuilder provides a very limited means of version control in the check-in and check-out facilities in the Library painter. This paradigm is borrowed straight from real libraries and the book control mechanism they use. By the judicious use of a good directory structure, you can isolate and maintain major version releases of an application, but if you are tackling any sort of large-scale application development, a proper version control tool, such as ObjectCycle, should be used.

NOTE

PowerBuilder does *not* maintain previous versions of the object for you; this you must do for yourself.

Using the PowerBuilder check-in and check-out facilities does not prevent other developers from opening the original object, but it does prevent them from overwriting it until the modified object is checked back in or the status is cleared.

The first time you check out an object in PowerBuilder you will be prompted to set the user ID to be used for the process. The mechanics of the various methods to use the check-in and check-out functions are discussed in Chapter 13, "The Library Painter."

WARNING

You need to choose an ID not already in use by another developer; otherwise, you can access each other's checked-out objects. This ID is best set to your login name to prevent duplication.

This ID is stored in the PB.INI file and is accessible using a text editor. This means that you can alter your ID and assume someone else's identity in order to check an object back in; you should, however, do this with caution and remember to immediately reset your ID.

The next (or first, if you have already been registered) dialog box to be displayed is the Check Out Library Entries dialog box (see Figure 20.2), which shows all the library files in the current working directory.

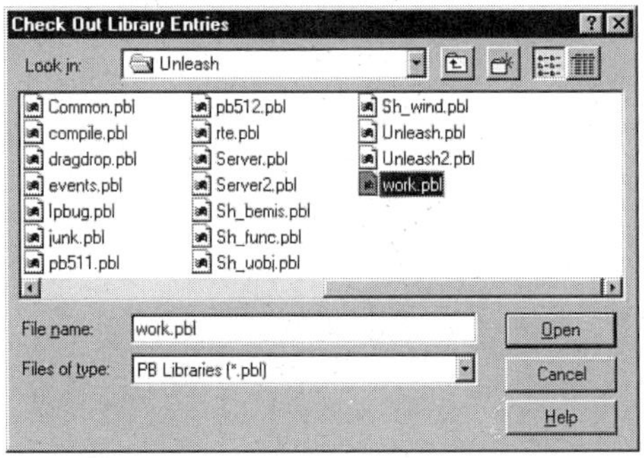

FIGURE 20.2.
The Check Out Library Entries dialog box.

Once you have selected a PBL, PowerBuilder will do one of two things. Normally, it will copy the object to the indicated PBL and mark both objects with a checked-out status. However, if the object is already checked out (see Figure 20.3), this is the point at which PowerBuilder will tell you. (Of course, this never happens because we all carefully watch the tiny icon by the side of the object name in the Library painter. Right?)

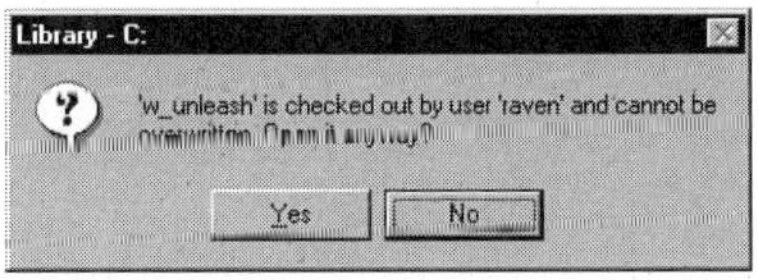

FIGURE 20.3.
The object-already-checked-out warning.

The Yes/No option on this dialog box allows you to continue processing a multiselection operation.

The object that has been copied to your working area is only accessible by you, and it will remain in that library until you either check it back in or clear its checked-out status. You can also copy the object if you wish, but you may not delete or move it.

PowerBuilder uses two different icons (see Figure 20.4) next to the object name in the Library painter to indicate that an object is checked out.

When you check an object back in, the original version of the object is overwritten, the working copy is deleted from your work area, and the check-out status is reset. The object can now be checked out by other developers. The new object is known as a *revision*.

FIGURE 20.4.
One icon indicates the working copy of the checked-out object, and the other icon indicates the original version of an object that is checked out.

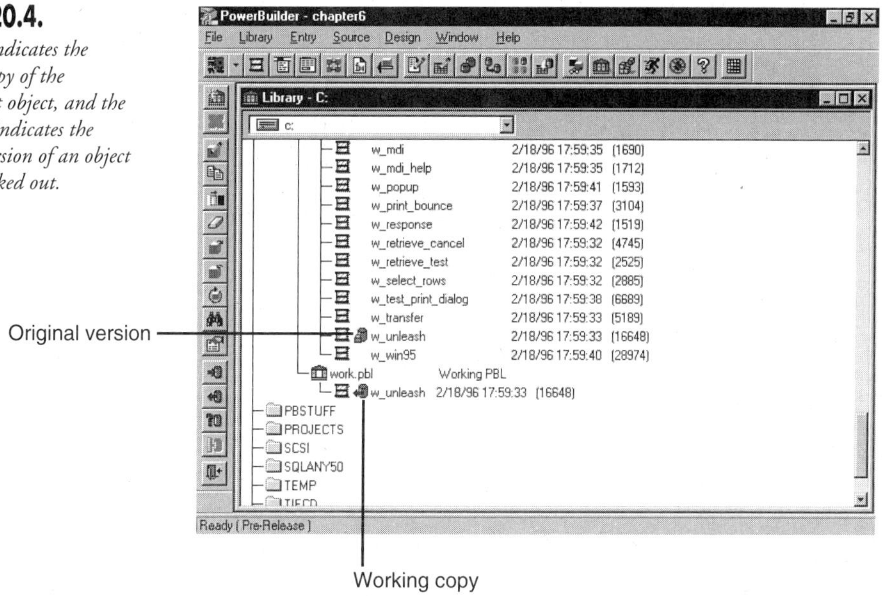

If you want to remove the checked-out status of an object and leave the original version, you need to select the Clear Check Out Status option. A dialog box asks you whether PowerBuilder should delete your working copy at the same time (see Figure 20.5).

FIGURE 20.5.
The clear check-out status dialog box.

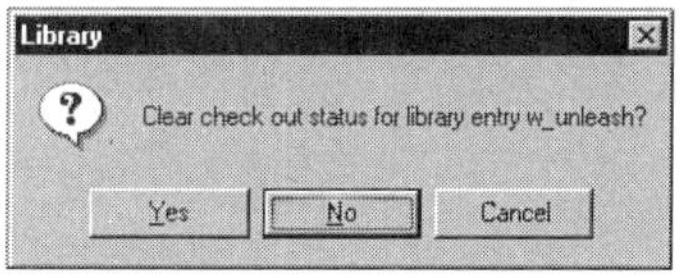

You can clear the check-out status of an object from either the working library or the originating library. This can be very useful to recover the original object if the working PBL is accidentally deleted!

A problem that seems to be less of an issue with the latest versions of PowerBuilder is that while you are checking in an object, for some reason it fails. The reasons seem to be based on the file system of the server and how many people are accessing the library and its objects concurrently. Whatever the reason, the result is the same. The original object maintains a checked-out status and the working copy remains in your working PBL but is no longer considered to be checked out. Powersoft seems to have made some modifications to PowerBuilder in this area, because this now occurs a lot less frequently.

Recovery from this situation is not as bad as you might think, and requires you to follow these steps:

1. Check all other objects into the original PBL.
2. Within the operating system rename the original PBL file.
3. Create a new PBL with the same name as the original.
4. Move all the objects (except the checked-out one) from the old original to the new.
5. Move the modified object from your work PBL to the new original PBL.
6. Delete the original PBL file.

Version Control Interfaces

As you can see, PowerBuilder only provides the barest means of version control—it protects against multiple overwriting of updates to the same object. To provide a means of full version control with the ability to provide phased implementations, auditing, and version back-out, you need to turn to one of the third-party tool vendors.

The PowerBuilder version control facilities are very limited. A number of third-party tool vendors provide full version control products that tightly integrate with PowerBuilder by use of the ORCA interface.

Before using one of the version control products, you must first register all your objects with the tool—this effectively checks them all out into the control system! You now carry out your check in and check out against this system through a vendor-supplied interface accessed from the Library painter.

These tools track every change that is made to a registered object in an archive, which can be reported against, and old versions of an object can be opened.

What follows is a concise breakdown of the major features for three of the most common version control products that integrate directly with PowerBuilder. These vendors, and their competitors, are always updating their product features and one may have a more appealing feature set than another that fits your development requirements and budget.

ObjectCycle

NEW 5 in PowerBuilder

ObjectCycle is Powersoft's new network-based source management and version control software for your PowerBuilder applications. ObjectCycle differs from many of the existing file-based version control packages in that it uses Sybase SQL Anywhere to store all its information. Registered versions of your application's objects are stored in the Sybase SQL Anywhere database. The following sections discuss the setup and use of ObjectCycle.

Installing ObjectCycle

There are two main components needed for installing ObjectCycle: the client and the server software. The server installation consists of Sybase SQL Anywhere and the ObjectCycle server software. The server components can be installed on an NT server Version 3.51 or higher or on a Windows 95 machine. ObjectCycle can be networked or can also run on a standalone machine as long as one of the two specified operating systems is in use.

The ObjectCycle Client Utilities can be installed on NT 3.51, Windows 95, or Windows 3.*x*. The client utilities consist of the ObjectCycle Manager and help files. ObjectCycle Manager allows you to manage projects, objects, and users by accessing the Sybase SQL Anywhere database.

> **NOTE**
>
> Remember that NT is case-sensitive and, therefore, so is the connection information.

Setting Up a Project

Once you have connected to the central repository of information, you are ready to set up any projects and users. A project is just a collection of objects that typically correlates to your application's name. To create a new project from the ObjectCycle Manager, select File | New | Project on the menu bar, which opens the New Project dialog box (see Figure 20.6).

FIGURE 20.6.
The New Project dialog box.

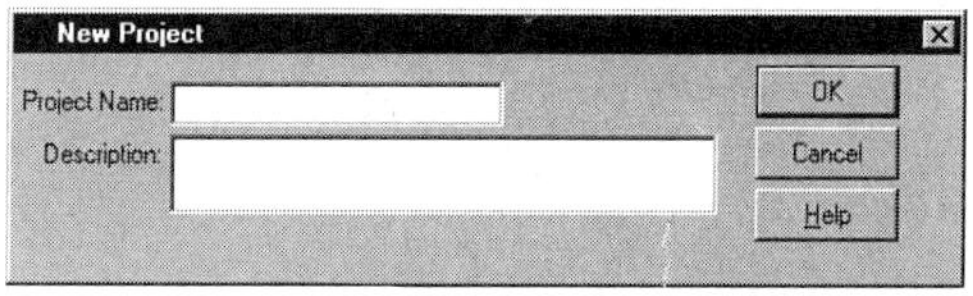

Specify the project name and a description and click OK. After you have created all the projects needed and you are in a multideveloper environment, you will need to create individual user accounts. This is done by selecting Users from the Configure menu, which opens the Configure Users dialog box (see Figure 20.7).

FIGURE 20.7.
The Configure Users dialog box.

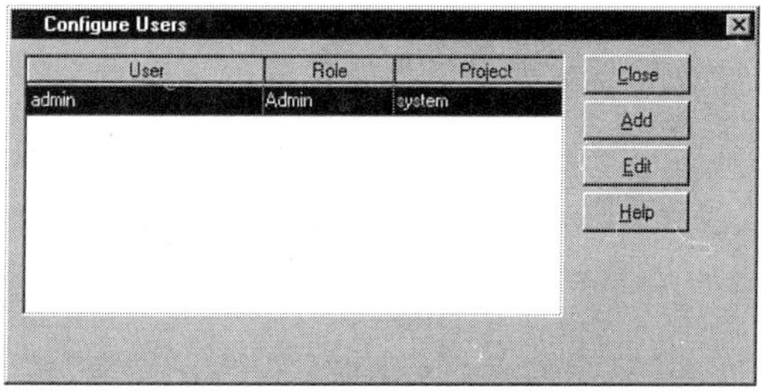

To create a new user account, click the Add button, which opens the User Profile dialog box (see Figure 20.8).

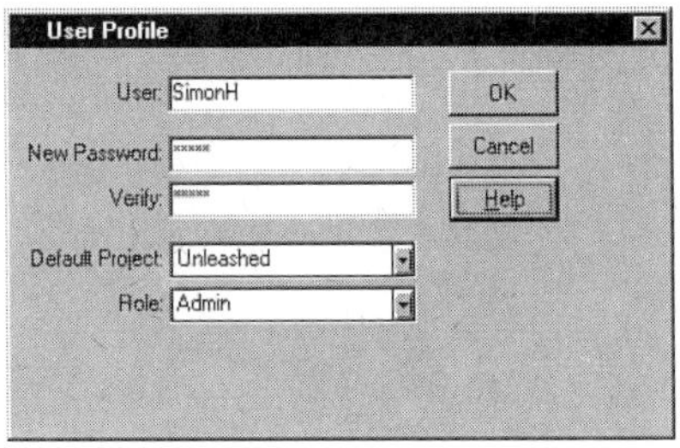

FIGURE 20.8.
The User Profile dialog box.

The User Profile dialog box asks you to specify a unique user ID, the user's password, the default project, and the user's role (either admin, user, or inactive). The different roles have the following abilities:

- User—Has the ability to perform version control functions.
- Admin—Has the ability to move objects, create and destroy projects, folders, and labels, and set up user accounts.
- Inactive—The user account is no longer active. An inactive user can browse projects but is not allowed to modify objects, folders, or projects.

After you click OK, the new user ID is added to the Configure Users dialog box. If you are modifying an existing account, any changes made will be applied the next time the user logs on to ObjectCycle.

After setting up your projects and user accounts, you are ready to create the ObjectCycle objects within each project.

Registering ObjectCycle Objects

ObjectCycle objects equate to the PowerBuilder objects that comprise your application. If your application is large enough to be dispersed across multiple library files, you might want to keep track of the object placement within ObjectCycle. By default, all objects will be placed in the main project folder (supplied by ObjectCycle). It is possible, and often desirable, to create additional folders within your project. Each folder would correspond to a specific PBL. Objects within a library file are then placed in the corresponding folder in ObjectCycle. These objects can be added from within the ObjectCycle Manager or from PowerBuilder. Since typically only one person (the administrator) will be able to access these options, we will focus on the alternative method most developers use, which is through PowerBuilder's Library painter.

To access ObjectCycle through the Library painter, select Connect from the Source menu, which opens the Connect dialog box (see Figure 20.9). In this dialog box you specify the name of the source management vendor you wish to use (in this case, ObjectCycle).

FIGURE 20.9.
The Connect dialog box.

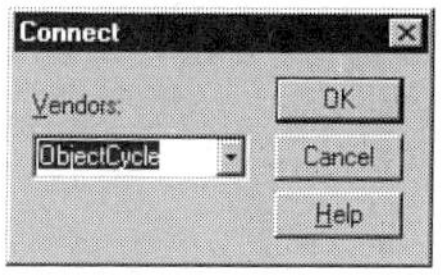

After you select ObjectCycle and click OK, the ObjectCycle Connect dialog box (see Figure 20.10) prompts you for the user ID, password, the ObjectCycle project you want to connect to, and the server that contains the Sybase SQL Anywhere database.

FIGURE 20.10.
The ObjectCycle Connect dialog box.

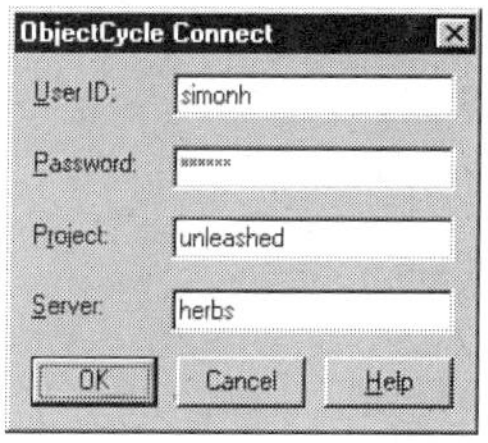

If this is the first time you are connecting to ObjectCycle from within PowerBuilder, you will be prompted to create a configuration file that stores your connection information.

If you have multiple library files that comprise your application, you should create folders in ObjectCycle (through the Object Manager) that correspond to each library file. To specify which folders you want available to place objects in, select the Configuration menu item under the Source menu, which opens the ObjectCycle Configuration dialog box (see Figure 20.11).

FIGURE 20.11.
The ObjectCycle Configuration dialog box.

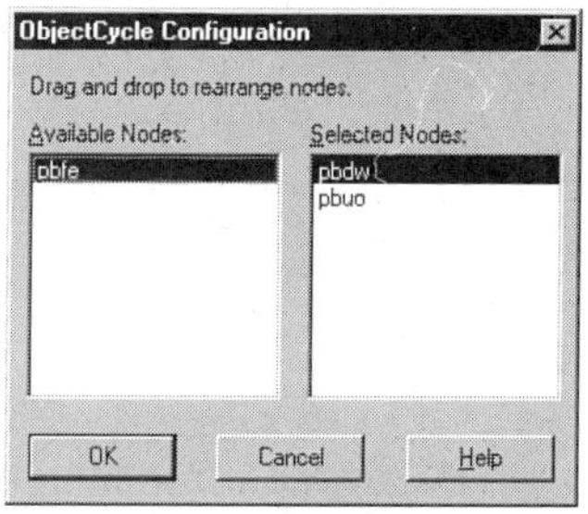

This dialog box lists all the available folders (nodes) and those to which you can register objects. To add a node to the list of selected nodes, click on a node in the Available list box and drag it to the Selected list box. Once you are connected to the server and have specified any nodes that you wish to access, you have to register your application's objects in ObjectCycle. Object Registration is performed to ensure that a centralized copy of each object is stored in the ObjectCycle repository. This way, the developers have to check out objects from ObjectCycle so that there is no accidental overlaying of one another's work. To do this, select the object(s) you want to register and select Register from the Source menu, which opens the ObjectCycle Registration dialog box (see Figure 20.12).

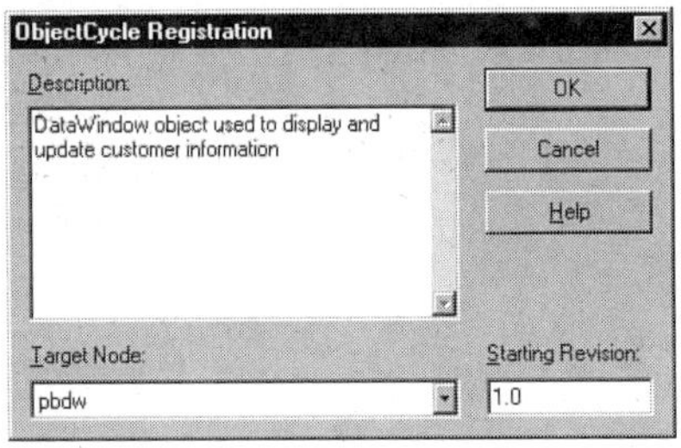

FIGURE 20.12.
The ObjectCycle Registration dialog box.

If the object was saved with comments, the comments will be used in the description field. In addition to supplying a description for the object, you need to specify the Target Node and the Starting Revision number. The Target Node is enabled if you have multiple ObjectCycle folders that the object could be registered with. The Starting Revision number is used to specify the desired version of the object. If you have more than one object selected, you will be prompted with the ObjectCycle Registration dialog box for each object. After an object has been registered, PowerBuilder places an icon next to the object to indicate that it has been registered (see Figure 20.13).

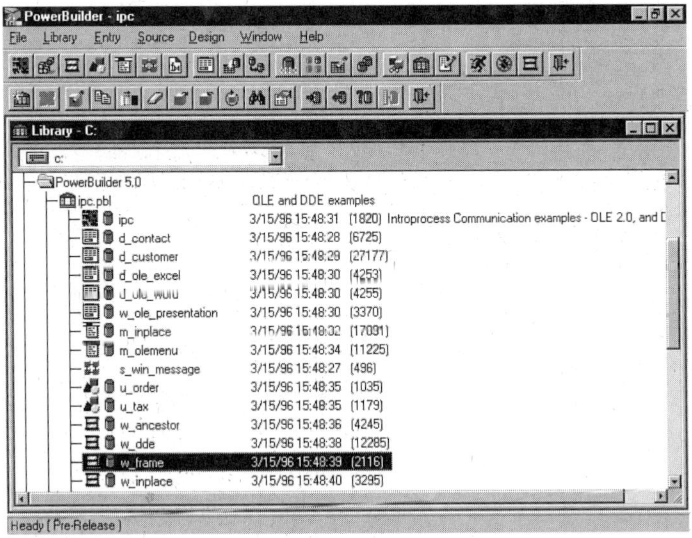

FIGURE 20.13.
The Library Painter with registered objects.

After the objects have been registered, all developers on the project team can check objects in and out as they normally would. The only difference is that the source and any changes are being maintained and tracked in the ObjectCycle SQL Anywhere database.

After modifications have been made to an object and you go to check it back in, in addition to the object description, you can indicate a new version label (see Figure 20.14). Project versions are covered in more depth in the upcoming section "ObjectCycle Version Control."

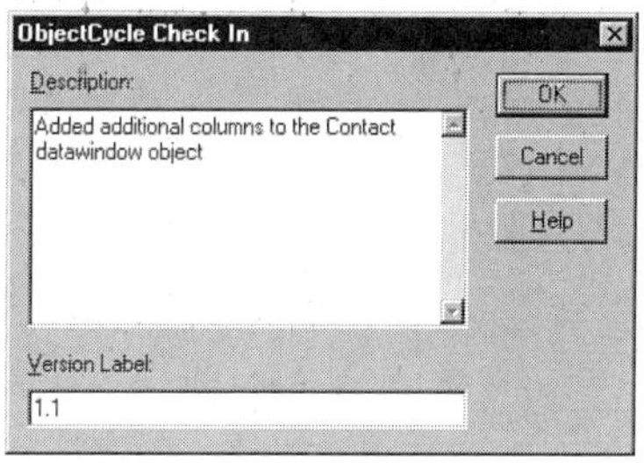

FIGURE 20.14.
The ObjectCycle Check In dialog box.

The versions are tracked within the ObjectCycle database. ObjectCycle provides a number of functions in the Library painter that allow you to track an object's history.

The Registration Directory

The easiest method of tracking an object's version history is to use the Registration Directory option under the Source menu. Clicking on this menu item opens the ObjectCycle Registration Directory dialog box (see Figure 20.15).

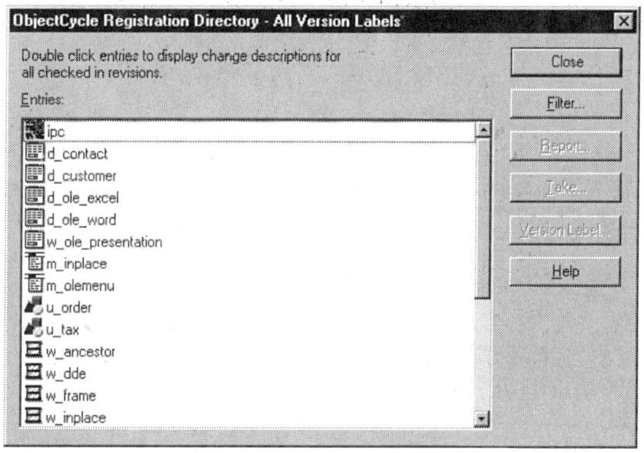

FIGURE 20.15.
The ObjectCycle Registration Directory dialog box.

In this dialog box you can view objects from a particular version, generate a status report for a particular object, restore an object from a specific version, and specify a new version label.

By clicking on the Filter button, you can specify a specific version label to view on the ObjectCycle Filter On Version Label dialog box (see Figure 20.16).

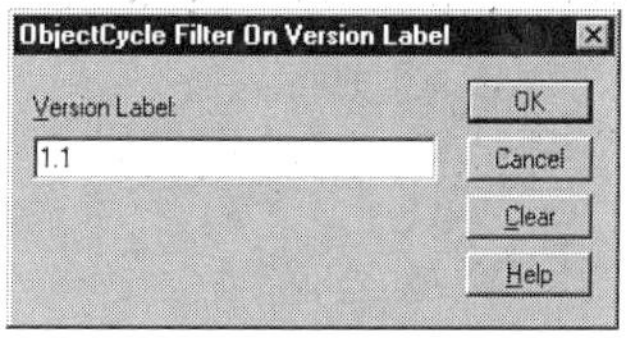

FIGURE 20.16.
The ObjectCycle Filter On Version Label dialog box.

This modifies the ObjectCycle Registration Directory dialog box so that it displays all objects for the specified version label (see Figure 20.17).

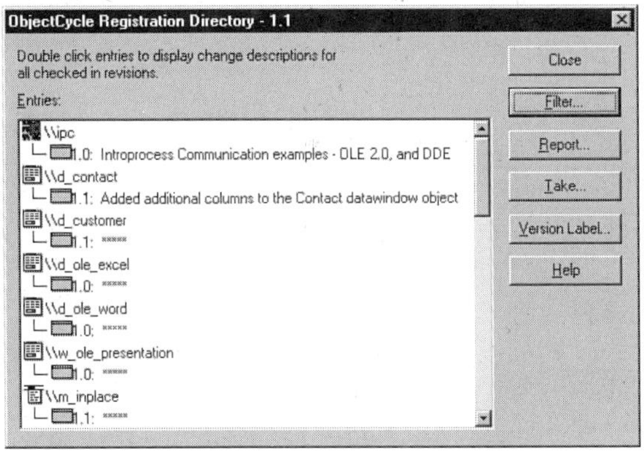

FIGURE 20.17.
The ObjectCycle Registration Directory dialog box, displaying a specific version label.

To display all objects again, click the Filter button and select Clear.

You can create a status report that displays the version history of the object, including the modification comments, the datetime stamps, the compiled size, and the check-out status. After selecting an object, click the Report button, which opens the ObjectCycle Object Report dialog box (see Figure 20.18) and gives you the ability to print the report.

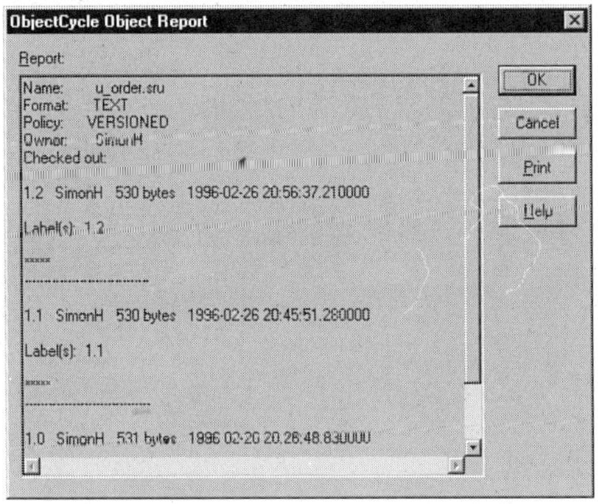

FIGURE 20.18.
The ObjectCycle Object Report dialog box.

You can also generate the ObjectCycle object report directly from the Library painter by selecting Registration Report from the Source menu.

The Take button in the ObjectCycle Registration Directory dialog box opens the Select Destination Library dialog box, which displays the libraries in the current application object's library search path. Specifying a library and clicking OK takes the current version of the object in the ObjectCycle database and places it in the specified library. The "taken" object is not checked out and can be modified, but it must be registered as a different object. This could be used to copy a registered object to be used as a template for a new object. The Version Label button opens the ObjectCycle Assign Version Label dialog box, which allows you to assign a new version label to the selected object.

In addition to the functionality available via the Registration Directory dialog box, there are several other options under the Source menu that assist you in source management and version control. The Synchronize menu item ensures that the library entry mirrors the ObjectCycle repository copy in case of "taken" objects or mismatched versions. The Clear Registration menu item removes the object from ObjectCycle.

ObjectCycle Version Control

One of the greatest benefits of using ObjectCycle is the ability to maintain different versions of an application. Not only does ObjectCycle provide a version history, but it also allows you to restore a prior version. This is often needed if the current version does not work correctly and needs to be backed out.

To create a new version of an application from within PowerBuilder, select Create New Release from the Source menu, which opens the ObjectCycle New Release dialog box (see Figure 20.19).

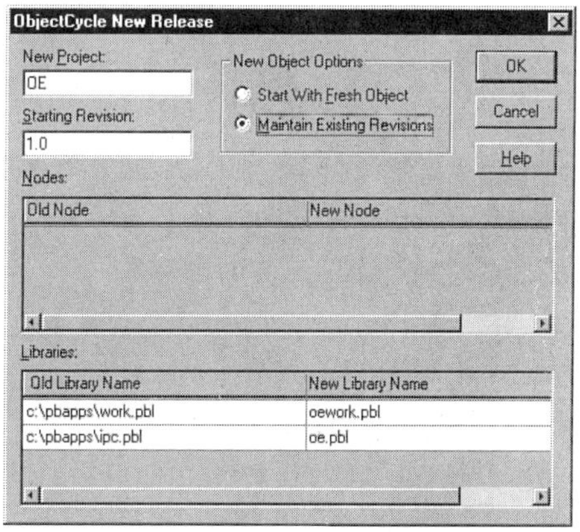

FIGURE 20.19.
The ObjectCycle New Release dialog box.

This dialog box allows you to create a new project in the ObjectCycle database using copies of the current project's objects. You can specify whether you copy the revision history of the objects, which nodes are included, and the name of the new library files that the objects will be copied to.

The Library painter only allows you to copy an existing project. The Object Manager provides you with additional methods of maintaining, restoring, and saving different versions of your application.

For any object in the Object Manager, you can bring up its property sheet, which enables you to view the object's version history (see Figure 20.20).

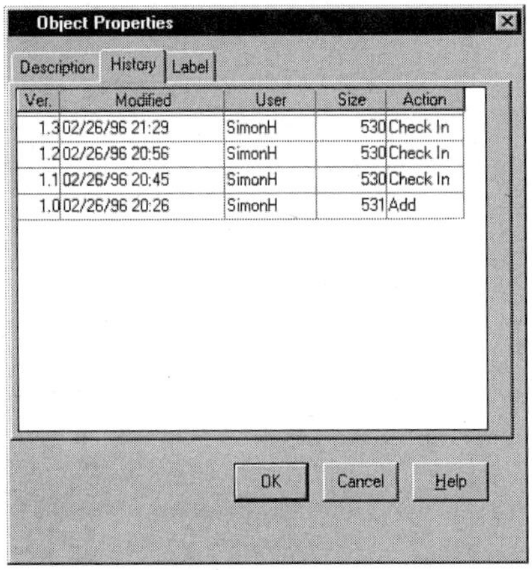

FIGURE 20.20.
The History tab page of the Object Properties property sheet.

To restore an existing object's version, select the object and click Get from the pop-up menu, which opens the Get Object to File dialog box (see Figure 20.21).

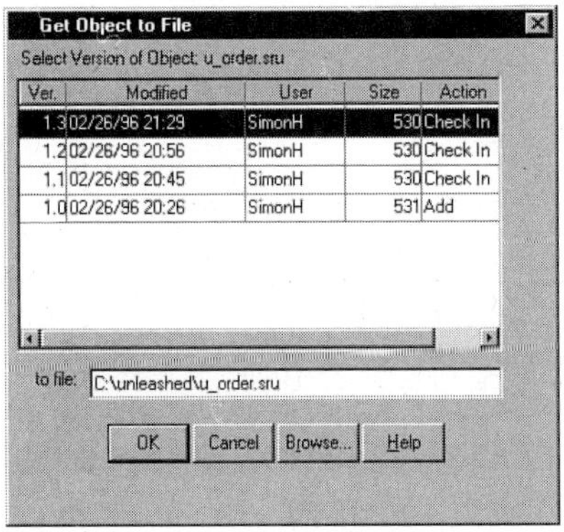

FIGURE 20.21.
The Get Object to File dialog box.

From this dialog box you can select a specific version and have the exported version of the object saved to a file. Once this is done, the exported object can be imported via the Library painter.

To overlay an existing object in the ObjectCycle repository with a different version of the object, select the object, right-click, and choose Put from the pop-up menu. Selecting this menu item opens the Put Object From File dialog box (see Figure 20.22).

Select the path of the exported object syntax that you wish to import into the ObjectCycle database, specify a description, and click OK. This moves the selected exported object syntax into the database as the current version.

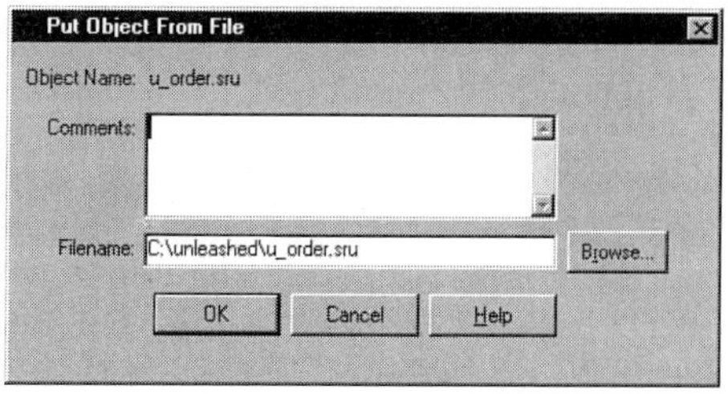

FIGURE 20.22.
The Put Object From File dialog box.

WARNING

The Get and Put options are not tracked as part of the object's version history and can only be performed by the administrator. These are destructive actions and are therefore potentially dangerous.

The Get and Put functions allow you to easily remove/insert objects to and from the ObjectCycle database without having to create new version labels.

ObjectCycle provides a tight interface into PowerBuilder via the Library painter and uses a different approach than many other version control software products by using a centralized database to store your application's objects.

ENDEVOR

The ENDEVOR product is produced by Legent Corporation and controls PowerBuilder objects within a repository controlled by ENDEVOR Workstation. The ENDEVOR interface requires the following software versions and disk space:

- ENDEVOR Workstation Release 5.2.2 or 5.2.3
- PowerBuilder 3.0 or greater
- At least 850KB available disk space

Powersoft and Legent provide integrated support, with Powersoft handling any problems that occur once the interface is installed.

ENDEVOR offers the following features:

- Automatic inventory
- Change and configuration management
- Release management for development and maintenance
- Compression of versions
- Source code merging with conflict notification

- Comprehensive reporting
- Security classes for users to manage developer privileges to code

You should not make any changes to PowerBuilder objects in the ENDEVOR Workstation program because this will corrupt the information being maintained.

SE/Open

LBMS (Learmonth and Burchette Management Systems) is probably one of the best-known CASE tool vendors in the industry, and its System Engineer (SE) product provides a number of interlinked components that can be used independently. One of these, SE/Open, integrates with PowerBuilder to provide version control, and provides the following features:

- A bidirectional link between the SE repository and PowerBuilder extended attributes
- A reuse management feature
- Reporting and impact analysis
- Access control to objects and administrative functions

These facilities are provided through the Library Service Application (LSA), with the PowerBuilder objects being stored in the SE/Repository. It is through the SE/Repository that SE/Open monitors the changes you make to an object. The PowerBuilder objects are stored as SE general forms along with the real PowerBuilder object image. Different SE general forms are created for the different PowerBuilder objects, and this is the representation used in the Systems Engineer product. This allows you to associate PowerBuilder objects with other SE/Repository objects such as requirement documents or data entities.

SE/Repository can also be used to carry out configuration control, which allows baselines to be archived, reported, promoted, demoted, and exported.

PVCS Version Manager

PVCS Version Manager from Intersolv has gained a large share of the version control market within the PC environment and is one of the most commonly used interfaces in PowerBuilder.

The PVCS interface has the following functionality:

- Registering objects
- Checking objects in and out
- Retrieving earlier revisions of objects
- Running reports
- Rebuilding earlier releases of your application
- Assigning version labels to your objects
- Creating a new release of your application

- Synchronizing your objects with PVCS archives
- Clearing object-registration status
- Clearing an object's checked-out status
- Viewing a list of objects that are checked out

PVCS tracks your changes within its archive and allows you to recover your PowerBuilder objects from disasters. Each time an object is checked into PVCS, it is assigned a new revision level. Version labels are assigned to groups of objects to indicate a particular phase in your project's life cycle.

Carrying Out Application Upgrades

The task of upgrading an existing system can be a very involved process, and a sound plan is a definite requirement. The following list provides a guide to the questions you need to address in your planned upgrade:

- Is the target group relatively small?
- Do you have physical access to the machines?
- Is the application run from a LAN, a WAN, or locally?
- How frequently will you be updating files?
- Where are the various files located?

For small groups of users that have physically accessible machines, there is nothing to stop you from carrying out an upgrade using a floppy disk carried to each machine. This does have a drawback if the machines are "diskless" workstations, if there is a corporate antivirus policy, or if you are updating a large number of files.

For large groups of users or large updates, you need to consider an automated approach to file distribution. There are a number of factors that you must also consider with this approach:

- The network connection is lost during an upgrade.
- The client or server machine fails during upgrade.
- The destination drive runs out of space.
- A file is already in use on the client machine.
- Your automated distribution program fails.

WARNING

If the application is currently running, the EXE and PBD files are "in use" by the operating system and cannot be replaced. Be careful that you do not get a partial upgrade of only some of the PBD or DLL files.

The following sections detail some suggested methods for upgrade distribution.

Auto-Update at Login

The first thing a user does upon arriving at work in the morning is turn on his or her computer and log in to the file server. This provides an ideal opportunity to copy new files to the desired location, because the user will rarely have any of the files being upgraded in use. The automation is simply an extension to the file server login batch file—to call a batch file or DOS program that you supply to make the copy. This will usually be transparent to the user, and the user will often not mind if takes a little longer to log in.

This approach does have some drawbacks, though. For example, not all users log on and off each day. Most times the user will log in only once per day and this will prevent you from carrying out incremental upgrades during the day.

Manual Update by the User

With this method you provide the user an icon on the desktop or a button on a toolbar that sits right next to the one the user uses to start the PowerBuilder applications you have deployed. Selecting this option causes a custom program to copy all updated files to the client area. This has the advantage of being accessible all day to the user. Update notices can either be e-mailed or broadcast from a file server. You could even make your PowerBuilder applications sensitive to an update situation and display a message box during an application `Idle` event.

Auto-Sensing by Application

During the `Open` event of an application, the application checks for either the existence of a program file or records in a certain database table. When the application detects that there is an update pending, it can then carry out one of three options.

- Inform the user to carry out a manual requested upgrade.
- Auto-load another Windows program to carry out the operation.
- Auto-generate a BAT file that can then be executed or used the next time the user logs in.

It should be obvious that if you go for the second option, it cannot be written using PowerBuilder because this will cause those files to be in use!

Third-Party Tools

You can use a third-party tool to take away the strain of upgrades. The most obvious choice at the moment is the Microsoft System Management Server (SMS). This allows you to carry out maintenance releases of your PowerBuilder application along with releases of other commercial packages, drivers, and so on.

Powersoft has also upgraded the PBSETUP program previously available; it is now a commercial program called InstallBuilder. There are a number of other installation builders available, and these types of programs are rarely application-language specific, and can be used for the installation of many types of files.

Upgrading PowerBuilder Itself

Powersoft has committed itself to a version release followed by three maintenance releases each year. Within the maintenance releases, Powersoft generally changes a number of the DLLs, and with each new version number, all the DLLs are released with new names. As your development team starts to use the new DLLs, you will need to start planning for your end user deployment of the same DLLs.

PowerBuilder DLLs are generally upward compatible, which means that your existing EXE and PBD files will work with the new DLLs. You should not totally rely on this; recompilation of EXE and PBD files is always a wise precaution.

Files generated using new DLLs are nearly never backward compatible, and as soon as your development team produces a release using upgraded DLLs, you should upgrade the end users' DLLs in one fell swoop.

Summary

This chapter shows why version control and release management need to be an integral part of a serious development effort. The three main version control products available for direct use with PowerBuilder are briefly introduced, along with suggested methods of application upgrade deployment.

Cross-Platform PowerBuilder

21

IN THIS CHAPTER

Today's businesses have a number of different hardware options. Therefore, many M.I.S. departments are facing the dilemma of creating applications that run on a number of different platforms. Since most software is created specifically for a particular environment (for example, Macintosh or Windows), M.I.S. must build multiple applications using different software for each of the required platforms. Another alternative is to convert all users to the same hardware system. Either resolution results in considerable cost for the company in either hardware or software. The need for development to occur across multiple platforms is usually a difficult undertaking that requires you to fall back to a language such as C++ and the cross-platform libraries available for it.

With the release of PowerBuilder Version 4.0, Powersoft gave us the ability to create PowerBuilder applications on a variety of platforms. PowerBuilder currently has the ability to run in Windows 3.*x*, Windows 95, Windows NT, Windows for pen computing, Macintosh, and UNIX Motif. This gives the developer the ultimate in flexibility. A developer needs to learn only one tool (PowerBuilder) and can use that tool to develop applications for multiple environments.

This chapter takes a look at the different platforms PowerBuilder runs on and the different approaches used for each of the platforms. In addition to each platform, the chapter gives examples of some coding techniques you can use to develop code that can be used across platforms.

PowerBuilder Platforms

The idea of the cross-platform functionality of PowerBuilder is to give the developer the ability to create an application in one environment (for example, Windows 3.11) and deploy the application to all of his users, regardless of the operating system being used. Also, two or more developers can work on the same PowerBuilder library files (PBLs) at the same time and use different platforms (for example, one Macintosh and one Windows developer). Once the application has been created, the executable must be created in its planned runtime environment (for example, Macintosh). The next sections examine each of the platforms and some of the specifics of working with each.

PowerBuilder's advanced object library and source manager introduce binary-format compatibility across multiple operating platforms. This allows teams of developers to share PowerBuilder objects and libraries with other PowerBuilder applications in a multiplatform environment that includes Intel-based Windows and Windows NT, DEC Alpha Windows NT, and Apple Macintosh. This allows developers to build a single application, deploy it across a heterogeneous environment, and provide users with a look and feel that complies with their native environment.

Windows 3.x

The most common of the PowerBuilder platforms is the first operating system PowerBuilder ran under. PowerBuilder has been a Windows 3.*x* product since its conception. Currently, most developers use this platform to create their applications. It is the most well-documented operating system for use with PowerBuilder, and Windows 3.1 and 3.11 are currently the industry standards for IBM-compatible PCs.

Windows 3.*x* implements an interface known as Program Manager that uses icons to represent applications. You launch an application by double-clicking on the appropriate icon. The most prevalent interface style in Windows 3.*x* is the multiple-document interface (MDI). MDI-style applications provide a means of handling several related windows (or documents) using a combination of menus and toolbars within the confines of a frame window. PowerBuilder is an example of an MDI application, as is the Program Manager itself. Several other application components that are available in Windows are object linking and embedding, dynamic data exchange, wizards, tooltips, pop-up menus, and access to the Windows 16-bit API function set.

Windows NT

Windows NT is Microsoft's server and high-powered workstation operating system. It provides multitasking and access to a 32-bit API. PowerBuilder for NT looks almost identical to the Windows 3.*x* version of PowerBuilder, and the application design approach should be the same.

Windows NT does have some special considerations (besides the 32-bit API access) that set it apart from Windows 3.*x*:

- NT does not support the pen computing API.
- Hardware usually must be upgraded to run NT because NT requires additional memory, more hard drive space, and so on.
- Some of the common Windows 3.*x* shortcut keys have different meanings under NT and should be avoided (for example, Ctrl+Alt+Del in Windows 3.*x* will reboot the PC, but in NT, Ctrl+Alt+Del opens a dialog with a number of options, one of which allows you to lock/unlock the workstation).

Windows 95

Windows 95 is the latest release from Microsoft in the Windows product family. In Windows 95 PowerBuilder acts almost exactly as it does in previous releases of Windows. There are some differences, though:

- Program Manager has been replaced with the Start Menu and TaskBar.

- Many of the controls used in PowerBuilder have a slightly different look and feel (the 3D look is very prevalent). New controls include progress indicators, trees, sliders, and rich text edit controls. The tab control was introduced in Windows 3.*x*, but is now a Windows 95 standard. Tab pages are used in property sheets to indicate settings for various objects.
- Microsoft has stated that the MDI common in Windows 3.*x* is considered a thing of the past because it does not conform to the new Windows 95 document-centric paradigm (although it has continued to be used in some of Microsoft's Office products). The new approach relies heavily on the use of OLE in your application development to create compound documents.
- The Windows help interface is significantly different and makes heavy use of context-sensitive help in the form of the What's This help menu.
- Pop-up menus as well as cascading menus are used throughout Windows 95, which makes it difficult to navigate without a mouse.
- The use of the Recycle Bin as a recovery area for deleted files affects file access applications. Files support the universal naming conventions (UNCs), which removes the limitation of the 8.3 filename.
- With Windows 95 you have access to the Windows 32-bit API.

The Microsoft product line design guide recommended reading is *The Windows Interface Guidelines for Software Design,* by Microsoft Press.

Macintosh

Apple's Macintosh line is the major desktop competitor to the different Microsoft Windows operating systems. The interface is similar to Windows 95, but the Macintosh uses a different architecture. PowerBuilder for the Mac has been based on the Apple Shared Library Manager (ASLM), which is similar to Windows's dynamic link libraries (DLLs). PowerBuilder for the Mac supports AppleScripts and automatic mapping of keys.

When designing an interface for the Mac, there are several things you must watch out for if you are currently a Windows developer:

- There is no tabbing between controls (other than edits) on a Mac.
- Application menus appear on the desktop. All applications share this desktop. This means that the MDI style behaves differently. A frame does not confine the sheets to its border.
- The mouse for the Mac has only one button. Therefore, there is no right mouse button functionality.

- You should be careful when deciding on keyboard commands. Not all the Mac keyboards have function keys, so you should avoid using them. Keyboard shortcuts should use the Mac command keys and not Ctrl and should also not use reserved command keys (such as Command+? for help).
- TrueType fonts should be used if possible so that the interpretation of fonts from one platform to another is minimized. To ensure that your application fonts are interpreted correctly on both the Mac and in Windows, it is recommended that you use AccuFonts. The following list displays the suggested AccuFonts and the recommended font sizes for cross-platform development:

PC Font	*Equivalent Mac Font*	*Point Size*
Accuat	Athens	18
Accuca	Cairo	18
Accushi	Chicago	12
Accujen	Geneva	9, 10, 12, 14, 18
Accula	Las Angeles	12
Accumo	Mobile	18
Accumon	Monaco	9, 10, 12
Accuny	New York	9, 10, 12, 14, 18
Password		12
Accusf	San Francisco	18
Accusm	Symbol	10, 12, 14, 18
		On the Macintosh, Symbol 12 point has a larger line height than 14 point; otherwise, character for character, Accusm matches Apple's Symbol font.
Accuve	Venice	12, 14

Do not use DDE, Windows API calls, and VBX controls because they are not supported on the Mac.

For more information on GUI design for the Mac, see *Human Interface Guidelines: The Apple Desktop Interface* by Apple Computer, Inc.

PowerBuilder also supports the use of AppleScripts in your applications via the `DoScript()` PowerScript function. `DoScript()` takes two string arguments: one indicating the AppleScript to be run and the second for any text that is returned from the script. The string indicating the script to be run can be one of three different options: the script text, the name of the file containing the script text (file type `TEXT`), or the name of the file containing the compiled script (file type `OSAS`). `DoScript()` returns an integer, with `0` indicating success and `-1` indicating failure.

NOTE

`DoScript()` can be used only with AppleScripts that have not been saved as applications. You must use the `Run()` function to execute these scripts.

The minimum system requirements for PowerBuilder for the Macintosh are

- 68030 or 68040 processor or PowerMac running in 68020 emulation mode Apple System Software 7.5.1
- 24MB of RAM (This can be accomplished by using Connectix's RAM Doubler (one copy is shipped with PowerBuilder for the Mac) with 12MB of RAM)
- 20MB of disk space for PowerBuilder and SQL Anywhere

UNIX Motif

PowerBuilder for UNIX was created to exploit the raw processing power of RISC technology that gives the developer extremely high throughput of data from server to client. PowerBuilder for UNIX provides a 32-bit development platform. It provides scalability and security often needed in a large, complex, and computation-intensive application. PowerBuilder for UNIX uses an extended Motif GUI environment including multiple screen displays.

The minimum system requirements are

- Sun Solaris 2.4 for Sparc
- X Window System X11R5
- Motif 1.2.3
- 16MB RAM
- 40MB swap space
- 45MB hard disk space

A good source for more information on UNIX Motif design is the *Motif Style Guide* by Open Software Foundation.

Building Cross-Platform Applications

Before you can create an application, you need to identify which platforms the users and developers will have access to. The difficulty in writing a cross-platform application is designing it so that it takes advantage of each different platform and complies to the standard behavior of the common applications for that environment.

Since your interface should comply with the standards for each environment, you will have to keep these in mind as you build the application. A very simple example is that in Windows, most applications have an Exit menu item under the File menu option. For a Macintosh, there is a Quit menu option under File. These subtle differences must be considered because they will be immediately obvious (and possibly confusing) to the end user.

Since each environment has its own special behavior and coding techniques, you might be tempted to create several different applications and deploy a different version of the same application to each platform. This would defeat the whole purpose of PowerBuilder's cross-platform capability. The next section addresses how to code one application so that it can dynamically incorporate the functionality required for each platform.

The Environment Object

Coding a multiplatform application depends on a PowerBuilder structure that gives you the ability to get information about the platform your application is running on. The `Environment` object has the following variables defined for it:

Variable	*Data Type*	*Values*	*Description*
`PBType`	PbTypes	`Desktop!` `Enterprise!`	Version of PowerBuilder product
`PBMajorRevision`	Int		Major version of PB
`PBMinorRevision`	Int		Minor version of PB
`PBFixesRevision`	Int		Maintenance version of PB

`OSType`	OsTypes	`AIX!`
		`HPUX!`
		`Macintosh!`
		`OSF1!`
		`SOL!`
		`Windows!`
		`WindowsNT!`
			Operating system or environment

`OSMajorRevision`	Int		Major version of operating system
`OSMinorRevision`	Int		Minor version of operating system
`OSFixesRevision`	Int		Maintenance version of operating system

continues

Variable	*Data Type*	*Values*	*Description*

`CPUType`	CpuTypes	`Alpha!`
		`Hppa!`
		`I286!`
		`I386!`
		`I486!`
		`M68000!`
		`M68020!`
		`M68030!`
		`M68040!`
		`Mips!`
		`Pentium!`
		`Powerpc!`
		`RS6000!`
		`Sparc!`
			CPU

`ScreenWidth`	Long		Width of the screen in pixels
`ScreenHeight`	Long		Height of the screen in pixels
`NumberOfColors`	Long		Number of colors on the screen (for example, 16 or 256)

Once an environment object has been declared, you need to populate the structure with values. This is done using the `GetEnvironment()` function. `GetEnvironment()` takes the name of your newly declared environment object as an argument. The function returns an integer, `1` for success and `-1` for failure. Once the function has been successfully called, you will want to evaluate the environment object's attributes to determine what processing you want to occur.

The next three sections deal with some common situations you might encounter when working in a multiplatform environment. Each section details a script that can be incorporated into a custom class user object for use with all your applications. In these examples, the user object example is implemented with an environment instance variable declared; it is called `i_Environment`. For more information on user objects, see Chapter 24, "Building User Objects."

Using an API Class User Object

If your application is designed to use API calls, it is a good idea to create a custom class user object called `u_n_externals`. This user object is the ancestor for each of your operating-system–specific API user objects (for example, `u_n_external_winapi` for Windows 3.*x* and `u_n_external_win32` for Windows 95 and NT). Depending on the operating system under which your PowerBuilder application is running, you will want to instantiate the appropriate API user object for that environment. The code in Listing 21.1 uses a user object instance variable—`externals`—of type `u_n_externals`.

Listing 21.1. Private subroutine `uf_SetEnvironment()`.

```
GetEnvironment(i_Environment)
Choose Case i_Environment.OSType
   Case Windows!
      Choose Case i_Environment.OSMinorRevision
         Case 4
            externals = Create u_n_externals_win32
         Case Else
            externals = Create u_n_externals_winapi
      End Choose
   Case WindowsNT!
      externals = Create u_n_externals_win32
   Case Else
      SetNull(externals)
End Choose
```

The Dynamic Library Search Path

Since one of the complexities of application development on multiple platforms is creating objects that take full advantage of the environment's functionality and appearance, it is often necessary to create different copies of the same object. As seen in the API user object example, you can use inheritance to assist in building your objects. Unfortunately, this is not always possible. Once you have developed your platform-specific objects, you most likely will maintain that platform's objects in their own library file (in other words, one PBL per platform).

Each library file would be specified in the library search path for your application (for example, common.pbl, windows.pbl, mac.pbl, unix.pbl). PowerBuilder uses the order in the search path to find objects requested by your application. If an object is located in the PBL listed last in the search path, PowerBuilder looks through all the other PBLs before looking in the last one. If you are using platform-specific objects that have the same name as other objects, you will always use the object first found in the library list. Therefore, you would never use any of your platform-specific objects.

This is also fine if you do not use objects in the last PBL very often. If you do need the objects in the last PBL often, your performance will be affected because all library files must be searched first. This would be true for the example if you needed objects from the Mac or UNIX PBLs. Therefore, performance would be fine for those people requiring objects from the windows.pbl, but users on different platforms would notice a slight performance degradation.

Most likely you would create a dynamic library (either PBD or DLL) for each PBL, and PowerBuilder would maintain the library search path for the dynamic libraries, which would affect the runtime environment as well as development. To alleviate this problem, you could deploy several different executables, each with a different search path defined. This would not be particularly efficient. A different approach would be to dynamically modify the library search path for your application using the function `SetLibraryList()`.

`SetLibraryList()`, a function of the application object, accepts a comma-separated list of dynamic libraries and uses this list to search for specified objects. This function will give you the ability to change the search path at runtime depending on the environment of the user.

To implement this functionality, you could hard code the dynamic library list into your application, but that would result in a new executable being created if you changed the library list. A better approach would be to create a function in a custom class user object that is instantiated in your application object. The best method of maintaining this list would be to place it in a table in your database. Then, based on the user's environment, read the table and assign the appropriate library order to the application. The idea is that only the table needs to be changed and the code can remain generic. You could also do this by reading information in from an INI file.

However the dynamic library list is maintained, the user object function in Listing 21.2 can be used to dynamically build the library search path. The application user object has an instance variable, `i_application`, of type `application` that is initialized to the current application object.

Listing 21.2. Public subroutine `uf_LibraryList()` in `u_n_application`.

```
string ls_libpath, ls_environ, ls_appname

//Populate the environment variable
GetEnvironment(i_environment)

//Get Application Name
ls_appname = GetApplication().AppName

Choose Case i_environment.OSType
   Case Windows!
      ls_environ = "WIN"
   Case WindowsNT!
      ls_environ = "NT"
   Case Macintosh!
      ls_environ = "MAC"
   Case Else  //Catch all for UNIX box
      ls_environ = "UNIX"
End Choose

SELECT libpath INTO :ls_libpath
FROM library
WHERE environ = :ls_environ
AND AppName = :ls_appname;

i_AppName.SetLibraryList(ls_libpath)
```

This function should be called from the `Open` event of your application object before any other objects are referenced so that the correct PBDs are placed at the top of the library search path.

Screen Width and Height

One problem of moving across platforms and even within the same platform is the resolution of the user's monitor. Applications should be developed using the least common denominator in terms of the resolution. If one of your users is running 640×480, the application should be developed for a 640×480 environment. If this is not done (for example, the application is developed for 800×600), objects may be too large and therefore cut off in a 640×480 display. The problem is that applications developed in lower resolutions will have windows appear in the upper-left corner of any higher-resolution environments. This produces a strange-looking application. The font is very important to the appearance of the window in this type of adjustment. You should use the AccuFonts mentioned in the "Macintosh" section earlier in the chapter. To see the code that can be used to center a window for different resolutions, see Chapter 33, "API Calls."

Menu Modification

One subtle difference between Windows and the Macintosh is that the word for the menu item to leave the application is Exit in Windows and Quit on the Mac. You need to consider the difference in interface design, and the code in Listing 21.3 gives you a base function to work from. The function, `wf_SetExitText()`, accepts an argument of type `m_ancestor`, which is the ancestor menu for all menus in your application.

Listing 21.3. Public window function `wf_SetExitText()`.

```
//Arguments: menu_id m_ancestor
//Returns: none

Environment l_environ

GetEnvironment (l_environ)

// Change menu "Exit" to "Quit" if on Mac
if l_environ.OSType = Windows! then
   menu_id.m_file.m_exit.text = "E&xit"
elseif l_environ.OSType = Macintosh! then
   menu_id.m_file.m_exit.text = "Quit"
end if
```

The code that calls this function should be placed in the window `Open` event and look something like this:

```
wf_SetExitText(this.menuid)
```

This assumes that the menu associated with the window has been inherited from `m_ancestor`.

TIP

An alternative method for achieving the same results is to use the Type option in the Menu painter or reference the `MenuItemType` attribute of the menu. It allows you to indicate that a menu object (for example, the Exit menu) is to be displayed differently depending on the platform. In the case of the Exit menu, specify a value of `MenuItemTypeExit!` for the `MenuItemType` attribute, which converts the text to Quit on the Macintosh platform.

Windows for Pen Computing

PowerBuilder also gives you the capability to make your applications pen aware, that is, recognize a computer pen input device. This is implemented using a library of PowerBuilder functions and windows called PBPenLib, which enables you to create an application that can run on a standard PC or on a hand-held pen computer. The hand-held computer must be running Microsoft Windows for Pen Computing Version 1.0.

PBPenLib enables you to include standard pen-computing functionality such as boxed edits, notes, and signature boxes in your application. To do this, you use several different user objects in PBPENLIB.PBL that encapsulate functionality to access Windows for Pen Computing. These user objects access the Windows for Pen Computing API, PENWIN.DLL. The external functions that call PENWIN.DLL can process both on the pen-computing device and on a standard PC. On a PC, the functions will not do anything. This enables you to have an application that runs on both machines and can take advantage of the pen device if it is used.

To use the user objects in PBPENLIB.PBL in your application, you must declare two global variables, one of type `uo_PBPenFunc` and a Boolean variable used to determine whether the application is running on a pen-computing device. In your application `Open` event, create an instance of the `uo_PBPenFunc` global variable (`guo_PBPenFunc`) as follows:

```
guo_PBPenFunc = CREATE uo_PBPenFunc
```

To make the application pen aware, call the `uf_Enable()` function in the user object `uo_PBPenFunc` and capture the return value in the Boolean global variable `gb_PenAware` declared earlier, as follows:

```
gb_PenAware = guo_PBPenFunc.uf_Enable()
```

The variable `gb_PenAware` can be used to determine which parts of your system will be used (pen computing or not).

Although this makes your application pen enabled, there is much more that needs to be incorporated. There are several design issues that you must consider to fully take advantage of the pen-computing device's features:

- Do not have multiple windows open. (They are difficult to handle with a pen.)
- Minimize text entry.
- Provide large handwriting areas.
- Leave ink when writing to provide feedback to your user.

These are just a few considerations in addition to deciding which controls can be enhanced by replacing them with the user objects in the PBPENLIB.PBL.

As the number of pen-computing devices increases, the sophistication and completeness with which PowerBuilder can create an application that runs on a PC and a pen computer will increase. The user objects PowerBuilder provides give you an easy way to make your application pen aware.

The System Registry

The Windows operating systems maintain a hierarchical database to store application information such as file associations and hardware and software configurations. This database is referred to as the Windows Registry and is accessed by the Registration Editor.

In Windows 3.*x* the Registry database mainly stores file associations and relies on the SYSTEM.INI and WIN.INI files to store application and hardware configurations. In Windows NT and Windows 95, the INI file information has been transferred to the Registry, thus increasing the Registry's importance and the need for developers to access the information stored within it.

In the Windows 3.*x* environment, many PowerBuilder applications utilize INI files to store system and user configurations. The INI files are accessed via several PowerScript functions such as `ProfileString()`. In the 32-bit Windows environments, the information previously stored in INI files should be maintained in the Registry.

The Registry database organizes information in a hierarchical format that is composed of keys. A key is an element within the Registry and each key is a subkey of the parent key above it in the database hierarchy. There are several predefined root keys supplied, such as `HKEY_CLASSES_ROOT`, `HKEY_CURRENT_USER`, `HKEY_LOCAL_MACHINE`, and `HKEY_USERS`. Each key is separated by slashes. The key to a field within the Registry database looks like a DOS pathname and can be treated as a path to a particular database entry. For example, the connection information for the Powersoft Demo database might be stored in `HKEY_CURRENT_USER\Software\Powersoft\PowerBuilder\Code Examples\sqlca`.

For a specific key, there are typically one or more entries referred to as value names (such as database or DBMS in the previous example). There are two types of value names that can be specified: one unnamed value name and multiple named value names. A value can be associated with each value name or with just the key. In Window 3.*x* there are no value names, only keys with their corresponding values.

PowerBuilder 5.0 provides several new functions that allow you to access and modify the Windows Registry.

NOTE

While the Registry is recommended for the 32-bit environment, it is not required. Many applications, including PowerBuilder, use both the Registry and INI files for backward compatibility and for those platforms that do not support the 32-bit Registry.

TIP

An alternative to using the PowerBuilder 5.0 functions is to call the underlying Windows functions. The can be useful if you need additional functionality/flexibility or have not migrated to PowerBuilder 5.0. For more information on the API calls, see Chapter 33.

RegistryGet()

`RegistryGet()` is used to extract a value from the Windows Registry. The syntax is

```
RegistryGet(Key, ValueName, ValueVariable)
```

`Key` is a string that identifies the key in the registry from which you want to extract the value. *`ValueName`* is a string indicating the value name within a key from which the desired information is stored. If you want to extract the value for an unnamed value name for a key, specify an empty string. *`ValueVariable`* is a string in which the retrieved value is stored. `RegistryGet()` returns `1` if successful and `-1` to indicate failure. The Registry can store string, numeric, and binary values. `RegistryGet()` converts numbers to strings and returns `-1` if the value retrieved is a binary value.

Here's an example using `RegistryGet()`:

```
String ls_key, ls_database
Int li_rtn

ls_Key =  "HKEY_CURRENT_USER\Software\Powersoft\PowerBuilder\Code Examples\sqlca"

li_rtn = RegistryGet( ls_key, "database", ls_database)
```

```
If li_rtn = 1 Then
   SQLCA.Database = ls_database
End If
```

For Windows 3.*x*, an empty string is always specified for `ValueName`.

RegistrySet()

`RegistrySet()` is used to modify values and/or add keys to the Registry. This is the syntax:

```
RegistrySet( Key, ValueName, Value)
```

`Key` and `ValueName` are the same as `RegistryGet()` and `Value` is a string containing the value to be placed into the Registry.

NOTE

The value placed in the Registry by the `RegistrySet()` function is always a string!

If the `ValueName` specified does not exist in the Registry, the new name is created and the value specified is stored. `RegistrySet()` returns an integer, with `1` indicating success and `-1` indicating failure.

RegistryDelete()

`RegistryDelete()` is used to delete a value for an entry or a key if no value is specified. This is the syntax:

```
RegistryDelete( Key, ValueName)
```

`Key` is the path to the desired registry key and `ValueName` is the name of the entry that you want to delete. This function removes the value and the value name. If you want to delete a key, specify the `Key` argument and pass an empty string in `ValueName`.

RegistryValues()

`RegistryValues()` is used to extract all the value names beneath a specified key. The following is the syntax:

```
RegistryValues( Key, ValueName[])
```

`Key` is a string containing the path of the desired Registry key of which you want to determine all the value names. `ValueName[]` is a string array that is used to store all the value names found for the specified `Key`. The array can be specified with an upper boundary or can be unbounded. If a fixed array is used, the upper bound should be high enough to incorporate all the value names found. `RegistryValues()` returns an integer, with `1` indicating success and `-1` indicating failure.

RegistryKeys()

While the `RegistryValues()` function returns the value names underneath a particular key, the `RegistryKeys()` function is used to determine the subkeys beneath a specified key. This is the syntax:

```
RegistryKeys( Key, SubKeys[])
```

Key is a string indicating the parent key for which you want to extract the subkeys. *SubKeys[]* is a string array (fixed or dynamic) that stores the names of the subkeys under the specified *Key*.

NOTE

The *SubKeys[]* argument only contains the names of the keys directly below the specified *Key*. Any subkeys further down the hierarchy are not part of the returned string array.

`RegistryKeys()` returns an integer, with `1` indicating success and `-1` a failure.

Summary

The need for a front-end development that crosses multiple platforms has been answered by PowerBuilder 5.0. With support for the Microsoft suite, the Macintosh, and UNIX Motif, PowerBuilder gives developers the ability to use the same product to develop applications that can be run on and take advantage of each platform. With the incorporation of the environment object, PowerBuilder allows you to modify your application at runtime to access each platform-specific object.

PART IV

Advanced PowerBuilding

IN THIS PART

Standards and Naming Conventions

22

IN THIS CHAPTER

Having standards for coding and conventions for naming objects and variables is as important for individuals as it is for team projects. Standards and naming conventions provide the following benefits:

- Objects and variables have consistent names.
- You can easily determine what an object is or where a variable is defined.
- Scripts have the same look.
- Scripts are easily maintainable.
- Objects and applications are easily maintainable.

The learning time required for a set of standards is small when you consider the advantages of their application over the life of the application and future applications.

PowerBuilder allows up to 40 characters for an *identifier* (an object or a variable name).

NOTE

The 40-character limit on identifiers is the value stated in the PowerBuilder online help, but you can declare an identifier of 99 characters before you get a compile error. Of course, it is unlikely that you would ever use 40 characters, let alone 99!

This chapter is broken into three sections for three types of standards and conventions. The first type is from the Powersoft manuals (even though Powersoft doesn't follow it very closely itself). The next two are from client projects that we have worked on. Each has something to add to the arguments about naming conventions, and you can pull a little from each and decide on your own.

The most common technique used in naming items is to use a prefix in the names of objects and variables that varies depending on the type of object, access level, and scope.

Powersoft Conventions

As mentioned previously, even though Powersoft has declared a set of standards and conventions, it has failed to follow them in code examples and online help. Powersoft has promised to define a clear set of conventions that it will use in all its sample code in future releases of PowerBuilder.

With PowerBuilder 5.0, Powersoft has introduced the PowerBuilder Foundation Class (PFC). As part of this effort, a set of naming standards has been put together and is available for your use. Tables 22.1, 22.2, and 22.3 detail the Powersoft suggested naming guidelines and are taken from the online help available for PFC.

Table 22.1. Object naming in PFC.

Class	*Prefix*	*Example*
Application	(none)	quickstart
DataWindow	d_	d_authors
Function	f_	f_get_symbol
Menu	m_	m_system
NonVisualObject	n_	n_book
Pipeline	pl_	pl_finance_refresh
Project	pr_	pr_quickstart
Query	q_	q_delivery_codes
Structure	s_	s_person
UserObject	u_	u_security
Window	w_	w_library

Table 22.2. Data type naming in PFC.

Data Type	*Prefix*	*Example*
Application	app_	app_myapp
Connection	cn_	cn_orders
ConnectionInfo	cninfo_	cninfo_orderusers
ConnectObject	cno_	cno_orders
DataStore	ds_	ds_servicereplist
DataWindow	dw_	dw_orders
DataWindowChild	dwc_	dwc_ordertype
DragObject	drg_	drg_anorder
DrawObject	drw_	drw_object
Dwobject	dwo_	dwo_dynamic
DynamicDescriptionArea	dda_	dda_mine
DynamicStagingArea	dsa_	dsa_mine
Environment	env_	env_mine
Error	err_	err_mine
ExtObject	ext_	ext_object

continues

Table 22.2. continued

Data Type	*Prefix*	*Example*
GraphicObject	`go_`	`go_current`
GrAxis	`grax_`	`grax_x`
GrDispAttr	`grda_`	`grda_attribute1`
ListViewItem	`lvi_`	`lvi_item`
MailFileDescription	`mfd_`	`mfd_attach1`
MailMessage	`mm_`	`mm_memo`
MailRecipient	`mr_`	`mr_to`
MailSession	`ms_`	`ms_error`
MdiClient	`mdi_`	`mdi_1`
Menu	`m_`	`m_frame`
Menucascade	`mc_`	`mc_edit`
Message	`msg_`	`msg_mine`
NonVisualObject	`nv_`	`nv_controller`
OleControl	`oc_`	`oc_clip`
OleObject	`oo_`	`oo_clip`
OleStorage	`ostg_`	`ostg_1`
OleStream	`ostm_`	`ostm_1`
OmControl	`omc_`	`omc_1`
OmCustomControl	`omcc_`	`omcc_1`
OmEmbedded control	`omec_`	`omec_1`
OmObject	`omo_`	`omo_1`
OmStream	`omstm_`	`omstm_1`
OmStorage	`omstg_`	`omstg_1`
Pipeline	`pl_`	`pl_transfer`
PowerObject	`po_`	`po_object`
RemoteObject	`rem_`	`rem_object`
RteObject	`rteo_`	`rteo_memo`
Structure	`str_`	`str_bagvalues`
TabPage	`tabpg_`	`tabpg_1`
Transaction	`tr_`	`tr_ordercursor`
Transport	`trp_`	`trp_mine`
TreeViewItem	`tvi_`	`tvi_item`

Data Type	*Prefix*	*Example*
UserObject	`uo_`	`uo_object`
WindowObject	`wo_`	`wo_object`
Window	`w_`	`w_frame`
Any	`a_`	`a_current`
Blob	`blb_`	`blb_word_doc`
Boolean	`b_`	`b_isselected`
Character	`ch_`	`ch_gender`
Date	`d_`	`d_payday`
DateTime	`dtm_`	`dt_logged_at`
Decimal	`dec_`	`dec_pi`
Double	`dbl_`	`dbl_result`
Enumerated (any type)	`enum_`	`enum_alignment`
Integer	`i_`	`i_count`
Long	`l_`	`l_row`
Real	`r_`	`r_fudge`
String	`s_`	`s_name`
Time	`tm_`	`tm_now`
UnsignedInteger	`ui_`	`ui_count`
UnsignedLong	`ul_`	`ul_count`
Custom	`cst_`	`cst_object`
External	`ext_`	`ext_object`
C++	`cpp_`	`cpp_object`

Table 22.3. Variable scope in PFC.

Variable or Function	*Scope Qualifier*	*Example*
Argument	`a`	`as_title`
Global	`g`	`gnv_app`
Instance	`i`	`ii_count`
Local	`l`	`ll_row`
Shared/Class	`s`	`si_height`

Object-level functions in PFC are all prefixed with of_ regardless of what type of object they are defined in. This is also true of structures that are prefixed with os_. User-defined events are prefixed with pfc_.

Single spaces are placed before and after all operators and the assignment verb (=), and after each comma in a function parameter list.

Tabs rather than spaces should be used to indent code to show inclusion in loops and other compound statements.

Function calls are coded in both upper- and lowercase. Variables are all lowercase.

Project B Conventions

As you can see from the previous section, Powersoft did not go to any great lengths to detail standard naming or coding conventions. Tables 22.4, 22.5, and 22.6 show the conventions we have used on a real-life project and provide a more complete and robust set of standards that you can follow.

Table 22.4. Object naming conventions in Project B.

Type	*Prefix*	*Example*
Application	(none)	order_entry
Application function	af_	af_CloseDown()
Application structure	as_	as_OpenWindows
Window	w_	w_frame
Window function	wf_	wf_SaveOrder()
Window structure	ws_	ws_order
Menu	m_	m_frame
Menu function	mf_	mf_CloseSheet()
Menu structure	ms_	ms_sheets
User object	u_	u_dw
Class user object	u_n_	u_n_transaction
C++ user object	u_cc_	u_cc_encryption
Visual external user object	u_vx_	u_vx_status
Visual VBX user object	u_vbx_	u_vbx_counter
User object function	uf_	uf_ChangeDataObject()
User object structure	us_	us_pointers
DataWindow object	d_	d_order_header

Type	*Prefix*	*Example*
DataWindow control	`dw_`	`dw_HeaderEdit`
Query	`q_`	`q_order_summary`
Project	same as application	`order_entry`
Pipeline	`p_`	`p_watcom_to_sybase`
Structure object	`s_`	`s_keys`
Function object	`f_`	`f_GenerateNumber()`
Function object structure	`fs_`	`fs_PriorNumbers`

Table 22.5. Data type naming conventions in Project B.

Data Type	*Prefix Qualifier*	*Example*
Blob	`bb`	`bbWordDoc`
Window	`w`	`wParent`
MenuItem	`m`	`mFrame`
DataWindow	`dw`	`dwOrderHeader`
DataWindowChild	`dwc`	`dwcServiceRep1`
ListViewItem	`lvi_`	`lvi_file`
TreeViewItem	`tvi_`	`tvi_file`
User object	`uo`	`uoButton`
Integer	`n`	`nCount`
Unsigned integer	`un`	`unCount`
Long	`l`	`lRow`
Unsigned long	`ul`	`ulRow`
Boolean	`b`	`bFlag`
String	`sz`	`szName`
Character	`c`	`cInitial`
Double	`d`	`dCost`
Real	`r`	`rCost`
Decimal	`dec`	`decCost`
Date	`dt`	`dtToday`
Structure	`s`	`sKeys`

continues

Table 22.5. continued

Data Type	*Prefix Qualifier*	*Example*
MailSession	`Pbmail`	`PBmailSession`
Transaction	`tr`	`trServiceReps`
Time	`t`	`tNow`
DateTime	`dtm`	`dtmCreated`

Table 22.6. Variable scope conventions in Project B.

Scope	*Prefix Qualifier*	*Example*
Global	`g_`	`g_szID`
Shared	`sh_`	`sh_nSheetNo`
Instance	`i_`	`i_nThisSheetNo`
Argument	`a_`	`a_wParent`

Local variables do not have a scope prefix because local variables are by far the most commonly used. Therefore, any variable you see without a prefix is a local variable. You also use the argument prefix when specifying arguments within the DataWindow and Custom Event painters.

Single spaces are placed before and after all operators and the assignment verb (=), and before each argument in a function parameter list.

Tabs rather than spaces should be used to indent code to show inclusion in loops and other compound statements.

Function calls and variables are coded in both upper- and lowercase.

Database commands (for example, `INSERT`, `SELECT`, and `DECLARE CURSOR`) should be all capitals, with field names in lowercase, and PowerBuilder bind variables should use the same convention as normal PowerBuilder variables. PowerScript functions and commands should be coded with the first letter of each word capitalized (for example, `If`, `RightTrim()`). User-defined objects should be in all lowercase (for example, `f_clear_mdi_children()`).

Line continuation should leave connecting tokens (for example, `AND`, +) at the end of the line, rather than at the beginning of the next line.

One-line structures should be broken into multiple lines:

```
If nRows > 6 Then
   dw_report.Retrieve()
EndIf
```

instead of appearing like this:

```
If nRows > 6 Then dw_report.Retrieve()
```

The interpreter (and now compiler) does not differentiate between these formats, and the suggested format removes any unnecessary errors when you want to actually include the next line in the `If` clause but forget to expand the control structure.

User Event Numbering

At the highest level of the object hierarchy, the events should be numbered `custom01` to `custom10`. For the next level of inheritance, numbering should start at `custom11` and go to `custom20`, and so on down the hierarchy. This allows for the addition of events at each level without interfering with modifications made in inherited or placed controls. For example, consider `u_edit_field`, which defines an edit field and adds three new events: `validate`, `InvalidEntry`, and `reset`, with the IDs `custom01`, `custom02`, and `custom03`, respectively. Now consider `u_required_field`, which is inherited from `u_edit_field` and adds a new event: `InputRequired`. This should be given the ID `custom10`. Further, consider that `u_edit_field` is used on a window and has a user event assigned at that level. This would also be given the ID `custom10`. If the object `u_required_field` were used instead, the new event would be given the ID `custom20`.

Inheritance

All objects used on a window or in construction of a user object are ideally inherited. This ensures consistency throughout development of the application and of future applications. Ideally, all windows are also inherited.

Application Objects

The application object is located in its own library. This object is controlled by one individual. A developer should make copies into his private PBL if he needs to make local changes. Any permanent changes must be coordinated through the authorized developer.

Because global variables and global external functions are a part of the application object, the authorized developer must make modifications to these functions.

Library Naming

PBL names conform to the format *AAA_EEEE*, where *AAA* is the project abbreviation (it can be just one or two characters if you want) and *EEEE* is either the object type or business function abbreviation (for example, OE_MAIN.PBL, PRS_DWIN.PBL).

In addition to these libraries are three more types. The first is the extension for application-independent objects or framework libraries and uses the abbreviation SH_ for shared. The second is for the application-specific ancestor objects and uses the prefix ANC_. The last is a library for each developer and should uniquely identify that person; the person's logon should be sufficient if it is eight or fewer characters.

The Search PBL Path

In the search PBL path, the developer's private PBL comes first, followed by shared PBLs, then ancestor PBLs, and finally the application-specific PBLs. The order of each section should be as follows: structures, functions, menus, DataWindows, user objects, and then windows.

A developer should check out objects into his private work library. All modifications to an object occur there, and once finished and tested, the objects are checked back into the originating library. See Chapter 20, "Application Maintenance and Upgrades," for further information on object check in and check out.

Project Z Conventions

Tables 22.7, 22.8, and 22.9 show more examples of a real-life naming convention. Notice that most of the naming is the same—only a few preferences have changed.

Table 22.7. Object naming conventions in Project Z.

Type	*Prefix*	*Example*
Window	`w_`	`w_frame`
Window function	`wf_`	`wf_saveorder()`
Window structure	`s_`	`s_kits`
Menu	`m_`	`m_frame`
Menu function	`mf_`	`mf_closesheet()`
Menu structure	`s_`	`s_menu_stuff`
Standard user object	`u_`	`u_dw`
Custom class user object	`u_cc_`	`u_cc_business_class`
Standard class user object	`u_cs_`	`u_cs_error`
Visual custom user object	`u_vc_`	`u_vc_group`
Visual external user object	`u_vx_`	`u_vx_outthere`
Visual VBX user object	`u_vv_`	`u_vv_progress`
User object function	`uf_`	`uf_changedataobject()`
User object structure	`s_`	`s_columns`
DataWindow object	`d_`	`d_order_header`
DataWindow control	`dw_`	`dw_header_edit`

Type	*Prefix*	*Example*
Structure object	s_	s_keys
Query	q_	q_getkits
Function object	gf_	gf_getnextnumber()

Table 22.8. Data type naming conventions in Project Z.

Data Type	*Prefix Qualifier*	*Example*
Window	w_	w_junk
MenuItem	m_	m_frame
DataWindow	dw_	dw_orderheader
User object	uo_	uo_button
Integer	i_	i_count
Unsigned integer	ui_	ui_count
Long	l_	l_row
Unsigned long	ul_	ul_row
Boolean	b_	b_flag
String	s_	s_name
Double	db_	db_cost
Real	r_	r_cost
Decimal	c_	c_cost
Blob	bb_	bb_bigblob
Character	ch_	ch_byte
DragObject	do_	do_custdrag
Nonvisual	nv_	nv_error
PowerObject	po_	po_powerobj
DataWindowChild	dwc_	dwc_child
Mail session	ms_	ms_mailit
Structure	str_	str_stuff
Transaction object	trans_	trans_objectone
Date	d_	d_today
Time	t_	t_now
DateTime	dt_	dt_created

Table 22.9. Variable scope conventions in Project Z.

Scope	*Prefix Qualifier*	*Example*
Local	`l?_`	`li_count`
Instance	`i?_`	`istr_structure`
Shared	`s?_`	`sl_long`
Global	`g?_`	`gr_real`
Argument passed by value	`v?_`	`vdw_datawindow`
Argument passed by reference	`r?_`	`rl_long`

Single spaces are placed before and after all operators and the assignment verb (=), and after each comma in a function parameter list.

Tabs rather than spaces should be used to indent code to show inclusion in loops and other compound statements.

Function calls and variables are coded in both upper- and lowercase.

Database commands (for example, `INSERT`, `SELECT`, and `DECLARE CURSOR`) should be coded in all capitals, with field names in lowercase and PowerBuilder bind variables using the same convention as normal PowerBuilder variables. PowerScript functions and commands should be coded with the first letter of each word capitalized (for example, `If`, `RightTrim()`). User-defined objects should be in all lowercase (for example, `f_clear_mdi_children()`).

Line continuation should leave connecting tokens (for example, `AND`, +) at the end of the line, rather than at the beginning of the next line.

Control Names

The prefix for controls is rarely changed from the PowerBuilder defaults that are displayed in the Preferences painter.

Table 22.10 lists each control and its default prefix.

Table 22.10. Default control prefixes.

Control	*Prefix*
CheckBox	`cbx_`
CommandButton	`cb_`

Control	*Prefix*
DataWindow	dw_
DropDownListBox	ddlb_
DropDownPictureListBox	ddplb_
EditMask	em_
Graph	gr_
GroupBox	gb_
HscrollBar	hsb_
Line	ln_
ListBox	lb_
ListView	lv_
MultiLineEdit	mle_
OLE 2.0	ole_
Oval	oval_
Picture	p_
PictureButton	pb_
PictureListBox	plb_
RadioButton	rb_
Rectangle	r_
RoundRectangle	rr_
RichTextEdit	rte_
SingleLineEdit	sle_
StaticText	st_
Tab	tab_
Tab Page	tabpage_
TreeView	tv_
User object	uo_
VScrollBar	vsb_

NOTE

In Powersoft's Foundation Class the following objects have different prefixes:

Object	*Prefix*
`OleControl`	`oc`
`Rectangle`	`rec`
`RoundRectangle`	`rrec`

Other Standards

These standards are used only within the PowerBuilder development environment; you also need to consider what the front end will look like. For this you need to set some GUI guidelines. Remember that they are only guidelines. They are not meant to be all-encompassing or too restricting, but to show what colors, 2D or 3D effects, and fonts to use.

An excellent reference for these kinds of guidelines is *The Windows Interface—An Application Design Guide,* published by Microsoft Press. This book covers the principles of user interface design, the keyboard, windows, menus, dialog boxes, and even OLE and pen computing.

NOTE

The Application Design Guide is mostly relevant to Microsoft Windows applications. For more information on using PowerBuilder in other environments, see Chapter 21, "Cross-Platform PowerBuilder."

By specifying GUI guidelines, you can eliminate randomly designed GUIs with inconsistent menus, dialog boxes, and buttons.

A number of companies are starting to sell GUI and naming guidelines, usually in an online format which you may want to examine. If you buy one of the commercial frameworks available, you will also be buying the GUI and naming standards that have been used in its development.

Summary

This chapter explains three types of naming and coding conventions. What you decide to use might be forced on you by a class library or framework, or you might stick with Powersoft's convention or define your own, drawing on various areas of the conventions detailed. If you do create your own, you need to be aware of the many areas that require definition of a standard or convention, such as GUI guidelines.

The User Object Painter

23

IN THIS CHAPTER

User objects are one of the most important components PowerBuilder provides for developing object-oriented applications. They are mainly used to carry out commonly used processing or functionality, which allows the developer to concentrate on the integration aspect of objects rather than the reconstruction and retesting of certain components across an application. A user object can be written to be used either as a visual control on a window object or as a non-visual object that can be used from anywhere in your PowerScript. This chapter explores the different types of user objects PowerBuilder provides, how they are created and used, and what special functions can be used with them.

Why User Objects?

A user object is an object that encapsulates a set of related scripts and properties that define a particular functionality.

So why use PowerBuilder user objects? Here are some of the advantages:

- They eliminate the need to code functionality in different places in your application. You can place the code in a central location and call it as required.
- You can collect visual controls that are always used together in a particular manner into one visual control that can be reused.
- They provide *the* method for enforcing a standard look and feel to visual controls by providing a user object for each control type with the desired font face and size, object color, and object size.
- You can encapsulate related functionality.
- They allow the extension of some of the system objects, such as the `Transaction` object, to incorporate your own functionality.

The keyword through most of these advantages is *encapsulation* (information hiding), which allows you to hide the actual workings of the user object and provide interaction through a flexible public accessible interface—this is a very important concept to remember when constructing user objects. If the user object needs to act on an object that is external to itself, you should provide a means to pass a reference to this other object into the user object. Once a user object has been heavily used throughout one or even many applications, you will inevitably have to enhance the functionality or even fix some minor problems or undesired characteristics. Since the user object was written to make the best use of encapsulation, this will allow the modification to be made without affecting the objects that are using it.

When you encapsulate this functionality into a user object, it becomes reusable, allowing you to accelerate application development with pretested objects that have a predefined functionality and interface. With reusability, you get the advantages of improved code quality and efficiency.

User objects are also one of the few objects that can be inherited from, which allows you to carry out further encapsulation by inheriting an ancestor object to create functionally specific descendants.

It cannot be emphasized enough that you should place your own user objects in place of the standard controls available in the Window painter. This allows you to place functionality into your user objects and immediately have it available throughout your application, rather than having to retro-fit each place a certain control is used. For example, consider a window that makes use of a number of single-line edit controls that hold a variety of data. After you have constructed the window, you find out that all the fields have to reset themselves to a particular value at some point in the window's life. If you have made use of a user object for each field, the functionality to achieve this can be coded in one place and is instantly available. If not, you have to visit each user object and place the same code in each. As you can see, using your own user objects will save you time, effort, and frustration later in the development life cycle.

Types of User Objects

User objects come in two distinct types: visual and class (or nonvisual). As you will see in the next couple sections, both of these types encompass a couple different styles.

Visual User Objects

A visual object comprises either a single control or multiple related controls that define a certain type of functionality. There are four types of visual user objects: custom, external, standard, and VBX. Visual user objects can only be used in either the Window painter or in a user object of the visual custom type. Visual user objects can only be modified in the User Object painter and not directly through the Window painter. You can set external properties of the user object that you place in a window object. These vary depending on the type of user object, but include position, size, background color, and scrollbars. You also have access to *at least* the following events for the user object, and the events available will vary between the different user object types: `Constructor`, `Destructor`, `DragDrop`, `DragEnter`, `DragLeave`, `DragWithin`, `Other`, `RButtonDown`, as well as any user events that you have added to the user object.

Standard Visual User Objects

A *standard visual user object* is in essence an inherited object from one of the base classes of visual controls supported by PowerBuilder. The definition of the original object is carried down to the user object, which includes all the properties and events. This type of user object is often used to extend the functionality of the normal control, the most common example being DataWindow controls. The standard user object based on a DataWindow usually has default behavior placed in some of the events (for example, error handling and processing in `DBError`). The standard type of visual user object is the most commonly used because it allows access to all the original properties and events of the object while extending it further. The standard visual controls that can be used to build a standard visual user object are CheckBox, CommandButton, DataWindow, DropDownList box, DropDownPictureList box, EditMask, Graph, GroupBox, HScrollBar, List box, ListView, MultiLineEdit, OLEControl, Picture, PictureButton, PictureList box, RadioButton, RichTextEdit, SingleLineEdit, StaticText, Tab, TreeView, and VScrollBar.

Custom Visual User Objects

Custom visual user objects contain multiple related controls that together provide a defined function. The user object area in the painter is akin to a miniature window and you use it as you would a window in the Window painter. This type of user object is often used when you notice that you are grouping a number of the same controls together over and over in different areas of the same, or even different, applications.

The user object acts as a single unit when placed on a window object, and is of class type UserObject!. You access the controls in the custom user object through a Control[] array in the same manner as you would a window's controls.

The one thing about the custom visual user object that is different from all the other user object types is that you have multiple controls within one package. This introduces some interesting problems regarding communication from the outside in and from the internal controls to outside the parent user object. There are a number of ways to achieve object communication, and the method you choose will depend on a couple factors. Mainly, what is the purpose of the communication? Other factors are based on the object-oriented concepts that the development team is working against. Consider the problem of a command button that is used to insert a row into a DataWindow control. The desired communication can be achieved in the following ways:

- Specifically name the DataWindow control that will be used. Obviously, this is a very poor solution, because it is not generic anymore. The object relies on the DataWindow to be called a particular name.
- Create a user event for the custom user object that is then triggered by the button. The event will then be coded with the specific DataWindow reference once it is placed in a window. If you use the arguments that are available in 5.0 event messages, you can even customize the row insertion to add the row at a specific position in the DataWindow control. This allows loose coupling of the custom user object to the parent, such that if the user object were used inside a different custom user object, you would still maintain flexibility in your processing.
- You can use an instance variable for the DataWindow control that is set in the Constructor event of the custom user object from within the window object that is using it. This has the advantage of providing you with a direct reference to an object

that can be used from many other scripts without having to trigger events that require code to be written externally to the user object. Just remember not to try using any of these references until all the `Constructor` events have finished executing.

To illustrate the concept of a custom user object, consider the Windows 3.*x* help system and the scrolling search window that allowed you to scroll through a list as you typed in the word. This can be constructed as a single-line edit control that is tied to a list box control. In order to encapsulate these two controls and the functionality required for reuse, this would be created as a custom visual user object.

External Visual User Objects

The *external visual user object* allows you to use objects that have been built by third-party companies or that you can create yourself using the operating system Software Development Kit (SDK). These are usually supplied in the form of DLLs. You must have the required information on the DLL that tells you about the classes, messages, and styles that the DLL understands. PowerBuilder supplies a 3D progress meter that is contained in the CPALETTE.DLL file as an example of an external visual user object.

The SDK custom control must contain a registered class and a window procedure. The window class ties instances of an object to a class definition, which includes color information, cursor and icon settings, and a window procedure. The window procedure is the entry point used every time a message is processed by a custom control. The window procedure must be named *`class`*`WndFn`, where *`class`* is the registered class name.

You can interact with a custom control using three methods: Windows messages (see Appendix E, "Mapping Windows Messages to PowerBuilder Event IDs," which is on the book's CD), style bits that allow access to particular object attributes, and functions that may have been defined for the object and are contained within the DLL.

VBX Visual User Objects

VBX visual user objects enable you to use the plethora of objects that compatriot developers using Visual Basic have available. PowerBuilder 4.0 supports VBX objects compatible with VB Version 1.0, and allows you to use VBX controls of a later version but provides limited access to the attributes and events. Many of the newer-version properties are accessible only at runtime, and you take the risk of a runtime error. Powersoft supplies an example of a VBX with PowerBuilder; you can find it (it is a diamond arrangement of arrows) in the VBDIA.VBX file. When you select a VBX in the User Object painter, the properties of the object, such as the class name and events supported, are retrieved.

NOTE

You can now access the VBX option of the User Object painter only using the 16-bit version of PowerBuilder 5.0. In the 32-bit environments VBX controls have been replaced by OCX controls. You place OCX controls directly on windows as you would a standard control, and you should see Chapter 36, "OLE 2.0 and DDE," for more information on how to use OCX objects.

Class User Objects

Class user objects allow the encapsulation of logic and functionality that do not have visual components. There are three types of class user objects: custom, standard, and C++. These types of user objects are used for the declaration of business logic components, specific management functions, calculations, and extending the nonvisual system objects. The third type of class user object, the C++ one, is only available after installing the Class Builder portion of PowerBuilder Enterprise.

The main advantage of a class user object is that it is truly nonvisual and therefore consumes no GUI resources and only the memory required for the object and its working structures and other dynamically created class objects. This also means that you use them a little differently than you do the visual user objects that were just introduced, and this is explained later, in the section "Creating a Custom Class User Object."

Auto-Instantiate

The class user objects that you create can now be made to be auto-instantiating. This is achieved by selecting the AutoInstantiate option from the pop-up menu in the User Object painter. This means that to use the class you now only have to declare a variable using that user object class. There is no need to do explicit `Create` and `Destroy` calls, as PowerBuilder handles the memory management as the object variable comes into and leaves scope.

Custom Class User Objects

You use custom class user objects for the encapsulation of processing that will not be visible to the user. These objects do not inherit any base-level definition from a PowerBuilder object and are shaped completely by the instance variables, functions, and events that you declare. They have two predefined events: `Constructor` and `Destructor`.

Standard Class User Objects

Standard class user objects take their definition from the standard PowerBuilder object that they are based on, and like standard visual user objects, they allow you to extend the default behavior with your own code to make them specific to your requirements.

The standard classes in PowerBuilder for which you can create standard class user objects are shown in Table 23.1.

Table 23.1. PowerBuilder's standard classes.

Standard Class	*Description*
`Connection`	Distributed PowerBuilder connection information.
`DataStore`	A nonvisual DataWindow object.
`DynamicDescriptionArea`	Stores information on the input and output parameters used in type 4 dynamic SQL.
`DynamicStagingArea`	Stores information for use in subsequent dynamic SQL statements, and is the only connection between the execution of dynamic SQL and a transaction object.
`Error`	Stores information on errors and where the errors occurred.
`MailSession`	The context in which MAPI processing occurs.
`Message`	Used during the processing of events.
`OLEObject`	A proxy for a remote OLE object.
`OLEStorage`	A proxy for an open OLE storage.
`OLEStream`	A proxy for an OLE stream.
`Pipeline`	The context in which a data pipeline is executed.
`Transaction`	The communication area between a script or DataWindow and the database.

An example of a standard class user object that is fully fleshed out in Chapter 24, "Building User Objects," is extending the transaction class to incorporate specific transaction management facilities.

To use a standard class user object, you need to declare it in the application object's property sheet on the Variable Types tab page (see Figure 23.1).

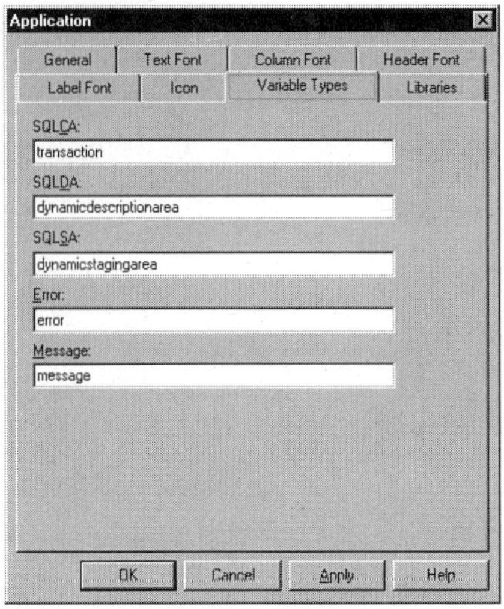

FIGURE 23.1.
The Variable Types tab page for an application's properties.

Transaction Objects and `RPCFUNC`

You can use database stored procedures (that do not produce a result set) using the same *`Object.Function`* notation that you use with other PowerScript functions. This syntax performs better than the multitude of dynamic SQL commands that you normally need to issue to carry out the same operation. This is because PowerBuilder prepares the SQL ahead of time.

You can declare database stored procedures to be used in this manner within transaction class user objects *only*. Within a standard class user object you can then enter the syntax required for the call in the Local External Functions dialog box. The syntax for declaring an RPC is similar to that of a normal external function, and conforms to the following:

```
FUNCTION ReturnDataType FunctionName({REF}{Datatype1 Arg1,...DatatypeN ArgN}) &
                                         RPCFUNC {ALIAS FOR DataBaseProcedureName}
```

If the stored procedure does not return a value, you should use the following syntax:

```
SUBROUTINE FunctionName( {REF} {Datatype1 Arg1, ... DatatypeN ArgN}) &
                         RPCFUNC {ALIAS FOR DataBaseProcedureName}
```

`FunctionName` is the name of the aliased stored procedure that you will use within your PowerScript call. If any of the arguments are being used as output parameters, you should prefix them with the keyword `REF` to indicate that they will be returning a value.

> **WARNING**
>
> You should pre-pad string output parameters, just as you would any other external function call that returns values by reference.

Instead of entering this syntax by hand, you can use the Procedures button to display a list of all the currently available stored procedures. When you select one, PowerBuilder automatically generates the `RPCFUNC` syntax for you.

Remember to change the default global variable type for the SQLCA from `Transaction` to the standard class user object you have created.

C++ Class User Objects

The C++ class user object allows the construction of very fast compiled versions of functions that are processor intensive into DLLs that can then be incorporated into your PowerBuilder application the same as the other types of class user objects. This type of object provides very fast execution as well as access to the large library of existing C++ code already in the programming community. The only drawbacks are that you need to know some C++, and the data types of parameters are a little restricting. The user object can accept the common data types (String, Integer, and so on), but it will not handle structures or enumerated data types.

Using the User Object Painter

You open the User Object painter by clicking on the user object button in the PowerBar. The first dialog box (see Figure 23.2) of the painter that displays is the Select User Object, which allows you to open an existing user object, create a new user object inherited from an existing one, or create a new one.

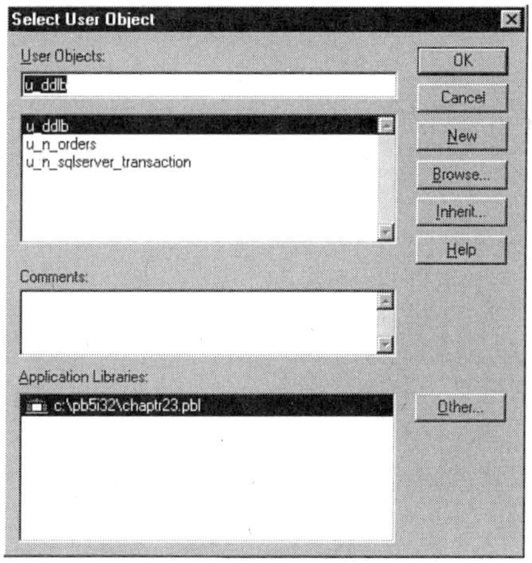

FIGURE 23.2.
The Select User Object dialog box.

Inheritance in user objects works with the same principles as in windows and menus: You cannot directly modify the scripts and controls that were inherited from the ancestor object.

The next dialog box (see Figure 23.3) you will see allows you to specify the type of user object that you want to create.

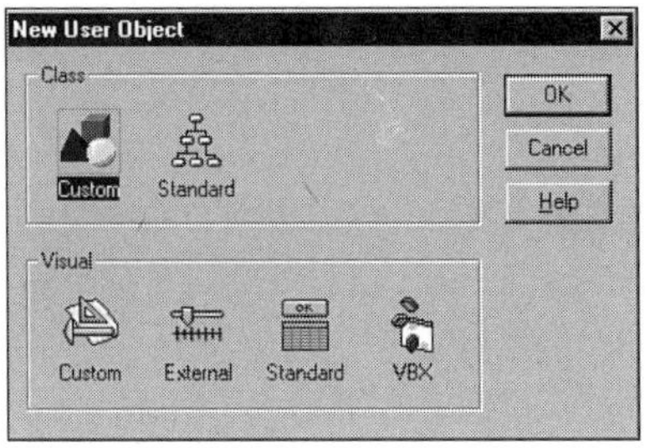

FIGURE 23.3.
The New User Object dialog box.

The available types will vary from platform to platform as will additional components you have loaded for use with PowerBuilder.

The next sections explore how to create and use each of the user object types that have already been introduced.

Creating a Standard Visual User Object

To create a standard visual user object, select the Standard icon in the Visual group box, which opens the Select Standard Visual Type dialog box (see Figure 23.4), where you select the object type on which you want to base the new user object.

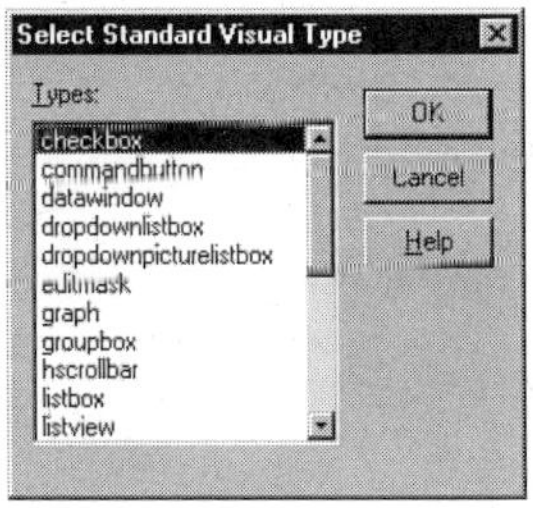

FIGURE 23.4.
The Select Standard Visual Type dialog box.

For this example, we will create a database-enabled drop-down list box control that populates its list based on a `SELECT` statement.

The drop-down list box control displays in the painter area and actually defines the area of the user object. As you stretch the user object, you are increasing the size at which the control will appear.

By using the properties sheet, you can set up the default style of the drop-down list box. In this case, the defaults are exactly what you want. As you explore the user object, you will notice that it contains the same events that you would see in a drop-down list box control placed on a window. The same is true of the functions that you can use on the user object. The events available for the object will be extended with the following custom events:

- `DropDown`—Traps when the user clicks on the arrow to display the drop-down list of the control.
- `Validate`—Coded in the parent object to allow validation of the edit area of the control.
- `InvalidEntry`—Used to provide a custom error message when the validation fails.
- `Refresh`—Can be used to refresh the list box control. This would usually be carried out by a broadcast message (see Chapter 24 for the code) to reload the list. The actual action is carried out by script written once the user object has been placed on a window or custom user object.
- `Reset`—Used to return the control to some predetermined state. Also another candidate for a broadcasted message.

The `DropDown` event is connected to the PowerBuilder `pbm_cbndropdown` event ID, while the remaining events use `pbm_custom01` through `pbm_custom04`.

You should also declare two Boolean instance variables:

- `i_bModified`—Used to flag that the edit field has been modified. Initially set to `FALSE`.
- `i_bValidated`—Used to indicate whether the value has been successfully validated. Initially set to `FALSE`.

The default events and some of the new ones are coded to handle validation of the data field, as well as some additional tasks.

To provide an auto selection of the edit field, similar to the edit styles in a DataWindow, you code the following line in the `GetFocus` event:

```
this.SelectText( 1, Len( this.text))
```

When the user makes a change in the edit field and moves the focus away (either using the mouse or the Tab key), you want to validate the entry. To achieve this you place the following code in the `Modified` event to call the validation code outside the focus change:

```
i_bModified = TRUE
this.Post Event Validate()
```

When the object is told to reset itself, the object-level variables need to be returned to a `FALSE` state and the edit field and list need to be emptied. This is done in the `Reset` event:

```
this.text = ""
this.Reset()
i_bModified = FALSE
i_bValidated = FALSE
```

The main reason you are creating this user object is so that it is database aware. For this you use an additional user event that will make use of the new PowerBuilder event style. Declare the event as `Populate` and click on the Args button. Change the return type to be a Long, so that this event conforms with the other PowerBuilder events. Specify one argument, `a_szSQLSelect`, of type String. In PowerBuilder 4.0 you can use the same method, except that you will need to process the `Message.LongParm` to extract the string. The code for this event is shown in Listing 23.1.

Listing 23.1. The `Populate` event for `u_ddlb_from_database`.

```
Integer nSQLCode
String szSQLText, szValue

// For PB4.0 declare a_szSQLSelect as a string and then
// populate the variable using
// szSQLSelect = String( Message.LongParm, "address")
// Remember when you call this event within PowerBuilder 4.0 to set
// the WordParm to a 0.

If a_szSQLSelect = "" Then
   Return -1
Else
   PREPARE SQLSA FROM :a_szSQLSelect;

   DECLARE dynamic_cursor DYNAMIC CURSOR FOR SQLSA;

   OPEN DYNAMIC dynamic_cursor;

   If SQLCA.SQLCode < 0 Then
      MessageBox( "Unable to open dynamic cursor in Populate event code", &
                                                      SQLCA.SQLErrText)
      Return SQLCA.SQLCode
   End If

   this.SetRedraw( FALSE)
   this.Reset()

   Do While SQLCA.SQLCode = 0
      FETCH dynamic_cursor INTO :szValue;

      If SQLCA.SQLCode = 0 Then
         this.AddItem( szValue)
      ElseIf SQLCA.SQLCode < 0 Then
         nSQLCode - SQLCA.SQLCode
         szSQLText = SQLCA.SQLErrText
         CLOSE dynamic_cursor;
         MessageBox( "Unable to fetch row from table specified", szSQLText)
         Return nSQLCode
      Else
         Exit
      End If
   Loop
```

```
    this.SetRedraw( TRUE)

    CLOSE dynamic_cursor;

    Return 0
End If
```

The same population technique could be used to create a list box user object that could then replace the standard list box you used in the scrolling lookup custom user object.

You can now save this user object and use it in windows and custom user objects to provide a list populated from the database. Obviously you can achieve the same results by using a drop-down DataWindow within a DataWindow. This is one of the advantages of using PowerBuilder—there are different ways to achieve the same goal. This user object is very useful for providing a simple lookup without requiring you to create two DataWindow objects and a DataWindow control that retrieves the data.

To cause the user object to populate, you could use the following code, possibly executed from a post-open event of the window, another control, or the user object's own `Constructor` event:

```
this.Trigger Event Populate( "SELECT name FROM employee")
```

Unlike in a drop-down DataWindow, you can only supply one column with this user object; you can of course concatenate multiple columns and place a known separator between them, which will then allow you to extract the various components of the list item if you need to.

Creating a Custom Visual User Object

To create a custom visual user object, select the Custom icon in the Visual group box, which will open the User Object painter with an empty canvas—an untitled custom visual user object.

For this example, you will actually create the scrolling lookup control that you used to describe this type of user object.

Have you ever used the search function in Windows 3.*x* help and thought, hey, that is just the kind of scrolling lookup I need in my application, then spent a few agonizing hours trying to get a drop-down list box to do just that? The simple fact is the drop-down list box cannot be made to carry out this kind of as-you-type scrolling lookup. This is because of the manner of interaction between the edit field and the list, which causes the highlight in the list to disappear whenever the edit field is typed in. The solution in PowerBuilder is to create a custom user object that contains a standard single-line edit object and a standard list box object.

To do this you just select the appropriate items from the control list on the toolbar. These controls will be called `sle_lookup` and `lb_lookup`. The first piece of code has the task of trapping the user's keystrokes in the single-line edit. For this you need to add a user event `EditChange` for the PowerBuilder event ID pbm_enchange to the single-line edit. This PowerBuilder-defined event message is fired off every time a change is made in a single-line edit. On each keypress, you need to use the current string in a search of the items in the list box. The function SelectItem(*ItemText*, *StartIndex*) will be used for this, with the starting index always being zero. This allows you to search the list from the beginning in case the user backspaced or deleted the previously entered letters.

To make the custom user object a little more open to the outside environment, you should also add a line of code to provide a message to indicate that a key was pressed. So this is the code for EditChange:

```
lb_lookup.SelectItem( this.text, 0)

Parent.TriggerEvent( "sle_keypress")
```

If the user is to tab away after entering a partial string, you will copy the current selection from the list box into the single-line edit. The following line of code is placed in the LoseFocus event of sle_lookup:

```
this.text = lb_lookup.SelectedItem()
```

Now, in order to prevent a tab away from the single-line edit going to the list box, you need to set the tab order of the list box to zero.

Whenever the user selects an item in the list box, you need to move this to the single-line edit. This provides object interaction in the reverse direction and only requires the following line of code placed in the SelectionChanged event of lb_lookup:

```
sle_lookup.text = this.SelectedItem()
```

If you look at the Windows 3.*x* help lookup again, you see that when you double-click on an item in the list, a set of matching topics appears in another list box. With a custom user object, you lose access to this event when the object is used in a window or another user object. Therefore, as you did for the single-line edit keypress event, you need to set up a list box_doubleclick user event. The code for the list box DoubleClick event is as follows:

```
Parent.Trigger Event list box_doubleclick( this.SelectedIndex(), &
                                          this.SelectedItem())
```

Notice that you pass back the index and associated text value from the list box for use external to the user object.

To put the finishing touches on this user object, you need to cause the single-line edit and list box to resize themselves so that the size of the custom user object is stretched when placed in a window or other custom user object. The resize code is placed in the Constructor events for sle_lookup and lb_lookup. For sle_lookup the code is

```
this.width = Parent.width - 10
```

This makes the single-line edit the same width as the user object. The `-10` brings the right edge of the single-line edit to the left of the user object border; otherwise, the single-line edit becomes clipped.

For `lb_lookup` you must deal with the fact that it is located below the single-line edit, and so the code is

```
this.width = Parent.width  - this.x
this.height = Parent.height - this.y - 10
```

Again, you have a `-10` factor to bring the bottom edge inside the border of the parent.

The attributes and related functions of `sle_lookup` and `lb_lookup` can be manipulated from outside the custom user object. The syntax is `userobjectname.sle_lookup.attribute`. Similarly, each control's functions can also be accessed externally. For example, to populate the list box with items on which to search, you would use this:

```
u_c_lookup.lb_list box.AddItem( "Albion")
```

The attributes for the controls are accessed in the same way. For example, say you wanted to change the 3D borders to a regular border; this would be the code:

```
u_c_lookup.sle_lookup.BorderStyle = StyleBox!
u_c_lookup.lb_lookup.BorderStyle = StyleBox!
```

This provides a completely encapsulated visual user object that you can place on a window or other user object to provide scrolling lookup functionality.

Creating an External Visual User Object

To create an external visual user object, select the External icon in the Visual group box, which will open the Select Custom Control DLL dialog box (see Figure 23.5), where you select the file that contains the object you want to use.

FIGURE 23.5.
The Select Custom Control DLL dialog box.

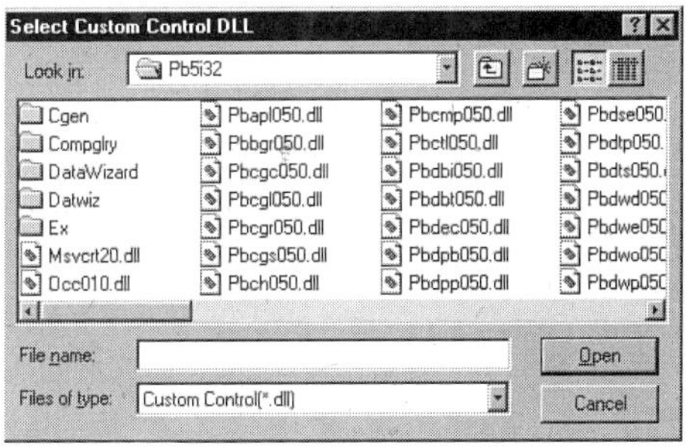

To illustrate this type of user object, select CPALETTE.DLL from your PowerBuilder examples directory. The DLL name and default class name are populated in the External User Object Style dialog box (see Figure 23.6), which appears next.

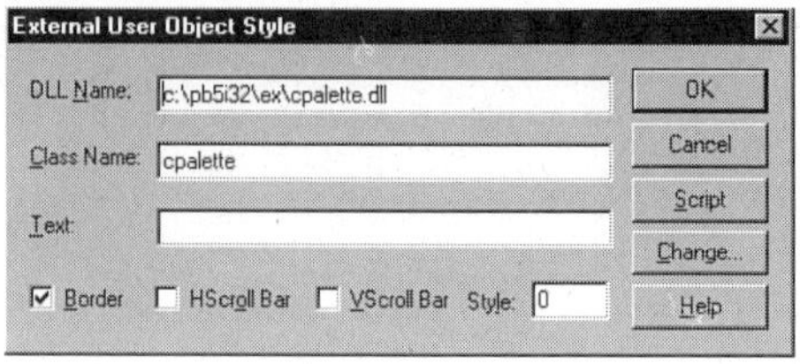

FIGURE 23.6.
The External User Object Style dialog box.

You will be using the progress meter control that is part of this DLL, so change the class name to `cpmeter` and the style to `3` (which changes the border). You can play around with different values for the style to change the border used by the control—when you buy a commercial DLL you will be provided with documentation on the various style settings. You can think of the style bits as attributes for the object, and for some settings you may be required to add style bits together.

The untitled user object is now shown in the painter, and you can return to the previous dialog by double-clicking on the object.

The only functionality you will add to this user object is to set the position of the progress bar. This is achieved by passing an integer value that is used to indicate the new increment to be made on the bar. The method of passing is by message, and the `cpmeter` object responds to a message ID of `4042`. Thus the code would be coded into a user object function, `uf_IncProgress()`, in this way:

```
Send( Handle( this), 4042, a_nIncrement, 0)
```

This function could then be used to indicate how far along a process is. For example, if the save of some information involved a number of integrated pieces that took more than a few seconds to save, you could use the progress bar within a status window and place calls to it using the following code:

```
w_status.u_x_progress.uf_IncProgress( 10)
```

This would allow you to place this same code in nine other locations to indicate 10% increment steps in the save process.

Some user objects trigger notification events; these are sent in the `wParm` parameter of the `WM_COMMAND` event to the parent of the external object. PowerBuilder intercepts these and translates them to event IDs `pbm_uonexternal01` through `pbm_uonexternal25` for notification messages 0 through 24.

Creating a VBX Visual User Object

To create a VBX visual user object, select the VBX icon in the Visual group box, which will open the Select VBX Control dialog box (see Figure 23.7), where you select the file that contains the object you want to use.

NOTE

VBX controls are now only supported under the 16-bit version of PowerBuilder.

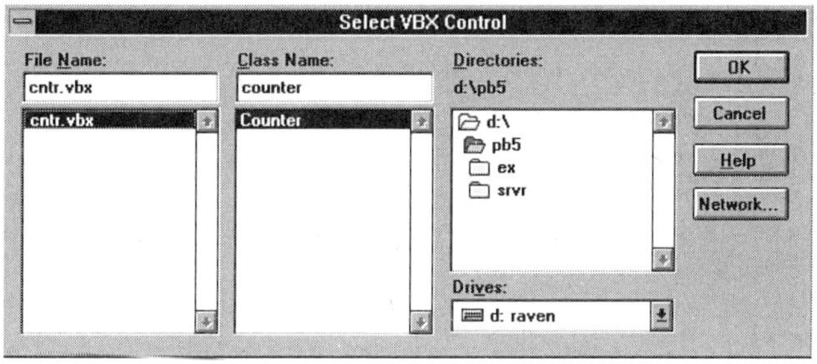

FIGURE 23.7.
The Select VBX Control dialog box.

To illustrate this type of user object, select CNTR.VBX from your PowerBuilder examples directory. The classes available in the VBX control are shown in the middle list box; for this control there is only one class—Counter. The untitled VBX control will now appear in the User Object painter work area (see Figure 23.8).

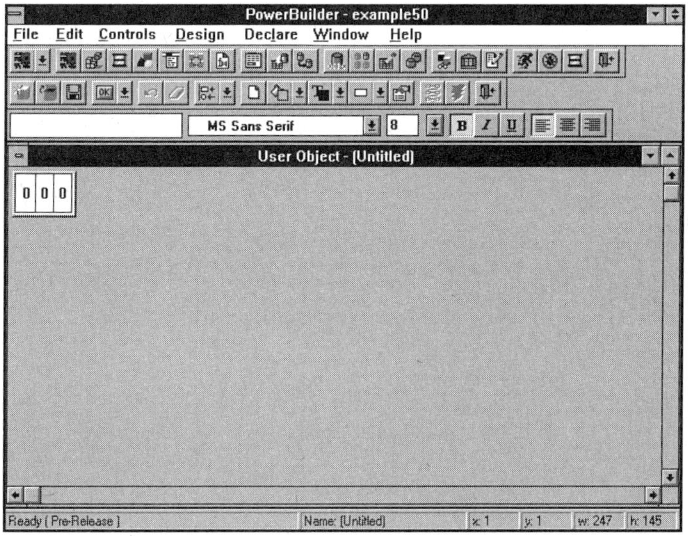

FIGURE 23.8.
The Counter VBX in the User Object painter.

Notice that PowerBuilder gives the control a default size. The first thing you will want to do is size the user object area to the desired height and width. The next step is to alter the properties of the VBX control. You open the VBX properties dialog box as you would any other objects (see Figure 23.9).

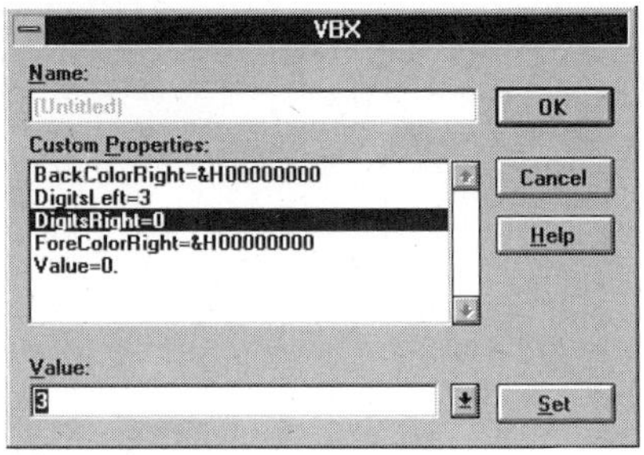

FIGURE 23.9.
The Counter VBX custom attribute dialog box.

You select an attribute from the list, use the Value area at the bottom of the dialog box to specify the new value, and then use the Set button to save the changes into the list. Change `DigitsLeft` to equal `5`, `DigitsRight` to equal `3`, and `Value` to be `12345.678`. When you close the Properties dialog box, you will see the altered VBX control (see Figure 23.10).

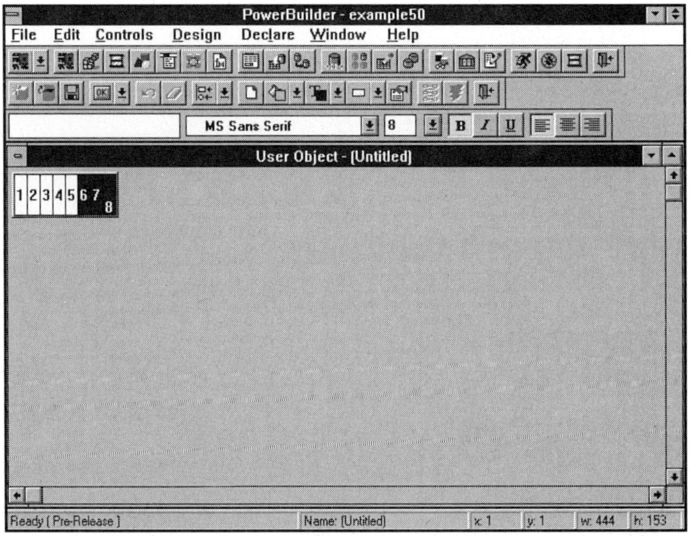

FIGURE 23.10.
The modified Counter VBX.

Now let's explore what events are defined for the VBX; PowerBuilder automatically reads their definition and adds them to the standard list of available events for the control. VBX-specific events are prefixed with `vb`, and the counter VBX only has two: `VBDragDrop` and `VBDragOver`.

NOTE

Different VBX objects have different properties and events defined for them. Some VBX controls have attributes that cannot be modified from within the PowerBuilder painter and must be set using PowerScript.

Some VBX events pass parameters to the control and you need to use two VBX-specific functions to retrieve them: `EventParmDouble()` and `EventParmString()`. This is the syntax for these two functions:

```
VBXUserObject.EventParmDouble( Parameter, ParmVariable)

VBXUserObject.EventParmString( Parameter, ParmVariable)
```

The *`Parameter`* argument indicates the number of the parameter of which you want the value, and *`ParmVariable`* is a variable of the appropriate data type used to store the value.

For example, in the `VBClicked` event for the Diamond VBX that comes with PowerBuilder you need to determine which of the four buttons was pressed:

```
Double dButtonNo
Integer nReturn

// 0 Up Arrow
// 1 Right Arrow
// 2 Down Arrow
// 3 Left Arrow

nReturn = EventParmDouble( 1, dButtonNo)

If nReturn <> -1 Then
   // Process button press
Else
   // Error retrieving event parameter
End If
```

The VBX controls gave developers a nice insight into the potential of external controls and objects that could be integrated with PowerBuilder; and now with PowerBuilder 5.0 we have access to OCXs and all that they provide.

Creating a Custom Class User Object

To create a custom class user object, select the Custom icon in the Class group box, which will open the User Object painter with an empty canvas. Because this is a nonvisual object, the standard controls are disabled, and you create this type of object using events, variables, structures, and functions.

To demonstrate this type of user object, you will be encapsulating all the rules required to create and manage an order number for an order entry system. This sample user object illustrates the use of events, variables, and object-level functions within a class object.

Before we start, let me first define what an order number is for this object. The order number is made up of a two-digit plant number (where the order was entered into the system), followed by a one-digit year representation, a one-character product code, and a four-digit sequence number.

To start with, declare three instance variables for the object:

Scope	*Data Type*	*Variable Name*
Public	Boolean	`i_bMaintainConnection`
Protected	String	`i_szPlantNo`
Protected	`u_n_sqlserver_transaction`	`i_trOrderNo`

The `i_szPlantNo` variable is used during the generation of the order number and can be set from outside using a provided method, which you will see later. Since this object will be carrying out database access, you will want to create and maintain your own connection. You do this in case this object is called by a script that already has a cursor open using the SQLCA, and the database access carried out by this object would cause problems in the caller. The `i_trOrderNo` variable is provided to maintain connection information for the object. Since keeping a connection open to the DBMS can itself cause problems, you allow the parent application to cause the object to make and break its connection as required using the `i_bMaintainConnection` variable.

NOTE

For the functionality demonstrated in the following code using the transaction object, you should refer to Chapter 24.

The real content of the class user object will be contained in object-level functions. The first function (see Listing 23.2) we will construct will create a new order number and is based on a key index table.

Listing 23.2. Public function string `uf_GetNextOrderNo()`.

```
String szOrderNo
Long lNextOrderSeqId

If Not i_bMaintainConnection Then
   i_trOrderNo.MakeConnection()
End If

UPDATE next_order_seq_id
SET order_seq_id = order_seq_id + 1
USING i_trOrderNo;

If i_trOrderNo.SQLCode <> 0 Then
   Return ""
End If

SELECT order_seq_id
INTO :lNextOrderSeqId
FROM next_order_seq_id
USING i_trOrderNo;
```

```
If lNextOrderSeqId > 99999 Then
   Error.Text = "Out of sequence numbers - report this to your supervisor!"
   Open( w_error)
   Return ""
End If

szOrderNo = i_szPlantNo + String( Today(), "yy") + String( lNextOrderSeqId)

If Not i_bMaintainConnection Then
   i_trOrderNo.CloseConnection()
End If

If Len( szOrderNo) <> 8 Then
   Return ""
End If

Return szOrderNo
```

The next three functions are provided to break down the order number into the encoded pieces and are shown in Listings 23.3–23.5.

Listing 23.3. Public function string `uf_ExtractPlantNo( String a_szOrderNo)`.

```
Return Right( a_szOrderNo, 2)
```

Listing 23.4. Public function string `uf_ExtractProductClass( String a_szOrderNo)`.

```
Return Mid( a_szOrderNo, 4, 1)
```

Listing 23.5. Public function string `uf_ExtractYear( String a_szOrderNo)`.

```
String szToday, szOrderYear, szPartial

szToday = String( Today(), "yyyy")

szPartial = Mid( a_szOrderNo, 3, 1)

szOrderYear = Right( szToday, 3) + szPartial

If szOrderYear > szToday Then
   szOrderYear = String( Integer( Left( szToday, 3)) - 1) + szPartial
End If

If Len( szOrderYear) <> 4 Then
   szOrderYear = ""
End If

Return szOrderYear
```

In order to allow external scripts to change the protected `i_szPlantNo` variable, we provide an access function (see Listing 23.6), which validates the new value before assigning it.

Listing 23.6. Public function Boolean `uf_SetPlantNo( String a_szNewPlantNo)`.

```
If Len( a_szNewPlantNo) = 2 And IsNumber( a_szNewPlantNo) Then
   i_szPlantNo = a_szNewPlantNo
   Return TRUE
Else
   Return FALSE
End If
```

Another piece of business logic states that "each order may be based on another order," which means that you have a one-to-many self relationship on the order table. To validate an order number that is about to be used as a parent identifier, you will provide an additional function (see Listing 23.7).

Listing 23.7. Public function Boolean `uf_ValidateOrderNo( String a_szOrderNo)`.

```
String szOrderNo
Boolean bReturn = FALSE

If Not i_bMaintainConnection Then
   i_trOrderNo.MakeConnection()
End If

SELECT order_no
INTO :szOrderNo
FROM order_header
WHERE order_no = :a_szOrderNo
USING i_trOrderNo;

If i_trOrderNo.SQLCode = 0 Then
   bReturn = TRUE
End If

If Not i_bMaintainConnection Then
   i_trOrderNo.CloseConnection()
End If

Return bReturn
```

Class user objects start with only two events: `Constructor` and `Destructor`. You will not be adding any additional events, but placing code in both of these.

Within the `Constructor` event you will set a default value for the plant number variable, using one of the methods that you just created, and clone the default transaction object, `SQLCA`, for use with the object:

```
this.uf_SetPlantNo( "10")

i_trOrderNo = SQLCA.CloneObject()
```

The `Destructor` event will carry out the cleanup of the database connection object that was created in the `Constructor` event:

```
If i_trOrderNo.IsConnected() Then
   i_trOrderNo.CloseConnection()
End If

DESTROY i_trOrderNo
```

This completes the functionality for the class object. To actually use it, you need to place the following code in the application:

```
u_n_orders i_Orders

// Instantiate an instance of the class
i_Orders = CREATE u_n_orders

// Get a new order number
i_Orders.uf_GetNextOrderNo()

// Destroy what we create
DESTROY i_Orders
```

The declaration, creation, and destruction of the object can occur anywhere throughout your application, maybe within the application object or a specific window.

Creating a Standard Class User Object

To create a standard class user object, select the Standard icon in the Class group box, which will open the Select Standard Class Type dialog box (see Figure 23.11), where you select the class object that you want to extend.

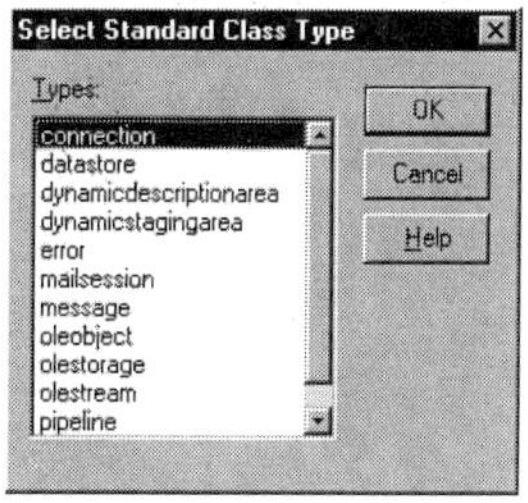

FIGURE 23.11.
The Select Standard Class Type dialog box.

To illustrate this type of user object, you will be extending the `Error` object, so select it from the list. The empty canvas in the User Object painter shows next, and you can begin to build your extensions. Each standard type has a different number of events that are predefined for it, and the `Error` object just has the basic two: `Constructor` and `Destructor`.

The standard error object contains the attributes shown in Table 23.2.

Table 23.2. Attributes of the standard `Error` object.

Attribute	*Data Type*	*Description*
`Line`	Integer	The script line number in which the error occurred
`Number`	Integer	The PowerBuilder error number
`Object`	String	The object name in which the error occurred
`ObjectEvent`	String	The event within the object
`ProxyName`	String	The name used to access this object in a distributed environment
`Text`	String	The PowerBuilder error text
`WindowMenu`	String	The window or menu name in which the error occurred

To further enhance the `Error` object, you will add four new attributes (public instance variables).

> **NOTE**
>
> When modifying any of the standard class objects, you might consider leaving off prefixes on either the variables or the new functions, so that they will look like part of the original object.

The variables are declared as the following:

Data Type	*Variable Name*	*Description*
Boolean	`AllowHalt`	Indicates whether the user should be given the option to halt the application from the error window.
Boolean	`SeriousError`	Indicates whether to use a "friendly" message window or a full-blown system error window.

String	`SpecialEmail`	Additional e-mail requirements for certain error messages (for example, to a DBA upon serious database errors).
String	`UserMessage`	The error message text that was retrieved from the database.

A very common method of providing user-friendly messages to error conditions is to store the actual messages in a database table. Of course, this means that you will need to check whether the error is a serious database error and handle it in a different fashion.

The method you will provide to fetch the message from the database will be called `RetrieveError()` (see Listing 23.8) and will take a numeric error code as its single parameter.

Listing 23.8. Public function `RetrieveError( Long a_lError)`.

```
SELECT error_message, special_email, serious_error, allow_halt
INTO :this.UserMessage, :this.SpecialEmail, :this.SeriousError, :this.AllowHalt
FROM error_messages
WHERE error_id = :a_lError
USING SQLCA;

If SQLCA.SQLcode = 100 Then
   this.UserMessage = "Unable to find the Error message for " + String( a_lError)
ElseIf SQLCA.SQLcode = -1 Then
   this.UserMessage = "SQL Error getting " + String( a_lError) + &
                     "~r~n~nSQL Error: " + SQLCA.SQLErrText
End If
```

Depending on the type of error that the object is currently processing, you may want it to open one of two different message windows—a comprehensive error reporting window for system type errors and a less intimidating message box–style window. To handle this you will provide the `OpenErrorWindow()` method (see Listing 23.9).

Listing 23.9. Public function `OpenErrorWindow()`.

```
If this.SeriousError Then
   Open( w_error)
Else
   MessageBox( "Error", this.UserMessage, StopSign!, Ok!)
End If

If this.SpecialEmail <> "" Then
   this.MailError()
End If
```

To provide direct, full, and detailed information on an error condition, you should provide the method `MailError()` (see Listing 23.10) that will allow the developer to post the message into the e-mail system. The recipient of the message may be someone in QA (quality assurance) or technical support, or the developers themselves.

Listing 23.10. Public function `MailError()`.

```
MailSession PBmailSession
MailMessage PBmailMessage
MailReturnCode PBmailReturn
String szRecipient, szSystem, szUser, szPhoneBook, szTitle

//
// Find out who the current user of the system is, and who should be notified
//
szUser = ProfileString( g_App.i_szINIFile, "Database", "UserId", "")
If this.SpecialEMail <> "" Then
   szRecipient = this.SpecialEmail
Else
   szRecipient = ProfileString( g_App.i_szINIFile, g_App.i_szApplication, &
                                                   "MailRecipient", "")
End If
szSystem = g_App.i_szApplicationName
szPhoneBook = ProfileString( g_App.i_szINIFile, "Errors", "PhoneBook", "FALSE")

If Trim( szRecipient) = "" Or IsNull( szRecipient) Then
   //
   // No-one has been specified to receive the mail - error out.
   //
   Return
End If
//
// Create and log into a mail session
//
PBmailSession = Create MailSession

PBmailReturn = PBmailSession.MailLogon()

If PBmailReturn <> mailReturnSuccess! Then
   szTitle = "Error - " + f_mail_error_to_string( PBmailReturn)
   MessageBox( szTitle, "Unable to notify administrator by specified mail " + &
                        "address. "Please notify the system administrator " + &
                        "of this problem.")
   Return
Else
   //
   // Setup the contents of the mail message
   //
   PBmailMessage.Subject = "An error has occured within " + szSystem
   PBmailMessage.NoteText = "System User:   " + szUser + "~n~n" + &
                            "Window Name:   " + this.WindowMenu + "~n" + &
                            "Object Name:   " + this.Object + "~n" + &
                            "Object Event:  " + this.ObjectEvent + "~n" + &
                            "Line Number:   " + String( this.Line) + "~n" + &
                            "Error Number:  " + String( this.Number) + "~n~n" + &
                                                this.Text
   //
   // Should the address "phone book" be opened for user to specify recipient
   //
   If Upper( szPhoneBook) = "TRUE" Then
```

```
        PBmailReturn = PBmailSession.mailAddress( PBmailMessage)
        If PBmailReturn <> mailReturnSuccess! Then
           szTitle = "Error - " + f_mail_error_to_string( PBmailReturn)

           MessageBox( "Error", "Unable to open the mail list. " + &
                            "Please notify the system administrator of " + &
                            "this problem.")
           Return
        End If
     Else
        //
        // Set the recipient of the message
        //
        PBmailMessage.Recipient[1].name = szRecipient
     End If
     //
     // Send the e-mail message and close down the session
     //
     PBmailReturn = PBmailSession.MailSend( PBmailMessage)
     If PBmailReturn <> mailReturnSuccess! Then
        szTitle = "Error - " + f_mail_error_to_string( PBmailReturn)

        MessageBox( szTitle, "Unable to notify admin by specified mail " + &
                          "address. Please notify the system administrator " + &
                          "of this problem.")
        Return
     End If
  End If

  PBmailReturn = PBmailSession.MailLogoff()
  If PBmailReturn <> mailReturnSuccess! Then
     szTitle = "Error - " + f_mail_error_to_string( PBmailReturn)
     MessageBox( "Error", "Unable to logoff from mail. " + &
                       "Please notify the administrator of this problem.")
  End If

  Destroy PBmailSession
```

Once you have saved the user object, you can use it in an application. By opening the property sheet for the application object and going to the Variable Types tab page, you can set the objects that will be used for `SQLCA`, `SQLDA`, `SQLSA`, `Error`, and `Message`.

Now you can call the new methods and access the new attributes as you would any of the standard properties of an `Error` object. For example, to retrieve a message, display it to the user, and then send an e-mail notification, this would be the code:

```
//
// Some code that produces a problem!
//
Error.RetrieveError( 1969)
//
Error.SeriousError = FALSE
Error.OpenErrorWindow()
//
Error.SpecialEmail = "[MHS:raven@iquest.net]"
Error.MailError()
```

This can make the task of adding error-checking code into your event scripts quite a bit easier.

NOTE

It is important to note that the `RetrieveError()` method uses the SQLCA to access the database. You will want to carry out the same functionality introduced in the Custom class user object example to maintain a separate database connection for the `Error` objects. This is especially true for this object over the custom class object as the `Error` object will often be handling SQL errors. The necessary code was not included in this example to allow focus to be maintained on the main points of the `Error` object.

Creating a C++ Class User Object

To create a C++ class user object, select the C++ option under the Class type in the New User Object dialog box (refer to Figure 23.2) and click the OK button. (This option only appears if you have installed the Class Builder component of the Enterprise Edition of PowerBuilder.)

The User Object painter is opened, and you are presented with a screen that looks just like the ones for the other two class user objects. Within this painter, you define the methods and variables that will be used by the C++ user object. To demonstrate this painter, you will use a string encryption and decryption module.

The first thing you do is create a definition for the encryption function. To do this, bring up the User Object Function painter and enter the name, return data type, and parameters (see Figure 23.12).

FIGURE 23.12.
The user object function declaration for `cf_encrypt()`.

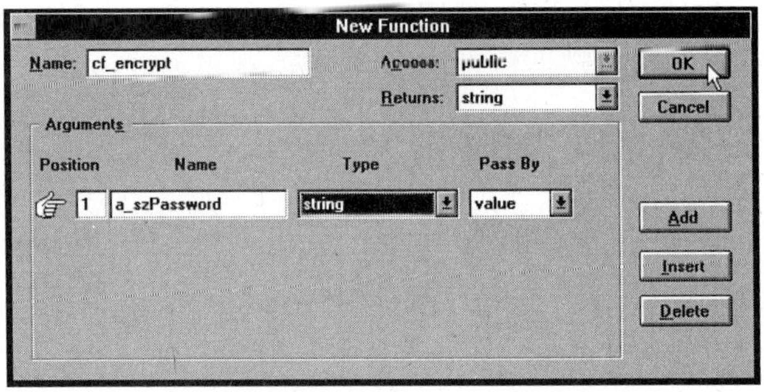

Notice that the function is prefixed with `cf_`, which indicates that a C function is being accessed. Create a similar function declaration for the decryption function and call it `cf_decrypt()`.

When you have finished declaring the variables and functions that will be part of the C++ class user object (as you have for this example), either right-click on the user object and select Invoke C++ Editor or select it from the Design menu. This causes a message box to appear that asks whether you want to name the user object (see Figure 23.13). Click the Yes button. This does not save any of the work done so far.

FIGURE 23.13.
The prompt for naming the user object.

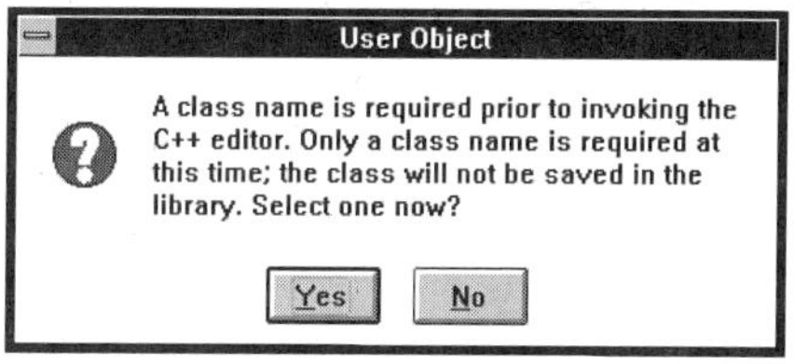

The Save User Object dialog box (see Figure 23.14) is now displayed, but you are only naming the object, not saving it. If something goes awry within the C++ Class Builder or when you return to PowerBuilder from the builder, the object will not have been saved.

FIGURE 23.14.
Naming the user object.

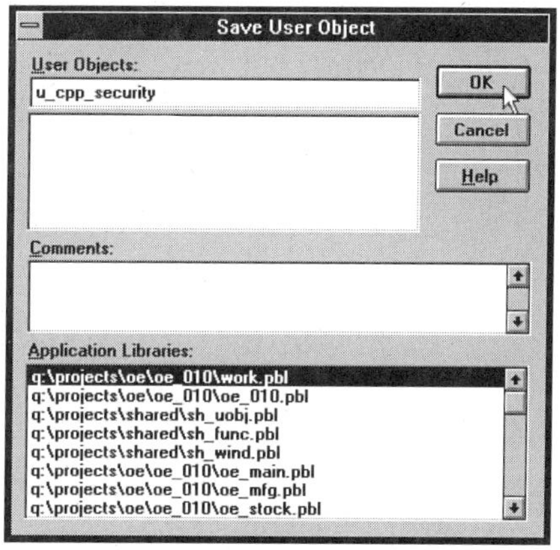

The actual C++ Class Builder is now invoked and you are placed in the Watcom IDE (integrated development environment). The Watcom IDE (see Figure 23.15) provides you with a shell from which you can call and use many different tools, such as a debugger or compiler.

When you invoke the C++ Class Builder, it generates some skeleton C++ code in the four files that are listed in Figure 23.15.

The first file listed is the first five letters of the user object name that you specified earlier, with a `c` character prefixing them and two random characters as a suffix. The reasoning behind this is to create a uniquely named file. This file contains declarations for the functions you will write, which can be accessed through PowerBuilder. You should not modify this file in any manner. Any changes you do make will be overwritten on each invocation of the Class Builder.

FIGURE 23.15.
The Watcom IDE, showing the three base files and the user-object-specific file.

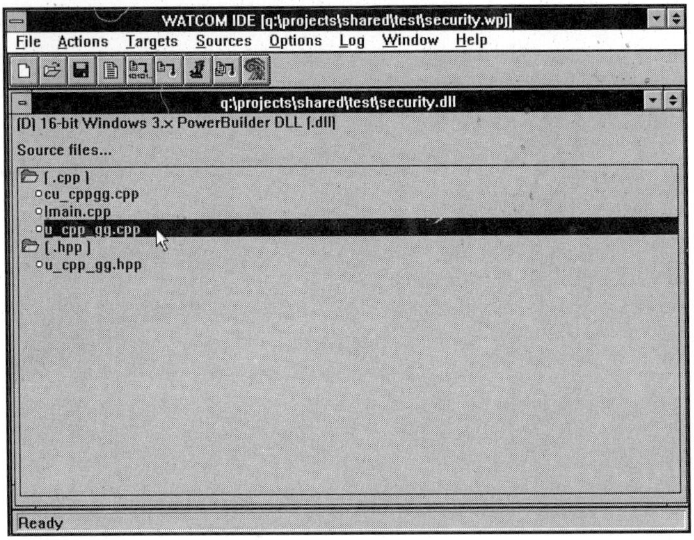

The next file in the list is lmain.cpp, which contains the DLL entry point and other essential code for generating a Windows DLL. It contains simple source for the Libmain and WEP. You will rarely, if ever, make any changes to this file.

The third file is the one that you will be actually editing, and it is called by the same name as your user object with a two-character unique identifier on the end. It initially contains only stub code for the functions you defined in the PowerBuilder User Object painter. There are a number of comments throughout this file, and you should not modify anything between `//$PB$` comments because it will cause the code generation to fail.

The final file contains the declaration and function prototype information and should only be modified if you are adding internal C++ functions or data declarations.

To access any of these files, just double-click on the filename. This opens the Watcom File Editor (see Figure 23.16) so that you can view and edit the file.

The Watcom File Editor provided some early insight into the promised new editor for PowerBuilder Version 5.0, although the final version of PowerBuilder has been implemented a little differently. A feature that has been available for some time in a number of other development packages is the capability to color code different types of scripts (such as making comments light gray so that they are less intrusive). The Watcom File Editor provides a drag-and-drop color palette for this purpose (see Figure 23.17).

FIGURE 23.16.
The Watcom File Editor.

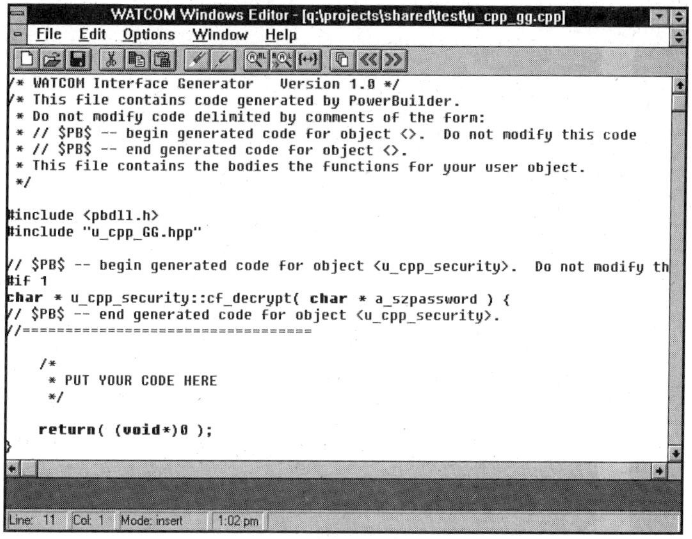

FIGURE 23.17.
The Watcom File Editor color palette.

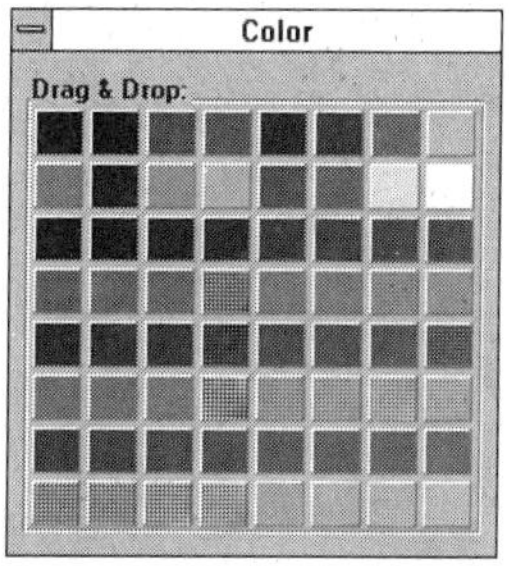

NOTE

The drag-and-drop color palette choices you make will not be saved unless you choose Save Configuration from the Options menu.

Modify the third file by adding the code in Listing 23.11.

Listing 23.11. Additional code added to the third file.

```
/* WATCOM Interface Generator  Version 1.0 */
/* This file contains code generated by PowerBuilder.
* Do not modify code delimited by comments of the form:
* // $PB$ — begin generated code for object <>. Do not modify this code
* // $PB$ — end generated code for object <>.
* This file contains the bodies the functions for your user object.
*/
#include <pbdll.h>
#include "u_cpp_GG.hpp"
// $PB$ — begin generated code for object <u_cpp_security>.
// $PB$ — Do not modify this code
#if 1
char * u_cpp_security::cf_encrypt( char * a_szpassword ) {
// $PB$ — end generated code for object <u_cpp_security>.
//==================================
   int nBreak = strlen( a_szpassword) / 2;
   char str1[8]="";
   char str2[8]="";
   char newstr1[8]="";
   char newstr2[8]="";
   char* newPass="";
   unsigned int i;

   strncpy( str1, a_szpassword, nBreak);
   strncpy( str2, &a_szpassword[ nBreak], strlen( a_szpassword) - nBreak);

   for( i = 0; i< strlen( str2); i++)
   {
      newstr1[ i] = str2[ i] - (char)7;
   }

   for( i = 0; i< strlen( str1); i++)
   {
      newstr2[ i] = str1[ i] - (char)6;
   }
   strcpy( newPass, newstr1);
   strcat( newPass, newstr2);
   return newPass;
}
#endif // PowerBuilder code, do not remove
// $PB$ — begin generated code for object <u_cpp_security>.
// $PB$ — Do not modify this code
#if 1
char * u_cpp_security::cf_decrypt( char * a_szpassword ) {
// $PB$ — end generated code for object <u_cpp_security>.
//==================================
int nBreak = strlen(a_szpassword) / 2;
char str1[8]="";
char str2[8]="";
char newstr1[8]="";
char newstr2[8]="";
char* newPass="";
unsigned int i;

   nBreak = nBreak + strlen( a_szpassword) % nBreak;
```

```
    if nBreak == 0 Then nBreak = 1

    strncpy( str1, a_szpassword, nBreak);
    strncpy( str2, &a_szpassword[ nBreak], strlen( a_szpassword) - nBreak);

    for( i = 0; i< strlen( str2); i++)
    {
       newstr1[ i] = str2[ i] + 6;
    }

    for( i = 0; i< strlen( str1); i++)
    {
       newstr2[ i] = str1[ i] + 7;
    }
    strcpy( newPass, newstr1);
    strcat( newPass, newstr2);

    return newPass;
}
#endif // PowerBuilder code, do not remove
```

Now you need to make this into a DLL that you can access from PowerBuilder. To do this, select the Make option from the Targets menu. This invokes the necessary compiler (and appropriate switches) and linker to create the DLL. The status of the compilation is shown in a window at the lower half of the screen (see Figure 23.18).

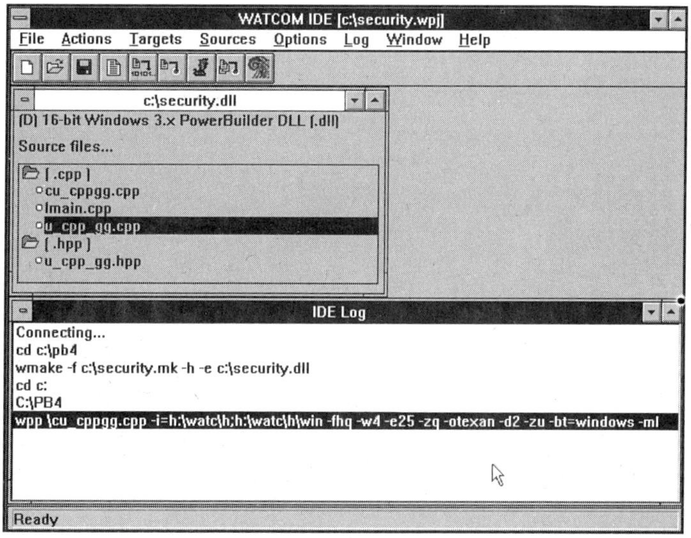

FIGURE 23.18.
Compiling the code to a DLL.

If you see an `Execution Successful` message at the bottom of this window, you can return to PowerBuilder and make use of this new user object. As you can see in Figure 23.19, the C++ class user object looks very much like any other user object.

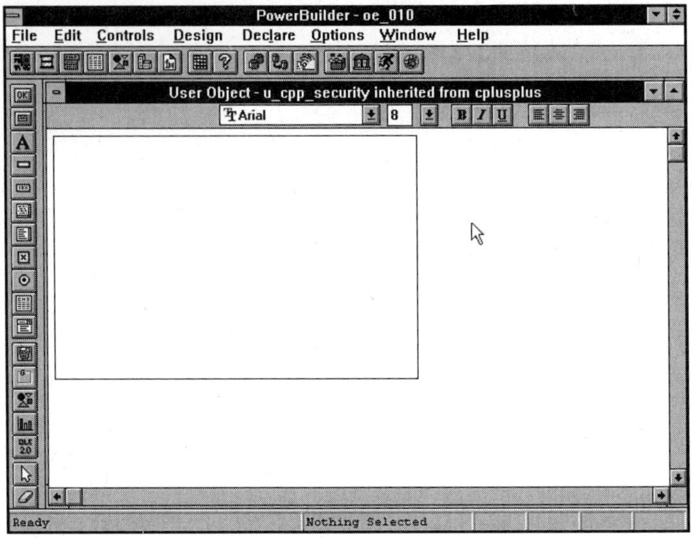

FIGURE 23.19.
The finished C++ class user object.

The following code creates an instance of the object and passes in a string to be encrypted:

```
String szPassword = "Gallagher", szEncrypted, szDecrypted

u_cpp_security ucppSecurity
ucppSecurity = create u_cpp_security

szEncrypted = ucppSecurity.cf_encrypt( Left( szPassword, 8))
szDecrypted = ucppSecurity.cf_decrypt( szEncrypted)

Destroy ucppSecurity
```

As you can see from this code, you instantiate and access the user object as you would any other user object. There are a number of pitfalls and restrictions associated with creating C++ class user objects, but they are beyond the scope of this introductory text.

Summary

This chapter provides some insight into how easy it can be to code outwardly complex functionality—visual or nonvisual—into manageable objects. Some of the techniques you need to use to create easily reusable objects are discussed, as is how each of the user object types should be used.

Building User Objects

24

IN THIS CHAPTER

This chapter introduces the user-object–specific functions in PowerScript and some of the most common user objects you will find in a framework.

Creating User Objects at Runtime

You can place visual user objects on a window using two different methods. You can either paint them on the window during development, as you would any other control, or dynamically create them during execution using the functions outlined in the following sections. In the following sections the relevant functions are introduced and you're given an actual example of how and where to use them.

The `OpenUserObject()` Function

To create and display a user object on a window, you need to use the `OpenUserObject()` function. This will make the attributes, controls, functions, and events available for use within the window.

There are two syntaxes for this function that parallel the `Open()` function used with windows. The first syntax opens an instance of a particular user object, and the second allows you to specify the class of the object to open.

The user object is drawn to the screen when the display is next updated; this can occur because of either another function call or display attribute change that causes the screen to be repainted or a function call at the end of the script. This is a useful feature if you are creating a number of objects because it won't cause a lot of screen flicker.

The `OpenUserObject()` Function: Format One

The first syntax is as follows:

```
WindowName.OpenUserObject( UserObjectVariable {, X, Y})
```

The *`UserObjectVariable`* parameter specifies either the user object data type or a variable declared of the desired user object data type. The function returns a reference to the opened user object and stores it either in the variable that was used in the argument or as the instance pool entry for that object class. The *`X`* and *`Y`* parameters are optional positions in the window to open the user object. If you call this function a second time with the same user object or variable, the user object is activated twice and you will not have two instances appearing.

For example, to dynamically open an instance of a single-line edit user object at coordinate `300,200` on the window, this would be the syntax:

```
u_sle sle_dynamic1

OpenUserObject( sle_dynamic1, 300, 200)
```

The `OpenUserObject()` Function: Format Two

With the second syntax you can open a user object by specifying the class type as an additional parameter:

```
WindowName.OpenUserObject( UserObjectVariable, UserObjectClass {, X, Y})
```

The parameter *`UserObjectVariable`* must be a variable, and it either can be declared as an ancestor class for all user objects you will be opening or must be type `DragObject`. The function places a reference to the opened user object in this variable. The *`UserObjectClass`* parameter is a string that specifies the name of the user object to display, which must be a descendant of the class *`UserObjectVariable`*. Just remember that you will be unable to access attributes, functions, or structures that belong to the class *`UserObjectVariable`*.

You use the second syntax of `OpenUserObject()` when you do not know the user object that will be opened when the script is executed.

For example, if a function is to be used to open a number of different classes of user objects you would pass a string representing the class:

```
// String a_szClassName
DragObject doNewUO

OpenUserObject( doNewUO, a_szClassName)
```

Or if you knew that the user objects were all inherited from a base class, say `u_sle`, then you could use that as the Variable data type:

```
// String a_szClassName
// which might contain "u_sle_numeric" or "u_sle_required"
u_sle doNewUO

OpenUserObject( doNewUO, a_szClassName)
```

This has the advantage of allowing you to access ancestor-level functions and attributes that you would have been unable to use with the first example that used `DragObject` as the variable data type.

NOTE

Using these functions does *not* add the new user object to the window's control array. PowerBuilder also does *not* include the object specified by `UserObjectClass` in an executable, and you must use a PBD to incorporate it into your finished application.

The `OpenUserObjectWithParm()` Function

This function is similar in purpose to the `OpenWithParm()` function used with windows. Using `OpenUserObjectWithParm()` not only can you carry out the same functionality as detailed in the section "The `OpenUserObject()` Function," but you can also pass parameters to the user object. As with `OpenWithParm()`, the parameter(s) are stored in the `Message` object.

There are again two syntaxes to mirror those available for `OpenUserObject()`.

This is the first syntax:

```
WindowName.OpenUserObject( UserObjectVariable, Parameter {, X, Y})
```

This is the second syntax:

```
WindowName.OpenUserObject( UserObjectVariable,Parameter,UserObjectClass {,X,Y})
```

The use of the `Message` object and retrieving information from it is covered in Chapter 11, "Windows and the Window Painter."

The same warnings that apply for opening windows with parameters and user objects hold:

- Access the `Message` object immediately in the user object in case the `Message` object is inadvertently used by another event.
- Check the `PowerObject` value for a `NULL` object reference before trying to use it.

The `CloseUserObject()` Function

By using the `CloseUserObject()` function you can close down and free up the resources of user objects you have opened. This causes the user object to be removed from the display and the `Destructor` event to be triggered in the user object. This is the syntax for this function:

```
WindowName.CloseUserObject( UserObjectName)
```

`UserObjectName` is the object name or instance to be closed.

NOTE

Remember to destroy all objects that *you* create. This should be part of your credo while developing PowerBuilder applications.

We will now examine an example that uses the functions that were just introduced to create a very useful addition to an MDI frame window.

A Dynamic User Object Example: An MDI Status Bar

A very useful window is included in the PowerBuilder sample libraries that allows you to create a status bar similar to the ones you can find on most commercial Windows applications. This effect is achieved using a window and dynamically creating user objects for different areas of the bar.

The Status User Object

The actual status area is a custom visual user object, `u_mdi_microhelp_item`, that contains a single static text control that is stretched to fill the user object area, along with one gray and one white line graphic control. The lines are placed at the far left end of the user object area to form a 3D-looking separator.

The user object has a single instance variable (Listing 24.1) and five functions that provide an interface to the attributes of the user object.

Listing 24.1. An instance variable for `u_mdi_microhelp_item`.

```
Private:
   // Specifies the action that the user object is to display, ie. Date and time
   Integer i_nAction
```

To change the width of the object, you provide a function, `uf_SetWidth()`, that is called with the new width and a text alignment enumerated type (see Listing 24.2). When the user object is resized, the static text control is also resized.

Listing 24.2. The public subroutine `uf_SetWidth()`.

```
//Parameters:
//     Integer a_nWidth
//     Alignment a_Align

this.Width = a_nWidth
st_1.Width = a_nWidth - st_1.X
st_1.Alignment = a_align
```

To maintain the total encapsulation of the user object, you also provide a function to set the `Text` attribute of the static text object (see Listing 24.3).

Listing 24.3. The public subroutine `uf_SetText()`.

```
//Parameters:
//     String a_szText

st_1.text = a_szText
```

To alter the color of the text displayed in the static text object, use the `uf_SetColour()` function (see Listing 24.4).

Listing 24.4. The public subroutine `uf_SetColour()`.

```
//Parameters:
//    Long a_nColour

st_1.TextColor = a_nColour
```

The next functions provide set and get access to the private instance variable of the user object. The set function is shown in Listing 24.5.

Listing 24.5. The public subroutine `uf_SetAction()`.

```
//Parameters:
//    Integer a_nAction

i_nAction = a_nAction
```

This is the get function:

```
Return i_nAction
```

This user object provides the basis of all the status items that will be displayed on the window that is attached to the frame.

The Frame Parasite Window

The window `w_frame_system_data` is of type Popup and is initially declared as invisible, disabled, and without a border.

Listing 24.6 shows the private instance variables that are declared for this window.

Listing 24.6. The private instance variables for `w_frame_system_data`.

```
Window i_wParent
Integer i_nItems, i_nWinHeight, i_nOffset
Integer i_nBorderHeight, i_nBorderWidth, i_nResizeableOffset
u_mdi_microhelp_item i_uoItems[]

// Constants
Integer SYS_TIME = 1, USER_HEAP = 2, GDI_HEAP = 3, SYS_MEMORY = 4, DB_SERVER = 5
Integer TOTAL_ITEMS = 5
```

The window is based on three event scripts: `Open`, `Close`, and `Timer`.

The `Open` event, shown in Listing 24.7, is used to set up the required pieces of the status bar. The window is opened with a numeric parameter, which is a bit representation (see Table 24.1) of the desired styles to add to the status bar.

Table 24.1. Bit styles for `w_frame_system_data`.

Bit Value	Decimal Value	Description
00001	1	Time
00010	2	User heap
00100	4	GDI heap
01000	8	Memory
10000	16	Database server and database (current)

To add a style to the list you simply add the decimal values together. For example, to display just the time and memory items you would open `w_frame_system_data` with the value 9.

NOTE

This method of passing style bits around is very useful if you don't want to deal with structures and the associated overheads.

Within the `Open` event, shown in Listing 24.7, the style bits are converted from a numeric representation into separate Boolean equality tests. As you can see in Table 24.1, each style overlays, without overwriting, the other styles, so you can determine each individual setting by successively dividing by 2, taking the result away from the total value, and checking for a remainder. Information about the environment in which the window will appear is gathered: screen height, window height, offset within window, and window border (and whether this border is resizable). The window function `wf_AddItem()` is called for each status item that was requested to be displayed. After all the status items have been created, the window is resized to show just these items and then attach itself to the correct area of the parent. A 30-second timer is then set to cause the status items to be refreshed at regular intervals.

Listing 24.7. The `Open` event for `w_frame_system_data`.

```
Integer nCount, nWork, nPrevious, nBorder

// Hold for later
nWork = message.Doubleparm

// Initialize and determine environment information
i_wParent = ParentWindow()

// This assumes standard PC screen dimensions
Choose Case g_App.i_Environment.ScreenHeight
   Case 480
      i_nWinHeight = 57
      i_nOffset = 16
```

continues

Listing 24.7. continued

```
   Case 600
      i_nWinHeight= 54
      i_nOffset = 18
   Case Else
      i_nWinHeight= 57
      i_nOffset = 10
End Choose
this.Height = i_nWinHeight

nBorder = ProfileInt( "win.ini", "windows", "borderwidth", 2)
i_nBorderHeight = 4 * nBorder
i_nBorderWidth = PixelsToUnits( nBorder, XPixelsToUnits!)

// If the window that was passed is resizable include additional border thickness
If Not i_wParent.Resizable Then
   i_nResizeableOffset = 8 * ( nBorder + 2)
End If

// Break out the bit pattern of the passed parm
nPrevious = nWork
For nCount = 1 to TOTAL_ITEMS
   nWork /= 2
   If (( nPrevious - ( nWork * 2)) = 1) Then
      If nCount = 1 Then wf_AddItem( 350, Center!, SYS_TIME, FALSE)
      If nCount = 2 Then wf_AddItem( 350, Center!, USER_HEAP, FALSE)
      If nCount = 3 Then wf_AddItem( 150, Center!, GDI_HEAP, FALSE)
      If nCount = 4 Then wf_AddItem( 250, Center!, SYS_MEMORY, FALSE)
      If nCount = 5 Then wf_AddItem( 350, Center!, DB_SERVER, FALSE)
   End If
   nPrevious = nWork
Next

wf_ParentResized()

this.TriggerEvent( Timer!)

// Every 30 seconds refresh the item text
Timer( 30, this)
```

The initial setting and subsequent refreshing of the status items is carried out in the `Timer` event (see Listing 24.8). There are five different types of status that can be displayed: `SYS_TIME`, `USER_HEAP`, `GDI_HEAP`, `SYS_MEMORY`, and `DB_SERVER`. Two user object functions, `uf_SetText()` and `uf_SetColour()`, are used to set each item's text and appropriate color.

Listing 24.8. The `Timer` event for `w_frame_system_data`.

```
Uint unResource
Ulong ulMem
Integer nCount
String szServerName

For nCount = 1 To i_nItems
```

```
    Choose Case i_uoItems[ nCount].uf_GetAction()
        Case DB_SERVER
            szServerName=Upper(Left(SQLCA.ServerName,1)) + Mid(SQLCA.ServerName,2)
            i_uoItems[nCount].uf_SetText(szServerName + " (" + SQLCA.Database+")")
        Case SYS_TIME
            i_uoItems[ nCount].uf_SetText( String( Today(), "m/dd/yy") + " " + &
                                          String( Now(), "h:mm am/pm"))
            i_uoItems[ nCount].uf_SetColour( RGB( 0, 0, 128))
        Case GDI_HEAP
            unResource = g_App.Externals.uf_GetFreeSystemResources(1)
            If unResource < 20 Then
                // Set the colour to red - indicate potential problem
                i_uoItems[ nCount].uf_SetColour( 255)
            Else
                // Normal black text colour
                i_uoItems[ nCount].uf_SetColour( 0)
            End If
            i_uoItems[ nCount].uf_SetText("GDI: " + String(unResource,"###")+" %")
        Case USER_HEAP
            unResource = g_App.Externals.uf_GetFreeSystemResources(2)
            If unResource < 20 Then
                // Set the colour to red - indicate potential problem
                i_uoItems[ nCount].uf_SetColour( 255)
            Else
              // Normal black text colour
              i_uoItems[ nCount].uf_SetColour( 0)
            End If
            i_uoItems[nCount].uf_SetText("User: "+ String(unResource,"###") +" %")
        Case SYS_MEMORY
            ulMem = g_App.Externals.uf_GetFreememory()
            If ulMem < 2 Then
                i_uoItems[ nCount].uf_SetColour( 255)
            Else
                i_uoItems[ nCount].uf_SetColour( 0)
            End If
            // Divide the value by 1024 * 1024 to convert from bytes to MB
            i_uoItems[nCount].uf_SetText("Mem: "+String(ulMem/1048576,"#.0")+" Mb")
    End Choose
Next
```

Think back to the start of this chapter, where we added a phrase to the developers' credo: destroy all objects that you create. In the `Close` event, shown in Listing 24.9, we put this into practice. Each user object that we had opened is now closed and the associated resources are recovered.

Listing 24.9. The `Close` event for `w_frame_system_data`.

```
Integer nCount

For nCount = 1 To i_nItems
    CloseUserObject( i_uoItems[ nCount])
Next
```

Four supporting window functions undertake a variety of tasks.

The function `wf_ParentResized()` (see Listing 24.10) is called by the parent window whenever a `Resize` event occurs. The width and height of `w_frame_system_data` has to be calculated in order to display the requested status areas. The height and width of the user objects are taken into consideration when calculating the new width, height, and position of the window in the parent frame.

Listing 24.10. The public subroutine `wf_ParentResized()`.

```
// Position window so it is over lower right hand portion of MicroHelp bar
Integer nWindowHeight, nWindowWidth, nTemp
Boolean bVisible

bVisible = this.Visible
this.Visible = FALSE

If i_wParent.WindowState = Minimized! Then
   Return
End If

wf_CalculateItemSizes()

nWindowHeight = i_wParent.Y + i_wParent.Height - &
                ( this.Height + i_nOffset + i_nBorderHeight)
nWindowWidth = i_wParent.X + WorkSpaceWidth( i_wParent) + &
               i_nBorderWidth - ( this.Width + 12)
If g_App.i_Environment.OSMajorRevision = 4 Then
   // Move the parasite more to the left because of the resize box in Win95
   nWindowWidth -= 45
End If

// Calculate smallest possible distance in from left edge of frame
nTemp = i_wParent.X + 2 * i_nBorderWidth + 16

// Is the window width less than the smallest possible frame size?
If nWindowWidth < nTemp Then
   // Then move the window to the left most edge of the frame.
   nWindowWidth = nTemp
   this.Width = WorkSpaceWidth( i_wParent) - ( i_nBorderWidth + 32)
End If

this.Move( nWindowWidth, nWindowHeight)
this.Visible = bVisible
i_wParent.SetFocus()
```

The function `wf_CalculateItemSizes()` (see Listing 24.11) is called to calculate the overall width of the visible status items and to adjust the spacing of the objects in case a status object has been created or destroyed since the last call. The width of the window is then adjusted to allow the status objects to be displayed.

Listing 24.11. The private subroutine `wf_CalculateItemSizes()`.

```
// Determine the overall width of the window and reposition the items them selves
Integer nCount, nTotalWidth

If i_nItems <= 0 Then Return

i_uoItems[ i_nItems].X = 0
nTotalWidth = i_uoItems[ i_nItems].Width

For nCount = (i_nItems - 1) To 1 Step -1
   i_uoItems[ nCount].X = i_uoItems[ nCount + 1].X + i_uoItems[ nCount + 1].Width
   nTotalWidth += i_uoItems[ nCount].Width
Next

this.width = nTotalWidth
```

The function `wf_AddItem()` (see Listing 24.12) demonstrates the `OpenUserObject()` function in use. The second format is used to open each instance of the `u_mdi_microhelp_item` class. The object reference is stored in the instance array `i_uoItems`. The attributes of the object instance are then set using the access functions that were provided.

Since we have just altered the number of visible status items, `wf_ParentResized()` is called to resize the window, and then a `Timer` event is caused to set the initial value of the new item.

Listing 24.12. The public function integer `wf_AddItem()`.

```
//Parameters:
//     Integer a_nItemWidth
//     Alignment a_Alignment
//     Integer a_nCode
//     Boolean a_bUpdate

// Add an item to the list of items, and appear to the left of the last
i_nItems ++

Choose Case a_nCode
   Case DB_SERVER
      a_nItemWidth = 450
   Case SYS_TIME
      a_nItemWidth = 450
   Case GDI_HEAP
      a_nItemWidth = 260
   Case USER_HEAP
      a_nItemWidth = 260
   Case SYS_MEMORY
      a_nItemWidth = 360
End Choose

OpenUserObject( i_uoItems[ i_nItems], "u_mdi_microhelp_item")

i_uoItems[ i_nItems].Height = i_nWinHeight
i_uoItems[ i_nItems].uf_SetAction( a_nCode)
```

continues

Listing 24.12. continued

```
i_uoItems[ i_nItems].uf_SetWidth( a_nItemWidth, a_Alignment)

If a_bUpdate Then
   wf_ParentResized()
   PostEvent( Timer!)
End If

Return i_nItems
```

The function `wf_DeleteItem()` (see Listing 24.13) is called to selectively remove status items from `w_frame_system_data`. The `CloseUserObject()` function is used to destroy the storage associated with the item, and the `i_uoItems` array is shuffled to fill the hole that's left. The `wf_ParentResized()` function is called to resize the window to the smaller number of visible status items.

Listing 24.13. The public function Boolean `wf_DeleteItem()`.

```
//Parameters:
//     Integer a_nPosition

// Delete the item at the passed position
Integer nCount

If (( a_nPosition > i_nItems) Or ( a_nPosition <= 0)) Then
    Return FALSE
End If

CloseUserObject( i_uoItems[ a_nPosition])

i_nItems --
// Remove the deleted item from the array of items
If i_nItems > 0 Then
   For nCount = a_nPosition To i_nItems
      i_uoItems[ nCount] = i_uoItems[ nCount + 1]
   Next
End If

wf_ParentResized()
Return TRUE
```

You can add a number of access functions to allow the frame window to query, and maybe set some of the private instance variables if you wish.

The finished MDI frame status bar is shown in Figure 24.1.

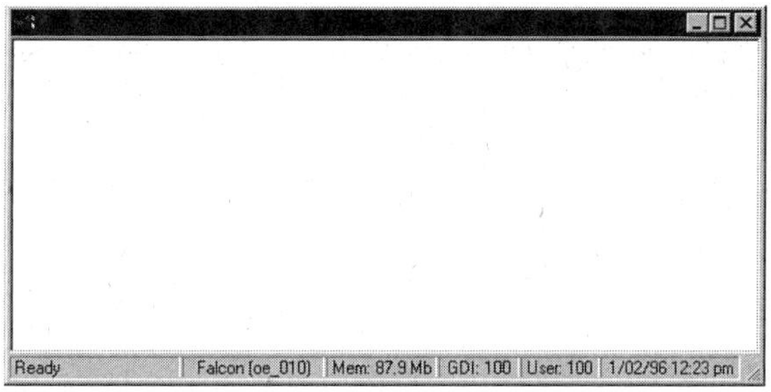

FIGURE 24.1.
The MDI frame status bar.

Transaction Class Objects

Along with the `DataWindow` standard visual user object, one of the most important user objects you can create is a standard class user object based on the system class `Transaction`. This allows you to encapsulate basic functionality into one object, instead of having to code the same statements over and over (for example, starting a transaction).

The transaction object we will build in this section will incorporate the transaction management practices introduced in Chapter 5, "SQL and PowerBuilder," as well as some additional object management functions.

The user object `u_n_transaction` is written as an abstract class and you will inherit concrete class objects for each of the database management systems you will be using. There are a few instance variables declared for the object (see Listing 24.14).

> **NOTE**
>
> The `This` keyword will not work in SQL statements in PowerBuilder 4.0 and you need to place a self-referencing variable in the user object. This is not the case for Version 5.0 and you can remove the instance variable and place self-references within the code.

Listing 24.14. Instance variables for `u_n_transaction`.

```
Protected:
   Error i_Error
   Integer i_nOpenTransactions = 0
   Boolean i_bConnected = FALSE, i_bBeginTran = FALSE, i_bSaveTran = FALSE
```

In the abstract class five functions are prototyped (see Listing 24.15) and are all set to return a zero value. These will be overridden in each concrete class for DBMS-specific transaction management.

Listing 24.15. Function prototypes for `u_n_transaction`.

```
public function integer SaveTran( String a_szTranName)
public function integer CommitTran()
public function integer BeginTran()
public function integer RollbackToSave( String a_szTranName)
public function integer RollbackTran()
```

Transaction Class Events

Within the `Constructor` event (see Listing 24.16) you will create the error object that will be used by this object's functions for error reporting. The private `Error` object allows you to set persistent values and make additional assignments without affecting the calling script's error object held by the application.

Listing 24.16. The `Constructor` event for `u_n_transaction`.

```
i_Error = Create Error
i_Error.Object = this.ClassName()
```

Before the object is destroyed, you need to ensure that the current connection has been closed down correctly. After that has been achieved, the private error object must be destroyed along with its parent (see Listing 24.17).

Listing 24.17. The `Destructor` event for `u_n_transaction`.

```
If i_bConnected Then
   this.CloseConnection()
End If

Destroy i_Error
```

Transaction Class Methods

A function that will be used throughout the object is `CheckForError()` (see Listing 24.18), which is called to check the `SQLCode` and open the standard error window if requested to. The `SQLCode` is returned by the function for additional processing in the calling function (see the `MakeConnection()` function in Listing 24.20 for an example).

Listing 24.18. The public function Integer `CheckForError()`.

```
//Parameters:
//    Error a_Error
//    Boolean a_bDisplayError
```

```
If this.SQLCode = -1 And a_bDisplayError Then
   error.WindowMenu = a_Error.WindowMenu
   error.Object = a_Error.Object
   error.ObjectEvent = a_Error.ObjectEvent
   error.Line = a_Error.Line
   error.Number = this.SQLDBCode
   error.Text = this.SQLErrText
   open( w_error)
   Return this.SQLCode
Else
   Return this.SQLCode
End If
```

`IsConnected()` is an access function that returns the current status of the connection:

```
Return i_bConnected
```

`InTransaction()` is an access function that returns whether the connection is currently in the midst of a transaction:

```
Return i_bBeginTran
```

`OpenTransactions()` is an access function that returns the current level of transaction nesting:

```
Return i_nOpenTransactions
```

The `ExecuteSQL()` function, shown in Listing 24.19, provides a controlled point to execute SQL code that is outside the commands that PowerBuilder recognizes.

Listing 24.19. The public function Integer `ExecuteSql()` for `u_n_transaction`.

```
//Parameters:
//    String a_szStatement
//    Boolean a_bShowError

EXECUTE IMMEDIATE :a_szStatement USING this;

If a_bShowError Then
   i_Error.ObjectEvent = "ExecuteSQL()"
   i_Error.line = 1
   Return CheckForError( i_Error, TRUE)
Else
   Return this.SQLCode
End If
```

The `MakeConnection()` function, shown in Listing 24.20, issues the `CONNECT` statement for you and carries out the error processing for you.

Listing 24.20. The public function Integer `MakeConnection()` for `u_n_transaction`.

```
i_Error.ObjectEvent = "MakeConnection()"
i_Error.Line = 4

If i_bConnected Then
   // Already connected!
   Return -1
End If

CONNECT USING this;

If CheckForError( i_Error, FALSE) = 0 Then
   i_bConnected = TRUE
End If

Return this.SQLCode
```

The `CloseConnection()` function, shown in Listing 24.21, issues the `DISCONNECT` statement and carries out any error processing for you. Also, rather than relying on PowerBuilder to carry out an implicit transaction rollback or commit, you know for certain that an explicit rollback of an open transaction will occur.

Listing 24.21. The public function Integer `CloseConnection()`.

```
If Not i_bConnected Then
   // Already disconnected!
   Return -1
End If

i_Error.ObjectEvent = "CloseConnection()"

// Currently have an open transaction roll it back.
If this.AutoCommit Then
   If i_bBeginTran Then
      this.RollbackTran()
      i_Error.Line = 10
      CheckForError( i_Error, TRUE)
   End If
Else
   ROLLBACK USING this;
   i_Error.Line = 15
   CheckForError( i_Error, TRUE)
End If

DISCONNECT USING this;
i_Error.Line = 17

If CheckForError( i_Error, TRUE) = 0 Then
   i_bConnected = FALSE
   i_nOpenTransactions = 0
End If

Return this.SQLCode
```

The Concrete Transaction Class: SQL Server

In each concrete class object inherited from `u_n_transaction`, the following methods should be defined. The sample code shown in Listing 24.22 is for a Microsoft or Sybase SQL Server transaction object.

The first function in Listing 24.22 was not prototyped in `u_n_transaction` because it would have served no purpose; the function is not used in the object itself, and the variable it uses is particular to each concrete class. The function `CloneObject()` creates and returns a new unconnected transaction object based on the current transaction object.

Listing 24.22. The public function `u_n_sqlserver_transaction CloneObject()`.

```
u_n_sqlserver_transaction trChildTransaction

trChildTransaction = create u_n_sqlserver_transaction

trChildTransaction.DBMS = this.DBMS
trChildTransaction.database = this.database
trChildTransaction.servername = this.servername
trChildTransaction.logid = this.logid
trChildTransaction.logpass = this.logpass
trChildTransaction.userid = this.userid
trChildTransaction.dbparm = this.dbparm
trChildTransaction.dbpass = this.dbpass
trChildTransaction.lock = this.lock
trChildTransaction.autocommit = this.autocommit

Return trChildTransaction
```

The remaining methods for this object are discussed in Chapter 5, and they are shown in their completed form here.

The `BeginTran()` function, shown in Listing 24.23, starts a database transaction based on the current value of the transaction's `AutoCommit` attribute, starting a true transaction if it is set to `TRUE`, and a PowerBuilder transaction if it is set to `FALSE`.

Listing 24.23. The public function Integer `BeginTran()`.

```
i_Error.ObjectEvent = "BeginTran()"

If this.AutoCommit Then
   EXECUTE IMMEDIATE "BEGIN TRANSACTION" USING this;
   i_Error.Line = 4
Else
   // There is no BEGIN TRANSACTION for PB with no AutoCommit
   COMMIT USING thid;
```

continues

Listing 24.23. continued

```
   i_Error.Line = 8
End If

i_nOpenTransactions ++
i_bBeginTran = TRUE

Return CheckForError( i_Error, TRUE)
```

The `CommitTran()` function, shown in Listing 24.24, completes an open database transaction and causes the changes to be committed to the database. The method used is dependent on the current value of the transaction's `AutoCommit` attribute.

Listing 24.24. The public function Integer `CommitTran()`.

```
i_Error.ObjectEvent = "CommitTran()"

If this.AutoCommit Then
   If i_bBeginTran Then
      EXECUTE IMMEDIATE "COMMIT TRANSACTION" USING this;
      i_Error.Line = 5
   End If
Else
   COMMIT USING this;
   i_Error.Line = 9
End If

i_bBeginTran = FALSE
i_bSaveTran = FALSE
i_nOpenTransactions —

Return CheckForError( i_Error, TRUE)
```

The `RollbackTran()` function, shown in Listing 24.25, completes an open database transaction and causes the changes made in it to be thrown away. The method used is dependent on the current value of the transaction's `AutoCommit` attribute.

Listing 24.25. The public function Integer `RollBackTran()`.

```
i_Error.ObjectEvent = "ExecuteSQL()"

If this.AutoCommit Then
   If i_bBeginTran Then
      EXECUTE IMMEDIATE "ROLLBACK TRANSACTION" USING this;
      i_Error.Line = 5
   End If
Else
   ROLLBACK USING this;
   i_Error.Line = 9
```

```
End If

i_bBeginTran = FALSE
i_bSaveTran = FALSE
i_nOpenTransactions = 0

Return CheckForError( i_Error, FALSE)
```

The next two functions are based on SQL Server's ability to save points in a transaction and allow partial recovery to these points to occur.

The `SaveTran()` function, shown in Listing 24.26, is used to label a position in the transaction so that recovery can occur to that point. There is no corresponding save transaction point command in the default PowerBuilder behavior, and everything must be committed or rolled back together.

Listing 24.26. The public function Integer `SaveTran()`.

```
//Parameters:
//    String a_szTranName

String szCommand

szCommand = "SAVE TRANSACTION " + a_szTranName

i_Error.ObjectEvent = "SaveTran()"

If this.AutoCommit Then
   EXECUTE IMMEDIATE :szCommand USING this;
   i_Error.Line = 8
Else
   // There is no SAVE TRANSACTION for PB with no AutoCommit
   // continue the existing transaction, and commit or rollback everything.
End If

i_bSaveTran = TRUE
i_nOpenTransactions ++

Return CheckForError( i_Error, TRUE)
```

The `RollbackToSave()` function, shown in Listing 24.27, is used to carry out a partial rollback of all commands issued since the save transaction label specified. Again, there is no corresponding partial rollback command in the default PowerBuilder behavior and everything must be committed or rolled back together.

Listing 24.27. The public function Integer `RollBackToSave()`.

```
//Parameters:
//    String a_szTranName

String szCommand

szCommand = "ROLLBACK TRANSACTION " + a_szTranName

i_Error.ObjectEvent = "ExecuteSQL()"

If this.AutoCommit Then
   If i_bBeginTran Then
      EXECUTE IMMEDIATE :szCommand USING this;
      i_Error.Line = 9
   End If
Else
   ROLLBACK USING this;
   i_Error.Line = 13
End If

i_nOpenTransactions —

If a_szTranName = "" Then
   i_bBeginTran = FALSE
   i_nOpenTransactions = 0
End If

i_bSaveTran = FALSE

Return CheckForError( i_Error, TRUE)
```

Application Class Objects

Another useful addition to any framework or class library is an abstract application class, from which you inherit for each application. This allows you to perform generic processing for each application, and also provides a location to store global variables. You can provide access functions to them if you want.

The application class object is constructed using a custom class user object as the base. The user object has a number of instance variables declared (see Listing 24.28) and they are all publicly accessible from within the application.

Listing 24.28. `u_n_application` variables.

```
u_n_externals Externals
Environment i_Environment
Application i_Application
Window i_hWndFrame
String i_szApplication, i_szApplicationName, i_szINIFile
```

The very first variable, `Externals`, is in fact another custom class user object and is further discussed in Chapter 33, "API Calls." Very simply, it references the appropriate class user object through which external calls should be made. During the initialization of the application user object the environment that the application is running in is determined, and `Externals` is instantiated with the appropriate API user object. This is the code:

```
uf_SetEnvironment()
```

As important as the `Constructor` event is the call in the `Destructor` event that is used to clean up the resources used by the application. This is the code:

```
uf_CleanUp()
```

The complete functionality of this user object is hidden behind object-level functions, and in some of the function descriptions shown in Listing 24.29 you will see comments where code previously introduced in Chapter 11 goes.

Listing 24.29. The public subroutine `uf_SetApplication()`.

```
//Parameters:
//    application a_application

i_application = a_application
//
// See Chapter 11- set the toolbar startup attributes
//
```

One of the user objects that will be introduced later in this chapter is a standard class transaction user object. If you use this user object, it needs to be instantiated with the correct type of transaction object. The function `uf_SetDBMS()` (see Listing 24.30) is used for this purpose. The function would be ideally called in a connection window, but the application `Open` event would serve just as well.

Listing 24.30. The public subroutine Boolean `uf_SetDBMS()`.

```
//Parameters:
//    String a_szDBMS

Boolean bSuccess = TRUE

Choose Case Lower( a_szDBMS)
    Case "hpallbase"
         SQLCA = Create u_n_allbase_transaction
    Case "ibm db2"
         SQLCA = Create u_n_db2_transaction
    Case "in4 - i-net v4.x",  "in5 - i-net v5.x"
         SQLCA = Create u_n_informix_transaction
    Case "mdi gateway"
         SQLCA = Create u_n_gateway_transaction
    Case "or6 - oracle v6.x", "or7 - oracle v7.x"
         SQLCA = Create u_n_oracle_transaction
    Case "syb - sql server v4.x"
         SQLCA = Create u_n_sqlserver_transaction
    Case "gupta"
         SQLCA = Create u_n_sqlbase_transaction
    Case "netgateway"
         SQLCA = Create u_n_netgateway_transaction
    Case "syc - sybase system 10"
         SQLCA = Create u_n_sybase_transaction
    Case "xdb"
         SQLCA = Create u_n_xdb_transaction
    Case Else
         // Failed to pick up a specific transaction object
         bSuccess = FALSE
End Choose

Return bSuccess
```

The return from this function should be checked to ensure that the DBMS string passed was recognized.

When the application is first run, the `uf_SetEnvironment()` function (see Listing 24.31) is called to set up the environment-related variables: the operating environment and the necessary API object that works in this environment. As you extend your applications across multiple platforms (see Chapter 21, "Cross-Platform PowerBuilder") you can extend the `Choose...Case` statement to make use of the API user objects that you create. Because of the way you construct the API object and call those functions, you will not need to change a single line of code elsewhere in your application.

Listing 24.31. The private subroutine `uf_SetEnvironment()`.

```
GetEnvironment( i_Environment)

Choose Case i_Environment.OSType
   Case Windows!
      If i_Environment.OSMajorRevision = 4 Then
```

```
         // Windows 95
         Externals = Create u_n_externals_win32
      Else
         // Windows 3.x
         Externals = Create u_n_externals_winapi
      End If
   Case WindowsNT!
      Externals = Create u_n_externals_win32
   Case Else
      SetNull( Externals)
End Choose
```

Just as you would like an application's toolbar to appear in the exact way that it did last time you used the application, making a window (well the main one at least) open with the previous size and position is also a nice feature. The `uf_SetMdiFrame()` function (see Listing 24.32) not only sets up the frame and toolbar to the last known settings, but also keeps a reference to the frame window for use throughout the application.

Listing 24.32. The public subroutine `uf_SetMdiFrame()`.

```
//Parameters:
//    window a_hWnd

String szAlignment

i_hWndFrame = a_hWnd

//
// See windows chapter - set the toolbar start up attributes
//

Choose Case Upper(ProfileString(i_szINIFile,"Application","FrameState","Top!"))
   Case "MAXIMIZED!"
      i_hWndFrame.WindowState = Maximized!
   Case "MINIMIZED!"
      i_hWndFrame.WindowState = Minimized!
      i_hWndFrame.X = ProfileInt( i_szINIFile, "Application", "FrameX", 0)
      i_hWndFrame.Y = ProfileInt( i_szINIFile, "Application", "FrameY", 0)
      i_hWndFrame.Height=ProfileInt(i_szINIFile,"Application","FrameHeight",600)
      i_hWndFrame.Width=ProfileInt(i_szINIFile,"Application","FrameWidth",400)
   Case "NORMAL!"
      i_hWndFrame.WindowState = Normal!
      i_hWndFrame.X = ProfileInt( i_szINIFile, "Application", "FrameX", 0)
      i_hWndFrame.Y = ProfileInt( i_szINIFile, "Application", "FrameY", 0)
      i_hWndFrame.Height=ProfileInt(i_szINIFile,"Application","FrameHeight",600)
      i_hWndFrame.Width=ProfileInt(i_szINIFile,"Application","FrameWidth",400)
End Choose
```

To maintain the last position and settings of toolbars and the frame, `uf_ClosingMdiFrame()` (see Listing 24.33) is called to inform the application that the frame is being closed and to sav the information and carry out any other shutdown procedures.

Listing 24.33. The public subroutine `uf_ClosingMdiFrame()`.

```
//
// See windows chapter - store the toolbar attributes
//

Choose Case i_hWndFrame.WindowState
   Case Maximized!
     SetProfileString( i_szINIFile, "Application", "FrameState", "Maximized!")
   Case Minimized!
     SetProfileString( i_szINIFile, "Application", "FrameState", "Minimized!")
     SetProfileString(i_szINIFile,"Application","FrameX",String(i_hWndFrame.X))
     SetProfileString(i_szINIFile,"Application","FrameY",String(i_hWndFrame.Y))
    SetProfileString(i_szINIFile,"Application","FrameHeight",String(i_hWndFrame.Height))
    SetProfileString(i_szINIFile,"Application","FrameWidth",String(i_hWndFrame.Width))
   Case Normal!
     SetProfileString( i_szINIFile, "Application", "FrameState", "Normal!")
     SetProfileString(i_szINIFile,"Application","FrameX",String(i_hWndFrame.X))
     SetProfileString(i_szINIFile,"Application","FrameY",String(i_hWndFrame.Y))
    SetProfileString(i_szINIFile,"Application","FrameHeight",String(i_hWndFrame.Height))
    SetProfileString(i_szINIFile,"Application","FrameWidth",String(i_hWndFrame.Width))
End Choose
```

Similar to the previous function (`uf_ClosingMDIFrame()`), `uf_ClosingApplication()` (see Listing 24.34) is called as part of the application shutdown process in order to save settings and perform any further clean up.

Listing 24.34. The public subroutine `uf_ClosingApplication()`.

```
If i_application.ToolbarText Then
   SetProfileString( i_szINIFile, "Application", "ToolbarText", "TRUE")
Else
   SetProfileString( i_szINIFile, "Application", "ToolbarText", "FALSE")
End If

If i_application.ToolbarTips Then
   SetProfileString( i_szINIFile, "Application", "ToolbarTips", "TRUE")
Else
   SetProfileString( i_szINIFile, "Application", "ToolbarTips", "FALSE")
End If
```

When the user object is closed, the clean-up routine, `uf_CleanUp()`, is called to clean up the resources used by any created objects:

```
Destroy this.Externals
```

Applicationwide Functionality

The previously detailed functions form the basic functionality that we require of the application object. Additional commonly used functions can be added to the user object. Some examples of functions you might want to add are described in the following sections.

Centering a Window

To center a window within the screen requires some simple calculations and conversions (see Listing 24.35), but it is tedious to keep repeating the same code in different places. This is an ideal candidate to add as an object-level function to `u_n_application` and allows you to encapsulate this code to just the one place in an application.

Listing 24.35. The public subroutine `uf_CenterWindow()`.

```
//Parameters:
//    window wToActOn

Long lScreenWidth, lScreenHeight

lScreenWidth = PixelsToUnits( i_Environment.ScreenWidth, XPixelsToUnits!)
lScreenHeight = PixelsToUnits( i_Environment.ScreenHeight, YPixelsToUnits!)

// Calculate central position
wToActOn.X = ( lScreenWidth - wToActOn.Width) / 2
wToActOn.Y = ( lScreenHeight - wToActOn.Height) / 2
```

Logging Application Events

Another useful function is to provide the capability to log an event to either a database or a flat file. The function shown in Listing 24.36 uses a stored procedure to make an entry in the appropriate database table. You use this so that you do not have to know anything about the underlying database structure; the only requirement is that a stored procedure called `sp_log_event` be available in each database. In SQL Server this would be a simple matter of adding the stored procedure and required tables to the `model` database so that each database subsequently created automatically has the necessary database objects.

Listing 24.36. The protected function `uf_LogEvent()`.

```
//Parameters:
//    String a_szSystemId
//    String a_szEventId
//    String a_szStatus
//    String a_szDescription
//
//Returns:
//    Boolean

DateTime dtNow
u_n_transaction trEventLog
Boolean bSuccess = TRUE

// Clone the SQLCA settings for our own transaction object
trEventLog = SQLCA.CloneObject()
```

continues

Listing 24.36. continued

```
// Connect the new transaction to the DBMS
trEventLog.MakeConnection()

DECLARE log_event PROCEDURE FOR sp_log_event
        @systemid = :a_szSystemId, @eventid = :a_szEventId,
        @eventdt = :dtNow, @status = :a_szStatus, @desc = :a_szDescription
USING trEventLog;

dtNow = DateTime( Today(), Now())

EXECUTE log_event;

If trEventLog.SQLCode <> 0 Then
   bSuccess = FALSE
End If
// Close the database connection
trEventLog.CloseConnection()

Destroy trEventLog

Return bSuccess
```

Broadcasting Messages

It is very useful to be able to broadcast a message to all of a window's or user object's controls. In PowerBuilder 4.0 you had to either write this as one function that takes a number of parameters, some of which are used only for certain calls, or as separate functions that provide a variety of methods. In PowerBuilder 5.0 you can now achieve the same result with one function and overloading; before, this would have taken six levels of unnecessary inheritance to provide just one polymorphic function.

The following three functions (all call `uf_Broadcast()` by using function overloading) are based on making calls to a window object's controls and can be copied directly for the `UserObject`-based ones. The first version of the `uf_Broadcast()` function (see Listing 24.37) is the simplest and only triggers the event for each object of the requested type. The other functions are all based on the exact same code with the only difference being the `TriggerEvent` call, and for the user-object–based functions, the calling parameter.

Listing 24.37. `uf_Broadcast()`, which takes a string message.

```
//Parameters:
//     Window a_hWindowParent
//     Object a_hObjects
//     String a_szMessage

Integer nNoControls, nAffected, nCount
```

```
nNoControls = UpperBound( a_hWindowParent.Control)

For nCount = 1 To nNoControls
   If TypeOf( a_hWindowParent.Control[ nCount]) = a_hObjects Then
      nAffected ++
      a_hWindowParent.Control[ nCount].TriggerEvent( a_szMessage)
   End If
Next

Return nAffected
```

The next version of the function (see Listing 24.38) allows the `WordParm` and `LongParm` attributes of the `Message` object to be sent as part of the broadcasted message.

Listing 24.38. `uf_Broadcast()`, which takes additional numeric parameters.

```
//Parameters:
//     Window a_hWindowParent
//     Object a_hObjects
//     String a_szMessage
//     Long a_lWordParm
//     Long a_lLongParm

Integer nNoControls, nAffected, nCount

nNoControls = UpperBound( a_hWindowParent.Control)

For nCount = 1 To nNoControls
   If TypeOf( a_hWindowParent.Control[ nCount]) = a_hObjects Then
      nAffected ++
      a_hWindowParent.Control[ nCount].TriggerEvent( &
                                    a_szMessage, a_lWordParm, a_lLongParm)
   End If
Next

Return nAffected
```

As you can see from each of the functions, they all share the same base code, with just minor alterations. You can choose to combine them into one function, but then there are optional parameters that *have* to be defined by anyone using the function, which you will usually require to be `NULL` so that you can determine the required functionality. This approach may require additional code but is much simpler to call. The code in Listing 24.39 shows the `uf_Broadcast()` function written for broadcasting messages to user object controls. As you can see, it contains only a few minor alterations to the code from the ones used for broadcasting to windows.

Listing 24.39. `uf_Broadcast()`, which takes a numeric and string parameter.

```
//Parameters:
//     UserObject a_hUserObjectParent
//     Object a_hObjects
```

continues

Listing 24.39. continued

```
//    String a_szMessage
//    Long a_lWordParm
//    String a_szLongParm

Integer nNoControls, nAffected, nCount

nNoControls = UpperBound( a_hUserObjectParent.Control)

For nCount = 1 To nNoControls
   If TypeOf( a_hUserObjectParent.Control[ nCount]) = a_hObjects Then
      nAffected ++
      a_hUserObjectParent.Control[ nCount].TriggerEvent( &
                                             a_szMessage, a_lWordParm, a_szLongParm)
   End If
Next

Return nAffected
```

The parameter for the parent object must be passed in as either type `Window` or `UserObject`. This is because these are the only two classes that have a `Control[]` array. It would be helpful if these were both subclassed so that you could use a generic data type in the parameter list and then pass either object type to the same function(s).

Here are two sample calls to these functions:

```
// Tell all window datawindows to refresh their contents
g_App.uf_Broadcast( this, Datawindow!, "Refresh")

// Tell all user object singlelineedit objects to set their
// values to the passed string
g_App.uf_Broadcast( uo_lookup, SingleLineEdit!, 0, "Undefined")
```

Using the Application Class Object

At the start of each new application that you create you should inherit from this user object to provide a concrete class object that can be modified for the specific processing required. This may include additional functions and most certainly globally accessible variables. The `uf_LogEvent()` function has been defined as protected, and within each inherited application object you can provide either a single access or multiple-point access to this function.

In order to make use of this user object you need to place function calls in very specific areas of your application. First, you must declare a global variable of the application class user object:

```
u_n_oe_application g_App
```

You should use the same variable name in each application (in this case `g_App`). In the `Open` event of the application object you need to instantiate this variable, assign values to the relevant variables, and then call the `uf_SetApplication()` function (see Listing 24.40).

Listing 24.40. The `Open` event for an application.

```
g_App = Create u_n_application

g_App.i_szApplication = "Order Entry "
g_App.i_szApplicationName = "Order Entry System - Version 1.3"
g_App.i_szINIFile = "PCS.INI"

g_App.uf_SetApplication( this)
```

With these commands issued you can now use the different functionality of the application object:

```
// Set the DataWindow error message window title to the application name
this.DWMessageTitle = g_App.i_szApplicationName

// Make an API call
hWnd = g_App.Externals.uf_FindWindow( "FNWNS040", szNull)
```

In the `Open` event of your MDI frame window you need to call `uf_SetMdiFrame()` to register the window with the application:

```
g_App.uf_SetMdiFrame( this)
```

More importantly, when the MDI frame and subsequently the application is closed, two very important function calls must be made. The first is in the `Close` event of the frame:

```
g_App.uf_ClosingMdiFrame()
```

The second is in the `Close` event of the application:

```
g_App.uf_ClosingApplication()
```

Standard DataWindow Objects

Probably *the* most important user object you will create, or use, is a standard visual user object based on the `DataWindow` control. In this user object you can encapsulate frequently used functionality. Any operation on or action that is required by a DataWindow should be done through an associated event or function.

The user object `u_dw` is declared with a number of instance variables for use in the various event and function scripts (see Listing 24.41).

Listing 24.41. Instance variables for `u_dw`.

```
Public:
   Boolean bFailedAccept = FALSE, i_bFailedSave = FALSE
   Boolean i_bAutoResizeHorizontal = FALSE, i_bAutoResizeVertical = FALSE
   Integer i_nBottomGap, i_nRightGap
   Integer i_nMinWidth, i_nMaxWidth = -1, i_nMinHeight, i_nMaxHeight = -1
```

continues

Listing 24.41. continued

```
   Window i_wParent

Private:
   Boolean i_bInAcceptText = FALSE
```

Whenever you change the `DataObject` attribute of a `DataWindow` object, the associated transaction object is disconnected and the row focus indicator is lost. `uf_ChangeDataObject()` provides a central point to change the value of this attribute, reconnect the transaction, and reset the row pointer (see Listing 24.42). You can overload the function so that either a picture object or pointer type can be passed in.

Listing 24.42. The public subroutine `uf_ChangeDataObject()`.

```
//Parameters:
//     String szDataObject
//     Version 1 of the function: RowFocusInd rfiPointerType
//     Version 2 of the function: Picture ptrPointer
//     Integer nXLocation
//     Integer nYLocation
//     Transaction trTransaction

this.DataObject = szDataObject

If IsValid( ptrPointer) Then
    this.SetRowFocusIndicator( ptrPointer, nXLocation, nYLocation)
Else
    this.SetRowFocusIndicator( rfiPointerType, nXLocation, nYLocation)
End If

this.SetTransObject( trTransaction)
```

Here are examples of a call to this function for both overloaded versions:

```
// Version 1 of the function - uses the pointer type as the 2nd argument
dw_1.uf_ChangeDataObject( "d_shipping_list", Hand!, pNull, 0, 0, SQLCA)
dw_1.TriggerEvent( "RetrieveData")

// Version 2 of the function - uses a picture object as the 2nd argument
dw_1.uf_ChangeDataObject( "d_shipping_list", p_pointer, pNull, 0, 0, SQLCA)
dw_1.TriggerEvent( "RetrieveData")
```

Customizing with DataWindow Events

Where better than the `Constructor` event (see Listing 24.43) of a DataWindow control to set up the transaction object? It is a task you do for every DataWindow control, so code it once and forget about it.

Listing 24.43. The `Constructor` event for `u_dw`.

```
If this.SetTransObject( SQLCA) <> 1 Then
   error.object = this.ClassName()
   error.objectevent = "Constructor"
   error.line = 1
   error.number = SQLCA.SQLDBCode
   error.text = SQLCA.SQLErrText
   // Open a standard error window
   open( w_error)
End If
```

Most DataWindows use the SQLCA as their transaction object. If you require alternative processing, you can override this script and copy the code to the descendant level.

Errors are a fact of life, and the `DBError` event (see Listing 24.44) is written to make handling DataWindow errors a little less painful. The standard error window is displayed with the error code and text supplied by the DataWindow. The `GetUpdateStatus()` function is used to find the row that caused the error, which is then scrolled into view and has the focus set to it.

Listing 24.44. The `DBError` event for `u_dw`.

```
Long lRow
dwBuffer ptrBuffer
// Open the standard error window, no values can be passed from this level
// any information displayed apart from error text will have to be defined
// at the child level

error.text = this.DBErrorMessage()
error.number = this.DBErrorCode()

Open( w_error)
//
// Scroll to the row causing the error, if it is in the visible, PRIMARY!, buffer
//
this.dwGetUpdateStatus( lRow, ptrBuffer)
If ptrBuffer = PRIMARY! Then
   this.ScrollToRow( lRow)
   this.SetFocus()
End If

// Do Not process message any further
this.SetActionCode(1)
```

Resizing the DataWindow

Some windows are laid out in such a manner that it makes sense to allow the controls within them to be resized to make use of additional window space if the window is itself resized.

By using two attributes of the attributes you added to `u_dw` you can tell the DataWindow control to resize with its parent; then you use some additional instance variables to finely control the resizing operation (see Listing 24.45). If you turn on the vertical and horizontal scrollbars of a DataWindow control, they will display if there is not enough space to show the whole DataWindow object.

Listing 24.45. The `ParentResize` event (`pbm_custom10`) for `u_dw`.

```
Integer nNewWidth, nNewHeight

this.SetRedraw( FALSE)

If i_bAutoResizeHorizontal Then
   nNewWidth = i_wParent.Width - this.X - i_nRightGap
   If nNewWidth >= i_nMinWidth And &
      ((this.X + nNewWidth) <= i_nMaxWidth Or i_nMaxWidth = -1) Then
      this.Width = nNewWidth
      this.HScrollBar = TRUE
   ElseIf nNewWidth < i_nMinWidth Then
      this.Width = i_nMinWidth
   End If
End If

If i_bAutoResizeVertical Then
   nNewHeight = i_wParent.Height - this.Y - i_nBottomGap
   If nNewHeight >=i_nMinHeight And &
      ((this.Y + nNewHeight) <= i_nMaxHeight Or i_nMaxHeight=-1) Then
      this.Height = nNewHeight
      this.VScrollBar = TRUE
   ElseIf nNewHeight < i_nMinHeight Then
      this.Height = i_nMinHeight
   End If
End If

this.SetRedraw( TRUE)
```

Two steps must be carried out to make it active. The first is coded in the DataWindow `Contructor` event and sets the values `i_wParent`, `i_nRightGap`, and `i_nBottomGap`. For example, in the `Constructor` event of a DataWindow the code might be this:

```
this.i_wParent = Parent
this.i_nRightGap = Parent.Width - this.X - this.Width
this.i_nBottomGap = Parent.Height - this.Y - this.Height
this.i_nMinWidth = this.width
this.i_nMaxWidth = dw_2.x - 20
this.i_nMinHeight = this.Height
this.i_nMaxHeight = dw_3.y - 20
this.i_bAutoResizeHorizontal = TRUE
this.i_bAutoResizeVertical = TRUE
```

The second requirement is that a parent (which could be either `Window` or `UserObject`) inform the DataWindow of a resize. This simply requires you to use the application custom class object and its associated methods. Here's an example:

```
this.SetRedraw( FALSE)
g_App.uf_Broadcast( this, DataWindow!, "ParentResize")
this.SetRedraw( TRUE)
```

This is the only code required in the `Resize` event, and it allows you to add, delete, and rename the DataWindows to your heart's desire and they will all still receive the message with no further coding or modification to code. The calls to `SetRedraw()` allow the window to paint correctly after all the object resizing has occurred.

Modifying DataWindow Rows

One of the common operations on a DataWindow is the deletion of a row. To do this you use the code in Listing 24.46, which can also be encapsulated in the object. This allows you to carry out extensive error checking and friendlier post scrolling without having to repeat a lot of code.

Listing 24.46. The `DeleteRow` event (`pbm_custom03`) for `u_dw`.

```
Long lRow

lRow = Message.WordParm

If lRow = 0 Then
   // Row NOT sent as parameter - get current row
   lRow = this.GetRow()
End If

If lRow = -1 Then
   error.object = this.ClassName()
   error.ObjectEvent = "DeleteRow"
   error.line = 3
   error.number = -1
   error.text = "Error get row information from the datawindow."
   open(w_error)
Else
   If this.DeleteRow( lRow) <> 1 Then
      error.object = this.ClassName()
      error.ObjectEvent = "DeleteRow"
      error.line = 12
      error.number = -1
      error.text = "Unable to Delete a new row into the datawindow."
      open( w_error)
   Else
      this.ScrollToRow( lRow - 1)
      this.SetFocus()
   End If
End If
```

Notice that you can either delete a specified or the current row. To delete a particular row, in this case the fourth, you would use the following code:

```
dw_1.TriggerEvent( "DeleteRow", 4)
```

In this case the second parameter of `TriggerEvent()` is the row number.

Another of the common operations on a DataWindow is the addition of a row. Using the code in Listing 24.47, you can encapsulate the whole operation in the object. This event makes use of the `Message` object in a similar manner to the code to delete a row.

Listing 24.47. The `NewRow` event (`pbm_custom02`) for `u_dw`.

```
Long lRow, lLongParm

lRow = Message.WordParm
lLongParm = Message.LongParm

If lLongParm = 1 Then
   lRow = this.GetRow() + lRow
End If

If lRow = -1 Then
   error.object = this.ClassName()
   error.ObjectEvent = "NewRow"
   error.line = 3
   error.number = -1
   error.text = "Error get row information from the datawindow."
   open( w_error)
Else
   lRow = this.InsertRow( lRow)
   If lRow = -1 Then
      error.object = this.ClassName()
      error.ObjectEvent = "NewRow"
      error.line = 12
      error.number = -1
      error.text = "Unable to insert a new row into the datawindow."
      open(w_error)
   Else
      this.SetColumn( 1)
      this.ScrollToRow( lRow)
      this.SetFocus()
   End If
End If
```

Here's the code to call this event for the various insert row configurations:

```
// New first row
dw_1.TriggerEvent( "NewRow", 1, 0)
//
// New last row
dw_1.TriggerEvent( "NewRow")
//
// New row after current
dw_1.TriggerEvent( "NewRow", 1, 1)
//
// New row before current
dw_1.TriggerEvent( "NewRow", 0, 1)
```

Data Retrieval Events

For generic retrieval calls, the following user-defined event provides the necessary functionality. For most calls you will be passing only a few arguments to the DataWindow, so you declare a total of 10 Any data type parameters for the event (see Listing 24.48). In PowerBuilder 4.0 your only course of action was to override the event and enter retrieval-specific code whenever the DataWindow expected arguments. In PowerBuilder 5.0 the DataWindow does not care if it is passed more arguments than it requires; this allows you to implement the retrieval function of many a PowerBuilder developer's dreams!

Listing 24.48. The `RetrieveData()` function for `u_dw`.

```
Long lRow

this.SetRedraw( FALSE)

SQLCA.BeginTran()

lRow = this.Retrieve( a_Arg0, a_Arg1, a_Arg2, a_Arg3, a_Arg4, a_Arg5, a_Arg6, &
                      a_Arg7, a_Arg8, a_Arg9)


SQLCA.CommitTran()

If lRow = -1 Then
    error.object = this.ClassName()
    error.ObjectEvent = "RetrieveData"
    error.line = 3
    error.number = -1
    error.text = "Unable to retrieve data into the datawindow."
    open( w_error)
End If

this.Title = String( this.RowCount()) + " records"

this.SetRedraw( TRUE)
```

You can then call this event with up to 10 different arguments. For example, to pass an integer ID, a string name, and a date of birth, this would be the call:

```
dw_employee.Trigger Event RetrieveData( 10, "Gallagher", Date("6/12/69"))
```

Saving Data

To save a DataWindow control's data to the database or elsewhere, you use the `SaveData` event (see Listing 24.49). A call to this event should be enclosed in a transaction begin and end, and the `i_bFailedSave` is provided for examination by the calling script. If you are saving the data somewhere other than a database, or even as well as the database, you can extend or override this event in the descendant and provide your own functionality.

Listing 24.49. `SaveData` (`pbm_custom04`) for `u_dw`.

```
Long lRow

lRow = this.Update()
If lRow <> 1 Then
    i_bFailedSave = TRUE
    error.object = this.ClassName()
    error.ObjectEvent = "SaveData"
    error.line = 7
    error.number = -1
    error.text = "Unable to save data from the datawindow."
    open( w_error)
Else
    i_bFailedSave = FALSE
End If
```

Accepting the Last Edit

Chapter 10, "DataWindow Scripting," discusses the process of detecting when a call to the `AcceptText()` function is required. The code required for the detection and execution of this functionality is detailed in the code in Listings 24.50 to 24.53.

Listing 24.50. `AcceptText` (`pbm_custom06`) for `u_dw`.

```
If Not i_bInAcceptText Then
    i_bInAcceptText = TRUE
    If this.AcceptText() = -1 Then
         bFailedAccept = TRUE
         this.SetFocus()
         this.PostEvent( "PostAcceptText")
         Return
    Else
         bFailedAccept = FALSE
    End If
End If

i_bInAcceptText = FALSE
```

Listing 24.51. The `LoseFocus` event for `u_dw`.

```
this.PostEvent( "accepttext")
```

Listing 24.52. The `ItemError` event for `u_dw`.

```
i_bInAcceptText = TRUE
```

Listing 24.53. `PostAcceptText (pbm_custom09)` for `u_dw`.

```
i_bInAcceptText = FALSE
```

Object Documentation

A useful user event to add to each of your user objects is one to document what the object is and how certain tasks are accomplished, possibly with required external calls and sample code (see Listing 24.54). When you compile the object, this event's contents are considered white space and will not be included in your final executable. Using this method, you have encapsulated the object's documentation as part of the object itself!

Listing 24.54. A documentation user event for any object.

```
// Copyright Simon Gallagher 1993-1996
//
// This DataWindow object contains the following functionality:
//
// Events:
//        DeleteRow - Handles deleting the current row
//        Yatta yatta yatta
```

The DataWindow user object introduced here is a good starting point from which you can add or inherit for additional functionality.

Summary

This chapter explores the functions that allow you to dynamically create visual user objects at runtime, and it gives examples of their use. It also explores some of the standard user objects that are found in frameworks and the functionality you would expect to be contained in them. You should make extensive use of user objects in your PowerBuilder applications to encapsulate the functionality that PowerBuilder does not provide and you find yourself duplicating.

Advanced DataWindow Techniques I

25

IN THIS CHAPTER

This chapter explores the basic syntax and functions that are used to query and modify a DataWindow object, and it gives some examples of how and where these techniques are used.

The direct access syntax that has been introduced with PowerBuilder 5.0 is discussed in Chapter 10, "DataWindow Scripting." Some of the examples in this chapter and Chapter 26, "Advanced DataWindow Techniques II," show you how to use this new access method and how this is used to work as a team with the `Modify()` and `Describe()` functions. Some of your existing calls to `Describe()` and `Modify()` can easily be transformed to the direct access syntax, often only requiring you to replace the function name with the `.Object` attribute reference and reorganize the quotation marks, in order to convert between the two forms.

The DataWindow Object

The DataWindow object contains attributes that are comparable to the DataWindow control's attributes; it also contains objects similar to the controls you place in a window. Before PowerBuilder 5.0, the manner in which these were accessed was a little different, and you may still want to use some of these old functions in 5.0. The main reason is that you can bundle up multiple attribute changes into one statement, which is more efficiently executed. Some expressions just cannot be expressed in the new direct access format, and you still need to use the `Modify()` and `Describe()` functions you currently have coded.

A specific syntax language is used with the three DataWindow object-description and modification functions: `Describe()`, `Create()`, and `Modify()`. The syntax is usually simple and obvious, but it can border on the stupefying. The `Describe()` function returns strings that consist of this syntax, as well as the values of DataWindow object attributes. The `Create()` and `Modify()` functions require only the DataWindow object's attributes as the function's parameters.

NOTE

To obtain a list of the attributes and objects that can be retrieved using `Describe()`, you can refer to the PowerBuilder help under the Describe or Modify PowerScript Function topics, and then click on the Valid Attributes for Describe and Modify line in the See Also section.

Most actions concentrate on columns in a DataWindow object. This is why it is good practice to give all columns, especially computed columns, meaningful names. Occasionally, the text label associated with a column is acted on; remember that for regular columns, the text label is the same name with a `_t` appended to the end.

In PowerBuilder, DataWindow functions are generally poor performers. To improve the speed of execution, you can collect actions into a single string using a tab character (`~t`) as a separator for some functions. For example, to hide a column and its associated text, this would be the string:

```
"ss_number.Visible=0 ~t ss_number_t.Visible=0"
```

Any number of actions can be concatenated into one string.

If the value in the assignment is a string rather than a number, you need to embed the quotes to denote a string value. You can do this a couple ways. The simplest method is to use the single quote ('):

```
"start_date.Format='mm/dd/yy'"
```

Alternatively, the double quote (") can be used if you first prefix it with an escape character (~) so that it isn't taken as the end of the string. Here's an example:

```
"start_date.Format=~"mm/dd/yy~""
```

The syntax becomes more convoluted when you need to embed more quotes inside the modification string:

```
"start_date.Format='mm/dd/yy;~~~"None Specified~~~"'"
```

The `~~~"` has become something of a legend in PowerBuilder circles. When the concept is understood there is little mystery. First, you need to think of the whole string as two smaller strings, like this:

```
"start_date.Format="
"mm/dd/yy;~"None Specified~""
```

At this level of quote embedding, you need to use `~"` only around `None Specified`, as you did in the first examples. Now, when you take the second string and embed it into the first, all quotes need to be taken down a level. This means that the string is now enclosed in quotes, either `~"` or `'` (the two are equivalent). The embedded string needs to become an embedded string. This is where the `~~~"` is used. The `~~~"` breaks down to a `~~` and a `~"`, which at the next level up gives a `~` and a `"`. Then, at the top level, you arrive at the lone quote ("). The escape sequence `~~~"` can also be written as `~~'`.

Fortunately, there is little need to embed to a level below this, but if you do require such a string, just add `~~` for each level. This equates to the `~` required to escape the following tildes and quote to the next level.

Finding DataWindow Information: Describe()

To query the DataWindow object for information about itself, use the `Describe()` function (previously known as `dwDescribe()`). The syntax for this function is

```
DataWindowName.Describe( AttributeEvaluationList )
```

`DataWindowName` can be either a DataWindow control or a child DataWindow. The *`AttributeEvaluationList`* is a space-separated list of attributes or evaluation expressions and is

used to report the values of attributes of columns and graphic objects. Expressions can be evaluated using values of a particular row and column.

`Describe()` returns a string containing the values of the attributes and expression results in a newline-separated (`~n`) list. If an expression or attribute returns more than one item, it does so in a tab-separated (`~t`) list.

If the attribute list contains an invalid item, `Describe()` returns the results up to that item position and then an exclamation point (`!`). The remainder of the attribute list is ignored. `Describe()` returns a question mark (`?`) if there is no value for an attribute.

Table 25.1 gives some examples of the `Describe()` function and the result string.

Table 25.1. Examples of `Describe()` expressions for a DataWindow.

Describe Expression	*Result String*
`"DataWindow.Bands DataWindow.Objects"`	`"header~tdetail~tsummary~t footer~nemp_id~temp_id_t"`
`"DataWindow.Band DataWindow.Objects"`	`"!"`
`"DataWindow.Bands DataWindow.Object"`	`"header~tdetail~tsummary~t footer~n!"`

If the value of an attribute would be ambiguous—for example, a string value that has an exclamation point, question mark, tab, or newline—it is enclosed in quotes.

The following line will return the string `""Name?""` if the label is `Name?` (note that the quotes are not `~"` but straight quotes):

```
dw_1.Describe( "l_name_t.Text")
```

When the first value in a list of values is enclosed in quotation marks, the rest of the list for that attribute is also enclosed in quotation marks.

An alternative syntax to specifying the column name is to use the column number. Be very careful when using this, and try to avoid it if possible, because the column's number may change on you if you alter the data source. For example, if `l_name` were column six, the `Describe()` function syntax could be

```
dw_1.Describe("#6.ColType")
```

This syntax is more often used in conjunction with the `GetColumn()` function to retrieve the current column's number, or when you wish to step through each column in the DataWindow. For example, the following code could be used to capture each column's data type:

```
Integer nColumn, nTotalColumns
String aszType[]

nTotalColumns = Integer( dw_1.Object.DataWindow.Column.Count)
aszType[ nTotalColumns] = ""
```

```
For nColumn = 1 To nTotalColumns
   aszType[ nColumn] = dw_1.Describe( "#" + String( nColumn) + ".ColType")
Next
```

This particular loop will be used in one of the code listings in Chapter 26.

> **WARNING**
>
> You should be aware that 5.0 has more data types for a DataWindow. This means that your old `Describe()` calls that return the column data type will be different for numbers. The new data types available are Long, Ulong, and Real. Any column type equal to `"number"` will have to be updated to work with the correct column data type!

NEW in 5 PowerBuilder

Evaluation Expressions

You use the `Evaluate()` function from within your PowerScript to carry out the evaluation of a DataWindow expression using data from the DataWindow. The syntax for this function is

```
Evaluate( 'Expression', nRowNumber )
```

`Evaluate()` is placed in the attribute evaluation list of `Describe()`. *`Expression`* is a DataWindow function or logical operation to be evaluated, and *`nRowNumber`* indicates the row within the DataWindow on which to evaluate the expression. For example, to evaluate an `If` statement that checks the field `print_upside_down` for row two and returns either `1` or `0`, the code is

```
szReturn = dw_1.Describe("Evaluate('If(print_upside_down = ~"T~", 1, 0)', 2)")
```

`Evaluate()` is used to execute functions that are unique to the DataWindow painter and cannot otherwise be accessed from PowerScript.

Obtaining the Display Value from a Code Table

One of the functions that cannot be directly called from PowerScript but can be included in an `Evaluate()` expression is `LookUpDisplay()`. With this function you can obtain the display value from a code table or a drop-down DataWindow. If the column uses a code table, the user sees the value from the display column, and `GetItem` functions (or direct access syntax) return the data value. The syntax is

```
LookUpDisplay( Column)
```

NOTE

Column used in the LookUpDisplay() expression is the actual column name, not a string containing the column name.

The function returns the display value or an empty string if an error occurs.

A drop-down DataWindow maintains a code table similar to a developer-generated code table attached to a simple edit. The following example queries a drop-down DataWindow column, service_rep, on row one of the control dw_header, for the name (display value) associated with the code (data value):

```
szServiceRep = dw_header.Describe( "Evaluate( 'LookUpDisplay( service_rep)', 1)")
```

Modifying DataWindow Information: Modify()

To make runtime modifications to DataWindow object attributes, instead of using the direct access syntax, you should use the Modify() function (formerly known as dwModify()). This is the syntax for the function:

```
DataWindowControl.Modify( ModificationString )
```

DataWindow objects can have their appearance, behavior, and database information changed at runtime using the appropriate syntax. You can even create and destroy objects within the DataWindow object by providing the complete specifications for the objects. *DataWindowControl* can either be a DataWindow control or a child DataWindow object.

Modify() returns an empty string if the modifications were successful. If an error was encountered in the modification syntax you tried to use, the return value will be in the form "Line *n* Column *n* incorrect syntax", where column *n* is the position of the error counted from the beginning of *ModificationString*.

There are three types of statements you can specify using the *ModificationString* parameter:

- CREATE
- DESTROY
- Attribute alteration

These formats are addressed in the following sections.

Creating Objects Using `Modify()`

To add an object (such as text, computed fields, and bitmaps) you use this syntax:

```
CREATE Object( Settings)
```

`Settings` defines a list of attributes and values for the object to be created; and you must provide enough information to define the object.

The best way to get the correct syntax for an object is to export a simple DataWindow containing the object. You can then cut and paste the object's syntax into your application. Another way is to use one of the many tools (which are becoming more commercial) that will display the syntax for specific objects in a DataWindow.

To illustrate this format, assume that you have just dynamically created a completely new DataWindow from scratch (how to do this is covered later in this chapter) and you now want to place a corporate logo in the header band. This would be the syntax:

```
String szModify, szReturn

szModify = "CREATE bitmap( band=background filename='c:\logo.bmp' x='60' y='8' "  &
          +"width='1308' height='513' border='0' name=logo)"

szReturn = dw_1.Modify( szModify)

If szReturn <> "" Then
   MessageBox( "Logo Creation Failure", szReturn)
End If
```

This code creates the logo in just the right position for the report DataWindow you just created. Figure 25.1 shows the DataWindow before you create the logo object, and Figure 25.2 shows the final state of the DataWindow.

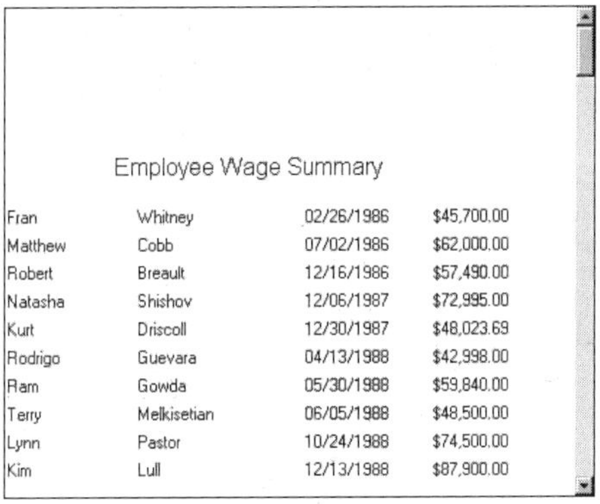
Employee Wage Summary
Fran Whitney 02/26/1986 $45,700.00
Matthew Cobb 07/02/1986 $62,000.00
Robert Breault 12/16/1986 $57,490.00
Natasha Shishov 12/06/1987 $72,995.00
Kurt Driscoll 12/30/1987 $48,023.69
Rodrigo Guevara 04/13/1988 $42,998.00
Ram Gowda 05/30/1988 $59,840.00
Terry Melkisetian 06/05/1988 $48,500.00
Lynn Pastor 10/24/1988 $74,500.00
Kim Lull 12/13/1988 $87,900.00

FIGURE 25.1.
The DataWindow before the logo is created.

FIGURE 25.2.
The dynamically created logo.

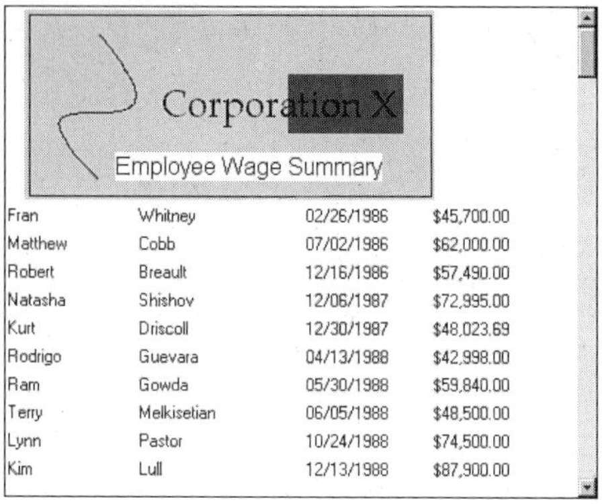

Destroying Objects Using `Modify()`

As well as creating objects within a DataWindow, you can also destroy objects, using the following syntax:

```
DESTROY [COLUMN] Object
```

`Object` is the name of the object in the DataWindow object to destroy. To remove a column and the column's data from the buffer you need to specify the `COLUMN` keyword.

For example, in the previous example you added a logo to the dynamically created reports. If you provide this as a runtime option, say via a check box, you need to be able to create and destroy the picture object. This would be the code for the destroy:

```
String szReturn

szReturn = dw_1.Modify( "DESTROY logo")

If szReturn <> "" Then
   MessageBox( "Logo Removal Failure", szReturn)
End If
```

Here's an example of removing a column and its associated label using this `Modify()` format:

```
String szReturn

szReturn = dw_1.Modify( "DESTROY COLUMN salary DESTROY salary t")

If szReturn <> "" Then
   MessageBox( "Column Removal Failure", szReturn)
End If
```

Attribute Alteration

The last format is probably the most commonly used of the three, but it most likely will be superseded for simple operations by the direct-access syntax of PowerBuilder 5.0. This is the syntax for this format:

```
ObjectName.Attribute=Value
```

Depending on the `Attribute` being affected, the value can be any of the following types:

- A constant—These are simple value changes of attributes that do not use expressions. Here's an example of this type of modification:

  ```
  ColumnName.Band = Footer
  ```

- A quoted constant—These are also simple value changes of an attribute, but for attributes that require an expression. Here's an example of this:

  ```
  ColumnName.Height = '65'
  ```

- An expression—This consists of a default value followed by an expression; it returns values of the same data type as the attribute. Here's an example:

  ```
  ColumnName.Protect='1~tIf(IsRowNew(),0,1)'
  ```

  Note the format of this expression. The whole expression is enclosed in single quotes and a default value (`1`) is required and is separated by a tab (`~t`) from the remainder of the expression. The expression returns either `0` or `1`, which are the valid values for the attribute.

You need to check the online help to determine whether the object's attribute requires a constant or quoted constant; this is indicated by the `(exp)` in the attribute description.

Using Expressions

As you just saw, one of the methods of changing or even setting a default value in the DataWindow painter is to use an expression. This is the syntax:

```
ColumnName.Attribute='DefaultValue~tExpression'
```

`Expression` can use any of the DataWindow functions and must evaluate to the appropriate data type for the attribute.

When you're setting an attribute using an expression, it is important that the expression be evaluated for *each* row in the DataWindow. This allows you to set properties for one row without affecting those settings for any other row.

The majority of the expressions you will build are based on the evaluation of a true/false statement. This is implemented using the DataWindow `If` function (do not confuse this with the PowerScript `If...Then` construct), which has this format:

```
If( BooleanExpression, TrueValue, FalseValue)
```

`BooleanExpression` is an expression that can be evaluated to either `TRUE` or `FALSE`. When the expression evaluates to `TRUE`, `TrueValue` is returned, and when `FALSE`, `FalseValue`. The return type of the `If()` is whatever the data type of `TrueValue` is, and `TrueValue` and `FalseValue` have to be of the same data type.

TrueValue or *FalseValue* can themselves be an `If()` expression, and this allows you to nest successive expression evaluations. Here's an example:

```
If( object_color='Red', 1, If( object_color='White', 2, If( object_color='Blue', 3,
0)))
```

This expression returns `1`, `2`, `3`, or `0`, depending on the current value of the column `object_color`.

The Boolean expression can be constructed using `AND`, `OR`, and `NOT` operators to provide for quite elaborate evaluations.

The following are some examples of expressions using the techniques and syntax that have just been introduced:

- Set the salary of a person to `red` if the person earns more than $80,000; otherwise leave it black:

  ```
  salary.Color='0~tIf( salary > 80000, 255, 0)'
  ```

- Hide the termination date for the rows that have an active or on-leave status:

  ```
  termination_date.Visible='1~tIf( status = ~~~'T~~~', 0, 1)'
  ```

- Flag a person on his or her birthday if the person's status is active by turning the last name column blue:

  ```
  Emp_lname.Color='0~tIf( birth_date = Today() And Status = ~~~'A~~~',
  16711680, 0)'
  ```

Referencing Relative Rows in Expressions

Occasionally, you will need to build an expression that uses information from another row for an action on the current row. To do this, you use a relative position syntax as follows:

```
ColumnName [RelativePosition] RestOfExpression
```

The relative position can be any positive or negative integer. The space before and after the brackets must exist or the expression is invalid. For example, if you wanted to find duplicate customers in your customer table, you could use the following expression for the color attribute of a name field:

```
'0~tIf( GetRow() <> 1 AND lname = lname[-1], 255, 0))'
```

Notice the use of the `-1` relative position combined with the `GetRow() <> 1` condition. This saves you from having to execute a `RowCount()` call for each row while checking for the special condition of the last row.

NOTE

For this example, as for most other applications of the relative row syntax, you will want to sort the data; in this case you'll sort by the `lname` column.

The following time trial was set up to find out just what speed difference there might be. A DataWindow containing a bitmap object was created and placed on a window with a controlling command button and display fields. When pressed, the button executed a 100-iteration loop for the direct access method and then the modify. The bitmap object had the `X`, `Y`, `Width`, and `Height` attributes modified to new values and then back to their original ones. These values were all hard coded. The time with the redraw left on was approximately 26 seconds for the direct access and 10 seconds for the modify. Of course, when the screen redraw for the DataWindow was turned off, the efficiency of each method was optimal, and the timing for direct access was 1.8 seconds and the modify 0.5 seconds. So don't throw away all your code just yet!

Filtering Data

To restrict the data that is displayed in a DataWindow, you can use three methods, either individually or together:

1. You can specify a `WHERE` clause for the DataWindow SQL `SELECT` statement. This restricts the rows that the DBMS returns and is covered in Chapter 5, "SQL and PowerBuilder," and Chapter 9, "The DataWindow Painter."
2. You can specify a filter condition using the `DataWindow.Table.Filter` attribute. This restricts the rows that are placed in the DataWindow buffers and is covered later in this chapter.
3. You can specify a DataWindow filter expression either within the DataWindow or using the `SetFilter()` and `Filter()` functions. This restricts the view of data already in the DataWindow buffer.

The `SetFilter()` function takes a valid string expression that defines the filtering that is desired, and has this syntax:

```
DataWindow.SetFilter( Expression)
```

`DataWindow` can be either a DataWindow control, a child DataWindow, or a DataStore object. *`Expression`* is constructed of columns and DataWindow functions to produce a Boolean value. If you specify *`Expression`* as `NULL`, PowerBuilder will open the Specify Filter dialog box (see Figure 25.3) for the user to enter the expression at runtime.

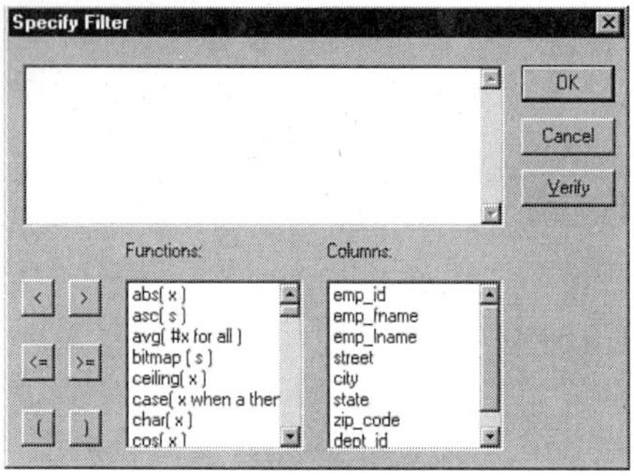

FIGURE 25.3.
The Specify Filter dialog box.

`SetFilter()` by itself does not cause any action other than setting the new filter for the DataWindow. To actually carry out the filtration you have to call the `Filter()` function, which has this syntax:

```
DataWindow.Filter()
```

When you call this function, the rows not matching the filter expression are transferred from the Primary to the Filter buffer of the DataWindow control.

For example, to show only the customers who are in the state of Colorado, you would specify and execute the filter using the following code:

```
dw_1.SetFilter( "state = 'CO'")
dw_1.Filter()
```

The filter expression is constructed using columns, relational operators, functions, and values, and you may want to use parentheses to control the evaluation order. For example, to extend the previous filter to include the customer NewMedia no matter what state in which it appears, this would be the `SetFilter()` expression:

```
"state = 'CO' OR fname = 'NewMedia'"
```

To reset the filter and return all the rows in the Filter buffer to the Primary, you simply call the `SetFilter()` function with an empty string (`""`) and then call `Filter()`.

Sorting Data

To sort the DataWindow data into a certain order you can also use three methods, again either individually or together. They are applied in the following order:

1. You can specify an `ORDER BY` clause for the DataWindow SQL `SELECT` statement. This sorts the rows that the DBMS returns.
2. You can specify sort criteria using the `DataWindow.Table.Sort` attribute. This sorts the rows that are placed in the DataWindow buffers and is covered later in this chapter.

3. You can specify a DataWindow sort expression either in the DataWindow or using the `SetSort()` and `Sort()` functions. This sorts the data in the DataWindow Primary buffer.

The `SetSort()` function takes a string expression that defines the sort criteria desired and has this syntax:

```
DataWindow.SetSort( Expression)
```

`DataWindow` can be either a DataWindow control, a child DataWindow, or a DataStore object. *`Expression`* is constructed of column names with the desired order. If you specify that *`Expression`* is `NULL`, PowerBuilder will open the Specify Sort Columns dialog box (see Figure 25.4) for the user to enter the expression at runtime.

FIGURE 25.4.
The Specify Sort Columns dialog box.

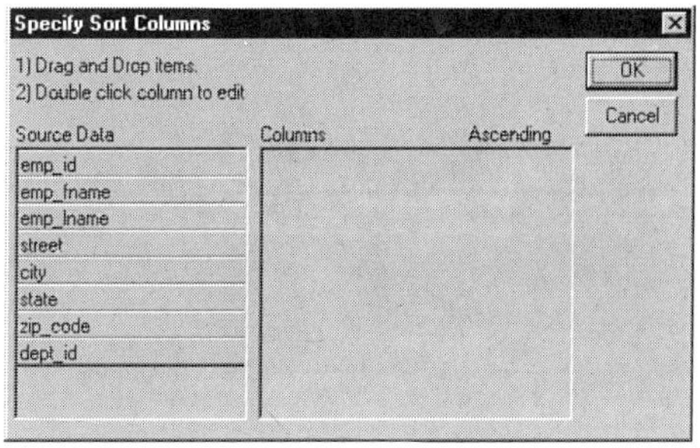

`SetSort()`, like the filter functions, does not cause any action to occur other than setting the new sort criteria for the DataWindow. To actually carry out the sort you have to call the `Sort()` function, which has this syntax:

```
DataWindow.Sort()
```

This function reorders the rows in the DataWindow to match the sort criteria.

For example, to sort on the employee's last name and then first name you would specify and execute the sort using the following code:

```
dw_1.SetSort( "emp_lname A, emp_fname A")

dw_1.Sort()
```

To sort in ascending order specify `A` after the column name, and for a descending-order sort specify `D`.

You will need to call the `Sort()` function to place the rows in a sorted order before you use the `GroupCalc()` function. This function is used to force a recalculation of the breaks in the grouping levels after you have modified a DataWindow's rows. This is the syntax for `GroupCalc()`:

```
DataWindow.GroupCalc()
```

`DataWindow` is either a DataWindow control or a child DataWindow.

DataWindow SQL Code

SQL code is the driving force behind most DataWindows, and there will be occasions when you need to extract and modify the SQL code that the DataWindow uses as part of its data retrieval and update.

In the next few sections you will learn about methods to obtain and to alter a DataWindow's SQL code.

Obtaining the DataWindow SQL Code

One of the most common uses of the `Describe()` function is to extract the `SELECT` syntax from a DataWindow so that it can be modified to add or remove conditions from the `WHERE` clause. The DataWindow stores the `SELECT` in a special format (called a `PBSELECT`). You can see this syntax if you export a DataWindow from the Library painter. This is important because if the application is not connected to a database when the `Describe()` function is executed, the `PBSELECT` statement is returned instead of the true `SELECT`. The syntax for extracting the SQL `SELECT` can be done one of four ways. You can also access the first three directly using the new access syntax of Version 5.0:

```
szSelect = dw_1.Describe("DataWindow.Table.Select")
szSelect = dw_1.Describe("DataWindow.Table.SQLSelect")
szSelect = dw_1.Describe("DataWindow.Table.Select.Attribute")
szSelect = dw_1.GetSQLSelect()
```

The value that is returned for each of these varies a little (see Figure 25.5). When the DataWindow is not connected to the database, the top two statements return column names and embedded quotes in tilde quotes. The bottom two statements return only embedded quotes in tilde quotes. All four display the `SELECT` as a `PBSELECT`. When connected, the top two statements return the true `SELECT`, with embedded quotes in tilde quotes. If the DBMS requires quotes (for example, Watcom-SQL's column names), these are placed in `~"`. The bottom statement returns the quotes without any tildes, and the third statement still returns the `PBSELECT`.

The `Select.Attribute` syntax is used only with `Describe()` and returns a string containing the `PBSELECT` statement for the DataWindow. This is formatted in a logical way with the table name and columns broken out, along with the `WHERE` clause and sorting criteria. You might want to use this if you want to reconstruct the SQL code for some reason. The `SQLSelect` syntax returns the most recently executed `SELECT` statement and cannot be set. Most often, the `GetSQLSelect()` function is used to capture the `SELECT` syntax.

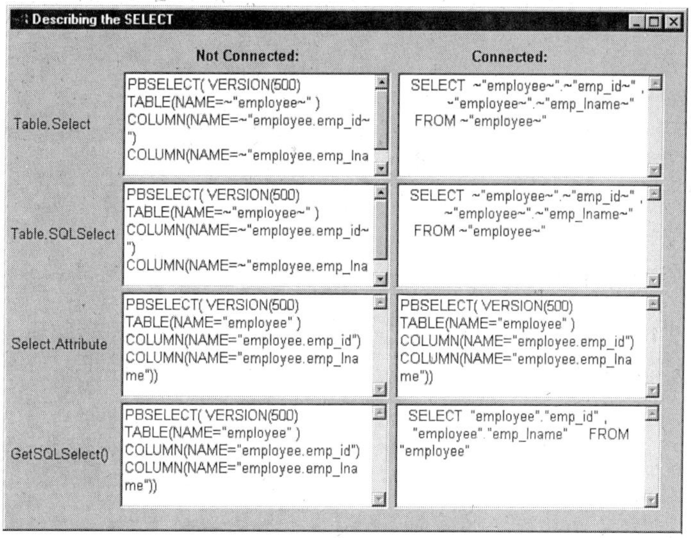

FIGURE 25.5.
DataWindow SQL `SELECT`*s extracted using the* `Describe()` *function.*

Modifying DataWindow SQL Code

The SQL code that is obtained using the methods introduced in the previous section can then be modified and reapplied to the DataWindow object. As with extraction of the syntax, a couple methods are available for placing the SQL back into the DataWindow: direct syntax, `Modify()`, and `SetSQLSelect()`.

This is the syntax for the `SetSQLSelect()` function:

```
DataWindow.SetSQLSelect( SQLStatement)
```

`DataWindow` is either a DataWindow control or child DataWindow to be modified. *`SQLStatement`* is a string that defines a valid SQL `SELECT` statement that must structurally match that of the original `SELECT` statement. This means that the same number of columns must be retrieved, with the same data type and in the same order. *`SQLStatement`* is validated when you call `SetSQLSelect()` only if the DataWindow is updateable. The function returns `-1` if the `SELECT` statement cannot be changed and `1` if it succeeds.

If the DataWindow object is updateable and the new `SELECT` statement uses a different table name in the `FROM` clause, PowerBuilder attempts to modify the update settings. PowerBuilder assumes that the key columns are still in the same positions as the original `SELECT`, and it will make the DataWindow not updateable if it runs into the following two conditions:

- More than one table is specified in the `FROM` clause
- A DataWindow update column is a database computed value

This will prevent you from executing an `Update()` function call for this DataWindow object, and you will get a runtime `DataWindow Not Updateable` error.

> **NOTE**
>
> Remember to associate the DataWindow control with a transaction object after calling `SetSQLSelect()`.

The `SetSQLSelect()` function does have a limitation: It cannot be used to modify a DataWindow object's SQL `SELECT` if it has retrieval arguments specified.

You can use the direct syntax to also change the `SELECT` statement. Here's an example:

```
dw_1.DataWindow.Table.Select="SelectStatement"
```

However, using this method (and the corresponding `Modify()` call) will not cause the `SELECT` statement to be validated, and it will not modify the update properties of the DataWindow. This makes it fast, but you must be careful that the syntax is perfect. You must use either of these methods when the DataWindow has defined arguments.

> **NOTE**
>
> Modifying the `WHERE` clause can be hard enough sometimes, so it is generally a good idea not to specify any additional SQL clauses (such as `ORDER BY`). This functionality can be implemented within the DataWindow on the client (`SetSort()` and `Sort()`).

DataWindow SQL Properties

As mentioned at the start of the section "DataWindow SQL Code," there are a number of SQL properties associated with a DataWindow and its columns. This section explores each one in turn, and shows you what it is and how to use it:

- `DataWindow.Retrieve.AsNeeded`—Determines whether the rows are retrieved into the DataWindow buffer as the user scrolls the visible portion of the DataWindow downward. This allows the user to access the first records of information before PowerBuilder has finished retrieving them all. The value is either Yes or No. Here's an example:

  ```
  dw_1.Object.DataWindow.Retrieve.AsNeeded='Yes'
  ```

- `DataWindow.Storage`—This property reports the amount of virtual storage (in bytes) taken up by the DataWindow object. This is a property to check if you allow your users to retrieve large volumes of data (within the `RetrieveRow` event). Here's an example:

```
Long lStorage

lStorage = Long( this.Object.DataWindow.Storage)

If lStorage > 50000 Then this.DBCancel()
```

- `DataWindow.Table.CrosstabData`—Specifies a tab-separated list of expressions that are used to calculate the column values for a crosstab DataWindow.
- `DataWindow.Table.Filter`—The filter expression used by the DataWindow. This filters records out before they reach the DataWindow buffers, whereas the `SetFilter()` and `Filter()` functions filter data already in the DataWindow. The filter expression must evaluate to either `TRUE` or `FALSE`. For example, you'd use the following to retrieve only items where the state field is set to `'IN'`:

```
dw_1.Object.DataWindow.Table.Filter = "state = 'IN'"
```

  Remember that this only applies to data before it reaches the DataWindow, so if you change this property, you need to retrieve the data afterward for it to take effect.
- `DataWindow.Table.Procedure`—You can use this property to either change which stored procedure is used by the DataWindow or to change the data source to make use of a stored procedure. For example, say you have a stored procedure that selects the same data but from a different database (possibly using different table columns and selection criteria); it could be swapped in using this code:

```
dw_1.Object.DataWindow.Table.Procedure = "EXECUTE sp_customers;0"
```

- `DataWindow.Table.Select`—This is the SQL `SELECT` statement used as the data source for the DataWindow, and is covered in the section "Obtaining the DataWindow SQL Code."
- `DataWindow.Table.Select.Attribute`—A read-only version of the `SELECT` statement, also covered in the section "Obtaining the DataWindow SQL Code."
- `DataWindow.Table.Sort`—Specifies the sort order of the data before it is loaded into the DataWindow. You use the `SetSort()` and `Sort()` functions to sort data already in the DataWindow. The sort string is specified by column name and direction in a comma-separated list. For example, to sort in ascending order of last name and descending order of state, this would be the expression:

```
dw_1.Object.DataWindow.Table.Sort = "emp_lname A, state D"
```

- `DataWindow.Table.SQLSelect`—A read-only property that returns the most recently executed `SELECT` statement for the DataWindow.

- `DataWindow.Table.UpdateKeyInPlace`—Specifies what type of SQL update PowerBuilder will generate if a key column has been modified. If the property is `'Yes'`, an `UPDATE` statement will be generated to modify the key in place. If it's `'No'`, `DELETE` and `INSERT` statements will be generated.
- `DataWindow.Table.UpdateTable`—This is the name of the table in the `FROM` clause that will be used when PowerBuilder generates data modification statements. You will use this property together with *`ColumnName`*`.Update` to allow updates to multiple tables from a single DataWindow. This is covered in Chapter 10.
- `DataWindow.Table.UpdateWhere`—This property is used to specify which columns are included in the `WHERE` clause of data modification SQL (see Chapter 9 for more information on the settings). The values for this property are Key Columns (`0`), Key and Updateable Columns (`1`), and Key and Modified Columns (`2`). For example, to set the update characteristics to Key and Updateable columns, you'd use this code:

```
dw_1.Object.DataWindow.Table.UpdateWhere=1
```

As well as specifying DataWindow-wide database requirements and settings, there are also three properties for individual columns:

- *`ColumnName`*`.Criteria.Dialog`—Determines whether PowerBuilder opens the Specify Retrieval Criteria dialog box (see Figure 25.6) when the `Retrieve()` function is called. If the column property is `'Yes'`, the column is included in the dialog. `'No'` is the default. For example, to allow specification of the employee's last name, this would be the code:

```
dw_1.Object.emp_lname.Criteria.Dialog = "Yes"
```

There must be at least one column specified with `'Yes'` for the dialog to open.

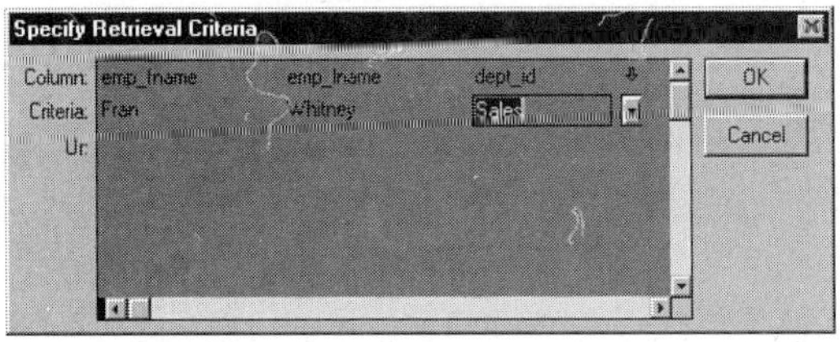

FIGURE 25.6.
The Specify Retrieval Criteria dialog box.

By specifying a criterion the user is appending to the end of any existing `WHERE` clause that might be specified for the DataWindow, you may cause conflicts with the conditions already specified, so you will want to provide a DataWindow without an existing `WHERE` clause.

- *`ColumnName`*`.Criteria.Override_Edit`—This property controls whether the column edit style should be used for entering data in the Specify Retrieval Criteria dialog box. It is also used when the DataWindow is in query mode. If the value is `'Yes'`, the user enters data in a standard edit box. The default is `'No'`, which restricts entry to that edit style. For example, to allow entry in a normal box, this is the code:

```
dw_1.Object.emp_lname.Criteria.Override_Edit = "Yes"
```

- `ColumnName.Criteria.Required`—This prevents the user from specifying operators other than equality (=) and inequality (<>) in the Specify Retrieval Criteria dialog box for a column. It also used when the DataWindow is in query mode. The default (`'No'`) allows the user to specify a relational operator in the dialog.
- `ColumnName.Update`—This property governs whether the column is included in the SQL data modification statements. All updateable columns *should* be in the same table. The value is `'Yes'` for inclusion and `'No'` for exclusion.

The Crosstab presentation style for a DataWindow has some of its own properties that can be looked at and modified:

- `DataWindow.Crosstab.Columns`—A string expression (either tab- or comma-separated list) of the column names for the crosstab columns.
- `DataWindow.Crosstab.Rows`—A string expression (either tab- or comma-separated list) of the columns to be used as row names in a crosstab.
- `DataWindow.Crosstab.SourceNames`—A string expression (either tab- or comma-separated list) of the column names that are displayed in the Crosstab Definition dialog box. This defaults to the column names from the database.
- `DataWindow.Crosstab.Values`—A string (either tab- or comma-separated list) that details the expressions used to calculate the values of the crosstab.

DataWindows can be placed in query by example (QBE) mode (see Figure 25.7 and 25.8), which allows the user to specify the retrieval criteria by using the DataWindow to enter conditions and values for columns, much like specifying a QuickSelect.

FIGURE 25.7.

A DataWindow in normal edit mode.

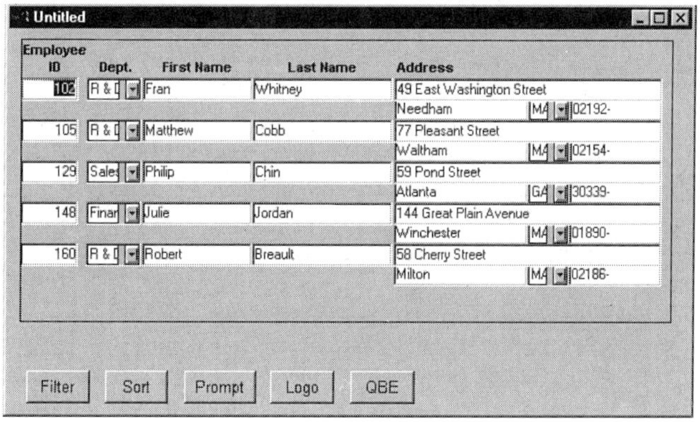

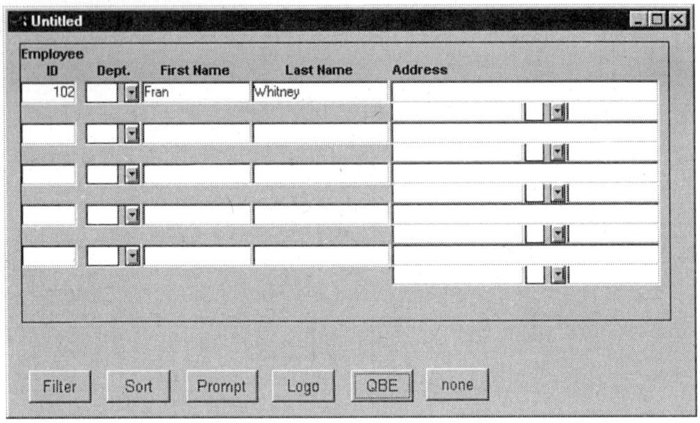

FIGURE 25.8.
A DataWindow in query mode.

There are two DataWindow properties used to control this behavior:

- `DataWindow.QueryMode`—This property turns the QBE mode on or off. Once the user specifies a criterion during query mode, this will be used in all future retrievals. The value is either `'Yes'` to place the DataWindow into query mode or `'No'` to disable the query mode. If the query mode is disabled, the criterion specified by the user is saved for use in the retrieve. For example, to enter query mode, this would be the code:

  ```
  dw_1.Object.DataWindow.QueryMode = "Yes"
  ```

- `DataWindow.QuerySort`—This property turns the first line of the DataWindow into a sort specification. The user can specify sorting criteria for the DataWindow if the value is `'Yes'`. If the DataWindow is not already in query mode, setting `QuerySort` to `'Yes'` also sets `QueryMode` to `'Yes'`. However, turning `QuerySort` off does not turn `QueryMode` off as well, and that must be done as a separate step.

Swapping DataWindows

There will be many occasions when you will want to use a single DataWindow control for many different DataWindow objects; a generic maintenance window is a good example. This is achieved by altering the `DataObject` attribute of the DataWindow control.

After you have changed this attribute, the DataWindow control no longer has a transaction object associated with it and you must issue a new `SetTransObject()` or `SetTrans()` call.

> **NOTE**
>
> If you have a row focus indicator set for the DataWindow, you will have to call `SetRowFocusIndicator()` again after the attribute modification.

If you are going to be swapping DataWindows and retrieving data into them, it is a good idea to set the redraw for the DataWindow control off until you have finished. This will prevent a lot of messy screen repaints.

In the ancestor DataWindow control, this functionality has been built into an object-level method, which handles reconnecting the transaction and resetting the row indicator.

Dynamically Creating DataWindows

In order to provide ultimate flexibility for your end users, you may want to consider allowing them to create a DataWindow object at runtime. This could be a DataWindow for reporting or even data modification. You can still maintain control over what users create by limiting the tables and columns that can be used.

To dynamically create a DataWindow you need to use the `Create()` function. This function has the following syntax:

```
DataWindow.Create( Syntax {, ErrorBuffer})
```

`DataWindow` is a DataWindow control that will be associated with the new DataWindow object. *`Syntax`* is a string that describes the exact syntax (DataWindow source code) to create a DataWindow, and *`ErrorBuffer`* is optionally used to hold any error messages that occur during creation. If you do not specify an *`ErrorBuffer`* a message box will be opened to display the error. The function returns `1` if it succeeds and `-1` if an error occurs

NOTE

If either of the arguments is `NULL`, the `Create()` function will return a `NULL`.

Since the `Create()` is replacing the `DataObject` attribute of the control, you need to carry out a `SetTransObject()` or `SetTrans()` call (as you saw in the section "Swapping DataWindows").

The first step is the creation of the *`Syntax`* argument used in the `Create()` call. The source code syntax of a DataWindow is very complex and is not something that you want to try to enter by hand. PowerBuilder provides two functions that will create the syntax for you: `LibraryExport()` and `SyntaxFromSQL()`.

Using Exported Syntax

The `LibraryExport()` function allows you to take a DataWindow object and export it to a textual representation that you can capture. This can then be used as the necessary argument for `Create()`. This is the syntax for the function:

```
LibraryExport( LibraryName, ObjectName, ObjectType)
```

`LibraryName` is the name of the PowerBuilder library that contains the object to be exported. If the full path is not specified, the file will be searched for, using the system's standard search order. `ObjectName` is the name of the object to be exported, and `ObjectType` is the type of that object. `ObjectType` is a value of the `LibExportType` enumerated data type. The function returns the syntax of the object. It's for use with DataWindows, and a sample call would look like this:

```
String szDWSyntax, szError

szDWSyntax = LibraryExport( "C:\PB5I32\UNLEASH.PBL", "d_employee",
ExportDataWindow!)

dw_1.Create( szDWSyntax, szError)
```

The syntax returned by the `LibraryExport()` function is the same as that generated in the Library painter, except that it does not include an export header. If any of the arguments is `NULL`, the function also returns a `NULL`.

TIP

Once you have the syntax for a DataWindow you can use the `LibraryImport()` function and other associated library functions to save the DataWindow to a library for future use. This allows the user to create and store DataWindows on-the-fly if you provide them with the interface to do so.

Syntax from SQL Code

The other method for generating syntax is the `SyntaxFromSQL()` function, which has the following syntax:

```
TransactionObject.SyntaxFromSQL( SQLSelect, Presentation, ErrorBuffer)
```

This function generates the source code required to create a DataWindow based on a SQL `SELECT` statement. `TransactionObject` is a connected transaction object. `SQLSelect` is a valid SQL `SELECT` statement string that the DataWindow syntax will be based on. `Presentation` defines the presentation style that will be used for the DataWindow and this is its simplest form:

```
Style( Type = PresentationStyle)
```

`PresentationStyle` can be Tabular (default), Grid, Form (for freeform), Crosstab, Graph, Group, Label, and N-up. `ErrorBuffer` is used to collect any error messages that occur during the function call.

As with `LibraryExport()`, the returned string from `SyntaxFromSQL()` can also be directly passed into a call to the `Create()` function. Here's an example:

```
String szSQLSelect, szError, szError2, szSyntax
```

```
szSQLSelect = "SELECT emp_id, emp_lname, emp_fname FROM employee"

szSyntax = SQLCA.SyntaxFromSQL( szSQLSelect, "Style( Type = Form)", szError)

dw_1.Create( szSyntax, szError2)
```

This sample code will create a DataWindow object that uses the FreeForm presentation style to display the `emp_id`, `emp_lname`, and `emp_fname` columns from the `employee` table.

WARNING

You should be aware that if the DBMS you use is SQL Server, PowerBuilder cannot determine whether the columns are updateable if transaction processing is on. It is assumed that the columns are not updateable in this case. You should therefore set the `AutoCommit` attribute to `TRUE` before calling `SyntaxFromSQL()`.

The *`Presentation`* argument for `SyntaxFromSQL()` can be extended to define other attributes and objects for the DataWindow than just the presentation style. The full format is this:

```
"Style( Type = Value Property = Value ...) &
DataWindow( Property = Value ...) &
Column( Property = Value ...) &
Group( GroupBy_Column1 GroupBy_Column2 ... Property ...) &
Text( Property = Value ...) &
Title('TitleString')"
```

As you can see, you can specify the styles of individual columns, the whole DataWindow, specific areas of the DataWindow, and the text used in the DataWindow.

The properties for the `Style` parameter are shown in Table 25.2.

Table 25.2. The properties for the `Style` parameter.

Property	*Description*
`Detail_Bottom_Margin`	Bottom margin of the detail area
`Detail_Top_Margin`	Top margin of the detail area
`Header_Bottom_Margin`	Bottom margin of the header area
`Header_Top_Margin`	Top margin of the header area
`Horizontal_Spread`	Horizontal space between columns in the detail area
`Left_Margin`	The left margin of the DataWindow
`Report`	Defines whether the DataWindow is a read-only report
`Type`	The presentation style
`Vertical_Size`	The height of the columns in the detail area
`Vertical_Spread`	The vertical space between columns in the detail area

The properties for the `Group` parameter are shown in Table 25.3.

Table 25.3. The properties for the `Group` parameter.

Property	*Description*
`NewPage`	Whether a change in a group column's value causes a page break to occur
`ResetPageCount`	A new value in a group column will cause the page numbering to reset

The *`Title`* keyword is used to assign *`TitleString`* as the title of the DataWindow object. The properties for the keywords *`DataWindow`*, *`Column`*, and *`Text`* are the standard properties that you would use either directly or with the `Describe()` and `Modify()` functions.

To illustrate how all these properties work, the following example builds a free-form DataWindow with a black background, with columns that have green labels (with a transparent background) and data with 3D lowered borders. The top border of the detail band was also modified to give more space:

```
String szSQLSelect, szSyntax, szStyle, szError, szError2

szStyle = "Style(Type=Form Detail_Top_Margin = 100) DataWindow(Color = 0) &
          Column(Border =5) Text( Color = 32768 BackGround.Mode = 1)"

szSQLSelect = "SELECT emp_id, emp_lname, emp_fname FROM employee"

szSyntax = SQLCA.SyntaxFromSQL( szSQLSelect, szStyle, szError)

dw_1.Create( szSyntax, szError2)
```

The resulting window might be familiar to some end users, because it looks a lot like a 3270 screen!

You can also use either the `Describe()` function or the direct access of DataWindow object attributes to get information that you can then use to reconstruct a DataWindow.

Sharing DataWindows

Data can be shared by two or more DataWindow controls using the `ShareData()` function. This allows you to use the same data in a different DataWindow without having to duplicate the data and worry how to update from both DataWindows.

There are three categories of data:

- Static data—This is often implemented by hard coding values into your application, as constants, predefined list box values, check box state values, and so on.
- Occasionally modified data—This encompasses system codes (for example, product codes) and is usually associated with database lookup tables.

- Volatile data—With this category of data, the data value changes or is added to multiple times a day (for example, order numbers).

The second and third categories of data are ideal candidates for a drop-down DataWindow, but only the second is truly worth sharing. This is because the volatile data might already have changed by the time the user uses a secondary DataWindow that has been shared to. This is especially so if the data has been cached for applicationwide use and the application is kept open for long periods of time.

There are two types of DataWindow controls in a sharing relationship: the primary and the secondary. The *primary* DataWindow actually contains the data within its buffers. *Secondary* DataWindows are those that are granted access to the data of a primary DataWindow.

Only the data is shared between the DataWindows. This encompasses each of the buffers as well as the current filter and sort order. Formatting, column placement, and so on are independent for each DataWindow. Since the data itself is shared, modification using any of these functions (or appropriate direct access syntax) will affect the primary and all related secondary DataWindows: `DeleteRow()`, `Filter()`, `ImportClipBoard()`, `ImportFile()`, `ImportString()`, `InsertRow()`, `Retrieve()`, `Reset()`, `RowsCopy()`, `RowsDiscrd()`, `RowsMove()`, `SetFilter()`, `SetSort()`, `Sort()`, and `Update()`.

NOTE

This also means that all events associated with these functions are triggered in only the primary DataWindow.

There is one important consideration you must make before trying to share data between DataWindows. The primary and secondary DataWindows must have the exact same result set description. This means they must have the same data types, column names, and column order. `SELECT` statements can vary in the tables and `WHERE` clauses and still be shareable. You can even share with an external data source DataWindow, as long as the columns are defined to be like the expected results.

NOTE

You will need to use the appropriate numeric data type for external source DataWindows. Otherwise, the share will fail.

To turn on data sharing you use the `ShareData()` function, which has this syntax:

```
PrimaryDataWindow.ShareData( SecondaryDataWindow)
```

You need to call this function for each share you want to make. Neither of these DataWindows can be a crosstab DataWindow, but they can be child DataWindows.

To turn off the sharing between a primary and secondary DataWindow, you need to call the `ShareDataOff()` function, which has this syntax:

```
DataWindow.ShareDataOff()
```

The results of calling this function depend on whether *`DataWindow`* is a primary or secondary DataWindow. If *`DataWindow`* is a primary DataWindow, all the related secondary DataWindow controls have their association dropped and are reset. When *`DataWindow`* is a secondary DataWindow, only its association is dropped and its data cleared.

NOTE

If you use `ShareData()` from a secondary DataWindow to a new DataWindow, the new DataWindow is then based on the original primary DataWindow. Therefore, when you issue a `ShareDataOff()` for the secondary DataWindow, the new secondary DataWindow does not become reset.

The `DataStore` Object

NEW in PowerBuilder 5

The `DataStore` object is the nonvisual DataWindow that PowerBuilder developers have been praying for. In previous versions of PowerBuilder data stores (more commonly known as *data caches*) were implemented using hidden windows together with user objects and DataWindow controls. These data stores were used to cache code tables and lookups and to hold result sets to allow different presentation styles of the same data. Now using the `DataStore` you not only get a nonvisual object but one that you can extend with variables, events, and functions and even inherit from.

NOTE

This is the only way to really make distributed PowerBuilder work by allowing you to easily control and transmit large amounts of data across distributed applications.

The `DataStore` has only three attributes (and they serve the same purpose for the `DataStore` as they do for a DataWindow):

- `DataObject` (String)—The name of the PowerBuilder DataWindow object (for example, `d_order_header`).
- `Object` (`dwObject`)—The DataWindow object and all of its attributes and objects.
- `ProxyName` (String)—The proxy name used in making the object distributed.

The DataStore object allows you to cache data for your application without consuming any graphics resources. You use the DataStore object very much as you would a normal DataWindow, only the setup and initialization are different. Your first step is to declare a variable at the scope at which you want the DataStore to exist (global, shared, instance, local). For example, in the instance variables section of a window, you'd use this:

```
DataStore i_dsDeparments
```

Then, in the appropriate event you need to instantiate the object (in this case the Open event of the window) and assign the DataWindow object that you want to associate it with:

```
i_dsDepartments = CREATE DataStore

i_dsDepartments.DataObject = "d_departments"
```

You can now do anything (except graphics operations) to i_dsDeparments that you would to a DataWindow. Here's an example:

```
// Insert a new row into the data store
//
i_dsDepartments.InsertRow( 0)
//
// Set the dept id of the new row
//
i_dsDepartments.Object.Data.dept_id[ 1] = nDeptId
//
// Delete the second row in the DataWindow
//
i_dsDepartments.DeleteRow( 2)
//
// Set the sort order to dept_name and sort
//
i_dsDepartments.SetSort( "dept_name D")
i_dsDepartments.Sort()
```

NEW in PowerBuilder 5

The DataStore object provides you with a very useful addition to your data processing tools. An important new feature with 5.0 DataWindows is the ability to cache data to disk, and you can also use this feature with your DataStore objects as well. You may want to consider making an ancestor user object of type DataStore and incorporating many of the same methods you have for your DataWindow ancestor for this.

Summary

This chapter looks at a number of advanced DataWindow programming techniques that you will commonly need in day-to-day DataWindow development. The Describe() and Modify() functions are introduced, as is the new direct access syntax. With these you have access to almost any DataWindow attribute. If you are not sure how to access a specific attribute, consult the PowerBuilder online help under "Attributes for the DataWindow Object."

Advanced DataWindow Techniques II

26

IN THIS CHAPTER

This chapter explores some additional advanced DataWindow techniques that you can use in your applications. The chapter covers how to carry out searches of data and extract object information from DataWindows and provides you with a number of reusable and useful functions. DataWindow printing and all the relevant functions are described in depth. Data transfer, the how-to's of drop-down DataWindows, and master/detail relationships round out the remainder of this chapter.

NOTE

The examples in this chapter, like those in Chapter 25, "Advanced DataWindow Techniques I," show you how the new direct syntax works together with the existing `Describe()` and `Modify()` functions.

Finding Data in a DataWindow

A common requirement from end users is the ability to search through large amounts of newly retrieved data. You could provide the users a way to restrict the data being retrieved, but this can be almost as complex as allowing them to retrieve the data and then providing search capabilities. Restricting data retrieval has been covered in other areas of this book, and in the following sections you will see how to search based on various criteria and what is entailed in providing an end user with a search function.

The `Find()` Function

At the heart of any search functionality you build for a DataWindow will be the `Find()` function. This function locates the next row, after a given starting row, that matches the specified criteria, and has this syntax:

```
DataWindow.Find( Expression, StartRow, EndRow)
```

You can search on both DataWindow controls and child DataWindows by specifying a valid search expression, *`Expression`*, and a start and end row, *`StartRow`* and *`EndRow`*. You can make `Find()` search backward by specifying an *`EndRow`* that is less than the *`StartRow`*. The function returns the first row matching the criteria, or `0` if no rows are found.

`Expression` must evaluate to a Boolean result, and is constructed using column names, data type comparison operators, and Boolean operators. The search is case-sensitive, so you must code your own case-insensitivity into the expression. All DataWindow expressions are constructed in the same manner and obey the same rules. The following are some examples of `Find()` expressions:

```
// Search for an employee without a lastname
dw_1.Find( "IsNull( emp_lname)", 1, dw_1.RowCount())
```

```
//
// Find any employees who earn more than $50k in department 501
dw_1.Find( "emp_salary > 50000 AND dept_id = 501", 1, dw_1.RowCount())
//
// Find an employee with a last name of O'Connor who start on 1/1/94
dw_1.Find( "emp_lname='O~'Connor' AND start_date='1/1/94'", 1, dw_1.RowCount())
```

The next section shows how to make good use of the `Find()` function to provide DataWindow-wide search capabilities.

A Data Search Window

There are a couple methods for supplying a scrolling lookup for DataWindows. One method you may have seen is to have a series of edit fields appear above the DataWindow for each of the columns you are interested in searching on. Another, and probably the more elegant, is to use a pop-up window similar to the Find windows of most other Windows applications. The advantage of the window over the other methods is that you do not lose any screen space to other controls, the window floats over the DataWindow, and the user can move it around as needed. This last method is described in detail in this section.

The finished window is displayed in Figure 26.1.

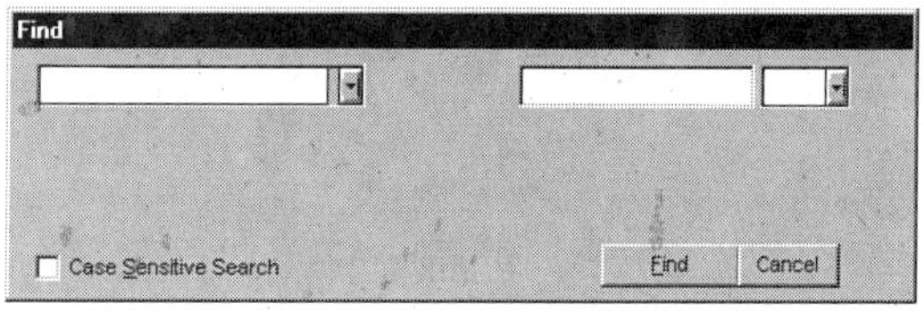

FIGURE 26.1.
The Find window.

The controls for the Find window are shown in Table 26.1. The attribute settings in this table refer to the actual attributes for the control type listed and the associated value assigned to the control's attribute.

Table 26.1. Controls for the Find window.

Control Name	*Control Type*	*Control Attribute Settings*
`cb_find`	CommandButton	`Text = "&Find"`
`cb_cancel`	CommandButton	`Text = "Cancel"`
		`Cancel = TRUE`
`cbx_case_sensitive`	CheckBox	`Text = "Case &Sensitive Search"`
`dw_criteria`	DataWindow	`DataObject = "d_find"`
		`VScrollBar = Yes`

The window is a pop-up and is called `w_datawindow_find`, and it has the following instance variables declared in it:

- `i_lRow`—A Long value that holds the current position in the DataWindow being searched and is used to continue searches from the previously located value.
- `i_aszTypes[]`—An array of strings that holds the searched DataWindow's columns data types.
- `i_szFind`—The current find expression. This is cached for reuse on a find next operation.
- `i_dwToActOn`—The DataWindow that is being searched.

There will be two main areas of code: in the `Open` event for the window and the `wf_Find()` window function. The other pieces of code are quite short and are either reactions to user interaction or supporting functionality.

The `Open` event first extracts the DataWindow argument from the `Message` object and assigns it to the instance variable `i_dwToActOn` (see Listing 26.1). The total number of columns in the DataWindow to be searched is ascertained and used to set an upper boundary for the column data type array, `i_aszTypes`. The child drop-down DataWindow for the `column_number` column is captured into a local variable, so you can insert rows for the searchable column information.

For each column in the search DataWindow you need to determine if it has a label (our only criterion for making a DataWindow searchable), which helps eliminate all those hidden ID and work fields of a DataWindow. When you find a valid column, a row is added to the drop-down DataWindow and the column's name and number are saved. The column data type is stored in the instance variable array `i_aszTypes`, using the column number as the index. You then add a row to the main DataWindow, `dw_criteria`, and await the user's interaction.

Listing 26.1. The `Open` event for `w_find`.

```
Integer nColumnCount, nColumnIndex
String  szColumn
Long lRow
DataWindowChild dwcColumns

i_dwToActOn = Message.PowerObjectParm

nColumnCount = Integer( i_dwToActOn.Object.DataWindow.Column.Count)
i_aszTypes[ nColumnCount] = ""

dw_criteria.GetChild( "column_number", dwcColumns)

For nColumnIndex = 1 To nColumnCount
   // Strip out any CR, LF, or tab control characters from the label.
   szColumn = f_strip( i_dwToActOn.Describe( i_dwToActOn.Describe( "#" + &
                       String(nColumnIndex) + ".Name") + "_t.Text"))
```

```
   If szColumn <> "!" Then
      lRow = dwcColumns.InsertRow( 0)
      dwcColumns.SetItem( lRow, "column_name", szColumn)
      dwcColumns.SetItem( lRow, "column_number", nColumnIndex)
      i_aszTypes[ nColumnIndex] = i_dwToActOn.Describe( "#" + &
                                  String(nColumnIndex) + ".ColType")
   End If
Next

dw_criteria.TriggerEvent( "NewRow")
```

The events for the check box and the cancel are very simple and are shown in Listings 26.2 and 26.3, respectively.

Listing 26.2. The `Clicked` event for `cbx_case_sensitive`.

```
wf_ResetFind()
```

Listing 26.3. The `Clicked` event for `cb_cancel`.

```
Close( Parent)
```

The main DataWindow for the Find window contains only two event scripts: `ItemChanged` (see Listing 26.4) and `NewRow` (a user event that is detailed in Chapter 24, "Building User Objects").

Listing 26.4. The `ItemChanged` event for `dw_criteria`.

```
Long lRow, lTotalRows, lIndex
String szValue

lRow = this.GetRow()
lTotalRows = this.RowCount()
szValue = this.GetText()

Choose Case this.GetcolumnName()
   Case "column_number"
      lIndex = Long( szValue)
      If lIndex > 0 Then
         If i_aszTypes[ lIndex] <> "" Then
            this.SetItem( lRow, "column_datatype", i_aszTypes[ lIndex])
         End If
      End If
   Case "join_operator"
      If lRow = lTotalRows And Not &
         IsNull( this.GetItemNumber( lRow, "column_number")) Then
         this.TriggerEvent( "NewRow")
      ElseIf Trim( szValue) = "" And lTotalRows > 1 And lRow <> lTotalRows Then
```

continues

Listing 26.4. continued

```
         dw_criteria.SetRow( lRow + 1)
         dw_criteria.TriggerEvent( "DeleteRow")
      End If
End Choose

wf_ResetFind()
```

The `ItemChanged` event of the DataWindow detects two types of user interaction: a change in the choice of column and the addition or subtraction of additional expressions. The first case is trapped to provide feedback to the DataWindow so that the operator drop-down list box can be switched to the correct list for the column's data type. This is achieved by defining three fields: one for numeric operators, another for date and time operators, and the last for string operators. The `Visible` attribute of each is then set to show them only when the appropriate data type value is in the `column_datatype` column. The `join_operator` column controls whether a new expression should be added (if the current row is the last in the DataWindow) or removed (the blank operator was selected).

This provides all the control scripts except for the actual code that carries out and manages the find: the `Clicked` event for `cb_find` (see Listing 26.5).

Listing 26.5. The `Clicked` event for `cb_find`.

```
If IsNull( dw_criteria.GetItemNumber( 1, "column_number")) Then
   // Only search when we have some criteria
   Return
End If

i_lRow ++

i_lRow = wf_find( i_lRow)

If i_lRow = 0 Then
   MessageBox( "Data Search", &
               "Unable to find any data matching specified criteria.")
   wf_ResetFind()
ElseIf i_lRow > 0 Then
   this.text = "&Find Next"
   i_dwToActOn.SetColumn( dw_criteria.GetItemNumber( 1, "column_number"))
   i_dwToActOn.SetRow( i_lRow)
   i_dwToActOn.ScrollToRow( i_lRow)
   i_dwToActOn.SetFocus()
End If
```

This script controls the continuation of a search by passing the `i_lRow` variable to the `wf_Find()` function, which is covered next. Depending on the return value of this function, the script can determine whether a row was found. When a row has been found that matches the user's criteria, the DataWindow searched is set to the column in the first expression and scrolled to the row so that the user is immediately presented with the data requested. The Find button changes its name to Find Next so that the user can continue to search for other matches.

The whole search process is achieved by one main and two supporting functions. The `wf_Find()` function (see Listing 26.6) is called to generate the expressions that are then used in a call to the PowerScript `Find()` function.

Listing 26.6. The `wf_find()` function for `w_find`.

```
// private function long wf_find( Long a_lStartRow)
//
Long lNoOfCriteria, lRow, lColumnNo
Integer nPos
String szColumn, szOperator, szValue, szExpression, szJoin, szFormat, szValue1,
szValue2, szValue3

If i_szFind = "" Then
   lNoOfCriteria = dw_criteria.RowCount()

   For lRow = 1 To lNoOfCriteria
      lColumnNo = dw_criteria.GetItemNumber( lRow, "column_number")

      szColumn = i_dwToActOn.Describe( "#" + String( lColumnNo) + ".Name")
      szJoin = dw_criteria.GetItemString( lRow, "join_operator")
      If IsNull( szJoin) Then szJoin = ""
      szValue = wf_escapechars( dw_criteria.GetItemString( lRow, "value"))

      If IsNull( szValue) Then
         szExpression = szColumn
      Else
         Choose Case Left( i_aszTypes[ lColumnNo], 4)
         Case "char"
            szOperator = Upper( dw_criteria.GetItemString( lRow, &
                                                           "string_operators"))
            If Right( szOperator, 4) = "LIKE" Then
               If Pos( szValue, "%") = 0 Then
                  szValue = szValue + "%"
               End If
            End If
            szExpression = szOperator + " '" + szValue + "' "

            If cbx_case_sensitive.Checked Then
               szExpression = szColumn + " " + szExpression
            Else
               szExpression = "LOWER( " + szColumn + ") " + Lower( szExpression)
            End If
         Case "date", "time"
            szOperator = Upper( dw_criteria.GetItemString( lRow, &
                                                         "datetime_operators"))
            If Right( szOperator, 7) = "BETWEEN" Then
               nPos = Pos( Upper( szValue), " AND ")
               If nPos > 0 Then
                  szValue1 = Left( szValue, nPos-1)
                  szValue2 = Mid( szValue, nPos + 5)
               End If
```

continues

Listing 26.6. continued

```
            Else
               nPos = 0
            End If

            If i_aszTypes[ lColumnNo] = "date" Then
               szFormat = "yyyymmdd"
               szValue = String( Date( szValue), szFormat)
               szValue1 = String( Date( szValue1), szFormat)
               szValue2 = String( Date( szValue2), szFormat)
            Else
               szFormat = "hhmmss"
               szValue = String( Time( szValue), szFormat)
               szValue1 = String( Time( szValue1), szFormat)
               szValue2 = String( Time( szValue2), szFormat)
            End If

            If nPos = 0 Then
               szExpression = "Long(String( " + szColumn + ", '" + szFormat + &
                              "')) " + szOperator + szValue
            Else
               szExpression = "Long(String( " + szColumn + ", '" + szFormat + &
                              "')) " + szOperator + &
                              " " + szValue1 + " AND " + szValue2
            End If
         Case Else
            szOperator = Upper( dw_criteria.GetItemString( lRow, &
                                                        "numeric_operators"))
            If szOperator = "IN" Or szOperator = "NOT IN" Then
               szExpression = szColumn + " " + szOperator + " (" + szValue + ") "
            Else
               szExpression = szColumn + " " + szOperator + " " + szValue + " "
            End If
         End Choose
      End If

      i_szFind = i_szFind + " ( " + Trim( szExpression) + ") " + szJoin
   Next
End If

lRow = i_dwToActOn.Find( i_szFind, a_lStartRow, i_dwToActOn.RowCount())

Return lRow
```

This function may seem a little overwhelming at first, but it can be logically broken down into four main parts: the acquisition of an expression's worth of information, and the construction of a numeric, string, or date and time expression from those component pieces.

The first step is to determine if you can use a cached expression, rather than rebuild it each time; if this expression has been reset, you need to create a new find expression. In this case, for each row in the Find window's criteria DataWindow you need to generate row expressions and then join them together.

With each row you extract the column's name (the name of the column in the DataWindow), the join condition if any (if there is no join condition, make it an empty string so you don't create a `NULL` final expression!), and the value the user entered for searching. If the user did not enter a search value, you should assume that the user entered a function expression for the column name. An example is `IsNull( emp_lname)`, although obviously this will require the user to have prior knowledge of the database structure and names, as well as an understanding of PowerScript functions. This is kind of a hidden feature for power users!

Each expression is then constructed based on the requirements of the data type and special operators that can be used. For example, strings are required to have the values enclosed in quotation marks, and the `LIKE` operator makes use of a percent sign. The date and time expressions are converted to Long values to make the comparison of the values easier.

At the bottom of the `For...Next` loop the whole expression is then joined to the overall find string, with each new expression being enclosed in parentheses. After each expression row has been analyzed and the find expression is complete, the actual call to the `Find()` function is made, starting from the current row in the DataWindow. The returned value is then passed back to the script that called the `wf_Find()` function.

The `wf_EscapeChars()` function (see Listing 26.7) is called from `wf_Find()` to place the PowerBuilder escape character (~) in front of any characters that would cause a problem in a string.

Listing 26.7. The `wf_EscapeChars()` function for `w_find`.

```
// Private Function String wf_EscapeChars( String a_szValue)
//
Char cChar
Integer nLength, nPos

nLength = Len( a_szValue)

For nPos = nLength To 1 Step -1
   cChar = Mid( a_szValue, nPos, 1)
   Choose Case cChar
      Case "~t", "~r", "~n", '"', "'", "~~"
         a_szValue = Replace( a_szValue, nPos, 1, "~~" + cChar)
   End Choose
Next

Return Trim( a_szValue)
```

The `wf_EscapeChars()` function is very straightforward and should require no commentary, except that you should note that the string is parsed backward (this enables you to add to the string without having to alter your position in it) and the escape character ~~ is inserted into the string.

The `wf_ResetFind()` function (see Listing 26.8) is used in a couple of the scripts and is simply used to reset the Find window, so it has to generate a completely new expression and search from the start of the DataWindow.

Listing 26.8. The `wf_ResetFind()` function for `w_find`.

```
// private subroutine wf_resetfind ();
//
i_szFind = ""
i_lRow = 0
cb_find.Text = "&Find"
```

These few lines of code that have been introduced for the various events and functions provide you with a completely flexible method for providing end user search capabilities for large result sets.

Drop-Down DataWindow Scrolling Lookup

The list box controls available in a window provide the standard behavior of scrolling to the first occurrence within the list whose first letter matches a typed letter. This section explores the simple code required to provide full word matching, as well as suggestions of the complete value for a DataWindow.

The complete functionality is contained in a single DataWindow event, `LookupDDDW` (see Listing 26.9), which is a custom user event. This function will only handle string values, because it is unlikely that you will want to carry out scrolling lookups on any other data type. You can easily expand it for numeric columns if you have a need for that capability.

Listing 26.9. The `LookupDDDW` event.

```
String szValue, szFoundValue, szColumnName, szDDDWColumnName, szColumnType
Long lRow
DataWindowChild dwcSearch

szColumnName = this.GetColumnName()

// Check to see if we are dealing with a DDDW
If this.GetChild( szColumnName, dwcSearch) = 1 Then
   // Find out the DropDownDataWindow name and column type
   szDDDWColumnName = this.Describe( szColumnName + ".dddw.DisplayColumn")
   szColumnType = dwcSearch.Describe( szDDDWColumnName + ".ColType")
   // Only operate on string based data columns
   If Left( szColumnType, 4) = "char" Then
      szValue = Trim( this.GetText())
      If szValue = "" Then
         Return
      End If
      // Capture the currently entered text-not the highlighted text that we
      // place there
      szValue = Upper( Left( szValue, Len( szValue)-this.SelectedLength()))
      // Case-insensitive search
      lRow = dwcSearch.Find( "Upper( " + szDDDWColumnName + ") LIKE '" + &
                             szValue + "%'", 1, dwcSearch.RowCount())
```

```
      If lRow > 0 Then
         // A match was found, scroll to it, and capture the text into the
         // edit field
         szFoundValue = dwcSearch.GetItemString( lRow, szDDDWColumnName)
         this.SetText( szFoundValue)
         this.SelectText( Len( szValue) + 1, Len( szFoundValue))
         dwcSearch.ScrollToRow( lRow)
         dwcSearch.SelectRow( lRow, TRUE)
      End If
   End If
End If
```

The script starts by ascertaining a number of facts about the drop-down DataWindow (initially that the column is in fact a drop-down DataWindow). The current value of the edit field of the DataWindow is captured. Since you will be providing a scrolling lookup that replaces the value being typed, you will also highlight the untyped portion of the value. This allows the user to keep typing to replace the value with additional letters, which are in turn searched on.

The actual search is carried out using the unselected part of the value, which has already been passed through the `Upper()` function to provide a search that is not case-sensitive. The column name is then built into the construction together with the `Like` operator (new to PowerBuilder 5.0) and a `%` wildcard indicator character.

If a matching value is found, the edit control is set to this value and the untyped part is highlighted. The DataWindow child is then scrolled to the appropriate row and the row is highlighted.

The `LookupDDDW` event is called from within another user event, `Key` (see Listing 26.10), which is mapped to the PowerBuilder `pbm_dwnkey` message ID. This event then posts a message to `LookupDDDW`, which allows PowerBuilder time to process the keystroke. There are two special conditions that you do not want to perform a search on: when the key is a backspace and when the user accepts the value using the Enter key.

Listing 26.10. The `Key` event used to trigger `LookupDDDW`.

```
If Key <> KeyBack! And Key <> KeyEnter! Then
   this.PostEvent( "LookupDDDW")
End If
```

You will probably want to build this into an ancestor DataWindow object for re-use throughout your application development.

PowerBuilder also allows you to search for other conditions within a DataWindow, not just on the data within it, and in the next two sections you will see two specialized search functions.

Required Fields

Before allowing the user to save the data from a DataWindow you need to check whether all the required fields have had data entered. This will prevent the database from rejecting an attempted save, if you match your required fields with the `NOT NULL` columns of the table. By forcing the user to enter these values, you won't generate unnecessary network or DBMS usage. You also won't have to trap the error message from the DBMS for this case; thus, you get a much cleaner and friendlier user interface.

PowerBuilder provides a function to help you carry out this check: `FindRequired()`. This function has the following syntax:

```
DataWindow.FindRequired( dwBuffer, Row, ColumnNumber, ColumnName, UpdateOnly)
```

`dwBuffer` specifies which of the DataWindow's buffers you want to check, and can be either `Primary!` or `Filter!`. *`Row`* and *`ColumnNumber`* specify the first row and column to start searching on. These two arguments, along with *`ColumnName`*, are passed by reference to the function, which the function then uses to return information on the first required field that has a `NULL` value. The `UpdateOnly` parameter allows you to boost the performance of the function by only requiring it to check modified columns and inserted rows (`TRUE`), rather than every row and column (`FALSE`). This function can only be used with DataWindow controls.

NOTE

You can make a column required by using the DataWindow painter and bringing up the column's properties and going to the Edit tab page.

The code shown in Listing 26.11 is built as a DataWindow object-level function, and returns either `TRUE` or `FALSE` to indicate whether all the required columns have values.

Listing 26.11. The `CheckRequiredFields()` object-level function.

```
Integer nColumn = 1
Long lRow = 1
String szColumn

// Ensure that the last data entry has been accepted into the DataWindow
If this.AcceptText() = -1 Then
   // Problem on the last edit-return focus to the DataWindow so the user
   // can fix it.
   this.SetFocus()
   Return FALSE
End If

// Find the first empty row and column
If this.FindRequired( Primary!, lRow, nColumn, szColumn, TRUE) < 0 Then
   // Search error
   Return FALSE
End If
```

```
// Was a row found with a missing value?
If lRow <> 0 Then
   // Get the label for the column
   szColumn = this.Describe( szColumn + "_t.Text")

   // Indicate problem field
   MessageBox( "Required Value Missing",
               "You must enter a value for '" + szColumn + ".", StopSign!, Ok!)

   // Make the problem field the current one
   this.SetColumn( nColumn)
   this.ScrollToRow( lRow)
   this.SetFocus()
   Return FALSE
End If

// Return success if all of the rows and columns have data
Return TRUE
```

This function would be called from within the save event script for the DataWindow. Here's an example:

```
If this.CheckRequiredFields() Then
   this.Update()
End If
```

By using this function you will avoid any errors generated by the DBMS for columns that have to be `NOT NULL`, and by providing this function in an ancestor DataWindow object, you only need to code it once.

NOTE

You can easily extend this function to search the Filter buffer as well. Of course, you must provide a means to display any problem rows to the user by moving/copying them out of the filter buffer.

Group Changes

If you have a DataWindow that uses required fields groups, you can search the groups using the `FindGroupChange()` function. This allows you to locate rows within the DataWindow, possibly for additional processing or focus. The syntax for this function is

```
DataWindow.FindGroupChange( Row, Level)
```

`DataWindow` can either be a DataWindow control or child DataWindow that you want to search, with *`Row`* indicating in which row to start searching for the break (a group break occurs when the value of a column defined for a group changes from one row to the next). The *`Level`* argument indicates the group level number that you want to search within (the groups are numbered in the order in which you defined them).

The function returns the number of the row where the change occurred and `0` if no value in the group changed. The return value also conforms to the following rules:

- If *Row* is the first row of a group, the returned row is *Row*.
- If *Row* is a row within a group (other than the last), the returned row is the first row of the next group.
- If *Row* is within the last group, the returned row is `0`.

To use this function you need to set *Row* to `0` and then continue to increment this value to find subsequent groups until you find the one you want. For example, to find an inclusive range of rows that match a certain criterion, the code would be

```
Boolean bFound = FALSE
Long lRow, lStartRow = -1, lEndRow

Do While Not bFound
   lRow = dw_1.FindGroupChange( lRow, 1)

   // If no breaks are found or error then exit the loop
   If lRow <= 0 Then Exit

   // Group break found-is it the one we are looking for?
   If dw_1.GetItemNumber( lRow, "manager_id") = 1293 Then
      lStartRow = lRow
   ElseIf lStartRow <> -1 Then
      lEndRow = lRow-1
      bFound = TRUE
   End If

   // Increment row to find next group break
   lRow ++
Loop

If bFound Then
   // Processing for Manager 1293 occurs here based on the rows lStartRow to
   // lEndRow inclusive
Else
   MessageBox( "Data Not Found",  "The requested manager was not found!")
End If
```

This is a fairly simple example, but it illustrates how the function should be used within a loop and how to capture the start and end row numbers of the group.

Printing DataWindows

PowerBuilder provides two functions to print a DataWindow. There are actually three ways to print, but the third method requires you to code your own print function that makes use of PowerBuilder's low-level print functions. Of course, you don't use that approach except in rare cases, and starting in PowerBuilder 4.0 you have access to composite reports that remove almost all need to resort to these functions.

Before venturing into the PowerBuilder print functions, you need to understand the following two terms: print cursor and print area.

The Print Cursor

Similar to a screen cursor, a print cursor is used when you open a print job to keep track of the current print location. The print cursor points to the top-left corner of the location where the next object will be printed on the page.

The Print Area and Margins

The print area is the available space on the printer's page, not counting the margins. The margins can be altered for DataWindows, but you have to use the `PrintSend()` function to send printer-defined escape sequences to alter them for any other print job.

Starting a Print Job

The `PrintOpen()` function opens a print job and assigns it a unique number that is used as an argument to other print functions. When you call `PrintOpen()`, the currently active window in the application is disabled. This is done to enable the Windows operating system to handle the printing request because the currently active window is assigned as the parent of a new window. This means that if you try to open a window—for example, a message box—after calling `PrintOpen()`, another application is assigned as the parent of the message box and becomes active. This can cause some very confusing behavior for the end user. The syntax is

```
PrintOpen( { JobName})
```

The function returns a Long value for the job number and `-1` if an error occurs. You have the option of naming the print job; this is the name that appears in the print queue.

When a new print job is started, the font is set to the printer's default, and the print cursor is positioned at the top-left corner of the print area.

At the end of the print job you must close it and allow PowerBuilder and Windows to clean up the resources used. It is therefore advisable to close the print job in the same event where you open it.

Closing a Print Job

Two functions can be used to close a print job. The `PrintClose()` function sends the current page to the print spool and closes the job. The syntax is

```
PrintClose( PrintJobNumber)
```

The `PrintCancel()` function cancels the print job and causes the spool file to be deleted. This function can be used in conjunction with either the `PrintDataWindow()` or the `Print()` function. The syntax for use with `PrintDataWindow()` is

```
DataWindowControl.PrintCancel()
```

The syntax for use with `Print()` is

```
PrintCancel( PrintJobNumber)
```

The `PrintClose()` and `PrintCancel()` functions are mutually exclusive. You cannot and should not call one after the other.

The PrintDataWindow() Function

The `PrintDataWindow()` function prints the contents of a DataWindow control as a single print job. PowerBuilder uses the fonts and layout as they appear in the DataWindow object. You can use this function to print multiple DataWindows in one print job. Unfortunately, each DataWindow control starts printing on a new page, so if you require a sequence of DataWindows to print on one page, you will need to make use of the low-level print functions or the new composite DataWindow presentation style. The syntax for the `PrintDataWindow()` function is

```
PrintDataWindow( PrintJobNumber, DataWindow)
```

PrintJobNumber is the Long data type returned by the `PrintOpen()` function that is used to identify a particular print job. *DataWindow* can be either a DataWindow control or a child DataWindow. The `PrintDataWindow()` function cannot be used in conjunction with any functions other than `PrintOpen()` and `PrintClose()`.

The following example makes use of the preceding functions to print four DataWindows as a single print job:

```
Long lJobNumber

lJobNumber = PrintOpen( "Example Print-4 DataWindows")

// Remember-Each DataWindow will print on separate pages
PrintDataWindow( lJobNumber, dw_1)
PrintDataWindow( lJobNumber, dw_2)
PrintDataWindow( lJobNumber, dw_3)
PrintDataWindow( lJobNumber, dw_4)

PrintClose( lJobNumber)
```

Occasionally you will need to make the page numbering between these DataWindows contiguous, unless of course you are making use of PowerBuilder's composite reports. You use a DataWindow expression with access to global functions to accomplish this. First, you need to declare a global Long (or Integer) variable for the application. Next, you write a one-line function that returns this global variable. Then, for each computed field, in each DataWindow that calculates the current page number, you add the value returned from the global function, as follows: `page() + f_global_page_no()`. Finally, in the `PrintEnd` event of each DataWindow, you increment the global variable by the amount in the computed column for the last row.

The `Print` Function

The other function that can be used to print a DataWindow is the `Print()` function. Because this is a general-purpose function, it can be used to print a wide variety of objects in addition to DataWindows.

The first syntax is used with DataWindows:

```
DataWindowControl.Print( { DisplayCancelDialog})
```

The DataWindow to be printed can be either a DataWindow control or a child DataWindow. `DisplayCancelDialog` is an optional Boolean that if `TRUE` causes a nonmodal print cancel dialog box to appear that enables the user to stop the print job. This version of the function handles the creation and destruction of a print job and does not require the use of `PrintOpen()` and `PrintClose()`. For this reason, you cannot batch multiple DataWindows into one print job unless you are using PowerBuilder's composite report style. The other versions of the `Print()` function require you to manage the print job programmatically.

WARNING

You should be aware that there is another subtle difference between `Print()` and `PrintDataWindow()`. The `PrintDataWindow()` function uses the current printer defaults as it prints and not, like the `Print()` function, the print specifications that you set within the DataWindow object. For example, if you have the DataWindow set up to print landscape and you use the `PrintDataWindow()` function when the current printer is set up as portrait, your DataWindow will print in portrait.

The second syntax is used to print a particular object—either a window or any control you can place on a window—to a specific region of the print area:

```
ObjectName.Print( PrintJobNumber, XLocation, YLocation {, Width, Height})
```

The *`Xlocation`* and *`Ylocation`* parameters control the coordinates of the left corner of the object and are measured in thousandths of an inch. You can use the optional parameters *`Width`* and *`Height`* to resize the object in the print area; they are also measured in thousandths of an inch.

When a new line is started, the X coordinate is reset to `0` and the Y coordinate is incremented by 1.2 times the character height, by default. The line spacing can be modified using the `PrintSetSpacing()` function, which enables you to set a new multiplication factor. The syntax is

```
PrintSetSpacing( PrintJobNumber, SpacingFactor)
```

The third syntax is used to print lines of text to the print job. With this syntax you can control the starting horizontal position of each line as well as the horizontal position of the following line. The syntax is

```
Print( PrintJobNumber, { Position1, } Text {, Position2})
```

`Position1` specifies, in thousandths of an inch, the distance from the left edge of the print area where the text should start. If this value is not greater than the current position, the text is printed from the current position. `Position2` specifies the position to which the print cursor should move after printing the text. The print cursor will move only if it is not already beyond this point. If `Position2` is omitted from the syntax, the print cursor will move to the start of the next line. If the text contains carriage returns and new lines, the string will be printed on multiple lines, but the positioning values will be ignored.

Because this syntax automatically increments the position down the page each time a line is created, it also handles all page breaks automatically.

Two additional print functions that you can use with the third syntax of `Print()` enable you to specify the font to be used when printing a string. These are `PrintDefineFont()` and `PrintSetFont()`.

The `PrintDefineFont()` function is used to create a new font definition for an existing printer font, which can then be used in calls to the `PrintSetFont()` and `PrintText()` functions. The syntax is as follows:

```
PrintDefineFont( PrintJobNo, FontNo, FaceName, Height, Weight, FontPitch, &
                 FontFamily, Italic, Underline)
```

`FontNo` can be a number from 1 to 8 that uniquely identifies the font. `FaceName` is a string that contains the name of a printer-supported typeface (for example, Prestige 20Cpi). `Height` of the font is specified in thousandths of an inch. `Weight` is the stroke weight (how thick the characters are) of the type: Bold is 700 and Normal is 400. `FontPitch` and `FontFamily` are enumerated types that further define the font styling. `FontPitch` can be `Default!`, `Fixed!`, or `Variable!`. `FontFamily` can be `AnyFont!`, `Decorative!`, `Modern!`, `Roman!`, `Script!`, or `Swiss!`. `Italic` and `Underline` are Booleans that specify whether the font should be italicized and underlined, respectively.

Use the `PrintSetFont()` function to make a previously defined font number the current font for the open print job:

```
PrintSetFont( PrintJobNumber, FontNo)
```

NOTE

Microsoft Windows uses the `FontFamily` parameter of `PrintDefineFont()` along with the font name to identify the desired font, or to substitute a similar font if it is not found. Macintosh, however, makes use of only the `FaceName`, `Height`, and `Weight` parameters to find the font and ignores the `FontFamily` and `FontPitch` values.

Following is an example of creating and using a font based on the Prestige 20Cpi font, 10 point, bold and underlined:

```
Long lJob

lJob = PrintOpen( "A test")
PrintDefineFont( lJob, 1, "Prestige 20Cpi", -10, 700, Default!, AnyFont!, &
                 FALSE, TRUE)
PrintSetFont( lJob, 1)
```

DataWindow `Print` Events

When the `Print()` function is used on a DataWindow, a `PrintStart` event is triggered. This event occurs before anything is sent to the print spool.

A `PrintPage` event is triggered before each page is formatted and sent to the print spool. Within this event you can force the page to be skipped by setting the return code as follows:

- `0`—Process the page normally (the default).
- `1`—Skip the current page.

The `PrintEnd` event is triggered at the end of the print job.

These events enable you to carry out specific printing requirements that cannot be addressed from the printer setup dialog box or through the DataWindow objects.

Building a DataWindow Print Preview Dialog Box

If you've ever printed DataWindows from PowerBuilder 3.0 and from later versions of PowerBuilder, you've probably noticed a much-improved Print dialog box provided by PowerBuilder (see Figure 26.2), which enables the specification of particular pages to print.

FIGURE 26.2.
The Print window.

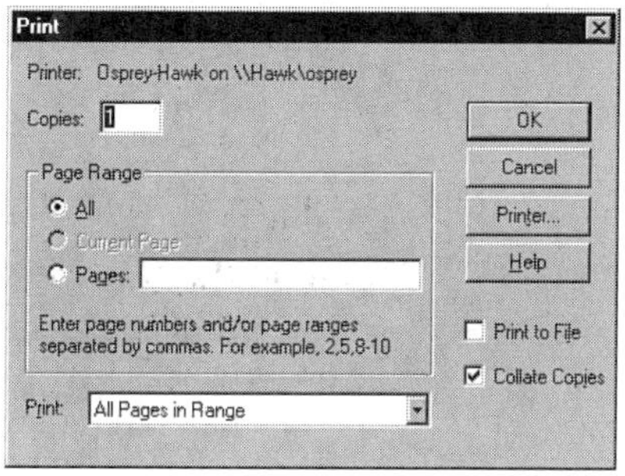

NOTE

The Windows 95 print dialog box is different from the one that Powersoft uses, and you might want to move the controls around for the window you will create next, so that they look more like the Windows 95 dialog box.

Table 26.2 lists all the available print attributes.

Table 26.2. Print attributes for DataWindow objects.

Attribute	*Value*	*Description*
`Collate`	`Yes` `No` (Default)	Indicates whether printing is collated.
`Color`	`1` (Color) `2` (Monochrome)	An integer indicating whether the printed output will be color or monochrome.
`Columns`	`1` (Default)	An integer specifying the number of newspaper-style columns the DataWindow will print on a page.
`Columns.Width`		An integer specifying the width of the newspaper-style columns in DataWindow units.
`Copies`		An integer indicating the number of copies to print.
`DocumentName`		A string containing the name that will display in the print queue.
`Duplex`	`1` (Simplex) `2` (Horizontal) `3` (Vertical)	An integer indicating the orientation of the printed output.
`Filename`		A string containing the name of the file to which you want to print the report.
`Margin.Bottom`		An integer indicating the width of the bottom margin on the printed page in DataWindow units.
`Margin.Left`		An integer indicating the width of the left margin on the printed page in DataWindow units.

Attribute	*Value*	*Description*
`Margin.Right`		An integer indicating the width of the right margin on the printed page in DataWindow units.
`Margin.Top`		An integer indicating the width of the top margin on the printed page in the units specified for the DataWindow.
`Orientation`	`1` (Landscape) `2` (Portrait) `0` (Use default)	An integer indicating the print orientation.
`Page.Range`		A string containing the numbers of the pages you want to print, separated by commas. You can also specify a range with a dash.
`Page.RangeInclude`	`0` (Print all) `1` (Print even pages) `2` (Print odd pages)	An integer indicating which pages to print within the desired range.
`Paper.Size`	`0` (Default) `1` (Letter 8$^1/_2$×11 in.) `2` (LetterSmall 8$^1/_2$ ×11 in.) `3` (Tabloid 17×11 in.) `4` (Ledger 17×11 in.) `5` (Legal 8$^1/_2$×14 in.) `6` (Statement 5$^1/_2$×8$^1/_2$ in.) `7` (Executive 7$^1/_4$×10 $^1/_2$ in.) `8` (A3 297×420 mm) `9` (A4 210×297 mm) `10` (A4 Small 210×297 mm) `11` (A5 148×210 mm) `12` (B4 250×354) `13` (B5 182×257 mm) `14` (Folio 8$^1/_2$×13 in.) `15` (Quarto 215×275 mm) `16` (10×14 in.)	An integer indicating the size of the paper that will be used for the output.

continues

Table 26.2. continued

Attribute	*Value*	*Description*
	`17` (11×17 in.)	
	`18` (Note $8^{1}/_{2}$×11 in.)	
	`19` (Envelope #9 $3^{7}/_{8}$×$8^{7}/_{8}$)	
	`20` (Envelope #10 $4^{1}/_{8}$×$9^{1}/_{2}$)	
	`21` (Envelope #11 $4^{1}/_{2}$×$10^{3}/_{8}$)	
	`22` (Envelope #12 4×$11^{1}/_{276}$)	
	`23` (Envelope #14 5×$11^{1}/_{2}$)	
	`24` (C-size sheet)	
	`25` (D-size sheet)	
	`26` (E-size sheet)	
	`27` (Envelope DL 110×220mm)	
	`28` (Envelope C5 162×229 mm)	
	`29` (Envelope C3 324×458 mm)	
	`30` (Envelope C4 229×324 mm)	
	`31` (Envelope C6 114×162 mm)	
	`32` (Envelope C65 114×229 mm)	
	`33` (Envelope B4 250×353 mm)	
	`34` (Envelope B5 176×250 mm)	
	`35` (Envelope B6 176×125 mm)	
	`36` (Envelope 110×230 mm)	
	`37` (Envelope Monarch 3.875×7.5 in.	
	`38` ($6^{3}/_{4}$ Envelope $3^{5}/_{8}$×$6^{1}/_{2}$ in.)	
	`39` (US Std Fanfold $14^{7}/_{8}$×11 in.)	
	`40` (German Std Fanfold $8^{1}/_{2}$×12 in.)	
	`41` (German Legal Fanfold $8^{1}/_{2}$×13 in.)	
`Paper.Source`	`0` (Default)	An integer indicating the bin that will be used as the paper source.
	`1` (Upper)	
	`2` (Lower)	
	`3` (Middle)	
	`4` (Manual)	
	`5` (Envelope)	
	`6` (Envelope manual)	

Attribute	*Value*	*Description*
	7 (Auto) 8 (Tractor) 9 (Smallfmt) 10 (Largefmt) 11 (Large capacity) 14 (Cassette)	
`Preview`	`Yes` `No` (Default)	Indicates whether the DataWindow object is displayed in preview mode.
`Preview.Rulers`	`Yes` `No` (Default)	Indicates whether the rulers are displayed when the DataWindow object is displayed in preview mode.
`Preview.Zoom`	`100` (Default)	An integer indicating the zoom factor of the print preview.
`Prompt`	`Yes` (Default) `No`	Indicates whether a prompt will display before the job prints so that the user can cancel the print job.
`Quality`	`0` (Default) 1 (High) 2 (Medium) 3 (Low) 4 (Draft)	An integer indicating the quality of the output.
Scale		An integer specifying the scale of the printed output as a percent.

Here are some additional considerations to be aware of when printing:

- `Collate`—Collating is usually slower because the print is repeated to produce collated sets.
- `FileName`—An empty string means send to the printer.
- `PageRange`—The empty string means print all.

Emulating the Print dialog box requires only a few of the attributes shown in Table 26.2. Some of them are directly influenced by the Printer Setup dialog box, to which you will provide access from your dialog box. There is also a smaller group of attributes that will be used in a Print Preview dialog box (which you will create later in this chapter).

The first step is to lay out the dialog window (see Figure 26.3) with the controls shown in Table 26.3. The attribute settings in Table 26.3 refer to the actual attribute for the control type listed and the associated value assigned to the control's attribute.

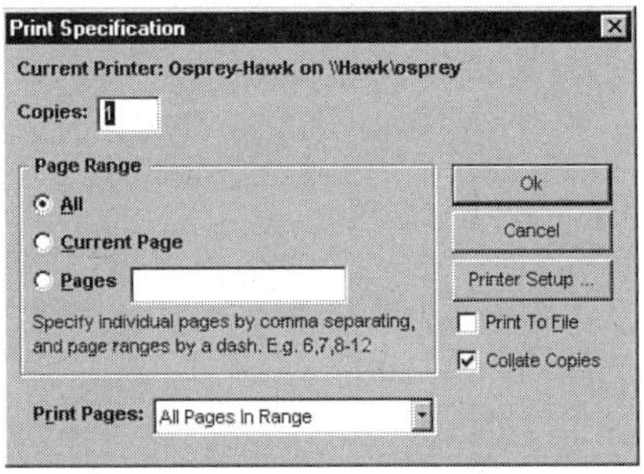

FIGURE 26.3.
The control layout for the Print Specification window.

Table 26.3. Controls for the Print dialog window.

Control Name	*Control Type*	*Control Attribute Settings*
`st_current_printer`	StaticText	`Text = "Current Printer:"`
`st_1`	StaticText	`Text = "Copies:"`
`st_2`	StaticText	`Text = "Specify individual pages by comma separating, and page ranges by a dash. For example: 6,7,8-12"`
`st_3`	StaticText	`Text = "Print Pages;"`
`em_copies`	EditMask	`Mask = "###"`
`cb_ok`	CommandButton	`Text = "OK"` `Default = TRUE`
`cb_cancel`	CommandButton	`Text = "Cancel"` `Cancel = TRUE`
`cb_printer_setup`	CommandButton	`Text = "Printer Setup..."`
`cbx_collate`	CheckBox	`Text = "Collate Copies"`
`cbx_print_to_file`	CheckBox	`Text = "Print To File"`
`gb_1`	GroupBox	`Text = "Page Range"`
`rb_all_pages`	RadioButton	`Text = "All"` `Checked = TRUE`
`rb_current_page`	RadioButton	`Text = "Current Page"`
`rb_pages`	RadioButton	`Text = "Pages"`

Control Name	Control Type	Control Attribute Settings
sle_page_range	SingleLineEdit	
ddlb_range_include	DropdownListBox	Item = {"All Pages In Range", "Even Pages", "Odd Pages"}

The window is of type Response, is called w_dw_print_dialog, and has two instance variables declared in it. i_dwToActOn of data type DataWindow will hold the DataWindow that is passed to the dialog box as a parameter. i_szFileName of data type String will hold the filename if the user specifies the print to file option.

There will be two main areas of code: in the Open event for the window and the Clicked event of the OK button. The remainder of the code will be short and result from user interaction or initial setup.

The Open event first extracts the argument from the Message object and assigns it to the instance variable i_dwToActOn (see Listing 26.12). The current default printer is extracted from the DataWindow using a Describe() call on the DataWindow.Printer attribute. The DataWindow current copy count is extracted, and if this is currently empty or 0, 1 is assigned to the edit field. The current state of the Collate attribute is extracted and compared in-line with the string YES to produce a Boolean value that can be used in the assignment of the Checked attribute. A similar statement is used on the print-to-file filename, except that a copy is kept in the instance variable i_szFileName.

Listing 26.12. The Open event for w_dw_print_dialog.

```
String szCopies

i_dwToActOn = Message.PowerObjectParm

st_current_printer.text = "Current Printer: " + &
                          String(i_dwToActOn.Object.DataWindow.Printer)

szCopies = String( i_dwToActOn.Object.DataWindow.Print.Copies)
If szCopies <> "" And szCopies <> "0" Then
   em_copies.Text = szCopies
Else
   em_copies.Text = "1"
End If

cbx_collate.Checked = ( Upper( String( &
                        i_dwToActOn.Object.DataWindow.Print.Collate)) = "YES")
i_szFileName = Trim( String( i_dwToActOn.Object.DataWindow.Print.FileName))
cbx_print_to_file.Checked = (i_szFileName <> "")
```

When the user clicks on the Print To File check box, you need to display a dialog box in which the user can specify the filename and path (see Listing 26.13). The GetFileOpenName()

function is used to enable the specification of the print file. (See Chapter 6, "The PowerScript Language," for more information.) A dummy value, `szFile`, is used to accept the filename because you want only the full path and filename. The full path is stored in the instance variable `i_szFileName`, which is blanked out if the user unchecks the box.

Listing 26.13. The `Clicked` event for `cbx_print_to_file`.

```
String szFile

If this.Checked Then
   GetFileSaveName( "Select Print File", i_szFileName, szFile, "PRN", &
                    "Print Files (*.PRN),*.PRN")
Else
   i_szFileName = ""
End If
```

In case the user wants to specify a page range for the print job, the window will automatically set the focus to the edit field (see Listing 26.14).

Listing 26.14. The `Clicked` event for `rb_pages`.

```
If this.Checked Then
   sle_page_range.SetFocus()
End If
```

To automatically select the first item in the drop-down list, you need to code a line in the `Constructor` event as follows:

```
this.SelectItem( 1)
```

If the user cancels out of the dialog box, you need to close the window and make no other changes. Do this by coding the following in the `Clicked` event of `cb_cancel`:

```
Close( Parent)
```

If the user wants to change the current printer or other more specific options for the current printer, open the Windows Print dialog box. Within this dialog box, the user can make changes to other `DataWindow.Print` attributes such as orientation and margins. The user can also change the printer. To catch this, you need to repopulate the static text `st_current_printer` as follows:

```
PrintSetup()
st_current_printer.text = "Current Printer: " + &
                          String( i_dwToActOn.Object.DataWindow.Printer)
```

All modifications to the DataWindow are made when the user clicks on the OK button (see Listing 26.15). A string, `szModify`, is built on through the code before being used in a `Modify()` call. The first part of the string takes the current value from the Copies edit field and concatenates it with the necessary syntax. The Collate check box is then queried, and the value of `Print.Collate` is set appropriately. The same happens for the Print To File check box. Setting the page range gets a little more involved. To print all pages, the attribute is set to the empty string, and for a specific page range the value is easily concatenated. To print just the current page requires you to execute a call to the `Describe()` function to evaluate an expression that will return a page number. The `Page()` DataWindow painter function is used in the expression for the current row, and it will return the desired page number. The drop-down list box is searched to find the appropriate index, which is decremented by 1 to give the value needed for the `RangeInclude` attribute. When the modification string is constructed, it is passed into the `Modify()` and the return value is checked. If the `Modify()` fails, an error window is opened to display the reason. The dialog box then closes.

Listing 26.15. The `Clicked` event for `cb_ok`.

```
Integer nIndex
String szModify, szPage, szReturn

szModify = "DataWindow.Print.Copies=" + em_copies.text
If cbx_collate.Checked Then
   szModify = szModify + " DataWindow.Print.Collate=Yes"
Else
   szModify = szModify + " DataWindow.Print.Collate=No"
End If

If cbx_print_to_file.Checked Then
   szModify = szModify + " DataWindow.Print.FileName=" + i_szFileName
Else
   szModify = szModify + " DataWindow.Print.FileName=''"
End If

If rb_all_pages.Checked Then
   szModify = szModify + " DataWindow.Print.Page.Range=''"
ElseIf rb_current_page.Checked Then
   szPage = i_dwToActOn.Describe( "Evaluate('Page()', " + &
                              String(i_dwToActOn.GetRow()) +")")
   szModify = szModify + " DataWindow.Print.Page.Range='" + szPage + "'"
Else
   szModify = szModify+" DataWindow.Print.Page.Range='"+sle_page_range.text+"'"
End If

nIndex = ddlb_range_include.FindItem( ddlb_range_include.Text, 0)

szModify = szModify + " DataWindow.Print.Page.RangeInclude=" + String(nIndex-1)

szReturn = i_dwToActOn.Modify(szModify)
If szReturn <> "" Then
   Error.Line = 36
   Error.Text = szReturn
   Open(w_error)
End If
//
// Turn the print window invisible while the system print dialog appears
```

continues

Listing 26.15. continued

```
//
Parent.Visible = FALSE
//
// Print the DataWindow and then set the focus back to this window, in case it
// was lost due to the print dialog.
//
i_dwToActOn.Print( TRUE)

this.SetFocus()
//
Close( Parent)
```

The dialog box is called using the `OpenWithParm()` function syntax, and it takes the DataWindow as the second argument. You can also modify this so that when the dialog box is closed, it returns a string with the button's name indicating whether it was closed from the OK or the Cancel button. The calling script could then decide what it wants to do to handle the error.

Building a DataWindow Print Zoom Dialog Box

One of the many enhancements made to DataWindows in PowerBuilder 3.0 was the addition of print preview and zoom modes. You access this functionality through some of the DataWindow attributes previously mentioned. To provide a consistent user interface to zoom and preview, you will create a reusable window that can be called from any DataWindow-bearing window.

To enable the user to specify a zoom value, you will provide four standard settings—200%, 100%, 50%, and 33%—as well as an area for the user to specify an exact value. The interface for this will be a group of radio buttons. To the right of the Custom option, an edit mask field with spin control styling will enable the user to set a specific value. The spin range will be from 1 to 999, with a spin increment of 10. The mask will be `###` and will restrict the user to the 1 to 999 range if he enters the zoom value by keyboard rather than by the spin control.

Another feature you will provide is the capability to show and hide rulers during preview. The rulers enable the user to interactively change the margins for the DataWindow. To turn this feature on and off, use a check box.

The buttons will enable users to make their selections and leave or cancel out of the window, returning the DataWindow to its original state.

The dialog box will act on a DataWindow passed in as a parameter via the `OpenWithParm()` function, so the DataWindow needs to be retrieved from `Message.PowerObjectParm` and placed into a window instance variable, `i_dwToActOn`. In the `Open` event for the dialog box, the `Describe()` function is used to extract the DataWindow's current state of preview, ruler visibility, and zoom:

```
szDescribe = i_dwToActOn.Describe( "DataWindow.Print.Preview " + &
                                   "DataWindow.Print.Preview.Rulers " + &
                                   "DataWindow.Print.Preview.Zoom")
```

Using the string returned, you can set initial states for the radio buttons and the ruler check box. This is done by using a global function, `f_get_token()`, that extracts tokens (see Listing 26.16). This function takes the `szDescribe` string by reference and returns a string that is the token for which the user is searching.

NOTE

Token is a term carried over from compilers, and refers to the individual elements of a larger object. In this case the tokens are the string values that are separated by spaces.

Listing 26.16. The `f_get_token()` function.

```
// ARGUMENTS:
//    szSource    (a string passed by reference-tokenized string)
//    szSeparator (a string passed by value-separator between tokens)
// RETURNS:
//    szReturn    (a string-first token)
Integer nPosition
String  szReturn

nPosition = Pos(szSource, szSeparator)
If nPosition = 0 Then          // if no separator,
   szReturn = szSource         // return the whole source string and
   szSource = ""               // make the original source of zero length
Else
   // otherwise, return just the token and
   // strip it & the separator
   szReturn = Mid(szSource, 1, nPosition-1)
   szSource = Right(szSource, Len(szSource)-nPosition)
End If

Return szReturn
```

Using the previous trick from the Print dialog box, you can compare two strings and return a Boolean for assignment:

```
cb_cancel.Enabled = ( Upper( f_get_token( szDescribe, "~n")) = "YES")
```

Passing the remainder of `szDescribe` back into the `f_get_token()` function, you get the ruler status:

```
cbx_rulers.checked = (Upper(f_get_token(szDescribe, "~n")) = "YES")
```

The remaining value will be a number representing the current zoom level, which you will use in a `Choose...Case` statement to determine the initial state of the radio buttons:

```
Choose Case szDescribe
   Case "200"
      rb_200.Checked = TRUE
   Case "100"
      rb_100.Checked = TRUE
   Case "50"
      rb_50.Checked = TRUE
   Case "33"
      rb_33.Checked = TRUE
   Case Else
      rb_custom.Checked = TRUE
End Choose

em_custom.Text = szDescribe
```

The initial value is also set in the edit mask field as a starting point for modification by the user. The value of the edit mask is set to the appropriate value so that whenever the user clicks on one of the radio buttons, you have a central location from which the final value can be extracted. The only exception is the custom radio button. Here, you want to move the focus to the edit mask field:

```
em_custom.SetFocus()
```

The Preview button does all the modifications to the DataWindow. In the `Clicked` event of this button, a modification string is built that will set the values for preview, ruler, and zoom. For optimal performance, all three attributes are built into one string and `Modify()` is called just once. The value for the zoom level is extracted from the `em_custom` control. The preview state will be yes, and the ruler visibility will be concatenated onto the end with an `If` statement, as follows:

```
szDescribe = "DataWindow.Print.Preview.Zoom=" + &
              em_custom.Text + " DataWindow.Print.Preview=Yes " + &
             "DataWindow.Print.Preview.Rulers="

If cbx_rulers.Checked Then
   szDescribe = szDescribe + "Yes"
Else
   szDescribe = szDescribe + "No"
End If
```

The constructed string is then passed into `Modify()`, and the return value is checked for an error, which is then displayed:

```
szReturn = i_dwToActOn.Modify( szDescribe)

If szReturn <> "" Then
   MessageBox( "Modify() Error", szReturn)
End If
```

The response window is then closed so that the user can see the DataWindow in preview mode. To cancel the preview mode, the user simply needs to reopen this window and select the Cancel Preview button. This sets the preview state to `No`:

```
i_dwToActOn.Modify( "DataWindow.Print.Preview=No")
```

To give access to this window, you can place a command button on the window or run it via a menu option.

Copying and Moving Data

PowerBuilder provides a set of functions that will move or copy DataWindow rows, either within the same DataWindow or to another. These functions, unfortunately, are not very intelligent and, therefore, will only copy a row if the receiving row's columns exactly match those of the source. The syntax for these functions is

```
DataWindow.RowsMove( StartRow, EndRow, SourceBuffer, TargetDW, BeforeRow, &
                     TargetBuffer)
DataWindow.RowsCopy( StartRow, EndRow, SourceBuffer, TargetDW, BeforeRow, &
                     TargetBuffer)
DataWindow.RowsDiscard( StartRow, EndRow, Buffer)
```

The functions `RowsMove()` and `RowsCopy()` act in similar ways. The only difference is that `RowsMove()` copies rows to the destination DataWindow and then discards (deletes) them from the source DataWindow, and `RowsCopy()` leaves the source rows alone. The *StartRow* and *EndRow* values specify the inclusive range that the operation will affect in the source DataWindow's buffer, indicated by *SourceBuffer*. The *BeforeRow* value specifies the row before which the new rows will appear; or, if the value is greater than the number of rows currently in the target DataWindow, the rows are appended. Rows being moved to a different DataWindow take on the `NewModified!` status. If the rows stay within the same DataWindow (even if in a different buffer), they retain their status. Here are some examples:

```
// Straight move of all rows from dw_1 to a mirror DataWindow dw_2
dw_1.RowsMove( 1, dw_1.RowCount(), Primary!, dw_2, 1, Primary!)
//
// Then append the rows that have been deleted
dw_1.RowsCopy( 1, dw_1.DeletedCount(), Delete!, dw_2, dw_2.RowCount() + 1, &
               Primary!)
```

NOTE

If the same DataWindow is used in a `RowsMove()` or `RowsCopy()` and the value of *BeforeRow* is less than (that is, `RowsMove()` does nothing) or equal to the number of rows in the buffer, you will get some strange results. You need to be careful when moving rows within the same DataWindow.

The `RowsDiscard()` function is used to completely and irrecoverably remove the rows in the inclusive *StartRow* and *EndRow* range from the DataWindow. For example, to enable any row changes that will generate `INSERT`s or `UPDATE`s but stop any `DELETE`s, the code would be

```
dw_1.RowsDiscard( 1, dw_1.DeletedCount(), Delete!)
```

NOTE

`SaveAs()` and `ImportClipboard()` can also be used to move data around, but they provide little benefit over the three functions just introduced.

As mentioned earlier, the copy-and-move functions just introduced require an exact match of columns between the source and target DataWindows. With most copy-and-move operations this is usually not the case, and a more intelligent method of transfer is required. The function (see Listing 26.17) that will be built in this section does a best guess on the intended column, based solely on the column name.

Listing 26.17. The `f_transfer_rows()` function.

```
// f_transfer_rows written by Simon Gallagher (1995)
// revised January 1996 to make use of new 5.0 features
// Parameters:
//    a_dwPrimary      -the DataWindow to copy data from
//    a_lPrimaryStart  -the row to start copying from
//    a_lPrimaryEnd    -the row to finish copying from
//    a_dwSecondary    -the DataWindow to copy data to
//    a_lSecondaryStart-the row to start copying to
//    a_bCreateNewRows -whether new rows should be added to the Secondary
//
Long lRowCount, lPrimaryRows, lDifference
Integer nColumn, nColumn2, anIndexes2[], nNocolumns

a_dwSecondary.SetRedraw( FALSE)

lPrimaryRows = a_lPrimaryEnd-a_lPrimaryStart
//
// Set the upper bound of the array
//
nNocolumns = Integer( a_dwPrimary.Object.DataWindow.Column.Count)
anIndexes2[ nNoColumns] = 0

If a_bCreateNewRows Then
   // The +1 is for the correction of the total of the primary rows, ie.
   // a_lPrimaryStart = 2 and a_lPrimaryEnd = 7,
   // then a_lPrimaryEnd-a_lPrimaryStart = 5
   // should be 6, but we use this lesser value later so add the 1 here.
   If a_dwSecondary.RowCount() = 0 Then
      lDifference = lPrimaryRows + 1
   Else
      lDifference = lPrimaryRows-a_dwSecondary.RowCount() + &
                    a_lSecondaryStart + 1
   End If

   For lRowCount = 1 To lDifference
      a_dwSecondary.InsertRow( 0)
   Next
End If
//
// Locate the matching column within the Secondary DataWindow
//
```

```
For nColumn = 1 To nNoColumns
   nColumn2 = Integer( a_dwSecondary.Describe(
                     a_dwPrimary.Describe( "#" + String( nColumn) + &
                                           ".Name") + ".id"))

   anIndexes2[ nColumn] = nColumn2
Next
//
// Carry out the copy using direct access of the 2 DataWindows
//
For lRowCount = 0 To lPrimaryRows
   For nColumn = 1 To nNoColumns
      If anIndexes2[ nColumn] <> 0 Then
         a_dwSecondary.Object.Data[ a_lSecondaryStart + lRowCount,
                                    anIndexes2[ nColumn]] = &
           a_dwPrimary.Object.Data[ a_lPrimaryStart + lRowCount, nColumn]
      End If
   Next
Next

a_dwSecondary.SetRedraw( TRUE)

Return lPrimaryRows + 1
```

This transfer function was introduced in the book *PowerBuilder 4.0 Unleashed* and has been dramatically improved using the new DataWindow object syntax and is more than 2.5 times faster.

Here are some points you should note from the function in Listing 26.17:

- Notice the use of the `Describe()` function to retrieve the corresponding column position within the secondary DataWindow. The column value is then stored in an array for use in the copy loop.
- Direct syntax is used in the actual copy loop to transfer between the two DataWindows. The `If` expression makes sure there is a column to copy to from the primary DataWindow.
- By placing a row loop outside the object loop, you will get better performance when copying only a few rows.
- If the source and destination DataWindows have exactly matched columns, use the PowerScript functions `RowsMove()` and `RowsCopy()`. They are significantly faster.
- The function took half a second to transfer 76 rows of 6 columns from one DataWindow to another. `RowsCopy()` and `RowsMove()` both take around 40 milliseconds. Half the time of the function can be contributed to the `InsertRow()` loop, because it is a slow function to execute.
- If you want to use this function to carry out a move, the fastest performance can be achieved by using `RowsDiscard()` to throw away the source rows, rather than coding `DeleteRow()` calls.

You can further enhance this function to transfer the edit status of each column and/or row from the source DataWindow to the target DataWindow.

Drop-Down DataWindow Techniques

Using drop-down DataWindows (also referred to as DDDWs) can greatly reduce the clutter with a DataWindow. This column edit style provides the functionality of a drop-down list box while being dynamically populated from a relational database. A drop-down DataWindow is quite simply a DataWindow, usually with the Grid or Tabular presentation style, that is used as a drop-down list within another DataWindow. It is automatically populated with data when you issue a retrieve or insert a new row into the parent DataWindow, and then it acts just like a drop-down list control.

WARNING

There is a bug in PowerBuilder 4.0 that acts up if you modify certain attributes of a column that you have obtained a child handle to. Changing attribute values with the `Modify()` function causes the reference returned by `Getchild()` to become invalid. After setting an attribute using `Modify`, you have to call `Getchild()` again to obtain a valid handle. The affected DataWindow attributes are `background.color`, `background.mode`, `dddw.case`, `dddw.datacolumn`, `dddw.displaycolumn`, `dddw.percentwidth`, and `dddw.name`.

Synchronizing Column Values

One trick I learned by accident while helping with another PowerBuilder project is the ability to display and synchronize multiple fields using a single drop-down DataWindow. The first step is to create the drop-down DataWindow with one visible column and as many other invisible data columns as you want. Then, within the parent DataWindow place multiple copies of the same column (name them differently so that you can refer to them within your PowerScript) and set all their edit styles to DropDownDataWindow with the same data value and whichever display value you want for each column.

This provides a very quick and easy way for the user to select numerous default values in one selection. One thing to be aware of is that since each of the columns is a drop-down DataWindow, PowerBuilder will be retrieving data for each. These are good candidates for setting up data sharing.

NOTE

If this concept seems a little alien, you should explore the `d_customer2` DataWindow that is part of this chapter's code and which you can find on the accompanying CD.

Problems and Solutions

Drop-down DataWindows do, however, have some pitfalls and issues that you should be aware of and be able to provide solutions for.

One of these undesirable behaviors is when a drop-down DataWindow is populated using a parameter, and you initially retrieve data or insert a row. If you do not specify the necessary arguments for the drop-down DataWindow's retrieval, PowerBuilder will prompt for them. This can be avoided by fooling the drop-down DataWindow into thinking that it already has data, and is achieved by inserting a blank row into the child DataWindow. For example, the DataWindow `d_order_product` uses a DropDownDataWindow edit style for the warehouse that is retrieved depending on the value of the `product_id` column; this means that you display only warehouse IDs that stock this particular product item. To prevent PowerBuilder from prompting for a `product_id` value when you initially set up the parent DataWindow, you have two methods available. The first method is set up using the following:

```
DataWindowChild dwcWarehouse

dw_order_product.GetChild( "warehouse_no", dwcWarehouse)
//
dwcWarehouse.InsertRow( 0)
//
dw_order_product.Retrieve()
```

You can then continue the script and base the drop-down DataWindow's retrieval on some value pulled back from the parent DataWindow, `dw_order_product`. For example, this code continues where the previous code leaves off:

```
//
szProductId = dw_order_product.GetItemString( this.GetRow(), "product_id")
//
dwcWarehouse.Retrieve( szProductId)
```

The second method requires you to set up a "dummy" value from within the DataWindow painter, using the Data menu item under the Rows menu. This method has the disadvantage of having the blank row in the child DataWindow until you carry out the child retrieve. The first method allows you to insert the dummy row and then retrieve over it or delete it when you have finished with the parent retrieve.

Another problem is that once a drop-down DataWindow is populated, PowerBuilder basically forgets all about having populated it, and further uses of the same drop-down DataWindow or even within the same parent DataWindow cause individual retrievals to occur. You can solve many of your data retrieval performance problems by caching the data using the new `DataStore` object, and then using the `ShareData()` function to connect each use of the drop-down DataWindow to this object. Most developers prior to Version 5.0 had to use a hidden window containing DataWindow controls to achieve the same functionality. This has been one of the main reasons behind the introduction of the `DataStore` object by Powersoft. Just remember that when using the cached data, any filtering, sorting, or other manipulation you do with `DataStore`'s data will be reflected in all other drop-down DataWindows that are using it.

Editable drop-down DataWindows can also cause some problems for the unwary. Since PowerBuilder attempts to match what the user types with an entry in the list, you will run into a problem if the data value of the drop-down DataWindow is not a string. This is due to the four levels of validation (see Chapter 10, "DataWindow Scripting"). The second level checks the column's data type and will fail before you can even begin to process it in the `ItemChanged` event. This will require you to carry out some special processing in `ItemError` if you want to provide a more friendly interface for the user. This processing will require you to check the column in error and the data currently in the edit control of the DataWindow; from this you should be able to ascertain if it is some other type of DataWindow error or one caused by the mismatch of data types for a drop-down DataWindow.

There will be times when the number of rows retrieved into a drop-down DataWindow becomes excessively large, and you should try to alleviate this problem by using retrieval arguments for the child DataWindow to restrict the result set. This may not always be possible, and you may want to investigate a method that allows the user to enter a partial string before carrying out a lookup. This could be done within a user event defined for the `pbm_dwndropdown` event ID that traps when a drop-down DataWindow has its drop-down arrow clicked on. The event script could then either take a partially entered value and look it up, or cause a dialog box to be opened to query the user for additional criteria that will limit the result set. If you create a good user interface, you should be able to remove any need to bring back a list of hundreds or even thousands of rows into the drop-down DataWindow.

Master/Detail Relationships

A commonly used association between DataWindows is master/detail. This is where one DataWindow is used as the main interface with one or more other DataWindows displaying supporting and related data. The master DataWindow is usually in a list format, and as the user scrolls and selects rows within it, the detail for the record is shown in a secondary (the detail) DataWindow.

Synchronization between the two DataWindows can be achieved using two different techniques: manual copy and sharing. The manual copy method is only really useful if the detail DataWindow is non-editable and there are only a few columns. You use a call to the `RowsCopy()` function within the master `RowFocusChanged` event to copy the new current row to the detail DataWindow.

More often you will make use of PowerBuilder's ability to share data between DataWindows using the `ShareData()` function. This function is covered in Chapter 25. Since two or more DataWindows are sharing data, you will only have to issue a single update to save any modified data. Other DataWindow management issues (for example, filtering or sorting) are also much easier to handle.

In the next two sections you will see how to ensure that the current master row is also displayed in the detail DataWindows and how to prevent a detail DataWindow from being scrolled.

Keeping the Detail DataWindow in Sync

In order to keep the detail DataWindows synchronized with the master, you need to trap two events: `RowFocusChanged` and `ScrollVertical`. These are used to spot either row-by-row changes or scrollbar manipulations, respectively.

The code for the `RowFocusChanged` event checks what row is current in the detail DataWindow against the new current row in the master by use of the `CurrentRow` event parameter. This is done because the `ScrollVertical` event may have been triggered first and might have already updated the detail. This is the code for the `RowFocusChanged` event:

```
If dw_2.GetRow() <> CurrentRow Then
   dw_2.ScrollToRow( CurrentRow)
End If
```

The `ScrollVertical` event is also quite simple. By determining the row number that appears on the page once the scroll has occurred, it sets the detail DataWindow to be the same value. This is the code for this event:

```
dw_2.ScrollToRow( Long( dw_1.Object.DataWindow.FirstRowOnPage))
```

Using both of these events will ensure that the detail DataWindows are kept synchronized with the master.

Preventing Detail DataWindow Scrolling

Most often the detail DataWindow is just that, detail of the master record, and you display only one record's data at a time. Unfortunately, since the data is actually being shared with the master, the detail also has access to the other rows of the data. This allows the user to scroll through the detail DataWindow using the Tab, Enter, arrow, and page up and down keys.

The method introduced next makes use of just two events to prevent the user from scrolling the detail DataWindow: a user event `KeyPressed` and `RowFocusChanged`.

The `KeyPressed` event (see Listing 26.18) makes use of the `pbm_dwnkey` PowerBuilder event ID and is triggered every time the user presses a key while in the detail DataWindow.

Listing 26.18. The `KeyPressed` event for a master/detail DataWindow.

```
Choose Case Key
   Case KeyEnter!, KeyDownArrow!, KeyUpArrow!, KeyPageDown!, KeyPageUp!
      // The default behavior in a DataWindow is to accept the value entered
      // so we carry out the same for the detail DataWindow.
      this.AcceptText()
      Return 1
   Case KeyTab!
      this.SetRedraw( FALSE)

      this.Post Function ScrollToRow( this.GetRow())
```

continues

Listing 26.18. continued

```
      If keyflags = 1 Then
         // An attempt has been made to Shift-Tab-trap it and capture the
         // focus back to the detail DataWindow whether the focus remains in
         // the DataWindow or had been set elsewhere.
         //
         dw_1.SetRedraw( FALSE)
         this.Post Function SetFocus()
         dw_1.Post Function SetRedraw( TRUE)
      End If

      this.Post Function SetRedraw( TRUE)
End Choose
```

As you can see from the code, you use the `Key` event parameter within a `Case` statement to trap one of three conditions:

- A key that causes a scroll (Enter, arrow, and page up and down keys).
- The Tab key. This is a valid keypress when you're moving between columns, but not when you're at the beginning or end of the row.
- Any other key.

In the first case, you return `1` for the event, which indicates that the key has been processed. Since you do nothing, the scrolling keys are effectively disabled with one line of code. The second condition occurs when the user tabs off the last column for the row. In normal DataWindow behavior, this would take you to the first column of the next row. Instead, you turn off the redraw for the detail DataWindow and post a call to scroll back to the current row (this makes use of the new 5.0 feature posting functions). At the end of the case, you turn back on the redraw for the detail DataWindow, also by posting a call to the function. The first column of a DataWindow is also part of a unique relationship with the Tab key. If the user holds down the Shift key and then presses Tab, the focus switches back to the master DataWindow. You may or may not want this to occur, and you might even want to send the focus to the other end of the detail DataWindow. In the code shown in Listing 26.18, you simply trap the Shift+Tab combination by checking the `KeyFlags` event parameter, and set the focus back to the detail DataWindow. You may choose to provide other functionality.

This one event provides all the functionality needed to prevent the user from scrolling the DataWindow.

Master/Detail Manager

As you can see from the event scripts in the previous two sections, you are required to know which DataWindow is the master and which is the detail. This may not be much of a problem if you are providing a base window with this functionality. But what happens when you need to add a second or third detail DataWindow? Suddenly you have to start going into multiple scripts to change DataWindow control references. A more concise and object-oriented approach to this is to create a master/detail DataWindow manager.

In this manager you provide the functionality to register the master DataWindow, as well as all the necessary detail DataWindows, possibly along with other information, such as the last column in each DataWindow, so that a Shift+Tab wraps within the DataWindow.

Summary

In this chapter you have learned about the many different advanced DataWindow programming techniques that are commonly needed in day-to-day programming. The DataWindow is a very powerful and complex control, and you have seen how to make use of some of its features. These include searching for various conditions in the DataWindow, providing flexible printing options for the end user, copying and moving data around, and using drop-down DataWindows.

Graphing

27

IN THIS CHAPTER

Graphs provide a means of presenting large amounts of data in different ways to provide summaries or overviews. Human beings can make better assessments of information if they are presented with a graphical representation rather than the individual pieces of data. In PowerBuilder, a graph can be used in three ways: as a DataWindow style, as a separate object in a DataWindow, or as a control in a window. Graphs can also be built as user objects, but they are accessed and controlled as they would be in a window (and, for the purposes of this discussion, they are considered the same). The definition of a graph is the same regardless of how you are using it; only the population and runtime manipulation of the graph are different. This chapter examines the components that make up a graph and the process to build one. Once we have created a graph (either via a DataWindow or a graph control), we will look at some coding techniques that can be used with graphs.

Principles of Graphing

Before diving into building a graph, there are some limitations you must be aware of. Graphs can only be built around certain data types. Each axis has different constraints. These data types are listed in Table 27.1.

Table 27.1. Graph axis data types.

Axis	*Possible Data Types*
Series	String
Value	Number, Date, DateTime, Time
Category	String, Number, Date, DateTime, Time

After you have determined what values you want to incorporate into your graph, you are ready to build your graph.

Components of a Graph

A PowerBuilder graph is made up of three parts: categories, values, and series. A *category* is the major division of the data, the *values* are the values of the data, and a *series* is a set of data. These components are shown in Figure 27.1, along with corresponding labels and text.

The *category axis* corresponds to the X axis in normal XYZ geometry. The *value axis* corresponds to the Y axis, and the *series axis* corresponds to the Z axis. Optionally, you can also specify a title and legend.

FIGURE 27.1.
Components of a graph.

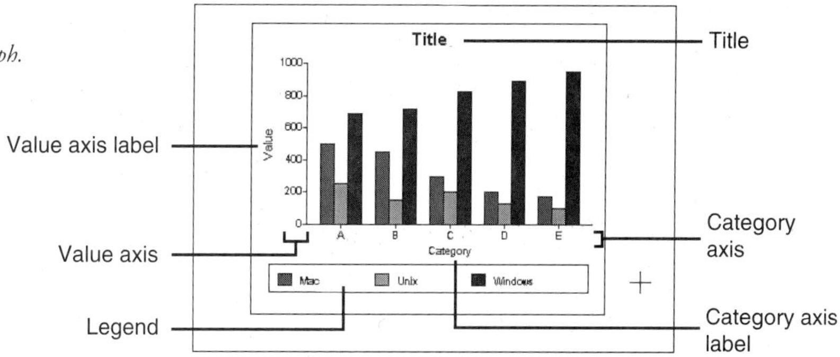

Types of Graphs

PowerBuilder provides a wide variety of graph types and varying styles within some of the types. The graph types can be broken down into three main groups.

The first group encompasses area, bar, column, and line graphs. The properties among these types are common, and they differ only in the method of presentation. The typical use for area and line graphs is for displaying continuous data. Bar and column graphs are used for non-continuous data.

Together with pie graphs, this group of styles can be displayed in two or three dimensions. Instead of appearing along the category axis, series now use the extra dimension as the series axis (see Figure 27.2).

FIGURE 27.2.
A three-dimensional graph.

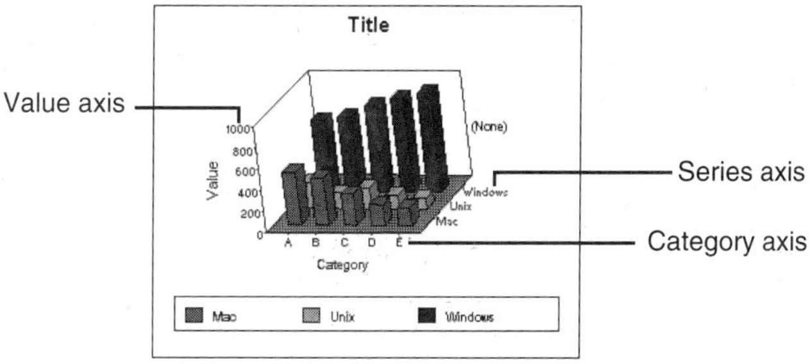

Bar and column graphs can also be presented in a stacked format (see Figure 27.3); another option is a solid, stacked style that looks three dimensional. Each category is represented as one bar for all series, rather than as separate bars for each individual series.

FIGURE 27.3.
A stacked graph.

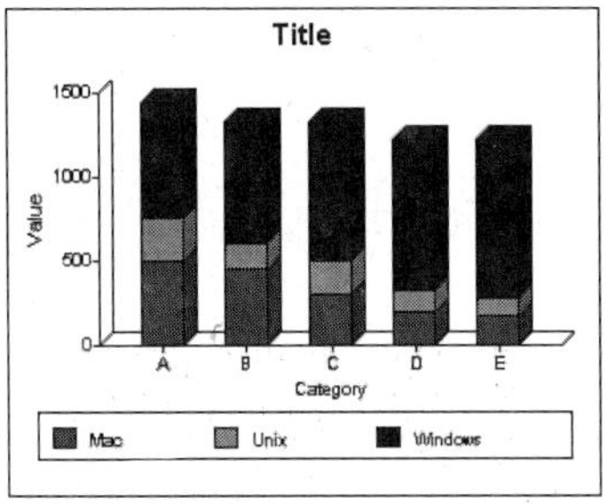

The second group consists of pie graphs (see Figure 27.4). Pie graphs show data as a percentage of the whole. Multiseries pie graphs (see Figure 27.5) display the series as concentric circles and are usually used in the comparison of data series.

FIGURE 27.4.
A three-dimensional pie graph.

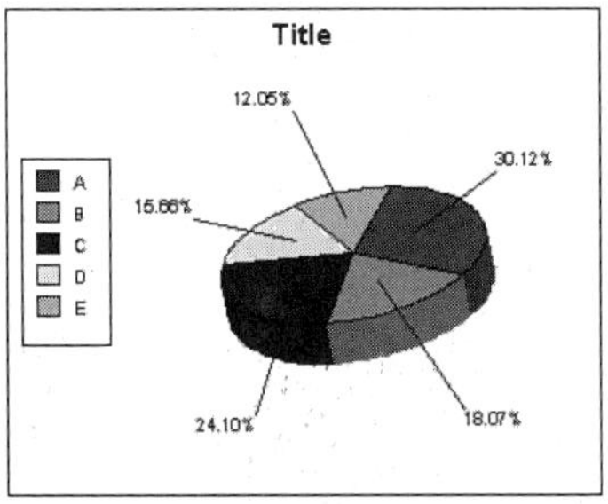

FIGURE 27.5.
A multiseries pie graph.

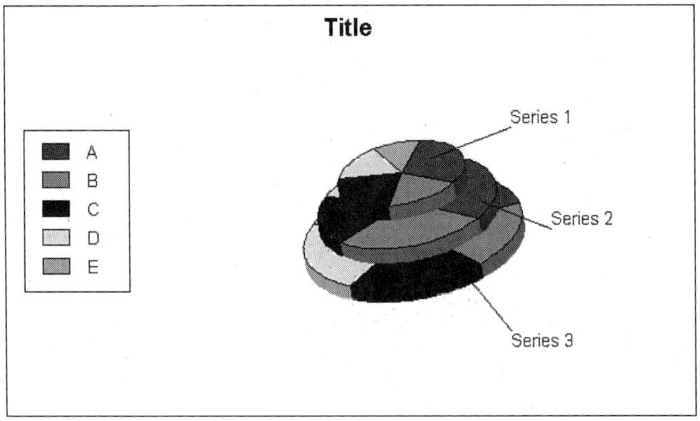

Scatter graphs make up the last group and are used to display X,Y data (see Figure 27.6). For this reason, scatter graphs do not use categories. This type of graph is usually used in the comparison of two numerical sets of data.

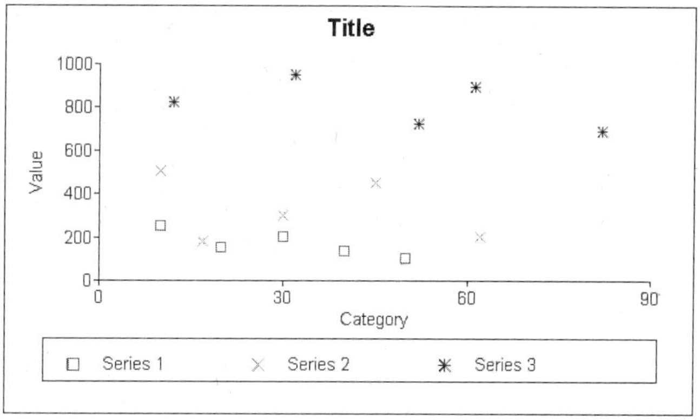

FIGURE 27.6.
A scatter graph.

Defining a Graph's Attributes

When you have decided on the type of graph presentation you want, you can enhance its presentation by changing the graph's attributes.

Initial Status

Recall the three ways a graph can be created: as a DataWindow presentation, an object in a DataWindow, or as a control (within a window or user object). When a graph is placed in a DataWindow, it can be positioned in the foreground to enable users to move and resize it during execution. If the graph is placed in a band, movement can be prevented. In windows, graphs are placed in the same way as other window controls. Regardless of how the graph is implemented, the interface for defining the graph is the same.

All graphs use the Graph property sheet (see Figure 27.7). As you modify the graph's attributes, the changes are reflected in the model graph on the Data and Graph tab pages. The labels you entered are used, and sample data is shown (not data from the DataWindow) to represent series, categories, and values.

The Graph property sheet automatically opens when you first create a DataWindow graph, but can be accessed any time during development (these methods all apply to a graph control as well). To open the property sheet, double-click anywhere on the graph, right-click on the graph and select properties from the pop-up menu, or click on the Properties icon on the PainterBar. For the most part, most of the tab pages are the same for both the DataWindow graph and the graph control. Let's take a look at the common tab pages that comprise the Graph property sheet.

FIGURE 27.7.
The Graph property sheet (Graph tab page).

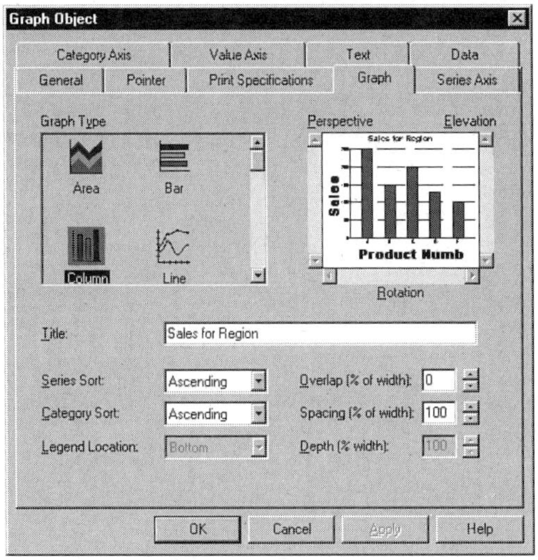

Text Attributes

There are a number of text objects connected with a graph, from the title to the axis labels. The attributes of each text element can be specified using the Text tab page (see Figure 27.8).

FIGURE 27.8.
The Text tab page.

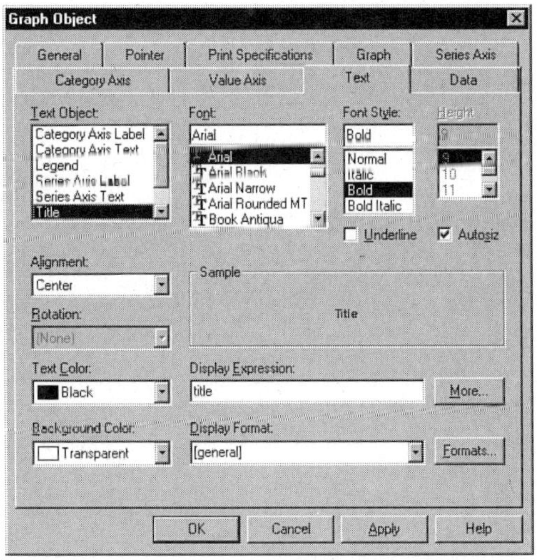

You can specify what text object you wish to modify using the Text Object list box in the upper-left corner of the tab page. The text's rotation, font, size, and color can be changed. The label can also be set to autoscale itself to be in step with the overall graph size. In addition to just a string literal, an expression can be used. This is specified by clicking on the More... button next to the Display Expression edit box. Clicking this button opens the familiar Modify Expression dialog box. Because you can build an expression that returns a Numeric data type, a display format can also be specified using the Display Format drop-down list box.

NOTE

To create text that spans multiple lines, use ~n at the position where you require the line break.

Axes

To modify axis attributes, three tab pages are provided (see Figure 27.9) that correspond to the category, value, and series axes. These tab pages enable the definition of the scaling required for a numeric axis, the major and minor divisions, and the line styles for each axis.

FIGURE 27.9.
The tab page for specifying axis attributes.

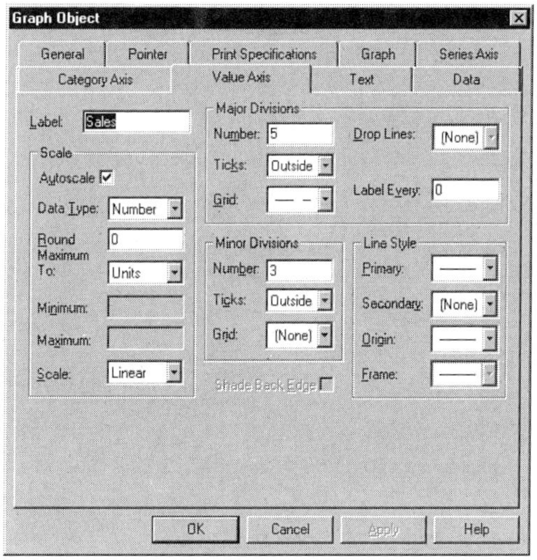

Table 27.2 describes the scaling attributes that can be specified for your axes.

Table 27.2. Scaling attributes.

Attribute	*Description*
Autoscale	PowerBuilder automatically scales the numbers along the axis based on the data values.
Data Type	Specifies the axis data type.

continues

Table 27.2. continued

Attribute	*Description*
Round Maximum To	The value to which you want to round the axis values.
Minimum	The smallest number to be used on the axis (used only if Autoscale is not set).
Maximum	The largest number to be used on the axis (used only if Autoscale is not set).
Scale	Linear or logarithmic scaling.

Axes are divided into *divisions*. The larger divisions, called *major divisions*, are supplied by default, and smaller breakdowns within each major division are called *minor divisions* (see Figure 27.10).

NOTE

The interface for specifying divisions is a little confusing the first time through. If you want a major tick mark at every 200 and minor tick marks at each 50, intuition tells you set major at 200 and minor at 50. If you do this, you will sit and watch PowerBuilder struggle and grind away for minutes trying to draw 200 major divisions, with each of these broken down further into 50 minor divisions. The number you specify is the number of divisions, not the value where the division will appear.

To specify minor divisions, you need to enter in the `Number` field a value that will be the minor ticks (which is `5` in Figure 27.10). You can also specify where the tick marks appear in reference to the axis: outside, inside, and straddle.

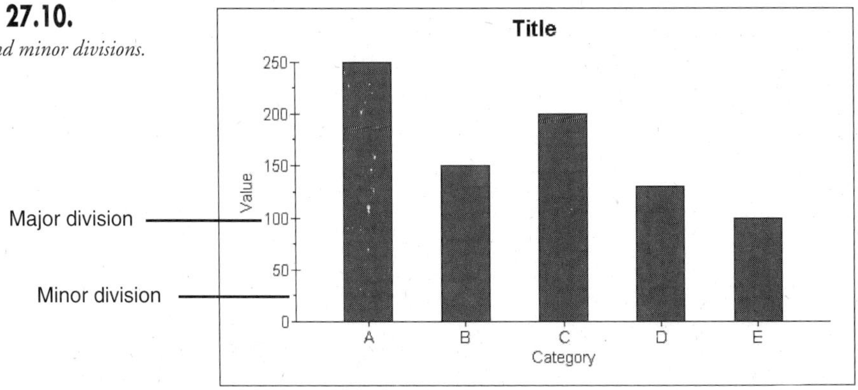

FIGURE 27.10.
Major and minor divisions.

Grid lines can be added for both major and minor divisions, with differing line styles. For the major divisions, drop lines can also be specified that display a line from the point to the opposing axis. These are useful for complex graphs where your users may need to line up different values for comparison (see Figure 27.11).

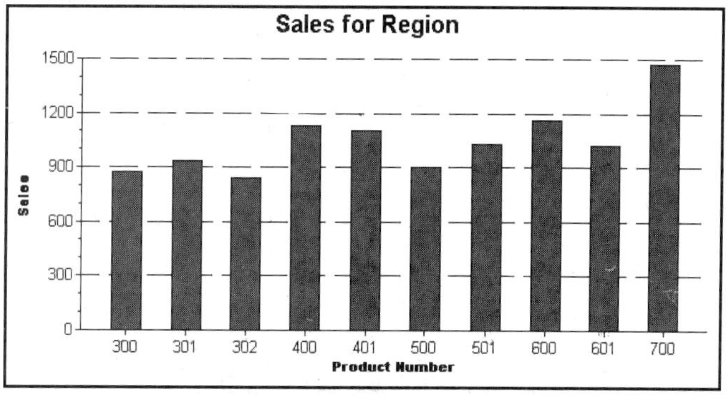

FIGURE 27.11.
A graph containing drop lines.

Once you have set some of the basic attributes for your graph, using some simple techniques described in the next sections, you can greatly enhance your graph.

Overlays

An *overlay* provides a way to call attention to the trend of a particular series in a graph. Overlays are usually used in the bar and column graph types and can provide information similar to that of the stacked style. The overlay is shown as a line passing through the column for each series.

If you are using a column for the overlay, use the following format:

```
"@overlay~t" + ColumnName
```

When you're specifying a label for the series, this is the format:

```
"@overlay~tSeriesLabel"
```

For example, to show the total salary for each department and the average salary within that range, the axes would be set up as follows:

Axis	*Value*
Category	`dept_id, dept_id`
Value	`sum(salary for graph), avg(salary for graph)`
Series	`"Total Salary", "@overlay~tAverage Salary"`

The resulting graph (see Figure 27.12) shows the total salaries as a green bar with the highest salary appearing as the line overlay.

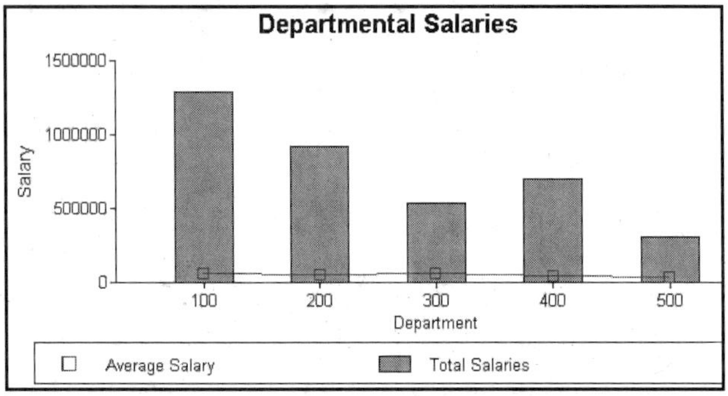

FIGURE 27.12.
A graph containing an overlay.

Bar and Column Charts

Additionally, you can set up bar and column graphs to overlap the bars or columns, or to space them apart (see Figure 27.13). The *overlap attribute* is the percentage of the current bar that is drawn over by the following bars. The default is no overlap. The *spacing attribute* is also a percentage. It is a percentage of the bar's width that appears as space between each group of bars. The width of the bars also changes to make use of the extra space or to make room for the spacing. As you change both attributes on the Graph tab page, the model graph reflects the new settings.

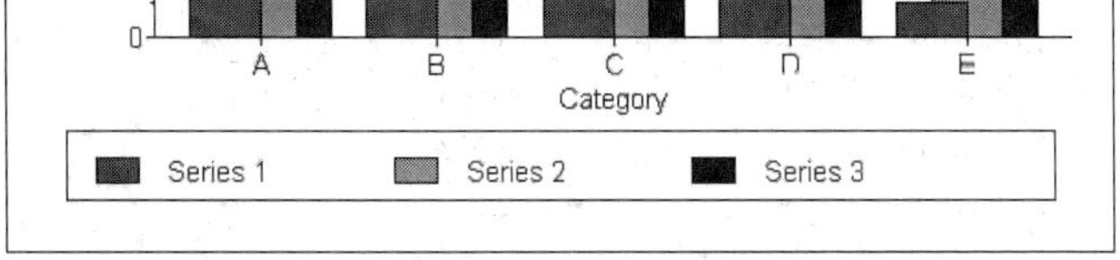

FIGURE 27.13.
A graph with overlapping bars.

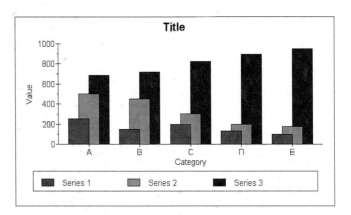

DataWindow Graphs

Graphs can be used in DataWindows in one of two ways: either as the presentation style for the DataWindow or as an object with a DataWindow of any other style. In the first case, the user will not see the underlying data. The second method is used to provide enhancements to the display of the information.

How to Create a DataWindow Graph

To add a graph to a preexisting DataWindow, click on the Graph button in the PainterBar, and then click on the area where you want the graph. PowerBuilder then displays the Graph Data property sheet for you to specify the columns and expressions to use for the graph. This property sheet can be closed and returned to at any time. The default is for the graph to be in the foreground and appear in front of retrieved data. It is also movable and resizable, and will remain so at runtime unless you turn off the appropriate attributes.

To create a DataWindow with the graph presentation style, select the graph option in the New DataWindow dialog box.

Populating a DataWindow Graph

The axes are associated with columns from the DataWindow or expressions involving columns. Changes to data within the DataWindow are reflected in the graph.

For the graph object, the range of rows for which the graph will display can be specified:

Value	*Description*
`All`	All rows of data in the primary buffer
`Page`	Only data currently displayed on the screen
`Group n`	Only data from the specified group *n*

If there are multiple groups, the graph should be moved to the appropriate group band with which the data is to be related.

If the column for the categories is based on a code table (such as a drop-down DataWindow), the graph will use the column's data values by default. To use the display values, make use of the `LookUpDisplay()` function when you define the column. For example, the `dept_id` column has a code table, and you want to use it as a category for a graph. To display the department name instead of the data values in the categories, enter the following into the Category box in the Graph Data dialog box:

```
LookUpDisplay(dept_id)
```

The drop-down list for the value axis shows all of the available columns, as well as `Count()` entries for all non-numeric columns and `Sum()` entries for all numeric columns. You can build any valid expression, such as `Sum(salary * 0.9 for graph)`.

For a single-series graph, leave the Series box empty. For multiple series, you need to check the box to the left of the field. You can select column names from the list box or enter them as an expression, or you can separate multiple entries with commas.

To see this in action, create a graph displaying the category `LookUpDisplay(sex)`, having the value `Avg(salary for graph)` (see Figure 27.14). The resulting graph is shown in Figure 27.15.

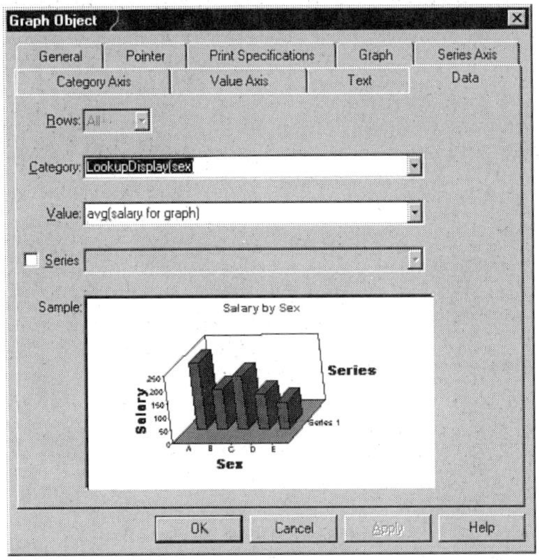

FIGURE 27.14.
The `LookUpDisplay()` *graph definition.*

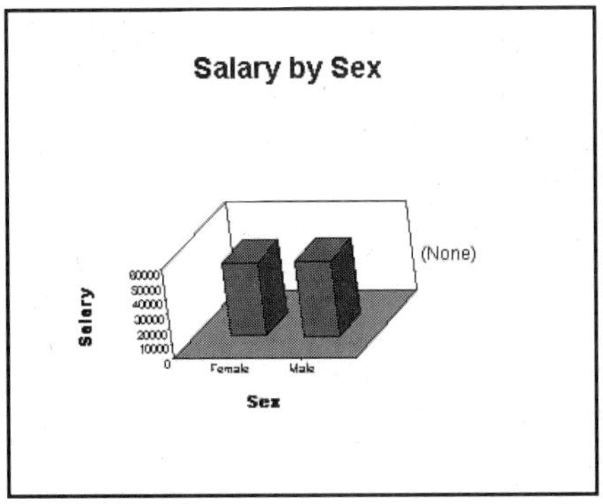

FIGURE 27.15.
A Graph demonstrating `LookUpDisplay()`.

Using the same graph, add a series by state (see Figure 27.16). The resulting graph is shown in Figure 27.17.

As you can see, there are a variety of techniques you can use to create graphs in a DataWindow. The next section shows how to implement a graph using the graph control.

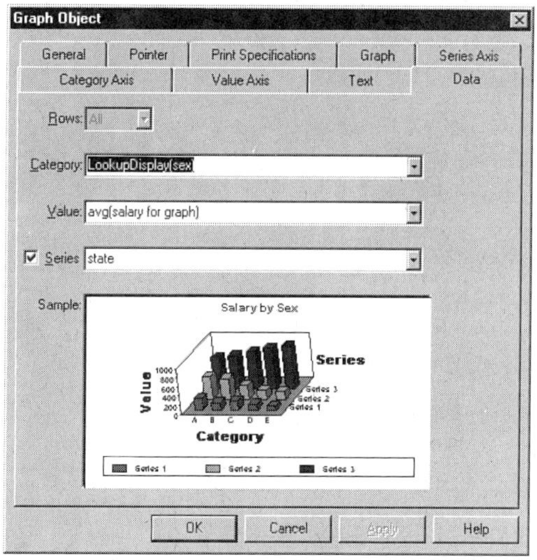

FIGURE 27.16.
A graph with state series definition.

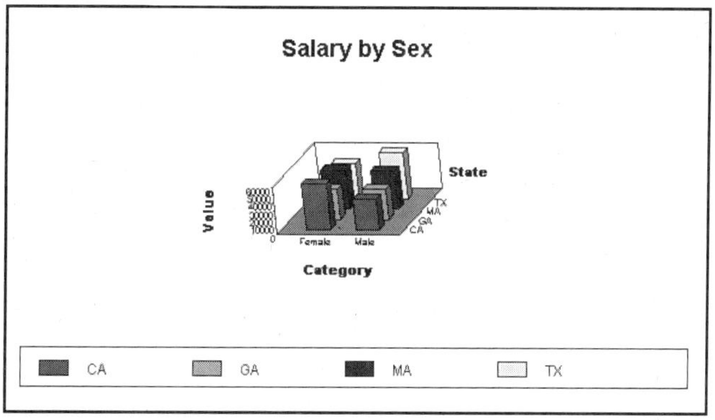

FIGURE 27.17.
A graph demonstrating the added state series.

Graph Controls

In addition to specifying a graph using DataWindows, you can create a graph on a window using a graph control.

Creating a Graph Control

To create a graph control click the Graph Control icon on the PainterBar or choose Graph from the Controls menu. You then add the control as you would any other window control by clicking on the desired window location. The property sheet can be accessed as mentioned earlier and many of the graph attributes can be set.

Populating a Graph Control

The graph control has one main difference from its DataWindow counterpart. The DataWindow graphs are populated by the specified data source (typically a SQL `SELECT` statement). The graph control does not have this underlying set of data to rely on, so it must be manually populated. Numerous PowerScript functions can be used to manipulate the data in the graph. These functions are used specifically for graph controls.

How you want your graph to appear will dictate which functions you use. The first functions that are needed are those that populate the graph with data.

The `AddSeries()` function is used to add a new series to a graph. The series is assigned a sequential number which can be used for reference later on. This is the syntax:

```
graph_control.AddSeries( SeriesName)
```

`AddSeries()` takes a string argument, *`SeriesName`*, that contains the name of the series you want to add to the graph control. The function returns an integer, which is the sequential number assigned to the series or `-1` for failure.

After creating a series, you need to add the actual data values. This can be done using the `AddData()` function. This is the syntax for all graph styles except scatter graphs:

```
graph_control.AddData( SeriesNumber, DataValue, {CategoryName})
```

The *`SeriesNumber`* argument is the sequential number of the series in which the data is to be inserted. *`DataValue`* is the actual data that is to appear on the graph, and the last optional argument is the name of the category for the data value being inserted. While *`CategoryName`* is optional, it is a good idea to specify a value; otherwise, the value will be added to the graph without a corresponding category. `AddData()` returns a Long data type containing the position of the new data value or `-1` for failure. If *`CategoryName`* does not already exist, the data is placed at the end of the series unless the axis is sorted. With sorting specified, the new category is placed in the appropriate location in the sort order. If *`CategoryName`* does exist, the data replaces the existing information.

For scatter graphs, the syntax for `AddData()` differs in the last two arguments. This is the syntax for a scatter graph:

```
graph_control.AddData( SeriesName, XValue, YValue)
```

The two arguments, *`XValue`* and *`YValue`*, are the data values for the corresponding X and Y values you wish to plot on the graph.

Listing 27.1 uses the functions `AddSeries()` and `AddData()` together to populate a graph.

Listing 27.1. Graph control population.

```
integer li_series_no

//Add first region
li_series_no = gr_1.AddSeries("Northeast")

If li_series_no <> -1 Then
   //Add sales and reps for series
   gr_1.AddData(li_series_no, 400, "Malcolm")
   gr_1.AddData(li_series_no, 350, "Jonathan")
   gr_1.AddData(li_series_no, 275, "Casiana")
End If
```

This creates three categories containing the sales reps' names and plots their sales for that region. The script would add more regions/reps in much the same manner. Of course, this example was simplified to demonstrate the functions. Most likely, you would not hard code the values in your script, but would retrieve the values from some other source (for example, an RPC call or a user entry).

If you wish to define the category values before placing the data values, you can do so with the `AddCategory()` function. This function takes a String value containing the name of the new category. Category names must be unique. One thing you need to keep in mind is that the category names are case-sensitive. This means that the same category name with different capitalization is considered two unique names.

In addition to the addition functions already discussed, Table 27.3 provides a description of some of the common graph functions for insertion, deletion, and modification of graph data. The functions work much the same way as the addition functions.

Table 27.3. Graph control functions.

Graph Function	*Description*
`InsertCategory`	Inserts a new category on the graph. All existing series are renumbered to remain in sequential order.
`InsertData`	Inserts a data point in a series of a graph. This is not used for scatter graphs.
`InsertSeries`	Inserts a series in a graph. All existing series are renumbered to remain in sequential order.
`ImportClipboard`	Inserts data into a graph control from tab-delimited data on the Clipboard.
`ImportFile`	Inserts data into a graph control from data in a file.
`ImportString`	Inserts data points into a graph from tab-delimited data in a string.
`DeleteCategory`	Deletes a category and associated data values from the category axis of a graph.

continues

Table 27.3. continued

Graph Function	*Description*
`DeleteData`	Deletes a data point from a series. The remaining data in the series is shifted left.
`DeleteSeries`	Deletes a series and its data values from a graph.
`ModifyData`	Modifies a data point value. Syntax is different for scatter graphs (must specify X and Y values).
`Reset`	Clears the contents of the graph. You can specify `All!`, `Category!`, `Data!`, and `Series!`.

Dynamic Graphs

The previous sections focus on the design of the graph and populating it with data. You can dynamically modify almost any component of your graph via your PowerScript code. The type of graph you are using will dictate how you interface with the graph. For a graph control, the attributes are accessed as with any other control:

```
gr_1.Title = "Regional Sales"
```

For DataWindows, you need to reference the `Object` attribute:

```
dw_1.Object.Title = "Regional Sales"
```

NOTE

In Version 4.0 you would need to use the `Modify()` function to achieve the same results.

For more information on how to dynamically reference a DataWindow object's attributes, see Chapter 10, "DataWindow Scripting."

In addition to manipulating the graph via its attributes, there are a number of functions that can be used. The graph functions can be grouped into three types of functionality: *informational*, *extraction*, and *modification*. These functions are listed in Table 27.4.

Table 27.4. Graph functions.

Action	*Function*	*Description*
Information	`CategoryCount`	Number of categories in a graph.
	`CategoryName`	Name of a category number.
	`DataCount`	Number of data points in a series.
	`FindCategory`	Number of a category for a given name.
	`FindSeries`	Number of a series for a given name.
	`GetData`	Value of data at a given series and position.
	`GetDataPieExplode`	Percentage of slice exploded.
	`GetDataStyle`	The visual property of a data point.
	`GetDataValue`	More flexible `GetData`.
	`GetSeriesStyle`	Visual property of a series.
	`ObjectAtPointer`	Graph element clicked on.
	`SeriesCount`	Number of series in graph.
	`SeriesName`	Name of a series number.
Extraction	`Clipboard`	Copies image of graph to Clipboard (not data).
	`SaveAs`	Saves underlying data in one of a number of formats.
Modification	`ResetDataColors`	Resets colors of a data point.
	`SetDataPieExplode`	Explodes a pie slice.
	`SetDataStyle`	Sets visual properties of a data point.
	`SetSeriesStyle`	Sets visual properties for a series.

Let's take a look at an example that uses several of these functions. The business functionality of the application is to create a graph displaying each region's sales as a percentage of the overall sales. When a user double-clicks on a region, he or she wants to see what products are selling well for the selected region. We will create this application (one window) using two DataWindow graphs.

The first thing we need to do is create the DataWindow graph that displays each region's percentage of overall sales. For this we create a 3D pie graph with a data source of the following SQL statement:

```
SELECT "sales_order"."region",
       sum("sales_order_items"."quantity")
FROM "sales_order",
     "sales_order_items"
WHERE ( "sales_order_items"."id" = "sales_order"."id" )
GROUP BY "sales_order"."region"
```

The category is the region and the value is the computed sum field. After specifying the axis's labels and title, you get the graph shown in Figure 27.18. The name of this DataWindow is d_regional_sales.

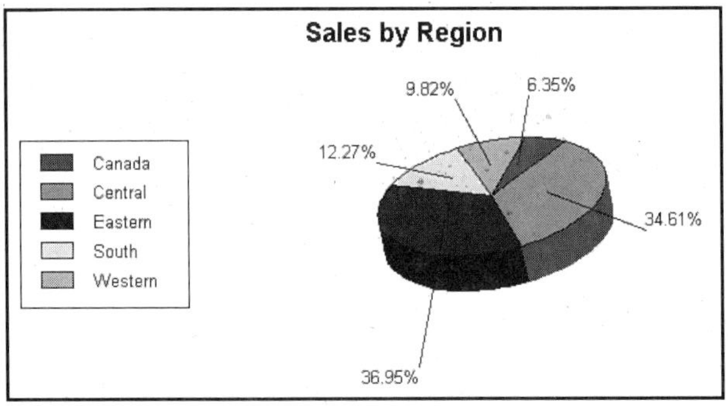

FIGURE 27.18.
The Sales by Region pie graph.

The next thing to do is to create the second DataWindow graph that will display the detail for a specified region. The SQL for this DataWindow is as follows:

```
SELECT "sales_order_items"."prod_id",
       sum("sales_order_items"."quantity")
FROM "sales_order",
     "sales_order_items"
WHERE ( "sales_order_items"."id" = "sales_order"."id" ) and
      ( ( "sales_order"."region" = :arg_region ) )
GROUP BY "sales_order_items"."prod_id"
```

Notice that the SQL statement contains a retrieval argument for the region name. The graph type initially is a column graph and is shown in Figure 27.19. The category is prod_id and the value is the computed column. The graph also has grid lines specified for the major division The name of this DataWindow is d_sales_for_region.

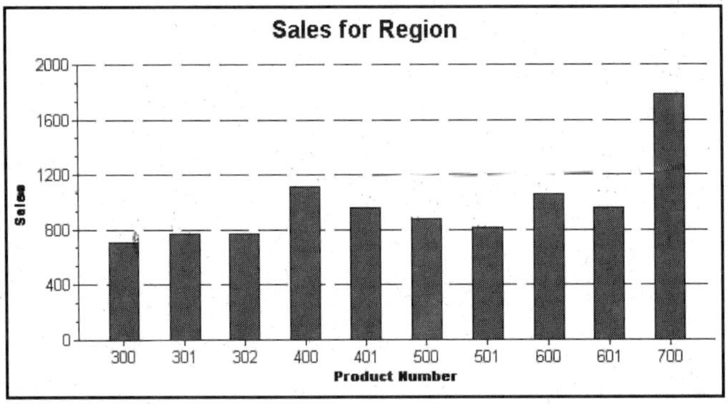

FIGURE 27.19.
Product sales details for a specified region.

Now that the two graphs are created, we are ready to synchronize the two graphs on the window. The window w_graphing contains two DataWindow controls: the top control (dw_total) is associated with `d_regional_sales` and the bottom control (`dw_detail`) is associated with `d_sales_for_region`. `dw_detail`'s `Visible` attribute is set to `FALSE`.

For the `Constructor` events for both DataWindow controls, the transaction object is set and the `Open` event of the window performs a `Retrieve()` for `dw_total`. The majority of the code is located in the `DoubleClicked` event for `dw_total`. The user can double-click on a piece of the pie graph, which will reveal the second graph, displaying the detail for the clicked region.

The first thing we need to do is find out where on the graph the user double-clicked. This can be done using the function `ObjectAtPointer()`, which has this syntax:

```
ControlName.ObjectAtPointer( {GraphControl,} SeriesNumber, DataPoint)
```

`ControlName` is the name of the graph control or the DataWindow control that contains the graph. *`GraphControl`* is used when dealing with a DataWindow graph. It is a String containing the name of the graph as it is defined on the DataWindow object. *`SeriesNumber`* is an Integer used to store the number of the series the user clicked. *`DataPoint`* is an Integer that stores the number of the data point that was clicked.

The return value of the `ObjectAtPointer()` function is of the `grObjectType` enumerated data type. A value of `grObjectType` is returned if the user clicks anywhere in the graph, including an empty area, and a `NULL` value is returned if the user clicks outside the graph. The return values of the enumerated data type `grObjectType` are defined in Table 27.5.

Table 27.5. Return values for the function `ObjectAtPointer()`.

Enumerated Data Type	*Description*
`TypeCategory!`	A label for a category
`TypeCategoryAxis!`	The category axis or between the category labels
`TypeCategoryLabel!`	The label of the category axis
`TypeData!`	A data point or other data marker
`TypeGraph!`	Any place within the graph control that isn't another `grObjectType`
`TypeLegend!`	Within the legend box, but not on a series label
`TypeSeries!`	The line connecting the data points of a series when the graph's type is a line or on the series label in the legend box
`TypeSeriesAxis!`	The series axis of a 3D graph
`TypeSeriesLabel!`	The label of the series axis of a 3D graph
`TypeTitle!`	The title of the graph
`TypeValueAxis!`	The value axis, including on the value labels
`TypeValueLabel!`	The user clicked the label of the value axis

`ObjectAtPointer()` should be called first in the `Clicked` or `DoubleClicked` event for your graph to ensure that the proper value is captured. In addition, the graph control has to be enabled or the `Clicked` event script won't be executed.

If the user clicks on a valid data point on `dw_total` (indicating a region), we want to extract the data value and use the region name as the argument value for `dw_detail`. On its own, this would provide the necessary functionality for our users, but with a little extra effort, we make the presentation something they won't soon forget.

It would be very easy for the users to remember what region was clicked on if the piece of the pie graph that was clicked on exploded out from the rest of the pie. This can very easily be implemented using the functions `SetDataPieExplode()` and `GetDataPieExplode()`.

`SetDataPieExplode()` causes a specified pie slice to be separated from the rest of the pie graph. This is the syntax:

```
ControlName.SetDataPieExplode({GraphControl,} SeriesNumber, DataPoint, Percent)
```

`ControlName` is either a graph control or a DataWindow control name. If you are using a DataWindow control graph, you must specify the *`GraphControl`* argument, which is a string indicating the name of the graph object. *`SeriesNumber`* is the number identifying the series. *`DataPoint`* is the number of the desired data point (or pie slice) that you want to have exploded out. The last argument, *`Percent`*, is the percentage of the pie's radius at which the pie slice is to be moved away from the center. The valid values are from `0` to `100`. `SetDataPieExplode()` returns an Integer, with `1` being a success and `-1` a failure.

`GetDataPieExplode()` is used to find out if a particular pie slice is exploded and at what percentage it is exploded from the center. This function has exactly the same arguments as `SetDataPieExplode()`. The only difference is that the *`Percent`* argument is an integer variable that is used to return the percent that the pie slice is exploded.

Listing 27.2 displays the script for the `DoubleClicked` event of `dw_total`.

Listing 27.2. The `DoubleClicked` event of `dw_total`.

```
int li_series, li_data, li_percent
string ls_region
grObjectType clicked_object

//Determine what part of the graph was clicked
clicked_object = this.ObjectAtPointer("gr_1", li_series, li_data)
//Turn the redraw off
this.SetRedraw( FALSE)

//Determine if pie was clicked before
If ii_series <> 0 and ii_data <> 0 then
   If li_series = ii_series and ii_data = li_data then
      //Same object was clicked, so do nothing
      this.SetRedraw( TRUE)
      Return
```

```
      Else
         //Reset previous pie explosion
         this.SetDataPieExplode("gr_1", ii_series, ii_data, 0)
      End If
   End If

   //Determine if the clicked object was a datapoint
   If clicked_object = TypeData! then
      //Find out if current object is exploded
      this.GetDataPieExplode("gr_1", li_series, li_data, li_percent)
      // If Not exploded
      If li_percent = 0 Then
         //Explode 50 percent
         this.SetDataPieExplode("gr_1", li_series, li_data, 50)

         //Set instance variable to remember series and data
         ii_series = li_series
         ii_data = li_data

         //Get the region
         ls_region = this.CategoryName("gr_1", li_data)

         //Retrieve data
         dw_detail.SetRedraw( FALSE)
         dw_detail.Retrieve(ls_region)

         //Set the title of the second datawindow
         dw_detail.object.gr_1.Title="Sales for the " + ls_region + " Region"
         dw_detail.Show()
      Else
         //Pie already exploded, reset
         this.SetDataPieExplode("gr_1", li_series, li_data, 0)
         dw_detail.Hide()
         dw_detail.Reset()
         ii_series = 0
         ii_data = 0
      End If
   Else //Clicked on anything else
      dw_detail.Hide()
      MessageBox("Not a Region", "Please click on a region")
   End If

   this.SetRedraw( TRUE)
   dw_detail.SetRedraw( TRUE)
```

A couple features were added to enhance the presentation even more. The two integer instance variables for `w_graphing`—`ii_series` and `ii_data`—are used to remember what pie slice was exploded last so that if the same pie slice is clicked, it is not reset and then exploded again. Also notice that the title of `dw_detail` is modified to reflect the clicked region name.

One thing to keep in mind is that in DataWindows, graphs are created and destroyed internally by PowerBuilder as the user pages through the data. The implication of this is that any changes you have made to your graph's appearance are continually lost. You can avoid this by trapping the graph creation event as a DataWindow user event mapped to the event ID, `pbm_dwngraphcreate`, and reissuing all necessary changes. This event is triggered after the graph has been created and populated with data, but before the graph is displayed.

TIP

As you probably noticed in Listing 27.2, you can improve performance and the user presentation by using the `ReDraw()` method. This will allow you to make numerous modifications to your graph without continuously repainting the graph. The other option is to toggle the `Visible` attribute on and off.

Summary

This chapter shows how to provide a graphical representation of data within a DataWindow and a window using a graph control. While much of the functionality that your user requires may be specified at design time, PowerBuilder gives you the ability to dynamically create and modify different components of your graph.

Frameworks and Class Libraries

28

IN THIS CHAPTER

Whether you build your own, work from someone else's, or purchase a commercial package, frameworks and class libraries can accelerate your development and reduce your debugging and maintenance time.

Frameworks and class libraries are completely different animals; you might be working with what you think is a framework, without realizing that it is in fact a class library. You need to decide which approach will work best for the project you are developing because each has its advantages and disadvantages. As you will see, frameworks provide many more advantages, so the majority of this chapter deals with that subject.

Consider this before you start: A true object incorporates attributes, services, and methods, and can be inherited. Some of PowerBuilder's "objects" do not conform to this definition. However, when you see the word *object*, you should interpret it as a general description that encompasses windows, structures, functions, and the rest of PowerBuilder's objects and controls.

A New Philosophy

Most developers must adjust their perspective on design and implementation methods; they must switch from having a project view to having a component (object) view. This is an important change for developers to make and will be what drives and directs the effort put into building and/or maintaining an organizationwide framework.

The focus of a developer shifts slightly away from the department and now considers how an object might be constructed to benefit development work on an organization level. The time taken to create a department-level application also includes time that invested in the modification and refinement of the framework used. This is where you really start to reuse objects, rather than simply copying "good" objects from one project to the next.

The following sections show how to spot and create objects that should be part of your framework, and what methods and mechanisms are available to develop these objects in an object-oriented manner.

Class Libraries

A *class library* is a collection of objects that are independent of each other and can usually be used without any other object in the library. Each object is essentially a black box with defined inputs and known outputs or effects, which gives you the capability to plug and play easily.

Because the objects in the class library are black boxes, you must code as much functionality and flexibility into them as possible. This means that the objects are generally much larger than they would be in a framework, because you have to provide additional parameters to switch functionality on and off.

Class libraries rarely, if at all, impose any kind of interface standards on a developer. Each object might have an interface that's consistent with the others, but there is little or no method for enforcement of standards.

The objects in a class library usually consist of the following:

- General-purpose functions such as for string handling and conversion.
- A concrete level of standard controls, most of them containing general-purpose code.
- Standalone windows such as a print dialog box and an import/export dialog box.
- An abstract level of windows, such as frames, dialog boxes, and sheets (but these libraries start to become hybrids).

Throughout this book, you have learned about windows, objects, and functions that you can easily add into a class library. Each of them is independent of the others and has no external requirements on an application.

Frameworks

Frameworks are also collections of objects, but because of their tight coupling, they cannot be used outside the framework. *Coupling* is a term used to describe the relationships between objects. Tight coupling is usually due to global and object instance variables, object-level functions, and object attributes. Each object is constructed with the intention of the developer inheriting and expanding the functionality. In contrast to class libraries, a framework object is a white box; the developer has access to the internal workings and can modify them if necessary.

By using a framework, you provide a foundation for all developers to work from; this usually leads to a consistent interface for applications built from the same framework.

Objects within a framework are built on specific application tasks—for example, managing the application object, database connections, and business rules. A framework is built to use explicit references to other objects. Therefore, it will be much tighter and faster code, because you will not provide for all cases that a developer might require (which you would have to do if the object were in a class library).

Frameworks can provide too much functionality, and you end up hiding controls and overriding excessive numbers of scripts to carry out simple tasks. There are occasions when it is more appropriate to copy and override some code rather than inherit and extend. The point at which you will need to do this depends on the functionality you want and how you can achieve that from the framework with the minimum of code. The advantages of frameworks generally outweigh these factors, and with careful and considered design you can minimize these effects.

Problem Domains

With a framework you can tackle a system by breaking down the areas into problem domains: user-interface domain, business domain, and system domain.

The *user-interface domain* deals with the look and feel of the application by providing standard controls in a consistent way.

The *business domain* encompasses the business rules and logic required for the system.

The *system domain* provides the management of the application, including object communication, database access and processing, and other system tasks and processing.

As you might already have realized, probably only the user and system domains are going to be reusable parts of the framework. Business domains are generally specific to an application and only provide some reusability if you are constructing a suite of applications within the same problem domain.

Hybrids

Hybrids of class libraries and frameworks also exist. These provide loosely coupled, standalone objects—in addition to some objects that require very tight coupling—for your application. These kinds of tools tend to be homegrown affairs that are built to tackle a particular type of project or fit a certain type of development group. Most often, they start out as a shareable library of objects, and as the project progresses, existing objects start to be coupled and new ones are added.

There are a number of experienced PowerBuilder developers that find commercial frameworks to be restrictive and carry too much overhead. These developers make use of a solid class library and build a framework based on that library to the requirements of the problem domain. This approach has a number of obvious advantages:

- Developers have a deep understanding of the objects available and how to use them.
- The framework can be easily extended. With commercial frameworks, you are often left wondering how future releases of the product will affect existing development work.
- Developers have a stake in providing the most optimal and useful objects—they will be the users of them!
- The framework does not carry the unused components that most frameworks do.

So how can you tell what you have?

If you can take an object and use it by itself in another application, you possibly have a class library. If you can do it with all the objects, you definitely have a class library. Otherwise, you have a hybrid. Do not include global functions in this testing process because they will mostly be transportable between applications no matter where their origins are.

Building a Framework

Now that you understand what frameworks and class libraries are, you can probably see the benefits of building or purchasing a framework. In the next section, you will see some of the requirements and structures involved in building a framework. The same information can be used in your evaluation and determination of which commercial framework to buy.

Classes

A *class* can be considered a template from which other objects are created; in fact, it can be a collection of objects that share similar attributes and behaviors. Every object in PowerBuilder is based on a class (for instance, all user objects are of the class `UserObject`).

According to Booch and Vilot, authors of *Object-Oriented Design: C++ Class Categories* (1991), there are five types of classes, two of which are appropriate for use with PowerBuilder: abstract and concrete. The *abstract* class is purely a definition and is never instantiated and used. A *concrete* class object is usually inherited from an abstract class object. The concrete class is an instantiation of an abstract class and provides the objects that will actually be used in an application. In your libraries, you should attempt to differentiate between abstract and concrete classes either by their placement in different PBL files or by their names.

An *instance* is an embodiment or one representation of a class, and the class is said to be *instantiated*. Depending on the method that instantiated a class, you will be able to create multiple instances of the same class. For example, the following code shows both methods of instantiating a window class:

```
w_sheet wInstance, wInstance2
//
// Open one instance of the class w_sheet
OpenSheet( wInstance, w_frame)
//
// Open a second instance of the class w_sheet
OpenSheet( wInstance2, w_frame)
//
// Open the one and only one direct instance of class w_report
// Note: we can still declare a variable of type w_report and
// open the window as we do above.
OpenSheet( w_report, w_frame)
```

A class definition incorporates attributes, services, and methods, which are all properties you will uncover during an object-oriented design and analysis phase. *Attributes* contain information about the class and its current state, and you will add to the attributes that are predefined by PowerBuilder using object-level instance variables. Controls placed in another object also become attributes of the parent object. The *services* of a class provide a defined functionality that is available to objects external to the class. *Methods* are provided to implement the services provided by the class; in PowerBuilder this is achieved through events and functions.

Abstraction

Abstraction is the process of designing and implementing objects at a high level. This removes the complexities of exactly how the functionality will be implemented and allows you to define the interface components of the object that will be used in performing the function.

This aids you in the creation of abstract class objects that are more stable and flexible, and that will make use of *polymorphism*, *encapsulation*, and *inheritance*.

Polymorphism

Polymorphism is a property that enables a single operation to have different effects on different objects. You could also look at this as the objects reacting differently to the same message. This property is an important part of building a framework; it is usually implemented using functions, but you can get a form of polymorphism by using message events.

At the abstract class level, the function might contain code, but usually it will be a virtual function. *Virtual function* means that the function is named and the parameters are specified, as is the return data type. The function does nothing except return a default value, if one is required. The concrete classes provide the actual code and can also redefine the input or output parameters. You write virtual functions in an abstract object so that other objects can make calls to methods for any of the concrete classes based on that abstract class. The calling object makes use of the abstract object as a data type and can then reference the method for any of the derived concrete classes. For example, all of the MDI sheets for an application (let's say there are two types, `w_mfg_sheet` and `w_stock_sheet`) are inherited from an abstract class `w_sheet`. In the application you can find the active sheet and assign it to a variable of type `w_sheet` and then make calls to methods that were prototyped in the abstract class and were coded in the concrete classes.

Function Overriding

Once you have defined a virtual function, you will re-declare the same function at the descendant levels with the same name, parameters, and return type. Within this descendant-level function you will actually carry out the required functionality. This is known as *function overriding.*

Function Overloading

Another alternative is to overload the function, and before PowerBuilder 5.0, the only mechanism for overloading was to use inheritance. At each level the function could be re-declared with the same name but different parameters. The function could then be called for an object, and depending on what parameters were passed, would determine which function was executed. In PowerBuilder 5.0 you can now overload functions at the same level, which saves you from resorting to multiple inheritance levels. `TriggerEvent()` is an example of an overloaded function in PowerBuilder.

Another form of polymorphism is one that is class based, with a number of different abstract classes defining the same function. Examples of this can be seen throughout the PowerBuilder object structure; for instance, the `Paste()` function is defined for `DataWindow` and `SingleLineEdit` (among others) but not at the next level up (`DragObject`), which is the ancestor to them both. This form forces you to repeat your code for each class, which is certainly less desirable.

Encapsulation

Encapsulation is the process of hiding the workings of an object and is implemented by using the `Private` and `Protected` keywords in variable and function declarations. Objects contain all the information they need to know about themselves and how other objects will interact with them, and this enables the object to become independent of other objects. All of an object's variables should be declared as one of these two types. There should be no `Public` variables declared. To provide access to a variable, you should code `Get()` and `Set()` functions, which enable you to validate the value being set and to carry out additional actions if required upon the change of the variable. As you might have guessed already, this also aids you in debugging your code, because you can place a break point in the `Set()` function and trace back to each caller to see which one is affecting the variable.

Inheritance

Inheritance is the mechanism that makes a framework operate and makes use of previously defined qualities. Inheritance enables an object to incorporate the definition of another object into its own definition. PowerBuilder enables you to inherit from windows, menus, and user objects. As you saw earlier, when you construct a window/menu/user object, you are inheriting from the appropriate abstract class.

There must also be a determination of what type of inheritance tree you will build for each class (see Figure 28.1).

With a single chain of inheritance, it is easy to construct an insulation layer (see the section "Insulation Layers" for a full description) and indicate from which class object a developer should inherit. However, because of the single-mindedness of the object, functionality that might not be required will be present. This redundant code will need to be maintained between the related classes. The objects are coded as solving all problems but being masters of none.

With multiple levels of inheritance, the objects are more specific to a task and methods. With a single chain of inheritance you can place attributes and events at the correct level in the inheritance tree rather than at inopportune or duplicate levels.

For example, if you needed to add a new function or attribute to all the related objects, you would have to tackle it in different ways, depending on the type of inheritance. With a single level, you would have to code the same modification in each object of the related classes. This is the class-based polymorphism that was discussed earlier. For multiple levels of inheritance, you can truly make use of the inheritance and code it at the ancestor level, which was the first type of polymorphism discussed (it's known as *inclusion polymorphism*—see Cardelli and Wegner, *On Understanding Types, Data Abstraction, and Polymorphism*, published in 1985).

FIGURE 28.1.
The levels of inheritance.

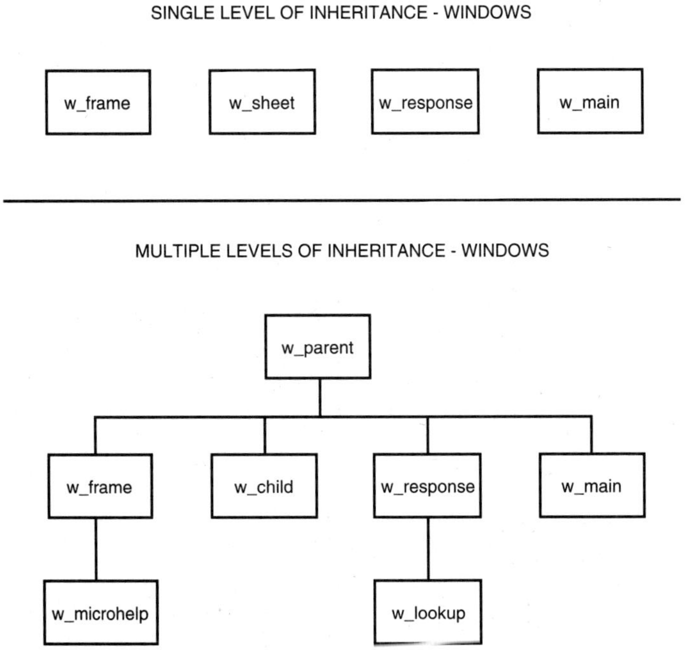

So far this chapter hasn't addressed inheritance in PowerBuilder object terms. In PowerBuilder only windows, user objects, and menus can be inherited. The latter can provide some performance problems when placed on windows within an inheritance chain, or if they themselves are inherited from and used. You should try to keep the inheritance of menus to one level at most, and you should be extremely wary of defining menus for abstract classes or concrete classes from which you're inheriting.

You have just seen single and multiple levels of inheritance for windows. Next, you will see how menus fit into this scheme (see Figure 28.2).

Users of PowerBuilder 4.0 should remember this one piece of information: When a menu item is made invisible at runtime, the whole menu is destroyed and reconstructed. Thus, if you make numerous changes to a menu, you will take some performance hits. Keep it simple or keep it visible! In Version 5.0 of PowerBuilder some considerable effort has gone into the performance of menus and this axiom is less relevant.

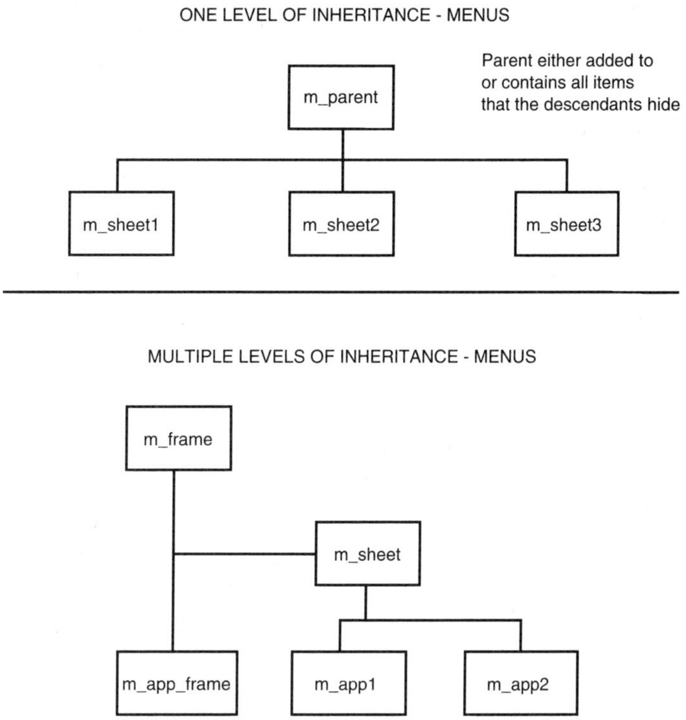

FIGURE 28.2.
The levels of inheritance for menus.

The diagram shown in Figure 28.2 does not conform with the ideas of the object-oriented approach. Menus can be considered to be attributes of a window, and if you look at some existing menus, you will see that they are usually tied closely with one particular window class. Therefore, your frameworks' menu hierarchies should closely match those of the windows they operate against (see Figure 28.3).

Memory Management

Classes, instances, and inheritance all have a profound effect on the way available memory is used. It is very important to understand how PowerBuilder manages memory when allocating resources for objects.

When a request is made to create an instance of a class, PowerBuilder allocates memory to hold the class definition (only on the first instance of the class to be created) and then allocates the memory for the instance to use. The memory used by the instance is for its instance variables and objects. On subsequent requests to create an instance of the class, only the memory required for the instance needs to be allocated. When an instance is destroyed, the memory allocated for just the instance is released.

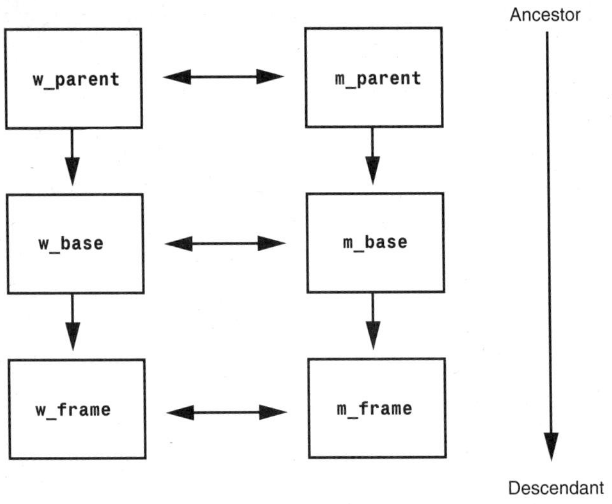

FIGURE 28.3.
The levels of inheritance for menus as they relate to windows.

Consider what happens when you start an application. First, PowerBuilder has to load the application object, which is a descendant of the PowerObject class. This means that PowerBuilder has to load the PowerObject class and allocate memory for it before loading the application object. The first window or menu created will cause the `GraphicObject` class to be loaded, followed either by the `Window` or `Menu` class, respectively, then the window or menu object class, and finally the instance of the class. Consider the example in Figure 28.4, which creates an instance of the window `w_connect` (in this example it is the first window to be opened in the application).

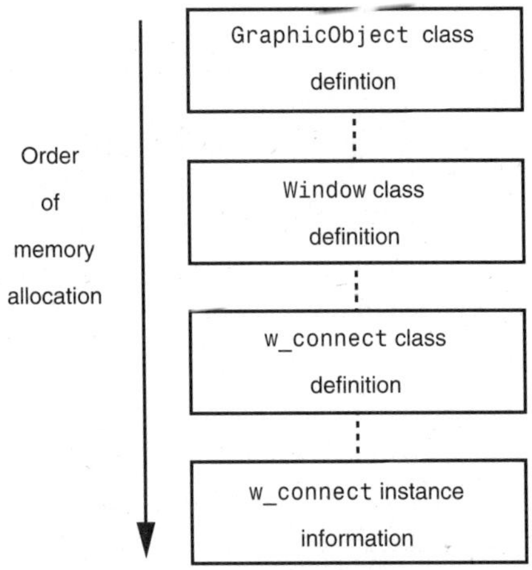

FIGURE 28.4.
Memory allocations during the creation of a window.

By carefully considering the hierarchy tree of your framework and applications, you can anticipate memory requirements and class usage. Plan on loading heavily used class hierarchies as soon as you can, because this will improve performance as the application is used.

Object Relationships

Object relationships are the particular properties that set frameworks apart from class libraries. The relationship can be based on association or ownership.

With an *associative relationship*, either object can exist without the other, and the actual relationship is achieved using reference variables (a pointer). This type of relationship can be constructed as one way or two way, with either one or both of the objects maintaining pointers to the other. For example, when you open two different windows, such as `w_mfg_sheet` and `w_stock_sheet`, PowerBuilder creates a global variable for each. This enables `w_stock_sheet` to reference `w_mfg_sheet` and vice versa. Within a framework, however, you must code this kind of behavior yourself and not rely on PowerBuilder's global help. This type of relationship enables many different objects to access one another.

An *ownership-based relationship* is one in which an object cannot exist without another object. The second object is the owner object. As with the associative relationship, this type of relationship is also usually implemented with reference variables. The best example is a control on a window; the window can exist without the control, but the control requires the window for its existence. The control is placed in the `Control[]` array attribute of the window, and this array provides the reference variable to the control. The owning object is then obligated to create and destroy the dependent object.

Making Sense of It All

You have been given a lot of definitions and advice in the past few sections, but how does this help you in the construction of your application?

Your first step is to explore any existing systems or prototypes that are accessible to you. By extracting common functionality and requirements from these, you begin the process of building an abstraction or an abstract class layer. This is where you will impose a consistent look and feel to all objects, especially if you have pulled code from various applications. Usually, when different project teams have created the applications, there will be a variety of coding and notation standards. Extracting common functionality into an abstract class gives you an ideal opportunity to standardize the code and carry out a code walkthrough at the same time. This code walkthrough gives you the opportunity to look at any optimizations or improvements in encapsulation that can be made.

The abstract class should include an MDI frame, a main window and a sheet window, menus for the MDI frame and sheet windows, and all of the controls as standard user objects. Probably the most important of all is the DataWindow user object.

We cannot stress how important it is to provide standard user objects for all of the controls and to use those instead of those directly available in the Window painter. This allows you to extend the functionality of your objects easily and with minimal changes to existing objects and code. This is very important when you do not initially know what functionality belongs in the ancestor object, and allows you to include and extend the object at a later date.

From this stage on, you should have a firm idea of who will be making use of the framework—whether it will be a single team, the whole department, or the whole enterprise. This will affect the kind of code that is placed at each level of the object inheritance tree. For single teams or departments, redundant code can easily be moved higher up the inheritance tree and will more often than not be used. However, at the enterprise level, you should keep the upper levels of the inheritance tree as generic as possible. You might also provide a slightly different inheritance tree because the additional abstract classes (mentioned in the next section) cannot be department specific. The investment in time and effort will be much greater to provide a good framework that everyone can use effectively. You may have come across the object-oriented term *thin objects*—this is what the term means.

From the abstract class windows, you might also want to inherit additional abstract class windows that are function or type based. For example, this could be a window that does master/detail browsing or a window that defines how all response windows will appear. Do not produce type-based abstract class objects just for the sake of doing it. If you are going to make an abstract `w_response` window for all dialog boxes, add something more to it than just setting the `WindowType` attribute to `Response`. With each of these abstract objects, try to encapsulate as much as possible. An ideal way to do this is to set up messages on the window that its controls can call to carry out communication between this window and other windows or objects.

Insulation Layers

For enterprise-level frameworks, the additional abstract classes might contain an extra layer that provides a buffer between the top-level object and a department's object (see Figure 28.5). Insulation layers are also often used as a buffer between a purchased framework and departmental objects.

The objects in the insulation layer are called an *insulation class*, which is also an abstract class. It effectively provides a department-level version of the master abstract class so that department-specific code can be added and other scripts can inherit from it.

As mentioned earlier, you should provide a standard class user object for each type of control, and you must impress on the development team that they should use these objects instead of the normal controls accessible in the painter. These user objects provide you with a consistent 2D or 3D look, the same font and font size, coloring, and labeling. Internally, these objects contain common code that you will always add, such as a `SetTransObject()` call in the `Constructor` event for a DataWindow.

Insulation layers are very important and an integral method that you should use to create a flexible framework. Consider the additional code and/or development group control that would be required to implement the departmental solutions shown in Figure 28.5.

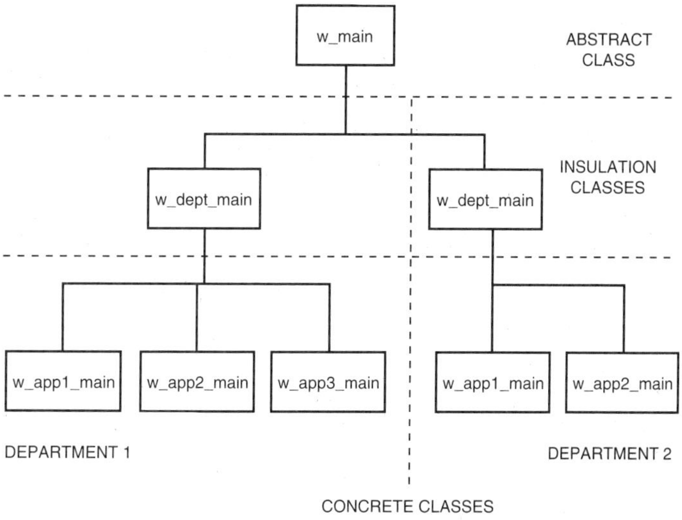

FIGURE 28.5.
An enterprisewide framework.

Object Coupling

The method used for communicating between objects can have a profound effect on the framework and how it is used. For tightly coupled objects, use direct referencing and functions; for loosely coupled objects, use indirect referencing, pronouns, PowerBuilder functions, and messages. There is a trade-off between having objects loosely coupled, which enables them to be more easily dropped in place, and the performance gains that come from direct references between objects.

Whether the referencing is direct or indirect, the pointer that is created by PowerBuilder takes up four words of memory (a *word* is the number of bits that are treated as a unit by the computer hardware, either 16 or 32 bits). This occurs regardless of whether it is a window, a DataWindow, or simply a command button. The pointer retains information on the class at which it is pointing, which PowerBuilder relies on during compilation within the Script painter. If you try to access an attribute of the object that does not belong to that class, the compilation will fail.

Direct Referencing

Direct referencing uses the actual name of the object to carry out some processing involving the object (for instance, `Open( w_mfg_sheet)`). After this particular operation is done, the object `w_mfg_sheet` can be used anywhere in the application. This obviously works only if the object is opened once; you will run into problems if you open additional instances of the window because the global pointer then points at the last instance opened. This kind of behavior is very undesirable in a framework and can lead to problems.

Indirect Referencing

Indirect referencing is used by frameworks to generically operate on an arbitrary object as directed by the application. These reference variables can be assigned from the pronoun keywords or other reference variables that are usually passed as parameters to the object.

When using reference variables, you must make sure that the variable is declared of the expected type. For example, if you execute the following code, you will get a compilation error:

```
Window wMfgSheet

wMfgSheet = w_mfg_sheet

wMfgSheet.wf_SaveOrder()
```

This happens because PowerBuilder has used the class definition of the variable and not the class referenced by the variable. To fix this, you would code it as follows:

```
w_mfg_sheet wMfgSheet

wMfgSheet = w_mfg_sheet

wMfgSheet.wf_SaveOrder()
```

Look at the second line of both pieces of code. Until the variable is referenced to an object, it points at nothing and you will get `Null Object` error messages.

As long as you have means to get to an object that is created, you do not need to maintain a pointer to it. For example, MDI sheets can be reached through `GetSheet()` and `GetNextSheet()`. Within objects, you can make use of the `This`, `Parent`, and `ParentWindow` pronouns. This is the preferred way to make reference to all objects, and the pronouns can be used in passing reference pointers to other objects. The function declaration must be set to pass by value, because you cannot use pronouns when the parameter is by reference.

Remember that object types other than windows can also be used as reference variables, but they require the use of the `Create` command to instantiate the object. Also remember this warning: You cannot make object assignments directly from one reference variable to another if the objects come from different levels of the inheritance chain. For example, if the object `u_n_oe_transaction` is inherited from `u_n_transaction`, the following will compile, but at runtime it will produce a cannot assign error:

```
u_n_transaction trCustomers
u_n_oe_transaction trSoldTo

trCustomers = Create u_n_transaction
trSoldTo = trCustomers
```

The statement made in the preceding paragraph is not strictly true. You can make assignments within the inheritance chain if they occur going back up the tree, as in this example:

```
u_n_transaction trCustomers
u_n_oe_transaction trSoldTo

trCustomers = Create u_n_oe_transaction
trSoldTo = trCustomers
```

Object Communication

Now that you know how to obtain references to other objects, how do you communicate requests between the objects? You can use either messages or direct function calls. Again, this gets back into loose and tight coupling. You can, of course, use a message to request that the receiving object execute one of its own functions.

Events execute from the topmost ancestor on down the inheritance chain to the descendant, unless you have set Event Override to on. If you send a message to an object that is not set up to receive it, you will not get a runtime error and the object will do nothing.

Object-level functions are used to strongly *type* (make certain that the correct function is called) the request. If the function's *signature* (function name and arguments) does not match that of the function being called, the ancestor chain is traversed from the descendant up until it is matched.

You can specify functions that override or overload at each level of the inheritance chain (starting at the first inherited level). Overriding a function requires you to define a function with the same name, arguments, and return value. You then code the function to carry out some behavior different from that of the ancestor. With function overloading, you call the function the same name, but you alter the number and type of arguments.

NOTE

You cannot overload the return type of a function.

Using functions or events provides the initiation of a conversation, but the whole idea is to pass information to, and sometimes from, the other object.

Events now support passing values other than just the `WordParm` and `LongParm` attributes of the message object. You can also use global variables and structures that are populated before the call, which can then be interrogated by the object receiving the message. You can also use globals or event return values using the new event calling syntax (see Chapter 6, "The PowerScript Language"). Events have an advantage in that they can be called both asynchronously (using `PostEvent()`) and synchronously (using `TriggerEvent()`). But they are also at a disadvantage because they are publicly accessible.

Functions, as you already know, can both receive and return values during a call. Access to functions (except global functions) can be as open or as restricted as you like, using the `Public`, `Protected`, and `Private` declarations.

You will make use of both events and functions in your framework, but you should pick the correct candidate for the job. Here are some tips for selecting the method to use:

Requirement	*Method*
Strong data typing	Function or parameterized events
Passing values back and forth	Function or parameterized events
Controlling access	Function
Loose coupling	Event (not parameterized)
Extendibility lower in inheritance chain	Event

When you use an event, or even a function, and you want to pass a number of values, there are a number of different ways to do it:

- Parameters to the event/function
- Global variables or application instance variables
- Single or multiple global structures
- Using a hidden window that is only used for communication purposes
- A class (nonvisual) user object

Obviously, the first and last two methods are more object-oriented because control can be placed on the modification and retrieval of values.

What Does Object Coupling Provide?

What does all this mean for your framework? If you have declared attributes at a high enough level, you can use a base class as the reference variable data type rather than a specific object. This enables you to use generic data type reference variables to affect a wider range of objects than if the variable has to be declared using a set class.

There is one more thing to remember before you continue to the next section. The PowerObject data type is the ancestor of all objects, and when you are using loose coupling, you can use `TriggerEvent()` and related functions to cause actions to be performed very easily when using control or object arrays.

Including Objects in a Framework

Not all objects or functions belong in a framework, and some that you may have already included may themselves have missing links in their own class structures. The following list of questions can be broken down into two areas (Is the object complete? and Is the object necessary?):

- Question: Does the object share the same or similar functionality with another object?
- Solution: Create a super-class object that you can then use to inherit this and other objects from that contains the duplicate functionality.
- Question: Does the object not carry out a well-defined function—is it trying to do more than one role?
- Solution: Determine if the object can be broken down into more distinct pieces. Revisiting the abstraction design for this object might also be worthwhile to see if you can clean up the object's definition.
- Question: Does the object rely on a lot of other objects to complete its own task? Are these supporting objects used by other objects?
- Solution: Determine if these objects can or should be combined into one object. This will be determined by the functionality being implemented. If the objects are themselves self-contained and reusable, they can be left alone.
- Question: Does the object have more than a few attributes and methods?
- Solution: Consider whether the object is actually necessary.
- Question: Does the object contain redundant functionality? Is the same functionality available in other objects?
- Solution: Consider whether the object is actually necessary.

The careful analysis of a problem domain and the design of object-oriented solutions will help you in the creation and inclusion of good objects into your framework.

Maintaining a Framework

When the framework is in use, you must treat any enhancements and additions to the framework with the greatest of care. Although it is easy to add a new function or other attribute to an object, when you are modifying existing code and attributes, you must ensure that any changes appear seamless to both inherited objects and developers.

However, do not feel that it is dangerous or unnecessary to examine and update the framework objects, because this is a necessary step in ongoing support and maintenance of the framework. Consider all the requests that come back from the development teams, but carefully consider the modifications and their implications before making a change.

Although a number of people might have been involved in writing the framework initially, the task of maintaining and modifying the code should be restricted to a single person: the framework guardian (object administrator and reuse coordinator are two of a number of titles for the same duty). The original members of the framework-development team will return to specific projects and can't be relied on to give subjective views of the needs of a framework, and they will rarely have the time to spend making carefully considered changes. The guardian will also be responsible for maintaining versions of the framework so that if a disastrous change is made, it can be quickly and painlessly reversed and the old copy can be reinstated. Other duties of the guardian include keeping good communication channels open between the various development teams, informing the teams of changes and additions to the objects, making the modifications to objects, removing old code and objects, and reviewing and updating object code.

Having a guardian in place should not exclude the original developers or other project members from contributing to the framework. Indeed, you will ideally set up regular meetings for discussion on problems, missing functionality, or enhancements the project teams that are actually using the framework in their developing have come across. These can then be discussed in a cross-team effort.

Other Considerations

Whatever methods you use to construct your framework, keep in mind that simple structures can lead to elegant products. Try to keep your inheritance trees under control and not too deep (around five or six levels is manageable). This will help your development teams in the long run and will make their debugging exercises that much easier.

Documentation cannot be stressed enough. If you construct your own objects, document them with the intention of making it easy for a developer to pick up an object and drop it into an application with a minimum of fuss.

NOTE

You can even incorporate the documentation for a window or user object into the object itself by declaring a user event called `Documentation` and placing the text there. Now that is true encapsulation!

The hierarchy of the PowerBuilder objects themselves provides a good base of investigation and learning. You can view this in the PowerBuilder Object Browser by selecting the System tab page and clicking on the hierarchy check box. From this list, you can see how and why objects are inherited and super-classed; they provide good indicators for your own framework.

NOTE

Even commercial frameworks are not above changing the hierarchy structure. PowerBuilder 4.0 moved `DynamicDescriptionArea`, `DynamicStagingArea`, `Error`, `MailSession`, and `Message` under a new super-class: `NonVisualObject`.

Your framework will only be as good as the time and resources you devote to it.

Commercial Products

If the previous sections have been sufficient to dissuade you from constructing your own framework, you are probably thinking about buying a commercial framework. The advantages of commercial products are that they are prebuilt and include pretested code. You get full documentation, tutorials, usually technical support, and even training if you require it. Even at the time of writing this book, there are an increasing number of frameworks and class libraries coming into the marketplace. The following sections contain information about some of the market leaders and a very brief overview of their products. (More information on the companies can be found in Appendix B, "PowerBuilder Resources, " which is on this book's CD.) Powersoft also provides its own framework and calls it the PowerBuilder Foundation Class (PFC).

You can use your knowledge from the previous sections to help you determine the worth that one of these frameworks or class libraries can add to your development effort.

CornerStone

This product is from Financial Dynamics, Inc. (FDI).

CornerStone is a collection of reusable objects that are intended as a foundation for an organization's own internal object library. The library was originally architected by Michael Horwith and has been enhanced by FDI's consultants with real-world experience. CornerStone comes with online help, standards and conventions, a sample application, and a tutorial. The library provides fully encapsulated windows, custom controls for security and navigation, and standard error reporting, trapping, and logging. Also included are a tab control, context-sensitive list box searching, pop-up calendars, and other useful widgets.

FDI has extended the base class library in its ClienTele product (available separately), which provides a telemarketing application framework.

ObjectStart

This product is from Greenbrier & Russel, Inc.

This company offers a whole line of PowerBuilder productivity tools, of which ObjectStart is their comprehensive PowerBuilder object toolkit. ObjectStart is a comprehensive class library of more than 100 reusable objects, including security objects. These objects are organized into three groups: Managers, Controllers, and Utilities. This product is highly object oriented; development teams should be well versed in object-oriented methodology before attempting to use this product.

PowerBase

This product is from Millennium, Inc.

PowerBase consists of a base library, a template library, custom objects, a sample application, a tutorial, online help, and standards and conventions. The objects in the base library are crafted to provide a consistent interface, online help support, testing modes, and SQL previewing. The template library contains a number of prebuilt objects such as data entry, searching, and login windows.

PowerBuilder Foundation Class Library

This product is from Powersoft Corporation, and was formerly known as the PowerBuilder Application Library in PowerBuilder 4.0. The two libraries are, however, radically different.

The Application Library is provided as part of the Enterprise Edition of PowerBuilder and consists of software and a reference book/tutorial.

The PowerBuilder Foundation Class is written in PowerBuilder using all the same objects and PowerScript that every other developer has access to. The product draws on the many object-oriented coding techniques that are applicable to PowerBuilder and features a thorough service-oriented architecture. Service-based architectures allow applications to use only the necessary amount of computer resources and provide an as-needed functionality model for developers to code against.

PFC isolates related types of processing into groups, which it calls *services*. The majority of the services are implemented as custom class user objects, and include the following:

- Window services
- DataWindow services
- File services
- DBMS services
- Date and Time services
- String services

The major advantages of this approach are that you have control over which services you load and use and it minimizes the application's overhead. Development is made easier for both using and extending the services and allows you to build simple as well as complex applications using the same techniques. PFC uses the new auto-instantiating feature for custom class user objects, so you don't even have to worry about cleaning up services after you have finished with them and the service has left scope.

The PFC product consists of a set of four main PBLs, which you must include in any PFC-based application's search path. These four PBLs contain ancestor objects and other important objects used by PFC:

- PFCMAIN.PBL—Basic PFC services
- PFCAPSRV.PBL—Application manager and application services
- PFCDWSRV.PBL—DataWindow services
- PFCWNSRV.PBL—Window services

These libraries are not intended to be modified by anyone but Powersoft, and you have to make use of extension-level libraries.

Since no class library is going to be able to meet your development needs straight out of the box, Powersoft has designed an extension layer. For example, if you modify the top-level objects to integrate some applicationwide functionality, when Powersoft releases the next version of PFC, all your changes will be gone. This would force you to manually reapply your changes.

Objects in the extension level are unmodified descendants of the corresponding objects in the ancestor library. You customize your application to use PFC by modifying objects at this extension level, as well as by inheriting from such objects. Powersoft has provided you with four extension-level libraries that match the ancestor libraries: PFEMAIN.PBL, PFEAPSRV.PBL, PFEDWSRV.PBL, and PFEWNSRV.PBL.

All in all, the PowerBuilder Foundation Class appears to be a well-thought-out and constructed framework whose use will become second nature to many PowerBuilder developers.

PowerClass

This product is from ServerLogic Corporation.

PowerClass provides an integrated framework that contains an extensive class library of reusable objects. The framework was originally architected by the person who is now president of ServerLogic. The company also provides two additional products that can be integrated with PowerClass or any other framework: PowerLock and PowerObjects. PowerLock is a security-implementation library, and PowerObjects provides a collection of advanced objects and utilities. PowerClass was written and designed for data-entry applications and includes skeleton code in the base class objects rather than just the comments some other frameworks provide.

PowerFrame

This product is from MetaSolv Software.

PowerFrame provides two modules: a library module and a development module. The library module serves as the foundation for the application. The development module consists of programming standards and a set of class libraries. A base MDI frame, menu, toolbar, and MicroHelp bar are provided to display additional information. The PowerFrame application loads site and user preferences to influence the execution of the application. Add-ons can be purchased for security and tab control processing.

PowerGuide

This product is from AJJA Information Technology Consultants, Inc.

PowerGuide is a PowerBuilder framework that consists of architectural guidelines, procedures, methodologies, sample applications, and object class libraries. PowerGuide is customizable to fit the organizational and technical environment in which you are working. The class library provides more than 150 visual and nonvisual reusable objects.

PowerTool

This product is from PowerCerv.

PowerCerv is another provider of a wide range of PowerBuilder products, including PowerTool, an award-winning class library. PowerTool promotes inheritance and provides navigational control and application-security features. The product provides support for MDI applications, application templates, naming conventions, and intersheet communication, and includes a comprehensive tutorial.

Summary

With the use of either a framework or a class library, you can increase the end-user community's involvement in the prototyping stages of an application because of the rapid development and changes that can be made. Frameworks and class libraries provide increased quality and more reliable applications that are much easier to maintain.

Data Pipelining

29

IN THIS CHAPTER

Developers often have problems moving data and data structures from one database to another. In the client/server environment, the need to copy tables and their data from a test database to a development database or from the server to a local database is constantly in demand. Depending on the tools available, this can be a fairly easy task or it can result in a lot of manual work that takes away from valuable development time.

The same problem occurs in the business community. With more and more people relying on computers to perform their day-to-day business activities, managing the data becomes a serious concern. As a growing number of business people use laptops and dial in to access remote information, M.I.S. professionals must find easier ways to move data from a centralized server to locally maintained machines. The solution to both development and runtime transfer of data and data structures is PowerBuilder's data pipeline object. It provides an easy method to transfer data from one database to another regardless of the DBMS.

This chapter examines how to transfer (or pipe) data and data structures from one database to another. The piping of information can be done during development using the Data Pipeline painter as well as implemented in your application for your users to use at runtime. After defining a pipeline object in the Data Pipeline painter, this chapter shows how to use the pipeline object in your application.

The Pipeline Object

As just mentioned, the data pipeline can be used to transfer data for developers or users. This is a very general definition of what a pipeline object can do for you. There are three main groups of tasks the data pipeline can perform that result in great time and effort savings for the developer.

The most obvious reason to use a pipeline object is to transfer data from one database to another. These databases can be the same DBMS or different DBMSs. The transfer of data can consist of inserts into an existing table or updates of existing data. The data in the source database remains the same and is only reproduced in the destination database. Although it is most common for the source and destination databases to be different databases, they can be the same database.

The entire database can be moved from one DBMS to another, one table at a time. This would allow you to create a copy of an existing database in another location (for example, replicate a SQL Server database to a Watcom database for local access). All extended attributes (for example, edit styles, displays formats, and labels) for a table can be chosen to be migrated for the whole table as can just the table and its data.

The last task you can use the data pipeline for is to make changes to a table that are not allowed using the Alter Table dialog box in the Database painter. For example, you might want to change the primary key definition or even allow certain columns to contain `NULLs` when they did not previously.

Whatever purpose you have for using the data pipeline, there are several pipeline options you must specify when creating a pipeline object:

- The source database
- The destination database
- The source tables from which to move data
- The destination table to which the data will be moved
- The piping operation to be performed
- The frequency with which commits are performed
- The maximum number of errors allowed
- The extended attributes that need to be included

All this information is combined to form your data pipeline or pipeline object. Once the definition of the pipeline object is complete, it can be run in PowerBuilder or used in an application. Either way, the definition can be saved to your library file and reused again and again. The pipeline object is created in the Data Pipeline painter.

The Data Pipeline Painter

You access the Data Pipeline painter by clicking on the icon on the PowerBar that displays two database cylinders connected with an arrow. Clicking on this icon opens the Select Data Pipeline dialog box (see Figure 29.1).

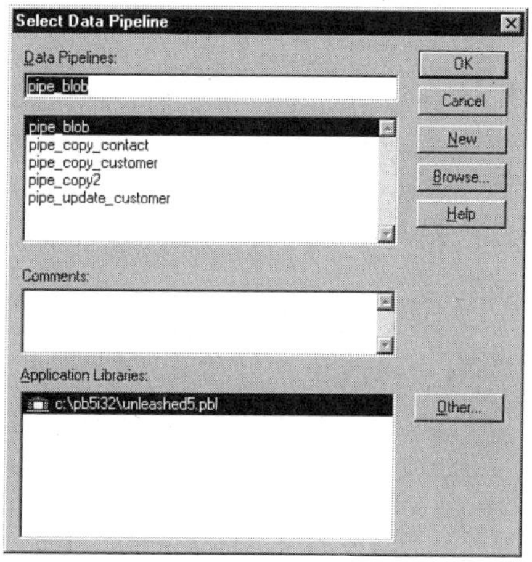

FIGURE 29.1.
The Select Data Pipeline dialog box.

After you click on the New button, PowerBuilder prompts you with the New Data Pipeline dialog box (see Figure 29.2).

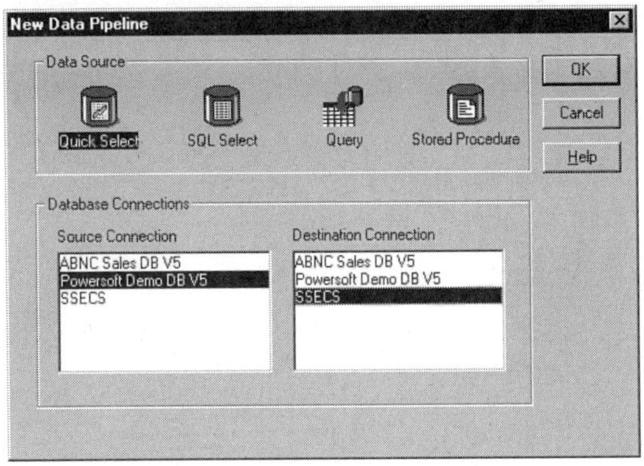

FIGURE 29.2.
The New Data Pipeline dialog box.

In this dialog box you must choose the database profile from which you want to migrate data, the source connection, and the database profile that you want the data migrated to (or the *destination connection*). If you have already connected to a database in the Database painter, it will be your default source database. If the database that you wish to migrate data from or to does not initially appear in either of the list boxes, you must define the profiles in the Database painter or using the Database Profiles icon on the PowerBar (for more information see Chapter 4, "Databases and the Database Painter").

New to 5.0 is the ability to choose the type of Data Source: Quick Select, SQL Select, Query, and Stored Procedure. All four options are different methods to generate the SQL `SELECT` statement needed to pipe your data. The different data sources act exactly as they do in the DataWindow painter. For more information on the how to use the data sources see Chapter 9, "The DataWindow Painter." After you click the OK button, the chosen data source painter/dialog will open, allowing you to specify the data you wish to migrate. To access a different database in the Pipeline painter, you must enter the Database painter and point to a different data source.

NOTE

The SQL Select painter functions exactly the same as it does in the DataWindow painter; it even has the capability to create *retrieval arguments*, which give you the ability to narrow the scope of the data that is migrated.

The `SELECT` statement you generate should specify the data you wish to migrate from the source database. The `SELECT` statement can be an entire table or a subset of one or more tables. Once you are satisfied with your `SELECT` statement, click the depressed Select PainterBar icon to enter the pipeline definition window (see Figure 29.3).

FIGURE 29.3.
The pipeline definition window.

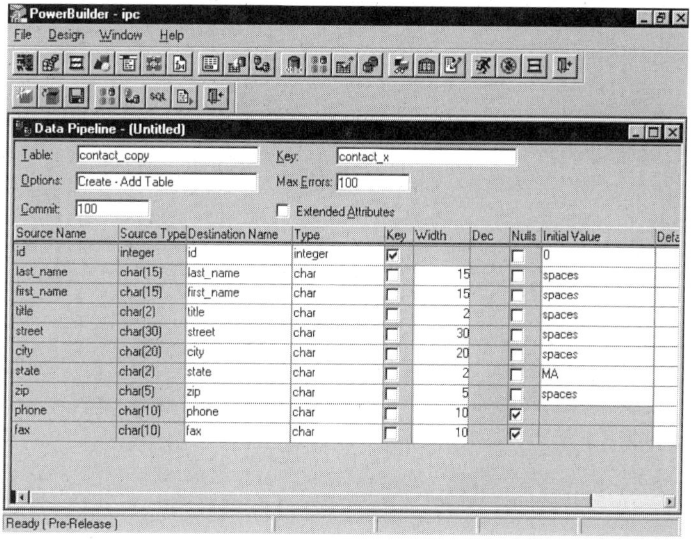

An alternate method to access the Data Pipeline painter is to right-click on a table title in the Database painter and select Data Pipeline from the pop-up menu or click the Data Pipeline icon on the PainterBar. Using this method, PowerBuilder defaults the source and destination database to your current connection. The `SELECT` statement generated retrieves all columns for the table chosen in the Database painter and automatically takes you into the pipeline definition window.

The pipeline painter is divided into several different sections: the source table, the destination table, and the pipeline options. The PainterBar for the Data Pipeline painter is shown in Figure 29.4.

The Source Table

The source table section of the Data Pipeline painter displays the information about the tables that are to be piped. This information is

- The name of the source column
- The data type (source type) of the column with the current size—the total number of significant digits—of the column specified in parentheses

These columns cannot be modified in the pipeline definition window. The only way to modify the source table information is to click on the Edit Data Source menu item under the Options menu or click the corresponding PainterBar icon (see Figure 29.4). Clicking this icon takes you back into the SQL Select painter.

Once you have made your modifications to the `SELECT` statement and return to the pipeline definition window, PowerBuilder notifies you that the pipeline definition will change. After you have specified all the source information, you need to define how the destination columns should appear.

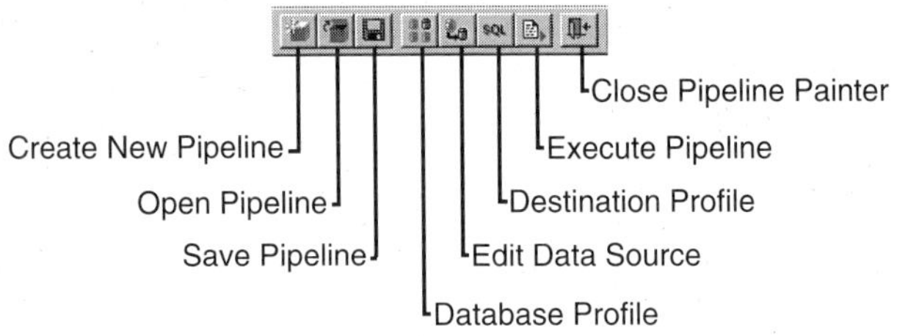

FIGURE 29.4.
The Data Pipeline PainterBar.

The Destination Table

The destination table section of the pipeline definition is used to indicate where the data is going to be migrated to. Using the destination table columns, you can specify what the new column names will be, the appropriate data types, and primary key information. The destination table section includes the following:

- The name of the destination column
- The data type of the destination column
- Whether each column should be included as part of the primary key
- Column width (if applicable)—the total number of significant digits
- Number of decimal (`DEC`) places if applicable
- Whether the column can have a `NULL` value
- An initial value for the column
- A default value for the column such as auto-incremented, current date or time, timestamp, `NULL`, or the user.

All this information can be modified to suit your particular needs. The data type column provides a drop-down list box displaying the valid data types for the destination database (since it could be a different DBMS with different data type definitions). If you choose that a column can contain `NULL` values, you cannot specify an initial value.

New to the data pipeline is support for blob (binary large object) columns. Select Database Blob from the Options menu, which opens the Database Binary/Text Large Object dialog box (see Figure 29.5).

In this dialog box you need to specify the name of the destination column name, the source table, and the name of the blob column. Once this information has been specified, the blob column is added to the list of columns in the pipeline definition window and a different data type and default value can be specified (all other columns are disabled). To edit the definition of the blob column, double-click the newly added row in the pipeline definition window or right-click the row and choose Properties from the menu. To remove the blob column, right-click on the row and select Clear from the pop-up menu.

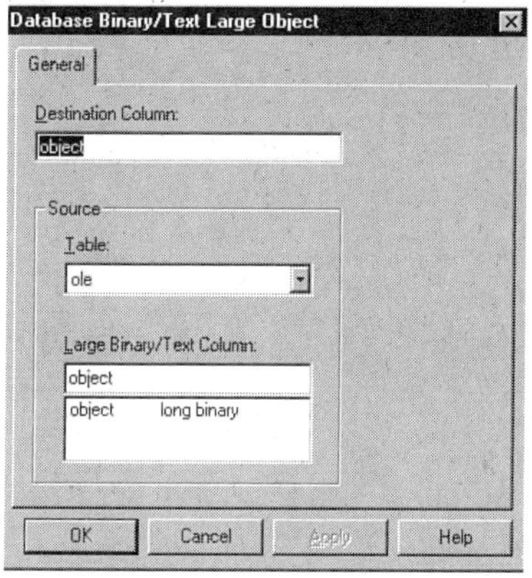

FIGURE 29.5.
The Database Binary/Text Large Object dialog box.

In Version 4.0 of PowerBuilder (in which blobs were not supported), the initial definition of the blob was assigned by searching the destination database for the closest match to the source database's data types. This is what appears as the initial values for the destination data type column. These can be modified to suit your needs.

An additional feature of the Data Pipeline painter is that at any point you can change the destination database. This would give you the ability to pipe data to one database and then modify the destination database profile and pipe the identical data to another database. To change the destination database, click on the Database Profile icon on the PainterBar, which opens the Database Profiles dialog box (see Figure 29.6).

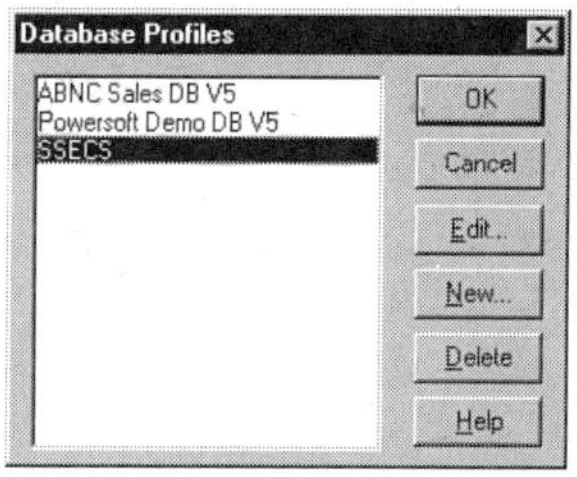

FIGURE 29.6.
The Database Profiles dialog box.

You can now select a new destination database and PowerBuilder will try to connect to the newly specified database. An alternative method of changing the destination database is to choose Destination Connect from the File menu and select one of the database profiles listed in the cascading menu. Once you have settled on a destination database, there are some pipeline options you can specify that further define how the pipeline object will perform.

The Pipeline Options

Above the source and destination column specifications are a series of options that indicate how you want the piping to occur. The pipeline options are

- The destination table name
- The primary key name for the destination table
- The piping options
- The maximum number of errors allowed
- The number of rows in a transaction that are committed
- Whether extended attributes are piped

The destination table name can be changed at any time. The primary key name can be modified if the piping option is either Create—Add Table or Replace—Drop/Add Table.

The piping options have the greatest effect on how you interact with the pipeline definition. There are five options available that affect how you pipe your data:

- Create—Add Table
- Replace—Drop/Add Table
- Refresh—Delete/Insert Rows
- Append—Insert Rows
- Update—Update/Insert Rows

The Create piping option creates the specified destination table in the destination database. If the table already exists in the destination database, PowerBuilder notifies you that the table exists. To continue, you must either rename the destination table or select another piping option. If the table does not already exist, PowerBuilder creates the new table and inserts the source rows into the destination table.

The Replace piping option also creates the specified destination table in the destination database and inserts the source rows into the new table. The difference between Create and Replace is that if the destination table already exists in the destination database, PowerBuilder will drop the existing table and create the new table. This option should be used with caution.

While the first two options allow you to modify the data structures, the last three options affect the actual data maintained in the tables.

> **NOTE**
>
> The last three piping options require that the destination table already exist in the destination database. If you specify a table name that does not exist, the destination table section of the painter is disabled.

The Refresh piping option deletes all rows in the destination table and then inserts the rows from the specified source. The difference between Refresh and Replace is that Refresh requires that the destination table exist and just deletes existing rows, whereas Replace will drop/create the destination table.

The Append piping option generates `INSERT` SQL statements for all the source rows and inserts them into the destination table. This option retains existing rows and does not delete the destination table's rows first.

The Update piping option generates an `UPDATE` SQL statement for a source row whose key matches the key of a row in the destination database. The source rows that do find a key match with the destination database generate `INSERT` SQL statements. The only option you can change in the destination table section is the key field check boxes. The primary key columns must be selected and must either match the primary key in the destination table or uniquely identify each source row in case the destination table has no primary key.

Once you have decided on the piping options, you also need to specify the maximum number of errors that you will allow, the number of rows processed before a commit is performed on the destination database, and whether you wish to copy extended attributes to the destination database.

The Max Error value is used to determine the number of errors that can occur during the execution of the pipeline object. Once the value specified is reached, the pipeline is halted. Depending on the number of anticipated errors, you may want to set a higher value or No Limit for the Max Errors value.

The Commit value determines the number of rows that make up one transaction. Once the number count specified is reached, a commit is performed on the destination database. The Commit value should reflect how often you want the data to be written to disk. If you specify a Commit value of All, a commit will only be performed after all source rows have been piped. If an error occurs during a transaction, all changes after the last commit are rolled back.

NOTE

New to Version 5.0 is the option to specify a value of None for a Commit value, which indicates that no commit will be performed after the data has been migrated.

The last option on the pipeline definition window is the Extended Attributes check box. If you wish to copy any of the extended attributes associated with the specified source columns, the check box should be checked. If an extended attribute definition already exists in the destination table with the same name as a source column, the source extended attribute definition is not copied. The column in the destination table will then use the existing extended attribute definition.

Executing the Pipeline

Once the definition of the pipeline object is complete, you can click on the Execute icon in the PainterBar (refer to Figure 29.4) or select Execute from the Design menu.

If you have specified any retrieval arguments in the SQL SELECT statement, PowerBuilder will prompt you for values when you try to execute the pipeline. PowerBuilder then generates the necessary SQL statements to migrate the data as specified by the piping options. PowerBuilder also indicates the number of rows read, the number of rows written, and the time elapsed in the MicroHelp.

After beginning execution of the pipeline object, you have the option to cancel the processing. After you have clicked the Execute icon, the icon changes to a red hand, and when clicked, it stops the pipeline processing. If you reach the maximum number of errors specified for your pipeline, PowerBuilder halts the processing and then displays the rows that were in error. For more information on handling pipeline errors see the following section, "Pipeline Errors."

Remember that since you are performing database processing, the database will ensure any integrity constraints via foreign keys or the execution of triggers. These can be the cause of errors in the data pipeline process.

Pipeline Errors

When PowerBuilder detects any pipeline errors, it displays them using a standard pipeline error DataWindow (see Figure 29.7).

FIGURE 29.7.
The pipeline error DataWindow.

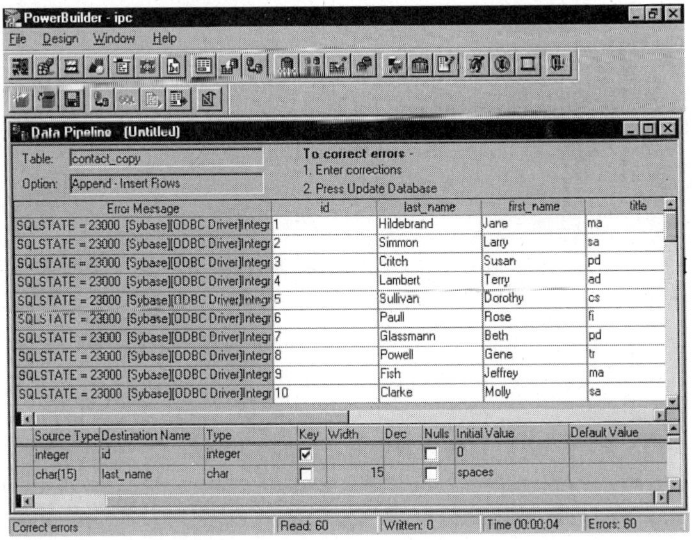

The pipeline error DataWindow displays all columns for each failed row and an error message indicating what the problem was. This DataWindow allows you to correct the errors by editing each of the problem columns or ignore the errors.

If you wish to ignore the errors, click on the Design PainterBar icon or select Design from the Options menu, which takes you back to the pipeline definition window. You cannot return to the error DataWindow once you have returned to the pipeline definition.

If you want to correct the pipeline errors, review each of the error messages and make the appropriate modifications to the problem columns. Since the error DataWindow is a grid presentation, you can resize the columns to view more or less of the column's value. After the errors have been corrected, click on the Update Database icon or select Update Database from the Design menu. PowerBuilder will try to repipe these rows to the destination database and displays any new or remaining errors after the process is complete. While the other PainterBar icons appear, only the Update Database and Design icons are enabled.

NOTE

If you reach the maximum error limit, you will be unable to continue the pipeline even after fixing the errors. To get around this problem, you must either fix the pipeline object's definition or fix the source data. You can then re-execute the pipeline.

The rest of the information on the window indicates the pipeline object's definition. This information cannot be modified.

Saving a Pipeline Object

A pipeline object is saved in the same way as any other PowerBuilder object. Select Save from the File menu or the new Save PainterBar icon, which opens the Save Data Pipeline dialog box (see Figure 29.8).

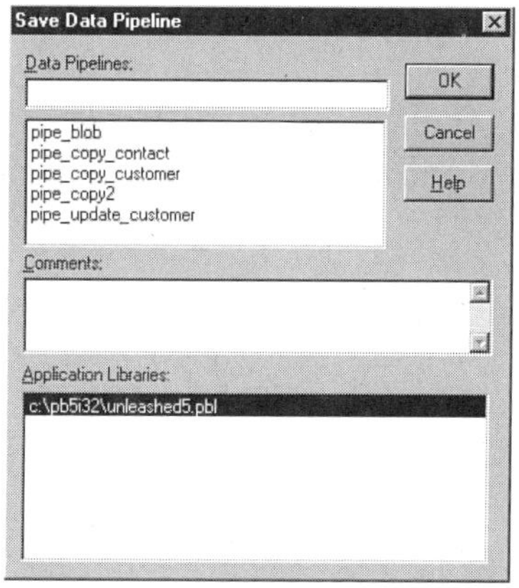

FIGURE 29.8.
The Save Data Pipeline dialog box.

By saving the pipeline object to a PowerBuilder library, you can reuse it later or incorporate the pipeline into any of your applications.

Using a Pipeline in Your Application

To implement a pipeline in any of your applications, there are several objects that you must create. The first, and most obvious, is the pipeline object created in the Pipeline painter. The other components are a standard class user object of type pipeline and a window containing a DataWindow control. Depending on your approach, runtime pipelines can be very simple, and with a little more effort, a pipeline can be a reusable object that can be utilized by many applications.

The Pipeline User Object

You create the pipeline user object by using the User Object painter and selecting a standard class of type pipeline. For a very simple application, all you need to do is save the user object and continue to create your window and pipeline object. This, of course, would be the easy way out and would force you to create a non–object-oriented solution as well as rework the code if you implement any additional pipelines in the application.

Pipeline Attributes

The pipeline user object has five attributes:

- `DataObject`
- `RowsInError`
- `RowsRead`
- `RowsWritten`
- `Syntax`

The `DataObject` Attribute

The `DataObject` attribute works in much the same way as the DataWindow control attribute of the same name. This attribute specifies the name of the pipeline object created in the Data Pipeline painter that you want to execute in your application. Unlike the DataWindow control attribute, this value may only be set at runtime using dot notation, as in this example:

```
iu_pipeline.DataObject = "pipe_copy_contact"
```

`iu_pipeline` is the instance of the pipeline user object and `pipe_copy_contact` is the name of the pipeline object.

WARNING

Since `DataObject` can only be assigned at runtime, the pipeline object will not get included into your executable. Pipeline objects must, therefore, be distributed using PowerBuilder dynamic libraries (PBDs or DLLs) since they cannot be specified in a PBR either.

The `RowsInError`, `RowsRead`, and `RowsWritten` Attributes

The `RowsInError`, `RowsRead`, and `RowsWritten` attributes are used to provide information about the number and status of the rows that are being processed by the pipeline. These values are typically displayed to the user via your application's pipeline window to indicate the pipeline's current status.

`RowsInError` is a Long that indicates the number of rows the pipeline found in error. For example, if your pipeline processed 100 rows and 7 of them were not accepted due to a duplicate key error, `RowsInError` would have a value of `7`.

`RowsRead`, also a Long, indicates the number of rows that the pipeline has read. In the previous example, `RowsRead` would be `100`.

`RowsWritten`, a Long, specifies the number of rows that have been written to the database (although not necessarily committed). Following the same example, `RowsWritten` would contain a value of `93`.

The `Syntax` Attribute

The `Syntax` attribute is a string that contains the syntax that was used to create the pipeline object. When you create a pipeline object in the Data Pipeline painter, this syntax is generated and assigned for you. Using a series of string manipulation functions (for example, `Mid()`, `Pos()`, and `Len()`), you can allow the user to query information about the pipeline's setup and modify its definition (such as the Commit value and Max Errors specified).

Events

In addition to the two standard events `Constructor` and `Destructor`, there are three events specific to the pipeline user object. They are `PipeStart`, `PipeMeter`, and `PipeEnd`.

The `PipeStart` event is triggered after the pipeline `Start()` or `Repair()` function is called. `PipeMeter` is triggered after a transaction (determined by the value of the Commit option in the Data Pipeline painter) is committed. `PipeEnd` is triggered when the process executed by `Start()` or `Repair()` has terminated.

These events can be used for several reasons. The most common usage of these events is to provide the user with status of the pipeline's processing either in terms of rows processed or time taken.

Methods

The pipeline user object also has several unique methods or functions that apply to it: `Start()`, `Repair()`, and `Cancel()`.The following three sections examine the syntax for each function and then incorporate the functionality into the pipeline user object.

The `Start()` Function

The `Start()` function is used to begin execution of the pipeline object. The syntax is

```
pipeline_user_object.Start(source_trans, dest_trans, dw_error, &
    {arg1, arg2,..., argn})
```

The first three arguments are required and every additional argument is optional, dependent on the data pipeline object's retrieval arguments. The first argument, *source_trans*, is the name of the transaction object that is connected to the database containing the source tables. The second argument, *dest_trans*, identifies the name of the transaction object that is connected to the destination database. The third required argument is the name of the DataWindow control that will contain any rows in error during the pipeline process. PowerBuilder generates a DataWindow object and assigns it to the DataWindow control passed to the `Start()` function. Each additional argument identifies any retrieval arguments that were defined in the data pipeline object's `SELECT` statement.

The `Start()` function returns an integer of one of the following values:

Value	*Meaning*
1	Function executed successfully
-1	Pipeline open failed
-2	Too many columns
-3	Table already exists
-4	Table does not exist
-5	Missing connection
-6	Wrong retrieval arguments
-7	Column mismatch
-8	Fatal SQL error in source
-9	Fatal SQL error in destination

Value	*Meaning*
`-10`	Maximum number of errors exceeded
`-12`	Bad table syntax
`-13`	Key required but not supplied
`-15`	Pipeline already in progress
`-16`	Error in source database
`-17`	Error in destination database
`-18`	Destination database is read-only

The error checking for a call to the `Start()` function will be implemented as another function in the pipeline user object, as detailed in the section "Building the Pipeline User Object."

The `Cancel()` Function

The `Cancel()` function is executed when you need to stop a pipeline already in progress. The syntax for the function is

```
pipeline_user_object.Cancel()
```

The function returns an integer with a value of `1` for success and `-1` for a failure.

The `Repair()` Function

The `Repair()` function is used after your application has executed a pipeline that has had some rows error out. The rows in error will be displayed in the DataWindow control that is passed as an argument to the `Start()` function. The user can correct the problems and reapply the fixes to the database using the `Repair()` function. The syntax for `Repair()` is

```
pipeline_user_object.Repair(dest_trans)
```

The argument *`dest_trans`* passed to this function is the name of the transaction object connected to the destination database. `Repair()` returns the following values:

Value	*Meaning*
`1`	Function executed successfully
`-5`	Missing connection
`-9`	Fatal SQL error in destination
`-10`	Maximum number of errors exceeded
`-11`	Invalid window handle
`-12`	Bad table syntax
`-15`	Pipeline already in progress

Value	Meaning
-17	Error in destination database
-18	Destination database is read-only

The error checking for `Repair()` is combined with the error processing for the `Start()` function in the pipeline user object.

Building a Pipeline in an Application

This section discusses some basic functionality that should be implemented in your pipeline user object so that you can reuse it in multiple applications. In addition to the pipeline user object, you will also use a window with a DataWindow control (required) and several other controls, as shown in Figure 29.9.

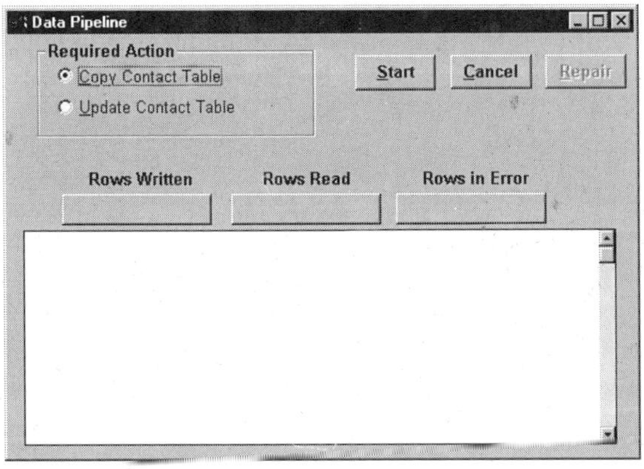

FIGURE 29.9.
The contact pipeline window `w_pipeline`.

The first thing you must do before you execute the pipeline is some initialization. In the window `Open` event, you need to create instances of the transaction objects and user object (defined as window instance variables), connect to the appropriate databases, and initialize several key variables. The script for the window's `Open` event is shown in Listing 29.1.

Listing 29.1. The `Open` event for `w_pipeline`.

```
SetPointer(HourGlass!)
//Instantiate instance variables
iu_pipeline = CREATE u_pipeline
itr_sourcetrans = CREATE u_transaction
itr_desttrans = CREATE u_transaction

//Connect to databases
If wf_connect() <> 0 Then
   Close(this)
End If
```

```
//PostEvent to initialize pipeline user object
this.PostEvent("PostOpen")
```

The window function `wf_connect()` connects your application to the source and destination databases. The code is shown in Listing 29.2.

Listing 29.2. Public function `wf_connect()` in `w_pipeline`.

```
// This script will read all the database values from PB.INI
//   and store them in itr_sourcetrans.

itr_sourcetrans.DBMS        ="ODBC"
itr_sourcetrans.Database    ="Powersoft Demo DB V5"
itr_sourcetrans.DbParm      = &
   "ConnectString='DSN=Powersoft Demo DB V5;UID=dba;PWD=sql'"

Connect Using itr_sourcetrans;

If itr_sourcetrans.SqlCode < 0 then
   MessageBox("Connect error","Could not connect to source db")
   Return -1
End If

// This script will read all the database values from PB.INI
//   and store them in itr_desttrans.

itr_desttrans.DBMS        ="ODBC"
itr_desttrans.Database    ="Pipeline"
itr_desttrans.DbParm      ="ConnectString='DSN=Pipeline;UID=sjah;PWD=sjah'"

Connect Using itr_desttrans;

If itr_desttrans.SqlCode < 0 then
   MessageBox("Connect error","Could not connect to destination db")
   Return -1
End If

Return 0
```

The function takes no arguments and returns an integer. If an error is encountered while connecting, a message box is displayed and `-1` is returned, causing the window to close. If the connection is successful, a custom event (`PostOpen`) is posted to, which initializes the pipeline user object's variables. The script for this is shown in Listing 29.3.

Listing 29.3. `PostOpen` for `w_pipeline`.

```
iu_pipeline.uf_initialize(itr_sourcetrans,itr_desttrans,dw_error)

iu_pipeline.ist_read = st_read
iu_pipeline.ist_written = st_written
iu_pipeline.ist_error = st_error
```

In order to make the pipeline user object as reusable as possible, you define a user object function that initializes all required variables. The instance variables for the pipeline user object are

```
transaction         itr_source, itr_dest
datawindow          idw_error
statictext          ist_rowsread, ist_rowswritten, ist_rowserror
```

After each of these instance variables has been declared, you must create the user object function `uf_Initialize()` to assign values to some of these variables (see Listing 29.4).

Listing 29.4. Public subroutine `uf_Initialize` for `u_pipeline`.

```
//Initialize the instance variables used in the pipeline
itr_sourcetrans = arg_sourcetrans
itr_desttrans = arg_desttrans
idw_error = arg_dwerror
```

The static text instance variables are not required to perform the basic pipeline processing and therefore are not included in the initialization function, but are assigned in the `PostOpen`.

Once all setup has been completed, the window is displayed to the user. The window contains two radio buttons that allow the user to specify what action to perform (in this example, the user can copy or update the contact table). In the `Clicked` events of the two radio buttons, the `DataObject` attribute of `iu_pipeline` is assigned to one of the data pipeline objects. Here's an example:

```
iu_pipeline.DataObject = "pipe_copy_contact"
```

The user can then click the Start button to begin the pipeline processing. The `Clicked` event for the Start button is shown in Listing 29.5.

Listing 29.5. The `Clicked` event for `cb_start` on `w_pipeline`.

```
Integer li_rtn

li_rtn = iu_pipeline.uf_Start()

//Check the value of the return code from Start()
If li_rtn <> 1 Then
   iu_pipeline.uf_error(li_rtn)
   cb_Repair.Enabled = TRUE
End If
```

The user object function `uf_Start()` starts the pipeline processing using the code shown in Listing 29.6.

Listing 29.6. Public function `uf_Start()` for `u_pipeline`.

```
//Execute the pipeline and return the value
Return this.Start(itr_sourcetrans, itr_desttrans, idw_error)
```

The function returns an integer that can be used to perform some standard error processing, which has been incorporated into the pipeline user object subroutine `uf_error()`. The repair command button, `cb_Repair`, is enabled so that the errors can be fixed. The function `uf_error()` is defined as shown in Listing 29.7.

Listing 29.7. Public function `uf_error()` for `u_pipeline`.

```
string ls_msg

Choose Case a_rtn_code
   Case -1
      ls_msg = "Pipe open failed"
   Case -2
      ls_msg = "Too many columns"
   Case -3
      ls_msg = "Table already exists"
   Case -4
      ls_msg = "Table does not exist"
   Case -5
      ls_msg = "Missing connection"
   Case -6
      ls_msg = "Wrong arguments"
   Case -7
      ls_msg = "Column mismatch"
   Case -8
      ls_msg = "Fatal SQL error in source"
   Case -9
      ls_msg = "Fatal SQL error in destination"
   Case -10
      ls_msg = "Maximum number of errors exceeded"
   Case -12
      ls_msg = "Bad table syntax"
   Case -13
      ls_msg = "Key required but not supplied"
   Case -15
      ls_msg = "Pipe already in progress"
   Case -16
      ls_msg = "Error in source database"
   Case -17
      ls_msg = "Error in destination database"
   Case -18
      ls_msg = "Destination database is read-only"
End Choose

If a_rtn_code <> 1 Then
   MessageBox("Pipeline Error", ls_msg, StopSign!, Ok!)
Else
   MessageBox("Pipeline Successful", "Operation completed")
End If
```

The subroutine takes one argument: the return value from `uf_Start()`.

If the user decides to cancel the pipeline processing at any time, he only needs to click the cancel command button, which executes the code shown in Listing 29.8.

Listing 29.8. The `Clicked` event for `cb_cancel` on `w_pipeline`.

```
If iu_pipeline.uf_cancel() < 0 Then
   MessageBox("Cancel","Cancel Failed")
End If
```

The function `uf_Cancel()` (shown in Listing 29.9) is declared in the user object and returns an integer indicating the function's success or failure.

Listing 29.9. Public function `uf_Cancel()` for `u_pipeline`.

```
Return this.Cancel()
```

In the `PipeMeter` event of the pipeline user object, use the code shown in Listing 29.10 to display status information to the user every time a transaction is committed to the database.

Listing 29.10. The `PipeMeter` event for `u_pipeline`.

```
ist_error.text = String(this.RowsInError)
ist_read.text = String(this.RowsRead)
ist_written.text = String(this.RowsWritten)
```

Finally, if there are any errors encountered during the pipeline execution, they will be displayed in the DataWindow control `dw_error`. The user can make changes to the data in error and then click on the Repair button, which contains the code shown in Listing 29.11.

Listing 29.11. The `Clicked` event for `cb_repair` on `w_pipeline`.

```
integer li_rtn

li_rtn = iu_pipeline.uf_Repair()

//Check the value of the return code from Repair()
If li_rtn <> 1 Then
   iu_pipeline.uf_error(li_rtn)
End If
```

The subroutine `uf_Repair()` is defined as shown in Listing 29.12.

Listing 29.12. Public function `uf_Repair()` for `u_pipeline`.

```
Return this.Repair(itr_desttrans)
```

Notice that the same error processing (`uf_Error`) is used for `uf_Repair()` as for `uf_Start()`.

This makes up the majority of the application. The only other processing that needs to be built into the window is one additional function. The function performs the disconnect from the databases and destroys the transaction objects and user object. This is implemented in `wf_Disconnect()`, which is called from the window's `CloseQuery` event.

Listing 29.13. Public function `wf_Disconnect()` for `w_pipeline`.

```
Disconnect Using itr_desttrans;

If itr_desttrans.SQLCode <> 0 Then
   MessageBox("Database Error","Could not disconnect from the destination")
   Return -1
End If

Disconnect Using itr_sourcetrans;

If itr_sourcetrans.SQLCode <> 0 Then
   MessageBox("Database Error","Could not disconnect from the source")
   Return -1
End If

//Destroy instance variables
Destroy itr_desttrans
Destroy itr_sourcetrans
Destroy iu_pipeline
Return 0
```

The `CloseQuery` event has the code shown in Listing 29.14.

Listing 29.14. The `CloseQuery` event for `w_pipeline`.

```
If wf_Disconnect() = -1 Then
   Message.ReturnValue = 1
End If
```

This processing lays the majority of the foundation for creating a reusable pipeline object. In addition to the processing found here, there is some functionality that can be incorporated into your user object if deemed necessary. This includes creating a series of user object functions that use string functions to manipulate the `Syntax` attribute of the pipeline user object. Information can be displayed to the user for any of the data pipeline object's definition (for example, the current value for `MaxErrors`).

Summary

As you have seen in this chapter, the data pipeline can be an extremely useful tool for a developer and for an end user. Using a data pipeline allows you to move data and data structures across databases with a minimal amount of work. The pipeline is useful at any time to the developer using PowerBuilder for working with relational database. The pipeline can also be implemented into an application using a pipeline user object. This allows for easy reuse of a pipeline in multiple applications.

Mail Enabling PowerBuilder Applications

30

IN THIS CHAPTER

The point of the client/server paradigm is to make data more available and accessible for end users. Mail enabling your application gives users the ability to communicate the results of their work to others. A number of reasons exist for mail enabling your application, however; sharing data is just one. One of these reasons is the ability to create a standard error-message window so that when errors occur they are directly relayed to a development coordinator. This is an attempt to ensure that problems are collated and can be acted on properly, because you cannot always rely on an end user to give a correct or accurate account of an application or a system error.

The Microsoft Messaging Application Program Interface

Microsoft defined a standard *messaging application program interface* (MAPI) in the early '90s in collaboration with a number of application and messaging service vendors and included it in the Windows API set. Before MAPI was available, developers had to write source code for each proprietary mail system's API. MAPI now provides a layer between the client application and the messaging service, enabling total independence. Messaging services are connected by service provider drivers to a subsystem using the MAPI service provider interface.

PowerBuilder provides an interface to MAPI through a number of functions, structures, and enumerated data types. None of the PowerBuilder-provided mail functions work on the Macintosh platform. The code listings introduced in this chapter were coded and tested against Microsoft Mail, but should work with other mail systems that support MAPI without any changes.

Other common messaging APIs are VIM and CMC. VIM stands for *vendor independent messaging* and was developed by Apple, Borland, Lotus, and Novell to provide a common set of functions across multiple platforms. Currently the VIM API only talks to cc:Mail and is not directly supported by PowerBuilder. To carry out mail operations using VIM you will need to use external function calls to the appropriate VIM DLLs.

All PowerBuilder interaction with the mail system is done through a single object, `mailSession`.

The `mailSession` Object

The `mailSession` object is the main mail object and consists of only two attributes: `SessionID` and `MessageID[]`. `SessionID` is a protected Long data type used for holding the handle of the mail session used in calls to external functions; `MessageID[]` is an array of strings. This array is used to hold message identities, which are used in arguments to mail functions. Before making any calls to mail functions, however, the `mailSession` object must be declared, created, and then connected using the `mailLogon()` function.

The mailLogon() Function

The `mailLogon()` function makes the connection between the PowerBuilder application and the mail system, by either creating a new session or making use of an already existing session. The syntax is

```
mailSession.mailLogon( { UserId, Password} {, LogonOption})
```

UserId and *Password* are the user's ID and password for the mail system. *LogonOption* is an enumerated value of the `mailLogonOption` data type (see Table 30.1) and specifies whether a new session should be started and whether new messages should be downloaded on connection. These three parameters are all optional, but if a user ID is specified, the password must also be included.

Table 30.1. `mailLogonOption` enumerated data types.

Enumerated Data Type	*Description*
`mailNewSession!`	Starts a new mail session, regardless of any current connections.
`mailDownLoad!`	Starts a new mail session only if the mail application is not already running and forces the download of any new messages from the server to the user's in box.
`mailNewSessionWithDownLoad!`	Starts a new mail session and forces the download of any new messages from the server to the user's in box.

The default action of `mailLogon()` is to use an existing session and not to force new messages to be downloaded.

`MailLogon()` returns a value of the `mailReturnCode` enumerated data type. For this function, it can be any of the following: `mailReturnSuccess!`, `mailReturnLoginFailure!`, `mailReturnInsufficientMemory!`, `mailReturnTooManySessions!`, or `mailReturnUserAbort!`. `mailReturnCode` has a number of other values that are used by other mail functions.

To display the error code after failing an error check, it is useful to have a function that converts `mailReturnCodes` to a string message that can be shown to the user. This function is detailed later in this chapter.

If a new session is not started, the PowerBuilder mail session makes use of the existing session and does not require the user ID and password. If a new session needs to be established, however, the mail system's login dialog box will open if the user ID and password are not supplied.

In the following example, a series of `mailLogon()` calls are made. Note that this is simply to illustrate the various manners of calling and that code would not look like this:

```
mailSession PBmailSession
PBmailSession = CREATE mailSession
//
// Try to connect to an existing session, o/w create a new one
PBmailSession.mailLogon()
//
// Create a new session - do NOT download new mail
PBmailSession.mailLogon( mailNewSession!)
//
// Create a new session and download new mail
PBmailSession.mailLogon( "sng", "secret6", mailNewSessionWithDownLoad!)
```

The `mailLogoff()` Function

The `mailLogoff()` function breaks the connection between the PowerBuilder application and the mail system. The syntax is

```
mailSession.mailLogoff()
```

If the mail application was running before PowerBuilder began its mail session, the mail system is left in the state in which it was found.

`mailLogoff()` also returns a value of the `mailReturnCode` enumerated data type, which for this function can be one of the following: `mailReturnSuccess!`, `mailReturnLoginFailure!`, or `mailReturnInsufficientMemory!`.

When you have finished with the mail session and have closed it, you need to release the memory being used by the `mailSession` object. For example, to close the mail session started by the previous examples, the code is

```
PBmailSession.mailLogOff()
DESTROY PBmailSession
```

The `mailHandle()` Function

Although PowerBuilder provides a basic set of functions you can use with the mail system, you might need to make calls to external functions that carry out a certain functionality that is not provided. As with some other API function calls, you need to pass a handle to the object on which you want to act. The `mailHandle()` function provides the handle of the mail object. The syntax is

```
mailsession.mailHandle()
```

The handle returned is of type `unsigned long`.

The mailAddress() Function

The `mailAddress()` function is used to check the validity of the recipients of a mail message. If there is an invalid entry in the `mailRecipient` array of the `mailMessage` object, `mailAddress()` opens the Address Book dialog box, shown in Figure 30.1, so the user can fix the problem address.

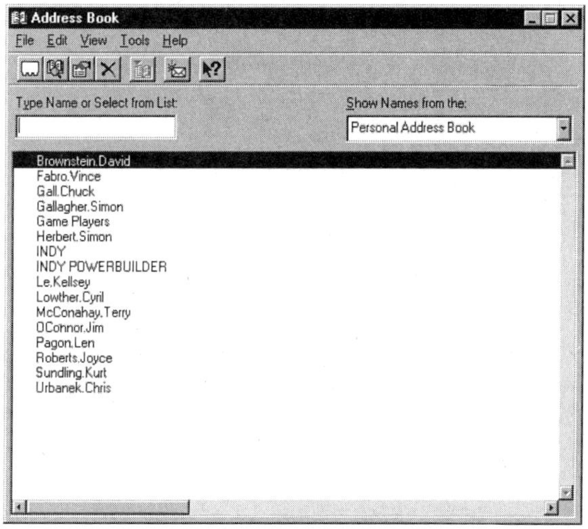

FIGURE 30.1.
The Address Book dialog box.

The `mailRecipient` array for the mail message is then updated. The syntax is

```
mailSession.mailAddress( { MailMessage})
```

If no *`MailMessage`* is specified, the Address Book dialog box is opened for the user to look for addresses and maintain his or her personal address lists. When this happens, the dialog box does not return addresses for use in addressing a message.

NOTE

The `mailRecipient` array contains information about recipients of a mail message or the originator of a message. The originator field is not used when you send a message.

`mailAddress()` returns a value of the `mailReturnCode` enumerated data type and takes one of the following values: `mailReturnSuccess!`, `mailReturnFailure!`, `mailReturnInsufficientMemory!`, or `mailReturnUserAbort!`.

To check that the address is valid for a previously constructed mail message, the code would be

```
If PBmailSession.mailAddress( PBmailMessage) <> mailReturnSuccess! Then
   MessageBox( "Sending Mail", "The addressing for this Message failed.")
   Return
End If
```

The `mailResolveRecipient()` Function

To enable the entry of partial names as addresses, the `mailResolveRecipient()` function is used to validate them and to retrieve the full address. The syntax is

```
mailSession.mailResolveRecipient( Recipient {, AllowUpdates})
```

The *`Recipient`* parameter is either a string variable or a `mailRecipient` structure. `mailResolveRecipient()` sets the string or the structure to the resolved address information. A string address variable is sufficient for users in a local mail system, but if the mail is to be sent through mail gateways, the full address details should be obtained in a `mailRecipient` structure. The *`AllowUpdates`* Boolean indicates whether the mail system updates the address list with the recipient's name; the default is `FALSE`. If the user doesn't have update privileges, *`AllowUpdates`* is ignored.

`MailResolveRecipient()` returns a value of the `mailReturnCode` enumerated data type and takes one of the following values: `mailReturnSuccess!`, `mailReturnFailure!`, `mailReturnInsufficientMemory!`, or `mailReturnUserAbort!`. If the name is not found, the function returns `mailReturnFailure!`.

If the partial address matches multiple addresses, the mail system opens a dialog box to enable the user to select the correct name. This is system dependent, however. See Figure 30.2 for the MS Mail dialog box.

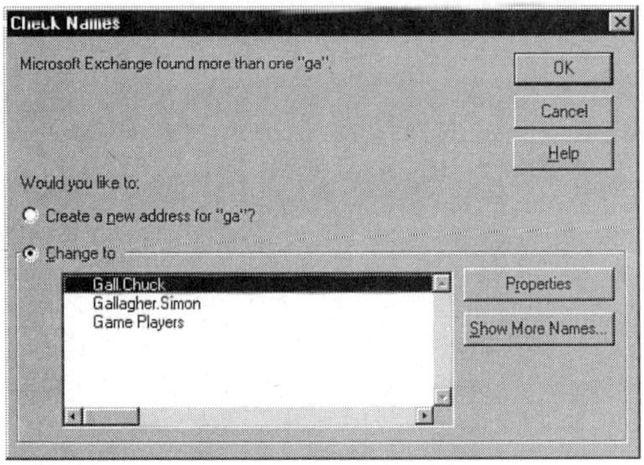

FIGURE 30.2.
The MS Mail dialog box to resolve a mail address.

In the following example, the single-line edit `sle_address` contains either a full or a partial recipient name. The value is assigned to a `mailRecipient` structure, and the function `mailResolveRecipient()` is called to find the address details. The resolved address is then placed back into the edit field:

```
mailRecipient PBmailRecipient

PBmailRecipient.Name = sle_address.Text

If PBmailSession.mailResolveRecipient( PBmailRecipient) <> mailReturnSuccess! Then
   MessageBox( "Address Resolution", sle_address.Text + " not found.")
Else
   sle_address.Text = PBmailRecipient.Name
End If
```

The `mailRecipientDetails()` Function

To display a dialog box with the specified recipient's address information, use the `mailRecipientDetails()` function (see Figure 30.3).

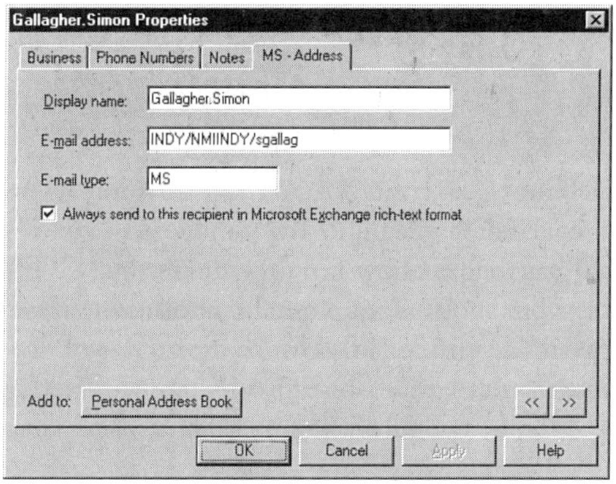

FIGURE 30.3.
The recipient information dialog box.

The syntax is

```
mailSession.mailRecipientDetails( MailRecipient {, AllowUpdates})
```

The *`MailRecipient`* structure contains a valid address recipient identifier returned by `mailAddress()`, `mailResolveRecipient()`, or `mailReadMessage()`. The *`AllowUpdates`* Boolean indicates whether the recipient's name can be modified, but only if the user has update privileges for the mail system.

`MailRecipientDetails()` returns a value of the `mailReturnCode` enumerated data type and takes one of the following values: `mailReturnSuccess!`, `mailReturnFailure!`, `mailReturnInsufficientMemory!`, `mailUnknownReturnRecipient!`, or `mailReturnUserAbort!`.

The following example builds on the example started in the `mailResolveRecipient()` function description. On a successful resolution it displays the address details by calling `mailRecipientDetails()`:

```
mailRecipient PBmailRecipient

PBmailRecipient.Name = sle_address.Text

If PBmailSession.mailResolveRecipient( PBmailRecipient)  <> mailReturnSuccess! Then
   MessageBox ("Address Resolution", sle_address.Text + " not found.")
Else
   PBmailSession.mailRecipientDetails( PBmailRecipient)
End If
```

The `mailGetMessages()` Function

You use the `mailGetMessages()` function to populate the `messageID` array of the `mailSession` object with the message IDs found in the user's in box. The syntax is

```
mailSession.mailGetMessages( { MessageType,} { UnreadOnly })
```

`MessageType` is a string that identifies the type of a message. The default type is InterPersonal Messages (IPM); use `"IPM"` or the empty string (`""`). Mail system interprocess messages can be accessed using `"IPC"`, as can other message types defined by the mail administrator. The *`UnreadOnly`* parameter is a Boolean that indicates whether only the IDs of unread messages (`TRUE`) or all messages (`FALSE`) are to be returned.

`mailGetMessages()` returns a value of the `mailReturnCode` enumerated data type and takes one of the following values: `mailReturnSuccess!`, `mailReturnFailure!`, `mailReturnInsufficientMemory!`, `mailReturnNoMessages!`, or `mailReturnUserAbort!`.

The message IDs that are returned are used as arguments to other mail functions to indicate which message should be acted on.

To retrieve the actual contents of a message specified by the ID held in the message ID array of a session object, the `mailReadMessage()` function is used. The syntax is

```
mailSession.mailReadMessage( MessageID, MailMessage, ReadOption, Mark)
```

The *`MailMessage`* parameter is a variable declared of type `mailMessage`. `mailMessage` is a MAPI structure that holds the fields listed in Table 30.2.

Table 30.2. Attributes of the `mailMessage` MAPI structure.

Attribute	*Data Type*
`ReceiptRequested`	Boolean
`MessageSent`	Boolean
`Unread`	Boolean

Attribute	*Data Type*
`Subject`	String
`NoteText`	String
`MessageType`	String
`DateReceived`	String
`ConversationID`	String
`Recipient[]`	`mailRecipient` array
`AttachmentFile[]`	`mailFileDescription` array

The fields of this structure are populated depending on the *`ReadOption`* parameter. This parameter uses the `mailReadOption` enumerated data type to control which parts of the message are retrieved, and can take the values in Table 30.3.

Table 30.3. Valid values for the `ReadOption` parameter.

Enumerated Data Type	*Description*
`mailEntireMessage!`	Obtain header, text, and attachments.
`mailEnvelopeOnly!`	Obtain header information only.
`mailBodyAsFile!`	Obtain header, text, and attachments. Treat the message text as the first attachment, and store it in a temporary file.
`mailSuppressAttach!`	Obtain only the header and text.

The *`Mark`* parameter is a Boolean that indicates whether the message should be marked as read (`TRUE`) in the user's in box, or unmarked (`FALSE`).

`mailReadMessage()` returns a value of the `mailReturnCode` enumerated data type and takes one of the following values: `mailReturnSuccess!`, `mailReturnFailure!`, or `mailReturnInsufficientMemory!`.

Attachment information is stored in the `AttachmentFile` attribute of the `mailMessage` object. The `AttachmentFile` attribute is itself an object of type `mailFileDescription`, which is structured as follows:

Attribute	*Data Type*
`FileName`	String
`PathName`	String
`FileType`	`mailFileType`
`Position`	Unsigned Long

The `PathName` attribute holds the location of the temporary file created for the attachment. This file is created in the directory specified by the environment variable `TEMP`.

The `FileType` attribute is of the `mailFileType` enumerated type. The values for this enumerated type are `mailAttach!`, `mailOLE!`, and `mailOLEStatic!`.

If the `Position` attribute is `1`, the attachment is placed at the beginning of the note, prefixed and suffixed by spaces. If the value of `Position` is greater than `1` or equal to `0`, the attachment replaces the character at that position in the note.

Recipient information is stored in the `Recipient` attribute of the `mailMessage` object. The structure is used to identify both senders and receivers. The `Recipient` attribute is itself an object of type `mailRecipient`, which is structured as follows:

Attribute	*Data Type*
`Name`	String
`Address`	String
`RecipientType`	`mailRecipientType`
`EntryID`	Protected Blob

The `RecipientType` attribute is of the `mailRecipientType` enumerated type. The values for this enumerated type are `mailTo!`, `mailCC!`, `mailOriginator!`, and `mailBCC!`. The suffixes stand for the following:

- `To`—The recipient of the message
- `CC`—The addressees receive carbon copies of the message
- `Originator`—The message sender (only used with received messages)
- `BCC` (blind carbon copy) These recipients are not shown to `To` and `CC` recipients

An example using the two functions introduced so far, `mailGetMessages()` and `mailReadMessage()`, populates a DataWindow with a list of all message headers currently in the user's in box:

```
mailSession PBmailSession
mailMessage PBmailMessage
Integer nCount, nTotalMsgs
Long lRow

PBmailSession = CREATE mailSession
If PBmailSession.mailLogon() <> mailReturnSuccess! Then
   Return
End If
PBmailSession.mailGetMessages()

nTotalMsgs = UpperBound( PBmailSession.MessageID[])
For nCount = 1 To nTotalMsgs
   PBmailSession.mailReadMessage( PBmailSession.MessageID[ nCount], &
```

```
PBmailMessage, mailEnvelopeOnly!, FALSE)
   lRow = dw_1.InsertRow( 0)
   dw_1.SetItem( lRow, "message_id", PBmailSession.MessageID[ nCount])
   dw_1.SetItem( lRow, "message_date", PBmailMessage.DateReceived)
   dw_1.SetItem( lRow, "message_subject", Left( PBmailMessage.Subject, 40))
Next
```

The `mailDeleteMessage()` Function

To delete a mail message from a user's in box, use the `mailDeleteMessage()` function. The syntax is

```
mailSession.mailDeleteMessage( MessageID)
```

`MessageID` is the string value ID of the message that has been previously retrieved with a call to `mailGetMessages()`.

`MailDeleteMessage()` returns a value of the `mailReturnCode` enumerated data type and takes one of the following values: `mailReturnSuccess!`, `mailReturnFailure!`, `mailReturnInsufficientMemory!`, `mailReturnInvalidMessage!`, or `mailReturnUserAbort!`.

The `mailSaveMessage()` Function

If you need to save a new message or replace an existing message in the user's in box, use the `mailSaveMessage()` function. The syntax is

```
mailSession.mailSaveMessage( MessageID, MailMessage)
```

`MessageID` is the string ID of the message to be replaced, or an empty string (`""`) if the message is to be a new one. `MailMessage` is a variable of the `mailMessage` type that has had its structure filled with the information to be saved. The message must be correctly addressed, even if it is replacing an existing message.

`MailSaveMessage()` returns a value of the `mailReturnCode` enumerated data type and takes one of the following values: `mailReturnSuccess!`, `mailReturnFailure!`, `mailReturnInsufficientMemory!`, `mailReturnInvalidMessage!`, `mailReturnUserAbort!`, or `mailReturnDiskFull!`.

In the following example a new message is being created and addressed. This message will be sent the next time the mail system checks for messages to send:

```
mailSession PBmailSession
mailRecipient PBmailRecipient
mailMessage PBmailMessage

PBmailSession = CREATE mailSession
If PBmailSession.mailLogon() <> mailReturnSuccess! Then
   // Error Handling - unable to startup
   Return
End If
```

```
PBmailRecipient.Name = "Gallagher, Simon"

If PBmailSession.mailResolveRecipient( PBmailRecipient) <> mailReturnSuccess! Then
   MessageBox( "Save New Message", "Invalid address.")
   Return
End If

PBmailMessage.NoteText = mle_note.Text
PBmailMessage.Subject = sle_subject.Text
PBmailMessage.Recipient[ 1] = PBmailRecipient

If PBmailSession.mailSaveMessage( "", PBmailMessage) <> mailReturnSuccess! Then
   MessageBox( "New Message", "The Save Failed.")
   Return
End If
```

The `mailSend()` Function

To send a previously created message or to open the mail system message entry dialog box, use the `mailSend()` function. The syntax is

```
mailSession.mailSend( { MailMessage})
```

If no message information is supplied, the mail system opens a dialog box so you can enter the information before sending the message.

`mailSend()` returns a value of the `mailReturnCode` enumerated data type, and takes one of the following values: `mailReturnSuccess!`, `mailReturnFailure!`, `mailReturnInsufficientMemory!`, `mailReturnLogFailure!`, `mailReturnUserAbort!`, `mailReturnDiskFull!`, `mailReturnTooManySessions!`, `mailReturnTooManyFiles!`, `mailReturnTooManyRecipients!`, `mailReturnUnknownRecipient!`, or `mailReturnAttachmentNotFound!`.

Mail Enabling a System Error Window

As mentioned at the start of this chapter, one use of mail enabling is the communication of application and system errors to a development team coordinator. In this section you will learn how to build the script that can be used as part of this process.

Listing 30.1 contains a very useful function that converts a mail return code, returned by all the mail functions, into a string that can then be used in a message box. This can be written either as a global function or as a method for a class user object based on `MailSession`.

Listing 30.1. The `MailErrorToString()` function.

```
// Parameters:
//           a_mailReturnCode     (mailReturnCode)
// Returns:
//           string               (the string representation)
```

```
Choose Case a_MailReturnCode
   Case mailReturnAccessDenied!
      Return "Access Denied"
   Case mailReturnAttachmentNotFound!
      Return "Attachment Not Found"
   Case mailReturnAttachmentOpenFailure!
      Return "Attachment Open Failure"
   Case mailReturnAttachmentWriteFailure!
      Return "Attachment Write Failure"
   Case mailReturnDiskFull!
      Return "Disk Full"
   Case mailReturnFailure!
      Return "Failure"
   Case mailReturnInsufficientMemory!
      Return "Insufficient Memory"
   Case mailReturnInvalidMessage!
      Return "Invalid Message"
   Case mailReturnLoginFailure!
      Return "Login Failure"
   Case mailReturnMessageInUse!
      Return "Message In Use"
   Case mailReturnNoMessages!
      Return "No Messages"
   Case mailReturnSuccess!
      Return "Success"
   Case mailReturnTextTooLarge!
      Return "Text Too Large"
   Case mailReturnTooManyFiles!
      Return "Too Many Files"
   Case mailReturnTooManyRecipients!
      Return "Too Many Recipients"
   Case mailReturnTooManySessions!
      Return "Too Many Sessions"
   Case mailReturnUnknownRecipient!
      Return "Unknown Recipient"
   Case mailReturnUserAbort!
      Return "User Abort"
   Case Else
      Return "Other - Unknown"
End Choose
```

In the framework I use for my applications, I include a global object, `g_App`, that is a holder for application-related objects. One of these objects is information about the application INI file. (I use one INI file for all of my applications because it makes it easy to collect related information into one area.) One of the entries specifies whether the user's address book should be opened, `szPhoneBook`, or whether there is a recipient address hard coded, `szRecipient`. A number of single- and multiline edit fields are populated with error information in the `Open` event script. A window function `wf_Notify()`, or if you are using the `Error` class user object you built in Chapter 23, "The User Object Painter," the `MailError()` function, is then called to check whether mail notification should be carried out, the condition being an empty mail recipient entry in the INI file. The function is shown in Chapter 23 and as you can see, most of the mail functions and a few of the structures and objects are used. The only thing worthy of note is that new lines can be embedded into the note field using the escape character (`~n`).

Mailing a DataWindow Object

A neat little feature to add to your application is the capability to e-mail a report or DataWindow to someone else. This is, in fact, quite straightforward and makes use of the `SaveAs()` DataWindow function.

The first step is to save the DataWindow in a Powersoft Report (PSR) file format using the `SaveAs()` function with the `PSReport!` enumerated type, as follows:

```
dw_1.SaveAs( "datadump.psr", PSReport!, FALSE)
```

This saves a description of the DataWindow and the currently retrieved data into a file in the first directory in the path list. The third parameter (include column headings) can be `TRUE` or `FALSE`—it makes no difference to the PSR format.

When you have created the mail session and logged on, the following code is issued:

```
mailFileDescription PBmailAttachment

PBmailAttachment.FileType = mailAttach!
PBmailAttachment.PathName = "datadump.psr"
PBmailAttachment.FileName = "datadump.psr"
PBmailAttachment.Position = -1

PBmailMessage.AttachmentFile[ 1] = PBmailAttachment
```

A variable of type `mailFileDescription` is created to hold the attachment file information. The type of file to be attached is normal (`mailAttach!`), and the filename used in the `SaveAs()` is assigned to the `PathName` and `FileName` attributes. The attachment is in the first position (I found that only `-1` actually worked successfully). The file description is then assigned to the first element of the `AttachmentFile` array, after which the message is ready for transmittal.

The only step left is to tidy up the temporary file used. This needs to be done on any error conditions as well as at the end of the script:

```
FileDelete( "datadump.psr")
```

When the recipient of the message opens it (providing he has set up the association in File Manager), he can simply double-click the attachment and have PowerBuilder or InfoMaker launch the Report painter and display the DataWindow pretty much as it was saved.

NOTE

You can easily add multiple attachments to a message by populating the `PBmailAttachment` structure with the next file's details and then assigning it to the next position in the `AttachmentFile[]` array.

Using the VIM API with PowerBuilder

Of course not everyone is using Microsoft's MS Mail or a MAPI-supported mail system. The most popular alternative to MS Mail is Lotus's cc:Mail, which uses the vendor-independent messaging (VIM) interface. This of course means that you cannot utilize the functions introduced in the first part of this chapter.

Required Components

There are three files that you need in order to communicate with cc:Mail. These are VIM.DLL, VIMVBWRP.DLL, and PBVIM.DLL. The first two are supplied by Lotus, VIM.DLL comes with cc:Mail, and VIMVBWRP.DLL comes with the Lotus Developer's Toolkit. PBVIM.DLL is supplied by Powersoft for developing against Lotus Notes. Both the cc:Mail files and these three DLLs should exist in the user's path.

The Code

The PowerBuilder Library for Lotus Notes consists of the following components:

- The PowerBuilder Library Application for Lotus Notes (PLAN)
- PowerBuilder Notes API libraries and a sample application
- PowerBuilder VIM API libraries and a sample application
- A sample database (DISCUSSN.NSF)

The pb_notes_vim application provides an excellent source from which to copy the function declarations. There are a number of complex structures used in many of the function calls, and to prevent a catastrophic runtime failure, you are well advised to include vimstrct.pbl in your application path. This library has all the structures predefined for you by Powersoft. Another useful library to include is vim_func.pbl, which provides you with PowerBuilder functions that access the external functions and hide some of what you need to know about the VIM API.

The code examples in the following section all make use of the functions and structures found in these two libraries.

Initialization

As with MAPI, the first step in sending a mail message requires you to initialize and open a mail session. Two functions are used for this purpose: `f_VIM_Initialize()` and `f_VIM_Open_Session()`. The following code shows how these functions should be used:

```
String szPathSpec, szName, szPassword
Ulong ulCharSet
```

```
f_VIM_Initialize()    // This calls the external function VIMInitialize

// Set the default value
ulCharSet = 16        // This is the valid code for MS-Windows

// The path should be set to the home directory of the user sending the message(s)
szPathSpec = "C:\CCMAIL\CCHOME"
szName = "sgallag"
szPassword = "password"

// The version of the cc:Mail VIM is 100
f_VIM_Open_Session( szPathSpec, szName, szPassword, 100, ulCharSet, i_ulSession)
```

The `ulSession` variable should be declared as an instance variable because it is used in other function calls and is the handle to the current cc:Mail session.

Sending a Message

The following code creates a mail message with one recipient, a short text message, and an attachment:

```
ULong ulClass, ulMessage
String szTemp, szType
// Message structure - defined in vimstrct.pbl
s_vb_vim_buff_file_desc sBufferFile, sBufferFile2
// Recipients structure - defined in vimstrct.pbl
s_vim_recipient sRecipient
s_buff_f

// Create the message and get a message handle
If Not f_VIM_Create_Message( i_ulSession, "VIM_MAIL", ulMessage) Then
Return
End If

// Add recipient to the message
ulClass = 97   // TO recipient

// Set recipient name
sRecipient.DName.SType = 55    // Native File System
sRecipient.SType = 101         // Unknown recipient type
SetNull( sRecipient.DName.AddressBook[1])
sRecipient.DName.Value = "kpenner"

// Set recipient address
sRecipient.Address.SType = 55
SetNull( sRecipient.Address.Value[1])

If Not f_VIM_Set_Message_Recipient( ulMessage, ulClass, sRecipient, &
                                    i_ulSession) Then
   Goto CloseMessage
End If

// Set subject - 91 for subject
szTemp = "This is the subject line"
If Not f_VIM_Set_Message_Header( ulMessage, 91, Len( szTemp), szTemp, &
                                 i_ulSession) Then
```

```
   Goto CloseMessage
End If

// Set the message body
szTemp = "This is the message body text"
sBufferFile.Size = Len( szTemp)
sBufferFile.Buffer = Left( szTemp, sBufferFile.Size) + Char(0)
sBufferFile.FileName[1] = Char(0)
sBufferFile.Offset = 0
szType = "VIM_TEXT"

// Part = 62 and No. Flags = 0
If Not f_VIM_Set_Message_Item_Note_Part( ulMessage, 62, szType,0,"Text Item", &
                                         sBufferFile, i_ulSession) Then
   Goto CloseMessage
End If

// Setup attachment
sBufferFile2.FileName = "c:\temp.psr"
sBufferFile2.Size = 0
szType = ""

// VIMSEL_ATTACH = 6 & VIMSEL_NATIVE = 55
If Not f_VIM_Set_Message_Item_File_Attachment( ulMessage, 6, szType, &
                                               sBufferFile2, i_ulSession) Then
   Goto CloseMessage
End If

// Send the message
If f_VIM_Send_Message( ulMessage, 0, 0, 2, i_ulSession) Then
   Return
End If

CloseMessage:
   f_VIM_Close_Message( ulMessage, i_ulSession)
```

You can easily add more recipients by populating the same structure and calling the `f_VIM_Set_Message_Recipient()` function each time.

If you compare this code to the MAPI example, you see that the basic steps are the same. You just have to jump through a few more hoops with VIM and need to be aware of the various codes, function names, and structures that you need to use.

Closing the Connection

Once you have opened a connection, you can send as many messages as you want using code similar to that just introduced. Like with MAPI, once you have finished with the connection, you should close it down and recover any resources in use. This is easily achieved by calling two functions:

```
f_VIM_Close_Session( i_ulSession)
f_VIM_Terminate()
```

Further Reading

This has only been a simple introduction and rapid overview of how to use VIM within your PowerBuilder applications. For further information, you should explore PowerBuilder Library for Lotus Notes Reference and Lotus VIM Developer's Toolkit Release 2.2.

Summary

The MAPI functions, structures, and enumerated data types available from within PowerBuilder enable you to create mail-enabled applications to better serve the end user. They can also be used to aid in the process of application deployment, tuning, and debugging by use of a mail-enabled error window. As you saw with the VIM example, PowerBuilder does not tie your development to just MAPI but allows you access to other messaging providers through external functions.

Drag and Drop

31

IN THIS CHAPTER

Drag and drop is a useful technique for moving, copying, and linking objects in your application. This chapter defines the components of drag and drop, guidelines for using drag and drop, and how to implement drag and drop in your PowerBuilder applications.

Defining Drag and Drop

Drag and drop is a method used to perform operations on an object by clicking on the object and holding the mouse button down while moving the mouse. This process is referred to as *dragging*. The object is then moved to a specified object and the mouse is released, which is referred to as *dropping* the object. Drag and drop is therefore a method of directly manipulating an object and its data via a mouse.

The most familiar example of drag and drop is the operating system's file management tool. In this case, we will take a look at the Windows Explorer in Windows 95. The Explorer allows you to click on a file or directory and drag it to a new location. The default behavior is to move the file/directory to the new directory location (see Figure 31.1).

FIGURE 31.1.
The Windows Explorer.

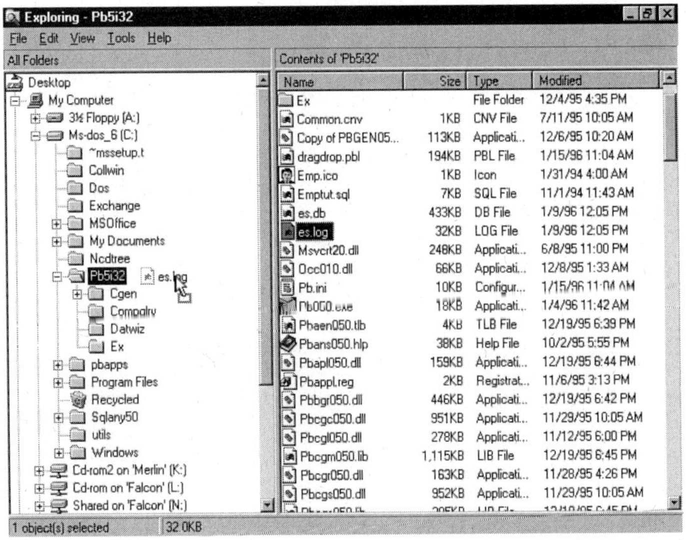

As you can see, the destination object (in this case, the directory) defines the action that will take place. This technique can be implemented in a number of different places in your application, such as copying information between DataWindows and providing a color palette for changing object colors.

Before looking at how to implement drag and drop, let's define all the components that make up drag and drop.

Drag and Drop Terminology

Drag and drop has two main components: the dragged object and the target object. The dragged object is the object on which you want to perform an action. The target object is the object on which the dragged object is dropped and defines what processing will occur. When an object that can be dragged has been clicked and the mouse button is held, you are said to be in *drag mode.*

Just about any PowerBuilder control can be used as the dragged or target objects. The only criteria is that they must be inherited from the system class `DragObject`. To determine if a control is derived from the `DragObject` class, use the Script or Library painter to open the Object Browser. From within the Object Browser, click on the System tab page. Right-click on one of the entries and make sure the Show Hierarchy option is selected. The entry for `DragObject` can be found under the `PowerObject\GraphicObject\WindowObject` hierarchy path (see Figure 31.2).

FIGURE 31.2.
The Object Browser system class hierarchy.

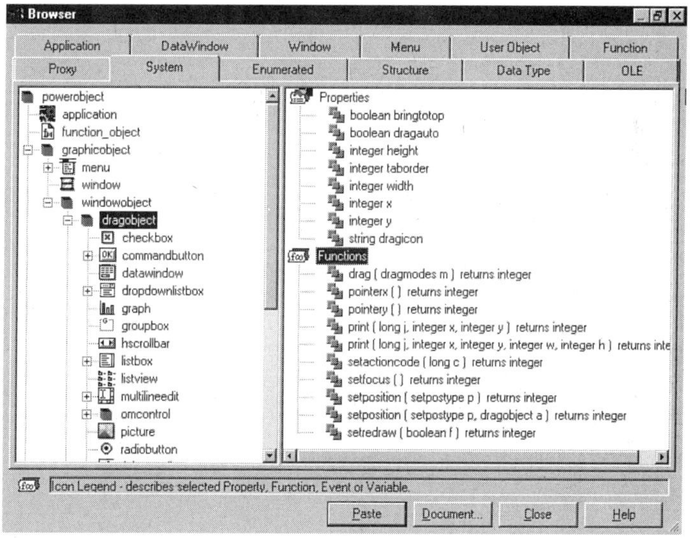

The only objects not inherited that cannot be involved in the drag/drop process are drawing objects: lines, ovals, rectangles, and round rectangles. This is because they are derived from the system class `PowerObject\GraphicObject\WindowObject\DrawObject` and not under `DragObject`, which renders them not draggable.

Now that you know what objects can be dragged and can be targets, it is important that you use the drag/drop paradigm with moderation. The following section discusses some guidelines for implementing drag and drop.

Drag and Drop Guidelines

Drag and drop can be an obvious method to carry out a task in your application, but there are some rules you should follow to ensure its success.

It is tempting to overuse drag and drop in your application. The main thing to keep in mind is that drag/drop is used to represent an action being performed on a particular object. The correlation between the source object and the action performed by the target should be intuitive and meaningful.

After a useful purpose for implementing drag/drop has been decided on, you need to identify which objects will be used for the dragged object and the target. Some good candidates for a dragged object are

- A DataWindow row or column
- A Picture control representing data
- An item in a list box

For the target objects, a good choice might be

- A DataWindow
- A list box or drop-down list box
- A Picture control representing an action
- A command button
- Any object whose attributes you want to modify

It is important that drag and drop not interfere with the control's normal usage. For example, a command button would be a poor choice for a dragged object. This is because you usually click the button to start some process, and not to begin a drag and drop session.

If you are using pictures on either the dragged or target objects, you should make sure that the pictures used are meaningful. This provides a more intuitive interface for the user. In addition, when you're dragging between two objects, an icon (referred to as the *drag icon*) is used to indicate that the object is in drag mode. The drag icon should be meaningful so the user knows exactly what's being dragged and where the object is going to be dragged to.

Finally, drag/drop should never be the only method to accomplish a task. There should always be a keyboard or menu option that allows the user to perform the same functionality. This gives your users more flexibility and does not tie them to a particular input device.

Keeping these guidelines in mind, take a look at how you can implement drag and drop in PowerBuilder.

Implementing Drag and Drop

Those objects derived from the system class `DragObject` have several attributes, events, and functions available to them to implement drag and drop.

Attributes

There are two important attributes needed in the drag/drop process: `DragAuto` and `DragIcon`. `DragAuto` indicates whether the selected control is automatically placed in drag mode when clicked. Drag mode, as discussed earlier, occurs when the user has clicked on the dragged object and continues to hold the mouse button down (almost always the primary mouse button).

`DragAuto` is a Boolean attribute, where a value of `TRUE` indicates that the control is placed in drag mode when clicked. A value of `FALSE` means that drag mode must be started via your PowerScript code. Therefore, there are two options for drag mode: Automatic and Manual. When a control is specified with `DragAuto` set to `TRUE`, the control no longer responds to any of the click events. More often than not, drag/drop is implemented using Manual drag mode so that the click events can still be utilized.

`DragIcon` is the icon that is used to indicate that an object is in drag mode. If no icon is specified, the default is a transparent rectangle the same size as the dragged object (`DragIcon` has a value of `None!`). Since the transparent rectangle does not look very professional (imagine a rectangle the size of a large DataWindow), an icon should always be specified.

> **NOTE**
>
> Remember to include the icons you use in a PBR file for distribution with your executable. Otherwise, the user *will* run into the transparent rectangles.

To specify both `DragAuto` and `DragIcon`, select the object to be dragged and open the Property sheet. Within the property sheet, select the Drag and Drop tab page (see Figure 31.3).

To set the drag mode to Automatic, make sure the Drag Auto check box is checked. For `DragIcon`, you can choose from one of the stock icon pictures or specify your own ICO file.

The `DragAuto` property usually retains the value set at design time, but `DragIcon` is typically changed at runtime from within the drag and drop events.

Events

There are four events that a `DragObject` control has defined for it: `DragDrop`, `DragEnter`, `DragLeave`, and `DragWithin`.

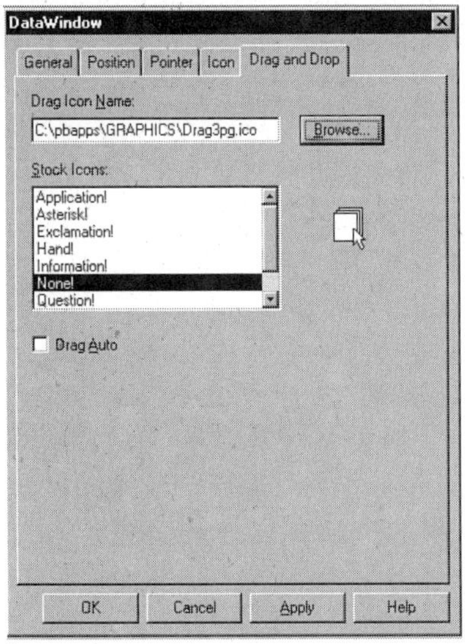

FIGURE 31.3.
The Drag and Drop tab page.

The most important event is the `DragDrop` event, which is triggered when your application is in drag mode and the primary mouse button is released when the mouse pointer is over the target object. It is in this event that you place the code for the target object's response to the dragged object being dropped on it.

The other three events are triggered when the application is in drag mode and the dragged object is being moved over the target object. The movement and position of the dragged object determine which event is fired:

- `DragEnter`—The center (also referred to as the "hot spot") of the dragged object crosses the edge into the target object.
- `DragLeave`—The center of the dragged object exits the target object.
- `DragWithin`—The center of the dragged object is within the target object.

These three events are typically used to change the `DragIcon` attribute of the dragged object. If the target is a picture, it too can be changed to indicate that the user can now release the mouse button.

Functions

There are several functions that you need to use when building a drag and drop application.

Drag()

`Drag()` is used to manually place an object in drag mode (in other words, `DragAuto` is set to `FALSE`). The syntax is

```
control.Drag( DragMode)
```

In this case `control` is the name of the dragged object and `DragMode` is one of the following values:

- `Begin!`—Place `control` in drag mode
- `Cancel!`—Stop drag mode, but do not cause a `DragDrop` event
- `End!`—Stop drag mode and if `control` is above a target object, trigger a `DragDrop` event.

`Drag()` returns an integer, with `1` indicating success and `-1` indicating a failure. This is true of all controls except for OLE 2.0 controls, which return the following:

Return Value	*Description*
`0`	Drag was successful
`1`	Drag was canceled
`2`	Object was moved
`-1`	Control was empty
`-9`	Unspecified error

Of the arguments passed to `Drag()`, `Begin!` is the most common. Typically, drag mode is started by clicking on a control and holding the mouse button down. It is possible to implement drag and drop by having the user click on an object, release the mouse button, and click on the target object to "drag" an object. In this case, `Cancel!` and `End!` are used to end drag mode without requiring the user to hold the mouse button down. While this is possible, it is not the standard method of implementing drag and drop.

The `Drag()` function can be called from several events. The most common events are `Clicked` and `MouseMove`. If the `Clicked` event is not being used, you can simply use `control.Drag( Begin!)` to start `control` dragging. If you are using the `Clicked` event to perform some other type of processing, `MouseMove` is your best alternative.

For the selected dragged object, define a user event mapped to event ID `pbm_mousemove` (for more information on creating user events, see Chapter 7, "The PowerScript Environment"). Before you exit the User Events dialog box, take a look at the parameters defined for `MouseMove` (see Figure 31.4).

The parameter `flags` is used to indicate the state of the primary mouse button when the event is triggered. A value of `1` indicates that the primary mouse button is being held down. This means that the user is moving the mouse and holding the primary mouse button down; in other words, the user is attempting to drag the object! The basic code for starting drag mode from the `MouseMove` event is

```
//Check to see if mouse button is down
If flags = 1 Then
   This.Drag( Begin!)
End If
```

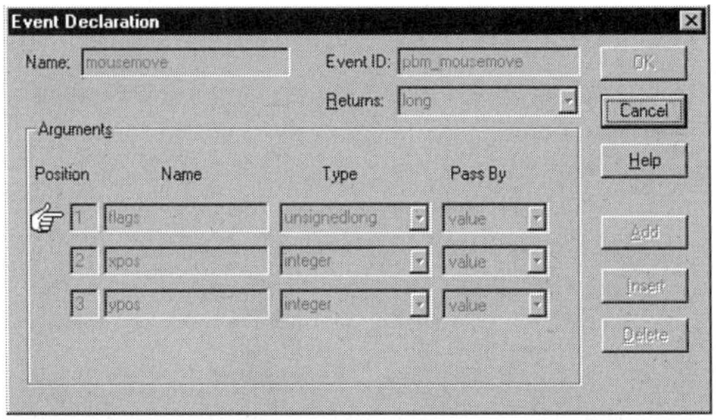

FIGURE 31.4.
Parameters for `pbm_mousemove`.

> **NOTE**
>
> In previous releases of PowerBuilder, the `flags` argument was not available. You can achieve the same functionality by checking for a value of `1` in `Message.WordParm`.

Once drag mode has begun, the icon specified for the `DragIcon` property is displayed. This is all that is required for the dragged object. The rest of the processing is done in the drag events for the target object.

DraggedObject()

`DraggedObject()` can be called from any of the drag events and returns a value indicating the control that triggered the event. The return value is of type `DragObject` and is actually a reference to the dragged object.

NEW 5 in PowerBuilder

> **NOTE**
>
> `DraggedObject()` has been replaced in Version 5.0 with an event parameter for all of the drag events. The parameter, `source`, is the same for all events and has a data type of `DragObject`. A mixture of both techniques will be used to familiarize you with the syntax.

A common use of the function when called from `DragEnter`, `DragLeave`, or `DragWithin` is to change the `DragIcon` attribute. The code for the `DragEnter` event would be this:

```
DragObject drag_control

drag_control = DraggedObject()

drag_control.DragIcon = "openfile.ico"
```

This code is insensitive to the type of dragged object (for example, a DataWindow versus a list box) and changes the `DragIcon` appropriately. Coding all your drag/drop events like this can be dangerous because you might want to take different actions depending on the object type or on a particular class. The next two sections examine some functions that can be used to refer to a specific object in drag and drop.

TypeOf()

The `TypeOf()` function is used to determine the system class that a control was inherited from. In drag and drop, this function can be used to provide processing based on a particular object type as opposed to a specific object. The syntax is

```
ObjectName.TypeOf()
```

`ObjectName` is the object or control for which you want to know the object type. The return value is of the enumerated data type `Object`. An example of using `TypeOf()` would be in the `DragDrop` event, to reset any object to its original values if it is dropped on the target (see Listing 31.1).

Listing 31.1. Generic control reset processing using the `TypeOf()` function.

```
DragObject drag_control
SingleLineEdit sle_drag
DataWindow dw_drag
DropDownListBox ddlb_drag

//Can use the event argument source in place of drag_control
drag_control = DraggedObject()

Choose Case drag_control.Typeof()
   Case SingleLineEdit!
      sle_drag = drag_control
      sle_drag.text = ""
   Case DataWindow!
      dw_drag = drag_control
      dw_drag.Reset()
      dw_drag.InsertRow(1)
   Case DropDownListBox!
      ddlb_drag = drag_control
      ddlb_drag.SelectItem(1)
End Choose
```

In this example the object type is determined and then the dragged object is set equal to a variable of the appropriate object type. This is done so that you have full access to the dragged object's attributes and functions. Otherwise, you are limited to the attributes and properties common to `DragObject` (such as `X`, `Y`, `Width`, and `Height`).

Using `TypeOf()` is useful when you are just concerned with receiving a generic reference to identify a particular system class. In the next section you will see how to directly reference a specific instance of a class.

ClassName()

The function `ClassName()` is used to retrieve the class (the name) of the object specified. The syntax is

```
ControlName.ClassName()
```

`ControlName` is the control you want to know the class for—in this case, it's the dragged object. `ClassName()` returns a string with the name of the control or an empty string to indicate that an error occurred. The function could be used this way:

```
DragObject drag_control

drag_control = DraggedObject()

Choose Case drag_control.ClassName()
   Case "dw_customer_list"
      //Do something
   Case "dw_customer_detail"
      //Do somthing else
   Case "sle_id"
      //Do this
End Choose
```

An alternative method of direct reference can be written like this:

```
Choose Case DraggedObject()
   Case dw_customer_list
      //Delete a customer
   Case dw_customer_detail
      //Add new data
   Case sle_id
      //reset value
End Choose
```

The benefit of these two methods is that you do not have to declare separate object variables to access the control's attributes and functions. The downside is that you are hard coding the control name into your script, which makes maintenance more involved.

Depending on the complexity of the application and the extent to which object-oriented development is adhered to, you might consider using a nonvisual user object. If you are dragging between DataWindows, the business object can be structured to include instance variables for each of the columns, arrays of column values, and functions used to set and extract the column data. While this would follow a more object-oriented approach by encapsulating the drag/drop functionality within the user object, it often overcomplicates the process and has unnecessary overhead. In addition, in most implementations of drag and drop, the target object is either directly related to the dragged object or the script is generic enough that it only cares about the object's type.

Drag and Drop Examples

The rest of the chapter looks at examples of implementing drag and drop in your application.

The Trash Can

The implementation of a trash can that is used to delete data is one of the most common uses of drag and drop. In this section, you will create a trash can similar to the Windows 95 Recycle Bin or the Macintosh Trash Can. The window `w_delete_contacts` contains three controls: a DataWindow displaying a list of contacts, a picture control displaying the trash can, and a command button for closing the window (see Figure 31.5).

FIGURE 31.5.
The trash can window.

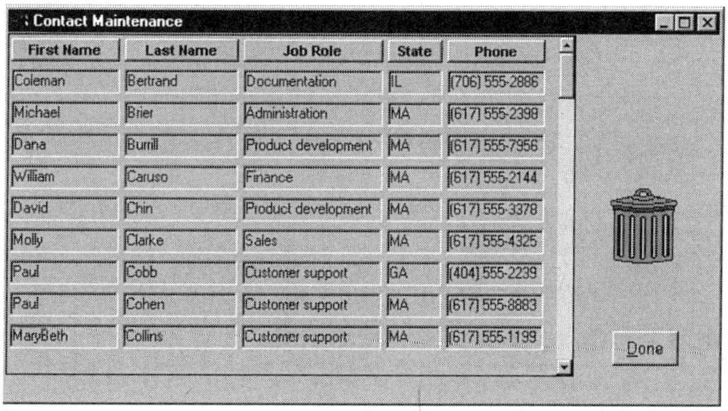

The purpose of the window is to display all contacts and allow the user to delete a customer by dragging a row to the trash can. The DataWindow is the dragged object and the picture control is the target. The window has one instance string variable defined, `is_dragicon`, which is used to hold the value of the `DragIcon` attribute of the DataWindow. Drag mode is started in the `MouseMove` event of the DataWindow using the `Drag()` function.

The picture control, `p_trash`, has scripts coded for the `DragEnter`, `DragLeave`, `DragDrop`, and `RButtonDown` events.

The `DragEnter` event for `p_trash` (see Listing 31.2) captures the intial value of the `DragIcon`. This is done in case the user drags back outside of the trash can and `DragIcon` needs to be reset. The icon is then changed to an open folder to indicate that the trash can is the target object.

Listing 31.2. The `DragEnter` event for the picture control `p_trash`.

```
//Capture the initial value for the DragIcon
is_dragicon = source.DragIcon
//Change the icon to an open folder
source.DragIcon = "folder.ico"
```

The effect on the mouse pointer due to the `DragEnter` event is shown in Figure 31.6.

FIGURE 31.6.

Dragging a row to the trash can.

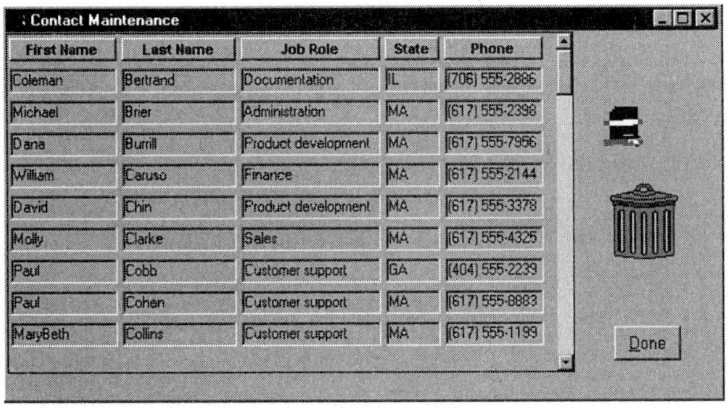

The `DragLeave` event (Listing 31.3) resets `DragIcon` back to the initial icon displayed before dragging over the trash can.

Listing 31.3. `DragLeave` for `p_trash`.

```
//Change the DragIcon property back to initial vlaue
source.DragIcon = is_dragicon
```

When the dragged DataWindow is dropped on the trash can (see Listing 31.4), the `DragDrop` event is triggered. In this event, the dragged object is identified, and if it is the DataWindow `d_contacts`, the current row is deleted. The trash can picture is changed to indicate that at least one row has been flagged for deletion.

Listing 31.4. `DragDrop` for `p_trash`.

```
If source = dw_contacts then
//Delete the current row
   dw_contacts.DeleteRow(0)
//Change the picture to a full trash can
   this.PictureName = "fatcan.bmp"
   //Change the DragIcon back to the initial value
   source.DragIcon = is_dragicon
End If
```

The enlarged trash can indicating a deleted row is shown in Figure 31.7.

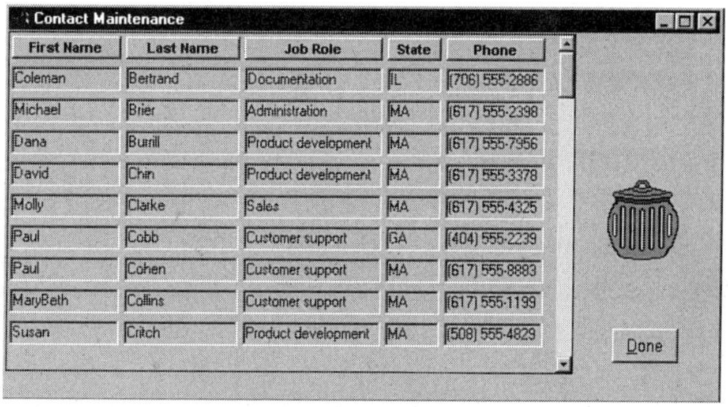

FIGURE 31.7.
A row dropped in the trash can.

As a final touch, right-clicking on the trash can displays a pop-up menu giving the options to empty the trash can (update the database) or undo the changes (restore deleted row). This is implemented using the `RButtonDown` event, as shown in Listing 31.5.

Listing 31.5. `RButtonDown` for `p_trash`.

```
m_drag_trash lm_popup

//Create a popup menu for clearing trash and undoing deletions
lm_popup = Create m_drag_trash

lm_popup.m_edit.PopMenu( Parent.PointerX(), Parent.PointerY())
```

The pop-up menu is shown in Figure 31.8.

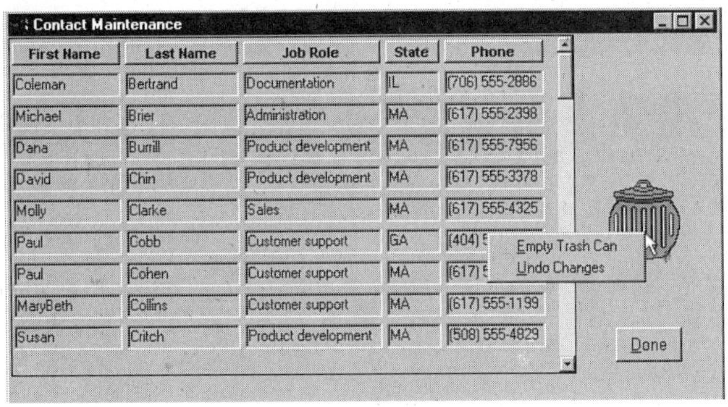

FIGURE 31.8.
A trash can pop-up menu.

The `DragEnter` and `DragLeave` events are used to toggle `DragIcon` to indicate that the picture control is the target object. The `DragDrop` event determines if the drag object is the DataWindow, `dw_contacts`. If it is, the current row is deleted, the trash can is made wider to indicate that it contains data, and `DragIcon` is reset for the next time drag mode is started. The last event, `RButtonDown`, captures a right mouse click on `p_trash` and displays a pop-up menu allowing the user to delete all data in the trash can or undo all changes.

In addition to the scripts written for `p_trash`, the `DragEnter` and `DragLeave` events were coded for the command button `cb_close` to indicate that it is not a valid target. The code is identical to that for `p_trash`, with the exception of a different icon specified. The result is shown in Figure 31.9.

As you can see, the trash can is easy to implement and provides a familiar metaphor to your users for deleting data.

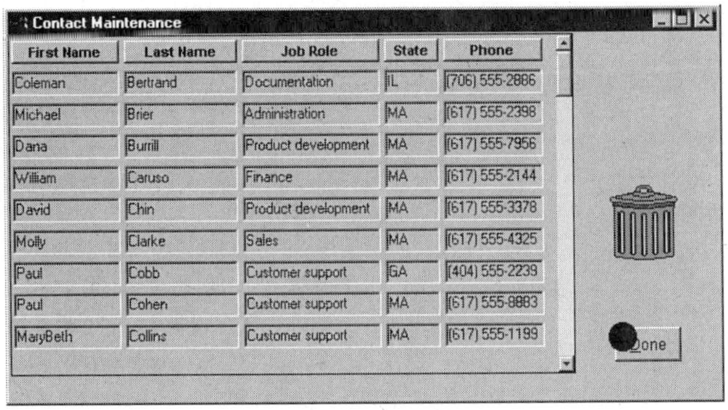

FIGURE 31.9.
An invalid target indication.

The Color Palette

The trash can drag and drop example provides a means of modifying data. In this section, you will use drag and drop to modify an object's attributes. The color palette is used to modify an object's color attributes (see Figure 31.10). The purpose of the color palette is to allow you to change an object's foreground and/or background color.

FIGURE 31.10.
The color palette.

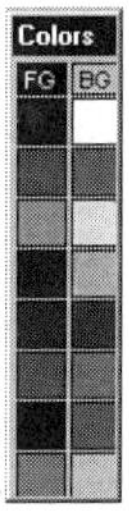

The color palette is composed of two PowerBuilder objects: a standard static text user object, `u_colour_square`, and a window, `w_colour_pallet`. The window contains 16 instances of the user object, each with a different background color. `DragAuto` is set to `TRUE` on all user objects, and `DragIcon` is the same for each user object. The name of each of the user objects is `st_color_##`, where `##` is a sequential number from 1 to 16. `w_colour_pallet` has a private instance Boolean variable defined for it (`i_bFG`) that has an initial value of `TRUE`. This variable is used to indicate whether the background or foreground is going to change on the target.

The window also contains two additional static text boxes. One is clicked to indicate that you wish to change the object's foreground color and the other is clicked to indicate a change in the background color. The `Clicked` events for these static texts are in Listings 31.6 and 31.7.

Listing 31.6. The `Clicked` event for the foreground static text.

```
this.BackColor = RGB( 0, 0, 0)// Black
this.TextColor = RGB( 255, 255, 255)// White

st_bg.BackColor = RGB( 192, 192, 192)// Light Gray
st_bg.TextColor = RGB( 0, 0, 0)// Black

i_bFG = TRUE
```

Listing 31.7. The `Clicked` event for the background static text.

```
this.BackColor = RGB( 0, 0, 0)// Black
this.TextColor = RGB( 255, 255, 255)// White

st_fg.BackColor = RGB( 192, 192, 192)// Light Gray
st_fg.TextColor = RGB( 0, 0, 0)// Black

i_bFG = FALSE
```

This code acts as an indicator as to whether you want to change the foreground or the background color of the target. Whichever is selected will have a black background with white lettering while the other static text will have a light gray background with black lettering. In addition to visually indicating to the user which option is selected, the value of `i_bFG` is changed.

Since `i_bFG` is a private variable, `w_colour_pallet` must provide a means for the developer to access its value to determine whether to change the target object's foreground or background color. This is done by declaring a window function called `wf_textcolor()` and is defined as

```
//No arguments
//Returns integer

Return i_bFG
```

Once this is defined, you can code the `DragDrop` event for the target object. If the target object is a window, the event should be coded, as in Listing 31.8.

Listing 31.8. The `DragDrop` event for a window.

```
statictext drag_text

//Determine if the dragged object is one of the color pallet static texts
If Left(Lower(source.ClassName()),8) = "st_color" then
   drag_text = source
   //Change the windows backcolor
   this.BackColor = drag_text.BackColor
End If
```

If you are changing the color scheme of a control, you must differentiate between changing the foreground and the background colors according to the value of `i_bFG`. Listing 31.9 shows the code needed to change the colors for a single-line edit.

Listing 31.9. The `DragDrop` event for a single-line edit.

```
statictext drag_text

// Determine if the dragged object is one of the color pallet static texts
If Left(Lower(source.ClassName()),8) = "st_color" then
   drag_text = source
   //Check the status of i_bFG to determine whether to change foreground
```

```
   // or background
   If w_colour_pallet.wf_textcolor() Then
      //Change the foreground color
      this.TextColor = drag_text.BackColor
   Else
      //Change the background color
      this.BackColor = drag_text.BackColor
   End If
End If
```

The same code can be used for most other standard PowerBuilder controls, with the only modification being the assignment of the dragged object. The only control that must be addressed differently is the DataWindow. Changing the background changes the whole background color of the DataWindow. Changing the foreground changes all the object's color attributes. The background modification is relatively simple, but changing all objects' foreground colors requires that you know the names of all the objects that are in the DataWindow. To accomplish this, you create a global function that will allow interrogation of a DataWindow (see Listing 31.10).

Listing 31.10. DataWindow object interrogation using the `f_list_objects()` function.

```
//ARGUMENTS:
//a_dwToActOn (the datawindow control passed by value)
//a_sObjectList (a string array passed by reference)
//a_sObjectType (a string passed by value)
//a_sColumnType (a string passed by value)
//a_sBand (a string passed by value)

String ls_Objects, ls_AnObject
Boolean lb_NotEOS = TRUE, lb_FoundEOS = FALSE   // EOS = End Of String
Integer li_ObjectCount, li_StartPos=1, li_TabPos, li_Count = 0

ls_Objects = a_dwToActOn.Describe( "datawindow.objects")

li_TabPos = Pos( ls_Objects, "~t", li_StartPos)

Do While lb_NotEOS
   ls_AnObject = Mid( ls_Objects, li_StartPos, ( li_TabPos—li_StartPos))
   If ( a_dwToActOn.Describe( ls_AnObject + ".type") = a_sObjectType &
   Or a_sObjectType = "*") And ( a_dwToActOn.Describe( ls_AnObject + ".band") &
   = a_sBand Or a_sBand = "*") And ( Left( a_dwToActOn.Describe( ls_AnObject  &
   + ".coltype"), 5) = Left( a_sColumnType, 5) &

      Or a_sColumnType = "*") Then
     li_Count ++
     a_sObjectList[li_Count] = ls_AnObject
   End If
   li_StartPos = li_TabPos + 1
   li_TabPos = Pos( ls_Objects, "~t", li_StartPos)
   If li_TabPos = 0 And Not lb_FoundEOS Then
```

continues

Listing 31.10. continued

```
      li_TabPos = Len( ls_Objects) + 1
      lb_FoundEOS = TRUE
   ElseIf lb_FoundEOS Then
      lb_NotEOS = FALSE
   End If
Loop

Return nCount
```

This function returns a list of the DataWindow objects using the `Describe()` function. You are allowed to specify which objects you want to filter, thus removing unwanted object types from the final list. If you want all objects returned, you must pass an asterisk (`*`) to the function. After an object has passed through the filter (the first `If` statement), it is placed into a string array that is returned from the function.

Once you have created the means to retrieve all of the DataWindow's objects, you are ready to code the `DragDrop` event for the DataWindow, as in Listing 31.11.

Listing 31.11. `DragDrop` for a DataWindow control.

```
statictext drag_text
string ls_PrimaryObjects[]
integer li_PrimaryObjects, li_count

If Left(Lower(source.ClassName()),8) = "st_color" then
   drag_text = source
   If w_colour_pallet.wf_textcolor() Then
      //Fill array with all objects on the DW
      li_PrimaryObjects = f_list_objects( this, ls_PrimaryObjects, "*","*","*")
      //Change the foreground color
      For li_count = 1 to li_PrimaryObjects
         this.Modify( ls_PrimaryObjects [li_count] + ".Color = " + &
         String( drag_text.BackColor))
      Next
   Else
      //Change the background color
      this.object.datawindow.color = drag_text.BackColor
   End If
End If
```

An alternative placement of this code would be in the user object as a function that accepts the object type as an argument.

Dragging Between DataWindows

A useful implementation of drag and drop is moving data from one DataWindow to another. Imagine how easy it would be for your user to click a row in one DataWindow, drag the data, and have it inserted into another DataWindow.

The window `w_orders` contains two DataWindows: a list of products and a sales order form. The product list, `d_products`, is populated with all valid company products by retrieving data from a table. The sales order form DataWindow, `d_sales_order`, initially has no rows in it. When the users want to order a particular product, they click on the product description and drag the product over to the sales order form. Once the product is dropped on the order form, a new line is inserted into `d_sales_order`, and the product ID, description, and unit price are filled in. The user can then enter a quantity, which is summed into the total cost (see Figure 31.11).

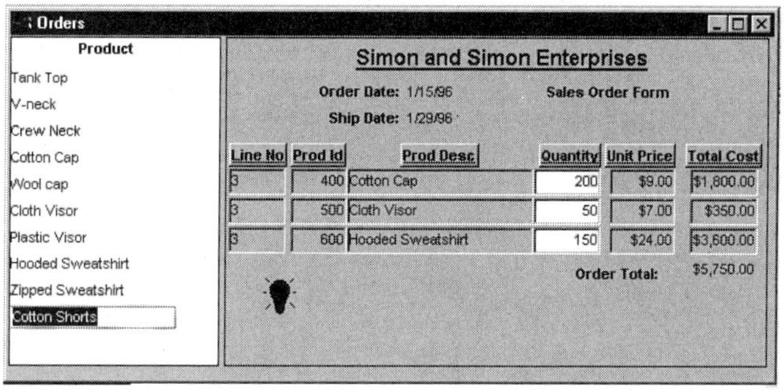

FIGURE 31.11.
Sales order form insertion.

The code follows the same pattern as many of the other examples in this chapter. The `DragDrop` event is shown in Listing 31.12.

Listing 31.12. The `DragDrop` event for `d_sales_order`.

```
long newnum, currow

//Make sure the products DataWindow is being dragged
If source = dw_product Then
   //Insert a new row
   newnum = this.InsertRow(0)
   currow = dw_product.GetRow()
   //Copy the information from the product DataWindow
   this.SetItem(newnum,"prod_id",dw_product.GetItemNumber&
         (currow, "id"))
   this.SetItem(newnum,"prod_desc",dw_product.GetItemString&
         (currow, "description"))
   this.SetItem(newnum,"unit_price",dw_product.GetItemNumber&
         (currow, "unit_price"))
End If
```

An alternative method of moving data from one DataWindow to another is using the `RowsCopy()` and `RowsMove()` functions, but only if they share the same result set.

Summary

Drag and drop is an application development technique that follows the object-to-action metaphor. In this chapter you have learned about the components needed to implement drag and drop and some guidelines about when and where to use it. Using the examples provided, you have a basis for developing sophisticated drag/drop-enabled applications.

Animation, Sound, and Multimedia

32

IN THIS CHAPTER

When an application is near completion, it is common for developers to spend a little time adding some interesting features. This can include the construction of some type of hidden "signature" such as displaying the developer's name in a fireworks presentation. A standard and fun way to accomplish this in an application is to use some sort of animation. Animation consists of changing pictures, moving objects, sound, or any other type of visual treat that goes beyond the functionality of the base system. Not only is this typically fun for the developer to create, but the end users often enjoy discovering and playing with the different features. Animation can also add value in applications to draw attention to an object on a window and is useful with drag and drop.

The use of sound in an application can also be fun as well as informative for the user. These two techniques, animation and sound, were about as visually complex as many Windows 3.*x* applications got. With the release of Windows 95 and 32-bit access, the realm of multimedia has become required application specification as opposed to a developer's toy.

This chapter shows several different techniques for creating animation, enabling sound, and implementing multimedia in your PowerBuilder applications.

Picture Animation

Probably the most common use of animation in an application is to make a picture seem to come to life. This can be accomplished in several different ways, depending on where you want the picture to be changing (such as a toolbar icon, picture control, or mouse pointer). The basic concept of picture animation is to use an object that contains a picture, and then at runtime change the `Picture` attribute of that object. Before you get too far into planning your picture animation, you must decide on the pictures you are going to use.

If you are not sure what picture to use in your application, there are a number of places where you can look. PowerBuilder comes with a series of stock icons for toolbars (available through the Menu painter) and bitmaps (BMPs) with its sample applications. If you can't find what you want there, explore the directories of other Windows applications and see whether you can find some there (for instance, \Windows\MORICONS.DLL). You can also purchase a number of different icon and bitmap libraries or use a third-party tool such as Snag-It to perform screen captures.

The last option for determining a picture for animation is to design and create your own. As with the icon and bitmap libraries, a number of tools exist for you to use to create pictures. The most accessible tool for a PowerBuilder developer is the Watcom image editor that ships with PowerBuilder (WIMGEDIT.EXE). The Watcom image editor enables you to create bitmaps, icons, and cursors. You can manipulate an existing picture to suit your needs (which is especially useful if you are not artistically inclined or just impatient), or you can create a brand-new one (see Figure 32.1).

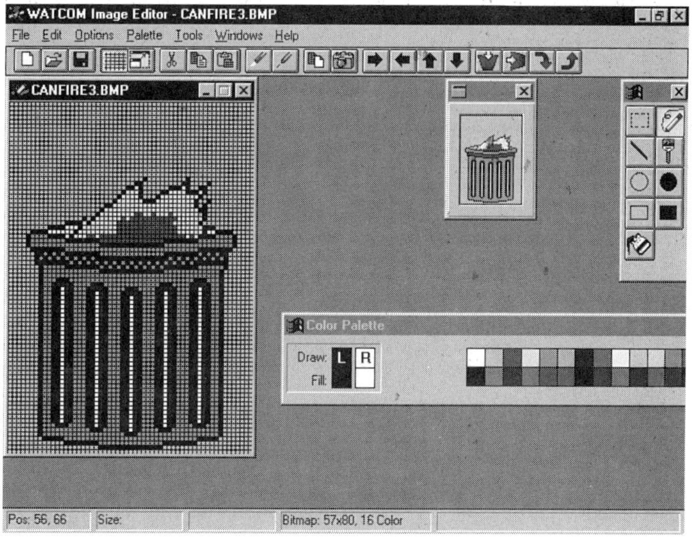

FIGURE 32.1.
The Watcom image editor.

Typically, you need a series of different pictures with subtle differences in each picture to give the appearance that the picture is animated. Determine the initial picture and then use an editor (such as the Watcom image editor) to change the picture and save it to a new picture file. After you have done this you can begin to implement the picture animation. Let's take a look at some different techniques, starting with the most simple and moving on.

Toolbar Icons

There are a couple methods you can use to manipulate the picture that appears in the toolbars associated with an MDI application. The easiest method is to specify a Picture and a Down Picture (when the button appears depressed) for the toolbar icon in the Menu painter (see Figure 32.2).

At runtime, whenever the user clicks on the toolbar icon, the picture changes from the up icon to the down icon and then back again (see Figure 32.3).

This is the easiest way to incorporate animation into your application because everything is done during design time.

NOTE

Unfortunately, if your users decide that they want to have the Show Text option on, PowerBuilder will not display the down picture.

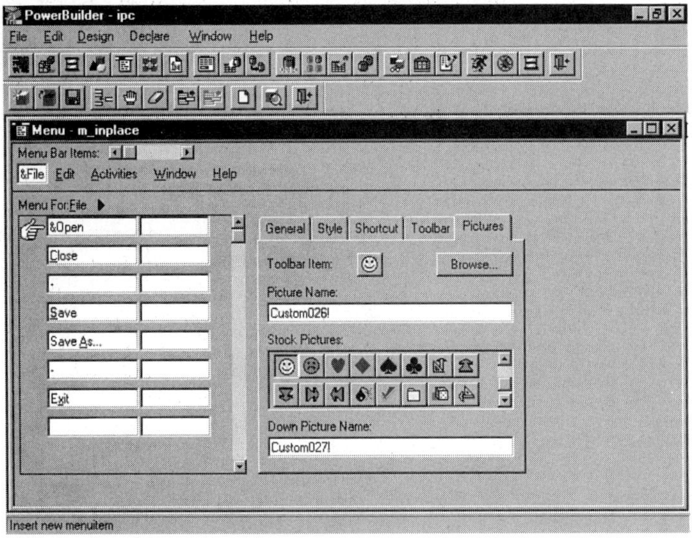

FIGURE 32.2.
Using the toolbar item dialog box to specify different pictures for the up and down states of the icon.

FIGURE 32.3.
The up and down pictures in the toolbar.

The only limitation to this method is that it is initiated by user interaction. The user has to click the toolbar icon to see anything happen. It is even more interesting to have the toolbar change without the user doing anything. To implement this type of functionality, you need to change the `ToolbarItemName` attribute of the associated menu object via your code. This requires no user interaction.

The sample application has a face on the toolbar that is cycled through to show a smile, no expression, and a frown. The first thing you need is a face bitmap. The bitmap (SMILE.BMP) in this example was created using the Watcom image editor (15×16 pixels) together with two additional bitmaps (NONE.BMP and FROWN.BMP). You will first associate these pictures with the menu toolbar (SMILE.BMP will be the default, because you want the users to be happy!), and then you'll be ready to write the code.

Another key ingredient to make the application animation work effectively is to utilize the `Timer` event.

Timers

With PowerBuilder and animation, you will need to rely extensively on a window's `Timer` event and the `Timer()` function. The `Timer()` function triggers a window's `Timer` event at the interval specified. The argument that the `Timer()` function takes is the number of seconds you want between `Timer` events, and optionally the window name (the current window is the default).

The number of seconds that can be specified ranges from 0 to 65. A zero interval turns off the timer so that `Timer` events are no longer executed. Note that the smallest time frame between time events is .055 ($^1/_{18}$ second), which is a Windows limitation.

When the `Timer()` function is called, PowerBuilder triggers the `Timer` event for the specified window and resets the timer. When the timer interval is reached, PowerBuilder executes the `Timer` event again. This continues to occur until `Timer(0)` is coded to turn the timer off.

The timer is very useful with animation because it gives you the capability to change the attributes of an object constantly (in this case, the object is the picture on the toolbar). Let's see how you would use the timer in conjunction with changing the toolbar icon.

The Timer and the Toolbar

Because the `Timer` event is going to be the heart of the code, take a look at the code that you need here. Remember, the toolbar only works for an MDI application, so this code will be in the MDI frame's `Timer` event. Declare an integer instance variable (`ii_toolbar`) with an initial value of `1`. This will be used to determine which picture is currently being displayed and which picture will be displayed next. Each of the three bitmaps will be associated with a value of `ii_toolbar`. You will use a `Choose...Case` statement to determine the value and swap the pictures in and out, as follows:

```
Choose Case ii_toolbar
   Case 1
      m_frame.m_file.m_open.m_report.toolbaritemname = "none.bmp"
      ii_toolbar = 2
   Case 2
      m_frame.m_file.m_open.m_report.toolbaritemname = "frown.bmp"
      ii_toolbar = 3
   Case 3
      m_frame.m_file.m_open.m_report.toolbaritemname = "smile.bmp"
      ii_toolbar = 1
End Choose
```

To reference the `ToolbarItemName` attribute for the menu, you must fully qualify the menu name. The bitmap must be in the directory from which the application is being run or in your DOS search path. At runtime, you can include these in your EXE or PBDs via a PBR. By changing the value of `ii_toolbar`, you change the picture that is being displayed to the user.

The only other code that is necessary is in the `Open` event of the MDI frame window. You need to trigger the `Timer` event using the `Timer()` function. For example,

```
Timer( .5, this)
```

will trigger the `Timer` event for the MDI frame window every half-second. Although animation can be fun, not all users are amused by icons changing on the screen. Some find it distracting, and because of this, you should always provide an option (a menu item) to turn off the animation. The following code stops the `Timer` event from being executed:

```
Timer( 0)
```

Picture Controls and Picture Buttons

Many times you do not want to change the icon on a toolbar. Using picture controls and picture buttons provides an alternative. Of the two controls, the picture control is more prevalent in animated applications. The same logic used with the toolbars is used for both of these controls. The only difference is that the attribute to change for the picture control and picture button is `PictureName`. Using a picture control on an About box is common, and having a changing picture adds a little extra excitement.

Window Icon Animation

If you don't want to place any potentially distracting animation in the application workspace, consider animating the window's icon when it is minimized to the Windows desktop.

Like for toolbars and picture controls, the basic premise of swapping pictures and using timers holds true. The code for the window `Timer` event would be as follows:

```
Choose Case ii_picture
   Case 1
      this.icon = "face1.ico"
      ii_picture = 2
   Case 2
      this.icon = "face2.ico"
      ii_picture = 3
   Case 3
      this.icon = "face3.ico"
      ii_picture = 4
   Case 4
      this.icon = "face0.ico"
      ii_picture = 1
End Choose
```

The variable `ii_picture` is again an instance integer variable initialized to a value of `1`. The main difference between the previous examples and this one is in how the `Timer` event is triggered. Because you only want the picture to change when the window is minimized to the desktop, you need to find out when the user has minimized the current window. This is accomplished through the window's `Resize` event:

```
If this.windowstate = Minimized! Then
   Timer( 1)
Else
   Timer( 0)
End If
```

When the user changes the size of the window, this code checks to see whether the user chose to minimize the window. The valid values for the window attribute `WindowState` are `Maximized!`, `Minimized!`, and `Normal!`. When `WindowState` is equal to `Minimized!`, the `Timer` event will be triggered every second. If the user sets the window to anything but minimized, the timer will be turned off until the next time the window is minimized.

Drag and Drop

The capability to drag an object (such as a filename or a record in a DataWindow) and drop it on a picture of a trash can is common in many applications. When the dragged object is released on the trash can, fire shoots out of the top of the trash can and the dragged object is consumed (which translates into a deleted record or file).

Although it might be disheartening for many, this is not magic but a simple case of animation combined with drag-and-drop techniques. (For more in-depth coverage of drag and drop, see Chapter 31, "Drag and Drop.")

You create the animation by using the different drag-and-drop events for the picture control. My sample application enables a user to click on a customer in a DataWindow control and drag that customer to a trash can, which deletes the row from the DataWindow. Therefore, the DataWindow control is my dragged object and the picture control is my target (see Figure 32.4).

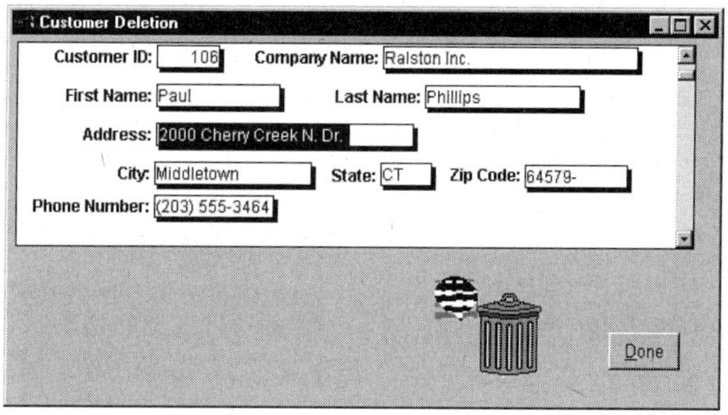

FIGURE 32.4.
Dragging a row from a DataWindow to a trash can picture control.

Drag mode is turned on in the `MouseMove` event (a user event for `pbm_dwnmousemove`) of the DataWindow control if the mouse button is still being held down. When it has been determined that the user wants to be in drag mode and the user drags a particular customer to the picture control, utilization of the `DragEnter`, `DragLeave`, and `DragDrop` events of the picture control provides the animation. Use the following three bitmaps to accomplish the animation: TRASH.BMP, OPEN.BMP, and FIRE.BMP. The drag icon of the DataWindow control is set at design time, so you don't have to worry about that one.

When the hot spot (the center) of the dragged object crosses the target, the `DragEnter` event triggers the following:

```
If DraggedObject() = dw_customer Then
   p_1.picturename = "open.bmp"
End If
```

If the DataWindow control is being dragged, the trash can picture appears to open (see Figure 32.5). If the user continues dragging and drags the object out of the picture control, the `DragLeave` event is triggered, which resets the `PictureName` attribute to TRASH.BMP.

FIGURE 32.5.
Opening the trash can.

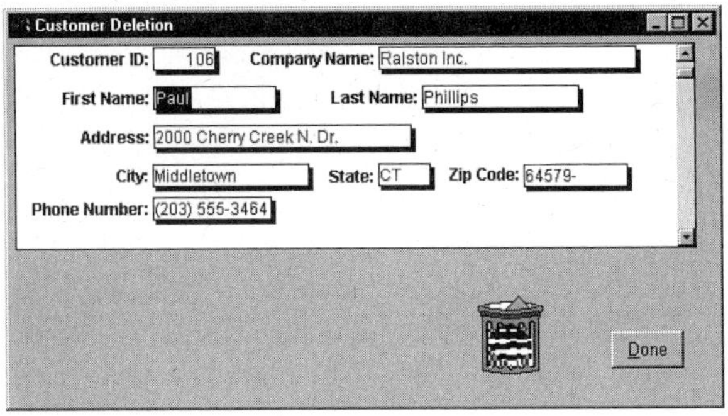

As is standard with drag-and-drop applications, the majority of the code appears in the `DragDrop` event of the target object (in this case, the picture control):

```
If DraggedObject() = dw_customer Then
   p_1.PictureName = "fire.bmp"
   dw_customer.DeleteRow(0)
End If

// You might need to place a delay in here, so that the user gets to see
// the FIRE.BMP. The delay can be anything from a For..Next loop to a
// While..Loop that checks for a certain time delay.

p_1.PictureName = "trash.bmp"
```

The `DraggedObject()` function determines whether the object dropped on the picture control is the DataWindow control. If it is, the picture is changed to the trash can with flames shooting out the top, burning the record that was dropped on the trash can (see Figure 32.6). The current row in the DataWindow control is deleted (but notice that the changes are not yet applied to the database). After the deletion is complete, the picture is changed back to the original trash can. To physically remove the rows from the databases, you can add a pop-up menu so that when the trash can is right-clicked to clear the trash, you call the `Update()` function.

FIGURE 32.6.
The emptying trash can animation.

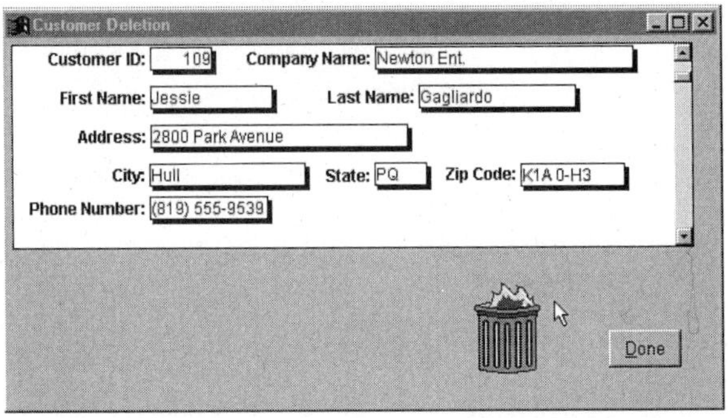

Your mouse pointer—like picture controls, buttons, and toolbars—can be changed at runtime to a different picture. For a window, the mouse pointer can be changed to several different stock cursor pictures. This is accomplished by using the `SetPointer()` function and specifying the enumerated data type for the particular pointer you want (see Figure 32.7 for a list of types).

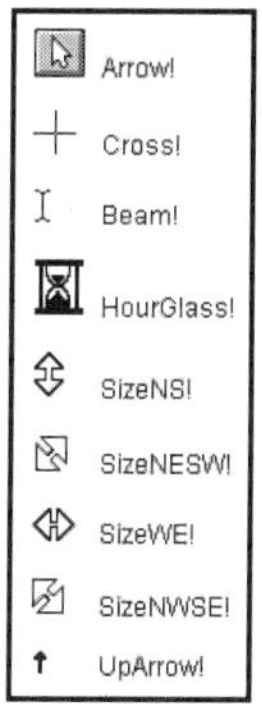

FIGURE 32.7.
The mouse pointers for `SetPointer()`.

The `SetPointer()` function only changes the pointer for the script in which it is called. After the script terminates, the pointer returns to an arrow. It is important to remember that you can only specify PowerBuilder's cursor pictures, and the changes are only for the current script.

At design time, you can specify a non-PowerBuilder cursor file (CUR) by referencing the window attribute `Pointer` and setting it to a string containing the name of the CUR file. You can change the `Pointer` attribute for most controls as well. You can also change the cursor that appears over a DataWindow or any object on a DataWindow to a specified CUR file at runtime. Use `Modify()` to change the `Pointer` attribute:

```
dw_order_detail.Object.DataWindow.Pointer = 'c:\pb4\no.cur'
```

The same enumerated data types that can be used with a window can also be used in a DataWindow.

Depending on where you want the mouse pointer to change (such as over the whole window or just over a particular control), you can use `SetPointer()` or the `Picture` attribute in conjunction with a timer to toggle the pointer that the user sees. Using the `SetPointer()` function in a `Timer` event to change from the `HourGlass!` to `Arrow!` pointers can be useful if you have a long-running procedure. However, if you have specified the `Yield()` function so that the user can still do some work while the procedure is executing, changing the pointer gives the user that information. You use the `Timer` event to flip-flop between setting `HourGlass!` and `Arrow!` pointers. Remember to turn off the timer at the end of the long-running code.

NOTE

Because all the examples you have seen are dynamically changing some `Picture` attribute of an object, it is important to remember that these picture files must be distributed with your application or incorporated in a PBR.

Object Movement

All the previously discussed examples utilize an object or control that has a constant location on the screen. All you have done is changed the picture that is being viewed. In addition to providing this functionality, you can code some additional scripts to manipulate the location/size of objects to give the appearance that the objects themselves are moving across a window.

Moving Pictures

A fun way to use animation in your application is to write script that is only triggered when a series of events occurs (usually not a common functionality in the system). For example, double-clicking on a static text control in an About box or on the window itself could be the event. This is a pretty good choice because the user might accidentally stumble across this new functionality of the system and not be exactly sure what he did. When the user has figured out what he did to activate your script, he will probably go and tell all the other users. It seems like an easy way to get your name out in a positive light with the users if you include it in your application. (But be sure that your company doesn't frown on such things before you implement this.)

Place a picture control on your window and associate the desired picture. Because you don't want users to see the picture until they have triggered the event with the animation script (such as `DoubleClicked`), make sure to set the `Visible` attribute to `FALSE` at design time. Access the script for which you want the animation to be triggered, and decide what you want the script to do.

You probably want the picture to move around the window and then display a message (maybe the developer's name). Your initial thought on how to accomplish this is probably to change the picture's `X` and `Y` attributes in order to move the picture in increments across the screen. You can do it this way, but the results might be less than satisfactory. To demonstrate this for yourself, create a window with a picture control and a static text control. Place the static text control in the middle to top half of the window and the picture control on the top left. Write the following script for the `DoubleClicked` event of the window:

```
int li_x,li_y

li_x = p_1.X
li_y = p_1.Y
```

```
Do While p_1.X < ( this.Width - 250)
   p_1.X = p_1.X + 1
Loop

Do While p_1.Y < ( this.Height / 2)
   p_1.Y = p_1.Y + 1
Loop

Do While p_1.X > li_x
   p_1.x = p_1.X - 1
Loop

Do While p_1.Y > li_y
   p_1.y = p_1.Y - 1
Loop
```

NOTE

The same thing can be accomplished using the `Move()` function to specify the X and Y coordinates. When you run the window, the picture does not paint crisply across the window. This is because the window must be repainted every time the picture control is moved. PowerBuilder actually re-creates a small window with the picture in it for each successive change.

To avoid the flickering encountered with the previous technique, use the PowerScript `Draw()` function. This function takes two arguments, which are the X and Y coordinates of where the image is to be drawn. The `Draw()` function moves the picture much more quickly and cleanly by drawing directly on the window. `Draw()` does not change the actual position of the picture control; rather, it just displays the control's picture at the position specified in the function. The function does, however, leave the image at the specified location. To avoid leaving trailing pieces of different images across the screen, move the image in small increments so that the next image covers up the prior image.

TIP

Make the background of your picture image the same color as the background of the window; otherwise, you will leave a trail across the window. This can also be avoided by having a second picture control the same color as the window background moving after the first picture control. Any color trail left by the first picture control will be overlaid by the second control.

A common example of this sort of animation that you've probably seen is a starship that flies across the window (see Figure 32.8). Let's incorporate the starship example in PowerBuilder and add some enhancements.

FIGURE 32.8.
The flying starship.

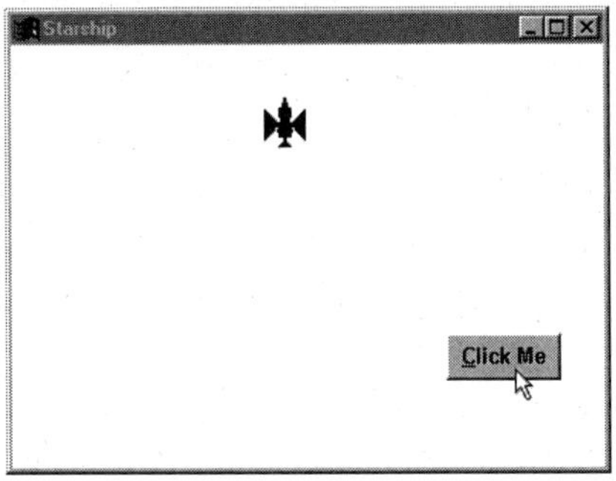

At design time, the actual location of the picture control is with the top of the control aligned with the top of the window. (This is the location where you want the picture control at the end.) The picture control and a static text control both have their `Visible` attributes set to `FALSE`. The Click Me command button contains the first part of the code that moves the picture control:

```
Long ll_Vertical = 880

Do Until ll_Vertical = 0
   ll_Vertical = ll_Vertical - 1
   p_starship.Draw( 750, ll_Vertical)
Loop

p_starship.PictureName = "destroy.bmp"
p_starship.Visible = TRUE
```

The variable `ll_Vertical` is the Y coordinate if the bottom of the picture control is aligned at the bottom of the window. When you specify this as the starting position, the starship begins at the bottom of the window; through each pass of the `Do...Until` loop, the vertical position is decreased by one. The starship will fly to the top of the screen until its Y coordinate is equal to zero (aligned with the top of the window).

After the starship has moved to the top of the screen, the picture is changed from the original, STARSHIP.BMP, to DESTROY.BMP. This picture shows the starship bursting into flames, and then the picture control is made visible.

If you want to add extra functionality, add the following code to the `Clicked` event of the command button:

```
Integer li_Count, li_Index

// Flash the window's background colors
For li_Count = 1 To 30
   Parent.BackColor = RGB( 46, 46, 46)
   Parent.BackColor = RGB( 0, 0, 0)
   li_Index = li_Index + 1
Next

p_starship.PictureName = "rubble.bmp"
st_unleashed.Visible = TRUE
```

```
For li_Index = 1 To 200
   FlashWindow( Handle( Parent), TRUE)
Next
```

The background color of the window is flashed by cycling through a loop 30 times, and then the picture control image is changed to RUBBLE.BMP to show the destroyed starship. After the rubble is displayed, a static text control is made visible to show the message underneath the destroyed starship (see Figure 32.9).

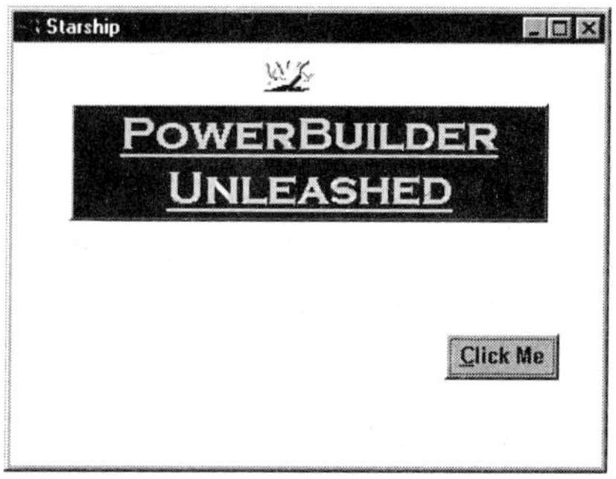

FIGURE 32.9.
The final effect after the starship has crashed.

The title of the window is then flashed using the Windows API function `FlashWindow()`, which is declared as

```
Function Boolean FlashWindow(int hWnd, Boolean bInvert) Library "user32.dll"
```

The starship example demonstrates some different ideas you can use in application animation. Not only can you move a picture, but you can also make use of hiding and displaying different controls. Changing the colors (particularly the window's background color) can add some flair to your application.

External Function Calls

In addition to using the PowerScript functions and changing the image that is viewed, you can also utilize several Windows API functions that are available for use in your application. You just saw an example of this usage when the `FlashWindow()` function in USER32.DLL (or USER.EXE in Windows 3.*x*) was utilized to make the window title bar flash on and off. You can use any applicable function in the Windows SDK (take a look at the library GDI32.DLL or GDI.EXE in Win16) or any third-party function library, or you can write your own DLLs. You will learn about using an external function call to enable sound for your application in the "Sound Enabling" section later in the chapter. For more information on using external function calls, see Chapter 33, "API Calls."

Moving Windows

The way a window is opened or closed can also add some interesting effects to your application. For example, when you open a window, it can start small and expand to its normal size. This exploding technique is fairly simple to implement; all you have to do is change four attributes of the window: `X`, `Y`, `Height`, and `Width`. The only difficulty is determining how fast you want the window to open and the size to which you want the window opened.

For this example, the window will be created small and then made to explode to fill most of the screen when it is opened. The majority of the code needed to make the window expand is in a user-defined event for the window called `ue_explode`. It maps to the `pbm_custom01` event ID (see Chapter 7, "The PowerScript Environment," on how to create user events). In the `Open` event of the window, the `PostEvent()` function is used to trigger `ue_explode`. This is done so that the resizing of the window will occur after the window has been displayed to the user. The `ue_explode` event contains the following code:

```
Do Until this.Height >= 1650
   this.Width = this.Width + 35
   this.Height = this.Height + 25
   this.X = this.X - 10
   this.Y = this.Y - 10
Loop
```

The window's height and width are incremented, while at the same time the X and Y coordinates of the upper-left corner of the window are moved. Both must be done; otherwise, your window will disappear off the right side and bottom of the screen. The only negative parts about making the window explode are controlling the way that any controls on the window look while the window is exploding and determining the incremental and decremental values of the `X`, `Y`, `Height`, and `Width` attributes. These values will vary depending on the size you want to make your window and how fast you want it to open. You might have to try several different values until you find what you like.

TIP

Do not increment the height and width by a number less than 10 because it takes too long for the window to open.

The other downside is the way controls appear, which is due to the window being repainted each time you resize it. Because the window is constantly being repainted, PowerBuilder does not have time to paint the controls and they end up looking like splotches on the window as it opens. You can avoid this by making all controls invisible initially and making them visible after the window has exploded to its desired size.

The same code, except in reverse, can be implemented to shrink a window when it is closed. Although this can be fun to play with, it would probably only be suitable for an unimportant window such as an About box. Due to the time taken to draw this, you might consider using a special window that has no controls, which you use for the purpose of exploding, and then hide it and show the intended window.

Sound Enabling

You can easily add sound to a PowerBuilder application by using Windows API calls. The actual mechanics of making API calls are discussed in Chapter 33, so you might want to explore that chapter first.

You can make use of sound to provide an audio cue as well as the visual cues you have already used within your application. Imagine in the drag-and-drop example that you not only drag a file to a trash can, which animates burning the trash, but you also play a sound clip at the same time. This can make even more of an impression. Granted, these are embellishments, but they can make the difference between just another application and one that users will enjoy.

The API call used to play sound requires you to have installed either specific drivers for a sound card or a generic sound driver that makes use of the computer's internal speaker.

The external function declaration for the API function that plays a wave file is

```
Function Boolean PlaySound( String szSound, uInt Hmodule, uLong Flags) &
   Library "winmm.dll"
```

> **NOTE**
>
> The `sndPlaySound()` function used in Win16 is still available in the Win32 environment but provides only a subset of the functionality of `PlaySound()`.

The `PlaySound()` function plays a sound specified in one of three ways: by filename, by resource, or by system event. A system event may be associated with a sound in the registry or in the WIN.INI file.

`szSound` specifies the sound to play. If this parameter is `NULL`, any currently playing waveform sound is stopped. Three flags (`SND_ALIAS`, `SND_FILENAME`, and `SND_RESOURCE`) determine whether `szSound` is interpreted as an alias for a system event, a filename, or a resource identifier. If none of these flags is specified, `PlaySound()` searches the registry or the WIN.INI file for an association with the specified sound name. If no association is found in the registry, the name is interpreted as a filename.

`hModule` should be `NULL` in all cases except when using the `SND_RESOURCE` flag (which is not covered in this book).

`Flags` indicates the flags that when combined give the desired method for playing the sound. The values shown in Table 32.1 can be combined using `OR` (by adding the decimal values) to carry out multiple functions during the same call.

Table 32.1. Valid argument values for the `PlaySound()` function.

Constant Name	*Hex Value*	*Decimal Value*	*Description*
`SND_ALIAS`	0x10000	65536	`szSound` is a system-event alias in the registry or the WIN.INI file.
`SND_ALIAS_ID`	0x110000	1114112	`szSound` is a predefined sound identifier.
`SND_ASYNC`	0x00001	1	The sound is played asynchronously and `PlaySound()` returns immediately after beginning the sound.
`SND_FILENAME`	0x20000	131072	The `szSound` parameter is a filename of a sound file.
`SND_LOOP`	0x00008	8	Plays repeatedly until `PlaySound()` is called again with `szSound` set to `NULL`.
`SND_MEMORY`	0x00004	4	`szSound` points to an image of a sound in memory.
`SND_NODEFAULT`	0x00002	2	If the sound cannot be found, `PlaySound()` returns without playing the default sound.
`SND_NOSTOP`	0x00010	16	Yield to another sound event that is already playing.
`SND_NOWAIT`	0x02000	8192	If the driver is busy, return immediately without playing the sound.
`SND_SYNC`	0x00000	0	Synchronous playback of a sound event. `PlaySound()` returns after the sound event completes.

The `SND_ASYNC` option will play the sound asynchronously until either it finishes or you call `PlaySound()` with `szSound` set to `NULL`. You must use the `SND_ASYNC` flag when using `SND_LOOP` to indicate that the sound event can be eventually stopped.

NOTE

`PlaySound()` searches for the sound file to play in the following directories: the current directory, the Windows directory, the Windows system directory, directories listed in the `PATH` environment variable, and the list of directories mapped in a network.

Therefore, you should package any sound files together with your application when you distribute it.

If `PlaySound()` cannot find the specified sound, the default system event sound entry is played instead. If neither the system default entry nor the default sound can be found, `PlaySound()` makes no sound and returns `FALSE`.

Using the `SND_ALIAS` flag you can make `PlaySound()` play sounds referred to by a keyname in the registry. This allows the end user to customize the system alerts and warnings with their own sounds.

NOTE

Sounds that are associated with system alerts and warnings are called *sound events.*

For example, to play the sound associated with the `SystemExclamation` entry and to wait for the sound to complete before returning, this would be the call:

```
Uint ui_Null
Ulong SND_SYNC = 0

SetNull( ui_Null)
PlaySound( "SystemExclamation", ui_Null, SND_SYNC)
```

The predefined sound events vary with the Win32 platform you are using. The following are the sound events that are defined for all Win32 implementations:

- `SystemAsterisk`
- `SystemExclamation`
- `SystemExit`
- `SystemHand`
- `SystemQuestion`
- `SystemStart`

To provide complete customization for end users you should have your application register its own sound events. This allows the user to configure the sound event using the standard Control Panel interface.

NOTE

The application sound event entries belong at the same position in the registry hierarchy as the rest of the sound events.

The `sndPlaySound()` function always searches the registry for a keyname matching the `szSound` argument before attempting to load a file with this name. On the other hand, `PlaySound()` uses the passed flags to specify the location of the sound.

To check the Windows system and make sure you can play sound files, a second function is used. Its declaration is

```
Function uInt waveOutGetNumDevs() Library "winmm.dll"
```

The two functions are used in the following code in a call to play the Windows TADA.WAV file continuously and synchronously:

```
uInt ui_NoOfDevices, ui_Null

ui_NoOfDevices = WaveOutGetNumDevs()

If ui_NoOfDevices > 0 Then
   SetNull( ui_Null)
   PlaySound( "TADA.WAV", ui_Null, 0+2+8+16)
End If
```

Note the use of the `SND_NODEFAULT flag (2)` to make sure that the wave exists before you attempt to play it. If you do not specify this, the application just makes the default beep at you indicating an error (but processing continues).

A great touch to your application is to play a welcome sound when your user starts the application. This can be made sensitive to the time of day and say "Good morning" or "Good afternoon." Similarly, when the application closes, a voice saying "Goodbye" or "Good night" is a nice touch. A voice saying "Error" is another one you could incorporate easily. You should keep the sound bites short because the user will often tire of hearing them and will become irritated at having to sit through 20 seconds of musical fanfare to leave the application.

Multimedia

PowerBuilder has the capability to write scripts for some of the Windows multimedia events. Multimedia capability has been vastly expanded with the introduction of Windows 95 and PowerBuilder for the Macintosh, as both platforms support a 32-bit architecture. PowerBuilder supports joystick input, enhanced timer services, multimedia file input and output, and audio control. The remainder of this section addresses multimedia applications for the Windows platform.

To interface with the multimedia capabilities of Windows, you need to have already installed the driver for the particular multimedia device that you want to use (such as CD audio or a joystick). Also, you must have the Windows translation file for multimedia, MMSYSTEM.DLL for 16-bit applications and WINMM.DLL for 32-bit applications.

Windows multimedia application development is done using the Media Control Interface (MCI). The MCI gives access to media devices with high-level methods (using standard human language commands) and a lower-level method (consisting of parameters). The high-level approach is very easy to implement into your applications using such commands as `Play welcome.avi`. The low-level method would be necessary for complex multimedia device communication, which requires you to detail specific operations and parameters.

PowerBuilder traps the multimedia Windows messages in a series of new events that you can add as user-defined events. These events are shown in Table 32.2.

Table 32.2. PowerBuilder event IDs for multimedia window messages.

Joystick
PBM_MMJOY1MOVE
PBM_MMJOY2MOVE
PBM_MMJOY1ZMOVE
PBM_MMJOY2ZMOVE
PBM_MMJOY1BUTTONDOWN
PBM_MMJOY2BUTTONDOWN
PBM_MMJOY1BUTTONUP
PBM_MMJOY2BUTTONUP
MCI
PBM_MMMCINOTIFY
Waveform Output
PBM_MMWOM_OPEN
PBM_MMWOM_CLOSE
PBM_MMWOM_DONE
Waveform Input
PBM_MMWIM_OPEN
PBM_MMWIM_CLOSE
PBM_MMWIM_DATA
MIDI Input
PBM_MMMIM_OPEN
PBM_MMMIM_CLOSE
PBM_MMMIM_DATA
PBM_MMMIM_LONGDATA
PBM_MMMIM_ERROR
PBM_MMMIM_LONGERROR

continues

Table 32.2. continued

MIDI Output
PBM_MMMOM_OPEN
PBM_MMMOM_CLOSE
PBM_MMMOM_DONE

For example, if you want your application to access a CD audio player, you might add the event ID `pbm_mmmcinotify`. This event is used by Windows to notify a window that an MCI device has completed a particular task. In PowerBuilder, the `WordParm` attribute of the `Message` object is used to return those values, as shown in Table 32.3.

Table 32.3. The `WordParm` attribute of the `Message` object used in MCI communications.

Value	*Meaning*
1	Task aborted
2	Task successful
4	Task superseded
8	Task failed

In conjunction with declaring the user event, you also need to declare two external functions, `mciSendStringA` and `mciGetErrorStringA`. These Win32 function declarations are shown in Listing 32.1.

Listing 32.1. MCI function declarations.

```
FUNCTION Long mciSendStringA( string lpstrCommand, &
ref string lpstrRtnString, int wRtnLength, uint hCallBack) LIBRARY "WINMM.DLL"

FUNCTION Boolean mciGetErrorStringA( long dwError, &
ref string lpstrBuffer, int wLength) LIBRARY "WINMM.DLL"
```

The `mciSendStringA()` function is used to pass a string request to the Windows multimedia translation layer (WINMM.DLL), which interprets it and sends off the request to the appropriate device drivers. The following is coded in a window function:

```
Long ll_Return
String ls_Return, ls_Message = "play_cdaudio_notify"

ls_Return = Fill( Char(0), 255)
```

```
ll_Return = mciSendStringA( ls_Message, ls_Return, 255, Handle( this))

If ll_Return <> 0 Then
   mciGetErrorStringA( ll_Return, ls_Return, 255)
   MessageBox( "CD Audio Error", ls_Return)
End If
```

The return value (`ll_Return`) from the `mciSendStringA()` function can be used to pass to `mciGetErrorStringA()` (if not equal to zero), which returns the MCI error message as a string.

Because the CD will now be playing, you must trigger the user event assigned to `pbm_mmmcinotify`; it will not be triggered until after the CD is done playing. You don't need any code in the `pbm_mmmcinotify` event, but you could check `Message.WordParm` for returned information. Instead, code a `Timer` event that triggers every half-second and calls `mciSendStringA()` using the message `status cdaudio mode wait`. The function will return the status of the CD player as a String value that can be displayed in the window title (such as `"Playing"`). When you use the `Timer` event, you are constantly checking to see what the status is of the CD player.

Now that you have been introduced to the basics of the MCI high-level method of multimedia programming, let's take a look at writing an application that plays Windows AVI (Audio Video Interleave) files.

Playing Windows AVI Files

Incorporating a Windows video clip into your application uses the same MCI high-level method you saw previously with the CD example. The two functions, `mciSendStringA()` and `mciGetErrorStringA()`, need to be declared as in Listing 32.1. Once these have been declared, the code in Listing 32.2 can be used to run your video file.

The video file can be run one of two ways: in a separate window or in a DataWindow control. You will implement the second method. After placing a DataWindow control on your window, declare a window function that will call `mciSendStringA()`. The function will receive a String variable containing the command that you want to process.

Listing 32.2. Public subroutine `wf_SendStringA()` calling external function `mciSendStringA()`.

```
//Argument:
//   String arg_message
//Returns Long

long ll_rtn
String ls_error, ls_string

//Initialize the return strings
ls_error = Space(128)
ls_string = Space(128)
```

continues

Listing 32.2. continued

```
//Execute the argument message
ll_Rtn = mciSendStringA( arg_message, ls_string, 127, 0)

//Check to see if execution was successful
If ll_rtn <> 0 then
   mciGetErrorStringA(ll_rtn, ls_error, Len(ls_error) - 1)
   MessageBox("Media error","Error message: ~r~n" + ls_error)
   return ll_rtn
End If

return 1
```

The window, thus far, could be used as an ancestor window from which all multimedia application windows can be inherited. Then, depending on what type of multimedia application you were building, the framework would be in place. In this case, you will create a series of command buttons that control the play of the AVI file.

If the AVI file is going to be constant, the filename can be hard coded into the application code. If the DataWindow will be used as a viewer for potentially several different AVI files, then you give the user a method of selecting the desired file. This can be done using `GetFileOpenName()`. Once the file has been determined, you need to send a series of commands calling the window function, `wf_SendStringA()`. This has been implemented in the `Clicked` event of an Open command button on the window, as shown in Listing 32.3.

Listing 32.3. The `Clicked` event of the command button `cb_Open`.

```
string ls_handle, ls_named
long ll_rtn_code

//Get the desired AVI file and store it in
//an instance variable, is_file_name
ll_rtn_code = GetFileOpenName("Select File", &
              is_file_name, ls_named, "DOC",&
              "AVI Files (*.AVI), *.AVI")

If ll_rtn_code = -1 Or Upper(Right(Trim(is_file_name),3)) <> "AVI" Then
   MessageBox("Selection Error","You must select an AVI file!")
   is_file_name = ""
   Return
End If

//Open the media device
ll_rtn_code = wf_SendStringA("Open " + is_file_name)

If ll_rtn_code <> 1 Then Return

ls_handle = String(handle(dw_1))

//Send the handle of the DataWindow Control
//To indicate where the AVI file will be displayed
```

```
wf_SendString("Window " + is_file_name + " Handle " + ls_handle)

//Expands the AVI display to fit the DataWindow Control
wf_SendString("Put " + is_file_name + " destination", ls_return)

//Specify that the AVI display intervals is frames
wf_SendString("Set " + is_file_name + " time format frames", ls_return)
```

The default frame to start with is the first frame. If all is successful, you are now ready for your user to interact with the AVI file. The window can also contain several other buttons such as one to play the AVI file, one to pause execution, one to rewind to the beginning, one to stop playing, and one to close the file. The code for the `Clicked` event for each button differs only slightly. This would be the script for the Play button:

```
If wf_SendStringA("Play " + is_file_name) <> 1 Then
   MessageBox("Play Failed","Could not play " + is_file_name)
End If
```

Table 32.4 shows the commands sent to `wf_SendStringA()` to perform the rest of the processing.

Table 32.4. The AVI command set for `wf_SendStringA()`.

Desired Functionality	*Commands*
Pause execution	`"Pause " + is_file_name`
Rewind to beginning	`"Seek " + is_file_name + " to 1"`
Stop execution	`"Stop " + is_file_name`
Close file	`"Close " + is_file_name`

Your users may not understand why they need to close a file and they shouldn't have to worry about consciously closing a file. Therefore, perform the `Close` command from the window's `CloseQuery` event to ensure that the file is properly closed and that all resources are released.

This section introduces you to the basic idea of multimedia interaction with PowerBuilder. For more information about all of the possible string values that can be sent to the Windows multimedia translation layer (WINMM.DLL), take a look at the books *Multimedia Programmer's Guide* and *Multimedia Programmer's Reference* in the Windows SDK documentation.

Summary

The use of animation and multimedia can make one application stand head and shoulders above another. Not only is it fun to write these parts of an application, but users enjoy discovering and playing with the different components. Unless animation is specifically requested, however, it is probably a good idea to minimize its use because it can be distracting and resource intensive.

If you do animate the application, give your users the capability to shut it off if they want to. There are several different techniques that can be used: pictures toggling in toolbars, picture controls, and picture buttons; object movement; sound; and external function calls.

In addition to animation, PowerBuilder now provides the capability to implement an application that utilizes many multimedia features. You can access a number of external devices and receive input from such devices as joysticks and CDs. Although many companies have not moved into multimedia application development, the desire is increasing and implementation is becoming easier. As time goes by, the need will increase and the topics discussed in this chapter will become more frequently used.

API Calls

33

IN THIS CHAPTER

PowerBuilder, like many other GUI development languages, gives the developer the capability to extend outside the constraints of the host language and make use of functionality inherent in the operating system and in third-party controls and functions. This process is referred to as making an API (Application Program Interface) call. In PowerBuilder 4.0 a common use of API calls occurs when the application is undertaking some math-intensive task, and due to the slowness of PowerBuilder's interpreted runtime code this time-consuming processing is moved into a dynamic link library (DLL). Obviously, the driving force for this has been somewhat removed with the introduction of PowerBuilder 5.0 compiled executables. You can write DLLs using any language that supports the Pascal calling sequence, but often you write them using C or Pascal. No matter which language is used, or what the requirements of using an API call are, you need to know how PowerBuilder provides an interface to the outside environment.

Declaring an External Function

There are two types of external functions: global and local. *Global* external functions can be declared and are available anywhere in the application. They are stored in the application object with the other global variables. *Local* external functions can be defined for a window, menu, user object, or global function and become part of that object's definition. These functions can be made accessible, or inaccessible, to other objects using the `Public`, `Private`, and `Protected` keywords, in the same manner as object instance variables.

You can only access local external functions by prefixing the external function name with the object's name using the dot notation, as follows:

```
ObjectName.ExternalFunction( Arguments)
```

For example, if you declared the local external function `FlashWindow()` for the window `w_connect`, you would call the function like this:

```
w_connect.FlashWindow()
```

As with PowerBuilder functions, there are two types of code blocks: functions, which return a value, and subroutines, which carry out specific processing and return no value (a `Void` data type return data type). However, PowerBuilder makes a distinction with the external code blocks and provides two different syntaxes:

```
{Access} FUNCTION ReturnDataType FunctionName({REF}{DataType1 Arg1,     ...}) &
LIBRARY LibraryName {ALIAS FOR ExternalName}
{Access} SUBROUTINE SubroutineName({REF}{DataType1 Arg1, ... } ) &
LIBRARY LibraryName {ALIAS FOR ExternalName}
```

The `Access` declaration is valid only for local external functions. `ReturnDataType` must be a supported PowerBuilder data type that matches the return data type of the external function (see Table 33.1 for the PowerBuilder-supported data types). `FunctionName/SubroutineName` is the name of the function as it appears in the DLL/EXE file. `LibraryName` is the name of the DLL or EXE file in which the function is stored.

NOTE

If you want to use a different name for the function in your PowerScript for the external function or if the name of the function contains invalid characters, you have to specify an alias. This is done using the `ALIAS FOR` keywords followed by a string containing the real name. This establishes the association between the PowerScript name and the external name.

TIP

If you are migrating an application originally written under the 16-bit version of Windows, you can use `ALIAS FOR` in your declaration lines to avoid having to change all the places you make external function calls. Of course, if you are using an API manager class, like the one detailed in the section "Building an API Controller User Object," this will not be a problem you have to face.

The library must be accessible to the application at runtime (in the DOS path); PowerBuilder does not parcel it with the application or ensure that you distribute it with the EXE.

NOTE

If you create your own external function libraries for use with PowerBuilder, you must declare them using `FAR PASCAL` (see the next section for an example).

External functions are declared from within most objects' Script painters under the Declare menu. This opens up a window with a multiline edit field where you type the function declaration using one of the previous syntaxes. When you close this window, PowerBuilder compiles the declaration and checks for syntax errors. You must fix any errors before you can save the function declaration.

NOTE

PowerBuilder will *not* inform you that the function does not exist in the DLL, or that the call arguments are incorrect during the statement's compilation. Instead, you will get runtime errors.

Data Type Translation

Table 33.1 lists the PowerBuilder-supported C data types and their PowerBuilder equivalents. PowerBuilder only supports passing FAR pointers, and the external function must have the FAR qualifier in its declaration. This table is from Watcom C++ Class Builder documentation.

Table 33.1. PowerBuilder-supported data types for external functions.

C++ Data Type	*PowerBuilder Data Type*	*Data Type Description*
BOOL	Boolean	2-byte signed integer
WORD	uInt	2-byte unsigned integer
DWORD	uLong	4-byte unsigned integer
HANDLE	uInt	2-byte unsigned integer
HWND	uInt	2-byte unsigned integer
LPINT	String	4-byte FAR pointer
LPWORD	String	4-byte FAR pointer
LPLONG	String	4-byte FAR pointer
LPDWORD	String	4-byte FAR pointer
LPVOID	String	4-byte FAR pointer
LPVOID	Char	4-byte HUGE pointer
BYTE	Char	1 byte
CHAR	Char	1 byte
CHAR CHARARRAY [10]	Char CHARARRAY [10]	10 bytes
INT	Int	2-byte signed integer
UNSIGNED INT	uInt	2-byte unsigned integer
LONG	Long	4-byte signed integer
UNSIGNED LONG	uLong	4-byte unsigned integer
DOUBLE	Double	8-byte double-precision floating-point number
DOUBLE	Decimal	8-byte double-precision floating-point number
FLOAT	Real	4-byte single-precision floating-point number
N/A	Time	Date and time structure
N/A	Date	Date and time structure
N/A	DateTime	Date and time structure

PowerBuilder does not support the C `NEAR` pointer data type—that is, `PSTR` and `NPSTR`—and the keyword `REF` must be used to provide a 32-bit `FAR` pointer to a PowerBuilder variable. For example, the API function is declared as follows:

```
BOOL FAR PASCAL VerQueryValue( ...., UINT FAR *lpBuffSize);
```

This would be declared in PowerBuilder like so:

```
FUNCTION Boolean VerQueryValue( ...., REF UINT lpBuffSize) LIBRARY "VER.DLL"
```

The following code could then be used to call the function:

```
// A pointer to a buffer
UINT lpBuffSize

// Other processing
If VerQueryValue( ...., lpBuffSize) THEN
   // Some processing
ELSE
   // Some other processing, function failed
END IF
```

PowerBuilder passes the internal memory address of the variable `lpBuffSize` to the DLL function, which fills in the value. This is known as *passing by reference*, which is the same principle as that used in PowerBuilder functions that have arguments passed by reference.

Passing Arguments

Sometimes it is enough to just call a function and maybe get a value returned, but more often than not the functions you are calling expect parameters. These parameters, as in PowerBuilder, can be passed either by value or by reference.

The syntax for arguments passed by value is

```
ParameterDataType Parameter
```

The syntax for arguments passed by reference is

```
REF ParameterDataType Parameter
```

Passing Numeric Data Types by Reference

The following statement is an example of passing Numeric data types by reference; it declares an external function `Increase()` in PowerBuilder. The function takes two integer values; the first is the value to be increased and the second is the modification factor. The function returns a Boolean, and the integer to be modified is passed by reference:

```
FUNCTION Bool Increase(REF Int nValue, Int nFactor) LIBRARY "MyLib.DLL"
```

The function's C declaration would look like this:

```
bool far pascal Increase(int far * value, int factor)
```

Passing Strings by Reference

Because PowerBuilder undertakes all memory management for you, you cannot receive a pointer to a string from an external function. This also affects how things happen—but not what happens—when you pass a string by reference. PowerBuilder actually passes the string—not a pointer to the string—and then changes the PowerBuilder string with the returned string.

For example, the external function of the following declaration expects a string as a parameter to be passed by reference:

```
char far * far pascal ExtractName( char far * bigstring)
```

The PowerBuilder external function declaration would be

```
FUNCTION String ExtractName(REF String szBigString) LIBRARY "MyLib.DLL"
```

Using the way PowerBuilder handles string arguments, you could also define the external function declaration as follows:

```
FUNCTION String ExtractName(String szBigString) LIBRARY "MyLib.DLL"
```

The only difference on the PowerBuilder side is that the `REF` keyword has been taken out. This, however, means that even though the `ExtractName()` function modifies the string, PowerBuilder does not update the string with the returned value.

WARNING

You must be very careful when you are passing strings or string buffers that are expected to be a certain size. When you declare the variables, you must use the `Space()` function to fill the string to the required size before the external function is called.

If the external function requires a string parameter not to be `NULL`-terminated, you can use an array of type Char.

Passing Structures

Some of the Windows API functions expect specific structures to be passed as parameters. If you know the exact makeup of the structure, it is then only a simple task of creating a PowerBuilder structure object in the same order with comparable data types. All that you have to do then is instantiate the structure before passing it into the function call.

For example, let's look at a call to the `GetSystemInfo()` function, available only in the Win32 API. This function obtains information on the current state of the system and takes only one parameter: a pointer to a structure of type `SYSTEM_INFO`.

You create the structure object `s_system_info` as shown in Table 33.2.

Table 33.2. The `s_system_info` structure.

Variable Name	*Variable Data Type*	*Target Type*
`ulOEMId`	uLong	DWORD
`ulPageSize`	uLong	DWORD
`szMinAppAddress`	String	LPVOID
`szMaxAppAddress`	String	LPVOID
`ulActiveProcessorMask`	uLong	DWORD
`ulNoOfProcessors`	uLong	DWORD
`ulProcessorType`	uLong	DWORD
`ulRes1`	uLong	DWORD
`ulRes2`	uLong	DWORD

The external function declaration would be

```
SUBROUTINE GetSystemInfo( REF s_system_info sSystemInfo ) LIBRARY "kernel32.dll"
```

First, you would need a declaration either at a global or an instance level:

```
s_system_info sSystemInfo
```

The actual call would be something like this:

```
GetSystemInfo( sSystemInfo)
MessageBox( "Processor Type", String( sSystemInfo.ulProcessorType))
```

Where to Find Further Information

The source of information you use depends on the kind of information you want to obtain.

You can find information on function names, the value of constants, and the construction of window structures by opening the windows.h file in a text editor. This file is included as part of any C/C++ compiler for Windows (for example, Visual C++). It is the file that contains all the prototype information for the Windows API. You use this with a `grep`-like utility to find pattern matches to a certain word. For example, if you were searching for a function to flash a window, you could easily find all references to the word *flash*.

Actually finding the DLL or EXE file where the function is located takes a little more effort. With Windows 3.1, your best bet is to start with USER.EXE, KRNL386.EXE, and GDI.EXE, and then any other DLL that looks like it might have a name similar to the function's. In the Win32 API the corresponding DLLs are USER32.DLL, KERNEL32.DLL, and GDI32.DLL, respectively. A few tools exist that can be used to dissect a Windows binary file and return the functions stored within it—for example, EXEHDR from Microsoft Visual C++, or TDUMP from Borland's C++ Windows compiler.

A more user-friendly, but not as easily searched, reference is the WIN31API.HLP, WIN31WH.HLP, and API32.HLP files that come with Windows C/C++ compilers and some other GUI development tools. These are Windows help files that provide the same sort of limited searching as the PowerBuilder help pages. You usually make use of these in conjunction with the output from one of the disassemblers mentioned, to provide further information after a function or structure is found.

TIP

If you are using the Windows 95 operating system, you can use the Quick View program to look at the functions available in DLL files.

You can find a number of books that deal with the Windows API—some are good, but some are very poorly written. A helpful book is Schildt, Pappas, and Murray's *Osborne Windows Programming Series Vol. 2, General Purpose API Functions*. This book includes a lot of the general API functions, structures, data types, and constants.

NOTE

In the Win32 API some of the functions have been renamed and some have been removed. Some function calls are suffixed with either an `A` or a `W`. This indicates whether the function is Unicode, "wide character" (`W`) enabled, or an ANSI (`A`) type of function.

Building an API Controller User Object

Now that PowerBuilder is a multiplatform development tool, you need to make your applications both environment aware and environment independent. To do this, you need to build and use class user objects; that is, build an ancestor user object that prototypes all the functions that can be defined for each of the environments. These functions are user-object functions and not the external declarations. The environment specifics—the actual external function declarations—are attached to descendant user objects of the main user object. Within an application or application object, you would declare an instance variable of the following type:

```
u_n_externals externals
```

In the Constructor event (shown in the following code) for the application user object, or in the Open event of the application object, you need to call an initialization function. This function is coded as follows:

```
private subroutine uf_initialize()

GetEnvironment( i_Environment)

Choose Case i_Environment.OSType
   Case Windows!
      If i_Environment.OSMajorRevision = 4 Then
         // Windows 95
         Externals = Create u_n_externals_win32
      Else
         // Windows 3.x
         Externals = Create u_n_externals_winapi
      End If
   Case WindowsNT!
        Externals = Create u_n_externals_win32
   Case Else
        SetNull( Externals)
End Choose
```

This function uses GetEnvironment() to query the application's environment and determine under which operating system it is running. In a Case statement, the Externals instance variable previously declared is assigned an instantiation of one of the descendant user object classes that provides API calls specific to the current operating system.

To access the user object functions for an application user object g_App, using the instance variable Externals, the code from anywhere within an application would be

```
g_App.Externals.uf_FlashWindow( this)
```

This ensures that no matter what the actual API function call is, the application is written to a consistent interface.

The base object of u_n_externals would contain a prototype function for uf_FlashWindow() that does nothing. The inherited objects u_n_externals_winapi or u_n_externals_win32 would also declare the same function and provide the appropriate calls to the local declared external functions.

Sample Code

The easiest way to relay information is to provide examples, so the following sections describe a number of the most common uses for API functions.

Registry Functions

Even though PowerBuilder provides you with access to the registry using four "wrapper" functions (functions that are defined to hide the complexities of other function calls), they are very limited in their flexibility. For example, the Powersoft functions only deal with string values. This section shows how to use some of the registry functions available through the Win32 API. For more information on the PowerScript functions provided by Powersoft, refer to Chapter 21, "Cross-Platform PowerBuilder."

A number of constants are used with the registry functions to indicate not only where to make a modification, but how and with what kind of values. Table 33.3 lists most of the commonly used constants and their corresponding numeric values.

Table 33.3. Win32 constants for registry functions.

Data Type	*Constant*	*Numeric Value*
Long	HKEY_CLASSES_ROOT	2147483648
Long	HKEY_CURRENT_USER	2147483649
Long	HKEY_LOCAL_MACHINE	2147483650
Long	HKEY_USERS	2147483651
Long	HKEY_PERFORMANCE_DATA	2147483652
Long	HKEY_CURRENT_CONFIG	2147483653
Long	HKEY_DYN_DATA	2147483654
uInt	REG_OPTION_RESERVED	0
uInt	REG_OPTION_NON VOLATILE	0
uInt	REG_OPTION_VOLATILE	1
uInt	REG_OPTION_CREATE_LINK	2
uInt	REG_OPTION_BACKUP_RESTORE	4
uInt	REG_NONE	0
uInt	REG_SZ	1
uInt	REG_EXPAND_SZ	2
uInt	REG_BINARY	3
uInt	REG_DWORD	4
uInt	REG_DWORD_LITTLE_ENDIAN	4
uInt	REG_DWORD_BIG_ENDIAN	5
uInt	REG_LINK	6
uInt	REG_MULTI_SZ	7

Data Type	Constant	Numeric Value
uInt	REG_RESOURCE_LIST	8
uInt	REG_FULL_RESOURCE_DESCRIPTOR	9
uInt	REG_RESOURCE_REQUIREMENTS_LIST	10
Long	SYNCHRONIZE	1048576
Long	READ_CONTROL	131072
Long	KEY_QUERY_VALUE	1
Long	KEY_SET_VALUE	2
Long	KEY_CREATE_SUB_KEY	4
Long	KEY_ENUMERATE_SUB_KEYS	8
Long	KEY_NOTIFY	16
Long	KEY_CREATE_LINK	32
Long	KEY_READ	131097
Long	KEY_WRITE	131078
Long	KEY_ALL_ACCESS	983103
Long	STANDARD_RIGHTS_READ	131072
Long	STANDARD_RIGHTS_WRITE	131072
Long	KEY_EXECUTE	131097

Five registry functions from the Win32 API allow you to create and query registry values. The first operation is querying existing registry values. For this you need to use the `RegQueryValueExA()` function, which has the following prototype:

```
Function Long RegQueryValueExA( Long hKey, String lpValueName, Long lpResvd, &
                                Ref Long lpType, Ref String lpData, &
                                Ref Long lpcbData)  &
                                Library "advapi32.dll"
```

The parameter *`lpValueName`* is the name of the value within the open key, *`hKey`*, that you are interested in obtaining the value of. The value of *`lpResvd`* is always `0`. *`LpType`* indicates the data type of the key value, which can range from a numeric (`REG_DWORD`) to a string (`REG_SZ`). The value of the name within the key is returned into *`lpData`*, and *`lpcbData`* indicates the size of the returned value.

The `RegQueryValueExA()` function, like most of the registry functions, acts on a handle to a key, *`hKey`*. This handle is obtained by using the `RegOpenKeyExA()` function, which has the following prototype:

```
Function Long RegOpenKeyExA( Long hKey, String lpSubKey, Long ulOptions, &
                             Long samDesired, Ref Long phkResult) &
                             Library "advapi32.dll"
```

The parameters `hKey` and `lpSubKey` specify the exact path to the values you are interested in. `samDesired` specifies the access mask for new keys that are created. The last parameter, `phkResult`, contains the handle used in the other function calls. As with other controlled resources, such as opening print jobs or files, you also need to close the resource when you have finished with it. The registry is no exception, and you make use of the `RegCloseKey()` function, which has the following prototype:

```
Function Long RegCloseKey(Long hKey) Library "advapi32.dll"
```

The following example illustrates the use and context of these functions and the parameters that are expected:

```
Long lReturn, lLen, lKey, lType
String szValue, szPath
//
//
//
szPath = "\Software\RavenSoft\Order Entry"

lReturn = RegOpenKeyExA( HKEY_CURRENT_USER, szPath, 0, KEY_ALL_ACCESS, lKey)

If lReturn = 0 Then
   szValue = Space( 30)

   // Add one for the null termination character
   lLen = Len( szValue) + 1

   lReturn = RegQueryValueExA( lKey, "Database", 0, lType, szValue, lLen)

   // Process the returned key value, in this case we will simply display it
   // we could just as simply assign it straight to SQLCA.Database
   MessageBox( "", szValue)

   lReturn = RegCloseKey( lKey)
End If
```

As you can see in this example, the key path `HKEY_CURRENT_USER\Software\RavenSoft\Order Entry` is opened and the value name `Database` is queried for its value. In this case you know that the database name will not be more than 30 characters, so you allocate only that much space in the receiving parameter for the value.

NOTE

If the return value, `lReturn`, is a value of 234 (`ERROR_MORE_DATA`), then the value of `lLen` indicates the size that `szValue` must be to accept the key. Otherwise, if the value is `0` (`ERROR_SUCCESS`), the operation completed successfully.

To create a key within the registry you need to use the `RegCreateKeyExA()` function, which has the following prototype:

```
Function Long RegCreateKeyExA( Long hKey, String lpSubKey, Long Reserved, &
                               String lpClass, Long dwOptions, &
                               Long samDesired, string lpSecurityAttribs, &
                               ref long phkResult, ref Long lpdwDisposition) &
                               Library "advapi32.dll"
```

The parameters `hKey` and `lpSubKey` specify the exact path of the key that you want to create. `lpClass` is a string representation of the data type for the new key. The parameter `dwOptions` is used to set whether the key is volatile (the key is stored in memory and is lost when the system is restarted) or nonvolatile (the key is preserved for future use). `samDesired` specifies the access mask for the new key, and `lpSecurityAttribs` can be used to specify the security attributes for the new key. If `lpSecurityAttribs` is `NULL`, the key receives a default security descriptor. The parameter `phkResult` contains the handle to the newly created key, which you can use in other function calls. The final parameter, `lpdwDisposition`, returns additional information about the creation operation: key did not exist and was created, `REG_CREATED_NEW_KEY` (1), or key existed and was just opened without changing it, `REG_OPENED_EXISTING_KEY` (2).

NOTE

For Windows NT Version 3.5 and later, as well as Windows 95, the value of `lpSubKey` should not start with a back slash (\).

The following code shows an example of creating a key within the current user's profile for an order entry application:

```
String szKey, szNull
Long lResult, lDisposition

SetNull( szNull)

szKey = "Software\RavenSoft\Order Entry"

RegCreateKeyExA( HKEY_CURRENT_USER, szKey,0,"REG_SZ", REG_OPTION_NON_VOLATILE,&
                 KEY_ALL_ACCESS, szNull, lResult, lDisposition)
```

To actually create and assign a value to a registry key, you have to use the `RegSetValueExA()` function, which has the following prototype:

```
Function Long RegSetValueExA( Long hKey, String lpValueName, Long Reserved, &
                              Long dwType, String lpData, Long cbData)  &
                              Library "advapi32.dll"
```

The `RegSetValueExA()` function uses the same parameters as used by the `RegQueryValueExA()` function. The only difference is that you are specifying the actual value for the key. An example of how to use this function is shown in the following code:

```
Integer nLen
String szValue, szPath
Long lReturn, lKey

szPath = "\Software\RavenSoft\Order Entry"

lReturn = RegOpenKeyExA( HKEY_CURRENT_USER, szPath, 0, KEY_ALL_ACCESS, lKey)

If lReturn = 0 Then
   szValue = "oe_010"

   // Add one for the null termination character
   nLen = Len( szValue) + 1

   RegSetValueExA( lKey, "Database", 0, REG_SZ, szValue, nLen)

   RegCloseKey( lKey)
End If
```

Determining Whether an Application Is Already Open

A common requirement is for an application to query the other open applications running on the host machine, usually to determine whether another application needs to be opened first. You can accomplish this task in one of two ways. The first uses the `FindWindow()` API function:

```
HWND FindWindow( LPCSTR lpszClassName, LPCSTR lpszTitle)
```

This translates to a PowerBuilder external function declaration of

```
// Win31
Function uInt FindWindow( String szClass, String szName) Library "user.exe"

// Win32
Function uInt FindWindowA( String szClass, String szName) Library "user32.dll"
```

Either of the parameters can be `NULL`, in which case the function matches on all classes and/or titles (you'll learn later in this section how to determine an application's class and title). The function returns the window handle of the window if it can be found, or `0` if no match is found.

For example, to see whether the Windows Calculator application is already open, the code would be as follows:

```
uInt hWnd

hWnd = g_App.Externals.uf_FindWindow( "scicalc", "calculator")

If hWnd = 0 Then
   Run( "calc")
Else
   g_App.Externals.uf_SetFocus( hWnd)
End If
```

Note the use of another API call to `SetFocus()` that enables you to bring an already open window to the front. The `SetFocus()` function takes a Windows handle and is defined inside PowerBuilder as

```
// Win31
Function uInt SetFocus( uInt hWnd ) Library "user.exe"

// Win32
Function uInt SetFocus( uInt hWnd ) Library "user32.dll"
```

To find whether a DOS prompt window has been opened, you set the class name parameter to `tty`. To find the DOS prompt window in particular, you look for a window by the name of MS-DOS Prompt. The case, spaces, and characters must match exactly with those of the window.

Determining a window's class can be a little tricky. A freeware program that gives you valuable information about windows is WinSnoop by D.T. Hamilton. WinSnoop displays the window's handle, title, creator, parent, class, and owner. A number of other programs will return the same information—for example, SPY.EXE and WSPY.EXE.

The second method can only be used in Win16 (this is because each Win32 application runs in its own address space, and therefore the `GetModuleUsage()` function has been removed) and requires the use of two functions, `GetModuleHandle()` and `GetModuleUsage()`, as follows:

```
HMODULE GetModuleHandle( LPCSTR lpszModuleName);
```

The `GetModuleHandle()` function returns the handle of the module specified by `lpszModuleName` if successful; otherwise, it returns `NULL`.

```
Int GetModuleUsage( HINSTANCE hInst);
```

The `GetModuleUsage()` function returns the usage count of the module specified by `hInst`. The Windows operating system increments a module's reference count every time an application is loaded. The count is decremented when an application is closed.

These functions are declared in PowerBuilder as

```
// Win31
FUNCTION uInt GetModuleHandle( String szModuleName) Library "krnl386.exe"
FUNCTION Int GetModuleUsage( uInt hWnd) Library "krnl386.exe"
```

For example, to check for the existence of an already running version of Word for Windows, the code would be as follows:

```
Uint uiModule
Integer nUsage

uiModule = GetModuleHandle( "winword.exe")

nUsage = GetModuleUsage( uiModule)

If nUsage = 0 Then
   Run( "winword.exe")
End If
```

You can use the optional parameter of the `Handle()` function to check for the existence of another PowerBuilder application of the same executable like this:

```
If Handle( this, TRUE) > 0 Then
   // Already running
   HALT CLOSE
End If
```

The Boolean value of the second parameter determines whether you want to obtain the current instance (`FALSE`—the default), or the handle of the previous instance (`TRUE`). You can use this method in either Win31 or Win32 environments.

Attracting Attention

Occasionally, you will need to draw the user's attention to a particular window in an application, either when it is open or when it's iconized. The accepted GUI standard is to cause the window title (or icon, if the window is iconized) to flash. You do this with the `FlashWindow()` function:

```
// Win31
Function Boolean FlashWindow( uInt handle, Boolean bFlash) Library "user.exe"

// Win32
Function Boolean FlashWindow( uInt handle, Boolean bFlash) Library "user32.dll"
```

The Boolean `bFlash` should be `TRUE` to cause the window to flash from one state to another, and `FALSE` to return the window to its original state (either active or inactive). For example, to attract attention to an error window, you first need to obtain the Windows handle for the window `w_error` and pass it to the external function, as follows:

```
uInt hWnd

hWnd - Handle( w_error)
g_App.Externals.uf_FlashWindow( hWnd, TRUE)
```

The call to `FlashWindow()` usually appears in a `Timer` event so that you get the window to truly flash. A timer interval of about half to a quarter of a second seems about right.

Centering a Window

A very common requirement when you open a window is to have it centered on the screen. Although PowerBuilder gives you access to the X and Y coordinates of the window, you need to know the current screen resolution to set these values. The width and height of the screen varies between resolutions, so Microsoft has provided a function, `GetSystemMetrics()`, that can be used to access these values, among others. Its syntax is

```
// Win31
Function int GetSystemMetrics( int nIndex) Library "user.exe"

// Win 32
```

```
Function int GetSystemMetrics( int nIndex) Library "user32.dll"
```

The `nIndex` parameter provides access to a number of different system constants (see Table 33.4). Note that all `SM_CX*` values are widths and all `SM_CY*` values are heights.

Table 33.4. `GetSystemMetrics` parameter constants.

Value	*Meaning*
SM_CMOUSEBUTTONS	Number of mouse buttons, or zero if no installed mouse
SM_CXBORDER, SM_CYBORDER	Width and height of window border
SM_CXCURSOR, SM_CYCURSOR	Width and height of cursor
SM_CXDLGFRAME, SM_CYDLGFRAME	Width and height of frame for dialog box
SM_CXFRAME, SM_CYFRAME	Width and height of frame for a resizable window
SM_CXFULLSCREEN, SM_CYFULLSCREEN	Width and height of the client area for a full-screen window
SM_CXHSCROLL, SM_CYHSCROLL	Width and height of arrow bitmap on horizontal scrollbar
SM_CXHTHUMB	Width of horizontal scrollbar thumb box
SM_CXICON, SM_CYICON	Width and height of an icon
SM_CXICONSPACING, SM_CYICONSPACING	Width and height of cell used in tiling icons
SM_CXMIN, SM_CYMIN	Minimum width and height of a window
SM_CXSCREEN, SM_CYSCREEN	Width and height of the screen
SM_CXSIZE, SM_CYSIZE	Width and height of bitmaps contained in the title bar
SM_CXVSCROLL, SM_CYVSCROLL	Width and height of arrow bitmap on vertical scrollbar
SM_CYVTHUMB	Height of vertical scrollbar thumb box
SM_CYCAPTION	Height of normal caption area
SM_CYMENU	Height of single-line menu bar
SM_MOUSEPRESENT	Zero if a mouse is not installed; non-zero otherwise
SM_SWAPBUTTON	Non-zero if the left and right mouse buttons are swapped

This function can be added to the external call controller user object that was previously mentioned with the following syntax in the `u_n_externals` object:

```
public function integer uf_GetSystemMetrics (integer a_nIndex);
   Return GetSystemMetrics( a_nIndex)
end function
```

You could then write a global function or application function to make use of one or all three of these functions, as follows:

```
//
// The window to centre is passed in as an argument to the function.
// Window wToActOn
//
Long lWidth, lHeight

// Query the system for the desktop size, and then convert to the
// PB unit system.
lWidth = this.Externals.uf_GetSystemMetrics(0) * (686/150)
lHeight = this.Externals.uf_GetSystemMetrics(1) * (801/200)

// Calculate central position
wToActOn.X = ( lWidth - wToActOn.Width) / 2
wToActOn.Y = ( lHeight - wToActOn.Height) / 2
```

The return value from `GetSystemMetrics()` is modified using a conversion factor that takes pixels and converts them to PowerBuilder units.

NOTE

This example only illustrates the use of the function. You would of course use the `GetEnvironment()` function and use the `ScreenHeight` and `ScreenWidth` properties from the returned structure. Therefore, the two lines would be

```
lWidth = PixelsToUnits( i_Environment.ScreenWidth, XPixelsToUnits!)
lHeight = PixelsToUnits( i_Environment.ScreenHeight, YPixelsToUnits!)
```

When all the code is in place, each window can then make a single call in the `Open` event. The following example makes use of an application user object and center function:

```
g_App.uf_CentreWindow( this)
```

It should be obvious that this code cannot be used to center a sheet within an MDI application, but will work on all other types of windows. To center a sheet you only have to reference the client area of the MDI frame; but remember that the sheet will always open according to the `ArrangeOrder` argument value and will automatically be visible.

Modifying a Window's Style

Whenever you open a sheet in an MDI frame, regardless of the window type and style bits you have set, they are overridden by PowerBuilder. This is done to produce a resizable, minimizable, and maximizable window with a system menu. There may be occasions when you would like to provide slightly different behavior, and this requires you to use the `SetWindowLongA()` function. The definition of this function is

```
// Win 31
Function Long SetWindowLong( uInt hWindow, Integer unIndex, Long lNewValue) &
                                                          Library "user.exe"

// Win 32
Function Long SetWindowLongA( uInt hWindow, Integer unIndex, Long lNewValue) &
                                                          Library "user32.dll"
```

The window to act on is passed as a handle using `hWindow`. The `unIndex` argument is used to specify what area of the window you will be changing; for the style changes that you might possibly want to make this value will always be `GWL_STYLE (-16)`. The `lNewValue` argument is a bit representation of the new styles (see Table 33.5).

Table 33.5. Values for the `lNewValue` argument.

Windows Constant	*Numeric Value*	*Description*
WS_BORDER	8388608	Window has a normal border.
WS_CAPTION	12582912	Window has a title bar (implies the WS_BORDER style).
WS_DLGFRAME	4194304	Window with a modal dialog box (no title).
WS_EX_TOPMOST	8	Window will appear above all non-topmost windows and stay above them even when the window is deactivated.
WS_EX_TRANSPARENT	32	Any windows beneath the window are not obscured by the window.
WS_HSCROLL	1048576	Window has a horizontal scrollbar.
WS_MAXIMIZE	16777216	The window has a maximized state.
WS_MAXIMIZEBOX	65536	Window has a maximize button.
WS_MINIMIZE	536870912	The window has a minimized state.
WS_MINIMIZEBOX	131072	Window has a minimize button.
WS_OVERLAPPED	0	Window has a caption and a border.
WS_POPUP	2147483648	Window is created as a pop-up.
WS_SYSMENU	524288	Window has a System menu box in its title bar.

WS_THICKFRAME	262144	Window has a thick resizable border.
WS_VSCROLL	2097152	Window has a vertical scrollbar.

The constants listed in Table 33.5 can be combined by adding the numeric values, although not all combinations are allowed and some require other specific constants to also be listed.

WARNING

Before you start altering the style of a window, you first need to capture the current settings; otherwise, you will need to specify *all* of the style bits that are required to make the window function correctly.

The current style is captured using the `GetWindowLongA()` function, which is defined as

```
// Win 31
Function Long GetWindowLongA( uInt hWindow, Integer unIndex) Library "user32.dll"

// Win 32
Function Long GetWindowLongA( uInt hWindow, Integer unIndex) Library "user32.dll"
```

In the following, you will alter the existing window by adding the minimize button and removing (disabling) the maximize button:

```
uInt hWindow
Integer GWL_STYLE = -16
Long WS_MAXIMIZEBOX = 65536, WS_MINIMIZEBOX = 131072, lOldStyle

hWindow = Handle( this)

lOldStyle = GetWindowLongA( hWindow, GWL_STYLE)

SetWindowLongA( hWindow, GWL_STYLE, lOldStyle + WS_MINIMIZEBOX - WS_MAXIMIZEBOX)
```

Notice that it is simply a matter of adding or subtracting the style value from the current window style setting.

Obtaining System Resource Information

Everyone knows that under Windows 3.*x* PowerBuilder can be quite a resource consumer, and that it often pays to provide an indication of the current system resources to the user. This enables the users to spot when they will need to start closing windows or applications, or even when to reboot Windows.

The external function declaration is as follows:

```
// Get system resource information
// Win 31
Function uint GetFreeSystemResources( uint resource) Library "user.exe"
```

As you are probably aware, Windows has two fixed-sized heaps of memory that it uses for tracking open windows, device contexts, and other system information. These two heaps are the graphic device information (GDI) and user heaps and can be obtained from the function `GetFreeSystemResources()` using the values `1` and `2`, respectively.

The function would be added to the user object as follows:

```
public function unsignedinteger uf_getfreesystemresources( Integer nParm)

//Query Windows API to get free Window resources
Return GetFreeSystemResources( nParm)
```

A call to obtain the free GUI heap percentage would be

```
Uint unResource

unResource = g_App.Externals.uf_GetFreeSystemResources(1)
```

A call to obtain the free user heap percentage would be

```
Uint unResource

unResource = g_App.Externals.uf_GetFreeSystemResources(2)
```

A call to obtain the free memory would require the following declarations:

```
//Get free memory
Function ulong GetFreeSpace( uint dummy) Library "krnl386.exe"

public function unsignedlong uf_getfreememory()

//Query Windows API to get free memory
Return GetFreeSpace( 0)
```

The code to call this function would then be

```
Ulong ulMem

ulMem = g_App.Externals.uf_GetFreememory()
MessageBox( "Free Memory", String( ulMem / 1048576, "###.0") + " Mb")
```

The manner in which resources are handled in the 32-bit Windows environments is a little different, but anyone who has worked just a little with Windows 95 knows that resources still get consumed and are not always released.

First, a little background on how the different memory management systems work.

Within Windows 3.*x*, there are two 64KB heaps from which resources are allocated. The User and Menu heaps are both limited to 64KB of data, which limits the maximum number of windows and menus to about 200.

Windows 95 naturally enhances this method, and adds an additional 32-bit heap, which can grow as large as available memory; the 16-bit heap is still limited to 64KB. Windows 95 stores data structures within the 16-bit heap, and physical objects such as fonts and bitmaps in the 32-bit heap. GDI regions have also been moved to the 32-bit, freeing up the 16-bit heap's responsibilities. When a process terminates, the GDI resources that were used in Windows 95 or NT are freed immediately, unless the application was a 16-bit application, in which case the resources are held until the last 16-bit application is closed. The user and menu heaps with Windows 95 have been increased to 2MB each, and the previous limit of 200 windows/menus is effectively eliminated.

You can check on Windows 95 memory usage with the API function, `GlobalMemoryStatus()`, which has this definition:

```
// Win32
Subroutine GlobalMemoryStatus( lpmemorystatus lpBuffer) Library "kernel32.dll"
```

This makes use of a single parameter, a pointer to a `_MEMORYSTATUS` structure, which was re-created in PowerBuilder, as shown in Table 33.6.

Table 33.6. The `s_memory_status` structure.

Variable Name	*Variable Data Type*	*Description*
`ulLength`	uLong	Length of the structure, which you should set before using.
`ulMemoryLoad`	uLong	A general idea of current memory utilization. Between 0 (no memory use) and 100 (full memory use).
`ulTotalPhys`	uLong	Total number of bytes of physical memory.
`ulAvailPhys`	uLong	Number of bytes of physical memory available.
`ulTotalPageFile`	uLong	Total number of bytes that can be stored in the paging file.
`ulAvailPageFile`	uLong	Number of bytes available in the paging file.
`ulTotalVirtual`	uLong	Total number of bytes in the virtual address space.
`ulAvailVitrual`	uLong	Number of bytes of unreserved and uncommitted memory in the virtual address space.

You can then call the `GlobalMemoryStatus()` function using the following code:

```
ws_memory_status sSystemInfo
```

```
sSystemInfo.dwLength = 32

GlobalMemoryStatus( sSystemInfo)
//
// Calculate percentage free of each memory resource
//
ulPhysicalFree = ( sSystemInfo.dwAvailPhys / sSystemInfo.dwTotalPhys) &
                 / 1024) * 100
ulPagingFree   = ( sSystemInfo.dwAvailPageFile / sSystemInfo.dwTotalPageFile) &
                 / 1024) * 100
ulVirtualFree  = ( sSystemInfo.dwAvailVirtual / sSystemInfo.dwTotalVirtual) &
                 / 1024) * 100
```

These values provide little meaningful information for the average user, though, because they only provide an indicator of the current state of memory available. In Windows 95 there is little reason to track the heaps anyway, so this is a moot point.

Making Connections

Three very useful functions are `WNetGetConnection()`, `WNetAddConnection()`, and `WNetCancelConnection()`. These enable you to make and break network connections within Microsoft Windows 3.*x*, and they can be used for printer connections as well as drive mappings. These functions have been made backward compatible from within the Win32 API, which includes enhanced versions of these functions under a different name.

NOTE

In the Win32 API the `WNet` functions have been superseded with newer versions. You can still use the versions shown in the following sections as is.

The function `WNetGetConnection()` is used to retrieve the name of a network resource associated with a local device name. The external function is

```
uInt WNetGetConnection( LPSTR lpszLocalName, LPSTR lpszRemoteName, &
                        UINT FAR *cbRemoteName)
```

The PowerBuilder declaration is

```
Function uInt WNetGetConnection( string szLocalName, ref char szRemoteName[], &
                                 ref uInt nRemoteSize) Library "user.exe"
```

The *`szLocalName`* parameter points to the local device on which you are querying. The *`szRemoteName`* parameter is used to receive the network name. *`nRemoteSize`* specifies the size (in characters) of the buffer pointed to by *`szRemoteName`*. If the function call fails because the buffer is too small, this parameter returns the required buffer size.

The function returns a value of `WN_SUCCESS` if it succeeds or the appropriate error message (see Table 33.7) upon failure.

Table 33.7. `WNetGetConnection()` return values.

Error	*Value*	*Meaning*
WN_SUCCESS	0	The function was successful
WN_NOT_SUPPORTED	1	The function is not supported
WN_OUT_OF_MEMORY	11	The system is out of memory
WN_NET_ERROR	2	An error occurred on the network
WN_BAD_POINTER	4	The pointer was invalid
WN_BAD_VALUE	5	The *szLocalName* value is not a valid local device
WN_NOT_CONNECTED	48	The *szLocalName* value is not a redirected local device
WN_MORE_DATA	53	The buffer is too small

You use the function `WNetAddConnection()`to make a new connection to a network resource and associate it with a local device name. The external function is

```
uInt WNetAddConnection( LPSTR lpszNetPath, LPSTR lpszPassword, &
                        LPSTR lpszLocalName)
```

The PowerBuilder declaration is

```
Function uInt WNetAddConnection( string szNetPath, string szPassword, &
                                 string szLocalName) Library "user.exe"
```

The *szNetPath* parameter points to the network device where you want to connect the local device, *szLocalName*. The *szPassword* parameter is used to supply the network password associated with the network device to be connected to. If this parameter is `NULL`, the network default password is used. If the string is empty, no password is used.

The function returns a value of `WN_SUCCESS` if it succeeds or the appropriate error message (see Table 33.8) upon failure.

Table 33.8. `WNetAddConnection()` return values.

Error	*Value*	*Meaning*
WN_SUCCESS	0	The function was successful
WN_NOT_SUPPORTED	1	The function is not supported
WN_OUT_OF_MEMORY	11	The system is out of memory

Error	Value	Meaning
WN_NET_ERROR	2	An error occurred on the network
WN_BAD_POINTER	4	The pointer is invalid
WN_BAD_NETNAME	50	The network resource name is invalid
WN_BAD_LOCALNAME	51	The local device name is invalid
WN_BAD_PASSWORD	6	The password is invalid
WN_ACCESS_DENIED	7	A security violation occurred
WN_ALREADY_CONNECTED	52	The local device is already connected to a remote resource

A successful connection made with this function is persistent. This means that Windows will re-create the connection every time you go through the login procedure.

The function `WNetCancelConnection()` is used to break an existing network connection. The external function is

```
uInt WNetCancelConnection(LPSTR lpszName, BOOL bForce)
```

The PowerBuilder declaration is

```
Function uInt WNetCancelConnection( string szName, Boolean bForce) Library
"user.exe"
```

The *szName* parameter is the name of either the redirected local device or the remote network resource that is to be disconnected. In the first case, only the redirection is broken, causing Windows not to restore the connection during future login operations. In the latter, only the connection to the network resource is broken. The *bForce* parameter is used to force a disconnection if there are open files or jobs on the connection. If *bForce* is `FALSE`, the function call will fail if there are open files or jobs and will return the `WN_OPEN_FILES` return code.

The function returns a value of `WN_SUCCESS` if it succeeds or the appropriate error message upon failure, as shown in Table 33.9.

Table 33.9. `WNetCancelConnection()` return values.

Error	Value	Meaning
WN_SUCCESS	0	The function was successful
WN_NOT_SUPPORTED	1	The function is not supported
WN_OUT_OF_MEMORY	11	The system is out of memory
WN_NET_ERROR	2	An error occurred on the network
WN_BAD_POINTER	4	The pointer is invalid

WN_BAD_VALUE	5	The lpszName value is not a valid local or network device
WN_NOT_CONNECTED	48	The lpszName value is not currently connected
WN_OPEN_FILES	49	Files were open and bForce is FALSE

An example that ties all three of these functions together is shown in the following script. In this example, the local printer connection of LPT1 is redirected to a different network printer queue for the duration of a piece of processing and printing; it is then reset to the original queue when the processing and printing have finished:

```
String szPassword, szOldQueue, szNewQueue = "\\RAVEN\HP-IV"
Uint nError = 40

szOldQueue = Space( 40)
g_App.Externals.uf_WNetGetConnection( "LPT1", szOldQueue, nError)
g_App.Externals.uf_WNetCancelConnection( "LPT1", TRUE)
g_App.Externals.uf_WNetAddConnection( szNewQueue, szPassword, "LPT1")
//
// Some processing - print to printer
//
g_App.Externals.uf_WNetCancelConnection( "LPT1", TRUE)
g_App.Externals.uf_WNetAddConnection( szOldQueue, szPassword, "LPT1")
```

You can alter the default printer setting very simply by making a modification directly to the WIN.INI file that is used by both Windows 3.*x* and Windows 95. You simply alter the `device` entry of the `[windows]` section and state the printer name, printer driver, and printer port or redirection of the desired printer. The entry looks like this:

```
 [windows]
load=c:\mouse\wbuttons.exe
run=
NullPort=None
device=Osprey-Hawk,PANSON24,\\Hawk\osprey
```

With the `WNet` functions, you can provide very flexible printing options to your end users. There are a number of additional functions in the `WNet` group that you might want to explore.

Copying a File

Copying and moving files in Windows 3.*x* has always been somewhat of a problem from within PowerBuilder applications. You had to resort to a trick using the `LZCopy()` function to fool it into making a copy of the file for you. This method is described next, and then you will see how much easier this and other file operations have been made in Win32.

The `LZCopy()` function is used to expand files that have been compressed with the Microsoft File Compression utility (COMPRESS.EXE) to create a decompressed destination file. When the original file is already uncompressed, it duplicates the original file. This is the function declaration:

```
Function Long LZCopy( uInt hSource, uInt hDestination) Library "lzexpand.dll"
```

The `hSource` and `hDestination` arguments specify handles that identify the source and destination files and must be defined by calling the `LZOpenFile()` function. The `LZCopy()` function returns the size of the destination file in bytes.

`LZOpenFile()` can be used to create, open, reopen, and delete files. This is the definition:

```
Function uInt LZOpen( String szFileName, Ref of_struct lpOpen, uInt unStyle) &
                                                    Library "lzexpand.dll"
```

The argument `szFileName` is a string containing the name and path of the file to act on. `of_struct` is used to hold the information returned by the function and is of the structure shown in Table 33.10.

Table 33.10. The `of_struct` structure.

Variable Name	*Variable Data Type*	*Description*
`cBytes`	Char	Length of the structure
`cFixedDisk`	Char	Whether file is on a fixed disk (non-zero)
`unErrorCode`	uInt	The MS-DOS error value
`cReserved`	Char[4]	Reserved for future use
`szPathName`	Char[128]	The path of the file

The results in the `of_struct` structure contain file information that results from opening that file, and you must open both the source and destination files required by the `LZCopy()` function.

The `unStyle` argument of `LZOpen()` controls how the function operates, including checking whether the file exists, deleting the file, and prompting the user with a dialog box if the file cannot be found.

The last function you need is `LZClose()`, which is used to close the files opened by `LZOpen()`. The definition for this function is

```
Subroutine LZClose( uInt hFile) Library "lzexpand.dll"
```

Using all three of these functions together will allow you to copy a file in Win16:

```
of_struct sSource, sDestination
String szSource = "raven.txt", szDestination = "raven.bak"
uInt hSourceFile, hDestinationFile
uInteger OF_READ = 0, OF_CREATE = 4096

/* Open the source file. */
hSourceFile = LZOpenFile( szSource, sSource, OF_READ)
```

```
/* Create the destination file. */
hDestinationFile = LZOpenFile( szDestination, sDestination, OF_CREATE)

/* Copy the source file to the destination file. */
LZCopy( hSourceFile, hDestinationFile)
/* Close the files. */
LZClose( hSourceFile)
LZClose( hDestinationFile)
```

Now wasn't that a lot of work? In Win32 we can all relax and let a single function call take all the strain. The one function is `CopyFileA()`, which is declared as

```
Function Boolean CopyFileA( String szExistingFile, String szNewFile, &
                            Boolean bFail) Library "kernel32.dll"
```

The code to use this function is very simply this:

```
String szSource = "c:\temp\raven", szDestination = "c:\temp\raven.cpy"
Boolean bFail = TRUE // Make the copy fail if the file already exists

CopyFileA( szSource, szDestination, bFail)
```

The `bFail` argument is used to prevent an existing destination file from being overwritten. If the value is `TRUE`, the function fails; otherwise, it continues and overwrites the file.

There is also a move function, `MoveFileA()`, that allows you to move a file or directory (including all child objects) instead. The function definition is

```
Function Boolean MoveFileA( String szExistingFile, String szNewFile) &
                            Library "kernel32.dll"
```

The only restrictions on this function are that the new name cannot already exist and a new directory must be on the same drive.

Capturing a Single Keypress in a DataWindow

You can capture keypresses within a DataWindow control using two external API functions. You examine the message queue for the floating edit control of the DataWindow control using the `PeekMessage()` function, as follows:

```
BOOL PeekMessage( MSG FAR *lpMsg, HWND hwnd, UINT uFilterFirst, &
                  UINT uFilterLast, UINT fuRemove)
```

The PowerBuilder function declaration for Win32 is as follows, and the Win16 function can be found in USER.EXE:

```
FUNCTION Boolean PeekMessage( REF s_win_message sMsg, uInt hWnd, &
uInt unFilterFirst, uInt unFilterLast, uInt unRemove) Library "user32.dll"
```

The *`sMsg`* parameter is a pointer to a Windows `MSG` structure. *`hWnd`* is the handle of the object whose message queue you want to check. The parameters *`unFilterFirst`* and *`unFilterLast`* are used to specify the range of messages to examine. The final parameter, *unRemove*, is used to specify whether the messages are removed from the queue at the end of the function call.

In PowerBuilder you create this as a normal structure object, `s_win_message`, with the fields listed in Table 33.11.

Table 33.11. The Windows `MSG` structure.

Variable Name	*Variable Data Type*	*Target Type*
`hWnd`	uInt	`HWND`
`unMessage`	uInt	`UINT`
`unWParm`	uInt	`WPARM`
`lLParm`	Long	`LPARM`
`lTime`	Long	`DWORD`
`nPt`	Int	`POINT`

Don't be concerned with the last two fields. The `hWnd` attribute specifies the handle of the edit control, `unMessage` contains the message number, `unWParm` contains the character pressed, and `lLParm` contains the state of the key pressed.

The other external function used is `GetWindow()`, which obtains the handle of the edit control so that it can be passed into the `PeekMessage()` call. This is the external function:

```
HWND GetWindow( HWND hWnd, UINT fuRelationship)
```

The `GetWindow()` function can be directed to retrieve a window's handle depending on the relationship between it, and the window that the call is issued with using the *hWnd* parameter. The function can be used to search the system's list of top-level windows, associated child windows, child windows of child windows, and siblings of a window.

The PowerBuilder declaration for Win32 is as follows, and the Win16 function can be found in USER.EXE:

```
FUNCTION uInt GetWindow( uInt hWnd, Int nRelationShip) Library "user32.dll"
```

The *hWnd* parameter specifies the window to use as the base to search from. The *nRelationShip* parameter specifies the relationship between the original window and the window to be returned. Its possible values are listed in Table 33.12.

Table 33.12. Relationship constants for `GetWindow()`.

Relationship	*Value*	*Meaning*

continues

Table 33.12. continued

Relationship	*Value*	*Meaning*
GW_CHILD	5	The window's first child window
GW_HWNDFIRST	0	The first sibling window for a child window; otherwise, the first top-level window in the list
GW_HWNDLAST	1	The last sibling window for a child window; otherwise, the last top-level window in the list
GW_HWNDNEXT	2	The sibling window that follows the given window in the window manager's list
GW_HWNDPREV	3	The previous sibling window in the window manager's list
GW_OWNER	4	Identifies the window's owner

The function returns the handle of the window if the function is successful. If it is not, a `NULL` is returned.

The code in a user event mapped to the `pbm_dwnkey` event for a DataWindow would be this:

```
uInt hDataWindowControl, hEditControl
Integer GW_CHILD = 5
Boolean bReturn
s_win_message sMsg

hDataWindowControl = Handle( this)

hEditControl = GetWindow( hDataWindowControl, GW_CHILD)

bReturn = PeekMessage( sMsg, hEditControl, 0, 0, 0)
```

The character code pressed will now reside in `sMsg.unWParm`, and further information on the key state is in `sMsg.lLParm`. To get the actual character representation, pass `sMsg.unWParm` in a call to the PowerScript function `Char()`.

> **NOTE**
>
> You can also trap keypresses using the user event of `pbm_dwnkey` and checking the virtual code using the `KeyDown()` function. This, however, requires you to write a `KeyDown()` call for each key on which you want to trap.

Summary

In this chapter you have been introduced to external functions, why you would use them, and where you need to declare them. The chapter lists PowerBuilder-supported data types and gives a number of examples that make use of several external functions. The Win32 API has introduced a considerable number of new functions that range from file operations to date and time

The Powersoft Open Library API: ORCA

34

IN THIS CHAPTER

In order to allow the PowerBuilder development community a wider choice of tools that integrate with the PowerBuilder development environment, Powersoft introduced the CODE (client/server open development environment) initiative. As part of this initiative, Powersoft developed an Open Library API called ORCA to provide access to PowerBuilder library objects.

This allows tool vendors to write their own interfaces between their products and PowerBuilder, and does not tie you into one particular vendor or its tools. ORCA allows the third-party tool vendors to integrate very closely to the underlying architectures of PowerBuilder to provide you with additional functionality without making you jump through hoops. If you look in Appendix B, "PowerBuilder Resources" (which is on the book's CD-ROM) you will find a list of all the current CODE partners, and you can see a number of competitors within the same tool market. By using ORCA, Powersoft is allowing you to make the tool decisions you want.

Function Groups in ORCA

The ORCA API functions can be divided into four logical groups: session management, library management, compilation, and object query.

The Session Management Functions

Interaction with ORCA exists within the context of a *session*. As with print and file operations, you are required to open a session before you carry out any operations and then close the session when you have finished. For some of the functions in other groups, you also must set the current library search path and application before calling them; these tasks are also carried out by session management functions.

NOTE

Library names should be fully qualified whenever possible.

PBORCA_SessionOpen()

The `PBORCA_SessionOpen()` function is used to open an ORCA session, which must be made before any other ORCA functions are called. This is the function prototype:

```
HPBORCA PBORCA_SessionOpen( void)
```

Powersoft recommends that you leave the session open as long as you might need to use it, and because it requires a minimum amount of resources (just the session pointer) and no overhead, this is perfectly viable. The handle returned is used in all future ORCA function calls. The return data type is prototyped in the PBORCA.H file as a LPVOID.

PBORCA_SessionSetLibraryList()

The PBORCA_SessionSetLibraryList() function is used to set the library search path for the session and must be called before any of the compilation or query functions. This is the function prototype:

```
int PBORCA_SessionSetLibraryList( HPBORCA hSession, LPSTR far *pLibNames,
                                                    int nNoOfLibs)
```

The *pLibNames* parameter is a pointer to an array of pointers to library names, with *nNoOfLibs* indicating the number of pointers in the array.

The return value from this function is one of the ORCA interface return codes; these are some common ones:

- PBORCA_OK—Success
- PBORCA_INVALIDPARMS—Invalid parameter list
- PBORCA_BADLIBRARY—Bad library name
- PBORCA_LIBLISTNOTSET—Library list not set
- PBORCA_LIBNOTINLIST—Library not found in the library list

For all of the following functions that return a value, this value is one of the ORCA return codes listed in the PBORCA_SessionGetError() function section.

PBORCA_SessionSetCurrentAppl()

The PBORCA_SessionSetCurrentAppl() function should only be called after the PBORCA_SetLibraryList() function and before any of the compilation and query functions because it sets the current application for the session. This is the function prototype:

```
Int PBORCA_SessionSetCurrentAppl( HPBORCA hSession, LPSTR lpszApplLibName,
                                                    LPSTR lpszApplName)
```

The *lpszApplLibName* parameter is a pointer to the name of the library that the application resides in, and the *lpszApplName* parameter is the application object name.

PBORCA_SessionClose()

When you have finished with an ORCA session, you must close it in order to free any allocated system resources. This is the function prototype for PBORCA_SessionClose():

```
void PBORCA_SessionClose( HPBORCA hORCASession)
```

PBORCA_SessionGetError()

When an error is returned by an ORCA function, you can use the `PBORCA_SessionGetError()` function to retrieve ORCA's own description of the error. This is the function prototype:

```
void PBORCA_SessionGetError( HPBORCA hSession, LPSTR lpszErrorBuffer,
                                                  int nErrorBufferSize)
```

The *lpszErrorBuffer* parameter is a pointer to a string buffer that the error text will be returned into. *NErrorBufferSize* tells the function how big the string buffer is. If there is no current error, *lpszErrorBuffer* is set to an empty string (""). The ORCA return codes that are used by most of the functions are shown in Table 34.1.

Table 34.1. ORCA return codes.

ORCA #define	*Value*	*Description*
PBORCA_OK	0	Operation successful
PBORCA_INVALIDPARMS	-1	Invalid parameter list
PBORCA_DUPOPERATION	-2	Duplicate operation
PBORCA_OBJNOTFOUND	-3	Object not found
PBORCA_BADLIBRARY	-4	Bad library name
PBORCA_LIBLISTNOTSET	-5	Library list not set
PBORCA_LIBNOTINLIST	-6	Library not in library list
PBORCA_LIBIOERROR	-7	Library I/O error
PBORCA_OBJEXISTS	-8	Object exists
PBORCA_INVALIDNAME	-9	Invalid name
PBORCA_BUFFERTOOSMALL	-10	Buffer size is too small
PBORCA_COMPERROR	-11	Compile error
PBORCA_LINKERROR	-12	Link error
PBORCA_CURRAPPLNOTSET	-13	Current application not set
PBORCA_OBJHASNOANCS	-14	Object has no ancestors
PBORCA_OBJHASNOREFS	-15	Object has no references

The Library Management Functions

The library management functions allow the manipulation of libraries and the objects they contain, from creating and destroying libraries to copying, exporting, and moving object entries.

> **NOTE**
>
> These functions can all be used outside the context that is set by the `PBORCA_SessionSetCurrentAppl()` and `PBORCA_SetLibraryList()` functions.

PBORCA_LibraryCreate()

You use the `PBORCA_LibraryCreate()` function to create a new PowerBuilder library file. This is the prototype for this function:

```
int PBORCA_LibraryCreate( HPBORCA hSession, LPSTR lpszLibName,
                                            LPSTR lpszLibComments)
```

The *lpszLibName* parameter specifies a pointer to the new library name, and the *lpszLibComments* parameter can be used to set the comments for the library when it is created.

PBORCA_LibraryDelete()

You use the `PBORCA_LibraryDelete()` function to delete an existing PowerBuilder library file. This is the prototype for this function:

```
int PBORCA_LibraryCreate( HPBORCA hSession, LPSTR lpszLibName)
```

The *lpszLibName* parameter specifies a pointer to the library to be deleted.

PBORCA_LibraryCommentModify()

You use the `PBORCA_LibraryCommentModify()` function to modify the comments of an existing PowerBuilder library file. This is the prototype for this function:

```
int PBORCA_LibraryCommentModify( HPBORCA hSession, LPSTR lpszLibName,
                                                   LPSTR lpszLibComments)
```

The *lpszLibName* parameter specifies a pointer to the library name to set the comments of using the *lpszLibComments* parameter.

PBORCA_LibraryDirectory()

To explode the directory of a library to see all of its contents, you use the `PBORCA_LibraryDirectory()` function in conjunction with a callback function. This is the prototype for this function:

```
int PBORCA_LibraryDirectory( HPBORCA hSession, LPSTR lpszLibName,
                             LPSTR lpszLibComments, int nBufferSize,
                             PBORCA_LISTPROC pListProc, LPVOID pUserData)
```

The *lpszLibName* parameter specifies a pointer to the library name, the *lpszLibComments* parameter points to a comments buffer, and *nBufferSize* details the size of that buffer. *pListProc* is a pointer to a callback function used by PBORCA_LibraryDirectory() to pass entry information to. The entry information includes entry name, comments, entry size, and last modification time. *PUserData* is a pointer to user data that will be passed to the callback function with each entry.

NOTE

Callback functions are functions that are called by the DLL or EXE file that you originally called in order to return information that you requested.

PBORCA_LibraryEntryCopy()

The PBORCA_LibraryEntryCopy() function is used to copy an object from one library to another. This is the prototype for this function:

```
int PBORCA_LibraryEntryCopy( HPBORCA hSession, LPSTR lpszSourceLibName,
                             LPSTR lpszDestLibName, LPSTR lpszEntryName,
                             BORCA_TYPE otEntryType)
```

The *lpszSourceLibName* and *lpszDestLibName* parameters specify the source and destination library, respectively. *lpszEntryName* is the name of the object entry to be copied and *otEntryType* is an enumerated data type that represents what type of object it is. The enumerated data type is defined in PBORCA.H as PBORCA_TYPE with the values PBORCA_APPLICATION, PBORCA_DATAWINDOW, PBORCA_FUNCTION, PBORCA_MENU, PBORCA_QUERY, PBORCA_STRUCTURE, PBORCA_USEROBJECT, and PBORCA_WINDOW.

PBORCA_LibraryEntryMove()

The PBORCA_LibraryEntryMove() function is used to move an object from one library to another. This is the prototype for this function:

```
int PBORCA_LibraryEntryMove( HPBORCA hSession, LPSTR lpszSourceLibName,
                             LPSTR lpszDestLibName, LPSTR lpszEntryName,
                             BORCA_TYPE otEntryType)
```

The parameters and usage are identical to PBORCA_LibraryEntryCopy().

PBORCA_LibraryEntryDelete()

The PBORCA_LibraryEntryDelete() function is used to delete an object from a library. This is the prototype for this function:

```
int PBORCA_LibraryEntryDelete( HPBORCA hSession, LPSTR lpszSourceLibName,
                               LPSTR lpszEntryName, BORCA_TYPE otEntryType)
```

The parameters and usage are similar to those of `PBORCA_LibraryEntryCopy()`.

PBORCA_LibraryEntryExport()

The `PBORCA_LibraryEntryExport()` function is used to export the source of an object from a library into a text representation. This is the prototype for this function:

```
int PBORCA_LibraryEntryExport( PBORCA hSession, LPSTR lpszLibName,
                               LPSTR lpszEntryName, PBORCA_TYPE otEntryType,
                               LPSTR lpszExportBuffer, long lExportBufferSize)
```

The *`lpszLibName`* and *`lpszEntryName`* parameters specify the library and entry to be used to export the source from, respectively. *`otEntryType`* is an enumerated data type that represents what type of object it is. *`lpszExportBuffer`* and *`lExportBufferSize`* specify the buffer and its size, which will be used to receive the exported code.

PBORCA_LibraryEntryInformation()

To retrieve information on an object entry within a library you use the `PBORCA_LibraryEntryInformation()` function. This is the prototype for this function:

```
int PBORCA_LibraryEntryInformation( HPBORCA hSession, LPSTR lpszLibName,
                                    LPSTR lpszEntryName, PBORCA_TYPE otEntryType,
                                    PPBORCA_ENTRYINFO pEntryInformationBlock)
```

The parameters are similar to previous parameters, except for the last one, *`pEntryInformationBlock`*. This parameter is a pointer to a structure of type `PBORCA_ENTRYINFO`, which will hold information on the entry, such as comments, size, and modification time.

The Compilation Functions

The compilation functions allow you to import source code to create object entries and to cause the regeneration of library entries.

NOTE

These functions must all be used inside the context that is set by the `PBORCA_SessionSetCurrentAppl()` and `PBORCA_SetLibraryList()` functions.

PBORCA_CompileEntryImport()

The `PBORCA_CompileEntryImport()` function imports source code into a PowerBuilder library entry and compiles it. This is the prototype for this function:

```
int PBORCA CompileEntryImport( PBORCA hSession, LPSTR lpszLibName,
                               LPSTR lpszEntryName,
                               PBORCA_TYPE otEntryType, LPSTR lpszComments,
                               LPSTR lpszEntrySyntax, long lBufferSize,
                               PBORCA_ERRPROC pCompErrorProc, LPVOID pUserData)
```

The *lpszLibName* and *lpszEntryName* parameters specify the library and entry names that will be used to import the source into, respectively. *otEntryType* is an enumerated data type that represents what type of object it is. *lpszComments* specify optional comments to place in the library for the object. *lpszEntrySyntax* is a pointer to the source syntax buffer and *lBufferSize* indicates the length of that buffer. *pCompErrorProc* is a pointer to a callback function to be used when a compile error occurs. The error information includes the error text and line number. *pUserData* is a pointer to user data that will be passed back with each compile error.

PBORCA_CompileEntryImportList()

Instead of using `PBORCA_CompileEntryImport()` in a loop to create a number of objects, you can use `PBORCA_CompileEntryImportList()` to import the source for a list of objects and compile them. This is the prototype for this function:

```
int PBORCA_CompileEntryImportList( PBORCA hSession, LPSTR far *pLibNames,
                                   LPSTR far *pEntryNames,
                                   PBORCA_TYPE far *otEntryTypes,
                                   LPSTR far *pComments,
                                   LPSTR far *pEntrySyntaxBuffers,
                                   long far *pEntrySyntaxBuffSizes,
                                   int nNoOfEntries,
                                   PBORCA_ERRPROC pCompErrorProc,
                                   LPVOID pUserData)
```

The parameters *pLibNames*, *pEntryNames*, *otEntryTypes*, *pComments*, *pEntrySyntaxBuffers*, and *pBufferSizes* are all arrays with *nNoOfEntries* elements, and have been defined in previous sections. *pCompErrorProc* is a pointer to a compile error callback function, and *pUserData* is user data returned with each compile error.

Entries are imported and their type definitions compiled (for use with objects occurring later in the list), and then when the complete list is in without an error, all the objects are fully compiled. This function is often used to import a number of related objects at one time.

NOTE

Objects used by other objects must occur in the list before the dependent object.

PBORCA_CompileEntryRegenerate()

The `PBORCA_CompileEntryRegenerate()` function causes the recompilation of a library entry. Within the PowerBuilder environment this is the regenerate operation. This is the prototype for this function:

```
int PBORCA_CompileEntryRegenerate( PBORCA hSession, LPSTR lpszLibName,
                                   LPSTR lpszEntryName, PBORCA_TYPE otEntryType,
                                   PBORCA_ERRPROC pCompErrorProc,
                                   LPVOID pUserData)
```

The parameter list is similar to that of the `PBORCA_CompileEntryImport()` function.

PBORCA_ExecutableCreate()

The `PBORCA_ExecutableCreate()` function is used to compile either a p-code or machine code executable. This is the prototype for this function:

```
int PBORCA_ExecutableCreate( PBORCA hSession, LPSTR lpszExeName,
                             LPSTR lpszIconName, LPSTR lpszPBRName,
                             PBORCA_LNKPROC pLinkErrProc,
                             LPVOID pUserData, INT FAR *iPBDFlags,
                             INT iNoOfPBDFlags, LONG lFlags)
```

The parameters *`lpszExeName`*, *`lpszIconName`*, and *`lpszPBRName`* are pointers to the names for the executable, optional icon, and optional PBR files, respectively. *`pLinkErrProc`* is a pointer to a link error callback function, and *`pUserData`* is user data returned with each compile error.

The parameter `lFlags` specifies the options to be used during the compilation of the executable (see Table 34.2).

Table 34.2. Compilation options.

Constant Defined in Header	*Hex Value*
`PBORCA_P_CODE`	0x00000000
`PBORCA_MACHINE_CODE`	0x00000001
`PBORCA_MACHINE_CODE_NATIVE` (default for 32-bit PowerBuilder)	0x00000001
`PBORCA_MACHINE_CODE_16`	0x00000002
`PBORCA_OPEN_SERVER` (machine code only)	0x00000004
`PBORCA_TRACE_INFO`	0x00000010
`PBORCA_ERROR_CONTEXT`	0x00000020
`PBORCA_MACHINE_CODE_OPT`	0x00000100
`PBORCA_MACHINE_CODE_OPT_SPEED`	0x00000100
`PBORCA_MACHINE_CODE_OPT_SPACE`	0x00000200
`PBORCA_MACHINE_CODE_OPT_NONE`	0x00000000

PBORCA_DynamicLibraryCreate()

The PBORCA_DynamicLibraryCreate() function is used to compile a single library into either a PBD or DLL. This is the prototype for this function:

```
int PBORCA_DynamicLibraryCreate( PBORCA hSession, LPSTR lpszLibraryName,
                                 LPSTR lpszPBRName, LONG lFlags)
```

The parameters *lpszLibraryName* and *lpszPBRName* are both pointers to the names for the executable and optional PBR files, respectively.

The parameter lFlags specifies the options to be used during the compilation of the executable (see Table 34.2).

The Object Query Functions

The object query functions give you the ability to query objects for references to other objects.

> **NOTE**
>
> These functions must all be used inside the context that is set by the PBORCA_SessionSetCurrentAppl() and PBORCA_SetLibraryList() functions.

PBORCA_ObjectQueryHierarchy()

You use the PBORCA_ObjectQueryHierarchy() function to query a PowerBuilder object about objects in its ancestor chain. This is the prototype for this function:

```
int PBORCA_ObjectQueryHierarchy( HPBORCA hSession, LPSTR lpszLibName,
                                 LPSTR lpszEntryName, PBORCA_TYPE otEntryType,
                                 PBORCA_HIERPROC pHierarchyProc,
                                 LPVOID pUserData)
```

All but the last two parameters are similar to all other ORCA function calls. *pHierarchyProc* is a pointer to a callback function that is used to return information on the hierarchy such as the ancestor object names. *pUserData* is used to pass user data to the callback function.

> **NOTE**
>
> The *otEntryType* parameter can only be PBORCA_WINDOW, PBORCA_MENU, or PBORCA_USEROBJECT; none of the other object types are allowed.

PBORCA_ObjectQueryReference()

You use the `PBORCA_ObjectQueryReference()` function to query a PowerBuilder object about objects that it references. This is the prototype for this function:

```
int PBORCA_ObjectQueryReference( HPBORCA hSession, LPSTR lpszLibName,
                                 LPSTR lpszEntryName, PBORCA_TYPE otEntryType,
                                 PBORCA_REFPROC pRefProc,
                                 LPVOID pUserData)
```

Again, all but the last two parameters are similar to all other ORCA function calls. *`pRefProc`* is a pointer to a callback function that is used to return information on the objects referenced such as the names, library, and object type. *`pUserData`* is used to pass user data to the callback function.

A Sample ORCA Function Call

The code example in Listing 34.1 shows the steps required to use the `PBORCA_CompileEntryImport()` function, with the required order of function calls.

NOTE

The code is not meant to be complete or provide extensive error checking, and the `WEP` and `LibMain` functions and required header files are not detailed.

A number of the functions that have just been defined are used in Listing 34.1, as is an example of a callback function.

Listing 34.1. Sample ORCA code.

```
/***********************************
* Limit this call to 100 libraries! *
***********************************/
typedef struct ArgumentsForImport
{
   HWND hWndParent;
   LPSTR lpszSourceFile;
   LPSTR lpszLibraryName[100];
   UINT nLibraries;
   LPSTR lpszEntryName;
   PBORCA_TYPE otEntryType;
   LPSTR lpszComments;
   LPSTR lpszApplLibName;
   LPSTR lpszApplName;
} ImportArgs, FAR *pImportArgs;
```

continues

Listing 34.1. continued

```
/***********************************************************************
* Declaration: int FAR PASCAL _export importEntry(pImportArgs)          *
*                                                                       *
* Purpose: Imports a source file into a specified PowerBuilder PBL file. *
***********************************************************************/
int FAR PASCAL _export importEntry( pImportArgs pArgs)
{
   HPBORCA hORCASession;
   LPSTR lpszImportSyntax;
   long lFileLength;
   HFILE hSourceFile;
   int nError;
   UINT nCharactersRead;
   PBORCA_ENTRYINFO  EntryInfo;
   char lpcMsg[500];

/* Open an ORCA Session */
hORCASession = PBORCA_SessionOpen();
if( hORCASession == NULL)
{
   return -1;
}

nError = PBORCA_SessionSetLibraryList( hORCASession, pArgs->lpszLibraryNames,
                                       pArgs->nLibraries);
if( nError != PBORCA_OK)
{
   /* Ooops, ran into a problem—close the session and return ORCA error number
   PBORCA_SessionClose( hORCASession);
   return nError;
}

nError = PBORCA_SessionSetCurrentAppl( hORCASession, pArgs->lpszApplLibName,
                                       pArgs->lpszApplName);
if (err != PBORCA_OK)
{
   /* Ooops, ran into a problem—close the session and return ORCA error number
   PBORCA_SessionClose( hORCASession);
   return nError;
}

nError = PBORCA_LibraryEntryInformation( hORCASession, pArgs->lpszLibraryName,
                                         pArgs->lpszEntryName,
                                         pArgs->otEntryType, &EntryInfo);

if( nError == PBORCA_OK )
{
   /* Uh oh, the object entry is already in the library */
   wsprintf( lpcMsg, "%s already exists! Do you wish to continue?",
             pArgs->lpszEntryName);

   if( MessageBox((HWND)NULL, lpcMsg,"Warning!", MB_YESNO | MB_ICONQUESTION |
                                                  MB_APPLMODAL) == IDNO)
   {
      PBORCA_SessionClose( hORCASession);
      return -1;
```

```
    }
}
else if( nError != PBORCA_OBJNOTFOUND)
{
   /* Ooops, ran into a problem—close the session and return ORCA error number
   PBORCA_SessionClose( hORCASession);
   return nError;
}

/* Open the source file and then allocate a buffer to hold the text */
hSourceFile = fopen( pArgs->lpszSourceFile, "r");
if( hSourceFile == NULL)
{
   PBORCA_SessionClose( hORCASession);
   return -1;
}

lFileLength = _filelength( hSourceFile);
if( lFileLength == -1)
{
   PBORCA_SessionClose( hORCASession);
   fclose( hSourceFile);
   return -1;
}

lpszImportSyntax = (LPSTR)_fmalloc((size_t) lFileLength + 1);
if( lpszImportSyntax == NULL)
{
   PBORCA_SessionClose( hORCASession);
   fclose( hSourceFile);
   return -1;
}

/* Copy Text into Buffer and then close the file */
nCharactersRead = fread( lpszImportSyntax, sizeof(char), lSrcFileLen,
                         hSourceFile);
if( nCharactersRead < 1)
{
   free( lpszImportSyntax);
   fclose( hSourceFile);
   PBORCA_SessionClose(hORCASession);
   return -1;
}

fclose( hSourceFile);

nError = PBORCA_CompileEntryImport( hORCASession, pArgs->lpszLibraryName,
                                    pArgs->lpszEntryName, pArgs->otEntryType,
                                    pArgs->lpszComments, lpszImportSyntax,
                                    lFileLength,
                                    (PBORCA_ERRPROC) CompileErrorHandler,
                                    (LPVOID) hORCASession);

if( nError == PBORCA_COMPERROR)
{
   /* Handle compile error */
}
```

continues

Listing 34.1. continued

```
if( nError != PBORCA_OK)
{
   free( lpszImportSyntax);
   PBORCA_SessionClose( hORCASession);
   return nError;
}

/* Woooo Wooo we made it—clean up and get out of here */
free( lpszImportSyntax);
PBORCA_SessionClose( hORCASession);
return 0;
}

/**********************************************
* Callback function to handle compiler errors *
**********************************************/
void FAR PASCAL CompileErrorHandler( PPBORCA_COMPERR pCompileError,
                                     LPVOID pUserData)
{
   /* Include whatever error processing you wish here.
      For example,
                 Open a MessageBox
                 Log it to a file
   */
}
```

After you have incorporated this code into a DLL, you can use this and other functions from within PowerBuilder by defining the prototypes in the local or global external function area of an object, populating the structure with the relevant information, and then calling it as you would any other function.

Summary

The Open Library API was first introduced with PowerBuilder Version 3.0 of the Enterprise Edition, and consists of the following files: PBORC0*x*0.DLL (where *x* is the PowerBuilder version, that is, 3, 4, or 5), PBORCA.H, and PBORCA.LIB. These last two files are used in the development of C programs that use ORCA to carry out additional functionality that is not directly accessible from within PowerScript. This is the interface used by third-party tool vendors that want to interface directly with PowerBuilder.

Configuring and Tuning

35

IN THIS CHAPTER

Many factors can affect the performance of a client/server-based application. You have to consider the configuration of the server, the network, and the client—and each of those areas can be further broken down into hardware and software pieces. The often-forgotten piece is the human factor, in other words, the end user or person for whom the system is being constructed in the first place.

This chapter covers some of the areas you will need to examine when tuning your application, and some PowerBuilder-specific coding traps into which you might have fallen.

A number of factors can affect performance:

- Server configuration
- Database structure
- Type and configuration of network
- Network load
- Environment parameters on servers and clients
- Capability of the development team
- Perception of the users

The Server

The database server or DBMS is the obvious place to look for a degradation in performance. Optimally, the database server will be only that and will not be used to provide additional file or print services. The more memory the DBMS has, the more data and code (triggers and stored procedures) it can place into memory cache and the less it has to share with the host operating system. The usual bottlenecks on database servers are the I/O channels and the network interface. Both of these can become clogged with multiple user requests, and it is well worth the extra money to purchase a high-performance network card and disk subsystem.

The disk subsystem increases in performance as the I/O requests become spread across multiple disk controllers and multiple disks. *RAID* (redundant array of inexpensive disks) drive arrays can provide additional performance and security. Some operating systems, notably Windows NT, provide duplexing at the software level, but you should always do this at the hardware level or you will take a performance hit.

When you have your high-performance hardware solution in place, you need to configure the software (operating system and database management system) to make best use of it. This involves two steps: optimizing the number of drivers and other miscellaneous programs that get loaded by the server, and attempting to get the smallest memory footprint possible for the operating system. In addition, some databases frequently run faster on certain operating systems (for example, MS SQL Server is specially optimized for NT).

The Database

How a database is structured, both physically and logically, can have a profound impact on the performance of both queries and data entry. The performance of a particular database is a function of the structure of the data and the size of the data sets. The development team should spend the necessary time and effort to complete all data-modeling stages to arrive at an optimized third normal form entity-relationship diagram (which is sometimes called *BNF*, or *best normal form*).

During the modeling stage, you will have determined whether the database is to be used for a decision support system (DSS), an executive information system (EIS), or data entry. Actually, it is not recommended that you write a reporting system against a database already involved in data entry because of the performance degradation and data locking that a report can have on data-entry processes. A database designed for DSS or EIS will make use of summarized data and can be populated at off-peak times from a data-entry database. This requires normalization techniques that produce data models that do not conform with the accepted normal forms, and this is acceptable if it yields higher performance and remains manageable.

The use of *indexes* can increase or decrease the performance of data accesses to a table. The benefit of indexes is that they provide quicker access to data. Indexes can cause problems with concurrency by causing pages or rows to become locked, so you should make judicious use of the number and type of column indexes.

Some DBMSs, notably SQL Server, carry out what are known as *deferred updates* when the table's columns accept `NULL`s or variable-length data types. Rather than the DBMS making the necessary changes to the data in the table's columns during an `UPDATE` command, it will cause the record to be first deleted and then reinserted into the table. Where possible, you should make use of NOT NULL columns and column defaults to solve this problem.

During the data-analysis phase of data modeling, you should have defined each entity attribute's data type and its valid range of values. Ideally, try to stay away from the variable-length data types in favor of the fixed-length ones. This will require some extra space to achieve, but it could be well worth the expense to gain better performance than you would have because of the problem with deferred updates.

A number of classes, books, and database-proficient consultants can provide you with tuning techniques for your particular database and operating system setup, but it is beyond the scope of this book to delve into any specifics of this field. Usually the best place to start looking is the documentation that comes with the DBMS itself.

The Network

The *network* is another of the forgotten, or not closely examined, areas of a client/server application that can have a profound effect on performance. The physical wiring of the network restricts the amount of information that can pass along it due to its power rating. The faster a network cable is, the more power required to transmit data through it and the higher the cost.

This type of network topology can cause bottlenecks or degradation as load increases. An Ethernet network might provide satisfactory performance for a small departmentwide system, but when you attach it to a companywide network there will be an increased number of data clashes and everyone's performance drops. A Token Ring topology, although more expensive, guarantees network performance with increasing load.

High-performance network cards are really worth getting for machines that are servers of one kind or another; they usually won't provide a noticeable performance gain for the individual client machines. Setting up the network cards and drivers with optimal settings can help solve a number of performance and error issues.

The Human Factor

The human factor of a client/server project can be the make-or-break point, and it includes not only the end users but the members of the project team.

The development team must be a highly motivated and technically minded group of people to bring a client/server project to fruition. Management and technical staff must have a partnership to ensure that all the necessary pieces of the project come together. If the team members are motivated and energetic in their approach, it will rub off on the end users during interviews and prototyping. If members of the project team are new to client/server, they should be provided with internal or external courses to bring them up to speed on the technology and development environment.

Unfortunately, regardless of the development team, the system's performance is ultimately only as good as the end user's expectations. If the end user has been given the misconception that the system will be much faster or contain more features than the existing one, he will usually be in for a surprise. That's because the great majority of client/server systems being installed are replacing mainframe sessions; and because the old programs are text-based and centrally run, it is more than likely that there will be a speed difference. The reverse is also true: If an end user is told by a project member that the system is going to be much slower, the user will form a hasty misconception that will probably be worse than the truth.

Before the Development Process

Because much of the configuration and tuning affects the development and testing process, there are several decisions you must make before you begin the development stage. This includes programming standards, PowerBuilder library organization, source code and version control, and client setup, to name a few. Some of these will directly affect performance; all will lead to more solid code being produced.

Programming Standards

One of the first things you must consider is the coding standards that you and your project team are going to follow. This includes naming standards for your objects and variables (see Chapter 22, "Standards and Naming Conventions," for common naming conventions). When you are consistent across the application, it is much easier for other developers to assist each other with problem areas, maintenance is considerably less cumbersome, and it is easy to determine which object is which.

You must also decide what approach you will take in creating the application. Are you going to develop a class library or use an existing framework? What objects can you steal from other development teams at your company? Are you going to use PowerBuilder's object-oriented capabilities (such as inheritance, polymorphism, and encapsulation)?

All these questions must be considered—if possible, before development—to make the process as smooth as it can be. For a first application, these types of questions can be very difficult to answer, because the answers quite often come from experience. Try to decide what objects can be utilized in all aspects of the application and start from there. Don't be discouraged if you find yourself knee-deep in code before you realize that the object would have been a good candidate for inheritance; you can always go back later. Development with a particular product becomes fine-tuned only with practice and experience.

Managing Your PowerBuilder Libraries

When creating your application, you should decide where the PowerBuilder library files should reside, both for performance reasons and source management. The following section covers some guidelines that can help you increase the performance and ease of use of your library files.

Library Guidelines

Before any development begins, there are several recommended guidelines for use with PowerBuilder library files, both for tuning and ease of use. These guidelines include library location, organization, size, and optimization.

It is important to decide where you are going to store the actual PowerBuilder library files (PBLs) (that is, on what drive and in which directory). There are some special considerations when several developers are creating an application versus when a single developer is creating an application. How the objects are distributed within your PBLs is important for ease of access and ease of use.

The library search path is also very important in the performance tuning of your PowerBuilder application. Frequently used objects should be placed near the top so that PowerBuilder does not have to search through multiple PBLs to find the requested object. The library search path can be modified at runtime using the function `SetLibraryList()` to get the optimal configuration for each user. Once you have organized your PBLs, it is important that your library files be optimized to prevent fragmentation of your objects. For a discussion of library file maintenance, see Chapter 13, "The Library Painter."

Configuring the Client

Another area that can greatly affect the performance of any application is the configuration of the machine on which it is running. Your application might run fine on your 486/66 with 16MB of RAM, but it is just a little bit slower on the user's 386/25 with 4MB of RAM, and you should consider this before implementation of the application. Although it might not be in the budget to upgrade your user's workstation, there are some things you can do to get better performance from the user's machine.

A simple change is to make sure that the machine is using a permanent swap file residing on a local drive, thus ensuring Windows knows where the swap file is located and its size. If you use a temporary swap file, do not place it on the network or have a TEMP directory on the network because it will cause access time to increase dramatically. Upgrading Windows 3.1 users to Version 3.11 or Windows 95 enables them to make use of 32-bit disk- and file-access features, and you will see quite a performance gain with local disk access.

Memory is also an area you can tune to improve performance. Depending on what else needs to be done on your user's workstation, consider using extended memory and loading drivers into high memory. Wallpaper used as a background in Windows is often popular with users but is also a resource hog. If you can convince them to get rid of it, do so. Similar to the resources that wallpaper takes up, higher resolution slows your application. The last thing to remember with memory is the more, the merrier! If you can't purchase a new machine for the user, see whether you can get him more memory. It's relatively inexpensive and can have a large impact on an application's performance.

There are settings in numerous DOS and Windows configuration files that can also negatively affect an application's performance. These include CONFIG.SYS, AUTOEXEC.BAT, WIN.INI, and SYSTEM.INI. If you don't know what everything in there means (many front-end developers do not), find someone who does (your network administrator, for starters). In the 32-bit environment, much of the same information is stored in the Windows Registry.

Many of these decisions that need to be considered before development begins do not take much time. Pull from the experience of other development teams to see what worked for them. Remember, these are guidelines, not hard-and-fast rules.

The Development Process

This section is a series of tips you can utilize to improve the performance of your application through your scripts, event usage, and implementation of object-oriented programming. The tips combine techniques that actually decrease process time and hints to give the appearance to the user that the application is running faster. It is surprising how a few seemingly simple modifications can have a dramatic impact on your application's actual and perceived speed.

PowerScript

In the 32-bit environment, you now have the ability to create machine-code executables and runtime libraries. This new feature of PowerBuilder will have the greatest effect on the speed of your PowerScript. To see a comparison of an application using p-code versus machine code, see Chapter 18, "Application Implementation, Creation, and Distribution." The following sections take a look at PowerScript statements that are commonly misused and lead to decreased performance.

Calling Functions

A frequent area of abuse concerns how various functions in PowerBuilder are utilized. You would be surprised at how often and how long some developers create a function that the PowerScript language already provides. PowerScript has over 400 different functions available, and chances are that what you want to do is incorporated in those functions. Even more prewritten functions are now available since the arrival of the FUNCky library of functions for use with PowerBuilder.

NOTE

The FUNCky library is currently only available in a 16-bit version.

If PowerScript does not provide the functionality that you need (for example, calculating current inventory), there are a couple of ways to go. If you plan to use the functionality more than once, create a user-defined function. If the function is only applicable to a specific object class, create an object-level function so that it is stored with the object it references. If the function is going to be called by multiple objects, create a global function or a nonvisual user object (especially if there are related functions or variables).

Intuition would tell you that the object-level function would be accessed more quickly than a corresponding global function. Depending on how it is coded, this may or may not be true. If you fully qualify the function name within your scripts with the object name, the object-level function will run faster than if you just state the function name. In the `Clicked` event of a Save command button, compare line one to line two:

```
(1)wf_update()

(2)w_parts.wf_update()
```

Line two will run faster than line one. This is because of the hierarchy that PowerBuilder uses to execute functions that are not fully qualified. This is the order in which PowerBuilder searches for an unqualified function:

- A global external function
- A global function
- An object function
- A local external function
- A system function

The first function found with the specified name is executed. As you can see, if you do not fully qualify an object-level function, PowerBuilder searches through the global functions first, which could adversely affect performance.

When you're using inheritance, PowerBuilder will begin at the bottom descendant and search upward for object and local external functions through the inheritance hierarchy until a match is found. Event order must also be considered when using inheritance. PowerBuilder also starts at the bottom descendant and looks up through the inheritance hierarchy until either the top-most ancestor script is reached or an event script is found that overrides the ancestor. Depending on the levels of inheritance and extension of events, PowerBuilder may have to traverse multiple layers of inheritance.

Similar to the function and event hierarchy is the precedence of variable scope for variables with the same name. PowerBuilder's order of precedence is local, shared, global, and then instance. Since everyone should use a naming standard that incorporates scope into the variable names, this should not be an issue!

TIP

It is also worth noting that you will see a small performance degradation when using dynamically bound methods as opposed to statically bound methods. This is because the dynamic reference has to be resolved at runtime.

Choose...Case

If you are moving from a mainframe environment to PowerBuilder, you are probably a big fan of the `If...Then` statement. Although this is more familiar to most programmers, consider using a `Choose...Case` statement instead. You will find that reading a `Choose...Case` statement is much easier than reading an `If...Then`, and it is much easier to maintain, as you can see in the following example:

```
If li_division_code = 10 Or li_division_code = 40 Then
   //Division 10 and 40 processing
```

```
ElseIf li_division_code = 20 Or li_division_code = 21 &
   or li_division_code = 22 Then
   //Division 20 , 21, and 22 processing
ElseIf li_division_code >= 50 Then
   //Division 50 and greater processing
Else
   //Default division processing
End If
```

Here's another example:

```
Choose Case li_division_code
   Case 10, 20
      //Division 10 and 20 processing
   Case 20 To 22
      //Division 20, 21, and 22 processing
   Case Is >= 50
      //Division 50 and greater processing
   Case Else
      //Default division processing
End Choose
```

In the second example, it is easier to determine which values are being evaluated and what logic is executed when. Regardless of which method you use to evaluate an expression, remember that the values that occur most often should be placed first and the least common values should be placed last in the test case list. This is true of both the `Choose...Case` and `If...Then` statements.

Loops

A mistake commonly made by beginners is to use a function that always returns the same value in a loop control statement (for example, `Do...While`). Take a look at the following code:

```
long ll_row, ll_cust_id


//Loop through the DataWindow looking for required customer id
Do Until ll_cust_id = Long( sle_cust_id.text)
   ll_row = ll_row + 1
   If ll_row > dw_customer.RowCount() Then
      MessageBox( "Customer Not Found", "Could not locate customer")
      Return
   End If
   ll_cust_id = dw_customer.GetItemNumber( ll_row, "customer_id")
Loop
```

The function `RowCount()`, which returns the number of rows in the DataWindow Primary buffer, is executed inside of the loop until the desired customer ID is found (also using the `Long()` function within the `Do...Loop`). Instead, the code should be written as follows (note that the changes appear in bold):

```
long ll_row, ll_row_count, ll_cust_id, ll_req_cust

ll_row_count = dw_customer.RowCount()
```

```
//Grab the desired customer id entered by the user
ll_req_cust = Long( sle_cust_id.text)

//Loop through the DataWindow looking for required customer id
DO UNTIL ll_cust_id = ll_req_cust
   ll_row = ll_row + 1
   If ll_row > ll_rowcount Then
      MessageBox( "Customer Not Found", "Could not locate customer")
      Return
   End If
   ll_cust_id = dw_customer.GetItemNumber( ll_row, "customer_id")
Loop
```

Using this code, `RowCount()` is executed once and then stored in a variable, reducing the overhead of multiple function calls.

Modify()

Several functions, such as `Modify()` and `Describe()`, can be easy targets for tuning. During development, you might typically have the following script:

```
dw_order.Modify( "received_date.background.color='9477526'")
dw_order.Modify( "received_date.border='5'")
dw_order.Modify( "ship_date.background.color='9477526'")
dw_order.Modify( "ship_date.border='5'")
```

This code would be desirable during development, because you want to make sure that each modification to the DataWindow object is correct and occurs as coded. Once the syntax is correct for these statements, the application should be modified (and, of course, retested) to the following:

```
dw_order.Modify( "received_date.background.color='9477526' &
                 ~treceived_date.border='5'~tship_date.background.color='9477526' &
                 ~tship_date.border='5'")
```

This reduces the script from four function calls to one. Also, with multiple commands being sent to one call of `Modify()`, Windows will only repaint the screen once.

With the introduction of 5.0, you now have the capability to directly reference the attributes of your DataWindow object. Just like each `Modify()` call, directly manipulating an attribute causes the DataWindow to repaint. To minimize the number of screen repaints, you should use the `SetRedraw()` function. The syntax is

```
ObjectName.SetRedraw( Flag)
```

`ObjectName` is the desired object (in this case a DataWindow control) and *`Flag`* is a Boolean value. A value of `TRUE` ensures a screen repaint after an attribute has been modified and a `FALSE` value specifies the object should not be repainted. With this in mind, the previous `Modify()` statement can be written as this:

```
dw_order.SetRedraw(False)
dw_order.object.received_date.background.color='9477526'
dw_order.object.received_date.border='5'
```

```
dw_order.object.ship_date.background.color='9477526'
dw_order.object.ship_date.border='5'
dw_order.SetRedraw(True)
```

Array Processing

If you are using arrays in your application, you might want to review your code to make sure that it is functioning as efficiently as it can. This is particularly true if you are using dynamic arrays. Every time the dynamic array grows in size, PowerBuilder requests a new block of memory from Windows that is the same size as the existing array plus the new elements to be added. The data from the old array is then copied into the new array in memory before the memory of the old array is released. Therefore, you use memory equal to at least double the size of the existing array. Although this makes dynamic arrays easier to program, it decreases the efficiency considerably (because of the processing overhead of maintaining and copying between two arrays and memory fragmentation).

You can use a couple techniques to reduce the effects of this problem. The easiest and most efficient technique is to not use dynamic arrays. But because static arrays are not always flexible enough, consider allocating more memory for the array than is first needed. For example, if you need 100 elements, specify 110 elements. This way, you have 10 more elements available to you and PowerBuilder does not have to request more memory for the next 10 elements that are added.

Another method is to step backward through the elements in the array in order to populate it. The first element should be high (say 100), which causes PowerBuilder to request the memory for 100 elements. Any access between 1 and 100 will not require Windows to allocate more memory. You can then work backward through the array, decreasing the index by 1, to assign the elements. This is particularly useful in loops that create and fill dynamic arrays, as shown in the following code:

```
Integer li_index, li_array_size
Decimal{2} lc_price

li_size = Integer( sle_max.text)

FOR li_index = li_array_size TO 1 STEP -1
        lc_price[li_index] = gc_original_price * .20
NEXT
```

When using a dynamic array, it is often necessary to find the lower or upper bound of an array. This is done using the functions `LowerBound()` and `UpperBound()`, respectively. Both of these functions are expensive in terms of processing times; use them minimally.

WARNING

Absolute care should be taken not to use these functions inside a loop construct.

If you are using a global dynamic array (maybe to track references to instances of a particular window class in an MDI application) or a shared dynamic array, PowerBuilder does not release the memory until the application is terminated. This is a problem if you are done using the array and you need the memory for other processing.

You need to return the dynamic array back to an empty state. To accomplish this, declare another array of the same type and set the original array equal to the new array. This clears out the original array. Calling the `UpperBound()` function after completing the processing will return a value of `0`. Here's an example of resetting an array to an empty state:

```
Long ll_order_no[]

//Empty out global array
gl_order_no[] = ll_order_no[]
```

Similar to the problem of memory allocation of dynamic arrays is passing arrays as arguments to a function. As you know, you can pass arguments by reference or by value. If you pass by reference, you pass the memory location of the array and the function can modify the array. If you pass by value, you make a copy of the array and pass it to the function. If you have a large array and pass it by value to a function, you could consume quite a bit of memory. If your function does not need to modify the array, make sure to pass the array by reference.

The Control Array

If you need to track the controls that have been placed on a window, you might consider creating an array. However, PowerBuilder already takes care of this and enables you to access it in your code.

PowerBuilder uses the control array to paint the window. The order in which the controls appear in the array is important in producing an even painting effect. Your application will look better if it paints across and down the screen instead of jumping to different locations. The default order of the control array is the order in which the controls were placed on the screen. If you want to change the order, send the controls to the back and then bring them to the front in the order in which you want them to be painted.

The control array can also be used in your code. You might find the array to be useful if you have a window that contains a Reset button that restores all controls to their initial states. The code would be as follows:

```
Integer li_index, li_count
SingleLineEdit sle_generic
DropDownListBox ddlb_generic
DataWindow dw_generic
CheckBox cbx_generic

li_count = UpperBound( parent.Control)

For li_index to li_count
Choose Case TypeOf( parent.Control[ li_index])
```

```
    Case SingleLineEdit!  //Clear text
       sle_generic = parent.Control[li_index]
       sle_generic.text = ""
    Case DropDownListBox! //Clear drop-down listbox
       ddlb_generic = parent.Control[li_index]
       ddlb_generic.SelectItem(0)
    Case DataWindow!       //Reset DataWindow and insert new row
       dw_generic = parent.Control[li_index]
       dw_generic.Reset()
       dw_generic.InsertRow(0)
    Case CheckBox!         //Uncheck all checkboxes
       cbx_generic = parent.Control[li_index]
       cbx_generic.checked = FALSE
 End Choose
 Next
```

Using the `TypeOf()` function, you can determine the type of control the array element is referencing and provide the appropriate code to the object type.

Miscellaneous Scripting Techniques

When you are finished with a window and the user no longer needs to access data from it, close it. Not only is leaving unneeded windows open a sloppy interface, but these windows consume resources that could be more effectively used by other parts of your application. The same is true of windows whose `Visible` attribute is `FALSE`.

Finally, any object that you create should also be destroyed. If you create any nonvisual user objects in your application using the `CREATE` statement, you should ensure that the object is properly removed from memory by using the `DESTROY` statement when you are done with the object.

NOTE

PowerBuilder now gives you some assistance in ensuring that objects get destroyed properly with the `AutoInstantiate` property for custom class user objects. If you set this property on, PowerBuilder will create and destroy the object for you.

Event Usage

You can easily tune the usage of functions to increase efficiency in your application, and the same situation applies to events.

The `Open` event of a window is an excellent target for improving the performance and perceived performance of your application. Many beginning PowerBuilder developers place a lot of code in this event, which means that the window takes a while to open and become visible to the user.

For example, if you need to populate a DataWindow or a drop-down list box for your user, you might think that the `Open` event is the perfect place to perform this logic. But if either script runs long, the user will have to wait to see the window. To get around this delay, create a user event tied to a `pbm_custom` event ID and place the retrieval or population logic there. Then, from the `Open` event, use the `PostEvent()` function to call the new user event. The message will be placed at the bottom of the Windows message queue and will permit the window to appear before the code finishes executing. This way, the user sees the window but will probably not be quick enough to do anything before the posted event finishes executing. If the script does take longer, use a status window indicating that initialization is still occurring so that the user will not feel like he is waiting.

The amount of code written in the `Open` event script should be kept to a minimum, but it is a good candidate for manipulating graphics. The objects on the window have already been constructed but not yet displayed, and can therefore be manipulated. By performing this manipulation before the window is opened, Windows only has to paint the window once. This increases performance and does not cause the screen to flicker, which is an unattractive user-interface feature. Long-running scripts should also be avoided for the `Activate` event so that the user does not have to wait for this event to finish before using the window.

The `Other` event should also be avoided because it is used to trap all Windows messages that are not associated with a specific object. If you want to trap a particular Windows message, create a user-defined event tied to the appropriate event ID. If PowerBuilder does not trap that message with a corresponding event ID, this will not be possible.

Object-Oriented Programming

PowerBuilder, unlike many front-end development tools, incorporates many object-oriented features that help to streamline the development process. By providing an object-based approach to development, you can easily reuse objects and create an application that is easier to maintain.

NOTE

For first-time PowerBuilder developers, the object-oriented features of PowerBuilder can actually increase the length of development. This is because these developers will not know what objects work well and can be reused—this is knowledge that comes with experience and a strong design.

The object-oriented features are inheritance, encapsulation, and polymorphism. For in-depth coverage of these topics, see Chapter 15, "Programming PowerBuilder."

Inheritance and encapsulation enable you to create an application that has cleaner code and objects that can be reused repeatedly. Code is located in one place and is not duplicated throughout the application, making maintenance a much simpler process.

Inheritance, in addition to providing reusable objects, can give you a performance gain at execution time. When an inherited object is loaded into memory at runtime, all of its ancestors are also loaded. If several objects are inherited from the same ancestors, the ancestor definitions are already loaded into memory, and therefore, each subsequent descendant object's load time is faster, as shown in the following example.

In this example, the application requires the development of three windows: `w_product_sales`, `w_sales_rep`, and `w_regional_sales`, which all contain DataWindows that retrieve data to display overall weekly sales figures, sales representative sales, and regional sales, respectively. If each window is created as a separate entity (no inheritance), the time taken to open each window is 10 seconds.

As the development of all windows nears completion, you realize that you have just written the same code for each window (updates, insert, deletes, error handling, and sales calculations). You decide that the common DataWindow processing (updates, insert, deletes, and error handling) can be placed in an ancestor window, `w_ancestor`. This window can be used by other applications, so you decide to inherit a new window from `w_ancestor` that will contain the specific sales calculations, `w_sales_ancestor`. After you build the two ancestor windows, `w_product_sales`, `w_sales_rep`, and `w_regional_sales` are inherited from `w_sales_ancestor` and modified to perform their own specific processing. The resulting inheritance chain is shown in Figure 35.1.

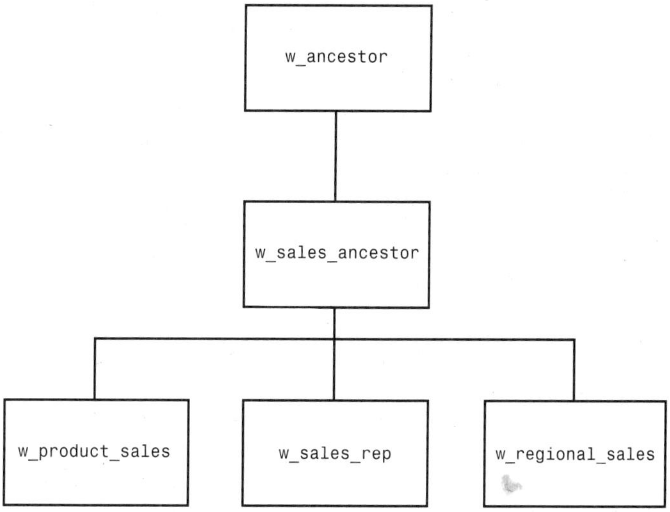

FIGURE 35.1.
A window inheritance tree.

When the user specifies that he wants to open `w_product_sales`, the class definitions for `w_ancestor` and `w_sales_ancestor` must be loaded into memory before `w_product_sales` can be loaded. The time taken to load `w_product_sales` is 15 seconds. This is an increase of 5 seconds from the standalone version of the same window. When `w_sales_rep` is opened, its ancestors, `w_ancestor` and `w_sales_ancestor`, are already loaded into memory so just `w_sales_rep`'s definition needs to be loaded. The open time necessary for the inherited windows `w_sales_rep` and `w_regional_sales` is only 5 seconds. This also means that each subsequent descendant window takes less time to load. For the three windows, you went from a combined open time of 30 seconds to 20 seconds using inheritance. This example, of course, is greatly simplified, but you can begin to see some of the performance benefits of inheritance.

Another object-oriented technique that is incorporated with inheritance is polymorphism. Polymorphism enables you to define a series of operations for different objects even if they behave differently. Consider this: A function is defined for a set of objects but acts differently based on the referenced object type. For example, an update function might update a database for one window and save to a file for another window. Using polymorphism can speed up your code by reducing the amount of code needed, as shown by the following example.

Suppose you have two sheets (`w_order_detail` and `w_customer`) open in an MDI application that update different tables. You could create a function in each to perform the update. In the `Clicked` event for a Save menu item, you could place the following code:

```
window lw_sheet
w_order_detail lw_order
w_customer lw_customer

lw_sheet = w_mdiFrame.GetActiveSheet()

If IsValid(lw_sheet) Then
   Choose Case ClassName(lw_sheet)
      Case "w_order_detail"
         lw_order = lw_sheet
         lw_order.wf_UpdateOrderTable()
      Case "w_customer"
         lw_customer = lw_sheet
         lw_customer.wf_UpdateCustTable()
   End Choose
End If
```

If another window is added that uses this menu, you must add it to the code. This, unfortunately, requires hard coding values in your script, which you should avoid. The polymorphic solution would be to create an ancestor window (`w_ancestor`) containing an object-level function called `wf_Update()` with no script in it. The Save menu item's `Clicked` script would then be much simpler:

```
w_ancestor lw_sheet

lw_sheet = w_mdiFrame.GetActiveSheet()

If IsValid( lw_sheet) Then
        lw_sheet.wf_Update()
End If
```

As you can see, the code is much easier to read. PowerBuilder does not have to evaluate multiple arguments, making the script process faster, and you do not have to modify the code if all new windows use `w_ancestor` through inheritance. Each descendant window would then override the ancestor function with its own specific update processing.

Another method of achieving the same functionality is to use the function `TriggerEvent()`. This function immediately executes an event for a specified object. From the `Clicked` event of the Save menu, you could code `ParentWindow.TriggerEvent("ue_filesave")`. This would attempt to execute the user-defined event `ue_filesave` in the menu's associated window. The beauty of doing this is that the event does not have to be defined for all windows. There are two reasons: First, since the event-name argument for `TriggerEvent()` is just a string, PowerBuilder cannot validate at compile time that the event exists. Second, if the event does not exist, `TriggerEvent()` does not cause an application-terminating runtime error, but just returns `-1`. This method should be used as a workaround for those occasions when you do not have the time to implement a polymorphic solution.

DataWindows

As if you didn't already know, the DataWindow is the main reason PowerBuilder is the popular application-development tool that it is today. The DataWindow incorporates much of the functionality that a developer needs with a minimum amount of code.

The DataWindow has many strengths:

- A variety of display formats
- Several different edit styles (for example, edit masks and radio buttons)
- An easy method for laying out a data-entry screen
- Built-in scrolling
- Multiple reporting techniques (graphing, crosstabs, groups, and layers)
- Data validation by both PowerBuilder and the developer
- Less resource-intensive than conventional controls
- Minimal script is required to retrieve data
- Updating a database is handled internally by the DataWindow object
- Increases performance

Obviously, by providing a control that requires minimal script to retrieve data, handle updates, scroll, and provide data validation, the performance of the application is going to increase as development time decreases. One of the reasons performance is increased is that to build the functionality of a DataWindow using standard controls would result in a considerable amount of code on the developer's behalf. The interpreted code will not be as fast (and potentially not as well structured) as the same compiled code built into PowerBuilder.

The DataWindow is also more efficient in terms of controls on a window and screen painting. If you had an application that displayed 10 columns and 10 rows from a database at one time and didn't have the DataWindow available, you would have to use 100 single-line edits and a lot of code. Imagine populating each control every time the user scrolled down. Even worse, if the user wanted to update the database, you would have to track what had been changed and generate the appropriate SQL statement.

Not only would this be tedious to code, but the amount of memory consumed by the 100 single-line edits would have an adverse effect on your application's performance. The DataWindow, on the other hand, tracks changes, generates the SQL statements, and is considered as one control that consumes significantly less memory. The fact that the DataWindow is considered to be only one control also means that when Windows repaints the screen, the DataWindow control is painted all at once, increasing the repainting speed.

Although the DataWindow is a powerful object that can increase the efficiency of your application, do not abuse it. For example, if you do not need to access a database, it might make more sense and provide better performance to use the standard PowerBuilder controls.

The following sections give some tips that will help you tune the performance of the DataWindow even more.

DataWindow Tuning

Avoid using the `RetrieveRow` event of the DataWindow control. `RetrieveRow` is triggered every time a row is retrieved from the database into the DataWindow (after a `Retrieve()` function call). PowerBuilder performs a Yield after each row, thus slowing down the retrieval process.

NOTE

Even if you only code a comment line in the `RetrieveRow` event, there is still an effect on performance.

You should also limit the amount of code placed in the `ItemChanged`, `ItemFocusChanged`, and `RowFocusChanged` events. For example, your application retrieves a product description from a database every time the product code changes (using the `ItemChanged` event). If the user has to wait more than a second for a response, you are guaranteed to get a phone call.

In addition to keeping the scripts short in the aforementioned events, you should keep the script brief in the `Clicked` event if you plan on using the `DoubleClicked` event as well. If you have too much code in the `Clicked` event, the script might still be running when the user clicks a second time. The second click will not be recognized and, therefore, the `DoubleClicked` event will not be triggered.

Data Retrieval

Although using a DataWindow is an efficient method of retrieving data, even it can be used to produce long-running queries and poor memory utilization. One thing that will improve application performance is to minimize the number of rows and columns that are returned to the client by making your queries as specific as possible. By bringing back unnecessary data (rows or columns), you are tying up resources on the server, the network, and the client. Several additional techniques exist to minimize the amount of data that is returned to the client. They are described in the following sections.

Limit the User

The easiest method of limiting what is retrieved is to make the user define the queries he will need and implement only those queries (you might have to force the user to choose a "top 10" list). By specifying the queries up front, you know exactly what will be retrieved and approximately the time needed. This information can then be shown to the user.

Although you won't get any surprises in what data is retrieved using this method, there are some serious disadvantages in this approach. Limiting your users to specific queries is not flexible, and users invariably want more functionality. Plus, when you implement the specific queries, you can ensure that the data retrieved is not too large, but the database might grow and then the queries will begin to take longer.

SQL `Count()`

Because limiting your users to a specific query could eventually result in a large amount of data being retrieved, it would be nice to know how many rows are going to be returned and to ask the user whether he wants to continue. This can be accomplished using the `Count` function in a SQL statement.

For example, if your DataWindow were going to execute this SQL statement:

```
SELECT order_num, customer_name, item_no, quantity, ship_date
FROM order_detail od, customer cs
WHERE od.cust_id = cs.cust_id
AND cs.cust_id = :a_cust_id
AND od.ship_date BETWEEN "07/11/93" AND GetDate()
```

you would probably want to know if the selected customer were going to retrieve a lot of orders. You could run the following first to find out the exact number of rows returned:

```
SELECT Count(*)
FROM order_detail od, customer cs
WHERE od.cust_id = cs.cust_id
AND cs.cust_id = :a_cust_id
AND od.ship_date BETWEEN "07/11/93" AND GetDate()
```

The `Count` statement will tell you exactly how many rows match the criteria specified in the `WHERE` clause. You can then display a message box telling the user how much data will be retrieved and ask whether he wants to continue.

The disadvantage of this approach is that you are executing the SQL statement twice. Although you do not have the overhead of bringing data across the network into memory, you still have a performance hit. Depending on the query, this is a fairly common method of limiting data retrieved.

The `RetrieveRow` Event

If performing a count takes too long, you can use the `RetrieveRow` event of the DataWindow control to count the number of rows returned from the database. Set a counter that is incremented every time a row is retrieved. After it reaches a certain number of rows (for example, 100), ask the user whether he wants to continue to query or cancel the retrieval.

This seems like a good approach, but it does have a negative effect on performance. The `RetrieveRow` event is executed each time a row is retrieved from the database. This will slow down all retrievals, even the small ones.

Database Cursors

If you want the ultimate in control, consider using a database cursor. A cursor enables you to manipulate one row at a time in a result set. By using a cursor, you can prompt the user to see whether he wants to continue after a certain number of rows has been reached. If the user says yes, you can continue the retrieval where you left off.

The downside to using a cursor is that you are bypassing most of the power given to you by the DataWindow. You have to manually place the data into the DataWindow (using `SetItem()` or the corresponding direct access syntax).

Retrieve As Needed

In the DataWindow painter under the Rows menu, there is an option named Retrieve As Needed. PowerBuilder retrieves as many rows as it takes to fill the DataWindow and presents the data to the user while the query is still returning data from the server. As the user scrolls or moves to see additional data, PowerBuilder continues to retrieve more data from the server. Retrieve As Needed gives the user immediate access to the data for even long-running queries.

NOTE

If you specify any client-side sorting, grouping, averages, or any other functions that act on the result set as a whole, Retrieve As Needed will be overridden.

The query has effectively finished! The database server is now just waiting on requests to send data to the client.

The downside to this option is that the user must wait as he scrolls down because PowerBuilder is retrieving additional data. PowerBuilder is also maintaining an open connection (by using an internal cursor) to the server. Maintaining this connection is dangerous because locks are being held. You also cannot commit to free these locks or the cursor will close and no more data will be returned. After presenting the data to the user following the initial retrieve, you might consider turning off Retrieve As Needed using the following syntax:

```
dw_1.Object.DataWindow.Retrieve.AsNeeded = 'NO'
```

This code will allow PowerBuilder to return the remaining data into the DataWindow.

NOTE

A new option in PowerBuilder 5.0 is the ability to specify that retrieved rows are saved to disk, which frees memory to your application. This should be used in cases where the user does not require constant access to the retrieved data; otherwise, performance will decrease due to the extra disk access.

NEW 5 in PowerBuilder

Query Mode

You can set the DataWindow to query mode, which enables the user to specify data-retrieval criteria for the `WHERE` clause in the DataWindow's SQL `SELECT` statement. This enables the user to tune a query to his precise requirements. Query mode is activated at runtime by coding the following:

```
dw_1.Object.DataWindow.QueryMode='Yes'
```

The interface is the same Query by Example look (see Figure 35.2) as shown in the Quick Select data source option.

FIGURE 35.2.
Query mode for a DataWindow.

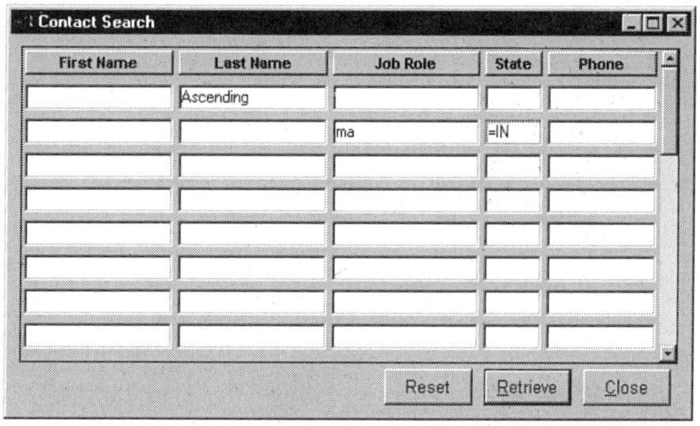

PowerBuilder clears the DataWindow object and enables the user to type criteria onto any of the lines. If you also want the user to have the capability to specify sort criteria, code a line like this:

```
dw_1.Object.DataWindow.QuerySort='Yes'
```

When using query mode, it is important that you initially create your DataWindow object with no `WHERE` clause; otherwise, you might have information from an existing `WHERE` clause that conflicts with information from the user specifications.

Prompt for Criteria

Prompt for Criteria is very similar to query mode, with a few minor differences. Prompt for Criteria can be turned on from the Rows menu in the DataWindow painter or by using `Modify()` or the appropriate direct object syntax. When you use Prompt for Criteria, you specify in which columns you want the user to be able to specify his criteria (see Figure 35.3), whereas query mode enables the user to specify criteria for all visible columns.

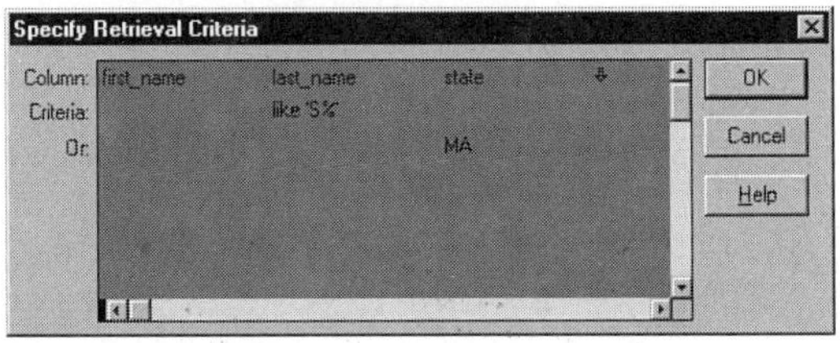

FIGURE 35.3.
The Specify Retrieval Criteria dialog box.

You cannot, however, specify a sort criteria using Prompt for Criteria. The only other important thing to note is that if the user does not specify any criteria, the SQL is still executed but with no `WHERE` clause. The downside to using both the query mode and Prompt for Criteria options is that PowerBuilder is required to compile the SQL for each DataWindow retrieval.

Additional DataWindow Considerations

The previous techniques to control the amount of data returned to the client are important. A number of additional techniques can be applied to the client that will assist in increasing your application's performance. You should perform data validation on the client to prevent bad data being sent across the network to the database only to be rejected. Data formatting should also be done by the client to provide interface consistency and keep unnecessary formatting characters from being stored in the database.

The client should also manage database connections and transaction processing. The number of times you connect and the number of connections to a database should be kept at a minimum. Issuing a `CONNECT` is an expensive operation and ties up resources on the server and client. To manage connections effectively, use the function `SetTransObject()` as opposed to `SetTrans()`. `SetTrans()` manages the database connections for you, going so far as to connect and disconnect after every `Retrieve()` and `Update()` function call. The application, using `SetTransObject()`, should perform `COMMIT`s after a logical unit of work has processed on the database to remove database locks and to free memory on the server.

Although the client has numerous responsibilities, the server also has its share. Aggregation should be performed on the server, because it is most likely a more powerful machine than the client. If the SQL needed to retrieve data is too complex for a DataWindow or a script to handle, consider using stored procedures (if supported by your DBMS) to execute the SQL. Stored procedures are particularly useful if you have complex multiple joins that the DataWindow cannot handle and when you want to make use of temporary tables to fine-tune your SQL.

In minimizing the number of times that data is retrieved, you might want to consider one of the following options. You can capture often-used static data one of two ways: caching it using arrays or in 5.0 you can now use the new DataStore object. You can also use hidden DataWindows to maintain static or large amounts of data. After the data has been retrieved, you can then use the `ShareData()` function so that the same data does not have to be maintained multiple times in memory for different DataWindows.

The User Interface

As mentioned earlier, the human factor can make or break any project. This is true of the development team, but also—more importantly—of the user. If the user does not like the application, you will have nothing but headaches. For that reason, get your user involved in every facet of the development and testing process. The user then can't complain about the end product and also has his reputation at stake if the application does not perform well.

The user interface has a huge impact on the perceived performance of the application. If the interface is not intuitive and the user has to spend time figuring out what he needs to do, it matters little whether the application runs at lightning speed. Therefore, it is important to spend time on developing and enforcing good GUI standards across your company's applications.

The number of menu items and objects on a window should not be excessive or the user will not know what to do. Also, people cannot comprehend as much on a computer screen as they can on a printed page (up to 50 percent less in some cases).

The density of items on a window is as important as is the placement of the controls. Microsoft publishes a list of CUA (common user access) practices and GUI guidelines that you should review before and after the development process. For more details on the guidelines for the Windows environment and other platforms (for example, the Macintosh), see Chapter 21, "Cross-Platform PowerBuilder."

Summary

As you can see, a number of places can be focal points for tuning. This chapter mainly points out some techniques that will help make your PowerBuilder application run more smoothly. You should make sure that you and other project team members configure all the components (that is, server, network, client, software, and hardware) in your client/server application. By doing so, you will provide a product that you can be proud of and that your users will love.

OLE 2.0 and DDE

36

IN THIS CHAPTER

In this chapter you will learn about a couple different methods and techniques that can be used for interprocess communication and application integration in the Windows environment. Although there are several ways to exchange information between Windows applications, this chapter focuses mainly on object linking and embedding (OLE) and dynamic data exchange (DDE).

In addition to being DDE compliant, PowerBuilder supports OLE 2.0 in the Window painter, and now in Version 5.0, also in the DataWindow painter. First, you will see the high-level definitions of the concepts of interprocess communication and application integration. Then you'll learn how to use DDE and OLE within your PowerBuilder applications.

Interprocess Communication

The term *interprocess communication* (IPC) is defined as the process used by two or more Windows applications running at the same time to send messages and data to one another. The most common methods of IPC are DDE, OLE, external function calls to dynamic link libraries (DLLs), file access, and the Windows Clipboard.

All of these methods enable different Windows applications to have conversations with one another. In PowerBuilder, you can build applications implementing all of these techniques, but the most prevalent methods to communicate are DDE and OLE.

DDE Overview

DDE was first implemented in Windows (pre-3.*x*) as a message-based protocol used to exchange data between different Windows applications. Unfortunately, in its initial form, DDE was complicated and therefore was not used much in actual application development. With the release of Windows 3.0, DDE was simplified and much easier to incorporate into an application. This was accomplished by making the DDE services available through an *Application Programming Interface* (API) called the *DDE Management Library* (DDEML). The physical file is named DDEML.DLL and comprises about 25 functions based on the same concepts as the initial message-based protocol.

In PowerBuilder, the PowerScript language provides a much easier method than using the message-based protocol or the API calls to DDEML.DLL. PowerScript provides a series of DDE functions that wrap around the DDEML functions and provide a simpler interface.

When you're using DDE, the interprocess communication, or *conversation*, takes place in much the same way as with a standard client/server application (such as a PowerBuilder application communicating with a database server). In DDE, one application is the client and the other is the server, and they communicate via transactions. A PowerBuilder application can be either the client, used to request and present data, or the server, used to provide data and functionality.

OLE Overview

OLE is a more recent development than DDE. It is a set of standardized interfaces that enables you to integrate multiple applications in the Windows environment. Using these standard interfaces, OLE permits applications to use each other's data or objects and call each other's services.

An OLE object can be any number of different types: a document, a spreadsheet, a graphical image, or a sound wave, to name just a few. Just like DDE, an operation using OLE is comprised of a client and a server application. The job of the server in OLE is to create and maintain the OLE object. A common example is a graph that has been created and saved using Microsoft Excel. This graph can then be placed as an object inside a Word for Windows document or another OLE client. For the Word example, the Excel graph is an embedded object in the Word document. Excel would be the server and Word for Windows would be the client application.

Dynamic Data Exchange

The following sections discuss the terminology involved in using dynamic data exchange and the common functions needed to implement it in your PowerBuilder application.

DDE Concepts

A *DDE conversation* occurs between a client application and a server application. The *client* is the application that makes the initial request to talk to the *server* application. When the connection is established, the client can continue to ask the server for data or use the functionality inherent to the server. An example is using Excel to perform the calculations to amortize a loan because that capability is built into Excel.

A client application can use the services of multiple server applications at the same time, and a particular server can have multiple clients requesting data from it. To make things even more challenging, a server can be a client at the same time that it is a server. For example, a PowerBuilder application could request data from a Word document and the Word document could be executing a function in Excel. In this example, Word would be a server to the PowerBuilder application and a client for Excel.

PowerBuilder can be used as both a client and a server application. For example, PowerBuilder could retrieve data from a database into a DataWindow and place a value from the DataWindow at a bookmark in a Word document. In this example, the PowerBuilder application would be acting as a server. An example of using PowerBuilder as a client is extracting values from a range of cells in an Excel spreadsheet and displaying them in a drop-down list box. It is also possible to have distinct PowerBuilder applications running simultaneously and conversing with each other, so that you have PowerBuilder acting as both a client and a server.

To successfully establish a conversation between the client and the server applications, a server needs to be uniquely identified to the client application. To accomplish this, DDE uses the following naming convention to identify the server application: *application name*, *topic*, and *item* (`appname.topic.item`).

Application Name

The *application name* uniquely identifies a particular application, such as Microsoft Excel. The name is a string and must be provided to establish the connection. A server typically has only one application name. For example, for Microsoft Excel the application name is EXCEL; Program Manager is PROGMAN; and Microsoft Word for Windows is WINWORD. The application name is often referred to as the *app name* and occasionally as the *service name*.

Topic

The *topic name* further defines the server with which the client wants to converse. The topic name is also a string and is used to identify a classification of data (for instance, in Excel, a topic name could be the filename of a spreadsheet). The topic does not have to be a specific file. It could be a file type, an object, or a special topic name called `System`. The `System` topic name is used to provide general information about the different types of information that can be supplied to the client application in a DDE conversation. The `System` topic name is a requirement for an application to be a DDE server.

Item

The *item name* further defines the application server. The item name is also a string used in a DDE function call from the client application to identify specific data. The item in a Word document might be the name of a bookmark, or in Excel it might be a cell reference (such as `R5C6`).

The Registration Information Editor

The Windows Registration Information Editor is a Windows utility program used in adding to and modifying the registration database, which contains information about application integration. To access the Registration Editor, run REGEDIT.EXE (located in the \WINDOWS directory). This opens the Registration Information Editor (see Figure 36.1).

The Registration Editor displays a list of all applications in a hierarchical registration database (\WINDOWS\REG.DAT, a hidden file). Most applications update the Windows registration on installation. If this doesn't happen, check the application's directory for a registration file (REG) and merge it into the registration database. If the application does not have a REG file, check the application's documentation for additional information or call the software vendor.

FIGURE 36.1.
The Registration Information Editor.

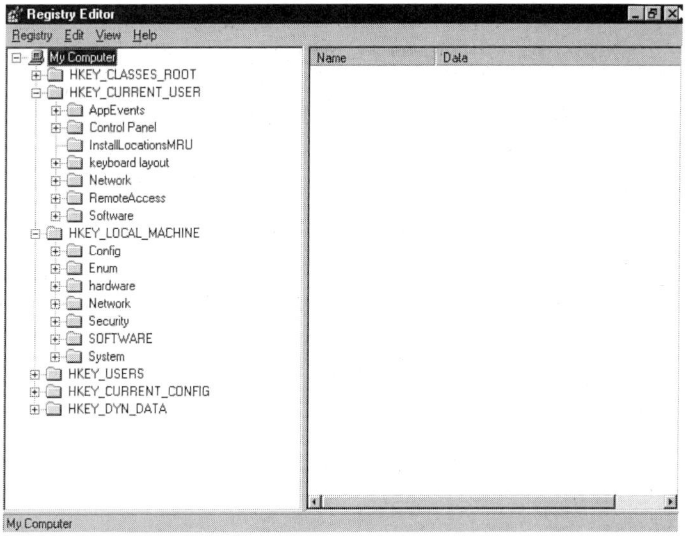

The registry is broken down into six different keys (all begin with `HKEY`). To find information about an application's DDE capabilities, locate the application name under `HKEY_CLASSES_ROOT` (see Figure 36.2).

FIGURE 36.2.
The `HKEY_CLASSES_ROOT` *expansion for Word for Windows.*

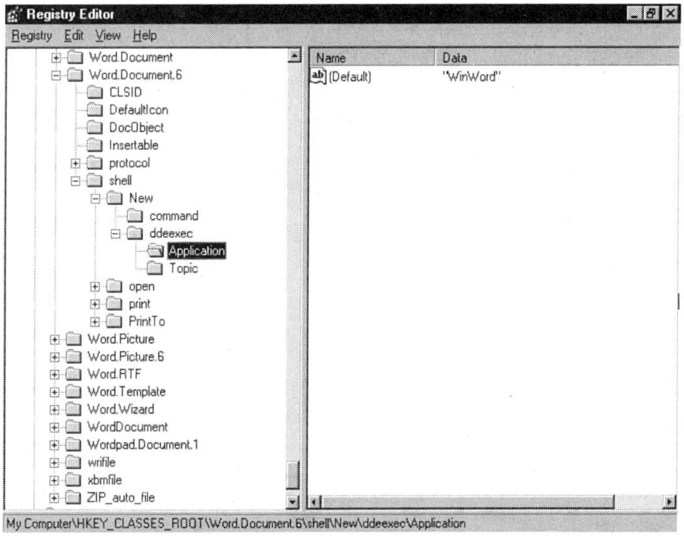

As you can see in Figure 36.2, if an application is DDE enabled, the application and topic names for the application are specified in the application tree under shell*command*\\ddeexec where *command* is a particular DDE command. These will be used later to establish your connection to the server. If you are unsure of where to look, you can use the Registration Editor's search engine, which allows you to look for a particular string.

The Registration Editor is a vital component needed to define your application to the operating system and has become increasingly more important in Windows NT and Windows 95.

NOTE

This chapter uses the Windows 95 Registry for its examples. The Windows NT Registry is very similar in its structure to Windows 95. There is, however, a considerable difference between these two registries and the Windows 3.*x* Registry. In Windows 3.*x*, if you just run REGEDIT.EXE, you will get a simplistic application that displays file associations and some DDE references. To access much of the same information in Windows 3.*x*, run `REGEDIT.EXE /v`.

The Complete DDE Process

After you have specified all the information for an application to be defined as a DDE server, the client is ready to begin a conversation with it. There are several steps involved in using DDE in your PowerBuilder application.

The first thing you must do is make sure that the server application is running in Windows. After the server is started, the client application must open a channel to the server, which is how the two applications share data and functions. When the channel has been established, the client sends commands or data to the server application to be processed. The server application processes whatever the client sends and responds appropriately. The client must handle the response from the server. This continues until the client application no longer needs to use any of the server's functionality. The client then closes the channel with the server, and the last step is for the client application to shut down the server application.

Starting the Server Application

Before the client application can establish a connection with the server application, the server must be up and running in the Windows environment. To load an application via PowerScript, use the `Run()` function. This function takes two arguments. The first is a string that identifies the filename of the application you want to execute. The string can also contain any parameters that the application might use (such as a data file that the program will use). The second argument is optional and indicates the window state in which you want the program to run. The valid enumerated data types are `Maximized!`, `Minimized!`, and `Normal!`. The `Run()` function returns an integer, with `-1` indicating failure and `1` indicating success. If the application is already running, PowerBuilder starts a new instance of it. To determine whether the application is currently running, you can use the `FindWindow()` API call. For more information on the correct usage of this call, see Chapter 33, "API Calls."

Initiating a Conversation

To start a DDE conversation between the client and server applications, use the function `OpenChannel()`, which establishes the link between the two applications. There are three arguments to the `OpenChannel()` function: the application name, the topic name, and, optionally, the window handle. As specified earlier, the *`app name`* argument specifies the DDE name of the DDE server as found in the Registration database. The *`topic name`* argument tells what instance or data of the application that you want to utilize. Table 36.1 shows several common Windows applications and their corresponding application names and topic names.

Table 36.1. Application and topic names for common Windows applications.

Application	`app name` *Argument*	`topic name` *Argument*
Excel	`Excel`	*`Spreadsheet_name`*`.XLS`
Lotus 1-2-3	`123W`	*`Spreadsheet_name`*`.WK(1,2,3,4)`
Program Manager	`PROGMAN`	`PROGMAN`
Word	`WinWord`	*`Document_name`*`.DOC`

For PowerBuilder, it is up to the developer to determine the app name and topic name for each application that is to be used as a DDE server. The last argument, the window handle, is optional and is used to indicate which window is the DDE client when there is more than one window open in your application. The following runs the server application (Word for Windows) and opens a channel to it:

```
integer li_rtn
string ls_program

ls_program = "c:\msoffice\winword\winword.exe " + &
"c:\msoffice\winword\unleash.doc"

li_rtn = Run( ls_program, Minimized!)

If li_rtn = -1 then
   MessageBox( "Run Error", "Could not start Word for Windows")
   Return
Else
   il_ddehandle = OpenChannel( "WINWORD", "c:\msoffice\winword\unleash.doc")
   If il_ddehandle < 0 Then
      MessageBox( "Connection Error", "Word is not responding!")
      Return
   End If
End If
```

An important consideration when using DDE is the possibility that it might take the server application some time before it responds. As a developer, you must allow for this delay in response time. The amount of time before the DDE client gives up trying to communicate is set in the `DDETimeOut` attribute of the application object. The amount of time is specified in seconds. The `DDETimeOut` attribute can be set anywhere in your application, but it must be fully qualified with the application object's name.

Communicating with the DDE Server

After the channel has been opened, you are ready to send data, request data, or execute commands on the server application. You accomplish these tasks through a series of PowerScript functions.

Sending Data

To send data to a DDE server, use the `SetRemote()` function. The `SetRemote()` function asks the DDE server to accept the data being passed and store it in a particular location (such as a document bookmark or a spreadsheet cell). There are two different syntaxes for the `SetRemote()` function depending on what type of DDE connection has been established.

The valid types of DDE connections are cold link, warm link, and hot link. A *cold link* is a single DDE command (such as `SetRemote()` or `GetRemote()`) that does not require that you open a channel. With a cold link, the client application does not know whether the data has changed in the DDE server. A *hot link* is a single-step process that opens the conversation channel and sends data in the same step. The hot link is useful if you need to know when data has changed since the server automatically notifies the client application. A warm link is a combination of the hot and cold links, depending on how it is coded by the developer. A *warm link* usually starts with `OpenChannel()` and ends with `CloseChannel()`. A warm link is most useful when you need to make several DDE requests.

The first syntax is used with a cold link, and the arguments for `SetRemote()` are *`location`*, *`value`*, *`app name`*, and *`topic name`*. *`location`* (a string) is the specific location in the DDE server where the data is to be placed. *`value`* is a string that contains the data being sent. *`app name`* and *`topic name`* are the same as defined earlier. The function returns `1` to indicate success, `-1` to indicate that the link was not started, and `-2` to indicate that the request was denied. The following is an example of the first syntax that updates a bookmark in a Word document:

```
SetRemote( "last_name", "Herbert", "Winword", "unleash.doc")
```

The second syntax is used with a warm DDE link. The arguments are the location, the value, the channel handle (returned from the `OpenChannel()` function), and, optionally, the window handle. The second syntax also has the same return values as the first syntax, with the addition of `-9`, which indicates that the handle is `NULL`. This code demonstrates the second syntax of `SetRemote()`:

```
long ll_ddehandle
integer li_count

ll_ddehandle = OpenChannel( "Winword","Unleash.doc")

Do While SetRemote( "last_name","Herbert", ll_ddehandle) <> 1
   li_count++
   If li_count > 10 then return
Loop
```

The `Do_While` loop handles the situation when Word for Windows is busy processing another request. The loop tries 10 times to process the request before exiting the script. The same thing could be managed using a timer or the `DDETimeOut` attribute.

Requesting Data

If you want to retrieve information from the DDE server application, use the `GetRemote()` function. Just like the `SetRemote()` function, `GetRemote()` has two formats—one for a cold link and one for a warm link. The arguments remain the same for both functions and formats, with the exception of the second argument. This string argument is the variable location where the requested data will be placed. The following demonstrates `GetRemote()`:

```
string ls_LastName

GetRemote( "last_name",ls_LastName,"Winword","unleash.doc")
```

Executing Commands

The other function typically used to communicate with a DDE server is `ExecRemote()`, which executes a specific command in the DDE server application. The commands are those used in the application's own scripting language (such as Word Basic). `ExecRemote()` uses two different syntaxes based on the link type and has three arguments. For the first syntax use `command`, `handle`, and, optionally, `window handle`. For the second syntax use `command`, `app name`, and `topic name`. The command argument is a string containing the command that you want the DDE server to process. The following is an example of the first syntax:

```
integer li_ddehandle, li_rtn

li_ddehandle = OpenChannel( "WinWord","Unleash.doc")
li_rtn = ExecRemote( "FileSave", li_ddehandle)
```

Typically, you will have a combination of sending data, requesting data, and executing functions. You do this using a warm link DDE conversation.

Using a Hot Link

If your application needs to know when changes have been made to the data in the server application and needs the new data, you must establish a DDE hot link. To start a hot link, you must use the function `StartHotLink()`. The arguments for this function are the location of the data that you want to monitor for changes (such as a bookmark or cell specification), the server application name, and the topic name for the specific application instance.

After the hot link has been established, the `HotLinkAlarm` event of the window is triggered whenever the data at the location specified is changed. You can use a series of functions in this event to communicate with the server application.

`GetDataDDEOrigin()` is used to determine which application triggered the `HotLinkAlarm` event. The function passes three empty strings, which will be filled with *app name*, *topic name*, and *item name* (all strings). These values are then used to determine the response that your PowerBuilder application will take.

`GetDataDDE()` passes an empty string in which the changed data from the server will be placed. The `RespondRemote()` function is used to notify the server application of whether the information received was acceptable. The argument is a Boolean variable indicating `TRUE` if the data was acceptable and `FALSE` if it was not.

After all processing is complete, you need to terminate the hot link with the server application. This is done using `StopHotLink()`. This function needs the location name, the app name, and the topic name that you want to terminate.

Terminating a Connection

After all transactions have been sent to the DDE server, it is up to the developer to free the resources being used by the open channel between the client and server applications. To close a DDE conversation, use the function `CloseChannel()`. This function takes the argument's handle and, optionally, the window handle. The handle is the long variable that was returned from the `OpenChannel()` function. The valid return values (integers) are `1` indicating success, `-1` indicating that the open failed, `-2` indicating that the channel would not close, `-3` indicating that there was no confirmation from the server, and `-9` indicating that the handle is `NULL`. The following would close the connection to Word:

```
integer li_rtn

li_rtn = CloseChannel(il_ddehandle)

If li_rtn <> 1 Then
   MessageBox("Close error","Unable to terminate conversation!")
End If
```

`il_ddehandle` is an instance variable containing the handle returned from the `OpenChannel()` function.

When using a warm link for your DDE conversation, a problem occurs when you need to close the DDE channel and close the server application. If you perform an `ExecRemote()` to close the server while maintaining the open channel, you'll hang your application and Windows. If you close the channel first, you no longer have the warm link to communicate to the server. The solution is to close the channel first and then use a cold link `ExecRemote()` to close the server application.

PowerBuilder as a DDE Server

In the previous examples, you saw how to use PowerBuilder as the client application requesting services from another Windows application. PowerBuilder applications also can be used as DDE server applications. To start a PowerBuilder application as a DDE server, use the function `StartServerDDE()`. The arguments are the app name, topic name, and optional item, as described earlier. When your application has been started as a DDE server, other Windows applications can send requests to your application. The requests for data from your application will be written in the scripting language for the client application (such as Word Basic or VBA).

Within your application, you need to utilize a series of functions and events to trap the requests of the client applications. What you code is dependent on the information that the client applications can request. For example, with the `RemoteRequest` event of a window, you can determine what item the client has requested and respond to the request by sending data back. `GetDataDDEOrigin()` is used to determine the application, topic, and item of the server making the request. If the server is recognized by your application, you can respond to the request and send data back using `SetDataDDE()`, which takes a string containing the data to be sent back.

OLE 2.0 Terminology

Because the computer industry is scattered with TLAs (three-letter abbreviations!), it is difficult enough to keep track of what the abbreviations stand for, let alone understand what they mean. This section defines what OLE really means. OLE (Version 1.0) was first introduced just before Windows 3.1 went to market. This version is limited and was introduced to get the Windows community familiar with the concepts. OLE 1.0 was built on dynamic data exchange and used Windows messages and callbacks to pass information between applications. All that it gave you was a fancy method to shell out to another application from your PowerBuilder application. The functionality has been greatly enhanced in OLE 2.0.

OLE 2.0 has extended functionality because it does not use DDE as a base for communication. It has been implemented using *lightweight remote procedure calls* (LRPC), which are similar to RPCs in the UNIX environment. Remote procedure calls enable applications to pass information to one another (not just messages). The lightweight adjective indicates that unlike UNIX RPCs, the OLE calls are limited to passing information within the same machine. The *Component Object Model* (COM) defines how OLE 2.0 applications interact. COM specifies the necessary interfaces for an object and how and when an object can be created and destroyed. COM defines the sharing of information using a defined set of interfaces referred to as *Uniform Data Transfer* (UDT). UDT enables the exchange of data by having the client application grab a pointer to the OLE interface of the server application and then execute the functions incorporated into the server's OLE interface.

OLE maintains a method for storing objects known as *structured storage*. Structured storage can be thought of in terms of the DOS file structure concept of files and directories. These files, called streams, and directories, called storages, can be moved and copied just like their DOS counterparts. Using OLE streams and storages allows you to construct a *compound document*. A compound document is simply a collection of objects (for example, a Word document and an Excel graph) within one container application.

Integral to understanding OLE (as well as DDE) is the fact that one application (probably your PowerBuilder application) is a client that shares data and functionality with a server application. The client application is more commonly known as the container application.

The most common question about OLE concerns the difference between an object being embedded and an object being linked. An *embedded object* is stored in your application. The OLE data object maintains the original OLE server application's full functionality, but the document physically resides in the container application. Embedding is useful for data that should not change (such as a letter template); although your users can edit the data in the embedded object, their changes cannot be saved because the object is physically part of your EXE (or PBD/DLL). If your users want to be able to change the embedded document, you must re-create the application. Note that users will still have the capability to make changes and save them with a new filename. This is only important if you want your users to see changes to the data made by other users.

If you need the capability to update the data of an OLE object and have the document retain the changes, you must link the document. When you link an object, the object physically resides outside your application. Your application maintains a reference to the data, but it does not contain the actual data itself. PowerBuilder provides a visual presentation of the OLE object for display purposes only. The advantage of this is that if any application changes the data of the OLE object, the changes are reflected in all documents maintaining a link to the document.

OLE 2.0 enables the user to activate the control and edit the OLE object using the built-in functionality of the server application, which DDE and OLE 1.0 don't allow. For example, a PowerBuilder application has a window with an OLE 2.0 control that contains an Excel spreadsheet. When the control is activated, the application has the full functionality of Excel (menus and all) without having to leave the application. (Excel is not opened as a separate window either!) This capability is referred to as *in-place activation*. You also have the capability to open the server application (as in OLE 1.0) and edit the document directly in the server application (which is called *offsite activation*). OLE standards state that linked objects are to be activated offsite and embedded objects are handled in-place.

You can also programmatically create an OLE object, manipulate it, and use the server application's capabilities without the visual component. This capability to use the server's commands to modify an object is referred to as *OLE automation*.

OLE in the DataWindow Painter

OLE version 2.0 is now supported in the DataWindow painter in Version 5.0 as a database column or as an OLE object. As a database column, you can add an OLE column to a DataWindow in order to store and retrieve *binary large object* (blob) data in your database. Blob data could include a spreadsheet from Microsoft Excel or a document from Word for Windows. The OLE object is similar to the OLE 2.0 container used in the Window painter and can be used to manipulate data in an OLE server application. The following sections discuss creating a blob column and using OLE objects.

Blob Columns

To create an OLE column in the DataWindow painter, the first thing you must have is a table in your database that has a blob data type. The data type name will vary from one DBMS to another. In Watcom, a blob is the long binary data type, and in SQL Server, the Image data type is used. A very common table structure for OLE objects is a numeric primary-key column (`id`), the blob column containing the OLE object (`object`), and a text description of the blob column. The table with the OLE object must contain at least one additional field other than the OLE object to uniquely identify a row in the table. In addition, the blob column should accept `NULL` values.

After the table has been created, specify SQL or Quick Selects and select a presentation style for your new DataWindow object. In your Selection List, specify the key columns for the table, but do not select the blob column as part of the data source (PowerBuilder will not let you anyway). The blob column will be added later in an additional step. The DataWindow object is displayed in design mode showing just the primary-key columns.

To add the blob column to your DataWindow object, click on the OLE Database Blob menu item in the Objects menu. Click on the DataWindow in the location where you want to place the blob object. This opens the Database Blob Object property sheet (see Figure 36.3).

The property sheet is opened with the Definition tab (Figure 36.3) displaying so that you can enter the column information. The Client Class (optional) defaults to the value of DataWindow and is used by some OLE server applications to create the title that is displayed at the top of the server's window. The Client Name single-line edit (also optional) defaults to Untitled and also is used by some OLE servers to create the title that is displayed at the top of the server application's window.

The Table list box contains a list of all tables that are contained in the current database. You scroll through the list box to locate the table containing the blob column and click on the table name. The Large Binary/Text Columns list box displays all of the columns for the selected table and is used to indicate the blob column (object). The Key Clause single-line edit is used to build the `WHERE` clause for the `SELECT` statement and for when the DataWindow is updated to the database. PowerBuilder defaults a key clause of `id = :id`, which will connect the primary key (`id`) specified in this dialog to the `id` field already placed on the DataWindow object.

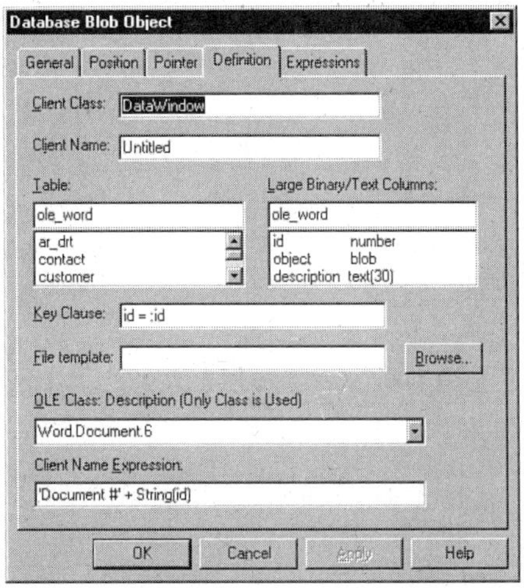

FIGURE 36.3.
The Database Blob Object property sheet.

The next two single-line edits, File Template and OLE Class Description, are used to specify the OLE server application that will generate the files for storage in the blob column. If you always want to open the same file in the OLE server, type the name into the File Template box. (Make sure that the file is in the current DOS path; if it is not, fully qualify the filename.) If you do not know the exact location or filename, click the Browse button to open the Select a File Name dialog box. Locate the file and click Open to place the filename and path in the File Template single-line edit.

If you want to open a different file each time, leave the File Template box empty and specify an OLE Class Description. Click on the drop-down list box to see the list of valid server applications that are a part of the Registration database. If your application does not appear, you must run the Registration Information Editor, as discussed earlier in this chapter, and merge the server application's registration file.

The last item to specify in this dialog box is an expression that will display in the OLE server application's title and can be used to specify the current row you are on in the DataWindow. The Client Name Expression must evaluate to a string. It's a good idea to create a unique name for each column (such as `'Excel Worksheet ' + String(id)`).

Just like most objects in the DataWindow painter, you can set values for the object's attributes using the Expression tab, change the pointer on the Pointer tab, specify the object's position on the Position tab, and name, tag value, and some formatting options on the General tab. On the General tab, the Name single-line edit is optional for naming your OLE object. A name is required if you are going to refer to the object in any of your scripts.

After specifying all the necessary information, click OK to display the DataWindow design with the new blob column. The column is displayed as a box with the label Blob on it. The blob column is often invisible to the user until the server application has been started. To accommodate this, a DataWindow drawing object (square or oval) can be placed behind the blob column so that the user knows where to double-click in order to activate the server application (see Figure 36.4).

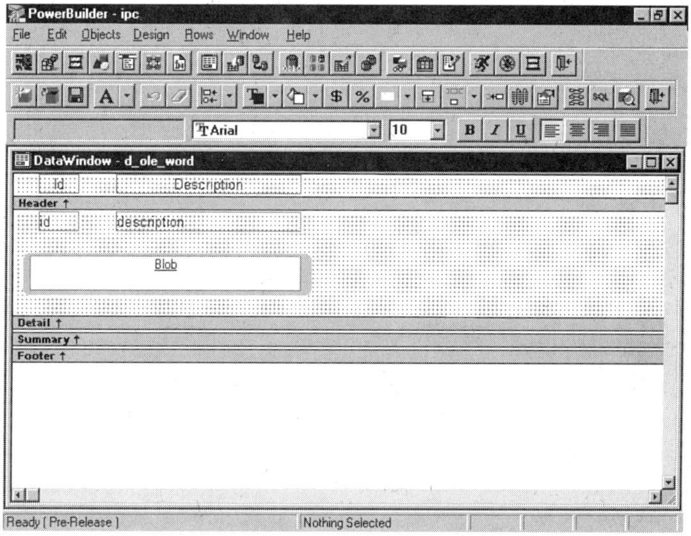

FIGURE 36.4.
The blob column with a drawing object behind it.

Click the Preview icon on the DataWindow PainterBar to view how the OLE column works in PowerBuilder. Insert a new row and enter a value for the key column (see Figure 36.5). The OLE column data is still edited using offsite activation. Therefore, when you double-click on the blob column (where the drawing object is) to activate the OLE server application, the server application is opened as a separate window. This window displays either the file you specified in the File Template box or an empty workspace if you chose an OLE Class Description (see Figure 36.6).

Make any changes that you want in the OLE server application. When you are done, the File menu contains a new menu item that is used to update the data in the server and in the client applications. Most of the time, the menu item text is Update. After you select Update, the new information is sent back to the DataWindow. Close the server file (or close the server) and you will be returned to the DataWindow painter. Notice that the blob column now displays the information you typed into the server application (if there is a significant amount of information, the data will be unreadable), as shown in Figure 36.7.

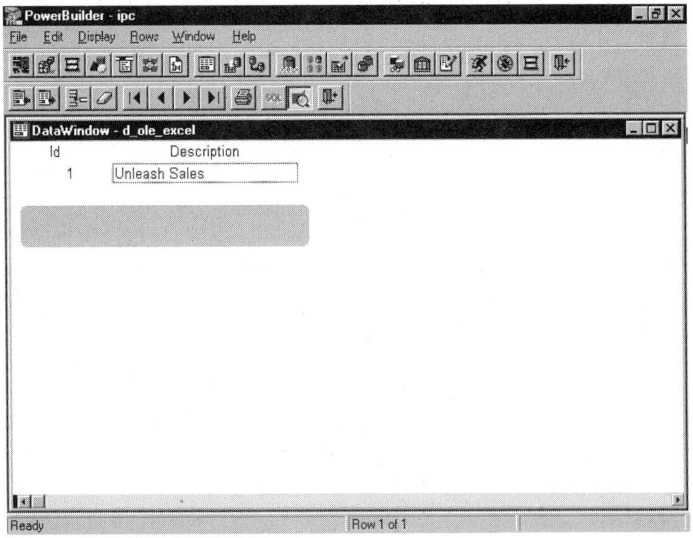

FIGURE 36.5.
A DataWindow object preview with OLE column.

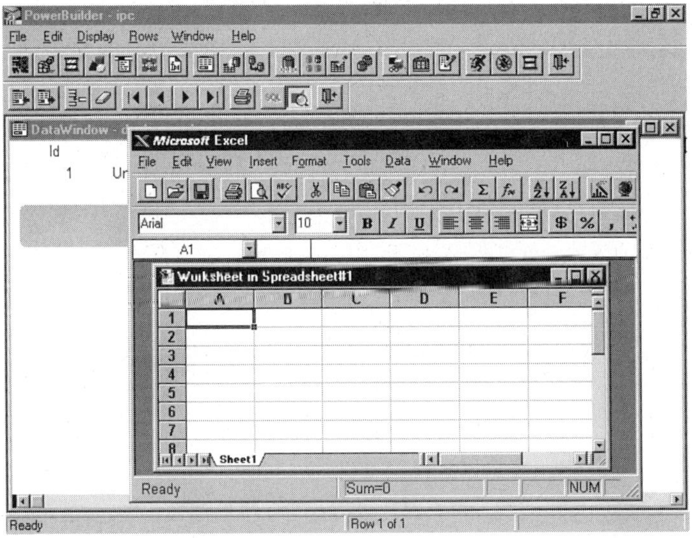

FIGURE 36.6.
An OLE object in the server application.

You can now save your changes back to the database. The blob column will be retrieved any subsequent time you use Preview, or at runtime when the DataWindow object is associated with a DataWindow control and the `Retrieve()` function is specified. At runtime, after the data is retrieved from the database, the user can interact with the data by double-clicking just as in preview mode.

FIGURE 36.7.
An OLE column with updated data.

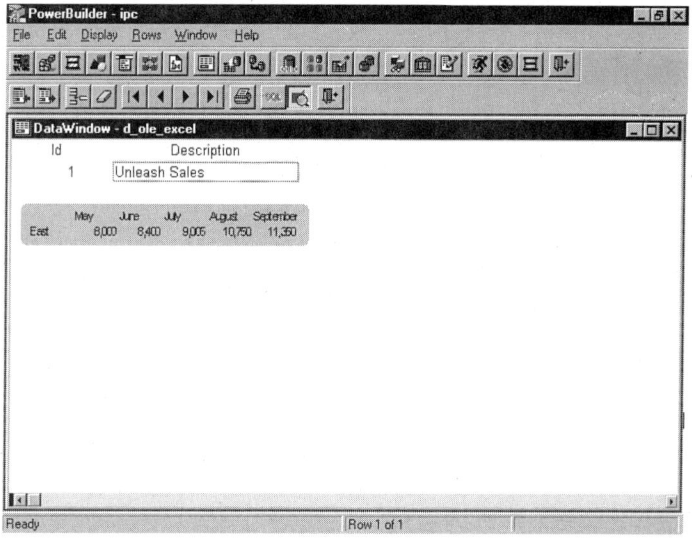

If you prefer to provide your user with a different means of opening the OLE server application instead of double-clicking, you can use the `OLEActivate()` function. This function is a method of a DataWindow control and takes three arguments. The first argument is a Long that identifies the row in the DataWindow of the desired OLE column. The second argument is the OLE column itself—either the column number (an integer) or, preferably, the column name (a string). The last argument is the action to pass to the OLE server application (commonly referred to as a *verb* in Windows). Most of the time, your user will want to edit the document in the server, which is typically a verb value of `0`. To find out the verbs supported by a specific OLE server application, you must run the Registration Information Editor and look at the verbs defined under `HKEY_LOCAL_MACHINE\SOFTWARE\Classes\`*`ClassName`*`\Protocol\StdFileEditing\Verb`, where *`ClassName`* is the object class of the server application (for example, `Excel.Sheet.5`). The following is an example:

```
dw_budget.OLEActivate( dw_budget.GetRow(), "object",  0)
```

This code can be placed in the script you want to use to activate the OLE object (for example, a command button `Clicked` event or the `Clicked` event of the DataWindow control).

In addition to placing a database blob column on your DataWindow, you now have the ability to create an OLE presentation style.

OLE DataWindow Presentation Style

New in PowerBuilder 5.0 is the OLE 2.0 DataWindow presentation, which allows you to combine data retrieved via SQL with an OLE server. After you have specified the data source for the DataWindow, the Insert Object property sheet appears (see Figure 36.8). It asks you to

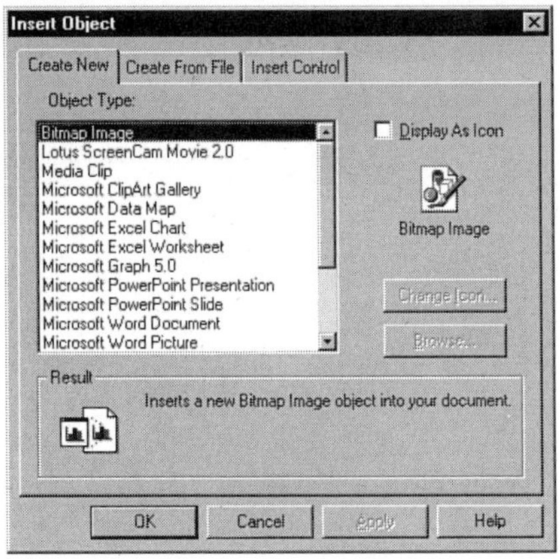

FIGURE 36.8.
The Insert Object property sheet.

specify what type of OLE object you want to create.

At this point, you have several options. You can choose a specific server application, a specific object or file, an OCX control, or nothing for the control. To create an empty OLE control, click the Cancel button.

To create an OLE object with a new object in a server application, select the Create New tab page (Figure 36.8). In the Object Type list box, a list of OLE server applications that have been registered with the Windows operating system appears. Choose a server application from the list box, indicate whether you want it displayed as the server application's icon, and click OK. PowerBuilder will activate the server application, enabling you to edit the new OLE object. By default, a new object is specified as embedded.

To create an OLE object from an existing file, click on the Create from File tab page (see Figure 36.9).

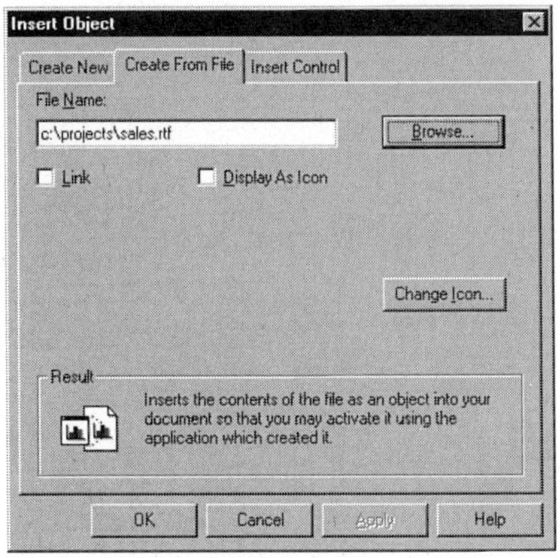

FIGURE 36.9.
The Create from File tab page.

The DataWindow now becomes tied to a specific file. You can type the name into the File single-line edit; or, if you do not know the path or filename, click on the Browse button. If you want the OLE object to be linked instead of embedded, click the Link check box. You can also specify if the object should be displayed as an icon. The default icon is the server application's icon, but you can specify another by using the Browse Icon button and choosing a new icon. You can also specify an OCX control, but these typically do not form the basis for a presentation style.

After you have specified the OLE server, PowerBuilder activates the server application in place in the DataWindow painter, allowing you to make any modifications you may require. Once you are done, click on the DataWindow outside of the hash-mark outline around the OLE object to return to the DataWindow design mode. Once you have clicked outside the OLE object, the OLE Object property sheet opens (see Figure 36.10).

FIGURE 36.10.
The OLE Object property sheet.

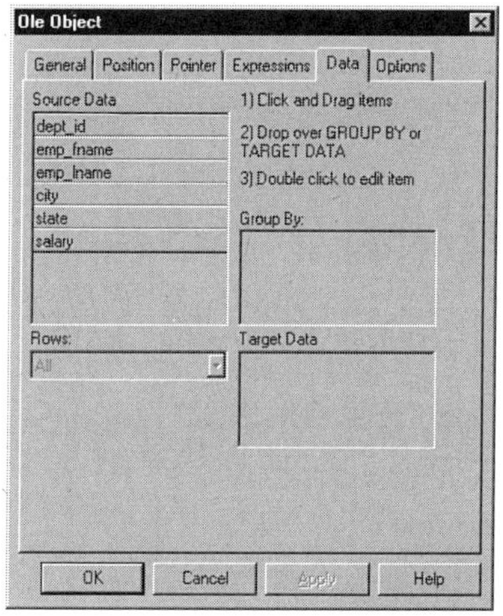

While the majority of the property sheet tab pages are consistent with most of the object property sheets in the DataWindow, the Data tab page is unique and asks you to specify the Target Data and Group By information. If you want data to be grouped, click the desired columns and drag them to the Group By list box. With one or more columns specified in the Group By list box, any columns dragged to the Target data are incorporated into a computed column (string columns are counted and numerics are summed). If there is no grouping to be performed, drag the desired columns to the Target data; the desired columns then appear as the column values (no computations).

If you decide that you want to change the OLE server associated with the DataWindow, right-click on the DataWindow to bring up the pop-up menu. The menu lists the options you have to manipulate the OLE connection. If a server application has not been specified, the Insert menu item is the only one available. Clicking Insert opens the Insert Object property sheet. To activate the object from the Window painter, select Open, which starts the server application and activates the OLE object offsite. Delete removes the connection to a server application. Paste Special allows you to paste the current information from the Clipboard into your OLE control.

You are now able to preview the DataWindow, which retrieves the data specified but does not automatically activate the OLE server. To view the data in the OLE server, double-click the DataWindow to activate the server in-place. The DataWindow can then be implemented and accessed just like any other DataWindow object.

If you want to integrate an existing DataWindow with an OLE server, you can do so using the new OLE object. To place an OLE object on your DataWindow, click the OLE icon from the control drop-down toolbar. This will open the Insert Object property sheet (refer to Figure 36.8). The process continues for data specification just as it did with the OLE presentation. The main difference is that the OLE control does not consume the whole DataWindow presentation.

If you want to access an OLE server without accessing a database, you can do so using the OLE 2.0 control.

The OLE 2.0 Container

OLE 2.0 is available in the Window and User Object painters as a container control. This chapter discusses a window OLE control that can be manipulated the same way as an OLE user object.

To place an OLE control on a window, click on the PainterBar icon that says OLE. PowerBuilder places an empty container (a rectangle) on the window and opens the Insert Object property sheet (refer to Figure 36.8).

Just as with the DataWindow presentation style, you can choose a specific server application, a specific object or file, an OCX control, or nothing for the control. To learn how to use the Insert Object property sheet, refer to the section "OLE DataWindow Presentation Style."

When you have made the association between the OLE control and the OLE server, you can specify the rest of the attributes of the OLE control. Double-clicking on the OLE control or selecting Properties from the pop-up menu or PainterBar causes the OLE property sheet to open (see Figure 36.11).

The OLE control has several standard attributes on the General tab page such as `Name`, `Visible`, `Enabled`, `FocusRectangle`, `Border`, `Color`, and `Resizable`. In addition to these common control attributes, there are several other attributes specific to the OLE 2.0 control.

The Contents drop-down list box enables you to specify whether the control is Linked, Embedded, or Any (the default). If you choose Any, the object can be either linked or embedded. The Display Type drop-down list box specifies what is displayed in the OLE 2.0 control—the contents or the icon. If you want to display a physical representation of the OLE object, choose the Contents option.

FIGURE 36.11.
The OLE 2.0 Control property sheet.

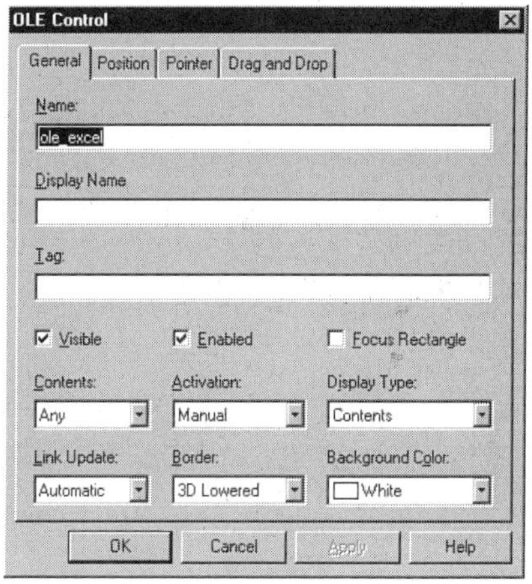

NOTE

The size of the OLE object is usually reduced so that it fits into the size of the OLE 2.0 control and, therefore, can be unreadable. If you use Word for Windows as your OLE server, it increases the control to the size of the document page.

The other Display Type option is Icon. The icon associated with the data contained in the OLE 2.0 control is displayed on the window. The icon is typically the icon used to represent the server application.

The Link Update drop-down list box is used to specify how an object is updated if the server object is specified as linked. If the link is broken and PowerBuilder is unable to find the file that was linked, the Automatic option will open a dialog box enabling the user to specify the file. When you're using the Manual option, if the link is broken, you cannot activate the OLE object. To reestablish the link to the file, you must code some script using the `LinkTo()` function.

The Activation drop-down list box determines how the OLE control is activated. The first two options correspond to the OLE 2.0 control events `DoubleClick` and `GetFocus`. Whenever the user double-clicks on the OLE control, or if the user clicks on or tabs to the control, the respective event triggers and activates the OLE object. The third option, Manual, requires that the control be activated using the `Activate()` function via a script.

NOTE

Even if one of the events is used for activation, the `Activate()` function can still be used.

If you decide that you want to change the object associated with the OLE 2.0 control, right-click on the OLE 2.0 control to bring up the pop-up menu. The Object cascading menu lists the options you have to manipulate the OLE connection. If a server application has not been specified, the Insert menu item is the only one available. Clicking Insert opens the Insert Object property sheet. To activate the object from the Window painter, select Open, which starts the server application and activates the OLE object offsite. Delete removes the connection to a server application. Paste Special allows you to paste the current information from the Clipboard into your OLE control.

Using the OLE 2.0 Control

When you have decided how you want the OLE object to be set up (Linked, Embedded, Any, or no object specified yet) in the Window painter, you need to think about a few other considerations:

- How will the object be activated—in place or offsite?
- How will the menus behave if the object is activated in place?
- How will the user activate the OLE object?

All these questions revolve around how the user will interact with the OLE 2.0 control.

In-Place Versus Off-Site Activation

Do you want your users to be able to invoke the server application's full functionality without leaving the current window (in-place activation)? Or do you want the users to open the server application and edit the data in the native server environment before returning to your application (offsite activation)? As mentioned previously, a linked object must be activated offsite.

With in-place activation, the control is activated by the value specified for the OLE 2.0 control's Activation attribute (in the control style dialog box). When the control is activated in place, the control has a wide, hatched border. The menus also can be changed, as you will see later in this chapter.

NOTE

Be aware that OLE 1.0 servers can be attached to OLE 2.0 controls, but they do not have the capability to have in-place activation.

Offsite activation will open the server and enable the user to edit the object in the server application window. The menus will be the standard server application's menus, with some additional menu items such as Update. The OLE control will also appear with a shaded border to indicate that the object is open.

How Is the Control Activated?

The default method for activating an OLE object, whether activated in-place or offsite, is to double-click on the control. This can be changed to the `GetFocus` event or to Manual at design time (in the Control Style dialog box). If the Manual option is chosen, you can specify when the OLE object is activated programmatically by using the `Activate()` function. This function takes one argument of data type `ActivationType`. The enumerated values are `InPlace!` and `OffSite!`. `Activate()` returns the integer values shown in Table 36.2.

Table 36.2. Return values for the `Activate()` function.

Value	*Meaning*
`-1`	Control is empty
`-2`	Invalid verb for object
`-3`	Verb not implemented by object
`-4`	No verbs supported by object
`-5`	Object cannot execute verb
`-9`	Other error

`Activate()` can be coded anywhere, but some common places are in the `Clicked` event of the OLE 2.0 control, the `Clicked` event of a command button, and the `Clicked` event of a menu item.

As you can see, the `Activate()` function will fail and return `-1` if there is no object specified for the control. You must assign an object before it can be activated. To do this programmatically, take a look at the `InsertObject()` function, discussed in the "OLE Automation" section later in this chapter. `Activate()` will also fail if you have a linked object and the corresponding linked file is not found (for instance, if the network crashed and the drive is no longer available). Depending on how the `Link Update` attribute is set (either Automatic or Manual), PowerBuilder will either prompt you with a dialog box (Automatic) or you will be forced to catch the error with PowerScript (Manual).

Menus and In-Place Activation

If you decide that you want to give your users the capability to activate the OLE object in place, you also need to consider how the server's menus will interact or merge with your application's existing menus. To specify how the two menus will merge, you need to become familiar with the Menu Merge Option drop-down list box in the Menu painter (see Figure 36.12).

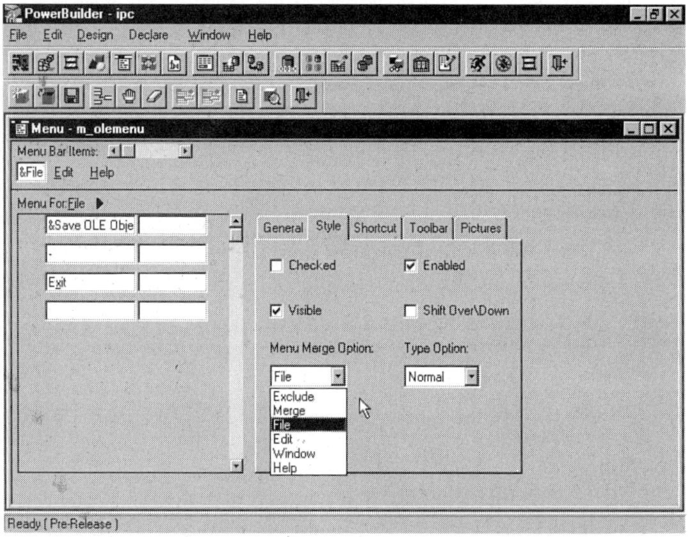

FIGURE 36.12.

The Menu Merge menu attribute in the Menu painter.

The Menu Merge drop-down list box is only activated when you are positioned on a menu title (such as File, Edit, or Help). You cannot combine individual menu titles from the different applications, but you can specify which menu displays. Menu settings and their uses are shown in Table 36.3.

Table 36.3. Menu Merge activation options in the Menu painter and their meanings.

Menu Setting	*How It Is Used*
Exclude	The menu will not be displayed when the OLE object is activated.
Merge	The menu from the container to be displayed after the first menu of the OLE server application.
File	The menu from the container application that will be placed first (farthest to the left) on the menu bar. (The File menu from the OLE server will not display.)
Edit	The menu from the container specified as Edit will not display. The Edit menu from the OLE server application will display.
Window	The menu from the container displaying the list of open sheets will be displayed. The OLE server's Window menu will not display.
Help	The menu from the container specified as Help will not display. The Help menu from the OLE server application will display.

Any menus specified as Merge will be included. The menu bar will also include additional menus that the server application has deemed appropriate. Figure 36.13 shows the PowerBuilder application's menus. Figure 36.14 shows Word's menus. Both sets of menus are in their natural states. In Figure 36.15, you see the result of the menu merge when the OLE 2.0 control was activated in place.

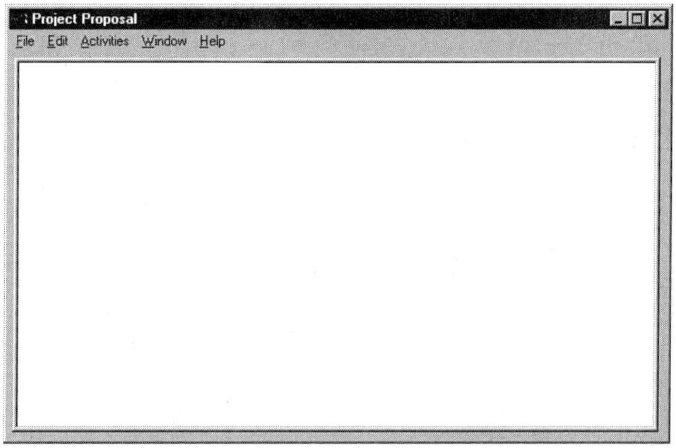

FIGURE 36.13.
A PowerBuilder application's menus.

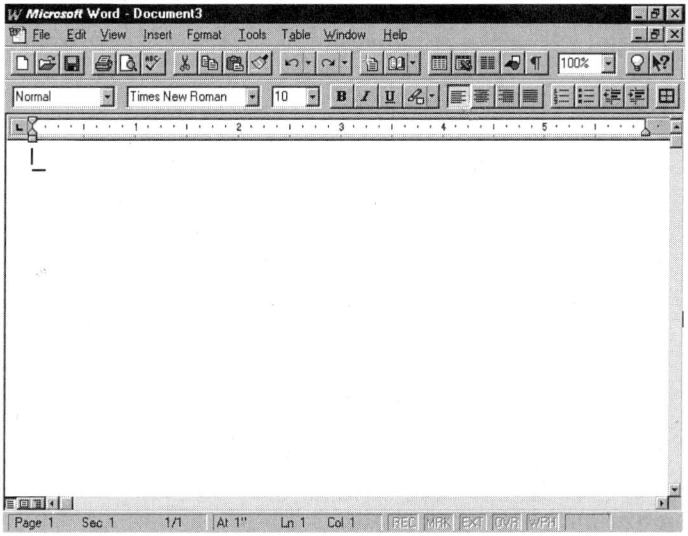

FIGURE 36.14.
An OLE server's menus (Word).

The aforementioned properties of an OLE object enable you to use the OLE server application without having to generate much code (with the exception of `Activate()`). Part of the beauty of OLE 2.0 is its capability to access the server application in your code.

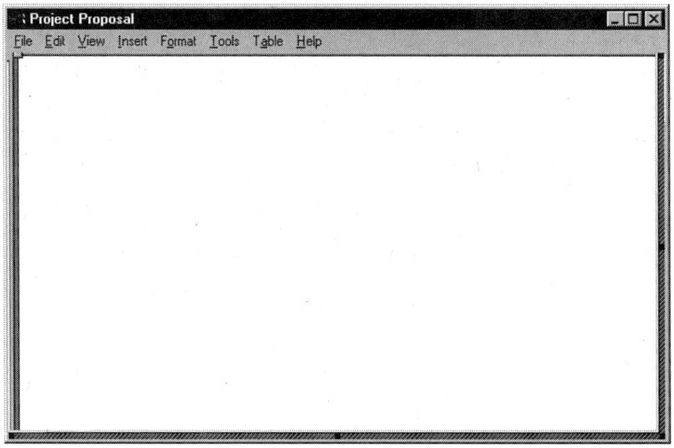

FIGURE 36.15.
A PowerBuilder application's menus with in-place activation.

OLE 2.0 Control Events

Table 36.4 shows several events specific to the OLE 2.0 control.

Table 36.4. Unique OLE 2.0 control events.

Event	*Occurs When*
`DataChange`	Data has been changed in the server application.
`Error`	Dot notation specified to access properties or data is invalid at runtime.
`ExternalException`	Dot notation specified to access properties or data is invalid at runtime. Occurs before the `Error` event.
`PropertyChanged`	A property of the object has been changed by the server (server specific).
`PropertyRequestEdit`	A property of the object is about to be changed and the server sends a notification (server specific).
`Rename`	The object has been renamed in the server application.
`Save`	The data has been saved from the server application.
`ViewChange`	The view shown to the user has been changed.

These events all notify PowerBuilder when some action has occurred or is going to occur in the server application that affects the OLE object. The changes that trigger these events are automatically reflected in the OLE 2.0 control. They are made available in case you need to perform additional processing in response to a server action.

If an error occurs in an OLE server call, the OLE control executes several levels of error handling. The first event triggered is `ExternalException`. The server application provides information about the error code and even passes the help topic context ID that documents the error. The event parameter, `Action`, is used to indicate how the OLE control responds to the error. `Action` is of the enumerated data type `ExceptionAction` and has the values listed in Table 36.5.

Table 36.5. Values of `ExceptionAction`.

Value	*Description*
`ExceptionFail!`	Error is not fixed and processing continues to the `Error` event.
`ExceptionIgnore!`	Ignore the error and continue processing.
`ExceptionRetry!`	Execute the last command again to ensure server readiness.
`ExceptionSubstituteReturnValue!`	Use the `ReturnValue` argument of the event instead of the value passed by the OLE server and stop the error processing.

NEW 5 in PowerBuilder

If the `ExternalException` script sets the `Action` argument to `ExceptionFail!` or there is no script written for the event, the `Error` event occurs. The `Error` event works in a similar fashion to `ExternalException`, but with not as much detail. The `Error` event also gives you the ability to set a default return value in response to an error. If the `Error` event is triggered and does not have script or sets the `Action` argument to `ExceptionFail!`, the `SystemError` event is triggered as your last line of defense before the application terminates.

These events are triggered not only for the OLE control, but also for the `OLEObject` standard class user object. To use either the `OLEObject` or OLE control in your application, most often, you will need to write some script. This scripting capability is referred to as *OLE automation.*

OLE Automation

OLE automation gives you the capability to use the OLE server application's command set within the context of your application. You can use this with an object in an OLE 2.0 control or by defining an `OLEObject` variable in your script without actually displaying the OLE object to the user.

Manipulating the OLE Control

You have seen that activation of the OLE object can be done by double-clicking, by the control receiving focus, or by manually coding the `Activate()` function. In addition, the `DoVerb()`

function can be used to initiate OLE actions. A *verb* is defined as an integer value used to specify the action that is to be performed, as defined by the server application. The default action for most servers is `0`, which means edit and also activates the OLE object:

```
ole_1.DoVerb(0)
```

You can find more information about a server's verbs in each server application's documentation and in the Windows registry.

If you create an OLE 2.0 control and don't assign an object to the control at design time, you must assign the object at runtime. You can use several different functions to do this. The first function is `*olecontrol*.InsertObject()`, which opens the Insert Object dialog box and enables the user to specify a new or an existing OLE object to be inserted into the OLE control. If the `Contents` attribute of the OLE 2.0 control is set to `Any`, the user can also specify whether the object is embedded or linked. The return codes are `0` if successful, `-1` if the user clicked Cancel, and `-9` for all other errors.

If you have a specific file that you want to embed into an existing OLE control, use the function `*olecontrol*.InsertFile()`. The argument for the function is a string containing the name and location of the file to be embedded in the OLE control. `0` means success, `-1` means that the file was not found, and `-9` is for all other errors.

A more specific case of `InsertFile()` is `LinkTo()`. This function also specifies a particular filename, but it enables you to link to a specific item within the file (such as a range of cells in an Excel spreadsheet). If an item name is not specified, the link is established with the whole file. The return codes are `0` for success, `-1` if the file was not found, `-2` if the item was not found, and `-9` for all other errors.

A function that is similar to `InsertFile()` is `*olecontrol*.InsertClass()`, which embeds a new object of the chosen OLE server into the OLE control. If you do not know the names of the registered OLE server applications installed, open the Object Browser from within the PowerScript painter and select the OLE tab page to list all OLE server applications (see Figure 36.16).

The OLE tab page is broken down into three headings: Insertable Objects, OLE Custom Controls, and Programmable Objects. You can expand each heading by double-clicking on it. The insertable objects are the different application servers that you can connect to. Some objects can be expanded to display the methods and properties that are available for you to access via your script. If you select one of the insertable objects listed and click the Paste button, the object's class is pasted into your script. The object class can then be used for the `InsertClass()` function. Common examples of the insertable objects are `Word.Document.6` and `Excel.Sheet.5` for WinWord and Excel, respectively. The `InsertClass()` function also returns `0` and `-9`, just like `InsertFile()`, and `-1` when an invalid class name is specified.

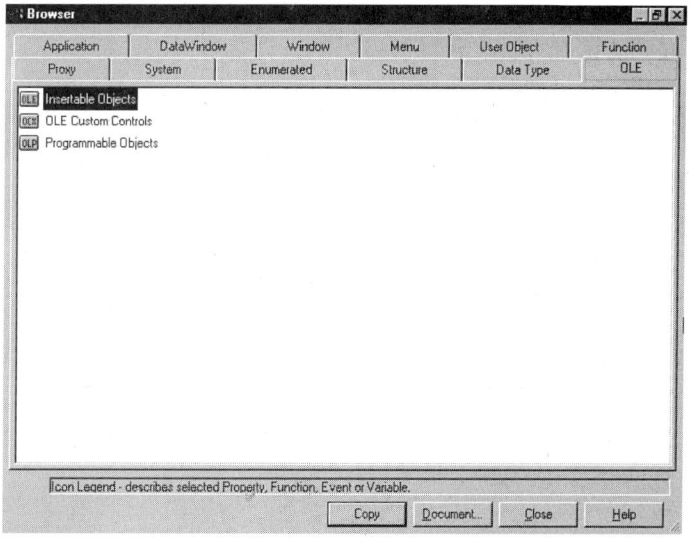

FIGURE 36.16.
The Object Browser OLE tab page.

You can also specify an OLE object stored as a blob variable to be assigned to the OLE control by referencing the `ObjectData` attribute, as follows:

```
Blob sales_blob

ole_1.ObjectData = sales_blob
```

Data can be cut, copied, or pasted into the OLE control using the Windows Clipboard. The functions that are used to paste Clipboard data into an OLE object or control are `Paste()`, `PasteLink()`, and `PasteSpecial()`. The difference between the functions, respectively, is how the object is placed in the OLE control: Embedded, linked, or give the user the option to embed or link the data via a dialog box. Chapter 12, "Menus and the Menu Painter," outlines the code that is needed to implement standard Cut, Copy, and Paste menu items.

Whether you assign the OLE object at design time or at runtime, in most cases the user will want to edit the data. If the object is embedded, the user cannot save the changes back to the file because it is part of your EXE or PBD. If changes are to be saved, they must be saved to either a database or another file.

To save the OLE object to a database, reference the `ObjectData` attribute of the OLE control and store the value in a blob variable. To update the database, you must use a special SQL statement, `UPDATEBLOB`.

NOTE

PowerBuilder writes blobs in 32KB chunks. If the last update is not a full 32KB, PowerBuilder appends NULL values at the end. Be sure to remember when retrieving the data that the NULLs must be stripped off programmatically so that garbage is not displayed in the server application.

To save the OLE object as a file, use the GetFileSaveName() function as follows to open the Save common dialog box and the SaveAs() function:

```
string ls_filename, ls_pathname
integer li_rtn

li_rtn = GetFileSaveName( "File Select", ls_pathname, ls_filename, "OLE", &
"OLE Files (*.OLE),*.OLE")

If li_rtn <> -1 then
   li_rtn = ole_1.SaveAs( ls_filename)
End If
```

The users can specify the filenames they want the objects to have when saved. Note that an OLE file cannot be opened using the server application; it can only be opened by using the OLE control in PowerBuilder and activating the server application.

Everything discussed so far has dealt with manipulating the OLE control and its assignment with an OLE object. Now you will see how to manipulate the OLE object.

Manipulating the OLE Object

Using DDE, you needed to issue functions such as ExecRemote() and SetRemote() that specified tasks for the server to perform. With OLE 2.0, you can specify those task commands explicitly in your scripts. This is done by referencing the Object attribute of the OLE 2.0 control. The syntax is as follows:

```
oleObjectName.Object.Method ( Arguments)
oleObjectName.Object.Attribute = Value
```

An easy example is assigning a bookmark value in a Word for Windows document, as follows:

```
ole_1.Activate( InPlace!)
ole_1.InsertFile( "c:\msoffice\winword\unleash\cover.doc")
ole_1.Object.application.wordbasic.editgoto( "last_name")
ole_1.Object.application.wordbasic.insert ( "Herbert")
```

PowerBuilder does not do syntax checking on any of the statements after the OLE control's Object attribute. The obvious reason for this is that PowerBuilder does not know the valid syntax for the server application. It is a good idea to test the script in the server application before placing it in PowerBuilder.

What if you don't know the server's command language (such as VBA or WordBasic)? Two methods are common and are usually used together to generate the commands to use in a PowerBuilder application. The standard method is to buy a book that details the server application's native script or macro language. In addition to this reference, most server applications enable you to record actions as you perform them. Record your movements and edit the recorded script (which is usually referred to as a *macro*). Sometimes you can copy the script verbatim, but it might need some additional tweaking to get it to work in your application's script.

In Version 5.0 of PowerBuilder you have access to information about a server's methods, properties, and events via the Object Browser. As shown in Figure 36.16, the OLE tab page of the Object Browser displays all the registered OLE servers in Windows. Depending on the server, you can drill down via the OLE tree and view the accessible methods, properties, and events for that object and paste them into your script (see Figure 36.17).

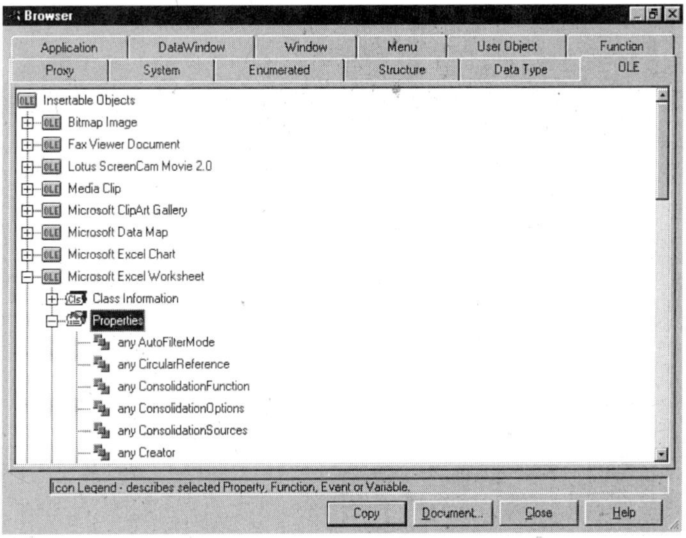

FIGURE 36.17.

Insertable object syntax in the Object Browser.

For Excel's `Delete` method, clicking the Paste button would place the following in your script:

```
OLEControl.Object.Delete()
```

With Word for Windows, the command language is WordBasic, which does not use a function format as does PowerBuilder. For example, the previous code example appeared in Word as follows:

```
EditBookmark .Name = "last_name", .SortBy = 0, .Goto
Insert "Herbert"
```

To use a WordBasic command in PowerBuilder, you must include the parentheses to indicate a function; otherwise, if you use the Word format, PowerBuilder assumes an attribute setting. (This is not an issue with applications that use VBA language.)

The same process is also true of any OCX (OLE custom control) that you might use in your application. If the OCX has been registered with Windows, it will appear in the OCX section of the Object Browser. You can then expand the tree view to see the class information as well as the different events, methods, and properties of the control (see Figure 36.18).

FIGURE 36.18.
OCXs in the Object Browser.

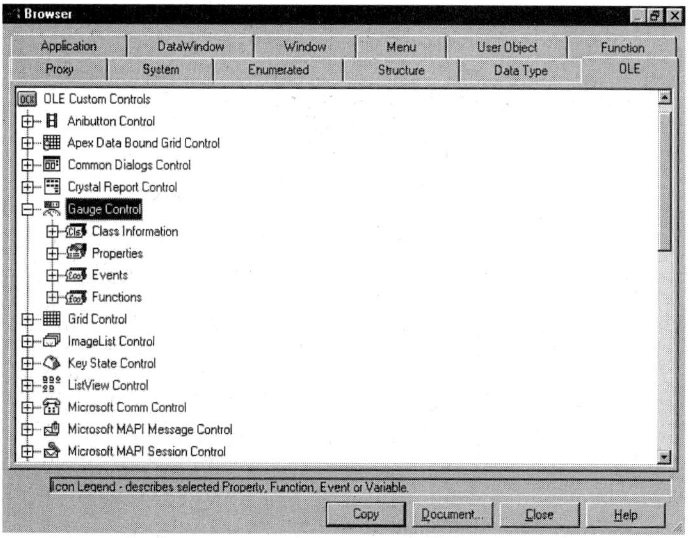

Once the desired value is located, clicking on the Paste button would place the following in your script:

```
OLECustomControl.object.Enabled
```

PowerBuilder works with OLE automation by executing one function at a time. This means that you cannot access the server's control statements (such as `If...Then` and `For...Next`). You must add this kind of logic into your PowerBuilder application.

TIP

You could execute a server macro from PowerBuilder with the control statements written in the server application. The only negative is that now you are maintaining code in multiple locations.

One thing to be careful of is how you qualify the server command—for instance, whether you use the name of the application. This depends on the server application and how the object is connected. The object hierarchy differs from one application to another and needs to be considered when writing your OLE commands. For example, in Excel, seemingly identical commands in PowerBuilder produce different results:

```
ole_1.Object.cells(5,5).value = dw_1.GetItemNumber(1, "unit_price")
```

This statement modifies the cell in an Excel spreadsheet located in the PowerBuilder OLE control. However, an error will occur if the document is not activated first:

```
ole_1.Object.cells(5,5).application.value = dw_1.GetItemNumber(1, "unit_price")
```

Although this statement appears to do exactly the same thing as the previous example, it does not. By referencing the application, the specified cell (row 5, column 5) will be changed in the active document regardless of whether the active document is the same one specified in your OLE control. Because you might be updating the wrong spreadsheet, the first method is preferred in Excel.

In contrast, Word for Windows approaches the object hierarchy differently. As seen in the Word example earlier, you must qualify your command statements with `application.wordbasic`. This also assumes that the OLE object has been activated.

OLEObject

What if you just want to use the functionality of a particular application and never let the user see the server application? The answer is to create an OLE object in your script that is independent of an OLE 2.0 control. You can create an OLE object with the data type `OLEObject` and connect your application to the server; then you have exactly the same capabilities to call functions and set attributes in the server application. You can also create a standard class user object with standardized processing. For some OLE server applications, you can even specify whether the user can see that the server application is open.

The following lines declare and instantiate an OLE object:

```
OLEObject ole_letter

ole_letter = CREATE OLEObject
```

This allocates memory for the OLE object, which is actually quite small because UDT ensures that the variable contains only a reference to the actual object. The object itself is stored with the server application. Note that depending on the kind of processing you will be doing in your application, you might declare the OLE object as an instance variable rather than a local.

After creating your OLE object, you need to establish a connection with a server application before doing any other processing. There are two functions to accomplish this: *`oleobject`*`.ConnectToNewObject()` and *`oleobject`*`.ConnectToObject()`.

`ConnectToNewObject()` is used like the `InsertClass()` function to create a brand new object for an OLE server. `ConnectToObject()` is used to connect to an OLE object using an existing file. With `ConnectToObject()`, you specify the filename and optionally the class name

(`ConnectToNewObject()` just needs the class name). If you do not specify a class name, PowerBuilder uses the filename's extension to determine which server application to start.

When the connection has been established, you can continue and use the server's commands to do your processing, as in this example that you saw earlier:

```
ole_letter.ConnectToNewObject( "word.basic")
ole_letter.EditGoto( "last_name")
ole_letter.Insert ( "Herbert")
```

Notice that you do not need to include the application qualifier for the commands (`application.wordbasic` no longer needs to be added). It was already specified when connecting to the server.

After all processing has been completed, you need to disconnect from the server application and release the memory that the OLE object is using (just like disconnecting from a database), as follows:

```
ole_letter.DisconnectOjbect()
DESTROY ole_letter
```

NOTE

Make sure to disconnect before your `OLEObject` variable goes out of scope; otherwise, there is no means to programmatically close the server application. If the server is visible, the user can close the server, but that would be sloppy programming.

The Any Data Type

Because PowerBuilder does not know the syntax of the server's command language, it also makes sense that it knows nothing of the data types that are returned from any of the commands executed. To handle this situation, PowerBuilder has a generic data type called Any, which can handle assignments from the server regardless of the data type. At runtime, when the Any data type is assigned a value, it becomes a variable of the appropriate data type (such as string or integer). To determine the true data type of the `any` variable, use the function `ClassName()` as follows:

```
OLEObject ole_excel
string ls_string
integer li_int
any la_any

ole_excel = CREATE OLEObject
ole_excel.ConnectToObject( "budget.xls")

la_any = ole_excel.application.cells(10,5).value
```

```
Choose Case ClassName( la_any)
Case "string"
   ls_string = la_any
Case "int"
   ls_int = la_any
Case Else
   MessageBox( "Retrieve Error","Unknown data type returned")
   Return
End Choose
```

Although the Any data type definitely has its use with OLE applications, it is not recommended to use it on a regular basis because of its high overhead.

OLEStorage and OLEStream

As defined earlier, OLE storages and streams make up the underlying structures of OLE and are how OLE objects are stored. Recall that OLE storages equate to DOS directories and streams equate to the files within a storage. For the most part, you can work with OLE objects and never have to worry about managing OLE storages. If you do need to perform some complex OLE functionality such as combining multiple OLE objects into one structure, PowerBuilder gives you the ability to manipulate OLE data.

PowerBuilder supplies two standard class user objects, `OLEStorage` and `OLEStream`. These objects are treated like any other nonvisual user objects in that they must be declared, instantiated, and destroyed. In addition, you will need to open and close the storages using the `Open()` and `Save()` or `SaveAs()` methods. Since streams are contained within a storage, you must remember to open the storage first.

In most cases, if you need to store OLE data, you will be able to by using a blob column from the database. If you are not using a database or your DBMS does not support blobs, you might consider using storages as an alternative.

OCXs

In Version 5.0, PowerBuilder supports the use of OCX technology via the OLE 2.0 control. OCXs are the OLE-based component now available with Visual Basic 4.0. After placing an OLE control on your window, user object, or DataWindow, you can select the Insert Control tab page on the Insert Object property sheet (see Figure 36.19).

This tab page displays all OCXs registered with Windows. If you have an OCX that does not appear, you can register via the Register New button, which opens a Browse dialog box allowing you to indicate the OCX file. You can also remove an OCX file via the Unregister button. Clicking on the Browse button opens the OLE Object Browser (see Figure 36.20).

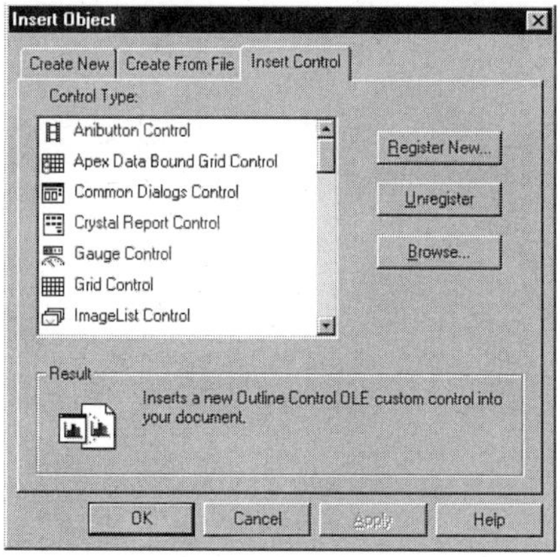

FIGURE 36.19.
The Insert Control tab page.

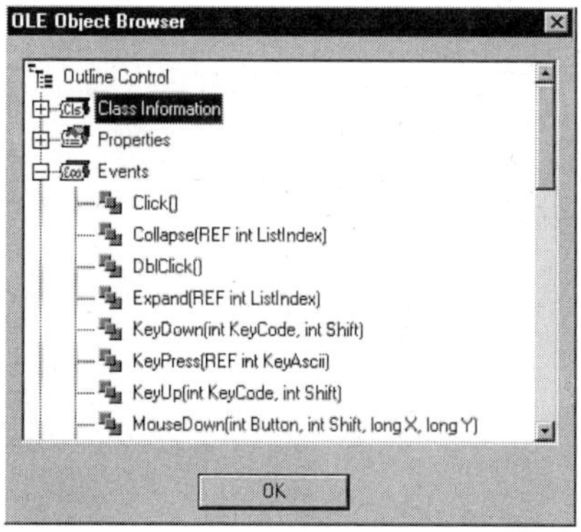

FIGURE 36.20.
The OLE Object Browser.

The browser allows you to view the methods, events, and properties for the selected OCX.

After specifying the desired OCX, click the OK button, which takes you back to the Window painter and allows you to place the OLE control.

Right-clicking on the control gives you the ability to set the standard control properties, but also gives you a menu option of setting the OCX properties. This menu item opens the property sheet for the specified OCX control (see Figure 36.21).

Here you can specify the desired settings for the control as detailed in the OCX's documentation. The OCX's events are then accessible from the Script painter in the Select Event drop-down list box.

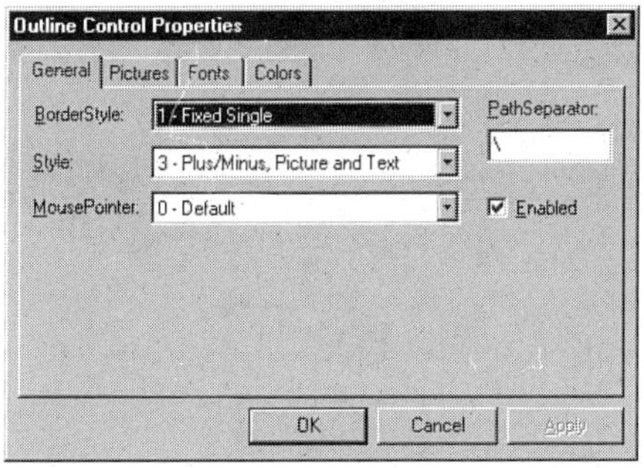

FIGURE 36.21.
The OCX property sheet (for the Outline OCX).

NOTE

Unlike VBXs in PowerBuilder, the OCX events are not discernible from the standard OLE control events. To determine which events are defined for the OCX, you can browse the OCX as discussed earlier or access the user event declarations. In the user event declarations, the OCX events are listed beneath the standard control events, have no event IDs associated with them, and are not grayed out.

To access an OCX's properties or methods, this is the syntax:

```
OLEControl.Object.PropertyOrMethodName
```

`OLEControl` is the name of the OLE 2.0 control and the `PropertyOrMethodName` is the desired property or method. You can find these in the OCX documentation or you can use the Object Browser. From the PowerScript painter, open the Object Browser and click the OLE tab page. Double-click the OCX entry to display a list of all the registered OCXs. Each OCX can be expanded to show its methods, events, and properties. Each of these can be expanded in turn and then pasted into your script (see Figure 36.22).

Select the desired category and click the Paste button to place the necessary syntax in your script, including placeholders for any arguments. The selected method above for the outline OCX (in Figure 36.22) would produce this:

```
OLECustomControl.object.Clear()
```

PowerBuilder has made OCX implementation a relatively seamless process by allowing OCXs to be accessed like any other control. PowerBuilder does include several of the lighter-weight OCX controls in its new Component Gallery, and additional controls can be purchased in the Component Pack.

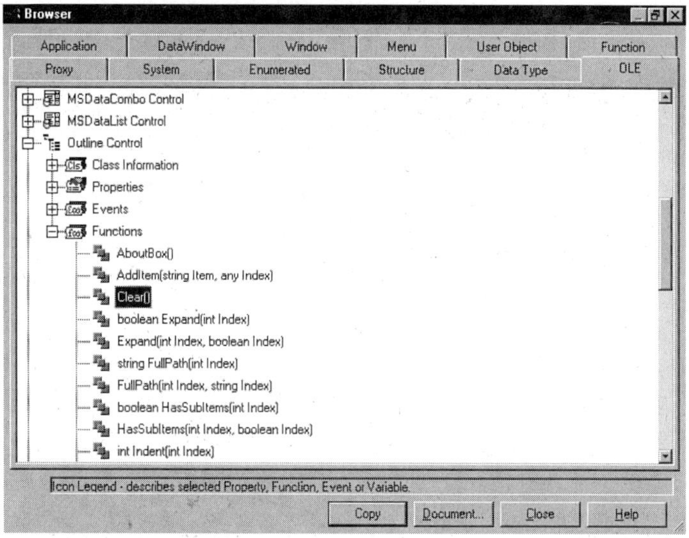

FIGURE 36.22.
The expanded OCX in the Object Browser.

PowerBuilder as an OLE Server

Many people wonder whether PowerBuilder can be a server application for another Windows application. In Version 5.0, PowerBuilder can now act as an OLE server via a nonvisual user object. In addition, the Powersoft product InfoMaker can be a server. InfoMaker generates Powersoft Reports (PSRs), which are embedded or linked to the OLE client application. These reports can be added to an application supporting OLE 2.0. When the OLE PSR is activated, InfoMaker is started and its full functionality can be used. On the other hand, unlike PowerBuilder, InfoMaker cannot be an OLE client and contain an OLE object in one of its reports. PSR files can also be generated from within PowerBuilder through the DataWindow painter or using the `SaveAs()` function.

The first step is to create the custom class user object with all attributes and functions you want to access via OLE automation defined as public. The user object needs to be compiled into a dynamic library (either machine code or p-code) from within PowerBuilder.

In order to implement the user object as an OLE server, it must be defined in the Windows Registry. This can be done one of two ways. The first method is to create a registry entry that helps OLE locate the user object. The entry takes the program identifier (the user object class name) and translates it into a global unique identifier. Once the global identifier has been created, additional entries are defined in the Registry to set the library list indicating the PowerBuilder dynamic library containing the user object and the executable type (machine code or p-code). Once this is done, each OLE client application can create an instance of the object in its application (in PowerBuilder, this is accomplished via `ConnectToNewObject()`).

The only problem with this approach is that translation information must be predefined in the registry. The second method does not require predefining the registry entries and allows you to generate the registry file via the OLE automation object `PowerBuilder.Application`. This object has three methods, `GenerateGUID()`, `GenerateRegFile()`, and `CreateObject()`, that you can use to create a global unique identifier (GUID) and then create the registry file to update the client machine's registry.

Before you can access any of the properties or methods, you have to create an instance of `PowerBuilder.Application`. This is done using the function `ConnectToObject()`. Here's the syntax:

```
OLEObject PBObject
long ll_rtn

PBObject = CREATE OLEObject

ll_rtn = PBObject.ConnectToObject("PowerBuilder.Application")
```

In addition to the three methods, there are two properties of `PowerBuilder.Application` that must be set after the OLE automation object has been instantiated. The `LibraryList` property is a string that contains a list of dynamic libraries that are searched to locate object classes when creating instances. The list must be set prior to the creation of the first object since it is fixed after the first object is instantiated. The second property is `MachineCode`, which is a Boolean value (the default is `TRUE`) that is used to indicate the library code type (machine code or p-code). Both properties are ignored once the first object is created.

`GenerateGUID()` is used to create the GUID and returns a string representing the identifier in a reference parameter. The return values are shown in Table 36.6.

Table 36.6. `GenerateGUID()` return values.

Value	*Description*
0	GUID successfully generated
-1	Could not load required DLL to generate GUID
-2	No network card found. GUID not generated.
-3	Create failed
-9	Unknown error

The string reference returned is passed to the `GenerateRegFile()` function to create the registration file. This is the syntax:

```
GenerateRegFile( GUID, ClassName, ProgId, MajorVersion, MinorVersion, &
   Description, TargetFile)
```

`GUID` is the string reference generated by `GenerateGUID()`. `ClassName` is a string containing the class name of the user object. `ProgId` is a string containing the OLE programmatic identifier (such as `Tax.Object`). `MajorVersion` and `MinorVersion` are used to indicate the major and minor releases of the OLE object. `Description` is a descriptive name displayed by OLE. `TargetFile` is a string specifying the name of the text registration file to create. `GenerateRegFile()` returns a Long with one of the values listed in Table 36.7.

Table 36.7. `GenerateRegFile()` return values.

Value	*Description*
0	Registry file created
-1	Memory allocation error
-2	No target file name specified
-3	Unable to open target file
-9	Unknown error

The whole process to create a registration file is shown in Listing 36.1.

Listing 36.1. Registration file generation.

```
OLEObject PBObject
String GUID
long ll_rtn

PBObject = CREATE OLEObject

ll_rtn = PBObject.ConnectToNewObject("PowerBuilder.Application")
If ll_rtn < 0 Then
   MessageBox("Connect Error","Could not connect to OLE Automation object")
   Return
Else
   //Set the library list
   PBObject.LibraryList = "c:\projects\tax\tax.dll"
   //Specify the library compilation type
   PBObject.MachineCode = True
   //Generate the GUID
   ll_rtn = PBObject.GenerateGUID( REF GUID)
   If ll_rtn < 0 Then
      MessageBox ("Generation Error","Could not generate GUID.")
      Return
   Else
      //Generate the registration file
      ll_rtn = PBObject.GenerateRegFile( GUID, "u_tax_calc", "Tax.Object", 1, 0, &
                                         "Tax calculations",
 "c:\projects\tax\tax.reg")
      If ll_rtn < 0 Then
         MessageBox( "Generation Error", "Could not generate registration file")
```

```
      End If
   End If
End If
```

Once the registration file is successfully created, you can merge it into the registration editor. This results in entries under the keys `HKEY_CLASSES_ROOT\CLSID` (see Figure 36.23).

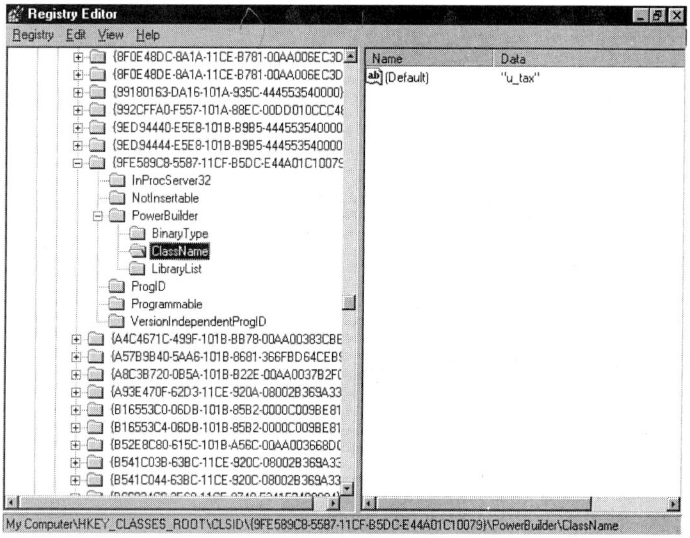

FIGURE 36.23.
The `HKEY_CLASSES_ROOT\CLSID` *Registry Editor entry.*

The registration file for the tax application generated the registration file shown in Listing 36.2.

Listing 36.2. The tax.reg file.

```
REGEDIT
;;;;;;;;;;;;;;;;
;
; Registry entries for tax.object
;
; CLSID = {9FE589C8-5587-11CF-B5DC-E44A01C10079}
;
;;;;;;;;;;;;;;;;

; Version independent entries:
HKEY_CLASSES_ROOT\tax.object = tax application
HKEY_CLASSES_ROOT\tax.object\CLSID = {9FE589C8-5587-11CF-B5DC-E44A01C10079}
HKEY_CLASSES_ROOT\tax.object\CurVer = tax.object.1
HKEY_CLASSES_ROOT\tax.object\NotInsertable

; Version specific entries:
HKEY_CLASSES_ROOT\tax.object.1 = tax application
```

continues

Listing 36.2. continued

```
HKEY_CLASSES_ROOT\tax.object.1\CLSID = {9FE589C8-5587-11CF-B5DC-E44A01C10079}
HKEY_CLASSES_ROOT\tax.object.1\NotInsertable

; CLSID entries:
HKEY_CLASSES_ROOT\CLSID\{9FE589C8-5587-11CF-B5DC-E44A01C10079} = tax application
HKEY_CLASSES_ROOT\CLSID\{9FE589C8-5587-11CF-B5DC-E44A01C10079}\ProgID =
tax.object.1
HKEY_CLASSES_ROOT\CLSID\{9FE589C8-5587-11CF-B5DC-
E44A01C10079}\VersionIndependentProgID = tax.object
HKEY_CLASSES_ROOT\CLSID\{9FE589C8-5587-11CF-B5DC-E44A01C10079}\InProcServer32 =
PBROI050.DLL
HKEY_CLASSES_ROOT\CLSID\{9FE589C8-5587-11CF-B5DC-E44A01C10079}\NotInsertable
HKEY_CLASSES_ROOT\CLSID\{9FE589C8-5587-11CF-B5DC-E44A01C10079}\Programmable
HKEY_CLASSES_ROOT\CLSID\{9FE589C8-5587-11CF-B5DC-
E44A01C10079}\PowerBuilder\ClassName = u_tax
HKEY_CLASSES_ROOT\CLSID\{9FE589C8-5587-11CF-B5DC-
E44A01C10079}\PowerBuilder\LibraryList =
HKEY_CLASSES_ROOT\CLSID\{9FE589C8-5587-11CF-B5DC-
E44A01C10079}\PowerBuilder\BinaryType = PCODE
```

Once this is done, you are ready to access the OLE object from your client automation application. For example, to call the tax object `u_tax_calc` from Visual Basic 4.0, you'd use this code:

```
Dim PBObject As Object
Dim Taxuo As Object
Dim GrossPay as Integer
Dim TaxRate as Integer

'Connect to the tax object
Set PBObject = CreateObject("PowerBuilder.Application")
   If pbobject Is Nothing Then
      MsgBox "Create of PB object failed"
      End Sub
   Else
      PBObject.LibraryList = "c:\pbi32\tax.pbd"
      Set Taxuo = PBObject.CreateObject("u_tax_calc")
      If Taxuo Is Nothing Then
         MsgBox "tax uo failed"
         End Sub
      Else
         'Call the tax bracket function
         TaxRate = Taxuo.uf_Tax (GrossPay)
         Set Taxuo = Nothing
        End If
    Set pbobject = Nothing
    End If
```

To have the ability to create PowerBuilder OLE servers, you need to merge PBAPPL.REG into the Windows Registry and you must update the path for PBROI050.DLL and PBAEN050.TLB to point to the installed directory.

Summary

In this chapter you have seen two different techniques to communicate among Windows applications. OLE 2.0 is receiving a lot of attention and is rapidly becoming the standard direction for IPC within the Windows environment. It has the unfortunate problem of being rather slow, occasionally unstable, and not supported by all applications, but these problems are being methodically addressed. For these reasons, DDE continues to be used and has its own niche in the interprocess communications arena.

INDEX

SYMBOLS

B

D

F

G

J

K

L

N

O

Q

R

T

U

V

X-Y-Z

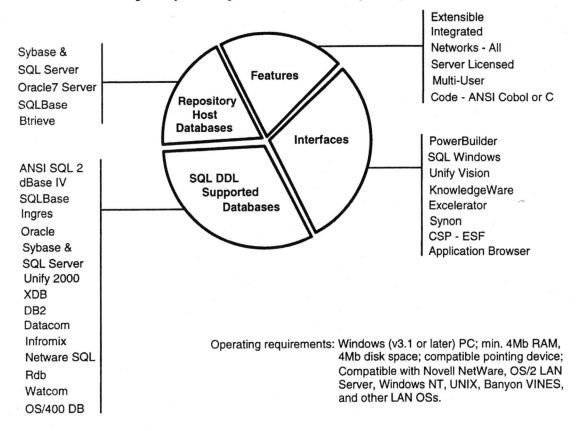

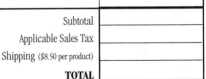

Book ISBN 0-672-30907-6